W9-ALJ-727

ON LOCATION: AT KNITMEDIA

MANAGING IN AN ERA OF RAPID CHANGE AND GLOBALIZATION

[small-print body text of boxed case study, largely illegible]

104 PART ONE Introduction to...

YOU BE THE CONSULTANT

IDENTIFYING TOP TALENT

As you might imagine, heading up an enterprise like Knit-Media requires an extraordinary range of decision-making skills. On the one hand are the relatively rational decisions like what banks to tap for loans and what locations to use for new Knit Factories; but on the other hand, much of Knit-Media's business depends (and has always depended) on finding top-notch talent, a process that is distinctly intuitive and creative. In the past, Michael and his colleagues have shown a keen ability for identifying talent such as John Zorn, Bill Frisell, and Indigo Girls; and in fact, one reason for KnitMedia's desire to expand is to allow Michael and his colleagues to get access to emerging talent in local markets. However, Michael would like to know if there is anything they can do to make even better talent-choice decisions.

Team Exercises and Questions

Use what you learned in this chapter to answer the following question:

1. What creativity-stimulating techniques do you think would be useful for helping Michael Dorf and his colleagues in their quest to identify top local talent?

2. What decision-making techniques discussed in this chapter would you recommend the KnitMedia managers use in finding top talent, and why do you recommend using these?

For the online version of this case, visit our Web site at: <www.prenhall.com/desslermgmt>.

How Is KnitMedia Used in This Text?

- **Video Cases** A six-part, integrative video case focuses on managers and management practices at KnitMedia. The corresponding videos were custom-produced specifically for use with this book.

- **CD-ROM** The KnitMedia custom videos are available on the free CD-ROM that is bound in the back of every copy of the book.

- **You Be the Consultant** A minicase at the end of each chapter focuses on a managerial challenge that KnitMedia faces, and asks you to act as a consultant by analyzing business opportunities and recommending actions to KnitMedia's manager.s

- **Internet Exercises** Web-based exercises let you apply to what you've learned to KnitMedia (and other companies, too!) by conducting electronic research on the World Wide Web. The exercises are found on the Dessler home page at

www.prenhall.com/desslermgmt

For more information on KnitMedia and its role in this text, please see "A Note to the Student on KnitMedia" following the preface.

< A band performing at the Knitting Factory's Main Performance Space.

Michael Dorf, CEO and Founder of KnitMedia >

MANAGEMENT

MANA

*Leading Peop
in the 21st C

ALABAMA CRIMSON TIDE

(Ch 1, 14), (3, 4, 13)
(10, 11, 15)

GARY DESSLER
Florida International University

Prentice Hall
Upper Saddle River, NJ 07458

Acquisition Editor: Stephanie Johnson
Editor-in-Chief: Natalie Anderson
Development Editor: Elisa Adams
Production Editor: Dee Josephson
Marketing Manager: Tamara Wederbrand
Supplements Editor: Lisamarie Brassini
Managing Editor: Dee Josephson
Design Director: Pat Smythe
Manufacturing Supervisor: Arnold Vila
Manufacturing Manager: Vincent Scelta
Cover & Interior Designer: Lorraine Castellano
Cover Illustration: Eric Kittelberger/Stock Illustration Source, Inc.
Photo Research: Melinda Alexander
Editorial Assistant: Dawn-Marie Reisner
Composition & Prepress: GTS Graphics, Inc.

© 1998 by Prentice Hall, Inc.
A Simon & Schuster Company
Upper Saddle River, NJ 07458

All rights reserved. No part of this book may be
reproduced, in any form by any means, without
permission in writing from the publisher.

Library of Congress has cataloged another edition as follows:

Dessler, Gary
    Management : leading people and organizations in the 21st century
/ Gary Dessler
      p. cm.
    Includes biliographical references and index.
    ISBN 0-13-862970-6
    1. Management. 2. Leadership. 3. Organization I. Title.
HD31.D4863   1997   97–32116
658.4'092--dc21   CIP

Prentice-Hall International (UK) Limited, London
Prentice-Hall of Australia Pty. Limited, Sydney.
Prentice-Hall Canada, Inc., Toronto
Prentice-Hall Hispanoamericana, S.A., Mexico
Prentice-Hall of India Private Limited, New Delhi
Prentice-Hall of Japan, Inc., Tokyo
Simon & Schuster Asia Pte, Ltd., Singapore
Editora Prentice-Hall do Brasil, Ltda., Rio de Janiero

Printed in the United States of America
10 9 8 7 6 5 4 3 2

To Natalie Anderson

Brief Table of Contents

Contents

Features of the Text

ORGANIZATIONAL BEHAVIOR IN ACTION

STRATEGY IN ACTION

MANAGING CHANGE

ENTREPRENEURS IN ACTION

Preface

Bill Gates recently discovered that Microsoft's basic focus on providing operating software for small computers was becoming dangerously outmoded. Users were increasingly using the Internet for computer assistance, and investors, seeing the Internet's popularity, briefly depressed Microsoft's stock while boosting Netscape's. In response, Gates tapped the enormous intellectual capital and flexibility of his huge firm. In less than a year he reoriented his company's strategy around the Internet, reorganized around new Internet-product oriented teams, and led a corporate transformation that virtually recreated his huge company and its product line, triggering a firestorm of opposition from competitors and regulators in the process.

Microsoft's transformation is one example of the changes in managing organizations taking place today. Globalization, deregulation, and technological advances mean that today's organizations must respond quickly to change if they are to thrive in intensely competitive environments. To achieve this responsiveness and competitiveness, new management methods and philosophies have emerged, such as boundaryless organizations, team-based structures, scenario planning, transformational leadership, and commitment-building to supplement conventional control devices. Managing—leading people and organizations in 21st century businesses—will depend on maintaining open, communicative, and responsive organizations, in large part by relying on the firms' human capital. It is this point of view that provides the foundation for this book.

This book provides students with a practical and concrete explanation of the management concepts and techniques they will need to manage today's new organizations. It is intended for use in undergraduate or graduate courses in management or in courses that combine management and organizational behavior. Adopters will find that the book's outline follows the familiar "planning, organizing, leading, controlling" process format, and that its contents and continuing themes stress the leading-edge management concepts and techniques that students will need to manage today's and tomorrow's organizations.

THEMES OF THE TEXT Within the planning, organizing, leading, and controlling framework of this text, we emphasize leading-edge management concepts and techniques by focusing on six themes. These themes, which are woven into each chapter, are:

1. **OB Is Part of Managing.** Particularly with today's emphasis on being responsive, managers like Bill Gates cannot separate their behavioral responsibilities from their managerial ones. Thus planning requires setting and getting acceptance of goals, and recreating the organization and product line of a firm like Microsoft requires enormous leadership and motivational skills. Because human capital is so important to managing change today, this book contains one to two more OB (organizational behavior) chapters than competing texts, as well as two to three **Organizational**

Behavior in Action features in every chapter to show how managers use OB in practice.

2. **Managing Requires Vision and Strategy.** With employees operating more autonomously today, managers like Bill Gates know it's important to formulate a vision for their firms, one that helps keep all employees focused in the same direction. Our book uses **Strategy in Action** features within most chapters, and a **Strategy Case** at the end of every chapter to illustrate the importance of vision and strategy as a touchstone for all the decisions a manager makes.

3. **Managing Change Is Crucial.** Understanding how to manage under conditions of rapid change is crucial today. Managing change is, therefore, a central theme of our book, implemented through special chapters such as "Designing Organizations to Manage Change" (chapter 8) and through **Managing Change** features in most chapters.

4. **Entrepreneurship Is Important.** Most college graduates today will go to work for smaller firms. Managing in a small business is, thus, our book's fourth theme. Although small business examples are sprinkled throughout the text, this theme is implemented primarily with an **Entrepreneurs in Action** box in each chapter, and with an end-of-chapter **Entrepreneurial Case.** In addition, all the features related to KnitMedia (videos, video cases, "You Be the Consultant" mini-cases, and Internet exercises) provide an in-depth look at an exciting, entrepreneurial company on a continuing basis throughout this book. (See "A Note to the Student on KnitMedia" on page xxx for more information.)

5. **Managing Is Cross-Functional.** Today's team-based managers have to take a cross-functional view at work, a fact recognized by the Business Schools accrediting agency (the AACSB) in its emphasis on encouraging more cross-functional teaching of courses. Our book uses several devices including **The Business Team, Inc.,** a continuing cross-functional case, to show how production, accounting, HR, and marketing have to work together within a small consulting firm.

6. **Diversity Must Be Managed.** As the workforce becomes increasingly diverse, it is important for managers to recognize that diversity is a positive force rather than a negative one. You will, therefore, find a portion of chapter 3 devoted to this topic, as well as numerous examples and a **Diversity Case** at the end of each chapter illustrating the need for techniques of effectively managing diversity.

MANAGERS MANAGE GLOBALLY Few changes in the past ten years have had more impact on managers than globalization, and this trend will no doubt continue into the 21st century. This text covers the impact of globalization with a full chapter right up front (chapter 2), to give students an early introduction to global issues. But because today's managers need to see all aspects of business and management from a global perspective, we also weave numerous discussions and examples of globalization into every chapter. Here are just a few of the many examples of the international/globalization material throughout the text:

Chapter 1 discusses the impact on management of changing political systems around the world, including the explosive opening of new markets with hundreds of millions of potential customers.

Chapter 2 is entirely devoted to the impact on managing of globalization. It covers the reasons companies expand operations abroad and their strategies for doing so; economic, legal, political, and other factors that influence a manager's decision to expand abroad; and how doing business internationally affects the way managers plan, organize, lead and control.

Chapter 3 discusses ways that ethics codes can help enable top management to expand globally, secure in the knowledge that even in subsidiaries far removed from the firm's home base, local managers will be more likely to adhere to the company's code of ethical practices.

Chapter 4 recognizes that, to some extent, a manager's approach to making decisions is culturally based, with examples describing why terms like "devil's advocate" or "loyal opposition" have no place in a Japanese auto manufacturing facility in Michigan.

Chapter 5 profiles how Shell Oil Company, a multinational corporation, uses scenario planning to better anticipate geopolitical changes and international economic changes that might impact the plans it makes.

Chapter 6 discusses how companies, like the one that publishes *The Wall Street Journal,* achieve above-average growth rates by aggressively expanding into new geographic markets, both domestic and overseas.

Chapter 7 includes a feature on how Cirque du Soleil organizes its 1,200 employees worldwide in seventeen different countries.

Chapter 8 discusses how multinationals such as Toyota establish team-based organizational structures abroad, as at the Camry facility in Lexington, KY.

Chapter 9 offers an extensive example of how Japan's Mazda Corporation uses employee selection techniques to help establish factories that are capable of maintaining high quality and productivity under conditions of rapid change.

Chapter 10 discusses the effective leadership skills of people like former British Prime Minister Margaret Thatcher, GE's Jack Welch, and India's Mahatma Gandhi.

Chapter 11 includes examples of how to build total quality-oriented cultures like those consistent with the International Standards Organization's ISO 9000 and Japan's Deming Award.

Chapter 12 shows how multinationals like Scandinavian Air Systems and Pratt & Whitney use empowerment to motivate employees.

Chapter 13 emphasizes that cross-cultural communication is a fact of business life, and it illustrates how to communicate in a culture not your own.

Chapter 14 offers examples of how companies use transnational teams, which are work groups composed of multinational members whose activities span many countries.

Chapter 15 discusses Sony CEO Idei's most "un-Japanese" way of sweeping Sony movie studio executives out of office and installing a new team of industry veterans with a mandate to fix Sony's movie business.

Chapter 16 points out that managing a globally dispersed workforce requires a particularly effective control system, in order to avoid problems such as the misbehavior of a rogue trader in Singapore that recently ruined a British banking firm.

Chapter 17 discusses total quality management programs that are used in a similar fashion in companies around the world, from the United States to Europe to Asia, to implement continuous improvement through people and through innovative manufacturing techniques.

Chapter 18 shows how many companies today are using information technology to compete in a global marketplace, and why most firms would find it almost impossible to compete globally without such technology.

PEDAGOGICAL AIDS   The pedagogical elements of this text have been carefully designed to reinforce the major themes of the text described above, and to encourage active learning for the student.

Management on the Web   Each chapter opens with a featured Web site that offers opportunities to explore online for more information about the chapter's topics.

Organizational Behavior in Action   Each chapter features two to three Organizational Behavior in Action sections that emphasize the importance of the "human" or behavioral aspects of managing. For example, chapter 4 includes an Organizational Behavior in Action feature on "How One Company Uses Teams to Make Better Decisions" (page 128). See page xvii for a complete list of all Organizational Behavior in Action features in this text.

Strategy in Action   Most chapters include a Strategy in Action feature that illustrates the importance of vision and strategy as a framework for all decisions a manager must make. For example, chapter 3 includes a section on "The Ethical Foundations of a Company's Strategy" (page 88). See page xix for a complete list of all Strategy in Action features.

Managing Change   Most companies today face the challenge of managing under conditions of rapid change. That's why we've included a section in most chapters called Managing Change, such as the one in chapter 6 on "The Virtual Corporation" (page 188). See page xix for a full list of Managing Change features.

Entrepreneurs in Action   Each chapter includes at least one box on Entrepreneurs in Action to emphasize the increasing significance of smaller companies in today's business environment. Chapter 4, for example, includes a box on USWeb, a 46-employee company that offers Web design franchises. See page xx for a full list of Entrepreneurs in Action features. *Questions listed for this feature on the Dessler Web site at <www.prenhall.com/desslermgmt> permit using each Entrepreneurs feature as a case assignment.*

Cases   Five different cases at the end of each chapter encourage students to apply that chapter's concepts to specific scenarios. The cases focus on the following issues:

- **Diversity Case** focuses on a different company, issue, or manager in each chapter, and emphasizes issues of diversity in today's workforce.

- **Strategy Case** profiles the strategic challenge facing a different company in each chapter, in the context of that chapter's topic.

- **Entrepreneurial Case** focuses on a different small business or entrepreneurial venture in each chapter, applying that chapter's topic to the business.

- **The Business Team, Inc.** is a continuing case that focuses on a small consulting firm started by recent college graduates. Each member of the team brings a different area of expertise, including accounting, finance, sales, production, and human resource management to the partnership. The team confronts different challenges in each chapter.

■ **You Be the Consultant** is a continuing case that focuses on KnitMedia, a music and entertainment company (see "A Note to the Student on Knit-Media" on page xxx for more information on this company). Students are asked to put themselves in the place of KnitMedia managers, and make decisions regarding the future direction of the company.

■ **Entrepreneurs in Action** Questions listed for each Entrepreneurs in Action feature on the Dessler Web site at <www.prenhall.com/desslermgmt> permit use of each feature as a case assignment.

Self Test Ten true/false and ten multiple-choice questions at the end of each chapter allow students to test their comprehension of each chapter's concepts.

Critical Thinking Exercises Two scenario-based questions per chapter encourage students to think more deeply about each chapter's concepts.

Experiential Exercises Two end-of-chapter exercises promote active learning on either an individual or a team basis.

Chapter Summary A concise summary reviews each chapter's major concepts.

Key Terms Key terms appear in bold within the text and are defined when used. The terms are also listed at the end of each chapter, and are defined again in the glossary at the end of the text.

Video Cases "On Location at KnitMedia" is a six-part, integrative video case that focuses on KnitMedia, a music and entertainment company. The cases correspond to video clips that were custom-filmed at KnitMedia's offices and edited specifically for use with this text. The video cases appear at the end of each major part of the text. The KnitMedia video clips are also available on the CD-ROM that accompanies this book.

SUPPORT MATERIALS

Instructor's Manual The *Instructor's Manual* has been designed to be an indispensable teaching tool. For every chapter it includes a topic introduction, learning objectives, an annotated outline that includes space for instructors' own notes, answers and suggestions for all in-chapter elements, and answers to all end-of-chapter materials. It also contains a video guide section that summarizes the accompanying ABC News video clips and the custom KnitMedia videos; and it provides suggestions for tying videos to the chapter content.

Instructor's Manual on Disk The *Instructor's Manual* is also available on disk in ASCII files for instructors who would like to tailor the material to their own teaching needs.

Test Item File The *Test Item File* contains over 100 questions per chapter, including multiple-choice, scenario-based, true/false, and discussion questions. Every question is page referenced to the text and is labeled easy, moderate, or challenging to satisfy all classroom needs.

Computerized Testing The *Test Item File* is designed for use with *PH Custom Test,* a computerized package that allows users to custom design, save, and generate tests. Instructors can add and delete questions. The *PH Custom Test* is available in either Windows or Macintosh format.

Video Cases: **On Location at KnitMedia** This customized video, shot and edited specifically for this text, focuses on a music and entertainment company called KnitMedia. The five video segments correspond to five integrative end-of-part video cases in the text, with an additional video segment that introduces students to KnitMedia. For more information on KnitMedia, see the section on page xxx on "A Note to the Student on KnitMedia."

ABC News/Prentice Hall Video Library Seventeen video clips from various ABC News programs like *World News Tonight, 20/20, Prime Time Live* and *Nightline* complement the topics of the text. Video notes that tie the clips to the text are found in the *Instructor's Manual.*

Color Transparencies Full-color acetates (100) based on key exhibits and concepts from the text add a visual element to your lectures. Teaching notes accompany all acetates to further enhance their ease of use.

Electronic Transparencies PowerPoint disks allow access to over 200 figures, exhibits, and text materials.

Study Guide Available for sale to students, this manual has been designed to reinforce key concepts of the text as well as to enhance understanding and application of the concepts. The *Study Guide* is also accessible online at the Dessler Web site at no charge to users.

Web Site The Dessler Web site is found at <www.prenhall.com/desslermgmt>. It offers information about the author, Internet exercises, an online *Study Guide,* and a link to PHLIP (Prentice Hall's Learning on the Internet Partnership). PHLIP provides links to additional management Web sites, up-to-date news articles that are page referenced to the text, and faculty support materials like PowerPoint slides and *Instructor's Manual* chapters (the faculty materials are password protected).

CD-ROM To encourage students' use of technology and the Internet to enhance their classroom experience, each copy of this text includes a free CD-ROM. The CD-ROM contains the full text of the book in Adobe Acrobat files; custom video clips from KnitMedia; and an Internet connection to the Dessler Web site, where students will find an interactive study guide, links to additional management Web sites, and up-to-date news articles that are page referenced to the text.

ACKNOWLEDGMENTS Creating this book required an exceptionally intensive effort from an extraordinarily dedicated team of Prentice Hall professionals, and I would be remiss if I did not acknowledge their extraordinary contributions. Natalie E. Anderson was, as usual, a gem, and as Management Editor had the vision and confidence to commit to the project, the intelligence and market knowledge to help set the direction of the book, and the energy and eye for detail when a partner was needed in the final stages of manuscript production, although by that time she was also adjusting to her new title as Editor-in-Chief. Along with Natalie, I benefited enormously at the early stages of this project from recommendations of a group at Prentice Hall comprised of Stephanie Johnson, then Marketing Manager and now Management Editor, who has continued to do an exceptional job of keeping this project on track; Sandy Steiner, President of the Business Publishing Division; Steve Rigolosi, Managing Editor for Development; Jim Boyd, Editorial Director; and Bill Oldsey, then President of the Business Publishing Division and now President of Silver Burdett Ginn. I would like to thank Brian Kibby, the Director of Marketing, Tamara Wederbrand, the Marketing Manager, Eve Adams, the Advertising Art Director, and Janet Ferruggia, the Marketing Communications Director, for their creativity and energy in promoting this book. I am also indebted to Elisa Adams, Development Editor, for the good humor, intelligence, and creativity with which she worked with me to make this a much better book than it might have been; Pat

Smythe, the Design Manager, Ann France, the Senior Designer, and Lorraine Castellano, the Designer, for their extraordinary work on the interior and cover design for this book; and Dee Josephson, Managing Editor, and Margaret Pinette at GTS Graphics, for an exceptional job of creating the final product and keeping it on schedule. Last but certainly not least, I am deeply grateful to all of the professionals in the Prentice Hall sales force, who have enthusiastically promoted my human resource management text over seven editions. The success of *Management: Leading People and Organizations in the 21st Century* rests in their capable hands, and I thank them in advance for their efforts.

The quality of this book has been vastly improved by the contributions of our reviewers, and I would like to thank and acknowledge them here:

Professor Clarence Anderson, Walla Walla College
Dr. James Bell, Southwest Texas State University
Professor Aleta Best, Texas A&M University
Professor Barbara Boyington, Brookdale Community College
Professor Monica Briedenbach, Devry Institute of Technology
Professor James H. Browne, University of Southern Colorado
Dr. John Carmichael, Union County College
Professor Bonnie Chavez, Santa Barbara City College
Professor R. J. Dick, Missouri Western State
Professor Paul Fadil, Valdosta State University
Professor Janice Feldbauer, Austin Community College
Professor Kevin McCarthy, Baker University
Professor Mike Peng, University of Hawaii
Professor Preston Probasco, San Jose State University
Professor Rajib Sanyal, The College of New Jersey
Mr. Tim Weaver, SVP Corporate Banking

At Florida International University I appreciate the moral support I received from all of my colleagues including Enzo Valenzi, Jan Luytjes, Earnest Friday, Mary Ann Von Glinow, and Bill Taggart as well as Bill Jerome's wise, practical, and always enthusiastic advice, and the support and advice of Richard Hodgetts.

I am grateful to Michael Dorf, CEO of KnitMedia, and his staff for giving us access to a fascinating business enterprise so that we could create the videos, video cases, Internet exercises, and You Be the Consultant features for this text. My thanks also to Dr. d. t. ogilvie of Rutgers University for her excellent work in helping to craft the KnitMedia videos, and for authoring the KnitMedia video cases that appear at the end of each part of this book.

On the home front I want to acknowledge the support of my wife, Claudia, and her willingness to tolerate my disappearance for more evenings and weekends than I should have been gone while I wrote this book. However, when all the acknowledgments are said and done, if there can be a single inspiration for a book entitled *Management: Leading People and Organizations in the 21st Century*, it was my son Derek, for whom I wrote this book in as practical and useful a way as I could, and whose unswerving support was the only motivation I needed.

A Note to the Student on KnitMedia

You are not going to learn how to be a manager by reading this book. You know that you can't learn how to do anything—play golf, do calculus problems, or make fine furniture—just by reading about it. Instead, you have to actually *apply* what you read; you have to *practice*. As one famous commentator once replied when asked how to get to Carnegie Hall, "Practice, practice, practice."

By the time you've completed this book, we'd like you to have had an opportunity to step into a manager's shoes, and to practice what it's like to plan, organize, lead, and control (in other words, to manage) an organization. To help you do this, we've created a number of features that focus on a company called KnitMedia.

I personally find the nature of KnitMedia's business interesting, and I hope that you will, too. KnitMedia is an alternative music and entertainment company whose businesses include an independent record label, and the Knitting Factory—a live music club in New York City that specializes in alternative jazz. As you move through the book you'll see that KnitMedia is involved in other businesses, too, including radio, TV, and Internet and video-conference interactive performances.

Understanding and explaining how to manage a huge enterprise like IBM or General Motors requires quite a stretch of the imagination for most of us, and by *us*, I mean myself and many of the students and professors who will be using this book. On the other hand, most of us can relate more easily to and "get our hands around" the sort of small business that Michael Dorf, the founder and president, is building in KnitMedia. Here are some of the features you'll find in this book that focus on KnitMedia.

You Be the Consultant (found at the end of each chapter) is a continuing case that focuses on different aspects of KnitMedia from chapter to chapter. As a result, you're going to become very familiar with just about everything about KnitMedia, its competitors, its strengths and weaknesses, its financial situation, and its managers' hopes and dreams. That way, you'll be able to make your decisions not in a vacuum but within the context of what you know about the company. For instance, you'll be able to propose a technique to help the president of the company, Michael Dorf, control his increasingly far-flung enterprise, in the context of what you know about his motives and how he likes to manage.

Integrative Video Cases (found at the end of each major part of the book) let you apply your knowledge of what you've learned from the preceding chapters. The cases are designed to help you think about management the way managers actually have to, in a more integrated, "it's all related" fashion.

KnitMedia Videos correspond to the end-of-part integrative cases, and will let you see and hear how KnitMedia's managers and employees are actually managing their company on a day-to-day basis. These videos can be accessed on the CD-ROM that you'll find at the back of your textbook.

Internet Exercises let you apply what you've learned in each chapter to KnitMedia, whose managers, products, services, and competitive situation will become very familiar to you. You can use Internet resources to research your solutions to the assigned exercises—such as zipping electronically across the Atlantic to learn more about what competition the Knitting Factory nightclub and its managers will face as they expand into London and beyond. You'll find the Internet Exercises on our Web site (www.prenhall.com/desslermgmt).

The multimedia nature of this KnitMedia component should provide you with a more realistic and concrete way to learn about making management decisions and managing companies. You'll be able to use the text, videos, CD-ROM, and Internet to read about KnitMedia, to actually see the participants at work, to interact with some of them, and to research your answers to the exercises. And, depending upon how your professor sets up your assignments, you may even be able to interact with others in your group electronically via the Internet, to develop realistic answers to the group assignments.

I hope and believe that this integrated package will provide you with an opportunity to apply in practice what you've learned, and thus to actually see what it's like to be a manager. After all, how do you become a manager? Practice, practice, practice.

About the Author

GARY DESSLER is Professor of Business in the College of Business Administration at Florida International University in Miami. He has a Bachelor of Science Degree from New York University, a Master of Science Degree from Rensselaer Polytechnic Institute, and a Ph.D. in Business Administration from the Bernard M. Baruch School of Business of the City University of New York.

In addition to *Management: Leading People and Organizations in the 21st Century,* Dr. Dessler has authored numerous other books, including, most recently, *Winning Commitment: How to Build and Keep a Competitive Workforce,* and *Human Resource Management,* Seventh Edition. He wrote the syndicated "Job Talk" column for the Miami Herald for 10 years and has written numerous articles on organizational behavior, leadership, and quality improvement. His recent consulting assignments have involved strategic planning, executive and management recruiting, establishing human resource management systems, and negotiating multinational joint ventures.

CHAPTER 1

MANAGING IN THE 21st CENTURY

What's Ahead?

Since starting his first copy shop near the University of California's Santa Barbara campus, Paul "Kinko" Orfalea, whose nickname refers to his kinky red hair, has become an expert at managing change. He began his career working nights, selling pens and spiral notebooks on the Santa Barbara campus, and borrowed $5,000 to open his first Kinko Copy Center. He built a loyal following nationwide by giving students 24-hour access to word processors and copiers for their reports. As PCs and campus copiers became more readily available, Orfalea shifted to offering more expensive office equipment like desk-

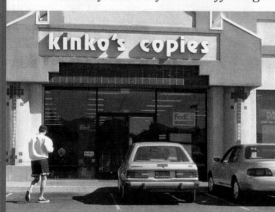

top color printers, and to services like duplicating teaching materials and compiling students' reports. Now, with color printers selling for under $300, he's shifting his company again, focusing on business firms and offering new services like KinkoNet: Work on your sales presentation until the last minute, zap it from your PC to Kinko's, and pick up your bound color copies when you arrive at the meeting on the opposite coast.[1] Orfalea's only question is, "What's in store for us next?"

Objectives

After studying this chapter, you should be able to

- **identify** the main environmental trends influencing managers like Paul Orfalea

- **explain**, with examples, what managers do

- **describe** why the behavioral or "people" side of managing is so important

- **discuss** the main trends today in how modern organizations are managed.

MANAGEMENT ON THE WEB

BEST PRACTICES

This site includes reports discussing the best practices used by U.S. Navy suppliers, based on one-week visits by best-practices teams. The company profiles outline practices in various areas of high performance. Visit the page and see what high-performance organizations are doing to develop a competitive advantage in an era of change. Could Kinko's use any of these practices? ■

http://www.bmpcoe.org/surveys/index.html

Managing in an Era of Change

The opportunities and challenges facing Kinko's illustrate the rapid change and unpredictability that all managers face today. Kinko's has survived and thrived because of the remarkable management talent of Paul Orfalea. However, not all companies have been so successful. Japanese firms have surpassed Chrysler as the third largest car maker, and Intel president Andy Grove predicts an industrywide shakeout among PC makers, noting that "there are 500 suppliers—and 450 should not exist."[2] Dozens of banks have been forced to merge to survive, and many U.S. airlines—Eastern, Braniff, USAir, Pan Am—have either gone out of business or been forced to merge.[3] In the process hundreds of thousands of employees have been thrown out of work ("downsized") as companies have tried to drive up their efficiency by squeezing more productivity from a smaller employee base.

The main purpose of this chapter is to explain what managers do, but in point of fact that's impossible to do until we first discuss the sorts of changes managers and their organizations must increasingly respond to. We turn to these changes next. They include: technological innovation; globalization; deregulation; new political systems; a new workforce; more service-oriented jobs; and a new emphasis on "knowledge work."

Technological Innovation

As Kinko's Paul Orfalea knows, technological innovations like information highways, the Internet, microprocessors, and automated factories are proliferating. The number of U.S. patents issued rose from 67,000 annually in the 1970s to 77,200 in 1985, and to over 100,000 per year in the 1990s. The number of U.S. trademarks issued has risen from almost 66,000 in the 1980s to over 120,000 per year in the 1990s. And this total reflects just U.S. patents and trademarks, not those issued in other industrial countries.

Technological innovations are changing the way companies compete. For example, Inter-Design of Ohio sells plastic clocks, refrigerator magnets, soap dishes, and similar products. Its president explains the impact of *information technology,* which merges communications systems with computers, this way: "In the seventies we went to the post office to pick up our orders. In the early 80s, we put in an 800 number. In the late 80s, we got a fax machine. In 1991, pressured by Target [stores, a customer], we added electronic data interchange." Now, just two years later, more than half of Inter-Design's orders arrive via modem, straight into company computers. Errors in order entry and shipping have all but disappeared.[4]

And that, of course, is just one of millions of examples. Netscape Navigator has changed how many companies do business and how people shop, almost overnight.[5] Amazon.com has gone from zero book sales to tens of millions, thanks to the Internet.[6] Jim Manzi, former head of Lotus, hopes to rebuild his new company Industry.Net, into a huge Internet-based market for businesses.[7]

Information technology like this has been a boon to many companies but a near-disaster for others. In the 1980s and 1990s, Wal-Mart ballooned in size, in part because its managers used information technology to directly link their stores with their suppliers: Levi Straus & Co., for instance, always knew exactly how many size-10, 501-style jeans were being sold and could replenish the stores' supplies almost at once. But Wal-Mart's technology advantage almost torpedoed K-Mart, which struggled for many years without the speed and cost-effectiveness of such a system.

Globalization

Globalization is the tendency of firms to extend their sales or manufacturing to new markets abroad. For businesses everywhere, the rate of globalization recently has been nothing short of phenomenal, as has the resulting rise in competition.

For instance, in the early 1980s General Electric, long accustomed to being the dominant lighting manufacturer in the United States, had a rude awakening. Its relatively weak competitor, Westinghouse, sold its lamp operations to Dutch electric powerhouse Philips Electronics; overnight GE's competitive picture changed. As one GE executive put it, "Suddenly we have bigger, stronger competition. They're coming into our market, but we're not in theirs. So we're on the defensive."[8]

As more and more firms expand abroad to make the business environment truly global, investment banking firm Goldman Sachs hopes to mine new business in Moscow under Evan Newmark's leadership.

GE did not stay there for long. It soon bought Hungary's Tungstram electronics and is fast moving into Asia through a partnership with Hitachi.[9] In 1990, GE lighting got less than 20 percent of its sales from abroad; by 1993, the figure was 40 percent, and for 1996 the estimate is more than half.

Globalization is manifesting itself in U.S. firms in many ways. The value of U.S. imports/exports grew from 9.4 percent of GNP in 1960 to almost 23 percent in the 1990s.[10] U.S. exports are also reaching new markets, with big gains since 1988 in sales to countries ranging from Uruguay and Mexico to the Netherlands, Hungary, and Kuwait.[11]

Production is becoming globalized, too, as manufacturers around the world put manufacturing facilities where they will be most advantageous. Thus, the Toyota Camry—what many would claim is "obviously" a Japanese car—is produced in Georgetown, Kentucky, and contains almost 80 percent U.S.-made parts. At the same time, the General Motors Pontiac LeMans ("obviously" a U.S. car) actually contains almost two-thirds foreign-made parts.[12]

Globalization of markets and manufacturing is important, in part because it has vastly increased international competition. Throughout the world, firms that formerly competed only with local firms—from airlines to car makers to banks—have discovered they must now face an onslaught of new foreign competitors.

Many firms have successfully responded to this new international environment, while others have failed. For instance, when Swedish furniture retailer Ikea built its first U.S. furniture superstore in New Jersey, its superior styles and management systems grabbed market share from numerous domestic competitors, driving several out of business.

Global competition is a two-way street, though. Ford and GM have huge market shares in Europe, for instance, while IBM, Microsoft, Apple, and countless smaller firms have major market shares around the world. As one international business expert puts it, "the bottom line is that the growing integration of the world economy into a single, huge marketplace is increasing the intensity of competition in a wide range of manufacturing and service industries."[13]

Deregulation

Meanwhile, the comfortable protection provided to thousands of businesses around the world by government regulations has been stripped away in country after country. In the United States, as mentioned earlier, a dozen airlines including Eastern, People's Express, Braniff, and Piedmont have either been bought up or gone bust as airline deregulation exposed inefficiencies that less-responsive competitors couldn't eliminate in time. In 1997, AT&T—formerly only a long-distance phone service provider—was poised to invade the regional Bells' local-phone service turf: in 1996 Congress had approved sweeping deregulation of local and long distance phone service, allowing carriers to invade each other's markets.[14] The Morris Air Entrepreneurs in Action box shows how one small firm dealt with deregulation.

Changing Political Systems

As nations ranging from the Philippines to Argentina, Russia, and Chile join the ranks of democracies, central planning and communism are being replaced by capitalism. This prompted Francis Fukuyama, a State Department planner, to declare "the end of history." Fukuyama characterized the conquest of capitalism over communism and its consequences as the end of the historical conflict between two economic ideologies.[15] To him, the overthrow of Marxist-Leninist ideology means the

Entrepreneurs in Action

MORRIS AIR

The business philosophy at tiny Morris Air was simple: offer low enough fares and travelers will dream up their own excuses to journey by air. Then all you have to do is operate efficiently, and the increased volume will translate into profits. But that last part is not as easy as it sounds.

Founder June Morris was the driving force behind Morris Air. With characteristic understatement, Morris says that in starting the company she simply identified a need and filled the niche. She believed she had talent, but perhaps more importantly, she found good people and let them use their own abilities in building Morris Air.

The Salt Lake City-based regional carrier grew to 2,000 employees, including Morris's son Rick Fendt, the airline's chairman, and a few others who went as far back as grade school with June Morris. She thinks Utah was a good place to find good employees; work ethics are solid and people are well educated and polite. That, too, is important, because despite low fares and cost-conscious operations, Morris insists customer service be the best. Since her management style focuses on the human side, she wants to hear about problems, too. Personally, Morris stays on top of what's happening by monitoring in-flight surveys, reading complaint letters, and occasionally fielding telephone calls.

One way the airline has managed to keep fares low—often below competitors' fare-war prices—was by leasing many of its planes and contracting flight crews. Another tactic was more ingenious, an advertising strategy that encourages fliers to see that their own best interests coincide with those of Morris Air. One of the company's promotional brochures summed it up: "A ticket on Morris Air is a vote for permanent low fares!" When the carrier began Salt Lake City to Denver service with four flights daily, Delta, American, and United had to slash fares as much as 50 percent.

The increased competition hit Delta the hardest. In mid-1992, 75 percent of passengers boarding flights in Salt Lake were Delta fliers. A little over a year later that number had dropped to 67 percent while Morris Air's market share rose from 8 to 14 percent. Analysts said the big airline underestimated Morris Air. Whatever the case, it's safe to assume Delta management was not amused, and retaliation was swift. Delta notified travel agents in mid-1993 that booking fliers on Morris Air could cost them lucrative commissions from the big carrier. Delta even gave away free tickets to loyal agents as a further inducement. Morris was forced to hire new reservation agents, but the small carrier quickly won back the 20 percent loss in business.

June Morris patterned much of her airline operations around Texas-based Southwest Airlines. The two carriers have much in common. Both flew 737 jets exclusively and concentrated on short flights of around 500 miles. Today, they have even more in common, as deregulation continues to churn airlines and their management. In December 1993, Southwest announced it was buying Morris Air. The relationship has proved to be very beneficial. For example, Morris Air helped show Southwest how to switch to a ticketless travel system in 1995, so it could keep up with rivals' competitive moves. ■

Source: John Accola, "Tiny Morris Air Is Making the Big Airlines Nervous with Its Cut-Rate Fares," *Rocky Mountain News,* 88A, 90A; Judy B. Rollins, "Morris Air Owner Says Every Cloud Has a Silver Lining," *Salt Lake Tribune,* 10 January 1993, F8, F9; Julie Schmit and Jefferson Graham, "When Morris Took Flight, Fares Fell," *USA Today,* 30 August 1993, B1; Carlene Canton, "Flying High," *The Costco Connection #6,* no. 8 (August 1992): 1 15; and Terry Maxon, "Southwest to Buy Carrier," *Dallas Morning News,* 14 December 1993, 1A, 10A; Ron Levine, "Southwest Soars with Ticketless Travel," *Lan Times On Line* (1995): (www.wcmh.com/lantimes/archive/605b031a.htm/)

victory of the principles of liberty and equality, and thus the strengthening of economic liberalism, capitalism, and competition. "Indeed," says Fukuyama, "the meaning of 'great power' will be based increasingly on economic rather than military, territorial, or other traditional measures of might."[16]

Such political changes have triggered an explosive opening of new markets, markets with hundreds of millions of potential customers in countries from Russia to Chile. For business firms, the opportunities are enormous: see for instance, the photo of Evan Newmark, head of investment banker Goldman Sachs' new Moscow office.[17] Yet with the burgeoning demand for goods and services comes increased global competition. See, for instance, the photo of the new Hungarian-built bus now cruising the streets of Portland, Oregon.[18]

Demographics and the New Global Workforce

The workforce is changing dramatically, too. During the 1990s, the white labor force will have grown less than 15 percent, while the black labor force will have grown by about 29 percent and the Hispanic by more than 74 percent. During the period 1986–2000, Hispanics will have accounted for nearly 29 percent of the labor force's growth; Asian and other nonwhite races (including Alaskan natives) will account for more than 11 percent.

These demographic changes are already changing how companies are managed. Special diversity-management programs are proliferating, equal opportunity protection laws are being aggressively applied, and organizations from IBM to the Citadel are instituting new training and other programs to assist in the assimilation of this new minority and multicultural workforce.[19]

At the same time, more U.S. firms are transferring their operations abroad, not just to seek cheaper labor but also to tap what *Fortune* magazine calls "a vast new supply of skilled labor around the world."[20] Even today, in fact, most multinational firms set up manufacturing plants abroad, partly to establish beachheads in promising markets and partly to utilize other countries' professionals and engineers. For example, ASEA Brown Boveri (a $30 billion-a-year Swiss builder of transportation and electric generation systems) has 25,000 new employees in former Communist countries and thus has shifted many jobs from Western to Eastern Europe.

Global competitors can reach new U.S. markets as well, as did a Hungarian bus company whose vehicles now ply the streets of Portland, Oregon.

Tapping such overseas labor markets is a two-edged sword for managers. Employers gain thousands of potential new highly skilled employees, but also the challenge of managing a geographically dispersed workforce.

Demographic changes like these are having repercussions that are making it more difficult for many types of organizations to manage change, as the following example illustrates.

Managing Change

MANAGING A GLOBALLY DISPERSED WORKFORCE

Does an increasingly diverse and globalized workforce mean that companies today must be better at managing change? It does, and companies are handling this challenge in several ways.

For one thing, employment managers in global companies are changing what they look for in job candidates. Just a few years ago, qualities like experience working or traveling abroad, flexibility, and multiple language proficiency were only really stressed when seeking candidates being hired to be sent abroad. Today, employment managers look for such "global awareness" skills in everyone they hire, not just those hired to go right overseas.

Why this change in how hiring is managed? First, as firms become more globalized, more of their employees are being asked to serve abroad, so it makes more sense to ensure you have many current employees with the skills required to successfully transfer abroad. Second, all employees in globalized firms—even those based at home—must be globally aware, because they'll be dealing almost daily with customers, suppliers, and coworkers from abroad. ■

Human Capital: A Shift to Service and Knowledge Work

Another characteristic change in companies today is the growing emphasis on human capital[21]—the knowledge, training, skills, and expertise of a firm's workers—at the expense of physical capital like equipment, machinery, and the physical plant.[22]

This shift is illustrated in Figure 1.1.[23] The U.S. human capital investment (including direct outlays for all forms of formal schooling and worker training) rose from about 42 percent of total productive investment to about 56 percent between 1950 and 1990. During the same time, the investment in physical capital as a percentage of total productive investment dropped from about 58 percent to about 44 percent.

The growing emphasis on education and human capital reflects several trends in the business environment. One is the growing importance of service work in today's society. Over two-thirds of the U.S. workforce is now involved in producing services, not things. And of the 21 million jobs added to the U.S. economy in the 1990s, virtually all will be in service industries like retailing, consulting, teaching, and law. Service jobs like these put a bigger premium on worker education and knowledge than do traditional jobs, and thus they add more to a company's "human capital." As James Brian Quinn, an expert in this area, puts it, "Intellect is the core resource in producing and delivering services."[24]

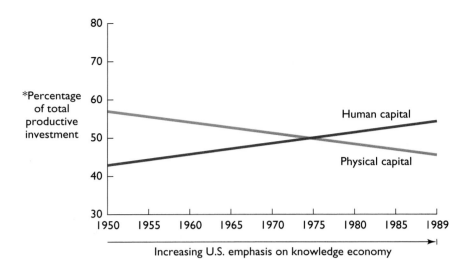

■ FIGURE 1.1

U.S. Investment in Human Capital Compared to U.S. Investment in Physical Capital, 1950 to 1989

The human capital investment in things like schooling and training has risen from about 42 percent of industry's total productive investments to about 58 percent between 1950 and 1989.

SOURCE: Adapted from Richard Crawford, *In the Era of Human Capital* (New York: Harper Business, 1991), 31.

Human capital is also more important today because manufacturing jobs are changing, too. Particularly in the United States, manufacturing-intensive jobs in the steel, auto, rubber, and textile industries are being replaced by knowledge-intensive high tech manufacturing in such industries as aerospace, computers, and telecommunications.[25] At Alcoa Aluminum's Davenport, Iowa, plant, for instance, a computer stands at each work station to help employees control their machines or communicate data. As *Fortune* magazine recently put it, "practically every package deliverer, bank teller, retail clerk, telephone operator, and bill collector in America works with a computer [today]."

Innovation, driven by competition, demands more highly skilled employees, too. It is not unusual for more than one-fourth of many firms' sales to come from products less than five years old. As a result, "innovating—creating new products, new services, new ways of turning out goods more cheaply—has become the most urgent concern of corporations everywhere."[26] This means that companies are relying more on employees' creativity and skills, thus placing more stress on employees' brain power. As *Fortune* magazine recently said:

> Brain-Power . . . has never before been so important for business. Every company depends increasingly on knowledge—patents, processes, management skills, technologies, information about customers and suppliers, and old-fashioned experience. Added together, this knowledge is intellectual capital.[27]

For managers, the challenge of human capital is that these "knowledge workers" must be managed differently than were those of previous generations. "The center of gravity in employment is shifting fast from manual and clerical workers to knowledge workers, who resist the command and control model that business took from the military 100 years ago."[28] Knowledge workers, in other words, cannot just be ordered around and closely monitored. New management skills will be required, and the behavioral side of managing will become more important.

What Managers Do

Managers can have the most remarkable effects on organizations. IBM floundered through much of the 1980s and early 1990s, losing market share, seeing costs rise, and watching its stock price dwindle from almost $180 per share to barely $50. Within three years, new chairman Louis Gerstner revamped the company's product line, dramatically lowered costs, changed the company's culture, and oversaw a rise in the firm's stock price from $50 back to almost $180 again. At American Airlines, Chairman Richard Crandall navigated his company to a position of profitable industry dominance in the 1990s, buying the right planes, picking the right routes, and keeping a vise-like grip on costs, even as slews of his airline's competitors struggled to stay aloft.

"Manager" effects like these don't happen just at giant corporations. At this moment—as you read these words—managers at thousands and thousands of small businesses—diners, drycleaning stores, motels—are running their business well, with courteous, prompt, and first-class service, high-morale employees, and a minimum of problems like "My dinner's cold," or "You didn't press my pants." What do you think would happen if you took the competent managers out of those small businesses and dropped in managers without the training or skills to do their jobs? You know the answer, because you've probably experienced the effects yourself—businesses with untrained or unprepared staff, orders not prepared on time, lost reservations, or dirty rooms. About 90 percent of the new businesses started this year will fail within five years, and Dun & Bradstreet says the reason is generally "poor management."

The effect of good management is nothing short of remarkable. Take an underperforming—even chaotic—organization and install a skilled manager, and he or she soon can have the enterprise humming like a well-tuned machine. Take a successful enterprise that's been managed well for years by its proprietor—say, a neighborhood stationery store—and watch as a new, less-competent manager takes over. Shelves are suddenly in disarray, products are out of stock, and bills go unpaid as the new owner tries in vain to run the little store and its handful of employees.

All these enterprises—IBM, American Airlines, the diner, the motel, and the neighborhood store—are organizations. An **organization** consists of people with formally assigned roles who must work together to achieve stated goals.

Organizations needn't just be business firms; obviously the definition applies equally well to colleges, local governments, and to nonprofits like the American Red Cross, as well as to many other institutions. The U.S. government is an organization—certainly a not-for-profit one—and its head manager, or chief executive officer, until 2000 is President Bill Clinton.

Organizations, by their nature, cannot simply run themselves—they can't just "run on compressed air," as an engineer might joke. Review the definition of an organization again and you'll see why. Who would ensure that each of the people actually knew what to do? Who would see that they are trained? Who would hire them? Who would ensure that they work together, more or less harmoniously? Who would decide what the organization's goals would be, and then monitor whether each employee was doing his or her share to reach those goals?

All organizations are run by managers. A **manager** is someone who plans, organizes, leads, and controls the people and the work of the organization in such a way that the organization achieves its goals. **Management** refers to two things: (1) collectively to the managers of an organization; and (2) to the study of what managers do. This is a book about management. It is our hope and belief that carefully studying it will put you well on the road to being a better manager.

The Management Process

Management writers traditionally refer to the manager's four basic functions of planning, organizing, leading, and controlling as the **management process.** Following is a synopsis of what each entails (the rest of the book will cover each of these in detail).

PLANNING.   Planning is setting goals and deciding on courses of action, developing rules and procedures, developing plans (both for the organization and for those who work in it), and forecasting (that is, predicting or projecting what the future holds for the firm).

ORGANIZING.   Organizing entails identifying jobs to be done, hiring people to do them, establishing departments, delegating or pushing authority to subordinates, establishing a chain of command (in other words, channels of authority and communication), and coordinating the work of the manager's subordinates.

LEADING.   Leading means influencing other people to get the job done, maintaining morale, molding company culture, and managing conflicts and communication.

CONTROLLING.   Controlling is setting standards (such as sales quotas or quality standards), comparing actual performance with these standards, and then taking corrective actions as required.

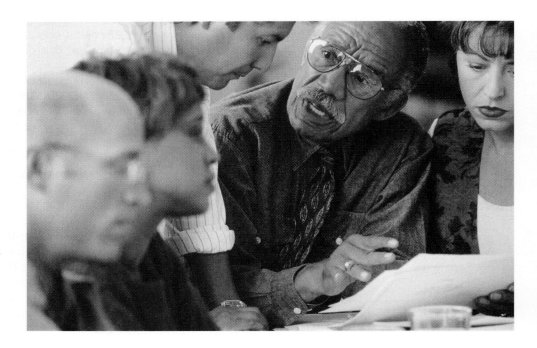

Managers get the job done by working with people, making leadership the key ingredient among many in the management task.

Types of Managers

Most organizations with which you are familiar contain several types of managers. In your college, for instance, there are presidents, vice presidents, deans, associate deans, and department chairs, as well as various administrators like human resource managers. At your place of work (if you work) you might find first-line supervisors, financial controllers, sales managers, plant managers, and top executives including the chief executive officer, president, and vice presidents. All these people are managers, because they all plan, organize, lead, and control the people and the work of that particular organization in such a way that their organization achieves its goals.

However, you would find that each of these managers spends his or her time quite differently depending on the specific type of manager he or she is. For convenience, we can roughly distinguish three types of managers, based on their *organizational level, position,* and *functional title*. They are illustrated in Table 1.1.

The managers at the top of an organization like IBM of course represent the firm's top management. These managers are usually referred to as **executives.** Functional titles include President, Chief Executive Officer, HR Vice President, and Chief Financial Officer.

Beneath this top management level and reporting to it may be one or more levels of middle managers, positions that typically have the term "manager" or "director" in their titles. (Particularly in larger companies like IBM, managers would report to directors, who in turn would report to top managers like vice presidents.) Examples of functional titles here include Production Manager, Sales Manager, HR Manager, and Finance Manager.

First-line managers are at the bottom management ladder rung. These managers are often called supervisors, and they might for instance include the Production Supervisors who actually supervise the assembly-line employees at Toyota as they carry out their day-to-day tasks.

■ TABLE 1.1 *Types of Managers*

BASED ON ORGANIZATIONAL LEVEL	BASED ON POSITION	BASED ON FUNCTIONAL TITLE (EXAMPLES)
Top Managers (Have managers as subordinates)	Executives	President Vice President, Production Vice President, Sales Vice President, HR Chief Financial Officer
Middle Managers (Have managers as subordinates)	Managers or Directors	Production Manager Sales Manager HR Manager Finance Manager
First-line Managers (Have non-managers as subordinates)	Supervisors	Production Supervisor Regional Sales Manager Assistant HR Manager Chief Bookkeeper

All managers have a lot in common. Whether top, or middle, or first-line, they all plan, organize, lead, and control the people and the work of their organizations in such a way that their organizations achieve their goals. And—of particular importance—all managers at all levels and with every functional title spend an enormous part of their day with people—talking, listening, influencing, motivating, and attending one-on-one conferences or committee meetings.[29] In fact, even chief executives (whom you might expect to be somewhat insulated from other people, up there in their executive suites) reportedly spend about three-quarters of their time dealing directly with other people.[30]

However, there are two big differences between the management levels. First, as you can see, executives and middle managers both have managers for subordinates; in other words, they are in charge of other managers. Supervisors have workers—non-managers—as subordinates.

Managers at different levels also use their time somewhat differently. Top managers typically spend more time planning and setting goals. Middle managers then take these goals (like "double sales in the next two years") and translate them into specific projects (like "hire two new salespeople and introduce three new products") for their subordinates to execute. First-line supervisors then concentrate on directing and controlling the employees who work on these projects.

Yet the manager's job is changing so fast that some—like Peter Drucker—say, "I'm not comfortable with the word manager anymore, because it implies subordinates."[31] Forces such as globalization and deregulation have so changed the nature of what managers do that in some respects the job today would be unrecognizable to a time traveler from the 1940s. For one thing, it is probably a lot more people-oriented, as the following examples illustrate.

The Behavioral Side of Management

Managing has always been a decidedly behavioral or people-oriented occupation, since managers do their work by interacting with others. Over 20 years ago, for instance, Professor Henry Mintzberg conducted a study of what managers actually do, in part by walking around and watching managers as they worked. Basically, Mintzberg found that as they went from task to task, managers wore various hats, and most of these hats or roles meant the managers had to deal with people:

The *Figurehead* Role: Every manager spends part of his or her time performing some duties of a ceremonial nature. For example, the president of the United States might have to greet representatives of the state legislature, a supervisor might attend the wedding of a front-desk clerk, or the sales manager might take an important client to lunch.

The *Leader* Role: Every manager must also function as a leader, motivating and encouraging his or her employees, for instance.[32]

The *Liaison* Role: Managers also spend a lot of time in contact with people outside their own departments, essentially acting as the liaison between their departments and other people within and outside the organization. For example, the assembly-line supervisor might field a question from the sales manager about how a new order is coming, or the vice president for sales might meet with the vice president of finance to make sure that a new customer has the credit required to place an order.

The *Spokesperson* Role: The manager is often the spokesperson for his or her organization. For example, the supervisor may have to keep the plant manager informed about the flow of work through the shop, or the president may make a speech to lobby the local county commissioners for permission to build a new plant on some unused land.

The *Negotiator* Role: Mintzberg found that managers also spend a lot of their time negotiating: the head of the airline tries to negotiate a new contract with the pilots' union, or the first-line supervisor negotiates a settlement to a grievance with the union's representative, for instance.

Managing Change

USING THE BEHAVIORAL SIDE OF MANAGEMENT TO MANAGE CHANGE AT ALLIED-SIGNAL

Chairman Lawrence A. Bossidy's people skills have had a remarkable effect on Allied-Signal, a huge industrial supplier of aerospace systems, automotive parts, and chemical products.[33] In 1991 he took over a troubled company that was "hemorrhaging cash."[34] After just three years under Bossidy, Allied-Signal's net income (profits) had doubled from $359 million to $708 million, profit margins had doubled, and the company's market value (the total value of its shares) had more than doubled as well, to almost $10 billion.

What did Bossidy do to bring about such a dramatic transformation in just three years? A lot of his changes were operational: under his guidance the company merged business units, closed factories, reduced suppliers from 9,000 to 3,000, and cut 19,000 salaried jobs from the payroll, for instance.[35]

But much of what Bossidy focused on was behavioral in nature. In other words, he focused on applying his knowledge of how people, as individuals and groups, act within organizations to help bring about change. For example, in his first two months on the job, "I talked to probably 5,000 employees. I would go to Los Angeles and speak to 500 people, then to Phoenix and talk to another 500. I would stand on a loading dock and speak to people and answer their questions. We talked about what was wrong and what we should do about it."[36] His job, as he saw it, was not just to cut jobs and merge operations, since actions like these would have only short-term effects on profitability. In the longer run, Bossidy knew, he had to excite his giant firm's many employees by promoting "our employees' ability to win," by uniting the top management team "with vision and values," and in general by convincing all his employees that there was a tremendous need to change—that their "platform was burning," as Bossidy put it.[37]

Trends like technological innovation, global competition, and deregulation have created an environment that's merciless to those companies and other organizations whose employees aren't fully committed to doing even more than their best, every day. That's why Bossidy says that when he looks for managers, he looks for ones who have a gift for working with and turning on employees:

> Today's corporation is a far cry from the old authoritarian vertical hierarchy I grew up in. The cross-functional ties among individuals and groups are increasingly important. There are channels of activity and communication. The

traditional bases of managerial authority are eroding. In the past, we used to reward the lone rangers in the corner offices because their achievements were brilliant even though their behavior was destructive. That day is gone. We need people who are better at persuading than at barking orders, who know how to coach and build consensus. Today, managers add value by brokering with people, not by presiding over empires.[38] ■

Building Three Core Processes

Two management experts, Sumantra Ghoshal and Christopher Bartlett, also emphasize the importance of the behavioral or people side of managing in creating a responsive and change-oriented company.[39] Successful managers today, say Bartlett and Ghoshal, can't afford to focus just on mechanical aspects of management work, like designing organization charts or drawing up plans. Instead successful managers cultivate three processes aimed at getting the company's employees to focus their attention on creating change. Specifically, these are the *entrepreneurial process,* the *competence-building process,* and the *renewal process.*

THE ENTREPRENEURIAL PROCESS. Entrepreneurship, say Bartlett and Ghoshal, refers to "the externally-oriented, opportunity-seeking attitudes that motivate employees to run their operations as if they own them."[40] In their study of 20 companies in Japan, the United States, and Europe, they found that successful managers focused much of their time and energy on getting employees to think of themselves as entrepreneurs, and on giving those employees the authority, support, and rewards that self-disciplined and largely self-directing employees should have to run their operations like their own.

THE COMPETENCE-BUILDING PROCESS. Bartlett and Ghoshal found that "in a world of converging technologies, large companies have to do more than match their smaller competitors' flexibility and responsiveness. They must also exploit their big-company advantages, which lie not only in scale economies but also in the depth and breadth of employees' talents and knowledge."[41] Successful managers therefore also devote much of their efforts to creating an environment that lets their employees' competence flourish: encouraging them to take on more responsibility; providing the education and training they need to build their self-confidence; and allowing them to make mistakes without fear of punishment, while coaching them and supporting them to learn from their mistakes. Part of the competence-building process, say these experts, is "shaping an environment for collaborative behavior."[42] This is done, for instance, by encouraging teamwork in which employees learn to work with one another, such that their confidence and competence rises, as does a football player's as the team successfully masters new plays and learns to anticipate each other's moves.

THE RENEWAL PROCESS. Successful managers also concentrate today on fostering what Bartlett and Ghoshal call a renewal process, one "designed to challenge a company's strategies and the assumptions behind them."[43] Managers, in other words, have to make sure they and all their employees guard against complacency. Employees should develop the habit of questioning why things are done

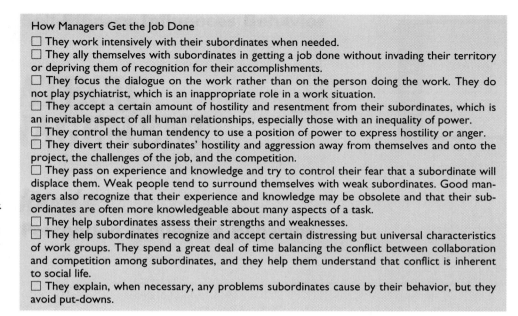

■ **FIGURE 1.2**
How Managers Get the Job Done

SOURCE: Reprinted by permission of *Harvard Business Review.* "How Managers Get the Job Done." From *Briefings from the Editors: Managing People, Ten Essential Behaviors,* January–February 1995.© 1995 by the President and Fellows of Harvard College; all rights reserved.

How Managers Get the Job Done
☐ They work intensively with their subordinates when needed.
☐ They ally themselves with subordinates in getting a job done without invading their territory or depriving them of recognition for their accomplishments.
☐ They focus the dialogue on the work rather than on the person doing the work. They do not play psychiatrist, which is an inappropriate role in a work situation.
☐ They accept a certain amount of hostility and resentment from their subordinates, which is an inevitable aspect of all human relationships, especially those with an inequality of power.
☐ They control the human tendency to use a position of power to express hostility or anger.
☐ They divert their subordinates' hostility and aggression away from themselves and onto the project, the challenges of the job, and the competition.
☐ They pass on experience and knowledge and try to control their fear that a subordinate will displace them. Weak people tend to surround themselves with weak subordinates. Good managers also recognize that their experience and knowledge may be obsolete and that their subordinates are often more knowledgeable about many aspects of a task.
☐ They help subordinates assess their strengths and weaknesses.
☐ They help subordinates recognize and accept certain distressing but universal characteristics of work groups. They spend a great deal of time balancing the conflict between collaboration and competition among subordinates, and they help them understand that conflict is inherent to social life.
☐ They explain, when necessary, any problems subordinates cause by their behavior, but they avoid put-downs.

as they are and whether it might not be better to disrupt the status quo and do things differently. And they need the people skills to deal productively with any arguments or conflicts that arise.

How Managers Get the Job Done— Through People

An ongoing study by Harvard business professor Renato Tagiuri also helps to illustrate how people-oriented is the job of managing today. How exactly do managers "get the job done"? As you can see in Figure 1.2, Tagiuri found that managers get their jobs done by working with and interacting with people—working intensively with their subordinates when needed, accepting that there's going to be a certain amount of hostility and resentment from their subordinates, helping subordinates assess their strengths and weaknesses, and dealing with the challenges of competition and conflict within their organizations, for instance.[44] Certainly planning, organizing, leading, and controlling are the basic functions that all managers perform. However, doing each of these things requires that the manager work with his or her people—that is the "behavioral side of management." Therefore, **leading** (which is the management function that focuses on the behavioral or people aspects of what managers do) can't just be viewed with planning, organizing, and controlling as one step in a sequence. "Leading" really applies to almost everything.

Rearranging the Management Process

This means we have to adjust our view of the management process, to see what managers actually do. Specifically (to repeat), the leading or behavioral side of what managers do is not just another step in the management process, but an integral part of almost everything the manager does. This is illustrated in Table 1.2.

MANAGEMENT FUNCTION	BEHAVIORAL (LEADERSHIP) SIDE OF THE MANAGEMENT FUNCTION: SOME EXAMPLES
Planning	Getting department heads to work together to craft a new strategic plan; working with small groups of employees to encourage more creative ways of looking at the company's situation; dealing with the interdepartmental conflicts that may arise when one department's plans may conflict with another's.
Organizing	Dealing with the questions of power and company politics that arise as employees in various departments jockey for positions of dominance; encouraging communication across departmental lines; understanding how personality, motivation, and skills can influence who should or should not be put in charge of various departments.
Controlling	Influencing subordinates to correct "out of control" behavior; dealing with the fact that employees may be motivated to subvert the control system to make themselves look better in the short run; and using effective interpersonal communication skills to encourage employees to change the way they do things.

NOTE: Leading, the management function that focuses on the behavioral or people aspects of what managers do, is not just another step in the management process but an integral part of everything the manager does.

Understanding Behavior at Work

Since the behavioral side of managing is so important to what managers do, much of this book will focus on understanding behavior at work.

WHAT IS ORGANIZATIONAL BEHAVIOR? **Organizational behavior (OB)** has been defined as ". . . the study and application of knowledge about how people—as individuals and as groups—act within organizations."[45] As used in this book, organizational behavior isn't simply a commonsense, seat-of-the-pants approach to dealing with people at work; it is a scientific discipline in which research studies are used to help show managers how to build effective practices in their own or others' organizations. OB, in other words, is an *applied* science.

As the study and application of knowledge about how people—as individuals and as groups—act within organizations, the science of OB gives managers a useful set of tools they can use at several different levels. For example, OB helps managers look at how and why *individuals* in organizations behave as they do—how, say, a subordinate's personality might make her particularly suited (or unsuited) for a job that has to be done.

OB also helps managers understand the dynamics of **interpersonal behavior**—such as when the manager and a subordinate seem to keep talking and talking although neither seems to hear what the other is saying. Managers are also always interested in OB's insights into what makes small **groups** behave as they do—such as when a worker restricts his or her output to win coworkers' approval. OB helps managers understand **intergroup behavior** as well, such as how to manage potentially lethal conflict between, say, the production and sales departments. OB findings and insights also help managers at the *overall organization* level, as when a manager uses the results of a companywide morale survey to better understand how to implement a major organizational change like that achieved by Allied-Signal's Lawrence Bossidy.

THE BUILDING BLOCKS OF OB.   What topics are included within the overall discipline of OB? A representative list would include the following.

- Individual differences between people, for instance in terms of needs, values, motivation, attitudes, personality, and perception.
- The sources and management of power and politics in organizations.
- Groups and teams within organizations and related topics like how to build group cohesiveness and reduce intergroup conflicts.
- Leadership, specifically how to influence subordinates to willingly attain goals that you've set for them.
- Conflict resolution, including the sources of interpersonal, group, and intergroup conflict and how to manage such conflicts.
- Organizational culture, and specifically how to influence the values that are the signposts employees use to decide what to do and what not to do within their organizations.
- Job satisfaction, for instance, why providing some employees with higher pay might temporarily make them more satisfied but not increase their motivation to do their jobs.
- Work stress, in particular the sources of stress and how to manage stress so that its effects are beneficial and not crippling to the people in the organization.
- Job design, for instance, the pros and cons of giving employees enlarged and more challenging jobs to do.
- Interpersonal and organizational communication, including barriers and ways to overcome them.
- Organizational change and development, including why employees may resist change and how to cultivate an atmosphere in which change can successfully be implemented.

The OB in Action Features

Managers cannot separate the leadership or behavioral parts of their jobs from the managerial parts. For example, planning is a management activity, but getting department heads to work together to cooperatively produce a new plan is a behavioral one. Much of the OB material you'll need as a manager to more effectively manage is concentrated in the six leadership chapters in part IV of this book, chapters 10 through 15. However, it is also important to see how OB applies to the manager's work in each and every chapter of the book.

This is why you'll find OB in Action features throughout all the chapters in this book. Each illustrates how OB studies have been used by real managers to do a better job of managing. Perhaps the best way to explain how these work is to turn to the following example.

Organizational Behavior in Action

DO YOU WANT TO BE A MANAGER?

If you're thinking of being a manager, there's a wealth of OB research to help you decide whether that's the occupation for which you're best suited.

PERSONALITY AND INTERESTS. Career counseling expert John Holland says that personality (including values, motives, and needs) is an important determinant of career choice. Specifically, he says there are six basic "personal orientations" that determine the sorts of careers to which people are drawn. Research with his Vocational Preference Test (VPT) suggests that almost all successful managers fit at least one of the two following personality types or orientations from that group.

> **Social orientation.** Social people are attracted to careers that involve working with people in a helpful or facilitative way (managers as well as others like clinical psychologists and social workers would exhibit this orientation). Generally speaking, socially oriented people find it easy to talk with all kinds of people, are good at helping people who are upset or troubled, are skilled at explaining things to others, and enjoy doing social things like helping others with their personal problems, teaching, and meeting new people.[46]

> **Enterprising orientation.** "Enterprising" people tend to like working with people in a supervisory or persuasive way, in order to achieve some goal. They especially enjoy verbal activities aimed at influencing others (not just managers but lawyers and public relations executives would exhibit this orientation). Enterprising people often characterize themselves as being good public speakers, as having reputations for being able to deal with difficult people, as successfully organizing the work of others, and as being ambitious and assertive. They enjoy influencing others, selling things, serving as an officer of a group, and supervising the work of others.

COMPETENCIES. It's not just your interests but your competencies too that will help determine how successful you might be at managing others. Professor Edgar Schein says that career planning is a continuing process of discovery—one in which a person slowly develops a clearer occupational self-concept in terms of what his or her talents, abilities, motives, and values are. Schein also says that as you learn more about yourself, it becomes apparent that you have a dominant **career anchor,** a concern or value that you will not give up if a choice has to be made.

Based on his study of MIT graduates, Schein concluded that managers had a strong **managerial competence** career anchor.[47] These people showed a strong motivation to become managers, "and their career experience enables them to believe that they have the skills and values necessary to rise to such general management positions." A management position of high responsibility is these people's ultimate goal. When pressed to explain why they believed they had the skills required to gain such positions, many said they saw their competencies in a combination of three areas: (1) analytical competence (ability to identify, analyze, and solve problems under conditions of incomplete information and uncertainty); (2) interpersonal competence (ability to influence, supervise, lead, manipulate, and control people at all levels); and (3) emotional competence (the capacity to be stimulated by emotional and interpersonal crises rather than exhausted or debilitated by them, and the capacity to bear high levels of responsibility without becoming paralyzed).

ACHIEVEMENTS. Organizational behavior research also suggests that you might gain some insight into your prospects as a manager by looking closely at your achievements to date. For example, industrial/organizational psychologists at AT&T conducted two long-term studies of managers to determine how their pre-management achievements were related to their managerial success on the job.[48]

Some of their findings were not too surprising. For example, employees who had gone to college showed much greater potential when first hired for middle and upper management positions than did those who had not gone to college, and eight years later the differences between these two groups were even more pronounced. Specifically, those who went to college rose (on average) much faster and higher in management than did those in the noncollege sample. College grades were important, too: People with higher college grades showed greater potential for promotion early in their careers, and in fact they rose higher in management than did those with lower college grades.

Also, perhaps not too surprisingly, the quality of the college the person attended meant a lot more early in the person's management career than it did later. Those who had attended what were considered to be better-quality colleges at first ranked higher as potential managers, but within several years "college quality" seemed to have little effect on who was promoted and who was not.

The manager's college major did seem to have a big effect, however, and here there were some surprises. Managers who had majored in humanities and social sciences initially scored higher as potential managers and eventually moved faster and further up the corporate ladder.[49] Business administration majors ranked second, and math, science, and engineering majors ranked third.

What accounted for the surprising performance of the humanities and social science majors? At least in this study, conducted in one company, these majors turned out to score the highest in decision making, intellectual ability, written communication skills, creativity in solving business problems, and motivation for advancement. Both the humanities and social science majors and the business administration majors ranked higher in leadership ability, oral communication skills, interpersonal skills, and flexibility than did the math, science, and engineering majors.[50] Findings like these obviously don't suggest that business and science majors are lost—do not switch majors! They may just be unique to this specific group of managers, or to AT&T. However, they may suggest that, whatever your major, it's important for future managers to work on improving things like their decision-making, creativity, and written communication skills. ▪

The Future Is Now: Snapshots of the Modern Organization

To fit today's fast-changing, globally competitive, and increasingly high-tech environments, a new breed of organization is arising. It goes by many names: the **postentrepreneurial organization,**[51] the **information-based organization,**[52] and the **postmodern organization.**[53] Whatever it is called, a new kind of business firm has been born, one for which *responsiveness* is a top priority. Probably no single firm exemplifies all the traits of a postmodern organization. However, examples of firms that exemplify specific features abound. Let's close this chapter by looking at a few.

ABB Asea Brown Boveri

Zurich-based electrical equipment maker ABB Asea Brown Boveri is a good example of a firm that "dis-organized itself to compete in the fast-moving global market."[54] ABB did four things to make itself super-responsive: It organized around mini-units, empowered its workers, flattened its hierarchy, and eliminated central staff. How did ABB do it?

First, within two years of taking over this $30 billion firm, former Chairman Percy Barnevik "dis-organized" its 215,000 employees into 5,000 minicompanies, each averaging only about 50 workers each.[55] For example, the ABB hydropower unit in Finland is a minicompany that serves just its own Finnish customers. Such direct customer contact transformed the unit into a highly customer-focused little business, one in which employees' efforts are all centered on its local market. Each of ABB's 50-person units is run by its own manager and three or four lieutenants. Such small units are very manageable; it's a lot easier to monitor what everyone is doing when there are only 50 people to keep track of than when there are 1,000 people, let alone 5,000 or 10,000.

Next, to speed decision making, the 5,000 minicompanies were made autonomous and their employees empowered with the authority to make most of their own business decisions. They also have the self-confidence and motivation to do so. For example, if a customer has a complaint about a $50,000 machine, a mini-company employee has the authority to approve a replacement on the spot, rather than having to wait for review by several levels of management. Giving employees this much authority means that ABB's 5,000 businesses must be staffed by, as management expert Tom Peters put it, "high-performance team members," highly skilled employees with the capacity and commitment to make those big decisions.

Third, unlike most big firms, ABB's 215,000-employee organization has only three management levels (a comparably sized company might have seven or eight). There is a 13-member top-management executive committee based in Zurich. Below this is a 250-member executive level that includes country managers and executives in charge of groups of businesses. Last is a third level consisting of the 5,000 mini-company managers and their management teams. ABB thus flattened the hierarchy or chain of command. By slicing out layers of management and letting lower-level employees make their own on-the-spot decisions, ABB empowered its employees to respond more quickly to customers' needs and competitors' moves.

Fourth, since decision making was pushed down to front-line ABB employees, ABB could eliminate most headquarters staff. For example, when Barnevik became CEO in 1980, he found a total of 2,000 people working at headquarters, basically reviewing and analyzing (and slowing down) the decisions of the firm's lower-level employees. Within a few months, Barnevik reduced the total headquarters staff to 200—and he reduced its advisory staff from 800 to 25. Similarly, he reduced German ABB headquarters staff in Mannheim from 1,600 to 100.

Responsiveness is the net effect of all these managerial changes: A lean, flat organization is staffed with highly committed employees organized into small, empowered teams, each able to quickly respond to competitors' moves and customers' needs with no need to wait for approval from headquarters.

Saturn Corporation

One of the most responsive and progressive companies today is part of the huge General Motors Corporation, which many management experts still use as an example of yesterday's unresponsive, bureaucratic organization.

Its team-based organization is one thing that sets the GM subsidiary, Saturn Corporation, apart. For example, virtually all the work on the shop floor is organized around work teams of 10 to 12 employees. Each team is completely responsible for a task, such as installing door units, checking electrical systems, or maintaining automated machines.

These work teams don't have supervisors in the traditional sense. Instead, the teams' highly trained workers do their own hiring, control their own budgets, monitor the quality of their own work, and generally manage themselves. Are too many of the door parts not fitting right? Then the team must find the problem and get the parts supplier to solve it. Is there a co-worker who is always late? Then the team must discipline him or her in order to manage its own (and its team members') time.

AT&T

AT&T has undergone tremendous management changes in the past decade. In 1984, the U.S. government split the huge AT&T local phone monopoly into seven regional operating companies (the "Baby Bells"). That left AT&T with the long-distance phone business, and with Western Electric, the telephone equipment maker.[56] Decades of operating as a regulated monopoly (with virtually no competition) had made AT&T slow and bureaucratic. Deregulation and divestiture meant that it had to get moving—and fast—if it wanted to compete with the likes of MCI. In the process, AT&T has moved to remake itself into a postmodern organization, by downsizing, improving internal communications, empowering workers, and changing employees' values.

Here's a synopsis of what AT&T did. First, the company eliminated 140,000 jobs—and the employees who went with them. Chairman Robert Allen also reorganized AT&T to promote communication between the firm's units and to dramatically speed up decision making. AT&T was organized into three major business groups: the telephone network itself, makers of equipment for the telecommunications network, and makers of user products (like telephones and answering machines). The heads of these three groups (along with the company's top financial officer) comprise a four-person presidency known as the "Operations Committee." Communication is also encouraged by having lots of interdepartmental teams. These teams "mix it up, get people talking, and figure out the businesses and structures that AT&T as a company will need."[57]

AT&T managers also empower their employees. For example, the president of AT&T's global business communications systems unit reportedly not only never shuts his office door—he had the lock removed.[58] He wants and expects his employees to interact with him often—"I am not a boss," he says—and prefers to be called "Coach." His job, as he sees it, is not to manage a group of subordinates. Instead, he wants to get what he calls his "associates" to focus on their customers' needs. His job is to make sure he gets employees the training, authority, resources, and self-confidence they need to satisfy those customer needs.

None of this, Allen knew, would be possible without instilling new business values throughout AT&T. Allen says that one of his highest priorities today is defining and disseminating the new values AT&T will need to compete in the new millenium. These include respect for individuals, dedication to helping customers, integrity, innovation, and teamwork.[59]

Today, AT&T continues to change, and fast. A new president, John R. Walter, lasted barely a year before being ousted by the board of directors. A top-to-bottom review of AT&T's most senior managers and business plans is taking place. At AT&T, as at most other firms today, change is the order of the day.[60]

Tomorrow's Management Today

Let's briefly summarize where we stand. Organizations today need to grapple with a number of revolutionary forces: accelerating product and technological change, globalized competition, deregulation, political instability, demographic changes, and trends toward a service society and the information age. Forces like these have changed the playing field on which firms must compete. In particular, they have dramatically increased the need for firms to be responsive, flexible, and capable of competing and reacting rapidly in a global marketplace.

Firms like ABB, Saturn, and AT&T are in the vanguard of thousands of other firms that are re-creating themselves to fit these new conditions. From their experiences, and from those of others, here is a summary of what management experts believe "the new management" will look like.

THE AVERAGE COMPANY WILL BE SMALLER, EMPLOYING FEWER PEOPLE. More people will set up businesses for themselves, and many firms like GM and IBM will continue to downsize or break themselves up. Even within big firms (like ABB), the operating units will be divided into small, self-contained mini-units.

Cypress Semiconductor is an example. Tom Rogers, president of this California firm, believes that large organizations stifle innovation. So when a new product must be developed he doesn't do it within the existing corporation. Instead, he creates a separate start-up company under the Cypress umbrella. "I would rather see our billion-dollar company of the 1990s be ten $100-million companies, all strong, growing, healthy and aggressive as hell," Rogers says. "The alternative is an aging billion-dollar company that spends more time defending its turf than growing." True to his words, Rogers already has four successful start-ups under development.[61]

THE TRADITIONAL ORGANIZATION STRUCTURE WILL BECOME MORE TEAM-BASED AND "BOUNDARYLESS."[62] As at AT&T, the new organization will stress cross-functional teams and interdepartmental communication. There will be a corresponding de-emphasis on "sticking to the chain of command" to get decisions made. At General Electric, Chairman Jack Welch talks of the boundaryless organization, in which employees do not identify with separate departments but instead interact with whomever they must to get the job done.

EMPLOYEES WILL BE EMPOWERED TO MAKE MORE DECISIONS. Work will require constant learning, "higher-order" thinking, and much more worker commitment. The result for employees will be more empowerment and less of a 9-to-5 mentality. Experts like Karl Albrecht argue for turning the typical organization upside down. They say today's organization should put the customer on top and emphasize that every move the company makes must be geared toward satisfying the customer's needs. To do so, management must empower its front-line employees—the front desk clerks at the hotel, the cabin attendants on the Delta plane, and the assemblers at Saturn—with the authority to respond quickly to the customer's needs. The main purpose of managers in this "upside-down" organization is to serve the frontline employees, to see that they have what they need to do their jobs—and thus to serve the customers.

FLATTER ORGANIZATIONS WILL BE THE NORM. Instead of the pyramid-shaped organization with its seven or more layers of management, flat organizations with just three or four levels will prevail. Many companies have already cut the management layers from a dozen to six or fewer, and with them the number of managers.[63] As the remaining managers are left with more people to supervise, they will be less able to meddle in the work of their subordinates, who will thus have more autonomy.

WORK ITSELF—ON THE FACTORY FLOOR, IN THE OFFICE—WILL BE ORGANIZED AROUND TEAMS AND PROCESSES RATHER THAN SPECIALIZED FUNCTIONS. On the plant floor, for instance, workers won't just have the job of installing the same door handle over and over again. Instead, they'll be part of multifunction teams, ones that manage their own budgets and control their own quality.

THE BASES OF POWER WILL CHANGE. In these new organizations, says management theorist Rosabeth Moss Kanter, leaders will no longer be able to rely on their formal positions or authority to get their jobs done.[64] Instead, "success depends increasingly on tapping into sources of good ideas, on figuring out whose collaboration is needed to act on those ideas, and on working with both to produce results. In short, the new managerial work implies very different ways of obtaining and using power."[65] Peter Drucker puts it this way: "You have to learn to manage in situations where you don't have command authority, where you are neither controlled nor controlling."[66] In other words, managers will have to win the respect and commitment of their highly trained and empowered employees.

THE NEW ORGANIZATION WILL BE KNOWLEDGE BASED. Management specialist Tom Peters says the new organizations will be "knowledge based," the way consulting firms and hospitals are today. Here teams of highly trained and educated professionals apply their knowledge to clients' problems, working in an atmosphere in which they direct and discipline their own activities.[67]

One thing this means is that managers' big role will be to help their employees get their jobs done by training and coaching them, removing roadblocks, and getting them the resources they need: You can't simply "boss" teams of professionals.

This highlights one big difference between the old and the new manager. Yesterday's manager thinks of himself or herself as a "manager" or "boss," whereas the new manager thinks of himself or herself as a "sponsor," "team leader," or "internal consultant." The old-style manager makes most decisions alone; the new one invites others to join in the decision making. The old-style manager hoards information to build his or her personal power. The new manager shares information to help subordinates get their jobs done.[68]

THE NEW COMPANY WILL STRESS VISION AND VALUES. Formulating a clear vision and values to which employees can commit themselves will be more important than ever. Managers will have to communicate clear values regarding what is important and unimportant, and regarding what employees should and should not do. As GE's CEO Jack Welch has said:

> Every organization needs values, but a lean organization needs them even more. When you strip away the support system of staffs and layers, people need to relearn their habits and expectations or else the stress will just overwhelm them . . . values [are] what enable people to guide themselves through that kind of change.[69]

Other experts agree. Peter Drucker says today's organizations—staffed as they are by professionals and other employees who largely control their own behavior—require "clear, simple, common objectives that translate into particular actions." In other words, they need a clear vision of where the firm is heading.[70] Even without a lot of supervisors to guide them, employees can then be steered by the company's vision and values.

MANAGERS MUST BE CHANGE AGENTS. As GE's Jack Welch puts it, "You've got to be on the cutting edge of change. You can't simply maintain the status quo, because somebody's always coming from another country with another product, or consumers' tastes change, or the cost structure does, or there's a technology breakthrough. If you are not fast and adaptable, you are vulnerable."[71]

LEADERSHIP WILL BE MORE IMPORTANT. Empowered workers, service jobs, and the need to get workers thinking like owners will put a premium on the

Explosion of Technological Innovation
- Vast numbers of new patents
- Three new Web sites "born" each minute
- New computers outdated in six months
- New high-tech factories

Globalization of Markets and Competition
- Staggering number of new competitors
- New pressures for quality and productivity
- New opportunities

Deregulation
- Banking
- Telecoms
- Airlines

Changing Demographics
- More diversity
- Two-wage-earner families
- Increasing global workforce

New Political Systems
- Former Soviet Union moves to capitalism
- Rise of European Union, NAFTA, Asia

Leads to

Uncertainty, Turbulence, Rapid Change
- More consumer choices
- Mergers and divestitures
- Joint ventures
- More complexity
- Short product life cycles
- Market fragmentation
- More uncertainty for managers
- Record number of business failures

So Companies Must Be

Fast, Responsive, Adaptive
- Flat organizations
- Downsized
- Quality-conscious
- Empowered
- Smaller units
- Decentralized
- Human-capital oriented
- Boundaryless
- Values- and vision-oriented
- Team-based

■ **FIGURE 1.3**
Fundamental Changes Facing Managers
A series of forces—globalized competition, technology revolution, new competitors, and changing tastes—are creating outcomes that include more uncertainty, more choices, and more complexity. The result is that the organizational winners of today and tomorrow will have to be responsive, smaller, flatter, and oriented toward adding value through people.

"leading" portion of the manager's job. Understanding how to work with and through people and how to use behavioral science concepts and techniques at work will be more important than ever before.

On to the Future

Figure 1.3 summarizes where **21st-century managing** is heading, and the forces propelling it there. All these forces (on the left of the figure), including deregulation, technological revolution, new competitors, and changing tastes are interacting with one another to create a new and rapidly changing context for doing business. This has led to outcomes like demands for more quality and responsiveness and to more uncertainty for managers. As a result, the company winners today and tomorrow will have to be designed and managed to be as fast and responsive as possible.

With that in mind, a main theme of this book is how managers can use planning, organizing, leading, and controlling to make their firms more responsive.

SUMMARY

1. Managers and the organizations they manage have to confront rapid change and unpredictability today. Trends contributing to this change and unpredictability include technological innovation, globalization, deregulation, new political systems, a new workforce, more service-oriented jobs, and a new emphasis on "knowledge work."
2. An organization consists of people who have formally assigned roles and who must work together to achieve the organization's goals. Organizations needn't be just business firms.
3. Organizations cannot simply run themselves. Instead, they are run by managers. A manager is someone who plans, organizes, leads, and controls the people and the work of the organization in such a way that the organization achieves its goals.
4. Management writers traditionally refer to the manager's four basic functions of planning, organizing, leading, and controlling as the management process.
5. We can classify managers based on an organizational level (top, middle, or first-line), position (executives, managers or directors, or supervisors), and functional title (vice president of production, sales manager, or chief bookkeeper). All managers get their work done through people and by planning, organizing, leading, and controlling. Top managers spend more time planning and setting goals, while lower-level managers concentrate more on implementing those goals and directing and controlling employees to achieve them.
6. Managing has always been a behavioral or people-oriented occupation, since almost everything a manager does involves interacting with and influencing people. The bottom line is that the leading, or "people," or behavioral, side of what managers do is not just another step in the management process, but an integral part of almost everything the manager does.
7. Organizational behavior is the study and application of knowledge about how people—as individuals and as groups—act within organizations. In this book we'll emphasize how managers can use organizational behavior knowledge to do a better job of managing.
8. Companies like ABB Asea Brown Boveri, Saturn, and AT&T illustrate the new organization of today and the 21st century, in which responsiveness is now a top priority and effective leadership is extraordinarily important.

KEY TERMS

globalization
organization
manager
management
management process
executives
first-line managers

leading
organizational behavior
  (OB)
interpersonal behavior
groups
intergroup behavior
career anchor

managerial competence
postentrepreneurial
  organization
information-based
  organization
postmodern organization
21st-century managing

SELF-TEST

TRUE / FALSE QUESTIONS

1 T F Only a few managers in the largest companies are facing rapid change and unpredictability in their environments.

2 T F One of the primary reasons for "downsizing" is so companies can improve their competitive efficiency.

3 T F The rate of globalization for businesses worldwide has been phenomenal in the last few years.

4 T F One aspect of change for organizations has been the increase in regulations being established in country after country.

5 T F The ethnic group estimated to grow the most as part of the U.S. labor force is African Americans.

6 T F The shift from an industrial economy to a service and knowledge-based economy is creating a growing emphasis on "human capital."

7 T F Competition-driven innovation demands more highly skilled employees than a stable environment with limited competition.

8 T F All organizations are run by managers.

9 T F Based on a study of what managers actually do, three roles emerged: the figurehead, the leader, and the liaison.

10 T F The organizational process consists of four basic processes: planning, organizing, leading, and controlling.

MULTIPLE-CHOICE QUESTIONS

1 Which of the following is not noted in the text as a major factor in "managing in an era of change"?
  a. technological innovation
  b. globalization
  c. stable political systems
  d. changing demographics and the new global workforce

2 According to the text, if we include non-Hispanic white women in our demographic projections, women and minorities will account for more than _____ percent of the labor force's recent growth:
  a. 25
  b. 47
  c. 73
  d. 90

3 The two primary reasons for U.S. firms transferring their operations abroad are:

  a. cheaper labor and more competitive labor markets.
  b. skilled labor and stable political climates.
  c. cheaper labor and skilled labor.
  d. skilled labor and limited growth in the U.S. economy.

4 A manager is someone who plans, organizes, leads, and _____ the _____ and the _____ of the organization so it can achieve its _____:
  a. manages, production, work, mission.
  b. controls, people, work, goals.
  c. controls, mission, goals, work.
  d. controls, people, production, competitive edge.

5 We can distinguish among three types of managers based on the managers':
  a. organizational level.
  b. position.
  c. functional title.
  d. all of the above are correct.

6 In Mintzberg's analysis of what managers actually do, the role that involves motivating and encouraging employees is called:
   a. figurehead.
   b. liaison.
   c. negotiator.
   d. leader.

7 According to management experts Sumantra and Bartlett, managers should cultivate all but which of the following processes in building the organization's core?
   a. bureaucratic process
   b. entrepreneurial process
   c. competence-building process
   d. renewal process

8 Which of the processes of management is "*not* just another step in the management process, but *an integral part of almost everything the manager does*"?
   a. planning

   b. organizing
   c. leading
   d. controlling

9 What has been defined as ". . . the study and application of knowledge about how people—as individuals and as groups—act within organizations"?
   a. organizational theory
   b. systems analysis
   c. organizational behavior
   d. none of the above

10 According to a recent study, managers who had majored in _____ and social sciences initially scored higher as potential managers and eventually moved faster and farther up the corporate ladder.
   a. humanities
   b. business
   c. engineering
   d. science

CRITICAL THINKING EXERCISES

1 The traditional organization is usually depicted as a pyramid-shaped hierarchy with authority and decision making flowing from the top down. As this chapter has pointed out, the changing environment demands that new forms of organization be designed. Your assignment is to graphically depict some new organizational designs. Draw whatever shapes you think represent the boundaryless, team-focused, and process-oriented organizations that are evolving. Then write a brief narrative describing what you have drawn and what you think the implications behind your designs are.

2 The world today is very different from the business world of even 10 years ago. Your audience is the newly "downsized" employees of IBM, AT&T, and other large companies that survived their companies' downsizing, but who are now confused by the new and evolving rules of the corporate game. As a student of today's perspective, explain to them the "new rules" for corporate survival based on the information presented in this chapter. Write a one-page report describing the business world today, and a second page predicting how it might evolve in the next 10 years.

EXPERIENTIAL EXERCISES

1 The Internet is a major feature of today's business world. Visit the Internet home page of one of the companies discussed in this first chapter and explore what it has to offer and what (if anything) it says about how the company is managed. Then write up a one-page description of the site, explaining to customers and shareholders how the firm is managed.

2 An excellent way to find out about entrepreneurship is to talk to an entrepreneur. By asking your professor, other professors, the Small Business Administration in your region, or another small business organization such as the Small Business Chamber of Commerce, you should be able to identify an entrepreneur or entrepreneurs who have started a business in the last five years. Contact the person

and conduct an informational interview. Some questions you might want to ask are: (1) What did it take to establish the business? (2) Did you have a business plan? (3) Where did you get your financing? (4) What management challenges do you face today? (5) How did you develop your human resource policies? Also ask any other questions that specifically fit the type of business. Then prepare a page on the major points you found out about entrepreneurship and be ready to present your findings in class or in a small group.

   You may want to do this project with two or three other students and divide the labor according to expertise.

   Use references like *Inc.* or *Fast Company* magazines that are devoted to entrepreneurship. These resources may help you find an entrepreneur or decide what questions you want to ask your entrepreneur.

DIVERSITY CASE

We saw in this chapter that the workforce and the customer base that most companies deal with are becoming increasingly diverse. Managers must, therefore, be skilled at understanding how to deal with people with diverse ethnic, gender, racial, cultural, and other backgrounds. To help you develop this skill, a Diversity Case like the following can be found at the end of each chapter.

WHAT IS THE FUTURE OF TREND MICRO?

Managing in the 21st century will not be like what it was in the previous 100 years or, certainly, the previous 10,000. A global, knowledge-based market has evolved.

No one knows that better than Steve Chang, native of Taiwan, graduate of Lehigh University (PA), and entrepreneur in California and Taipei. Founder of Trend Micro, Chang is a computer "virus doctor." Realizing the threat from the more than 5,000 known computer viruses (programs that intentionally disrupt a computer's normal functions) and the potential profit in thwarting that threat, Chang used money from the sale of another business to start Trend Micro in Los Angeles. Once the company was up and running, he moved back home where there is a labor pool of skilled engineers at salaries about half the level of their U.S. counterparts. In August 1996 alone, 800,000 people logged onto his "virus alert" Web site to protect their computers. In all, over 7 million computer users rely on Chang's protective software.

After much trial and error Chang has become a global force, licensing his products to Intel and Novell, who sell it under their names. Facing the endless challenge from some 200 new viruses discovered every month, Chang sells his new program for Microsoft Windows 95 software, called PC-cillin, in 18 languages under the Trend brand name. Chang has also given Netscape the right to use Trend's antivirus software in its server products. A Japanese conglomerate, Softbank, plans to buy a 40 percent stake in Chang's company.

Questions

1 In what ways is Trend Micro a model of 21st century management?
2 What issues facing U.S. companies are reflected in the story of Trend Micro?
3 How does the United States compete with the salary differences and mobility of Chang's organization?
4 What do you think the future holds for Trend Micro? Why?

Source: Louis Kraar, "Trend Micro," *Fortune,* 28 October 1996, 162–63.

STRATEGY CASE

Every company needs a strategy. A strategy is a plan that states how the company is going to use its strengths to compete with other firms in its industry. For example, the strategy of the Coca Cola Company is basically to specialize in producing and selling through bottlers the ingredients for high-quality drinks, such as Coca Cola and Minute Maid juices.

One reason a strategy is important is that it provides a framework within which the manager makes his or her other decisions. For example, Coca Cola's managers know that their strategy means they should not waste much time thinking about selling products other than high-quality drinks. That is because selling other products would not be consistent with their company's strategy. It's therefore important for managers and future managers to get used to thinking about how their management decisions—such as who to hire and how to motivate employees—fit with or are consistent with the company's strategy. You'll find a Strategy Case like the following at the end of each chapter.

UNITED WE OWN, DIVIDED WE LOSE

When the airline industry was deregulated in 1978 there was a predictable fallout. Companies went bankrupt, merged, and struggled to realign themselves. Price wars, strikes, and competition from tiny air carriers such as Morris Air and innovators like Southwest made the market very competitive. What strategies do companies use to survive in such a dynamic environment?

Many traditional carriers were looking for ways to stay alive. United was in trouble, and a radically new strategy called employee ownership was needed. In 1994 the employees agreed to take pay cuts averaging 17 percent in return for 55 percent ownership of the company and three seats on the board of directors. Through this new arrangement, United's skies have become much friendlier, with efficiency rising, grievances falling, market share inching up, and profit margins holding strong.

However, making major changes in a company isn't like waving a magic wand. For starters, the flight attendants refused to take a pay cut and join the team. In addition, the pilots are at loggerheads with management rather than working as a team. They want more money and more workplace initiatives to improve morale, while management wants competitive compensation and would like to put some employee pay at risk through profit sharing. Management and the pilots are now trying to negotiate, and the stakes are high for the firm's 84,000 employees and their $5 billion company.

Questions

I   What impact do you think United's strategy has on the firm's planning, organizing, leading, and controlling?

2   What do you think is changing United's problems?

3   What do you think management should do?

4   Do you think the turmoil in the airline industry is typical of most industries today? Why or why not?

SOURCE: Susan Chandler, "United They Don't Stand," *Business Week*, 3 March 1997, 86–88.

THE BUSINESS TEAM, INC.

THEIR FIRST ASSIGNMENT

Like most professors who teach the business program's final, capstone course in strategic management, Professor Cynthia Thomas liked to split her class into groups of five or six students, who then spent the rest of the semester analyzing cases and developing a strategic plan for a company in the vicinity of State University.

From the day they got together to analyze their first case and create their presentation, the five members of Group 1—Maria, Sid, Len, Hal, and Ruth—seemed to hit it off, and during the rest of the semester their friendship grew. Maria was a specialist in accounting and planned on earning her CPA and then perhaps joining a "big six" accounting firm. Sid was a finance major, whose professors described him as "one of the sharpest students ever." Len was a sales and marketing major with a particularly strong interest in small businesses. Hal was majoring in production and operations management and was also a skilled mathematician. Ruth's specialty was human resource management, an area in which her intelligence and understanding of people made her especially effective.

Something students generally learn in analyzing strategy management cases is that problems and solutions rarely affect only one department in a company. For example, one case this team of students worked on involved developing a new strategy for K-Mart, the large discount firm that was being battered by the increasingly successful Wal-Mart. When group members thought about changing K-Mart's computer systems to make the company more competitive, they immediately found that other departments would feel the change. For instance, the HR department would have to hire new computer people and retrain current employees to use the new systems; the finance department would have to determine if buying new computers was cost effective; and the accounting department would have to change most of the accounting control paperwork in the company to make it consistent with the new computer system. The group also learned the importance of teamwork. As the team analyzed company after company, the confidence of these five young business majors grew. By the end of the semester they'd decided that after graduation they wanted to set up a consulting firm together.

The Business Team, Inc., is the company they formed. The idea behind the company was to create a consulting firm in which each person on the five-person team would bring his or her expertise to the analysis of client problems. Clients would get complete and comprehensive top-down solutions. A Business Team, Inc., Case can be found at the end of each chapter.

The Business Team, Inc., didn't have to wait long for their first client. The hurricane that blew away thousands of homes in Dade County, Florida, created a tremendous demand for plumbing supplies. The storm turned out to be a boon to Len's parents, who ran a small plumbing-supply business. Sales mushroomed from $4 million before the hurricane to almost $8 million two years after. Hernandez Plumbing Supply Company went almost overnight from a traditional "mom-and-pop" operation to a sizable company with nearly 100 employees. Len's parents, who ran the company, knew they needed some management advice, and fast. They had never had the advantages of college and formal management training. Here are the questions Len's parents posed to The Business Team, Inc. Help the team answer them.

Questions

I   "What do managers do? Exactly which of the management functions described in management textbooks do we as business owners need to address as we look at our company?"

2   "We have almost 100 employees, split between plumbing-parts retail-store employees and delivery people. Most of our employees work in the store or the adjacent warehouse. How do you think we should organize our company, and what sorts of managers would you appoint to run a company like ours?"

3   "We already see that by getting bigger we're losing a lot of the personal contact we used to have with each of our employees, and morale is beginning to become a problem. What are the sorts of 'people' issues you think we should be addressing as our company grows?"

KNITTING MUSIC IS UP AND RUNNING

When it comes to managing a business, the rubber really hits the road, so to speak, when the business is a small, fast-growing enterprise. Managing a large company like an IBM or GE is a complex task, since decisions about how to organize, hire, motivate, and keep track of the activities of tens of thousands (and sometimes hundreds of thousands) of employees are required. Sometimes a better way to see what managing is like is to focus on someone who has to start and manage a small firm, since for most of us the kinds of things that a manager does are easier to grasp than the kinds of sweeping decisions that the president of IBM must make.

At the end of every chapter in this book, you'll have an opportunity to meet Michael Dorf and apply that chapter's materials to the challenges faced by KnitMedia, LLC. KnitMedia is an alternative music and entertainment company. Its businesses include an independent record label and the Knitting Factory, a live performance club. But, as we'll see, Michael Dorf and his company are involved in other businesses, too. These include touring and festival promotion, music publishing, and multimedia, including radio, TV, and Internet and video conference interactive performances. You'll find a good deal of information about KnitMedia and its businesses in each of these end-of-chapter Web exercise cases, and more information on our Web site <www.prenhall.com/desslermgmt> as well as on KnitMedia's Web site <www.KnitMedia.com>.

KnitMedia began, to some extent, as a result of economic necessity. In 1985, while still a college student in Madison, Wisconsin, Michael began managing the band Swamp Thing. He and the band started Flaming Pie records to record and distribute their songs. After struggling for two years to get Swamp Thing some exposure, Michael and his partner Louis Spitzer found themselves in New York's SoHo district (an area so-named because it is the area south of Houston Street in southern Manhattan). They found a dilapidated office on Houston Street between the Bowery and Broadway, and they were in business: The Knitting Factory was born. The initial idea (as Michael Dorf describes in his book *Knitting Music*) was to have an art gallery/performance space that sold coffee, tea, and a small assortment of foods. As they said in their first press release,

The Knitting Factory is primarily a showcase. Our aim is to weave strands of art mediums into a congruent whole, from the Wednesday night poetry series to the works on the walls. The Knitting Factory is also a café. It serves interesting forms of food like a fondue with fresh fruit. The Knitting Factory considers many things art and is open to suggestions. Hope to see you soon.[1]

Michael's real motivation at the time was ". . . to earn enough money to live and to cover the rent for Flaming Pie records."

Ten years ago there wasn't, strictly speaking, much "managing" to do since KnitMedia had few employees. Today, however, is a different story: As you'll see on the WEB exercise for chapter 1, KnitMedia, LLC includes several separate businesses and at least seven executive personnel, as well as numerous other key personnel. The executive staff in 1997 included Michael Dorf, President and Chief Executive Officer; Kenneth Ashworth, Executive President and Chief Operating Officer; Mitchell Goldman, Director, Knitting Factory Productions; Rachel McBeth, Business Manager; Edwin Greer, Director, KnitWork Operations; Mark Perlson, Record Label Manager; and Arthur Phillips, Director European Operations.

These managers know that they are in a competitive business that is changing very fast. They want to know about the competitive challenges they can expect to face in the next few years.

Team Exercises and Questions

Use what you learned in this chapter to answer the following questions:

1 Few industries are undergoing as much rapid change as music, entertainment, and Internet/new media—industries that KnitMedia is in. Compile a list of the trends (such as consolidation of the music companies) taking place today for which Michael and his colleagues will have to plan.

2 Using WEB resources, make a list of the competitors in New York City for the Knitting Factory Club.

For the expanded online version of this case, visit our Web site at <www.prenhall.com/desslermgmt>.

---

[1]Michael Dorf, *Knitting Music* (New York: Knitting Factory Works, 1992), 4.

For Internet exercises, interactive study questions, news updates and more, visit the Dessler Web site at

www.prenhall.com/desslermgmt

If you're using the CD-ROM that accompanies this text, simply click on the "Web Site" button to access the site.

APPENDIX

Foundations of Modern Management

THE EARLY FOUNDATIONS OF MANAGEMENT

It would be impossible to imagine a modern society without organized effort or the managers who help to synchronize that effort, but the roots of management can actually be traced back to antiquity. Hunters banded into tribes for protection; the Egyptians used organizations to build pyramids and control the rise and fall of the Nile; and the Romans relied on organizing to build their armies and control their empire. Management is thus a very old idea.

Some recurring themes become apparent when we view management over the ages. First, many of the management concepts we take for granted today, such as dividing employees into departments, can be traced to the earliest organizations including those of the Egyptians and the ancient Greeks. Similarly, the close supervision and reliance on coercion and rules that management expert Peter Drucker has called "command and control" is also a product of earlier times, in particular of the militaristic organizations of Egypt and ancient Rome.

Second, we will see that the forms organizations take and the ways managers manage have always been a product of the environments of the time. As futurist Alvin Toeffler has said (in describing nineteenth-century management):

> Each age produces a form of organization appropriate to its own tempo. During the long epic of agricultural civilization, societies were marked by low transcience. Delays in communication and transportation slowed the rate at which information moved. The pace of individual life was comparatively slow. And organizations were seldom called upon to make what we would regard as high-speed decisions.[1]

So management is also an evolutionary process. Let us look back to the beginning of modern management theory.

SCIENTIFIC MANAGEMENT

Management theory as we know it today is an outgrowth of the first attempts to view the management process with new and almost scientific rigor.

The Industrial Revolution

By 1750, with the advent of the Industrial Revolution, what Toeffler referred to as "the long epic of agricultural civilization" was about to end. The Industrial Revolution was a period of several decades during which machine power was increasingly substituted for hand labor. During these years several major trends converged. Scientific and technological discoveries, including the invention of the steam engine and the use of electricity, all contributed to the rise of industrialization. England, generally recognized as the epicenter of the Industrial Revolution, at that time had a stable, constitutional government, a sensitivity to laissez-faire (hands-off) economics, and a strong spirit of self-reliance. In his book *The Wealth of Nations*, Adam

Smith described the division and specialization of work as a pillar of the burgeoning competitive market system and accurately predicted that it would lead to enormous increases in productivity and output.[2]

The Industrial Environment

For firms in the 1800s, industrialization meant emphasizing resource accumulation and company growth. Division of work and specialization—two pillars of industrialization—required the high volume and stability that only growth could bring. Growth led to higher profits; as sales, volume, and stability increased, unit costs decreased.

But enlarged operations created new problems for the entrepreneurs of the 1800s. They needed management techniques through which they could run their new, large-scale enterprises. These industrialists therefore quickly adopted the structures and principles followed by managers of an earlier day, such as centralized decision making, a rigid chain of command, specialized division of work, and autocratic leadership. All of these had been born and nurtured in military and religious organizations like those of ancient Rome and Egypt.

Frederick Winslow Taylor and Scientific Management

The race to grow and accumulate resources was particularly pronounced in the United States. The War of 1812 severed the United States from England economically and spurred the growth of domestic manufacturing operations. Technological advances flourished and included the steamboat, the cotton gin, the iron plow, the telegraph, the electric motor, and the expansion of a railroad and canal network that opened new markets for producers. In turn, these new markets provided the volume that was a basic requirement for effective division of work.

Historian Alfred Chandler has pointed out that by the late 1800s many new industries were completing the resource-accumulation stage of their existence and beginning to move into what he calls a rationalization stage.[3] The management focus shifted from growth to efficiency. As organizations became large and unwieldy, and as competition became more intense, managers needed better ways to utilize the resources they had accumulated. They sought new concepts and techniques that would cut costs and boost efficiency. It was out of this industrial environment that the *classical school of management* emerged.

Frederick W. Taylor was among the first of what historians today call the "classical management writers"; he specifically developed a set of principles that became known as *scientific management*. Taylor's basic theme was that managers should study work scientifically to identify the "one best way" to get the job done. This framework for scientific management was based on four principles:

1. The "one best way." Management, through observation and "the deliberate gathering . . . of all the great mass of traditional knowledge, which in the past has been in the heads of the workmen . . . ," finds the "one best way" for performing each job.
2. Scientific selection of personnel. This principle requires "the scientific selection and then the progressive development of the workmen." Management must uncover each worker's limitation, find his or her "possibility for development," and give each worker the required training.
3. Financial incentives. Taylor knew that putting the right worker on the right

job would not by itself ensure high productivity. Some plan for motivating workers to do their best and to comply with their supervisors' instructions was also required. Taylor proposed a system of financial incentives, in which each worker was paid in direct proportion to how much he or she produced, instead of according to a basic hourly wage.

4. Functional foremanship. Finally, Taylor called for a division of work between manager and worker such that managers did all planning, preparing, and inspecting while the workers did the actual work. Taylor proposed using specialized experts, or functional foremen, who would be responsible for specific aspects of the worker's task, such as choosing the best machine speed, determining job priorities, and inspecting the work. The worker was to take orders from each of these foremen, depending upon whether the matter concerned machine speed, planning, or inspecting, for example.[4]

Frank and Lillian Gilbreth

The work of the husband-and-wife team Frank and Lillian Gilbreth also exemplifies the techniques and points of view of the scientific management approach. Born in 1868, Frank Gilbreth passed up an opportunity to attend MIT, deciding instead to enter the contracting business. He began as an apprentice bricklayer and became intrigued with the opportunities for improving bricklayers' efficiency. By carefully studying bricklayers' motions he developed innovations—in the way bricks were stacked, in the way they were laid, and in the number of motions bricklayers used, for instance—that nearly tripled the average bricklayer's efficiency.[5]

In 1904 Frank married Lillian, who had a background in psychology, and together they began to develop the principles and practices to more scientifically analyze tasks. In addition to using stopwatches to improve production efficiencies, these experts developed various tools, including *motion-study principles,* to assist them in their quest for efficiency. They concluded, for example, that:

1. The two hands should begin and complete their motions at the same time.
2. The two hands should not be idle at the same time except during rest periods.
3. Motions of the arms should be made at opposite and symmetrical directions and should be made simultaneously.[6]

Therbligs, another example of the tools used by the Gilbreths, were elemental motions like searching, grabbing, holding, and transporting. (The Gilbreths created the term therblig by using their last name spelled backward and transposing the *th.*) *Micromotion study* was the Gilbreths' process of taking motion pictures of a worker doing his or her job and then running the film forward and backward at different speeds so that details of the job could be examined and re-examined. Used in conjunction with timing devices, micromotion study made it possible to determine precisely how long it took to complete each component activity of a task. The worker's performance could then be improved by modifying or eliminating one or more of these components.

Henri Fayol and the Principles of Management

The work of Henri Fayol also illustrates the classical approach to management and behavior at work. Fayol had been a manager with a French iron and steel firm for 30 years before writing his book *General and Industrial Management.* In it, Fayol said that managers performed five basic functions: planning, organizing, commanding, coordinating, and controlling.

He also outlined a list of management principles that he found useful during his years as a manager. He argued that other managers should use these principles in planning, organizing, commanding, coordinating, and controlling. Fayol's 14 principles are summarized in the list below and include his famous principle of *unity of command:* "For any action whatsoever, an employee should receive orders from one superior only."[7]

1. Division of work. The worker, always on the same part, and the manager, concerned always with the same matters, acquired ability, sureness, and accuracy, which increased their output.
2. Authority and responsibility. Authority is the right to give orders and the power to exact obedience. Distinction must be made between a manager's official authority, deriving from office, and personal authority, compounded of intelligence, experience, moral worth, and ability to lead.
3. Discipline. The best means of establishing and maintaining [discipline] are: good superiors at all levels; agreements as clear and fair as possible; sanctions [penalties] judiciously applied.
4. Unity of command. For any action whatsoever, an employee should receive orders from one superior only. . . .
5. Unity of direction. There should be one head and one plan for a group of activities serving the same objective.
6. Subordination of individual interests to general interests. This principle means that in a business, the interests of one employee or group of employees should not prevail over those of the concern. . . . Means of effecting it are: firmness and good example on the part of superiors; agreements as far as is possible.
7. Remuneration of personnel. Remuneration should be fair and as far as possible afford satisfaction to both personnel and firm.
8. Centralization. The question of centralization or decentralization is a simple question of proportion; it is a matter of finding the optimum degree for the particular concern. What appropriate share of initiative may be left to intermediaries depends on the personal character of the manager, on his moral worth, on the reliability of his subordinates, and also on the condition of the business. The degree of centralization must vary according to different cases.
9. Scalar chain. The scalar chain is the chain of superiors ranging from the ultimate authority to the lowest ranks. . . . It is an error to depart needlessly from the line of authority, but it is an even greater one to keep to it when detriment to the business ensues.
10. Order. For social order to prevail in a concern, there must be an appointed place for every employee and every employee must be in his appointed place.
11. Equity. For the personnel to be encouraged to carry out its duties with all the devotion and loyalty of which it is capable, it must be treated with kindliness, and equity results from the combination of kindness and justice. Equity excludes neither forcefulness nor sternness. . . .
12. Stability of tenure of personnel. Time is required for an employee to get used to new work and succeed in doing it well, always assuming that he possesses the requisite abilities. If, when he has gotten used to it, or before

then, he is removed, he will not have had time to render worthwhile service.

13. Initiative. Thinking out a plan and ensuring its success is one of the keenest satisfactions for an intelligent man to experience. . . . This power of thinking out and executing is what is called initiative. . . . It . . . represents a great source of strength for business.

14. Esprit de corps. "Union is strength." Harmony, union among the personnel of a concern, is a great strength in that concern. Effort, then, should be made to establish it.

Max Weber and Bureaucratic Organization Theory

Max Weber was a contemporary of Taylor, Fayol, and the Gilbreths. His work, first published in Germany in 1921, provides further insight into the ideals of the classical management writers, but unlike most of these writers, Weber was not a practicing manager but an intellectual. He was born in 1864 to a well-to-do family and studied law, history, economics, and philosophy at Heidelberg University.

During the 1920s, Weber saw the growth of the large-scale organization and correctly predicted that this growth would require a more formal set of procedures for how to administer organizations. Managers, at the time, had few principles they could apply in managing their organizations. He, therefore, created the idea of an ideal or "pure form" of organization, which he called *bureaucracy*. This term, as developed by Weber and his followers, did not refer to red tape and inefficiency as it often does today. Indeed *bureaucracy,* for Weber, was the most efficient form of organization. Weber described bureaucracy as having certain characteristics:

1. A well-defined hierarchy of authority.
2. A clear division of work.
3. A system of rules covering the rights and duties of position incumbents.
4. A system of procedures for dealing with the work situation.
5. Impersonality of interpersonal relationships.
6. Selection for employment, and promotion based on technical competence.[8]

Summary: The Classical Approach to Management

The classical approach to management generally focused on boosting efficiency. To Taylor, Fayol, Weber, and the Gilbreths, an efficiently designed job and organization were of prime importance. These writers, therefore, bent their efforts on developing analytical tools, techniques, and principles that would enable managers to create efficient organizations. Human work behavior was not unimportant to the classical writers; they simply assumed its complexities away by arguing that financial incentives would suffice to ensure motivation. As a result, intentionally or not, the classicists left the impression that workers could be treated as givens in the system, as little more than appendages to their machines. "Design the most highly specialized and efficient job you can," assumed the classicist, and "plug in the worker who will then do your bidding if the pay is right."

THE BEHAVIORAL SCHOOL OF MANAGEMENT

The Environment

In the 1920s and 1930s, many changes swept across the United States, and indeed the world. Increasing numbers of people moved from farms to cities and thus became more dependent on each other for goods and services. Factories became more mechanized and the jobs became more specialized and interdependent.[9] Instead of continuing its hands-off policy, government became more deeply involved in economic matters, and a number of lawsuits were filed to break up big industrial monopolies. Many social movements aimed at giving women the right to vote, electing senators by direct popular vote, establishing a minimum wage, and encouraging trade unions. Even the literature of the period became more anti-individualistic, as people questioned whether a philosophy based on hard work, individualism, and maximizing profits—the building blocks of the classical management era—might actually have some drawbacks.

The Hawthorne Studies

In 1927, the *Hawthorne Studies* began at the Chicago Hawthorne Plant of the Western Electric Company, and these eventually added an entirely new perspective to the management of people at work. Three main sets of studies took place, one of which became known as the "relay assembly test studies." A group of workers was isolated and studied as a series of changes was made, such as modifying the length of the workday and altering the morning and afternoon rest breaks. Researchers noted with some surprise that these changes did not greatly affect worker performance, underscoring their growing belief that performance depended on factors other than physical conditions or rate of pay.

The relay assembly test studies led the researchers to conclude that the *social* situations of the workers, not just the *working* conditions, influenced their behavior and performance at work. The researchers discovered, for instance, that in countless ways, their observations had inadvertently made the workers feel they were each "special." The observer had changed the workers' situation by "his personal interest in the girls and their problems. He had always been sympathetically aware of their hopes and fears. He had granted them more and more privileges."[10]

These results have been codified as the Hawthorne effect. The *Hawthorne effect* is what happens when the scientist, in the course of his or her investigation, inadvertently influences the subjects so that it is not the scientist's intended changes that affect the subject's behavior but the way the scientist acts. In the relay assembly test, for instance, the researchers wanted to schedule rest periods where they would be most advantageous. They, therefore, called a meeting during which they showed the workers their output curves and pointed out the low and high points of the day. "When asked at what times they would like to have their rest, they unanimously voted in favor of ten o'clock in the morning and two o'clock in the afternoon." Accordingly, the investigators agreed to schedule the rests at these times. In retrospect, however, the researchers concluded that the subsequent rise in employee morale and performance was due to more than just the rest breaks; it was also due to the fact that the researchers had inadvertently involved the workers in the decision.

Hawthorne's Consequences

The Hawthorne studies were a turning point in the study of management. As the research became more widely known, managers and management experts began to recognize that human behavior at work is a complex and powerful force to be dealt with. The *human relations movement,* inspired by this realization, emphasized that workers were not just givens in the system but instead had needs and desires that the organization and task had to accommodate.

Environment, Increased Diversity, and Change

Historian Alfred Chandler has suggested that after accumulating and then rationalizing resources, managers traditionally moved to a third stage in which they attempted to better utilize their organizational resources by developing new products and new markets—by diversifying. In the United States, movement into this third stage was hampered in the 1930s by the Depression. However, excess production capacity did ultimately stimulate research and development activities. Coupled with the technological and managerial advancements that emerged in the years surrounding World War II, this excess capacity finally shifted most U.S. industries into Chandler's third, *diversification* stage.[11]

To understand the evolving management theory, it is important to recognize that this period was characterized by differentiated, complex, and rapidly changing environments. Even before World War II, many firms had embarked upon extensive research and development activities to utilize their resources by developing new products. For example, at General Electric and Westinghouse, research and development activities resulted in the manufacture of plastics as well as a variety of other products based on electronics. The automobile companies had begun to produce airplane engines, electrical equipment, and household appliances before the war. After the war, companies in the rubber industry—such as United States Rubber and BFGoodrich, which had concentrated on tire manufacturing—entered into systematic research and development and began to market such items as latex, plastics, and flooring.

These changes in the business environment contributed to the development of management theory in several ways. First, the increased rate of change and novelty triggered by diversification meant that managers and management theorists could no longer view organizations as closed systems that were essentially operating within the predictable, unchanging environments.[12] Second, efficiency was no longer a manager's main concern. It was eclipsed by the drives to diversify and then to monitor the activities of previously unrelated companies. Third, the shift toward making organizations more responsive to their environments was characterized by a trend toward *decentralization,* which in essence meant letting lower-level employees make more of their own decisions. Decentralization, though, required a new managerial philosophy: allowing subordinates to do more problem solving and decision making meant that managers had to rely on their employees' self-control. This change (coming as it did just after Hawthorne's results became popularized) led to a new emphasis on participative, people-oriented leadership and a more behavioral approach to management.

Douglas McGregor: Theory X, Theory Y

The work of Douglas McGregor is a good example of this more behavioral approach to management. According to McGregor, the classical organization (with its highly specialized jobs, centralized decision making, and top-down communications) was not just a product of the need for more efficiency. Instead, McGregor said it was a reflection of certain basic managerial assumptions about human nature.[13] These assumptions, which McGregor somewhat arbitrarily classified as *Theory X,* held that most people dislike work and responsibility and prefer to be directed; that they are motivated not by the desire to do a good job but simply by financial incentives; and that, therefore, most people must be closely supervised, controlled, and coerced into achieving organizational objectives.

McGregor questioned the truth of this view and asked whether management practices such as specialized division of work are appropriate for the sorts of tasks faced by more modern organizations. He felt that management needed new organizations and practices to deal with diversification, decentralization, and participative decision making. These new practices had to be based on a revised set of assumptions about the nature of human beings, which McGregor called *Theory Y*. Unlike Theory X, Theory Y held that people could enjoy work and that an individual would exercise substantial self-control over his or her performance if the conditions were favorable. Implicit in Theory Y is the belief that people are motivated by the desire to do a good job and by the opportunity to affiliate with their peers, rather than just by financial rewards.

Rensis Likert and the Employee-Centered Organization

Researcher Rensis Likert's work is another example of the trends in management theory during these post-war years. Likert concluded that effective organizations differ from ineffective ones in several ways. Less effective *job-centered companies* focus on specialized jobs, efficiency, and close supervision of workers, he said. More effective organizations, on the other hand, "focus their primary attention on endeavoring to build effective work groups with high performance goals."[14] As Likert noted, in these *employee-centered companies:*

> The leadership and other processes of the organization must be such as to insure a maximum probability that in all interactions and all relationships with the organization, each member will, in the light of his background, values and expectations, view the experience as supportive and one which builds and maintains his sense of personal worth and importance.[15]

Chris Argyris and the Mature Individual

Chris Argyris reached similar conclusions but approached the problem from a different perspective.[16] In his view, the classical command and control approach to managing was unhealthy for workers. Argyris argued that healthy people go through a maturation process. As they approach adulthood, they move to a state of increased activity, greater independence, and stronger interests, and they pass from the subordinate position of a child to an equal or superordinate position as an adult. Gaining employees' compliance by assigning them to highly specialized jobs with no decision-making power and then closely supervising them inhibits these normal maturation processes by encouraging workers to be dependent, passive, and subordinate. Argyris concluded that it would be better to give workers more responsibility and broader jobs.

The Behavioralist Prescriptions

Behavioral scientists like Argyris, McGregor, and Likert soon translated their ideas into practical methodologies that became the heart of the emerging subject of organizational behavior. Likert, for example, emphasized leadership style and group processes. "The low-producing managers, in keeping with the traditional practice, feel that the way to motivate and direct behavior is to exercise control through authority."[17] In contrast, "the highest-producing managers feel, generally, that this manner of functioning does not produce the best results, that the resentment created by direct exercise of authority tends to limit its effectiveness."[18] Therefore, said

Likert, "widespread use of participation is one of the more important approaches employed by the high-producing managers."[19] Likert found that the value of participation applied to all aspects of the job and of work, "as, for example, in setting work goals and budgets, controlling costs, organizing the work, etc."[20]

McGregor had his own prescriptions, too. He said decentralization and pushing decision making down should be the norm in order to free people from the "too-close control of conventional organization." Management should encourage job enlargement (in which the variety of tasks an employee performs is increased), so that workers' jobs are made more challenging and more interesting. Participative management (which McGregor said would give employees some voice in decisions that affect them) would similarly enhance self-control. Finally, McGregor urged using management by objectives (MBO) to encourage self-control. In MBO, subordinates set goals with their supervisors and are measured on the accomplishment of these goals, thus avoiding the need for close day-to-day supervision.

Bridging the Eras: Chester Barnard and Herbert Simon

The work of Chester Barnard and Herbert Simon does not fit neatly into any one school of management theory. Their research actually spanned several schools and contributed to the development of an integrated theory of management.

CHESTER BARNARD. Chester Barnard used his experience as an executive to develop an important new management theory. He was the president of New Jersey Bell Telephone Company and, at various times, president of the United Service Organization (the USO of World War II), president of the Rockefeller Foundation, and chairman of the National Science Foundation.

Barnard was the first major theorist after the Hawthorne studies to emphasize the importance and variability of the individual in the work place. He said, for example, that "an essential element of organizations is the willingness of persons to contribute their individual efforts to the cooperative system." And he added that "the individual is always the basic strategic factor in organization. Regardless of his history or obligations, he must be induced to cooperate, or there can be no cooperation."

Barnard, therefore, set about developing a theory of how to get workers to cooperate. According to Barnard the question is, how do you get the individuals to surrender their personal preferences and to go along with the authority exercised by their supervisors?[21]

Barnard believed the answer could be found in what he called the person's *zone of indifference,* a range within each individual in which he or she would willingly accept orders without consciously questioning their authority.[22] Barnard saw willingness to cooperate as an expression of the net satisfactions or dissatisfactions experienced or anticipated by each person. In other words, organizations had to provide sufficient inducements to broaden each employee's zone of indifference and thus increase the likelihood that the boss's orders would be obeyed.

But Barnard, in a clear break with the classicist, said that material incentives by themselves were not enough: "The unaided power of material incentives, when the minimum necessities are satisfied, in my opinion, is exceedingly limited as to most men."[23] Instead, said Barnard, several other classes of incentives, including "the opportunities for distinction, prestige, [and] personal power" are also required.

HERBERT SIMON. Whereas Barnard wrote from the vantage point of an executive, Herbert Simon was a scholar who had mastered organization theory, economics, natural science, and political science, and who went on to win the Nobel

Prize in economics. Like Barnard, Simon viewed getting employees to do what the organization needed them to do as a major issue facing managers. He proposed two basic ways to gain such compliance, which can be paraphrased as follows:

> Decisions reached in the highest ranks of the organization hierarchy will have no effect upon the activities of operative employees unless they are communicated downward. Consideration of the process requires an examination of the ways in which the behavior of the operative employee can be influenced. These influences fall roughly into two categories:
>
> First, the manager can establish in the employee him or herself the attitudes, habits and state of mind that lead him or her to reach the decision that is advantageous to the organization. In other words, the manager somehow gets the worker to want to do the job. Or, second, the manager can impose upon the employee decisions reached elsewhere in the organization, for instance by closely supervising everything the person does.[24]

Thus, according to Simon, managers can ensure that employees carry out tasks in one of two ways. They can *impose control* by closely monitoring subordinates and insisting that they do their jobs as they have been ordered (thereby using the classicist' command and control approach to managing). Or managers can foster employees' *self-control* by providing better training, encouraging participative leadership, and developing commitment and loyalty. As rapid change forced employers to depend more and more on employee initiative, developing such self-control would soon become a major theme in management writings. First, we should discuss The Quantitative School

THE QUANTITATIVE SCHOOL

After World War II, a trend developed among management theorists to apply quantitative techniques to a wide range of managerial problems. This movement is usually referred to as *operations research* or *management science* and has been described as "the application of scientific methods, techniques, and tools to problems involving the operations of systems so as to provide those in control of the system with optimum solutions to the problems."[25]

The Management Science Approach

Management science has three distinguishing characteristics. First, management scientists generally deal with well-defined problems that have clear and undisputable standards of effectiveness. They want to know, for instance, whether inventory costs have been too high and should be reduced by 20 percent, or whether a specific number of items should be produced at each of a company's plants to minimize transportation costs to customers.

Second, management scientists generally deal with problems that have well-defined alternative courses of action. Thus, a company might have four different plants from which to ship products, or various levels of product A and product B that can be produced to maximize sales revenues. The management scientist's task is to recommend a solution. Finally, management scientists must develop a theory or model describing how the relevant factors are related. Like any scientist, management scientists must understand the problem and relationships clearly enough to formulate a mathematical model.

Historian Daniel Wren points out that operations research/management science has "direct lineal roots in scientific management."[26] Like Taylor and the Gilbreths, today's management scientists try to find optimal solutions to management problems. As Taylor and his people used scientific methods to find the one best way to do a job, management scientists use the scientific method to find the best solution to industrial problems. The difference in the two approaches is twofold. First, modern-day management scientists have at their disposal much more sophisticated mathematical tools and computers. Second, management science's goal is not to try to find a science of management (as did Taylor) so much as it is to use scientific analysis and tools to solve management problems.

The Systems Approach

The management science approach is closely associated with what is called the systems approach to management. A *system* is an entity—a hospital, a city, a company, or a person, for instance—that has interdependent parts and a purpose. *Systems approach* advocates argue that viewing an organization as a system helps managers to remember that a firm's different parts, departments, or subsystems are interrelated and all must contribute to the organization's purpose.

According to systems advocates like C. West Churchman, all systems have four basic characteristics.[27] First, they operate within an environment, which is defined as those things outside and important to the organization but largely beyond its control. For a company these include clients, competitors, unions, and governments.

Second, all systems are composed of building blocks called elements, components, or subsystems. In an organization, these basic building blocks might be departments, like those for production, finance, and sales. The subsystems may also cut across traditional departmental lines. For example, the marketing subsystem might include sales, advertising, and transportation, because each of these elements has an impact on the marketing task of getting the product to the customer.

Third, all systems have a central purpose against which the organization's efforts and subsystems can be evaluated. For example, the optimal inventory level for a firm that serves top-of-the-line customers would probably be higher than for a firm whose customers want the best buy in town and are willing to wait for shelves to be restocked.

Fourth, focusing on the interrelatedness among the subsystems (and between the subsystems and the firm's environment) is an essential aspect of systems thinking. For example, interrelatedness emphasizes the fact that a manager can't change one subsystem without affecting the rest—hiring a new production manager might have repercussions in the sales and accounting departments, for instance. Similarly, managers and management theorists need to be sensitive to the way changes taking place in industrial environments affect the organization and management of the firm, a point to which we now turn.

TOWARD A SITUATIONAL MANAGEMENT THEORY

In the early 1960s, at about the same time the systems approach was popular, organizational research studies in England and the United States began to underscore the need for a situational or contingency view of management, one in which the appropriateness of the organization and its management principles were contingent on the rate of change in an organization's environment and technology. In one such study, Tom Burns and G.M. Stalker analyzed a number of industrial firms in England. They concluded that whether what they called a "mechanistic" or an "organic" management system was appropriate depended on the nature of the organization's environment.

Burns and Stalker argued that a *mechanistic management system* was appropriate if the company's tasks were routine and unchanging. Thus, in a textile mill they studied, it was important to have long, stable production runs that kept surprises to a minimum and thereby prevented the necessity of shutting down huge machines. In such unchanging conditions, Burns and Stalker found that a mechanistic (or classical) management approach—characterized by an emphasis on efficiency, specialized jobs, elaborate procedures for keeping behavior in line, and an insistence that everyone play by the rules—was appropriate.

On the other hand, Burns and Stalker found that the more behavioral *organic management system* was appropriate if innovative, entrepreneurial activities were important. In high-tech electronic firms, for instance, companies and their employees are constantly under pressure to come up with new devices so that they can compete effectively with rival firms. Burns and Stalker found that management often ran such firms with an organic approach that emphasized creativity rather than efficiency. These firms placed less emphasis on specialized jobs and issued fewer rules and procedures. Instead, they delegated decisions to employees who then exercised self-control in getting their jobs done.

Also in England, Joan Woodward and researchers from the Tavistock Institute analyzed a group of firms to discover the relationship between an organization and its production technology. The organic, flexible system described by Burns and Stalker again appeared to be more appropriate where dealing with unexpected, unpredictable occurrences was of paramount concern. Thus it was used in small, custom-made job shops, and in large factories that were built to run continuously and in which unexpected breakdowns were a main concern. On the other hand, Woodward and her team found that the mechanistic, classical approach was appropriate where predictability and efficiency were paramount, such as where mass production technologies and assembly lines were utilized.[28] These findings and others like them culminated in what came to be called a situational, or contingency, approach to management theory, the main findings of which we will address in chapter 8.

CHAPTER 2

MANAGING IN A GLOBAL ENVIRONMENT

What's Ahead?

arry Harris, recent college graduate and founder of the Pollo Tropical fast-food restaurant chain, had a problem. Restaurants in cities like Miami with heavy Hispanic populations were doing great. Those outside Miami had to be closed to stem further losses. It seemed obvious that the best way to expand was internationally, south from the company's Miami base, to Mexico and South and Central America.[1]

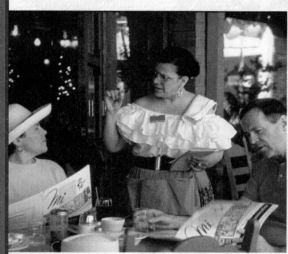

Objectives

After studying this chapter, you should be able to

- **explain** why companies expand operations abroad; discuss strategies for expanding abroad, such as exporting and licensing
- **give** examples of the economic, legal, political, sociocultural, and technological factors that influence a manager's decision to expand abroad
- **discuss** how doing business internationally affects the ways managers plan, organize, lead, and control.

MANAGEMENT ON THE WEB

INTERNATIONAL BUSINESS RESOURCES ON THE WWW

The International Business Resources on the WWW site provides a wealth of international business information. Links are maintained to news/periodicals, journals/research papers/articles, regional and country specific information, international trade information, international listservs, statistical data and information resources, company listings/directories/yellow pages, government resources, and international trade shows/seminars/business events. Is there any information there that Larry Harris could use now? ■

http://ciber.bus.msu.edu/busres.htm

Understanding International Business

The Language of International Business

The terms **international business, international trade,** and **international investment** are central to any discussion of managing in a global environment. An *international business* is any firm that engages in international trade or investment.[2] International business also refers to those activities, like exporting goods or transferring employees, that require the movement of resources, goods, services, and skills across national boundaries.[3] Most generally, international business refers to all business transactions that involve two or more countries.[4] *International trade* refers to the export or import of goods or services to consumers in another country. Similarly, *international investment* refers to the investment of resources in business activities outside a firm's home country. **International management** is the performance of the management functions of planning, organizing, leading, and controlling across national borders. If Pollo Tropical's owners decide to expand to Mexico, for instance, they will begin to engage in international management.

The multinational corporation is one type of international business enterprise. A **multinational corporation** (or **MNC**) may be defined as an internationally integrated business that is controlled by a parent corporation, owned and managed essentially by the nationals of its home country. Basically, the multinational corporation operates manufacturing and marketing facilities in two or more countries; these operations are coordinated by a parent firm, whose owners are mostly based in the firm's home country. Firms like General Electric, General Motors, and ITT have long been multinational corporations. The Entrepreneurs in Action box shows that even small firms like resourceful VeriFone, Inc., can go global, too.

Marketing expert Theodore Levitt contends that the multinational corporation is slowly being displaced by a special type of multinational enterprise that he calls the global or transnational corporation. The multinational corporation, says Levitt, operates in a number of countries and adjusts its products and practices to each. This is a relatively expensive procedure, since products must be "fine-tuned" to the needs of the consumers in each separate country.

The **global corporation**, on the other hand, operates as if the entire world (or major regions of it) were a single entity, says Levitt. Global corporations sell essentially the same things in the same way everywhere. Thus a global corporation such

Entrepreneurs in Action

VERIFONE, INC.

Getting a handle on where VeriFone, Inc., chief executive Hatim Tyabji is on any given day isn't easy. Hong Kong is a possibility, and Marseilles or Copenhagen would also be good bets, but Bangalore, India, shouldn't be ruled out either. "Being at [San Francisco] headquarters is irrelevant to me," he says, summing up the philosophy of the global manager.

VeriFone manufactures the terminals used for credit-card transactions, and Tyabji takes literally the notion that he and his 2,500 employees must stay close to their customers. That's why each new employee is issued a laptop computer. "There is my office," Tyabji says, indicating his own laptop. And even though it sounds like hyperbole, employees learn to "modem in regularly," as one manager put it. Managers average 60 VAX-mail and Internet messages a day, and for them to receive 200 isn't uncommon.

Requiring employees to hopscotch around the globe might be a disaster for some firms, but not for VeriFone. Despite formidable competitors such as IBM and GTE, the company has a 60 percent market share for card authorization services in the United States. It has also outdistanced rivals in Europe, Asia, and South America, the source of 22 percent of company revenues.

Hatim Tyabji, CEO of VeriFone, Inc., regularly travels around the world without losing touch with his 1,500 employees. Computers play a major role in his employee communications.

VeriFone employees even use global time differences to their advantage. When VeriFone was competing to design a payment authorization system for German banks, company employees around the globe joined in a cooperative effort. At day's end, the team concluding its work would forward it on in the direction of the rising sun, and another VeriFone team picked up where the first team left off. The effort continued around the clock until completion, at which time the pleasantly surprised bankers awarded the company 80 percent of the business.

SOURCES: David H. Freedman, "Culture of Urgency," *Forbes,* 25–28; William Tyler, "At VeriFone It's a Dog's Life," *Fast Company, 1,* no. 1 (Premiere Issue, 1995).

as Sony sells a standardized Walkman throughout the world, with components that might be made in or designed in different countries.[5]

Economic Integration and Free Trade

The concept of free trade helps to explain why business today is increasingly international. **Free trade** means that all trade barriers among participating countries are removed.[6] The classic explanation for the advantages of free trade was presented by the economist Adam Smith in his famous book *The Wealth of Nations.* Smith argued that each country, if unhindered by subsidies and tariffs, would end up specializing in the goods and services it could produce best. For instance, Ireland might produce fine glass, Switzerland might manufacture watches, and Japan might specialize in electronics. Such specialization would lead to higher productivity and efficiency, which would lead to higher income, which in turn could be used to purchase imports from abroad. **Economic integration** occurs when two or more nations obtain the advantages of free trade by minimizing trade restrictions between them.

Free trade area

Customs union

Common market

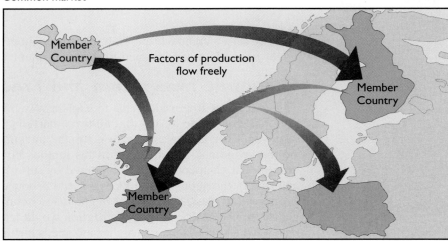

■ **FIGURE 2.1**
Levels of Economic
Integration

Economic integration occurs on several levels. In a **free trade area,** all barriers to trade among member countries are removed, so that goods and services are freely traded among the member countries. At the next higher level of economic integration, members of a **customs union** dismantle barriers to trade among themselves while establishing a common trade policy with respect to nonmembers. In a **common market,** no barriers to trade exist among members and a common external trade policy is in force; in addition, factors of production, such as labor, capital, and technology move freely between member countries, as in Figure 2.1.

- **Europe.** Several examples of economic integration exist today. In 1957, the European Economic Community (now called the European Union or EU) was established by founding members France, West Germany, Italy, Belgium, the Netherlands, and Luxembourg (Figure 2.2). The main provisions of their agreement, the Treaty of Rome, called for the formation of a free trade area, the gradual elimination of tariffs and other barriers to trade, and the formation of a customs union and (eventually) a common market. By 1987, the renamed European Community had added six other countries (Great Britain, Ireland, Denmark, Greece, Spain, and Portugal) and signed the Single Europe Act. This act "envisages a true common market where goods, people, and money move among the twelve EC countries with the same ease that they move between Wisconsin and Illinois."[7]

  In a 1991 meeting in Maastricht, Netherlands, the twelve countries agreed to submit to their respective legislatures' plans for cementing even closer economic ties between them, including plans for a single European currency by 1999 and free movement of labor. The Maastricht Accord was approved by each country by 1993.

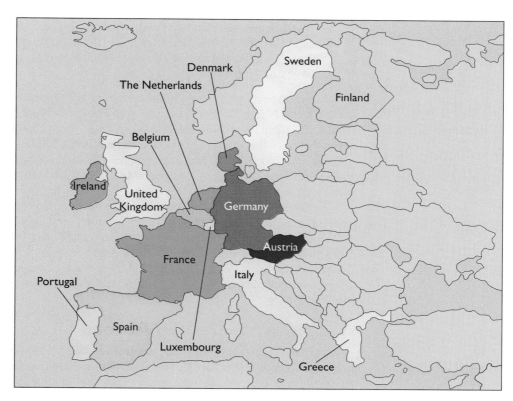

■ **FIGURE 2.2**
EU Member Countries

FIGURE 2.3
ASEAN member countries

- **Asia.** Considerable free-trade cooperation has occurred in Asia, too. For example, the Association of Southeast Asian Nations (ASEAN) was organized in 1967 (Figure 2.3). It includes Brunei, Indonesia, Malaysia, the Philippines, Singapore, and Thailand. These countries are cooperating in reducing tariffs and in attempting to liberalize trade, although the results at this point have been limited.[8]
- **North America.** Canada, the United States, and Mexico have together established a North American Free Trade Agreement (NAFTA) (Figure 2.4). NAFTA will create the world's largest free market, with a total output of about $6 trillion.

Some experts predict a global economy will evolve with a triad of three economic hubs: North America, the EU, and East and Southeast Asia (including Japan, India, and China).[9] Of the three, Asia is widely predicted to have the fastest growth over the next few years—in particular, mainland China, South Korea, Taiwan, Singapore, and Hong Kong. For example, the Chinese economy is growing at an annual rate of about 11.4 percent, compared to about 4 percent for Japan and about 3 percent for the United States.[10]

Economic integration has a big effect on company managers. It can, for example, enhance the rate of growth of the country and its markets. But there are also potential negative side effects. For instance, some fear that the EU's existence will lead to a "fortress Europe to which non-EU firms will find it increasingly difficult to export goods."[11] As a result, many U.S. managers are entering joint ventures with European partners to establish local beachheads from which they can sell throughout the EU.

Why Companies Go Abroad

Firms expand internationally for several reasons.[12] "Finding cheap labor" is usually *not* a main motive for most firms' internationalization efforts (although for some it is certainly a motive). Instead, *sales expansion* is usually the main goal. Firms like GE are moving resources to Asia because of the relatively fast growth rate of the

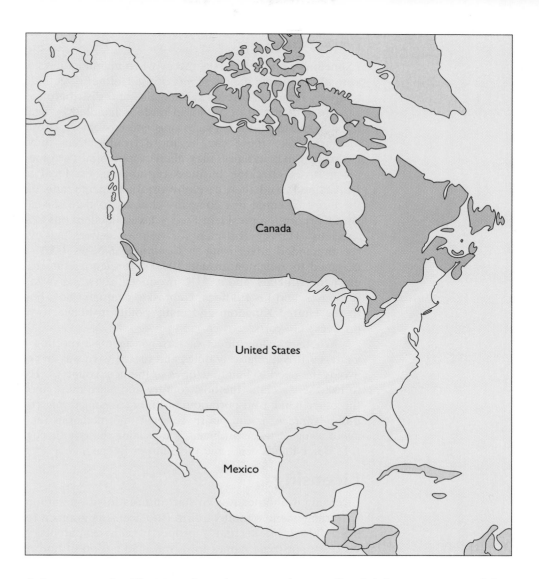

■ FIGURE 2.4
NAFTA Member
Countries

Asian economies. That translates into more income for Asia's consumers and fast sales increases.

Firms go international for other reasons. Manufacturers and distributors also seek out foreign products and services to reduce their costs. For example, Florida apparel manufacturers have items assembled in Central America, where the labor costs are relatively low. In many cases it is high quality that drives firms overseas. For example, U.S.–based Apple Computer enlisted Sony's aid in producing parts for its new notebook computer. Companies can also smooth out sales and profit swings by going overseas. For example, a manufacturer of snowblowers might sell in Chile, knowing that as demand for its products in the United States is dropping off in the spring, it is rising in Chile where the seasons are reversed.

Types of International Strategies

There are several strategies a company can use to expand internationally. Let's look now at the main alternatives.

Exporting

Exporting is often the first strategy when manufacturers decide to expand their sales abroad. Exporting means selling abroad, either directly to target customers or indirectly by retaining foreign sales agents and distributors.[13]

More than half of all world trade is handled by agents and distributors familiar with the local market's customs and customers. However, poorly selected intermediaries like these can be more trouble than they are worth, for instance if, through inexperience, they alienate potential customers. Carefully selecting representatives, checking business reputations via local agencies of the U.S. State Department, and then carefully drafting agency and distribution agreements are therefore essential if a company chooses to take this route.[14] For example, when Bird Corporation president Fred Schweser sought out Commerce Department trade specialist Harvey Roffman for help in generating overseas business, Roffman recommended advertising in *Commercial News USA,* a government publication designed to enlighten around 100,000 foreign agents, distributors, buyers, and government officials about U.S. products. Schweser was very soon deluged with responses, and his Elkhorn, Nebraska, company now boasts customers from Japan to the United Kingdom and many points in between. What is Bird Corporation's product? Go-carts.[15]

Whether selling direct or through agents, exporting has advantages and disadvantages. It is a relatively quick and inexpensive way of "going international," since it avoids the need to build factories in the host country.[16] Exporting is also a good way to test the waters in the host country and learn more about its customers' needs. On the other hand, transportation, tariff, or manufacturing costs can put the exporter at a disadvantage, as can poorly selected intermediaries (as noted above). One way to avoid some of these problems is by selling directly through mail order. For example, L.L. Bean, Lands' End, and the Sharper Image all export globally via their catalogs.[17]

Licensing

Licensing is another way to start international operations. International licensing is an arrangement whereby a firm (the licensor) grants a foreign firm the right to use intangible ("intellectual") property such as patents, copyrights, manufacturing processes, or trade names for a specified period of time, usually in return for a percentage of the earnings, called royalty.[18]

Licensing arrangements have their pros and cons. For example, consider a small, underfunded U.S. inventor of a new material for reducing pollution. Working out a licensing agreement with a well-established European environmental products company could allow the U.S. firm to enter the expanding Eastern European pollution control market without any significant investment. On the downside, the U.S. firm might not be able to control the design, manufacturing, or sales of its products as well as it could if it set up its own facilities in Europe. It is also possible that by licensing its knowledge and know-how to a foreign firm, the small U.S. firm could eventually lose control over its patented property.

Franchising

As anyone who has eaten at McDonald's on the Champs Élysées knows, franchising is another way to start operations overseas. Franchising is the granting of a right by a parent company to another firm to do business in a prescribed manner.[19]

Franchising is similar to licensing, but it usually involves a longer time commitment by both parties. Furthermore, franchising usually requires the franchisee to

We're happy you're joining us, and we're out to make you feel at home.

U.S. direct marketer Land's End sells casual wear around the world with mail-order catalogs customized for different overseas markets.

follow much stricter guidelines in running the business than does licensing. In addition, licensing tends to be limited to manufacturers, while franchising is more popular with service firms such as restaurants, hotels, and rental services.

The advantages here are generally the same as those for licensing: Franchising is a quick and relatively low-cost way for a firm to expand its sales in other countries. The one significant disadvantage is maintaining quality control. For example, one early French McDonald's franchisee was forced by McDonald's to close down its Paris restaurants for failing to maintain McDonald's well-known quality standards.

Foreign Direct Investment and the Multinational Enterprise

Exporting, licensing, and franchising get most firms only so far. At some point, they find that taking full advantage of foreign opportunities requires making a substantial, direct investment in another country. **Foreign direct investment** refers to operations in one country that are controlled by entities in a foreign country. A foreign firm might build new facilities in another country, as Toyota did when it built its Camry manufacturing plant in Georgetown, Kentucky. Or a firm might acquire property or operations in a foreign country, as when Matsushita bought control of Rockefeller Center in New York City. Strictly speaking, a foreign direct investment means acquiring control by owning more than 50 percent of the operation. But in practice, it is possible for any firm to gain effective control by owning less. In any event, a foreign direct investment turns the firm into a multinational enterprise, one that controls operations in more than one country. Joint ventures and wholly owned subsidiaries are two examples of foreign direct investment.

Joint Ventures

The terms joint venture and strategic alliance are often used interchangeably, although strictly speaking they aren't the same thing. **Strategic alliances** refer to "cooperative agreements between potential or actual competitors."[20] For example, several years ago, Boeing combined with a consortium of Japanese companies to produce the 767 commercial jet. However, most experts would probably define strategic alliances as "any agreements between firms that are of strategic importance to one or both firms' competitive viability."[21] Used in that sense, even licensing or franchising agreements may come under the umbrella of strategic alliances.

A joint venture is a specific type of strategic alliance. In fact, it is the classical example of such an alliance.[22] A **joint venture** is "the participation of two or more companies jointly in an enterprise in which each party contributes assets, owns the entity to some degree, and shares risk."[23]

The joint venture of General Motors and Toyota called New United Motor Manufacturing, Inc. (NUMMI) is an example. Toyota needed to sharpen its U.S. marketing skills and gain direct access to U.S. customers. General Motors, faced with anemic productivity and morale compared to Japanese car manufacturers, needed to learn more about Japanese manufacturing systems and technology. The two firms formed NUMMI and had it take over a chronically troubled GM plant in Freemont, California. Within two years, the Japanese management methods had made this plant GM's most productive.

As at NUMMI, joint ventures have advantages. Consultant Kenichi Ohmae points out that "in a complex, uncertain world filled with dangerous opponents, it is best not to go it alone."[24] A joint venture arrangement lets a foreign firm (like Toyota) gain useful experience in a foreign country while using the expertise and resources of a locally knowledgeable company. Joint ventures also help both companies share what may be the substantial cost of starting a new operation. But, as in licensing, the joint venture partners also risk giving away proprietary secrets to each other. Furthermore, joint ventures almost always mean sharing control. Each partner thus runs the risk that the joint venture may not be managed in the manner each would have chosen on its own.

Organizational Behavior in Action

THE PEOPLE FACTOR IN MULTINATIONAL JOINT VENTURES

Behavioral factors can be crucial to a joint venture's success. For example, experts believe that cultural differences caused the failure of a joint manufacturing venture in Mexico between Corning Company and Mexico's Virto. Organizational culture is the shared values, beliefs, and behaviors that characterize an organization. As it turned out, the values of the joint venture's Mexican and U.S. managers were quite different. The Mexican managers sometimes saw the Corning managers as too direct, but the Mexican managers themselves were often reluctant to criticize anyone, especially their Corning partners. Corning managers were dynamos, even gobbling down lunch at their desks, whereas their Virto counterparts took very long lunch breaks. Corning managers were used to making decisions on the spot, while their Mexican colleagues had to wait until their top managers made all the decisions. In the end, it wasn't political, economic, or technical factors that torpedoed this joint venture. It was the people factor and in particular a clash of company cultures.[25]

Wholly Owned Subsidiaries

As the name implies, a *wholly owned subsidiary* is owned 100 percent by the foreign firm. Thus, in the United States today, Toyota Motor Manufacturing, Inc., and its facility in Georgetown, Kentucky, is a wholly owned subsidiary of Toyota Motor Corporation, which is based in Japan. (NUMMI is a separate and independent operation.) In Japan, Toys-R-Us, Inc. was the first large U.S.–owned discount store, and the company is expanding its wholly owned subsidiary there.[26]

Wholly owned subsidiaries have pros and cons. They provide for the tightest controls by the foreign firm. That firm also does not have to fear losing any of its rights to its proprietary knowledge. However, this is a relatively costly way to expand into foreign markets.

The Business Team in a Global Economy

Expanding abroad entails a coordinated effort by the company's business team, including the marketing, manufacturing, and HR managers. Each must analyze how best to manage their functions abroad, while working together to ensure they meet their company's overall goals.

Global Marketing

For most companies, marketing abroad is a necessity today. As one expert says, "Even the biggest companies in the biggest countries cannot survive on their domestic markets if they are in global industries. They have to be in all major markets."[27] At the same time, mass media, telecommunications, and air travel help blur the distinctions that once separated one country's market from another. So for many products "the tastes and preferences of consumers in different nations are beginning to converge on some global norm. Thus, in many industries it is no longer meaningful to talk about the 'German market,' 'the American market,' or the 'Japanese market'; there is only the 'global market.'"[28]

The result has been an explosion of exports for U.S. firms. This is illustrated in Figure 2.5.[29] Between 1990 and 1995, U.S. exports to China jumped by 150 percent, while exports to India jumped by 36 percent; exports to Germany rose by 59 percent; exports to the ASEAN countries doubled. As one economist sums up, "the global marketplace surely has arrived when villagers in the Middle East follow the Gulf War on CNN, via Soviet government satellite, and through a private subsidiary of a local government enterprise."[30]

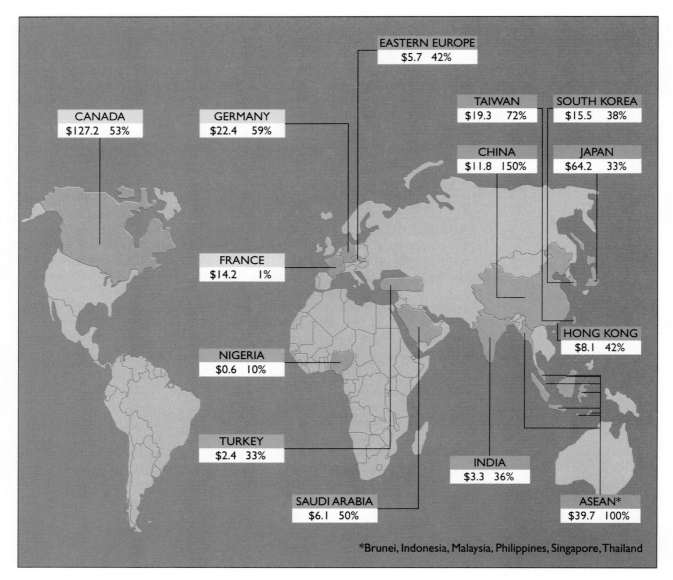

EASTERN EUROPE
$5.7 42%

CANADA
$127.2 53%

GERMANY
$22.4 59%

TAIWAN
$19.3 72%

SOUTH KOREA
$15.5 38%

CHINA
$11.8 150%

JAPAN
$64.2 33%

FRANCE
$14.2 1%

NIGERIA
$0.6 10%

HONG KONG
$8.1 42%

TURKEY
$2.4 33%

INDIA
$3.3 36%

SAUDI ARABIA
$6.1 50%

ASEAN*
$39.7 100%

*Brunei, Indonesia, Malaysia, Philippines, Singapore, Thailand

■ **FIGURE 2.5**
U.S. Exports
Generally Increasing
Most Quickly to Newly
Developed Countries
($Billion/% Change,
1990–1995).

SOURCE: Office of Trade and
Economic Analysis, U.S. Department of Commerce.

Organizational Behavior in Action

COMMUNICATING IN CHINA

While consumers' preferences may be merging in many instances, marketing managers know that behavioral differences still loom large. For example, foreign companies trying to win a share of the booming China market must adapt to *Quo Qing* (pronounced "gwor ching"), which means "Chinese characteristics." For example, typical Chinese consumers do not want to be among the first to try a new product, so setting up trials by early buyers is especially important. What to communicate is extremely important too. In the United States, marketing programs often communicate a product's "image" or "lifestyle." In China it is imperative to communicate the basics, such as "What is it?" "What is it called?" "And what does it do?" The interpretation of the message is important too. For example, Coca-Cola changed the phonetic spelling of its drink in China when it discovered that the previous translation roughly meant "wax mouth."

Given such cultural differences, marketing managers must work hard to find the right opportunities abroad for their companies' products. In other words, they have to find the right foreign marketing strategy—the right combination of products and promotion, given the needs of the overseas customers and the firm's ability to supply these products.

The easiest approach—and the one most often used by firms like McDonald's—is to supply abroad essentially the same products as at home, with only modest adaptation, at most, such as supplying sparkling water in some stores in France. At the other extreme, entirely new products might have to be supplied, as when McDonald's decided to build its restaurants in India around non-beef burgers, in deference to India's cultural requirements.[31]

Globalization of Production

Globalizing production means putting parts of a firm's production process in various locations around the globe. One aim is to provide manufacturing and supply support for the company's marketing efforts abroad. Another is to take advantage of national differences in the cost or quality of production.

It's usually important to integrate these global operations into a unified and efficient system of manufacturing facilities around the world.[32] Xerox Corporation's worldwide manufacturing system is an example. In the late 1970s and early 1980s, each Xerox company in each country had its own suppliers, assembly plants, and distribution channels. Production managers in each country's plants gave little thought to how their production plans fit into Xerox's global needs.

This approach became unworkable as international competition in the copier market grew more intense in the 1980s. Canon, Minolta, and Ricoh penetrated Xerox's U.S. and European markets with low-cost copiers. Between 1983 and 1985, Xerox's market share dropped from 57 percent to 52 percent.[33]

The competitive threat prompted Xerox's senior managers to coordinate their global production processes. For example, they created a central purchasing group to consolidate raw material sources and thereby cut worldwide manufacturing costs. They instituted a "leadership through quality" program to improve product quality, streamline and standardize manufacturing processes, and cut costs. Xerox managers eliminated over $1 billion of inventory costs by installing a system that linked customer orders more closely with worldwide production capabilities.

THE ROLE OF STRATEGIC GLOBAL PRODUCTION

Strategy therefore plays a big role in why companies globalize production. As at Xerox, many managers use their global production capability to build their competitive advantage. For example, here is how Whirlpool CEO David Whitman puts it:

> To me, "competitive advantage" means having the best technologies and processes for designing, manufacturing, selling, and servicing your products at the lowest possible costs. Our vision at Whirlpool is to integrate our geographical business wherever possible, so that our most advanced expertise in any given area—whether it's refrigeration technology, financial reporting systems, or distribution strategy—isn't confined to one location or one division. We want to be able to take the best capabilities we have and [apply] them in all of our operations worldwide.[34]

Global Staffing

Companies around the world are also tapping a vast new supply of skilled labor from wherever in the world that labor might be.[35] Thus, 3M makes tapes, chemicals, and electrical parts in Bangalore, India, for instance, and Hewlett-Packard assembles computers and designs memory boards in Guadalajara, Mexico. In Jamaica, 3,500 office workers make airline reservations, process tickets, and handle calls to toll-free numbers via satellite dishes for U.S. companies. Back in Bangalore, India, an educated workforce has drawn Texas Instruments and 30 more firms, including Motorola and IBM, to set up software program offices in the area.[36] Firms like these aren't just chasing after cheap labor. Instead, they are moving their plants and jobs overseas to tap into the pool of highly skilled employees that is becoming more available in Latin America and Asia.

Any decision to do business abroad therefore triggers global staffing questions. For example, setting up factories abroad requires analyzing employment laws in the host country and establishing a recruiting office. However, even a more modest expansion abroad requires a global staffing outlook. For example, sending the company's own sales manager abroad for several months to close a deal means deciding how to compensate her for her expenses abroad, what to do with her house here, and how to make sure she is trained to handle the cultural demands of her foreign assignment.

Organizational Behavior in Action

GLOBALIZATION IN MEXICO

Managers must carefully weigh behavioral factors when staffing their far-flung production facilities.[37] For example, consider some of the following OB factors in setting up a factory in Mexico.

WORKPLACE HARMONY. Compared to that of the United States, the Mexican workplace has a low tolerance for adversarial relations. While "getting along with others" is important in U.S. factories, Mexican employers put a much higher emphasis on hiring employees who have a record of working cooperatively with authority. Mexican employers, according to one expert, ". . . tend to seek workers who are agreeable, respectful, and obedient rather than innovative and independent."[38] This can lead to counterproductive behavior, even on the part of supervisors. For example, in attempting to preserve the appearance of harmony, supervisors may hide defective work from the department rather than have to confront the problem or report it to a manager.

ROLE AND STATUS. Mexican employees often put a relatively heavy emphasis on social order and on respecting one's status. In one factory in Chihuahua, Mexico, for instance, a U.S. manager wore jeans and insisted that everyone call him Jim. He assumed those around him would prefer that he reduce the visible status gap between himself and the Mexicans. He was therefore amazed to learn that the local employees considered him "uncultured and boorish."[39]

EXERCISING AUTHORITY. Mexican employees tend to have a more rigid view of authority than do their U.S. counterparts. Therefore, attempts by U.S. managers to encourage input and feedback from employees may just cause confusion. As an expert puts it:

> [Mexican] supervisors see their role as strictly following orders to the best of their ability, never questioning nor taking matters into their own hands, and this is exactly how they view the proper role of their subordinates. The Mexican supervisor's style is to supervise closely, and look for willing obedience. Opinions expressed by employees are often regarded as backtalk.[40] ■

The Global Manager

Globalization of markets, production, and labor is coinciding with the rise of a new type of manager—the global manager. To global managers like GE's Jack Welch, the bonds between company and country are thinning. A global manager is a manager who views markets and production globally and who seeks higher profits for his or her firm on a global basis.[41]

Global managers must be comfortable anywhere in the world: They must be cosmopolitan.[42] Webster's Dictionary defines cosmopolitan as "belonging to the world; not limited to just one part of the political, social, commercial or intellectual spheres; free from local, provincial, or national ideas, prejudices or attachments." The schedule of Manuel Diaz, president and general manager of Relsed Americas Corporation (shown in Figure 2.6), helps illustrate this cosmopolitan management style.[43] On the 13th, Diaz is in Hong Kong to lead a joint venture with a firm in Chiang Hai, China. In Chian Gai, he checks out Relsed's manufacturing facility. On the 18th, he is in Beijing for meetings with Chinese political leaders. Then, on the 20th, he's back at U.S. headquarters in Stamford, Connecticut, for meetings with other Relsed managers. In each location, he has to negotiate and finalize major decisions—opening new plants, hiring top managers, making financial commitments—with an understanding of the cultural differences from country to country.

Global managers like
Manuel Diaz must be
comfortable circling the
globe doing business with
people of many countries.

A MONTH IN THE LIFE OF
Frequent Flier
Manuel Diaz
President and General Manager
Relsed Americas Corporation

SEPTEMBER
13 Hong Kong, Relsed regional office
16 Shanghai. Relsed manufacturing complex
18 Beijing. Meetings
20 U.S. headquarters, Stamford, CT
22 Sao Paulo, Brazil
24 Buenos Aires, Argentina
27 Chile
29 Venezuela
OCTOBER
1   U.S. headquarters
6   Brazil
ONCE A MONTH: VISIT BRAZIL, MEXICO, AND CANADA
EVERY 3 OR 4 MONTHS: VISIT FAR EAST

Organizational Behavior in Action

COMMUNICATION AROUND THE WORLD

To manage globally, it also helps a manager to be a wizard at adapting his or her communications to the demands of different countries. Cultural differences play a big role in the way people in different countries "hear" what the manager is going to say. In the United States, for instance, people like a "comfort zone" around them and are uncomfortable when someone stands too close. In many Middle Eastern countries, on the other hand, it's not unusual for two managers to stand just a few inches apart when having a discussion at work. Similarly, in the United States the familiar "A-OK" sign formed when someone forms a circle with his or her index finger and thumb is meant to be positive, while in other countries it is a sign of deep disrespect.

Communicating can also create problems for unsuspecting managers in Japan. For example, just because a Japanese manager is smiling and nodding politely does not necessarily mean he or she is committing to anything. Similarly, one Japan expert suggests, "Don't ask questions too directly." She says that bombarding Japanese managers with too many questions can actually backfire. "This does not mean that you should not ask any questions, but take it slow."[44]   ■

The manager's philosophy about international business will influence his or her willingness to take a company global. An ethnocentric management philosophy may manifest itself in an **ethnocentric** or home-market-oriented firm. A **polycentric** phi-

Successful marketers like Coca-Cola tailor their communications and advertising when they sell their products abroad.

losophy may translate into a company that is limited to several individual foreign markets. Finally, a **regiocentric** (or **geocentric**) philosophy may lead the manager to create more of an integrated worldwide production and marketing presence.

Organizational Behavior in Action

WOULD YOUR COMPANY PICK YOU TO BE AN INTERNATIONAL EXECUTIVE?

Of course, there's going to be much more involved in getting picked to be a global manager than just having the capacity to travel the world and having the right international business philosophy. What do companies look for when trying to identify international executives, and do you think you might have what it takes? If you'd like to know, read on.

A recent study by behavioral scientists at the University of Southern California provides some insights into these questions. They studied 838 lower-, middle-, and senior-level managers from six international firms and 21 countries, focusing particularly on the managers' personal characteristics. Specifically, the researchers studied the extent to which personal characteristics such as "sensitivity to cultural differences" could be used to distinguish between managers who had high potential as international executives, and those whose potential was not so high.

Fourteen personal characteristics successfully distinguished the managers identified by their companies as high potential from those identified as not high-performing in 72 percent of the cases. To get an initial, tentative impression of how you would rate, the fourteen characteristics (along with sample items) are listed

SCALE	SAMPLE ITEM
Sensitive to Cultural Differences	When working with people from other cultures, works hard to understand their perspectives.
Business Knowledge	Has a solid understanding of our products and services.
Courage to Take a Stand	Is willing to take a stand on issues.
Brings Out the Best in People	Has a special talent for dealing with people.
Acts with Integrity	Can be depended on to tell the truth regardless of circumstances.
Is Insightful	Is good at identifying the most important part of a complex problem or issue.
Is Committed to Success	Clearly demonstrates commitment to seeing the organization succeed.
Takes Risks	Takes personal as well as business risks.
Uses Feedback	Has changed as a result of feedback.
Is Culturally Adventurous	Enjoys the challenge of working in countries other than his/her own.
Seeks Opportunities to Learn	Takes advantage of opportunities to do new things.
Is Open to Criticism	Appears brittle—as if criticism might cause him/her to break.*
Seeks Feedback	Pursues feedback even when others are reluctant to give it.
Is Flexible	Doesn't get so invested in things that he/she cannot change when something doesn't work.

*Reverse scored.

above. For each, indicate (by placing a number in the space provided) whether you strongly agree (number 7), strongly disagree (number 1), or fall somewhere in between.

Generally speaking, the higher you score on these fourteen characteristics, the more likely it is you might have been identified as a high potential international executive in this study.[45] The average would be about 50. ■

The Manager in an International Environment

Going international presents the manager with new and often perplexing problems. He or she must now be adept at assessing a wide array of economic, legal, political, sociocultural, and technological factors. Let's look at some of these.

The Economic Environment

Managers engaged in international business need to be familiar with the economic systems of the countries in question, the level of each country's economic development, and exchange rates.

THE ECONOMIC SYSTEM.   For example, consider the dilemma facing business managers in Hong Kong today. In 1997 the People's Republic of China, with its completely different economic system, resumed governing Hong Kong. How will this affect Hong Kong's existing economic structure, and how will foreign firms react?

At the present time, Hong Kong is an example of a market economy. In a pure market economy, the quantities and nature of the goods and services produced are not planned by anyone. Instead, the interaction of supply and demand in the market for goods and services determines what is produced, in what quantities, and at what prices.

At the other extreme, the People's Republic of China (PRC) until very recently has been entirely an example of a command economy. In a command economy, government *central planning agencies* try to determine how much is produced by which sectors of the economy, and by which plants and for whom these goods are produced. Countries like these (and they included, until recently, the former Soviet Union) usually base their yearly targets on five-year plans. They then establish specific production goals and prices for each sector of the economy (for each product or group of products) and for each manufacturing plant.

It is conceivable that some time in the future, the PRC might move to a mixed economy. In a **mixed economy,** some sectors of the economy are left to private ownership and free market mechanisms, while others are largely owned by and managed by the government.[46]

Hong Kong became part of the PRC in 1997. Firms now must decide whether to maintain, increase, or decrease their investments in Hong Kong, given its takeover by a traditionally command-economy–oriented country.

ECONOMIC DEVELOPMENT.   Countries also differ—often dramatically—in their rate of economic development. For example, Figure 2.7 illustrates that growth of gross domestic product—an indicator of economic growth—is estimated to be about 1.8 percent in the United States during 1996.[47] The figure for Hong Kong (5.7 percent) is over twice as large, while the growth rate in other Southeast Asian countries is even higher. This helps to explain why managers at firms like GE are shifting resources to Asia.[48]

EXCHANGE RATES.   Managers engaged in international business must also juggle exchange rates. The **exchange rate** for one country's currency is the rate at which it can be exchanged for another country's currency. As the foreign exchange chart in Figure 2.8 shows, in April 1997, one Brazilian real was worth about 94 cents in U.S. currency. Similarly, a French franc was worth about 17 cents. Exchange rates can have a big impact on a company's performance. For example, a dramatic drop in the value of the dollar relative to the pound could have a devastating effect on a small U.S. company that suddenly found it needed 30 percent more dollars to build its factory in Scotland than it had planned.

The Political and Legal Environment

The international manager also must consider the legal and political environments of the countries in which he or she is to do business. Consider the uneven playing field between Japan and the United States, for example. A Chrysler

		1994	1995 proj.	1996 proj.	1996 GDP projections Billions, U.S.
Mature Economics	CANADA	4.3	4.3	2.9	$633
	GERMANY	2.8	3.4	3.7	$2,311
	BRITAIN	3.9	3.1	2.3	$1,150
	U.S.	4.0	2.7	1.8	$7,383
	FRANCE	2.4	3.2	2.9	$1,503
	JAPAN	0.8	3.4	3.9	$5,252
	ITALY	2.5	3.0	2.4	$1,171
Asia	CHINA	11.3	9.9	8.2	$739
	SINGAPORE	10.2	8.6	6.8	$84
	MALAYSIA	8.8	8.5	7.2	$97
	THAILAND	8.1	8.5	6.2	$177
	SOUTH KOREA	7.9	7.4	6.3	$491
	TAIWAN	6.2	6.7	6.2	$287
	INDONESIA	6.3	6.2	5.3	$184
	HONG KONG	5.7	6.0	5.7	$167
	INDIA	4.9	5.0	4.9	$368
Latin America	ARGENTINA	6.3	5.6	6.1	$356
	CHILE	4.4	5.8	6.2	$58
	BRAZIL	2.6	4.5	6.2	$949
	MEXICO	3.2	0.7	2.1	$377
Europe	POLAND	6.3	6.0	5.8	$100
	CZECH REPUBLIC	4.3	6.8	6.0	$49
	HUNGARY	5.1	3.2	5.7	$45

Growth Rates

FIGURE 2.7
Growth of Gross Domestic Product in the United States— 1994

SOURCE: *Fortune Magazine* (March 20, 1995).

LeBaron sells for $18,176 in the United States but for $33,077 in Japan.[49] How could this be?

TRADE CONTROL. The answer is that trade controls can dramatically distort the price companies must charge in other countries. **Trade controls** are governmental influences usually aimed at reducing the competitiveness of imported products or services. *Tariffs,* the most common type of trade control, are governmental taxes levied on goods shipped internationally.[50] The exporting country collects export tariffs, the importing country collects import tariffs, and the country through which the goods are passed collects transit tariffs.

A multitude of nontariff barriers exist, too. For example, in addition to Japan's high automobile import tariffs, cars not made in Japan must meet a complex set of regulations and equipment modifications. Side mirrors must snap off easily if they come into contact with a pedestrian, and any manufacturer selling 1,000 or fewer cars of a particular model annually in Japan must test each car individually for gas mileage and emission standards.

Some countries make direct payments to domestic producers. These are called *subsidies* and can make an otherwise inefficient producer more cost competitive than it would be otherwise. Other countries impose quotas—legal restrictions on the import of particular goods—as further barriers to trade.[51]

POLITICAL RISKS. The international manager must be concerned not just with governmental influences on trade but with political risks as well. For example, com-

FOREIGN EXCHANGE

WEDNESDAY, APRIL 16, 1997

Currency	Foreign Currency in Dollars		Dollars in Foreign Currency	
	Wed.	Tue.	Wed.	Tue.
f-Argent (Peso)	1.0002	1.0002	.9998	.9998
Australia (Dollar)	.7711	.7741	1.2968	1.2918
Austria (Schilling)	.0824	.0820	12.137	12.190
c-Belgium (Franc)	.0281	.0280	35.56	35.73
Brazil (Real)	.9390	.9437	1.0650	1.0597
Britain (Pound)	1.6244	1.6316	.6156	.6129
30-day fwd	1.6236	1.6281	.6159	.6142
60-day fwd	1.6229	1.6273	.6162	.6145
90-day fwd	1.6221	1.6265	.6165	.6148
Canada (Dollar)	.7160	.7161	1.3966	1.3965
30-day fwd	.7179	.7177	1.3930	1.3933
60-day fwd	.7192	.7192	1.3904	1.3905
90-day fwd	.7206	.7205	1.3878	1.3880
y-Chile (Peso)	.002393	.002395	417.80	417.55
China (Yuan)	.1201	.1201	8.3261	8.3265
Colombia (Peso)	.000945	.000945	1058.73	1058.76
c-CzechRep (Koruna)	.0326	.0333	30.72	30.05
Denmark (Krone)	.1523	.1518	6.5640	6.5885
ECU (ECU)	1.13190	1.13290	.8835	.8827
z-Ecudr (Sucre)	.000262	.000262	3820.00	3820.00
d-Egypt (Pound)	.2947	.2947	3.3934	3.3934
Finland (Mark)	.1931	.1927	5.1775	5.1900
France (Franc)	.1721	.1722	5.8105	5.8085
Germany (Mark)	.5786	.5790	1.7283	1.7270
30-day fwd	.5799	.5807	1.7244	1.7220
60-day fwd	.5811	.5819	1.7208	1.7185
90-day fwd	.5824	.5832	1.7169	1.7147
Greece (Drachma)	.003681	.003693	271.67	270.80
Hong Kong (Dollar)	.1290	.1290	7.7490	7.7490

ECU: European Currency Unit, a basket of European currencies.
The Federal Reserve Board's index of the value of the dollar against 10 other currencies weighted on the basis of trade was 96.92 Wednesday, off −0.04 points or −0.04 percent from Tuesday's 96.96. A year ago the index was 87.93

a-fixing, Moscow Interbank Currency Exchange.
c-commercial rate, d-free market rate, f-financial rate, y-official rate, z-floating rate.
Prices as of 3:00 p.m. Eastern Time from Dow Jones Telerate and other sources.

■ **FIGURE 2.8**
Foreign Exchange
International travelers should be familiar with exchange rates between various countries. For example, on April 16, 1997, one Brazilian real was worth about $0.94.

panies doing business in South Africa wonder how the new majority rule will affect their businesses. U.S. manufacturers in Peru must be ever vigilant against terrorist attacks. In 1994, the ethnic violence in the former Yugoslavia brought economic activities for many companies exporting to those countries to a virtual standstill.[52]

LEGAL SYSTEMS. There are also important differences in legal systems. Many countries adhere to a system known as common law, based on tradition and depending more on precedence and customs than on written statutes. England is one example of a country that uses common law.

Other countries have a code law system, or a comprehensive set of written statutes. Some countries use a combination of common law and code law. For example, the United States adheres to a system of common law in many things but to a written Uniform Commercial Code for governing the activities of businesses.

International law is another consideration. International law is not so much an enforceable body of law as it is agreements embodied in treaties and other types of agreements that countries have agreed to respect. For example, international law governs intellectual property rights (such as whether U2's music can be reproduced in Japan without its permission).

Legal issues can influence how the manager expands abroad.[53] For example, a joint venture can help a U.S. firm achieve a market presence with the aid of a local partner. However, joint venture laws vary. In India, for instance, a foreign investor may own only up to 40 percent of an Indian industrial company, while in Japan up to 100 percent of foreign ownership is allowed.[54] Some managers, as we've seen, go global by appointing sales agents or representatives in other countries. But in some countries this is not an option: in Algeria, for instance, agents are not permitted to represent foreign sellers, and in other countries agents are viewed as employees subject to the employment laws of those countries.[55]

The Sociocultural Environment

People who travel to other countries quickly learn that they must also adapt to societal differences. In Latin America, for instance, *machismo* ("maleness") is defined by virility, zest for action, daring, competitiveness, and the will to conquer. This is translated into daily business life by demonstrating forcefulness, self-confidence, courage, and leadership.[56] The differences between the Japanese and U.S. culture manifest themselves in thousands of small ways. In Japan, saving face and achieving harmony are very important. As a result, indirect and vague communication is preferred, with sentences frequently left unfinished so the other person may draw his or her own conclusions. In the Middle East, the people of Arabia, it is said, love the spoken word and tend not to get to the point quickly. This can frustrate U.S. managers, who must be careful not to exhibit impatience or annoyance. And in France, a firm and pumping handshake may be considered uncultured; instead, a quick shake with some pressure on the grip is more appropriate.

VALUES.   Research by Geert Hofstede suggests that a society's values are among the most influential cultural differences. *Values* are basic beliefs we hold about what is good or bad, important or unimportant. Values (such as West Point's famous "duty, honor, country") are important because they shape the way we behave.

Hofstede argues that cultural differences among countries reflect the following four basic values.

- **Power distance.**[57] According to Hofstede, power distance is the extent to which the less powerful members of institutions accept and expect that power will be distributed unequally.[58] Hofstede concluded that the institutionalization of such a view of inequality was higher in some countries (such as Mexico) than it was in others (such as Sweden).
- **Individualism vs. collectivism.** The degree to which ties between individuals are normally loose or close is measured as individualism or collectivism. In more individualistic countries, "all members are expected to look after themselves and their immediate families."[59] Individualistic countries include Australia and the United States. In collectivist countries, people are expected to care for each other more. Indonesia and Pakistan are examples of collectivist countries.

- **Masculinity vs. femininity.** According to Hofstede, societies differ also in the extent to which they value assertiveness (which he called "masculinity") or caring ("femininity"). Japan and Austria ranked high in masculinity; Denmark, Costa Rica, and Chile ranked low.
- **Uncertainty avoidance.** Uncertainty avoidance refers to whether people in the society are uncomfortable with unstructured situations in which unknown, surprising, or novel incidents occur. In other words, how comfortable are people in this society when it comes to dealing with surprises? The people in some countries (such as Sweden, Israel, and Great Britain) are, according to Hofstede, relatively comfortable dealing with uncertainty and surprises. On the other hand, people living in other countries (including Greece and Portugal) tend to be uncertainty avoiders.[60] Those more comfortable with uncertainty "are more tolerant of opinions that are different from what they are used to; they [also] try to have as few rules as possible."[61]

LANGUAGE AND CUSTOMS. The international manager also needs to deal with differences in language. (One airline's "Fly in Leather" slogan was embarrassingly translated as "fly naked" for the company's Latin American campaign.)[62] The country's traditional manners and customs can also be important. For instance, Campbell's learned that Japanese drink soup mainly for breakfast. A country's predominant religions, cultural orientations (such as styles of music and art), and educational methods can also influence how business should be conducted in the country.

The Technological Environment

A country's technological environment—and in particular the relative ease or difficulty with which technology can be transferred from one country to another—can determine a product's success abroad. **Technology transfer** is the "transfer of systematic knowledge for the manufacture of a product, for the application of a process, or for the rendering of a service, and does not extend to the mere sale or lease of goods."[63]

Successful technology transfer depends on several things. First, there must be a *suitable technology* to be transferred, for instance, filtration devices. Second, *social and economic conditions* must favor the transfer. Thus, pollution-reducing technology that might be effective in the United States might be useless in a less-developed country where political, social, and economic conditions do not encourage pollution reduction. Finally, successful technology transfer depends on the *willingness and ability* of the receiving party to use and adapt the technology.[64] If the successful application of pollution control techniques required trained chemical engineers to whom the receiving country had no access, the technology transfer would not be successful.

The Process of International Management

International management means carrying out on an international scale the management functions of planning, organizing, leading, and controlling. Doing business internationally obviously affects the way each of these functions is carried out. We will present several examples here and then continue our discussion of international management in each chapter, as appropriate.

Multinational Planning Issues

Planning means setting goals and identifying the courses of action for achieving those goals. It therefore requires identifying opportunities and threats, and balancing these with the strengths and weaknesses of the enterprise. Planning in an international arena uses the same basic approach. However, global planning also means dealing with several unique issues.

For one thing, as we've seen, the international planners must address special political, legal, and technological issues. There is the possibility of political instability, since many countries have frequent changes of government.[65] Similarly, currency instability, competition from state-owned enterprises, and pressures from national governments (including changing tariff barriers) can all throw even the best-laid plans into disarray.

Instabilities like these are not just a characteristic of developing countries. Between 1993 and 1995, Italy embarked on a sweeping privatization of its nationalized businesses. During that time, Italy sold banks and companies worth about $60 billion, including some of the country's largest telecommunications, oil and gas, and insurance companies.[66] At the same time, sweeping criminal investigations created havoc among the country's political and managerial elite. The resulting upheaval created enormous opportunities for foreign firms doing business in Italy. But it also increased the risks by boosting both the competitiveness of the newly privatized Italian firms and the uncertainties of dealing with the country's political institutions.

Other complications arise in international planning.[67] A domestic (U.S.) planner faces a relatively homogeneous home market, while international planners face a relatively fragmented and diverse set of foreign customers and needs. For U.S. planners, data are usually available and are relatively accurate and easy to collect. Internationally, collecting information—about demographics, production levels, and so on—can be a formidable task, and the actual data are often of questionable accuracy.

Organizing the Multinational Business

As companies evolve from domestic to multinational enterprises, they typically go through several organizational stages.[68] Figure 2.9 illustrates the typical organizational alternatives, which include the domestic organization, the export-oriented organization, the international organization, and the multinational organization.

These alternatives differ in how they maintain authority over foreign operations. In the *domestic organization,* each division handles its own foreign sales, which may come largely from unsolicited overseas orders. Next, in response to increasing orders from abroad, the firm may move up to an *export-oriented organization* structure. Here, a department (often called an import-export department) coordinates all international activities such as licensing, contracting, and managing foreign sales. In an *international organization,* the company is divided into separate domestic and international divisions. The international division focuses on production and sales overseas, while the domestic division focuses on domestic markets. This describes the organization announced by Reynolds Metals in March 1997. The company was reorganized into six worldwide businesses with a U.S.–focused group and a separate international group.[69]

Finally, the firm may be pushed toward a *multinational form.* Here, each country in which the firm does business may have its own subsidiary. The oil firm Royal Dutch Shell is organized this way. It has separate subsidiaries for Shell Switzerland and Shell U.S.A. (as well as many other countries), for instance.[70]

Traditional Division Structure	Export-Oriented Division Structure	International Division Structure	Multinational Division Structure

Here each division handles the minimal existing sales to each market itself.

Here the export division or department helps to coordinate foreign sales, for instance by assisting with freight forwarding arrangements.

Here each domestic division produces and sells for the local market. The international division may handle production and sales for foreign markets, or possibly just market abroad products produced in domestic factories.

Here each country of geographic region is the responsibility of its own officer and division, which handles sales and production within its own geographic boundaries. Increasingly, as we'll see, companies are consolidating production facilities, so that, for instance, more efficient plants in, say, Asia, might supply products worldwide.

■ **FIGURE 2.9**
International Organizations

As firms evolve from domestic to multinational enterprises, their increasing international operations necessitate a more globally oriented organization.

Globalization also affects the firm's human resource staffing methods. Here policy issues range from how to select, train, and compensate managers who are to be sent to foreign posts to how to deal with inter-country differences in labor laws. For example, one expert says, "When international executives' relocations fail, they generally fail either because expatriates can't fathom the customs of a new country or because their families can't deal with the emotional stress that a company's relocation entails."[71] Global companies therefore should provide training that focuses on the impact of cultural differences, on raising trainees' awareness of the impact on business decisions of these cultural differences, and on other matters like building language and adaptation skills. Addressing inter-country differences in labor laws, such as the fact that what may be sexual harassment in one country might not be in another, is another example.[72] Yet few firms actually provide such intercultural-difference training to their employees.[73]

Leading the International Enterprise

Globalizing influences the behavioral side of leading the firm, too. In Latin America, for instance, bosses are expected to be more autocratic, so participative management (in which employees are encouraged to make work-related decisions) can backfire. At the other extreme, Japanese managers value consensus and rarely welcome the kind of take-charge leader who wants to personally make all the decisions.

In their book *Working for the Japanese,* Joseph and Suzy Fucini describe the cultural problems between the Japanese and U.S. workers that eventually caused

Denny Pawley, the highest-ranking American at the Michigan plant, to leave for a new job with United Technologies Corporation:

> Pawley did not quit for the money. He left Mazda because he had become frustrated with the constraints that the company's Japanese management had placed on him. After two years and one month with Mazda, it had become obvious to the burly, high-spirited car man . . . that because he was an American he would never be given real authority at Flatrock. He had, he believed, worked patiently with the Japanese to learn their system, in the belief that one day he would be combining this knowledge with the experience he brought with him from General Motors to create the "third-culture plan" that Mazda's executives had so often talked about. But, as he would later observe, "it started looking more and more to me [like] the real decision making would always come out of Hiroshima, and [this] just didn't offer me the opportunity to use my broad-based management experience."[74]

Issues in Controlling the Multinational Enterprise

Maintaining control means monitoring actual performance to ensure it is consistent with the standards expected. Doing so is difficult enough when the manager is around the corner. The problems can be even more complex in the global enterprise, since geographic distance, language, and cultural barriers can hinder communications and therefore control.

In summary, globalizing confronts the manager with new international management issues and challenges. The effectiveness through which he or she deals with these new issues—whether they involve planning, organizing, leading, managing human resources, controlling, or managing the behavioral side of his or her firm—will determine whether or not the decision to internationalize turns out to be a good one.

SUMMARY

1. An international business is any firm that engages in international trade or investment. Firms are globalizing for many reasons, the three main ones being to expand sales, to acquire resources, and to diversify sources of sales and supplies. Sales expansion is usually the primary motivation. Other reasons for pursuing international business include reducing costs or improving quality by seeking out products and services produced in foreign countries and smoothing out sales and profit swings.

2. Free trade means that all barriers to trade among participating countries are removed. Its potential benefits have prompted many nations to enter into various levels of economic integration, ranging from a free-trade area to a common market.

3. Companies can pursue several strategies when it comes to extending operations to foreign markets. Exporting is often the route chosen by manufacturers, but licensing and franchising are two popular alternatives. At some point, a firm may decide to directly invest its own funds in another country. Joint ventures and wholly owned subsidiaries are two examples of foreign direct investments.

4. Globalizing production means dispersing parts of a firm's production process to various locations around the globe. The aim is to take advantage of national differences in the cost and quality of production and then integrate these operations in a unified system of manufacturing facilities around the world. Companies also are tapping a new supply of skilled labor in various countries. The globalization of markets, production, and labor coincides with the rise of a new type of global manager, who can function effectively anywhere in the world.

5. International managers must be adept at assessing a wide array of environmental factors. For example, managers must be familiar with the economic systems, exchange rates, and level of economic development of the countries in which they do business. They also must be aware of import restrictions, political risks, and legal differences and restraints. Important cultural differences will also affect the way people in various countries act and expect to be treated. Values, languages, and customs are all examples of elements that distinguish people of one culture from those of another. Finally, the relative ease with which technology can be transferred from one country to another is an important consideration in conducting international business.

KEY TERMS

international trade
international business
international
   management
multinational corporation
   (MNC)
global corporation
free trade

economic integration
free trade area
customs union
common market
exchange rate
trade controls
technology transfer
ethnocentric

polycentric
regiocentric
geocentric
exporting
foreign direct investment
strategic alliance
joint venture
mixed economy

SELF-TEST

TRUE / FALSE QUESTIONS

1 **T F** Taking advantage of cheap labor is the primary reason most firms go overseas.

2 **T F** A polycentric management philosophy leads to the creation of home-market–oriented firms.

3 **T F** In a common market, no barriers to trade exist among members, but no common external trade policy is in force.

4 **T F** NAFTA will create the world's largest free market.

5 **T F** Asia has not yet developed free trade agreements.

6 **T F** Due to international accounting standards, exchange rates don't affect international companies.

7 **T F** The United States is considered to rank high on collectivism.

8 **T F** Franchising usually requires the franchisee to follow much stricter guidelines in running the business than does licensing.

9 **T F** Wholly owned subsidiaries are a relatively inexpensive way to expand into foreign markets.

10 **T F** Most firms provide cross-cultural training to employees taking on an overseas assignment.

MULTIPLE-CHOICE QUESTIONS

1 The export or import of goods or services to consumers in another country is called
  a. international investment.
  b. international trade.
  c. multinational commerce.
  d. multinational investment.

2 An internationally integrated production system, over which equity-based control is exercised by a parent corporation that is owned and managed essentially by the nationals of the country in which it is domiciled, is called a(n)
  a. multinational corporation.
  b. MNC.
  c. international investment.
  d. both a and b.

3 Which of the following is an example of an MNC?
  a. General Electric
  b. General Motors
  c. ITT
  d. all of the above

4 Which of the following is not a reason for today's increasing globalization?
  a. Domestic markets are too limited.
  b. Television, telecommunications, and air travel have combined to blur the distinctions among countries and their markets.
  c. It is a relatively cheap expansion strategy.
  d. All of the above are reasons for increasing globalization.

5 _____ means dispersing parts of a firm's production process to various locations around the globe.
  a. Globalizing production
  b. International investment

c. International trade
  d. None of the above

6 In a _____, some sectors of the economy are left to private ownership and free market mechanisms, while others are largely owned by and managed by the government.
  a. command economy
  b. market economy
  c. mixed economy
  d. all of the above

7 Southeast Asia's growth of GNP is _____ that of the United States'.
  a. substantially higher than
  b. substantially lower than
  c. equal to
  d. marginally lower than

8 _____ refer(s) to governmental influences that are usually aimed at reducing the competitiveness of imported products or services.
  a. Trade control
  b. Trade embargoes
  c. Trade subsidies
  d. Tariffs

9 Which of the following is not a type of trade control?
  a. tariffs
  b. subsidies
  c. quotas
  d. embargoes

10 _____ are government taxes levied on goods shipped internationally.
  a. Tariffs
  b. Subsidies
  c. Quotas
  d. Embargoes

CRITICAL THINKING EXERCISES

1 At the end of the nineteenth century, an admiral of the U.S. Navy predicted that as the Mediterranean had been the sea of the past and the Atlantic the sea of the present, so the Pacific would be the sea of the future. What do you think he meant? Is the Pacific Rim the leading market for goods and services in the twenty-first century? Write your own version of the admiral's prediction looking ahead to the year 3000.

2 "While a typical Western individual 'conceptualizes' things from an objective vantage point, a Japanese person does so by relating her- or himself to other things and persons. Therefore, the Japanese perspective is 'tactile' [almost as if he or she can 'touch' it] and 'interpersonal'. . . . Although Western societies promote the realization of the individual self as the goal of life, the Japanese ideal of life is to

exist among others harmoniously as a collective self."—Ikujiro Nonaka and Hirotaka Takeuchi, *The Knowledge-Creating Company* (New York: Oxford University Press, 1996), 31.

Japan has become an economic powerhouse over the last 50 years. From the above analysis, draw your own conclusions about what some basic differences are between U.S. and Japanese culture and what they might mean in terms of how each nation does business.

3 As a salesperson for an insurance firm, you have just been transferred from Fargo, ND, to San Francisco, CA. Your new supervisor has shared some very interesting figures with you. According to a recent issue of *Money* magazine, the total purchasing power of Asian Americans, Hispanics, African Americans, and gay adults runs into billions of dollars. San Francisco has a large population of each of these groups.

Your task is to come up with a strategy to sell insurance in the area. Write a one- to two-page report on your strategy. Include a paragraph about how your experience working in this city might help you with any international assignments in your future with the firm.

4 You work for a health-care technology firm interested in expanding internationally. Among the countries under consideration are Russia, China, Brazil, Kenya, New Zealand, Italy, Poland, Israel, Syria, Turkey, France, and Bulgaria. Your CEO has asked you to pick three countries, research them, and recommend one. Write a two-page report giving your recommendation and your reasons.

DIVERSITY CASE

DEALING WITH DIVERSITY ABROAD

Solving diversity-related problems is challenging enough for U.S.–based managers. Their U.S. counterparts overseas may face even more complex choices. While equal opportunity and individual civil rights are the law of the land here, that frequently isn't the case abroad. So when moral and legal issues run counter to host-country customs, problems are bound to arise.

Cultural differences are among the most difficult to address. AT&T asked New York–based consultants Cornelius Grove and Willa Hallowell to analyze gender and race issues around the world. Among their findings, Grove and Hallowell wrote that the ethical underpinnings that drive diversity issues at home don't always exist abroad. Many societies consider ethnic differences an appropriate criterion for employee selection. For example, European descendants in Mexico are loathe to promote indigenous races to management posts. Japanese managers are only rarely and reluctantly comfortable with East Indian employees, even those in positions of responsibility. Despite these findings, the two consultants recommend that U.S. managers abroad ignore cultural norms and continue placing a premium on equality.

Ali Boureslan has had some practical experience with discriminatory treatment overseas. When the Arabian American Oil Company (Aramco) engineer was transferred to Saudi Arabia, he says he was relentlessly ridiculed by his supervisor because he was of Lebanese extraction and a practicing Muslim. "As an American society, we are not free of this disease," Boureslan says. He was eventually fired, filed suit against Aramco, and lost. Higher courts sustained the verdict, concurring that Congress never intended to extend anti-bias laws overseas. "It is a chauvinistic and imperialistic view that U.S. law is always better," says Aramco's attorney Paul L. Friedman.

Questions

1 Do you think U.S. civil rights laws should apply to U.S. companies' foreign operations? Why or why not?
2 If you were setting policy for a U.S. company operating overseas, what approach would you suggest managers take in dealing with diversity issues outside the United States?
3 Discuss the contention that it is chauvinistic and imperialistic to believe that U.S. law is always better.

SOURCES: Leon E. Wynter, "Multiculturalism Stalls at the National Divide," *Wall Street Journal,* 19 January 1994, B1; Susan B. Garland, "Were Civil Rights Meant to Travel?" *Business Week,* 31 January 1991, 36.

STRATEGY CASE

BLOCKBUSTER VIDEO

For many years, the growth of the Blockbuster Video chain more than lived up to its name. Blockbuster's former chairman H. Wayne Huizenga and some close business associates bought out Blockbuster's founders and franchise holders in 1987 and began expanding rapidly across the United States. Video rental sales were booming. In 1982 rentals and sales of home videos in the United States were about $700 million. By 1991 sales had boomed to $11 billion, and by 1994 they were almost $14 billion, heading to an estimated $19 billion by the end of the decade. During this period Blockbuster opened thousands of stores across North America and began its international expansion in early 1992. Overseas it began by purchasing City Vision PLC, which at the time was the largest home video retailer in the United Kingdom. That foray abroad was followed by a joint venture in Japan with Fugita & Company as well as store openings in Austria, Australia, Canada, Chile, Guam, Mexico, Puerto Rico, Spain, and Venezuela. By 1994, Blockbuster had over 4,000 stores and was adding more daily. It was at that point that Huizenga and

Blockbuster were approached by the top management of Viacom (the owners of MTV). A deal was struck and Viacom purchased Blockbuster.

Strategically, the deal made a lot of sense. Viacom needed a source of cash for its expansion and Blockbuster rental stores were "cash cows," businesses that generate lots of cash without much continuing investment. Viacom was already in the business of showing music videos and was about to purchase Simon & Schuster publishers, another business that generally seemed to "fit" with the video rental business.

However, no industry's sales can go straight through the roof forever, and over the past year or so video rental sales growth has slowed. Blockbuster's management therefore is reconsidering its strategic options. For example, should it *diversify* its in-store product offerings and begin renting and selling books as well as videos? Should it *vertically integrate* and begin producing movies and music videos? Would it be enough for Blockbuster to pursue a *market penetration* strategy and simply increase the money it spends on advertising to take sales away from competing video rental stores? Or is Blockbuster's best strategic option to *expand geographically* into the many countries where viewers don't have the cable, movie-house, and entertainment options that U.S. consumers currently have?

Questions

1 Which strategy would you recommend top management follow? For example, do you think diversification makes sense, and, if so, what products would you add? Similarly, do you think vertical integration is an option? Market penetration? Global expansion? (You might want to do some research by first visiting a Blockbuster Video rental store.)

2 If Blockbuster did decide to put most of its resources into expanding abroad, what legal-political and cultural differences would be significant? How would you advise the company to adapt to these differences?

3 What strategic options in going international does Blockbuster seem to have followed up until now? What strategies would you recommend it follow from this?

4 Suppose you were the HR officer for Blockbuster's global headquarters here in the United States. You are about to recommend someone from headquarters to go to Japan to open several Blockbuster outlets. What would you look for in your candidate, what sort of training do you think this person would need, and what other HR issues in general (such as compensation) do you think would have to be taken into consideration, and why?

SOURCES: Based on James A. Kidney, "Blockbuster Entertainment Corporation," a case study included in John A. Pearce, II and Richard B. Robinson, Jr., *Strategic Management* (Burr Ridge, IL: Irwin, 1994), 518–29; and Marshall Loeb, "There's No Business Like Show Business," *Fortune,* 8 August 1994, 111–12; and Stephen Robbins and Mary Coulter, *Management,* 5th ed. (Upper Saddle River, NJ: Prentice Hall, 1996), 139.

ENTREPRENEURIAL CASE

RAFAEL'S BODEGAS GOES GLOBAL

The owners of Rafael's Bodegas had a problem. After several years of rapid U.S. expansion it was obvious that Rafael's Bodegas outside of those cities with high concentrations of Hispanics were not going to be successful. Several things accounted for this, they believed, including the chain's Hispanic name and its heavy emphasis on Hispanic-type food products. The owners felt it was unrealistic to even consider changing the product line or the name since these gave the chain its unique difference. They decided to close the unprofitable stores and to regroup.

After reviewing several strategic options (including merging with other grocery chains) the owners decided to pursue a strategy of global expansion. In particular they decided to look south instead of north and to begin the process of expanding their fledgling chain into Mexico and South America and Central America. It quickly became apparent, though, that this new strategy brought enormous risks of its own.

Questions

1 What new risks would expanding outside the United States bring the owners over and above the sorts of risks they would face by just expanding in the United States?

2 What strategies could they use to expand their chain south of the border, and which would you recommend and why?

3 List two or three specific ways in which Rafael's Bodegas's planning, organizing, leading, and controlling activities would be affected by or would have to be adapted in some way to expanding the company's operations abroad.

THE BUSINESS TEAM, INC.

STARR FILTER CORP.

Starr Filter Corp. is owned and run by Martin Starr, who invented a new material for filtering noxious gases out of the chimneys of chemical plants and fertilizer factories. Today the patents on several of Starr's main products are starting to run out, and Martin wants to aggressively build market share while the patents are still in force. To do this, he has decided to embark on a strategy of aggressive global expansion.

He knows that doing so will require a coordinated cross-functional effort. For example, how should he sell and market abroad, and which countries should he start with? Should he produce everything in the United States and ship it abroad or set up factories in other countries and, if so, where? And how should he go about financing the expansion? To help him and his managers evaluate these decisions he decided to retain The Business Team, Inc., the small consulting firm that specializes in bringing a cross-functional point of view to the solution of a company's problems.

The Business Team, Inc. partners must keep several things in mind when formulating recommendations for Martin and his company. First, selling Starr Filters anywhere tends to be a very specialized task: The salespeople generally must be trained in chemical engineering and are almost always dealing with sophisticated engineering plant managers. The latter are generally very concerned about meeting pollution-control standards, which vary widely from country to country. Given the special nature of these products, designing an application for a particular filter for a plant requires very specialized engineering know-how and may not be transferable abroad. Similarly, the manufacturing process for the filter material must be kept a secret.

Questions

1. If you were part of The Business Team, Inc., what types of international expansion strategies would you tell Martin are available for expanding overseas? If you decided to recommend using sales agents, how would you advertise and recruit them?

2. As the production expert, what strategic issues would you tell Martin to keep in mind when deciding how to set up production facilities abroad?

3. As the HR expert, what OB issues do you think the marketing and production managers should keep in mind?

YOU BE THE CONSULTANT

GOING GLOBAL WITH MICHAEL DORF AND KNITMEDIA

When it comes to the music industry, "abroad" is one place a company must be. About one-third of the $35.5 billion in global recorded music sales comes from outside the United States, and all the major record firms, including Sony, Warner, and Universal, are therefore expanding into foreign markets with joint ventures and by setting up company owned offices. They've done so, not just to sell American acts like Madonna overseas, but also to identify and develop local talent, since it's that local talent that music lovers abroad want to hear. That helps explain, for example, why Senegalese singer Youssou N'Dour sold 700,000 copies of his latest album and 1.5 million copies of his single hit in Africa, Europe, and Asia, although he sings not in English but in his native Wolof.

Michael Dorf and his music companies have been doing business overseas since 1990, starting with a 24-city European tour with bands like Sonny Sharrock, The Jazz Passengers, and Miracle Room. It was a good start to introducing European music lovers to Knit's artists, but not everything went smoothly on that first tour. For one thing, a first-time agent booked the tour for a few nights into a pub in Helsingbourg, Sweden, that held only 30 people—barely enough for Knit's three bands, let alone customers. And a gig in East Berlin just before the Wall fell ended up losing money when German Chancellor Helmut Kohl decided to start reuniting Germany by offering three East German marks for one Deutsch mark instead of the six or seven East-to-West mark exchange rate that existed at that time. However, the tour was successful in introducing Europeans to the KnitMedia artists and name, and the company's next tours were much more successful.

A lot of the company's other activities and plans involve globalizing their business. They have an office in Holland (e-mail: KFEURO@Knitting.factory.com) and will be opening Knitting Factory clubs around the world, with the first, a strategic alliance with the South Bank Centre in London, scheduled to open in 1997. As more clubs are added they'll be linked into a digital KnitMedia Community, and the clubs should provide a global outlet for the company's artists and products. And that's not all: other European tours and festivals are planned, the company is working with MCI to develop global Internet music broadcasting, and alliances with companies like Sony Music should help the company further expand, to South America, Asia, Africa, and the South Pacific. They would like some advice on how to further expand abroad.

Team Exercises and Questions

Use what you learned in this chapter to answer the following questions:

1. What international strategies have Michael and his company used so far to "go global"? How would you suggest he build on his success to date abroad?

2. Briefly explain how the economic, sociocultural, and technological components of the international environment have affected KnitMedia to date.

3. What "international management" challenges has Michael had to face to date in planning, organizing, leading, and controlling the company's expansion abroad, and what challenges do you anticipate as he opens new Knitting Factory clubs overseas?

4. What competition do you see Michael and his company facing abroad in Europe as they expand abroad? How do you suggest they address that competition?

For the online version of this case, visit our Web site at: <www.prenhall.com/desslermgmt>.

For Internet exercises, interactive study questions, news updates and more, visit the Dessler Web site at

www.prenhall.com/desslermgmt

If you're using the CD-ROM that accompanies this text, simply click on the "Web Site" button to access the site.

MANAGING ETHICS, DIVERSITY, AND SOCIAL RESPONSIBILITY

What's Ahead?

Volkswagen chairman Ferdinand Piech was thrilled to win the bidding war to hire José Ignacio López, the brilliant purchasing and production executive, away from General Motors. But although Mr. López (pictured at left) had immediate and extraordinarily beneficial effects on VW, these accomplishments were clouded by accusations that arose almost at once about the possible theft by Mr. López and his colleagues of General Motors' plans and documents. When Mr. López was subsequently indicted for allegedly stealing those documents, Mr. Piech had to make a number of ethical decisions, including what to do with Mr. López and how to respond to GM's demand for an apology.[1]

Objectives

After studying this chapter, you should be able to

- **explain** the nature of ethical decisions, including what makes a decision a moral one
- **discuss** the factors that influence whether specific people in specific organizations make ethical or unethical decisions
- **describe** two ethics programs currently in use and the steps companies take to foster ethics at work
- **explain** the main approaches to corporate social responsibility
- **discuss** techniques managers can use to manage workforce diversity so that its benefits outweigh potential drawbacks.

MANAGEMENT ON THE WEB

INSTITUTE FOR BUSINESS AND PROFESSIONAL ETHICS

The Institute for Business and Professional Ethics at DePaul University contains a wide variety of ethics resources. Resources include: *The Online Journal of Ethics; The Newsletter of the Institute for Business & Professional Ethics;* links to ethics resources on the WWW; links to ethics resources for teachers; links to other institutes; recent newspaper and journal coverage of ethical issues; and book reviews. Which could Mr. Piech use? ■

http://www.depaul.edu/ethics/

The Ethical Challenge at Work

Managers face ethical choices like these every day, sometimes with questionable results. For example, senior General Dynamics managers allegedly added $64 million of improper overhead expenses (including country-club memberships and dog-kennel fees) to their company's bill for defense contracts in the early 1980s.[2] Sales executives at an artificial eye-lens firm offered doctors "free use of a yacht off Florida, travel in Europe, all-expenses paid, week-long training seminars in the Bahamas, second homes, and cash rebates for buying their lenses rather than their competitors'." What guides our notions of what is or is not ethical?

The Nature of Ethics

Ethics refers to "the principles of conduct governing an individual or a group,"[3] and specifically to the standards used to govern conduct. Ethical decisions always involve normative judgments.[4] A **normative judgment** implies "that something is good or bad, right or wrong, better or worse."[5] Thus, "You are wearing a skirt and blouse" is a non-normative statement; "That's a great outfit!" is a normative one.

Ethical decisions also always involve **morality,** in other words, society's accepted norms of behavior. Moral standards differ from non-moral ones in five main ways:[6]

1. Moral standards address matters of serious consequence to human well-being. Moral standards against murder, lying, slander, or price-fixing exist because there is a consensus that such actions pose a serious threat to individuals' or society's well-being.
2. Moral standards cannot be established or changed by decisions of authoritative bodies like legislatures. Instead, the question of what is morally right or wrong transcends the actions of authoritative bodies.[7]
3. Moral standards should override self-interest. Thus, if you have a moral obligation to do something, you are expected to do it even if doing so might (for instance) impede your career or cost you money.
4. Moral judgments are never situational. Something that is morally right (or wrong) in one situation is right (or wrong) in another. For example, the fact that your company will benefit if you pay a bribe does not make the bribe right.

5. Moral judgments tend to trigger strong emotions. For example, violating moral standards may make you feel ashamed or remorseful. If you see someone else acting immorally, you may feel indignant or resentful.[8]

Ethics and the Law

The law itself is not an adequate guide to whether or not a decision is ethical. You can make a decision that involves ethics (such as firing an employee) strictly based on what is legal. However, that doesn't guarantee that the decision will be ethical, because a legal decision can be unethical (and an ethical one illegal). For example, firing a 38-year-old employee just before she has earned the right to her pension may be unethical, but generally it is not illegal. Similarly, charging a naive customer an exorbitant price may be legal but unethical.

Some retailers survey their customers' buying habits by using a variety of electronic and infrared surveillance equipment.[9] For example, Videocart, Inc. of Chicago, uses infrared sensors in store ceilings to track shopping carts; other firms compile information from credit card purchases to determine individual customers' buying habits. These activities are not illegal at the present time. But many believe that such encroachment into one's privacy is unethical.

What Determines Ethical Behavior at Work?

Several factors influence whether specific people in specific organizations make ethical or unethical decisions.

It may not be illegal, but is it unethical for stores to monitor their customers for reasons other than security?

The Individual Applies His or Her Own Standards

The individual should shoulder most of the credit (or blame) for any ethical decisions he or she makes, because people bring to their jobs their own ideas of what is morally right and wrong. Every decision they make and every action they take will reflect, for better or worse, the application of their moral standards to the question at hand. For example, a national survey of CEOs of manufacturing firms was conducted to identify factors explaining CEOs' intentions to engage in two questionable business practices: soliciting a competitor's technological secrets and making payments to foreign government officials to secure business. Based on their findings, the researchers concluded that the ethical intentions of the CEOs may have been more strongly affected by their personal predispositions than by environmental pressures or organizational/situational characteristics.[10]

CHARACTERISTICS OF ETHICAL PEOPLE. It's hard to generalize about the characteristics of ethical or unethical people. In one study, 421 employees were surveyed to measure the degree to which age, gender, marital status, education, dependent children, region of the country, and years in business influenced responses to ethical decisions. Decisions included "doing personal business on company time," "not reporting others' violations of company rules and policies," and "calling in sick to take a day off for personal use." With the exception of age, none of the variables were good predictors of whether a person would make the "right" decision. However, older workers in general had stricter interpretations of ethical standards and made more ethical decisions than younger employees, other things being equal.

This "generation gap" in business ethics also has been found by other researchers.[11] One study by Baylor University researchers surveyed 2,156 individuals who were grouped by age; those aged 21–40 represented the younger group and those aged 51–70 represented the older group. As in the previous study, respondents were asked to rate the acceptability of a number of ethics-related vignettes, such as "an executive earning $50,000 a year padded his expense account about $1,500 a year."[12]

The following are several of the 16 vignettes used in the study. For each, indicate whether you would find it acceptable or unacceptable.

1. A company president found that a competitor had made an important scientific discovery which would sharply reduce the profits of his own company. He then hired a key employee of the competitor in an attempt to learn the details of the discovery.
2. In order to increase profits, a general manager used a production process which exceeded legal limits for environmental pollution.
3. Because of pressure from his brokerage firm, a stockbroker recommended a type of bond that he did not consider to be a good investment.
4. A small business received one-fourth of its gross revenue in the form of cash. The owner reported only one-half of the cash receipts for income-tax purposes.
5. A company paid a $350,000 "consulting" fee to an official of a foreign country. In return, the official promised assistance in obtaining a contract that should produce a $10 million profit for the contracting company.
6. A corporate director learned that his company intended to announce a stock split and increase its dividend. On the basis of this information, he bought additional shares and sold them at a gain following the announcement.

7. A corporate executive promoted a loyal friend and competent manager to the position of divisional vice president in preference to a better-qualified manager with whom he had no close ties.

8. An engineer discovered what he perceived to be a product design flaw that constituted a safety hazard. His company declined to correct the flaw. The engineer decided to keep quiet, rather than taking his complaint outside the company.

9. A comptroller selected a legal method of financial reporting that concealed some embarrassing financial facts which would otherwise have become public knowledge.

10. An employer received applications for a supervisor's position from two equally qualified applicants but hired the male applicant because he thought that some employees might resent being supervised by a female.

In virtually every case, the older group viewed the ethically questionable decision as more unacceptable than did the younger group. This is illustrated in Figure 3.1. A larger percentage of older respondents chose "never acceptable" to describe the managerial choices to be made. Such findings do not suggest that all older employees are ethical, or that younger ones are unethical. However, they do raise the question of whether the relative lack of experience of younger employees leaves them more open to making the "wrong" decision. Also, believing that one is ethical may not be much of a guide: Most people view themselves as being more ethical than others; people, therefore, tend to have a distorted view of just how ethical they really are.[13]

■ **FIGURE 3.1**
Ethical Vignettes "Never Acceptable" Responses by Age Group
This figure shows the percentage of each age group (young and old) that responded "never acceptable" to each of the "ethically questionable" vignettes.

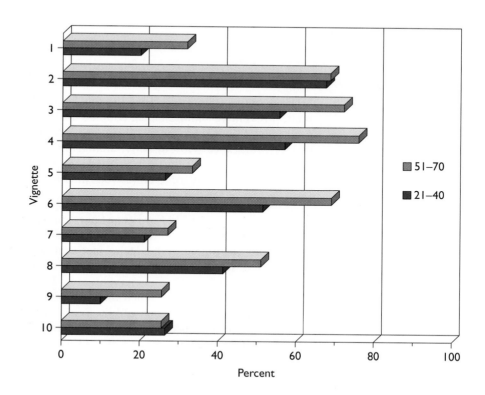

The Organization Shapes Individuals' Behavior

Although ethical crises are sometimes caused by unscrupulous employees, most often that isn't the case. It's rarely just one employee's character flaws that cause corporate misconduct. More typically, says one ethics expert:

> Unethical business practice involves the tacit, if not explicit, cooperation of others and reflects the values, attitudes, beliefs, language, and behavioral patterns that define an organization's operating culture. Ethics, then, is as much an organizational as a personal issue.[14]

The ethical crisis at Sears, Roebuck and Company several years ago provides a good example.[15] In 1992, consumers and attorneys general in more than 40 states accused Sears of misleading customers; the specific complaint was that Sears service writers had sold customers unnecessary parts and services, from brake jobs to front-end alignments. What could have triggered such a companywide crisis? Could so many Sears mechanics and service writers have had ethical lapses?

In this case the answer was "no." Instead, research by Sears management and by outside experts suggest that a number of organizational factors contributed to the problem.

Here's what apparently happened. Faced with declining revenues, Sears management tried to boost the financial results of its auto centers by introducing new quotas and incentives for auto-center employees. They gave mechanics new minimum work quotas and told service advisers they had specific sales quotas—sell so many shock absorbers per week, for instance. Advisers later reported that those failing to meet quotas would not only lose commissions but might be transferred to other jobs or have their work hours reduced.

While the pressure was building for sales, Sears management apparently didn't do enough to establish a company culture in which ethical decisions could flourish. As Sears' then-CEO Edward Brennan acknowledged, management was responsible for installing a compensation and goal-setting system that "created an environment in which mistakes did occur."[16] As one expert summarized:

> Management's failure to clarify the line between unnecessary service and legitimate preventive maintenance, coupled with consumer ignorance, left employees to chart their own courses through a vast gray area, subject to a wide range of interpretations. Without active management support for ethical practice and mechanisms to detect and check questionable sales methods and poor work, it is not surprising that some employees may have reacted to contextual forces by resorting to exaggeration, carelessness, or even misrepresentation.[17]

There is no reason to believe that Sears management or any Sears employees embarked on this new sales incentive program with any intent to deceive or mislead any Sears customers. Indeed, the fact that the program was probably put in place as an honest attempt to boost sales and market share is perhaps the scariest lesson to be learned from the Sears experience: That honest people with good intentions can create conditions in which unethical decisions can flourish.

Once the allegations became public, Sears' top management took steps to try to ensure that ethical lapses wouldn't occur again. For example, they eliminated commissions for service advisers and discontinued sales quotas for specific parts and services. And they instituted unannounced audits by undercover Sears shoppers, and made plans to expand its methods for monitoring the service operation. Unfortunately for Sears and its stockholders, though, the total cost of settling the various lawsuits against Sears and providing customer refunds was an estimated $60 million.[18]

Is Sears an isolated case? Psychologist Saul Gellerman would say "No." He describes how more than 40 years ago, information began to reach John Manville Corporation's medical department—and through it the firm's top executives—indicating that asbestos inhalation was a cause of asbestosis (a debilitating lung disease) among its employees. Subsequent testimony in a California court revealed that Manville had hidden the asbestos danger from its employees rather than looking into safer ways to handle it.[19] A New Jersey court was blunt. It "found that Manville had made a conscious, cold-blooded business decision to take no protective or remedial action, in flagrant disregard of the rights of others."[20] After reviewing all the evidence, Gellerman concluded that it is inconceivable that for 40 years all Manville managers could have been immoral. Instead:

> The people involved were probably ordinary men and women for the most part, not very different from you and me. They found themselves in a dilemma, and they solved it in a way that seemed to be the least troublesome, deciding not to disclose information that could hurt their product. The consequences of what they chose to do—both to thousands of innocent people, and, ultimately, to the corporation—probably never occurred to them. . . . The Manville case illustrates the fine line between acceptable and unacceptable managerial behavior.[21]

The Entrepreneurs in Action box shows how one entrepreneur, at Intuit Corporation, created the right ethical tone for his growing business.

The Leader Influences Others' Ethics

The behavior of one's superiors is another factor influencing ethical decisions.[22] In fact, many managers seem to feel that unethical actions are acceptable if their superior knows about them and says nothing. One writer gives these examples of how supervisors knowingly (or unknowingly) lead subordinates ethically astray.

- Tell staffers to "do whatever is necessary" to achieve results.
- Overload top performers to ensure that work gets done.
- Look the other way when wrongdoing occurs.
- Take credit for others' work or shift blame.
- Play favorites.[23]

Organizational Behavior in Action

CREATING THE RIGHT CULTURE

It's usually not just what the leader says but what he or she does that shapes employees' decisions. As at Sears and Intuit, the leader creates a particular **organizational culture,** and employees then take their signals from it.

As we will explain in more detail in chapter 14, culture represents the values and behaviors that are common to the organization and that tend to perpetuate themselves, sometimes over long periods of time.[24] A **value** is a basic belief about what you should and should not do, and what is and is not important. Organizational culture is important to ethics because a firm's culture reflects its shared

Entrepreneurs in Action

INTUIT

Ethical decisions usually come relatively easy when business is good; hard times are often a different matter altogether. Scott Cook faced hard times when he founded Intuit, a software company based in Menlo Park, California. His start-up bankroll of $151,000 was devoured almost instantly as Intuit developed its Quicken check-writing software. Cook's two principal competitors collectively spent $7 million on marketing alone.

Partly because of the hard times, Cook faced tough ethical questions. What could he promise customers? What could he promise employees? How could he window-dress the financial condition of his company without flagrantly abusing the truth?

Cook had heard the conventional arguments about the necessity of shading the truth for start-up operations. He disagreed. His view was that any enterprise should be based on being truthful and straightforward with customers.

Therefore, despite his financial concerns, Cook urged dealers and retailers to buy less of his software than they might have originally requested. Such advice was unusual in an industry that has long believed oversupplied dealers are loyal dealers, because they will have to work harder getting rid of excess copies.

But Cook calls oversupplying dealers both a bad ethical decision and a bad business one. It's a bad ethical decision because it basically involves tricking retailers into buying and stockpiling more than they need. On the other hand, keeping customers' inventories at the proper levels has several business ben-

Scott Cook, of maverick software maker Intuit, refused to allow customers of his fledgling firm to order more than he could deliver. His honesty won their loyalty— and their business.

efits. Consistent sales levels mean manufacturing schedules can be smoothed out. Ensuring that retail customers are properly supplied also reduces customers' inventory costs. Perhaps most important over the long term, Cook says Intuit customers develop a trusting relationship with the company that translates into loyalty. Recommendations from Intuit salespeople are then taken seriously, and vendors become partners.

Therefore, although Intuit suffered more than its share of adversity in its first three years of existence, Cook never wavered from one conviction: The ethics established and adhered to from day one would outlast him. "If you've got a choice about the culture you create," asks Cook, "why build it on a foundation of fraud?"

SOURCE: Scott Cook, "The Ethics of Bootstrapping," *Inc.,* September 1992, 87–95.

values, and it is values that help guide and channel people's behavior. At Sears, for instance, the service advisers and mechanics apparently had little to go by in making their sales decisions other than the incentive plan and quotas that top management had put in place. There was not a strong enough set of shared values throughout the company, shared values that said, for instance, "Potentially unethical sales practices will not be tolerated," and "The most important thing is to provide our customers with the top-quality services that they really need."

Leaders play a major role in creating and sustaining a firm's culture, through the actions they take, the comments they make, and the visions they espouse. Following are three specific ways in which leaders can shape their organization's culture.

CLARIFY YOUR EXPECTATIONS.   First, make it clear what your expectations are with respect to the values you want your subordinates to follow. For example, the investment banking firm Goldman Sachs has long been guided by a set of "principles," such as "Our client's interests always come first," and "We take great pride in the professional quality of our work."

USE SIGNS AND SYMBOLS.   Remember that when you are a leader, it's not just what you say but what you do that your subordinates will pick up on. At Sears, for instance, it was important that top management not just pay lip service to the importance of top quality ethical service. They also had to engage in those practices that symbolized those values. For example, they eliminated the service quotas and the commission incentive plan for service advisers. More important, perhaps, they instituted the unannounced shopping audits, a sure sign that they were serious about cracking down on unethical sales practices.

USE RITES AND CEREMONIES.   Scheduling recurring ceremonies is one way to "practice what you preach." At Sears, for instance, this might have involved the CEO instituting a yearly ceremony at which employees who most symbolized ethical practices that year received congratulations and a reward. JC Penney has a yearly ceremony in which new managers are inducted into the "Penney Partnership," which is based on the values of honor, confidence, service, and cooperation. ■

Ethics Policies and Codes Make Standards Concrete

The leader's actions may be "the single most important factor in fostering corporate behavior of a high ethical standard," but surveys rank an ethics policy as very important, too.[25] An ethics policy signals that top management is serious about ethics and wants to foster a culture that takes ethics seriously.

Many firms do have ethics codes. One study surveyed corporate management accountants. The researchers found that 56 percent of the respondents' firms had corporate codes of conduct, but the existence of these codes seemed to depend on firm size. For example, 77 percent of the firms with net worth greater than $100 million had corporate codes of conduct, compared with about half of midsize firms, and just fewer than one-fourth of smaller firms. Here are some other conclusions from this survey.[26]

Impact of Code. Top management must make it clear that it is serious about code enforcement.[27] Top management also must ensure that customers, suppliers, and employees are all aware of the firm's stress on ethics.

Approval of Code. The researchers concluded that "it is important for the code to be endorsed by executives at or near the top of the organization chart and by employees throughout the organization."[28] In 95 percent of the firms with codes, the code had been approved by the CEO, the board of directors, or both.

Communication of Code. To influence employee behavior, the ethics code must be communicated. The researchers found that the first step was generally to have top management assign responsibility for implementation of the code to a high-ranking manager. He or she in turn communicates the ethics code to employees. Although this is an important step, only about 57 percent of the firms actually sent a copy of their conduct codes to all employees.

Today's increased workforce diversity may make ethics codes even more important in the future than they have been in the past. One expert contends that, with the flow of immigrants across national borders, it may become increasingly difficult to rely on a common, shared organizational culture to control ethical behavior. In other words, to the extent that it is more difficult to infuse common values and beliefs in a diverse workforce, it may become more necessary to emphasize explicit rules, expectations, and ethics codes.[29]

Recent changes in U.S. federal sentencing guidelines also make it more important than in the past to have an ethics code. Under the new guidelines, the more effort management can show it made to ensure ethical behavior, the lower the fine they can expect to pay if they are sued for unethical practices and lose. For example, if a company had a published ethics code and program, discovered and reported a violation of law, and then cooperated with authorities and accepted responsibility for the unlawful conduct, the firm might be fined only five percent of the loss suffered by customers. If it had no program and no reporting, offered no cooperation, and took no responsibility, the fine might be 200 percent of the loss suffered by customers.[30]

Organizational Behavior in Action

ETHICS AND DECISION MAKING

A recent study suggests that the nature of the moral issue, and its intensity, can also influence the ethical decision the manager makes.[31] The subjects in this study were 259 managers enrolled in a part-time MBA program. They ranged from 22 to 41 years, and most held entry-level or middle management positions with medium or large sized organizations. About 60 percent were male.

The basic question in this study was this: In making an ethical decision, how do the nature of the potential harm and the magnitude of the potential consequences influence the rationales managers give for their decision? The managers were presented with several short scenarios describing ethical dilemmas. (We'll present examples below.) For each ethical dilemma they had to (1) make a decision, and then (2) provide their rationale. The rationales they could choose were the following:

1. The decision was made *to avoid punishment:* The decision the subject made was based on simply wanting to avoid physical punishment or on seeking personal satisfaction. This was the "lowest level" ethical rationale, since it involved no moral judgment on the person's part.
2. The decision was made *to uphold others' expectations:* The subject wanted to gain the approval of or maintain the expectations imposed by the person's family, group, or country.

3. The decision was made *to comply with moral conscience:* In this "highest-level" rationale, the subject's decision was based on universal moral principles, by which the researchers meant the dictates of the decision maker's conscience.

The subjects were asked to read three scenarios, which we can summarize as follows.

Scenario 1. In Europe, a woman was near death from a rare form of cancer. There was one drug that the doctors thought might save her, but the drug was too expensive for the woman's husband to buy. The husband told the druggist his wife was dying, but the druggist refused to sell him the drug at a reduced cost. The husband had to decide whether to break into the man's store to steal the drug for his wife. What should the husband do now?

Scenario 2. A woman worked for an automobile steel casting company. She was part of a small group asked to investigate the cause of an operating problem that had developed in the wheel castings of a new luxury automobile and to make recommendations for its improvement. The problem didn't involve safety but did lead to irritating sounds. The woman's boss terminated the investigation and submitted a report that "proved" metal stress was responsible for the problem. The woman's own research proved that this was not the cause. What should she do now?

Scenario 3. A man worked for a small auditing firm and conducted an annual audit of a machinery manufacturer. During the audit he discovered that the firm had received a large loan from the local savings and loan association (S&L). It was illegal for a savings and loan association to make a loan to a manufacturing firm; at that time S&Ls were restricted by law to mortgages based upon residential real estate. When the accountant went to his boss with this finding, his boss said, "I will take care of this privately. We simply cannot afford to lose a client of this status." He apparently planned to shred the evidence. What should the accountant do now?

What decisions would you have made and what rationales would you have given for your decisions?

In this study, remember that the researchers wanted to know whether the seriousness of the consequences influenced the type of rationale the subjects gave, and the researchers found that the answer was "Yes." Specifically, the more serious the potential consequences of the ethical decision, the more likely it was that the subjects considered their decisions in terms of higher-level moral reasoning. For example, in the life-and-death situation of the woman with cancer, it was most likely that the subjects would make their decisions based on the universal moral principles as symbolized by their consciences (rationale 3). Where the ethical decision involved economics and the possibility that the accountant would lose his job if he shredded the accounting papers, rationale 2—a concern for doing what would be expected by the decision maker's family, group, or country—was the most likely rationale. In the case of the noisy wheel casing, the most likely rationale was number 1—namely just sizing up the pros and cons in terms of the consequences to oneself.

These findings suggest that there was a good deal of practicality in the way these subjects arrived at their ethical decisions. In this study, at least, there was a tendency for the managers to use universal ethical principles and conscience as the basis for those ethical decisions that had the most serious consequences, such as the woman dying of cancer. At the other extreme, most of the subjects in the study took a more pragmatic approach when the potential consequences weren't very serious, as in the case of the noisy wheel; here they focused more on the pros and cons to them personally and on their careers than they did on their consciences. ▪

Ethics Programs in Practice

We can get a better perspective on how to encourage ethical behavior by looking more closely at how several firms actually manage their corporate ethics programs. We will look specifically at two firms, Johnson & Johnson and Norton.

The Johnson & Johnson Program

Ethical decision making at Johnson & Johnson has long been symbolized by what the company calls "our credo." The credo, presented in Figure 3.2, provides the ethical pillars on which the firm is built and on which it continues to produce its pharmaceutical and health products. It begins with the statement that "we believe our first responsibility is to the doctors, nurses and patients, to mothers and all others who use our products and services."[32] Other elements include "in meeting their needs, everything we do must be of high quality," and "our suppliers and distributors must have an opportunity to make a fair profit."

Stories abound about how the credo provides the moral standards that guide the firm. One story describes how Johnson & Johnson reacted when a few poisoned Tylenol capsules were discovered some years ago. Because "our first responsibility is to the doctors, nurses and patients . . . ", Johnson & Johnson decided to recall all outstanding capsules. The decision cost the firm hundreds of millions of dollars in lost sales.

The brief credo has also been described as the glue that helps hold the firm together.[33] Johnson & Johnson is a widely diversified international company with over 160 businesses in 50 countries. Its products range from baby powder to toothbrushes to contact lenses.[34] It is also very decentralized, with the presidents of its subsidiaries "usually left very much on their own in terms of the way in which they will manage their particular company."[35] By evaluating, promoting, and continually reminding all employees of the credo's importance, the company has used its credo to help give all its far-flung managers a common focus and set of standards. Whether the managers are working in Asia, South America, France, or the United States, the firm's home office can be assured that the company's ethical values will be adhered to by employees around the world.

Managing Change

THE ROLE OF ETHICS CODES IN MANAGING CHANGE

An ethical code like Johnson & Johnson's credo can therefore be a powerful tool for helping managers manage change. Change often requires decentralizing decisions and establishing far-flung subsidiaries around the globe. Inability to maintain

Our Credo

We believe our first responsibility is to the doctors, nurses and patients,
to mothers and fathers and all others who use our products and services.
In meeting their needs everything we do must be of high quality.
We must constantly strive to reduce our costs
in order to maintain reasonable prices.
Customers' orders must be serviced promptly and accurately.
Our suppliers and distributors must have an opportunity
to make a fair profit.

We are responsible to our employees,
the men and women who work with us throughout the world.
Everyone must be considered as an individual.
We must respect their dignity and recognize their merit.
They must have a sense of security in their jobs.
Compensation must be fair and adequate,
and working conditions clean, orderly and safe.
We must be mindful of ways to help our employees fulfill
their family responsibilities.
Employees must feel free to make suggestions and complaints.
There must be equal opportunity for employment, development
and advancement for those qualified.
We must provide competent management,
and their actions must be just and ethical.

We are responsible to the communities in which we live and work
and to the world community as well.
We must be good citizens — support good works and charities
and bear our fair share of taxes.
We must encourage civic improvements and better health and education.
We must maintain in good order
the property we are privileged to use,
protecting the environment and natural resources.

Our final responsibility is to our stockholders.
Business must make a sound profit.
We must experiment with new ideas.
Research must be carried on, innovative programs developed
and mistakes paid for.
New equipment must be purchased, new facilities provided
and new products launched.
Reserves must be created to provide for adverse times.
When we operate according to these principles,
the stockholders should realize a fair return.

Johnson & Johnson

■ **FIGURE 3.2**
Johnson & Johnson's Corporate Credo

SOURCE: Courtesy of Johnson & Johnson.

ethical standards throughout this broad network can be a major factor limiting further expansion and change, and the possibilities for corruption and misconduct expand as firms decentralize and globalize.[36]

Because a code of ethical conduct provides a standardized set of values to which all the firm's managers are committed, such codes can help reduce the undesirable effects of decentralization and looser control. They do this by enabling top management to expand globally, secure in the knowledge that however far removed subsidiaries are from the firm's home base, local managers will be more likely to adhere to the company's code of ethical practices. Goldman Sachs, for instance, is a global investment banker with offices throughout the world. How can the firm's managing partners be sure that all their far-flung employees will do the right thing? In part by steeping them in the firm's basic guiding principles, such as "Our clients' interests always come first." ■

The Norton Company

The Norton Company is a diversified, multinational manufacturer of industrial products including grinding wheels, abrasives, and advanced ceramics and plastics. Sales today are about $1.5 billion, and the firm has manufacturing plants in 27 countries.

The three main features of the Norton Ethics Program are a code of conduct, an ethics committee of the board of directors, and an annual ethics review.[37] The code itself, called "the Norton Policy of Business Ethics," is 12 pages of general guidelines with specific rules regarding responsibility to employees, customers, suppliers, shareholders, local communities, and the general public. It is currently printed in eight languages and distributed to every Norton manager. New employees receive a copy of the policy almost immediately. No formal ethics training occurs during the firm's management training program. However, frequent ethics seminars emphasize the importance of ethics and the company's ethics code.

Code compliance is monitored in two ways. First, top management annually solicits letters from the top 100 managers worldwide asking them to "specify any significant violations of the ethics policy which have occurred and any important cases which might be regarded as controversial."[38] At the same time, managers are required to review the performance of their subordinates on ethics. Then, the ethics committee of the firm's board of directors meets to review the annual ethics letters, to discuss and resolve any unresolved ethics issues, and to prepare a final report to the full board of directors.

Strategy in Action

THE ETHICAL FOUNDATIONS OF A COMPANY'S STRATEGY

As at firms like Norton and Johnson & Johnson, the strategic decisions managers make reflect the values and ethical principles to which they subscribe.[39] For example, you would hardly expect the head of a company like Johnson & Johnson to formulate a strategy that would lead the firm to intentionally manufacture products that were not of the highest quality, simply so he or she could boost the company's market share or rate of return. On the other hand, the strategy briefly pursued at Sears—to pump up sales by reformulating quotas and incentives—probably backfired in part due to management's failure to consider the strategy's potential ethical consequences.

Several strategic management experts contend that ethics poses two key questions that need to be answered when formulating strategy:

1. Are the values that underlie the strategy defensible?
2. Are the effects of the strategy on the firm's stakeholders moral?[40]

Formulating a strategy therefore involves more than just matching strengths and weaknesses to opportunities and threats. If there is a lesson to be learned by examples like Norton, Johnson & Johnson, or Sears, it is that managers must consider the ethical foundations and consequences of their strategies.

In Summary: How to Foster Ethics at Work

After a review of the ethics programs at eleven major firms, one study concluded that fostering ethics at work involved five main steps.

1. *Emphasize top management's commitment.* "In the experience of these companies with regard to corporate ethics, no point emerges more clearly than the crucial role of top management. To achieve results, the chief executive officer and those around the CEO need to be openly and strongly committed to ethical conduct, and give constant leadership in tending and renewing the values of the organization."[41]

2. *Publish a "code."* Firms with effective ethics programs set forth principles of conduct for the whole organization in the form of written documents. These generally cover areas such as fundamental honesty and adherence to laws; product safety and quality; health and safety in the workplace; conflicts of interest; employment practices; fairness in selling/marketing practices; and financial reporting.[42]

3. *Establish compliance mechanisms.* Establish mechanisms to ensure compliance with the firm's ethical standards. For example: pay attention to values and ethics in recruiting and hiring; emphasize corporate ethics in training; institute communications programs to inform and motivate employees; audit to ensure compliance; establish "ethics hot lines" to help employees report instances of unethical behavior; and enforce the ethics code, including discipline and dismissal.[43]

4. *Involve personnel at all levels.* Developing effective corporate ethics programs requires involving those whose behavior the ethics policies are to influence. For example, use roundtable discussions among small groups of employees regarding corporate ethics and employees surveys of attitudes regarding the state of ethics in the firm.[44]

5. *Measure results.* Although the end results cannot be precisely measured, all eleven firms used surveys or audits to monitor compliance with ethical standards.[45] The results of the audit should then be discussed among board members and employees to be effective.[46]

Social Responsibility at Work

Ethics and Social Responsibility

Corporate **social responsibility** refers to the extent to which companies should and do channel resources toward improving one or more segments of society other than the firm's own stockholders. Socially responsible behavior thus might include creating jobs for minorities, controlling pollution, or supporting educational facilities or cultural events.

Social responsibility is essentially an ethical issue, since it involves questions of what is morally right or wrong with regard to the firm's responsibilities. As you will see, though, there is less unanimity regarding what is right or wrong in this area than there is with respect to traditional ethical issues such as bribery, stealing, and corporate dishonesty. Many perfectly ethical people strongly believe that a company's only social responsibility is to its shareholders.

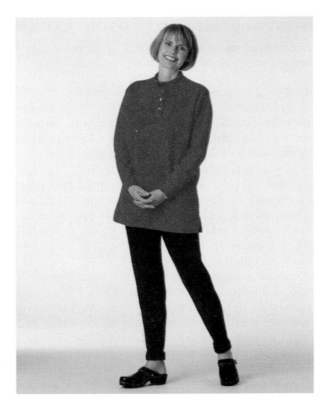

Firms with a strong sense of social responsibility include the children's clothing manufacturer Hanna Andersson. Used "hannas" can be returned to the company for distribution to the children's charities and credit on the customer's next order.

To Whom Should the Corporation Be Responsible?

The link between ethics and social responsibility is perhaps clearest when the social responsibility is to the firm's customers or employees. In 1993, Dow Corning replaced its top executive and released hundreds of internal memos revealing years of complaints about its breast implants. In 1984, when a Union Carbide chemical plant in Bhopal, India, began spewing poisonous methyl isocyanate gas into the surrounding town, the firm's managers were amazed to learn that most of the human and mechanical controls aimed at avoiding such disasters had been compromised.[47]

When chemical plants hurt thousands, the ethical mistakes are quite clear, and most would agree that firms have a social responsibility to serve their various nonowner constituencies. But to many social philosophers, a firm's social responsibilities go far beyond such clear-cut ethical rights and wrongs. They extend, they say, to such questions as whether firms should be responsible for creating jobs for minorities, or for supporting educational and cultural events in their communities.

MANAGERIAL CAPITALISM. The classical view of social responsibility is that a corporation's primary purpose is to maximize profits for its stockholders. Today, this view is most often associated with economist and Nobel laureate Milton Friedman, who has said:

> The view has been gaining widespread acceptance that corporate officials and labor leaders have a "social responsibility" that goes beyond the interest of their stockholders or their members. This view shows a fundamental misconception of the character and nature of the free economy. In such an economy, there is one and only one social responsibility of business—to use its resources and

engage in activities designed to increase its profits so long as it stays within the rules of the game, which is to say, engages in open and free competition, without deception and fraud. . . . Few trends could so thoroughly undermine the very foundation of our free society as the acceptance by corporate officials of a social responsibility other than to make as much money for their stockholders as possible.[48]

Friedman's position is built on two main arguments.[49] First, stockholders are owners of the corporation and so the corporate profits belong to them and to them alone. Second, stockholders deserve their profits because these profits derive from a voluntary contract among the various corporate stakeholders—the community receives tax money, suppliers are paid, employees earn wages, and so on. Everyone gets their due and additional social responsibility is not needed, Friedman says.

STAKEHOLDER THEORY. An opposite view is that business has a social responsibility to serve all the "corporate stakeholders" affected by its business decisions. A **corporate stakeholder** is "any group which is vital to the survival and success of the corporation."[50] As in Figure 3.3, six stakeholder groups are traditionally identified: stockholders (owners); employees; customers; suppliers; managers; and the local community (although conceivably others could be identified as well).[51]

Whereas Friedman's corporation focuses on maximizing its profits, stakeholder theory holds that:[52]

the corporation should be managed for the benefit of [all] its stakeholders: its customers, suppliers, owners, employees, and local communities. The rights of these groups must be ensured, and, further, the groups must participate, in some sense, in decisions that substantially affect their welfare.[53]

THE MORAL MINIMUM. Between the extremes of Friedman's capitalism and stakeholder theory is an intermediate position known as the **moral minimum.** Moral minimum advocates would agree that the purpose of the corporation is to maximize profits, but subject to the requirement that it must do so in conformity with the moral minimum,[54] meaning that the firm should be free to strive for profits so long as it commits no harm. By this view, a business would certainly have a social responsibility not to produce exploding cigarette lighters or poisonous chemical plants. However, it is unlikely that the social responsibilities of the business would extend beyond this moral minimum, to donating profits to charity or educating the poor, for instance.

SOCIAL RESPONSIBILITY AT BEN & JERRY'S HOMEMADE. Managers must make up their own minds regarding where on the social responsibility scale their

■ **FIGURE 3.3**
A Corporation's Major Stakeholders
One view of social responsibility is that a firm must consider and serve all the stakeholders that may be affected by its business decisions.

firm should lie. For Ben & Jerry's Homemade ice cream company, though, the decision was never in doubt. Founders Ben Cohen and Jerry Greenfield founded a company that had, as part of its mission,

> To operate the company in a way that actively recognizes the central role that business plays in the structure of a society by initiating innovative ways to improve the quality of life of a broad community: local, national and international.[55]

How does Ben & Jerry's put its socially responsible mission into practice? In many ways. The firm has "green teams" responsible for assessing the firm's environmental impact, and for developing and implementing programs to reduce any negative impact. The firm donates 7.5 percent of its pretax earnings to the Ben & Jerry's Foundation. (This is a nonprofit institution established by personal contributions from founders Cohen and Greenfield.) And, in explaining Ben & Jerry's choice of suppliers, Ben Cohen says:

> Wild Maine Blueberry is another step in how we are defining what caring capitalism is all about. Our goal is to integrate a concern for the community in every business decision we make. We are trying to develop a system that improves the quality of life through socially conscious purchasing of our ingredients. The brownies in Chocolate Fudge Brownie benefit the employment of underskilled persons, the nuts in Rain Forest Crunch benefit the preservation of the rain forest, the peaches in Fresh Georgia Peach support family farms, and the blueberries in Wild Maine Blueberry support traditional native American economy.[56]

How to Improve Social Responsiveness

Although few firms are as socially progressive as Ben & Jerry's, many have established mechanisms to improve their social responsiveness.

CORPORATE SOCIAL MONITORING: THE SOCIAL AUDIT. Given a commitment to being socially responsible, how can firms ensure that they are in fact being socially responsive? Some firms monitor how well they measure up to their social responsibility aims using a rating system called a **corporate social audit.**[57]

The Sullivan Principles for Corporate Labor and Community Relations in South Africa[58] was one of the first such rating systems. The Reverend Leon Sullivan was an African-American minister and General Motors board of directors member. For several years during the 1970s he had tried to pressure the firm to withdraw from South Africa, whose multiracial population was divided by the government-sanctioned racist policies known as apartheid. As part of that effort, Sullivan formulated the code that came to be named for him, the purpose of which was "to guide U.S. business in its social and moral agenda in South Africa."[59] The code provided for measurable standards by which U.S. companies operating in South Africa could be audited, including nonsegregation of the races in all eating, comfort, and work facilities, and "equal pay for all employees doing equal or comparable work for the same period of time."[60] In the 1990s he proposed a new code for companies returning to South Africa after apartheid, stressing the protection of equal rights and the promotion of education and job training.

WHISTLE-BLOWING. Many firms have a reputation for actively discouraging **whistle-blowing,** the activities of employees who try to report organizational wrongdoing. Yet many arguments can be made for actually *encouraging* whistle-blowers.

In a firm that adheres to the "moral minimum" view of social responsibility, for instance, such whistle-blowers can help the company avoid doing harm. As one writer has put it, whistle-blowers "represent one of the least expensive and most efficient sources of feedback about mistakes the firm may be making."[61] Other firms find the "benefit of muffling whistle-blowers is illusory."[62] Once the damage has been done—whether it is asbestos hurting workers or a chemical plant making hundreds of people ill—the cost of making the damage right can be enormous.

Yet firms often retaliate against whistle-blowers, either by firing them or by moving them to marginal jobs.[63] Some are preoccupied with maximizing profits, while others may not have strong enough ethics codes. But there is also the lingering belief in some firms that whistle-blowers are either disloyal or "kooks," or both. Such views are probably myopic; many firms can and do benefit from creating an environment that permits (and perhaps encourages) employees who observe corporate wrongdoing to report their observations to the highest levels of the firm.[64]

Managing Diversity

The workforces of countries around the world are becoming increasingly diverse. Almost half the net addition to the U.S. workforce in the 1990s will be nonwhite, and almost two-thirds female.[65] Similarly, it's been estimated that minorities comprise 8–10 percent of the population in France, 5 percent in the Netherlands, and a growing proportion in Italy, Germany, and much of Europe.[66] Even Japan, historically a homogeneous society averse to immigration, will have to find ways to accommodate many more women in its workforce.[67]

Such diversity will confront managers with challenges—ethical and otherwise—of epic proportions. In 1996, for instance, the entire U.S. Army command was shaken by allegations that dozens of sergeants at several Army bases took unethical and illegal liberties with female trainees; at the same time, the giant Texaco Corporation was forced to settle a huge lawsuit in the face of tape recordings that allegedly showed top-ranking Texaco officers making disparaging remarks about various ethnic groups.

But along with the challenges, we'll see that diversity creates enormous opportunities. There is, for instance, the opportunity to attract and retain the best possible human talent, and to boost creativity and innovation by bringing different points of view to bear on problems. **Managing diversity** means "planning and implementing organizational systems and practices to manage people so that the potential advantages of diversity are maximized while its potential disadvantages are minimized."[68]

Bases for Diversity

A workforce is **diverse** when it is comprised of two or more groups, each of whose members are identifiable and distinguishable based on demographic or other characteristics. The bases upon which groups can be distinguished are numerous. However, when managers talk of "diversity," they usually do so based on at least the following groups:[69]

- *Racial and ethnic groups.* African Americans, Pacific Islanders, Asian Americans, Native Americans, and other people of color now comprise about 25 percent of the U.S. population.

- *Women.* Almost two-thirds of the 15 million new entrants into the job market in the 1990s will be women, making them the largest and fastest-growing diversity group.
- *Older workers.* By the year 2000, the average age of the U.S. workforce will be 39, up from today's average of 36 years and reflecting the gradual aging of the workforce and the larger number of older people remaining at work.
- *People with disabilities.* The Americans with Disabilities Act makes it illegal to discriminate against people with disabilities who are otherwise qualified to do the job, and this act has thrown a spotlight on the large number of people with disabilities in the workforce.
- *Sexual/affectional orientation.* It has been estimated that about 10 percent of the population is gay, which may make gays a larger percentage of the workforce than some racial and ethnic minorities.[70]

Barriers in Dealing with Diversity

Any attempt at managing diversity has to begin with an understanding of the barriers that may prevent a company from taking full advantage of the potential in its diverse workforce. Among the more important barriers are the following.

STEREOTYPING AND PREJUDICES. Stereotyping and prejudice are two sides of the same coin. **Stereotyping** is a process in which specific behavioral traits are ascribed to individuals on the basis of their apparent membership in a group.[71] **Prejudice** is a bias that results from prejudging someone on the basis of some trait.

Most people form stereotyped lists of behavioral traits that they identify with certain groups. Unfortunately, many of these stereotypes (in addition to being inaccurate) carry negative connotations. For example, stereotypical "male" traits might include strong, cruel, aggressive, and loud, while "female" traits might include weak, softhearted, meek, and gentle.[72] When someone allows stereotypical traits like these to bias them for (or against) someone, then we say the person is prejudiced.

ETHNOCENTRISM. Ethnocentrism is prejudice on a grand scale. It can be defined as a tendency "for viewing members of one's own group as the center of the universe and for viewing other social groups (out-groups) less favorably than one's own." Ethnocentrism can provide a very significant barrier to managing diversity. For example, white managers have been found to attribute the performance of blacks less to their ability and effort and more to help they received from others; conversely, white managers attributed the performance of whites to their own abilities and efforts.[73]

DISCRIMINATION. Whereas prejudice means a bias toward prejudging someone based on that person's traits, **discrimination** refers to taking specific actions toward or against the person based on the person's group.[74] Of course, in many countries, including the United States, many forms of discrimination are against the law. Thus, in the United States it is generally illegal to discriminate against someone solely based on that person's age, race, gender, disability, or country of national origin. However, discrimination continues to be a barrier to diversity management. (For example, many argue that there is an invisible "glass ceiling," enforced by an "old boys' network" and friendships built in places like exclusive clubs, that effectively prevents women from breaking into the top ranks of management in many companies.)

TOKENISM. **Tokenism** refers to the tendency of some companies to appoint a relatively small group of women or minority-group members to high-profile positions rather than more aggressively achieving full work-group representation for that group. Tokenism is a diversity management barrier in part because it slows the process of hiring or promoting more members of the minority group. Furthermore, the "token" employees often fare poorly in the organization. Research suggests, for instance, that tokens face obstacles to full participation, success, and acceptance in the company. There is also a tendency for their performance, good or bad, to be magnified because of the extra attention their distinctiveness creates.[75]

GENDER ROLES. In addition to problems like glass ceilings and sexual harassment, working women confront **gender-role stereotypes,** in other words, the tendency to associate women with certain (frequently nonmanagerial) jobs. For example, in one study of job interviewers, attractiveness was advantageous for female interviewees only when the job was nonmanagerial. When the position was managerial, there was a tendency for a woman's attractiveness to work against her in terms of recommendation for hiring and suggested starting salary.[76]

Boosting Performance by Managing Diversity

We've defined managing diversity as maximizing diversity's potential advantages while minimizing the potential barriers described above. In practice, diversity management includes both compulsory and voluntary management actions. There are, first, many legally mandated actions employers must take to minimize discrimination at work. For example, since discrimination against many minority groups and women is illegal in the United States, employers should avoid discriminatory employment advertising (such as "young man wanted for sales position") and prohibit sexual harassment.

However, while such actions can reduce the more blatant diversity barriers, blending a diverse workforce into a close-knit and thriving community also requires

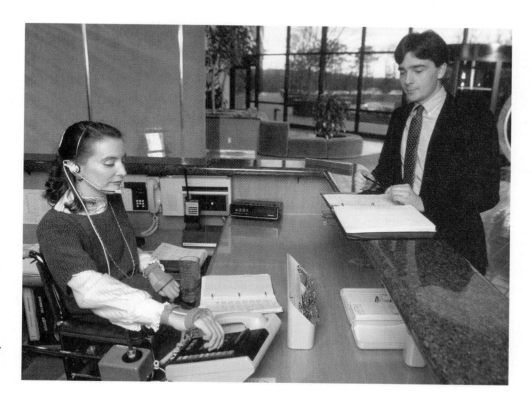

Advances in technology have enabled many disabled people to work productively. Nancy Thibeault, telephone operator and receptionist at PAC Corporation, uses specially designed equipment on the job.

that management take a number of other steps. These are illustrated in Figure 3.4. Based on his review of research studies, one diversity expert concludes that five sets of organizational activities are at the heart of any managing diversity program. These can be summarized as follows.

PROVIDE STRONG LEADERSHIP.   Companies that have exemplary reputations in managing diversity are typically led by chief executives who champion the cause of diversity. Such leaders include John Houghton of Corning and David Kearns, the former Chairman of Xerox Corporation. Leadership in this case means: taking a strong personal stand on the need for change; becoming a role model for the behaviors required for the change; and providing the mental energy and financial and other support needed to implement the actual changes (for instance, in hiring practices).

RESEARCH: ASSESS THE SITUATION.   The company has to assess the current state of affairs with respect to diversity management. For example, this might entail administering surveys to measure employees' current attitudes and perceptions toward different cultural groups within the company, and about relationships between the groups.

PROVIDE DIVERSITY TRAINING AND EDUCATION.   One expert says that "the most commonly utilized starting point for . . . managing diversity is some type of employee education program."[77] Employers typically use several types of programs, most often a one- to three-day workshop aimed at increasing employees' awareness and sensitivity to diversity issues.

CHANGE CULTURE AND MANAGEMENT SYSTEMS.   Ideally, education programs should be combined with other concrete steps aimed at changing the orga-

■ **FIGURE 3.4 Activities Required to Better Manage Diversity**

SOURCE: Reprinted with permission of the publisher. From *Cultural Diversity in Organizations: Theory, Research and Practice,* copyright © 1993 by Taylor Cox, Jr. Berrett-Koehler Publishers, Inc., San Francisco, CA. All rights reserved.

The Activities at the Heart of a Diversity Management Program

LEADERSHIP	RESEARCH/ MEASUREMENT	EDUCATION	CHANGES IN CULTURE AND MANAGEMENT SYSTEMS	FOLLOW-UP
• Top management commitment and support • Steering and advisory groups • Communications strategy	• Comprehensive organizational assessment • Baseline data • Benchmarking	• Awareness training • Development of in-house expertise • Orientation programs • Advanced training	• Recruitment • Orientation • Performance appraisal • Compensation and benefits • Promotion • Training and development development	• Evaluation process • Accountability • Ensuring continuous improvement

nization's culture and management systems. One important step is to review every aspect of the employer's human resource management system, to identify potential diversity barriers, and to eliminate them. For example, the performance appraisal procedure might be changed to emphasize that supervisors will henceforth be appraised based partly on their success in reducing inter-group conflicts. As another example, many companies institute mentoring programs. **Mentoring** has been defined as " . . . a relationship between a younger adult and an older, more experienced adult in which the mentor provides support, guidance, and counseling to enhance the protégé's success at work and in other arenas of life."[78]

Mentoring can contribute to a company's diversity management efforts. For example, it does little good to attract a racially or ethnically diverse workforce and then to simply leave the new people out there to "sink or swim." A good mentor can provide the advice and counsel needed to deal with challenges at work, particularly for those who may be new to the workforce or to the competitive environment of corporate life. Having a mentor can also kick-start one's career and help clear a path for a junior manager's promotion.[79]

EVALUATE THE MANAGING DIVERSITY PROGRAM. The follow-up or evaluation stage is aimed at measuring the results of the managing diversity program. For example, do the employee attitude surveys now indicate any improvement in employees' attitudes toward diversity? How many employees have entered into mentoring relationships, and do these relationships appear to be successful?

SUMMARY

1. Managers face ethical choices every day. Ethics refers to the principles of conduct governing an individual or a group. Ethical decisions always include both normative and moral judgments.

2. Being legal and being ethical are not necessarily the same thing. A decision can be legal but still unethical, or ethical but still illegal.

3. Several factors influence whether specific people in specific organizations make ethical or unethical decisions. The individual making the decision must ultimately shoulder most of the credit (or blame) for any ethical decision he or she makes. However, the organization itself—including its leadership, culture, and incentive/compensation plan—will also shape an individual employee's ethical behavior.

4. Ethics policies and codes are important as well. They send a strong signal that top management is serious about ethics and are a sign that it wants to foster a culture that takes ethics seriously.

5. There are several concrete steps managers can take to foster ethics at work. These include emphasizing top management's commitment; publishing a code; establishing compliance mechanisms; involving personnel at all levels; and measuring results.

6. Social responsibility is essentially an ethical issue, since it involves questions of what is morally right or wrong with regard to the firm's responsibilities. Good people differ in answering the question, "To whom should the corporation be responsible?" Some say solely to stockholders; some say to all

stakeholders; and some take an intermediate, "moral minimum" position: They agree that the purpose of the corporation is to maximize profits, but subject to the requirement that it must do so in conformity with the moral minimum.

7. As the workforce becomes more diverse, it becomes more important to manage diversity so that the benefits of diversity outweigh any potential drawbacks. Potential barriers to managing include stereotyping, prejudice, and tokenism. Managing diversity involves taking steps such as providing strong leadership; assessing the situation; providing training and education; changing the culture and systems; and evaluating the program.

KEY TERMS

ethics	corporate stakeholder	stereotyping
normative judgment	moral minimum	prejudice
morality	corporate social audit	discrimination
organizational culture	whistle-blowing	tokenism
value	managing diversity	gender-role stereotypes
social responsibility	diverse	mentoring

SELF-TEST

TRUE / FALSE QUESTIONS

1 **T F** The principles of conduct governing an individual or group are called ethics.

2 **T F** Ethical judgments, that is, the standards of right and wrong, are usually situational.

3 **T F** The law is an adequate guide to ethical conduct.

4 **T F** Leaders can shape their organization's culture by using signs and symbols.

5 **T F** An important factor shaping ethical behavior in the organization is your own supervisor's behavior.

6 **T F** Organizational culture has a minor impact on the ethical behavior of company members.

7 **T F** Because of workforce diversity, establishing codes of ethics is increasingly important.

8 **T F** A step in supporting ethics at work is to emphasize top management's commitment to ethical behavior.

9 **T F** Corporate social responsibility is defined as the extent to which companies should and do channel resources toward improving one or more segments of society other than the firm's own stockholders.

10 **T F** Milton Friedman's view is that a corporation's primary purpose is to maximize profits for all of the company's stakeholders.

MULTIPLE-CHOICE QUESTIONS

1 According to the text, moral standards differ from non-moral ones in a number of ways. Which of the following is *not* one of those ways?
a. Moral judgments tend to trigger strong emotions.

b. Moral standards should never override self-interest.
c. Moral judgments are never situational.
d. Moral standards address matters of serious consequences to human well-being.

2 According to a study, all the following were poor indicators of "whether a person would or would not make the 'right' decision" except:
a. marital status
b. gender
c. education
d. age

3 What does the following describe: "a basic belief about what you should and should not do, and what is important and what is not"?
a. culture
b. value
c. social responsibility
d. leadership

4 What is considered by many as "the single most important factor fostering corporate behavior of a high ethical standard"?
a. the leader's actions
b. the subordinate's moral character
c. how well employees are recruited
d. the company's mission statement

5 Many firms do have codes of ethics. Which size firm is the least likely to have an ethics code?
a. large
b. middle-sized firms
c. smaller firms
d. all have ethical codes

6 In Johnson & Johnson's "Our Credo," which stakeholders are of chief importance?
a. stockholders
b. employees
c. community
d. customers

7 The three main features of the Norton Ethics Program consist of all but which of the following?
a. a code of conduct
b. an ethics committee of the board of directors
c. an annual ethics review
d. a customer ethics audit

8 Which of the following statements would best fit with the views of Milton Friedman?
a. Business should be concerned with the community it works in.
b. Business should value its employees first and foremost.
c. The business of business is business.
d. The business of companies is to serve the common good.

9 An opposite view to classical theory argues that "business has a social responsibility to serve all the 'corporate stakeholders' affected by business decisions." A corporate stakeholder is best defined by which of the following:
a. any group vital to the survival and success of the corporation
b. any group lobbying the company for a change in products
c. any person who might be troubled by a corporate action
d. none of the above

10 A corporate _____ is a rating system used to evaluate the corporation's performance with regard to meeting its social obligations.
a. ranking
b. Chamber of Commerce rating
c. Department of Commerce approval
d. social audit

CRITICAL THINKING EXERCISES

1 Humans have faced ethical dilemmas throughout history. Every civilization has questioned the ability of humankind to balance peace and freedom:

> You could have freedom, but then you would have to forsake peace. Conflicts would necessarily arise, it seemed, among men who were free to seek their different goals. Or you could have peace, but at the cost of freedom, for how could peace endure if it were not imposed from above by a supreme power which alone would remain free, while others bore the yoke of tyranny.[80]

The whole world is now open to commerce, and because of that, business plays an increasingly powerful role in shaping the world. As business students, you may face these issues. Using the chapter, answer the following questions.
a. What are the ethical and social responsibility dilemmas facing businesses as they become increasingly powerful and influence behavior around the globe?
b. How can you address the balance of peace and freedom in the management of organizations as well as in society?
c. What role does each organizational member have in shaping an ethical future in his or her firm?

2   A key to ethical perception is realizing that all people bring different views, experiences, and other relevant influences to decisions. This is particularly true in our diverse society. Read the following narratives about perception and relate them to ethical decision making examples in the workplace.

> First narrative, by Taoist writer Lieh-tse: A man noticed that his axe was missing. Then he saw the neighbor's son pass by. The boy looked like a thief, walked like a thief, behaved like a thief. Later that day, the man found his axe where he had left it the day before. The next time he saw

the neighbor's son, the boy looked, walked and behaved like an honest, ordinary boy.[81]

> Second narrative, by Taoist writer Chuang-tse: An archer competing for a clay vessel shoots effortlessly, his skill and concentration unimpeded. If the prize is changed to a brass ornament, his hands begin to shake. If it is changed to gold, he squints as if he were going blind. His abilities do not deteriorate, but his belief in them does, as he allows the supposed value of an external reward to cloud his vision.[82]

EXPERIENTIAL EXERCISES

1   In class, select one or more of the following television programs: *ER, Chicago Hope, Homicide, Law and Order, NYPD Blue, New York Undercover, The X-Files, Star Trek: Voyager, Party of Five, JAG, Dangerous Minds.* Then divide the class into groups of five people each. Try to create as much diversity in the groups as possible. Each group should watch the program together, discuss the ethical and social responsibilities addressed in the show, and prepare a brief presentation for the class. After each group has presented its perspective, the whole class must come up with one set of ethical guides for the television programs situations discussed.

2   You were taking a month's holiday in Europe. In your first week there, you became very ill with a recurring ailment for which you have been treated with limited success in the States. In fact, it is a chronic condition that is inhibiting your ability to advance your career. The doctors who treated you in Europe have given you some medication that is legal there but has not been approved by the U.S. Food and Drug Administration. You feel better than you have in years and feel able to enjoy the remainder of your trip. Because the European drug restrictions allow this drug to be purchased across the counter without a prescription, you are able to buy a year's supply. However, you know that it is listed as an illegal drug in the United States and you must pass through customs. What would you do? What are the ethical and moral dilemmas facing you? Is there any action you can take as an individual to change the situation? If your decision is to smuggle the drug in and you are successful, what will you do in a year?

ENTREPRENEURIAL CASE

APEX FUEL OIL'S BATTLE AGAINST DRUGS

Five years after he started Apex Fuel Oil, Daniel Green suspected that some of his employees had drug problems. The number of on-the-job accidents was mounting, as workers injured themselves in what Green calls "stupid ways." One employee driving a fork lift hit a coworker and broke her leg. On separate occasions, two of the company's drivers ran into each other in the driveway.

Apex's health care and insurance costs rose as the number of accidents increased. Worker's compensation costs more than doubled, and the insurance costs for workers and vehicles skyrocketed. "There were rumors that people were on drugs," recalls Green. "We suspected that the broken leg accident was drug related, but we couldn't prove it. We didn't have a mechanism in place for drug testing."

Today, that is no longer true. Apex now has substance abuse and drug-testing policies in place. The company tests all job applicants, and it also tests employees when it has reasonable cause to do so. Because the company operates heavy trucks on highways, Apex also is able to randomly test employees in potentially hazardous occupations, for example, those operating heavy equipment. Although there was some resistance initially, employees have gradually accepted the system, and many workers who have been involved in accidents now voluntarily come forward for testing.

Employees with a positive test result get only one chance for rehabilitation through an employee assistance program (EAP). During the standard 30-day rehabilitation period, the company pays half of the employee's salary. If the program requires more than 30 days, Apex pays one-quarter of the worker's salary for up to 60 more days.

The results from Apex Fuel's substance abuse program have been significant. Since the program has been put in place, worker's compensation costs have dropped from $87,000 to $32,000. Likewise, insurance rates have fallen from $325,000 to $180,000. The insurance company used to see them as an insurance risk. Now they offer them competitive rates. Best of all, accidents and employee injuries are way down. Among other things, Apex Fuel's experience shows that although business owners may not want to believe drug abuse is a problem in their firms, it may well be.

Questions

1. What ethical questions and issues does a drug testing policy such as Chamberlain's raise? Do you think Daniel and Harold handled the issues properly? Why or why not?
2. What stakeholders did the partners have to consider in formulating their drug-testing policy?
3. What social responsibility issues are raised by this case? Did the partners do the socially responsible thing? Why or why not?

SOURCES: Adapted from Doreen Mangan, "An Rx for Drug Abuse," *Small Business Reports,* May 1992, pp. 28–38; Michael A. Verespej, "Drug Users—Not Testing—Anger Workers," *Industry Week,* February 17, 1992, pp. 33–34.

DIVERSITY CASE

BUSINESS REVOLUTIONARIES IN A DIFFICULT ENVIRONMENT

How does a nation manage to build an economy where the average farmer can make five times more money growing illegal drug crops than legal crops? What kinds of management issues do managers face in a country that has been under intense U.S. scrutiny for drug trafficking? How do you develop "principled private initiative" in a country rampant with corruption?

The CESA (Colegio de Estudios Superiores Administración) in Bogotá, Colombia, has some of the answers. Founded in 1974 by a group of business leaders who assumed responsibility for instilling business leadership capabilities in the community, CESA's mission is to revitalize Colombia by cultivating pragmatism and idealism. The school recruits young people of high moral character and awareness, people who love Colombia and want to create a better community through economic opportunity.

A married couple, Beatriz and Eduardo Marcia, started their own business, Crepes & Waffles, after attending CESA. They now have 14 stores throughout Colombia, Ecuador, and Panama. The company's growth rate has been 30 percent for each of the last five years, and it currently employs 700 people.

Although they have been financially successful, the Marcias believe that life is not just about making money. Beatriz notes, "To be a leader is not just to build a business, but rather to contribute to the country's development. To raise the quality of life in every way." To this end, the Marcias

have helped to finance more than 80 homes for their employees, provide free health insurance after one year of service, and make a social worker available for some consultations.

Part of the CESA curriculum involves taking students out of the classroom and putting them into the community. The first order of study is the preparation of a business plan. Students spend nine 22-week terms working in business in the home country and around the globe. When they graduate, they are well prepared to manage a business. As one CESA administrator notes, "Our professors talk from real life. . . . And in doing so, they give to the students what we call 'hidden studies' that deal with morality and social responsibility."

Questions

1. Compare and contrast attitudes toward social responsibility and their impact on management in the United States and at CESA.
2. What barriers do you think CESA might face in Colombia?
3. What management issues do the Marcias confront in developing their business?
4. How could U.S. universities use the CESA model to address issues of poverty and homelessness? What barriers might stand in their way?

SOURCE: David Benson, "Colombia's School for Business Revolutionaries," *Inc.,* August–September 1996, 28–30.

STRATEGY CASE

DID BASING ITS STRATEGY ON BEING SOCIALLY RESPONSIBLE BANKRUPT CA-CE-LEN?

Globalization has been the watchword over the past decade. The emerging global competition has created opportunities for some businesses and threats for many more. Many have not survived.

Ca-Ce-Len Manufacturing Co. of Granger, Texas, was in part a victim of globalization. Founded in 1975, it closed its doors in 1995. Until its demise, it provided employment to 125 people and at its peak in 1979 posted revenues of $1.5 million. The company grew in the relatively sheltered economy of the 1970's, which was characterized by trade barriers and protectionist policies. Competing in the crowded women's apparel industry, Ca-Ce-Len's strategy was to produce high-quality garments and pay above-average wages while earning a healthy profit. The company was not the traditional sweatshop notorious in this industry. Rather, good working conditions were the norm. The workday ran from 7:30 A.M. to 4 P.M. so that moms could drop off their kids at school and pick them up.

Then, in 1993, along came NAFTA (the North American Free Trade Agreement), which eliminated trade barriers between Mexico and the United States. GATT (General Agreement on Tariffs and Trade) also allowed for greatly expanded international competition. Ca-Ce-Len lost its orders to overseas shops, where labor was cheaper. Other work was lost to illegals working at home. In the end, unable to compete, Ca-Ce-Len was forced to call it quits.

Questions

1. What might Ca-Ce-Len's management have done differently in the face of changing times?
2. What social responsibility issues are involved in this case?
3. Did Ca-Ce-Len's strategy help do it in?

SOURCE: Tom Ehrenfeld and David Whitford, "Sweatshops, Free Trade Force Owner to Call It Quits," *Inc.*, November 1996, 23.

THE BUSINESS TEAM, INC.

DIVERSITY AT TEXACO

In all businesses, large and small, cash flow is the company's lifeblood, and the team has a comfortable monetary cushion at the moment. However, most consulting businesses go through up-and-down cycles, experiencing both good times and bad. The team wants to be socially responsible and ethical in all its dealings, but the partners know that the cash flow from their last few jobs has left them with a growing problem. Because good business practice dictates a careful evaluation of the implications of taking on new assignments, they want to carefully review each offer. But opportunities have been in the down cycle for a few months and the bills still need to be paid.

On Friday, Len got a call from a college fraternity brother. Jason had gone to work for Texaco right out of college, where he'd been assigned to a team of engineers developing international strategies. In the phone call, he asked if Len knew about the recent $175 million settlement Texaco had agreed to pay as a result of promotion discrimination charges brought by 1,400 African-American employees. Jason said that his multi-function planning team was in turmoil about the settlement and its implications for everyone's future at Texaco. He asked if Len's company would be willing to do a financial and performance audit of the impact of di-

versity on their planning team. As a big corporation, Texaco has deep pockets to pay well. The company is actively seeking to change its image, and its new CEO is stressing diversity and ethics training for everyone. Jason has told Len that he would like to show top management that his team is doing a good job of diversity management.

On Monday morning's agenda, Len puts Jason's inquiry on the table. He asks each member of the group to assess the issues presented by the potential Texaco contract from the perspective of each of their disciplines, and to discuss the ethical and social responsibility concerns such a contract might present.

Questions

1. What do you think the team members would say are the issues involved at Texaco, given their diverse backgrounds?
2. What types of ethical and social responsibility concerns might you come up with? On what would you base these concerns?
3. What is the relationship of organizational survival to ethical behavior?
4. What are the potential implications of going forward with this contract for future business?

ETHICS AND CONEDISON

In his book *Knitting Music*, Michael Dorf describes how ConEdison, New York City's electric utility, came close to putting the Knitting Factory out of business, at least for one long weekend. With bills topping off at about $2,000 a month, the Knitting Factory occasionally paid their bills a little late. ConEdison reacted by demanding an $800 deposit, and even Michael Dorf's letters, formal complaints, and visit to the local ConEd office wasn't enough to get ConEd to change its mind. Then one Friday afternoon at 5:45, a ConEdison employee came into the bar and explained that he was there to read meters. Instead, he secretly turned off the Knitting Factory's electric current, just before the start of the Knitting Factory's heavy weekend schedule of events and with four refrigerators filled with chilled products.

Team Exercises and Questions

Use what you learned in this chapter to answer the following questions:

1. Assume that it is possible that the Knitting Factory could have incurred a substantial loss without electric power for that weekend, and that ConEdison was aware of that. Do you believe that ConEd's decision to cut them off was an ethical one? Regardless of the decision to cut off the power, do you think the manner in which they did cut off the power was ethical?

2. Given the fact that ConEd could not be contacted until the following Monday, what would you have done if you were Michael Dorf? Would that have been ethical?

For the online version of this case, visit our Web site at: <www.prenhall.com/desslermgmt>.

For Internet exercises, interactive study questions, news updates and more, visit the Dessler Web site at

www.prenhall.com/desslermgmt

If you're using the CD-ROM that accompanies this text, simply click on the "Web Site" button to access the site.

MANAGING IN AN ERA OF RAPID CHANGE AND GLOBALIZATION

Managers plan, lead, organize, and control organizations and organizational behavior. Michael Dorf, founder, president, and chief executive officer of Knit-Media, performs all these functions on a daily basis. Currently, he is focused on preparing to lead a fast-growing global organization into the 21st century. KnitMedia recently raised funds to make its vision of a global music business a reality. It plans to double in size over the next year by expanding its record label globally and launching a network of Knitting Factory Clubs both domestically and internationally, which it is calling the Knitwork. The Knitwork will first open clubs in Los Angeles and London, with other clubs to be opened each year thereafter.

Michael's vision of KnitMedia's future is compelling and has attracted a very capable staff who share the same values about the music, artistic integrity, and a work ethic based on excellence. They envision KnitMedia's organizational culture spreading around the world. Michael has created an organization that encourages independence, creativity, and innovation among its employees in how they handle their work. It's a flat organization with Michael at the center.

Ken Ashworth, executive vice president and chief operating officer, says, "It"s different from other companies I've worked at, because it's a small business, . . . so it is a . . . day-to-day business, where it sort of survives on . . . the income and outflow of daily business. It is an entrepreneurial business where . . . the strategy of the company sometimes changes from a day-to-day basis and it's constantly moving with, changing with technology and entertainment and information. So, it's a strong company in the sense that it could change itself and keep growing, but keep the same direction. . . . It doesn't have the bureaucracy that ties down bigger companies, but it also doesn't have the capital structure that allows bigger companies to operate. So, it's as different as night and day."

As a manager helping his employees meet the organization's goals, Michael finds, hires, and promotes staff, and coaches and directs them. In his interpersonal role, he is a figurehead in ceremonial situations such as meetings. He gathers information in his informational role and disseminates it to those inside and outside the organization. In his controller role, he monitors KnitMedia's performance. In his decisional role, he commits the company to courses of action, initiating new projects, resolving conflicts, allocating resources, and negotiating. He is also something of a be-havioral scientist, understanding, developing, and motivating his employees.

Michael is building a multinational organization in which there are central controls of those areas of the organization that need to be standardized because of economies of scale and maintenance of the KnitMedia flavor, but local control of those areas based on distinct market considerations. This means that the financial function of KnitMedia's international clubs will be centralized in New York but will respond to local musical tastes, thus retaining their essence as a Knitting Factory Club. Daily tracking of each club's financial position will be made possible by using Internet technology and a customized accounting system. "So we can plug a club into [London]," explains Michael, "and we get a download every hour of their ticket sales, and of our bar sales; . . . we are thinking about it in these ways. And if we do it right, I think it's very, very manageable. But we have to make sure that we're completely on top of the controls." Michael can monitor the financial information to make informed decisions for the management of his clubs.

KnitMedia has a diverse, multicultural organization. Sascha von Oretzen, the Recording Studio Manager, is from Germany; Ed Greer, the Operations Manager, is from Scotland. They have an out-of-work lawyer working for them because he loves the music business and the Knitting Factory. Musicians from around the world perform at the Knitting Factory. It has an international reputation, and its music is enjoyed around the world.

Expanding into other countries presents a challenge to organizations, often due to their ignorance of cultural differences. To avoid these types of problems, Michael opened an office in Amsterdam to organize European tours and to develop relations with local European bands, music agents, promoters, and retailers. The KnitMedia has its multicultural staff's knowledge of local customs in their native countries on which to draw. The increasing popularity of KnitMedia music in Japan made it apparent to Michael that they needed to expand to Japan. He, therefore, took Japanese lessons so he could better understand the Japanese culture.

Michael is known for his integrity. He has refused sponsorship from vendors, such as Budweiser, that violate his sense of artistic integrity. He's also been very careful to pay his taxes and to generously pay the musicians who play for him, even though he loses money. (Clubs often take advantage of musicians and don't pay them fairly.) Because of his artistic integrity, instead of catering to pop artists, he continues to book cutting-edge avant-garde musicians, even though he could make more money with the former. Following his mother's advice, he avoids paying for anything with cash. He has hired homeless people to do chores in the club and he is sensitive to the neighborhood's concerns. Even though it is sometimes costly, Michael feels he personally needs to affect KnitMedia's integrity.

KnitMedia is all about new music around the world, experimental alternative pop and jazz. The Knitting Factory Club is a conduit between the artists who create, explore, and develop this avant-garde music and the consumers of music entertainment. As Michael enthuses, "The clubs are still going to be where live music is most likely to be experienced . . . so that's an important base of our business. But how the other medias develop over time, I don't know; and that's exciting because. . . . I'm glad I don't know where we're going to be in 10 years. That's exciting. That's what makes it all very exciting." He looks forward to leading KnitMedia in the 21st century.

Questions

Based on the cases, the videos, the textbook you've looked at thus far, and your knowledge from other sources, answer the following questions.

1. Is KnitMedia an organization for which you'd like to work? Would you be motivated to excel? Why or why not? Explain.

2. Based on what you've learned from the text, what is your assessment of Michael Dorf's efforts to expand to other countries and become global?

3. Based on your reading thus far, how would you characterize Michael's management style? How is it effective or ineffective? Explain.

4. What role does Michael's ethics play in the development of KnitMedia? In what ways is this manifested?

SOURCE: End-of-part video cases prepared by d. t. ogilvie, Rutgers University.

CHAPTER 4

MAKING DECISIONS

What's Ahead?

Tiny Micro Vision and its president Richard Rutkowski had some decisions to make. The company had developed a new way to display computer information, not on a screen, but by implanting images directly onto the retina of the human eye using low-level laser beams. Who should Micro Vision approach as the first customers for its $50,000 displays? Where were its potential markets? And how should it go about getting the funding for further development of its products?[1]

Richard Rutkowski

Objectives

After studying this chapter, you should be able to

- discuss the decision-making process
- compare "rational" decision making with decision making in practice
- identify the barriers to effective decision making
- utilize at least three techniques for making better decisions
- use groups more effectively in the decision-making process.

MANAGEMENT ON THE WEB

GROUP DECISION MAKING

This home page for Northeastern University's College of Business Administration offers practical information on group decision making and other aspects of teamwork. Could Micro Vision use any of them? ■

www.cba.neu.edu//%7Eewertheim/teams/ovrvw2.htm

Understanding Decision Making

While the issues facing Micro Vision may be a bit unusual, making decisions is a daily occurrence. Everyone is continually faced with the need to choose—the route to school, the job to accept, the computer to buy, for instance. A **decision** is a choice from among the available alternatives. **Decision making** is the process of developing and analyzing alternatives and making a choice.

Most decisions are prompted by problems. A *problem* is a discrepancy between a desirable and an actual situation. For example, if you need fifty dollars for a show and you only have ten, you have a problem. A decision doesn't necessarily involve a problem, although this is often the case. On the other hand, problem solving always involves making decisions, so we'll use the terms "decision making" and "problem solving" interchangeably in this book. *Judgment* refers to the cognitive or "thinking" aspects of the decision-making process.[2] We'll see in this chapter that the decision-making process is often subject to distortions and biases, precisely because it is usually a judgmental, not a purely mechanical, process.

Decisions and the Management Process

Decision making is at the heart of what all managers do. Planning, organizing, leading, and controlling are the basic management functions. However, as illustrated in Table 4.1, each of these calls for decisions to be made—which plan to implement, what goals to choose, and which people to hire, for instance.

DECISIONS AND THE BUSINESS TEAM. Every manager in the company's business team makes decisions. This is illustrated in Table 4.2. The accounting manager must decide what outside auditing firm to use, and how many days a customer can be allowed to wait before it pays its bills. The sales manager must decide which sales representatives to use in each region, and which advertising agency to hire. The production manager must choose between alternative suppliers and whether or not to recommend building a new plant. Nearly everything a manager does brings him or her to a decision that must be made, as the founders of USWeb illustrate in the Entrepreneurs in Action box.

Programmed and Nonprogrammed Decisions

Any decision a manager makes can be classified as either a **programmed decision** or a **nonprogrammed decision**. The two differ in the extent to which the decision must be handled as a completely new situation.[3]

TABLE 4.1 Decisions in the Management Functions

MANAGEMENT FUNCTION	TYPICAL DECISIONS MANAGERS FACE
Planning	What are the organization's long-term objectives? What strategies will best achieve these objectives? What should the organization's short-term objectives be? How difficult should individual goals be?
Organizing	How many subordinates should I have report directly to me? How much centralization should there be in the organization? How should jobs be designed? When should the organization implement a different structure?
Leading	How do I handle employees who appear to be low in motivation? What is the most effective leadership style in a given situation? How will a specific change affect worker productivity? When is the right time to stimulate conflict?
Controlling	What activities in the organization need to be controlled? How should these activities be controlled? When is a performance deviation significant? What type of management information system should the organization have?

SOURCE: Stephen P. Robbins, and Mary Coulter. *Management*, 5 ed. Upper Saddle River, N.J.: Prentice-Hall, (1996), 193.

TABLE 4.2 Some Decisions Business-Team Managers Make

MANAGER	EXAMPLES OF DECISIONS THESE MANAGERS FACE
Accounting Manager	What accounting firm should we use? Who should process our payroll? Should we give that customer credit?
Finance Manager	What bank should we use? Should we sell bonds or stocks? Should we buy back some of our company's stock?
Human Resource Manager	Where should we recruit for employees? Should we set up a testing program? Should I advise settling the equal employment complaint?
Production Manager	Which supplier should we use? Should we build the new plant? Should we buy the new machine?
Sales Manager	Which sales rep should we use in this district? Should we start this advertising campaign? Should we lower prices in response to our competitor's doing so?

PROGRAMMED DECISIONS. Luckily for managers, not every decision they make must be handled as a brand-new situation. Instead, many decision-making situations can be classified as programmed decisions. Programmed decisions are decisions that are repetitive and routine and that can be solved through mechanical procedures such as by applying rules. For example, to expedite the refund process, a

Entrepreneurs in Action

USWEB

When it comes to illustrating the fact that "nearly everything a manager does brings him or her to a decision that must be made," the founding managers of USWeb certainly fill the bill. USWeb is a 46-employee company, founded in 1995 in Santa Clara, California, that offers Web site design franchises.

The basic idea of USWeb is to create a world-wide chain of franchised Web design firms. CEO Joe Firmage, 25, believes this will be a growth business, because typical Web sites are often poorly organized, poorly designed, and often downright dull. It is hard for companies to design their own top-notch Web sites because hiring professional designers can be costly, and few Web sites right now are generating very high profits. Joe and his colleagues at USWeb also believe that many of today's Web design boutiques are staffed with people who haven't the training or experience to turn out first-class Web sites. Thus, their idea for Web-designing franchises.

Although the company is small and has fewer than ten franchisees so far, the number of decisions Joe Firmage and his management team make is enormous. At the same time, almost every decision the team makes is potentially a "life-and-death" decision, because until USWeb is big enough, even small decisions have the potential to sink the firm.

For example, the company is racing to sift through more than 1200 applications for its franchises, and Joe knows that ultimately, like McDonald's, the strength of his franchise company will rest on the individual abilities and strengths of the franchisees chosen to join his network. Similarly, he and his colleagues have been working overtime to hire and train a team of software, network hardware, marketing, and finance experts, and they know that these hiring decisions will help determine USWeb's ability to market a superior service. Indeed, the decisions to be made are virtually endless: Which type of computer hardware and Internet hookups should USWeb prescribe? Should they expand overseas at once, given the global nature of the Internet? How can USWeb continue to provide its franchisees with a competitive advantage so that individually they can compete effectively with independent Web site designers who don't have to pay USWeb's 7-percent-of-revenues fee?

At USWeb, nearly everything a manager does brings him or her to a decision point. The need to make the right decisions may be even more critical when the firm is very small, since there isn't much cash flow to keep the company going if a few bad decisions are made.

SOURCE: Tim Carvell, "USWeb," *Fortune*, 8 July 1996, 102.

department store may use this rule: "If the customer returns a jacket, you may give that person a refund if the tag is not removed, if the jacket is not damaged, and if the purchase was made within the past two weeks."

Some writers estimate that up to 90 percent of management decisions are of the programmed variety.[4] In many universities, for example, the question of which students to admit is a programmed decision made by mathematically weighting each candidate's test scores and grades. In most companies, the calculation of overtime pay and weekly payroll benefits is made by preprogrammed computer software. In fact, the advent of computers has dramatically boosted the number of organizational decisions that can now be "programmed." For example, when your credit card is "swiped" at a point of purchase, the decision to accept it is generally made by preprogrammed computers, which refer the decision to a credit manager only if your credit limit has been exceeded. It usually makes sense to try to determine whether particular decisions can be programmed, and if so, to free managers from having to make those decisions themselves; the decisions can be left to subordinates.

NONPROGRAMMED DECISIONS. In contrast, nonprogrammed decisions are unique and novel, and mechanical procedures are not available for making them. Crisis decisions—like managing the rescue work for a plane crash—are one example.

Nonprogrammed decisions don't always involve crises, but they are generally "...the kinds of [major] decisions which managers are paid to address..."[5] Viacom's purchase of Blockbuster Video and Boston Chicken's decision to broaden its product line and rename its stores "Boston Market" were both nonprogrammed decisions. Generally speaking, nonprogrammed decisions rely heavily on judgment and focus on the firm's long-term strategic development and survival. With the big and unexpected changes of the past few years—deregulation, global competition, and downsizings, for instance—such nonprogrammed decisions are increasingly prevalent.

Table 4.3 compares and contrasts programmed and nonprogrammed decision making. Programmed decisions are recurring decisions, ones for which there are clear-cut procedures and decision rules for finding a "best" solution. Nonprogrammed decisions involve exceptional, nonrecurring, often crisis or strategic decisions with so many imponderables that no specific procedures or "programs" are available. As in Table 4.4, programmed decisions are usually made by applying procedures, rules, and computerized computations. Managers making nonprogrammed decisions usually must rely more on judgment, intuition, and creativity, as in the example on the following page.

■ TABLE 4.3 *Comparing Programmed and Nonprogrammed Decisions*		
	PROGRAMMED	**NONPROGRAMMED**
Type of Decision	Programmable; routine; generic; computational	Nonprogrammable; unique; innovative
Nature of the Decision	Procedural; predictable; well-defined information and decision criteria	Novel; unstructured; incomplete channels information; unknown criteria
Strategy for Making Decision	Reliance on rules and computation	Reliance on principles; judgement; general problem-solving processes

■ TABLE 4.4 *Decision-Making Techniques Used*		
Type of Decision	Programmed, routine decisions	Unprogrammed, nonroutine decisions
General Nature of the Situation	Relatively unchanging; few novel events	Rapidly changing; much novelty
Decision-Making Techniques Emphasized	Management science; capital budgeting; computerized solutions; rules	Judgment; intuition, creativity

Managing Change

ADVANCED RISC MACHINES:
NONPROGRAMMED DECISION TO STAY FLEXIBLE

You are faced with the following problem: How does your firm navigate a path through the unpredictable peaks and valleys of semiconductor chip demand, and escape getting stuck with millions of surplus microchips? The decision for one firm in this fast-changing industry was to let other firms make the chips it designed.

Advanced RISC Machines (ARM) of Cambridge, England, is one such chip-making company. ARM decided to create a company based on what it perceived as the changes occurring in the semiconductor marketplace. A private company of 140 employees with $16 million in annual revenues, ARM focuses on supplying chips for products with "embedded intelligence"—cyberspeak for things like smart telephones, Internet TVs, pocket computers, and "intelligent" kitchen devices. Because such devices need to be light and portable, their microprocessors must be tiny and energy efficient, running for hours on a few volts of battery power.

Chips built by bigger semiconductor companies (such as Motorola and IBM) tend to be more powerful, but also bigger and more expensive—and thus impractical for carry-anywhere devices like the Apple Newton. ARM chips don't work quite so fast but are much cheaper. ARM's simplest chip is two to three times cheaper than competing products and one-tenth the price of Intel's Pentium chip.

The company currently has this niche almost to itself, and the future looks rosy. However, the product life of most of the devices that use ARM's chips is quite short. The company's managers must therefore continually apply good judgment lest ARM itself get stuck with excess chips.[6] ARM's nonprogrammed decision to subcontract production has helped it land big-name customers, including Texas Instruments and Samsung, while allowing it a profit almost from its first day in business. ■

■ **FIGURE 4.1**
Top managers tend to confront more ill-structured, ambiguous situations ("What will our competitors do?"), and so make more nonprogrammed decisions; lower managers tend to confront more structured decisions ("How many items should we produce today?"), and make more programmed decisions.

SOURCE: *Management* 5th Ed. by Robbins/Coulter, © 1996. Reprinted by permission of Prentice-Hall, Inc., Upper Saddle River, NJ.

Top-level managers tend to face more nonprogrammed decisions, while lower-level managers face more programmed ones. This is illustrated in Figure 4.1. Lower-level managers tend to spend more time addressing programmed decisions.

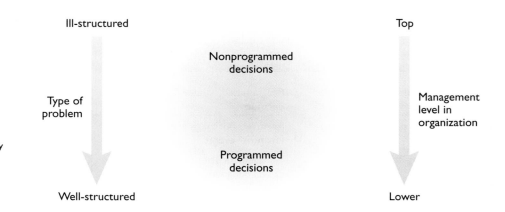

In other words, they focus more on decisions for which well-defined rules and procedures can be used to make the choice (such as determining how much inventory to order for next month). Entrepreneurs make almost all decisions at every level in their small firms at first, as the Entrepreneurs in Action box on Chris Zane shows.

The "Rational" Decision-Making Process

Suppose you are the owner of a big retail store and must decide which of several cars to buy for your deliveries. What process would you use in selecting among the many possible alternatives? The answer depends on how rational you believe you are. The idea that managers are entirely rational has a long and honorable tradition in economic and management theory. Early economists needed a simplified way to explain economic phenomena, like how supply and demand were related. Their solution was to accept a number of simplifying assumptions about how managers made decisions. Specifically, they assumed that the rational manager

1. had complete or "perfect" information about the situation including th : full range of goods and services available on the market and the exact price of each good or service;
2. could perfectly define the problem and not get confused by symptoms or other obstacles;
3. could identify all criteria and accurately weight all the criteria according to their preferences;

Entrepreneurs in Action

ZANE'S CYCLES BREAKS AWAY

Do you have a passion you can turn into a business? Chris Zane pursued his passion for bicycles and devoted his energy to becoming a leader in the industry. As a boy, he started repairing bikes in his parents' Connecticut garage. Later he went to work in a bicycle shop, and when it was about to close, he convinced his parents to help him buy it. Thus, Zane's Cycles was born.

As the company's chief decision maker, Chris found himself facing the routine and not-so-routine challenges of owning a small business. His first decision was to offer a one-year service guarantee, much more enticing than the 30 days offered by his competitors. When the competitors matched Zane, he countered with two years. His competitors matched

him again, and he now offers a lifetime guarantee that pays for itself in goodwill and repeat business.

Another of Zane's strategies was to charge nothing for any item that costs less than a dollar. The company also does extensive community outreach and service, offers scholarships, produces its own catalog, gives a 90-day price guarantee, and maintains a play area and coffee bar for customers. Most of Zane's competitors have gone out of business, and if you call them on the phone, you will be connected directly to Zane's.

Zane has made the right decisions involving even the smallest details of his customers' needs, and this has enabled him to become "*the* bike shop in New Haven County."

SOURCE: Donna Fenn, "Leader of the Pack," *Inc.,* February 1996, 31–38.

4. knew all possible alternatives and could accurately assess each against each criterion; and

5. could accurately calculate and choose the alternative with the highest perceived value.[7]

The "rational" manager's approach to making a decision would thus include the following six steps:

1. **Define the problem.**[8]

Managerial decision making is usually sparked by the identification of a problem. Perhaps you need to expand your retail chain, or you are faced with the problem of increased advertising by competitors. These challenges and a multitude like them are the sorts of problems managers face daily.

Identifying the problem is not always easy, however. Common mistakes here include emphasizing the obvious, or being misled by symptoms.[9]

Here is a classic example that illustrates these decision-making mistakes. A consulting team was retained by the owners of a large office building. The office workers were upset because they had to wait so long for an elevator to pick them up, and many tenants were threatening to move out. The owners called in the consulting team and told them the problem was that the elevators were running too slowly.

How would you have attacked the problem if you were one of the consultants? If you assume, as did the owners, that the problem could be defined as "slow-moving elevators," then the alternative solutions are both limited and expensive. The elevators were running about as fast as they could, so speeding them up was not an option. One solution might be to ask the tenants to stagger their work hours, but that could cause more animosity than the slow-moving elevators. Another alternative might be to add one or two more elevators, but this would be tremendously expensive.

The point of this example is that the alternatives you develop and the decision you make are both linked to the way you define the problem. What the consultants actually did in this case was to disregard "slow-moving elevators" as the problem. Instead, they defined the problem as "the tenants are upset because they have to wait for an elevator." Given that, the solution they chose was to have full-length mirrors installed by each bank of elevators so the tenants could admire themselves while waiting! The solution was both inexpensive and satisfactory, and the complaints virtually disappeared. This case shows that managers must be careful about how they define problems.

2. **Identify the criteria.**

In most decisions you'll want to achieve several objectives or satisfy several criteria. This is illustrated in Figure 4.2. In buying a computer, for instance, you may want to maximize reliability, minimize cost, obtain adequate support, and so on. An entirely rational decision maker will try to identify all the decision criteria.

3. **Weight the criteria.**

Some criteria may be more important to you than others. (For example, minimizing cost may be more important than having continuing service support.) Rational decision makers will weight each of the decision criteria, as in Figure 4.2.

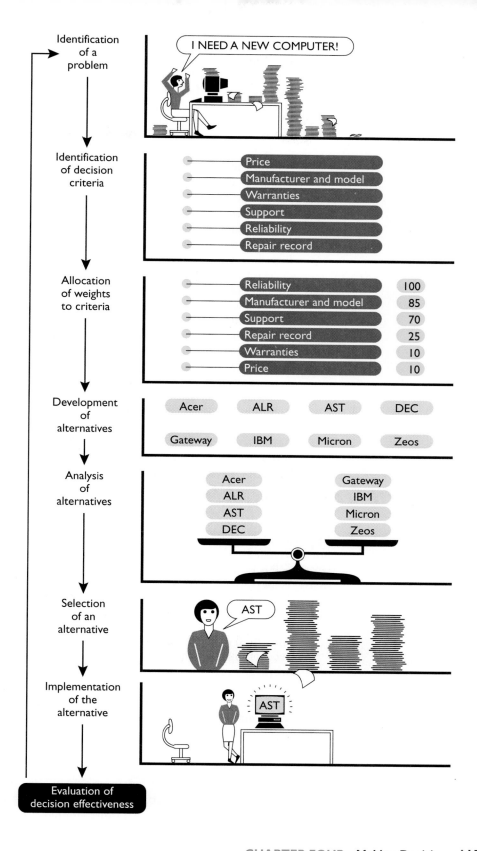

■ **FIGURE 4.2**
The Rational Decision-making Process

SOURCE: *Management* 5th Ed. by Robbins/Coulter, © 1996. Reprinted by permission of Prentice-Hall, Inc., Upper Saddle River, NJ.

4. **Develop alternatives.**

Whether we are choosing between alternative plans, job candidates, cars, or computers, the existence of some choice is a prerequisite to effective decision making. In fact, when a manager has no choice, there really isn't any decision to make—except perhaps to "take it or leave it."

Developing good alternatives may be easy in a completely rational world. But as often as not, developing good alternatives is no easy matter; it takes a great deal of creativity and judgment, as we'll see later in this chapter.

5. **Analyze the alternatives.**

The next step is to analyze the alternatives. Should you buy the IBM or the ACER? Should the factory buy machine A or machine B? How does each alternative stack up, given the criteria on which the decision is to be based? One expert says that "this is often the most difficult part of the decision-making process, because this is the stage that typically requires forecasting future events."[10] Under the most perfectly rational conditions, a decision maker would be able to carefully assess the potential consequences of choosing each alternative. However, as we'll see, such perfect conditions rarely exist.

6. **Make a choice, and then implement and evaluate decision.**

Under perfect conditions, making the choice should be a straightforward matter of computing the pros and cons of each alternative relative to your decision criteria and choosing the one that maximizes your benefits. However, in practice, as you know, making a decision—even on a relatively clear-cut matter like the choice of a computer—usually can't be done so accurately or rationally. To see why, let us move on to decision making in practice.

How Managers Make Decisions: The Limits to Rationality

In practice, many factors limit just how rational any decision maker can be. That is not to say that the foregoing rational model is useless: Most managers probably do try to make rational analyses. Furthermore, many decisions (particularly programmable ones) do lend themselves to the relatively mathematical precision of the rational decision-making process. But in practice we know that there are many limits or barriers to rationality. These include the following:

- individual differences
- decision-making shortcuts (heuristics)
- decision biases
- the framing of the problem
- escalation of commitment
- functional fixedness
- psychological set
- organizational decision-making barriers

Individual Differences

First, people's ability to absorb, analyze, and generally "process" information varies from person to person, and is also quite limited. In one series of lab studies, subjects were required to make decisions based on the amount of information transmitted on a screen.[11] Most people quickly reached a point at which "information overload" occurred, and they then began adjusting in several ways. For example, some people omitted or ignored some of the information transmitted on the screen; others began committing errors by incorrectly identifying some of the information; and others gave only approximate responses (such as "about 25" instead of "24.6").

Problems like these occur in the real world too. Managers, says decision-making expert Herbert Simon, have to juggle so many problems and assimilate so much information that even an approximation to complete rationality is hard to achieve. In organizations, information overload and managers' inability to cope with it manifest themselves in much the same kinds of distortion and omission that occurred in the lab. In one study, about 80 percent of the information in a message was lost by the time it had made its way down through five management levels.[12]

Organizational Behavior in Action

PERCEPTION IN PRACTICE

The way a person perceives a situation is a big example of how individual differences influence the way decisions are made. *Perception* is the selection and interpretation of information we receive through our senses and the meaning we give to the information. We'll see at a later point that many things, including our individual needs, influence how we perceive a stimuli. (Thus, a thirsty person in the desert may perceive the faraway heat waves as a mirage, whereas his healthy rescuer sees nothing but sand.) In organizations, a manager's prior experiences and position in the company can have a big effect on how the manager both perceives a problem and reacts to it.

The classic study of this phenomenon was carried out a number of years ago.[13] Twenty-three executives, all employed by a large manufacturing firm, were asked to read a business case. The case described the activities of a company of moderate size specializing in manufacturing seamless steel tubes. The executives were told to read the case and to individually write a brief statement of what they considered to be the most important problem facing the company—the problem "a new company president should deal with first." The 23 executives differed in terms of their functional backgrounds: Six were sales managers, five were production managers, four were accounting managers, and the rest included members of the legal, research and development, public relations, medical, HR, and purchasing departments.

The researchers found that a manager's position influenced the way he or she identified the "most important problem" facing the company. For example, of six sales executives, five thought the most important problem was a sales problem. "Organization problems" were mentioned by four out of five production executives, but by only one sales executive and no accounting executives. ■

SYSTEMATIC VS. INTUITIVE DECISION STYLES. Apart from (or perhaps because of) differences in perception and ability, individuals also differ in their approaches to decision making. People who are *systematic decision makers* tend to take a more logical, structured, step-by-step approach to solving a problem.[14] At the other extreme, *intuitive decision makers* use more of a trial-and-error decision-making approach, disregarding much of the information available and rapidly bouncing from one alternative to another to get a feel for which seems to work best.

Decision-Making Shortcuts: Heuristics

Heuristics—decision-making shortcuts—also undermine the economists' ideal of a perfectly rational, optimizing decision maker. Specifically, people take shortcuts when solving problems, by applying rules of thumb or **heuristics.** For example, a banker might follow the heuristic, "People should only spend 30 percent of their disposable income for mortgage and interest expenses."[15] Applying her rule of thumb may expedite the banker's decision making. However it probably will also undermine the rationality of her decisions, if, for instance, it means that an otherwise qualified applicant is rejected.

Managers apply several general types of heuristics. One is the **similarity heuristic** by which a manager might predict someone's performance based on that person's similarity to other individuals that the manager has known in the past. There is also the **availability heuristic** by which a manager might base a decision on the aspects of the situation that are most readily "available" in memory. A common problem in appraising a person's performance, for instance, is to evaluate the person based mostly on recent performance—the last few weeks rather than the whole year—because those experiences are more available in memory.

Decision-making shortcuts like these can lead to faster decisions, but also to errors. For example, the similarity heuristic can lead to discriminatory decisions, and the availability heuristic might lead to an appraisal that disregards the subordinate's earlier performance, good or poor. Either way, the shortcut has reduced the rationality of the manager's decisions.

Decision Biases

Two types of biases can also distort the decision a person makes. First, there are **person-specific biases,** which are defined as biases specific to particular people or groups. For example, someone biased in favor of a particular ethnic group might consciously or unconsciously decide to hire more people from that group.

Second, most people are influenced by what psychologists call **cognitive biases,** which are defined as standard errors in reaching a decision. For example, people tend to be overconfident and to overestimate their ability in answering moderately to extremely difficult questions. People are usually most overconfident in solving problems with which they are quite familiar. The problem is they do not correspondingly reduce their confidence level when solving relatively difficult problems that are outside their areas of expertise.[16]

The *confirmation trap* is a second example of a cognitive bias. It means that people tend to seek confirmatory information for what they think is true and neglect to search for disconfirmatory evidence. For example, most people tend to look for confirmatory evidence once they've tentatively decided to buy something. Suppose you have tentatively decided to buy a new computer or a new car. If you are like most people, your research now will tend to focus more on information that supports your initial decision than on information that does not support it. Like most people, you are the unwitting victim of a cognitive decision bias.

The Framing of the Problem

The way the problem is presented, or the **framing** of the problem, can also significantly influence the rationality of the decision. Here's an example. A company president is told she has a choice: Settle a lawsuit out of court for $10 million and thus accept a *sure loss* of $10 million, or go to court and have a 50 percent *chance* of a $20 million loss. When presented with a problem framed like this, most people choose to go to court. But suppose the problem is framed this way: The company can settle out of court for $10 million and thus *save* $10 million, or it can go to court and have a 50 percent *chance* of losing $20 million. Here most people pick the first option—settling out of court. Thus, managers must be aware of the fact that while they may believe they are making rational decisions, their judgment can actually be distorted by the way the problem is presented to them.

Escalation of Commitment

Have you ever had to negotiate with someone only to find that both of your positions became more and more entrenched the more you negotiated? *Escalation of commitment* means people tend to increase commitment to their positions when decisions need to be made step by step, as they are during a series of negotiating sessions. Price wars—say, between competing gas stations—are one example. Here both owners may continue to drop their prices even when the decision to do so is irrational, such as when prices drop below their actual costs.

Functional Fixedness

Functional fixedness "is the inability to see that an object can have a function other than its stated or usual one."[17] This decision-making barrier can limit a manager's ability to discover alternative solutions. For example, for many years the Arm & Hammer Company sold its baking soda for one purpose—baking. A new management team was able to expand upon the usual way of viewing the product. It is now marketed for dozens of other uses, including absorbing refrigerator odors, brightening teeth, and diminishing cat litter box odor.

Psychological Set

The tendency to focus on a rigid strategy or approach to certain types of problems is called **psychological set.**[18] This mental trait can severely limit a manager's ability to find alternative solutions. A classic example is presented in Figure 4.3. Your

Price wars are a form of escalation of commitment, in which step-by-step decision making leads each party to become more and more entrenched in a position that may even be irrational.

assignment is to connect all nine dots with no more than four lines running through them, and to do so without lifting your pen from the paper. Hint: Don't fall into the trap of taking a rigid strategy or approach to viewing and solving the problem. The answer is provided on page 123.

Organizational Decision-Making Barriers

Sometimes it's the organization itself that inhibits the adequate evaluation of a problem and its possible solutions. For example, employees tend to be reluctant to bring bad news to their managers, and one result, says organizational learning expert Chris Argyris, is that many decisions become "sealed in." In one company, for instance, Argyris found that although lower-level managers knew a product was in serious trouble, they were reluctant to tell their superiors. The reason was that their superiors had done the production and marketing studies leading to the decision to produce the product; the lower-level managers knew their bosses would therefore resist and disapprove of any advice that seemed to criticize their original decision. As a result, the product was carried for six years beyond the time it should have been dropped, resulting in a loss of over $100 million.[19]

Decision Making in Practice: Bounded Rationality

We have seen that many things stand in the way of a manager making a perfectly rational decision. Individual differences and the nature of human decision making lead to information overload if a manager tries to pursue every bit of information about the problem at hand. Heuristics or decision-making shortcuts lead to faster decisions but not necessarily to the best solution to the problem. Cognitive biases like overconfidence can make the manager jump to the wrong conclusion. The way the problem is framed or presented will influence the solution that the manager chooses. Escalation of commitment can lead to irrational decisions. Functional fixedness and psychological set can limit the manager's ability to discover all the possible solutions. And the nature of organizational life (including the realities of the superior–subordinate relationship) can seriously distort decisions made at each level of the organization.

Decision Making: How It Should Be Versus How It Actually Is

The existence of these decision-making barriers means that the ideal "rational" model of what management decision making *should be* must be modified to take into consideration how managers *actually do* make decisions. Herbert Simon and his associates say that, in practice, "bounded rationality" more accurately represents

■ TABLE 4.5 Rationality and Bounded Rationality: Assumptions

RATIONALITY	BOUNDED RATIONALITY
Can perfectly define problem	Decision maker lacks information to completely define problem
Identify and weigh all decision criteria	May not be able to knowledgeably weigh all criteria
Know and assess all alternatives based on criteria	Hasn't the time or money to assess all alternatives completely
Review all solutions until can make optimal choice	Satisfices by taking first good alternative

how managers actually make decisions. **Bounded rationality** means that a manager's decision making is only as rational as his or her unique values, capabilities, and limited capacity for processing information permit him or her to be—rationality is bounded or limited, in other words.

The differing assumptions of rationality and bounded rationality are compared in Table 4.5. The completely rational decision maker is able to perfectly define the problem, identify and accurately weight all the criteria, know all the relevant alternatives, and accurately assess all those alternatives to make the optimal choice based on his or her criteria. In contrast, bounded rationality accepts the fact that decision makers often lack important information about how to define the problem and the relevant criteria, and that time and cost constraints limit their ability to get all the required information. Decision making in practice is also limited by managers' ability to retain only a relatively small amount of information in their usable memory and by the sorts of decision-making barriers and biases we discussed in the previous section.[20]

Satisficing Versus Optimizing

A particularly important difference between the rational and the bounded rational decision maker is this: The rational manager continues to review solutions until he or she finds the optimal choice, while in contrast, managers in practice often "satisfice." To **satisfice** means that managers in practice tend to be concerned with just discovering and selecting *satisfactory* alternatives, and only in exceptional cases with finding *optimal* alternatives.[21] This is not to say that managers don't try to be rational; it is simply recognizing the fact that, in practice, their attempts to be rational will be limited or "bounded" by the sorts of decision-making barriers we discussed above. Luckily, several decision-making tools are available to help minimize the adverse effects of these barriers and thus improve a manager's decisions.

How to Make Better Decisions

Some people assume that good judgment is like great singing—either you can do it or you can't. But overcoming the many decision-making barriers we've identified can lead to better decisions by almost anyone. Techniques like those we discuss next can help you to avoid problems at every step of the decision-making process.

Increase Your Knowledge

Many bad decisions stem from the decision maker's lack of experience with the problem at hand. For example, we saw that people tend to be most overconfident about the correctness of their answers when asked to respond to more difficult questions (in other words, to questions about which their experience is relatively limited). Imagine the consequences: Through a lack of experience you make a questionable decision and through overconfidence you blindly stick to it, becoming increasingly more committed (due to people's tendency to escalate commitment to their preliminary decisions).

The first step in avoiding this sad outcome—whether the decision involves buying a computer, a car, a house, or another company—is to acquire experience. The more you know about the problem and the more facts you can marshal, the more likely it is that your confidence in your decision will not be misplaced.[22] You can acquire the necessary experience yourself, or through your own research. Many managers use management consultants: The consultants' experience with some area (such as personnel testing or strategic planning) can then be used to supplement the manager's lack of experience in that specific area. Talking the problem over with other people can also help, particularly if they've had some experience solving similar problems.

De-bias Your Judgment

We've seen that a number of cognitive or decision-making biases tend to distort a manager's judgment. These biases include overconfidence, the tendency to seek confirmatory information, and escalation of commitment. Managers also bring personal values and biases to the decision (for instance, for or against a particular ethnic group), and of course these personal biases can also influence the person's decisions.

De-biasing your judgment—reducing or eliminating biases from your judgmental processes—is therefore a crucial step toward making better decisions. Research studies show that de-biasing, while difficult, can be achieved.[23] It requires at least four steps: (1) understand that the possibility of bias exists; (2) understand how the bias can affect your judgment; (3) analyze previous decisions you've made to give yourself feedback on whether and how bias has influenced your judgment; and (4) accept the fact that such biases exist but can be reduced or eliminated through your diligent efforts.

Be Creative

Creativity plays a major role in making better decisions. *Creativity*—the process of developing original, novel responses to a problem—is essential for decision-making activities like developing new alternatives and correctly defining the problem. (For example, recall the consultant's creative redefinition of the "slow-moving elevators" problem, which led them to install mirrors to occupy the time of those waiting so they would no longer complain.) The trouble is that creativity itself is often hampered by the same sorts of barriers and biases (like functional fixedness) that stymie other aspects of the decision-making process. However, creativity *can* be cultivated, and there are several things you can do in this regard.

CHECK YOUR ASSUMPTIONS. The same decision-making barriers that hamper decision making in general can undermine your ability to be creative, too. For example, let us look again at the problem of the nine dots, which is reproduced in Figure 4.4. Remember your instructions were to connect all nine dots with no more

■ **FIGURE 4.4**
Looking at the Problem in Just One Way

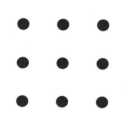

SOURCE: Lester A. Lefton and Laura Valvatine, *Mastering Psychology*, 4th ed. Copyright © 1992 by Allyn & Bacon. Reprinted by permission.

■ **FIGURE 4.5**
The Advantage of Not Just Looking at the Problem in One Way

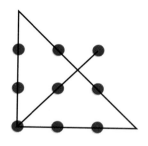

SOURCE: Max H. Bazerman, *Judgment in Managerial Decision Making.* Copyright © 1994 John Wiley & Sons, Inc., p. 93. Reprinted by permission of John Wiley & Sons, Inc.

than four lines running through them, and to do it without lifting your pen from the paper.

Psychological set is the decision-making barrier at work here. (Recall that this is the tendency to take a rigid view of a problem.) Most people's tendency is to view the nine dots as a square, but this of course limits your solutions. In fact, and you can try this, there is no way to connect all the dots with just four lines as long as you assume you must limit your drawing to a perfect square.

Figure 4.5 shows one creative solution. Notice that the key to this solution was breaking through assumptions about the problem and how it needed to be solved. In fact, one managerial decision-making expert refers to creativity as, in essence, " . . . an assumption-breaking process."[24] Now try to solve the problem in Figure 4.6. Remember, in this and all your other decisions, force yourself to *be creative:* always check your assumptions.

THINK THROUGH THE PROCESS. Forcing yourself to think through the whole process step by step can also help you be more creative. Consider this problem: An extraordinarily frugal person named Joe can make one whole cigar from every five cigar butts he finds. How many cigars can he make if he finds twenty-five cigar butts? Before you answer "five," think through Joe's cigar-making process, step by step. There he sits on his park bench, making (and smoking!) each of his five cigars. As he smokes each cigar, he ends up with one new cigar butt. Thus, in smoking his five hand-made cigars, Joe ends up with five new butts which of course he combines into his sixth, and in this case final, whole new cigar.[25]

This problem illustrates how "process analysis" can boost your creativity and insight. Process analysis means solving a problem by thinking about the processes that are involved.[26] In this case, process analysis involved more or less envisioning

■ **FIGURE 4.6**
Using Creativity to Find a Solution

How many squares are in the box? Now, count again. Only sixteen? Take away your preconception of how many squares there are. Now, how many do you find? You should find thirty!

SOURCE: *Applied Human Relations,* 4/e by Benton/Halloran, © 1991. Reprinted by permission of Prentice-Hall, Inc., Upper Saddle River, NJ.

FIGURE 4.7
Are You More Rational or More Intuitive?

SOURCE: Adapted and reproduced by special permission of the Publisher, Psychological Assessment Resources, Inc., Odessa FL 33556, from the Personal Style Inventory by William Taggart, Ph.D., and Barbara Hausladen, Copyright 1991, 1993 by PAR, Inc.

What Is My Orientation?

You can get a rough idea of your relative preferences for the rational and intuitive ways of dealing with situations by rating yourself on four items. For each statement, rank yourself on a six point scale from 1 (never), 2 (once in a while), 3 (sometimes), 4 (quite often), 5 (frequently but not always), to 6 (always) and place your response in the box to the right of the item:

1. When I have a special job to do, I like to organize it carefully from the start. ☐

2. I feel that a prescribed, step-by-step method is best for solving problems. ☐

3. I prefer people who are imaginative to those who are not. ☐

4. I look at a problem as a whole, approaching it from all sides. ☐

Now add the values for the first two items for one total and for the last two items for another total. Subtract the second total from the first. If your total has a positive value, your preference is Rational by that amount, and if your total has a negative value, your preference is Intuitive by that amount. Ten represents the maximum possible rational or intuitive score from the equally preferred midpoint (0). Mark your position on the range of possible scores:

Intuitive ◄—————————— | ——————————► Rational

−10 −9 −8 −7 −6 −5 −4 −3 −2 −1 0 1 2 3 4 5 6 7 8 9 10
|—|—|—|—|—|—|—|—|—|—|—|—|—|—|—|—|—|—|—|—|

These items are taken from a thirty item Personal Style Inventory (PSI) assessment of preferences for Rational and Intuitive behavior created by professor William Taggert.

Joe sitting on a park bench, and thinking through each of the steps he would go through. By using process analysis to look over his shoulder in this way, we boosted our creativity and discovered that he made a sixth cigar.

Use Your Intuition

Many behavioral scientists argue that overemphasizing rationality and logic can actually backfire by blocking you from using your intuition. *Intuition* can be defined as a cognitive process whereby we unconsciously make a decision based on our accumulated knowledge and experiences. For example, here is what the psychiatrist Sigmund Freud had to say about making important decisions:

> When making a decision of minor importance I have always found it advantageous to consider all the pros and cons. In vital matters, however, such as the choice of a mate or a profession, the decision should come from the unconscious, from somewhere within ourselves. In the important decisions of our personal life, we should be governed, I think, by the deep inner needs of our nature.[27]

Another expert says you can usually tell when a decision accords with your inner nature, for it brings an enormous sense of relief. Good decisions, he says, are the best tranquilizers ever invented; bad ones often increase your anxiety. Therefore, consult your inner feelings: Do not disregard your intuition.[28]

Intuitiveness can be measured. Figure 4.7 presents a short test that provides an approximate reading on whether you are more rational or intuitive in your decision making.[29]

◎ ◎ ◎ **Strategy in Action** ◎ ◎ ◎

STRATEGIC DECISION MAKING

Understanding the decision-making process and how to improve it is especially important when it comes to strategic decision making. There are two main reasons for this. First, intuition plays an especially important role in strategic decision making. For example, Professor Henry Mintzberg made a study of 25 top-level strategic decision makers. He found that in only 18 of 83 decisions did managers mention using explicit step-by-step analyses in arriving at a choice. Sometimes the choice was arrived at after considerable bargaining and debate among managers. More often, a more intuitive process seemed to be used. As Mintzberg says, "Typically, the options and all kinds of data associated with them were pumped into the mind of the manager, and somehow a choice later came out. How was never explained."[30]

Second, the fact that many people may have a hand in the strategic decision means that the effects of decision biases will be magnified. Typically, for instance, various executives, line and staff managers, and members of the board of directors will give some advice. As a result, the process of creating a strategy is not always neat and tidy. For example, an employee in the firm's R&D department may attend an industry conference where a new product is discussed. That person may mention the product to her supervisor, who passes it along to her own boss. Eventually, the idea may be discussed by the firm's production and sales managers for possible recommendation as part of the firm's new strategy.[31]

The point is that for strategic decision makers like the CEO, the decision-making process and its barriers may all have taken their toll, even before he or she gets the advice. Decision biases, heuristics, framing, and functional fixedness are just some of the factors that will influence each of the firm's decision makers, from the R&D employee to the members of the board. Unless the manager understands the decision-making problems that can arise and the questions to ask, his or her strategic decisions could end up based on inaccurate or incomplete information.

Don't Overstress the Finality of Your Decision[32]

Very few decisions are forever; there is more "give" in more decisions than we realize. While many major strategic decisions are certainly hard to reverse, most poor decisions won't lead to the end of the world for you, so it's not necessary to become frozen in the finality of your decision.

Make Sure the Timing Is Right

Most people's decisions are affected by their passing moods. For example, researchers in one study found that when subjects felt "down," their actions tended to be aggressive and destructive. Yet when they felt good, their behavior swung toward tolerance and balance. People tend to be lenient when they are in good spirits, and "tough" when they are grouchy. Managerial decision makers should therefore take their emotions into account before making important decisions, and not let their decisions be swayed by passing moods.

Using Groups to Make Better Decisions

Groups at Work

Whether they are called work groups, teams, or committees, groups accomplish much of the work in organizations. Since we've focused on individual decision making up to now, it's important that we turn our attention to how to use the power of groups to make better decisions.

Although we'll discuss groups in more detail at a later point in this book, some working definitions are in order now. A **group** is defined as two or more persons who interact together for some purpose and in such a manner that each person influences and is influenced by each other person. Thus the Board of Directors of Microsoft is a group, as is the Lexington, Kentucky work team that installs the dashboards on Toyota's Camry line.

Groups are important at work in part because of the effect they have on their members. For example, pressure by other group members can cause a member to raise or lower his or her output. In turn, the extent to which a group can influence its members depends on several things, including the **cohesiveness** of the group—the attraction of the group for its members—and on the group's **norms**—the informal rules that groups adopt to regulate and regularize group members' behavior.[33]

Pros and Cons of Group Decision Making

You probably have found from your own experience that groups to which you belong—whether work groups, social clubs, or some other kind—can and do influence how you behave and the decisions you make. It is therefore not surprising that having groups make decisions has its pros and cons as far as the employer is concerned. These pros and cons are summarized in Figure 4.8.

ADVANTAGES OF USING GROUPS TO MAKE DECISIONS. The old saying that "two heads are better than one" can be true when you bring several people together to arrive at a decision. Pooling the experiences and points of view of several people can lead to more points of view regarding how to define the problem, more possible solutions, and more creative decisions in general. Groups that analyze a problem and come up with their own decisions also tend to "buy into" those decisions; this acceptance boosts the chance that the group will work harder to implement the decision once it's put into effect.[34]

DISADVANTAGES OF USING GROUPS TO MAKE DECISIONS. Although group decision-making advocates say "two heads are better than one," detractors say "a camel is a horse put together by a committee." This is a reference to the fact that using a group can sometimes actually short circuit the decision process.

PROS	CONS
• "Two heads are better than one" • More points of view • Fosters acceptance • Group may work harder to implement decisions	• Pressure for consensus • Dominance by one individual • Escalation of commitment: pressure to "win your point" • More time consuming • Groupthink

■ **FIGURE 4.8**
Summary of Pros and Cons of Using Groups to Make Decisions

Better decisions sometimes result from consultation with others, particularly if they are more knowledgeable or more experienced in dealing with similar problems.

Several things can go wrong when groups are formed to make decisions. The desire to be a good group member and to be accepted tends to silence disagreement and to favor consensus, a fact that can actually reduce creative decisions instead of enhancing them.[35] In many groups, a dominant individual emerges who effectively cuts off debate and channels the rest of the group to his or her point of view. Escalation of commitment can be a problem here too: When groups are confronted by a problem, there is often a tendency for individual group members to become committed to their own pet solutions, and then the goal becomes winning the argument rather than solving the problem. Groups also take longer to make decisions than do individuals. The group decision-making process can therefore be inherently more expensive than having an individual make the decision.

The net effect of several of these disadvantages is a problem called groupthink. **Groupthink** has been defined as "a mode of thinking that people engage in when they are deeply involved in a cohesive group, when the members' desire for unanimity overrides their personal motivation to realistically appraise alternative courses of action."[36] The classic groupthink example involved the Kennedy Administration's decision to invade Cuba at the Bay of Pigs. Midway through the National Security Council's discussions of the pros and cons of the invasion, then-Attorney General Robert Kennedy reportedly told one detractor, "You may be right and you may be wrong, but President Kennedy has made his decision so keep your opinions to yourself."

However, the Bay of Pigs is by no means the only such example. When the *Challenger* space shuttle tragically exploded, one of the causes was reluctance on the part of the launch crew to recognize and accept the potential risk of a cold-weather launch. (The cold weakened the fateful O-ring connectors.) And we could speculate that the uproar over campaign financing in the 1996 U.S. presidential race was triggered at least in part by a White House fund-raising group whose desire for unanimity and commitment to winning distracted them from the possible harm that could result from their zeal. The common denominator in all these examples is that desire for unanimity overrode the potential advantage of including more varying points of view and contributed to what turned out to be bad decisions. A list of the warning signs of groupthink are presented in Figure 4.9.

■ **FIGURE 4.9**
Signs That Groupthink May Be a Problem

SOURCE: Adapted from information provided in Irving James, *Group Think: Psychological Studies of Policy Decisions and Fiascos*, 2nd ed. Boston: Houghton Mifflin, 1982.

"Don't ask, don't question."	Group members censor themselves, refuse to ask probing questions, and withhold disagreement.
"You must conform."	Someone, probably a group member, pressures others to withhold dissent and to go along with the group decisions.
"We all agree."	Group members press on with making their decisions, on the erroneous impression that all group members agree—possibly due to dissenters' silence.
"We're on a mission."	Group members frame their arguments in terms of what's right for the group's mission—electing the U.S. president, attacking a country, or beating a competitor, for instance—and assume therefore that what they're doing is right and ethical.
"Masters of the world"	Group members come to believe that the group is totally in command of the mission and can therefore do anything, regardless of the risks—they come to feel invulnerable.

Organizational Behavior in Action

HOW ONE COMPANY USES TEAMS TO MAKE BETTER DECISIONS

Many employers use the power of group decision making by creating problem-solving teams. A problem-solving team is a special type of work group, the purpose of which is to solve work problems which are either assigned to them or chosen by them.

IDS, the financial-services subsidiary of American Express, provides a good example.[37] With increased competition several years ago, IDS executives knew that dramatic improvements in the efficiency of their procedures were required if they were to remain competitive. Rather than trying to bring in consultants to suggest changes that would then be forced on employees, IDS executives set up a number of teams. The teams worked on reorganizing various company operations, from the way orders were processed to the way stocks were bought and sold.

Like many (but not all) such problem-solving teams, the IDS program was quite successful. For example, paperwork processing accuracy rose from 70 percent before the teams to over 99 percent after their suggestions were implemented. ■

Tools for Improving Group Decision Making

As at IDS, the manager's job is to use groups in such a way that the advantages of group decision making outweigh the disadvantages. For this there are several group decision-making tools in the manager's tool box.[38]

BRAINSTORMING.   **Brainstorming** is one way to amplify the creative energies of a group. It has been defined as a group problem-solving technique whereby group members introduce all possible solutions before evaluating any of them.[39] The technique is aimed at encouraging everyone to introduce solutions without fear of criticism, and the process typically has four main rules: (1) avoid criticizing others' ideas; (2) share even wild suggestions; (3) offer as many suggestions and supportive comments as possible; and (4) build on others' suggestions to create your own.[40] Interestingly, brainstorming can produce more creative solutions even if group members feel too inhibited to make wild suggestions.[41]

A recent and effective innovation is to use electronic brainstorming, for instance by letting group members interact via groupware (a type of software) and PCs instead of face-to-face. Doing so results in a relatively large increase in the number of high-quality ideas generated by the group, as compared with face-to-face brainstorming groups.[42]

DEVIL'S-ADVOCATE APPROACH.   One way to guard against the tendency for one group member's efforts to stifle debate is to formalize the process of criticism. The devil's-advocate approach is one way to do this. An advocate defends the proposed solution while a second, "devil's" advocate is appointed to prepare a detailed counterargument listing what is wrong with the solution and why it should not be adopted.

Brainstorming is a group problem-solving technique in which members of the group raise any and all possible solutions before any evaluation of those solutions takes place. Creativity is encouraged; criticism is discouraged.

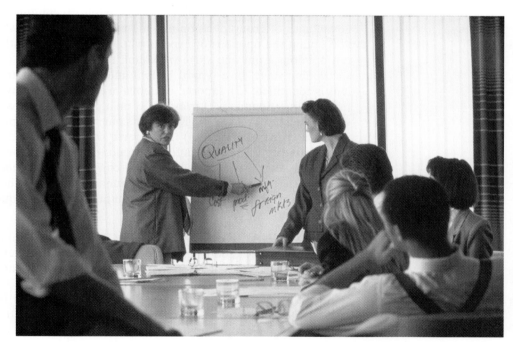

Organizational Behavior in Action

MAKING DECISIONS THE JAPANESE WAY, BY CONSENSUS

Compared with the confrontational devil's-advocate approach, the consensus decision-making approach at Mazda's Flatrock, Michigan facility seems a world apart, which is not surprising, given the factory's Japanese owners.

Flatrock's decision-making-by-consensus approach says a lot about cultural differences in how group decisions should be made.[43] Terms like "devil's advocate" or "loyal opposition" had no place in Flatrock's consensus process. Nor did voting, which the Japanese felt polarized people (as in, "either you're with me or against me"). Similarly, the idea that "majority rules"—so ingrained in much of what North Americans do—was foreign to the Japanese managers, who felt that a small majority like 51 percent shouldn't be able to impose its will on a large minority, say 49 percent.

At Mazda, consensus doesn't necessarily mean that discussions go on until everyone agrees. Instead, it's been defined as "working together . . . being willing to bend, being willing to argue your point, but being willing to be convinced."[44] In practice, this often means that a work group's manager won't make a decision until he or she has drawn out all the opinions of everyone in the group and then, if there isn't a clear consensus on a joint unified action, the manager will go ahead and make the decision. At Mazda, about half the decisions apparently are made that way, while half are purely consensus decisions.[45] ∎

THE DELPHI TECHNIQUE. The Delphi Technique aims to emphasize the advantages of group decision-making while minimizing its disadvantages. Basically, you obtain the opinions of experts who work independently, with the expert's written opinions from one stage providing the basis for the experts' analyses of each succeeding stage. In a typical Delphi analysis, the steps are as follows: (1) a problem is identified; (2) experts' opinions are solicited anonymously and individually through questionnaires (for example, on a problem such as "What do you think are the five biggest breakthrough products our computer company will have to confront in the next five years?"); (3) the experts' opinions are then analyzed, distilled, and resubmitted to other experts for a second round of opinions; (4) this process is continued for several more rounds until a consensus is reached.

This can obviously be a time-consuming process; on the other hand (as in electronic brainstorming), problems like groupthink can be reduced by eliminating face-to-face meetings.

THE NOMINAL GROUP TECHNIQUE. The nominal group technique is another process for reducing group decision-making barriers like groupthink. It can be defined as a group decision-making process in which participants do not attempt to agree as a group on any solution, but rather meet and secretly vote on all the solutions proposed after privately ranking the proposals in order of their preference.[46] It is called the "nominal" group technique because the "group" is a group in name only: Group members vote on solutions not as a group but individually.

The process is this: (1) each group member writes down his or her ideas for solving the problem at hand; (2) each member then presents his or her ideas orally and those ideas are written on a board for the other participants to see; (3) after all ideas have been presented, the entire group discusses all ideas simultaneously; (4) group members individually and secretly vote on each proposed solution; and (5) participants do not attempt to get a face-to-face consensus; instead the solution with the most individual votes wins.

THE STEPLADDER TECHNIQUE. The stepladder technique also aims to reduce the potentially inhibiting effects of face-to-face group meetings. Group members are added one by one at each stage of the decision-making process so that their input is untainted by the previous discussants' points of view. The process involves these steps: (1) individuals A and B are given a problem to solve and each produces an independent solution; (2) A and B then meet, develop a joint decision, and meet with C, who had independently analyzed the problem and arrived at a decision; (3) A, B, and C jointly discuss the problem and arrive at a consensus decision, and they are joined by person D who has individually analyzed the problem and arrived at his or her own decision; (4) A, B, C, and D meet and arrive at a final group decision.[47]

HOW TO LEAD A GROUP DECISION-MAKING DISCUSSION. The person leading the group discussion can have a big effect on whether the group's decision is useful or not. For example, if a committee chairperson monopolizes the meeting and continually shoots down others' ideas while pushing his or her own, it's likely that other members' points of view will go unexpressed. According to a classic series of group decision-making studies, an effective discussion leader therefore has a responsibility to do the following.

1. See that all group members participate. As a discussion leader, it is your responsibility to see to it that all group members actively participate in the discussion by having an opportunity to express their opinions. Doing so can help ensure that different points of view emerge and that everyone "takes ownership" of the final decision.
2. Distinguish between idea getting and idea evaluation. These studies conclude that evaluating and criticizing proposed solutions and ideas actually inhibit the process of getting or generating new ideas. Yet in most group discussions, there's a tendency for one person to present an alternative and for others to begin immediately discussing its pros and cons. As a result, group members quickly become apprehensive about suggesting new ideas. Instituting brainstorming rules—in particular, forbidding criticism of an idea until all ideas have been presented—can be useful here.
3. Do not respond to each participant or dominate the discussion. Remember that the discussion leader's main responsibility is to elicit ideas from the group, not to supply them. As a discussion leader, you should therefore work hard to facilitate a free expression of ideas and to consciously avoid dominating the discussion.
4. See that the effort is directed toward overcoming surmountable obstacles. In other words, focus on solving the problem rather than on discussing historical events that cannot be changed. For example, some discussion groups make the mistake of becoming embroiled in discussions concerning who is to blame for the problem or what should have been done to avoid

the problem. Such discussions can't lead to solutions, because the past can't be changed. Instead, as a discussion leader, your job is to ensure that the group focuses on obstacles that can be overcome and on solutions that are implementable.[48]

SUMMARY

1. A decision is a choice from among available alternatives. Decision making is the process of developing and analyzing alternatives and making a choice.
2. Decisions can be either programmed (repetitive and routine) or nonprogrammed (unique and novel). Nonprogrammed decisions require more intuition and judgment of decision making.
3. "Rational" decision making assumes ideal conditions such as accurate definition of the problem and complete knowledge about all relevant alternatives and their values.
4. In contrast, decision making in reality is bounded by differences in managers' ability to process information, reliance on heuristics or shortcuts, bias, framing, escalation of commitment, functional fixedness, psychological set, and factors in the organization itself.
5. "Bounded rationality" describes decision making in reality and often implies satisficing, or accepting satisfactory (as opposed to optimal) alternatives.
6. Guidelines for making better decisions include: increase your knowledge, de-bias your judgment, use creativity, use intuition, don't overstress finality, and make sure the timing is right.
7. A group consists of two or more persons who interact for some purpose and who influence each other in the process. Group decision making can result in the pooling of resources and strengthened commitment to the decision, but it can also be flawed by groupthink, or an overwhelming desire for unanimity.
8. Tools for better group decisions include brainstorming, the devil's-advocate approach, the Delphi and nominal group techniques, and the stepladder technique.

KEY TERMS

decision
decision making
programmed decision
nonprogrammed decision
heuristics
similarity heuristic
availability heuristic

person-specific biases
cognitive biases
framing
functional fixedness
psychological set
bounded rationality
satisfice

group
cohesiveness
norms
groupthink
brainstorming

TRUE / FALSE QUESTIONS

I **T** **F** A decision is a choice made from the available alternatives.

2 **T** **F** Creativity is at the heart of what all managers do.

3 **T** **F** The great advantage of making nonprogrammed decisions is that there are mechanical programs available for generating them.

4 **T** **F** The first step in the rational decision-making process is to identify criteria.

5 **T** **F** A rule of thumb or heuristic is a shortcut for problem solving.

6 **T** **F** Biases inhibit the adequate evaluation of the problem and the development of alternatives.

7 **T** **F** The concept of satisficing is integral to the process of rational decision making.

8 **T** **F** A manager's judgment can be biased by over-confidence.

9 **T** **F** Norms are informal rules that groups adopt to regulate and standardize group members' behavior.

10 **T** **F** Groupthink is one of the potential disadvantages of group decision making.

MULTIPLE-CHOICE QUESTIONS

I A _____ is a discrepancy between a desired and an actual situation.
 a. decision
 b. problem
 c. judgment
 d. cognitive thinking

2 Decisions that are repetitive and routine are called _____ decisions.
 a. irrational
 b. nonprogrammed
 c. nonrational
 d. programmed

3 Which of the following does *not* characterize a decision that is programmed?
 a. rules
 b. programs
 c. computerized computations
 d. one-time occurrences

4 The final step in the rational decision process is to _____.
 a. generate alternatives
 b. identify the problem
 c. analyze alternatives
 d. make a choice

5 The process whereby people tend to seek information for what they think is true and neglect the search for evidence that does not support their position is called _____.
 a. groupthink
 b. confirmation trap
 c. conflict trap
 d information snare

6 The inability to see that an object can have a function other than its stated or usual one is called _____.
 a. escalation of commitment
 b. framing a problem
 c. functional fixedness
 d. frozen vision

7 Decision making in practice is often referred to as _____ rationality.
 a. ideal-type
 b. irrational
 c. bounded
 d. top-up

8 _____ occurs when managers try to find acceptable alternatives and look for optimal alternatives only in exceptional cases.
 a. Satisficing
 b. Limiting
 c. Nonrationalizing
 d. None of the above

9 Which is a disadvantage of group decision making?
 a. More creativity may emerge.
 b. People accept group decisions.
 c. Escalation of commitment.
 d. More points of view are possible.

10 The _____ technique is a group-decision process in which participants do not attempt to agree on any solution but rather meet face to face and vote on all the solutions proposed after privately ranking the proposals in order of preference.
 a. Delphi
 b. nominal
 c. ordinal
 d. consensus

CRITICAL THINKING EXERCISES

1 In discussing business education, twentieth-century philosopher Alfred North Whitehead wrote that the world needs people with both imagination and the knowledge of experience: "Fools act on imagination without knowledge; pedants [scholars] act on knowledge without imagination." According to Whitehead, the task of the university or college is to develop managers who combine imagination and experience in building a vital society.[49] Whatever field of work in which you may labor, you will most probably become a manager of people, and at the very least you will need to manage your own career and life. How can the models and processes of decision making presented in this chapter help us address Whitehead's concern? Try to evaluate your university or college in light of Whitehead's charge to universities.

2 In his provocative book, *Managing as a Performing Art,* Peter Vaill argues that there are seven myths in managing organizations. Three are as follows.

a. The myth of a single person called "the manager" or "the leader." Vaill contends that all kinds of people without the title or power have opportunities for management and leadership in modern organizations.

b. The myth that what the leader leads and the manager manages is a single, freestanding organization. Vaill states that thinking of organizations as singular things allows us to ignore the fact that organizations are a part of their environment and must therefore be aware of their impact on that environment.

c. The myth of rational analysis as being the primary means of understanding and directing organizations. Intuition is important; change is so constant and discontinuous that we must be creative constantly and there is much mystery in our decisions today.

Analyze and discuss the points made by Vaill in light of what you now know about decision making and organizations from chapter 4.

EXPERIENTIAL EXERCISES

1 The world is becoming more competitive every day. Management expert Rosabeth Moss Kanter uses an analogy of "Alice in Wonderland" in her *When Giants Learn to Dance* to explain her perspective on the "game of change" that managers find themselves playing.

> To some companies, the contest in which they are now entered seems increasingly less like baseball or other traditional games and more like the croquet game in *Alice in Wonderland*—a game that compels the player to deal with constant change. In that fictional game, nothing remains stable for very long, because everything is alive and changing around the player—an all-too-real condition for many managers. The mallet Alice uses is a flamingo, which tends to lift its head and face in another direction just as Alice tries to hit the ball. The ball, in turn, is a hedgehog, another creature with a mind of its own. Instead of lying there waiting for Alice to hit it, the hedgehog unrolls, gets up, moves to another part of the court, and sits down again. The wickets are card soldiers, ordered around by the Queen of Hearts, who changes the structure of the game seemingly at whim by barking out an order to the wickets to reposition themselves around the court.

> Substitute technology for the mallet, employees and customers for the hedgehog, and everyone else from government regulators to corporate raiders for the Queen of Hearts, and the analogy fits the experience of a growing number of companies.

Divide the class into teams of five to seven. Assign one of the following companies to each group: Microsoft, Apple, GM, Gillette, GE, RJR-Nabisco, Levi Strauss, Home Depot, Intel, Johnson & Johnson, Coca-Cola, Pepsi, McDonalds, Mirage Resorts, Merck, Pfizer, United Parcel Service, New York Times, Kmart, TWA, and Berkshire Hathaway. Each group is to research its company, applying the, "Alice in Wonderland" analogy, and generate a two- to three-page analysis to be presented in class describing examples of how the Alice analogy applies and how it impacts organizational decision making.

2 People from other countries are often puzzled and intrigued by the complexity and enigmas of U.S. culture. Here are some examples from Nancy J. Adler's, *International Dimensions of Organizational Behavior.*

- **India:** "Americans seem to be in a perpetual hurry. Just watch them walk down the street. They never allow themselves the leisure to enjoy life; there are too many things to do."

- **Kenya:** "Americans appear to us rather distant. They are not really close to other people—even fellow Americans—as Americans overseas tend to portray. It's almost as if an American says, 'I won't let you get too close to me.' It's like building a wall."

- **Turkey:** "Once we were out in a rural area in the middle of nowhere and saw an American at a stop sign. Though he could see in both directions for miles and no traffic was coming, he still stopped."

- **Colombia:** "The tendency of the United States to think that life is only work hits you in the face. Work seems to be the one type of motivation."

- **Indonesia:** "In the United States everything has to be talked about and analyzed. Even the littlest thing has to be 'Why, Why, Why?' I get a headache from such persistent questions."

- **Ethiopia:** "The American is very explicit; he wants a 'yes' or 'no.' If someone tries to speak figuratively, the American is confused."

- **Iran:** "The first time . . . my (American) professor told me, 'I don't know the answer, I will have to look it up,' I was shocked. I asked myself, 'Why is he teaching me?' In my country, a professor would give the wrong answer rather than admit ignorance."[50]

There are two parts to this exercise. Part one is to discuss and analyze how decision making is made more complex when representatives of different cultures are attempting to make decisions and do business together.

Part two is to discuss how you would manage the group decision-making process if all these parties were represented around a table and needed to make a decision that would affect your organization as well as theirs.

DIVERSITY CASE

KENTUCKY FRIED CHICKEN

Consider the plight of Kentucky Fried Chicken (KFC) in India. In 1995, a New Delhi court ordered the city's KFC outlet closed for health code violations. Were those opposed to KFC's presence using the law to impose their own desires? The fight against KFC appears to have emerged as one of the major battlegrounds in determining whether India's future will be with the freewheeling global economy or in the Gandhian tradition of self-reliance.

India has over one billion citizens and is the leading vegetarian culture in the world. The cow is sacred and 70 percent of the population is employed in agriculture (compared to 3 percent in the United States). A coalition of health activists, farmers, doctors, environmentalists, and consumers do not want Western production methods and foods in their land.

Questions

1. Identify the problems facing KFC and then take the company through the rational decision process to determine whether it should maintain its investment in India.
2. What additional information would help you in deciding what KFC managers should do next?
3. Use this case to explain why the cultural context is important to decision making.

SOURCE: Bill McKibben, "Chicken Sutra," *Utne Reader,* July–August 1996, 11–12.

STRATEGY CASE

BELLY-UP AT PALM ISLAND BANK?

The president of Palm Island Bank had to make the sort of decision that bank presidents don't even want to think about. There is an old adage in banking that goes like this: "When a customer owes you a thousand dollars the customer has a problem, but when the customer owes you a million dollars the bank has the problem."

In this case, it was the small, one-branch, family-owned Palm Island Bank that had the problem.[51] About a year ago, a seemingly good credit risk came to the bank president and asked for a quarter-million-dollar loan to purchase several very large washing machines used to "stone wash" jeans. The firm's owner had several contracts from major jeans makers and convinced the bank president that the loans could be repaid with interest within two years. Now the owner was back in the lender's office with bad news. The jeans suppliers, under pressure from big department store chains, were astonishingly slow in paying their bills. If the business owner

didn't get another $250,000 within two weeks, he could not pay off his own suppliers and would have to go bankrupt, thus possibly ruining the bank, too. The banker had a strategic decision to make: To lend the extra $250,000, or not.

Questions

1. Of the many decision biases and barriers the bank president faces in this situation, which is the one you think should most concern her, and why?
2. Do you think this is the time for the bank president to take a "rational" or a "bounded-rational" approach to the problem? Why?
3. What is the first thing you would do now if you were the bank president and wanted to make as good a decision as possible under the circumstances? Why?
4. What decision would you make if you were the bank president?

ENTREPRENEURIAL CASE

DILBERT FINDS HIS OWN WAY

Perhaps no one has taken a funnier perspective on business than Dilbert's creator, Scott Adams. His 10-year-old comic strip has looked humorously at the world of business from his bird's-eye view of management practices while he worked at Pacific Bell. Nonetheless, on June 30, 1996, Adams was downsized like thousands of his big-company colleagues.

However, the ever-clever cartoonist already had a thriving business on the side with his comic strip *Dilbert* and also now a host of best-selling books. Adams has chosen full-time entrepreneurship. In an e-mail interview with *Inc.* (allowing only one question a day), Adams revealed his transition to self-employment. An example of his perspective is captured in this interchange.

Inc.: Now that you're the boss, do you find yourself with an uncontrollable urge to write memos, create more task forces, and hire consultants? Do you fantasize about hiring someone, just so you can "right-size"?

Adams: It's hell being the boss and the only employee. I keep telling myself to "work smarter, not harder," but it only makes me bitter and cynical. The weird part is that I didn't see it coming. I'm resisting the hassle of having a real employee, but I do reorganize my [cartoon] cast often just to keep them focused on the core competencies.

Questions

1 What do you think you can learn from Scott Adams about how entrepreneurs make decisions?
2 What are some humorous consequences of decisions made in an organization with which you are familiar that Dilbert might use?
3 Do you have an idea for a business you can start? What concepts in this chapter might help you make your decision?

SOURCE: George Gendron, "Dilbert Fired! Starts New Biz," *Inc.*, July 1996, 9–11.

THE BUSINESS TEAM, INC.

CAN WOMENS' PROFESSIONAL BASKETBALL BE SUCCESSFUL?

The Business Team Inc.'s Maria played basketball in her college days and loves the game. She has followed women's basketball from the 1996 Olympics to the newly formed Women's National Basketball Association. Now a good friend of hers, Vonnette, has been drafted by the newly formed women's professional team in Phoenix.

When Vonnette found out that Maria was part of a consulting firm, she wanted her new head coach, Cheryl Miller, the Hall of Famer who played and coached at U.S.C., to hire the Business Team. While there is great hope for the new league, there are also many potential barriers to women's basketball taking off as a big-league sport. Not only is there the competition with the NBA, there is also still some resistance to women as professional athletes in general. Everyone involved in the new league knows they must make good decisions from day one to build the sport, especially in this

difficult first year. In addition, the season starts in June, right in the middle of the baseball season. Vonnette believes Miller and the WNBA should at least have the Business Team help it develop a list of the barriers it can anticipate confronting this year.

Maria has promised Vonnette that she will talk to her colleagues and see what proposal they can come up with to present to Miller and the general manager.

Questions

1 How would you frame the problems facing the new WNBA?
2 What decision-making techniques would you suggest the Business Team propose to uncover the potential barriers?
3 What operational, financial, marketing, and organizational problems do you believe the WNBA will face in its first year?

IDENTIFYING TOP TALENT

As you might imagine, heading up an enterprise like Knit-Media requires an extraordinary range of decision-making skills. On the one hand are the relatively rational decisions like what banks to tap for loans and what locations to use for new Knit Factories; but on the other hand, much of Knit-Media's business depends (and has always depended) on finding top-notch talent, a process that is distinctly intuitive and creative. In the past, Michael and his colleagues have shown a keen ability for identifying talent such as John Zorn, Bill Frisell, and Indigo Girls; and, in fact, one reason for KnitMedia's desire to expand is to allow Michael and his colleagues to get access to emerging talent in local markets. However, Michael would like to know if there is anything they can do to make even better talent-choice decisions.

Team Exercises and Questions

Use what you learned in this chapter to answer the following questions:

1 What creativity-stimulating techniques do you think would be useful for helping Michael Dorf and his colleagues in their quest to identify top local talent?

2 What decision-making techniques discussed in this chapter would you recommend the KnitMedia managers use in finding top talent, and why do you recommend using these?

For the online version of this case, visit our Web site at: <www.prenhall.com/desslermgmt>.

For Internet exercises, interactive study questions, news updates and more, visit the Dessler Web site at

www.prenhall.com/desslermgmt

If you're using the CD-ROM that accompanies this text, simply click on the "Web Site" button to access the site.

Quantitative Decision-Making Aids

Many decisions (and particularly programmed ones) lend themselves to solution through quantitative analysis. This appendix discusses several of the more popular quantitative decision-making techniques.

BREAKEVEN ANALYSIS

In financial analysis, the breakeven point is that volume of sales at which revenues just equal expenses. Here you have neither a profit nor a loss. **Breakeven analysis** is a financial analysis decision-making aid that enables a manager to determine whether a particular volume of sales will result in losses or profits.[1]

Breakeven Charts

Breakeven analysis makes use of four basic concepts: fixed costs, variable costs, revenues, and profits. Fixed costs (such as for plant and machinery) are costs that basically do not change with changes in volume. In other words, you might use the same machine to produce 10 units, 50 units, or 200 units of a product. Variable costs (such as for raw material) do rise in proportion to volume. Revenue is the total income received from sales of the product. For example, if you sell 50 dolls at $8 each, then your revenue is $8 × 50 or $400. Profit is the money you have left after subtracting fixed and variable costs from revenues.

A **breakeven chart,** as in Figure A4.1, is a graph that shows whether a particular volume of sales will result in profits or losses. The fixed costs line is horizontal, since fixed costs remain the same regardless of level of output. Variable costs, however, increase in proportion to output and are shown as an upward sloping line. The total costs line is then equal to variable costs plus fixed costs at each level of output.

The **breakeven point** is the point where the total revenue line crosses the total costs line. Beyond this point (note the shaded area in Figure A4.1), total revenue exceeds total costs. So in this example, an output of about 4,000 units is the breakeven point. Above this, the company can expect to earn a profit. But if sales are fewer than 4,000 units, the company can expect a loss.

Breakeven Formula

The breakeven chart provides a picture of the relationship between sales volume and profits. However, a chart is not required for determining breakeven points. Instead, you can use the breakeven formula:

$$P(X) = F + V(X)$$

where

F = fixed costs

V = variable costs per unit

X = volume of output (in units)

P = price per unit

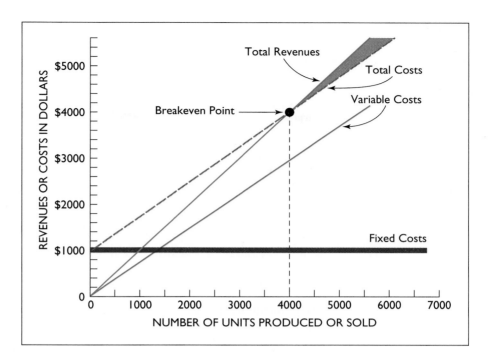

■ FIGURE A4.1
A Breakeven chart
The breakeven point is
that number of units sold
at which total revenues
just equal total costs.

Rearranging this formula, the breakeven point is $X = F/(P - V)$. In other words, the breakeven point is the volume of sales where total costs just equal total revenues. If, for example, you have a product in which:

F = fixed costs = $1,000.00

V = variable costs per unit = $.75

P = price per unit = $1.00 per unit

then the breakeven point is $1,000/$1.00 − $.75 = 4,000 units.

LINEAR PROGRAMMING

Breakeven analysis is only one of many techniques that are used for making better-programmed decisions. Decision-science techniques represent a second category of programmed decision-making aids, all of which are distinguished by their reliance on mathematics. For example, **linear programming** is a mathematical method used to solve resource allocation problems. These arise "whenever there are a number of activities to be performed, but limitations on either the amount of resources or the way they can be spent."[2] For example, it can be used to determine the best way to do the following:

- distribute merchandise from a number of warehouses to a number of customers;
- assign personnel to various jobs;
- design shipping schedules;
- select the product mix in a factory to make the best use of machine and labor hours available while maximizing the firm's project;
- route production to optimize the use of machinery.

In order for managers to successfully apply linear programming, the problem must meet certain basic requirements: There must be a stated, quantifiable goal, such as "minimize total shipping costs"; the resources to be utilized must be known (a firm could produce 200 of one item and 300 of another, for instance, or 400 of one or 100 of another); and finally, the firm must be able to express all the necessary relationships in the form of mathematical equations or inequalities, and all these relationships must be linear in nature. An example can help illustrate a typical linear programming application:

> Shader Electronics has five manufacturing plants and twelve warehouses scattered across the country. Each plant is manufacturing the same product and operating at full capacity. Since plant capacity and location do not permit the closest plant to fully support each warehouse, Shader would like to identify the factory that should supply each warehouse in order to minimize total shipping costs. Applying linear programming techniques to this problem will provide an optimum shipping schedule for the company.

WAITING-LINE/QUEUING TECHNIQUES

Waiting-line/queuing techniques are mathematical decision-making techniques for solving waiting-line problems. For example, bank managers need to know how many tellers they should have. If they have too many, they are wasting money on salaries; if they have too few, they may end up with many disgruntled customers. Similar problems arise when selecting the optimal number of airline reservations clerks, warehouse loading docks, highway toll booths, supermarket checkout counters, and so forth.

STATISTICAL DECISION THEORY TECHNIQUES

Statistical decision theory techniques are used to solve problems for which information is incomplete or uncertain. Suppose a shopkeeper can stock either brand A or brand B, but not both. She knows how much it will cost to stock her shelves with each brand, and she also knows how much money she would earn (or lose) if each brand turned out to be a success (or failure) with her customers. However, she can only estimate how much of each brand she might sell, so her information is incomplete. Using statistical decision theory, the shopkeeper would assign probabilities (estimates of the likelihood that the brand will sell or not) to each alternative. Then, she could determine which alternative—stocking brand A or brand B—would most likely result in the greatest profits.

Three Degrees of Uncertainty

Statistical decision theory is based on the idea that a manager may face three degrees of uncertainty in making a decision. Some decisions are made under conditions of **certainty**. Here, the manager knows in advance the outcome of the decision. From a practical point of view, for example, you know that if you buy a $50 U.S. savings bond, the interest you will earn to maturity on the bond is, say, 6 percent. Managers rarely make decisions under conditions of certainty.

At the opposite extreme some decisions are made under conditions of **uncertainty.** Here, the manager cannot even assign probabilities to the likelihood of the various outcomes. For example, a shopkeeper may have several new products that could be stocked but no idea of the likelihood that one brand will be successful or that another will fail. Conditions of complete uncertainty are also relatively infrequent occurrences.

Most management decisions are made under conditions of **risk**. Under conditions of risk, the manager can at least assign probabilities to each outcome. In other words, the manager knows (either from past experience or by making an educated guess) the chance that each possible outcome (like product A's being successful or product B's being successful) will occur.

Decision Tree

A **decision tree** provides one technique for making a decision under conditions of risk. With a decision tree like the one in Figure A4.2 an expected value can be calculated for each alternative. **Expected value** equals (1) the probability of the outcome multiplied by (2) the benefit or cost of that outcome.

For example, in the figure, it pays our shopkeeper to stock brand B rather than brand A. Stocking brand A allows a 70 percent chance of success for an $800 profit, so the shopkeeper has to balance the $560 profit she could make against the possibility of the $90 loss (.30 × possible loss of −$300). The expected value of stocking brand A is thus $470. By stocking brand B, though, the expected value is a relatively high $588.

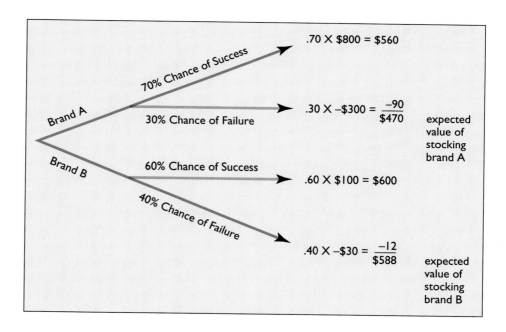

■ **FIGURE A4.2**
Example of a Decision Tree
The expected value of each alternative is equal to (1) the chance of success or failure, times (2) the expected profit or loss.

KEY TERMS

breakeven analysis
breakeven chart
breakeven point
linear programming
waiting-line/queuing
   techniques

statistical decision theory
   techniques
certainty
uncertainty
risk
decision tree

expected value

CHAPTER 5

PLANNING AND SETTING OBJECTIVES

What's Ahead?

Back in 1994, when Jeff Bezos was a young senior vice president at a thriving Wall Street firm, most of his business plans revolved around which assets to invest in. Two years later, Jeff was founder and CEO of the Internet bookstore Amazon.com, and now the business plans he has to make are much more extensive. He worked out his first business plan for Amazon.com on his laptop, while his wife MacKenzie drove him and the family car to Seattle where his business would be based.[1]

Jeff Bezos

Objectives

After studying this chapter, you should be able to

- **define planning and describe the different types of plans companies use**
- **explain each of the five steps in the planning process**
- **formulate effective objectives**
- **explain three techniques for producing the premises on which plans are built.**

MANAGEMENT ON THE WEB

COMPETITIVE INTELLIGENCE GUIDE

The basic premise of this site is that "virtually all organizations have the same access to information, but it is the ones who convert that information into actionable intelligence that will end up gaining a competitive advantage." Visit the site and you will gain an understanding of what competitive intelligence is and how someone like Jeff Bezos can use it. ■

http://www.fuld.com

The Nature and Purpose of Planning

Why Plan?

Plans, as Jeff Bezos knows well, are methods formulated beforehand for achieving a desired result. All plans specify goals (such as "boost sales by 10 percent") and courses of action (such as "hire a new salesperson and boost advertising expenditures by 20 percent"). Plans should specify (at a minimum) what you will do, how you will do it, and by when you'll get it done.[2] **Planning,** therefore, is "the process of establishing objectives and courses of action, prior to taking action."[3] **Goals,** or **objectives,** are specific results you want to achieve.

Planning is often called the "first among equals" of the four management functions (planning, organizing, leading, and controlling), because it establishes the goals which are (or should be) the basis of all these functions.[4] The people you hire, the incentives you use, and the controls you institute all relate to what you want to achieve and to the plans and goals you set.

Planning is an activity in which we all engage every day, often without giving it much thought. For example, if you are like most readers of this book, you're probably reading it as part of a management course. And why are you taking this course? Chances are the course is part of your program of studies. This program (it is hoped) is *planned*. It identifies your goal (say, getting a degree in business in two years), and it identifies how you will get that degree by specifying the courses you'll need to graduate.

Your plans may not end with earning the degree (although for many students, just doing so while working may be hassle enough for now). You may also have a broader goal, a vision of where you're headed in life. If you do, then your degree may just be one step in a broader- and longer-term plan. For example, suppose you have a dream or a vision of running your own management consulting firm by the time you are 35. Now (you ask yourself), "What do I have to do to achieve this goal?" The answer may be to work for a nationally known consulting firm, thus building up your experience and your reputation in the field. So here is your plan: Take this course to get the degree, get the degree to get the consulting job, and then work hard as a consultant to achieve your dream.

Types of Plans

There are many types of plans.

DIFFERENT FORMATS. Plans differ in format, or the way they are expressed. Perhaps the most familiar plans are **descriptive plans;** like the career plan above, they state in words what is to be achieved and how. Plans stated in financial terms are called **budgets. Graphic plans** show in charts what is to be achieved and how.

DIFFERENT TIME HORIZONS. Plans also differ in the spans of time they cover. Top management usually engages in long-term (five- to ten-year) strategic planning. A **strategic plan** specifies the business or businesses the firm will be in, and the major steps it must take to get there. Middle managers typically focus on developing shorter-term tactical plans (of up to five years' duration). **Tactical plans** (also sometimes called **functional plans**) show how top management's plans are to be carried out at the departmental level, for instance by the managers responsible for sales, finance, and manufacturing. First-line managers then focus on shorter-term **operational,** or detailed day-to-day, **planning.** These might show, for instance, exactly which workers are to be assigned to which machines or exactly how many units will be produced on a given day.

DIFFERENT FREQUENCY. Some plans are **programs** established to lay out in an orderly fashion all the steps in a major one-time project, each in its proper sequence. Thus, when JCPenney moved its offices from New York City to Dallas several years ago, it needed a program outlining the steps to be taken and the goals to be achieved in this one-time move.

In contrast to such single-use programs, **standing plans** are plans made to be used repeatedly, as the need arises.[5] Policies, procedures, and rules are examples of standing plans. **Policies** usually set broad guidelines for the enterprise. For example, it might be the policy at Saks Fifth Avenue that "we sell only high-fashion apparel and top-of-the-line jewelry." **Procedures,** as the name implies, specify how to proceed if some specific situation arises. For example, "Before refunding the customer's purchase price, the salesperson should carefully inspect the garment and then obtain approval from the floor manager for the refund." Finally, a **rule** is a highly specific guide to action. For example, "Under no condition will the purchase price be refunded after 30 days."

What Planning Accomplishes

Implemented properly, planning can provide several advantages.

PLANNING PROVIDES DIRECTION. Planning provides direction and a sense of purpose for the enterprise. Several years ago, R.R. Donnelley Company was mostly in the business of printing documents and other materials for clients such as investment bankers. Donnelley's planning led its managers to anticipate a change caused by telecommunications and the globalization of its customers. Donnelley then decided to reinvent itself. The company invested heavily in advanced technology and expanded overseas. Now, with the help of satellites, Donnelley can print a securities prospectus simultaneously in locations around the globe.[6] Its new vision and strategy provided a renewed sense of direction for the firm, one that all its managers and employees could rally around.

PLANNING REDUCES PIECEMEAL DECISION MAKING. A plan also provides a unifying framework against which decisions can be assessed. The result, as one expert put it, is that "planning channels effort toward desired results, and by providing a sequence of efforts, [it] minimizes unproductive behavior."[7] For instance, it would have been wasteful for R.R. Donnelley to spend its investment dollars building ever-bigger printing factories at its main U.S. location. The globalization of its customers demanded—and technological advances made possible—that it be capable of transmitting and creating documents via satellite around the globe. Its plan for doing so helped ensure that the firm channeled all its resources toward those desired results, thus avoiding activities—such as building unneeded domestic printing plants—that were inconsistent with the firm's overall direction.

PLANNING REVEALS FUTURE OPPORTUNITIES AND THREATS. Management theorist Peter Drucker says that planning can help identify potential opportunities and threats and at least reduce long-term risks.[8] For example, Donnelley's planning process helped identify the opportunity for satellite-based global printing.

PLANNING FACILITATES CONTROL. Control means ensuring that activities conform to plans; it is a three-step process in which standards are set, performance is measured against these standards, and deviations are identified and corrected.

Planning is the first step in this cycle—specifying what is to be achieved. For example, a company's five-year plan may specify that its profits will double within five years. This goal can then be a standard against which to measure and control the president's performance.

The Management Planning Process

Steps in Planning

As summarized in Figure 5.1, the management-planning process consists of a logical sequence of five steps.

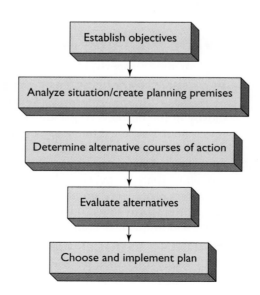

■ FIGURE 5.1
The Planning Process

Step 1: Establish objectives.

Plans are methods formulated beforehand for achieving a desired result. In a business, the first step in planning is therefore to establish objectives for the entire enterprise and then, through the process of planning, to establish goals in turn for subordinate units, each of which will develop its own plans.

For example, Albert J. Dunlap (called, not too affectionately, "Chainsaw Al" for his record of boosting shareholder value by taking over and downsizing companies) recently took over the struggling Sunbeam Corp., maker of household appliances. His first task was to develop a plan for turning the company around. He knew he had to set some objectives, and quickly, because the company was hemorrhaging cash. As objectives, he knew that within one year he had to make the company profitable, reduce expenses by at least 20 percent, and decide which products to keep and which to discard.

Step 2: Analyze situation and create planning premises.

The second step is to develop the forecasts and planning premises on which the plan will be built. At Sunbeam, Dunlap retained a team of assistants and management consultants, who developed sales forecasts for various products and thoroughly analyzed each of the company's plants and products.

Step 3: Determine alternative courses of action.

For any objective there should be more than one way to proceed. At Sunbeam, for instance, Dunlap's alternative might have been to merge with a larger appliance company rather than to dramatically downsize. As explained in the decision-making chapter, decision makers like Dunlap must have several alternatives, or the only real choice is to "take it or leave it." Creating alternatives is essentially a decision-making activity. Brainstorming and other group decision-making techniques such as the Delphi technique are some of the tools managers use here.

Step 4: Evaluate alternatives.

As in any decision, the next step is to evaluate each alternative relative to the manager's objectives. In Dunlap's case, a major evaluative question would have been, "Which alternative—downsizing or merging—results in the most substantial financial gain for Sunbeam's owners?" Based on their analysis, Dunlap and his team could then develop their plan to cut the number of employees in half, roll out 30 new products a year, and shrink the number of factories and warehouses from over 40 to just 13.

Step 5: Choose and implement the plan.

The final step is to choose an alternative and implement it. For example, Dunlap and his team decided on the downsizing plan and immediately set about determining which plants to close, which employees to dismiss, and what new products to roll out.

The Planning Hierarchy

In some respects, Step 5 is not the final step in the planning process. It is actually just the beginning, because top management's goals then become the targets for which subsidiary units must formulate derivative plans. (Thus, to implement Dunlap's overall plan at Sunbeam, the sales manager had to decide what products to introduce and develop plans for introducing them; the manufacturing manager had to identify the plants to close and develop plans for closing them; and the HR manager had to assist the other managers in deciding which employees to retain.)

THE HIERARCHY OF PLANS. In practice, one result of the management planning process is, therefore, a **hierarchy of plans.** The hierarchy of plans includes (1) the enterprise-wide plan and objectives, and (2) the chain of subsidiary units' derivative plans and objectives, each of which contributes to achieving the enterprise-wide plans and objectives. As Koontz and O'Donnell put it:

> Managers of each segment of the company make and execute the plans necessary for making a basic plan a reality, and this chain reaction must continue on down until there is a specific plan for each derivative activity of a main plan.[9]

Organizational Behavior in Action

THE NEED FOR TEAMWORK IN PLANNING

Because each manager's plans should complement those of his or her colleagues and also contribute to making the company's overall goals a reality, effective planning is enhanced by teamwork.

Chrysler Corporation's recent success in introducing new models while boosting profitability provides an example.[10] Many credit Chrysler's recent strong performance (including increased market share and a dramatic rise in profit per vehicle) to the close-knit camaraderie of Chrysler's top management team. In the car business, where huge investments are required, product planning requires especially close teamwork.

At Chrysler, product planning starts with market research information from sales head James Holden. That information helped design head Thomas Gale and his group design the successful "cab-forward" design, which in turn was implemented by engineering head François Castaing and his department. They then work closely with parts supply chief Thomas Stallkamp and manufacturing head Dennis

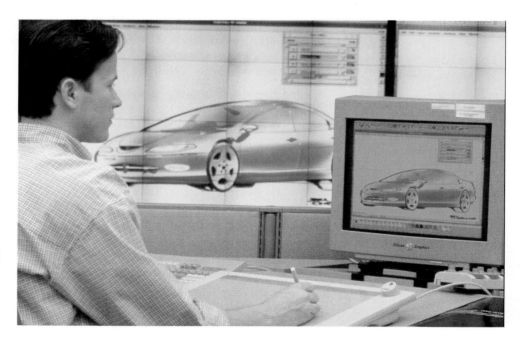

The first stage in the cab-forward design of Chrysler's 1998 Concorde. Cross-functional planning teams are responsible for implementing new designs like this one.

Pawley to develop a comprehensive product design/engineering/production/sales plan.

Anything less than close cooperation—disruptive interdepartmental rivalries, for instance, or political maneuvering by any of the department heads—could have slowed development and led to a less-successful product launch. At Chrysler, as at other enterprises, successful plans are usually the result of close cooperation among members of a cross-functional planning team. ■

Table 5.1 shows an executive assignment action plan for linking management's goals at one level to the derivative plans at the next level down.[11] In this case, one of top management's long-term objectives is to "have a minimum of 55 percent of sales revenue from customized products by 1999." The action plan on page 150 summarizes the derivative targets to be achieved by each department if that long-term objective is to be met. Thus, the vice president of marketing is to "complete market study on sales potential for customized products" within one year. The VP for manufacturing is to "convert Building C to customized manufacturing operation" within a year.

Each vice president's assigned goals then become the target for which they must develop their own plans. This is illustrated in Table 5.2 on page 151. Here the manufacturing vice president's goal of converting Building C to customized manufacturing is the target for which derivative plans must be formulated. For instance, converting Building C will entail completing a feasibility study, purchasing and installing new equipment, and training a production staff.

THE HIERARCHY OF GOALS. As you can see, the planning process therefore produces a hierarchy, or chain, of goals from the top to the lowest-level managers.[12] This is illustrated in Figure 5.2 on page 152. At the top, the president and his or her staff set strategic goals (such as to have a minimum of 55 percent of sales revenue from customized products by 1999), to which each vice president's goal (such as convert Building C to customized manufacturing operation) is then tied. Similarly, a hierarchy of supporting departmental goals down to tactical/functional goals and finally short-term operational goals is then formulated, as illustrated on page 152.

The Entrepreneurs in Action feature on page 153 shows that a practical hierarchy of goals doesn't have to be complicated, as Gregg Foster and the management team of his small business discovered.

How to Set Objectives

Why Set Objectives?

If there is one thing on which every manager can expect to be appraised, it is the extent to which he or she achieves his or her unit's goals or objectives. Whether it's a work team or a giant enterprise, the manager in charge is expected to move his or her unit ahead, and this means visualizing where the unit must go—and helping them get there. Organizations exist to achieve some purpose, and if they fail to move forward and achieve their aims, to that extent they have failed. As Peter Drucker puts it, "There has to be something to point to and say, we have not worked in vain."[13]

Effectively setting goals is important for other reasons. Objectives are the targets toward which plans are aimed, and the anchor-points around which the hierarchy of objectives is constructed. Objectives can also aid motivation. Employees—

■ TABLE 5.1 *Executive Assignment Action Plan for Achieving Long-Term Objective*

LONG-TERM OBJECTIVE: HAVE A MINIMUM OF 55 PERCENT OF SALES REVENUE FROM CUSTOMIZED PRODUCTS BY 1999.

Executive assignments/ derivative objectives	Accountability		Schedule		Resources Required			Feedback Mechanisms
	Primary	**Supporting**	**Start**	**Complete**	**Capital**	**Operating**	**Human**	
1. Complete market study on sales potential for customized products	VP Marketing	VP Sales	Year 1	**Year 1**		$10,000	500 hrs.	Written progress reports
2. Revise sales forecasts for Years 1, 2, and 3 to reflect changes	VP Sales	VP Marketing		**Year 1**			50 hrs.	Revised forecasts
3. Convert Building C to customized manufacturing operation	VP Mfg.	VP Engineering VP Administration	Year 1	**Year 2**	$500,000	$80,000	1100 hrs.	Written progress reports
4. Change compensation structure to incentivize customized sales	VP HR	VP Sales	Year 1	**Year 1**		$50,000	100 hrs.	Revised structure report
5. Train sales staff in new technology	Director of Training	VP Sales	Year 2	**Year 2**		$50,000	1000 hrs.	Training plan reports
6. Expand production of customized products — to 25 percent — to 30 percent — to 40 percent — to 50 to 55 percent	VP Mfg.	VP Engineering	Year 1	**Year 2** **Year 2** **Year 3** **Year 3**		Budgeted	Budgeted	Production reports
7. Increase sales of customized products — to 25 percent — to 30 percent — to 40 percent — to 55 percent	VP Sales	VP Marketing	Year 1	**Year 2** **Year 2** **Year 3** **Year 3**				Sales reports
8. Revise sales forecasts	VP Sales	VP Marketing		**Year 3**				Revised forecasts

NOTE: This executive assignment action plan shows the specific executive assignments required to achieve top management's long-term objective, "Have a minimum of 55% of sales revenue from customized products by 1999."

individually and in teams—focus their efforts on achieving concrete goals with which they agree, and usually perform better with goals at which to aim. In fact, when performance is inadequate, it is often not because the person or team is loafing, but because the individual or team doesn't know what the job's goals are. Therefore, all managers today require a good working knowledge of how to set objectives.

TABLE 5.2 Action Plan for Specific Executive Assignment

EXECUTIVE ASSIGNMENT: CONVERT BUILDING C TO CUSTOMIZED MANUFACTURING OPERATION BY 1999.

Assignments/ derivative objectives	Accountability		Schedule		Resources Required			Feedback Mechanisms
	Primary	Supporting	Start	Complete	Capital	Operating	Human	
1. Complete feasibility study on conversion requirements	Director Engineering	VP Manufacturing	Year 1	**Year 1**		$10,000	100 hrs.	Written progress reports
2. Complete converted production line design and equipment specifications	Director Engineering	VP Manufacturing		**Year 1**		$50,000	500 hrs.	Design review meetings
3. Purchase and install new equipment	Purchasing	VP-Manufacturing	Year 1	**Year 1**	$400,000		100 hrs.	Written progress reports
4. Modify existing equipment	VP Mfg.	VP Engineering	Year 1	**Year 1**	$100,000	$10,000	100 hrs.	Written progress reports
5. Train production staff	Director of Training	VP Manufacing	Year 1	**Year 1**		$10,000	300 hrs.	Training plan reports
6. Initiate customized production line	VP Mfg.	VP Engineering				Budgeted	Budgeted	Production reports
7. Increase production of customized products — to 25 percent — to 30 percent — to 40 percent — to 50 to 55 percent	VP Mfg.	VP Engineering	Year 1	**Year 2** **Year 2** **Year 3** **Year 3**		Budgeted	Budgeted	Production reports
8. Reassess future production capacity	VP Mfg.	VP Engineering		**Year 3**				Production forecast

SOURCE: Reprinted with permission from George Morrisey: *A Guide to Long-Range Planning.* Copyright © 1996 Jossey-Bass, Inc., Publishers. All rights reserved.
NOTE: This action plan shows the subsidiary assignments required to achieve the specific executive assignment, "Convert Building C to customized manufacturing operations by 1999."

Types of Objectives

The range of activities for which objectives may be set is virtually limitless. For example, in a classical analysis of planning objectives, Peter Drucker listed eight areas in which objectives should be set:

1. market standing
2. innovation
3. productivity

Note: A hierarchy of goals like this is one important byproduct of the planning process. This figure shows some (not all) of the supporting goals that need to be formulated to help achieve the company's overall goal of having a minimum of 55% of its sales revenue from customized products by 1999.

■ **FIGURE 5.2**
Hierarchy of Goals

4. physical and financial resources
5. profitability
6. managerial performance and development
7. worker performance and attitude
8. public responsibility[14]

Many other options are possible. For example, one planning expert lists over a dozen other areas in which objectives may be set, including:

1. market penetration
2. future human competencies
3. revenue/sales
4. employee development
5. new product/service department
6. new/expanded market development
7. program/project management
8. technology
9. research and development
10. customer relations/satisfaction
11. cost control/management
12. quality control/assurance
13. productivity
14. process improvement
15. production capability/capacity
16. cross-functional integration
17. supplier development/relations
18. unit structure[15]

One thing apparent from these lists is that "profit maximization" is not by itself a good enough guide to management action. It is true that in economic theory, and in practice, managers aim to maximize profits (although other goals, including social

Entrepreneurs in Action

GOAL SETTING MADE SIMPLE AT ELYRIA

When Gregg Foster purchased the troubled metal-converting Elyria foundry, he knew the key to long-term prosperity was setting strategic goals and then making employees—from the shop floor to the executive suite—committed to achieving them. He believed that setting goals would give all his employees targets that would guide them, "They're specific, but they also create a picture of how we want to be."

Foster used a hierarchical approach, but nothing complicated. First, he set a few strategic goals to point out a broad direction for the firm. He next turned to his department managers, who each sub-

mitted five to ten supporting goals. Foster then condensed those goals. In turn, input from lower-level employees yielded goals ranging from retirement plan participation to qualifying for ISO 9000 (international quality management) certification.

The resulting hierarchy of goals formed a chain, showing how each level's efforts contributed to attaining the goals at the next higher level and for the foundry as a whole. It also helped to identify the literally dozens of things that employees and managers felt needed fixing, if the firm were to achieve Foster's overall goals. ■

SOURCE: Leslie Brokaw, "One-Page Company Game Plan," *Inc.,* June 1993, 111–13.

responsibility, are crucial too). However, managers also require specific objectives in areas like market penetration and customer service if they are to have any hope of boosting profits.

How to Set Motivational Goals

Goals are only useful to the extent that employees are motivated to achieve them; managers can do several things to ensure that the goals they set do motivate employees. Organizational behavior research known as the **goal-setting studies** provides useful insights into setting effective goals, as do a number of practical suggestions made by planning experts. Let's look at the studies first.

Organizational Behavior in Action

THE GOAL-SETTING STUDIES

Studies conducted by psychologists Edwin Locke and Gary Latham and their associates provide a vivid picture of how managers should set goals. We can summarize the implications of these studies as follows.

ASSIGN SPECIFIC GOALS. Employees who are given specific goals usually perform better than those who are not. One study that illustrates this was conducted in an Oklahoma logging operation.[16] The subjects were truck drivers who had to load logs and drive them to the mill. An analysis of the truckers' performances showed that they often did not fill their trucks to the maximum legal net weight.

The researchers believed this occurred largely because traditionally the workers were urged just to "do their best" when it came to loading the truck to its maximum legal net weight. Therefore, the researchers arranged for a specific goal ("94 percent of a truck's net weight") to be communicated to each driver. The drivers were told that this was an experimental program, that they would not be required to make more truck runs, and that there would be no retaliation if performance suddenly increased and then decreased. No monetary rewards or benefits, other than verbal praise, were given for improving performance. The drivers and their supervisors got no special training of any kind.

The results of the study were impressive. Performance (in terms of weight loaded on each truck) jumped markedly as soon as the truckers were assigned specific high goals, and it generally remained at this much higher level. This and other evidence shows that setting specific goals with subordinates, rather than setting no goals or telling them to "do their best," can substantially improve performance in a wide range of settings.[17]

ASSIGN MEASURABLE GOALS.[18] Wherever possible, goals should be stated in quantitative terms and include target dates or deadlines for accomplishment. In that regard, goals set in absolute terms (such as "an average daily output of 300 units") are less confusing than goals set in relative terms (such as "improve production by 20 percent"). If measurable results will not be available, then "satisfactory completion"—such as "satisfactorily attended workshop" or "satisfactorily completed his or her degree"—is the next best thing. In any case, target dates or deadlines for accomplishment should always be set.

ASSIGN CHALLENGING BUT DOABLE GOALS. Researcher Gary Yukl says goals should be challenging but not so difficult that they appear impossible or unrealistic.[19] Particularly in areas such as sales management, where immediate and concrete performance is both obvious and highly valued, goals consistent with past sales levels—realistic yet high enough to be challenging—are widely espoused.[20]

When is a goal too difficult or too hard? Yukl recommends considering prior performance by the same person, performances by people in comparable positions, available resources, likely conditions that will affect performance, and the amount of time until the deadline. As he suggests:

> A goal is probably too easy if it calls for little or no improvement in performance when conditions are becoming more favorable, or if the targeted level of performance is well below that of most other employees in comparable positions. A goal is probably too difficult if it calls for a large improvement in performance when conditions are worsening, or if the targeted level of performance is well above that of people in comparable positions.[21]

ENCOURAGE PARTICIPATION WHERE POSSIBLE. Should managers assign their subordinates' goals, or should they permit their subordinates to participate in developing their own goals? Research evidence on this point has been mixed, but we can reach five conclusions concerning the relative superiority of participatively set versus assigned goals.

First, employees who participate in setting their goals do in fact tend to perceive themselves as having had more impact on the setting of those goals than do employees who are simply assigned goals.[22] *Second,* participatively set goals tend to be higher—more difficult—than the goals the supervisor would normally have assigned.[23] *Third,* even when goals set participatively are more difficult than the assigned ones, they are not perceived as such by the subordinates.[24] *Fourth,* participatively set goals do not consistently result in higher performance than assigned goals nor do assigned goals consistently result in higher performance than participatively set ones. However, when the participatively set goals are higher and more difficult than the assigned goals, as is usually the case, then the participatively set goals usually lead to higher performance. (The fact that the goal is more difficult seems to account for the higher performance, not the fact that it was participatively set.)[25] *Finally,* goals unilaterally assigned by managers can trigger employee resistance, regardless of the goal's reasonableness. Insofar as participation creates a sense of ownership in the goals, it can reduce resistance.[26] ■

How to Express the Goal

Knowing how to express the goal is important, too. As illustrated in Table 5.3, it is important to distinguish between an *area to be measured* (such as sales), a *yardstick* (such as sales revenue), and a *goal* (such as $85,000 per month). There are usually several possible yardsticks for any measurable area. For example, the area of "sales" could be measured in terms of sales revenue or market share. Remember to state any goal in measurable terms, if possible.

Planning expert George Morrisey presents a four-point model for use in formulating objectives. This is presented in Table 5.4 on page 156, along with several examples. According to Morrisey, a well-crafted goal should contain four types of information:

To (1) (*action verb*) . . . (2) (single measurable *result*)

By (3) (*target* date/time span) . . . at (4) (*cost* in time and/or money)

■ **TABLE 5.3** *Example of Yardsticks and Goals*

AREA	YARDSTICK	STANDARD/GOAL
Sales	Sales revenue	$85,000 per month
Accounts payable	Discounts received	Obtain all possible discounts
Production	Productivity	Produce at least five units per labor hour
Customer reactions	Satisfactions	Zero complaints
Quality	Number of rejects	No more than three rejects per 100 items produced
Employee behavior	Absenteeism Accidents Turnover	No more than 3% absences/week No serious accidents permitted 10% turnover maximum
Finances	Profitability Turnover	20% profit margins Sales − inventory = 8%
Expenses	Phone bill Raw materials Supplies	$300 per month maximum 20% of sales 5% of sales
Cash collections	Dollars collected from customers	90% of sales dollars collected per month

■ TABLE 5.4 *Model and Examples of Well-Stated Objectives*

MORRISEY'S FOUR-POINT MODEL

To (1) *(action/verb)*	(2) (single measurable *result*)
by (3) *(target date/time span)*	(4) *at* (cost in time and/or energy)

EXAMPLES OR OBJECTIVES THAT FOLLOW THE MODEL

■ To (1, 2) complete the Acme project by (3) December 31 at a (4) cost not to exceed $50,000 and five hundred work-hours.

■ To (1) decrease the (2) average cost of sales by a minimum of 5 percent, effective (3) June 1, at an (4) implementation cost not to exceed forty work-hours.

■ To release (1, 2) product A to manufacturing by (3) September 30 at a cost not to (4) exceed $50,000 and five thousand engineering hours.

■ To (1) reduce (2) average turnaround time on service requests from eight to six hours by (3) July 31 at an implementation cost (4) of forty work-hours.

SOURCE: Reprinted with permission from George Morrisey, *A Guide to Tactical Planning*. Copyright © 1996 Jossey-Bass, Inc., Publishers. All rights reserved.

Another example goal based on Morrisey's model is this: "To complete the cable TV project by December 31 at a cost not to exceed $50,000 and 500 work-hours."

Managing Change

CHANGING TIMES FOR DOCTORS

The medical profession has been under tremendous pressure to change. With rising health care costs being borne by business, individuals, and society alike, there is plenty of incentive to improve the planning and lower the cost of health care services. The strategy of Intensia HealthCare of Beech Grove, Indiana, is to take on the patients most hospitals can't afford to keep: the long-term acute cases. Operating within the walls of St. Francis Hospital, the company has taken advantage of an insurance quirk that allows it to collect higher reimbursement for such cases; but the real key to Intensia's success is its meticulous planning and goal-setting process. By focusing on a single business—caring for long-term acute cases—and then setting specific and measurable goals that are then closely monitored, Intensia's costs are 50 percent lower than those of typical intensive care wards. Intensia's success illustrates how setting measurable performance goals can help a company thrive in a fast-changing industry.[27] ■

Using the Management by Objectives Goal-Setting Technique

Management by objectives (MBO) is a technique used by many firms to assist in the process of setting organizationwide objectives and goals for subsidiary units and their employees. It is defined as a technique in which supervisor and subordinate jointly set goals for the latter and periodically assess progress toward those goals. A manager may engage in a modest MBO program by setting goals with his or her subordinates and periodically providing feedback. However, the term MBO almost always refers to a comprehensive organizationwide program for setting goals, one usually reserved for managerial and professional employees. As you will see, one advantage of this technique (in terms of the goal-setting studies just reviewed) is that, if implemented properly, it can lead to specific, measurable, and participatively set challenging objectives.

The MBO process generally consists of five steps:

1. *Set organization's goals.* Top management sets strategic goals for the company.
2. *Set departments' goals.* Department heads and their superiors jointly set supporting goals for their departments.
3. *Discuss departments' goals.* Department heads present departments' goals and ask all subordinates to develop their own individual goals.
4. *Set individual goals.* Goals are set for each subordinate, and a timetable is assigned for accomplishing those goals.
5. *Feedback.* The supervisor and subordinate meet periodically to review the subordinate's performance and to monitor and analyze progress toward his or her goals.[28]

Managers can do several things to make an MBO program more successful. They can state the goals in measurable terms, be specific, and make sure each person's goals are challenging but attainable. Most experts also agree that goals should be reviewed and updated periodically, and that the goals should be flexible enough to be changed if conditions warrant.[29]

Again, however, an effective formal MBO program requires more than just setting goals. Integrating the goals of the individual, of the unit in which the individual works, and of the company as a whole is absolutely essential. As Peter Drucker, an early MBO proponent, says:

> . . . the goals of each manager's job must be defined by the contribution he or she has to make to the success of the larger unit of which they are part. The job objectives of district sales managers should be defined by the contribution they and their district sales forces have to make to the sales department. The objectives of the general manager of a decentralized division should be defined by the contribution his or her division has to make to the objectives of the parent company.[30]

Organizational Behavior in Action

WINNING GOAL COMMITMENT

Drucker's comment above emphasizes the need to tightly integrate companywide, departmental, and individual employees' goals in such a way that employees feel they can achieve their own goals by achieving the company's goals. The manager's task, then, is to enhance **goal commitment,** which is the strength of one's determination to reach a goal.[31]

Several factors enhance goal commitment. Goal commitment is higher when an authority figure such as the boss is physically present, supportive, and trusted.[32] This is one reason you'll almost never see a smart gymnast or tennis player compete without his or her coach nearby. Group norms and peer pressure can also strengthen goal commitment, as can external rewards such as incentive pay and pay raises.

Goal commitment is also influenced by intrinsic factors, in other words, what is "inside" the employee. People with a stronger need to achieve and who are more aggressive, competitive, and higher in self-esteem tend to have higher goal commitment.[33] **Self-efficacy** (the expectation that one can master a task) may partly explain this: People who believe they are more capable of achieving the goals may be more likely to try to do so.[34] Supervisory behaviors such as building employees' self-esteem, providing training, and offering support can also, therefore, translate into higher goal commitment. ■

Techniques for Developing Planning Premises

Managers use several techniques to produce the premises on which they build their plans. Three popular techniques are forecasting, marketing research, and competitive intelligence.

Sales Forecasting Techniques

Plans are based on **planning premises,** which are the assumptions we make about the future. Thus, IBM's strategy in the late 1990s reflects the assumptions it made regarding what the demand would be for mainframe computers. **Forecast** means to estimate or calculate in advance or to predict.[35] According to one expert a forecast is "a service whose purpose is to offer the best available basis for management expectations of the future, and to help management understand the implications for alternative courses of action."[36]

In business, forecasting often means predicting the direction and magnitude of the company's sales. This section describes several popular sales forecasting methods.

There are two broad classes of sales forecasting methods: quantitative and qualitative. These are illustrated in Figure 5.3.[37] **Quantitative forecasting** methods use statistical methods to examine data and find underlying patterns and relationships. They can be either time-series methods or causal models. **Qualitative forecasting** methods emphasize human judgment. They include various judgmental methods.

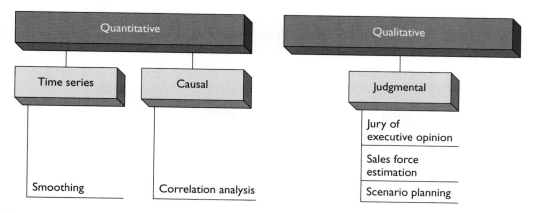

■ FIGURE 5.3

Forecasting Methods
We can distinguish between two broad classes of forecasting methods, quantitative and qualitative, each with specific techniques.

QUANTITATIVE FORECASTING METHODS. Quantitative methods like time-series methods and causal models forecast by assuming that past relationships will continue into the future.

TIME-SERIES ANALYSIS. A **time series** is a set of observations taken at specific times, usually at equal intervals. Examples of time series are the yearly or monthly gross domestic product (GDP) of the United States over several years, a department store's total monthly sales receipts, and the daily closing prices of a share of stock.[38]

If you plot time-series data on a graph for several periods, you may note various patterns. For example, if you were to plot monthly sales of Rheem air conditioning units, you would find seasonal increases in late spring and summer and reduced sales in the winter months. For some types of time series, there may also be an irregular pattern, such as a sudden "blip" in the graph that reflects unexplained variations in the data. The basic purpose of all time-series forecasting methods is to remove irregular and seasonal patterns so that management can identify the fundamental trend the data are taking.

Several methods are used to isolate a time series' underlying trend. **Smoothing methods** average the data in some way to remove seasonal and random variations. One of the simplest smoothing techniques is called simple smoothing average. With a **simple smoothing average** you take an average of, say, the last five months' sales, and the forecast for that next month's sales will be that average. Then every month you drop the first month's sales so that your forecast for the following month is continually an average of the past five months' sales.

CAUSAL METHODS. Managers often need to understand the causal relationship between two variables, such as (1) their company's sales, and (2) an indicator of economic activity, such as disposable income. **Causal methods** develop a projection based on the mathematical relationship between a company factor and those variables that management believes influence or explain the company factor.[39] The basic premise of causal models is that a particular factor—such as your company's sales of television sets—is directly influenced by some other, more predictable, factor or factors—such as the number of people unemployed in your state, or the level of disposable income in the United States. The basic assumption is that if you know the historical relationship between, say, TV sales and the level of unemployment, you will be able to project your TV sales if you know what unemployment is now, and what it is projected to be in the immediate future.[40] **Causal forecasting** thus estimates the company factor (such as sales) based on other factors (such as advertising expenditures, or level of unemployment). Statistical techniques such as correlation analysis (which shows how closely the variables are related) are generally used to develop the necessary relationships.

QUALITATIVE FORECASTING METHODS. Time series and causal forecasting have three big limitations. They are virtually useless when data are scarce, such as for a new product with no sales history. They assume that historical trends will continue into the future.[41] They also tend to disregard unforeseeable, unexpected occurrences. Yet it is exactly these unexpected occurrences that today often have the most profound effects on companies.

Qualitative forecasting techniques emphasize and are based on human judgment. They gather, in as logical, unbiased, and systematic a way as possible, all the information and human judgment that can be brought to bear on the factors being forecast. Techniques here include jury of executive opinion, sales-force estimation, and scenario planning.[42]

JURY OF EXECUTIVE OPINION. The **jury of executive opinion** technique involves asking a "jury" of key executives to forecast sales for, say, the next year. Generally, each executive is given data on forecasted economic levels and changes anticipated (in the firm's product or service, for instance). Each jury member then makes an independent sales forecast. Differences can be reconciled by the president or during a meeting of the executives. In an enhancement of this approach, experts from various departments of the company gather to make the forecast.

This is a straightforward way to forecast sales. However, its accuracy is reportedly almost always inferior to that of the more rigorous quantitative methods.[43] As discussed in chapter 3, the resulting forecast may also be biased by an influential group member, and the experts' subjective opinions may all be swayed by general business conditions (they may all be optimistic in boom times, for instance).

SALES FORCE ESTIMATION. The **sales force estimation** method is similar to jury of executive opinion, but it gathers the opinions of the sales force regarding what they think some factor—generally sales—will be in the forthcoming period. Each salesperson estimates his or her next year's sales, usually by product and customer. Sales managers then review each estimate, compare it with the previous year's data, and discuss changes with each salesperson. The separate estimates are combined into a single sales forecast for the firm.

This method has pros and cons. It facilitates management by objectives by involving each salesperson in setting his or her sales quota. It can also be advantageous to get sales estimates from the people who are most familiar with local conditions. On the other hand, a salesperson may underestimate sales if he or she knows the estimate will become his or her quota. Furthermore, salespeople may not be knowledgeable about influential economic trends.

Managing Change

SCENARIO PLANNING

Some companies such as Shell Oil must make major investments, although the firm's future may be very unpredictable. One way to manage change under such conditions is to make projections based on scenario planning. **Scenarios** have been defined as hypothetical sequences of events constructed for the purpose of focusing attention on causal processes and decision points. They answer two kinds of questions: (1) precisely how might some hypothetical situation come about, step by step, and (2) what alternatives exist, for each situation at each step, for preventing, diverting, or facilitating the process?[44]

Shell Oil Company is one firm that uses scenario planning. As one of its officers has said, "the Shell approach to strategic planning is, instead of forecasting, to use scenarios, which are 'stories' about alternative possible futures. These stories promote a discussion of possibilities other than the 'most likely' one, and encourage the consideration of 'what-if' questions."[45]

In developing its current scenarios, Shell looked at "the world . . . in terms of geopolitical change, international economics, and the environment." It saw such things as international economic tensions (as symbolized by some increase in trade tariffs) and increasing pollution concerns. Out of its analysis came two scenarios: "global mercantilism" and "sustainable world."

These two scenarios are summarized in Figure 5.4. In **global mercantilism,** the new post–cold war "international order proves to be too weak to withstand serious political and economic shocks and setbacks." As a result, regional conflicts and frustration with similar international failures lead to more government intervention in managing international trade. For a company like Shell (whose crude oil is a key traded commodity), this managed system could lead to "intermittent overcapacity and undercapacity and a price 'roller coaster.'" In the **sustainable world** scenario, international economic frictions are resolved, and economic trade flows freely. But here, concern about environmental problems leads to tightened emissions regulation and higher quality standards for energy products. In either case, scenario planning provides Shell managers with a better basis for managing change, by letting them view various futures and the consequences these futures might have for the firm and its products.

■ **FIGURE 5.4**
Scenarios Used by Royal Dutch Shell
Scenario planning involves looking at the events of the world and creating likely scenarios (such as "sustainable world" and "global mercantilism") along with the implications each of these scenarios would have for the company.

SOURCE: Reprinted from Adam Kahan, "Scenarios for Energy: Sustainable World vs. Global Mercantilism," *Long Range Planning,* vol. 25, no. 4, pg. 41 with permission from Elsevier Science.

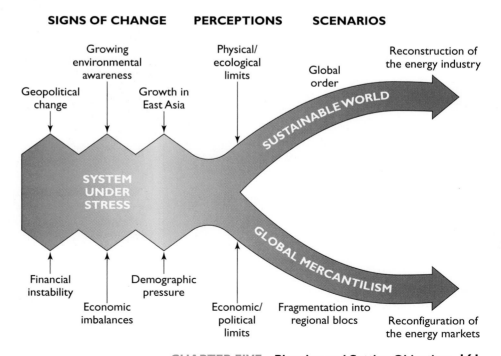

Marketing Research

Tools like causal models and scenario planning can help managers explore the future to develop more accurate planning premises. However, there are times when, to formulate plans, you want to know not just what may happen in the future, but what your customers are thinking right now. **Marketing research** refers to the procedures used to develop and analyze new customer-related information that helps managers make decisions.[46]

Marketing researchers depend on two main types of information, as summarized in Figure 5.5. One source is **secondary data,** information that has been collected or published already. Good sources of secondary data include libraries, trade associations, and company files and sales reports. **Primary data** refer to information specifically collected to solve a current problem. Primary data sources include mail and personal surveys, in-depth and focus-group interviews, and personal observations (like watching the reactions of customers who walk into a store).[47]

Competitive Intelligence

Developing useful plans often depends on knowing as much as possible about what competitors are doing or are planning to do. **Competitive intelligence** is a systematic way to obtain and analyze public information about competitors. Although "competitive intelligence" sounds (and is) a lot like legalized spying, it's become much more popular over the past few years. According to one report the number of large companies with competitive intelligence groups has tripled since 1988 to about 10 percent.[48]

Competitive intelligence (CI) practitioners use a variety of techniques to find out what their clients' competitors are doing. These include keeping track of existing and new competitors by having specialists visit their facilities, and hiring their workers and questioning their suppliers and customers. CI firms also do sophisticated Internet searches to dig up all available Internet-based information about competitors, as well as more mundane activities like reading stock analysts' reports

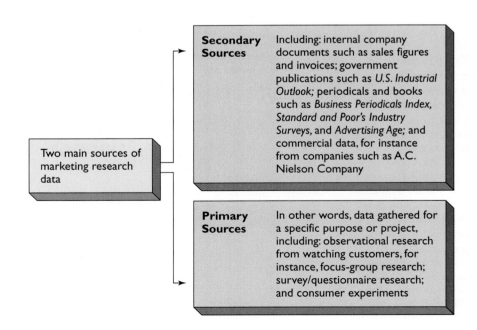

■ FIGURE 5.5
Sources of Secondary and Primary Data

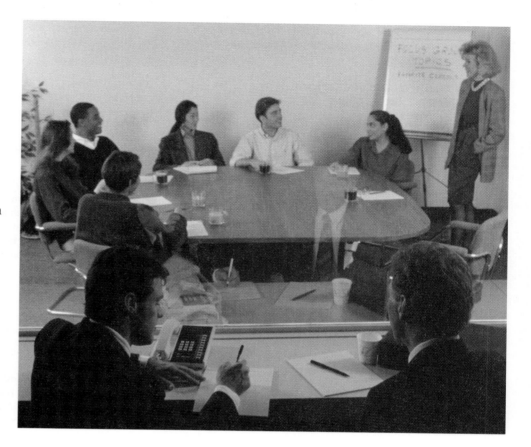

Focus groups, in which a moderator leads a group of typical customers in a discussion or trial of the firm's products, are a good source of primary marketing research information. Sometimes, as here, special rooms equipped with one-way observation windows allow executives to monitor the process.

on the competitors' prospects. Several private CI consulting firms, including Kroll Associates, have built successful businesses using prosecutors, business analysts, and former FBI and Drug Enforcement Agency employees to ferret out the sorts of information one might want before entering into an alliance with another company or before deciding to get into their business.

As illustrated in Table 5.5, CI consultants provide a range of information. For example, this particular firm can help client companies learn more about competitors' strengths and vulnerabilities, product strategies, investment strategies, financial capabilities, and current or prior anticompetitive behavior. Other CI services include evaluating the capabilities, weaknesses, and reputation of potential or existing joint-venture partners; identifying the major players in a new market or industry that the firm is thinking of entering; and helping planners boost sales opportunities, for instance by identifying the decision makers who actually do the purchasing and the critical factors they look for in vendors.

Managers using competitive intelligence must beware of slipping into activities that are ethically, morally, or legally wrong. Reading brokers' analytical reports on a competitor or finding information about it on the Internet would probably be viewed as legitimate activities by almost everyone, for instance. However, when CI practitioners dig through the target's trash on public property to search for planning memos, or hire former employees to pick their brains, ethical alarms start ringing. Some activities, like stealing customer lists and plans, are clearly illegal and would be shunned by any ethical CI advocate. As

CI CAN ADDRESS FOUR CRITICAL MANAGEMENT CONCERNS	BY PROVIDING INTELLIGENCE LIKE THIS ON COMPANIES, INDUSTRIES, AND COUNTRIES
COMPETITION: Learning enough about competitors to devise proactive and reactive strategies, including competitors' strengths and vulnerabilities, product strategies, investment strategies, financial capabilities, operational issues, and anti-competitive behavior.	**Operations:** Nature of business, sales, locations, headcount. **Financial:** Ownership, assets, financing, profitability.
BUSINESS RELATIONSHIPS AND TRANSACTIONS: Evaluating the capabilities, weaknesses, and reputation of potential or existing joint venture partners, strategic alliances, acquisitions, distributors, licensees/licensors, critical suppliers/vendors, and project finance participants.	**Management:** Organization structure, decision makers, integrity/reputation, management style, history as partner, political connections. **Marketing/Customers:** Market position, major accounts, pricing, distribution, sales force, advertising.
ENTRY INTO NEW MARKETS: Developing entry strategies into new geographic and/or product markets, including identifying players in an industry, analyzing industry structure and trends, assessing local business practices, ascertaining entry barriers, government regulation, and political risk.	**Manufacturing:** Plant and equipment, capacity, utilization, sourcing materials/components, shifts, labor costs, unions. **Technology:** New products and processes, R&D practices, technological assessment.
SALES OPPORTUNITIES: Maximizing opportunities to win contracts, develop major new customers, or maintain existing ones, including identifying purchasing decision makers and critical factors, determining current suppliers, understanding the competition, and assessing the status of bids.	**Strategic Directions:** Line of business priorities, diversification, geographic strategy, horizontal/vertical integration, strategic relationships. **Legal:** Lawsuits, judgments, potential liabilities, environmental exposure.

an unfortunate example, Volkswagen A.G.'s president, José Ignacio López de Arriortua, resigned in the face of allegations that he had committed what some viewed as industrial espionage by allegedly taking plans from his former employer, General Motors.[49]

Planners in Action

Who Does the Planning?

Over the past few years, most companies have made dramatic changes in the way they do their planning. For example, in the 1980s General Electric had a 350-member planning staff that churned out voluminous and detailed planning reports.[50] Today, GE is down to fewer than 20 full-time players. The real planning these days is done by the heads of GE's 13 businesses. Every year, each of these business heads develops five one-page "charts." These charts are actually memos listing possible business opportunities and obstacles over the next two years. So, when Hungary decided to let foreign firms take over state-run companies, GE needed just 60 days to buy 50% of Tungsram, Hungary's leading lighting company, because Tungsram had been on GE's "charts" for years.

As at General Electric, most companies have moved from centralized to decentralized planning in the past few years.[51] Today, in other words, the planners themselves are generally not specialists housed in large, centralized, headquarters planning departments. Instead, the actual planning is carried out by product and divisional managers, often aided by small headquarters planning advisory groups.

This redistribution of planning assignments parallels similar changes taking place in industry today. These changes include flattening organizational hierarchies, pushing down decisions to lower levels of management, and generally trying to position firms to be as responsive as possible to increasingly unpredictable competitive forces. Pushing planning down from centralized headquarters planning departments to product managers reflects the fact that the latter are usually in the best position to sense changes in customer, competitive, and technological trends and react to them.

What Planners Do

The idea that planning is done by lower-level managers rather than a planning department is in fact somewhat misleading, since the actual process involves much give and take. Based on input from product and divisional managers and other sources, top management sets an overall strategic direction for the firm; the resulting objectives then become the targets for which the product and divisional managers formulate specific tactical and operational plans. Thus, strategic planning and direction setting are still mostly done by top managers, usually with their planning unit's assistance. However, more of the premising, alternative generating, and product-planning input goes up the hierarchy than it did in previous years.

Most large companies still do have small headquarters planning departments, and these planners still play a crucial planning role. For example, the planning departments of multinational firms like GE reportedly engage in about ten basic planning-related activities.[52]

- *Act as information resource.* Headquarters planners typically compile and monitor all planning-related data, including that for divisions. This information might include divisions' progress toward meeting planned financial targets, competitor intelligence, regional and global economic summaries, and other data reporting the degree to which divisions are achieving their goals;
- *Conduct competitor and market research.* Headquarters planners help the divisions analyze global competition, for instance, by identifying major global competitors, developing scenarios, and monitoring competitors' strategies;
- *Develop forecasts.* Headquarters planners develop forecasts that are applicable companywide. For example, they typically develop forecasts of basic economic activity, such as gross domestic product or inflation rates around the world;
- *Provide consulting services.* For example, some headquarters planning staffs help divisions conduct industry analyses and provide divisional planners with training in the planning techniques they could or should be using;
- *Create a common language.* Headquarters planners usually devise standardized corporatewide planning reports and forms, so that the divisions' plans are comparable in terms of the information they provide and the way they provide it;
- *Communicate values.* The headquarters planning unit is often the one charged with promulgating those basic values and ethical standards that characterize the firm and provide its identity;

- *Communicate companywide objectives.* The headquarters planning unit generally is the intermediary that communicates companywide objectives to divisional managers. The latter then formulate plans for achieving their assigned objectives under those corporate objectives;
- *Serve as planning-process guardian.* Headquarters planners are generally charged with ensuring that the company's planning process and procedures are functioning smoothly;
- *Develop planning methods.* Some headquarters planning units develop special analytical planning tools and methods aimed at making their companies' planning processes more effective;
- *Lead planning teams.* Finally, the headquarters planning unit is generally responsible for ensuring that the managers involved with planning throughout the company are working together effectively as a team. Headquarters planners, therefore, engage in activities such as organizing and coordinating planning meetings and conferences. These are aimed at fostering close cooperation among all the managers involved in the planning process.

Organizational Behavior in Action

HOW TO BUILD A COHESIVE PLANNING TEAM

Having a close-knit management team doing the planning can translate into better and more effective plans. Disagreements aren't necessarily bad: They can help unearth new points of view and challenge questionable assumptions, for instance. However, a close-knit management team is probably in the best position to work out differences and minimize intramural politics and rivalries in such a way that a

If a planning team is separated by distance, videoconferencing can offer an effective way to communicate and thereby build cohesiveness, as for this group of Chase executives.

plan that's best for the whole company emerges.[53] Building a cohesive management team—one whose members are close, who desire to remain in the group, and who are committed to the group and its goals—can therefore contribute to better planning.[54]

How do you create a more cohesive management team? Based on OB and small-group studies, here are several things a manager can do.[55]

- *Put a high price on team membership.* The more difficult it is to be selected for a management position in the company and the more difficult it is to become one of those involved with developing the company's plans, the more "special" the team members will feel and the more cohesive the team will tend to be;

- *Boost opportunities for interaction.* Proximity and frequent contact and interaction tend to boost group cohesiveness (unless the number of meetings becomes excessive). Therefore, providing enough opportunities (including via videoconferencing) for the planners to interact and to meet formally and informally will tend to boost cohesiveness;

- *Crystallize the team's purpose.* When team members understand and agree on what they are to accomplish, cohesiveness tends to increase;

- *Emphasize the urgency of producing a top-notch plan.* One way to do this is to emphasize the threat of competition. Group cohesiveness tends to rise under conditions of high external threat or competition, for instance, when managers clearly understand that there's a "common enemy" that may threaten their company (and their jobs). Emphasizing the competitive threat (for instance by dramatically presenting information about your firm's declining market share or a competitor's new products) will tend to reduce petty disagreements and cause the planning team members to work together more closely;

- *Reward based on team results.* An incentive system that rewards only on individual or departmental results can lead to personal competition and reduce feelings of closeness. Those involved in creating the plan should therefore be appraised on and have a personal financial stake in the team's ability to produce a workable plan, as well as in the success of the resulting plan;

- *Foster success.* The degree of success a team has in meeting its goals will influence its cohesiveness. Success boosts cohesiveness and failure undermines it. Therefore, foster success. For example, provide clear instructions and training in planning techniques and premises that the planners will need to succeed in producing good plans.[56]

- *Limit team size.* Limit the size of each planning team to about seven people. Cohesiveness diminishes as the group becomes too large.

Planning in a Real Firm

BAT Industries (originally British American Tobacco Company and now a major financial services firm) has a planning process typical of many larger firms. The company has a presence in 50 countries, and is based in London. Its enormity notwithstanding, BAT's corporate planning has a staff of just four.[57] The head of corporate planning reports to BAT's chairman. In turn, BAT's subsidiaries (each of which is also very large) have their own planning groups.

At BAT, corporate planning's major role is designing and administering the planning process, for instance by "monitoring the business plans as they come in from the subsidiaries."[58] The corporate planning head says his department's main roles are (1) formulating policies—in particular, determining in what businesses BAT Industries wants to be involved; (2) formulating objectives, in terms of "where we're trying to get"; and (3) formulating companywide strategies, which answer the question, "How will we get there?"

The planning process at BAT illustrates the interplay between headquarters and divisional planning in a larger enterprise. Corporate planning controls BAT's planning cycle. In April, the divisions complete reviews of their businesses, covering matters such as competitive trends that may be affecting their businesses, and forward these to corporate planning. In June, the board adopts a set of planning assumptions based on recommendations prepared by the corporate planning department. (These assumptions might include, for instance, political, economic, and new business projections.) At the same time, headquarters planning prepares a financial forecast for BAT, based on projections from the individual BAT units. In July, the board reviews the financial objectives, as compiled and assessed by the corporate planning department. Modified financial objectives then go out in early August as a set of guidelines to each business unit. The business units, in turn, rely on these targets in preparing their own plans, which are then submitted to the board for approval by January. Once adopted, "plans are monitored [by headquarters] in quarterly progress reports submitted by the operating units."[59]

The BAT headquarters planning unit also helps maintain what BAT calls "cultural harmony." In such a geographically dispersed company, there's always a risk that employees may tend to identify first with their local business units rather than with BAT as a whole. Several BAT programs resist such tendencies. Top managers and senior directors travel widely and immerse themselves in the local division's businesses so as to "carry the flag" of the firm to all its far-flung outposts. BAT also has a strong internal accounting/audit group; it monitors each division's compliance with BAT policies regarding matters such as business ethics. Finally, headquarters planning plays a role here, by helping to standardize and publicize both the planning process and the overall sense of strategic mission that all divisions are to share.

SUMMARY

1. Plans are methods formulated beforehand for achieving desired results. Planning is the process of establishing objectives and courses of actions prior to taking action. We distinguish several types of plans: Plans differ in format, time horizon, and frequency.

2. The management-planning process consists of a logical sequence of five steps: establish objectives; conduct situation analysis (develop the forecasts and planning premises); determine alternative courses of action; evaluate alternatives; and choose and implement the plan. In practice, this produces a planning hierarchy because top management's goals become the targets for which subsidiary units must formulate derivative plans.

3. Teamwork is essential in business planning, because each manager's plans should complement those of his or her colleagues and also contribute to making the company's overall goals a reality.

4. Every manager can expect to be appraised on the extent to which he or she achieves assigned objectives, which makes setting objectives an essential management skill. The areas for which objectives can be set are virtually limitless, ranging from market standing to innovation and profitability. The goal-setting studies of Edwin Locke and Gary Latham and their associates suggest these guidelines for goal setting: assign specific goals; assign measurable goals; assign challenging but doable goals; encourage participation where feasible. In setting goals, remember also to distinguish between an area to be measured, a yardstick, and an objective, and to specify what is to be done, by when, and at what cost or in what time period. Management by objectives can be used to create an integrated hierarchy of goals throughout the organization.

5. Among the techniques for developing planning premises are forecasting, marketing research, and competitive intelligence. Forecasting techniques include quantitative methods such as time-series analysis and causal methods. Qualitative forecasting methods such as scenario planning, sales-force estimation, and jury of executive opinion emphasize human judgment. Competitive intelligence is a systematic way to obtain and analyze public information about competitors.

6. Most companies have moved from centralized to decentralized planning in the past few years, in part to place the planning responsibility with those product and divisional managers who are probably in the best position to understand their customers' needs and competitors' activities. However, the central planning units in larger companies, though dramatically downsized, still carry out important planning-related activities such as competitor and market research, communicating companywide objectives, and providing planning-related consulting services to the divisions.

KEY TERMS

plans
planning
goals
objectives
descriptive plans
budgets
graphic plans
strategic plans
tactical plans
functional plans
operational planning
programs
standing plans
policies

procedures
rule
hierarchy of plans
goal-setting studies
management by
  objectives (MBO)
goal commitment
self-efficacy
planning premises
forecast
quantitative forecasting
qualititative forecasting
time series
smoothing methods

simple smoothing average
causal methods
causal forecasting
jury of executive opinion
sales-force estimation
scenarios
global mercantilism
sustainable world
marketing research
secondary data
primary data
competitive intelligence

TRUE / FALSE QUESTIONS

1 **T F** Plans are methods devised in advance to achieve a desired outcome.

2 **T F** Planning is the second of the four basic management functions.

3 **T F** Middle management usually does most of the five- to ten-year strategic planning.

4 **T F** The role of policies is to set broad guidelines for the company.

5 **T F** One of the primary functions of planning is to identify potential opportunities and threats and to try to minimize long-term risks.

6 **T F** The first step in the management-planning process is to establish objectives.

7 **T F** Employees generally work better when they have goals to reach.

8 **T F** Research has unequivocally shown that the only way for subordinates to reach goals is to have them participate in developing their own goals to guide work.

9 **T F** The last step in the MBO process is feedback on the subordinate's performance.

10 **T F** Plans are based on the assumptions we make about the future.

MULTIPLE-CHOICE QUESTIONS

1 Planning departments of multinational firms like GE engage in about ten basic planning-related activities. Which of the following is *not* one of those functions?
a. Act as an information resource.
b. Develop forecasting.
c. Communicate values.
d. Create diverse languages throughout the company.

2 Which of the following are types of plans?
a. budgets
b. tactical
c. strategic
d. all of the above

3 Which of the following is best contrasted with single-use plans?
a. procedures
b. standing plans
c. rules
d. policies

4 A plan provides a _____ framework against which decisions can be assessed.
a. unifying
b. disintegrated
c. simplified
d. none of the above

5 The result of the management planning process is a _____ of plans.
a. bundle
b. hierarchy
c. processes
d. horizontally spaced

6 In Greg Foster's plans to turn around his troubled metal-converting foundry, one of the major goals was qualifying for the international quality-management certification or the _____.

a. H-P Seal of Approval
b. EU Stamp
c. ISO 9000
d. none of the above

7 Which of the following is listed by management expert Peter Drucker as a classical area in which objectives should be set?
a. market standing
b. productivity
c. profitability
d. all of the above

8 Which of the following is evidence for encouraging employee participation in goal setting?
a. Goals tend to be lower than the supervisor would have assigned.
b. Harder goals are not seen as so difficult by the employees.
c. Set goals do not consistently result in higher performance than assigned goals.
d. Employees have more impact on goals.

9 _____ is a technique used by many organizations to operationalize the process of setting organizationwide objectives and objectives for subsidiary units.
a. MBO
b. TBS
c. ISO
d. NBC

10 Quantitative forecasting methods are statistical methods to examine data and find underlying patterns and relationships. All of the following are methods *except:*
a. smoothing
b. time series
c. simple smoothing average
d. causal methods

CRITICAL THINKING EXERCISES

1 Consider an ancient country with a long tradition of religious philosophy, an ethic of hard work, and strong warrior instincts. Imagine this country emerging into the world marketplace almost overnight, a country with over 1.2 billion consumers. Many of its citizens have a per capita income of only $500, but economists estimate that as many as 200 million middle-class consumers have disposable income to spend on a variety of products. There are believed to be at least one million millionaires in this socialistic-capitalistic country.

This country has had most-favored-nation trade status since 1980. However, because it does not allow freedom of emigration as called for by a 1974 U.S. amendment, it must have its trade privileges reauthorized by the president every year. Many Americans are concerned with the civil and intellectual rights of the people of this country, which has imposed government sanctions on demonstrators and has a history of human-rights violations. Bilateral trade between the United States and this country reached $57 billion in 1995. U.S. investment rose from $358 million in 1990 to $25 billion in 1996.

The country, of course, is the world's largest: China. There is great potential and opportunity for business here. However, there are also threats. Using the concepts presented in the chapter, explain how you would go about developing a plan for doing business in China for the next five years.

2 Technology can be a very useful tool. Ask Randy Fields, cofounder (with his wife, Debbi) of Mrs. Fields Cookies. Fields argues for running a business on a clear set of rules, for instance, about how much dough to use in a cookie. Others say such rules remove the spontaneity and creativity of the company's individual employees. Fields believes that rules can set you free, as in this interview with *Inc.* in November of 1996.

Question: Debbi Fields as Big Sister?

Answer: No, but I'll admit that it's a paradox. Computerizing our rules has made our stores and our corporate culture not more impersonal but more humane. The technology frees employees to relate to customers and to one another. People think of computer technology as cold and depersonalizing, but we don't. It's one of the greatest tools we have for building corporate goals, vision, and understanding—which is to say, our culture, the glue that holds everything together. The computers tell managers: Here are the guidelines, here is how we do this now. You don't have to figure all that out. Your job is to implement as creatively as you know how. There's a great comfort in knowing that if A occurs, someone has already figured out what the best Bs are.

How can the Fields' approach to planning be used in other companies? What concepts used in this chapter relate to what Fields is saying? How do you think computer technology will impact planning, and how much will it do so in the future?

EXPERIENTIAL EXERCISES

1 One of the chronic complaints of employers about prospective employees, especially those just out of the university with limited work experience, is that they don't have well-honed presentation skills. A recent issue of *Fast Company* outlines an eight-point program for presentations guaranteed to keep your listeners on the edge of their seats.[60] The eight points are as follows.

- Incite, don't inform—effective presentations don't end with nodding heads and polite applause. They end with *action.*

- Don't talk to strangers—know your audience by doing research prior to the presentation.

- First (and last) impressions are everything—the two most important parts of your presentation are the first 30 and the last 15 seconds.

- Simpler is better. Make your presentations shorter and more candid.

- Perform, don't present. The impact of a typical presentation is 55% visual (how you look), 38% vocal (how you talk), and only 7% verbal (what you say). In other words, you don't deliver presentations, you *perform* them.

- The show must go on. Concentrate on the performance factor.

- There's one in every crowd—that is, a hostile member you must handle. The first rule is to disagree without being disagreeable and don't pick a fight.

- Practice, practice, practice—practice, practice, practice.

Select a topic from this chapter on planning and prepare a five-minute presentation following the rules outlined here. Be ready to give your presentation to your class.[61]

2 As noted in the chapter, we plan all day long without really knowing we are doing it. So, for the next three days, keep track of your days. On the first day, write down what, how, when, and where you accomplished the goals you had informally set out for the day. That night write out what goals you wish to accomplish the next day. At the end of the second day, write down what happened. Now write out what goals you wish to accomplish and a specific, hour-by-hour plan to accomplish those goals. At the end of the day, see how you have done on each of the three days and what you have learned about how you do or do not plan, and how planning can help you manage your time better. If you already plan your time, try not planning so carefully and see what happens. What new things did you learn about yourself?

DIVERSITY CASE

MARGARET F. GONZALES AND ACHIEVING GOALS

All good sales managers devote a big part of their energies to prospecting for new business. And when they find good prospects, they work hard to overcome barriers and close the sale. For Margaret F. Gonzales, director of Los Angeles' East Side enterprise zone, things don't always get easier after the deal is done. Her primary goal is to attract industries and create jobs in an area blighted by a host of urban problems. She must also constantly plot strategies and devise methods to keep them there.

A quarter of the warehouse space in Gonzales's state-mandated territory is empty. Unemployment is a chronic problem and is probably even higher than official estimates because the actual number of illegal alien residents is unknown. Gonzales brings an arsenal of employer incentives to the table: tax credits for each employee hired, low-interest loans, cut-rate utility bills, and a motivated labor force that comes cheap by surrounding standards. She's up against the predictable obstacles of crime, a decaying infrastructure, and concerns about maintaining a safe workplace, among others. Her staff and budget aren't adequate either.

To achieve her goals, Gonzales has enlisted the professional assistance of real-estate agents from other areas. She has taken her presentation to some of the fancier addresses to the north as well. Not long ago, she pitched the benefits of her Boyle Heights district to several accountants at the Beverly Hills Racquet Club, where the tax-shelter highlights of investing in her enterprise zone were discussed.

Her success stories include a salsa manufacturer's decision to move its factory to the area. An importer also plans on expansion, thanks to Gonzales's efforts to help the company obtain a $1 million Small Business Administration loan. But for every two steps forward, it seems Gonzales has to take a step back. One manufacturer is considering moving out of the area and relocating to Idaho. And United Parcel Service backed out of a plan to construct a distribution center there. The setbacks are not enough to deter Gonzales. "My job is to find out what's making them unhappy and to see if I can fix it," she says.

Gonzales knows hers will always be an ongoing effort. She has to continually develop plans to attract new businesses, as well as methods to keep them there over the long haul. The job is challenging and thought-provoking, but the economic payoff for her constituents makes it worthwhile.

Questions

1 Describe Gonzales's task using the five-step planning cycle outlined in the chapter.

2 Develop a hypothetical set of goals for Gonzales that is clear and specific, measurable and verifiable, and challenging but realistic.

3 How would you tackle the task of getting companies to invest in an economically disadvantaged area? What do you think are some of the unstated objections the firm's top managers want answered but may not ask?

SOURCE: Ronald Grover, "Local Heroes Making a Difference," *Business Week/Reinventing America,* 1992, 214–20.

STRATEGY CASE

THE CLASS ISSUES OF TOYS

A major strategic issue facing toy makers today is planning to meet the increasingly diverse demands of consumers, kids included.

In Brookline, Massachusetts, No Kidding has made its choice: It has built an educated, professional clientele from the affluent suburbs by stocking hard-to-find items with an educational focus and offering ready advice from a staff of moonlighting teachers. In an industry where more than 100 independent toy stores closed in 1995, No Kidding is thriving, even with 100% markups and none of the licensed products found in large commercial toy stores.

Co-owners Judy Crockerton and Carol Nelson have a vision of No Kidding as an educational toy business with close ties to the educational community. When asked whether she is an entrepreneur, founder Cockerton says, "I'm taken aback . . . no, . . . I'm a teacher."

Questions

1 What management and planning barriers might No Kidding face given its owners' philosophy?

2 What suggestions would you make to No Kidding about its plans for the future? Why?

3 How can planning help small, focused stores like No Kidding compete against larger, more commercial stores?

SOURCES: Cover Story, "Two-Tier Marketing," *Business Week,* 17 March 1997, 82–89; Joseph Pereira, "A Small Toy Store Manages to Level the Playing Field," *Wall Street Journal,* 20 December 1996, A1, A8.

ENTREPRENEURIAL CASE

CIN-MADE, INC.

The main thing Bob Frey learned during his career at a big consumer-products company was that he hated bureaucracy. So when he bought Cin-Made he decided that at his new paper and cardboard package manufacturing company he would shun formal training and keep track of everything in his head.

That turned out to be a mistake. For the next three years Cin-Made careened through the market from product to product while profit margins shrank. It finally dawned on Frey that he needed a business plan.

He started by making an analysis of the packaging market and where his company might fit in. One thing he discovered was that Cin-Made was one of many firms making a standard commodity that was subject to cutthroat pricing from the lowest-cost producers. He also discovered a big change in one of his prime packaging markets that made him think he could set his company apart.

Specifically, when motor oil cans went from paper to plastic containers, Frey decided to make the investment required to convert to manufacturing plastic chemical canisters. Since customers for such canisters wanted custom features, they usually didn't quibble about price as long as Frey could deliver the goods. He decided to refocus his company's mission on providing specialty packaging needs that his non-custom competitors couldn't provide. With the growing success of his new strategy, it became easier for Frey to make the decisions that had to be made. For instance, he eventually decided to permit bales of standard packages to diminish so he could concentrate on custom products and utilizing his new custom-built machinery.

Other decisions followed from Frey's new focus on custom packaging. For example, "To properly exploit our premium niche strategy, we have to plow more into R&D," Frey says. "That yields products with higher price tags to reflect our larger investment in custom-built machines."

Not surprisingly, Cin-Made's operations are now directed by very specific business-planning summaries that Frey creates. These one-page synopses circulate from the shop floor to the boardroom. While each plan covers targets up to five years out, the plans are updated at least monthly, and sometimes more often.

His plans reflect the sort of step-by-step approach that's usually required to achieve objectives over time. For example, Cin-Made is committed to premium pricing, in keeping with its emphasis on custom products, so it won't be drawn into a pricing war for its high-end products. Because the firm had previously spent a lot of money on noncustom packaging equipment before Frey adopted his custom-niche strategy, he still has a plan to compete for high-volume, traditional packaging business. His aim is to recoup his investment until Cin-Made's newer custom products carve out enough of a market to carry the firm.

Cin-Made's new strategy and planning have paid off. Pretax profit margins have increased fivefold. Even better, new products may double the company's revenues. And today, Frey seems to enjoy the new discipline that comes from being a planner instead of a manager who tries to keep all his ideas in his head.

Questions

1 In what ways does Bob Frey's planning approach differ from the more formal five-step process outlined in this chapter?

2 Based on what you know about Cin-Made, create several objectives using the Morrisey model discussed earlier in this chapter.

3 Overall, what do you think of Frey's planning method? Do you think it could be improved using any of the methods discussed in this chapter? How?

SOURCE: Teri Lammers, "The One-Page Strategy Guide," *Inc.*, September 1992, 135–38.

THE BUSINESS TEAM, INC.

PLANNING FOR THE FAMILY FUTURES

Business Team Inc. member Sid, and his wife, Jane, also a graduate of State University (in engineering), both have busy jobs. Jane works for a large engineering firm with clients all over the globe. She travels at least two months per year and will travel more as she moves up the corporate hierarchy.

Jane is pregnant with twins. She and Sid are ecstatic, but they know that raising kids and balancing professional careers is an enormous challenge. They have been trying to figure out what they will do once the babies come. Neither of them has immediate family in the area. There are a number of child-care centers in their community, but they are not sure that this is the option they want to pursue, nor how to evaluate the centers. Sid and Jane are the first of their friends to start a family, so the experience of others is not readily available. They've decided to let the Business Team Inc. give them some advice.

As a finance major, Sid knows there are many monetary and other matters to be considered for his own family. He wants to start planning now so he and Jane will be prepared when the twins arrive.

Questions

1 What are the planning issues that should be addressed by the Team?

2 What goals would you set for Sid and Jane?

3 What type of plans will be needed as all of the Business Team members start families or make lifestyle changes that affect the other team members?

YOU BE THE CONSULTANT

KNITMEDIA MAKES PLANS TO EXPAND

As you can see from budgets and other information on the Web site associated with this chapter, Michael Dorf and KnitMedia have formulated very careful and specific budgetary plans for the next few years. For example, sales for the Knit Factory clubs are estimated to grow for several years and then level off. In turn, all these plans are built on certain assumptions, such as the assumption that two additional Knitting Factory clubs will have been opened by the fourth quarter of 1997 (in Toronto and London), with additional clubs opening in North America and abroad for several years thereafter. Similarly, the sales assumptions for the touring operation are based on current and past touring activity and industry standards. KnitMedia would like to make sure that these plans are reasonable.

Team Exercises and Questions

Use what you learned in this chapter to answer the following questions:

1 Based on the information at your disposal, do you believe the projections that you have seen for KnitMedia are optimistic, pessimistic, or about right? Why?

2 List all of the assumptions that you can think of that are relevant to KnitMedia's plans.

3 Prepare a short proposal for Michael Dorf listing the sources of assumptions and premises he could use in developing his next plans for KnitMedia.

For the online version of this case, visit our Web site at <www.prenhall.com/desslermgmt>.

For Internet exercises, interactive study questions, news updates and more, visit the Dessler Web site at

www.prenhall.com/desslermgmt

If you're using the CD-ROM that accompanies this text, simply click on the "Web Site" button to access the site.

CHAPTER 6

STRATEGIC MANAGEMENT

What's Ahead?

Driven by the growing popularity of Java, the new Internet-based programming software, California's Silicon Valley computer companies are racing to form strategic alliances with Java application developers. At the center of much of this activity is Sun Microsystems, Inc., and its president Scott McNealy. To maintain its lead as Java's developer, Sun may well strike strategic alliances with other companies, with the aim of helping Sun to maintain its competitive advantage in the fast-changing Java applications market.[1]

Scott McNealy

Objectives

After studying this chapter, you should be able to

- **describe** the strategic management process
- **discuss** the three main types of strategies
- **explain** how to develop a strategy
- **use** three strategy-development tools.

MANAGEMENT ON THE WEB

CORPORATE REPUTATIONS: 1997

Which are the most- and least-admired companies in the United States and why? Where do companies rank in their own industries? What are the secrets of America's most admired corporations—how do they get to the top? Is there a relationship between financial performance and company reputation? The answers to these questions and more are found in *Fortune*'s 1997 Survey of Corporate Reputations. Use the information at this site as a starting point to discuss the interrelationships among management practices, corporate reputation, and organizational effectiveness. Could Sun use such information in forming alliances? ■

http://pathfinder.com/@@0@v@ogUAn4VCNxeo/fortune/1997/970303/tro.html

The Strategic Management Process

How do firms like Sun Microsystems know what strategy they should pursue to stay competitive? Management expert Peter Drucker has said that the primary task of top management is

> thinking through the mission of the business, that is, of asking the question "What is our business and what should it be?" This leads to the setting of objectives, the development of strategies and plans, and the making of today's decisions for tomorrow's results.[2]

Strategic management is the process of identifying and pursuing the organization's mission by aligning the organization's internal capabilities with the external demands of its environment.[3] As shown in Figure 6.1, the strategic management process consists of five tasks: defining the business and developing a vision and mission; translating the mission into specific strategic objectives; crafting a strategy to achieve the objectives; implementing and executing the strategy; and evaluating performance, reviewing the situation, and initiating corrective adjustments.

We'll look at each step in turn.

THE FIVE STRATEGIC MANAGEMENT STEPS

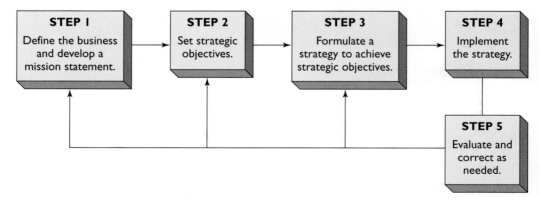

■ **FIGURE 6.1**
The Five Strategic Management Steps

Step 1: Define the business and develop a mission statement[4]

Two companies can compete in the same industry but still answer the question "What is our business?" in different ways. For example, Ferrari and Toyota both make cars, but there the similarity ends. Ferrari specializes in high-performance cars, and its competitive advantage is built on handmade craftsmanship and high-speed performance. Toyota produces a wide range of automobiles, as well as many of its own supplies and parts; its competitive advantage is built on cost-efficient production and a strong worldwide dealer network.

Similarly, Wal-Mart and K-Mart are in the same industry. Wal-Mart, however, distinguished itself from K-Mart by concentrating its stores in small southern towns, and by building a state-of-the-art satellite-based distribution system. K-Mart, on the other hand, opened stores throughout the country (where it necessarily had to compete with a great many other discounters, often for expensive, big-city properties). K-Mart also based its competitive advantage on its size, which it (erroneously) assumed would provide it with the economies of scale necessary to keep its costs below those of competitors.

The first step in strategic management is to define the business. It is not enough to say, "We make cars." Toyota and Ferrari both make cars, for instance, but their missions are quite different.

These examples underscore the idea that top managers must first define their business. In turn, answering the question, "What business should we be in?" usually results in both a vision statement and a mission statement (although the two are often the same). The organization's **vision** is a "general statement of its intended direction that evokes emotional feelings in organization members."[5] As Warren Bennis and Bert Manus say:

> To choose a direction, a leader must first have developed a mental image of a possible and desirable future state for the organization. This image, which we call a vision, may be as vague as a dream or as precise as a goal or mission statement. The critical point is that a vision articulates a view of a realistic, credible, attractive future for the organization, a condition that is better in some important ways than what now exists.[6]

For example, Dr. Edwin Land, who invented the Polaroid camera, had a vision of a company built on providing instant photographs in self-contained cameras. Rupert Murdock has a vision of an integrated global news-gathering, entertainment, and multimedia firm. Bill Gates had a vision of a software company serving the needs of the then-fledgling microcomputer industry.

The firm's **mission statement** further defines the company's purpose and operationalizes the top manager's vision. A mission statement "broadly outlines the organization's future course and serves to communicate 'who we are, what we do, and where we're headed.'"[7] Examples of mission statements are presented in Figure 6.2.

APEX ELEVATOR
   To provide a high reliability, error-free method for moving people and products up, down, and sideways within a building.

NICHOLLS STATE UNIVERSITY (COLLEGE OF BUSINESS)
   The principal mission of the College of Business is to prepare students to participate in society and the work force as educated individuals able to compete in a dynamic global economy. In order to enrich the learning process, the College also contributes to scholarship through applied research and instructional development. In addition to providing support to the employer community through the development of marketable skills in potential employees, the College also enhances the competitive capabilities of regional businesses by providing continuing education courses and consulting services through the Small Business Development Center (SBDC) and the individual efforts of faculty. The faculty advances the welfare of the University, the community, and academic and professional organizations through professional interactions.

UNITED TELEPHONE CORPORATION OF DADE
   To provide information services in local-exchange and exchange-access markets within its franchised area, as well as cellular phone and paging services.

JOSEPHSON DRUG COMPANY, INC.
   To provide people with longer lives and higher-quality lives by applying research efforts to develop new or improved drugs and health-care products.

GRAY COMPUTER, INC.
   To transform how educators work by providing innovative and easy-to-use multi-media-based computer systems.

■ **FIGURE 6.2**
Examples of Mission Statements
Note that mission statements usually crystallize the purpose of the company.

SOURCE: Nicholls mission courtesy of Nicholls State University, College of Business.

Step 2: Translate the mission into strategic objectives

The next strategic management task is to translate top management's broad vision and mission into operational strategic objectives. For example, strategic objectives for Citicorp include building shareholder value through sustained growth in earnings per share; continuing commitment to building customer-oriented business worldwide; maintaining superior rates of return; building a strong balance sheet; and balancing the business by customer, product, and geography.[8]

Step 3: Formulate a strategy to achieve the strategic objectives

A **strategy** is a course of action that explains how the enterprise will move from the business it is in now to the business it wants to be in (as stated in its mission), given its opportunities and threats and its internal strengths and weaknesses. For example, Wal-Mart decided to pursue the strategic objective of moving *from* being a relatively small southern-based chain of retail discount stores *to* becoming the national leader in low costs and prices. One of Wal-Mart's strategies was to reduce distribution costs and minimize inventory and delivery times through a satellite-based distribution system. The firm's strategic plan is comprised of its strategies and strategic objectives.

Step 4: Implement the strategy

Strategy implementation means translating the strategy into actions and results. Doing so requires drawing upon all the functions in the management process, namely, planning, organizing, leading, and controlling. For instance, employees will have to be hired and motivated and budgets formulated so progress toward the strategic goals can be measured.

Step 5: Evaluate performance and correct as required

Finally, **strategic control**—assessing the firm's progress toward its strategic objectives and taking corrective action as needed—operates to keep the company's strategy up-to-date. Strategic control should also ensure that all parts and members of the company are contributing in a useful way toward the strategy's implementation.

Managing strategy is thus an ongoing, not a stagnant, process. Competitors introduce new products, technological innovations make production processes obsolete, and societal trends reduce demands for some products or services while boosting demands for others. As a result, managers must be alert to opportunities and threats that might require modifying or, in some cases, totally redoing their strategic plans.

Managing Change

JUGGLING AT NOVELL

Managing change therefore requires continuing attention to the tasks of strategic management, and nowhere is this more apparent than in the fast-changing world of Silicon Valley. A popular saying there is, "Either we obsolete ourselves, or the competition will."[9] As a result, companies such as electronic equipment manufacturer Hewlett-Packard have continuously evolved their product lines, for instance, from medical equipment to calculators to laser-jet printers. One director of several Silicon Valley firms puts it this way: "A master strategic decision" is taken at virtually every board meeting.[10]

The strategic changes at Novell provide another example. Novell's network software helps a firm knit its computers together into local area networks so employees can more easily interact with and send messages to one another. In 1994 Novell made the strategic decision to branch out by buying WordPerfect, which markets word-processing programs.[11] When that purchase proved unprofitable it sold WordPerfect two years later to Corel, a Canadian firm, for a billion-dollar loss. Then, in March 1996, Novell announced it was forming a joint venture with Netscape to jointly market network software for use on the Internet.

Often, in other words, managing change goes hand in hand with strategic management. This is because adapting to competitive change requires assessing what those changes mean for the company's future, and then responding with the appropriate strategic change. ■

The Strategic Planning Process

Strategic planning is part of the overall strategic management process. As illustrated in Figure 6.3, it represents the first three of the strategic management tasks: defining the business and developing a mission, translating the mission into strategic objectives, and crafting a strategy or course of action to move the organization from where it is today to where it wants to be. Strategic planning is, therefore, the process of identifying the business of the firm today and the business it wants for the future, and then identifying the course of action or strategy it will pursue, given its opportunities, threats, and weaknesses. In the rest of this chapter we'll focus on how companies like King's Medical (see the Entrepreneurs in Action box) develop strategic plans.

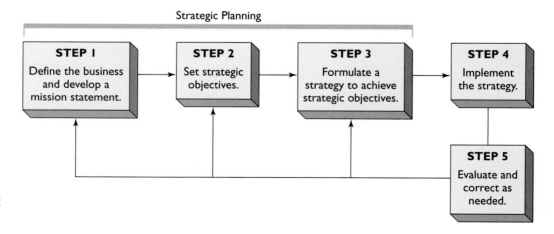

■ **FIGURE 6.3**
Strategic Management's Strategic Planning Components

Entrepreneurs in Action

STRATEGIC PLANNING AT KING'S MEDICAL COMPANY

King's Medical Company of Hudson, Ohio, is a 13-year-old company currently implementing its third three-year strategic plan. General manager and chief planner William Patton considers the decision-making discipline of the plan and the follow-through it promotes to be one reason for the company's success. "A lot of literature says there are three critical issues to a small company and they're all cash flow. [Cash flow] is critical, but the reason a small company survives is planning."

King's is both an owner and a manager of magnetic resonance imaging (MRI) equipment, expensive machinery that produces X-ray images for the health-care industry. Started in 1981, the company grew to more than $13 million in sales by 1992. Company founder Albert Van Kirk, who admits he used to do little planning, wholeheartedly concurs with Patton's views.

According to Van Kirk and Patton, plans are important for several reasons. Plans inspire evaluation and discussion in the formulation stage. Once in place, plans set the company course for the medium term. Managers across the company get involved in the decision-making process and develop an idea of how their work integrates in the overall company scheme.

At King's Medical, the planning process begins with the establishment of a planning group. This group is aimed at answering some basic questions like why the firm is in business, where it is currently, and where it hopes to be at the end of the planning period. The answers are reduced to a mission statement, which is then distributed to all employees.

Next, a strategic plan is produced through analysis of the industry. Patton considers this to be an essential exercise for a planner. "It's abbreviated SWOT—evaluating your strengths, weaknesses, opportunities, and threats," he says.

At the department level, strategic planning results in each division developing a tactical plan that matches the company's objectives. "I want to see how these more specific plans fit into our long-range objectives," says Patton. "That helps us create the vertical integration of our planning, to have a set of common ends we're all going after."

At King's, every tactical plan, regardless of where it originates, must address five issues: which objectives it aims to meet; the measurable outcomes, or what it will achieve; the time frame; the cost; and who will be held responsible. Department managers canvas their staffs to formulate plans, and Patton helps fine-tune them. Van Kirk has final veto power and monitors the results.

Van Kirk says everything at King's Medical comes back to three questions: How does the tactical plan—the proposed activity—fit with company goals? Where does this department want to be in the future? And how do you know when it has gotten there? Perhaps ironically, Van Kirk also feels the emphasis on planning makes the company more flexible. Changes in the marketplace that in the past might have led to a ruinous change can be avoided, because the vision or broad direction spelled out in the plan remains intact. "The key," Van Kirk says, "is keeping on track."

Source: Leslie Brokaw, "The Secrets of Great Planning," *Inc.*, October 1992, 51.

Situation Analysis

Situation analysis plays a central role in strategic planning. A strategic plan's purpose is to balance the internal strengths and weaknesses of a company with its external opportunities and threats. The purpose of situation analysis is to assess the

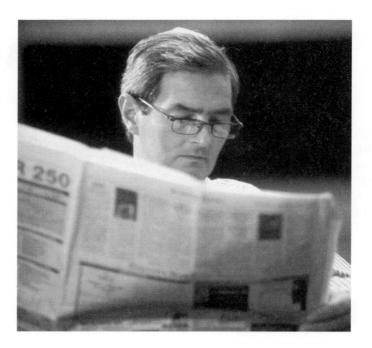

Foreign editions have offered new geographic markets to many international publications with growth strategies, like *The Wall Street Journal.*

internal features of and external forces on a company that will most directly affect its strategic options and opportunities.[12] Strategy management experts have devised several situation-analysis aids, including SWOT analysis, environmental scanning, and benchmarking.

SWOT Analysis

SWOT analysis is a technique for summarizing a company's *s*trengths, *w*eaknesses, *o*pportunities, and *t*hreats. SWOT analysis is used to list and consolidate information regarding the firm's external opportunities and threats, and internal strengths and weaknesses. As illustrated in Figure 6.4, potential strengths typically include adequate financial resources, economies of scale, and proprietary technology. Potential internal weaknesses include lack of strategic direction, obsolete facilities, and lack of managerial depth and talent.

Formulating a strategic plan is largely a process of identifying strategies or strategic actions that will balance (1) these strengths and weaknesses with (2) the company's external opportunities and threats. Opportunities might include the possibility of serving additional customers (market penetration), the chance to enter new markets or segments (market development), or falling trade barriers in attractive foreign markets. Threats might include the likely entry of new lower-cost foreign competitors, rising sales of substitute products, and slowing market growth. The manager considers all such facts, summarizes them on the four quarters of a SWOT chart, and uses this information to help develop a corporate strategy and then (as we'll see) a competitive strategy based on his or her analysis.

The Environmental Scan

The external environment of an organization is defined as the set of forces with which that organization interacts.[13] These external forces include all those things—like economic trends, regulatory policies and laws, and competitors' actions—that may influence a company by providing an opportunity for it to expand or a threat

■ FIGURE 6.4
Examples of a
Company's Strengths,
Weaknesses,
Opportunities, and
Threats

POTENTIAL STRENGTHS
- Market leadership
- Strong research and development
- High-quality products
- Cost advantages
- Patents

POTENTIAL WEAKNESSES
- Large inventories
- Excess capacity for market
- Management turnover
- Weak market image
- Lack of management depth

POTENTIAL OPPORTUNITIES
- New overseas markets
- Falling trade barriers
- Competitors failing
- Diversification
- Economy rebounding

POTENTIAL THREATS
- Market saturation
- Threat of takeover
- Low-cost foreign competition
- Slower market growth
- Growing government regulation

to which it must plan to react. **Environmental scanning** means obtaining and compiling information about those environmental forces that might be relevant to the company's strategic planners.

In general, six key areas of the company's environment are "scanned" to identify the environmental forces or factors that may represent areas of concern, or represent opportunities or threats.

1. *Economics:* These are factors related to the level of economic activity and to the flow of money, goods and services, information, and energy. For example, recently there has been a trend for people living in Asia to hoard more of their money in gold and gold items. What opportunities and threats would such a trend imply, for instance, for bankers or for companies in the business of selling gold items?

2. *Politics:* These are factors related to the use or allocation of political power among people, including dealings with local, national, and foreign governments. For example, major cigarette manufacturers like R. J. Reynolds must closely monitor trends in the regulation of cigarette smoking around the globe.

3. *Social trends and demographics:* These are factors that affect and reflect the way people live, including what they value. In the United States, for instance, the proportion of people who are Hispanic is rising quickly: What impact might such trends have on major advertising companies and on makers of consumer products?

4. *Technology:* This category includes all those factors related to the development of new or existing technology, including electronics, machines, tools, processes, and know-how in general. Several years ago, Microsoft's Bill Gates noticed that the Internet's explosive growth provided both opportunities and threats to his company. The threat lay in the possibility that computer users might increasingly rely on the Internet itself for computer processing and thus need less-sophisticated personal computers and Microsoft programs. The opportunity lay in the possibility of linking more and more Microsoft programs directly to the Internet, thus making Microsoft, instead of competitors like Netscape, the gateway to the Internet.

5. *Competition:* Included here are all those factors that involve actions taken or possibly taken by current and potential competitors, as well as related questions regarding, for instance, market share. For example, the trend toward increased consolidation in the airline industry, as evidenced by American Airline's partnership with British Air, is driving more and more airlines such as Delta and Continental to consider partnerships or mergers.

6. *Geography:* This includes factors related to topography, climate, natural resources, and so forth. In the state of Florida, for instance, an apparent long-term cooling trend has reduced the growing area for oranges, so that "Florida oranges" now increasingly come from South America.

Managers in practice use several techniques to gather this sort of information—to "scan" their environments, in other words. Premise-building techniques like forecasting, marketing research, and competitive intelligence (discussed in chapter 5) are certainly useful. Several experts also conclude that "experience shows that environmental scanning is most productive when it consists of a brainstorming session by a group."[14] (We discussed brainstorming in chapter 4.) Benchmarking, to which we now turn, can also provide useful input here.

Benchmarking

Sometimes it is important to build plans and strategies based on a knowledge of the very best that your competitors and others have to offer. **Benchmarking** is a process in which a company learns how to become the best in one or more areas by carefully analyzing the practices of other companies who excel in that practice. For example, numerous manufacturers come to the Saturn car company plant in Springhill, Tennessee, in order to study the human resource management practices that have created a unique partnership between management and labor.

The basic benchmarking process typically adheres to several guidelines:[15]

1. Focus on a specific problem and define it carefully. For example, a specific problem might be, "What order-fulfillment technology do best-practices companies use in the mail-order business?" (Best-practice companies are those that are widely agreed to excel in a particular process or practice. For instance, L. L. Bean is viewed as a best-practice company for the way it expeditiously and courteously answers prospective customers' questions and fulfills their orders.)

2. Use the employees who will actually implement those changes in your company to identify the best-practices companies and to conduct the on-site studies of their best practices. For example, companies interested in benchmarking the best order-fulfillment technology might plan visits to L. L. Bean and Dell Computers. Having employees who will actually implement the best practices do the study can help ensure their commitment to the changes.

3. Studying best practices is a two-way street, so be willing to share information with others.

4. Avoid sensitive issues such as pricing, and don't look for new product information.

5. Keep information you receive confidential.

Types of Strategies

There are three main types of strategies, as summarized in Figure 6.5. Many companies consist of a portfolio of several businesses. For instance the PepsiCo Corporation includes Pepsi, Frito-Lay, and Pizza Hut. These companies therefore need a corporate-level strategy. A **corporate-level strategy** identifies the portfolio of businesses that will comprise the corporation, and the ways in which these businesses will relate to each other.

Each of these businesses (such as Pizza Hut) then has its own business level/competitive strategy. A **competitive strategy** identifies how to build and strengthen the business' long-term competitive position in the marketplace.[16] It identifies, for instance, how Pizza Hut will compete with Domino's or how Microsoft will compete with Netscape.

Each business is in turn comprised of departments, such as manufacturing, marketing, and HR. **Functional strategies** identify the basic courses of action that each of the business' functional departments will pursue to contribute to attaining the business' competitive goals. We'll look at each type of strategy in turn.

Corporate-Level Strategies

Every company must choose the number of businesses in which it will compete and the relationships that will exist among those businesses. These decisions are driven by the firm's corporate-level strategy, which identifies the portfolio of business that will comprise the company. Companies can pursue one or more of the following standard or "generic" corporate strategies when deciding what businesses to be in and how these businesses should relate to each other.

CONCENTRATION. A concentration/single business corporate strategy means the company focuses on one product or product line, usually in one market. Organizations that have successfully pursued a single-business strategy include McDonald's, Kentucky Fried Chicken, and WD-40 Company, makers of the spray lubricant.

A concentration strategy has pros and cons. The main advantage is that the company can focus its strengths on the one business it knows well, allowing it to do that one thing better than competitors (for instance, Gerber's baby foods stresses

■ **FIGURE 6.5**
Relationships among Strategies in Multiple-Business Firms
Companies typically formulate three types of strategies. Corporate strategies identify the mix of business in which the firm will engage. The business level/competitive strategies identify how each of the firm's businesses will compete; and each business then has several functional strategies identifying how the unit's manufacturing, sales, and other functions will contribute to the business' strategy.

that "baby foods are our only business"). The main disadvantage is the risk inherent in putting all one's eggs into one basket. Therefore, concentrators must always be on the lookout for signs of decline. McDonald's Corporation, after years of concentrating in the hamburger franchise business, tried (unsuccessfully) to diversify into franchising children's play areas in covered shopping malls.

Concentrating in a single line of business need not mean that the firm won't try to grow. Indeed, some traditional concentrators like the Coca-Cola Company have achieved very high growth rates through concentration.

Four strategies can contribute to such growth.[17] Single business companies can grow through **market penetration.** This means taking steps to boost sales of present products by more aggressively selling and marketing into the firm's current markets. **Geographic expansion** is another strategic growth alternative. *The Wall Street Journal* has achieved above average growth rates while concentrating on its traditional business by aggressively expanding into new geographic markets, both domestic and overseas. Growth can also be achieved through **product development,** which means developing improved products for current markets with the goal of maintaining or boosting growth. **Horizontal integration,** acquiring ownership or control of competitors who are competing in the same or similar markets with the same or similar products, is another option. For example, the Humana hospital chain has grown rapidly while remaining a concentrator by acquiring hundreds of hospitals.

VERTICAL INTEGRATION. Instead of staying in one business, a firm can expand into other businesses through a strategy of vertical integration. **Vertical integration** means owning or controlling the inputs to the firm's processes and/or the channels through which the firm's products or services are distributed. (The former is backward integration, while the latter is forward integration.) Thus, Ford owns Libby-Owens glass, which supplies it with windshields; major oil companies like Shell not only drill and produce their own oil but also sell it through company-controlled outlets.

DIVERSIFICATION. **Diversification** means a strategy of expanding into related or unrelated products or market segments.[18]

Diversifying helps to move the organization into other businesses or industries or perhaps just into new product lines. In any case, it helps the firm avoid the problem of having all its eggs in one basket by spreading risk among several products or markets. However, diversification adds a new risk of its own: It forces the organization and its managers to split their attentions and resources among several products or markets instead of one. To that extent, diversification may undermine the firm's ability to compete successfully in its chosen markets.

Several forms of diversification are widely used. **Related diversification** means diversifying into other industries in such a way that a firm's lines of business still possess some kind of fit.[19] When women's-wear maker Donna Karan expanded into men's clothing, that was related diversification. When Campbell's Soup purchased Pepperidge Farm Cookies, it did so because it felt that Pepperidge Farm's customer base and channels of distribution were a good fit, related to its own.

Conglomerate diversification, in contrast, means diversifying into products or markets that are *not* related to the firm's present businesses or to one another. For example, Getty Oil diversified into pay television, and several years ago, Mobil Oil Company purchased (and then sold) the Montgomery Ward retail chain.

STATUS QUO STRATEGIES. Unlike other growth-oriented strategies, a stability or status-quo strategy indicates that the organization is satisfied with its rate of growth and product scope. Operationally, this means it plans to retain its present strategy and, at the corporate level, to continue focusing on its present products and markets for the foreseeable future.

INVESTMENT REDUCTION STRATEGIES. Whether due to over-expansion, ill-conceived diversification, or some other financial emergency, investment reduction and defensive strategies are corrective actions. They are taken to reduce the company's investments in one or more of its lines of business. For example Delta Airlines, when suffering from route over-expansion because of its purchase of Pan Am, made the first employee cutbacks in its history.

Several options are available to reduce investment. **Retrenchment** means the reduction of activity or operations. IBM engaged in a massive retrenchment effort, dramatically reducing (downsizing) its number of employees and closing a multitude of facilities. **Divestment** means selling or liquidating individual businesses. (Divestment usually denotes the sale of a viable business, while liquidation denotes the sale or abandonment of a nonviable one.) The OB in Action feature illustrates some of the behavioral drawbacks of downsizing a company.

Organizational Behavior in Action

DOWNSIZING HITS MORALE AT U.S. WEST

Staff reductions can boost efficiency, but they can also hurt morale among employees who remain.

U.S. West Communications, Inc., is one of many companies that have felt the double-edged blade of downsizing. Facing competitive pressure that resulted from a changing marketplace and changing technology, U.S. West began reducing its staff in 1989. In 1993, it announced further cuts that amounted to 14 percent of its 63,000-person workforce over three years. Altering operations made streamlining possible, but eliminating so many people made those workers who stayed behind fearful of losing their jobs.

U.S. West faced the problem squarely. The company clearly spelled out its future direction, and employees were informed about their prospects. Teams were formed to encourage worker involvement. With goals—and the methods of achieving them—clearly defined, workers were instilled with the sense that they once again had control of their own destinies. An investment in employee development and education helped to facilitate worker involvement and increase productivity. Having met the morale problems of downsizing, U.S. West addressed them. It now relies on a committed workforce that understands company goals and will take personal responsibility for achieving them.[20]

STRATEGIC ALLIANCES AND JOINT VENTURES. Sometimes the advantages of a corporate strategy can be obtained by forming a partnership with another company, rather than by growing internally. In such cases, strategic alliances and joint ventures are corporate strategic options. As we noted in chapter 2, either term generally refers to a formal agreement between two or more separate companies, the purpose of which is to enable the organizations to benefit from complementary strengths. For example, a small cash-poor Florida-based company with a patented industrial pollution control filter might form a European joint venture with a subsidiary of a major European oil firm. In this case, the joint venture might be a separate corporation based in Europe to which each partner contributes funds and other resources. The oil firm gets access to a product that could revolutionize its distilling facilities; the filter company gets access to the oil firm's vast European marketing network.[21]

Managing Change

THE VIRTUAL CORPORATION

For many firms encountering rapid change, the ultimate strategic alliance is the **virtual corporation,** "a temporary network of independent companies—suppliers, customers, even erstwhile rivals—linked by information technology to share skills, costs, and access to one another's markets."[22] Virtual corporations don't have headquarters staffs or organization charts or the organizational trappings (like HR departments) that we associate with traditional corporations. In fact, virtual corporations are not "corporations" at all, in the traditional sense of common ownership or a chain of command. Instead, virtual corporations are networks of companies, each of which lends the virtual corporation/network its special expertise. Information technology (computer information systems, fax machines, electronic mail, and so on) then helps the virtual corporations' often far-flung company constituents stay in touch and quickly carry out their contributions.[23] When managed correctly, the individual contributors to a virtual corporation aren't merely impersonal suppliers or marketers. Instead, successful virtual corporation-relationships are built on trust and on a sense of "co-destiny." This means that the fate of each partner and of the virtual corporation's whole enterprise is dependent on each partner's doing its share.[24]

Virtual corporations of some significance exist today. For example, AT&T called on Japan's Marubeni Trading Company to help it link up with Matsushita Electronic Industrial Company when it wanted to speed production of its Safari notebook computer (itself designed by Henry Dreyfuss Associates).[25] Unable to produce its entire line of PowerBook notebooks, Apple turned to Sony Corporation to manufacture one version, thus merging Sony's miniaturization manufacturing skills (its core competencies) with Apple's easy-to-use software.[26]

Similarly, when start-up company TelePad came up with an idea for a hand-held, pen-based computer, a virtual corporation was its answer for breathing life into the idea: An industrial design firm in Palo Alto, California, designed the product; Intel brought in engineers to help with some engineering details; several firms helped develop software for the product; and a battery maker collaborated with TelePad to produce the power supply.[27] ■

The Entrepreneurs in Action feature (page 189) shows how one entrepreneurial company used a virtual corporation to grow into a major firm.

CORPORATE STRATEGY PORTFOLIO ANALYSIS TOOLS. In formulating a corporate strategy, how do you decide which businesses to keep in the portfolio?

Entrepreneurs in Action

KINGSTON TECHNOLOGY AND THE VIRTUAL CORPORATION

John Tu and David Sun, cofounders of Kingston Technology, do business on a handshake, seldom use contracts, and have never hired a lawyer.

Kingston, located in Fountain Valley, California, is a world leader in upgrading personal computers. Sales in 1992 were $240 million, up from $140 million the year before, and would soon double. Tu and Sun took a look at how the huge, diversified companies of the United States were run, and their reaction was, "No, thank you." Instead they created a virtual corporation, a network of independent company partners working together in complementary roles. They share capital and know-how and still enjoy economies of scale that smaller firms can't match.

Here's an example of how it works. Early one week, a Los Angeles ComputerLand store phoned Kingston. It had an order from a bank for 100 IBM PC's with extra memory and other upgrades. Within hours, Kingston had designed the upgrade system and passed the specs along to a principal partner, Express Manufacturing. Express filled the order and sent it back before the end of the day. Kingston checked everything out and shipped the order, via Federal Express, to ComputerLand the same day. The bank had its new system in place before the weekend. "You've heard of just-in-time inventory?" asks Sun. "This is just-in-time manufacturing."

Both Kingston and Express work with other companies, but they maintain a primary commitment to one another. "You always have to think of your partners. They are there when we need them, and we are there when they need us." And that's the essence of a virtual corporation.

David Sun (left) and John Tu used commitment and know-how in the strategy that built Kingston Technology, their successful virtual corporation.

SOURCE: Michael Meyer, "Here's a Virtual Model for America's Industrial Giants," *Newsweek,* 23 August 1993, 40.

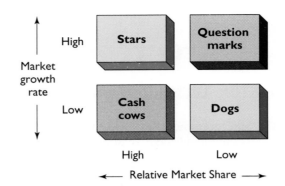

■ FIGURE 6.6
BCG Matrix
Once the position of each of the company's businesses is plotted, a decision can be made regarding which business will be cash sources and which will be cash users.

Several portfolio analysis aids are used to help managers decide. These include the BCG Matrix and GE Business Screen.

The *BCG Matrix,* developed by the Boston Consulting Group (BCG), helps to identify the relative attractiveness of each of a firm's businesses. As in Figure 6.6, it compares business growth rate and relative competitive position (market share) for each of the company's businesses. Each business is usually placed in a quadrant and represented by a circle proportional to the size of the business.

Once all businesses have been plotted on the matrix, a decision can be made as to whether each one is a "star," "question mark," "cash cow," or "dog," to use the technique's terminology. **Stars** are businesses in high-growth industries in which the company has a high relative market share. For example, Intel's microprocessor business (microprocessors are the heart of computers such as IBM's pentium-driven PC's) has a high growth rate, and Intel has a relatively high market share. Star businesses usually require large infusions of cash to sustain growth. However, they generally have such a strong market position that much of the needed cash can be generated from sales and profits.

Question marks are businesses in high-growth industries, but with low market shares. These business units (such as the computer business started by Exxon Oil several years ago) face a dilemma: They are in attractive high-growth industries, but they have such low market shares that they lack the clout to fend off larger competitors. The company must either divert cash from its other businesses to boost the question-mark business' market share or get out of the business.

Cash cows are businesses in low-growth industries that enjoy high relative market shares. Their being in a low-growth, unattractive industry argues against making large cash infusions into these businesses. However, their high market share generally allows them to generate high sales and profits for years, even without much new investment. Cash cows can thus be good cash generators for the company's question-mark businesses.

Finally, **dogs** are low-market-share businesses in low-growth, unattractive industries. Having a low market share puts the business in jeopardy relative to its larger competitors. As a result, dogs can quickly become "cash traps," absorbing cash to support a hopeless and unattractive situation. They are usually sold to raise cash for stars and question marks.

The *GE Business Screen,* shown in Figure 6.7, is another strategic portfolio analysis aid. This is a nine-cell matrix originally used by GE to analyze its own business portfolio. Each company is plotted into the appropriate cell according to its (1)

■ FIGURE 6.7 Company Position/Industry Attractiveness (GE) Screen

SOURCE: Michael Porter, *Competitive Strategy: Techniques for Analyzing Industries and Competitors* (New York: The Free Press, 1980), 365.

industry attractiveness and (2) business unit position. Industry attractiveness (as illustrated) reflects criteria such as industry size, market growth, and industry profitability. Business unit position reflects criteria such as relative size, market share, and profitability.

Like the BCG matrix, the GE Business Screen focuses on whether or not the company will boost or reduce its investment in each business. For this reason, it is also called the GE Stop Light Strategy. As in the upper left of Figure 6.7, businesses in attractive industries that are relatively strong competitors justify further investment and a growth strategy like market development. Businesses in the purple cells in the lower right of the matrix no longer deserve investment: They either become cash cows or are divested. Those falling in the three blue (diagonal) cells need to be monitored for any changes in industry attractiveness or business strengths that might signal the need for increased or decreased investment.

Competitive Strategies

Whether a company decides to concentrate on a single business or to diversify into several different ones, it should develop competitive strategies for each of its businesses. Strategic planning expert Michael Porter defines competitive strategy as a plan to establish a profitable and sustainable competitive position against the forces that determine industry competition.[28] Basically, the competitive strategy specifies how the company will compete, for instance, based on low cost or high quality. Porter says three basic or generic competitive strategic options are possible: cost leadership, differentiation, and focus.

COST LEADER. Just about every company tries to hold down its costs. In this way, a company can price its products and services competitively. **Cost leadership** as a competitive strategy goes beyond this. A business that pursues a cost leadership competitive strategy is aiming to become *the* low-cost leader in an industry. The unique characteristic of the cost leadership strategy is its emphasis on obtaining absolute cost advantages from any and all possible sources. Wal-Mart is a typical industry cost leader. Distribution costs are minimized through a satellite-based warehousing system, store location costs are minimized by placing most stores on relatively low-cost land outside small- to medium-sized southern towns, and the stores themselves are not plush.

Pursuing a cost leadership competitive strategy requires a tricky balance between relentlessly pursuing lower costs and maintaining acceptable quality. Southwest Airlines, for instance, manages to keep its cost per passenger mile below those of most other major airlines while still providing service as good as or better than those of its competitors.

DIFFERENTIATOR. In a **differentiation strategy,** a firm seeks to be unique in its industry along some dimensions that are valued by buyers.[29] In other words, it picks one or more attributes of the product or service that its buyers perceive as important, and then it positions itself to meet those needs. In practice, the dimensions along which a firm can differentiate itself range from the "product image" offered by some cosmetics firms, to concrete differences such as product durability as emphasized by Caterpillar Tractor. Similarly, Volvo stresses the safety of its cars, Apple stresses the usability of its computers, and Mercedes-Benz emphasizes reliability and quality. As Mercedes-Benz does, firms can usually charge a premium price if they successfully stake out their claim to being substantially different in some relevant way.

FOCUSER. Differentiators like Volvo and low-cost leaders like Wal-Mart generally aim their business at all or most potential buyers. In contrast, a business pursuing a **focus strategy** selects a market segment and builds its competitive strategy on serving the customers in its market niche better or more cheaply than its competitors. The basic question in choosing whether or not to pursue a focus competitive strategy is this: By focusing on a narrow market, can we provide our target cus-

Cost leadership is Wal-Mart's competitive strategy.

tomers with a product or service better or more cheaply than can our generalist competitors?

Examples of focusers abound. A Pea in the Pod, a chain of maternity stores, focuses on selling stylish clothes to pregnant working women. By specializing in "working woman maternity clothes," the company is able to provide a much wider range of such clothes to its target customers than those customers would find in generalist competitors such as Macy's or JCPenney.

Competitive Analysis: The Five Forces Model

To formulate a specific competitive strategy, the manager must understand the competitive forces that together determine how intense the industry's competitive rivalries are and how to best compete. Based on that analysis, the company then must find a sustainable **competitive advantage,** that is, a basis upon which to identify a relative superiority over competitors. Strategy expert Michael Porter argues that the way a company competes—its competitive strategy—depends largely on the nature and intensity of the competition in an industry. Thus, when competition was not so keen in the auto industry years ago, GM was not so concerned with competing on cost and quality.

Competitive intensity, says Porter, reflects five competitive forces, which are shown in Figure 6.8. The task in competitive analysis is to analyze these for the specific company. Management can then decide how best to compete in that industry. The major planning aid for conducting such an analysis is the Porter Five Forces Model shown in Figure 6.8.[30] We'll look at each of the five forces.

1. THREAT OF ENTRY. Intensity of industry competition depends first on the threat of new entrants to the industry. For instance, the competitive landscape for NBC, CBS, and ABC changed when Fox introduced a fourth network.

In general, the more easily new competitors can enter the business, the more intense the competition. However, several things can make it harder for new competitors to enter an industry. For example, it's not easy to enter the auto industry,

■ **FIGURE 6.8 Forces Driving Industry Competition**

SOURCE: Reprinted with the permission of The Free Press, a division of Simon & Schuster from *Competitive Strategy:Techniques for Analyzing Industries and Competitors* by Michael E. Porter. Copyright © 1980 by The Free Press.

where the investment in plant and equipment is high. Making it more expensive for customers to switch to a competitor is another entry barrier: For instance, once a travel agent signs up for American Airlines' computerized reservation system, it's expensive for that agent to switch to another system like Delta's.

2. INTENSITY OF RIVALRY AMONG EXISTING COMPETITORS. How intense is the rivalry among competitors? Rivalry among existing competitors manifests itself in tactics like price competition, advertising battles, and increased customer service.[31] Furthermore, the rivalry in some industries is more intense and warlike than it is in others. For example, for many years the rivalry among law firms and CPA firms could be characterized as cordial. More recently, it has turned quite cutthroat. This in turn has motivated many law firms to emphasize efficiency and to offer special pricing plans to clients.

3. PRESSURE FROM SUBSTITUTE PRODUCTS. Intensity of competition also depends on the availability of substitute products. For example, frozen yogurt is a substitute for ice cream, and rayon is a substitute for cotton. Like these examples, substitute products perform the same or similar functions. The more substitute products, then, in effect, the more competitive the industry. To the extent that few substitutes are available (as would be the case with certain patented heart medicines), rivalry is reduced and the industry is more attractive and less cutthroat to current competitors.

4. BARGAINING POWER OF BUYERS. The buyers' power is another factor contributing to intensity. For example, a buyer group is powerful if it purchases large volumes relative to the seller's sales: Toyota has a lot of clout with its suppliers, for instance. Similarly, when the products purchased are standard or undifferentiated (such as apparel elastic), and when buyers face few switching costs or earn low profits, then buyers' bargaining power (over suppliers) tends to be enhanced.

5. BARGAINING POWER OF SUPPLIERS. Finally, suppliers in turn can influence an industry's competitive intensity and attractiveness, for instance by threatening to raise prices or reduce quality. Several factors contribute to a supplier group's bargaining power. Suppliers tend to have greater bargaining power when they are dominated by a few firms and are more concentrated. Similarly, when few substitute products are available, when the buying industry is not an important customer of the supplier group, and when the supplier's product is an important input to the buyer's business, then the supplier's power rises.

APPLYING THE FIVE FORCES MODEL. Analyzing an industry using the five forces model helps a company choose competitive strategy options. For example, where rivalry among existing competitors is very intense or there is a real threat of new entrants, a competitive strategy of boosting product differentiation is a sensible option. That's one reason law firms now try to stress their differences, and why image-oriented advertising is important with cosmetics firms. Boosting switching costs (as American Airlines did when it convinced thousands of travel agents to use its SABER computerized reservation system) can also reduce rivals' (or new entrants') ability to compete, even when the product or service itself is fairly undifferentiated.

FORMULATING A COMPETITIVE STRATEGY: AN EXAMPLE. The success of Russ Leatherman and his colleagues at MovieFone illustrate how a smart entrepreneurial company put these competitive strategy ideas into practice. Leatherman dreamed up the idea for MovieFone in 1989, as an interactive telephone movie guide. Callers in many cities get complete up-to-the-minute listings of movie theaters and show times in their area and can even purchase tickets over the phone. Leatherman's task, once his firm was launched, was to build barriers to keep potential competitors like Ticketmaster at bay.

To build these competitive barriers, the MovieFone managers sought the following:

1. *Exclusivity*. For example, MovieFone acquired highly desirable phone numbers in each of its area codes, such as 777-FILM, and registered these as trademarks. The numbers make it easy for callers to remember and call MovieFone's lines, differentiating MovieFone and keeping competitors out.

2. *Focus*. By focusing on movie listings instead of branching out into other markets such as theaters or sporting events, MovieFone has become the industry expert when it comes to supplying movie listings and tickets. It knows its customers' profiles and has mastered the hardware, software, and logistics required to obtain, compile, and deliver listings and tickets better than anyone else.

3. *Expert systems*. MovieFone has developed what it calls expert systems comprising special hardware, software, and electronic "will-call windows" where customers can automatically pick up tickets. These systems further differentiate MovieFone and create substantial barriers to any new competitors that might be considering entering the market.

4. *Strategic alliances*. Many of the electronic "will-call windows" are placed in movie theaters, with which MovieFone has formed strategic alliances for this purpose. The alliance provides an additional source of income for the theaters and strengthens MovieFone's relationship with them.[32]

Organizational Behavior in Action

STRATEGY AND THE CEO'S PERSONALITY

Although managers certainly do use rational, analytical means to formulate strategies, it should come as no surprise that a top manager's values and personality may often have a prevailing effect on the strategy he or she chooses. For example, reports about various possible airlines mergers generally described Delta's top managers as cautious and conservative when making major strategic decisions, as opposed to American Airlines' more aggressive Robert Crandall.[33]

Sometimes the effects of the top manager's personal traits are subtle, and sometimes not. For example, when Stephen M. Wolf was CEO of United Airlines (and before that of several other carriers), he had all the planes painted a distinctive dark gray and blue. When he took over as chairman of U.S. Air, several commentators noted that if he took over any more U.S. airlines, the nation's entire fleet would soon all be the same colors.

Although the comments about Wolf were made in jest, they do underscore the important fact that the CEO's personality and values shape his or her perceptions and the actions that he or she takes. Building on this premise, two researchers, R. E. Miles and C. C. Snow, have found that there are four characteristic types of strategy makers, each of which pursues a characteristic strategy.[34]

These four types can be summarized as follows.

Defenders. Defender managers pursue concentrator/specialization strategies; their main aim seems to be to become the best at producing and marketing one specialized product or service. These top managers, not surprisingly, are highly expert in their organization's limited area of operation and do not search outside their traditional domains for new opportunities. Their personality and experience lead them to focus almost exclusively on improving the efficiency of their existing operations.

Prospectors. Prospectors run companies that are continually searching for new market opportunities and experimenting with new products and services. These managers are especially adept at finding product and market innovations, rather than at refining further efficiencies.

Analyzers. More cautious than prospectors are analyzers, who are unwilling to let new products overshadow their desire to maintain stable and efficient operations for their traditional products and services. They therefore try to combine (1) the efficiency advantage of defenders with (2) the innovation and new-product development advantage of prospectors, although the innate cautiousness of analyzers tends to make them emphasize efficiency when a choice needs to be made.

Reactors. Reactors run the most cautious companies of all. Top managers in these companies tend to pursue "status quo" strategies. Miles and Snow found that these types of managers frequently did perceive changes occurring in their environment, much as IBM's top managers saw the rapid growth of domestic and international PC clones rapidly eroding their markets in the 1980s. However, due either to their innate cautiousness or to misjudgments or some inadequacies in their management skills, top managers like these are unwilling or unable to respond effectively. They therefore continue to do business as usual even as the market for their goods undergoes profound changes.

Functional Strategies

At some point, each business' choice of competitive strategy (be it low-cost leader, differentiator, or focuser) is translated into supporting functional strategies for each of its departments to pursue. (Note that in some very large firms like GE, similar businesses are first grouped into strategic business units [SBUs] for control purposes. A **strategic business unit** is an organizational entity that contains several related businesses. For instance, the forest products SBU at a firm might include separate fine papers, newsprint, and pulp businesses.)

A **functional strategy** is the basic course or courses of action that each department is to follow in enabling the business to accomplish its strategic goals. For example, Wal-Mart has chosen to compete as the industry's low-cost leader. In order to implement this competitive strategy, it had to formulate departmental functional strategies that made sense in terms of moving Wal-Mart toward its desired position as low-cost leader. Thus, the distribution department pursued a strategy (satellite-based warehousing) that ultimately drove distribution costs down to a minimum; the company's land development department found locations that fit the firm's customer profile and kept construction costs to a minimum; and the merchandise buyers found sources that were capable of providing good quality merchandise at the lowest possible prices. Notice that functional strategies cannot be formulated intelligently unless the business has a clear direction in terms of the competitive strategy it wants to pursue. Then those functional strategies must "fit" the competitive strategy.

Implementing the Strategy

Formulating a strategic plan is just the first part of the strategy management process. Whether at the corporate or competitive level, the strategy must then be implemented. Implementation requires several things, including (1) achieving a strategic "fit" between the strategy and the company's functional activities, (2) leveraging the firm's core competencies, and (3) providing the top management leadership required to implement the plan.

Achieving "Strategic Fit"

Strategic planning expert Michael Porter says that managers can't just formulate a competitive strategy and expect it to be implemented. Instead, all the firm's activities must also be tailored to or "fit" that strategy, because this is how firms create competitive advantage. As he says, "All differences between companies in cost or price derive from the hundreds of activities required to create, produce, sell, and deliver their products or services, such as calling on customers, assembling final products, and training employees. Cost is generated by performing activities, and cost advantage arises from performing particular activities more efficiently than competitors."[35]

Let's look at an example.[36] Southwest Airlines is a low-cost leader that "tailors all its activities to deliver low-cost convenient service on its particular type of short-haul route."[37] By getting fast, fifteen-minute turnarounds at the gate, Southwest can keep its planes flying longer hours than rivals and have more departures with fewer aircraft. It also shuns the frills like meals, assigned seats, and premium classes of service on which other full-service airlines build their own competitive strategies.

Figure 6.9 illustrates the idea that its successful competitive strategy is the result of activities that all "fit both each other and Southwest's low-cost competitive strategy." The heart of Southwest Airlines' low-cost activity system is shown in the darker circles. It includes limited passenger services; frequent reliable departures; lean, highly productive ground and gate crews; high aircraft utilization; very low ticket prices; and short-haul, point-to-point routes. However, note how each of these activities is itself the focal point of subsidiary activities and decisions that Southwest Airlines managers make. Limited passenger service means things like no meals, no seat assignments, no baggage transfers, and limited use of travel agents. Lean, highly productive ground and gate crews require high compensation of employees, flexible union contracts, and a high level of employee stock ownership. Together, these activities combine to create a successful low-cost strategy.

Ideally, the relationship between competitive strategy and the firm's activities is reciprocal. In formulating the strategy, the manager considers the company's unique "core competencies" or strengths and weaknesses, such as a highly trained workforce. In the other direction, implementing the strategy then requires managing every activity so that it contributes to achieving the competitive strategy.[38]

Achieving strategic fit is important at the corporate strategy level, too. For example, consider McDonald's competitive strategy of expanding overseas. Pursuing this strategy meant that employees with knowledge and skills in the new markets had to be recruited and trained, and that new reward systems were needed to

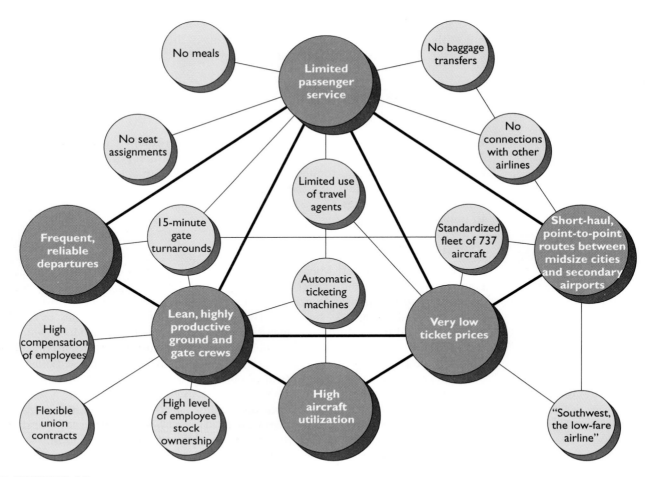

■ FIGURE 6.9
Southwest Airlines'
Activity System
NOTE: Companies like
Southwest tailor all their
activities so that they "fit"
and contribute to making
their strategies a
reality.

SOURCE: Reprinted by permission of *Harvard Business Review.*
"Southwest Airlines' Activity
System." From "What Is Strategy?" by Michael E. Porter, November–December 1996.
Copyright © 1996 by the President and Fellows of Harvard
College; all rights reserved.

inspire and motivate employees (for instance, to move overseas). For finance and accounting, it meant that control systems had to be modified to control what were now far-flung facilities around the globe. Entrepreneurs must also implement strategies, and the accompanying Entrepreneurs in Action feature explains how successful entrepreneurs do so.

Strategy as Stretch and Leverage

Strategy experts Gary Hamel and C. K. Prahalad caution that in planning and implementing strategy, firms should not be preoccupied with strategic fit, however.[39] They agree that every company "must ultimately effect a fit between its resources and the opportunities it pursues."[40] However, they argue that a preoccupation with fit can unnecessarily limit a company's growth. In practice, the concept of "stretch" should supplement that of "fit." Hamel and Prahalad argue that leveraging resources—supplementing what you have, and doing all that's possible, or more, with what you have—can be more important than just fitting the strategic plan to the firm's current resources.

For example, "if modest resources were an insurmountable deterrent to future leadership, GM, Phillips, and IBM would not have found themselves on the defensive with Honda, Sony, and Compaq."[41] Similarly, K-Mart would not have found

Entrepreneurs in Action

HOW ENTREPRENEURS CRAFT STRATEGIES

As one planning expert recently put it, "However popular it may be in the corporate world, a comprehensive analytical approach to planning doesn't suit most start-ups. Entrepreneurs typically lack the time and money to interview a representative cross-section of potential customers, let alone analyze substitutes, reconstruct competitors' cost structures, or project alternative technology scenarios."

As we've seen, this scarcity of time and money does not mean that entrepreneurs don't plan and don't have strategies. However, it does mean that they often take an abbreviated approach to planning and to creating a strategy for their firms. For example, interviews with the founders of 100 of the fastest-growing private companies in the United States and research on 100 other thriving ventures suggests that entrepreneurs use the following three general guidelines in formulating their strategies.

1. *Screen out losers quickly.* Entrepreneurs typically generate lots of ideas for new products and services, but successful entrepreneurs know how to quickly discard those that have low potential. This decision requires judgment and reflection rather than new data, as illustrated in Figure 6.10, on page 200.

Notice that entrepreneurs usually get ideas for their businesses by replicating or modifying an idea encountered in their previous employment. For example, apparel designer Ralph Lauren reportedly got the kernel of his idea for classic men's and women's wear when he began his career as a salesperson with Brooks Brothers. Notice also that only about 4 percent of entrepreneurs report discovering the ideas for their businesses by unearthing new data through systematic research for opportunities.

2. *Minimize the resources devoted to researching ideas.* With limited resources, entrepreneurs can obviously do only as much planning and analysis as seem useful; they then make subjective judgment calls, sometimes based on very limited data. Says this planning expert:

> In setting their analytical priorities, entrepreneurs must recognize that some critical uncertainties cannot be resolved through more research. For example, focus groups and surveys often have little value in predicting demand for products that are truly novel.

3. *Don't wait for all the answers, and be ready to change course.* Large corporations often make a clear distinction between planning and execution, and in established companies this can make sense. For example, managers in large companies must be concerned with "fit" and in particular with whether the proposed strategy fits, or can be made to fit, the company's existing activities.

However, entrepreneurs often start with a clean slate, so they "don't have to know all the answers before they act." In a sense, many entrepreneurs change the traditional motto "Ready, aim, fire" to "Ready, fire, aim." They try a product or service based on the most preliminary market data and then quickly move to drop or modify the product if it doesn't click with the customers. (Although it is not your traditional small start-up, consider how the Boston Chicken restaurant chain changed its business to Boston Market within six months when initial feedback from its first few stores suggested the need to offer more products.)

SOURCES: Amar Bhide, "How Entrepreneurs Craft Strategies that Work," *Harvard Business Review,* March–April 1994, 150–160. Unfortunately, one recent study suggests that about two-thirds of entrepreneurs—at least owners of family businesses—do not have written strategic plans. See "Planning Lessons from Family Business Owners," *Infoseek/Reuters,* 26 March 1997.

itself overtaken by Wal-Mart. Companies, they say, can **leverage** their resources, for instance, by concentrating them more effectively on key strategic goals. Thus, Wal-Mart focused its relatively limited resources on building its satellite-based distribution system and gained a competitive advantage that helped it overtake K-Mart.

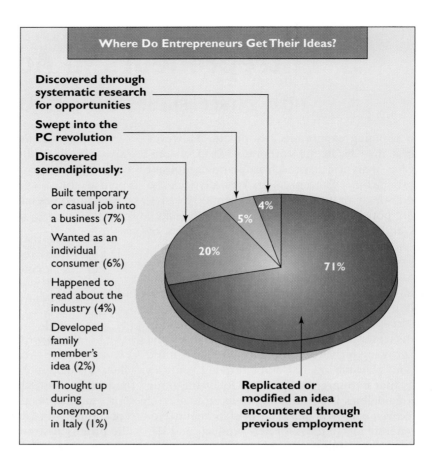

FIGURE 6.10
Most Entrepreneurs Get Most of Their Ideas for New Products by Modifying Existing Ideas They Had Gotten as Employees.

SOURCE: Reprinted by permission of *Harvard Business Review*. From "How Entrepreneurs Craft Strategies That Work." March–April 1994. Copyright © 1994 by the President and Fellows of Harvard College; all rights reserved.

Managing Change

THE STRATEGIC ROLE OF CORE COMPETENCIES

Hamel and Prahalad believe that it's a company's **core competencies** that should be leveraged. They define core competencies as "the collective learning in the organization, especially [knowing] how to coordinate diverse production skills and integrate multiple streams of technologies."[42]

Canon Corporation provides one example. Over the years it has developed three core competencies, in precision mechanics, fine optics, and micro-electronics. These core competencies reflect collective learning and skills that cut across traditional departmental lines. They result, for instance, from hiring and training in such a way as to create accumulated knowledge and experience in these three core competency areas.

Canon draws on its core competencies to produce core component products such as miniature electronic controls and fine lenses. Its businesses—its camera business, computer business, and fax business, for instance—are then built around such core products. The businesses use the core products to create end products such as electronic cameras, video still cameras, laser printers, and the laser fax.

"Growing" its businesses out of a handful of core competencies this way makes it easier for Canon's managers to quickly change its product mix. Regardless of how demand for products shifts—for instance from one type of fax machine to another—Canon's "eggs" aren't all in its products but in its core competencies of precision mechanics, fine optics, and micro-electronics. Canon can thus quickly sense changes in customer demand and reach across departmental lines to marshal its core competencies. For example, suppose Canon's managers sense the need for a tiny new consumer electronic product like a compact "fashion" camera. Its managers can reach across departmental lines and "harmonize know-how in miniaturization, microprocessor design, material science, and ultra thin precision casting—the same skills it applies in its miniature card calculators, pocket TVs, and digital watches—to design and produce the new camera."[43]

In 1996 the computer world was shown another example of how such an ability to "consolidate corporatewide technologies and production skills into competencies that empower individual businesses to adapt quickly to changing opportunities"[44] can work in practice. Microsoft, the giant of the PC operating system and computer software business, realized that its dominance was being challenged by Netscape. Microsoft saw that it was suddenly possible that the functions of Microsoft's software programs would be accomplished via the Internet rather than on an owner's PC.

Within a month or two, chairman Bill Gates reformulated his company's entire strategy, basically changing his company's mission to include making Microsoft the user's bridge to the Net (a position then held by Netscape). What transpired over the next few months was an extraordinary example of using core competencies to reorient a company's direction. Microsoft had emphasized hiring the brightest and most highly skilled programmers, who were, of course, spread throughout its various product divisions. Gates and his managers were able to reach across those divisions, putting together task forces whose skills became powerful new core competencies. The teams worked day and night, seven days a week, to create the "bridging" software that now permits users of Windows 95 (for instance) to access the Internet directly, without benefit of Netscape. Many of Microsoft's other products, including networking software and even learning and educational software, were similarly Internet linked. By the end of 1996, Microsoft was poised to take the lead in Internet browsing software and to regain its dominant position.

Achieving strategic fit and leveraging the firm's core competencies are just two elements in implementing the strategic plan. Providing top management leadership is also required, a point to which we now turn. ■

Organizational Behavior in Action

LEADERSHIP AND STRATEGIC CHANGE

The quality of the company's leadership will ultimately determine whether the new strategy succeeds or fails. Using core competencies and achieving fit are certainly important. Ultimately, however, each employee must be motivated to focus on and contribute to accomplishing the company's strategies, and for this effective leadership is required. **Leadership** may be defined as one person influencing another to work toward some predetermined objective.

Although leadership is explored more fully in chapter 10, several aspects of leadership particularly apply to implementing strategic change such as we have discussed in this chapter. These include the following.

PROVIDE A VISION. Leaders should provide a vision or dream of what the company can and will be, one that each employee can understand and link his or her activities to. For example, Raymond Gilmartin, CEO of medical equipment maker Bection Dickinson, knew his firm needed a way to encourage its employees to take the initiative and form teams to innovate and go after new business in new ways.[45] To keep employees and teams working toward the same goal, he laid out a broad vision to "develop innovative new products and beat the competition to the market with them." He then let his fifteen divisions and their employees develop their own business strategies to meet their individual needs. We'll see later that vision-setting is essential to what behavioral scientists today call transformational leadership. **Transformational leadership,** as discussed in chapter 10, is the process of influencing major changes in the attitudes and assumptions of organization members and building commitment for the organization's mission, objectives, and strategies.[46]

SET AND COMMUNICATE LIMITS.[47] Michael Porter points out that "deciding which target group of customers and needs the company should serve is fundamental to developing a strategy. But so is deciding *not* to serve other customers or needs and *not* to offer certain features or services." The leader therefore must set limits in order to channel his or her managers' decisions. Doing so involves (1) clarifying the company's business and mission, (2) teaching managers when to say "no" when something doesn't fit with that mission, and (3) providing the policies to ensure that managers have guidelines to follow (such as "fifteen-minute gate turnarounds" at Southwest Airlines).

COMMUNICATE THE STRATEGY. The leader also communicates the strategy (such as "minimizing costs by sticking with low-rent sites" at Wal-Mart). As Porter puts it, "one of the most important functions of an explicit communicated strategy is to guide employees in making choices. . . ."[48]

OVERCOME RESISTANCE TO CHANGE. A number of years ago social psychologist Kurt Lewin formulated a model of organizational change that emphasized what he called the need for "unfreezing" the organization. By unfreezing, he meant reducing the forces that are striving to maintain the status quo. Overcoming resistance to change is an important part of leading strategic change. Such resistance may stem from many sources, including a preference for a habitual way of doing things or a feeling that one's personal power or security is at stake. In any case, leaders can and should influence employees so that resistance is eliminated or at least reduced. In chapter 15 (Managing Organizational Change), we'll explain some techniques used to overcome resistance to change.

DEVELOP POLITICAL SUPPORT. A new strategy can threaten the balance of power in an organization, thus resulting in political conflicts and struggles.[49] For example, Louis Gerstner's strategy of downsizing IBM meant dismissing tens of thousands of long-term IBM employees. As chairman, Gerstner certainly was in a powerful position. However, as a shrewd leader, he also understood the wisdom of building political support for the downsizing strategy—among his top managers and other IBM board members, for instance.

MOTIVATE EMPLOYEES.   The most brilliant strategy is worthless unless the company's managers and employees are motivated to implement it. In chapter 12, we'll see that leaders use many techniques to motivate employees. One simple but powerful technique, say two change experts, is for the leader to convey "credible positive expectations" for the change, in terms of specific behavioral outcomes that the manager expects from his or her employees. Another is to express his or her confidence that the employees can achieve those outcomes.[50]

SUMMARY

1. A primary task of top management is to think through the mission of the business and ask the question "What is our business, and what should it be?" Strategic management is the process of identifying and pursuing the organization's mission by aligning the organization's internal capabilities with the external demands of its environment.

2. There are five steps in the strategy management process: define the business and develop a mission; translate the mission into strategic objectives; formulate a strategy to achieve the strategic objectives; implement the strategy; and evaluate performance and initiate corrective adjustments as required. Strategic planning includes the first three steps of this process.

3. A situation analysis assesses the internal and external features of a company that will most directly affect its strategic options and opportunities. Useful techniques here include SWOT analysis, environmental scanning, and benchmarking.

4. There are three main types of strategies. The corporate-level strategy identifies the portfolio of businesses that in total will comprise the corporation and the ways in which these businesses will relate to each other; the competitive strategy identifies how to build and strengthen the business's long-term competitive position in the marketplace; and functional strategies identify the basic courses of action that each of the business's functional departments will pursue to contribute to the attainment of its goals.

5. Each type of strategy contains specific standard or generic strategies. Generic corporate strategies include concentration, market penetration, geographic expansion, product development, horizontal integration, vertical integration, and diversification, as well as status quo and several retrenchment strategies. Portfolio analysis tools for formulating corporate strategy include the BCG Matrix and the GE Business Screen methods.

6. Generic competitive strategies include being a low-cost leader, differentiator, or focuser. Formulating a specific competitive strategy then requires understanding the competitive forces that determine how intense the competitive rivalries are and how best to compete. Useful here is the Porter Five Forces model. This model helps managers understand the five big forces of competitive pressure in an industry: threat of entry; intensity of rivalry among existing competitors; pressure from substitute products; bargaining power of buyers; and bargaining power of suppliers.

7. Implementing the organization's strategy involves several activities, among them achieving strategic fit, leveraging the company's core competencies, and effectively leading the change process.

KEY TERMS

strategic management
vision
mission statement
strategy
strategic control
strategic planning
SWOT analysis
environmental scanning
benchmarking
corporate-level strategy
competitive strategy
functional strategies
market penetration

geographic expansion
product development
horizontal integration
vertical integration
diversification
related diversification
conglomerate
  diversification
retrenchment
divestment
stars
question marks
cash cows

dogs
cost leadership
differentiation strategy
focus strategy
competitive advantage
functional strategy
leverage
core competencies
leadership
transformational
  leadership

SELF-TEST

TRUE / FALSE QUESTIONS

1 **T F** According to management expert Peter Drucker, the primary task of top management is thinking through the mission of the business, that is, asking the question: "What is our business and what should it be?"

2 **T F** Strategic management is the process of identifying and pursuing the organization's mission by aligning the organization's internal capacities with the external demands of government.

3 **T F** The first step in the strategic management process is to formulate a strategy to achieve the strategic objectives.

4 **T F** Once you have formulated a strategy, managing the strategy is a passive process.

5 **T F** SWOT analysis is a technique for evaluating a company's internal and external environment.

6 **T F** Companies that excel in a particular area of management are used by other companies as a benchmark for Total Quality Management.

7 **T F** Diversification is a strategy of expanding into related or unrelated products or market segments.

8 **T F** One of the major issues faced by any company downsizing its workforce is the morale problems created.

9 **T F** In the language of BCG's portfolio analysis tool, the BCG Matrix, question marks are businesses in low-growth industries which have high relative market shares.

10 **T F** A basic criterion of functional strategies is that they must "fit" the competitive strategy.

MULTIPLE-CHOICE QUESTIONS

1 Which of the following is the first step in the strategic management process?
a. Define the business and develop a mission.
b. Translate the mission into strategic objectives.
c. Formulate a strategy to achieve the strategic objectives.
d. Implement the strategy.

2 Which of the following does "S" stand for in the SWOT analysis?
a. strategy
b. symbols
c. strengths
d. stocks

3 Environmental _____ is a systematic method of obtaining and compiling information about those environmental forces that might be relevant to the company's strategic planners:
a. decision
b. scanning
c. surfing
d. brainstorming

4 According to strategic planning expert Michael Porter, there are three basic competitive strategic options. Which of the following is *not* one of them?
a. cost leadership
b. differentiation
c. focus
d. diffusion

5 Which of the following is *not* a way that single-business companies can grow?
  a. market penetration
  b. geographic expansion
  c. horizontal integration
  d. all the above are ways

6 Under the BCG Matrix, businesses in high-growth industries with high relative market share are called
  a. stars.
  b. question marks.
  c. cash cows.
  d. dogs.

7 According to Porter, competitive intensity reflects five competitive forces. Which of the following is *not* one noted by Porter?
  a. threat of entry
  b. pressure from substitute products
  c. lack of bargaining power of buyers
  d. intensity of rivalry among existing competitors

8 Of the four characteristic types of strategy makers identified by Miles and Snow, which characteristic describes managers who run companies that are continually searching for new market opportunities and experimenting with new products and services?
  a. defenders
  b. prospectors
  c. analyzers
  d. reactors

9 What strategy is described by the following: the basic course or courses of action that each department is to follow in enabling the business to accomplish its strategic goals?
  a. regional
  b. corporate
  c. functional
  d. none of the above

10 Leadership is key to effective strategic change. Which of the following is *not* a factor in providing leadership toward implementing strategic change?
  a. Provide a vision.
  b. Set and communicate the lack of limits.
  c. Communicate a strategy.
  d. Overcome resistance to change.

CRITICAL THINKING EXERCISES

1 You have just been appointed to a strategic planning committee for Apple Computer. You know the company has been having a difficult time with its strategies and you want to know why. Do some research on the history of Apple as well as its recent problems. (Both *Fortune* and *Business Week* have had many recent articles on Apple.) Using this information, apply the ideas, concepts, and approaches discussed in chapter 6 to develop a strategic plan for Apple to redesign itself and manage in an increasingly competitive environment.

2 Imagine an organization where everyone is involved in strategic planning. Seasoned managers are on committees with new employees so that the experience of the past can be blended with fresh impressions and new ideas. On other committees, retirees, customers, stockholders, and managers from all parts of the company participate. How might this approach challenge the traditional approaches to strategic planning? How might it create management problems as well as strengths?

EXPERIENTIAL EXERCISES

1 With three to four other students in the class, form a strategic management group for your college or university. In a two-hour time period, identify what "business" your college or university is in, where it is in terms of implementing a strategy, and where it needs to be strategically headed. Prior to meeting to develop your plan, look at what your college or university has developed in the way of a strategic plan by interviewing some administrators, faculty, and students about their knowledge of the strategic plan. From the information gathered, prepare a database for the other students to use assessing the strategy in a class "brainstorming" session.

2 Develop a personal strategic plan using the concepts presented in the chapter to guide you to the year 2008. Be prepared to discuss in class how this exercise might help position you to be competitive in an increasingly aggressive and global world environment. Use this exercise to question what your strategies are today in comparison to what they may need to be for you to succeed in the future.

DIVERSITY CASE

STRATEGIC MANAGEMENT AT AMIGOS CANNING COMPANY

During his more than 20 years in the Mexican food business, Amigos Canning Company CEO Ralph Velasco, Jr., has had to change strategic direction more than once. Soon after joining the San Antonio-based food producer in 1970, he helped engineer the switch from tortilla manufacturing to canning. Lots of diversification followed, and by the mid-1980s, the company founded by Velasco's father was producing a number of private-label canned food lines for major companies. In 1989, however, Amigos lost nearly $500,000, and Velasco began experiencing *déjà vu* all over again. He would have to redirect the company once more, and this time the entire business was at stake.

Before making a move, Velasco consulted with management and marketing experts. Smaller companies like Amigos are attracted to producing under the private labels of the food giants they contract with because no money is required for a sales force. The downside is hard price bargaining and an uncertain future. Big regional food distributors are frequently merged or bought, and past business relationships aren't always continued by new owners or managers. Together with the consultants, Velasco decided its strategy would be to market Amigo products under his own label.

Besides exhibiting an underdog's courage at a level that is seldom seen, Velasco made two other shrewd moves. He hired a seasoned national sales manager and gave him a substantial stake in the company. He also spent a considerable sum on an aluminized label that differentiated his primary product, bean dip.

Velasco recognized that dips had long been blithely regarded by big chip makers like Frito Lay and Borden's as merely a complementary item. Through consumer taste tests and careful quality control, he ensured that Amigos produced only the best. Velasco always considered himself a numbers man, so he took the process a step further. Because he didn't know who actually used Amigos products, he invested in finding out exactly which consumers were buying what products. The data helped him fine-tune the company's marketing strategy more effectively.

Perhaps not surprisingly, Velasco's next move is another new strategic objective. It will be a lot like the others, only more risky. After more market research to define his targets, he plans to launch more new product lines.

Questions

1. Using the five-step process outlined in the chapter, how does the strategic management approach Velasco took in 1989 compare?
2. How did Amigos' corporate-level strategy change over the years?
3. In what ways did and could Velasco take advantage of the United States' increased diversity in formulating his new strategy?

SOURCE: Rick Mendosa, "Amigos Canning Company," *Hispanic Business.*

STRATEGY CASE

FROM SMALL REGIONAL AIRLINE TO GLOBAL COMPANY

How do you make a regional airline with annual revenues of $10 million into an international carrier making $3 billion a year? For Canadian Airlines, the answer lies in an entrepreneurial culture that encourages risk-taking, finds opportunities in problems, permits failure, and supports an action-oriented environment.

When large Canadian air carriers moved from a downtown airport, leaving it nearly vacant and its commuters facing a long ride to the new terminal, small Pacific Western Airlines started a new air shuttle. It was an instant success. When a large carrier abandoned a specific air route, PWA stepped in. In one instance, flight attendants designed their own outfits, and everyone became part of a sales team. To expand their routes, employee and management teams traveled all over the world looking for revenue-generating ideas.

In 1984, Canada deregulated its airline industry and gave PWA more room to maneuver. The company restructured its fleet, purchased Canadian Pacific Air Lines, and grew from fewer than 3,000 employees to a combined workforce of 13,000. Although the new Canadian Airlines faced financial restructuring, rising oil costs, and disrupted routes, the carrier's entrepreneurial model is one way to prosper in unsettled times.

Questions

1. What strategies helped the airline grow?
2. What strategies can keep the firm entrepreneurial?
3. Conduct a SWOT analysis of Canadian Air's strategic future.

SOURCE: Rhys Eyton, "Making Innovation Fly," *Business Quarterly,* Autumn 1996, 59–64.

ENTREPRENEURIAL CASE

HARRISON PRODUCTS AND THE QUESTION OF ALLIANCES

Edward Harrison and his management team had some important strategic decisions to make. While the company had the best products on the market for filtering poisonous gases from special chemical processes, its marketing efforts were limited by its small size and the enormous clout of some of its bigger competitors. While competitors like Dow Chemical might not have superior products, they did have global sales networks, and their salespeople generally overwhelmed the meager efforts of the independent sales reps who represented Harrison Products.

Over the past two months, however, something interesting had been happening at Harrison. Officers of three separate competitors had met with Edward Harrison and his management team. Each of these officers basically made the same pitch, which was as follows: "We now offer many types of filters but want to fill in the holes in our product line by adding your excellent sophisticated filters. However, if you go into partnership with us it must be on an exclusive basis, so you won't be able to sell through anyone else—we'll do all your marketing for you. A big advantage for you and for us is that we'll become a one-stop shop: Unlike your small company, we can provide not just filters but the entire housing and piping that goes into the installation."

Edward and his management team had some decisions to make.

Questions

1 Assuming these suitors want to create, as they say, "one-stop shops," what sort of corporate strategies are they really recommending for Harrison Products?
2 Use Porter's Five Forces model to try to develop a competitive strategy that you think would work for Harrison if it decided not to form a partnership with one of the three larger firms.
3 Based on this brief case incident, and on whatever you may know about environmental protection and pollution control trends, complete an environmental scan for Harrison Products. Explain what implications your conclusions might hold for Edward Harrison and his management team.

THE BUSINESS TEAM, INC.

CAN PEPSI WIN?

As the Business Team sits at their round conference table drinking sodas, Ruth brings up an issue now near to her heart. She has just become engaged to Jake, who works for PepsiCo. Jake is worried about his new job. Coke's CEO Robert Goizueta has created more wealth for shareholders than any CEO in history with the single focused strategy of making Coke *the* domestic and international drink. On the other hand, Pepsi is a conglomerate with domestic and international drinks; restaurants such as Taco Bell, KFC, and Pizza Hut; domestic and international snacks; and bottling operations. While Coke has been focused on selling Coke, Pepsi has diversified, pouring billions of dollars into other capital-intensive businesses. Some think Pepsi has lost the cola wars, both here and overseas.

Jake wants the team's advice about what strategic help he can give his new boss.

Questions

1 Taking the steps in the strategic process in order, what advice do you think the Team should give Jake?
2 What factors do you think have led Pepsi to choose its strategy instead of Coke's strategy?
3 What strategic planning changes would you recommend to Pepsi and why?

KNITMEDIA'S STRATEGIES FOR GROWTH AND EXPANSION

KnitMedia hopes that the synergies created by the integration of the company's various divisions (recording, clubs, touring, and so on) will enable the company to better compete in the marketplace and to provide a single source of management, promotion, and distribution of its products and services. As explained elsewhere and on the Web site, the company itself is comprised of several divisions including the Knitting Factory Club, Knitting Factory Works, record distribution, touring agency and festival promotion, broadcasting, music publishing, and new media. The company's basic strategies for growth and expansion include: offering a broad integrated family of products and services; leveraging existing products, artists, and expertise; expanding international businesses; expanding and strengthening merchandising business; expanding and strengthening product licensing; and continuing to target consumers, especially Gen Ex and Next Gen consumers (those aged 25 to 49).

The question is whether a company this size can do so much while competing with giants like Warner Music Group and Sony Music. On the one hand, these giant businesses are, as Michael Dorf has said, relatively slow and ponderous when it comes to finding new talent and getting decisions made. But, on the other hand, they do have the financial and human resources to buy top talent and then market it effectively.

KnitMedia has to make sure it doesn't end up getting steamrolled by these giants while it spreads itself across its various businesses.

Team Exercises and Questions

Use what you learned in this chapter and the WEB sources listed for Chapter 6 on the Dessler Management Web site to answer the following questions (other questions will be found at the Web site):

1 Of the generic corporate strategies we discussed in this chapter, which is (are) KnitMedia pursuing? Do you think this is a good idea? Why or why not?

2 Do you think the company will be able to achieve the sorts of "vertical integration" synergies it desires, for instance, by running Knit Factory Clubs that spotlight talent that can then be put under contract and recorded and sent out on music tours? Why or why not? What problems should the company anticipate?

For the online version of this case, visit our Web site at: <www. prenhall. com/desslermgmt>.

For Internet exercises, interactive study questions, news updates and more, visit the Dessler Web site at

www.prenhall.com/desslermgmt

If you're using the **CD-ROM** that accompanies this text, simply click on the "Web Site" button to access the site.

PLANNING AND DECISION MAKING IN A RISKY ENVIRONMENT

Everyone at KnitMedia is constantly making decisions. Michael Dorf has given everyone lots of freedom to do their jobs, and this freedom to accomplish the task using their skills and creativity leads to the need for employees to make lots of decisions. As Mark Pearlson tells it, "There's sort of an anything-goes culture going on here. The beauty of what we're doing is you're free to do pretty much whatever you want. When I was in Amsterdam, . . . I was given this office and told to run with it and pretty much the same thing with the record label. I'm handed a record contract. He [Michael] tells me I just sign this and I have to turn it into a CD that goes to stores all over the world. So, it's very much of a free kind of environment for you to be as creative and innovative as you can.

"Michael has a very aggressive style of management. He hands you a project, and then he walks away. And he expects it to get done right, [to go] figure it out for yourself. . . . It's a pretty loose structure. [Michael] does give you guidelines. Not as many as some people would like, but of course, that leads into the freedom I was talking about earlier."

Although Michael gives the staff a lot of freedom to make decisions, he still makes many of the decisions himself. Michael often makes nonprogrammed decisions. They are based on his vision, intuition, and judgment, and, as Michael explains, "Some of the long-range decisions are going to be risky." Examples are his decision to expand the club concept to Europe and the rest of the world; to develop an interactive, multimedia presentation of the music; to put the Knit's music on the radio; to tour in Europe.

Others in the organization sometimes make nonprogrammed decisions, as when Mark was told to go run the Amsterdam office or to run the record label. However, many decisions that started as nonprogrammed become programmed over time as people making them gain more experience. Although they started making risky decisions "from the beginning," says Michael, "I believe ten years of experience has made a lot of the gut decisions become more empirical. So, it's less instinctual in terms of the daily decision making." Thus, the Knit now has procedures for producing a show or a CD, for running the club—bands have to be booked, the show needs to be promoted, provisions have to be made to tape the show. The bar has to be stocked, the place cleaned up, and so on. These are now fairly routine activities.

Perhaps one of the most critical roles that Michael Dorf performs is to plan and set goals for the Knit. He describes his first goal, which was to find a way to make it in the record business: "It was really about trying to figure out a way to sell muffins and tea. . . . So I needed to open up an elaborate lemonade stand, essentially, to go into the record business. Thank goodness I opened up a profitable lemonade stand, because we were selling alcohol, and I was able to spend more money on records and essentially build a business from there." Many of Michael's plans derived from his goal to make that business successful, to improve his cash flow. "Right around 1990, maybe three years into it, " he says, "we realized the key word for us was synergy, because we're going to have to work really hard to take this niche music—a very niche product—and get it out and start making a living from it. And so we needed to look at every stream possible." Thus he planned to open more clubs, go on tour, start the record label, do radio shows, and put the Knit on the Internet. The idea of synergy gave the Knit a unifying framework and helped shape the vision and direction of the business.

In order to get loans to support the business, Michael had to develop written plans and budgets. The early plans were more proposals than formal business plans. However, these proposals had to justify the need for the money and indicate how it would be spent, the returns expected, and so forth. More recently, Michael and Ken Ashworth, the executive vice president and chief operating officer, took these proposals and developed the Knit's first formal strategic business plan to present to potential investors to gain funds needed for the next stage of the company's growth.

Michael's father got him into the habit of writing his plans and goals. Because he was a young entrepreneur who was creating an entirely new business, Michael was unable to get bank financing without his father's cosignature. As a result, says Michael, "There was some discipline created to submit in writing, in a more formal proposal, that I had to defend what I put in writing to show the bank, and to show him [my father] in order for him to cosign [the loans I needed].

"And that process helped develop the [strategic] plan. When we moved to the new club, I had to take out a $350 thousand loan. And it wasn't going to come from me calling him on the phone and saying, you know, 'Hey, will you cosign a loan that potentially could screw up the rest of your life?' I needed to prove it. And I needed to have pro formas. I had to pretend to know what we were going to sell at the bar. I had to pretend to know what our ticket sales were going to be, based on some formulation, and put it in writing. And by doing that, I think, over time, certain sections became clear, that are in our [strategic] business plan now."

Michael and the Knitting Factory created a franchise in the mind of the consumer, and one of his core strengths is that he knows his customers and how to promote his products as a conduit between the artists who create the music and the public that consumes it. Music stores now have a category called "Knitting Factory Music," indicating that music lovers have a clear idea of what kind of music the club stands for. This reflects the embodiment of Michael's and the Knitting Factory's artistic integrity, an essential core value of KnitMedia.

Questions

Based on the cases, the videos, the textbook you've looked at thus far, and your knowledge from other sources, answer the following questions.

1 Compare and contrast the nature of decision making at the entrepreneurial KnitMedia and the general prescriptions for decision making at larger, more established companies.

2 How would you characterize planning and goal setting at the Knit? How does this differ from the textbook approach to planning and goal setting? How is it similar?

3 Describe Michael Dorf's strategic planning process. What do you see as its strengths? Limitations?

4 Should entrepreneurial firms in fast-moving businesses follow a traditional strategic planning process? Why or why not?

SOURCE: End-of-part video cases prepared by d.t. ogilvie, Rutgers University.

FUNDAMENTALS OF ORGANIZING

What's Ahead?

For many people, a latte and scone per day is a $1,400-a-year habit, and that's music to the ears of Howard Schultz, head of Starbuck's Coffee.[1] But with over 1,000 Starbucks in the United States, organizing the company so it will maintain its innovativeness is no easy task. There must be training departments to turn college students into café managers (every espresso must be pulled within 23 seconds or be thrown away), and departments to sell coffee to United Airlines and supermarkets. How to organize is, therefore, not just an academic issue to Howard Schultz.

Objectives

After studying this chapter, you should be able to

- define organizing
- describe the basic alternatives for organizing departments
- identify the types of authority in organizations and demonstrate how authority can be delegated
- illustrate what is meant by decentralization.

MANAGEMENT ON THE WEB

ORGANIZATIONAL KNOWLEDGE MANAGEMENT AND ORGANIZATIONAL LEARNING

This page contains links to knowledge management articles and books, other knowledge management resources on the WWW, tools for knowledge management, and knowledge and organizational learning. ■

http://www.brint.com/OrgLrng.htm

What Is Organizing?

There are probably as many types of organizations as there are companies in the world. Johnson & Johnson is an example of a huge, highly decentralized organization that produces a wide array of products and does so successfully. Starbucks is an example of a relatively small organization.

Organizing means arranging the activities of the enterprise in such a way that they systematically contribute to the enterprise's goals. An **organization** consists of people whose specialized tasks are coordinated to contribute to the organization's goals.

The usual way of depicting an organization is with an **organization chart,** as shown in Figure 7.1 on page 213. It shows the structure of the organization, specifically, the title of each manager's position and, by means of connecting lines, who is accountable to whom and who is in charge of what department.

The organization chart also shows the **chain of command** (sometimes called the *scalar chain* or the *line of authority*) between the top of the organization and the lowest positions in the chart. The chain of command represents the path a directive

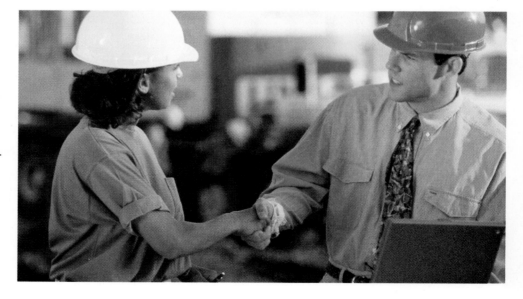

The informal organization, which does not appear on any organizational charts, consists of the informal contacts among themselves that employees use to get the job done.

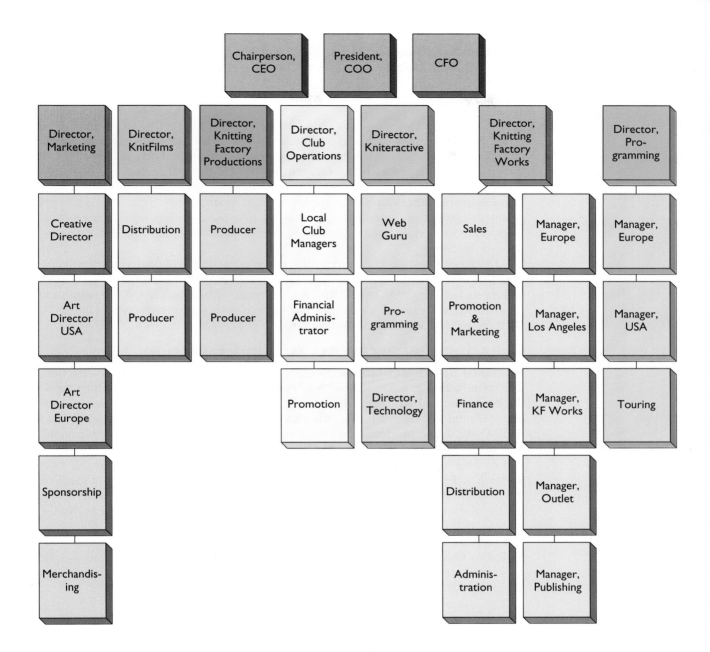

■ **FIGURE 7.1   KnitMedia Organization, 1996–1997**
An organization chart like this one shows the title of each manager's position and the departments they manage, as well as who reports to whom. Source: KnitMedia Prospectus, p. 37.

should take in traveling from the president to employees at the bottom of the organization chart or from employees at the bottom to the top of the organization chart.

One thing the organization chart does not show is the informal organization that has evolved in the enterprise. The **informal organization** means the informal, habitual contacts, communications, and ways of doing things that employees always develop. Thus, a salesperson might develop the habit of calling a plant production supervisor to check on the status of an order. The salesperson might find this quicker than adhering to the chain of command, which would entail having the sales manager check with the plant manager, who in turn checks with the supervisor.

Creating Departments

Every enterprise must carry out various activities to accomplish its goals. In a company, these activities might include manufacturing, selling, and accounting. In a city, they might include the activities of agencies like the fire, police, and health protection departments. In a hospital, they include nursing, medical services, and radiology. **Departmentalization** is the process through which an enterprise's activities are grouped together and assigned to managers; it is the organizationwide division of work. Departments—logical groupings of activities—are often called divisions, units, or sections.

The basic question in departmentalization is, around what activities should we organize departments? For example, should departments be established for sales and manufacturing? Or should there be separate departments for industrial and retail customers, each of which then has its own sales and manufacturing units? As we'll see next, many options are available.

Creating Departments Around Functions

Functional departmentalization means grouping activities around basic functions like manufacturing, sales, and finance. This is illustrated in Figure 7.2, which shows the organizational structure for the ABC car company. Each department is organized around a different business function, in this case, sales, finance, and production. At ABC, the production director reports to the chairperson and other members of the managing board. He or she manages ABC's domestic production plants and its one foreign-based assembly plant. On the other hand, note that the sales function is divided into domestic sales and overseas sales so that ABC can focus on the different needs of foreign and domestic customers. One manager is responsible for the domestic market's sales. The second is in charge of overseas subsidiaries' sales, including the considerable sales of the firm's U.S. company.[2]

Service businesses can be built around business functions, too. For example, the basic business functions around which banks are often departmentalized include operations, control, and loans. Similarly, in a university, the "business functions" might include academic affairs, business affairs, and student affairs.

■ **FIGURE 7.2**
Functional Departmentalization ABC Car Company
This organizational chart shows a *functional* organization with departments for basic functions like finance, sales, and production.

(a)

(b)

(c)

(d)

Functional areas include but are not limited to (a) sales, (b) finance, (c) human resources, and (d) manufacturing.

Some firms organize around managerial functions or technological functions. Building departments around managerial functions means putting supervisors in charge of departments like planning, control, and administration. As illustrated in Figure 7.3, departmentalization based on technological functions means grouping together activities such as plating, welding, or assembling. Again, the basic idea of any functional departmentalization is to group activities around the elemental functions the enterprise must carry out.

ADVANTAGES. Organizing departments around functions has several advantages. It is simple, straightforward, and logical; it makes sense to build departments around the basic functions in which the enterprise must engage. Functional organizations

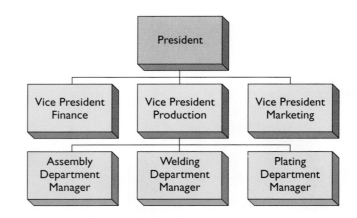

■ **FIGURE 7.3**
Departmentalization
Based on Technology
This chart shows a special
type of functional orga-
nization called a tech-
nological functional organization, with separate
departments for techno-
logical functions such as
assembly and welding.

also usually have single departments for sales, production, and finance that serve all the company's products, rather than duplicate facilities for each product. Because the volume in these departments is relatively high, the firm typically gets increased returns to scale—in other words, employees become more proficient (from doing the same job over and over again), and the company can afford larger plants and more efficient equipment. Functional organizations are therefore often associated with greater efficiency.

Functional organization has several other advantages. The managers' duties in each of the functional departments tend to be more specialized (a manager may specialize in finance or production, for instance); the enterprise therefore needs fewer general managers—those with the breadth of experience to administer several functions at once. This can simplify both recruiting and training. Functional department managers also tend to receive information on only part of the big picture of the company, that which concerns their own specialized functions. This can make it easier for top management to exercise tight control over the department managers' activities.

DISADVANTAGES. Functional organizations also have disadvantages. Responsibility for the enterprise's overall performance lies on the shoulders of one person, usually the president. After all, he or she may be the only one in a position to coordinate the work of the functional departments, each of which is only one element in producing and supplying the company's product or service. This may not be a serious problem when the firm is small or does not work with a lot of products. But as size and diversity of products increase, the job of coordinating, say, production, sales, and finance for many different products may prove too great for one person; the enterprise could lose its responsiveness. Also, the tendency for functional departments to result in specialized managers (finance experts, production experts, and so forth) makes it more difficult to develop managers with the breadth of experience needed for general management jobs like president. These advantages and disadvantages are summarized in Table 7.1.

Creating Departments Around Products

With product departmentalization, departments are organized for each of the company's products or for each family of products. Department heads in this type of organization are responsible for both producing and marketing a product or family of products. Figure 7.4 shows the organization chart for one such company. As you can see, a president heads North Atlantic operations. Three product divisions report to this person: one for drugs and pharmaceuticals, one for personal care products,

■ TABLE 7.1 *Advantages and Disadvantages of Functional Departmentalization*

ADVANTAGES	DISADVANTAGES
1. Managers functionally specialized and, therefore, more efficient	1. Responsibility for overall performance with chief executive only
2. Less duplication of effort than in other types of organization	2. Can overburden chief executive and lead to slower decision making and less responsiveness
3. Increased returns to scale	3. Reduces the attention paid to specific products, customers, markets, or areas
4. Simplifies training	4. Results in functionally specialized managers rather than general managers
5. Simple and proven over time	
6. Facilitates tight control by chief executive	

and one for stationery products. Each of these three product divisions then has its own staff for activities such as production and sales.

Arranging departments around products in this way is often called **divisionalization.** Divisionalization means the firm's major departments are organized so that each can manage all the activities needed to develop, manufacture, and sell a particular product or product line. The head of such a division usually has functional departments—say, for production, sales, and personnel—reporting to him or her. To the extent that he or she does so, each of these product divisions is self-contained. Each has control of all or most of the resources it needs to create, produce, and supply its product or products.

Managing Change

FOCUSING INTELLECTUAL CAPITAL IN KODAK'S PRODUCT DIVISIONS

Kodak's recent reorganization helps to illustrate how reorganizing can facilitate change. When he became CEO in 1993, George Fisher found that almost every department in the company had its own task force working to find a way to use digital (electronic) photography in its product line. The problem was that all the firm's intellectual capital—the creativity and energy of the engineers and scientists in these task forces—was dispersed and unfocused. Fisher found that Kodak had already spent $5 billion on digital photography, with little to show for it.

The first thing he did was dismantle the departmental task forces. In their place he created a new product-oriented Digital and Applied Imaging Division, and most of the dispersed task forces' engineers and scientists were asked to join its staff. Now all the intellectual capital could be focused, like light through a magnifying glass, on the challenge of creating new digital photography products. Sales of such products have since doubled in two years, to $1 billion.[3] ■

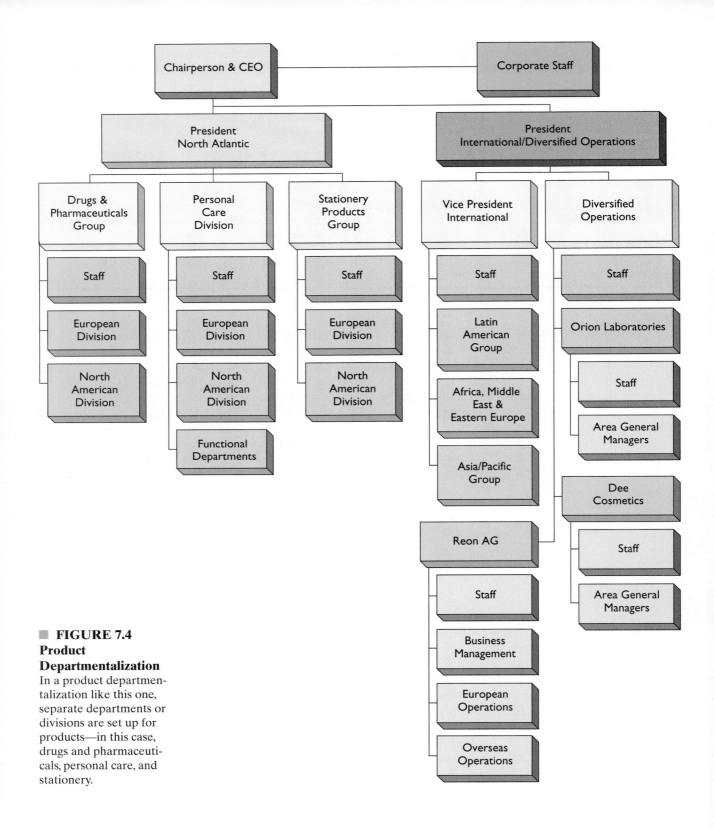

FIGURE 7.4
Product Departmentalization
In a product departmentalization like this one, separate departments or divisions are set up for products—in this case, drugs and pharmaceuticals, personal care, and stationery.

ADVANTAGES. As at Kodak, divisionalization can be advantageous. A single manager is charged with overseeing all the functions required to produce and market each product. Each product division can therefore focus its resources on being more sensitive and responsive to the needs of its particular product or product line. (The manager in charge of the North American personal care group in Figure 7.4, page 218, for example, has his or her own research, manufacturing, and sales departments. As a result, his or her division can usually respond quickly when, for instance, a competitor brings out a new and innovative product.) The manager need not rely on research, manufacturing, or sales managers who are not within his or her own division. Divisionalization is thus appropriate where quick decisions and flexibility (rather than efficiency) are paramount.

Divisionalization has other advantages. First, performance is more easily judged. If a division is doing well (or not doing well), it is clear who is responsible, because one person is managing the whole division. Related to this, being put in charge of the whole ball game can help motivate the manager to perform better. Self-contained divisions can also be good training grounds for an enterprise's executives because they are exposed to a wider range of problems, from production and sales to personnel and finance. Finally, divisionalization helps shift some of the management burden from top management to division executives. For example, imagine if the North American president in Figure 7.4 had to coordinate the tasks of designing, producing, and marketing each of the company's many products, which range from drugs to stationery. The diversity of problems he or she would face would be enormous. Therefore, virtually all very large companies, as well as many small ones with diverse products and customers, have divisionalized.[4]

Managing Change

THE DIVISIONAL STRUCTURE AT INTUIT

Even smaller companies are switching to divisionalized structures, in part because the divisional units are easier to manage and tend to be more innovative. That helps to explain why Bill Harris, executive vice president of the software company Intuit, praises the company's divisional structure:

> Two years ago, it was becoming clear that the bigger we got, the more being organized by functions was a liability. . . . The executive team had become a real bottleneck. We needed a new structure [and decided] to bust the organization apart. [Our new CEO] created eight business units, each with its own general manager and customer mission. The basic goal was to flatten the organization and fragment the decision-making process. Each business unit would be the size that Intuit had been a few years ago, and each would focus on one core product or market.

The effects of the reorganization have been dramatic. The new organization forces Intuit's top managers to give more decision-making authority to the individual business units. The executive team used to make or approve most product-related decisions. Today these decisions are left to the business units, and within these units they are usually left to the individual product teams. Intuit has become more responsive and effective at managing change.[5] ■

TABLE 7.2 *Advantages and Disadvantages of Product Departmentalization*	
ADVANTAGES	**DISADVANTAGES**
1. One unit is responsible for giving continuous, undivided attention to the product, so the unit is more sensitive and responsive to the unique needs of the product.	1. Duplication of effort, perhaps reduced efficiency. In some situations, customers may also be bothered by representatives of more than one division.
2. Part of the burden is lifted from the shoulders of the top manager.	2. Finding and training people to head each division is a more difficult job.
3. Performance is more easily identified and judged; this in turn may motivate performance.	3. Since division heads now do their own coordinating without checking with the top manager, the latter could begin to lose control. He or she no longer coordinates and oversees the day-to-day *activities* by which managers do their jobs, just the *ends*—like whether or not the division makes a profit at the end of the year.
4. Provides a good training ground for future top executives.	

DISADVANTAGES. However, organizing around divisions can also produce disadvantages. For one thing, divisions breed an expensive duplication of effort. The fact that each product-oriented unit is self-contained implies that there are several production plants instead of one, several sales forces instead of one, and so on. Related to this, the company's customers (such as a drugstore) may become annoyed at being visited by many salespeople representing different divisions.

Divisionalization may also diminish top management's control. As at Intuit, the division heads often have great autonomy because they are in charge of all phases of producing and marketing their products. Top management, therefore, tends to have less control over each division's day-to-day activities. For example, a division might run up excessive expenses before top management discovers there is a problem. In fact, striking a balance between providing each division head with enough autonomy to run the division and still maintaining top management control is crucial.

Divisionalization also requires more managers with general management abilities. Each product division is, in a sense, a miniature company, with its own production plant, sales force, personnel department, and so forth; therefore, divisional managers cannot just be sales, production, or personnel specialists. Companies with divisional structures and strong executive development programs therefore tend to be prime hunting grounds for executive recruiters. For example, GE is often listed as the place where recruiters look first when trying to find CEOs for other companies.

The advantages and disadvantages of product (divisionalization) departmentalization are summarized in Table 7.2.

Creating Departments Around Customers

Customer departmentalization is similar to divisionalization except that departments are organized to serve the needs of specific customers. Figure 7.5, for instance, shows the organization chart for the Grayson Steel Company. Notice how the company's main divisions are organized to serve the needs of particular customers, such as metals and chemicals customers, packaging systems customers, aerospace and industrial customers, and the international group.

**FIGURE 7.5
Customer
Departmentalization
Grayson Steel
Company**
With customer depart-
mentalization, separate
departments are orga-
nized around customers
such as aerospace and
metals and chemicals cus-
tomers.

ADVANTAGES AND DISADVANTAGES. Organizing around customers has
several advantages. As in product divisionalization, a manager is charged with giving his or her continuous, undivided attention to a customer or group of customers.
This can result in faster, more satisfactory service to each of the company's customers, particularly when their needs are substantially different. However, as in
product departmentalization, the main disadvantage is duplication of effort. The
company may have several production plants instead of one and several sales managers, each serving the needs of his or her own customers, instead of one. This can
reduce overall corporate efficiency.

Creating Departments Around Marketing Channels

With **marketing-channel departmentalization,** top-level departments are organized
around each of the firm's marketing channels. A **marketing channel** is the conduit
(wholesaler, drugstore, grocery, or the like) through which a manufacturer distributes its products to its ultimate customers.

Marketing-channel departmentalization is illustrated in Figure 7.6. As you can
see, it is similar to customer departmentalization, but there are several differences.
In customer departmentalization, each customer-oriented department is usually
responsible for both manufacturing and selling its own product to its own customers.
In marketing-channel departmentalization, the same product (such as Ivory Soap)
is typically marketed through two or more channels. Usually one department is chosen to manufacture the product for all the other marketing-channel departments.

Organizing around marketing channels assumes that it is the marketing channel's unique needs (rather than the ultimate customer's needs) that must be catered
to. For example, Revlon may sell through both department stores and discount drugstores. Yet the demands of these two channels are quite different: The department
store may want Revlon to supply specially trained salespeople to run concessions
in its stores, for instance. The discount druggist may just want quick delivery and
minimal inventories. Putting a manager and department in charge of each channel

FIGURE 7.6
Marketing Channel
Departmentalization
With marketing channels, the main departments are organized to focus on particular marketing channels such as drugstores and grocery stores.

NOTE: Only the department-store channel produces the soap, and each channel may sell to the same ultimate consumers.

can help ensure that such diverse needs are met quickly and satisfactorily. As in product and customer departmentalization, the resulting duplication—in this case, of sales forces—is the main disadvantage.

Creating Departments Around Geographic Areas

With geographic or territorial departmentalization, separate departments are organized for each of the territories in which the enterprise does business. Like product, customer, and marketing-channel departments, territorial departments are examples of divisional departmentalization in that each geographic area tends to be self-contained, perhaps with its own production, sales, and personnel activities.

Territorial departmentalization is illustrated in Figure 7.7, which shows the organization chart of one large company's international group. Notice that the group vice president, international, has several managing directors reporting to him or her, each for a different geographic area, including Australia, Mexico, and Europe.

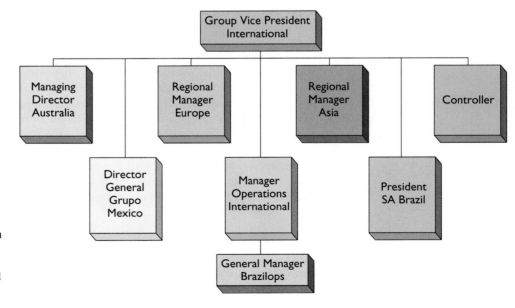

FIGURE 7.7
Geographic
Organization
This is one possibility for a geographic organization with separate departments for geographic areas, such as Europe and Asia.

ADVANTAGES AND DISADVANTAGES. As is the case with other types of divisional organizations, the main advantage of territorial departmentalization is that one self-contained department is charged with focusing on the needs of its particular buyers—in this case, those in its geographic area. This can lead to speedier, more responsive and satisfactory service. Thus, a department store chain like JCPenney's might organize territorially so as to cater to the tastes and needs of customers in each geographic area. Like product, customer, and marketing-channel departmentalization, territorial departmentalization is advantageous insofar as it ensures quick, responsive reaction to the needs of the company's clients. Also like these forms, however, territorial departmentalization may create duplication of effort. And, again, these types of divisions need to hire and train general managers capable of managing several functions (like production, sales, and personnel).

■ **FIGURE 7.8**
Matrix Departmentalization
With a matrix organization, a project structure is often superimposed over a functional organization.

Creating Matrix Organizations

A **matrix organization** (also known as **matrix management**) is defined as the superimposition of one or more forms of departmentalization on top of an existing form.[6] In one familiar form, illustrated in Figure 7.8, product departments are superimposed

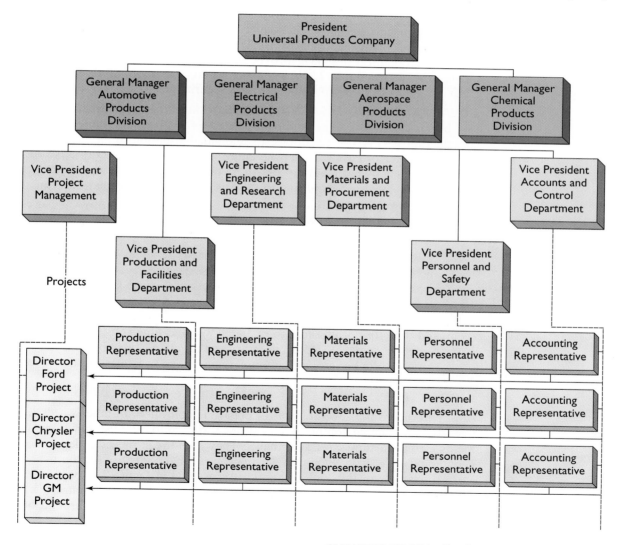

over a functional departmentalization. This company's automotive products division is functionally organized, with departments for functions like production, engineering, and personnel. But superimposed over this functional departmentalization are three product groups—for the Ford project, the Chrysler project, and the GM project. Each of these product groups has its own product manager (or project leader). One or more employees from each functional department (like production and engineering) is temporarily assigned to each project.

Dual reporting along product and geographic lines is another common matrix approach.[7] For example, one bank is organized geographically, with separate officers in charge of the bank's operations in each of several countries. At the same time, the bank has a customer structure superimposed over this geographic organization. Project heads for major bank customers such as IBM lead teams comprised of bank employees from each country who concentrate on the local and worldwide financial interests of IBM. Bank employees in each country may report to both their country managers and their project head managers.

Some matrix organizations are more formal than others. Sometimes information liaisons or temporary project managers are assigned to provide coordination across functional departments with regard to some project or customer. Other firms formalize their matrix organizations, sometimes by adding a matrix director to assist each of the project managers and a semipermanent administrative structure (including, for instance, project employee appraisal forms) to help build the project teams' authority.[8]

Matrix organizations have proved successful in a wide range of companies, including Citicorp Bank, TRW Systems, NASA and many of its subcontractors, UNICEF, and various accounting, law, and security firms, to name a few.[9]

ADVANTAGES AND DISADVANTAGES. Matrix departmentalization can help give bigger companies some of the advantages of smaller ones. For example, a self-contained project group can devote its undivided attention to the needs of its own project, product, or customer, yet the entire organization need not be permanently organized around what may turn out to be temporary projects. Another advantage is that management avoids having to establish duplicate functional departments for each of the several projects.

However, matrix organizations can also trigger problems that, although avoidable, are potentially serious. These problems can be summarized as follows:

- *Power struggles and conflicts.* Since authority tends to be more ambiguous and up for grabs in matrix organizations, struggles between managers who head the functional and project groups may be more commonplace than in traditional organizations.
- *Lost time.* Matrix organizations tend to result in more intragroup meetings and therefore often seem to be indecisive and time consuming.
- *Excessive overhead.* Research indicates that matrix organizations may tend to raise costs because hiring more managers and secretaries raises overhead.

Departmentalization in Practice: A Hybrid

Most enterprises use several forms of departmentalization: In other words, they are hybrids. For example, top management might decide to establish functional departments for production, sales, and finance. They then break the sales department into geographic areas, with separate sales managers for the north, east, south, and west.

An example of this type of hybrid is presented in Figure 7.9 (pages 226–227). This shows a large multinational's organization. Within the United States, this is basically a divisional structure, with separate departments organized around business systems, programming systems, and so forth. However, this firm also uses territorial departmentalization, for instance, with separate officers in charge of Asia, the United States, and the Middle East. As is often the case with divisional structures, the headquarters itself is organized around managerial functions (general counsel, finance and planning, and law, for instance).

Managing Change

ROSENBLUTH TRAVEL FINDS OUT
WHAT FARMERS KNOW ABOUT ORGANIZING

Rosenbluth Travel is a fast-growing 1,000-office global travel agency, but the way it is organized is based on what CEO Hal Rosenbluth learned on a cow farm.

Standing on a cowpat-spotted field in rural North Dakota several years ago, Rosenbluth made a discovery: "The family farm is the most efficient type of unit I've ever run across, because everybody on the farm has to be fully functional and multifaceted." He decided to look for an organizational design that would embody that approach to getting everyone's full involvement in helping to run the company. He knew doing so would help his managers better manage change.

His company now is a good example of how smart managers blend several organizational styles to build fast-moving and successful firms. The first thing Rosenbluth did was to break his company into more than 100 business units, each functioning like a "farm" serving specific regions and clients. Corporate headquarters became more like what Rosenbluth calls "farm towns," where "stores" like human resources and accounting remain centralized so all the "farms" can use them. Its computerized Global Distribution Network links every one of its travel agents to the company's minicomputers in Philadelphia, where centralized data on all the company's clients help ensure that the work of all the offices is coordinated to serve the needs of Rosenbluth's clients.[10] ∎

Achieving Coordination

The Nature and Purpose of Coordination

When work has been divided among units, it then needs to be coordinated. **Coordination** is the process of achieving unity of action among interdependent activities. It is required whenever two or more interdependent individuals, groups, or departments must work together to achieve a common goal.

In organizations, some departments are more interdependent than others, and so the difficulty of achieving coordination varies from situation to situation.[11] Some departments are highly interdependent. For example, review the ABC organizational chart in Figure 7.2. Notice that there are separate directors for the sales, finance, and production functions. For a new ABC product to be produced, each department's activities must be closely coordinated by the chairperson and managing board. If the sales director projects sales of 50,000 units next year, then the production director must take steps to produce that many cars, and the finance director must be sure

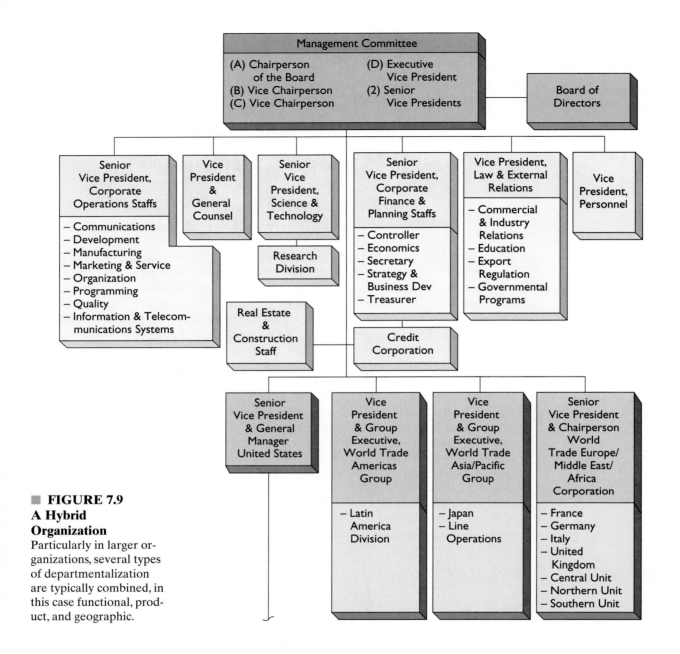

■ FIGURE 7.9
A Hybrid Organization
Particularly in larger organizations, several types of departmentalization are typically combined, in this case functional, product, and geographic.

that the funds are available to produce and sell that many cars. Therefore, the chairperson and his or her managing board closely coordinate each of these functional departments.

At the other extreme, in some organizations the work of different departments involves almost no interdependence. For example, the separate customer divisions established by Grayson (Figure 7.5) are pretty much self-contained. Although not shown, each division—such as those for metals and chemicals, and aerospace—has its own research, production, and sales units. In such a divisionalized organization, each division can be managed more or less as an independent, autonomous business. Here, the job of achieving coordination between the autonomous divisions

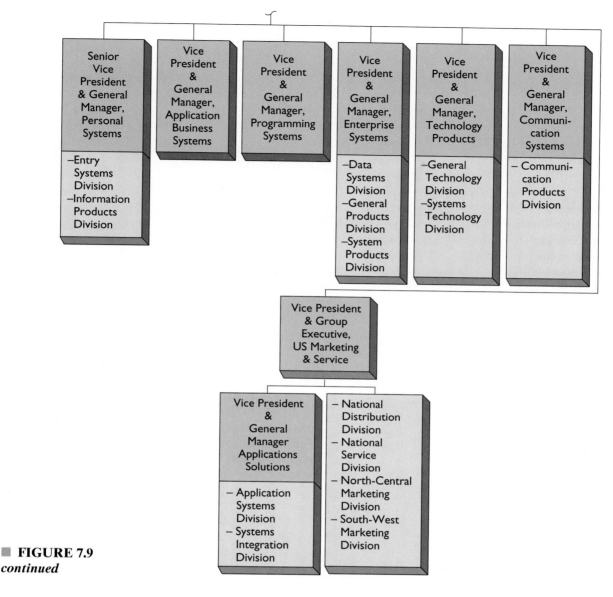

FIGURE 7.9
continued

would be relatively simple, because it is not essential for the divisions to work in unison on most day-to-day matters.

Techniques for Achieving Coordination

Theorists Jay Galbraith[12] and Henry Mintzberg,[13] working independently, have described the techniques managers use to achieve coordination. These techniques are summarized next.

COORDINATION THROUGH MUTUAL ADJUSTMENT. Mutual adjustment achieves coordination by relying on interpersonal communication. Mutual adjustment is used for coordination in both the simplest and most complex situations. In a simple situation such as two people moving a heavy log, coordination could be

The coordination of effort needed for complex tasks like this barn-raising is the result of a communication process called mutual adjustment.

achieved by having one person count "one, two, three, lift," at which time both people lift the log in unison.

But mutual adjustment is also used in highly complex situations. In these cases the situation changes so quickly and the work to be done is so unpredictable that using standard procedures and following the chain of command will not suffice. A platoon of marines planning its attack, for instance, may follow formal procedures and stick to the chain of command. But when the marines hit the beach, most coordination will likely take place through an ongoing process of mutual adjustment, with the marines continually interacting with and responding to each other as they respond to and anticipate problems.

COORDINATION THROUGH RULES OR PROCEDURES: STANDARDIZATION OF WORK PROCESSES. If the work to be done is predictable and can be planned for in advance, a supervisor can specify ahead of time what actions his or her subordinates should take. Rules and procedures are thus useful for coordinating routine, recurring activities. They specify in detail, ahead of time, what course of action each subordinate should take if a particular situation should arise. Thus, a restaurant manager could have a rule that bussers will bus tables as soon as customers finish eating. This ensures that the table is clear before the next course is served and that the work of the waiters and bussers is coordinated.

COORDINATION THROUGH DIRECT SUPERVISION: USING THE HIERARCHY. Direct supervision achieves coordination by having one person coordinate the work of others, issuing instructions to them and monitoring their results.[14] Thus, when problems arise that are not covered by rules or procedures, subordinates are trained to bring the problem to their manager. In addition to using rules and mutual adjustment, all managers use the chain of command to achieve coordination.

COORDINATION THROUGH DIVISIONALIZATION. Organizing around divisions can facilitate coordination. As a rule, functional departmentalization creates additional demands for presidential coordination, since the functional departments are interdependent. Product (or customer, market-channel, or area) departmentalization reduces such interdependence and makes it easier for the president to achieve coordination. For example, in a divisional organization, the president does not have to work as hard coordinating the efforts of his or her product divisions because they are not as interdependent as the production, finance, and sales departments are in a functional organization.

COORDINATION THROUGH STAFF ASSISTANTS. Some managers hire a staff assistant to make the job of coordinating subordinates easier. When subordinates bring a problem to the manager, the assistant can compile information about the problem, research it, and offer advice on what alternatives are available. This effectively boosts the manager's ability to handle problems and coordinate the work of his or her subordinates.

COORDINATION THROUGH LIAISONS. When the volume of contacts between two departments grows, some firms use special liaisons to facilitate coordination. For example, the sales department manager might appoint a salesperson to be his or her liaison with the production department. This liaison is based in the sales department but travels frequently to the factory to learn as much as possible about the plant's production schedule. When an order comes in to the sales department, the sales manager can then quickly determine from this liaison what the production schedules are and will know whether a new order can be accepted and delivered when promised.

COORDINATION THROUGH COMMITTEES. Many firms achieve coordination by appointing interdepartmental committees, task forces, or teams. These are usually composed of representatives of five or six interdependent departments. They meet periodically to discuss common problems and ensure interdepartmental coordination.

COORDINATION THROUGH INDEPENDENT INTEGRATORS. An **independent integrator** is an individual or group that coordinates the activities of several interdependent departments.[15] Integrators differ from liaison personnel in that integrators are independent of (not attached to) the departments they coordinate. Instead, they report to the manager who oversees those departments.

This technique has proved useful in high-tech firms where several interdependent departments must be coordinated under rapidly changing conditions. In the plastics industry, for instance, developing new products requires close coordination between the research, engineering, sales, and production departments in a situation where competitors are always introducing new and innovative products. Some firms have thus established new-product development departments. Their role is to coordinate (or integrate) the research, marketing analysis, sales, and production activities needed for developing and introducing a new product.

COORDINATION THROUGH STANDARDIZED TARGETS, SKILLS, OR SHARED VALUES. Firms also achieve coordination by standardizing the efforts of their employees. This can be accomplished in three ways. First, you can standardize the *goals or targets* the employees are to reach. For example, as long as the sales, finance, and production managers reach their assigned goals, the president can be reasonably sure that their work will be coordinated, because adequate financing and production will be provided to meet the sales target.

Standardizing *skills* also facilitates coordination. That's one reason why firms like Saturn spend millions of dollars training their workers. Whether a work team is installing door panels or solving a problem, training ensures that each team member knows how his or her efforts fit with the others and how to proceed. Standardized skills thus reduce the need for outside coordination.[16]

Finally, many firms facilitate coordination by creating *shared values* among their employees. They do this by carefully screening and socializing their employees and by establishing a set of values and a philosophy that permeate the organization and guide what employees do. For example, every year Unilever brings 300 to 400 of its managers to its executive development center and also gives 100 to 150 of its most promising overseas managers temporary assignments at corporate headquarters.[17] This gives the visiting managers a strong sense of Unilever's strategic vision and values. Such knowledge helps to ensure that, wherever they are around the world, Unilever managers will contribute in a coordinated way to that vision, while adhering to the values of the firm. As one of its managers put it, "The experience initiates you into the Unilever club and the clear norms, values, and behaviors that distinguish our people—so much so that we really believe we can spot another Unilever manager anywhere in the world."[18]

Organizational Behavior in Action

BUILDING TEAMWORK

No amount of coordination can compensate for the fact that a company's managers have decided for some reason not to work together as a team. Conversely, managers who are members of a cohesive team and who are all committed to working together for the good of the company and the team can ensure that their work is coordinated even without formal efforts like staff assistants, liaisons, or committees.

What can a manager do to build a sense of teamwork among his or her subordinates? We'll discuss building successful teams in more detail in Chapter 12, but important things to keep in mind include the following guidelines.

HIRE THE RIGHT PEOPLE. Begin building team effectiveness before, not after, the team is organized. Good football coaches do not choose players at random and then hope they will be effective athletes. Two team-building experts put it this way: "No team succeeds without all the skills needed to meet its purpose and performance goals."[19] This applies not just to business skills but to interpersonal skills as well: Teamwork is enhanced when the team comprises people who can work together amicably and who have the skills to do the job.

CREATE A SENSE OF PURPOSE. Whether it is a management team or a football team, the essence of teamwork is goal direction—in other words, ensuring that every team member knows what the team is supposed to accomplish. Through techniques like management by objectives, each member of the management team should understand what the company and his or her team are to accomplish and what his or her own contribution must be.

PROVIDE TEAM-BUILDING TRAINING. Many companies today use special team-building training methods to enhance teamwork and build more cohesive and committed management teams. Wilderness experiences and outdoor team-building sessions are interesting examples of this and are typically run by training organizations such as Outward Bound.[20]

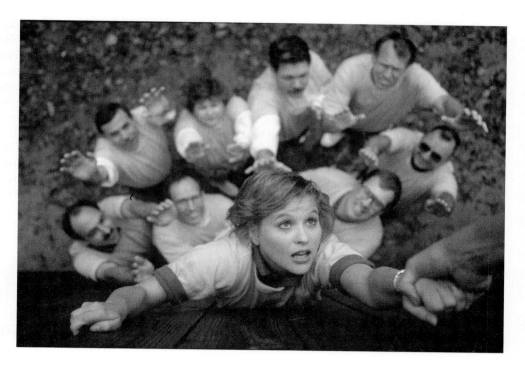

Team-building training programs typically ask participants to engage in risk-taking activities that build trust within the team.

These programs take managers into wilderness settings in order to build trust and teamwork through a series of outdoor activities. For example, team members might be required to participate in a "trust fall," where participants stand on a ledge, perhaps 15 feet high, with their backs to the ground. A group of seven to ten of their colleagues wait below with stretched palms, and the team member on the ledge is expected to fall backward into the waiting arms of his or her colleagues. The general idea of such programs is that after navigating trust falls and five-person canoe trips through white-water rapids, the individuals who started the program emerge as a close-knit and cohesive team.

Not every training director thinks that such team building really creates better work teams back on the job, and others caution against making participation mandatory; however, the programs on the whole do seem useful.

Authority in Organizations

Sources of Authority

Authority is the right to take action, to make decisions, and to direct the work of others. It is an essential part of organizing because managers and employees must be authorized to carry out the jobs assigned to them.

Authority derives from several sources, one of which is the person's position or rank. For example, the president of Intuit, a software manufacturer, has more authority based on rank than does one of his senior vice presidents.

But authority can stem from other sources, too. Some people are able to command authority because of their personal traits, such as intelligence or charisma. Others are acknowledged experts in some area or have some knowledge that requires others to depend on them. Thus, even the president of Intuit might have to defer on some highly technical matters to the head of R&D.

Some management writers argue that authority must come from the bottom up and be based on the subordinate's acceptance of the supervisor's orders. Theorist Chester Barnard was an early proponent of this view. Barnard argued that for orders to be carried out they must lie within the subordinate's "zone of acceptance" (in other words, they must be viewed as acceptable). From a practical point of view, there is a great element of truth in this. A president might have considerable authority based on rank but be unable to get anyone to follow his or her orders unless those orders are viewed as acceptable. Experts such as Rosabeth Moss Kanter and Tom Peters argue that getting employees' acceptance is increasingly important today, given the growing emphasis on empowered workers and team-based organizations.

Organizational Behavior in Action

POWER AND POLITICS AT WORK

The words "authority," "power," and "influence" are often used interchangeably. However, although they are interrelated, they do not all mean the same thing. *Influence* can be defined as the potential for producing an effect—the effect of somehow getting someone or something to take some action. **Power** was defined by Max Weber, a famous sociologist who wrote many years ago, as "the probability that one actor within a social relationship will be in a position to carry out his own will despite resistance, regardless of the basis on which this probability rests."[21] Authority, like power, refers to a person's potential for influencing others, but the word *authority* "has implicit in it the notion of legitimacy or ethical sanctification."[22] In organizations, in other words, the sources of authority are usually "legitimate." For example, they may stream down from the authority the owners decide to invest in the company's managers. Or they can percolate up from the acceptance of the governed.

Power, in organizational behavior, does not have to be "legitimate," and in fact, social scientists distinguish among at least five bases or sources of power.[23] These are reward power, coercive power, legitimate power, referent power, and expert power.

Reward power is defined as power whose basis is the ability to reward. In other words, a person has power over another to the extent that he or she can significantly influence the positive rewards (such as money) that the other person gets or significantly reduce the negative rewards (like poor working conditions) that the other person might otherwise have to endure.

The **coercive power** of one person over another stems from the real or imagined expectation on the part of the latter that he or she will be punished for failing to conform to the powerful person's attempts at influence. In organizations, coercive power is a familiar ingredient in group pressure. Groups are famous, for instance, for keeping "rate busters" in line by coercing them with fears of ostracism or physical violence. Unfortunately, some bosses depend on coercive power, too, and attempt to get their way through threats and intimidation.

Legitimate power is roughly synonymous with what we have called authority and refers to power that stems from a person feeling that someone has a legitimate right to influence him or her and that he or she has an obligation to accept this influence. The actual source of this legitimate power might be tradition (as in the case of a monarch) or it may derive from the office the superior holds. For example, on agreeing to join a company, its salespeople accept the right of the sales manager to assign them work, because this is a legitimate right of the office of "sales manager" in the organizational structure.

Referent power is power that stems from a person's identification with another. Thus the new presidential assistant might say of the president, "I want to be like that person, and therefore I shall behave or believe as the president does."

Finally, **expert power** derives from a person being viewed as an expert in some area and on whom others must therefore depend for advice and counsel. The way the organization is structured has a big influence on who will have expert power. For example, expert power in a company often stems from a person's position in the communications network and from that person's ability to control access to coveted information. Many public institutions such as universities have employees called budget officers. Although not high in the organization's chain of command, these people typically wield enormous expert power because every request for funds must be funneled through these financial gatekeepers.

For better or worse, the authority a manager has often doesn't translate into power. The vice presidents for sales and MIS may both seem to have about the same amount of authority, but if one is the president's son, you know he's probably going to have a lot more power than the other.

In organizations, the acquisition and use of power is called **politics.**[24] The existence of power and politics can make an organization chart with its neat boxes and lines a bit misleading. Unseen on that tranquil grid is the very real jockeying for power that often goes on in real companies as managers jostle each other for position.

WINNING AT OFFICE POLITICS

What can you do to win at office politics? Here are some suggestions:[25]

1. *Control vital information.* Remember that controlling vital information is a big source of expert power (recall the low-echelon budget officer with the high-echelon power). Other twists on this suggestion include finding out all you legitimately can about your competitors inside the organization and being selective in the information you disclose.

2. *Hook your career to a star.* A direct way to obtain more power is to find a powerful sponsor. There's a good chance that the lowly assistant sales manager who everyone knows is being watched over by the president will have more influence than his or her position would normally indicate. In terms of building a power base, therefore, don't view the organization chart as necessarily limiting you from communicating with and gaining the sponsorship of powerful individuals high up in the chain of command.

3. *Minimize power vacuums.* If reducing politics is your aim, you can minimize power vacuums. At General Electric Corporation, for instance, chairman Jack Welch was silent for many years regarding who was next in line to succeed him. This was probably necessary to give the ten or so possible candidates enough time to be tested. However, one effect of such a power

vacuum is to increase the jockeying and politicking among all the candidates as each surrounds himself or herself with coalitions of supporters, each trying to dislodge the other.

4. *Open communication channels.* The person organizing the company can reduce opportunities for politicking by opening communication channels and minimizing opportunities for secretiveness. For example, when no one knows how the budget is put together or exactly how much money is available in each account, there's more opportunity for a power-hungry budget officer to make himself or herself the budget gatekeeper and grab power as a result. Ensuring a free flow of information about all topics among all departments and levels helps minimize such covert actions. ■

Line and Staff Authority

Managers distinguish between line and staff authority. The way the terms are generally used, two basic differences exist between the two. First, **line managers,** like the president, production manager, and sales manager, are always in charge of essential activities, such as sales. Second, they are always authorized to issue orders to their subordinates down the chain of command. **Staff managers,** on the other hand, generally cannot issue orders down the chain of command (except in their own departments); staff managers can only assist and advise line managers. For example, an HR manager—even a senior vice president—can advise a production supervisor regarding the types of selection tests to use. However, it would be unusual for the human resource manager to order the supervisor to hire a particular employee. On the other hand, the production supervisor's boss—the production manager—usually could issue such orders.

There is an exception to this rule: A staff manager such as an HR manager may have functional authority. **Functional authority** means that the manager can issue orders down the chain of command within the very narrow limits of his or her authority. For example, the president might order that no screening tests be administered without first getting the HR manager's approval, who then has functional authority over the use of personnel tests.

Line and Staff Organizations

Although some organizations use only line managers, most have departments that are headed by staff managers too. Figure 7.10 illustrates a large line and staff organization, in this case for a large multinational corporation. The division heads have line authority; these are therefore all line divisions. However, staff departments have also been established, in this case for corporate planning, corporate finance, and corporate legal.

Line–staff conflict refers to disagreements between a line manager and the staff manager who is giving him or her advice. For example, a production manager may want to use a particular personnel test but the HR manager insists that the test not be used. Conflict usually results when line managers feel that staff managers are encroaching on their duties and prerogatives. For their part, staff managers may feel that line managers are unnecessarily resisting their good advice. One way to reduce such conflict is to make it clear who is responsible for what, in this case with respect to personnel testing.

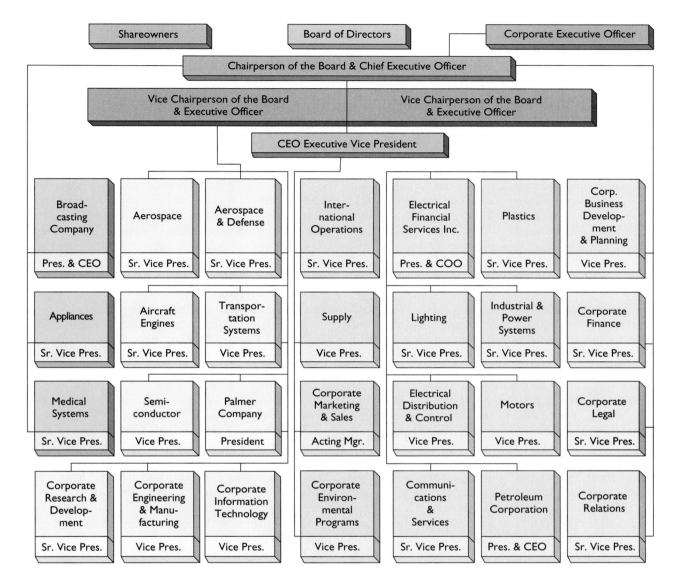

■ FIGURE 7.10
Typical Line and Staff Organization
Here the CEO and aerospace managers are line officers, while the heads of corporate development and planning and finance are staff managers.

The Delegation Process

Organizing departments would be impossible without **delegation,** which we can define as the pushing down of authority from supervisor to subordinate. The assignment of responsibility for some department or job traditionally goes hand in hand with the delegation of authority to get the job done. It would be inappropriate, for example, to assign a subordinate the responsibility for designing a new product and then deny him or her the authority to hire designers to create the best design.

But although authority can be delegated, responsibility cannot. A manager can assign responsibility to a subordinate. However, the manager is still ultimately responsible for ensuring that the job gets done properly. Since the supervisor retains the ultimate responsibility for the job's performance, delegation of authority always entails the creation of accountability. Thus, subordinates become accountable—answerable—to the supervisor for the performance of the tasks assigned to them, particularly if things go wrong.

Entrepreneurs in Action

DELEGATING AT WESTHAVEN SERVICES COMPANY

Mary Lou Fox is an enigma. Her greatest gifts—an entrepreneur's spirit and an innate sense for both marketing and problem solving—are also her greatest handicaps. The problem: No one to whom she delegates ever seems to react the way she would have, and the way she would have reacted is always the best way. Just ask her!

"I've spent years saying, 'How hard would it be to clone me?' I keep thinking, if I can do this, a high school graduate from an idiot town, why can't you?" she asks.

Under Fox's near-sole stewardship, Westhaven Services Company, an institutional pharmacy that sells to such clients as hospitals, has risen from nothing to an $18 million company in 15 years. Fox took over Westhaven from her husband on one condition: She wanted absolute control. Admittedly not a businessperson, Fox got a rough baptism the first year. She was sued once, had to sue a computer company herself, and came to work one day to find state licensing board investigators, working on an anonymous tip, perusing her in-house files. "It was all harassment and politics," she says. "I was not a pharmacist and the pharmacists hated me for it."

Those institutional pharmacies, her nameless competitors, generally emphasized price when trying to attract business. Occasionally they sent fruit baskets. Fox intuitively sensed their dearth of marketing zip and did what she knew how to do best—she marketed. Fox sent out poinsettia arrangements and pens that nurses could wear around their necks. "It says we are thinking of you," she says. "The best way for us to deliver quality care is to be in good communication with the nursing staff." She also threw bashes that became part of the Perrysburg, Ohio, lore. Fox knew what she wanted customers to feel, and she drew on her own life experiences to design ways to make them feel it.

In terms of her management style, Fox decided to get her employees to manage themselves. She would grow her own executives and instill in them what she already knew: that Westhaven sold service, not drugs. Once indoctrinated, she assumed they would achieve departmental objectives in support of Westhaven's corporate goals. But something went wrong. Fox said they couldn't delegate; the executives said she wouldn't. Nearly all of them burned out and left. Todd Herzog, one of the original appointees, said, "You get so much piled on you that you cannot survive. It pulls you to the bottom of the pond and you can't get back to the top."

Next Fox tried hiring experienced managers. She tapped Garth Tebay, an accountant. He discovered that managing for Fox meant dealing with an endless stream of problems but never having the authority to keep them from recurring. He lost 35 pounds and even Fox said he looked like a gray ghost. He left.

Fox's next tactic was an effort to create four teams of the company's key people, each led by a marketing representative, to concentrate on about 35 nursing homes each. Fox had selected four team captains. All left within a year, grousing that they were given plenty of responsibility, but little authority. Fox in turn said that none of them tackled problems like she would have.

Fox is alone again. She refuses to hire anyone, saying she's no good at it. A remaining subordinate says Fox is starting to let certain authority trickle down. Another says that she has even started to delegate real authority. Someone suggested that Fox is nearing the conclusion that there might even be another, maybe better, way to run Westhaven.

"This business is a reflection of me, and I personally care about what our customers think," Fox says. "What I know isn't hard to identify. But it takes time to mold it into something I can [delegate]. Maybe it's just too tough."

SOURCE: Hyatt, "No Way Out," *Inc.,* November 1991, 78–92.

Today, the terms *delegation* and *empowerment* are closely intertwined; they differ in that empowerment is the broader term. Specifically, as the term is increasingly being used, **empowerment** means authorizing and enabling workers to do their jobs. Thus, the assembly workers at Toyota do not just have the authority to solve problems on the line. In addition, they are given the training, tools, and management support required to enable them to solve their problems. In this way, Toyota workers are empowered to continuously improve production quality.

The Entrepreneurs in Action feature on Westhaven Services illustrates some of the problems managers encounter when trying to delegate.

The Decentralized Organization

A **decentralized organization** is one in which authority for most decisions is delegated to the department heads (usually the heads of product divisions), while control over essential companywide matters is maintained at the headquarters office.

Decentralization at successful decentralized companies like Rosenbluth Travel always represents a shrewd balance between delegated authority and centralized control. On the one hand, local managers have considerable autonomy and the means for quickly servicing their local customers. On the other hand, headquarters maintains control of its global company by centralizing (retaining control over) major decisions regarding activities such as making capital appropriations, managing incoming cash receipts, and setting profitability goals. Thus, decentralization always includes both selective delegation of authority and centralized control over essential matters.

There is both a communication aspect and a delegation aspect to decentralizing.[26] The communication aspect refers to the extent to which employees must channel all their communications directly through the head or hub of the organization.[27] For example, must the finance, production, and sales managers communicate with each other *only* through the president, or are they permitted to communicate directly when arriving at a joint decision? The more that communications must be channeled through the president, the more centralized the firm is. The more that managers can communicate directly with each other, the more decentralized the firm is.

The delegation aspect of decentralization can be summed up as follows: The more decisions and the more areas in which authority is delegated from the president to his or her subordinates, the more decentralized the organization is.

⇒ ⇒ ⇒ Managing Change ⇒ ⇒ ⇒

CIRQUE DU SOLEIL MANAGES GLOBALLY

It is a great challenge to manage an organization globally. For example, employment laws that apply in one country may not apply in another. What if your organization operates from Las Vegas to Amsterdam, from Montreal to Asia? One company that does is Cirque du Soleil, Inc., producer of an internationally celebrated traveling circus of sophisticated and daring performers.

Cirque du Soleil is headquartered in Montreal, with 1,200 employees worldwide and offices in Amsterdam and Las Vegas. How do you manage such an enterprise? The answer for this firm is combining decentralization with a small-company atmosphere.

Most of the 1,200 people are attached to local "product division" tours, with two-thirds of the workforce outside headquarters. Employees represent 17 different countries and speak 13 languages. Decision making for such areas as human resources is decentralized to the tour managers because employment law, for example, can vary drastically from country to country. The company maintains cohesion through its strong culture of shared beliefs. Open jobs are posted on the Internet, employees write the company newspaper, and members of, say, Las Vegas' finance department can videotape themselves on the job and swap tapes with the casting crew in Montreal to keep the community feeling.[28]

Companies organized around product divisions are, therefore, usually referred to as "decentralized." Managers of product divisions are often in charge of what amounts to their own miniature companies, as we've seen. Decisions that have anything to do with their product are delegated to them and can be made with little or no communication to the other divisions or the firm's CEO.

Strategy in Action

STRATEGY AND ORGANIZATIONAL STRUCTURE

People who study organizations today generally agree that the way a company is organized depends (or should depend) on that company's strategy.[29] The classic, and still the most influential, study in this area was conducted by economic historian Alfred Chandler a number of years ago; his findings have received recent and widespread empirical support.[30]

Chandler's study analyzed the histories of about 100 of the largest U.S. industrial enterprises. Information was obtained from sources such as annual reports, articles, and government publications, as well as interviews with senior executives. Chandler was fascinated by the fact that some companies like General Electric had adopted decentralized, divisionalized organizational structures, while others such as steel industry firms had remained functionally departmentalized.

Based on his analysis of these companies, Chandler concluded that "structure follows strategy," in other words, that a company's organizational structure had to fit or be appropriate to the nature of its strategy. He concluded, for instance, that

> The prospect of a new market or the threatened loss of a current one stimulated [strategies of] geographical expansion, vertical integration, and product diversification. Moreover, once a firm had accumulated large resources, the need to keep its men, money, and materials steadily employed provided a constant stimulus to look for new markets by moving into new areas, by taking on new functions, or by developing new product lines. [In turn] expansion of volume . . . growth through geographical dispersion . . . [and finally] the developing of new lines of products . . . brought the formation of the divisional structure. . . .[31]

Chandler explained the strategy-structure link in terms of the amount of diversity, new-product development, and technological change with which the company's strategy required its managers to cope. In the steel industry, for instance, managers followed a strategy of concentrating on just one product, and the main strategic objective was to boost the company's efficiency. Here the sorts of duplication inherent in setting up separate product divisions was unnecessarily inefficient, so these companies generally stayed with functional departmentalizations.

At the other extreme, Chandler found that companies in the electronics and chemical industries emphasized research and development, product development, and a strategy of expansion through product diversification. This meant that companies in these fast-changing industries had to market an increasingly diverse range of products to an increasingly diverse range of customers. Having to deal with so many diverse products and customers rendered these firms' original functional structures obsolete. As one early Westinghouse executive pointed out to Chandler, for example:

> All of the activities of the company were [originally] divided into production, engineering, and sales, each of which was the responsibility of a vice president. The domain of each vice president covered the whole diversified and far-flung operations of the corporation. Such an organization of the corporation's management lacks responsiveness. There was too much delay in the recognition of problems and in the solution of problems after they were recognized.[32]

"What is our strategy; what do we want to accomplish?" is, therefore, a question managers should ask in deciding how to organize. Pursuing a new strategy means that top management should consider whether a change in structure is required too, as it was when Westinghouse switched from a functional to a divisional organization.

However, the strategy-structure link is a two-way street, and managers can actually foster a new strategy by changing structure first. For example, decentralizing—pushing down more decision making from the top to the bottom—can empower lower-level employees and enable them to develop new products faster and get them to the market more quickly; this can help a CEO promote a new strategy of diversification.

Tall and Flat Organizations and the Span of Control

Flat Versus Tall Organizations

When he became CEO of General Electric (GE) in the late 1980s, Jack Welch knew he had to make some dramatic organizational changes—and fast. Welch had climbed the ranks and seen how GE's chain of command was draining the firm of its creativity and responsiveness. For instance, business heads had to get approval from the headquarters staff for almost every big decision they made: In one case, the light bulb business managers spent $30,000 producing a fancy film to demonstrate the need for some production equipment they wanted to buy. The old GE, Welch knew, was wasting hundreds of millions of dollars and missing countless opportunities because managers at so many levels were busily checking and re-checking each others' work.

Therefore, the first thing he did as CEO was strip away unneeded organizational levels. Before he took over, "GE's business heads reported to a group head, who reported to a sector head, who reported to the CEO. Each level had its own staff in finance, marketing, and planning, checking and double checking each business."[33] Welch disbanded the group and sector levels, thus dramatically flattening the organizational chain of command. No one stands between the business heads and the CEO's own office now. In disbanding those two levels Welch got rid of the organizational bottlenecks they caused, and the salaries of the almost 700 corporate staff that composed them. Now that it is flatter and leaner, GE is a much more responsive company, and its corporate results reflect its new effectiveness.

The restructuring at GE has been repeated tens of thousands of times in the past few years at tens of thousands of companies. Everywhere you look, from GM to IBM to Levi Strauss to Pratt and Whitney, CEOs are hammering down their chains of command and pushing authority down to lower levels.[34]

Management experts have long known the advantages of flat organizations. One of the first and most extensive empirical studies on the effects of flat and tall organizations was carried out by James Worthy many years ago in the Sears, Roebuck Company.[35] Worthy found that in many Sears units the merchandising vice president and store managers each had more than 40 managers reporting directly to them. As we'll see, this was an extraordinarily high number of subordinates: Early management writers had suggested keeping the number of subordinates reporting to a manager down to a more manageable seven or eight. (They felt that way the supervisors could more closely monitor the work and make most of the decisions.)

Worthy found, however, that because each vice president and store manager had so many managers reporting to them, subordinates all ended up with more autonomy and therefore with higher morale. The managers couldn't demand that all their subordinates keep coming to them for approval of their actions; if they did, they would have been swamped. So at Sears (and increasingly today at thousands of other firms) the organization chart is kept flat. There are relatively few levels and each manager has a relatively high number of subordinates reporting to him or her. The result is an organization in which employees tend to have high autonomy, and the ability to respond faster to customers' needs. Perhaps because of this, morale tends to be higher, too.[36]

The Span of Control

The **span of control** is the number of subordinates reporting directly to a supervisor. In the country-based geographic organization shown in Figure 7.11, the span of control of the country general manager is 13. There are 6 business managers, 6 directors, and 1 innovation manager.

A correlation exists between the number of people reporting to a manager and the number of management levels in an organization. For example, if an organization with 64 workers to be supervised contains a span of control of 8, there will be 8 supervisors directing the workers and 1 manager directing the supervisors (a flat organization). If, on the other hand, the span of control were 4, the same number of workers would require 16 supervisors. They would in turn be directed by 4 managers. These 4 managers would in turn be directed by 1 manager (a tall organization). There would be an extra management level.

FIGURE 7.11
Spans of Control in Country-Based Organization
In this chart, the span of control of the general manager is 13—6 business managers, 6 directors, and 1 manager.

Classic management theorists such as Henri Fayol believed that tall organizational structures (with narrow spans of control) improved performance by requiring close supervision.[37] However, as recent experience at firms like Rosenbluth Travel and Intuit has shown, taller organizations and narrow spans are not panaceas; they can backfire by slowing decision making. Therefore, as the rate of technological change and new-product introductions has increased, many more firms have opted for flatter structures and wider spans.[38] We will pursue this point in the following chapter.

Organizational Behavior in Action

ORGANIZING'S IMPACT ON EMPLOYEE STRESS

How would you feel if, after you had reported to a vice president for two years, your company reorganized and you ended up reporting to one of her subordinates? For many people, organizational changes like these can create stress.

Excessive employee stress can be a serious problem at work. Stress—which psychologists define as the psychological state that develops when an individual is confronted with situations that exceed his or her perceived ability to handle them—often results in a predictable sequence of reactions.[39] Physically, the body exhibits numerous physical changes including elevated heart rate, blood pressure, and respiration.[40] If the stress is perceived as sufficiently severe and unrelenting it can at worst lead to physical, behavioral, and psychological problems and decreased performance.[41] Under the worst of conditions the stress may prove so debilitating that the employee actually must escape the workplace, either by physically leaving it or by retreating into a shell and basically isolating himself or herself from the source of the problem.

We'll see in later chapters that many factors—called *stressors*—can trigger stress and its consequences. Some jobs, such as air traffic controller, are inherently more stressful than are others. The physical work environment (such as extreme heat or cold) can cause stress, too. Excessive corporate politics and a particularly loathsome boss are some other obvious stressors.

The way the company is organized—its structure—is a particularly important potential source of stress, but one that is manageable if the person doing the organizing knows what to look for. Some guidelines for managing organization-based stressors follow.

REDUCE ROLE CONFLICT. Even "management experts" in antiquity advised against putting anyone in the position of having to "serve two masters." Most people become uncomfortable when they receive incompatible instructions from two or more bosses. **Role conflict** is defined as a situation in which two or more sets of demands are placed on an employee in such a manner that compliance with one demand makes it difficult to comply with the other.[42]

The way companies organize can trigger role conflict in several ways, since there are several types of role conflict.[43] There may be conflict between the person and the role, such as when someone's personality or training doesn't fit the job: Introverts tend to make poor salespeople, for instance. Interrole conflict means demands are placed on an employee such that complying with one makes it hard to comply with the other: Having your boss tell you to complete a report by tomorrow morning and then having her boss tell you to finish another project instead is an example.

Such role conflicts can't always be eliminated, nor do they necessarily have to be. But, in general, reducing role conflict is advisable. Doing so includes ensuring that employees have clear job assignments, that employees are properly screened and trained for their jobs, and that employees feel secure enough to express their discomfort if they do receive contradictory orders.

MAKE JOB ASSIGNMENTS CLEAR. Sometimes the problem is a lack of clarity regarding what the employee is to do or how he or she is to do it; this is called **role ambiguity.** For example, consider how you would feel if you took a college class and weren't told the basis on which you were to be graded, or what you could do to get a better grade: You would probably exhibit some of the stress associated with role ambiguity.

EMPOWER EMPLOYEES. Stress can also be triggered by the perception that one has little or no control over important aspects of one's job, such as work schedule, work pace, or the decisions one can make. For example, consider the plight of a newly appointed sales manager who has just discovered that she doesn't have the authority to hire or fire salespeople, develop sales plans, or evaluate the sales staff in any way.

This sales manager would probably experience the stress associated with not having enough authority to do her job. Empowerment is one solution. In this case, empowerment might include (1) delegating more authority to the sales manager and allowing her to appraise her salespeople, to hire new ones, and (with her supervisor's approval) to dismiss those who are underperforming; (2) providing her with supervisory training in the areas of employee appraisal and interviewing; and (3) reinforcing with other managers the fact that she is now in charge of appraising, hiring, and dismissing members of her sales force. ■

SUMMARY

1. Organizing is the arranging of an enterprise's activities in such a way that they systematically contribute to the enterprise's goals. An organization consists of people whose specialized tasks are coordinated to contribute to the organization's goals.

2. Departmentalization is the process through which an enterprise's activities are grouped together and assigned to managers. Departments can be grouped around functions, customer groups, marketing channels, or geographic areas.

3. A matrix organization, or matrix management, is defined as the superimposition of one or more forms of departmentalization on top of an existing one. In practice, most enterprises use several forms of departmentalization and are called hybrids.

4. Coordination is the process of achieving unity of action among interdependent activities. It is required when two or more interdependent entities must work together to achieve a common goal. The techniques for achieving coordination include mutual adjustment; the use of rules or procedures; direct supervision; departmentalization; the use of a staff assistant, a liaison, a committee, or independent integrators; and the standardization of targets, skills, or shared values.

5. Authority is the right to take action, to make decisions, and to direct the work of others. Managers usually distinguish between line and staff authority. Departments could not be organized without delegation, which is defined as the pushing down of authority from superior to subordinate. In a decentralized organization, authority for most decisions is delegated to the department heads.

6. Many companies are adopting flatter structures in an effort to eliminate duplication of effort, inspire creativity, and increase the responsiveness of the company. The span of control in a company is the number of subordinates reporting directly to a supervisor.

KEY TERMS

organizing
organization
organization chart
chain of command
informal organization
departmentalization
functional
    departmentalization
divisionalization
customer
    departmentalization
marketing-channel
    departmentalization

marketing channel
matrix organization
    (matrix management)
coordination
mutual adjustment
independent integrator
authority
power
reward power
coercive power
legitimate power
referent power
expert power

politics
line manager
staff manager
functional authority
line–staff conflict
delegation
empowerment
decentralized
    organization
span of control
role conflict
role ambiguity

SELF-TEST

TRUE / FALSE QUESTIONS

1 **T F** Johnson & Johnson is an example of a highly structured, centralized bureaucracy.

2 **T F** An organization is defined as consisting of people whose specialized tasks are coordinated to contribute to the goals of the organization.

3 **T F** One of the most useful aspects of an organization chart is that it reflects the informal organization that has developed in the company.

4 **T F** One of the major advantages of organizing departments around functions is that it is a simple, straightforward, and logical way to organize.

5 **T F** A major disadvantage of organizing around divisions is duplication of effort.

6 **T F** A complexity of the matrix model is that you can have dual reporting lines across more than one area, such as product and geography.

7 **T F** Authority in organizations is basically legitimate power.

8 **T F** Referent power occurs when a person identifies with another person and is highly attracted to that person.

9 **T F** Staff managers can always issue orders to subordinates down the chain of command.

10 **T F** The strategy-structure link is one-way; that is, structure should always follow strategy.

MULTIPLE-CHOICE QUESTIONS

1 What does the following describe: "the informal, habitual contacts, communications, and ways of doing things that employees always develop"?
  a. formal organization
  b. outside customer relations
  c. informal organization
  d. none of the above

2 Grouping activities around basic functions like manufacturing, sales, human resources, finance, and marketing is called _____
  a. functional departmentalization.
  b. divisionalization.
  c. network organization.
  d. virtual corporation.

3 Which of the following is *not* an advantage of divisionalization?
  a. Performance is more easily judged.
  b. Divisionalization can shift some management responsibilities from top management to divisional management.
  c. Divisionalization can provide motivation for the manager to perform better.
  d. Sales can be more easily coordinated.

4 What type of organization is defined as the superimposition of one or more forms of departmentalization on top of an existing one?
  a. bureaucracy
  b. flat
  c. matrix
  d. none of the above

5 Which of the following is an example of a successful matrix organization?
   a. NASA
   b. Citicorp Bank
   c. UNICEF
   d. All of the above

6 Which of the following is *not* a disadvantage of matrix departmentalization?
   a. power struggles and conflict
   b. lost time
   c. avoidance of duplicate functional departments
   d. excessive overhead

7 _____ is the process of achieving unity of action among interdependent activities.
   a. Power relations
   b. Coordination
   c. Delegation
   d. Authority

8 Which of the following are ways to build teamwork?
   a. Hire the right people.
   b. Create a sense of purpose.
   c. Provide team-building training.
   d. All of the above

9 What is described by the following: The ability of A to get B to do something that A wants done even when B resists?
   a. authority
   b. power
   c. delegation
   d. none of the above

10 Organizations like GE that are redesigning themselves are adopting which of the following models?
   a. tall
   b. bureaucratic
   c. flat
   d. vertical

CRITICAL THINKING EXERCISES

1 The book *Creative Organization Theory* offers a series of mind-stretchers. Among them is the following exercise.

Conventional texts on management often define organizations as groups of people united by a common goal. This kind of definition eliminates almost all the interesting features of organizations in practice. They are rarely so rational and so united as the definition suggests. How would *you* define an organization?

2 Think about the university or college you are attending. How is it organized? Could it be organized more efficiently using the concepts discussed in this chapter? How would you reorganize the organization to be more effective and efficient for all stakeholders?

EXPERIENTIAL EXERCISES

1 You have been hired to reorganize and redesign the ABC corporation, which has had a single product line, women's dress shoes, for over four decades. It is a traditional tall organization with authority at the top (the CEO is a former designer) and a functional structure of sales, design, marketing, human resources, customer relations, finance and accounting, and production. Lately, sales have been falling off because styles in women's shoes have changed. Using the information provided in the chapter, propose how a new organization might help avoid further dips in sales.

2 By the time the office opens at 8:45 A.M., the line of people waiting to do business at the Registry of Motor Vehicles (RMV) in Watertown, Massachusetts, will be 25 deep. By midday, especially if it is near the end of the month, the line may extend around the building. Inside, motorists wait in slow-moving rows before poorly marked windows to get a driver's license or to register an automobile. When someone gets to the head of the line, he or she is often told by the clerk that it is the wrong line. The customers grumble impatiently. The clerks act harried and sometimes speak brusquely, even rudely.

Not far away, people also wait in line at a McDonald's fast-food restaurant. There are several lines; each is short and moves quickly. The menu is clearly displayed on attractive signs. The workers behind the counter are invariably polite. If someone's order cannot be filled immediately, he or she is asked to step aside for a moment while the food is prepared, and then is brought back to the head of the line to receive the order. The atmosphere is friendly and good natured. The room is immaculately clean.

What might the RMV learn from McDonald's? What are some of the issues and problems in redesigning the RMV to be more like McDonald's? What concepts discussed in the chapter might help the RMV and maybe even improve McDonald's?

SOURCE: James Q. Wilson, *Bureaucracy* (New York: Basic Books, 1989), 112.

DIVERSITY CASE

MONSANTO CHEMICAL GROUP

Several years ago, Monsanto Chemical Group of St. Louis, Missouri, awakened to the discovery that a lot of talented women and minorities were leaving because they had the sense that management neither appreciated nor really understood them. The company had a three-year-old diversity-management program under way, but it was obvious that something else was needed. After some statistical analysis and a lot of deliberation, management settled on the use of consulting pairs. The hope was that cross-cultural communication channels could be enhanced by the employees themselves and that the effort itself would signal Monsanto's commitment to its entire workforce.

In a given company setting, problems between employees of differing ethnic backgrounds are often grounded in erroneous, and perhaps more important, unarticulated perceptions. When ethnic, gender, racial, or similar conflicts arise at Monsanto, consulting pairs of trained volunteers are assigned to mediate. Ideally, the consulting pair selected will very closely reflect the backgrounds of both of the workers who are unable to come to agreement. Thus, a young Hispanic female who can't come to an accord with a 57-year-old white male can expect to see, as nearly as is possible, a consultant partner of the same age, gender, and ethnicity as herself. Matters are kept confidential when the quartet of two combatants and two mediators get together. The focus of these meetings is to get at the heart of the matter, whatever it may be.

Most of the efforts are focused on an aspect of the program called "join-up." Designed to smooth the supervisor-subordinate relationship, join-ups occur whenever an employee begins reporting to a new boss. Although it takes time for any employee to fully understand what a new boss expects of him or her, research has shown that the process is three to four times more difficult when the worker is a woman or minority. Consulting pairs moderate a two-hour get-together where expectations are outlined and the foundations of effective communication laid. Even if such meetings don't result in an outstanding level of rapport, they do allow both sides to put their cards on the table and avoid unexpected surprises later on.

Consulting pairs and the join-up program provide Monsanto employees with an avenue for airing grievances and for learning both what they can expect and what is expected of them. One of the primary reasons it has been effective is that employees know it's available. The company's turnover rate for the target group of women and minorities has flattened. Another benefit that might be even more important is that every employee now realizes there is a forum where he or she can be heard.

Questions

1 List some possible reasons why the relationship between a new boss and a subordinate is even more difficult when the employee is a woman or a minority.
2 What do you consider the primary benefits of a program such as Monsanto's consulting pairs?
3 How could the consulting pairs program be used to facilitate coordination at Monsanto?

SOURCE: Jennifer J. Laabs, "Employees Manage Conflict and Diversity," *Personnel Journal,* December 1993, 30–6.

STRATEGY CASE

THE NEW VISA ORGANIZATION

In the late 1960s the credit card industry was in a state of disaster. In their rush to win new customers, banks were issuing cards galore—even pets, children, and convicted felons became inadvertent credit card holders, and deliberate fraud became rampant.

In the midst of this chaos one of the major firms, Bank of America, decided to revise its strategy. Dee Hock, a member of the planning group, believed that command-and-control organizations were "archaic and increasingly irrelevant." Given the opportunity, he set out to shape a new organizational structure to carry out a new corporate strategy. After almost two years of brainstorming and planning, a new entity that came to be called Visa International was formed, with Dee Hock as its CEO.

Following Hock's suggestion, the organization was highly decentralized and collaborative, with authority, initiative, decision making, and profits pushed to the outside of the organization—its member banks.

Questions

1 What does "management" mean in this new decentralized context?
2 Do you agree with Dee Hock that command-and-control organizations are irrelevant to the postindustrial economy? What might be the advantage of decentralizing for an organization such as Visa?
3 Is it practical to implement a totally flat organization with just one boss, in which everyone is responsible for the welfare of the organization and for each other?

SOURCE: M. Mitchell Waldrop, "The Trillion Dollar Vision of Dee Hock," *Fast Company,* October–November, 1996, 75–86.

ENTREPRENEURIAL CASE

THE DESIGN AND DESIRES OF ST. LUKE'S

Every one of the 55 employees of St. Luke's, a creative London ad agency, is an owner, from the switchboard operator to the creative director.

A five-person council governs the company. Two of the council members are elected from among the employees. A new creative director who joins the firm receives shares in the company, but fewer than a receptionist who's been with the agency since the beginning.

Just one year old, St. Luke's generates annual billings of $72 million and is the fastest growing agency in London.

Questions

1 How does St. Luke's structure differ from that of a traditional organization?
2 What management problems might be encountered in such a flat structure?
3 What structural problems might St. Luke's find in the future? What concepts presented in the chapter might help the firm solve those problems?

SOURCE: Steven Alburty, "The Ad Agency to End All Ad Agencies," *Fast Company*, December–January 1997, 116–24.

THE BUSINESS TEAM, INC.

THE NEW MEDICAL MARKETPLACE

Hal has just returned from a trip to his health care clinic for his annual checkup. He had made an early appointment so he would not miss a client luncheon at noon, but unfortunately, he had to call the prospective client and cancel because the examination process was taking so long.

Hal had already waited four months for this appointment and he was experiencing some symptoms that might indicate an ulcer. So he decided to hang in there all day if necessary. And it was necessary. He was kept waiting for hours as the staff used triage to prioritize their cases. Hal's case was "just routine," so he was held up at the many stations he had to visit, from chest x-ray to blood and urine samples. Hal even had to walk from building to building within the facility to get the correct services. Only once did he see a doctor; the rest of his contacts were technicians or clerks who needed insurance information.

By the time he reached home at 6 o'clock that night, Hal was exhausted and frustrated. As a productions and operations specialist, he was appalled at how disorganized the clinic was. He was well aware that there are many pressures on health-care professionals, from demands for health-care reform to rising health-care cost. He felt that the disorganization masquerading as an organized business needed help from The Business Team, Inc.

Questions

1 How might the Team go about approaching the clinic with its reorganization needs?
2 What types of problems do you think the Team would find if it tried to change the organization of the clinic and consequently the authority relations among the staff?
3 Do you think a matrix structure would work in a medical clinic?
4 How would you approach the redesign problem if you were a member of The Business Team, Inc.?

YOU BE THE CONSULTANT

ORGANIZING KNITMEDIA

By the end of 1997, KnitMedia expected its employee count to increase from about 30 employees the year before to 48 staff and 20 contract employees. In addition to the executive personnel formerly listed (Michael Dorf, Kenneth Ashworth, Mitchell Goldman, Rachel McBeth, Edwin Greer, Mark Pearlson, and Arthur Phillips), the company employs other key personnel, as well as support and administrative staff.

The KnitMedia organization chart for 1996–1997 is presented in Figure 7.1 on page 213. As you can see, this shows three top-level executives (CEO, COO, and CFO) and, below these three positions, directors for each of the basic divisional activities in which KnitMedia engages (such as Knitting Factory Works). Although this organization chart was more than adequate while the company was small, as KnitMedia expands quickly in the late 1990s a number of changes might be necessary: For instance, there may be a need for greater clarity regarding exactly to whom each of the second-level directors reports—is it the CEO, COO, CFO, or to all three, as a committee?

Team Exercises and Questions

Use what you learned in this chapter to answer the following questions:

1 What type of organization is represented by the KnitMedia 1996–1997 organization chart?

2 What do you think accounts for the fact that there are no lines connecting any other directors to any of the three top-level managers?

3 How (if at all) would you reorganize KnitMedia, and why?

For the online version of this case, visit our Web site at: <www.prenhall.com/desslermgmt>.

For Internet exercises, interactive study questions, news updates and more, visit the Dessler Web site at

www.prenhall.com/desslermgmt

If you're using the CD-ROM that accompanies this text, simply click on the "Web Site" button to access the site.

CHAPTER 8

DESIGNING ORGANIZATIONS TO MANAGE CHANGE

What's Ahead?

Hewlett-Packard (HP) was the Silicon Valley trendsetter for progressive management and technological breakthroughs for over 45 years. But by the early 1990s, HP's unique management system, designed to encourage communication and break down the chain

of command, had solidified into an unresponsive giant. It once took seven months and 100 people on nine separate committees just to name a new computing package. "There was a lot of decision overhead," is how HP CEO John A. Young put it. HP thus found itself in an organizational straitjacket that was diminishing its responsiveness. Regaining its ability to manage change would clearly require redesigning the organization.

Objectives

After studying this chapter, you should be able to

- **discuss** the factors affecting how organizations are designed and structured
- **explain** the initial redesign steps for making organizations more responsive
- **explain** how to organize and lead team-based organizations
- **discuss** what is meant by network-based and boundaryless organizations
- **describe** the horizontal corporation.

MANAGEMENT ON THE WEB

JOURNAL OF ORGANIZATIONAL CHANGE MANAGEMENT

This online journal addresses how to manage change positively. It is international and inter-disciplinary in approach. What suggestions would you find there for Hewlett-Packard? ■

http://www.mcb.co.uk/cgi-bin/mcb_serve/table1.txt&jocmt.journal1.htm

A Wave of Reorganizations

Hewlett-Packard was not alone in needing to reorganize. A wave of reorganizations—actually, deorganizations—is sweeping industry as managers grapple with the challenge of managing rapid change.[1] In the early 1990s, Zurich-based ABB Asea Brown Boveri cut its headquarters staff by 95 percent and "deorganized" 215,000 people into 5,000 largely independent "profit centers" (individual minicompanies) that average only 50 people each. At IBM, CEO Louis Gerstner, Jr., is stripping away the ponderous central staff and bureaucratic procedures that helped to slow IBM's responsiveness, substituting instead decentralized decision making and smaller organizational units.[2] At GM's Saturn Corporation plant in Spring Hill, Tennessee, the "organization" is hardly an organization at all: Instead, almost all activities are carried out by self-managing work teams within the culture of quality and teamwork that drives this firm. And Hal Rosenbluth, as we saw in chapter 7, broke his company into more than 100 business units, each serving specific regions and clients of his travel firm.[3]

Factors Affecting Organizational Structure

To understand why today's rapid change is causing traditional structures to be replaced by more responsive ones, it is useful to understand the factors that influence how companies should be structured. Two important factors are the rate of change of the firm's *environment,* and the *technology* the firm uses to produce its work.

Organization and Environment: The Burns and Stalker Studies

Researchers Tom Burns and G. M. Stalker studied about 20 industrial firms in the United Kingdom a number of years ago. Their purpose was to determine how the nature of a firm's environment affected the way the firm was organized and managed. They believed that a stable, unchanging environment demanded a different type of organization than did a rapidly changing one.[4] We can illustrate Burns and Stalker's findings by focusing on two contrasting environments that they studied: the stable environment and the innovative environment.

ORGANIZING IN A STABLE ENVIRONMENT. A stable environment can be characterized as follows:

1. Demand for the organization's product or service is stable and predictable.
2. There is an unchanging set of competitors.
3. Technological innovation and new product developments are evolutionary rather than revolutionary, in that necessary product changes can be predicted well in advance and the required modifications made at a leisurely pace.
4. Government policies regarding regulation and taxation of the industry change little over time.

Burns and Stalker found that a rayon manufacturer they studied operated in a stable environment. To be successful in this industry, the parent firm had to keep costs down and be as efficient as possible. Its existence, therefore, depended on keeping unexpected occurrences to a minimum, to facilitate maintaining steady, high-volume production runs.

Burns and Stalker found that the rayon mill's organizational structure seemed to reflect this stable, unchanging environment and emphasis on efficiency. The organization was a "pyramid of knowledge" in that top management made most decisions and communicated them downward. Decision making in the plant was highly centralized, and the plant was run on the basis of an elaborate network of policies, procedures, rules, and tight production controls. Job descriptions were carefully defined, and everyone from the top of the organization to the bottom had a very specialized job to do.[5] Coordination was accomplished via the chain of command.

ORGANIZING IN AN INNOVATIVE ENVIRONMENT. At the other extreme, an innovative environment is characterized by:

1. Demand for the organization's product or service can change drastically, sometimes overnight, as competitors introduce radically improved products.

Innovative business environments like the bioengineering industry are characterized by rapid new product development and unexpected change. These factors have a profound effect on organizational structure.

2. Sudden, unexpected changes in the nature of the organization's competitors.[6]
3. An extremely rapid rate of technological innovation and new product development. Organizations in innovative environments usually rely heavily on research and development for their survival.
4. Quickly evolving government policies regarding regulation and taxation that try to keep pace with the stream of new and more technologically advanced products being introduced by firms.

Innovative environments are typical of industries such as Internet software, electronics, and computers, the space industry (satellites, space platforms), the deep-sea industry (new sources of food and minerals), and the gene industry (high-yielding crops, "oil-eating" bacteria).

Burns and Stalker found that several of the electronics firms they studied were competing in this sort of innovative environment. Their existence depended on their ability to continually introduce innovative electronic components. They also had to be constantly on the alert for innovations by their competitors, so responsiveness and creativity (rather than efficiency) were paramount for these companies.

In these firms, the researchers found a "deliberate attempt to avoid specifying individual tasks."[7] Each worker's job, in other words, might change daily, as employees rushed to respond to the "problem of the day." Most important, all employees recognized the need for sharing common beliefs and goals, and these common goals (such as "Let's make sure we only produce first-rate products") helped ensure that all could work together with little or no guidance. In turn, this pervasive self-control helped the firm adapt quickly and unbureaucratically to its rapidly changing environment. When a problem arose, an employee took the initiative to solve it, or took it to the person he or she felt was in the best position to solve it. This often meant bypassing the formal chain of command. The head of one such firm

> attacked the idea of the organization chart as inapplicable in his concern and as a dangerous method of thinking about the working of industrial management. The first requirement of management, according to him, was that it should make the fullest use of the capacities of its members; any individual's job should be as little defined as possible, so that it will 'shape itself' to his special abilities and initiative.[8]

MECHANISTIC AND ORGANIC ORGANIZATIONS. Their findings led Burns and Stalker to distinguish between two types of organizations, which they called **mechanistic** and **organic**. The rayon firm was typical of mechanistic, classic organizations; the electronics firms were typical of the organic, behavioral ones. Mechanistic organizations, they said, are characterized by:

- Close adherence to the chain of command.
- A functional division of work, through which the problems and tasks facing the concern as a whole are broken down into specialized activities.
- Highly specialized jobs.
- Use of the formal hierarchy for coordination.
- Detailed job descriptions that provide a precise definition of rights, obligations, and technical methods for performing each job.
- A tendency for interaction between employees to be vertical, "between superior and subordinate."
- A tendency for behavior to be governed by the instructions and decisions issued by superiors.

On the other hand, organic organizations are characterized by:

- Little preoccupation with the chain of command.
- A more self-contained, divisionalized structure of work.
- Job responsibility not viewed by employees as a limited field of rights, obligations, and methods. (Employees do not respond to requests by saying, "That's not my job," for instance.)
- Jobs that are not clearly defined in advance but instead are continually adjusted and redefined as the situation demands.
- A network or matrix structure of communication.
- Lateral rather than vertical communication and an emphasis on consultation rather than command. Communication generally consists more of information and advice rather than instructions and decisions.
- A pervasive commitment to the organization's tasks that motivates employees to maintain self-control (as opposed to having performance controlled solely through a system of rewards and penalties, as is often the case in mechanistic organizations).[9]

SUMMARY. In terms of organizational structure, the Burns and Stalker findings can be summarized as follows:

1. *Lines of authority.* In mechanistic organizations, the lines of authority are clear and everyone closely adheres to the chain of command. In organic organizations, employees' jobs are always changing and the lines of authority are not so clear. Here there is less emphasis on sticking closely to the chain of command and much more emphasis on speaking directly with the person who might have an answer to the problem.

2. *Departmentalization.* In mechanistic organizations (with their emphasis on efficiency), functional types of departmentalization prevail. In organic organizations (where flexibility is the rule), a product/divisional type of departmentalization prevails.

3. *Degree of specialization of jobs.* In mechanistic organizations, each employee has a highly specialized job at which he or she is expected to become an expert. In organic organizations, "job enlargement" is the rule.

4. *Delegation and decentralization.* In mechanistic organizations, most important decisions are centralized. In organic ones, more important decisions are made at lower levels; they are more decentralized.

5. *Span of control.* The span of control is narrow in mechanistic organizations, and there is close supervision. Spans are wider in organic organizations, and supervision is more general.

Organization and Technology: The Woodward Studies

British researcher Joan Woodward's contribution lies in her discovery that a firm's production technology (the processes it uses to produce its products or services) affects the way the firm should be organized.

Almost from the outset the studies by Woodward and her associates were aimed at trying to understand why a firm's organizational structure seemed at first to have no relationship to success for the firms they studied. The research team spent months analyzing volumes of data on each company's history and background, size, and policies and procedures. None of these factors seemed to explain why some successful firms had classic, mechanistic structures while others had behavioral, organic ones. Finally, the Woodward team decided to classify the companies according to their production technologies, as follows:

1. *Unit and small-batch production.* These companies produced one-at-a-time prototypes and specialized custom units to customers' requirements (like fine pianos). They had to be very responsive to customer needs.
2. *Large-batch and mass production.* These companies produced large batches of products on assembly lines (like Ford cars). Here efficiency was emphasized.
3. *Process production.* These companies produced products such as paper and petroleum products through continuously running facilities. Here highly trained technicians had to be ready to respond at a moment's notice to any production emergency.

Once the firms were classified it became clear that a different type of organizational structure was appropriate for each type of technology. Some of Woodward's findings are summarized in Table 8.1. Note that organic structures were usually found in the unit and process production firms; mass production firms usually had mechanistic structures.

In terms of organizational structure, the Woodward findings can be summarized as follows:

1. *Lines of authority.* The lines of authority and adherence to the chain of command are rigid in mass production firms, but more informal and flexible in unit and process production firms.

Joan Woodward's studies of organizational structure identified three types of production technologies that affect the way firms are organized: (a) unit or small-batch production, used for handmade luxury goods such as this Cartier watch; (b) mass production, like airplane manufacture; and (c) process production, like oil refining.

(a)

(c)

(b)

	UNIT AND SMALL-BATCH FIRMS (EXAMPLE: CUSTOM-BUILT CARS)	LARGE-BATCH AND MASS PRODUCTION (EXAMPLE: MASS-PRODUCED CARS)	PROCESS PRODUCTION (EXAMPLE: OIL REFINERY)
Chain of Command	Not Clear	Clear	Not Clear
Span of Control	Narrow	Wide	Narrow
Departmentalization	Product	Function	Product
Overall Organization	Organic	Mechanistic	Organic

NOTE: Summary of findings showing how production technology and organization structure are related.

2. *Departmentalization.* There is a functional departmentalization in mass production firms, and a product type of departmentalization in unit and process production firms.
3. *Degree of specialization of jobs.* Jobs are highly specialized in mass production firms, and less so in unit and process production firms.
4. *Delegation and decentralization.* Organizations tend to be centralized in mass production firms, and decentralized in unit and process production firms.
5. *Span of control.* Unit and process production firms have narrower supervisory-level spans of control than do mass production firms.

Synthesis: A Contingency Approach to Organizing

The Burns and Stalker findings, and Woodward's, suggest that different organizational structures are appropriate for, or contingent on, different tasks.[10] At one extreme are organizations dealing with predictable, routine tasks like running a rayon firm.[11] Here, efficiency is emphasized, and successful organizations tend to be mechanistic. They stress adherence to rules and to the chain of command, are highly centralized, and have a more specialized, functional departmentalization. At the other extreme, some organizations have more unpredictable tasks and are constantly faced with the need to invent new products and respond quickly to emergencies. Here creativity and entrepreneurial activities are emphasized, and to encourage these activities such organizations tend to be organic. They do not urge employees to "play it by the rules" or to abide closely to the chain of command. Similarly, decision making is more decentralized and jobs and departments less specialized.[12] These differences are summarized in Table 8.2, on page 256.

How Are Managers Moving Beyond Organic Organizations?

Early, "classical" management theorists were not oblivious to the fact that organizations had to be responsive—at least occasionally. Most of these experts, such as Henri Fayol, Frederick Taylor, and Luther Gulick, were managers or consultants. They were therefore experienced enough to know that there are times when sticking to the

■ TABLE 8.2 *Summary of Contingency Approach to Organizing*

CHARACTERISTICS	TYPE OF ORGANIZATION	
	Mechanistic	**Organic**
Type of Environment	Stable	Innovative
Comparable to	Classical Organization	Behavioral Organization Emphasis on Self-Control
Adherence to Chain of Command	Close	Flexible—Chain of Command Often Bypassed
Type of Departmentalization	Functional	Divisional
How Specialized Are Jobs	Specialized	Unspecialized—Jobs Change Daily, with Situation
Degree of Decentralization	Decision Making Centralized	Decision Making Decentralized
Span of Control	Narrow	Wide
Type of Coordination	Hierarchy and Rules	Committees, Liaisons, and Special Integrators

chain of command simply results in too ponderous a response. Henri Fayol, for instance, said that orders and inquiries should generally follow the chain of command. However, in very special circumstances a "bridge" communication could take place, say between a salesperson and a production supervisor, if a decision was required at once.

Prescriptions like these worked fairly well as long as abnormal situations were not the rule. If a company was operating in an environment in which novel, unexpected occurrences were minimal, then giving every employee a specialized job and achieving coordination by making most people stick to the chain of command was an effective way to do things. But as the number of unexpected problems and issues—new competitors, new product or technological innovations, customers suddenly going out of business, and so on—becomes unmanageable, a mechanistic organization gets overloaded and errors start to mount. Today, says management expert Tom Peters, success in the marketplace "is directly proportional to the knowledge that an organization can bring to bear, how fast it can bring that knowledge to bear, and the rate at which it accumulates knowledge."[13] In other words, companies must be organized to respond to rapid change, and to respond very quickly.

As a result, today you might say that we are moving beyond even organic organizations. Product divisions, flexible lines of authority, less specialized jobs, and decentralized decisions—all the features of organic structures—are often not enough today to provide the fast response time that companies need.

Managers—even those whose firms already had organic types of structures—initially reacted to today's more rapid change in several ways. Many downsized. **Downsizing** means dramatically reducing the size of a company's workforce.[14] Often, at the same time, they and others took their existing structures and then (1) reduced the levels of management, thus flattening their companies' structures; (2) reorganized around small mini-units; (3) reassigned support staff from headquarters to the divisions, thus decentralizing decisions; and (4) further decentralized by empowering workers. We'll address these initial attempts at boosting responsiveness next, and then move on to the team- and network-based structures that define designing organizations for managing change in the following three sections.

Reduce Layers of Management

Reducing management layers is perhaps the most widespread tactic used to manage change. When he took over the troubled Union Pacific Railroad (UPRR), former CEO Mike Walsh found an extremely bureaucratic and sluggish organization. Consider this typical example from Mr. Walsh:

> Suppose a customer was having difficulty [finding] a railroad car—it was either not the right one, or wasn't where the customer needed it for loading or unloading. The customer would go to his UPRR sales representative—who "went up" to the district traffic manager, who in turn "went up" to the regional traffic manager. The regional boss passed the problem from his sales and marketing organization, across a chasm psychologically wider than the Grand Canyon, to the operations department's general manager. The general manager then "went down" to the superintendent, who "went down" to the train master to find out what had gone wrong.[15]

After that, of course, the whole cumbersome approval process was repeated in reverse. The information went up the operations hierarchy, then down the sales and marketing hierarchy until the annoyed customer finally got his or her answer—often several days later. Multiplied hundreds or thousands of times a week, that sort of unresponsiveness, Walsh knew, helped to explain why Union Pacific was losing customers, revenues, and profits.

The first thing Walsh did was flatten the railroad's 30,000-person operations department, squeezing out five layers of middle management. The results are shown in Figure 8.1. When Walsh arrived, there were nine layers of managers between the

▣ FIGURE 8.1
Union Pacific Railroad Hierarchy: 1987 and 1990

Source: From *Liberation Management* by Tom Peters. Copyright © 1992 by Excel, a California Limited Partnership. Reprinted by permission of Alfred A. Knopf, Inc.

FIGURE A	FIGURE B
PRIOR TO 1987 REORGANIZATION	**1990**
Executive VP Operations	*Executive VP Operations*
VP Operations	VP Field Operations
General Manager	Superintendent Transportation Services
Assistant General Manager	Manager Train Operations
Regional Transportation Superintendent	Yardmaster
Division Superintendent	*Railroaders*
Division Superintendent Transportation	
Trainmaster/Terminal Superintendent	
Assistant Trainmaster/ Terminal Trainmaster	
Yardmaster	
Railroaders	

executive vice president of operations and the railroaders themselves. After the reorganization, only four levels remained. In about three months, Walsh stripped out five layers and 800 middle managers from the operations chain of command.[16]

Establish Mini-Units

Many managers reacted to the need to better manage change by reorganizing their companies into smaller minicompanies. These smaller units tended to be more entrepreneurial: Everyone (including the top executive) knew everyone else, layers of management weren't required for an approval, and interactions and communications were more frequent, given the greater likelihood of employees knowing each other and working in close proximity.

Many companies therefore took this route, at least initially. At ABB the CEO "deorganized" his 215,000 employees into 5,000 smaller profit centers averaging about 50 people each. At Intuit the new CEO, as we've seen, broke the company into eight separate businesses, each with its own general manager and mission.[17] And Hal Rosenbluth of Rosenbluth Travel broke his company into more than 100 business units, each focused on special regions and clients.[18]

Reassign Support Staff

Many firms also move headquarters staff such as industrial engineers out of headquarters and assign them to the divisional officers of their business units. For example, candy maker Mars, Inc., is a $7 billion company with only a 30-person headquarters staff. Mars does have staff employees. But, as is true in more and more firms, these staff employees are assigned directly to the individual business units. Here they can help their business units be successful in the marketplace rather than act as gatekeepers who check and recheck divisional managers' plans for the firm's top executives. When Percy Barnevik took over as CEO of Sweden's ASEA, it had a central staff of 2,000, which he quickly reduced to 200. When his firm then acquired Finland's Stromberg company, its headquarters staff of 880 was reduced within a few years to 25.[19]

Widen Spans of Control

Squeezing out management layers results in wider spans of control. Not too long ago, one researcher found that the average span of control in the United States was 1 supervisor to 10 nonsupervisors. The Japanese ratio was 1 to 100 (and often 1 to 200).[20] Today, flattening the hierarchy has widened U.S. spans by eliminating managers.

Organizational Behavior in Action

EMPOWERING EMPLOYEES

If the supervisors are not there to supervise, then who makes all their decisions? The answer, increasingly, is the employees themselves. Thus, at firms like ABB, GE, and Scandinavian Air Systems, employees who previously had to consult supervisors before taking some action (like approving a refund) are now making the decisions themselves: They are *empowered*.

The Pratt and Whitney engine division of United Technologies Corporation provides one example. When CEO Bob Daniell took over, he first had to address Pratt and Whitney's deteriorating reputation with its customers. American Airlines and United Airlines threatened they would never buy another Pratt engine unless they started getting faster responses to their complaints. Pratt soon saw its engine orders slip by over 25 percent. Part of Daniell's solution was to boost the number of service representatives in the field by nearly 70 percent. Then these field reps were given authority to approve multimillion dollar warranty replacements on the spot, instead of waiting weeks for headquarter's approvals. Customers found the improvements startling, and Pratt and Whitney quickly turned around.[21]

Building Team-Based Structures

Increasingly today, steps such as empowering, widening spans, or establishing mini-units are no longer enough. Managers are therefore using teams, networks, and "boundaryless" structures to redesign their organizations so as to better manage change. Many firms boost responsiveness by organizing most of their activities around self-contained and self-managing work teams. A **team** is a group of people who work together and share a common work objective.[22]

For example, at Johnsonville Foods in Wisconsin, CEO Ralph Stayer organized most of the firm's activities around self-managing, 12-person work teams. Teams like these have primary assignments, as do any work groups. At Johnsonville, some work teams were responsible for maintaining the firm's packaging equipment, for instance. But under traditional management structures, if something went wrong or the team wanted to change one of its practices, the issue would have to go up the chain of command for approval.

Not in self-managing work teams. At many firms like Johnsonville such teams are empowered to manage themselves and thus make fast, on-the-spot decisions.

Self-contained work teams, like this one at a publishing company, are proving to be more responsive and more productive in many industries than traditional organizational structures.

For example, some of the duties of a typical 12-person Johnsonville work team include:

- recruit, hire, evaluate, and fire (if necessary)
- formulate, then track and amend, its own budget
- make capital investment proposals as needed
- handle quality control, inspections, subsequent troubleshooting, and problem solving
- develop and monitor quantitative standards for productivity and quality
- suggest and develop prototypes of possible new products and packaging
- routinely work on other teams with counterparts from sales, marketing, and product development[23]

Under a similar program at Chesebrough-Ponds USA, a functional organization was replaced with multiskilled, cross-functional, self-directed teams that now run the plant's four production areas. Hourly employees make employee assignments, schedule overtime, establish production times and changeovers, and even handle cost control, requisitions, and work orders. They are also solely responsible for quality control under the plant's Continuous Quality Improvement Challenge, a program in which employees can post suggestions or challenges to improve quality. Employee Sherry Emerson summed up employee sentiments: "The empowerment is exciting. If we see something that will affect the quality to customers, we have the freedom to stop a process. They [management] trust us."

The results have been extraordinary. Quality acceptance is 99.25 percent. Annual manufacturing costs are down $10.6 million, work-in-process inventory has been reduced 86 percent, and total inventory is down 65 percent.[24]

Nature of Team-Based Organizations[25]

As these examples suggest, team-based organizations are different from the traditional departmentalized and hierarchical organizations described in chapter 7. Companies were traditionally organized with individuals, functions, or departments as their basic work units. This is evident in the typical organization chart, which might, for example, show separate boxes for each functional department, down to separate tasks for individual workers at the bottom of the chart.

In team-based organizations, however, the team is the basic work unit. The employees, working together as a team, will do much of the planning, decision making, and implementing required to get their assigned jobs done, and be responsible for activities like receiving materials, installing parts, and dealing with vendors who ship defective parts.

Designing Organizations to Support Teams[26]

No manager can create a team-based organization without providing the supporting mechanisms that will allow the teams to flourish. Management has to provide at least five organizational supporting mechanisms to enable work teams to do their jobs and therefore ensure the proper functioning of the team-based organization: organizational philosophy, structure, systems, policies, and skills (Figure 8.2). In a nutshell, here is what each entails:

- **Organizational philosophy.** Companies in which work teams flourish are characterized by a management philosophy and core values emphasizing high employee involvement and trust. For example, many companies like

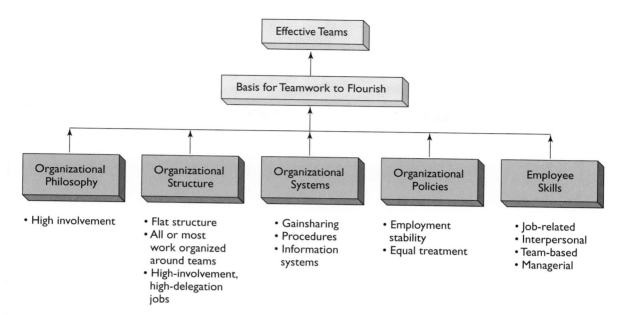

**FIGURE 8.2
Designing
Organizations to
Manage Teams**

SOURCE: Adapted from James
H. Shonk, *Team-Based Organizations* (Homewood, IL: Irwin,
1997), p. 36.

Saturn and Toyota emphasize values such as "People can be trusted to make important decisions about their work activities."

- **Organizational structure.** Team-based organizational structures are characterized by flat structures with few supervisors and delegation of much decision-making authority to the work teams themselves. In turn, the work teams in firms like Chesebrough-Ponds carry out tasks ranging from scheduling overtime to actually doing the work. Organizational charts are often nonexistent.

- **Systems.** The company's systems (and especially its reward systems) should also support the team-based approach. For example, in team-based companies like Johnsonville Foods and Toyota, "gainsharing" incentives—which pay employees a portion of the savings incurred by their hard work—are paid to the team as a whole rather than to individual employees. This supports the idea that teamwork is rewarded. Other important, team-oriented systems decisions include internal TV systems to keep employees informed, and team-friendly procedures such as "Consult those making a product before making engineering changes to the product."

- **Policies.** Building close-knit cohesive work teams takes time and therefore requires company policies that support and encourage teamwork. For example, "equal treatment" policies—no reserved parking spaces, minimal status differences in offices and dress, employees' evaluations of supervisors, and vice versa—help encourage a sense of community. Most team-based organizations also emphasize policies of employment stability. At Toyota's Camry facility in Lexington, Kentucky, for instance, slack demand might mean that more employees spend time being trained to develop new skills rather than being laid off.

- **Skills.** Work teams typically have wide-ranging responsibilities (such as scheduling their own time, hiring their own team members, installing their own units, and so on); it is, therefore, important that all team members have a wide range of skills. This includes: (1) the job skills to actually do the job (such as welding); (2) the interpersonal skills to work in a healthy manner with and in the team (listening, communicating, and so on); (3) team skills (such as problem solving and running decision-making meetings); and (4) management skills (including planning, leading, and controlling, for instance).

Organizational Behavior in Action

SPECIAL SKILLS FOR LEADING TEAM-BASED ORGANIZATIONS

Managers leading team-based organizations also need several skills.[27] In fact, one of the biggest problems of switching to team-based organizations is resistance from the company's existing managers and supervisors, many of whom are not accustomed to the sort of "support-and-coach" role that managers often play in such organizations. They may be more used to simply giving orders and controlling how things get done. However, that kind of "command-and-control" approach doesn't work well in organizations in which the work teams themselves are supposed to be making the decisions.

Leading a team-based organization is, therefore, different in several ways, including most notably the following:

The leader should be a *coach*. Leading teams is similar to coaching: "It involves assessing the team's skills and helping them use them to the fullest."[28]

The leader should be participative. Many of the benefits of the team-based organization derive from having the team itself identify and analyze problems and make its own decisions. Leaders in team-based organizations must therefore work in a highly participative style, which means soliciting the team's input, sharing decision-making responsibility, and delegating such decisions as hiring new team members.

The leader should be a boundary manager. One of the leader's most important roles is to see that the team's decisions are made and supported. This often means managing the interaction of the team with the environment beyond its own boundaries. The team itself makes the majority of its day-to-day operating decisions (for instance, who is scheduled to do what tasks that day). The "boundary manager" then must see to it that the work flows smoothly from one team to another and that if the team needs additional resources from top management, it receives them.

Network-Based Organizations

Many firms today superimpose "organizational networks" over their existing structures. In general, an *organizational network* is a system of interconnected or cooperating individuals.[29] In this section we describe three types: formal organizational networks, informal organizational networks, and electronic information networks. The network is, in essence, superimposed over the existing organizational structure, thus enhancing the likelihood that the work of far-flung units can be carried out promptly and in a coordinated way if quick decisions on some matters must be made.

Whether formal or informal, organizational networks share the same basic idea: to link managers from various departments, levels, and geographic areas into a multidisciplinary team whose members communicate across normal organizational boundaries. Let us first compare informal and formal networks.

Formal Networks

A **formal organizational network** has been defined as "a recognized group of managers assembled by the CEO and the senior executive team. . . . The members are drawn from across the company's functions, business units, and geography, and from different levels of the hierarchy. The number of managers involved almost never exceeds 100 and can be fewer than 25—even in global companies with tens of thousands of employees."[30]

The cross-functional nature of formal networks is illustrated in Figure 8.3. Note the number of organizational levels and departments represented by the blue boxes.

Formal networks differ from teams, cross-functional task forces, or ad hoc groups in three ways.[31] First, unlike most task forces, networks are *not temporary.* In fact, it is each manager's continuing experience in the network that helps build the shared understanding among members and explains the network's effectiveness.

Second, unlike most teams and task forces, networks *take the initiative* in finding and solving problems. In other words, they do not just solve the specific problems they are given.

Third, the existence of the formal network changes—or should change—the nature of top management's job. With the networks in place, CEOs "no longer define their jobs as making all substantive operating decisions on their own."[32] Instead, although CEOs still make many decisions, the network can handle more of the interunit coordinating that the CEO might otherwise have to do, leaving him or her more time for strategic planning.

One such formal network is used at the railroad firm Conrail. Here, 19 middle managers from various departments and levels constitute the firm's operating

■ FIGURE 8.3
How Networks Reshape Organizations— For Results
The members of a formal network may be selected from various departments and organizational levels.

SOURCE: Reprinted by permission of *Harvard Business Review.* From "How Networks Reshape Organizations—For Results," by Ram Charan, September–October 1991. Copyright © 1991 by the President and Fellows of Harvard College; all rights reserved.

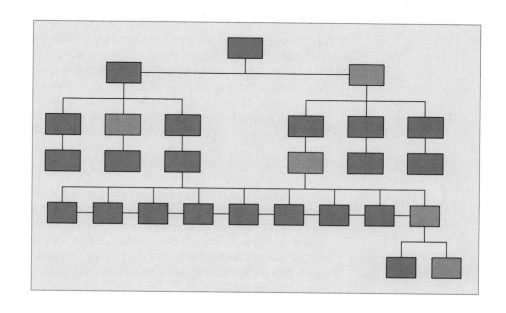

committee, which is actually a formal network. The managers influence most of the firm's key operating decisions through this committee. They meet for several hours on Monday mornings. Here they review and decide on tactical issues (delivery schedules and prices, for instance) and work on longer-term issues such as five-year business plans.[33]

The experience of Electrolux provides another example and illustrates how networks can be used to support a company's strategy. When Leif Johansson took over an Electrolux division that stretched from Norway to Italy, he inherited a daunting task. Electrolux's line included 20 products, numerous acquired companies, and more than 200 plants in many countries. Each presented unique market positions, capabilities, plant capacity, and competitive situations. Johansson recognized that his strategy had to be to create strengths across functional and geographic borders if he was to derive maximum economies of scale from the multiproduct, multiplant, multinational operation.

Local managers convinced him that abandoning local brands would jeopardize existing distribution channels and customer loyalty. But how could he derive the benefits of Electrolux's large multicountry scale while maintaining local brands' autonomy? His solution was to appoint a *formal network* comprising managers from various countries. Johansson's network structure helped to keep operations flexible and responsive. Local managers still had wide authority to design and market local brands. But the formal network helped provide the overall multinational and multi-product coordination that helped Electrolux obtain economies of scale.[34]

Informal Networks

Networks needn't be formally assigned, and indeed many firms, particularly multinationals, encourage the growth of informal organizational networks. "Here," as one expert puts it, "creating confidence in the work of colleagues around the world and building up personal relationships are the key factors."[35] Unlike formal networks with their assigned membership and purpose, **informal organizational networks** consist of cooperating individuals who are interconnected only informally. They share information and help solve each other's problems based on their personal knowledge of each other's expertise.

There are several ways to nurture the personal relationships on which informal networks are built. For example, multinationals like Phillips and Shell build personal relationships through international executive development programs, bringing managers from around the world to work together in training centers in New York and London. Other firms, like Olivetti, have international management development centers in their home cities, to which they bring their managers.

Moving managers from facility to facility around the world is another way to build informal networks. Transferring employees enables managers to build lasting relationships all around the globe, and some firms, such as Shell, transfer employees around the world in great numbers. In one case, for instance:

> [International mobility] has created what one might call a "nervous system" that facilitates both corporate strategic control and the flow of information throughout the firm. Widespread transfers have created an informal information network, a superior degree of communication and mutual understanding between headquarters and subsidiaries and between subsidiaries themselves, as well as a stronger identification with the corporate culture, without compromising the local subsidiary cultures.[36]

Development programs like these help build informal networks in several ways. Perhaps most notably, the socializing that takes place builds personal relationships among managers from the firm's facilities around the world. Such personal relationships then facilitate global networking and communications. So, if a new Shell Latin America sales manager needs to get in to see a new client, she might call a Shell Zurich manager she knows who has a contact at the client firm.

Electronic Networking

The rise of the Internet and of special "collaborative computing" networking software lets companies make better use of existing formal and informal networks and, indeed, encourages all employees throughout the firm to network. The advantages of such computer-based networking aren't limited to businesses, of course. For example,

> science advisors to state legislators joined together with technical professional societies, federal labs and public interest research groups to form Legitec Network. . . . [Using the network], for example, one frost-belt state posed the question: "What are alternatives to road salt for dealing with icy highways without polluting water supplies?" Another state, having recently dealt with the problem, responded, as did associations and labs that knew of relevant research on the topic. Other frost-belt states joined the topic to get the benefit of inquiry responses that might help their states as well. . . .[37]

Electronic networking is at the heart of many business organizations today. For example, Price Waterhouse's 18,000 accountants stay in touch with each other thanks to electronic bulletin boards on over 1,000 different subjects. Thus, a Dublin employee with a question about dairy plant accounting might have her question answered by a networked colleague half a world away.[38] Group decision support systems allow employees—even those in different countries—to brainstorm ideas and work together on projects.[39]

Boundaryless Organizations

"Old-style" organizations have various boundaries. Vertically, the chain of command implies clearly defined authority boundaries: The president gives orders to the vice president, who gives orders to the managers, and so on down the line. There are also clearly delineated horizontal or departmental boundaries such that most companies are separated into what some call "smokestacks": the production department has its responsibilities, the sales department has its own, and so on. Similarly, if the company happens to be divisionalized, then the work of each division is self-contained and each division often proceeds on the assumption that it can (and should) do its job with little or no interaction with the other product divisions.[40]

We've seen that such boundary-filled organizations once served a useful purpose. Jobs were specialized, lines of communication were well defined, and the slow-arriving problems could be solved in a relatively mechanical, step-by-step manner by an organization in which everyone knew exactly where they stood.

For most firms, things are different today. Rapid change demands a more responsive organization. As a result, yesterday's neat organizational boundaries need to be pierced, as they are with teams and formal and informal networks. As two experts summarized it, "Companies are replacing vertical hierarchies with horizontal networks; linking together traditional functions through interfunctional teams; and forming strategic alliances with suppliers, customers, and even competitors."[41] In so doing, they are creating boundaryless organizations.

What Are Boundaryless Organizations?

A **boundaryless organization** is one in which the widespread use of teams, networks, and similar structural mechanisms means that the boundaries that typically separate organizational functions and hierarchical levels are reduced and made more permeable.[42] In fact, taken to the extreme, the boundaryless company is one in which not only internal organizational boundaries are stripped away but also those between the company and its suppliers and customers. (Recall our discussion of the virtual corporation in chapter 6.) The Entrepreneurs in Action box illustrates a boundaryless small business.

How to Pierce the Four Organizational Boundaries

In practice, four specific boundaries must be pierced if the company is to obtain full advantage of teams and networks: the authority boundary, the task boundary, the political boundary, and the identity boundary.[43] A summary of these four boundaries and the managerial tensions and feelings that must be addressed in order to pierce them is shown in Figure 8.4.

THE AUTHORITY BOUNDARY. Superiors and subordinates—even those found in self-managing teams or formal networks—always meet at an **authority boundary,** in every company.

Therein lies the problem: To achieve the responsiveness required of a team-based or network structure, just issuing and following orders "is no longer good

■ **FIGURE 8.4**
The Four Organizational Boundaries That Matter

In setting up a boundaryless organization, four boundaries must be overcome, but doing so means dealing with the resulting tensions.

SOURCE: Reprinted by permission of *Harvard Business Review.* "The Four Organizational Boundaries that Matter." From "The New Boundaries of the 'Boundaryless' Company," by Larry Hirschorn and Thomas Gilmore, May–June 1992. Copyright © 1992 by the President and Fellows of Harvard College. All rights reserved.

	KEY QUESTIONS	TENSIONS DEVELOPING DUE TO THIS BOUNDARY
Authority Boundary	"Who is in charge of what?"	How to lead but remain open to criticism. How to follow but still challenge superiors.
Task Boundary	"Who does what?"	How to depend on others you don't control. How to specialize yet understand other people's jobs.
Political Boundary	"What's in it for us?"	How to defend one's interests without undermining the organization. How to differentiate between win-win and win-lose situations.
Identity Boundary	"Who is—and isn't—'us'?"	How to feel pride without devaluing others. How to remain loyal without undermining outsiders.

Entrepreneurs in Action

ATMOSPHERE PROCESSING, INC.

Gail Hering of Atmosphere Processing, Inc., brought an innovative hub-and-spoke form of organizational design to her firm. The customer has the prime position in this design—at the center. Another positive result is a better flow of cross-department communication.

Atmosphere Processing, Inc., CEO Gail Hering was never big on hierarchical organizational structures. She believes that employees in such organizations focus too much on pleasing managers, who are either peering over shoulders or building alliances and protecting their turf. "That mentality dooms a company," she says. The problem, says Ms. Hering, is that pleasing superiors may be good for an employee's longevity, but doesn't do much to improve output or creativity. In fact, making the immediate boss happy often supplants meeting the company's goals.

The old organization chart had another flaw, in Hering's view. Boosting profits and satisfying customers often became secondary to devising Machiavellian exercises aimed at helping one's career. Managers wanted bigger departments to boost their egos, but customers often complained about the layers they had to penetrate to get a decision.

Hering's solution was a boundaryless organization. She says her newly flattened organization is now full of unclassifiable, cross-trained workers because she convinced everyone, herself included, to focus on what makes a company really work: good products and happy customers.

In place of the traditional hierarchical chart, Hering adopted a hub-and-spoke chart. At its center is customer satisfaction. Positioned around the hub in slices are functions like engineering, scheduling, staffing, shipping, billing, and paying. Encircling that comes customer service, followed by CEO and COO, and finally the company board of directors. Generally, new employees are totally confused, but during a two-week orientation, they discover that they will learn and be responsible for a lot more than they might have under the traditional setup. "We require that new employees understand how the entire company earns a profit. We teach that if [they] don't understand something, instead of referring it to a supervisor, go directly to the person from whom it came and solve the confusion," Hering says.

"Customer satisfaction displaces the CEO at the center of the circular chart. Surrounding this with company functions illustrates the need to bring about customer satisfaction through employees without regard to traditional departmental boundaries, if need be," says Hering. Putting all the functions side by side promotes cross-department boundaryless communication channels.

Hering seems satisfied. "Now," she says, "API is a flattened organization. No one's productivity is constrained by the structure." Customers are happier, and she has control of her organization again.

SOURCE: Teri Lammers, "The New, Improved Organization Chart," *Inc.*, October 1992, 29–37.

enough."[44] For example, a manager in a formal network who happened to be a vice president would inhibit the network's effectiveness if she demanded the right to give orders based solely on the fact that she was the highest-ranking person in the network. Doing so would undermine the collaboration and the reliance on experts that are two advantages of teams and networks.

Piercing the authority boundary thus requires three things. Bosses must learn how to lead while remaining open to criticism. They must be willing to accept "orders" from lower-ranking employees who happen to be experts on the problems at hand. And "subordinates" must be trained and encouraged to follow but still challenge superiors if an issue must be raised.

THE TASK BOUNDARY. Creating a boundaryless organization also requires managing the **task boundary,** which means changing the way employees feel about who does what when employees from different departments must divide up their work. Specifically, managing the task boundary means training and encouraging employees to rid themselves of the "It's not my job" attitude that typically compartmentalizes one employee's area from another's:

> Indeed, their own performance may depend on what their colleagues do. So, while focusing primarily on their own task, they must also take a lively interest in the challenges and problems facing others who contribute in different ways to the final product or service.[45]

THE POLITICAL BOUNDARY. Differences in political agendas often separate employees as well. For example, manufacturing typically has a strong interest in smoothing out the demand for its products and in making the firm's products as producible as possible. Sales, on the other hand, has an equally legitimate interest in maximizing sales (even if it means taking in a lot of custom or last-minute rush orders). The result of such opposing agendas in a traditional organization can be a conflict at the departments' **political boundary.**

Members of each special-interest group in a boundaryless firm may still ask, "What's in it for us?" when a decision must be made. But they have to be encouraged to take a more collegial, consensus-oriented approach, defending their interests without undermining the best interests of the team, network, or organization.

THE IDENTITY BOUNDARY. Everyone identifies with several groups. For example, a General Motors accountant might identify with her colleagues in the accounting profession, with her co-workers in the GM accounting department, and perhaps with the General Motors Corporation itself, to name a few. The **identity boundary** means that we tend to identify with those groups with which we have shared experiences and with which we believe we share fundamental values.

Unfortunately, such identification tends to foster an "us" versus "them" mentality. The problem at the identity boundary arises because people tend to trust those with whom they identify but distrust others. Attitudes like these can undermine the free-flowing cooperation that responsive, networking, or team-based organizations require.

Achieving boundarylessness thus also means piercing the identity boundary, and there are several ways to do this. One is to train and socialize all the firm's employees so they come to identify first with the company and its goals and ways of doing things: "The company comes first" becomes their motto. Another is to emphasize that while team spirit may be laudable, employees must avoid "devaluing the potential contribution of other groups."[46]

Organizational Behavior in Action

BUILDING EMPLOYEE COMMITMENT TO THE MISSION

Piercing the boundaries and creating a boundaryless organization in which employees interact with each other throughout the company is futile unless employees are all on the same wavelength, that is, committed to supporting the company and its goals. What steps can managers take to foster such commitment?

One large study of managerial practices concluded that companies traditionally associated with committed employees generally engaged in seven practices that together seemed to contribute to building a committed workforce:[47]

- *Emphasize people-first values.* The companies emphasized respect for the individual and a commitment to their own employees.
- *Base communication on trust.* These firms instituted two-way communication systems and made it easy for employees to express concerns and gripes and to get answers to matters that bothered them, while assuring all employees that they would be treated fairly.
- *Set effective objectives.* The high-commitment companies excelled at formulating effective strategies, missions, values, and objectives and in communicating these to their employees.
- *Do high-competency hiring.* High-commitment firms didn't take a lackadaisical approach to hiring or just look at applicants' job-related skills. Instead, they tried to get a sense of the person and his or her personal qualities and values and to identify common experiences and values that might predict how the applicant's values fit the firm's.
- *Provide security.* While they did not guarantee lifetime employment, most of these employers recognized that it would be difficult to get commitment without showing that they were committed to their own employees. They therefore did their best not to lay off employees.
- *Promise attractive compensation packages.* All these firms offered packages of above-average pay combined with incentives and extensive benefits.
- *Be all you can be.* These employers did their best to help their employees to *self-actualize,* in other words, to become all they were capable of becoming. For example, they emphasized promotion from within and provided the educational and training opportunities employees needed to be promotable.

The Horizontal Corporation

In many firms today, boundarylessness translates into what management experts call a horizontal corporation. As illustrated in Figure 8.5, the **horizontal corporation** is a structure organized around customer-oriented processes such as new-product development, sales and fulfillment, and customer support. Employees work together in multidisciplinary teams; each team performs one or more of the processes. In its purest form, a horizontal corporation structure is one that eliminates functional departments, instead sprinkling functional specialists throughout

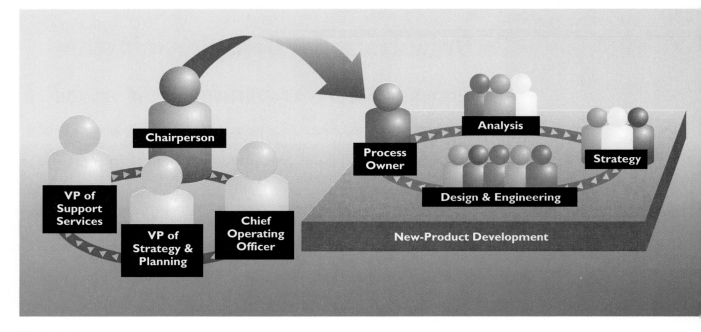

FIGURE 8.5

■ **FIGURE 8.5**
The Horizontal Corporation
In the horizontal corporation the work is organized around cross-functional processes with multifunction teams carrying out the tasks needed to service the customer.

SOURCE: John A. Byrne, "The Horizontal Corporation," *Business Week*, Dec. 20, 1993, 80.

the key process teams. They then work together on those teams with other functional specialists to accomplish the process-oriented team's mission, be it product development, sales and fulfillment, customer support, or some other goal. The horizontal structure usually has a small team of senior executives to ensure strategic direction and to provide essential staff support functions like human resource management.[48]

HORIZONTAL CORPORATIONS IN PRACTICE. Companies organize horizontally for several reasons. Many firms (including AT&T and Dupont) found that downsizing did not change the fundamental way their departments accomplished their work. The work of the organization—from getting the sales order to processing an invoice—was still handed from department to department like a baton in a relay race. At truck rental firm Ryder Systems, for instance, purchasing a vehicle for subsequent leasing required as many as 17 handoffs, as the relevant documents made their way from one department to another. Since such handoffs occurred both horizontally and vertically, the amount of time and energy wasted was enormous until Ryder reduced it by establishing a multispecialist horizontal "vehicle purchase" group.

Horizontal structures also help to obliterate the organizational boundaries we mentioned earlier. Even in divisionalized firms, functional areas tend to grow into fiefdoms in which protecting one's own turf takes priority over satisfying customer needs. Such territorial thinking is less likely to occur where the "departments" are not departments at all, but essentially multifunctional teams organized to provide basic customer-oriented processes. Thus the horizontal new-product-development process team might replace the new-product-development sequence, in which each department (such as engineering, production, and sales) did its part and then passed the responsibility to the next department.

Several companies are moving toward the horizontal model. For example, AT&T's Network Services division, with 16,000 employees, identified 13 core processes around which to reorganize. General Electric's lighting business similarly

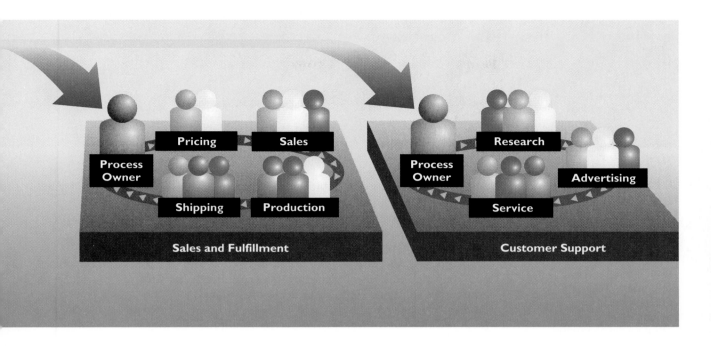

organized around multidisciplinary teams, each carrying out more than 100 processes, from new-product design to improving manufacturing machinery efficiency.

As shown in Figure 8.6, the essence of creating a horizontal corporation is defining the firm's core processes and then organizing teams around these while linking each process team's performance to specific customer-related objectives. Once the horizontal heart of the organization is in place, the firm eliminates the functions, levels, and staff departments that do not directly contribute to the work of the process-oriented teams.

Organizational Behavior in Action

THE PEOPLE SIDE OF ORGANIZING HORIZONTALLY

Creating horizontal, process-oriented organizations is not a panacea. Many companies today have "reengineered" their organizations, which essentially means that they've reorganized in such a way that teams of employees work together to carry out all the activities required to accomplish a single customer-oriented process such as getting an order processed and delivered to a customer.[49] Interestingly, many of these process-oriented reorganizations have not proved satisfactory, and a recent study helps to show why this is so.[50]

Many companies organize around complete, horizontal processes so as to speed decision making and get orders out faster to the customers, but doing so requires more than just reorganizing. In the successful reorganizations, management had fostered what these researchers call a "collective sense of responsibility." In other words, the employees took an active interest in their colleagues and in improving the outcome of their mutual efforts. They were willing to offer

Identify strategic objectives.

Analyze key competitive advantages to fulfill objectives.

Define core processes, focusing on what's essential to accomplish your goals.

Organize around processes, not functions. Each process should link related tasks to yield a product or service to a customer.

Eliminate all activities that fail to add value or contribute to the key objectives.

■ **FIGURE 8.6**
How to Create a Horizontal Corporation

Creating a horizontal organization involves several steps, starting with determining the firm's strategic objectives, and including such steps as flattening the hierarchy and using teams to accomplish the work.

SOURCE: Reprinted from December 20, 1993, issue of *Business Week* by special permission. Copyright © 1993 by the McGraw-Hill Companies, Inc.

their colleagues a helping hand and to work hard so the team would not be let down.

How do you cultivate that kind of collective responsibility in a horizontal organization? In four ways, these researchers found:[51]

■ *Make responsibilities overlap.* Design individual jobs as broadly as possible and keep the number of job titles to a minimum. That way, responsibility boundaries blur, and employees are more inclined to pitch in and help each other.

■ *Base rewards on unit performance.* In this study the most successfully reorganized companies based employees' rewards (salaries, incentives, recognition) on the performance of the units to which they belonged. That helped to emphasize the importance of everyone working together.

■ *Change the physical layout.* In other words, don't just reorganize. Change the physical layout so it promotes collective responsibility, such as by letting people see each other's work.

■ *Redesign work procedures.* Work procedures should encourage collective responsibility. For example, provide computer terminals so employees can communicate more readily; use the e-mail network to keep employees informed of how they're doing as a team; and make sure managers are available if the team or any member has an issue to discuss.

The "managing" and the "people" sides of organizations are really quite inseparable. Designing organizations for managing change—for instance, by creating a horizontal corporation—is crucial today and can be done successfully. However, the human element must be taken into consideration. The following Managing Change feature regarding the job stress that may accompany redesigned jobs is further proof of this. ■

Managing Change

CAN A JOB BE TOO INTERESTING?

OB experts tend to assume that the interesting and "enriched" jobs that result from change-oriented team-based structures are on the whole a good thing. For example, psychologist Frederick Herzberg recommends **job enrichment,** by

| Cut function and staff departments to a minimum, preserving key expertise. | Appoint a manager or team as the "owner" of each core process. | Create multidisciplinary teams to run each process. | Set specific performance objectives for each process. | Empower employees with authority and information to achieve goals. | Revamp training, appraisal, pay, and budgetary systems to support the new structure and link it to customer satisfaction. |

which he means building opportunities for achievement into the job by making it more interesting and challenging. This is often accomplished by giving a worker more autonomy and allowing him or her to do more of the planning and inspecting normally done by the person's supervisor.[52] And, of course, such job enrichment often results when decisions are pushed down to decision-making teams.

Unfortunately, having a more interesting job is not always what it's cut out to be. For one thing, there's considerable evidence that putting too many demands on someone can actually lead to so much stress it can backfire.

One recent study of 418 full-time employees illustrates the problem. The researchers focused on the extent to which the scope of employees' jobs—for instance, how many skills were needed to perform the jobs and how much autonomy employees had—was related to the amount of job stress the employees reported. The findings suggest that in managing change managers should use caution before dumping too much autonomy on employees.

The researchers basically drew three conclusions from their findings:

1. There is a U-shaped relationship between job scope and stress (Figure 8.7). In other words, when the job is too narrow, too boring, and too routine, job stress is high, but the opposite is true too: If the job is too enriched and the employee has too much responsibility and autonomy, that also triggers job stress. Managers have to design in the right level of autonomy, decision-making authority, and responsibility to keep job stress to a minimum.

■ **FIGURE 8.7**
The Relationship between Job Scope and Stress

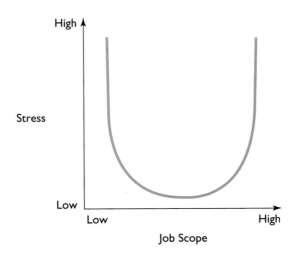

2. Particularly when dealing with wide-scope jobs, it's crucial to have a good fit between (1) the demands of the job and (2) the employee's ability to handle them. The more employees perceived a misfit between the two, the more stress they experienced. Managers must therefore be particularly careful to put people into jobs that they can do and then provide the training to ensure they then can do their jobs well.

3. It's not just the broader jobs and increased autonomy of team-based structures that can lead to job stress; downsizing can do it too. The process is as follows: A company downsizes; several layers of middle managers are squeezed out; the remaining employees each end up doing their previous work plus the work of one or more of their former colleagues; and job stress rises.

Job stress and its accompanying emotional exhaustion are not problems to be taken lightly. Quite aside from the very considerable human cost of exposing employees to job stress, the financial impact in terms of absences, hospitalization, and so on can be enormous.[53]

How can such adverse results be avoided? We'll discuss this further in later chapters, but based on this study the implications for managers are as follows:

1. Don't assume that more autonomy is always a good thing. Giving too much autonomy too fast can trigger job stress.

2. Provide adequate training, raise competence levels, and help ensure that employees have the skills they need to do their jobs.

3. Monitor the enrichment program carefully for signs of stress.

4. Be prepared to provide special support (counseling, for instance) for employees remaining with the firm after it downsizes.[54]

SUMMARY

1. Research suggests that different organizational structures are appropriate for, or contingent on, different tasks. Routine, efficiency-oriented tasks seem best matched with mechanistic organizational structures. These are characterized by adherence to rules and to the chain of command, centralization, and more specialized, functional departmentalizations. At the other extreme, rapid change and technological innovation seem more suited to organic organizational structures. Here employees are not urged to "play it by the rules" or to abide closely to the chain of command. Decision making is more decentralized and jobs and departments less specialized.

2. Managers can make a number of basic structural changes to rid their companies of ponderous decision making and make their organizations operate more responsively. Simplifying or reducing structure by reducing layers of management, creating mini-units, reassigning support staff, and widening spans of control while empowering workers are examples of these changes.

3. Some managers find that to manage change, innovative organizational structures are advisable. Team-based organizations built around self-managing teams are an example. Here the team is the basic work unit, and teams do much of the planning, decision making, and implementing required to get their assigned jobs done.

4. Many firms superimpose organizational networks over their existing structures. A network is a system of interconnected or cooperating individuals and can be formal or informal; either can also be electronically based. The basic idea is always to link managers from various departments, levels, and geographic areas so they form a multidisciplinary team whose members communicate across normal organizational boundaries.

5. Taken to its logical conclusion, such a networked organization results in a boundaryless organization. Boundaryless networked organizations are those in which managers have taken the steps required to pierce the organizational boundaries that often inhibit networked communications and decision making. These are the authority boundary, the task boundary, the identity boundary, and the political boundary.

6. The horizontal corporation is a structure organized around basic processes such as new-product development, sales fulfillment, and customer support. Everyone works together in multidisciplinary teams, with each team assigned to perform one or more of the processes.

KEY TERMS

mechanistic organization
organic organization
downsizing
team
formal organizational
   network

informal organizational
   network
boundaryless
   organization
authority boundary
task boundary

political boundary
identity boundary
horizontal corporation
job enrichment

SELF-TEST

TRUE / FALSE QUESTIONS

1 T F The new move toward reorganization or deorganization is occurring because managers are trying to wrestle with the challenge of managing fast change.

2 T F Two important factors affecting the structure of organizations are the company's environment and technology.

3 T F With a stable environment, technological innovation and new-product development are revolutionary.

4 T F A mechanistic organization uses lateral communication and consultation as the primary modes of management.

5 T F The studies by Woodward and Burns and Stalker suggest that different organizational structures are contingent on different tasks.

6 T F Downsizing means to reduce the size of a company's workforce dramatically.

7 T F Japanese firms have a wider span of control than do U.S. firms.

8 T F Employee trust and involvement are fundamental values of team-based organizations.

9 T F In influencing a team-based organization, the leader should use a command-and-control style so that power is not shared or undermined.

10 T F A key attribute of networks is that they are permanent.

MULTIPLE-CHOICE QUESTIONS

1 Which of the following are examples of an organization going through deorganization?
  a. ABB Asea Brown Boueri
  b. IBM
  c. Saturn
  d. all of the above

2 A stable environment is characterized by all but which of the following?
  a. predictable demand for the firm's product
  b. unchanging set of competitors
  c. rapid rate of technological innovation
  d. secure regulatory environment

3 Mechanistic organizations are based on all but which of the following?
  a. tight chain of command
  b. highly decentralized jobs
  c. detailed job descriptions
  d. formal hierarchy

4 In an organic organization, which of the following behaviors is highly prized?
  a. routine and rule following
  b. power held and self-assertion
  c. creativity and entrepreneurial activities
  d. none of the above

5 During a downsizing, the management hierarchy in a company often means:
  a. slimming down the chain of command
  b. less direct supervision
  c. narrower spans of control
  d. greater role in decision making

6 The term used to describe employees making more decisions for themselves and their company is _____ .
  a. delegation
  b. influence
  c. new wave power
  d. empowerment

7 A self-contained or self-managed work team is likely to
  a. recruit, hire, evaluate, and fire on its own.
  b. make capital investments proposals.
  c. formulate and track its own budget.
  d. all of the above

8 What is the leadership/management style that works well in mechanistic organizations but not well in team-based organizations?
  a. command-and-control
  b. coach
  c. supporter
  d. cheerleader

9 A _____ organization is one in which there is a great use of teams, networks, and similar structural arrangements to open up the organizational functions and make it more permeable, with less levels of hierarchy.
  a. bureaucratic
  b. mechanistic
  c. functional
  d. boundaryless

10 Which is *not* at the heart of creating a horizontal corporation?
  a. defining the firm's core processes
  b. organizing teams around core elements
  c. linking performance to customers
  d. depending on departmental development processes

CRITICAL THINKING EXERCISES

1 This chapter introduced new organizational structures that were created to deal with accelerated changes in technology and the environment. Here are three examples that illustrate many of those structures.

- At American Express, a program called "One Enterprise" led to a range of projects where peers from different divisions worked together on cross-marketing, joint purchasing, and cooperative product and market innovation. Employees' rewards were tied to their One Enterprise efforts. Executives set goals and could earn bonuses for their contributions to the results of other divisions.
- Security Pacific National Bank in California entered a joint venture with local auto dealers to sell fast financing for car purchases. The MIS department also became a profit center, selling its services outside the bank.
- At Alcan, the Canadian giant, managers and professionals from line divisions formed screening teams to consider new-venture proposals to aid the search for new uses and applications for its core product, aluminum. A venture manager chosen from the screening team took charge of concepts that passed muster, drawing on Alcan's worldwide resources to build a new business. In one case of global synergy, Alcan created a new product for the Japanese market using Swedish and U.S. technology and Canadian manufacturing capacity.[55]

What types of organizational restructuring are illustrated by the above examples?

2 Max Weber, the German sociologist, is considered by most to be the "Father of the Mechanistic or Bureaucratic Organization." Writing in the late 1800s and the early 1900s, Weber was analyzing the ushering in of what 1990s management expert Charles Handy has called "The Century of Organizations." For Weber it was a time when the new revolution of large-scale organizations would emphasize the importance of authority in the system: "In the past the man has been first, in the future the system must be first." What do you think he meant by that statement? How would he see the new revolution of today's boundaryless organizations? How might today's new structures change the relationship between the system and the human beings?

EXPERIENTIAL EXERCISES

1 William Pape, cofounder of VeriFone Inc., a virtual corporation, suggests we will need virtual workers to staff virtual companies. This new worker should

- have strong communications skills
- be a good problem solver
- agree with the goals and values of the company
- have a strong work ethic
- feel secure about her or his ability to do the job
- have a good sense of humor
- be able to cope with technology[56]

Break into teams of five students each. First, discuss what it would mean to all of you to be virtual workers. Second, sketch out what your team thinks the personality of a virtual worker is like and what the structure of a virtual corporation looks like.

Third, imagine your team has just been hired by a firm that is lagging behind in technology. It has no strategic plan, and there has been virtually no new-product development for the last 10 years. Few of the staff are computer literate. The strengths of the company are a strong work ethic, good communication among the functionally organized departments, and confidence about its ability to get the job done through the stability of its traditional, top-down management style. Your team's task is to come up with a plan for this company to become successful at managing change by becoming virtual in every respect (two pages at most). Be ready to discuss your findings in class.

2 There is a new system of organizing that gets every employee thinking like a businessperson, that is, like a competitor. Called "open-book management,"[57] it is getting remarkable results for companies such as Springfield Remanufacturing Corp., Case Company, and Cin-Made. In a nutshell, open-book management is a way of running a company that gets everyone to focus on helping the business make money. There are three essential differences between this approach and conventional approaches to management: (1) every employee sees—and learns to understand—the company's financial records, along with all the other numbers that are critical to tracking the business's performance; (2) employees learn that, whatever else they do, part of their job is to move those numbers in the right direction; and (3) employees have a direct stake in the company's success: If the company makes a profit, they get a share, and if it doesn't, they don't.

You work for an old-line industrial firm with a mechanistic organizational structure that has been managed by basically the same management team for the last 30 years. The company has developed a paternalistic culture where employees are expected to do their jobs, but not question the whys and wherefores. Financial data, including salaries and compensation packages, are kept secret. In fact, if you share information about your pay with others, you may be fired. Your competitors seem to have a very motivated workforce and aggressive sales and marketing people as well as technologically sophisticated products. As the newest member of the management team, you are very interested in introducing new ideas (like those in this chapter) about organizational design, including open-book management.

Your assignment is to write a brief report on *how* you would introduce these new concepts into this organization. The report should only be two pages and basically outline the issues and your recommendations based on concepts from the chapter. You should be ready to present your report either to a group in class or to the whole class.

DIVERSITY CASE

DISABILITY HIRING INITIATIVE BY CEOS

Even before the Americans with Disabilities Act pushed the recruitment and hiring of disabled persons to the forefront of public consciousness, a group of top corporate executives had already undertaken their own initiative. Called the Disability 2000-CEO Council, the group ambitiously set as its goal to double the number of disabled persons employed by the year 2000. But the group isn't simply focusing on filling slots and presenting statistics. Their aim is to enhance communication between disabled workers and their colleagues, upgrade their skill levels, and bring about changes in perception that in the past have effectively been boundaries to their development and growth. So far, an admirable cooperative effort between government and the corporate United States has taken place.

Similarly, U.S. West Corporation founded its FRIENDS program several years ago. Designed to attract applicants with disabilities, this support group now has almost 100 members companywide. The effort begins with human resource personnel visiting campuses to focus recruitment efforts on qualified graduates with disabilities. To get the most from these new hires, career assistance and developmental counseling is available on an ongoing basis. Disabled employees also actively deal with customers who have similar impairments, creating what the company considers a competitive advantage.

Westinghouse received the Opportunity 2000 Award in 1992 from the U.S. Department of Labor. The award is presented to the company that best exemplifies in-place affirmative action programs such as skills training, upward mobility, and work and family life programs. Among other achievements, the company created specialized medical equipment specifically designed to assist disabled workers. Westinghouse designed a stand-up wheelchair, a blink switch with a voice synthesizer that allows communication strictly by eye movement, and a computer-aided design workstation for quadriplegic employees.

The Target Corporation actively recruits disabled workers, and some stores appoint current staffers to be mentors for new employees in a "buddy system." The set-up affords the new hires the benefit of their mentor's experience when problems or unfamiliar tasks arise. Target believes the program is beneficial not only to customers but also to the employees who serve as buddies to disabled workers.

The Disability 2000-CEO Council believes that promoting higher employment among qualified persons with disabilities makes good business sense besides coming into compliance with the law. It also thinks eliminating the kind of tunnel vision in which employees only communicate with and relate to their own narrow peer groups will create all sorts of ideas and opportunities.

Questions

1. What effect will the efforts of the Disability 2000-CEO Council have on the identity boundary in the workplace?
2. Is it possible to completely eliminate an "us" versus "them" mentality among diverse workers? Why or why not?
3. US West, Westinghouse, and Target have developed programs aimed at integrating disabled employees into the workforce. Can you think of any other approaches companies could take? Might these approaches also be useful for piercing the organizational boundaries discussed in this chapter?

SOURCES: "The Disability 2000-CEO Council," *Business Week,* 28 October 1991, 32–3; *Willing and Able,* National Organization on Disabilities.

STRATEGY CASE

THE FUTURE IS NOW: HOW TO FINE-TUNE YOUR CRYSTAL BALL

Skandia Group is a 140-year-old Swedish financial services giant with $7 billion in revenue in 1996. In 1992, the company appointed Lief Edvinsson the world's first director of intellectual capital. He rapidly set out to revolutionize corporate accounting by establishing a framework for measuring such "intangibles" as customer relations and organizational knowledge. Edvinsson has now moved on to reinventing strategic planning.

He started a new unit, Skandia Futures Centers (SFC), with a handpicked team of 30 people from around the world. Their mission is to explore five driving forces of the business environment: the European insurance market, demographics, technology, the world economy, and organization and leadership. Their goal is to present a vision of the future to Skandia's corporate council, which consists of 150 of the company's senior managers.

The team represents diverse functional roles, organizational experiences, and cultural backgrounds, and every age from 20 to 60. In Edvinsson's experience, some of the most potent lessons have come from the young and inexperienced—those typically excluded from such ventures. As Edvinsson notes: "We need people who can understand the archeology of the future. . . . That's why we have these 25-year-olds in our program. They already have that vision—they carry the icons of tomorrow with them."

Questions

1. How might other companies implement Edvinsson's approach and prosper? Why have not more done so?
2. What resistance might his approach meet in traditional companies?
3. In what ways has Edvinsson redesigned Skandia to analyze strategic alternatives and better manage change?

SOURCE: Polly LaBarre, "How Skandia Generates Its Future Faster," *Fast Company,* December–January 1997, 58.

ENTREPRENEURIAL CASE

WE'RE ALL THINKERS AND DOERS HERE!

When Bob and Tom Jagemann took over the leadership of their $5 million family-owned tool-and-die shop, Jagemann Stamping Co., in 1985, they looked to their line employees for insight into quality problems.

They decided to send line workers on calls to customers, but first they trained them in interpersonal skills. Now at new-product introductions and research-and-development sessions, the engineers and salespeople who meet the customers are typically accompanied by several line workers who know the specific technology well. This approach improves communication and has helped to raise the line employees' commitment to the customers. If there is a problem, groups of line workers are sent out on their own to deal with the problem.

In 1995, the company's fiftieth year, its revenues were $28 million. Bob Jagemann attributes part of that growth to a culture that avoids the distinction between management and labor and builds a lifetime customer base.

Questions

1. How would such an approach work at a large organization like GE?
2. In what ways are Jagemann using boundaryless organization concepts?
3. What lessons about change might other companies learn from the Jagemanns?

THE BUSINESS TEAM, INC.

TEAMING WITH OTHERS

The Business Team has been operating very successfully from its domestic base. However, from its environmental scans, it is increasingly clear that being truly successful in the long run means going global. Sid has just read a Request for Proposal (RFP) from the Australian government asking for the firm to assist the government with the further privatization of its prison system. It is a lucrative contract calling for a total assessment from human resources to operations, with provisions for on-site analysis of currently privatized prisons in Australia.

The Team is very interested. This would open a window to government contracting. Designing and managing private prisons is a booming business in the United States as well as around the globe. They have excellent business skills to bring to the project. But the Team has no direct experience with

government contracting or with Australian culture or politics.

There are four U.S. firms doing this type of analysis. Maria and Len suggest establishing a networked organization with them, linked by the Internet, to respond to the bid.

Questions

1. How could the Team use the concepts of boundaryless, organizations to help them put together an organization for REP?
2. What are the main processes involved in fulfilling a consulting job such as this? How applicable would a horizontal organization be for accomplishing them?
3. What organizational arrangements would you recommend to the Team prior to entering into any contract with another company here or abroad?

REDESIGNING KNITMEDIA TO MANAGE CHANGE

KnitMedia is at the epicenter of several industries that are undergoing very rapid change. Record distribution and music publishing are two related industries that are rapidly consolidating, with giants such as Warner, Sony, and Universal responsible for over two-thirds of the total industry revenues. New media, including music Web sites and music cybercasts, is undergoing similar explosive growth: Not only are substantial players like KnitMedia increasingly active in this industry, but so are tiny "one-person bands" with their own Web sites and—at the other extreme—the Web sites and networks of giants like Viacom, Sony, and Apple Computer.

KnitMedia, therefore, finds itself competing in a marketplace dominated by both multinational corporations and smaller independent corporations. The large competitors have enormous resources, but their great size may also be their greatest weakness. As KnitMedia has said, "Due to the enormity of the multinationals' international structures, they are restricted in their ability to react quickly to market demands. This has historically caused late entry for major record labels in many new markets. Because the size of the large organizations also precludes them from a certain familiarity with the consumer, this has created an inability to see shifts in the market place."[1]

One of the things KnitMedia has to guard against, however, is having the same sort of institutional isolation set in as it grows larger. In other words, it has to do something to redesign its organization to make sure that Michael Dorf and his colleagues don't become so isolated from the consumer that they are no longer able to sense shifts in the mar-

ket-place and react quickly to them with the right artists at the right time. The question is, how should they do this?

Team Exercises and Questions

Use what you learned in this chapter to answer the following questions:

1 Do you think KnitMedia's 1996–1997 organization chart (review the Web Exercise for chapter 7) will provide KnitMedia with the ability to manage rapid change? Why or why not?

2 Of the techniques discussed in chapter 8, which do you think are particularly appropriate for helping Michael Dorf redesign KnitMedia for managing change? Explain why you chose these.

For the online version of this case, visit our Web site at <www.prenhall.com/desslermgmt>.

---

[1]KnitMedia Prospectus, 31–32.

For Internet exercises, interactive study questions, news updates and more, visit the Dessler Web site at

www.prenhall.com/desslermgmt

If you're using the CD-ROM that accompanies this text, simply click on the "Web Site" button to access the site.

STAFFING AND HUMAN RESOURCE MANAGEMENT

What's Ahead?

After a yearlong search in which candidates were invited to write essays explaining why they'd like to be president of Ben & Jerry's Homemade Ice Cream Company, the firm's owners, Ben Cohen and Jerry Greenfield, finally hired a president, only to have him leave in just over a year. In explaining his short tenure, Robert Holland, Jr., said that he had substantially improved the company's production operations and introduced a few new products and it was now time to move on. However, it seemed to most outside observers that next time Ben & Jerry's would have to take a more traditional approach to hiring a president if they wanted that person to stick around for the long haul. The question was, how exactly should they go about doing that?

Ben Cohen (right) and Jerry Greenfield

Objectives

After studying this chapter, you should be able to

- **explain** why effective human resource management (HR) is increasingly important today
- **discuss** the types of laws that affect a company's HR activities such as testing and interviewing candidates

- **explain** the importance of carefully developing job descriptions and then recruiting a pool of good candidates
- **discuss** how to use several employee selection techniques, including testing and interviews
- **describe** some of the important aspects of appraising and compensating employees.

MANAGEMENT ON THE WEB

SHRM ONLINE

This site is devoted to human resource management. Maintained by the Society for Human Resource Management, it provides HR-related links to online news, *HR Magazine,* job openings, bulletin boards, listservs, and resources on the Internet. How could Ben & Jerry have used this site? ■

http://www.shrm.org/

Human Resource Management as a Core Function

Ben & Jerry's took a rather unusual approach to the basic management task of hiring a president. Why is it so important to select the right person for the job? Because the organization chart supplies only the skeleton of the organization; *employees* are then needed to bring the company to life. **Human resource management** (also sometimes called **HRM,** staffing, or personnel management) is the management function devoted to acquiring, training, appraising, and compensating employees. All managers are, in a sense, personnel managers, because they all get involved in activities like recruiting, interviewing, selecting, and training. But most larger firms also have HR departments with their own human resource managers. Figure 9.1 on pages 284–285 illustrates the personnel functions of such a department.

Companies are flattening their pyramids, relying more on self-managing work teams, and getting closer to their customers, in part by empowering employees and giving them more authority to handle customer complaints and requests. Actions like these boost the need for motivated, self-directed, and committed employees. As workers become more fully empowered, the HR function thus grows in importance. We'll see in this chapter that HR plays a central role in molding a company's workforce into a motivated and committed team, one that can help the company and its management manage change more effectively.

FedEx's human resources—its employees—provide the firm with its competitive advantages of superior customer service and on-time deliveries. For this firm, human resource management is the key to the strategic plan.

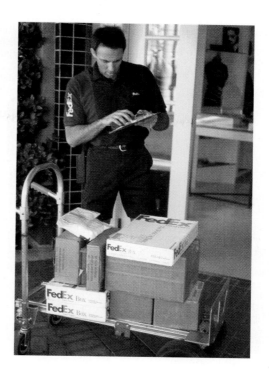

Strategy in Action

HR'S ROLE AS A STRATEGIC PARTNER

The fact that employees today are central to helping companies achieve competitive advantage and manage change has led to the emergence of strategic human resource management. **Strategic human resource management** has been defined as "the linking of HRM with strategic goals and objectives in order to improve business performance and develop organizational cultures that foster innovation and flexibility...."[1] Strategic HR means accepting the human resource function as a strategic partner in formulating the company's strategies, as well as in executing those strategies through HR activities like recruiting, selecting, training, and rewarding personnel.

HR'S ROLE IN FORMULATING STRATEGY. In many companies, HR management already plays a crucial role in formulating strategy. For example, several years ago both United Airlines and American Airlines considered and then rejected the opportunity to acquire USAir, a smaller and relatively weak airline. Although both American and United had several reasons for rejecting a bid, HR considerations loomed large. Specifically, both American and United had doubts about their abilities to successfully negotiate new labor agreements with USAir's employees, and both felt the problems of assimilating them might be too great.

Similarly, HR management is in a unique position to supply competitive intelligence that may be useful in the strategic planning process. Details regarding

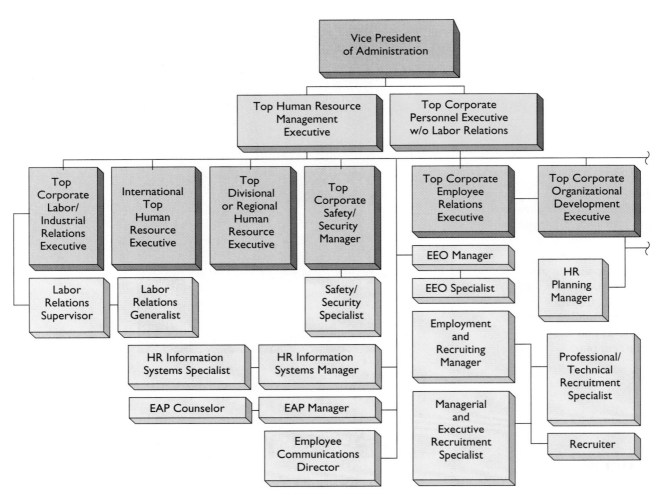

■ FIGURE 9.1
Human Resource Department in a Large Organization

This shows the organizational chart of the human resource department in a very large firm. Even in a small firm, however, the same personnel functions, such as labor relations, safety, equal employment, and training must be addressed.

SOURCE: Adapted from Bureau of National Affairs, *Datagraph*, July 27, 1995, pp. 236–237.

advanced incentive plans being used by competitors, opinion surveys from employees that elicit information about customer complaints, and information about pending legislation like labor laws or mandatory health insurance are some examples.

HR also participates in strategy formulation by supplying information regarding the company's internal strengths and weaknesses. For example, IBM's decision to buy Lotus was prompted in part by IBM's conclusion that its own human resources were inadequate to enable the firm to reposition itself as an industry leader in networking systems, or at least to do so quickly enough.

HR'S ROLE IN EXECUTING STRATEGY. Human resource management also plays a pivotal role in successfully executing a company's strategic plan. For example, Federal Express's competitive strategy is to differentiate itself from its competitors by offering superior customer service and guaranteed on-time deliveries. Since basically the same technologies are available to UPS, DHL, and FedEx's other competitors, it is FedEx's workforce that necessarily gives FedEx a crucial competitive advantage. This means the firm's HR processes and its ability to create a highly committed, competent, and customer-oriented workforce are crucial to FedEx being able to execute its strategy.

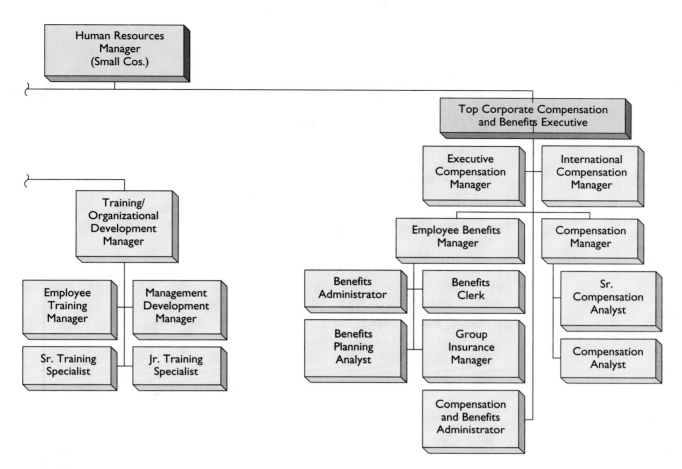

■ FIGURE 9.1
Human Resource
Department in a Large
Organization
(*continued*)

Human resource management supports strategic implementation in numerous other ways. For example, HR today is heavily involved in the execution of most firm's downsizing and restructuring strategies through outplacing employees, instituting pay-for-performance plans, reducing health care costs, and retraining employees. And in an increasingly competitive global marketplace, instituting HR practices that build employee commitment can help improve a firm's responsiveness. In summary, HR today plays a central role as a strategic partner, helping top management formulate and then implement its strategies.[2]

Human Resource's Legal Framework

The U.S. Army is accused of sexual harassment, and Texaco of racial discrimination. Time Warner's Home Box Office unit is being sued by a 58-year-old who charges that HBO turned him down for a job because he was too old.[3] Cases like these emphasize a fact of life of HR management: More than any other management function, personnel is subject to the constraints of numerous federal, state, and local laws.

Equal Employment Laws

The equal employment laws prohibiting employment discrimination are among the most important personnel laws. For example, *Title VII* of the 1964 Civil Rights Act bars discrimination because of race, color, religion, sex, or national origin (see Table 9.1). Its requirements are enforced by the federal Equal Employment Opportunity Commission. This is a five-member commission appointed by the president with the advice and consent of the Senate. It receives, investigates, and may file charges regarding job discrimination complaints on behalf of aggrieved individuals.

Other important antidiscrimination laws include the *Equal Pay Act* of 1963, which requires equal pay for men and women performing similar work; the *Pregnancy Discrimination Act* of 1978, which prohibits discrimination in employment against pregnant women; and the *Americans with Disabilities Act* of 1990, which requires employers to make reasonable accommodations for disabled employees at work.

At work, antidiscrimination laws mean employers should adhere to certain procedures. For example, employers should confirm that the selection tests they use do not unfairly screen out minorities, and in interviews they should avoid inquiring about an applicant's ethnic, racial, or marital status.

NONDISCRIMINATION IN PRACTICE. The main purpose of all these equal employment laws is to ensure that everyone has an equal opportunity of getting a job or being promoted at work, regardless of age, race, sex, disability, or national origin. What does this mean in practical terms? Although equal employment law is a complex and specialized field, here are some general guidelines a manager might find useful.

When recruiting employees:

- Do not rely solely on word of mouth to publicize job opportunities among current employees when your workforce is substantially white or some other class, because doing so might reduce the likelihood that people of other backgrounds will become aware of the jobs and thus apply for them.
- Do not place "Help wanted—male" or "Help wanted—female" ads, or any ads that limit the job according to age (such as "Younger worker preferred").

In selecting employees:

- Remember that if you use a selection standard, you may be called on to prove that it is absolutely required for performing the job satisfactorily. For example, do not insist that applicants for a supervisor's position must have a college degree, or that applicants for maintenance worker must be at least six feet tall unless you are sure that these requirements are prerequisites for performing the job satisfactorily (the former might discriminate against some minorities, the latter against most women).
- In the interview or on the application blank do not ask about or use a person's arrest record to disqualify him or her automatically for a position, because there is always a presumption of innocence until proven guilty.
- In general, do not ask about a person's religious preferences, age (as long as the applicant is old enough to have working papers), or country of national origin. Do not ask women questions that might suggest you will discriminate against them because they are women, such as "What will your husband think of all the traveling you'll need to do with this job?" or

ACTION	WHAT IT DOES
Title VII of 1964 Civil Rights Act, as amended	Bars discrimination because of race, color, religion, sex, or national origin; instituted EEOC
Executive orders	Prohibit employment discrimination by employers with federal contracts of more than $10,000 (and their subcontractors); establish office of federal compliance; require affirmative action programs
Federal agency guidelines	Guidelines used by federal agencies covering enforcement of laws barring discrimination based on sex, national origin, and religion, as well as employee selection procedures; for example, they require validation of tests
Supreme court decisions: *Griggs* v. *Duke Power Co., Albemarie* v. *Moody*	Ruled that job requirements must be related to job success; that discrimination need not be overt to be proved; that the burden of proof is on the employer to prove the qualification is valid
Equal Pay Act of 1963	Requires equal pay for men and women for performing similar work
Age Discrimination in Employment Act of 1967	Prohibits discriminating against a person 40 or over in any area of employment because of age
State and local laws	Often cover organizations too small to be covered by federal laws
Vocational Rehabilitation Act of 1973	Requires affirmative action to employ and promote qualified disabled persons and prohibits discrimination against disabled persons
Pregnancy Discrimination Act of 1978	Prohibits discrimination in employment against pregnant women, or related conditions
Vietnam Era Veterans' Readjustment Assistance Act of 1974	Requires affirmative action in employment for veterans of the Vietnam war era
Wards Cove v. *Atonio; Patterson* v. *McLean Credit Union*	These Supreme Court decisions made it more difficult to prove a case of unlawful discrimination against an employer
Morton v. *Wilks*	This case allowed consent decrees to be attacked and could have had a chilling effect on certain affirmative action programs
Americans with Disabilities Act of 1990	Strengthens the need for most employers to make reasonable accommodations for disabled employees at work; prohibits discrimination
Civil Rights Act of 1991	Reverses *Wards Cove, Patterson,* and *Morton* decisions; places burden of proof back on employer and permits compensatory and punitive money damages for discrimination

SOURCE: Gary Dessler, *Human Resource Management,* 7th ed. (Upper Saddle River, NJ: Prentice-Hall,1997), 47.

"How will you take care of the children if you take this job?" Do not ask a person whether he or she is disabled, although employers may ask applicants whether they are able to perform the essential functions of the job.

Affirmative Action Programs

Whereas equal employment opportunity aims to ensure equal treatment at work, **affirmative action** requires the employer to make an extra effort to hire and promote those in a protected group (women or minorities). Affirmative action thus includes taking specific actions (in recruitment, hiring, promotions, and compensation) that are designed to eliminate the present effects of past discrimination. An example would be setting a goal of promoting more minorities to middle management jobs.

Though illegal, sexual harassment is a widespread problem and one that the courts prefer firms to prevent.

Sexual Harassment

Sexual harassment doesn't have to mean insisting on sexual favors in return for some reward, as many people believe. Instead, it is defined as unwelcome sexual advances, requests for sexual favors, and other verbal or physical conduct of a sexual nature that occurs under conditions including the following: when such conduct is made, either explicitly or implicitly, a term or condition of an individual's employment; when submission to or rejection of such conduct by an individual is used as the basis for employment decisions affecting the individual; or when such conduct has the purpose or effect of unreasonably interfering with an individual's performance or creating an intimidating, hostile, or offensive work environment. In other words, if it makes the other person feel uncomfortable, it may be sexual harassment.

Managers should keep two facts in mind concerning sexual harassment. First, in addition to being unfair and detestable, it is also illegal. In one famous case, *Meritor Savings Bank, FSB v. Vinson,* the U.S. Supreme Court indicated that employers should establish meaningful complaint procedures and head off charges of sexual harassment before they occur.

Second, such harassment is also a widely occurring problem. Almost 60 percent of female employees (as well as a large percentage of male employees) report having experienced sexual harassment.[4] In 1997 several male cadets at the Citadel were disciplined for harassing female cadets, for instance. And at Stanford University, Dr. Frances Conley, one of the first female neurosurgeons in the United States, recently resigned from the School of Medicine saying she had endured years of subtle and not-so-subtle sexual harassment at the school.[5]

AVOIDING AND DEALING WITH SEXUAL HARASSMENT AT WORK. There are a number of steps that employers and individuals can take to avoid or deal with sexual harassment when it occurs. Here are some strategies.

What the employer should do:

1. First, take all complaints about harassment seriously. As one sexual harassment manual for managers and supervisors advises, "When confronted with sexual harassment complaints or when sexual conduct is observed in the workplace, the best reaction is to address the complaint or stop the conduct."[6]

2. Issue a strong policy statement condemning such behavior.
3. Inform all employees about the policy prohibiting sexual harassment and of their rights under the policy.
4. Establish a complaint procedure so that employees understand the chain of command when it comes to filing and appealing sexual harassment complaints.
5. Establish a management response system that includes an immediate reaction and investigation by senior management when charges of sexual harassment are made.
6. Begin management training sessions with supervisors and increase their own awareness of the issues.
7. Discipline managers and employees involved in sexual harassment.

An employee who believes he or she has been sexually harassed can also take several steps to eliminate the problem:

1. Make a verbal request to the harasser and the harasser's boss that the unwanted overtures cease because the conduct is unwelcome.
2. Write a letter to the accused providing a detailed statement of the facts and a statement that the person wants the harassing activities to end immediately (the letter should be delivered in person and, if necessary, a witness should accompany the writer).
3. Report the unwelcome conduct and unsuccessful efforts to get it to stop to the harasser's manager or to the HR director (or both) verbally and in writing.
4. Finally, consult an attorney about suing the harasser and possibly the employer.

Organizational Behavior in Action

PERCEPTIONS OF SEXUAL HARASSMENT

There's virtually no doubt about the fact that certain behaviors constitute sexual harassment. For example, behavior of the quid pro quo variety (in which, say, a supervisor tells a subordinate that the person either performs a sexual favor or is terminated) is clearly sexual harassment. But where the behaviors are not so blatant, the question of defining how a reasonable person would interpret the behavior becomes more important.[7]

One problem, however, is that there are gender-based differences in the way men and women perceive various behaviors. Based on various studies, for instance, females are more likely than males to report that they experienced some form of unwelcome sexual attention and to define more social-sexual behaviors as sexual harassment than are males.[8] Similarly, males are less likely to attribute responsibility for sexual harassment to the alleged harasser than are females, and men are more likely to place blame on the female target than are females.

A study of federal employees illustrates the important role that gender differences play in defining sexual harassment. The survey queried 8,523 people employed in 24 governmental agencies who were asked to assess the extent to which five different behaviors constituted sexual harassment: (1) uninvited letters, telephone calls, or materials of a sexual nature; (2) uninvited and deliberate touching, leaning over, cornering, or pinching; (3) uninvited sexually suggestive looks or gestures; (4) uninvited pressure for dates; and (5) uninvited sexual teasing, jokes, remarks, or questions.

The study's results indicated that males and females did indeed perceive sexual harassment in significantly different ways.[9] As the researchers conclude:

> Females are more likely than males to view letters, telephone calls, or materials of a sexual nature, touching, leaning over, cornering, or pinching, sexually suggestive looks or gestures, pressure for dates, sexual teasing, jokes, remarks, or questions as sexually harassing. In addition, females are consistently more likely than males to view the behaviors as sexually harassing regardless of whether the harasser is a supervisor or a co-worker.[10]

One implication of this study is that employers must do a better job of sensitizing their employees regarding the possibility of such gender-based differences in perceptions. A comment that a male supervisor may perceive as merely complimentary might be perceived by a female target as uncomfortable and insulting and create the basis for a sexual harassment charge. ■

Occupational Safety and Health

The *Occupational Safety and Health Act* was passed by Congress "to assure so far as possible every working man and woman in the nation safe and healthful working conditions and to preserve our human resources." It sets safety and health standards that apply to almost all workers in the United States. The standards themselves are contained in five volumes and cover just about any hazard one could think of at work, including, for instance, what sorts of ladders to use, appropriate fire protection, and ways to guard against accidents when using machines and portable power tools. They are administered by the Occupational Safety and Health Administration (OSHA), a U.S. government agency.

ENSURING OCCUPATIONAL SAFETY IN PRACTICE. Companies can take a number of steps to improve the safety and health of their workforces. Important examples include:

- *Reduce unsafe conditions that can lead to accidents.* This is an employer's first line of defense. A brief checklist like that in Figure 9.2 can be useful. For example, is material piled in a safe manner? Are there safety feet on straight ladders? Do stairways have guardrails?
- *Hire safety-prone people.* Employee selection and testing can be used to hire people who are less likely to have accidents, particularly on accident-prone jobs like driving heavy equipment. For example, psychological tests—especially tests of emotional stability—have been used to screen out accident-prone taxi drivers.[11] Similarly, tests of muscular coordination are important for jobs such as lumberjack, and tests of visual skills are important for drivers and employees operating machines.
- *Emphasize safety.* Use safety posters and continual reminders from top management that safety is paramount.
- *Use training to improve safety.* Safety training, such as instructing employees in safe practices and procedures and warning them of potential hazards, can help employees act more safely at work. The Subaru-Isuzu automotive plant in Lafayette, Indiana, has employees engage in a series of stretching

I. GENERAL HOUSEKEEPING

Adequate and wide aisles—no materials protruding into aisles

Parts and tools stored safely after use—not left in hazardous positions that could cause them to fall

Even and solid flooring—no defective floors or ramps that could cause falling or tripping accidents

Waste and trash cans—safely located and not overfilled

Material piled in safe manner—not too high or too close to sprinkler heads

All work areas clean and dry

All exit doors and aisles clean of obstructions

Aisles kept clear and properly marked; no air lines or electric cords across aisles

II. MATERIAL HANDLING EQUIPMENT AND CONVEYANCES

On all conveyances, electric or hand, check to see that the following items are all in sound working conditions:

Brakes— properly adjusted

Not too much play in steering wheel

Warning device—in place and working

Wheels—securely in place; properly inflated

Fuel and oil—enough and right kind

No loose parts

Cables, hooks or chains—not worn or otherwise defective

Suspended chains or hooks conspicuous

Safely loaded

Properly stored

III. LADDERS, SCAFFOLD, BENCHES, STAIRWAYS, ETC.

The following items of major interest to be checked:

Safety feet on straight ladders

Guardrails or handrails

Treads, not slippery

No splintered, cracked, or rickety

Properly stored

Extension ladder ropes in good condition

Toeboards

IV. POWER TOOLS (STATIONARY)

Point of operation guarded

Guards in proper adjustment

Gears, belts, shafting, counterweights guarded

Foot pedals guarded

Brushes provided for cleaning machines

Adequate lighting

Properly grounded

Tool or material rests properly adjusted

Adequate work space around machines

Control switch easily accessible

Safety glasses worn

Gloves worn by persons handling rough or sharp materials

No gloves or loose clothing worn by persons operating machines

V. HAND TOOLS AND MISCELLANEOUS

In good condition—not cracked, worn, or otherwise defective

Properly stored

Correct for job

Goggles, respirators, and other personal protective equipment worn where necessary

VI. ELECTRICITY

No frayed, cracked, or deteriorated cords

All portable, as well as fixed machinery grounded by three-wire connectors

No dangling wires

Ground-fault circuit interrupters used in humid conditions

VII. SPRAY PAINTING

Explosion-proof electrical equipment

Proper storage of paints and thinners in approved metal cabinets

Fire extinguishers adequate and suitable; readily accessible

Minimum storage in work area

VIII. FIRE EXTINGUISHERS

Properly serviced and tagged

Readily accessible

Adequate and suitable for operations involved

■ **FIGURE 9.2**
Checklist of Mechanical or Physical Accident-Causing Conditions

SOURCE: Courtesy of the American Insurance Association. From "A Safety Committee Man's Guide," 1–64.

exercises before starting work, in part to keep work-related injuries to a minimum.

- *Set specific loss-control goals.* Analyze the number of accidents and safety incidents and then set specific safety goals to be achieved, for instance, a maximum of time lost due to injuries.
- *Formulate and enforce safety rules.* Set specific safety rules, such as "Safety hats must be worn in construction area" and "Oil spills must be wiped up promptly," and actively enforce these rules.
- *Conduct safety and health inspections regularly.* Similarly, investigate all accidents and "near misses" and have a system in place for letting employees notify management about hazardous conditions.

Labor-Management Relations

Under the laws of the United States and many other countries, employees are permitted to organize into unions. In the United States, the Norris-LaGuardia Act guarantees each employee the right to bargain with employers for union benefits. The Wagner Act outlaws unfair labor practices such as employers interfering with, restraining, or coercing employees who are exercising their legally sanctioned rights of organizing themselves into a union. The Taft–Hartley Act prohibits unfair labor practices by unions against employers (like refusing to bargain with the employer). The Landrum-Griffin Act protects union members from unfair practices perpetrated against them by their unions.

Other Employment Law Issues

Other employment-related laws affect virtually every personnel-related decision that managers make at work. The Fair Labor Standards Act specifies a minimum wage ($5.15 per hour as of 1997), as well as child-labor and overtime pay rules. The Employee Polygraph Protection Act of 1988 outlaws almost all uses of the polygraph or "lie-detector" machine for employment purposes. Under certain legislation such as the Federal Privacy Act of 1974 and the New York Personal Privacy Protection Act of 1985, employees may have legal rights regarding who has access to information about their work history and job performance. Under the Whistle-Blower Protection Act of 1989, some employees who blow the whistle on their employers for the purpose of publicizing dangerous employer practices are entitled to legal protection.

Staffing the Organization

The term **staffing** is often used to refer to actually filling a firm's open positions, and it includes six steps (as summarized in Figure 9.3): job analysis, personnel planning, recruiting, interviewing, testing and selection, and training and development.

Job Analysis

Developing an organization chart (discussed in chapters 7 and 8) results in creating jobs to be filled. **Job analysis** is the procedure used to determine the duties of the jobs and the kinds of people (in terms of skills and experience) who should be hired for them.[12] These data are then used to develop a **job description,** or a list of duties showing what the job entails, and **job specifications,** a list of the skills and aptitudes

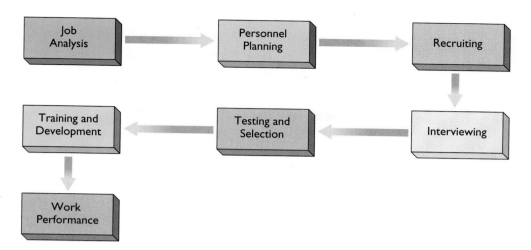

**■ FIGURE 9.3
Steps in the
Staffing Process**
The term "staffing" is often used to refer to the steps taken to actually fill a position—from job analysis to training and development.

sought in people hired for the job. A job description like the one in Figure 9.4 identifies the job, provides a brief job summary, and then lists specific responsibilities and duties of the job.

JOB ANALYSIS IN PRACTICE. How do managers determine the duties and functions of a job? A **job analysis questionnaire,** such as the one in Figure 9.5, (on pages 295–296) is often used. This one requires employees to provide detailed information on what they do, such as briefly stating their main duties in their own words, describing the conditions under which they work, and listing any permits or licenses required to perform duties assigned to their positions.

Managing Change

WILL COMPANIES BECOME "JOBLESS"?

Many of the trends that we've discussed so far in this book suggest that someday the job as we know it may disappear. Workers won't get jobs with neat listings of duties on job descriptions, say some experts.[13] Instead, they may be assigned to teams on which their duties may shift from day to day, and on which the lines between what's "my" job and "yours" may blur and disappear.[14]

We've already seen evidence of this shift in previous chapters. Flattening organizations and establishing self-contained mini-units often make employees' responsibilities much broader and less confined. Similarly, reengineering business processes and organizing the work to be done around teams usually mean that workers' jobs are designed to overlap so that they'll all pull together. Boundaryless organizations similarly foster a willingness on the part of employees to think of their jobs in terms of what the worker must do to get the work done.

Job descriptions will undoubtedly be around for some time. However, increasingly HR managers must help the company manage change by designing "jobs" that are broad and flexible enough to encourage team-based employees to work together and share each others' load. And HR has to see that the right employees are hired and properly trained for these more demanding jobs. ■

RELSED COMPUTER CORPORATION

Supervisor of Data Processing Operations	*Exempt*	*012.168*
Job Title	Status	Job Code

July 3, 1997	*Main Office*
Date	Plant/Division

Arthur Allen	*Information*
	Data Processing—Systems
Written By	Department/Section

Juanita Montgomery	*12*	*736*
Approved By	Grade/Level	Points

Manager of Information Systems	*16,800–Mid 14,760–20,720*
Title of Immediate Supervisor	Pay Range

SUMMARY

Directs the operation of all data processing, data control, and data preparation requirements.

JOB DUTIES*

1. Follows broadly-based directives.
   (a) Operates independently.
   (b) Informs Manager of Information Systems of activities through weekly, monthly, and/or quarterly schedules.
2. Selects, trains, and develops subordinate personnel.
   (a) Develops spirit of cooperation and understanding among work group members.
   (b) Ensures that work group members receive specialized training as necessary in the proper functioning or execution of machines, equipment, systems, procedures, processes, and/or methods.
   (c) Directs training involving teaching, demonstrating, and/or advising users in productive work methods and effective communications with data processing.
3. Reads and analyzes wide variety of instructional and training information.
   (a) Applies latest concepts and ideas to changing organizational requirements.
   (b) Assists in developing and/or updating manuals, procedures, specifications, etc., relative to organizational requirements and needs.
   (c) Assists in the preparation of specifications and related evaluations of supporting software and hardware.
4. Plans, directs, and controls a wide variety of operational assignments by 5 to 7 subordinates; works closely with other managers, specialists, and technicians within Information Systems as well as with managers in other departments with data needs and with vendors.
   (a) Receives, interprets, develops, and distributes directives ranging from the very simple to the highly complex and technological in nature.
   (b) Establishes and implements annual budget for department.
5. Interacts and communicates with people representing a wide variety of units and organizations.
   (a) Communicates both personally and impersonally, through oral or written directives and memoranda, with all involved parties.
   (b) Attends local meetings of professional organizations in the field of data processing.

*This section should also include description of uncomfortable, dirty, or dangerous assignments.

■ **FIGURE 9.4**
Sample Job Description

JOB QUESTIONNAIRE
OZARK MANUFACTURING COMPANY

YOUR NAME _____ PRESENT JOB TITLE _____
DEPARTMENT _____ EMPLOYEE NUMBER _____
SUPERVISOR'S NAME _____ SUPERVISOR'S TITLE _____

1. SUMMARY OF DUTIES: State briefly, in your own words, your main duties.
   _____
   _____
   _____

2. SPECIAL QUALIFICATIONS: List any licenses, permits, certifications, etc.
   required to perform duties assigned to your position.
   _____
   _____

3. EQUIPMENT: List any equipment, machines, or tools (e.g., computers, motor
   vehicles, lathes, fork lifts, drill presses, etc.) you normally operate as a part of
   your position's duties.

   MACHINE   AVERAGE NO. HOURS PER WEEK

   _____
   _____
   _____
   _____

4. REGULAR DUTIES: In general terms, describe duties you regularly perform.
   Please list these duties in descending order of importance and give the percent
   of time spent on them per month. List as many duties as possible and attach
   additional sheets, if necessary.
   _____
   _____
   _____
   _____

5. CONTACTS: Does your job require any contacts with other department
   personnel, other departments, outside companies or agencies? If yes, please
   define the duties requiring contacts and how often.
   _____
   _____

6. SUPERVISION: Does your position have supervisory responsibilities? ( ) Yes ( )
   No. If yes, please fill out a Supplemental Position Description Questionnaire for
   Supervisors and attach it to this form. If you have responsibility for the work of
   others but do not directly supervise them, please explain.
   _____
   _____
   _____

7. DECISION MAKING: Please explain the decisions you make while performing
   the regular duties of your job.
   _____
   _____
   _____

   (a) What might be a likely result of your making (a) poor judgment(s) or
   decision(s), or (b) improper actions?
   _____
   _____

(continued)

■ **FIGURE 9.5**
Job Analysis
Questionnaire for
Developing Job
Descriptions
A questionnaire like this
one can be used to inter-
view job incumbents or
may be filled out by them.

8. REPORTS AND RECORDS: List the reports and files you are required to prepare or maintain. State for whom each report is intended.

    (a)   REPORT   INTENDED FOR

    (b)   FILES MAINTAINED

9. FREQUENCY OF SUPERVISION: How frequently must you confer with your supervisor or other personnel in making decisions or in determining the proper course of action to be taken?

    ( ) Daily   ( ) Weekly   ( ) Monthly   ( ) Never

10. WORKING CONDITIONS: Please describe the conditions under which you work—inside, outside, air conditioned area, etc. Be sure to list any disagreeable or unusual working conditions.

11. JOB REQUIREMENTS: Please indicate the minimum requirements you believe are necessary to perform satisfactorily in your present position.

    (a) Education: (b) Experience:

        Minimum schooling _____   Type _____

        Number of years _____   Number of years _____

        Specialization or major _____

    (c) Special training:

                    TYPE   NUMBER OF YEARS

    (d) Special Skills:

        Computer programs: _____

        Other: _____

12. ADDITIONAL INFORMATION: Please provide additional information, not included in any of the previous items, which you feel would be important in a description of your position.

EMPLOYEE'S SIGNATURE_____ DATE:_____

■ **FIGURE 9.5**
Job Analysis Questionnaire for Developing Job Descriptions (*continued*)

Personnel Planning

Personnel planning consists of three activities: (1) forecasting personnel requirements (in terms of future open positions); (2) forecasting the supply of outside candidates and internal candidates; and (3) producing plans that describe how candidates will be hired, trained, and prepared for the jobs that will be opening up.

Thanks to computers, personnel planning today is becoming increasingly sophisticated. Many firms maintain computerized data banks containing information about hundreds of employee traits (like special skills, product knowledge, work experience, training courses, relocation limitations, and career interests).[15] The availability of so much employee data facilitates planning for and filling positions in big companies. It also has intensified the need to protect the privacy of the personal data that are sorted in the firm's data banks.

Employee Recruiting

Recruiting—attracting a pool of viable job applicants—is very important. If you only have two candidates for two openings, you may have little choice but to hire them. But if 20 or 30 applicants appear, you can use techniques like interviews and tests to hire the best. The main sources of applicants are discussed next.

INTERNAL SOURCES OF CANDIDATES. Although recruiting often brings to mind employment agencies and classified ads, current employees are often the largest source of recruits.

Filling open positions with inside candidates has both benefits and drawbacks. On the plus side, employees see that competence is rewarded and morale and performance may thus be enhanced. Inside candidates are also known quantities in terms of their performance and skills, and they may already be committed to your company and its goals. On the other hand, current employees who apply for jobs and do not get them may become discontented. Furthermore, promotion from within can lead to inbreeding: When an entire management team has been brought up through the ranks, there may be a tendency to maintain the status quo when innovation and a new direction could be needed.

ADVERTISING AS A SOURCE OF CANDIDATES. As you know from the many help-wanted ads that appear in your local newspaper, advertising is a major source of attracting applicants. The main issue here is selecting the best advertising medium, be it the local paper, the *Wall Street Journal,* or a technical journal. The medium chosen depends on the type of job. The local newspaper is usually the best source for blue-collar help, clerical employees, and lower-level administrative employees. For specialized positions, employers can advertise in trade and professional journals like *American Psychologist, Sales Management,* and *Chemical Engineering.* Executive jobs are often advertised in the *Wall Street Journal.*

EMPLOYMENT AGENCIES AS A SOURCE OF CANDIDATES. An employment agency is basically an intermediary whose business is to match applicants with employers' open positions. There are three types of agencies: (1) those operated by federal, state, or local governments; (2) those associated with nonprofit organizations; and (3) those that are privately owned.

Public state employment agencies exist in every state and are often referred to as job service or unemployment service agencies. Agencies like these are a major free source of hourly blue-collar and clerical workers and are increasingly establishing themselves as agents for professional and managerial-level applicants as well.

Other employment agencies are associated with nonprofit organizations. For example, most professional and technical societies, such as the American Institute of Chemical Engineers, have units to help their members find jobs.

Private agencies charge fees for each applicant they place. These fees are usually set by state law and are posted in the agencies' offices. Whether the employer or the candidate pays the fee is mostly determined by market conditions. However, the trend in the last few years has been toward "fee-paid" jobs in which the employer and not the candidate pays the fees. Such agencies are important sources of clerical, white-collar, and managerial personnel.

EXECUTIVE RECRUITERS AS A SOURCE OF CANDIDATES. **Executive recruiters** (also ominously known as *head hunters*) are agencies retained by employers to seek out top management talent. They fill jobs in the $40,000 and up category, although $50,000 is often the lower limit.

These firms can be very useful. They have many business contacts and are especially adept at contacting qualified candidates who are employed and not actively looking to change jobs. They can also keep a client firm's name confidential until late in the search process. The recruiter saves management time by doing the preliminary work of advertising for the position and screening what could turn out to be hundreds of applicants.

The executive recruiting process typically starts with the executive recruiter meeting with the client's executives to formulate a clear written description of the position to be filled and the sort of person needed to fill it. The recruiter will then use various sources and contacts to identify viable candidates, interview these people, and present a short list of three or four candidates to the client's executives for final screening.

REFERRALS OR WALK-INS AS A SOURCE OF CANDIDATES. Particularly for hourly workers, *walk-ins*—people who apply directly at the office—are a major source of applicants. Encouraging walk-in applicants may be as simple as posting a handwritten Help Wanted sign in your office or plant window. On the other hand, some organizations encourage walk-in applicants by mounting employee referral campaigns. Here, announcements of openings and requests for referrals are made in the company's newsletter or posted on bulletin boards.

OLDER WORKERS AS A SOURCE OF JOB CANDIDATES. Fewer 18- to 25-year-olds have been entering the workforce. This reduction has caused many employers to begin looking to alternative sources to help meet their employment needs.[16] For many U.S. employers this means harnessing the country's "gray power" by encouraging current retirement-age employees to stay with the company or actively recruiting applicants who are at, near, or beyond retirement age.[17]

THE INTERNET AS A SOURCE OF JOB CANDIDATES. A growing number of employers are recruiting using the Internet, the World Wide Web, and commercial on-line services like America Online.[18] For example, Winter, Wyman & Co., a Boston-based recruiting firm, posts job descriptions on its Web page. Similarly, Honeywell uses America Online's E-span service to recruit for applicants for jobs such as programmers. American Contract Services spends about $3,500 per year to run employment ads on the Internet. Another Web site called The Internet's Online Career Center (http://www.occ.com/occ/) lists open positions as well as résumés submitted by individual job-seekers.

Selection and Placement Techniques

With a pool of applicants, the employer can turn to screening and selecting. These processes use one or more techniques, including application blanks, interviews, tests, and reference checks, to assess and investigate an applicant's aptitudes, interests, and background. The company then chooses the best candidate, given the job's requirements.

Employee selection is important for several reasons. For a manager, his or her job performance will always hinge on the subordinate's performance. A poor performer will drag a manager down, and a good one will enhance the manager's performance. Therefore, the time to screen out undesirables is before they have their foot in the door—not after.

Screening applicants is also expensive, so it is best to do it right the first time. Hiring a manager who earns $60,000 a year may cost as much as $40,000 or $50,000 once search fees, interviewing time, and travel and moving expenses are added up. In fact, the cost of hiring even nonexecutive employees can be $3,000 to $5,000 each or more.

Organizational Behavior in Action

BUILDING COOPERATION AND TEAMWORK

It's hard to overemphasize the value of effective selection and placement, especially in today's team-based and networked organizations. By definition teamwork and networking depend on cooperation. If you hire uncooperative employees to begin with, then your chances of building a successful team-based organization are practically nil.

You have probably noticed that some people are generally more cooperative than others, and your observations are supported by behavioral science research findings.[19] The findings suggest that when it comes to cooperation, most people seem to fall into one of four distinct categories: competitors, individualists, cooperators, and equalizers.

Here's a brief snapshot of how each of these types of people behaves. **Competitors** are people whose primary motive is doing better than others—beating them or outperforming them in open competition. **Individualists,** on the other hand, simply want to gain as much as possible for themselves. In extreme situations competitors may actually prefer seeing others end up badly rather than maximizing their own gains; individualists have little interest in what happens to their competitors as long as they themselves gain as much as they can.

Cooperators are primarily concerned with maximizing joint outcomes—the total received by themselves and others. In a negotiating situation, for instance, cooperators would be interested in maximizing the size of the pie, so that everyone involved walked away with as much as possible. **Equalizers** have equality of outcomes as their primary concern: They want to make sure that everyone they work with receives the same basic results.

It will not surprise you that these different types of people behave differently at work. For instance, competitors tend to cooperate only when they see no other choice and to push for all they can get. Cooperators, on the other hand, would rather work with their co-workers than against them.

This being the case, managers in general (and HR managers in particular) have to be careful about how they match candidates with jobs. For example, a highly competitive person might make a terrific outside salesperson but would gradually reduce the sense of teamwork in any team he or she had to work with over time. Equalizers could be disasters as managers if they ended up inaccurately evaluating all their subordinates as about the same, but they might excel in a negotiation in which it's important for some resource (like office space) to be allocated equitably.

In summary, particularly in today's team-oriented organizations, managers must have the ability to select the right employees and then place them in the right jobs.

Managers should therefore never be nonchalant when making hiring decisions; instead, they need to be skilled in the use of the selection and placement techniques we turn to next. ■

Application Blanks

The selection process usually starts with an application blank, although some firms first require a brief prescreening interview. The **application blank** is a form that requests information about factors like education, work history, and hobbies.[20] It is a good means of quickly collecting verifiable and therefore fairly accurate historical data from the candidate.

Testing for Employee Selection

A **test** is basically a sample of a person's behavior. It is used in personnel management for predicting a person's success on the job. The use of tests for hiring, promotion, or both has increased in recent years after two decades of decline.[21] It appears that about half of all employers use tests of some sort for employee screening: about two thirds use skills tests (such as typing tests), while only about 17 percent use so-called personality tests.

Many types of tests are available to be used at work. For example, intelligence (IQ) tests are designed to measure general *intellectual abilities*. Common ones are the Stanford-Binet test or the Wechsler or Wonderlic tests.

For some jobs, managers will also be interested in testing an applicant's other abilities. For example, the Bennett Test of Mechanical Comprehension (illustrated in Figure 9.6) helps to assess an applicant's understanding of basic mechanical prin-

■ **FIGURE 9.6**
Bennet Test of Mechanical Comprehension, Example
Human resource managers often use personnel tests, like this one, to measure a candidate's skills and aptitudes.

SOURCE: Gary Dessler, *Human Resource Management*, 6th ed. (Englewood Cliffs, NJ: Prentice-Hall, 1994), 164.

Look at Sample X on this page. It shows two men carrying a weighted object on a plank, and it asks, Which man carries more weight? Because the object is closer to man B than to man A, man B is shouldering more weight; so blacken the circle under B on your answer sheet. Now look at Sample Y and answer it yourself. Fill in the circle under the correct answer on your answer sheet.

X
Which man carries more weight? (If equal, mark C.)

Which letter shows the seat where a passenger will get the smoothest ride?

ciples and might be useful for predicting success on a job such as machinist or engineer. A test like the Stromberg Dexterity Test is used to measure the applicant's speed of finger, hand, and arm movements. This would be useful if the job in question involves manipulating small items (for instance, assembling computer circuit boards).

It is also sometimes useful to measure the applicant's *personality and interests*. For example, you probably would not want to hire someone for an entry-level job as an accounting clerk if he or she had no measurable interest in working with figures.[22] With the burgeoning number of service workers these days, service management expert Karl Albrecht says that jobs with high levels of emotional labor will increase. *Emotional labor* is any work in which the employee's feelings are the tools of his or her trade (for instance, an airline reservation clerk would be expected to deal courteously with each and every caller). Most of us have had some experience dealing with service people who are obviously not well suited psychologically for such jobs. A personality test might have screened them out.

A **management assessment center** is another approach to selection. In such centers, about a dozen management candidates spend two or three days performing realistic management tasks (like making presentations) under the observation of expert appraisers. Each candidate's potential for management is thereby assessed.[23] The center's activities might include individual presentations, objective tests, interviews, and participation in management games. Here participants would engage in realistic problem solving, usually as members of two or three simulated companies that are competing in a mock marketplace.

Organizational Behavior in Action

HIRING HAPPY EMPLOYEES

With all the aptitudes, skills, and traits for which managers can test applicants, there is still one thing that's usually not tested for but that perhaps should be—at least if some recent research findings are valid. Particularly in companies being rocked by downsizings and competitive pressures, there's something to be said about hiring people who are inclined to remain happy even in the face of unhappy events. And, a recent line of research suggests that it may be possible to do so.

Basically, this line of research suggests that happiness seems to be largely determined by the person's genetic makeup—that, in other words, some people are simply born to be somewhat happier than are others.[24] The theory, in a nutshell, says that people have a sort of "set-point" for happiness, a genetically determined happiness level to which the person quickly gravitates, pretty much no matter what failures or successes the person experiences. So, confront a high-happiness-set-point person with the prospect of a demotion or unattractive lateral transfer and he or she will soon return to being relatively happy once the short blip of disappointment has dissipated. On the other hand, send an inherently low-set-point, unhappy person off on a two-week vacation or give him or her a sizable raise or a new computer and chances are he or she will soon be as unhappy as before the reward.

Several lines of research lend support to this set-point theory. For example, a study of lottery winners found that they were on the whole no happier a year after their good fortune than they were before. Several studies show that even people with spinal-cord injuries tend to rebound in spirits.[25] Studies of identical twins led one psychologist to conclude that life circumstances like salary, education, or marital status predicted only two percent of the happiness variation within each pair of twins, and that much of the rest was simply determined by the person's genes. In fact, the results of several long-term studies that followed people over many years suggest that the people who are happiest today will also be the happiest 10 years from now.

Like testing employees for any traits, coming up with a set of tests or interview questions to identify happier, high-set-point people requires careful consideration and probably the help of a licensed psychologist. However, following are several questions that may help provide some insight into a person's tendency to be relatively happy.

Indicate how strongly (high, medium, low) you agree with the following statements:

- "When good things happen to me, it strongly affects me."
- "I will often do things for no other reason than they might be fun."
- "When I get something I want, I feel excited and energized."
- "When I'm doing well at something, I love to keep at it."

Agreeing with more statements, and agreeing with them more strongly, *may* correlate with a higher happiness set-point.[26]

Interviews

Both before and after any testing occurs, several interviews will usually be in order. Although the interview is probably the single most widely used selection device, its usefulness is often questioned. One doubt centers on reliability: Will different people interviewing the same candidate come to similar conclusions about the applicant's acceptability for the job? A second question concerns validity: Do the results of the interview accurately predict success on the job?

HOW TO BE A BETTER INTERVIEWER. A manager can boost the reliability and validity of selection interviews by following sound interviewing procedures.[27] These can be summarized as follows:

Plan the interview. Begin by reviewing the candidate's application and résumé, and note any areas that are vague or may indicate strengths or weaknesses. Review the job specification and plan to start the interview with a clear picture of the traits of an ideal candidate.

If possible, use a structured form. Interviews based on structured guides like those in Figures 9.7 (pages 303–305) and 9.8 (page 306) usually result in the best interviews.[28] At a minimum, you should write out your questions prior to the interview.

The interview should take place in a private room where telephone calls are not accepted and interruptions can be minimized.

Also, plan to delay your decision. Interviewers often make snap judgments even before they see the candidate—on the basis of his or her application form, for instance—or during the first few minutes of the interview. Plan on keeping a record of the interview and review this record afterward. Make your decision then.[29]

Establish rapport. The main purpose of the interview is to find out about the applicant. To do this, start by putting the person at ease. Greet the candidate and start the interview by asking a noncontroversial question—perhaps about the

APPLICANT INTERVIEW GUIDE

To the interviewer: This Applicant Interview Guide is intended to assist in employee selection and placement. If it is used for all applicants for a position, it will help you to compare them, and it will provide more objective information than you will obtain from unstructured interviews.

Because this is a general guide, all of the items may not apply in every instance. Skip those that are not applicable and add questions appropriate to the specific position. Space for additional questions will be found at the end of the form.

Federal law prohibits discrimination in employment on the basis of sex, race, color, national origin, religion, disability, and in most instances, age. The laws of most states also ban some or all of the above types of discrimination in employment as well as discrimination based on marital status or ancestry. Interviewers should take care to avoid any questions that suggest that an employment decision will be made on the basis of any such factors.

Job Interest

Name _____ Position applied for _____

What do you think the job (position) involves? _____

Why do you want the job (position)? _____

Why are you qualified for it? _____

What would your salary requirements be? _____

What do you know about our company? _____

Why do you want to work for us? _____

Current Work Status

Are you now employed? _____Yes _____ No. If not, how long have you been unemployed? _____

Why are you unemployed? _____

If you are working, why are you applying for this position? _____

When would you be available to start work with us? _____

Work Experience

(Start with the applicant's current or last position and work back. All periods of time should be accounted for. Go back at least 12 years, depending upon the applicant's age. Military service should be treated as a job.)

Current or last
employer_____ Address _____

Dates of employment: from _____ to _____

Current or last job title _____

What are (were) your duties? _____

Have you held the same job throughout your employment with that company? _____Yes _____ No. If not, describe the various jobs you have had with that employer, how long you held each of them, and the main duties of each. _____

_____

What was your starting salary? _____ What are you earning now? _____ Comments _____

_____

Name of your last or current supervisor _____

What did you like most about that job? _____

What did you like least about it? _____

Why are you thinking of leaving? _____

   Why are you leaving right now? _____

   Interviewer's comments or observations _____

_____

What did you do before you took your last job? _____

   Where were you employed? _____

   Location _____ Job title _____

(continued)

■ **FIGURE 9.7 Structured Interview Guide**

Source: Copyright © 1992 The Dartnell Corporation, 4660 N. Ravenswood Ave., Chicago, IL, 60640. (800)621-5463. Adapted with permission.

Duties ———

Did you hold the same job throughout your employment with that company? ____Yes ____ No. If not, describe the jobs you held, when you held them and the duties of each. ————————————————————————————————————

———

What was your starting salary? ———————— What was your final salary? ————————————————————

Name of your last supervisor ——

May we contact that company? ____Yes ____ No

What did you like most about that job? ——————————————————————————————————

What did you like least about that job? ——————————————————————————————————

Why did you leave that job? ——

Would you consider working there again? ————————————————————————————————

Interviewer: If there is any gap between the various periods of employment, the applicant should be asked about them.

———

Interviewer's comments or observations ————————————————————————————————

———

What did you do prior to the job with that company? ————————————————————————————

What other jobs or experience have you had? Describe them briefly and explain the general duties of each.

———

Have you been unemployed at any time in the last five years? ____Yes ____ No. What efforts did you make to find work?

———

What other experience or training do you have that would help qualify you for the job you applied for? Explain how and where you obtained this experience or training. ——

———

Educational Background

What education or training do you have that would help you in the job for which you have applied? ————————————

———

Describe any formal education you have had. (Interviewer may substitute technical training, if relevant.) ————————————

———

Off-Job Activities

What do you do in your off-hours? ___ Part-time job ___ Athletics ___Spectator sports ___Clubs ___Other

Please explain. ——

Interviewer's Specific Questions

Interviewer: Add any questions to the particular job for which you are interviewing, leaving space for brief answers.

(Be careful to avoid questions which may be viewed as discriminatory.)

———

———

———

Personal

Would you be willing to relocate? ————Yes ———— No

Are you willing to travel? ————Yes ————No

What is the maximum amount of time you would consider traveling? ———————————————————————

———

Are you able to work overtime? ——————————————————————————————————————

What about working on weekends? ————————————————————————————————————

Self-Assessment

What do you feel are your strong points? ——————————————————————————————————

———

What do you feel are your weak points? ——————————————————————————————————

■ **FIGURE 9.7   Structured Interview Guide** *(continued)*

Interviewer: Compare the applicant's responses with the information furnished on the application for employment. Clear up any discrepancies. _____

_____

Before the applicant leaves, the interviewer should provide basic information about the organization and the job opening, if this has not already been done. The applicant should be given information on the work location, work hours, the wage or salary, type of remuneration (salary or salary plus bonuses, etc.), and other factors that may affect the applicant's interest in the job.

Interviewer's Impressions

Rate each characteristic from 1 to 4, with 1 being the highest rating and 4 being the lowest.

Personal Characteristics	1	2	3	4	Comments
Personal appearance					
Poise, manner					
Speech					
Cooperation with interviewer					
Job-related Characteristics					
Experience for this job					
Knowledge of job					
Interpersonal relationships					
Effectiveness					

Overall rating for job

1	2	3	4	5
_____ Superior	_____ Above Average (well qualified)	_____ Average (qualified)	_____ Marginal (barely qualified)	_____ Unsatisfactory

Comments or remarks _____

_____

_____

Interviewer _____ Date _____

■ **FIGURE 9.7**
Structured Interview Guide (*continued*)

weather or the traffic conditions that day. As a rule, all applicants—even unsolicited drop-ins—should receive friendly, courteous treatment, not only on humanitarian grounds but also because your reputation is on the line.

Be aware of the applicant's status. For example, if you are interviewing someone who is unemployed, he or she may be exceptionally nervous and you may want to take additional steps to relax the person.[30]

Ask questions. Try to follow your structured interview guide or the questions you wrote out ahead of time. A menu of questions to choose from (such as "What best qualifies you for the available position?") is presented in Figure 9.9, page 307.

Some suggestions for actually asking questions include these:

Avoid questions that can be answered "yes" or "no."

Don't put words in the applicant's mouth or telegraph the desired answer (for instance, by nodding or smiling when the right answer is given).

Don't interrogate the applicant as if the person were a criminal, and don't be patronizing, sarcastic, or inattentive.

Don't monopolize the interview by rambling, or let the applicant dominate the interview so you can't ask all your questions.

CANDIDATE RECORD

NAP 100 (10/77)

CANDIDATE NUMBER	NAME (LAST NAME FIRST)	COLLEGE NAME	COLLEGE CODE
I ☐☐☐ U 921 (1–7)	☐☐☐☐☐☐☐☐☐☐☐☐☐☐☐☐☐☐☐☐ (8–27)		☐☐☐ (28–30)

INTERVIEWER NUMBER
☐☐☐☐ 0 ☐☐☐ (33–40)

INTERVIEWER NAME
_____

SOURCE (41)
Campus ☐ C
Walk-in ☐ W
Intern ☐ I
Agency ☐ A

RACE (42)
White ☐ W
Black ☐ B
Asian ☐ A
Hispanic ☐ H
Native Am. ☐ NA

SEX (43)
Male ☐ M
Female ☐ F
Init.
Cont.
Date ☐☐☐☐☐

DEGREE (53)
Bachelors ☐ B
Masters ☐ M
Law ☐ L
Majors

AVERAGE
(A = 4.0)
Overall ☐☐ (54-55)
Acctg. ☐☐ (56-57)

CLASS STANDING
(59–59)
Top 10% ☐ 10
Top 25% ☐ 25
Top Half ☐ 50
Bottom Half ☐ 75

CAMPUS INTERVIEW EVALUATIONS

ATTITUDE – MOTIVATION – GOALS

POOR ☐   AVERAGE ☐   GOOD ☐   OUTSTANDING ☐

(POSITIVE, COOPERATIVE, ENERGETIC, MOTIVATED, SUCCESSFUL, GOAL-ORIENTED)
COMMENTS:

COMMUNICATIONS SKILLS – PERSONALITY – SALES ABILITY

POOR ☐   AVERAGE ☐   GOOD ☐   OUTSTANDING ☐

(ARTICULATE, LISTENS, ENTHUSIASTIC, LIKEABLE, POISED, TACTFUL, ACCEPTED, CONVINCING)
COMMENTS:

EXECUTIVE PRESENCE – DEAL WITH TOP PEOPLE

POOR ☐   AVERAGE ☐   GOOD ☐   OUTSTANDING ☐

(IMPRESSIVE, STANDS OUT, A WINNER, REMEMBERED, LEVELHEADED, AT EASE, AWARE)
COMMENTS:

INTELLECTUAL ABILITIES

POOR ☐   AVERAGE ☐   GOOD ☐   OUTSTANDING ☐

(INSIGHTFUL, CREATIVE, CURIOUS, IMAGINATIVE, UNDERSTANDS, REASONS, INTELLIGENT, SCHOLARLY)
COMMENTS:

JUDGMENT – DECISION MAKING ABILITY

POOR ☐   AVERAGE ☐   GOOD ☐   OUTSTANDING ☐

(MATURE, SEASONED, INDEPENDENT, COMMON SENSE, CERTAIN, DETERMINED, LOGICAL)
COMMENTS:

LEADERSHIP

POOR ☐   AVERAGE ☐   GOOD ☐   OUTSTANDING ☐

(SELF-CONFIDENT, TAKES CHARGE, EFFECTIVE, RESPECTED, MANAGEMENT MINDED, GRASPS AUTHORITY)
COMMENTS:

CAMPUS INTERVIEW SUMMARY

INVITE (Circle) Yes No	AREA OF INTEREST (Circle)	SEMESTER HRS.	OFFICES PREFERRED:	SUMMARY COMMENTS: _____
DATE AVAILABLE	AUDIT TAX	Acct'g. _____	No. 1 _____	
	MCS ABC	Audit _____	No. 2 _____	
	OTHER	Tax _____	No. 3 _____	

■ **FIGURE 9.8   Structured Interview Form for College Applicants**

■ **FIGURE 9.9**
Interview Questions to Expect

SOURCE: H. Lee Rust, *Job Search, The Complete Manual for Job Seekers* (New York, AMACOM, 1991), pp. 232–233.

1. Did you bring a résumé?
2. What salary do you expect to receive?
3. What was your salary in your last job?
4. Why do you want to change jobs or why did you leave your last job?
5. What do you identify as your most significant accomplishment in your last job?
6. How many hours do you normally work per week?
7. What did you like and dislike about your last job?
8. How did you get along with your superiors and subordinates?
9. Can you be demanding of your subordinates?
10. How would you evaluate the company you were with last?
11. What were its competitive strengths and weaknesses?
12. What best qualifies you for the available position?
13. How long will it take you to start making a significant contribution?
14. How do you feel about our company—its size, industry, and competitive position?
15. What interests you most about the available position?
16. How would you structure this job or organize your department?
17. What control or financial data would you want and why?
18. How would you establish your primary inside and outside lines of communication?
19. What would you like to tell me about yourself?
20. Were you a good student?
21. Have you kept up in your field? How?
22. What do you do in your spare time?
23. What are your career goals for the next five years?
24. What are your greatest strengths and weaknesses?
25. What is your job potential?
26. What steps are you taking to help achieve your goals?
27. Do you want to own your own business?
28. How long will you stay with us?
29. What did your father do? Your mother?
30. What do your brothers and sisters do?
31. Have you ever worked on a group project and, if so, what role did you play?
32. Do you participate in civic affairs?
33. What professional associations do you belong to?
34. What is your credit standing?
35. What are your personal likes and dislikes?
36. How do you spend a typical day?
37. Would you describe your family as a close one?
38. How aggressive are you?
39. What motivates you to work?
40. Is money a strong incentive for you?
41. Do you prefer line or staff work?
42. Would you rather work alone or in a team?
43. What do you look for when hiring people?
44. Have you ever fired anyone?
45. Can you get along with union members and their leaders?
46. What do you think of the current economic and political situation?
47. How will government policy affect our industry or your job?
48. Will you sign a noncompete agreement or employment contract?
49. Why should we hire you?
50. Do you want the job?

Listen to the candidate and encourage him or her to express thoughts fully.

Draw out the applicant's opinions and feelings by repeating the person's last comment as a question (such as "You didn't like your last job?").

When you ask for general statements of a candidate's accomplishments, also ask for examples.[31] Thus, if the candidate lists specific strengths or weaknesses, follow up with, "What are specific examples that demonstrate each of your strengths?"

Close the interview.   Toward the close of the interview, leave time to answer any questions the candidate may have and, if appropriate, to advocate your firm to the candidate.

Try to end the interviews on a positive note. The applicant should be told whether there is an interest in him or her and, if so, what the next step will be. Similarly, rejections should be made diplomatically, for instance, with a statement like "Although your background is impressive, there are other candidates whose experience is closer to our requirements." If the applicant is still being considered but a decision can't be reached at once, say this. If it is your policy to inform candidates of their status in writing, do so within a few days of the interview.

Review the interview.   After the candidate leaves, review your interview notes, fill in the structured interview guide (if this was not done during the interview), and review the interview while it's fresh in your mind.

Remember that snap judgments and negative emphasis are two common interviewing mistakes: Reviewing the interview shortly after the candidate has left can help you minimize these two problems.

Organizational Behavior in Action

GUIDELINES FOR INTERVIEWEES

Before you get into a position where you have to interview applicants, you will probably have to navigate some interviews yourself. Here are some hints for excelling in your interview.

The first thing to understand is that interviews are used primarily to help employers determine what you are like as a person. In other words, information regarding how you get along with other people and your desire to work is of prime importance in the interview; your skills and technical expertise are usually best assessed through tests and a study of your educational and work history. Interviewers will look first for articulate answers. Specifically, whether you respond concisely, cooperate fully in answering questions, state personal opinions when relevant, and keep to the subject at hand are by far the most important elements in influencing the interviewer's decision.

There are seven things to do to get that extra edge in the interview.

1. PREPARATION IS ESSENTIAL.   Before the interview, learn all you can about the employer, the job, and the people doing the recruiting. At the library or on the Internet, look through business periodicals and Web sites to find out what is happening in the employer's company and industry.

2. UNCOVER THE INTERVIEWER'S REAL NEEDS.   Spend as little time as possible answering your interviewer's first questions and as much time as possible getting him or her to describe his or her needs. Determine what the person is looking to get accomplished and the type of person he or she feels is needed. Use open-ended questions such as "Could you tell me more about that?"

3. RELATE YOURSELF TO THE INTERVIEWER'S NEEDS.   Once you know the type of person your interviewer is looking for and the sorts of problems he or she wants solved, you are in a good position to describe your own accomplishments *in terms* *of the interviewer's needs.* Start by saying something like, "One of the problem areas you've said is important to you is similar to a problem I once faced." Then state the problem, describe your solution, and reveal the results.

4. THINK BEFORE ANSWERING. Answering a question should be a three-step process: pause, think, speak. *Pause* to make sure you understand what the interviewer is driving at, *think* about how to structure your answer, and then *speak*. In your answer, try to emphasize how hiring you will help the interviewer solve his or her problem.

5. REMEMBER THAT APPEARANCE AND ENTHUSIASM ARE IMPORTANT. Appropriate clothing, good grooming, a firm handshake, and the appearance of controlled energy are important.

6. MAKE A GOOD FIRST IMPRESSION. Studies show that, although they should wait, in most cases interviewers make up their minds about the applicant during the early minutes of the interview. A good first impression may turn to a bad one during the interview, but it is unlikely. Bad first impressions are almost impossible to overcome. Remember: you only have one chance to make a good first impression. One expert suggests paying attention to these key interviewing considerations:

    a. Appropriate clothing
    b. Good grooming
    c. A firm handshake
    d. The appearance of controlled energy
    e. Pertinent humor and readiness to smile
    f. A genuine interest in the employer's operation and alert attention when the interviewer speaks
    g. Pride in past performance
    h. An understanding of the employer's needs and a desire to serve them
    i. The display of sound ideas
    j. Ability to take control when employers fall down on the interviewing job

Sample questions you can ask are presented in Figure 9.10. They include "Would you mind describing the job for me?" and "Could you tell me about the people who would be reporting to me?"

7. WATCH YOUR NONVERBAL BEHAVIOR. Remember that your *nonverbal behavior* may broadcast more about you than the verbal content of what you say. Maintaining eye contact is very important. Speak with enthusiasm, nod agreement, and remember to take a moment to frame your answer (pause, speak) so that you sound articulate and fluent.[32]

Other Selection Techniques

Various other selection techniques are used to screen applicants.

CHECKING REFERENCES. Most employers (estimates range up to 93 percent) do at least some reference checking on final candidates. These background checks can take many forms. However, most companies at least try to verify an applicant's current or previous position and salary with his or her current employer by telephone. Others call current and previous supervisors to discover more about the person's motivation, technical competence, and ability to work with others. Some employers also get background reports from commercial credit-rating companies;

1.	What is the first problem that needs attention of the person you hire?
2.	What other problems need attention now?
3.	What has been done about any of these to date?
4.	How has this job been performed in the past?
5.	Why is it now vacant?
6.	Do you have a written job description for this position?
7.	What are its major responsibilities?
8.	What authority would I have? How would you define its scope?
9.	What are the company's five-year sales and profit projections?
10.	What needs to be done to reach these projections?
11.	What are the company's major strengths and weaknesses?
12.	What are its strengths and weaknesses in production?
13.	What are its strengths and weaknesses in its products or its competitive position?
14.	Whom do you identify as your major competitors?
15.	What are their strengths and weaknesses?
16.	How do you view the future for your industry?
17.	Do you have any plans for new products or acquisitions?
18.	Might this company be sold or acquired?
19.	What is the company's current financial strength?
20.	What can you tell me about the individual to whom I would report?
21.	What can you tell me about other persons in key positions?
22.	What can you tell me about the subordinates I would have?
23.	How would you define your management philosophy?
24.	Are employees afforded an opportunity for continuing education?
25.	What are you looking for in the person who will fill this job?

■ **FIGURE 9.10**
**Interview Questions
to Ask**

SOURCE: H. Lee Rust, *Job
Search, The Complete Manual
for Job Seekers* (New York,
AMACOM, 1991), pp. 234–235.

this can provide information about an applicant's credit standing, indebtedness, reputation, character, and lifestyle.

HONESTY TESTING.   With so many employees working in jobs in which honesty is important—such as in banks, retail stores, and restaurants—paper-and-pencil "honesty testing" has become an important mini-industry.[33] Several psychologists have expressed concern about the proliferation and potential misuse of such tests. However, the American Psychological Association recently reported that "the preponderance of the evidence" supports the notion that some of the tests work, meaning that they can predict which prospective employees may prove undependable or dishonest.[34]

These tests ask questions aimed at assessing a person's tendency to be honest. For instance, a test might ask a series of questions such as "Have you ever made a personal phone call on company time?" Sometimes the test assumes that someone who answers all such questions "no" may not be entirely honest, although the person may actually be telling the truth.

HEALTH EXAMS.   A physical examination and drug screening are often two of the final steps in the selection process. A preemployment medical exam is used to confirm that the applicant qualifies for the physical requirements of the position and to discover any medical limitations that should be taken into account in placing the applicant. By identifying health problems, a physical exam can also reduce absenteeism and accidents and detect communicable diseases that may be unknown to the applicant.

Drug abuse, unfortunately, is a serious problem at work. Counselors at the Cocaine National Help Line polled callers of the 800-COCAINE hotline. They found that 75 percent admitted to occasional cocaine use at work, 69 percent said they regularly worked under the influence of a drug, and 25 percent reported daily use at work.[35] As a result, more employers are including drug screening as part of their prehiring program. In one survey, testing rose from 21 percent of surveyed firms in 1986 to 48 percent several years later.[36]

Entrepreneurs in Action

CAREFUL SELECTION IN TWO SMALL BUSINESSES

Hatteras Hammocks of Greenville, North Carolina, needed a new controller. Executive vice president Jay Branch picked a standout from a big field of applicants: His choice had received his undergraduate degree in accounting, earned an MBA from Indiana University, and worked as a CPA. The applicant was recommended by a personal friend, so after a brief chat with his former employer, Branch brought him aboard.

Six months later the man was gone. Soon after that, Branch discovered that the firm was missing about $60,000. The impressive résumé and credentials were fabricated. Apparently, the new controller had omitted his areas of greatest expertise: fraud, forgery, and embezzlement.

"The whole episode taught me the necessity of checking thoroughly," says Branch, "no matter how good a recommendation is."

The nightmare at Hatteras Hammocks underscores the importance of screening and background checks when selecting new employees. However, the potential for lawsuits against references who give derogatory statements can make reference checking useless. So how does a human resource manager determine if the reference is reliable? By applying sound judgment, using common sense, and sticking to queries that have a factual relevance to the particular job being filled.

For example, Voca Corporation of Columbus, Ohio, provides care to mentally retarded and developmentally disabled persons. Patient safety is naturally one of the paramount concerns, so applicants who will be in direct contact with residents are carefully screened for any history of abuse, neglect, or mistreatment. As the process begins, staffers give applicants the opportunity to explain or clarify anything that might come to light later. Fingerprinting follows. "It's our way of . . . demonstrating we're serious," says Hilary Franklin, director of human resources. "And it's pretty darn effective."

The company protects itself by adhering to strict guidelines throughout the process. Checks are run only on people to whom a job offer has been extended. Adverse discoveries, such as felony convictions, are kept strictly confidential. A prospective employee who would be in charge of transporting clients could expect his or her driving record to be scrutinized; a receptionist applicant would not. Everyone signs a release giving the company permission to verify the information the applicant has provided.

Source: Michael Cronin, "This Is a Test," *Inc.,* August 1993, 65–6.

The Entrepreneurs in Action feature above describes the screening steps two small businesses now take and suggests what can happen when no precautions are taken.

Managing Change

THE ROLE OF SELECTION IN MANAGING CHANGE

Managing change requires high-potential employees, people who have the potential to step into empowered jobs in self-managing teams. How do firms select such high-potential employees?

The selection process at Mazda's Flatrock, Michigan, plant provides a good example.[37] Almost from the day that Mazda announced it was building a plant in

Michigan, the company's managers emphasized that they would be very selective in choosing employees. Mazda would evaluate applicants more intensively than any U.S. automaker had ever evaluated hourly employees before, to ensure they hired high-potential employees who could work in self-managing teams.[38]

THE APPLICATION AND APTITUDE TESTS. Consider applicant Wayne Dodd. After mailing in a Mazda job application that had appeared in the local newspaper, Dodd received a letter from Mazda inviting him to come to an abandoned school just outside Flatrock for a series of written aptitude tests.

Dodd breezed through the two-hour battery of tests (which dealt mostly with basic math and reading comprehension) and did well enough on a test that evaluated his ability to detect quality defects (a crucial skill in the quality-oriented Mazda plant). In this test, applicants were shown illustrations (such as six light bulbs) and had to pick out the quality defect (such as the one with the small crack in its base).

THE PERSONAL INTERVIEW. Dodd did well enough to be invited back for a personal interview. The interview lasted 30 minutes, during which a man and woman inquired about Dodd's enthusiasm and asked questions about how he liked working as part of a team at Burger King (his current employer). He was asked whether he would have trouble at the auto plant if his supervisor asked him to pitch in to help out another team member who was having trouble completing a job on time. The interviewers, both Americans, wore the same blue and khaki Mazda uniform and introduced themselves by their first names. There were still two steps to go in Mazda's screening process.

THE PROBLEM-SOLVING ASSESSMENT. In the next screening process step, Dodd was asked to come to the Flatrock auto plant for a group problem-solving assessment. Dodd and several other employees were organized into teams of varying sizes and put through a six-hour series of problem-solving exercises aimed at evaluating traits like the applicant's ability to contribute to a consensus decision. The teams were asked to solve problems such as how to create a rewards program that ranked perfect attendance, a flawless safety record, and other achievements in their order of importance. Mazda's assessors then ranked each team's (and individual's) performance. They were looking for things like how well the applicants expressed their ideas, how well they listened to one another, and how well each applicant participated in the group's discussions.

In the second problem-solving exercise, Dodd was asked to join a new team in what Mazda called "*kaizan* (constant improvement) projects." Group members were issued toy blocks and told to work together as a team to assemble "air boats." The group was then instructed to use the *kaizan* process of constant improvement to find ways of more efficiently assembling the boats. For example, could the piles of toy blocks be arranged more efficiently so blocks could be found more quickly? The group problem-solving sessions went on for six hours.

THE SIMULATED WORK EXERCISE. In the final series of tests, Dodd had to pass a simulated work exercise. Applicants who had already showed that they had the intelligence and interpersonal skills required of Mazda team members now had to exhibit the physical coordination and endurance needed to build cars. Dodd did, and he got the job.

Why such a big investment of time in hiring employees? According to David Merchant, the personnel vice president at Flatrock, it was justified because Mazda would be investing so heavily in developing each employee. Merchant and Mazda were looking for very bright, flexible, and motivated team members who could help top management manage change in the intensely competitive and quality-oriented auto industry. They sought to screen out the inflexible and often alienated workers often associated with auto industry plants in the past.[39]

Orientation and Training

Once employees have been recruited, screened, and selected, they must be prepared to do their jobs; this is the purpose of employee orientation and training.

Employee **orientation** means providing new employees with basic information about the employer. In many companies, employees receive an orientation handbook to facilitate this. It contains information like that summarized in Figure 9.11, pages 314–315. Orientation aims to familiarize the new employee with the company and his or her co-workers; provide information about working conditions (coffee breaks, overtime policy, and so on); explain how to get on the payroll, how to obtain identification cards, and what the working hours are; and generally reduce the sorts of first-day jitters that are commonly associated with starting a new job.

This initial orientation is usually followed by a **training program,** one aimed at ensuring that the new employee has the basic knowledge required to perform the job satisfactorily. Traditional techniques include on-the-job training, lectures, and perhaps other methods using, for example, audiovisual tools and computers.[40]

Starbucks is a good example of a company that invests a great deal of effort in training employees. "Brewing the perfect cup" is one of five classes that all "partners" (as employees are called) complete during their first six weeks with the company.[41] What are some of the things they learn? Milk must be steamed at temperatures of at least 150°F; orders are "called out," such as "triple-tall nonfat mocha"; and coffee never sits on the hot plate for more than 20 minutes. At firms like Starbucks and Mazda, training means more than just teaching basic facts and skills, though. As in the following example, its aim is also to instill in new employees the basic attitudes and values that help to make the company's product or service unique.

Managing Change

ORIENTATION AND TRAINING AT MAZDA

Many employers use orientation and training to start the process of developing a committed and flexible high-potential workforce and of socializing new employees. **Socializing** means transforming new employees into effective organizational members by steeping them in the values and traditions of the organization.

To appreciate how such socialization works in practice, consider again the experience of Wayne Dodd and other workers hired at Mazda's Flatrock facility.[42] At Mazda, the aim of orientation and training is not just to familiarize workers with their new jobs. Instead, it is to socialize new employees and thus foster a high level of commitment to and identification with Mazda's values, traditions, and goals.

At Mazda, this process involves teaching employees such core Mazda values as standing behind the company, taking the initiative, and being able to work in teams.

STANDING BEHIND THE COMPANY. At Mazda, the socializing begins with the initial interviews. Interviewers often begin by asking job applicants questions like, "What

Orientation Checklist
(Small western supply company)

HOURLY & SALARIED EMPLOYEE ORIENTATION GUIDE CHECKLIST

NOTE: ALL INFORMATION MUST BE DISCUSSED
WITH EACH NEW EMPLOYEE

SUPERVISOR: This form is to be used as a guide for the orientation of new employees in your department.

In order to avoid duplication of instruction the information indicated below has been given to the employee by the Personnel Department.

PERSONNEL DEPARTMENT

EEO BOOKLET	PAY, SALARY, PROMOTIONS, AND TRANSFERS	
INSURANCE PROGRAM BOOKLET	TRANSPORTATION	
SALARY CONTINUANCE INSURANCE BOOKLET	TIME SHEET	
SAFETY BOOKLET	PERSONAL RECORDS	
PENSION PLAN BOOKLET	BULLETIN BOARDS	
EMPLOYEE HANDBOOK/LABOR AGREEMENT/RULES BOOKLET	PERSONAL MAIL E-MAIL	
MATCHING GIFTS	PARKING FACILITIES	
EDUCATIONAL ASSISTANCE PROGRAM	ABSENCES, TARDINESS	
PATENT AGREEMENT	VETERANS RE-EMPLOYMENT RIGHTS & RESERVE STATUS	
I.D. CARD	CHARITABLE CONTRIBUTION	
CREDIT UNION	VACATIONS	
STOCK PURCHASE PLAN	JURY DUTY	
SAVINGS BOND PLAN	SICK BENEFITS — A & S — LIMITATIONS, ETC.	
PROBATIONARY PERIOD	LEAVE OF ABSENCE, MATERNITY, MEDICAL, BEREAVEMENT, ETC.	
SERVICE AWARDS	DIFFICULTIES, COMPLAINTS, DISCRIMINATION & GRIEVANCE PROCEDURES	
VISITORS	MILL TOUR	
HOLIDAYS	TERMINATION NOTICE AND PAY ESP. VACATION ALLOWANCE (VOLUNTARY RESIGNATION)	
FOOD SERVICES	INTRODUCTION TO GUARDS	

■ **FIGURE 9.11**
Contents of Orientation Program
In many organizations, new employees receive a package of orientation materials or a handbook, containing information on matters like the ones shown in this checklist.

SOURCE: Joseph Famularo, *Handbook of Modern Personnel Administration* (McGraw-Hill, © 1985).

FIRST AID & REQUIREMENTS OF REPORTING INJURY	(OTHERS)	
SIGNATURE OF EMPLOYEE:	WITNESS:	DATE

SUPERVISOR: The following is a checklist of information necessary to orient the new employee to the job in your department. Please check off each point as you discuss it with the employee and return to the Personnel Department within three days following employee placement on the job:

INTRODUCTION TO FELLOW EMPLOYEES	HOURS OF WORK, OVERTIME, CALL IN PROCEDURES	
TOUR OF DEPARTMENT	REST, LUNCH PERIODS	
EXPLANATION OF NEW EMPLOYEE'S JOB. RESPONSIBILITIES AND PERFORMANCE EVALUATIONS	SUPPLY PROCEDURES	
LAVATORY	LINE OF AUTHORITY	
PHONE CALLS — PERSONAL/COMPANY		
SIGNATURE OF SUPERVISOR:		DATE

I have received a copy of the appropriate materials listed above and have had explained to me the information outlined. I understand this information concerning my employment with (Company name). Also, in case of voluntary separation (resignation) I understand the Company's policy, that in order to be eligible for any due vacation allowance, I must give my supervisor at least two weeks' notice in writing prior to my last day of work.

SIGNATURE OF EMPLOYEE:	WITNESS:	DATE

■ FIGURE 9.11 Contents of Orientation Program (*continued*)

would you do if your neighbor was having trouble with a Mazda automobile?"[43] Initially, candidates are taken aback by such questions. But by the end of Mazda's 12-week orientation/training/socialization program the answer becomes clear:

> Those Americans who had been hired by Mazda would, it was expected, answer this question without hesitation: "I would try to solve the problem, and I would apologize to my neighbor on behalf of Mazda." By then they would understand that standing behind a company and its products was the only correct thing for a worker to do. They would have grown to identify with their company, Mazda, in a way that was less American and more Japanese.[44]

TAKING THE INITIATIVE. Another thing Mazda's orientation and training program stresses is taking the initiative. For example, when the top HR officers spoke to the new employees, they emphasized that:

> It may have been okay to just follow orders where you worked before, but at Mazda things would be different. Here, everyone will be expected to take the initiative and participate in the management of the plant. This participation will take many forms: not only will workers be contributing ideas to the design and

Lexus, the luxury-car division of Toyota, uses state-of-the-art technology, like this computerized simulation called Fact Lab, for sales training. Computerized video simulations enable sales consultants to practice handling a variety of sales scenarios.

constant improvement of their own jobs, they will be expected to help maintain quality control standards throughout the shop floor.[45]

KNOW HOW TO WORK IN TEAMS. Mazda also emphasizes that to work effectively in self-managing teams, new employees require problem-solving and analysis skills. Their new-employee program, therefore, includes 100 to 750 hours of training, including time spent learning to read balance sheets (the company expects employees to know how their operations are doing profit-wise).[46]

From Mazda's point of view, the net effect of such a program is to make it easier for the company to respond to and manage change. Flexibility results because committed and highly trained employees require less supervision and can respond more readily if manufacturing processes or procedures must be changed. ■

Appraising and Compensating Employees

Employee Appraisal

Once employees have been at work for some time, their performance should be **appraised,** or evaluated. Such appraisal serves several purposes. People want and need feedback regarding how they are doing; appraisal provides an opportunity for management to give employees that feedback. And, if performance is below par, the appraisal conference provides an opportunity to review a subordinate's progress and map out a plan for rectifying any performance deficiencies.

Managers use several techniques to appraise their employees' performance. Probably the most familiar is a performance appraisal form like the one shown in Figure 9.12. This form lists several job characteristics (like quality of work) and provides a rating scale from outstanding to unsatisfactory along with short definitions of each rating. This particular appraisal form is relatively objective, because it calls

Performance Appraisal for:

Employee Name _____ Title _____

Department _____ Employee Payroll Number _____

Reason for Review: ☐ Annual ☐ Promotion ☐ Unsatisfactory Performance
                    ☐ Merit   ☐ End Probation Period ☐ Other _____

Date employee began present position _____ / _____ / _____

Date of last appraisal _____ / _____ / _____   Scheduled appraisal date _____ / _____ / _____

Instructions: Carefully evaluate employee's work performance in relation to current job requirements. Check rating box to indicate the employee's performance. Indicate N/A if not applicable. Assign points for each rating within the scale in the corresponding points box. Points will be totaled and averaged for an overall performance score.

RATING IDENTIFICATION

O – Outstanding – Performance is exceptional in all areas and is recognizable as being far superior to others.

V – Very Good – Results clearly exceed most position requirements. Performance is of high quality and is achieved on a consistent basis.

G – Good – Competent and dependable level of performance. Meets performance standards of the job.

I – Improvement Needed – Performance is deficient in certain areas. Improvement is necessary.

U – Unsatisfactory – Results are generally unacceptable and require immediate improvement. No merit increase should be granted to individuals with this rating.

N – Not Rated – Not applicable or too soon to rate.

GENERAL FACTORS	RATING	SCALE	SUPPORTIVE DETAILS OR COMMENTS
1. Quality – The accuracy, thoroughness, and acceptability of work performed.	O ☐ V ☐ G ☐ I ☐ U ☐	100–90 90–80 80–70 70–60 below 60	Points
2. Productivity – The quantity and efficiency of work produced in a specified period of time.	O ☐ V ☐ G ☐ I ☐ U ☐	100–90 90–80 80–70 70–60 below 60	Points
3. Job Knowledge – The practical/technical skills and information used on the job.	O ☐ V ☐ G ☐ I ☐ U ☐	100–90 90–80 80–70 70–60 below 60	Points

■ **FIGURE 9.12**
Performance Appraisal Chart
This is a page from a typical performance appraisal form. Supervisors use it to rate the employee's performance on factors like quality and productivity.

SOURCE: *Human Resource Management: 7/E* by Gary Dessler, © 1997. Reprinted by permission of Prentice-Hall, Inc., Upper Saddle River, NJ.

4. Reliability – The extent to which an employee can be relied upon regarding task completion and follow up.

			Points
O	☐	100–90	
V	☐	90–80	
G	☐	80–70	
I	☐	70–60	
U	☐	below 60	

5. Availability – The extent to which an employee is punctual, observes prescribed work break/meal periods, and the overall attendance record.

			Points
O	☐	100–90	
V	☐	90–80	
G	☐	80–70	
I	☐	70–60	
U	☐	below 60	

6. Independence – The extent of work performed with little or no supervision.

			Points
O	☐	100–90	
V	☐	90–80	
G	☐	80–70	
I	☐	70–60	
U	☐	below 60	

■ **FIGURE 9.12**
Performance Appraisal Chart (*continued*)

for specific ratings. However, also note that (as is often the case) the form provides space for more subjective examples of particularly good or particularly bad incidents of the employee's performance.

TOWARD MORE FLEXIBLE RATINGS. The trend is to move away from using forms like that in Figure 9.12 and instead to focus more on specific job-related outcomes and behaviors. For example, in their book *Workplace 2000,* Joseph Boyett and Henry Conn say that many companies are already revising their approach to performance appraisal, and we may even soon see that

> instead of a rating form, most companies will use nothing more than a blank sheet of paper on which employees and their bosses list specific objectives to be accomplished during the appraisal period. These objectives will encompass areas including learning and development goals (such as training programs in which the employee will participate and skills to be developed and used); teamwork goals (such as personal contributions the employee agrees to make to help his or her team improve feedback); problem-solving goals (such as participating on a problem-solving task force); taking on leadership responsibility in meetings; and plans for personal contribution to team goals such as quality improvement, cost reduction, or improvements in customer service.[47]

Basic Forms of Compensation

Employee compensation refers to all work-related pay or rewards that go to employees.[48] It includes direct financial payments in the form of wages, salaries, incentives, commissions, and bonuses, and indirect payments in the form of financial fringe benefits like employer-paid insurance and vacations.

A **fixed salary** or **hourly wage** is the centerpiece of most employees' pay. For example, blue-collar workers and clerical workers are often paid hourly or daily wages. Some employees—managerial, professional, and often secretarial—are salaried. They are compensated on the basis of a set period of time (like a week, month, or year), rather than hourly or daily.

Financial incentives are increasingly important and today are often referred to as "pay for performance." A **financial incentive** is any financial reward that is contingent on a worker's performance. Thus, salespeople are often paid financial incentives called *commissions,* which are generally proportional to the items or services they actually sell. Production workers are often paid a financial incentive called *piecework:* Piecework means that an employee is paid a standard sum for each item he or she produces. Many employees periodically receive merit pay or a merit raise, which is any salary increase that is awarded to an employee based on his or her individual performance. Merit pay differs from a bonus, which represents a one-time financial payment.

Managers have sought to formulate effective incentive plans for many years. One such plan was developed many years ago by Joseph Scanlon, a union official for the United Steel Workers. In his plan, workers participate in making cost-savings suggestions and then share whatever benefits result from these suggestions. The Scanlon plan is an early version of what today is known as a **gainsharing plan,** an incentive plan that engages many or all employees in a common effort to achieve a company's productivity objectives; the resulting cost-savings gains are shared among employees and the company.[49] Like the Scanlon plan, virtually all gainsharing plans have two components: the participation and cooperation of employees in making cost-cutting suggestions, and a formula by which employees then share in any resulting cost-savings gains.

Employee Benefits

Employee benefits are any supplements to wages or pay that employees get based on working for the organization. They typically include health and life insurance, vacation, pension, and education plans.

Many of these benefits are legally mandated. For example, under federal and state law, **unemployment insurance** is available to most employees and is paid by state agencies to workers who are terminated through no fault of their own (the funds come from a tax on the employer's payroll). **Worker's compensation,** another legally mandated benefit, is a payment aimed at providing sure, prompt income and medical benefits to work-related accident victims or their dependents, regardless of fault. Social Security is another federally mandated benefit paid for by a tax on an employee's wages (a total of 15.02 percent of pay as of 1997); employees and their employers share equally to pay this tax, up to a set limit. Among other things, Social Security provides beneficiaries with retirement benefits after they leave the company.

Employers also offer benefits voluntarily, or because they want to stay competitive with what other firms are offering. Most employers today offer hospitalization, medical, and disability insurance because of the expense employees would have to absorb if they had to obtain such insurance themselves. Many companies also offer their employees membership in a health maintenance organization (HMO). This is a medical organization consisting of several specialists (surgeons, psychiatrists, and so on) who provide routine, round-the-clock medical services at a specific site. Sick leave, vacations, and severance pay (a one-time payment when an employee is terminated) are other frequently used benefits.

USING BENEFITS TO BUILD LOYALTY. Starbucks is a good example of how managers can use benefits to help build a loyal workforce. Most retailers like to avoid paying benefits because of high turnover. Starbucks, on the other hand, wants loyalty. "Our only sustainable competitive advantage is the quality of our work force. We're building a national retail company by creating pride—and a stake in the outcome of our labor," says Howard Schultz, the firm's CEO. To get it, Schultz places a big emphasis on a benefits package that features fully company-paid physicals, dental coverage, eye care, and company-paid disability and life insurance. Also included are stock options, training programs, career counseling, and product discounts for all employees, full-time and part-time.

If that sounds like a potential financial hemorrhage, it hasn't been so far. Even though the benefits are generous, they make up only a quarter of Starbucks' labor costs and have stabilized there. Schultz sees stock options and benefits as the bond that ties workers to the company and inspires loyalty. Perhaps more important, he thinks employees who are treated right treat customers with the same kind of care. "The future of Starbucks," says Schultz, "lies in increasing shareholder value—and increasing employee value will [do that]."[50]

Promotions, Terminations, and Discipline

Performance appraisal often leads to personnel actions such as promotion, termination, and discipline. A **promotion** generally means rewarding the employee's efforts by moving that person to a job with increased authority and responsibility. Ideally, promotions (like rewards in general) should be awarded based on proven competence.

Unfortunately, that is often not the case today, for two reasons. First, with the downsizings and consolidations of the past few years, there are often not enough middle management (and higher) positions available into which a firm can promote worthy employees. As a result, companies today are relying more on lateral "promotions" to broaden employees' experiences and to help them gain additional skills. Being transferred from a post such as sales manager to one such as personnel manager may not have the same impact as a traditional promotion. However, it can at least reignite the initial interest and excitement that the employee felt in his or her first job, and it gives the person additional skills that may be useful later.

DISCIPLINE AND GRIEVANCES. A **grievance** is a complaint that an employee lodges against an employer, usually regarding wages, hours, or some condition of employment like unfair supervisory behavior. Most union contracts contain a grievance procedure that provides an orderly system of steps, whereby employer and union determine whether or not some clause of the contract has been violated. Steps typically include discussing the problem with one's supervisor, then referring the matter to the department head, the personnel department, and finally to the employer's head of the facility. Thus, a supervisor may fire an employee for excessive absences. The employee might then file a grievance stating that the supervisor had issued no previous warnings or discipline related to excessive absences as was called for in the union agreement and that the firing was thus unwarranted. Many nonunionized companies also offer grievance procedures.

Supervisors sometimes have to discipline subordinates, usually because a rule or procedure was violated. A company should have clear rules (such as "No smoking allowed when dealing with customers") as well as a series of progressive penalties that all employees know will be enforced if the rule is broken.

One way to set up a discipline system is to follow the so-called FRACT model: Get the *facts*, obtain the *reason* for the infraction, *audit* the records, pinpoint the *consequences*, and identify the *type* of infraction before taking remedial steps.

A recent innovation in this area is called **discipline without punishment.** With this disciplinary technique, for example, an employee first gets an oral reminder for breaking the rule and then a written reminder if the rule is broken again. Then a paid one-day "decision-making leave" is mandated if another incident occurs in the next few weeks. If the rule is broken again, then the employee may be dismissed.

Dismissal—the involuntary termination of an employee's employment with the firm—is the most dramatic disciplinary step an employer can take toward an employee. In general, the dismissal should be *just,* in that sufficient cause should exist for it. Furthermore, the dismissal should occur only after all reasonable steps to rehabilitate or salvage the employee have failed. However, there are undoubtedly times when immediate dismissal is required—such as for gross insubordination.

However, actual dismissals don't always follow such straightforward guidelines. For example, after John Walter took over as president of AT&T, several top managers, including Chief Financial Officer Richard Miller, said they were leaving. In one case—that of Joe Nacchio, head of AT&T's consumer long-distance business—Walter said Nacchio left because Walter "took him out of his job." Nacchio, for his part, said he wasn't pushed but simply left for a better job.[51] Several months later, Walter was himself pushed out by AT&T's board of directors.

SUMMARY

1. Human resource management is the management function devoted to acquiring, training, appraising, and compensating employees. As workers become more fully empowered, the HR function has grown in importance.

2. The HR function is subject to the constraints of numerous federal, state, and local laws. The equal employment laws prohibiting employment discrimination are among the most important of these personnel laws and include Title VII of the Civil Rights Act, various executive orders, the Equal Pay Act of 1963, and the Americans with Disabilities Act. The Occupational Safety and Health Act sets safety and health standards that apply to almost all workers in the United States. Other laws govern union-management relations and include the Wagner Act, which outlaws unfair labor practices such as employers interfering with employees who are exercising their legally sanctioned rights of organizing themselves into a union.

3. Staffing—filling a firm's open positions—starts with job analysis and personnel planning. Job analysis means determining the duties of the job and the kinds of people who should be hired. Once this has been done, personnel planning involves forecasting personnel requirements and the supply of outside and internal candidates and producing plans that describe how candidates will be hired, trained, and prepared for the jobs that will be opening up. Recruiting—including the use of internal sources, advertising, employment agencies, recruiters, referrals, and older workers—is then used to create a pool of applicants.

4. With a pool of applicants, the employer can turn to screening and selecting, using one or more techniques including application blanks, interviews, tests, and reference checks to assess and investigate an applicant's aptitudes, interests, and background.

5. Once employees have been recruited, screened, and selected, they must be prepared to do their jobs; this is the role of employee orientation and training. Orientation means providing new employees with basic information about the employer; training ensures that the new employee has the basic knowledge required to perform the job satisfactorily. Techniques traditionally used here include on-the-job training, lectures, and perhaps other methods relying on visual tools and computers.

6. Once they've been on the job for some time, employees are appraised. Many firms use a performance appraisal form like the one shown in Figure 9.12; it lists several job characteristics and provides a rating scale for each.

7. Employee compensation refers to all work-related pay or rewards that go to employees. It includes direct financial payments in the form of wages, salaries, incentives, commissions, and bonuses, and indirect payments in the form of financial fringe benefits like employer-paid insurance and vacations.

8. Performance appraisal often leads to personnel actions such as promotion, termination, and discipline. A promotion generally means rewarding the employee's efforts by moving that person to a job with increased authority and responsibility. A grievance is a complaint an employee lodges against an employer.

KEY TERMS

human resource management (HR)
strategic human resource management
affirmative action
staffing
job analysis
job description
job specifications
job analysis questionnaire
personnel planning
recruiting
executive recruiters

competitors
individualists
cooperators
equalizers
application blank
test
management assessment center
orientation
training program
socializing
appraisal
employee compensation

fixed salary
hourly wage
financial incentive
gainsharing plan
employee benefits
unemployment insurance
worker's compensation
promotion
grievance
discipline without punishment
dismissal

SELF-TEST

TRUE / FALSE QUESTIONS

1 T F Human resource management, or HR, is the management function that deals with recruiting, training, evaluating, and compensating employees.

2 T F The human resources function grows less important as workers become more empowered.

3 T F One of the most important equal employment laws is Title VII of the 1964 Civil Rights Act that prohibits discrimination based on race, color, religion, sex, or national origin.

4 T F A key aspect of the Americans with Disabilities Act of 1990 is that employees must make any and all accommodations for the disabled.

5 T F Affirmative action requires that employers make a positive effort to hire and promote the pro-

tected groups covered by Title VII of the Civil Rights Act.

6 T F Due to proactive policies adopted by most companies, sexual harassment is no longer a widely occurring problem in U.S. organizations.

7 T F A federal agency to ensure that every working person in the nation has safe and healthful working conditions is the Equal Employment Opportunity Commission (EEOC).

8 T F There are no laws that give employees legal rights to information about their work history and job performance.

9 T F Older workers have become a rich source of job candidates.

10 T F Paper-and-pencil honesty tests are illegal.

MULTIPLE-CHOICE QUESTIONS

1 More than any other management function, human resources is affected by many _____ laws.
   a. state
   b. federal
   c. local
   d. all of the above

2 Which of the following is *not* covered by Title VII of the Civil Rights Act?
   a. race
   b. age
   c. sex
   d. religion

3 Which of the following are types of sexual harassment?
   a. quid pro quo
   b. hostile environment
   c. reasonable behavior
   d. both (a) and (b)

4 Occupational safety practices include all but which of these?
   a. reduce unsafe conditions
   b. hire safety-prone people
   c. set specific loss-control goals
   d. make unannounced safety and health inspections

5 Labor-management relations in the United States are governed by laws. Which of these makes unfair labor practices illegal?
   a. Roosevelt-Truman
   b. Wagner
   c. Kennedy-Johnson
   d. none of the above

6 _____ is the procedure used to determine the duties of the job and the kind of person who should be hired to do them.
   a. Job description
   b. Job specification
   c. Job analysis
   d. Work flow

7 Attracting a pool of viable applicants is called _____.
   a. pooling
   b. marketing
   c. recruiting
   d. none of the above

8 Which of the following is *not* a type of employment agency?
   a. government
   b. nonprofit
   c. private
   d. personal

9 The average cost of hiring a manager who earns $60,000 a year can be as much as _____.
   a. $5,000
   b. $15,000
   c. $30,000
   d. $50,000

10 Which is a key to being a better interviewer?
   a. plan the interview
   b. establish rapport
   c. ask questions
   d. all of the above

CRITICAL THINKING EXERCISES

1 The United States is a heterogeneous nation. In states like California there is a rich mixture of natives and immigrants from other states as well as from many ancient and emerging nations. Please read the following final thoughts from Ronald Takaki's book on human diversity and our nation, *A Different Mirror* (Boston: Little, Brown & Company, 1993, 428), from a human resource management context. Then write a brief analysis on what the quote means for managing human resources in the 21st century:

> As Americans, we originally came from many different shores, and our diversity has been the center of the making of America. While our stories contain the memories of different communities, together they inscribe a larger narrative. Filled with what Walt Whitman celebrated as the "varied carols" of America, our history generously gives all of us our "mystic chords of memory." Throughout our past of oppressions and struggles for equality, Americans of different races and ethnicities have been "singing with open mouths their strong melodious songs" in the textile mills of Lowell, the cotton fields of Mississippi, on the Indian reservations of South Dakota, the railroad tracks high in the Sierras of California, in the garment factories of the Lower East Side, the canefields of Hawaii, and a thousand other places across the country. Our denied history "bursts with telling." As we hear America singing, we find ourselves invited to bring our rich cultural diversity on deck, to accept ourselves. "Of every hue and caste am I," sang Whitman. "I resist any thing better than my own diversity."

2 As quoted in John Aram's *Presumed Superior,* affirmative action has different meanings to different people. One observer comments on the double meaning of affirmative action as a means of institutional change: "If civil rights is defined as quotas, it's a losing hand. If it's defined as protection against discrimination and efforts to promote opportunity, then it will remain a mainstream value in American life." John Aram points out, "The dilemma is that progress on civil rights both restricts and opens opportunity. No single, definitive moral premise exists."[52]

What do you think Aram is trying to say? What aspects of human resource management can be related to his comments? What are your thoughts and feelings about civil rights and affirmative action as they affect organizational management and jobs?

EXPERIENTIAL EXERCISES

1 Human resource management is an increasingly challenging area. As the following scenario describes, human resources can be pulled into very difficult circumstances.

It's midday in Kuwait, but it's unnaturally dark. As far as the eye can see, blazing oil-field fires spew up tornadoes of black smoke. A blanket of sooty, acid clouds seal in the hundreds of miles of desert. On the ground, an army of Bechtel Corporation workers toil amid the heat, providing support activities to the actual fire fighters. They construct roads for the trucks, create pipelines pumping water, build hospitals for the workers, and cook and serve meals to the cadre of smoke-coated personnel.

More than 7,000 miles away from the flame and wreckage of the Gulf War, in a 14th-floor office in San Francisco's financial district, men and women of Bechtel Corporation sweat over 30,000 employee files and resumes. Culling through 105,000 phone-in inquiries, the HR staff works frantically to supply the necessary manpower to the Middle-East operation. The debris here isn't burned rubber and charred metal: it's fax paper and plastic coffee cups used by the HR staff as it dispatches calls from San Francisco to Bangkok, so that it can hire and assign foreign-contract personnel. Gathering and transferring employee information from headquarters to ground operations in Kuwait, human resources managers mobilize more than 16,000 Americans, Britons, Filipinos, Australians—people from 37 countries in all—to rectify the Kuwait disaster.[53]

Your task as human resources recruiter for Bechtel is to devise a plan to recruit, select, and deploy your resources and then explain how you would implement it. You may wish to form a team of experts from your class for this exercise.

You may want to visit the Internet and research this specific case. Go to: http://www.bechtel.com. Then click on Bechtel project <u>experience.</u> Once you are there, click on Search. Type in the word "Kuwait" and read the information presented. Include this information in your analysis.

2 You are the human resource director for Manugistics, Inc., a Maryland-based, highly successful software company employing 600 people. Your HR department has 12 employees, representing all areas of human resources. In less than a decade, your company has made a major domestic acquisition and a global acquisition, added new employees, sold off a product line, and seen two of the founders leave. How has it managed to remain competitive through all this?

It has "institutionalized change" through its three "elements of excellence": (1) We treat others as we would like to be treated, (2) partnership with our clients results in superior products, and (3) team success is more important than personal glory.[54]

Your department has developed a wide variety of flexible options for employees; for example, 50 percent of your staff are women with flexible schedules. Thirty to forty percent of your employees telecommute.

In March 1997 the company announced a joint venture with Information Resources Inc. (IRI), based in Chicago. The companies will collaborate on the development of an innovative product that integrates point-of-sale data and supply-chain planning, with 20 IRI employees from offices in Chicago, Atlanta, and Waltham, Massachusetts, joining the Manugistics workforce.

Your task as the HR director is to develop an orientation and training program for this joint venture.

DIVERSITY CASE

WILL THE GLASS CEILING EVER BE SHATTERED?

Since the 1960s, when many of the barriers to women entering the workforce were struck down by legislation, an increasing number of women of all ages have joined the ranks of workers and managers. In fact, approximately half the workforce is female, and women are starting their own small businesses at twice the rate of men. But where are the women CEOs and senior managers in the corridors of corporate power? Is the glass ceiling, the invisible barrier that is said to keep women out of the top management positions, firmly in place?

The outlook in 1997 was discouraging, according to Catalyst, a nonprofit research group. Only 10 percent of the most senior jobs at the nation's 500 largest companies are held by women. When you arrive at the elite tier of chairperson, president, CEO, and executive vice president, the number goes down to 2.4 percent. But there is some progress. At major corporations such as Motorola, Colgate-Palmolive, and JCPenney, women are moving up the corporate ladder in large numbers. At Pitney Bowes, women hold five of the top ten jobs, and at Avon Products, 44 percent of the most senior posts are held by women.

As the experience of a few trailblazing companies

shows, women can break through the glass ceiling into upper management. But what will it take for barriers to fall in the rest of corporate America?

Questions

1 Why do you think there are still barriers to women advancing in the workplace?

2 What changes would you recommend for companies that want to advance qualified women, and what would you recommend to women who want to advance to the highest echelons?

3 How important an issue is the glass ceiling for human resources? Do you think there is a corresponding glass ceiling for the disabled and racial minorities?

SOURCE: "Women Must Have a Champion at the Top," *Business Week,* 17 February 1997, 110.

STRATEGY CASE

ONLY ASIANS WANTED HERE

It was a human resource manager's nightmare. IBM Japan Limited, IBM's Japanese subsidiary, seemed to have been recruiting in Japanese magazines in the United States in a discriminatory fashion. Although IBM Japan insists it never instructed its employment agency to screen out whites and African Americans in favor of Asians, it does seem that some discriminatory actions might have taken place.

The problem revolved around the employment agencies owned by a Japanese firm called Recruit. According to allegations made by Recruit USA's former staffers, Recruit USA had set up a fairly formal system to see that only Asians were hired for the IBM Japan jobs. According to one memo submitted by a former staffer to the EEOC, Recruit officials summarized the hiring policy as: "Foreigners, no good—IBM current rule . . . white people, black people, no, but second-generation Japanese or others of Asian descent o.k." Another Recruit agency in the United States allegedly set up a system of code words to discriminate against people it didn't want to hire. For example, if the job order said "see Adam," it meant the client only wanted a male employee. If the job order said "talk to Haruo," it meant the client only wanted a Japanese worker.

The whole story first broke when former Recruit employees took their allegations to the *San Francisco Chronicle.* Then the EEOC got involved and more allegations were made. Japanese firms and other multinationals are therefore learning the truth of the old saying, "When in Rome, do as the Romans do." But in this case it means that when you're doing business in a certain country, you'd better know and follow the laws of the land.

Questions

1 Do you think a client (in this case IBM Japan) should be held responsible for the actions of an independent employment agency it hires? Why or why not?

2 Could the people of Recruit have believed that IBM Japan required such discriminatory hiring in order to achieve its strategic goals of expanding operations in Japan? Why or why not? In what ways must who a firm hires be consistent with its strategic plan?

ENTREPRENEURIAL CASE

ANTICIPATING STAFFING AND DEMOGRAPHIC CHANGES AT CIBA ADDITIVES

Ciba Additives (CA) is an 800-person division of Ciba U.S.A. that manufactures and sells specialty chemicals. To remain competitive, CA decided it must improve its career planning, compensation, training, and management development programs. Demographic trends mean the company and its competitors will be vying for the same small pool of qualified people. In the 1990s there were fewer high school and college graduates in the sciences, while a higher proportion of positions required a college education. By 2000, almost one third of all U.S. workers will be nonwhite, and while the largest increases in the workforce will be among Latinos, Asian Americans, and African Americans, these groups have not typically been attracted to chemistry and chemical engineering, essential fields for CA.

Ciba Additives built good contacts with educational in-stitutions in its area by providing scholarships, offering research grants, visiting schools, and generally becoming more visible. Internally, CA has changed its compensation program to include gainsharing and has moved its human resources function down the line, increasing the employee's responsibility for her or his own career. Since these changes began in the late 1980s, its employees have begun to think in terms of *we,* rather than *I.*

Questions

1 What HR challenges will Ciba face with the increasing diversity of its workplace?

2 What HR issues at Ciba are faced in most industries?

3 What, in brief, do you think "HR's strategy for the next century" should be at CA?

SOURCE: Stanley R. Kase, "Ciba Creates an HR Strategy for the Next Century," *Personnel Journal* (October 1995):109–12.

THE BUSINESS TEAM, INC.

SEXUAL HARASSMENT AND THE MILITARY

The military is still a very male-dominated organization. Even though women were finally accepted into the ranks, they were not allowed to carry weapons until very recently.

On Monday morning, the Team got a call from the local division headquarters of the Army's 4th battalion. There had been a sexual assault on Saturday night, and in fact there had been a series of recent complaints about verbal and physical assaults on female soldiers. The base commander wanted the Team to come in and assess the situation. Not only was he concerned about the overall morale of the soldiers, he feared for the safety of the women and for the reputation of the Army if any of them decided to sue the military.

The officers in the Human Resources Department had tried several training sessions with personnel, but now they were asking for help.

Questions

1 What human resources advice would you give the Team?
2 What are the pitfalls for a consulting firm of young professionals becoming engaged in such an incident?
3 Should the whole team tackle the problem or only select members of the team, and why?

YOU BE THE CONSULTANT

IMPLEMENTING AN HR PROGRAM AT KNITMEDIA

If you will again review KnitMedia's 1996–1997 organization chart, you will probably note one department conspicuous by its absence. Like most companies with under 100 employees, KnitMedia has no separate HR/Personnel department. There are simply not enough employees yet to make having an HR manager economically feasible. However, KnitMedia has plans to grow and needs to begin giving some more thought to how the company and its divisions should handle the various aspects of the HR function.

Team Exercises and Questions

Use what you learned in this chapter to answer the following questions:

1 In general, what HR activities do you think Michael Dorf and his management team now have to engage in, and how do you think these activities are getting done now?
2 Develop a proposal for Michael explaining how you believe the HR function should be administered at KnitMedia, and why.

For the online version of this case, visit our Web site at <www.prenhall.com/desslermgmt>.

For Internet exercises, interactive study questions, news updates and more, visit the Dessler Web site at

www.prenhall.com/desslermgmt

If you're using the CD-ROM that accompanies this text, simply click on the "Web Site" button to access the site.

ORGANIZING FOR FLEXIBILITY

KnitMedia has a formal organizational chart and an informal organization structure. It has developed organically. As the organization has grown, the work has changed, requiring new skills. When that happens, Michael Dorf, founder of the Knitting Factory and KnitMedia, finds the person the organization needs. When new personnel are added, job tasks are divided among more people and become more focused. Michael realizes this and does not judge new people's work performance on the basis of the previous job description. Despite the same title, the work is actually very different.

The Knit has a relatively flat organizational structure with little middle management. Some areas, such as the club division, have more levels. Others have only a few. Although the formal chart shows only a few people reporting to Michael, he actually interacts with just about everyone on a daily basis.

Michael has two views of the organization. He has described it as a campfire with himself at the middle spitting out sparks and as a pyramid with himself at the top. His staff describe the organization in different terms.

Sascha von Oertzen, Recording Studio Manager, says the organization's structure is "kind of informal . . . there is . . . the owner. There are managers who know about everything. And then there are . . . all kinds of people working on whatever their job is. . . . But it's pretty much up to yourself to . . . create the situation you want to work in and then just have enough contact with everybody and take responsibility, and then it works."

Steve Gratzer, Web site Manager, says, "In different ways it's very unorganized. You know? But somehow, we still get things done."

Mark Perlson, Knitting Factory Record Label Manager, describes the organization as a pie. "The Knitting Factory is set up in a kind of unusual way," he says. "I kind of picture it as a pie with Michael in the middle and pretty much everybody branching out in their own division around him. . . . As the company's grown, there's been satellite pies coming off. For instance, the record label—I now have some employees that report to me . . . and the club, of course, as well, has several employees who go through Ed Greer, the Manager of the club. And as we grow, it's gonna have to expand, and it's gonna be a learning process for everybody involved."

Rachel McBeth, Business Manager, thinks that "Michael—the founder and current . . . chief operator

here—is . . . the guiding force, the guiding principal, and all things have developed from . . . his fertile mind. And I don't think that it's been a very formal . . . development . . . it's developed in a very natural and organic way. When he's seen a need, he's found someone to work a particular angle. And for that reason, I would say that it's probably rather informal, but I think with any organization certain principles come to bear on a situation so that people can be effective in what they've been hired to do."

Ken Ashworth, the Executive Vice President and Chief Operating Officer, explains that the organizational structure is "fairly flat in that . . . the . . . head of the company is Michael Dorf . . . and I guess, if you'd look at it in terms of there's a record-label side and there's the club side . . . , each of those sort of separate businesses, each has somebody who runs them on a day-to-day basis, reporting up to Michael."

"Well, to some extent, a lot of those separate businesses are more, sort of, future projected separate businesses than current . . . separate businesses. And even though it's conceived that they are separate businesses, they're all . . . fully integrated into the company and . . . they all . . . support different aspects of the company. I mean, it's all integrated in the sense that it's all music; it's all going towards the same object, which is . . . promoting the Knitting Factory brand, or the music or the artists who work within the company. So . . . I guess it's conceived that each division operates separately, whether it's an office in Amsterdam or a club in Los Angeles, or . . . here on the record label, but they all . . . integrate in the sense that . . . artists who are on the record label could be touring through different clubs, or in Amsterdam. And it's all communication information that ties all those separate divisions together and is able to move our products through all those different divisions."

Michael Dorf, like most entrepreneurs, has problems letting go. But he has started giving decision-making authority to a few proven and trusted associates. Michael ponders, "And so I know that there's the ability deeper inside, once I feel comfortable with the manager, to have them control a lot of people. And obviously for it to grow that needs to happen and be scaled on a much, much bigger level. Everything, though, is still sort of new and in the . . . molding process. Liz [Leggett, the Art Director] is an example in art, I feel very comfortable with her aesthetic decisions." He trusts Rachel with the company's finances; Ed Greer, Club Manager and Operations Director, to make the operating decisions for the Knitting Factory Club and the Knitting Factory Works recording studio; and other employees with their areas of responsibility. He gives his staff a lot of autonomy in how they reach their goals.

Michael tries to hire "mature individuals looking to make a commitment. . . . It's not about having attended Harvard. . . . Obviously that's good background, but it's about the person, you know. And . . . how you get into the music business or into the art world. Everyone takes different directions. And it's really about how good and how enthusiastic and how intelligent you are [for instance,] how quickly you can pick up a new software program on a computer. If you're working . . . in advertising here, you know, collecting ads, how successful are you going to be selling an ad? I don't know if business school teaches you how to sell. It might give you some ideas, but in the end it's about the person and how enthusiastic they're going to be. It's . . . how enthusiastic you are."

Everyone is independent but comes together as teams to work on various projects. These ad-hoc teams are cross-functional areas, depending on the skills needed. Some people, like Liz, are on a lot of teams. In fact, Liz is on any team that has to do with artwork, whether for the Knitting Factory Club, the Knitting Factory Works record label, or the Knitting Factory music festivals. Sascha works on teams to produce a recording: "If I work on a production . . . everybody has to work as a team," she says. Teams give the Knit the flexibility to meet challenges as they arise.

Questions

Based on the cases, the videos, the textbook you've looked at thus far, and your knowledge from other sources, answer the following questions.

1 Describe how KnitMedia is organized. What are the strengths and weaknesses of its organizational structure?

2 Explain whether and how the KnitMedia organization is designed to manage change. If you were hired by Michael Dorf as a consultant to advise him how to be better organized to respond to change, what advice would you give him?

3 What are the strengths and weaknesses of the Knit's staffing operations (that is, recruiting, selecting, and training employees)?

SOURCE: End-of-part video cases prepared by d.t. ogilvie, Rutgers University.

CHAPTER 10

BEING A LEADER

What's Ahead?

When former Burger King CEO Barry Gibbons took over Spec's Music Stores, Spec's was a company in crisis. Faced with the buying and marketing power of huge chains like Blockbuster, Spec's had tried and failed to fight back, opening several money-losing music superstores of its own. Gibbons took over and in four short months closed the loss-making stores, arranged large bank loans, rallied his troops, and changed Spec's strategy, driving it to diversify into related businesses like sponsoring music concerts. In short, Gibbons brought Spec's the strong leadership it needed in its time of crisis. What made Barry Gibbons such an effective leader?

Barry Gibbons

Objectives

After studying this chapter, you should be able to

- think and assess a situation like a leader
- describe the foundations of leadership
- discuss how to provide a vision for an organization
- compare and contrast the various styles a leader can use
- list the specific attributes of being a leader.

MANAGEMENT ON THE WEB

PHIL JACKSON: ZEN AND BASKETBALL

Explore the topic of leadership from a different perspective. Combine iGuide's online interview of Phil Jackson, coach of the Chicago Bulls, with material from his latest book, *Sacred Hoops: Spiritual Lessons of a Hardwood Warrior,* to discuss the relevance of Native American and Eastern Philosophies to leadership practice. Is Jackson's successful use of Zen and spirituality on the basketball court applicable to more traditional organizational settings like Spec's? ■

http://www.iguide.com/sports/jackson2.htm

The Challenge of Leading

Leadership is an easy concept to define but a difficult one to study and understand. It is easy to define since leadership means influencing others to work willingly toward achieving objectives. When Gibbons took over Spec's, for instance, and got its owners, employees, and bankers to work enthusiastically toward downsizing the firm and diversifying it, he symbolized the essence of being a leader. What makes leadership a challenging concept to master, on the other hand, is the need to understand a variety of leadership theories, and to translate these into leadership skills through application and practice. In outline form, the leadership theories and skills we'll discuss in this chapter are as follows:

1. *How to think like a leader.* How to review a leadership situation in which you find yourself and identify what is happening, account for what is happening, and formulate leader actions.
2. *What are the foundations of leadership?* Two important foundations or prerequisites of leadership are *power* and the right mix of leadership *traits,* such as drive and self-confidence.
3. *How leaders provide a vision.* In other words, they provide a general statement of their organization's intended direction and, often, a "roadmap" for how to get there.
4. *How leaders act like leaders.* To influence followers to work toward the vision, leaders engage in a number of characteristic leader behaviors, such as providing *structure* and *consideration,* being *participative* when the situation warrants, and adapting their leadership style to the situation.

Leaders Fill Many Roles

Being a leader requires more than having a command of leadership theories like those covered in this chapter. That's why all of part IV of this book is called "Leading," although it also covers chapters on motivating, culture, groups, conflict, and change. Figure 10.1 helps to illustrate why these other topics are also part of *leading.*[1] As you can see, as a leader you will simultaneously fill many roles, interacting with and motivating individual subordinates, leading a group whose members are interacting with each other and in which conflicts might arise, and being one of several subordinates in a group reporting to your own leader, for instance. As a result the leadership knowledge contained in the present chapter is only part of what you must know to be a leader. This chapter will get you started; to really get on the road

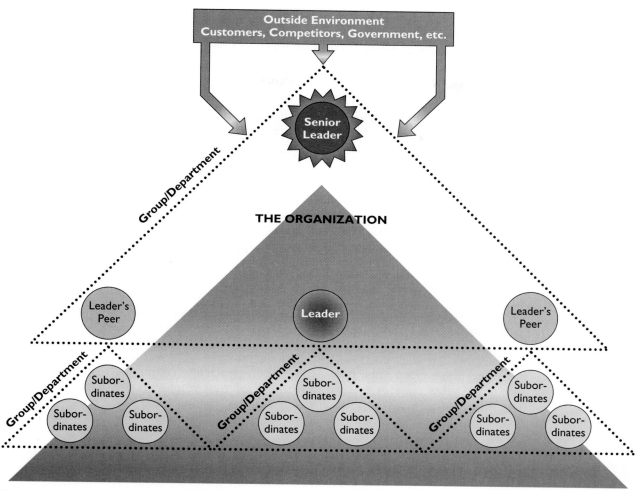

■ FIGURE 10.1   Leaders Fill Many Roles
Note: Leaders fill many roles, interacting with bosses and peers, motivating subordinates, and managing groups and teams of subordinates, for instance. These roles require not just "leadership" skills, but culture-building, motivating, communicating, team-building, and change-leadership skills as well.

SOURCE: Adapted from Jeffrey A. McNally, Stephen J. Gerra, and R. Craig Bollis, "Teaching Leadership at the U.S. Military Academy at West Point," *Journal of Applied Behavioral Science*, 32:2, p. 181, copyright © 1996 by Sage Publications. Reprinted by permission of Sage Publications, Inc.

to being a leader you'll need the following chapters, too. In a nutshell, here's what they'll cover:

Chapter 10: Being a Leader. Thinking like a leader, understanding the foundations of leadership, providing a vision, and acting like a leader.

Chapter 11: Organizational Culture and Shared Values. The leader's role in creating the organization's culture—in other words, the values and beliefs its employees share—and the physical symbols of that culture, such as the types of procedures and appraisal systems the company puts into place.

Chapter 12: Influencing Individual Behavior and Motivation. Individual differences (for example, in aptitudes and skills) that help to account for why people do what they do, and several theories that help to explain how leaders motivate employees.

Chapter 13: Influencing Interpersonal and Organizational Communications. The barriers that can undermine effective communications, and what a manager has to know about communicating to be an effective leader.

Chapter 14: Leading Groups and Teams. What a leader can do to create a more cohesive team, and the group dynamics the leader should take into account in supervising his or her team.

Chapter 15: Leading Organizational Change. Theories and techniques a leader can use to implement changes required to improve an organizational situation.

Do not be overwhelmed by the large number of leadership and behavioral science theories, each helping to explain how the effective leader should act. Instead, think of each theory as a tool in your leadership toolbox, each useful in its way and under the right conditions.

Leaders and Managers

Managers plan, organize, lead, and control, so that "leading" and "managing" are inseparable in management theory. Leading is part of managing: Managing means planning, organizing, leading, and controlling the work of others so the company's aims are achieved. But if you can't influence and inspire those people to work toward those aims, then all your planning and organizing will be for naught. "Leading" is thus the distinctly behavioral and "influencing" part of what managers do.

Similarly, managing is part of leading: Setting a direction and saying, "Here's where we've got to go" is usually not enough. In other words, no matter how inspiring you happen to be, management skills—such as ensuring that salaries, incentives, and other rewards make it worthwhile for your employees to try hard, and ensuring that they have the organization, abilities, and tools to do their jobs—are crucial too.[2] Let's start building our leadership skills by learning how to think like a leader.

Thinking Like a Leader

Being a leader requires more than possessing book knowledge about leadership theories; the leader also needs **critical leadership thinking skills.** These allow the leader to look at a situation and dig out the underlying assumptions and values that are motivating subordinates, evaluate the evidence, and think through how to apply what he or she knows about leadership theory to solve the problem.

One way to view such critical leadership thinking skills is in terms of a three-step framework (see Figure 10.2). Specifically, review the leadership situation and (1) identify what is happening, (2) account for what is happening, and (3) decide on the leadership actions you will take.[3]

Identify What Is Happening

The first step is to identify issues or areas of concern that compel you as a leader to resolve an organizational problem. For example: "The employees here refuse to divulge bad news to their supervisors."

Account for What Is Happening

This and the next few chapters contain behavioral science theories and concepts that leaders need. For example, in this chapter you'll find a number of leadership theories that aim to explain what makes leaders effective, and in the following chap-

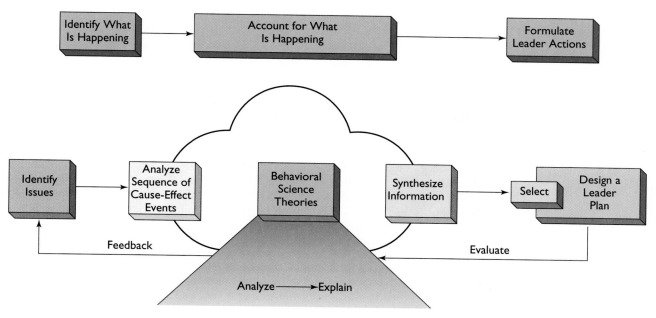

FIGURE 10.2
How to Think Like a Leader

SOURCE: Adapted from Jeffrey A. McNally, Stephen J. Gerra, and R. Craig Bollis, "Teaching Leadership at the U.S. Military Academy at West Point," *Journal of Applied Behavioral Science*, 32:2, p. 178, copyright © 1996 by Sage Publications. Reprinted by permission of Sage Publications.

ter are theories that explain how to motivate employees. The main purpose of the step "accounting for what is happening" is to use behavioral science theories and concepts like these to account for *why* the issues you identified (like employees refusing to divulge bad news) are occurring.

Accounting for what is happening in a situation means asking yourself which theory or theories best explains what you see happening by linking a leadership or other behavioral concept or theory to the issue. In other words, this step identifies a cause-effect relationship between what has occurred and why. For example, "The employees here refuse to divulge bad news because they are punished when they do by having the supervisors yell at them." The *effect* here is the employees' refusal to divulge bad news; the behavioral *cause*—in this case a motivational one—is the fact that they are "punished" when they do.

To account for what is happening you should view the situation as a coherent whole, while at the same time looking for a logical sequence of cause-effect events. You have to try to identify the root cause of the situation. For example, are the supervisors temperamentally unsuited for their jobs? Or are they just copying their own bosses' behavior, reacting quickly and harshly to any negative news?

In accounting for what is happening, you may well find that more than one leadership or behavioral science theory or concept applies. In this case, for instance, the supervisors may lack the required personality traits to do the job. Their own leaders may have inadvertently created a blame-oriented culture that signals that it is okay to dump on employees when they bring you negative news.

There often is more than one way to explain or solve a leadership problem. This isn't a bad thing: Don't be put off because there may be more than one behavioral science theory or concept you could apply to explain and solve the problem. You may combine several, or choose the one you'll take action on first.

Decide on the Leadership Actions You Will Take

After you have identified and accounted for what is happening, the next step is to decide on the leadership actions that will remedy the situation. Doing so will require applying all the knowledge you gain in this and our other chapters, such as those on how to motivate employees and how to resolve and manage intergroup conflicts.

For example, what actions would you take to help resolve the problem of the gun-shy employees who are afraid to report negative news to their supervisors? Your assessment of the situation is that (1) some of the current supervisors may be temperamentally unsuited for their jobs, and (2) there is a pervasive blame-oriented culture throughout the department. What actions would you take? Good possibilities include the following:

- Reassess the personality-based qualifications of the existing supervisors, to transfer or dismiss potential hotheads.
- Administer an attitude survey to all departmental employees to develop data that describe the current feelings about the blame-oriented atmosphere.
- Present this data to the top managers to encourage them to engage in a training program aimed at making them more open to getting bad news and criticism.

Learning to think like a leader is just one step in developing leadership skills. Leaders also need a sound understanding of what leaders do and what makes them successful. We turn to these issues in the next few pages, specifically:

- What are the foundations of leadership?
- How do leaders provide a vision?
- How do leaders act like leaders?

What Are the Foundations of Leadership?

Psychologists Shelley Kirkpatrick and Edwin Locke say that *power* and personal *traits* are two important foundation components of leadership—in other words, two important prerequisites you'll need before you can lead.[4]

Power

Perhaps you've had the unfortunate experience of being told you are in charge of something, only to find that your subordinates laughingly ignore you when you try to boss them around. Such an experience underscores an important fact of leadership: A leader without power is really not a leader at all, since he or she has zero chance of influencing anyone to do anything. Understanding the sources of leadership power is therefore important.

From what sources can a leader's power derive? You may recall from our discussion in chapter 7 that the sources of power are the following. A leader's authority most commonly stems, first, from the *position* to which he or she is appointed. In other words, positions like sales manager or president have formal authority attached to them that followers are generally expected to respect as part and parcel of keeping their jobs. As a leader you will also have power based on your authority to *reward* employees who do well or coerce or *punish* those who don't do well, for instance by dismissing them or sending them home for the day. As head of, say, the research lab you may also have *expert power* and be such an authority in your area that your followers do what you ask because of their respect for your expertise. If you are really lucky, you'll possess *referent power* based on your personal magnetism so that your followers will follow you just because of your charisma.

Notice that whatever your source of power, it must be legitimate if you are to call yourself a leader. A mugger on the street may have a gun and the power to threaten your life but hardly qualifies as a leader, because leading means influencing people to *willingly* work toward achieving your objectives.

That is not to say that a little fear can't be a good thing, at least occasionally. The most famous comment on fear was made in the 16th century by the Italian writer Niccolo Machiavelli, in his book *The Prince:*

> One ought to be both feared and loved, but as it is difficult for the two to go together, it is much safer to be feared than loved . . . for love is held by a chain of obligation which, men being selfish, is broken whenever it serves their purpose; but fear is maintained by a dread of punishment which never fails.

But remember that while there's more than a germ of truth in what Machiavelli said, there's a danger in becoming too Machiavellian and relying on fear. A shrewd executive named Chester Barnard wrote in his classic work *The Functions of the Executive* that managers are essentially powerless unless their followers grant them the authority to lead.[5] The reality of leading is that you're going to have to muster all the legitimate power you can get, and that will often include convincing your followers that you have earned the right to lead them.

The issue of power and fear is especially tricky in today's downsized, flattened, and empowered organizations. Increasingly, as we've seen, the tendency is to delegate authority and organize around horizontal, self-managing teams, teams in which the employees themselves have the information and skills they need to control their own activities. Influencing your people to get their jobs done by relying too heavily on your own formal authority or even on fear is therefore probably a much more imprudent tactic today than it would have been in the 1980s.

The Leader's Traits

To be a leader, a manager also needs the personality traits to do the job. Having "the right stuff" is thus a second important foundation component of being a leader. Identifying what exactly those traits are is the aim of the **trait theory** of leadership.

The idea that leaders are characterized by certain traits was initially inspired by a "great man" concept of leadership. This concept held that people like General Norman Schwarzkopf and California Senator Diane Feinstein are great leaders because they were born with certain definable personality traits. Early researchers believed that if they studied the personality and intelligence of great leaders, they would sooner or later stumble on the combination of traits that made these people outstanding.

Most of the early research on leadership traits was inconclusive. Specific traits were related to leadership effectiveness in some situations, but none was found to be consistently related in a variety of different studies and situations. However, recent research using a variety of methods "has made it clear that successful leaders are not like other people. The evidence indicates that there are certain core traits which significantly contribute to business leaders' success."[6] Six traits on which leaders differ from nonleaders include drive, the desire to lead, honesty/integrity, self-confidence, cognitive ability, and knowledge of the business. Let's see why each of these matters.

LEADERS HAVE DRIVE.   They are action-oriented people with a relatively high desire for achievement, which means they get satisfaction from successfully completing challenging tasks and attaining standards of excellence. Leaders are more ambitious than nonleaders. They have high energy, because "working long, intense work weeks (and many weekends for many years) requires an individual to have

According to the trait theory of leadership, definable personality traits make a great leader like Norman Schwarzkopf, the hero of Operation Desert Storm.

physical, mental, and emotional vitality."[7] Leaders are also tenacious and are better at overcoming obstacles than nonleaders.[8] Susan Lammers, CEO of Headbone Interactive, is a good example, as explained in the Entrepreneurs in Action box.

LEADERS WANT TO LEAD. Although at first this may seem obvious, not everyone has a strong desire to take charge. Leaders are motivated to influence others. They prefer to be in a leadership rather than a subordinate role and willingly shoulder the mantle of authority.

A LEADER HAS HONESTY AND INTEGRITY. Here's another way to state this: If your followers can't trust you, why should they follow you? Studies have found that leaders are generally rated more trustworthy and reliable in carrying out responsibilities than followers.[9]

A LEADER HAS SELF-CONFIDENCE. As two experts summarize, "Self-confidence plays an important role in decision-making and in gaining others' trust. Obviously, if the leader is not sure of what decision to make, or expresses a high degree of doubt, then the followers are less likely to trust the leader and be committed to the vision."[10]

LEADERS MAKE GOOD DECISIONS. By definition, a leader is the one who must pick the right direction and then put into place the mechanisms required to get there. Leaders, therefore, tend to have more cognitive ability than nonleaders, and a leader's intelligence and the subordinates' perception of his or her intelligence are generally highly rated leadership traits.[11] Behavioral scientists Shelley Kirkpatrick and Edwin Locke put it this way: "If someone is going to lead, followers want that person to be more capable in some respects than they are. Therefore, the followers' perception of cognitive ability in a leader is a source of authority in the leadership relationship."[12]

THE LEADER KNOWS THE BUSINESS. Effective leaders are extremely knowledgeable about the company and the industry; their information lets them make informed decisions and understand the implications of those decisions.[13]

Entrepreneurs in Action

LEADING HEADBONE

Susan Lammers is a good example of a leader. She's spent four months in Alaska working as a carpenter, was a book editor in San Francisco, and became a millionaire by developing multimedia software while with Microsoft Corp. She's always been driven to lead the way. "I've always been this way," she says, "willing to go for it." So now she's off and running with her new company, Headbone Interactive.

Thanks in large part to Lammers' leadership drive, Headbone is off to a good start. The company produces "edutainment" CDs for children, and so far she's sold 25,000 copies of each of her firm's new titles. Being an entrepreneur in a relatively new industry like this isn't easy: As one writer puts it, "Making a go of it in the CD-ROM business is tough." However, Susan Lammers seems to have the leadership drive and tenacity to get her company off the ground and to make it a success.

SOURCE: Janice Maloney, "Headbone Interactive," *Fortune*, 8 July 1996, 106.

There are exceptions: Louis Gertsner, Jr., became IBM's chairman with no computer experience, and he has excelled at the job. However, these exceptions make the rule: Gerstner has high cognitive ability and quickly immersed himself in absorbing the details of IBM's business.

Organizational Behavior in Action

WHAT ARE PERSONALITY TRAITS?

Leadership qualities like cognitive ability are actually specific types of personality traits. A **personality trait** is any persisting characteristic or dimension of personality according to which individuals can be rated or measured.[14] Introversion, sociability, aloofness, and impulsiveness are examples of traits.

Personality traits are just one means by which psychologists explain what personality is and why people act as they do. For example, you are probably somewhat familiar with the psychoanalytic personality theory of Sigmund Freud. Freud used building block concepts that he called *id, ego,* and *superego* to explain human personality and behavior, basically in terms of our desire to maximize gratification while minimizing punishment or guilt. His personality theory did not depend on the concept of personality traits.

Personality trait theories are another approach that psychologists use to explain personality. To trait theorists, someone's personality is basically the sum total of the behaviors which a person with those traits persistently exhibits. Psychologist Raymond Cattell viewed personality traits as sets of polar opposites. Examples of so-called Cattell traits include honest vs. dishonest, infantile vs. emotionally mature, thoughtful vs. unreflective, sociable vs. shy, responsive vs. aloof, deliberate vs. impulsive, and tidy vs. disorderly.[15] More recently, industrial psychologists have focused on what some call the "big five" personality dimensions. The big five are extroversion, emotional stability, agreeableness, conscientiousness, and openness to experience.[16]

As was already mentioned, traits such as honesty, integrity, self-confidence, and the desire to lead seem especially important if a person is to succeed as a leader. Like other personality traits, these leadership traits manifest themselves in behaviors that successful leaders persistently exhibit; they are, therefore, important prerequisites to effective leadership. ■

Power and the requisite leadership traits are not sufficient for successful leadership—they are only a foundation, a precondition. If you have the traits and you have the power, then you have the *potential* to be a leader.[17] As Kirkpatrick and Locke put it: "Traits only endow people with the potential for leadership. To actualize this potential, additional factors are necessary...."[18] Specifically, say Kirkpatrick and Locke, the leader must also have the skill to provide a vision and then engage in the behaviors required to implement that vision.

How Leaders Provide a Vision

Barry Gibbons knew when he took over Spec's that one of his first tasks was to clarify and communicate a vision for the company. Employees, owners, bankers—in fact, all Spec's stakeholders—knew the company was floundering and were looking to Gibbons for direction.

Showing the way out of the wilderness—providing direction—has always been a crucial task of leaders. Each year when he teaches seasoned executives in the Advanced Management Program and the International Senior Management Program at the Harvard Business School, Professor Renato Tagiuri polls them to compile what he calls a list of conditions for effective leadership. "Clarify the mission, purposes, or objectives of your employees' assignments" and "describe assignments clearly" head the list.[19]

The leader must provide a direction that his or her followers can work toward. Whether that "direction" is a statement of vision, mission, or objectives depends largely on what the leader wants to achieve and the level at which he or she is acting.

Sometimes what's required is a **vision,** a general statement of the organization's intended direction that evokes positive emotional feelings in organization members. Barry Gibbons' vision of a leaner Spec's offering a diversified blend of concerts and retail music helped provide the sense of direction employees, owners, and bankers all required, and around which they could rally.

Setting a Direction: Visions, Missions, Objectives

Many experts believe that communicating a vision is especially important in today's rapidly changing environment, where business conditions are "volatile and carry in them the seeds of rapid and potentially hostile change."[20] Here, "the faster the chief executive officer can conceive a future vision where new products are positioned within emerging product markets the greater is the ability of the firm to control its destiny and affirm a sense of direction."[21]

We've seen that the firm's **mission statement** defines and operationalizes the top manager's vision. A mission statement "broadly outlines the organization's future course and serves to communicate 'who we are, what we do, and where we're headed.' "[22] Mission statements like one elevator firm's ("Our mission is to provide any customer a means of moving people and things up, down, and sideward over short distances. . . .") are meant to communicate a specific sense of direction. It specifies the purpose of the company.

The leader's task might require that he or she provide **objectives,** which are specific results he or she wants the group to achieve. Even CEOs in their leadership role set (or should set) objectives for the members of their management teams. Thus, Barry Gibbons might have told his managers that within one year he expected to see 30 percent of Spec's profits coming from concerts the company had organized.

Setting a direction with a vision, mission, or goal is one area in which the roles of leader and manager clearly converge. Planning, the process of establishing objectives and courses of action, prior to taking action, is the first of the manager's functions. But in providing direction and showing the way, the manager is wearing his or her leadership hat, too: Leading means influencing others to work toward some aim, and the first step in doing so is to show the way.

The Leader's Style: How Leaders Act Like Leaders

■ **FIGURE 10.3**
The Building Blocks of Being a Leader
Note: Leaders with the power and personal traits required to be effective can provide leadership by engaging in four sets of activities: Provide a vision, think like a leader, use the right leadership style, and then use the OB leadership skills such as influencing culture and motivating, as explained in the next five chapters.

SOURCE: Adapted from an idea presented in Shelley Kirkpatrick and Edwin A. Luke, "Leadership: Do Traits Matter?" *Academy of Management Executive*, 5, no. 2 (May 1991) 47–60.

Having shown the way, the leader next must influence his or her subordinates to work toward achieving the stated aims. There is no generally accepted or proven theory describing how leaders actually do this. However, Figure 10.3 summarizes an approach that you may find useful for organizing your thoughts. Leaders with the power and personal traits required to be effective in a leadership situation can provide leadership by engaging in four sets of activities: Provide a vision; think like a leader; use the right leadership style; and then use organizational behavior

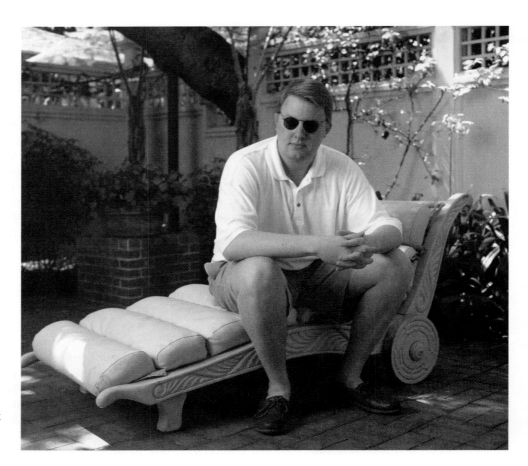

Marc Andreessen is the visionary leader who spearheaded the technical development of the Netscape Web browser.

leadership skills such as influencing culture and motivating, explained in the following five chapters. In this chapter we have already discussed the foundations of leadership (power and traits) as well as thinking like a leader and providing a vision. We'll turn next to choosing the right leadership style. Then, in chapters 11–15, we will turn to OB topics such as influencing culture and motivating.

The Leader's Behavior

Leadership researchers have formulated several theories to explain how the leader's style or behavior is related to his or her effectiveness as a leader, and we can make two generalizations about their theories. First, they all focus on what the leader *does* and how he or she behaves in trying to influence his or her followers. (Trait theory instead attempts to explain leadership on the basis of what the leader *is*.) Second, the basic assumption underlying all the behavioral leadership theories is that leaders perform two major functions—accomplishing the task and satisfying the needs of group members. Generally speaking, the functions of a task-oriented leader are to clarify the jobs to be done and force people to focus on their jobs. The role of a social or people-oriented leader is to reduce tension, make the job more pleasant, boost morale, and crystallize and defend the values, attitudes, and beliefs of the group. Most experts believe that the task and people dimensions of leader behavior are not mutually exclusive. In other words, most leaders exhibit degrees of both people and task orientation simultaneously.[23]

A number of different leadership styles are associated with these basic "tasks" and "people" dimensions. In the remainder of this section we'll describe some of the more popular leadership behavior theories, as well as several offshoots of them.

Structuring and Considerate Styles

Initiating structure and *consideration* have been two of the most frequently used descriptions of leader behavior. They developed out of a research project launched many years ago at Ohio State University.[24] A survey called the Leader Behavior Description Questionnaire (LBDQ) was developed and was further refined by subsequent researchers.[25] The two leadership factors it measures—consideration and initiating structure—have become synonymous with what experts call The Ohio State Dimensions of Leadership:

Consideration: Leader behavior indicative of mutual trust, friendship, support, respect, and warmth.

Initiating structure: Leader behavior by which the person organizes the work to be done and defines relationships or roles, the channels of communication, and ways of getting jobs done.

RESEARCH RESULTS. The research results, unfortunately, tend to be somewhat inconclusive. With respect to employee satisfaction, the findings led researcher Gary Yukl to conclude that "in most situations, considerate leaders will have more satisfied subordinates."[26] However, the effects of such considerate leadership on employee performance are inconsistent.

The effects of initiating structure are also inconsistent with respect to performance and on satisfaction too. In one representative study, structuring activities by the leader and employee grievance rates were directly related: The more structuring the leader was, the more grievances were filed. However, where the leader was also very considerate, leader structure and grievances were *not* related.[27]

How can we explain such inconclusive findings? Part of the explanation—as we'll see below—is that the leader style that is right for one situation might be wrong for another.

Participative and Autocratic Leadership Styles

Leaders can also act in either a participative or autocratic style. Faced with the need to make a decision, the autocratic leader solves the problem and makes the decision himself or herself, using information available at the time.[28] At the other extreme, the participative leader shares the problem with his or her subordinates as a group, and together they generate and evaluate alternatives and attempt to reach consensus on a solution.[29]

We know that encouraging employees to get involved in developing and implementing decisions affecting their jobs can have positive benefits. For example, employees who participate in setting their goals tend to set higher goals than the supervisor would normally have assigned.[30] We've also seen that participation brings more points of view to bear and can improve the chances that participants will "buy into" the final decision. On the other hand, there are obviously some situations (like a sinking ship) in which a captain being participative is inappropriate and too time consuming, so the tricky part is deciding when to be participative and when not. The Strategy feature illustrates this point in a not-for-profit setting.

Strategy in Action

REFORM WITHOUT PARTICIPATION

The buildings of the school district in Chelsea, Massachusetts, needed repair after years of bad management and chronic underfunding. Many of its 5,000 students are poor immigrants in an area of high unemployment and inadequate city services.

Enter Boston University (BU). In 1989 BU took over the management of the district with a strategy to install competent new administrators, bring basic education to students and their parents, and improve the quality of the curriculum and teachers with the help of BU scholars. The idea was to do so without the years of participative community involvement meetings that had plagued other such efforts.

Eight years into the experiment, even the critics are pleased. In the fall of 1996 the students walked into sparkling new buildings, the area's first new facilities since 1908. A new program offers literacy lessons to 900 immigrant parents, and teaches them how to help with their children's homework. The dropout rate had declined from 20% to 8%.

A relatively autocratic leadership approach was a primary key used by the BU leaders to achieve their strategy in a system that prides itself on collegial and community participation. According to New York University education expert Robert Berne, BU's autocratic approach sidesteps the community participation that is often a hallmark and strength of U.S. public education. Clearly, though, Chelsea is better off because BU's leadership improved a dismal system.

In November 1996 the Chelsea School Board unanimously extended BU's contract for another five years.[31]

Clearly leadership style can make a difference. But how do managers decide when to encourage participation and when not to?

Organizational Behavior in Action

A MODEL FOR DECIDING WHEN TO BE PARTICIPATIVE

Leadership experts Victor Vroom, Arthur Jago, and Philip Yetton have developed a technique that enables a leader to analyze a situation and decide whether it is right for participation. The technique consists of three components: (1) a set of management decision styles, (2) a set of diagnostic questions, and (3) a decision tree for identifying how much participation the situation calls for.

THE MANAGEMENT DECISION STYLES. Being participative is usually not an either/or decision, because there are different degrees of participation. These are summarized in Figure 10.4, which presents a continuum of five possible management decision styles. At one extreme is style I, no participation. Here the leader solves the problem and makes the decision himself or herself. Style V, total participation, is at the other extreme: Here the leader shares the problem with his or her subordinates and together they reach an agreement. You can see in Figure 10.4 that

I. You solve the problem or make the decision yourself, using information available to you at that time.

II. You obtain the necessary information from your subordinates, then decide on the solution to the problem yourself. You may or may not tell your subordinates what the problem is when getting the information from them. The role played by your subordinates in making the decision is clearly one of providing the necessary information to you, rather than generating or evaluating alternative solutions.

III. You share the problem with relevant subordinates individually, getting their ideas and suggestions without bringing them together as a group. Then you make the decision, which may or may not reflect your subordinates' influence.

IV. You share the problem with your subordinates as a group, collectively obtaining their ideas and suggestions. Then you make the decision, which may or may not reflect your subordinates' influence.

V. You share a problem with your subordinates as a group. Together you generate and evaluate alternatives and attempt to reach agreement (consensus) on a solution. Your role is much like that of a chairperson. You do not try to influence the group to adopt "your" solution, and you are willing to accept and implement any solution that has the support of the entire group.

between these two extremes are style II, minimum participation; style III, more participation; and style IV, still more participation.

THE DIAGNOSTIC QUESTIONS. In this leadership theory, the appropriate degree of participation depends on several attributes of the situation that can be quantified by asking a series of diagnostic questions (see Table 10.1). These situational

■ **TABLE 10.1** *Diagnostic Questions Used in the Vroom-Jago-Yetton Model*

PROBLEM ATTRIBUTES (THESE DETERMINE THE DEGREE OF PARTICIPATION THAT IS APPROPRIATE)	DIAGNOSTIC QUESTIONS (THESE ENABLE YOU TO DIAGNOSE THE PRESENCE OR ABSENCE OF EACH ATTRIBUTE)
A. The importance of the quality of the decision	Is there a quality requirement such that one solution is likely to be more rational than another?
B. The extent to which the leader possesses sufficient information/expertise to make a high-quality decision by himself	Do I have sufficient information to make a high-quality decision?
C. The extent to which the problem is structured	Is the problem structured?
D. The extent to which acceptance or commitment on the part of subordinates is critical to the effective implementation of the decision	Is acceptance of decision by subordinates critical to effective implementation?
E. The prior probability that the leader's autocratic decision will receive acceptance by subordinates	If you were to make the decision by yourself, is it reasonably certain that it would be accepted by your subordinates?
F. The extent to which the subordinates are motivated to attain the organizational goals as represented in the objectives explicit in the statement of the problem	Do subordinates share the organizational goals to be obtained in solving this problem?
G. The extent to which subordinates are likely to be in conflict over preferred solutions	Is conflict among subordinates likely in preferred solutions?

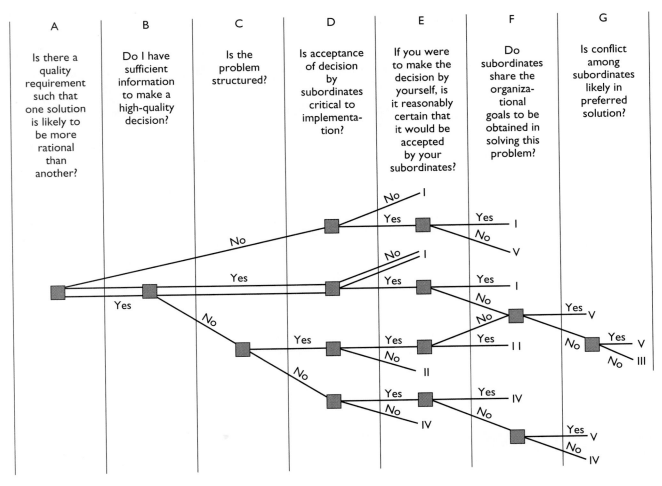

FIGURE 10.5
The Vroom-Jago-Yetton Model: Deciding Employee's Degree of Participation

attributes include the importance of the quality of the decision and the extent to which the leader possesses sufficient information to make a high-quality decision himself or herself. A typical diagnostic question is, "Do I have sufficient information to make a high-quality decision?"

THE DECISION TREE. The decision tree is actually a chart that enables the leader to determine the appropriate level of participation. It is presented in Figure 10.5. By starting on the left of the chart and answering each diagnostic question with a "yes" or "no," the leader can work his or her way across the decision tree and thus arrive at a decision regarding which style of participation (I–V) is best.

The University of Michigan Studies

At about the same time that researchers at Ohio State were developing their Leader Behavior Description Questionnaire for measuring initiating structure and consideration, a similar series of programs was beginning at the University of Michigan. Two sets of leadership styles emerged from the University of Michigan studies.

PRODUCTION-CENTERED AND EMPLOYEE-CENTERED LEADERSHIP STYLES. Rensis Likert and his associates at Michigan identified two leadership styles. **Employee-oriented leaders** focus on the individuality and personality needs of their employees and emphasize building good interpersonal relationships. Production or **job-centered leaders** focus on production and the job's technical aspects. Based on his review of the research results, Likert concluded the following:

> Supervisors with the best record of performance focus their primary attention on the human aspects of their subordinates' problems and on endeavoring to build effective work groups with high performance goals.[32]

CLOSE AND GENERAL LEADERSHIP STYLES. Other University of Michigan researchers conducted studies on what they called close and general leadership styles. **Close supervision,** according to these researchers, is at "one end of a continuum that describes the degree to which a supervisor specifies the roles of subordinates and checks up to see that they comply with these specifications."[33] The **laissez-faire leader** who takes a completely hands-off policy with subordinates is at the other extreme, while a **general leader** is somewhere in the middle of the continuum.

The research findings here are much clearer with respect to how close and general leaders affect employee morale than they are with respect to employee performance. Generally speaking, people do not like being closely supervised or having someone frequently checking up on them and telling them what to do. Close supervision is therefore usually associated with lower employee morale.[34] However, no consistent relationship emerged between closeness of supervision and employee performance.

Situational Theories of Leadership

If only one conclusion could be drawn from studies of these various leadership style theories, it would be that the style of leadership right for one situation might not be right for another. Whether the styles are initiating structure and consideration, participative and autocratic, employee-centered and job-centered, or close and general, it seems apparent that the style that's best depends on the situation. This dependency helps to explain why structuring or job-centered leaders sometimes have high-performing groups and sometimes don't, for instance.

Research in subsequent years, therefore, focused on trying to identify the situational factors that determined when one style or another was best. The Vroom-Yetton-Jago Theory discussed earlier is one example. Several other well-known situational leadership theories are presented next.

FIEDLER'S CONTINGENCY THEORY OF LEADERSHIP. Working at the University of Illinois, psychologist Fred Fiedler originally sought to determine whether a leader who was lenient in evaluating associates was more likely or less likely to have a high-producing group than the leader who was demanding and discriminating.[35] At the core of this research is the "least preferred co-worker" (or LPC) scale. The person who fills it out is asked to think of all the people with whom he or she has ever worked and to focus on the one person with whom he or she had experienced the most difficulty in getting a job completed, that is, on his or her least preferred co-worker. The rater is then asked to describe this person via a series of descriptive scales, for instance as:

Pleasant	**Unpleasant**
Smart	**Stupid**

Those who describe their least preferred co-worker favorably (pleasant, smart, and so on) are scored as "high LPC" and considered more people oriented. "Low LPCs" describe least preferred co-workers unfavorably and are less people oriented and more task oriented.

According to Fiedler's theory, three situational factors combine to determine whether the high-LPC or the low-LPC leader style is appropriate:

1. *Position power:* the degree to which the position itself enables the leader to get his or her group members to comply with and accept his or her decisions and leadership.
2. *Task structure:* how routine and predictable the work group's task is.
3. *Leader–member relations:* the extent to which the leader gets along with workers and the extent to which they have confidence in and are loyal to him or her.

Fiedler initially concluded that the appropriateness of the leadership style "is contingent upon the favorableness of the group-task situation."[36] Basically, he argued that where the situation is either favorable or unfavorable to the leader (where leader-member relationships, task structure, and leader position power all are either very high or very low), a more task-oriented, low-LPC leader is appropriate. On the other hand, in the middle range, where these factors are more mixed and the task is not as clear-cut, a more people-oriented, high-LPC leader is appropriate. (These relationships are summarized in Figure 10.6.) Many research findings cast doubt on the validity of Fiedler's conclusions, and the usefulness of the theory, including its more recent variants, remains in dispute.[37, 38]

PATH-GOAL LEADERSHIP THEORY. This leadership theory is based on the expectancy theory of motivation. *Expectancy theory* states that whether a person will be motivated depends on two things: whether the person believes he or she has the ability to accomplish a task, and his or her desire to do so. Leadership expert Robert J. House, who developed path-goal leadership theory, says that in keeping

■ **FIGURE 10.6**
How the Style of Effective Leadership Varies with the Situation

SOURCE: Adapted and reprinted by permission of the *Harvard Business Review.* "How the Style of Effective Leadership Varies with the Situation" from "Engineer the Job to Fit the Manager" by Fred E. Fiedler, September–October 1965. Copyright © 1965 by the President and Fellows of Harvard College; all rights reserved.

Relationship-motivated leaders perform better

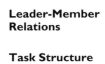
Task-motivated leaders perform better

Leader-Member Relations	Good	Good	Good	Good	Poor	Poor	Poor	Poor
Task Structure	Structured		Unstructured		Structured		Unstructured	
Leader Position Power	Strong	Weak	Strong	Weak	Strong	Weak	Strong	Weak
	I	II	III	IV	V	VI	VII	VIII

with expectancy motivation theory, leaders should increase the personal rewards subordinates receive for attaining goals, and make the *path* to these *goals* easier to follow, for instance, by clarifying it and reducing roadblocks and pitfalls.

Under this theory, the style a leader uses depends on the situation, so that leaders must be flexible and adopt the style that is required. For example, if subordinates lack confidence in their ability to do the job, they may need more consideration and support. If the leader finds himself in a situation in which subordinates are unclear about what to do or how to do it, he or she should provide structure (in terms of instructions, for instance) as required.[39] But in highly structured situations (such as might be found on an assembly line), a leader's additional attempts to structure the situation by closely supervising it and providing what might be redundant instructions could backfire and reduce both morale and performance.[40] Path-goal leadership theory in general has received minimal support, in part possibly because of the difficulty of measuring concepts such as "path."[41]

LEADER-MEMBER EXCHANGE (LMX) THEORY. Although a leader may have one prevailing style like "participative" or "autocratic," you have probably noticed that most leaders don't treat all their subordinates the same way. Most of the leadership style theories we've discussed to this point imply that a leader exhibits a similar leadership style toward all members of his or her work group. The **leader-member exchange (LMX) theory** says that leaders may use different styles with different members of the same work group.[42, 43]

This theory suggests that leaders tend to divide their subordinates into an "in" group and an "out" group, and you can imagine who gets the better treatment. The in group gets more attention and a larger share of the resources than the out group followers, of course. What determines whether you're part of your leader's in or out group? The leader's decision is often made with very little real information, although perceived leader-member similarities—gender, age, or attitudes, for instance—can be enough.[44]

A recent study helps to illustrate what makes a follower (or member) fall into a leader's in group or out group.[45] In this study, completed questionnaires were obtained from 84 full-time registered nurses and 12 supervisors in 12 work groups at a large hospital in the southern United States. Eighty-three percent of the supervisors (leaders) were women with an average age of 39.4 years; the nurses (followers) were mostly women (88.1 percent), with an average age of 36.7 years. Various things were measured, including the strength and quality of leader-member relationships or exchanges (friendliness between leader and member, rewards given to members, and so on).

The quality of leader-member exchanges was found to be positively related to a leader's perceptions of two things: similarity of *leader-follower attitudes* and follower *extroversion*. Leaders were asked to assess the similarity between themselves and their followers in terms of their attitudes toward six items: family, money, career strategies, goals in life, education, and overall perspective. Perhaps not surprisingly, leaders were more favorably inclined toward those followers with whom they felt they shared similar attitudes. Followers were also asked to complete questionnaires that enabled the researchers to label them as introverted or extroverted. The extroverted nurses were more likely to have high-quality leader-member exchanges than were the introverts, presumably because they were more outgoing and sociable in general.

Findings like these suggest at least two practical implications. First, because members of the in group can be expected to perform better than those in the out

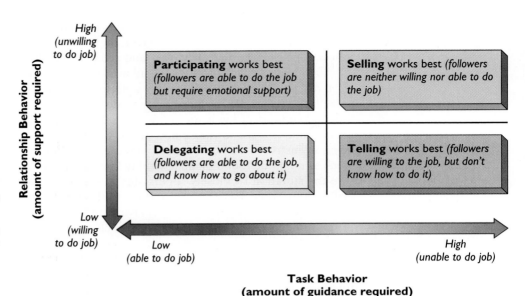

**FIGURE 10.7
Situational Leadership
Model**

SOURCE: *Managing Behaviour in
Organizations: Science in Service*
by Jerald Greenberg, © 1996.
Reprinted by permission of
Prentice-Hall, Inc., Upper
Saddle River, NJ.

group, leaders should strive to make the in group more inclusive. For followers the
findings emphasize the (obvious) importance of being in your leader's in group and
underscore the value of emphasizing similarities rather than differences in attitude—in politics, for instance—between you and your supervisor.

THE SITUATIONAL LEADERSHIP MODEL APPROACH.   Other behavioral
scientists have developed what they call a *situational leadership model* to describe
how the leader should adapt his or her style to the task; their model is presented
above in Figure 10.7.[46] They identify four leadership styles:

- The *delegating* leader lets the members of the group decide what to do
  themselves.
- The *participating* leader asks the members of the group what to do but
  makes the final decisions himself or herself.
- The *selling* leader makes the decision himself or herself but explains the
  reasons.
- The *telling* leader makes the decision himself or herself, telling the group
  what to do.

According to the situational leadership model, each style is appropriate in a specific situation, as follows:

- Delegating works best where followers are willing to do the job and know
  how to go about doing it.
- Participating works best when followers are able to do the job but are
  unwilling to and so require emotional support.
- Selling works best where followers are neither willing nor able to do the
  job.
- Telling works best where followers are willing to do the job but don't know
  how to do it.

Figure 10.8 presents a self-assessment exercise you can use to get a perspective
on whether you are primarily a delegating, participating, selling, or telling manager.

Determining Your Leadership Style

To be able to identify and enact the most appropriate style of leadership in any given situation, it is first useful to understand the style to which you are already predisposed. This exercise will help you gain such insight into your own leadership style.

DIRECTIONS

Following are eight hypothetical situations in which you have to make a decision affecting you and members of your work group. For each, indicate which of the following actions you are most likely to take by writing the letter corresponding to that action in the space provided.

A. Let the members of the group decide themselves what to do. (Delegating)

B. Ask the members of the group what to do, but make the final decision yourself. (Participating)

C. Make the decision yourself, but explain your reasons. (Selling)

D. Make the decision yourself, telling the group exactly what to do. (Telling)

_____ 1. In the face of financial pressures, you are forced to make budget cuts for your unit. Where do you cut?

_____ 2. To meet an impending deadline, someone in your secretarial pool will have to work late one evening to finish typing an important report. Who will it be?

_____ 3. As coach of a company softball team, you are required to trim your squad to 25 players from 30 currently on the roster. Who goes?

_____ 4. Employees in your department have to schedule their summer vacations so as to keep the office appropriately staffed. Who decides first?

_____ 5. As chair of the social committee, you are responsible for determining the theme for the company ball. How do you do so?

_____ 6. You have an opportunity to buy or rent an important piece of equipment for your company. After gathering all the facts, how do you make the choice?

_____ 7. The office is being redecorated. How do you decide on the color scheme?

_____ 8. Along with your associates you are taking a visiting dignitary to dinner. How do you decide what restaurant to go to?

SCORING

1. Count the number of situations to which you responded by marking A. This is your _delegating_ score.

2. Count the number of situations to which you responded by marking B. This is your _participating_ score.

3. Count the number of situations to which you responded by marking C. This is your _selling_ score.

4. Count the number of situations to which you responded by marking D. This is your _telling_ score.

QUESTIONS FOR DISCUSSION

1. Based on this questionnaire, what was your most predominant leadership style? Is this consistent with what you would have predicted in advance?

2. According to Situational Leadership theory, in what kinds of situations would this style be most appropriate? Have you ever found yourself in such a situation, and if so, how well did you do?

3. Do you think that it would be possible for you to change this style if needed?

4. To what extent were your responses to this questionnaire affected by the nature of the situations described? In other words, would you have opted for different decisions in different situations?

■ **FIGURE 10.8   Self-Assessment Exercise**

SOURCE: _Managing Behaviour in Organizations_ by Jerald Greenberg, © 1996. Reprinted by permission of Prentice-Hall, Upper Saddle River, NJ.

TRANSFORMATIONAL LEADERSHIP BEHAVIOR

A number of years ago James McGregor Burns wrote a book called *Leadership* that had a major impact on the course of leadership theory.[47] Burns argued that leadership could be viewed as either a transactional or a transformational process.[48] Leader behaviors like initiating structure and consideration, he suggested, are essentially based on *quid pro quo* transactions. Specifically, **transactional** behaviors are "largely oriented toward accomplishing the tasks at hand and at maintaining good relations with those working with the leader [by exchanging promises of rewards for performance]."[49] The key here is that transactional behaviors tend to focus more on accomplishing the tasks at hand, and perhaps on doing so by somehow adapting the leader's style and behavior to accommodate the follower's expectations.

In today's rapidly changing world, Burns argued, it's often not a transactional but a **transformational** style of leadership that is required to manage change. "Transformational leadership refers to the process of influencing major changes in the attitudes and assumptions of organization members and building commitment for the organization's mission, objectives and strategies."[50] Transformational leaders are those who bring about "change, innovation, and entrepreneurship."[51] They are responsible for leading a corporate transformation that "recognizes the need for revitalization, creates a new vision, and institutionalizes change."[52]

WHAT DO TRANSFORMATIONAL LEADERS DO? Transformational leaders engage in several specific behaviors. They encourage—and obtain—performance beyond expectations by formulating visions and then inspiring their subordinates to pursue them. In so doing, transformational leaders cultivate employee acceptance and commitment to their visions.[53] They "attempt to raise the needs of followers and promote dramatic changes of individuals, groups, and organizations."[54] Transformational leaders do this by articulating a realistic vision of the future that can be shared, stimulating subordinates intellectually, and paying attention to the differences among these subordinates. Transformational leaders also provide a plan for attaining their vision and engage in "framing," which means giving subordinates the big picture so they can relate their individual activities to the work as a whole.[55]

From the vantage point of the followers, transformational leaders come across as charismatic, inspirational, considerate, and stimulating:[56]

- Transformational leaders are *charismatic.* Employees often idolize and develop strong emotional attachments to them.
- Transformational leaders are also *inspirational,* in that "the leader passionately communicates a future idealistic organization that can be shared. The leader uses visionary explanations to depict what the employee work group can accomplish."[57] The inspired employees are then motivated to achieve these organizational aims.
- *Individual consideration* goes beyond being considerate. Transformational leaders treat employees as individuals and stress developing them in a way that encourages the employees to self-actualize and become all they can be.
- Transformational leaders use *intellectual stimulation* to "encourage employees to approach old and familiar problems in new ways."[58] This enables

employees to question their own beliefs and use creative ways to solve problems by themselves.

Questions used by researchers like psychologist Bernard Bass to assess these four characteristics are:

1. *Charisma.* "I am ready to trust him or her to overcome any obstacle."
2. *Individualized consideration.* "Treats me as an individual rather than just as a member of the group."
3. *Intellectual stimulation.* "Shows me how to think about problems in new ways."
4. *Inspirational leadership.* "Provides vision of what lies ahead."[59]

Many leaders—some of whom you've probably heard—have been described as transformational leaders. Former British Prime Minister Margaret Thatcher took over an industrially drifting nation and by the power of her will helped to transform it into a nation fitting her vision of a more privatized, competitive, hard-working nation. In the 1980s and again today, GE's chairman Jack Welch is transforming his giant company into a highly competitive and "lean machine," one that's increasingly offering not just products but services, too.[60] Transformational leaders of an earlier day include former Chrysler chairman Lee Iacocca, India's Mahatma Gandhi, and Martin Luther King, Jr.[61]

STUDIES OF TRANSFORMATIONAL LEADERS. Transformational leadership has been studied in many settings.[62] In one study, researchers found that high-performing managers in an express delivery firm used significantly more transformational leader behaviors than did less successful managers in the firm.[63] Another study found that successful champions of technological innovations—the men and women charged with carrying a technological change through an organization to its completion—used more transformational leader behaviors than did less successful champions.[64] Other studies suggest that transformational leadership tends to be more closely associated with leader effectiveness and employee satisfaction than were transactional styles of leadership such as general or laissez-faire leadership.[65] It seems clear that a transformational style of leadership can be very effective, especially in those situations that require managing dramatic change. ∎

Are There Gender Differences in Leadership Styles?

Although the number of women in management jobs has risen to almost 40 percent, barely 2 percent of top management jobs are held by women.[66] Most women managers are having trouble breaking through to the top executive ranks. Research evidence suggests on the whole that this disparity is caused not by some inherent inability of women to lead, but by institutional biases known as "the glass ceiling" and persistent, if inaccurate, stereotypes. In other words, while there *are* a few differences in the way men and women lead, they would not account for the slowed career progress of most women managers. We can summarize some of the more relevant research findings as follows.

PERSISTENCE OF INACCURATE STEREOTYPES. Promotions of women tend to be hampered first by inaccurate stereotypes. Managers tend to identify "masculine" (competitive) characteristics as managerial and "feminine" (cooperative and

Dynamic and innovative leaders like Kim Polese, a founder of Marimba, Inc., belie stereotypes about women leaders. Polese hopes her new firm's products will turn the personal computer into a "real consumer device," with "channels" instead of software.

communicative) characteristics as nonmanagerial.[67] Women, therefore, tend to be seen as less capable of being effective managers; men are thus traditionally viewed as "better" leaders than women. Another stereotype is that women managers tend to fall apart under pressure, respond impulsively, and have difficulty managing their emotions.[68] However, such stereotypes usually don't hold up under the scrutiny of the researchers' microscope, a fact to which we now turn.

LEADER BEHAVIORS.   Studies suggest few measurable differences in the leader behaviors that women and men managers use on the job. Women managers were found to be somewhat more achievement oriented, and men managers more candid with co-workers.[69] In another study the only gender differences found were that women were more understanding.[70] Women and men who score high on the need for power (the need to influence other people) tend to behave more like each other than like people with lower-power needs.[71]

PERFORMANCE.   How are women managers rated in terms of performance when compared with men? On the job and in joblike work simulations, women managers perform similarly to men. In actual organizational settings, "women and men in similar positions receive similar ratings."[72] In a special joblike simulation called an assessment center in which managers must perform realistic leadership tasks (such as leading problem-solving groups and making decisions), men and women managers perform similarly. It is only in several off-the-job laboratory studies that men have scored higher in performance.[73]

ON TO THE FUTURE.   Interestingly, one often-noticed and scientifically supported difference between men and women leaders may actually prove to be a boon to women managers. Women often score higher on measures of patience, relationship development, social sensitivity, and communication, and these may be precisely the skills that managers need today and tomorrow—for instance, to manage diversity and to manage the empowered members of self-managing teams.[74]

Being a Leader

Being a leader means taking the steps required to boost your effectiveness at filling the leader's role. No formula can guarantee that you can be a leader. However, based on the research presented in this chapter, there are some powerful actions you can take to improve the chances that in a leadership situation you will be a leader. These can be summarized as follows.

Think Like a Leader

It is important to think like a leader, so that you can bring to bear what you know about leadership and behavioral theories rather than just react with a knee-jerk response.

Thinking like a leader means doing at least these three things:

1. Apply the three-step model: Identify what is happening, account for what is happening by bringing to bear all your knowledge of leadership and behavioral theory and concepts, and formulate a leadership response to address the issue.
2. Remember that behavioral science knowledge about leading is not limited to the material contained in this chapter; you will need to be able to apply the knowledge from the subsequent chapters on culture, motivating, groups, conflict, and change, fitting it into your assessment of the issues as you account for what is happening and decide how to influence your followers to deal with the situation. Don't be overwhelmed by the number of theories and concepts that might apply; think of them as tools in your leadership toolbox. There may be—and probably is—more than one way to solve the problem.
3. In influencing your followers to move toward some goal, remember that you cannot ignore managerial planning, organizing, and controlling. In practice, moving followers from where they are to where you want them to be will require all your management skills. To achieve your goals you will have to implement procedures, assign jobs, and monitor performance, for instance.

Develop Your Judgment

Possessing the traits of leadership gives someone the potential to be a leader. Your ability to be a leader can thus be improved by enhancing your existing leadership traits.

Some traits are easier to enhance than others, but all of them can be modified. For example, the leader's judgment is important because people will not long follow a leader who makes too many bad decisions. In chapter 4, we saw that several steps can improve your decision-making ability:

- *Increase your knowledge.* The more you know about the problem and the more facts you can marshall, the more likely it is that your confidence in your decision will not be misplaced.
- *De-bias your judgment.* A number of cognitive or decision-making biases can distort a manager's judgment. De-biasing your judgment—reducing or eliminating biases like stereotyping from your judgment process—is, therefore, a crucial step toward making better decisions.

- *Be creative.* Creativity plays a big role in making better decisions. The ability to develop novel responses—creativity—is essential for decision-making activities like developing new alternatives and correctly defining the problem.
- *Use your intuition.* Many behavioral scientists argue that a preoccupation with analyzing problems rationally and logically can actually backfire by blocking someone from using his or her intuition.
- *Don't overstress the finality of your decision.* Remember that very few decisions are forever; there is more give in more decisions than we realize. Even major, strategic decisions can often be reversed or modified as situations warrant.
- *Make sure the timing is right.* Most people's decisions are affected by their passing moods. Managerial decision makers should therefore take their emotions into account before making important decisions. Sometimes it's best just to sleep on the decisions.

Develop Your Other Leadership Traits

Good judgment is just one of the leadership traits that you can enhance. For example, leaders also exhibit self-confidence. Although developing self-confidence may be a lifelong process, you can enhance it in several ways. One is to focus more on those situations in which you are more self-confident to begin with, such as those in which you are an expert: A stamp collector might exhibit more self-confidence as president of his or her stamp club than in coaching a baseball team, for instance. You can act like a leader by exhibiting self-confidence—by making decisions and sticking with them, and by acting dignified rather than cracking jokes constantly with your subordinates. Your knowledge of the business is probably the easiest trait to modify; immerse yourself in the details of your new job and learn as much about the business as you can, as fast as you can.

Organizational Behavior in Action

ARE YOU READY TO BE A LEADER?

The following self-assessment exercise can give you a feel for your readiness and inclination to assume a leadership role.

INSTRUCTIONS. Indicate the extent to which you agree with each of the following statements, using the following scale: (1) disagree strongly; (2) disagree; (3) neutral; (4) agree; (5) agree strongly.

1. It is enjoyable having people count on me for ideas and suggestions.	1	2	3	4	5
2. It would be accurate to say that I have inspired other people.	1	2	3	4	5
3. It's a good practice to ask people provocative questions about their work.	1	2	3	4	5
4. It's easy for me to compliment others.	1	2	3	4	5

5. I like to cheer people up even when my own spirits are down.	1	2	3	4	5
6. What my team accomplishes is more important than my personal glory.	1	2	3	4	5
7. Many people imitate my ideas.	1	2	3	4	5
8. Building team spirit is important to me.	1	2	3	4	5
9. I would enjoy coaching other members of the team.	1	2	3	4	5
10. It is important to me to recognize others for their accomplishments.	1	2	3	4	5
11. I would enjoy entertaining visitors to my firm even if it interfered with my completing a report.	1	2	3	4	5
12. It would be fun for me to represent my team at gatherings outside our department.	1	2	3	4	5
13. The problems of my teammates are my problems too.	1	2	3	4	5
14. Resolving conflict is an activity I enjoy.	1	2	3	4	5
15. I would cooperate with another unit in the organization even if I disagreed with the position taken by its members.	1	2	3	4	5
16. I am an idea generator on the job.	1	2	3	4	5
17. It's fun for me to bargain whenever I have the opportunity.	1	2	3	4	5
18. Team members listen to me when I speak.	1	2	3	4	5
19. People have asked me to assume the leadership of an activity several times in my life.	1	2	3	4	5
20. I've always been a convincing person.	1	2	3	4	5

Total score: ___

SCORING AND INTERPRETATION. Calculate your total score by adding the numbers circled. A tentative interpretation of the scoring is as follows:

=	90–100	high readiness for the leadership role
=	60–89	moderate readiness for the leadership role
=	40–59	some uneasiness with the leadership role
=	39 or less	low readiness for the leadership role

If you are already a successful leader and you scored low on this questionnaire, ignore your score. If you scored surprisingly low and you are not yet a leader or are currently performing poorly as a leader, study the statements carefully. Consider changing your attitude or your behavior so that you can legitimately answer more of the statements with a 4 or a 5.[75]

Build Your Power Base

Remember that a powerless leader is not a leader at all. Conversely, you can strengthen the foundation of your leadership by taking steps to enhance your authority and power.

Organizational Behavior in Action

RATING A MANAGER'S POWER

The following self-assessment exercise can give you a better feel for the steps you can take to enhance your power.

DIRECTIONS. Circle the appropriate number of your answer, using the following scale: 5 = strongly agree, 4 = agree, 3 = neither agree nor disagree, 2 = disagree, 1 = strongly disagree.

As a manager, I can (or, if I'm not a manager now, my manager can or former manager could) . . .

	Strongly Agree				Strongly Disagree
Reward Power					
1. Increase pay levels.	5	4	3	2	1
2. Influence getting a raise.	5	4	3	2	1
3. Provide specific benefits.	5	4	3	2	1
4. Influence getting a promotion.	5	4	3	2	1
Coercive Power					
5. Give undesirable work assignments.	5	4	3	2	1
6. Make work difficult.	5	4	3	2	1
7. Make things unpleasant here.	5	4	3	2	1
8. Influence getting a promotion.	5	4	3	2	1
Legitimate Power					
9. Make others feel they have commitments to meet.	5	4	3	2	1
10. Make others feel they should satisfy job requirements.	5	4	3	2	1
11. Give the feeling that others have responsibilities to fulfill.	5	4	3	2	1
12. Make others recognize that they have tasks to accomplish.	5	4	3	2	1
Expert Power					
13. Give good technical suggestions.	5	4	3	2	1
14. Share considerable experience and/or training.	5	4	3	2	1
15. Provide sound job-related advice.	5	4	3	2	1
16. Provide needed technical knowledge.	5	4	3	2	1

Referent Power	Strongly Agree				Strongly Disagree
17. Make employees feel valued.	5	4	3	2	1
18. Make employees feel that I approve of them.	5	4	3	2	1
19. Make employees feel personally accepted.	5	4	3	2	1
20. Make employees feel important.	5	4	3	2	1

Total score: ___

SCORING AND INTERPRETATION. Add all the circled numbers to calculate your total score. You can make a tentative interpretation of the score as follows:

90+	high power
70–89	moderate power
below 70	low power

Also, see whether you rated much higher on one type of power than on the others.[76]

Make Sure Your Followers Share Your Vision

Leading means influencing people to work enthusiastically toward achieving an objective. Ensure that your subordinates know and understand the vision, mission, or objective and that you have clarified their assignments.

Adapt Your Leadership Style and Actions to the Situation

We've seen in this chapter that no one leadership style is going to be appropriate for every situation in which you find yourself. The art of being a leader lies in your being able to identify the leadership-related issues and then being able to determine whether one or more leadership theories and concepts (including what you know about considerate and structuring styles, participative leadership, the Vroom-Yetton-Jago model, and so on) can be applied, and if so, how.

Substitutes for Leadership: Use Your Other Management Skills to Help You Lead

As we saw earlier in this chapter, leadership and management are inseparable: to get things done leaders have to use their management skills too. Research suggests that various management actions can actually function as effective "substitutes" for the leadership you may otherwise have to provide.[77] Here are a few examples.

CHOOSING THE RIGHT FOLLOWERS CAN REDUCE THE NEED FOR LEADERSHIP. If you select and train your followers well, there may be less reason for you to have to exercise leadership on a day-to-day basis. For example, the greater your subordinates' ability, the more their experience, the better their training, and the more professional their behavior, the less direct supervision they will need. Some followers are inherently more effective than others: Choose followers who are cooperative, flexible, and trustworthy and who have initiative and are good at problem solving.[78]

ORGANIZING THE TASK PROPERLY CAN REDUCE THE NEED FOR LEADERSHIP. You may also be able to modify organizational factors to reduce the need for day-to-day leadership. For example, jobs for which the performance standards are clear, or for which there is plenty of built-in feedback, may require less leadership.[79] Similarly, employees engaged in work that is intrinsically satisfying (work they love to do) require less leadership.[80] Cohesive work groups with positive norms also require less leadership (as do, by definition, self-managing teams). The reward system is important too: Some reward systems, like gainsharing programs that pay employees a percentage of any productivity improvement, leave the supervisor virtually out of the loop about controlling rewards. Conversely, merit pay plans in which the leader's rating has a big impact on each follower's end-of-year raise requires the leader to closely monitor performance and conduct appraisals.[81]

SUMMARY

1. Leadership means influencing others to work willingly toward achieving objectives. Being a leader requires more than having a command of leadership theories, however. It also means managing organizational culture; motivating employees; managing groups, teams, and conflict; and facilitating organizational change.

2. Thinking like a leader means reviewing a leadership situation and identifying what is happening, accounting for what is happening (in terms of leadership and other behavioral science theories and concepts), and formulating leader actions.

3. Legitimate power and authority are elements in the foundation of leadership, because a leader without power is not a leader at all. Sources of leader power include position, rewards, coercion, expertise, and referent power or personal magnetism.

4. To be a leader one must also have the potential to be a leader, which means having "the right stuff" (in terms of personality traits) is the second foundation component. Fixed traits on which leaders differ from nonleaders include drive, the desire to lead, honesty/integrity, self-confidence, cognitive ability, and knowledge of the business.

5. The leader must provide a direction that his or her followers can work toward. This direction may be a statement of vision, mission, or objectives, depending largely on what the leader wants to achieve and the level at which he or she is acting.

6. Influencing employees to work toward that vision involves several things. It requires the management skills of planning, organizing, and controlling. It calls for applying the behavioral theories and concepts presented in the following chapters. And, it means using the right leadership style in the right situation. Leadership styles or behaviors we discussed in this chapter include structuring and considerate styles; participative and autocratic styles; employee-centered and production-centered styles; close and general styles; and transformational behavior. Situational leadership theories like those of Fiedler and House and the leader-member exchange (LMX) theory underscore the importance of the leader's fitting his or her style to the situation.

7. Although there are some differences in the way men and women lead, these do not account for the slowed career progress of most women managers. Institutional biases such as the glass ceiling and persistent, if inaccurate, stereotypes are contributing factors.

KEY TERMS

leadership
critical leadership
  thinking skills
trait theory
personality trait
vision
mission statement

objectives
consideration
initiating structure
employee-oriented leader
job-centered leader
close supervision
laissez-faire leader

general leader
leader-member exchange
  (LMX) theory
transactional
  leadership
transformational
  leadership

SELF-TEST

TRUE / FALSE QUESTIONS

1 **T F** Leading and managing are inseparable in management theory; you cannot have one without the other.

2 **T F** Vision is the objective toward which all leaders want their followers to move.

3 **T F** A leader can be influential without power.

4 **T F** Referent power is based on expertise.

5 **T F** The trait theory of leadership assumes that a leader must have identifiable personality traits that effective leaders have and ineffective leaders do not.

6 **T F** One way to define and operationalize a leader's vision is through a mission statement.

7 **T F** The behavioral leadership studies focus on whether a leader's style is "task oriented" or "people oriented."

8 **T F** A decision tree is a chart that enables the leader to decide the correct level of authoritarianism.

9 **T F** A general leader is somewhere between the close supervision and the laissez-faire leader.

10 **T F** The key to Fiedler's contingency theory of leadership is his scale called the "most desirable manager context."

MULTIPLE-CHOICE QUESTIONS

1 The building blocks of leadership include which of the following?
a. vision
b. power
c. personality traits
d. all of the above

2 His or her leadership _____ describes how a leader acts.
a. style
b. communication
c. control
d. power

3 Which of the following is *not* one of the types of power presented in the chapter?
a. coercive
b. spiritual
c. expert
d. referent

4 Which of the following traits distinguishes leaders from nonleaders?
a. self-confidence
b. honesty and integrity
c. cognitive ability
d. all of the above

5 A _____ is any readily identifiable and continuing behavior that characterizes the way an individual varies from other people.
a. trait
b. physical attribute
c. cultural relativity
d. none of the above

6 Two of the most frequent tasks of leader behavior are _____ .
a. smoothing attitudes and consideration
b. initiating structure and task viability
c. hierarchy and consideration
d. initiating structure and consideration

7 Under the situational leadership model, which of the following is *not* identified as one of the four levels of participation?
a. delegating
b. participating
c. selling
d. advertising

8 The key to understanding Fiedler's explanation of leader effectiveness is what he calls _____ co-workers.
a. cognitive
b. least preferred
c. verbal
d. path-goal–oriented

9 _____ leadership is required in our day of rapid change, according to James MacGregor Burns.
   a. Transactional
   b. Transformational
   c. Autocratic
   d. Laissez-faire

10 About what percentage of women are part of top management?
   a. 2
   b. 12
   c. 24
   d. 46

CRITICAL THINKING EXERCISES

1 Guidance, vision, culture, empowerment, personality, power, influence, charisma, the "right stuff," revolutionizing the behavior of others: These seem to be evolving elements of leadership as we enter the next millennium. Rather than life-long work in one company, we are also increasingly becoming independent workers or contractors, tied more to our own profession and skills than to any one company, or country for that matter.

   Using the research presented in this chapter, develop a profile for the types of leaders needed for the following companies or leadership positions:

   ▪ President of the United States
   ▪ CEO of Microsoft
   ▪ Coach of an NFL team
   ▪ Owners of a small business
   ▪ CEO of Ford Motor Company in Brazil
   ▪ Director of the Food and Drug Administration
   ▪ President of the National Organization for Women
   ▪ CEO of Disney

   Be prepared to compare your profiles with those of others in the class.

2 As a group, compare and contrast the perspectives on leadership presented below.[82] What concepts from the chapter would help you in understanding their various perspectives? Which style do you like best and why?

   Leaders can't succeed if they care more about how people feel than how they perform. So focus on output, not attitude. Employees who get results should be taken at face value. Sincerity and competence rarely share a soul. Reward the latter and forget the former.

   Marilyn Moats Kennedy, Managing Partner, Career Strategies, Wilmette, Illinois

   I find it amusing, frustrating, and often, quite appalling, how few business leaders recognize that people should share in the economic value they create. At LifeUSA, our employees have options on 2 million shares of company stock. It seems like common sense to us. So why is it still so uncommon in most companies?

   Sharing the wealth with everyone creates a vested interest for everyone to succeed. It's also a powerful mechanism for accountability. And it encourages people to innovate and provide unbeatable service.

   Nobody wins unless everybody wins.

   Maggie Hughes, COO, LifeUSA Holdings, Inc., Minneapolis, Minnesota

   CEOs are always searching for vision, and I'm no different. But I've come to appreciate the value of bifocals—the kind that let me move from a close up view of Merix to one farther away, and then back again. I try to wear my corporate bifocals regularly, alternating my view so I can get a better look at where we are as an organization and where we are going in the future.

   Sometimes what you see depends on how you look.

   Debi Coleman, Chair and CEO, Merix Corporation, Forest Grove, Oregon

EXPERIENTIAL EXERCISES

1 Leaders come in all sizes, shapes, genders, and races. Your task is to research five of the following people and then write a brief analysis of what made them leaders. After you have completed that portion of the task, explain what you think an "ideal" leader is and identify someone you think fits that profile best. Write no more than two pages of analysis.

   The leaders are George Bush, former president; Andrew Young, politician; Cezar Chavez, labor leader; Golda Meir, former leader of Israel; Bill Clinton, U.S. president; Mao Zedong, late communist leader of China; Rosa Parks, civil rights leader; Madeline Albright, secretary of state; Bill Gates, CEO of Microsoft; Louis Gerstner, CEO of IBM; Robert Allen, CEO of AT&T; Helmut Kohl, chancellor of Germany; Jesus Christ, leader; and Michael Jordan, basketball player.

2 The world of corporate America has clearly changed in the last few decades. As the March 17, 1997, cover story of *Fortune* states: "For families to maintain their standard of living, it has been essential for women to get in the labor market and stay there much longer. This is not pin money. It is not fulfillment of stated ambitions. This is driving economic necessity."

   If we are to remain competitive, the mixture of work and family is an issue we should address as a nation.

   In groups of four to six, including men and women, discuss the following questions: What type of leadership do you think is needed in today's highly competitive workplace? Are men and women using the same leadership styles? Should they? Can women take their place in leadership positions under the current conditions?

DIVERSITY CASE

BUSINESS REVOLUTIONARIES IN A DIFFICULT BUSINESS ENVIRONMENT

Founded in 1974 by a group of Colombian business leaders to "give business leadership capabilities to the community," Colegio de Estudios Superiores Adminstracion (CESA) wants to revitalize Columbia by recruiting "young people of high moral character and awareness, who love Columbia and want to create a better community through economic opportunity."

The heart of CESA's curriculum is propelling students out of the classroom and into the community. The first thing they study is how to prepare a business plan. Students then spend nine 22-week terms working in business at home and around the globe. When they graduate, they are well prepared to manage a business. As director Rocha notes, "Our professors talk from real life. . . . And in doing so, they give to the students what we call 'hidden studies' that deal with morality and social responsibility."

Beatriz and Eduardo Marcia started their own business,

Crepes & Waffles, after attending CESA. They now have 14 stores throughout Columbia, Ecuador, and Panama. Their growth rate has been 30 percent for each of the last five years and they now employ 700 people with generous benefits.

Questions

1 Compare the views of social responsibility and its impact on management in the United States and at CESA.
2 What leadership theories do you think CESA should stress? Why?
3 What leadership issues do the Marcias face in developing their new businesses?
4 How could our universities use this model to address issues of poverty and homelessness here? What might some of the barriers be?

SOURCE: David Benson, "Columbia's School for Business Revolutionaries," *Inc.*, August–September 1996, 28–30.

STRATEGY CASE

FOOD FOR THOUGHT

Here is what two business leaders recently had to say about leadership:

- *Dee Hock, Founder and CEO Emeritus, Visa:*
  Given the right circumstances, from no more than dreams, determination, and the liberty to try, ordinary people consistently do extraordinary things. To lead is to create those circumstances, then go before and show the way.

- *Hatim Tyabji, President and CEO, VeriFone, Inc:*
  The first principle of leadership is authenticity: "Watch what I do, not what I say." If you want your company to exude a sense of urgency and a drive to get things done, then act that way on a daily basis. If you want your people to put the needs of the customer first, then do that too—in every situation. If you want your people to be

frugal, then don't spend money on perks designed to make your life more comfortable. Leadership requires moral authority. You can't have moral authority if you behave differently from your people.

Questions

1 What can you learn from leadership from the leaders here?
2 Compare and contrast the ideas about leadership here with the transformational leadership theory you read in the chapter.
3 Explain how a leader could apply the ideas of Dee Hock and Hatim Tyabji to help his or her company do a better job of implementing its strategy.

SOURCE: "The Fast Company Unit of One Anniversary Handbook," *Fast Company*, February–March 1997, 97–106.

ENTREPRENEURIAL CASE

THE ULTIMATE ENTREPRENEUR

Who is he? This entrepreneur started with little money but built a company up to $42 billion in revenues, created hundreds of thousands of jobs, and established a world-class name brand, all without charisma or big connections. High-

tech whiz? Biotech inventor? No, he is Konosuke Matsushita, creator of Matsushita Electric, whose annual sales eventually exceeded the combined sales of Bethlehem Steel, Colgate-Palmolive, Gillette, Goodrich, Kellogg, Olivetti, Scott Paper, and Whirlpool.

Matsushita made a fortune and spent it on civic projects such as a Nobel-prize like organization and the founding of a school of government to reform Japan's political system. Today his spirit is still part of the company he created. Its 265,000 workers worldwide start their day with the company song and from time to time recite Matsushita's six business principles:

1. Treat the people you do business with as if they were a part of your family.
2. After-sales service is more important than assistance before sales.
3. Don't sell customers goods they are attached to; sell them goods that will benefit them.
4. To be out of stock is due to carelessness.
5. Think of yourself as being completely in charge of and responsible for your own work.
6. If we cannot make a profit, we are committing a crime against society, using precious resources that could be better used elsewhere.

Perhaps among all his lessons about business, the greatest was that life is growth—as a human being, as a business person, and as a leader.

Questions

1. How does Matsushita illustrate the traits and skills of a leader?
2. Do you think Matsushita's culture made a difference in his leadership style? If so, how?
3. What are the lessons of leadership taught by Matsushita?
4. What do you think it would be like to work at Matsushita Electric?
5. What do you think it was about Matsushita that made him such a successful entrepreneur?

Source: John P. Kotter, "Matsushita: The World's Greatest Entrepreneur?", *Fortune*, 31 March 1997, 105–11.

THE BUSINESS TEAM, INC.

TROUBLE IN TEAMLAND?

The Business Team has been working together very successfully as a partnership until recently. Many of the consulting jobs available seem to be a combination of finance and production and operations. Because Sid and Hal majored in these areas, they have asserted themselves as the leaders. Maria, Len, and Ruth are becoming concerned. They argue that the vision for the Team was that each of them would bring his or her own perspective to the client's problem to ensure a comprehensive, not a specialized, analysis. Sid and Hal argue that their expertise is more valuable given the content of the projects, and that while the vision of comprehensiveness is laudable, they have the expert knowledge in those areas and should be in charge.

These differing perspectives have led to several heated discussions. The partners are still in conflict about what is important and what approach they should take. They know they need to solve this impasse to survive and they all want to keep working together.

Questions

1. Thinking like a leader, what do you think they should do? Why?
2. What leadership theories might help them to solve their impasse?
3. In the context of this case, why is the concept of leadership easy to define, but difficult to study and understand?

MICHAEL DORF LEADS KNITMEDIA

If you were to fast-forward through KnitMedia's history, you'd find that it embodied the leadership of Michael Dorf: Michael and the band Swamp Thing start Flaming Pie records in Madison, Wisconsin, in 1985; the first Knitting Factory is opened with Louis Spitzer in 1987 on Houston Street between the Bowery and Broadway to "... weave strands of art mediums into a congruent whole ..."; the first band to play on the Knitting Factory stage is Swamp Thing—the show is attended by 20 friends from Madison; by April 1987 Michael is booking every single night, mostly improvisers and artists in a jazz vein who need work; to publicize the early shows, Michael makes a number of different posters using copies of jazz greats and puts these up all over downtown New York; Michael soon buys a cassette deck, begins recording the live Knitting Factory performances, and offers them as a "Live at the Knitting Factory" radio series, in part by persuading 30 radio stations to pay $5 a week for the cost of duplication and mailing; by 1990, Michael is engaged in negotiations with Steve Ralbovsky (at the time, head of A&R for A&M records) to hammer out a contract that will allow the Knitting Factory to buy and install a digital recording studio in the club, record shows, and provide A&M with several records; and by 1997 KnitMedia is a multimillion-dollar operation, planning to raise capital to support the global expansion of Knitting Factory Clubs, multimedia broadcasts, tours, and KnitMedia's record label.

As the company grew, however, one question was how Michael Dorf's vision could continue to penetrate every nook and cranny of the company's worldwide operations so that he could continue to provide the sort of leadership that he did during the firm's first ten years of existence.

Team Exercises and Questions

Use what you learned in this chapter to answer the following questions:

1 How would you characterize Michael Dorf as a leader, based on the various styles and approaches to leadership discussed in this chapter?
2 How would you describe Michael Dorf's vision for KnitMedia? How would you suggest he ensure that his vision continues to provide the necessary guidance to KnitMedia managers and employees?

For the online version of this case, visit our Web site at <www.prenhall.com/desslermgmt>.

For Internet exercises, interactive study questions, news updates and more, visit the Dessler Web site at

www.prenhall.com/desslermgmt

If you're using the CD-ROM that accompanies this text, simply click on the "Web Site" button to access the site.

CHAPTER 11

INFLUENCING ORGANIZATIONAL CULTURE AND SHARED VALUES

What's Ahead?

When Marvin Runyon became head of the newly privatized U.S. Postal Service, he knew the prevailing culture had to be changed. Morale was low, and local post office workers often chatted on the job, apparently disdainful of the long lines of waiting customers. Behind the scenes some employees fought every suggested procedural change, so productivity remained in the doldrums. Runyon knew his only hope for dragging this organization into the 21st century was to dramatically change the values that permeated almost every nook and cranny and almost every employee. The question was, how to do so?[1]

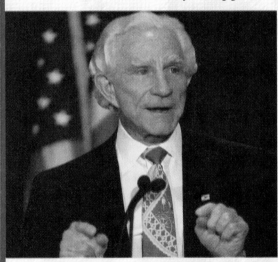

Marvin Runyon

Objectives

After studying this chapter, you should be able to

- **define** organizational culture and values
- **give** examples of healthy and unhealthy corporate cultures
- **explain** with specific examples how to create and sustain a corporate culture
- **discuss** the importance of using the corporate culture in managing change
- **explain** how a manager can change an organization's culture.

MANAGEMENT ON THE WEB

E-ZINE FOR THE HIGH PERFORMANCE COMPANY

This monthly "E-Zine" releases information about the "best practices" employed by high-performance companies and unions. How could Mr. Runyon make use of this site?■

http://www.fed.org/Leading-Companies/index.html

What Is Organizational Culture?

The challenge facing Marvin Runyon at the Postal Service is similar to the problems that have faced leaders like British Prime Minister Margaret Thatcher, Microsoft's Bill Gates, IBM's Louis Gerstner, and countless others over the past few years. Leaders today must inspire and manage change, but to do so they must also manage (and sometimes change) the values and culture of the companies they are leading. **Organizational culture** can be defined as the characteristic traditions, norms, and values that employees share. Values and norms (such as "Be honest," "Be thrifty," and "Don't be bureaucratic") are basic beliefs about what you should or shouldn't do, and what is or is not important. Norms and values guide and channel people's behavior; leading and influencing people therefore depends in part on influencing the norms and values they use as behavioral guides.

In keeping with Figure 11.1, we'll see in this chapter that leaders can and do have profound effects on their companies' cultures, and thus on their employees' shared values and behavior. However, leaders have to understand that such values can be a force for good or for ill: "Be candid" may be a laudable value for many firms, for instance, while "Be secretive" could stifle communications and trust.

■ FIGURE 11.1
Culture in an Organization

Leaders (as well as other factors discussed in this chapter) influence an organization's culture. Leaders influence culture by how they act, by the core-values statements they formulate, by the management practices they put in place, and by the signs, symbols, and stories they encourage.

SOURCE: Reprinted with the permission of The Free Press, a division of Simon & Schuster from *Corporate Culture and Performance* by John P. Kotter and James L. Heskett. Copyright ©1992 by Kotter Associates, Inc. and James L. Heskett.

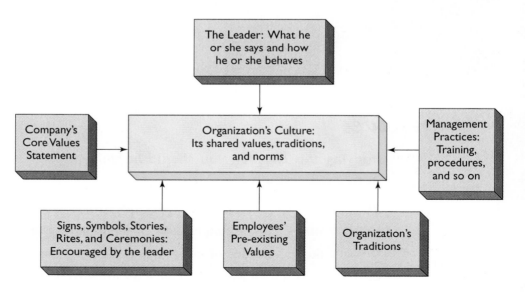

Whether the leader's influence on culture is positive or negative depends on the values the leader espouses and on how he or she molds the company's culture.

A Closer Look at What Organizational Culture Means

Let's take a closer look at what organizational culture means. To do that, think for a moment about what comes to mind when you hear the word "culture" applied to a country. In France, or China, or the United States, you'd probably think of at least three things. Culture means, first, the *physical aspects* of the country's society, things like the country's art, music, and theater. Culture also means the sorts of *values* that country's citizens share—for instance, the emphasis on "equality" and "fraternity" in France, or on "democracy" and "hard work" in the United States. By "culture" you'd also probably mean the characteristic way the people of that country behave—the patience of the people in England, or the emphasis on fine food and art among the people of France, for instance.

We can apply that sort of country analogy to get a better feel for what OB experts mean by organizational culture. Professor James Hunt says there are several layers to a company's culture. In layer 1 (see Figure 11.2) are **cultural artifacts,** the

■ FIGURE 11.2
Hunt's Peeled-Onion View of Organizational Culture
Studying culture requires sifting through several layers. "Artifacts" or physical manifestations of culture, include the organization's (or society's) technology and art. These in turn emerge from patterns of behavior (layer 2), which in turn are based on values and beliefs (layer 3). At the core, said Hunt, are people's basic assumptions.

SOURCE: Based on Schein (1985), Ott (1989), and Rousseau, as presented in James Hunt, *Leadership: A New Synthesis* (Thousand Oaks, CA: Sage Publications, 1991), 221, copyright © 1991 by Sage Publications. Reprinted by permission of Sage Publications, Inc.

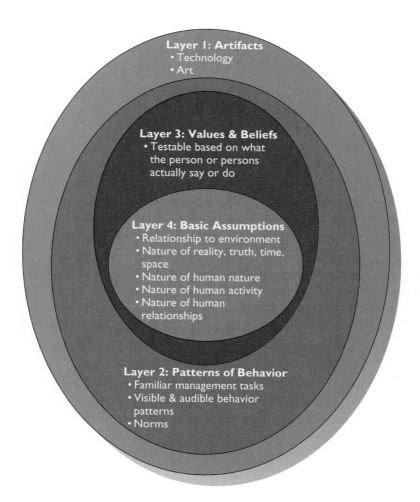

Layer 1: Artifacts
• Technology
• Art

Layer 3: Values & Beliefs
• Testable based on what the person or persons actually say or do

Layer 4: Basic Assumptions
• Relationship to environment
• Nature of reality, truth, time, space
• Nature of human nature
• Nature of human activity
• Nature of human relationships

Layer 2: Patterns of Behavior
• Familiar management tasks
• Visible & audible behavior patterns
• Norms

obvious signs and symbols of corporate culture, such as written rules, office layouts, organizational structure, and dress codes.[2]

Supporting this layer of obvious cultural signs lie **patterns of behavior.** These include the company's ceremonial events, written and spoken comments, and the actual behaviors that the firm's managers and other employees engage in (such as hiding information, politicking, or expressing honest concern when a colleague needs assistance).

In turn, these corporate cultural signs and behaviors are a product of the **values and beliefs** in layer 3. Values and beliefs (such as "The customer is always right" or "Don't be bureaucratic") are guiding standards that lay out "what ought to be, as distinct from what is."[3] Management's *stated* values and beliefs sometimes differ from what the managers actually value and believe; if so, this will show up in their behavior. Therefore, you can infer the manager's values from the actions he or she takes. For example, Fred Smith, the founder and chairman of Federal Express, says that many firms *say* they believe in respecting their employees and putting their people first.[4] But in a lot of these firms it's not what the managers say but the way they behave—insisting on time clocks, routinely downsizing, and so on—that makes it clear what their values really are.

Management's basic assumptions—such as their assumptions about human nature—are at the core of a firm's culture, says Hunt. Sample assumptions are presented in Figure 11.3. For example, does top management assume in general that people can or cannot be trusted? That people are inherently good or bad? Assumptions, says Hunt, influence values, which in turn influence behavior and actions. This chain of influences can be diagrammed something like this:

$$\text{Assumptions} \rightarrow \text{Values} \rightarrow \text{Behavior} \rightarrow \text{Artifacts}$$

Artifacts are the concrete results of the culture that you can see, such as time clocks, appraisal forms, and rules that say "Lateness will not be tolerated."

■ **FIGURE 11.3**
Five Basic Types of Assumptions
Assumptions mold values, which in turn mold behavior and the physical manifestations of a person's behavior, like policies and rules.

SOURCE: Based on Schein (1983), 16. As presented in James Hunt, *Leadership: A New Synthesis* (Thousand Oaks, CA: Sage Publications, 1991), 223, copyright © 1991 by Sage Publications. Reprinted by permission of Sage Publications, Inc.

1. Organization's Relationship to Environment. Extent to which key organizational members see this relationship as one of dominance, submission, harmonizing, finding an appropriate niche, and the like.

2. Nature of Reality, Truth, Time, Space. The linguistic and behavioral rules that define what is real and what is not, what is "fact," how truth ultimately is to be determined, and whether truth is "revealed" or "discovered"; basic concepts of time as linear or cyclical, monochronic (one kind only) or polychronic (several different kinds); basic concepts such as space as limited or indefinite and property as communal or individual; etc.

3. Nature of Human Nature. What does it mean to be "human," and what attributes are assumed to be intrinsic or ultimate? Is human nature evil, good, or neutral? Are human beings perfectible? Is Theory X or Y more appropriate?

4. Nature of Human Activity. What is the "right" thing for humans to do, on the basis of the above assumptions; should they be active, passive, self-developmental, fatalistic, or what? What is work and what is play?

5. Nature of Human Relationships. What is assumed to be the "right" way for individuals to relate to each other, to distribute power and love? Is life cooperative or competitive; individualistic, group, collaborative, or communal; based on traditional lineal authority, law, or what?

Informality is one of the most highly valued behaviors evident in the healthy corporate culture of Microsoft, Inc.

Organizational Behavior in Action

CORPORATE CULTURE AT PROCTER & GAMBLE

Procter & Gamble provides a good example of corporate culture in action. P&G's culture reflects what one management theorist has called the firm's legendary emphasis on "thoroughness, market-testing, and ethical behavior," values that are transmitted to new employees through the firm's selection, socialization, and training processes.[5]

THE UNDERLYING VALUES. Procter & Gamble has a strong corporate culture, which means its values exert a powerful influence on all P&G employees. The basic elements of its culture go back to the firm's founders, William Procter and James Gamble. They founded P&G in Cincinnati in 1837 with the mission of producing relatively inexpensive household products that were technically superior to the competition, quickly consumed, and an integral part of their customer's lifestyle.[6] The founders' intention was to "foster growth in an orderly manner, to reflect the standards set by the founders, and to plan and prepare for the future."[7]

This philosophy was translated into several core P&G values. The emphasis on orderly growth manifests itself in "tremendous conformity."[8] A new recruit soon learns to say "we" instead of "I."[9] One P&G manager was quoted as saying, "Everyone at P&G is like a hand in a bucket of water—when the hand is removed, the water closes in and there is no trace."[10] In turn, this conformity bolsters the thoroughness and methodical approach desired by the company's founders. Its result, according to one past chairperson, is a "consistency of principles and policy that gives us direction, thoroughness, and self-discipline."[11]

A focus on testing is also part of P&G's culture. Scientific research is an integral part of P&G's thoroughness, as well as part of its aim of "removing personal judgment from the equation" by continually testing and retesting all its products. P&G's aim is to produce products that consistently win in consumer blind tests.

The emphasis on written rather than oral communication is another manifestation of the firm's stress on the value of thoroughness. All significant events are preserved in writing and all records can be recreated at any point. Managers are taught to condense their comments to fit a one-page format. New P&G recruits reportedly tell horror stories about their first memos being ripped to shreds by the boss.[12]

Secrecy is another element of the P&G culture. As far back as the late 1800s, the firm tried to stop giving detailed financial reports to its stockholders; as recently as the late 1980s, reports confirmed that financial information was still very closely held and that the firm "maintains a mistrust of outsiders who are overly curious about P&G."[13] New employees are instructed not to talk about the company to outsiders.

MANAGEMENT PRACTICES AND CULTURE. As is usually the case, Procter & Gamble's culture manifests itself in and is sustained by various management practices. College graduates are recruited and placed in highly competitive situations, and those who can't learn the system are quickly weeded out; the remainder enjoy the benefits of promotion from within. As a result, no one reaches middle management without 5 to 10 years of close scrutiny and training. This in turn creates what one researcher called "a homogeneous leadership group with an enormous amount of common experience and strong set of shared assumptions."[14]

Other management practices contribute to creating and sustaining P&G's culture. New recruits may assume major responsibility for projects almost immediately, but the authority for most big decisions is made far up the chain of command, usually by committees of managers. Nearly everything must be approved through the memo process. Stories and legends abound that reinforce this process; one describes the decision about the color of the Folger's coffee lid, supposedly made by the CEO after four years of extensive market testing.[15]

Internal competition is fostered by the brand management system at P&G. Brands compete for internal resources, have their own advertising and marketing, and act as independent cost centers. The extensive use of memos, the continual rechecking of each other's work, and the rigid timeline for promotions also contribute to (and reflect) P&G's strong culture and emphasis on thoroughness.

In summary, corporate culture represents a firm's shared values and characteristic behaviors. These shared values often have their roots within the firm's founders and subsequent top executives, whose behaviors and policies then help to mold and sustain the firm's culture. The firm's shared values manifest themselves in characteristic behaviors, such as the emphasis on research and development at P&G. ■

Unhealthy Organizational Culture

A company's culture can be a force for good or for ill. Procter & Gamble's strong culture has helped make P&G a firm that dominates its industry. Yet, in other firms, corporate cultures have led to much less satisfactory results. Xerox is reportedly a case in point. According to several reports, Xerox was long known for its social responsibility and innovation, and for its founders' principles of "faith in people, concern for customers, and economic power through innovation, marketing, patents and world-wide presence."[16]

But by the 1970s (and into the early 1980s, when a turnaround began), Xerox's culture became unhealthy in terms of its effects on the company. The firm reportedly became increasingly insular and "most of the decisions (were) made around issues of turf, career advancement and those kinds of things."[17] Gradually, "the culture of Xerox also became intolerant of initiatives and leadership from the ranks . . . experimentation was often discouraged, and error was not tolerated well."[18]

Xerox is reportedly recovering, but damage was done. Clearly, unhealthy corporate cultures can undermine a firm's effectiveness. During the decades in which the firm's culture was insular and anti-innovative, Xerox's market share in duplicating machines dropped dramatically.

CAUSES OF UNHEALTHY CULTURES. In Figure 11.4, Professors John Kotter and James Heskett summarize the origins of unhealthy organizational cultures.

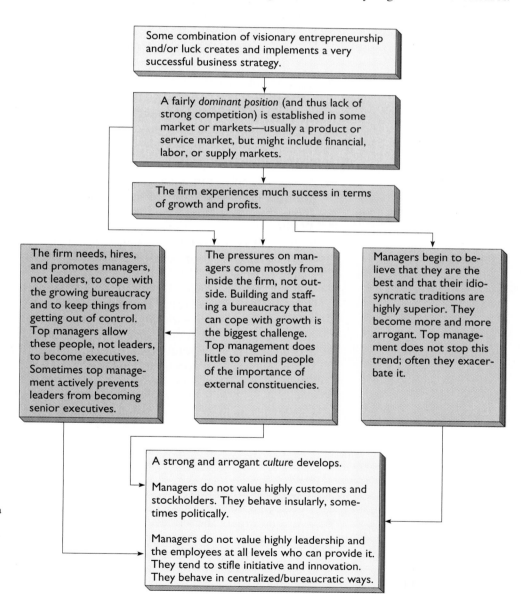

■ **FIGURE 11.4**
The Origins of Unhealthy Corporate Cultures

Success can lead to unhealthy, unresponsive organizational cultures if the pressure causes management to focus on building the internal bureaucracy rather than on serving the customer.

SOURCE: Reprinted with the permission of The Free Press, a division of Simon & Schuster from *Corporate Culture and Performance* by John P. Kotter and James L. Heskett. Copyright © 1992 by Kotter Associates, Inc., and James L. Heskett.

They say a firm's initial success creates pressure to manage the growing firm and (perhaps) a misplaced self-confidence on the part of the managers that they are unbeatable. The need to manage success drives management to permit an administrative bureaucracy to develop in which shuffling papers and protecting one's turf become more important than providing and following a visionary direction for the firm. As a result, a strong but arrogant corporate culture develops as managers concentrate on the internal administration and politics of the firm rather than on the company's outside customers, stockholders, and competitors. Gradually, the company's forward motion falters.

Organizational Behavior in Action

VALUES IN SUCCESSFUL COMPANIES

However, it is not unsuccessful but successful companies' values we are interested in. Two researchers conducted a four-year study in order to identify specific values in a number of successful companies; their findings help to illustrate in concrete terms what some successful managers mean by "values."[19] Based on their study, these researchers suggest that "the foundation of successful management is the active and persistent pursuit of" twelve values:[20]

- *Power.* The successful management understands the inherent power of its position and takes charge of the organization's destiny. It adopts this "power" value: Managers must manage.
- *Elitism.* The successful organization understands the vital importance of getting the best possible candidates into management jobs and of continuously developing their competence. It adopts this "elitism" value: Cream belongs at the top.
- *Reward.* The successful organization identifies and rewards success. It adopts this "reward" value: Performance is king.
- *Effectiveness.* A successful organization is able to focus resources on activities that get results. It adopts this "effectiveness" value: Do the right thing.
- *Efficiency.* The successful organization relentlessly searches for better ways to do things, and it constantly builds pride into the job. It adopts this "efficiency" value: Do things right.
- *Economy.* Every activity costs money; someone, somewhere, has to pay. The successful organization understands the importance of facing economic reality. It adopts this "economy" value: No free lunches.
- *Fairness.* The successful organization realizes that people's views, perceptions, and feelings are important. It adopts this "fairness" value: Who cares, wins.
- *Teamwork.* The successful organization ensures that it derives the benefits of effective teamwork. It adopts this "teamwork" value: Pull together.
- *Law and order.* The successful organization devises and honorably administers an appropriate system of rules and regulations. It adopts this "law and order" value: Justice must prevail.
- *Defense.* The successful organization studies external threats and then formulates a strong defense. It adopts this "defense" value: Know thine enemy.
- *Competitiveness.* The successful organization takes all necessary steps to be

competitive. It knows that in the world of commerce, it is the best who survive and the weakest who go to the wall. It adopts this "competitiveness" value: Survival of the fittest.

■ *Opportunism.* Opportunities have to be seized quickly, even though this may involve risks. The successful organization is a committed opportunist. It adopts this "opportunism" value: Who dares, wins. ■

How to Create and Sustain the Corporate Culture

Managers can take concrete steps to create and sustain a healthy corporate culture. These steps include publishing a core values statement, exercising leadership, using management practices, and establishing signs, symbols, and ceremonies.

Publish a Core Values Statement

Publishing a formal core values statement is a logical first step in creating a culture. For example, Figure 3.3 (see page 91) summarizes the core values credo of Johnson & Johnson: "We believe our first responsibility is to the doctors, nurses, and patients, to mothers and all others who use our products and services. In meeting their needs, everything we do must be of high quality."[21]

A firm's values should then guide the company's behavior. Thus, you may recall that Johnson & Johnson faced a crisis several years ago when someone tampered with its Tylenol capsules. According to one manager, "Crisis planning did not see us through the tragedy nearly so much as the sound business management philosophy that is embodied in our credo. It was the credo that prompted the decisions that enabled us to make the right early decisions."[22] From their credo, it was clear what management had to do: put their responsibility to "patients, to mothers . . ." first; emphasize high quality; and "be good citizens." In five months, the firm had produced a new tamper-resistant Tylenol product and regained 70 percent of its market share; within several years, its market share was fully restored.

It's important to include a balanced set of values in that cores values statement. Kotter and Heskett found that successful firms formulate values that support three key constituencies: customers, employees, and shareholders. Albertson's Markets, for instance, has a "corporate creed" stating the firm's responsibility to customers, employees, community, shareholders, and society. American Airlines' commitment to all its constituencies—stockholders, passengers, and employees—is part of its corporate vision statement. As Kotter and Heskett emphasize:

> When managers do not care about all three key constituencies and about leadership initiatives throughout the management hierarchy, the net results always seem to be less effective adaptation [to competitive pressures]. This is perhaps most obvious when a high concern for customers and/or leadership is lacking. But this is also true in a firm with a strong customer orientation but without much concern for employees or stockholders.[23]

Exercise Leadership

Leaders play a role in creating and sustaining a firm's culture, through the actions they take, the comments they make, and the visions they espouse.

The process of influencing shared values often starts with the company's founders. As Professor Edgar Schein has said:

By far the most important for cultural beginnings is the impact of founders. Founders not only choose the basic mission and the environmental context in which the new group will operate, but they choose the group members and bias the original responses that the group makes in its efforts to succeed in its environment and to integrate itself.[24]

The Wal-Mart discount chain is a good example of the founder's influence. As Harry Cunningham (who founded competitor Kmart stores while CEO of SS Kresge Company) said of Sam Walton:

> [His] establishment of a Wal-Mart culture throughout the company was the key to the whole thing. He is the greatest businessman of this century.[25]

The foundations of Wal-Mart's values can be traced to the late Sam Walton's personal values of "hard work, honesty, neighborliness, and thrift."[26] Under Walton's leadership, for example, the firm developed an almost religious zeal for doing things efficiently, and hard work became a requirement for getting promoted. Wal-Mart stressed honesty (for instance in identifying the sources of its merchandise), and its neighborliness was epitomized by the greeters at its doors. The entire thrust of its strategy—from low prices and locations away from the center of town to satellite-aided distribution—was aimed at making "Wal-Mart" synonymous with "thrift." Walton also worked hard to underscore his company's emphasis on thrift by downplaying his own billionaire status: Until the day he died he drove an old pickup truck, a decision he explained with the rhetorical question, "If I drove a Rolls Royce, what would I do with my dog?" He also worked hard to make sure other Wal-Mart employees (many of whom had become millionaires on company stock) did not flaunt their wealth. As he said, "Maybe it's none of my business, but I have done everything I can to discourage our folks from getting too extravagant with their homes, their meals and their lifestyles."[27]

But there was more to Wal-Mart's culture than hard work, honesty, neighborliness, and thrift. Walton wanted to create a culture that emphasized values like enthusiasm, fun, and unpredictability, and the way he did it says a lot about how cultures are formed. Walton would fly from store to store in his own plane to lead Wal-Mart's employees in their morning cheer ("Give me a W! Give me an A! Give me an L!" and so on). When Walton lost a bet to president David Glass, he had to pay up by donning a grass skirt and doing the hula on Wall Street. Store managers became known for what Walton called "crazy kinds of things." For example, the Nairbury, Nebraska, store had a "precision shopping cart drill team" that marched in local parades. The members all wore Wal-Mart's smocks and pushed their carts through a routine of whirls, twists, and circles.[28]

Use Management Practices

Managers use concrete planning, organizing, leading, and controlling management practices to foster the culture they desire. One crucial practice is the founder's tendency to hire people whose values, ideas, and beliefs are similar to his or her own. These "right-type" people then move into management positions and attract new generations of right-type people, who in turn become socialized into the firm's way of doing things. Training is important too: At Toyota (where quality and teamwork are essential), much of the training focuses on how to work in teams and how to solve quality problems. The Entrepeneurs in Action feature provides another example.

Even the way you organize can be important. Flat structures and empowered workers send a signal that self-control and fast decisions are encouraged, for instance.

Entrepreneurs in Action

ROSENBLUTH INTERNATIONAL

Rosenbluth International believes first impressions can be lasting. That's why the company spends a lot of time getting a few basic core values—customer service, sincerity, and respect for the individual—across to new hires.

An innovative two-day orientation helps to instill the right values. What differentiates the management company—elegant customer service—is stressed first. Sincerity is the basis of the company slogan, "Live the Spirit." Although it may sound empty, associates learn that this value is strictly upheld by ensuring that all company messages are both consistent and honest.

Finally, company president and CEO Hal

Rosenbluth values respect for the individual and feels strongly that the time and energy invested in his staff reaps enhanced customer service. He makes new associates the focal point of a formal ceremonial tea party at the conclusion of the orientation process, and he keeps a handle on the sentiments of his staff through his twice-yearly Happiness Barometer survey. Information gleaned from this survey has led to a number of useful improvements.

All this has resulted in Rosenbluth International's gaining an excellent reputation. In one recent year the company received 21,000 job applications for 800 openings, for example.

SOURCE: Nancy K. Austin, "Wacky Management Ideas That Work," *Working Woman,* November 1991, 42–4; Ellyn E. Spraging, "First Impressions," *Inc.,* December 1991, 157; and Rob Walker, "Down on the Farm," *Fast Company,* February–March 1997, 112–22.

Use Signs, Symbols, Stories, Rites, and Ceremonies

Tom Peters and Robert Waterman, in their book *In Search of Excellence,* emphasize that it is the leader's responsibility to create strong cultures by shaping norms, instilling beliefs, inculcating values, and generating emotions.[29] We've seen that one way leaders do this is by establishing management practices—training programs, plans, and organizations, for instance—that embody and symbolize the firm's core values. Another way they do this is by using symbols, stories, rites, and ceremonies.

Many believe that the symbolsm—what the manager says and does and the signals he or she sends—ultimately does the most to create and sustain the company's culture. At Saturn Corporation—known for its culture of quality, teamwork, and respect for the individual—one of the firm's top managers said this about company culture:

> Creating a value system that encourages the kind of behavior you want is not enough. The challenge is then to engage in those practices that symbolize those values [and] tell people what is really O.K. to do and what not [to do]. Actions, in other words, speak much more loudly than words.[30]

Signs, symbols, stories, rites, and ceremonies are concrete examples of such actions.

Signs and **symbols** are used throughout strong-culture firms to create and sustain the company's culture. At Ben & Jerry's, for instance, the "joy gang" is a concrete symbol of the firm's values (charity, fun, and goodwill toward fellow workers). The joy gang is a voluntary group that meets once or twice a week to create new ways to inject fun into what the Ben & Jerry's people do, often by giving out "joy grants," which are "five hundred quick, easy, no-strings attached dollars for long-term improvements to your work area."[31] Sam Walton's hula dance on Wall Street is another example of a culture-building symbol.

Stories illustrating important company values are also widely used to reinforce the firm's culture. Thus, at Procter & Gamble there are many stories about relatively trivial decisions going all the way to the top of the company.[32] IBM has similar stories, such as how IBM salespeople took dramatic steps (like driving all night through storms) to get parts to customers.

Rites and **ceremonies** can also symbolize the firm's values and help convert employees to them. At JCPenney (where loyalty and tradition are values), new management employees are inducted at ritualistic conferences into the "Penney Partnership." Here they commit to the firm's ideology as embodied in its statement of core values. Each inductee solemnly swears allegiance to these values and then receives his or her "H.C.S.C. lapel pin." These letters symbolize Penney's core values of honor, confidence, service, and cooperation.

◎ ◎ ◎ Strategy in Action ◎ ◎ ◎

SYNCHRONIZING CULTURE AND STRATEGY

Corporate culture plays a crucial role in formulating and implementing a company's strategy. For one thing, corporate culture can influence a company's openness to considering strategic alternatives. For example, we've seen that managers in adaptive corporate cultures tend to care deeply about customers, stockholders, and employees and to value the people and processes that can create useful change. Managers in unadaptive corporate cultures—such as GM and IBM in the 1980s—tend to focus on procedures more than on customers and to value orderly and risk-reducing management actions more highly than leadership initiatives.[33]

A company's culture also sometimes provides the competitive advantage on which to build a successful strategy. Maytag Corporation's lifelong commitment to quality, for instance, reflects the shared values established by founder F. L. Maytag and was recently mentioned by Maytag's past CEO Daniel Krumm as one of the company's sources of competitive advantage: "That, of course, has been Maytag's hallmark for as long as any of us can remember. We believe quality and reliability are, ultimately, what the consumer wants."[34]

As another example, implementing a major strategic change such as a merger can be disastrous if the merging companies' cultures aren't compatible. For example, merging potentially incompatible cultures was one of the challenges facing top managers when NCNB and C&S/Sovrain successfully merged to create NationsBank. According to news reports at the time, NCNB was highly centralized with a hard-charging, maverick style of management, whereas C&S/Sovrain was decentralized and conservative.[35]

On the other hand, the 1994 purchase of Snapple Beverages by Quaker Oats seems to have been partly derailed by incompatible corporate cultures. Seeking to squeeze more profits from its $1.7 billion purchase, Quaker Oats tried to force Snapple to revamp the laid-back way in which it produced and distributed its beverages and to use Quaker's own distribution channels. This apparently alienated Snapple's employees, "who prefer their more idiosyncratic ways of making and selling refreshments."[36]

Similarly, the 1993 merger of Price Club and Costco Wholesale became problematic in less than a year, in part because their vastly different cultures didn't blend well. On the other hand, Southwest Airlines' purchase of Morris Air in 1993 was highly successful, in part because Southwest first "weighed the likely effect of a takeover on everything from Morris' systems and schedules to its entrepreneurial culture; in effect, Southwest undertook a comprehensive cultural due diligence."[37]

The recent merger of investment companies Morgan Stanley and Dean Witter provides another example. The two companies reportedly represented vastly different cultures. Morgan Stanley's senior executives were described as Gucci-loafer-wearing managers with Armani suits, making millions of dollars per year and jetting to Tokyo, London, and other financial centers.[38] Their counterparts at Dean Witter wore less expensive suits and made much less money "hawking plain vanilla mutual funds."[39] Similarly, Dean Witter for the past few years has stayed away from the sorts of risky computerized trading practices that Morgan Stanley has thrived on. How will the high-risk "blue-blood" Morgan Stanley culture blend with the "just plain folks" approach at Dean Witter? After about a year the merger seemed to be blending well, but only the future will tell for sure.

Corporate Culture's Role in Managing Change

Company Culture and the Responsive Organization

Culture may be less tangible than other aspects of a firm such as plant and equipment, but it can still have very real effects on the firm's performance and responsiveness.[40] Corporate culture affects a company's responsiveness in two main ways.

SOME VALUES SUPPORT RESPONSIVENESS. First, some values support responsiveness better than others. For example, the apparent emphasis on values like "Politicking is good," and "Withhold information" at Xerox hampered the firm's ability to make a coordinated and rapid response to its competitors' moves. At the other extreme, GE's stress on the values of agility, candor, and openness facilitates interdepartmental communication and emphasizes to employees the need for fast decision making in a rapidly changing world.

VALUES FACILITATE DELEGATION. Shared values can help managers manage change in another way: they can enable managers to delegate more authority and let employees make more quick decisions, secure in knowing that they have shared values to guide them.

Peters and Waterman have described how shared values can provide the guidelines employees need to keep themselves on track under fast-changing conditions. Such firms' basic beliefs and values, say Peters and Waterman, provided the glue the firms needed to stay "tight but loose." They were loose in terms of letting everyone have a lot of authority for decisions and in terms of not relying on lots of close supervision of the decision-making process; decisions could thus be spontaneous, and the companies responsive. Yet such looseness required an inherent "tightness" on the part of employees: Top management could delegate plenty of authority as long as it knew the employees' decisions would be consistent with the firm's basic values. As a result, the best employees in such responsive firms "are those who have internalized the organization's goals and values—its culture—into their cognitive and effective make-up and therefore no longer require strict and rigid external control."[41] A strong culture, in other words, fosters responsiveness by enabling the firm to depend on employees' self-control. Sociologist Amitai Etzioni has said that while mechanistic organizations rely on traditional control like rules and procedures, responsive ones depend more on "normative control." **Normative control** means the required efforts of a company's employees are elicited and directed through control of the underlying values, thoughts, beliefs, and feelings that guide their actions. As one expert put it:

> Under normative controls, members act in the best interest of a company not because they are physically coerced, nor purely from an instrumental concern with economic rewards and sanctions. It is not just their behaviors and activities that are specified, evaluated and rewarded or punished. Rather, they are driven by internal commitment, strong identification with company goals, [and] intrinsic satisfaction from work.[42]

In other words, employee behavior in responsive firms is guided by a strong set of shared values, beliefs, and traditions—a strong culture.

Comparing Responsive and Unresponsive Cultures

Based on their study of corporate culture, Kotter and Heskett conclude that "only cultures that can help organizations anticipate and adapt to environmental change will be associated with superior performance over long periods of time."[43] They say the message from their data is clear:

> In the firms with more adaptive cultures, the cultural ideal is that managers, throughout the hierarchy, should provide leadership to initiate change in strategies and tactics whenever necessary to satisfy the legitimate interest of not just stockholders, or customers, or employees but all three. In less adaptive cultures, the norm is that managers behave cautiously and politically to protect themselves, their product or their immediate work groups.[44]

These researchers found several differences between adaptive and unadaptive cultures. The values and traditions of adaptive cultures emphasized risk taking, trust-

■ **FIGURE 11.5**
Characteristics of Adaptive Versus Unadaptive Corporate Cultures

SOURCE: Reprinted with permission of The Free Press, a division of Simon & Schuster from *Corporate Culture and Performance* by John P. Kotter and James L. Heskett. Copyright © 1992 by Kotter Associates, Inc., and James L. Heskett.

	Adaptive Corporate Cultures	Unadaptive Corporate Cultures
Core Values	Most managers care deeply about customers, stockholders, and employees. They also strongly value people and processes that can create useful change (such as risk-taking leadership initiatives).	Most managers care mainly about themselves, their immediate work group, or some product (or technology) associated with that work group. They value the orderly and risk-reducing management process much more highly than leadership initiatives.
Common Behavior	Managers pay close attention to all their constituencies, especially customers, and initiate change when needed to serve their legitimate interests, even if that entails taking some risks.	Managers tend to behave somewhat insularly, politically, and bureaucratically. As a result, they do not change their strategies quickly to adjust to or take advantage of changes in their business environments.

ing, and a proactive approach to identifying problems and implementing solutions.[45] On the other hand, unadaptive cultures were bureaucratic: Employees were reactive, quick to blame, risk averse, and not very creative. Similarly, communications were hampered, in part because negative values like "Guard your turf" were emphasized over "Get the job done."

Figure 11.5 summarizes such differences between adaptive and unadaptive corporate cultures. As you can see, core values in adaptive, responsive cultures emphasize caring deeply about customers, stockholders, and employees and highly valuing people and the processes that can create useful change. As a result, certain common behaviors typically exemplify adaptive cultures: Change is encouraged, and managers make it clear by their actions that they pay close attention to employees, stockholders, *and* customers (not just one or the other). They willingly initiate change when needed, even if this might entail some risks. For example, under the transformational leadership of Chairperson Bob Crandall, American Airlines, when faced with a drastic change in its industry, made hundreds of risky changes in the early 1980s.[46] "The firm cut costs, created hubs, altered routes, rewrote labor contracts, grounded a fleet of 707s, invented frequent flyer programs, automated processes, and consolidated functions and facilities."[47]

Organizational Behavior in Action

BUILDING A TOTAL QUALITY-ORIENTED CULTURE

In today's competitive international arena, *responsiveness* often goes hand in hand with total quality management. **Total quality management (TQM)** has been defined as "a people-focused management system that aims at continual increase in customer satisfaction at continually lower real cost."[48] TQM programs are organization-wide programs that integrate all functions of the business and related processes, such that all aspects, including design, planning, production, distribution, and field service, are aimed at maximizing customer satisfaction through continuous improvements.

Many companies today have found that a total quality orientation is not just laudable but essential for survival. Increasingly, for instance, suppliers of components ranging from auto parts to computer programs find that they must be internationally total quality certified in order to compete for buyers like Ford or IBM. A variety of total quality certification programs now exist, ranging from the International Standards Organization's ISO 9000 to Japan's Deming Award and the Baldrige Award in the United States. In other words, many companies just cannot compete today without a total quality program.

As we'll discuss in more detail elsewhere, implementing a total quality management program entails a number of concrete steps. For example, systems are required for continually monitoring and measuring customers' needs and reactions to your company's products. And, procedures are required for quickly translating what you learned about the customer's needs and reactions into modifications in your products or services and the way they are designed and produced.

The company's culture and shared values play a big role in creating a successful total quality management program. Particularly when it comes to matters like being quality conscious, it's not just what top management wants employees to do but what employees believe should be done—in other words, their values—that is going to guide their behavior. Down on the assembly line, in other words, the employees' commitment to quality-conscious values guides their behavior in doing things right and flagging quality flaws as much as (or more than) top management's prodding or the company's quality-checking procedures.

Several shared values characterize total quality–oriented companies. A sample of these values includes the following:[49]

Focus on what customers want not what management thinks they need. This has been called "perhaps one of the most telling indicators" of quality con-

Tampa Bay Vending founder Marie Bartholomew found out what customer service can be when her banker Holly Thomas (left) of First Union Bank asked to ride in one of her trucks to learn about the vending machine trade.

sciousness, because "too often managers assume that they know what customers value, when they really do not."[50] For example, Ricoh Company designers included three special keys in the keyboard of the company's fax machines, only to find out in a later survey that 95 percent of their customers never used these keys.

Focus on the customer, not on your own organization. In many companies, there's a tendency to focus on your own company's needs and ways of doing things rather on the customers' needs. For example, after three visits by IBM managers several years ago, one IBM customer was quoted as saying, "They never asked about our needs. They don't listen. All they do is talk and show you the charts they've brought along."[51]

Emphasize continuous improvement, not working to specification or maintaining the status quo. In today's highly competitive business environment, maintaining the status quo or even meeting specifications isn't enough, since all your competitors are continually striving to beat yesterday's performance and improve their results. Employees therefore should share the value of continually striving to improve quality and processes.

Seek out root causes of problems rather than addressing the symptoms. Addressing symptoms may help to keep the assembly line running, but over the long haul doing so is inherently more costly than eliminating the problem's root cause. In one company, for instance, wheels were being produced that had empty areas or voids inside them, a problem the employees got around by filling them with a plastic resin. Unfortunately, the resin gradually gave way under use, leading to numerous customer complaints. In this case the root cause of the problem was a design flaw: Once the wheel was redesigned, it could be produced and used properly.

Figure 11.6 illustrates one approach to identifying whether a company has a total quality–oriented culture. For example, TQM companies are "driven by customer needs," while traditional companies are "driven by company wants." You might want to fill in the survey for a company in which you've worked, or for another organization with which you do business.[52]

Changing Organizational Cultures

The challenges faced by Jan Timmer, former CEO of Phillips Electronics, illustrate why corporate cultures sometimes must be changed—and why change can be difficult. Taking over in 1990, Timmer reportedly eliminated 45,000 jobs, consolidated and sold off businesses, and put his firm on the offensive with innovative new consumer electronic products. Yet a recent drop in earnings and delays in launching new products made it clear that Europe's last big integrated electronics group wasn't changing fast enough. With all his cuts, Timmer's firm was reportedly slow moving and bureaucratic. Their digital compact cassette that should have been introduced in mid-1992 was months behind schedule and getting mixed reviews; partners were talking about abandoning Phillips' satellite-based television system in favor of another one (developed in the United States) that could send signals by cable as well as by satellite.

■ FIGURE 11.6 Do You Have the Right Corporate Culture for TQM?

SOURCE: "Total Quality Management: a Step-by-Step Guide to Making TQM Work for You," National Seminars brochure, 1992. As reproduced in Andrew J. DuBrin, *Leadership: Research Findings, Practice and Skills* (Boston: Houghton Mifflin Co., 1995), 312.

Do You Have the Right Corporate Culture for TQM?

Directions: To evaluate whether your company has a culture ideally suited to total quality, check whether the description in the left-hand or right-hand column best describes your firm. Confer with another person who works for the same employer to increase the accuracy of your ratings. If you are not currently working, speak to someone who is employed and evaluate his or her company. It would be helpful to interview more than one person from the same organization.

TQM Companies	*Traditional Companies*
_____ Driven by customer needs	_____ Driven by company wants
_____ Prevention of problems before they happen	_____ Detection of problems after the fact
_____ Nothing less than 100 percent will do	_____ Established maximum acceptable levels of error, waste
_____ Committed to quality at the source	_____ Belief that inspection is key to quality
_____ Cooperative, interdepartmental teams	_____ Autonomous, independent departments
_____ High employee participation— empowered workforce	_____ Top-down, management-directed workforce
_____ Long-term staying power a primary goal.	_____ Short-term profit a primary goal.

Interpretation: Seven check marks in the left-hand column would indicate that the firm you have evaluated is probably a world-class quality company. Seven check marks in the right-hand column suggest that the company you have evaluated might be at a competitive disadvantage in a quality-conscious economy. Check marks to the right can also be used as indicators of where organizational improvement is called for.

The bottom line seems to be that Timmer may not have made his company nimble enough fast enough. "You just can't change a deep-rooted corporate culture in one or two years," he says. "It takes at least five years or longer." After more than five years on the job, he ran out of time.[53]

When Cultures Must Be Changed

Leaders like Timmer have probably always had to grapple with the need for cultural change, but that need is even more urgent in today's chaotic times. In the United States, for instance, deregulation meant that airlines had to become lean and adaptive almost overnight. One of the distinguishing differences between successful firms (like American Airlines) and those that failed was probably the latter's inability to change their cultures fast enough. The highly politicized, antiunion, bureaucratic culture at Eastern Airlines contributed to the firm's demise.

Many things can force a firm to try to change its culture.[54] A crisis—such as deregulation or the introduction of an entirely new technology by a competitor—can force the firm's leaders to confront the need for cultural change. Turnover in top management provides the firm with another opportunity for new values and beliefs to be introduced. The firm's stage in its life cycle—whether growth, maturity, or decline—can also create the need for cultural change: Thus, the laid-back and somewhat crazy culture that defined Apple Computers during its formative years gradually gave way to a more formal, restricted, and hierarchical way of doing things as the computer business matured. Management needs to be cognizant of such events and then take steps to change the culture if the situation warrants.

Implementing Cultural Change

In our rapidly changing world, many companies have had to implement major cultural changes. They range from General Electric to Nissan, American Express, Bankers Trust, and British Airways.[55]

Two experts conclude that regardless of the industry, "the single most visible factor that distinguishes major cultural changes that succeed from those that failed was competent leadership at the top."[56] The competent leaders "knew how to produce change and were willing to do just that."[57] In each instance the leader

> created a team that established a new vision and set of strategies for achieving that vision. Each new leader succeeded in persuading important groups and individuals in the firm to commit themselves to that new direction and to energize the personnel sufficiently to make it happen, despite all obstacles. Ultimately, hundreds (or even thousands) of people helped to make all the changes in strategies, product structures, policies, personnel and (eventually) culture. But often, just one or two people seemed to have been essential in getting the process started.[58]

THE STEPS IN CULTURAL CHANGE. Implementing cultural change requires addressing the same management practices and activities that are involved with creating and sustaining corporate culture. Thus a logical first step is to publish a new formal core values statement and to publicize it widely, as Johnson & Johnson does with its credo. Leadership—influencing others to work willingly to achieve some goal, which in this case is to behave in a manner consistent with the desired culture and values—is crucial, too: The activities of Sam Walton provide a good example of how this is done. Beyond this, managers also use concrete planning, organizing, leading, and controlling to foster the culture they desire—such as selecting employees whose values are consistent with those desired by the firm and instituting incentive plans that reward behaviors (like teamwork) that the culture is designed to encourage. Signs, symbols, stories, rites, and ceremonies are used by the company's managers to emphasize the desirable new values and to encourage employees to adopt these values as their own.

Managing Change

CULTURAL CHANGE AT GENERAL ELECTRIC

The transformation of General Electric in the 1980s from "a sluggish, diverse set of businesses into a lean, cohesive market leader" is a good example of cultural change, one driven by the need to make the company more competitive.[59]

The chief strategist and transformational leader in this case was Chairperson John Welch, Jr. Welch spent the early 1980s downsizing the firm, a process that, for better or worse, left him with the nickname "Neutron Jack" (after the neutron bomb, which destroys the people but leaves the equipment and hardware standing). But Welch knew that downsizing wasn't enough—he had to change the company's culture and instill in employees the values that would foster change.

One of his first steps in establishing a new GE culture was to create a new GE values statement. Values to be stressed included teamwork, openness and candor of communications, passion for excellence, hatred of bureaucracy, trust, and being number one. Welch then turned to "living" each of these values by instituting management practices that epitomized them. He pushed authority down while fostering teamwork by promoting values like candor and trust. He instituted a training center in Crotonville, New York, that helps turn GE's managers into people who thrive on turmoil. He pushed hard to make GE managers "win-aholics," strong competitors who are driven to make their divisions number 1 or 2 in their industries.[60] He also instituted hundreds of "work-out" sessions aimed at supporting values like candor and openness throughout the firm.

The results have been dramatic. In 1996, GE had its best year ever, with revenues up 13% to $79.2 billion, and earnings up 11 percent to a record $7.3 billion.[61]

SUMMARY

1. Organizational culture may be defined as the characteristic traditions, norms, and values that employees share. Values are basic beliefs about what you should or shouldn't do, and what is and is not important.

2. There are several layers embodying a company's culture. In layer one are cultural artifacts, the obvious signs and symbols of corporate culture such as written rules and office layouts. Beneath this layer lie patterns of behavior, and underlying these are values and beliefs (such as "The customer is always right"). Finally, management's basic assumptions—for instance, about human nature—are at the core of a firm's culture.

3. A company's culture can be a force for good or ill. For example, P&G's strong corporate culture emphasizes quality, technical superiority, and thoroughness and has contributed to the company's success. On the other hand, Xerox's culture during the 1970s apparently emphasized politics and reportedly prevented the company from responding as effectively as it might have to competitive threats.

4. Several things contribute to creating and sustaining the corporate culture. One is a formal core values statement such as Johnson & Johnson's credo. Leaders also play a role in creating and sustaining culture, a process that often goes back to the firm's founders, who establish, in a sense, the firm's cultural beginnings. In any case, one of a leader's most important functions is to influence the culture and shared values of his or her organization, as Sam Walton did to create the Wal-Mart culture. Managers also use concrete planning, organizing, leading, and controlling management practices to foster the culture they desire. For example, training can be used to emphasize to employees the importance of teamwork and quality. Managers also use signs, symbols, stories, rites, and ceremonies to create and sustain their companies' cultures.

5. A company's culture can be an important force in helping managers manage change. For one thing, some values support responsiveness—such as

GE's emphasis on candor, openness, and interdepartmental communications. A strong culture can also aid responsiveness by enabling the firm to depend on employees' self-control: The shared values provide the guidelines that permit managers to decentralize more completely than they might otherwise.

6. Many things can force a firm to change its culture. For example, a dramatic crisis such as deregulation or the introduction of an entirely new technology by a competitor can force the firm's leaders to confront the need for cultural change. Many managers, like GE's Jack Welch, have successfully achieved cultural change. Doing so involves the same functions and activities that are always involved in creating and sustaining corporate culture: creating and publishing a core values statement; exercising leadership; engaging in planning, organizing, leading, and controlling management practices that foster the culture that is desired; and using signs, symbols, stories, rites, and ceremonies to clarify for all employees what the right values are.

KEY TERMS

organizational culture	signs	ceremonies
cultural artifacts	symbols	normative control
patterns of behavior	stories	total quality management
values and beliefs	rites	(TQM)

SELF-TEST

TRUE / FALSE QUESTIONS

1 T F Signs and behaviors within a corporate culture are outgrowths of its values and beliefs.

2 T F Procter & Gamble has a weak corporate culture.

3 T F A company's culture is basically value neutral, that is, it cannot be a force for good or for ill.

4 T F The successful organization adopts the value that performance is king and should be rewarded.

5 T F One of the keys to creating and sustaining a healthy corporate culture is to have middle management take the lead.

6 T F Leadership vision is the key to creating a corporate culture.

7 T F Managers use explicit planning, organizing, leading, and controlling management practices to support the culture they want.

8 T F A strong set of shared values helps managers guide behavior.

9 T F A key factor of TQM is to learn what customers want, not what management thinks they need.

10 T F Culture does not influence corporate strategies for change.

MULTIPLE-CHOICE QUESTIONS

1 Cultural _____ are the apparent signs and symbols of a corporate culture as found in written rules, organizational structure, and dress codes.
  a. artifacts
  b. relics
  c. red tape
  d. informal networks

2 Organizational _____ is defined as the characteristic traditions, norms, and values that employees share.

  a. mission
  b. opportunity
  c. culture
  d. none of the above

3 Management's _____ values and beliefs sometimes differ from what the managers _____ value and believe.
  a. desired; truly
  b. stated; really
  c. maintained; state they
  d. none of the above

4 _____ are guides to values that in turn influence behaviors.

   a. Assumptions
   b. Ideas
   c. Missions
   d. Thoughts

5 An important cultural factor at Procter & Gamble is _____ .

   a. communication
   b. people
   c. sales
   d. secrecy

6 Origins of unhealthy cultures include all but which of the following?

   a. turf fights
   b. politics
   c. concentration on stakeholders
   d. devotion to internal administration

7 There are ways of identifying a company's values. For example, when one adopts the value that "Cream belongs at the top," one is establishing _____ in management.

   a. reward
   b. power
   c. elitism
   d. effectiveness

8 Which among the following are specific steps for creating and sustaining a healthy corporate culture?

   a. publish a core values statement
   b. use signs and symbols
   c. exercise leadership
   d. all of the above

9 While mechanistic organizations rely on traditional systems like rules and procedures, responsive organizations depend more on _____ control.

   a. prescriptive
   b. empirical
   c. philosophical
   d. normative

10 TQM stands for

   a. total quality management
   b. total quantifiable management
   c. technical quality management
   d. total quality measures

CRITICAL THINKING EXERCISES

1 Why would companies open their financial books to their employees? Open book management would say that if each employee thinks like an owner then the company will more likely prosper. To do so the employees must have the financial information pertinent to managing the company. Others believe that it is not the business of employees to know the financials, that it can create more problems than it solves, and that it is management's prerogative to "own" the information and keep it secret. Whatever path management takes, quite different cultures may be created.[62]

Milton Lee, co-owner of Optics 1 Inc., an optical-engineering firm in Westlake Village, California, has 23 employees and close to $10 million in sales. Lee decided that the open book approach would help his highly educated employees understand how the company functions. But it did not quite work out that way. Although many employees have advanced degrees—even MBAs—Lee found they did not necessarily understand cash-flow management. This lack of sophistication about cash flow led to some unfortunate results, such as employees using the information against Lee or asking what was in it for them when he used profits to finance new product lines. Lee's conclusion was that if your employees misinterpret financial information, it's more damaging than their not having it.

Leslie Fishbein, president of Kacey Fine Furniture in Denver, has five retail stores, 170 employees, and over $30 million in revenues. At first she was reluctant to share financial data. But in the belief that it was better for employees to have more information, she adopted open book management, producing simplified versions of the financials and offering accounting classes. To motivate people, she tied learning about the financials to bonuses. For Fishbein, open book management has been a success.

Compare and contrast the cultures represented here. In which would you feel more comfortable and why? Could you give the firms some advice about their cultures based on the information given in this chapter? If so, what would it be?

2 Corporate culture is not new in our understanding of organizations, but our heightened awareness of its power may be. In groups of three to four, discuss, analyze, and critique the culture of your college or major department and the academic unit in which it is housed. Then compare your information with profiles of other majors on campus. Once you have gathered comparative materials, be prepared to discuss the differences you found and what they might mean.

EXPERIENTIAL EXERCISES

1 3M has long been known for its strong culture of teamwork, sharing of ideas, and innovation. 3M also values its people, and does not abandon employees when the going gets rough.

One 3M policy is to increase the research and development (R&D) budget and raise expectations of people's innovative capacities. 3M has a 30 percent new-products rule, meaning that 30% of 3M sales each year must come from new products. The results in one recent year were that

50 new products were identified and more than half were brought to market. 3M's culture also breeds almost fanatical loyalty and staying power. As one observer noted: "The Mafia gets more resignations than 3M."[63]

If you were a new employee of 3M, how would its culture affect you? Would you feel comfortable there or would you prefer a more individualistic organization? Why or why not? In teams of five to seven, compare your answers and then create an ideal organizational culture for your team based on your collective responses.

2 GSD&M, an advertising agency in Austin, Texas, understands that clients do not want advertising; they want to increase their market share. They want marketing effectiveness, measured by the attainment of specific, well-defined objectives.

GSD&M counts Wal-Mart stores and Southwest Airlines among its 22 clients and boasts a 90 percent client-retention rate. Part of its pitch is measurable goals. The physical manifestation of this culture of client centeredness is the War Room, the agency's command center where employees concentrate on a particular client. They often paint the room with the client's colors and set up red phones to and from the client's offices. All sorts of relevant materials, from earnings reports to weekly sales figures, are posted on the walls, with paraphernalia from the client's industry on the shelves. The War Room raises the intensity level of the project and gives the firm a mental edge. As GSD&M's president Roy Spence notes: "Clients see that we're 100% focused. And as we build their business, they build ours."

What would you experience if you worked in this intense environment? Would you manage culture as GSD&M does? How can the company maintain such intensity without burning everyone out? What might be some of the side effects of such a culture? What advice about culture and its impact on people would you give someone wishing to join this high-powered firm? After answering these questions, write a general description for what you see as the corporate culture at GSD&M.

DIVERSITY CASE

DYNAMIC DUO, FROM VIETNAM TO THE UNITED STATES

Finding gold today near the site of its first discovery almost 150 years ago are Trong Nguyen and Mai Pham, bakers and restaurateurs in Sacramento, California. Their story is like that of many immigrants and is a tale of determination, hard work, overcoming prejudice, and using their skills, knowledge, and ability to do what they do well. The company started with three employees and one small baker and now employs 375 people at 26 stores. Trong started A World of Good Taste Inc. with no business training, but he and Mai work daily in the stores, believing that no detail is too big or too small for them. Trong has done every job and believes that the dishwasher is just as important as the manager, and Mai helps out busy staff members during the lunch crunch. Both oversee all phases of construction during the building of a new store.

Questions

1. What diversity-based cultural barriers might have greeted these two immigrants from Vietnam?
2. What type of corporate culture do you think Trong and Mai created? What values do you think they espouse?
3. What internal barriers might there be to maintaining their corporate culture in their company?

SOURCE: Gilbert Chan, "Dynamic Duo," *Sacramento Bee,* 10 March 1997, 1, 16–7.

STRATEGY CASE

WHERE THERE'S SMOKE, MUST THERE BE FIRE?

The tobacco industry represents approximately 700,000 jobs and about $55 billion in gross domestic product in the United States alone. The world market for U.S.-made tobacco products is enormous. But the tobacco industry is under attack. Countless lawsuits are pending against every firm in the industry based on smokers' claims that smoking has damaged their health.

One of the most damaging events occurred in March 1997. The Liggett Group, smallest of the five leading tobacco producers, broke with the decades-long tradition of silence in the industry and admitted that smoking is addictive and that cigarettes contain cancer-causing chemicals. This admission set the stage for an accelerated war against the tobacco companies. Liggett's pledge to release a storehouse of internal documents was expected to provide damaging evidence in lawsuits still pending against other cigarette makers.

Not surprisingly, the other firms originally denounced the Liggett agreement and were able to block the release of the papers. However, victory was expected to be short lived if the Liggett documents already released showed that fraud had occurred.

The internal culture of the industry has always been a

stone wall of silence against any admission of the risks of tobacco smoking. Industry leader Philip Morris declared that the Liggett agreement "changes nothing. Philip Morris . . . will continue to defend vigorously against the meritless lawsuits filed by the states." Several months later Philip Morris joined other tobacco firms in signing their own agreement with the states.

Questions

I How would you describe the culture of the tobacco industry in general?

2 What do you think of Liggett's idea of breaking with the other companies?

3 What impact do you think the tobacco industry culture has had on the behavior of its employees as well as of other stakeholders?

4 How do you think the tobacco firms' cultures supported their strategies?

SOURCE: Sacramento Bee News Service Washington, "Tobacco Firm's Admission Sets Stage for Legal Battle," *Sacramento Bee,* 21 March 1997, A1, A24.

ENTREPRENEURIAL CASE

HERE COME THE CLOWNS!

Does the business of business always need to be serious, or can a laugh or two help build an entrepreneurial company? If you ask Robert Stillman, CEO of Cognex, he might go through a routine from the Three Stooges to make his point. A former professor at MIT, Shillman established Cognex 16 years ago with $100,000 of his life savings. The company's software systems monitor quality on assembly lines. With $131 million in sales, Cognex recently ranked No. 52 in a recent *Fortune* survey of the fastest growing U.S. companies. Shillman's philosophy is "Our antics break down barriers between managers and workers."

The CEO does a Three Stooges routine to welcome new employees, and he has dreamed up dozens of similar stunts to motivate his troops. He leads his workers, called "Cognoids," in the corporate anthem accompanied by an employee rock band. In one gig, he tossed moneybags with cash bonuses of up to $10,000 from a Brink's truck. In another, 15-year veterans were rewarded with trips to one of the world's seven wonders.

Questions

I What do you think is the key to Cognex's success?

2 Using concepts from this chapter, discuss the culture Shillman has created.

3 Suppose you were hired at Cognex. Evaluate whether or not you would like to work in this culture.

4 What do you think other companies might learn from Cognex?

SOURCE: *Fortune,* "Nyuck, Nyuck, Nyuck," 31 March 1997, 113.

THE BUSINESS TEAM, INC.

HELPING AMY'S ICE CREAM

The Business Team has been asked by an old friend from college days to help out with future strategies for Amy's Ice Cream, a seven-store chain of premium ice cream shops in Austin and Houston, Texas. Amy Miller is the owner, whose idea was to sell great products and provide superior service as a way of cutting a niche in the competitive world of premium ice cream. Amy decided that the qualitative approach would make the difference, so she made visiting her stores an "experience."

At Amy's you are likely to see employees performing, from juggling their serving spades to break-dancing on the freezer top. When the line is out the door on a Friday night, they may pass out free ice cream samples to anyone who will sing or dance or recite a poem or mimic a backyard animal. Their dress code is unique. If it's Sleep-Over-Night, the employees might wear pajamas.

To date, Amy has done well, but there is always urgency in the competitive marketplace to be out in front of the competitors. One of the questions for the Business Team is whether entertainment is enough of a difference for the stores to continue to be on the cutting edge.

Questions

I What would you recommend as techniques for maintaining the culture Amy has built?

2 If you wanted to change this culture, how would you go about it?

3 How do you think this type of culture affects both employees and customers?

4 How do you think each of the Team's production, marketing, finance, HR, and accounting experts will view Amy's approach?

SOURCE: John Case, "Corporate Culture." *Inc.,* November 1996, 42–4.

THE KNITMEDIA CULTURE

As befits a company that began as a small club showcasing avant-garde musicians on New York's lower East Side, Knit-Media has developed a culture all its own. Here are some snapshots of how Michael Dorf and his colleagues describe KnitMedia, which help provide a picture of what that culture is: "The Knitting Factory is primarily a showcase. Our aim is to weave strands of art mediums into a congruent whole, from the Wednesday night poetry series to the works on the walls. The Knitting Factory is also a café. It serves interesting forms of food, like a fondue with fresh fruit. The Knitting Factory considers many things art and is open to suggestions." "In Wisconsin we'd listened occasionally to John Coltrane, Thelonious Monk, and Elvis Costello, [but] now that I was in New York, though, I wanted to have as much of the Jack Kerouac smoky-jazz club experience as possible. Thus the need for 'Jazz on Thursdays.' " "But we always allow, we hope, for caprice, spontaneity and the un-expected . . . the secret is improvisation, and constant improvising." It is very interesting that the recording side of the Knitting Factory has come full circle—from the days of Flaming Pie records to Knitting Factory Works. Our ambition, however enlarged, is essentially the same—to try to get this unheard new music in front of an audience."

The problem for KnitMedia is that a culture becomes increasingly difficult to sustain as companies grow, as each employee becomes further removed from the visionary leader—in this case, Michael Dorf. The last thing a company like this wants is to begin developing an unhealthy, bureaucratic culture, although that's always a risk as more and more managers and employees are brought in.

Team Exercises and Questions

Use what you learned in this chapter to answer the following questions:

1 Write a short paper answer the question "What is KnitMedia's culture?" Make sure to specify the underlying values and assumptions, as well as any of the artifacts or other physical or procedural manifestations of that culture.

2 Do you see any need to change KnitMedia's culture? Why or why not? If so, what suggestions would you make for changing it?

3 Using the concepts and techniques explained in this chapter, how would you suggest that Michael Dorf ensure that KnitMedia's culture continues to provide the guidance for all employees that it has in the past?

For the online version of this case, visit our Web site at <www.prenhall.com/desslermgmt>.

For Internet exercises, interactive study questions, news updates and more, visit the Dessler Web site at

www.prenhall.com/desslermgmt

If you're using the CD-ROM that accompanies this text, simply click on the "Web Site" button to access the site.

CHAPTER 12

INFLUENCING INDIVIDUAL BEHAVIOR AND MOTIVATION

What's Ahead?

How do you motivate people to do a job that many would find objectionable? That was the question Jennifer Carter, newly appointed president of her father's chain of laundromats and dry cleaning stores, had to answer. All the employees in the stores—the managers, pressers, and cleaners—worked in excessively hot conditions doing monotonous jobs over and over again, often dealing with chemicals as hot as 150°F. "How can I motivate people under such abominable conditions?" Jennifer asks.

Objectives

After studying this chapter, you should be able to

- analyze **Jennifer's situation like a leader**
- understand **the role of personality, abilities, and perception in behavior**
- describe **three need-based approaches to motivating employees**
- explain **the role of equity, goal setting, and expectations in motivation**
- discuss **the behavior modification approach to motivation**
- explain **ten methods for influencing behavior and motivating employees.**

MANAGEMENT ON THE WEB

THE KEIRSEY TEMPERAMENT SORTER

Use the Keirsey Temperament Sorter site to develop a better understanding of your personality and how it shapes your behavior and satisfaction. Start with the *test*, then explore where their test results place you among the *four temperaments* and *sixteen types*. A *general explanation of the underlying logic of the test* and related *resource materials on personality typing* are also available. How might Jennifer Carter use this site? ∎

http://www.keirsey.com/cgi-bin/keirsey/newkts.cgi/

What Managers Should Know About Individual Behavior

Faced with a leadership situation like Jennifer's, managers have to think like leaders. Recall that this means being able to (1) identify the leadership-related things that are happening, (2) account for what is happening by bringing to bear knowledge of behavioral theory and concepts, and (3) formulate a leadership response to address the issues.

When it comes to identifying what is happening, accounting for what is happening, and formulating leader actions, no behavioral concepts and theories are as crucial as those relating to individual behavior and motivation. As you know from personal experience, for each of us the world revolves around who we are and what we want; any leader who ignores the individuality of his or her people and the needs and wants that drive them will have limited influence, to say the least.

Everyone Is Different

One of the paradoxes leaders face is that what motivates one person might not motivate another. Any stimulus—an order from the boss, an offer of a raise, or the threat of being fired—will have different effects on different people. One person might leap at the chance for a $100 raise, while another might shun it. One might emerge from training with excellent skills, while another will learn nothing. One might jump whenever the boss gives orders, while another will laughingly ignore them.

HOW PEOPLE DIFFER. To a large extent, these anomalies occur because of what psychologists call the **law of individual differences,** namely the fact that people differ in their personalities, abilities, values, and needs. As illustrated in Figure 12.1, these factors act much like filters, adding to, detracting from, and often distorting the effect of any stimulus. It is therefore important for managers to understand the nature of each of these factors.

Personality Influences Behavior

Personality is probably the first thing that comes to mind when most people think about what determines behavior. We tend to classify people as introverted, dominant, mature, or paranoid, for instance, and by and large these labels conjure up visions of particular kinds of behavior.

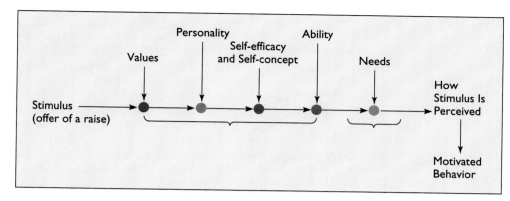

**■ FIGURE 12.1
Some Individual Determinants of Behavior**

A particular stimulus may evoke different behaviors among individuals, because each person's perceptions, personality, abilities, and needs will influence how he or she reacts to the stimulus.

PERSONALITY DEFINED.   One way to define **personality** is as "the characteristic and distinctive traits of an individual, and the way the traits interact to help or hinder the adjustment of the person to other people and situations." Psychologist Raymond Cattell used observations and questionnaires to identify sixteen primary personality traits,[1] which he then expressed in pairs of words, such as reserved/outgoing, submissive/dominant, and trusting/suspicious. Based on his work, Cattell and his colleagues developed a questionnaire that produced a personality profile for individuals. Figure 12.2 shows the average personality profiles for people in two sample occupational groups: airline pilots and business executives.

Traits do not just represent characteristics that people possess: People do not possess "submissiveness" or "sensitivity." Instead, they act and feel submissive or sensitive under most circumstances (although they may act in a dominant way in others). Thus, one way to define personality is in terms of traits, since traits will generally influence how someone will act in a given situation.

Recent studies of personality traits have tended to focus on the so-called big five traits: extroversion/introversion, emotional stability, agreeableness, conscientiousness, and openness to experience.[2] Extroverts tend to be outgoing and gregarious, whereas introverts are shy. Emotional stability reflects low levels of anxiety and insecurity. Agreeable people tend to be cooperative and flexible. Conscientiousness reflects behaviors such as thoroughness and dependability. Individuals open to experience tend to be imaginative and curious.[3] Having the right traits is also important for entrepreneurs, as the Entrepreneurs in Action box (page 397) illustrates.

PERSONALITY THEORIES.   Actually, defining personality in terms of traits is not the only option: Several theories aim to explain the basic components of personality and the way people's personalities develop. We can illustrate these by summarizing three theories: psychoanalytic, trait, and humanistic.

PSYCHOANALYTIC THEORY.   This theory is most closely associated with Sigmund Freud, the famed Austrian physician. In using hypnosis to treat his patients, Freud developed a theory of personality that placed a heavy emphasis on the role of sexual frustrations and the person's subconscious. Freud emphasized *psychic determinism,* namely, the idea that all thoughts, feelings, and actions are determined by events that happened to the individual in the past. He also emphasized *unconscious motivation,* which accounted for present thoughts and behaviors by linking them to thoughts and feelings buried deep in the person's unconscious mind.[4] In the unconscious, said Freud, are three basic building blocks of personality, which

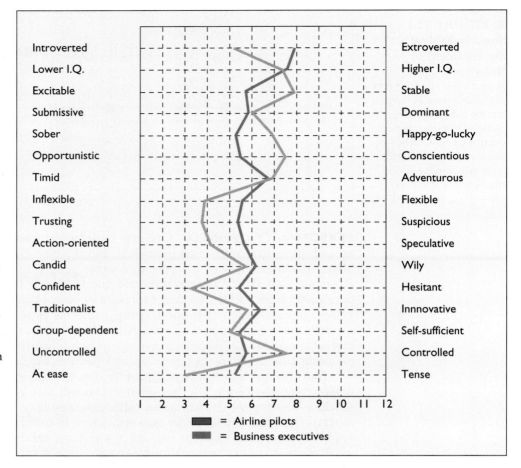

**FIGURE 12.2
Cattell's 16 Personality
Factors**

The personalities of various people and even various groups of people are characterized by particular packages of traits, such as introverted, dominant, excitable, and innovative.

SOURCE: Adapted from Gregory Northcraft and Margaret Neale, *Organizational Behavior* (Fort Worth, TX: The Dryden Press, 1994), 87.

together determine personality and behavior: the *id* works through the pleasure principle and drives the person to try to maximize immediate gratification by satisfying raw impulses. The *ego* works via the reality principle and basically tells the person, "You'd better be realistic before acting on that impulse: you can speed but you'll probably get caught." The *superego* is the ethical base of personality. It attempts to control the id, in part by creating feelings of guilt and anxiety.

TRAIT THEORIES. As mentioned earlier, psychologists like Raymond Cattell and Gordon Allport describe an individual's personality in terms of a unique set of personality traits. Trait theories hold that someone's traits are a function of both genetic factors and learning, and that, as we saw above, behavior reflects the person's traits—he or she is "extroverted," "agreeable," or "conscientious," for instance.

HUMANISTIC THEORIES. Humanistic psychologists like Abraham Maslow and Carl Rogers assume that people are motivated by the desire to fulfill the potential they see themselves as having. For example, Carl Rogers emphasized that what he called fulfillment—an inborn tendency driving people to "actualize" (realize) their inherent nature and attain their potential—is the main driving force in personality development. For Rogers, the notion of **self-concept**—the perceptions people have of themselves and of their relationships to people and other aspects of life—is crucial in determining who a person is and how he or she interacts with other people

Entrepreneurs in Action

THE PERSONALITY OF A PIRANHA

Machiavelli, the 16th century Italian management guru, used to say that "life is war," and never is that more true, perhaps, than when it comes to being an entrepreneur. Therefore, with many managers leaving the safe confines of corporate life to become entrepreneurs, it's important to keep in mind what one entrepreneur-watcher says: "Don't try it unless you've got the personality of a piranha."

Indeed, one recent story by the Hagberg Consulting Group outlines the behavioral traits of a typical entrepreneur, and that person does seem to be a breed apart. The research found that people who run their own businesses tend to be opinionated, focused, optimistic, aloof, aggressive, autonomous risk takers. In other words, there seems to be a bit of the piranha in most of them.

SOURCE: Justin Martin, "Take This Job and . . ." *Fortune,* 9 Dec. 1996, 216.

and other things, in other words, the person's personality. If something that happens to the individual is inconsistent with his or her self-concept, that person will either distort his or her perceptions to make them compatible with the self-concept, become very unhappy, or both. If Jane does not get the promotion she thinks she deserves, her tendency may be to explain the event in terms of her supervisor's ignorance or the promoted colleague's political activity, for instance.

PERSONALITY TYPES.   At work, you will of course come across many unique personalities, but the following two types are useful examples. The **authoritarian personality** has been studied for at least 50 years. Such a person is rigid, is intolerant of ambiguity, tends to stereotype people as automatically being good or bad, and conforms to the requirements of authority, perhaps while being dictatorial to subordinates. The **Machiavellian personality** (the name refers to the writings of the 16th-century political advisor Niccoló Machiavelli) tends to be oriented toward manipulation and control, with a low sensitivity to the needs of others.[5]

MEASURING PERSONALITY.   A test and scale known as the Myers-Briggs Type Indicator (MBTI) is one of the most popular tools for measuring personality, particularly in the work setting. The MBTI classifies people as extroverted or introverted (E or I), sensing or intuitive (S or N), thinking or feeling (T or F), and perceiving or judging (P or J). The person's answers to a questionnaire are classified into 16 different personality types (a 4 by 4 matrix); these 16 types are in turn classified into one of four cognitive (thinking or problem-solving) styles:

Sensation-thinking (ST)

Intuition-thinking (NT)

Sensation-feeling (SF)

Intuition-feeling (NF)

Classifying personality types and cognitive styles in this way has several applications at work. For example, some employers have found they can match the MBTI cognitive styles to particular occupations. This is illustrated in Figure 12.3. People with the sensation-thinking approach to problem solving are often well suited to occupations like auditor and safety engineer, for instance.

	Thinking Style	*Feeling Style*
Sensation Style	People with this combined thinking/sensation style tend to be *thorough, logical,* and *practical* and to make good *CPAs* or *safety engineers*.	People with this combined sensation/feeling style tend to be *conscientious* and *responsible* and to make *good social workers* and *drug supervisors*.
Intuitive Style	People with this combined intuitive/thinking style tend to be *creative, independent,* and *critical* and to make good *systems analysts, professors,* and *lawyers*.	People with this combined intuitive/feeling style tend to be *people-oriented, sociable,* and often *charismatic* and to make good *human resource managers, public relations directors,* and *politicians*.

■ **FIGURE 12.3**
Four Examples of MBTI Styles and Some Corresponding Occupations

Organizational Behavior in Action

DO YOU REALLY WANT TO SUCCEED?

Everyone probably does something that's self-defeating once in a while, but for some people such behavior is an ingrained part of their personality. For example, most people have probably procrastinated until a crucial deadline was past, or arrived inexcusably late for a crucial job interview. The question is, does that behavior occur so often that the person seems to be almost begging to fail?

In her book *The Success-Fearing Personality,* co-author Donnah Canavan says that Freud's personality theory helps to explain why some people actually seem to need to fail.[6] Freud believed that unresolved unconscious conflicts between parent and child would often leave the child with feelings of guilt and with a need to fail to make the guilty feelings go away.

Feeling a little guilty today? Perhaps you should take the following quiz.

The quiz is adapted from a questionnaire developed at Boston College (and published in *The Success-Fearing Personality,* by Donnah Canavan, Katherine Garner, and Peter Gumpert). The test isn't foolproof, but it should give you some idea of where you stand. If these statements apply to you, answer yes. Then figure your score as described below.

1. I generally feel guilty about my own happiness if a friend tells me that (s)he's depressed.
2. I frequently find myself not telling others about my good luck so they won't have to feel envious.
3. I have trouble saying no to people.
4. Before getting down to work on a project, I suddenly find a whole bunch of other things to take care of first.
5. I tend to believe that people who look out for themselves first are selfish.

6. When someone I know well succeeds at something, I usually feel that I've lost out in comparison.
7. I rarely have trouble concentrating on something for a long period of time.
8. When I have to ask others for their help I feel that I'm being bothersome.
9. I often compromise in situations to avoid conflict.
10. When I've made a decision, I usually stick to it.
11. I feel self-conscious when someone who "counts" compliments me.
12. When I'm involved in a competitive activity (sports, a game, work), I'm often so concerned with how well I'm doing that I don't enjoy the activity as much as I could.
13. A sure-fire way to end up disappointed is to want something too much.
14. Instead of wanting to celebrate, I feel let down after completing an important task or project.
15. Mostly, I find that I measure up to the standards that I set for myself.
16. When things seem to be going really well for me, I get uneasy that I'll do something to ruin it.

Scoring: Give yourself one point for every question to which you answered yes, except questions 7, 10, and 15. For each of those, subtract one point if you answered yes. Anything under 5 points means you're basically okay. Between 5 and 10 points, you're moderately at risk for self-sabotaging behavior. Between 10 and 16 points, you may have a problem that perhaps you should give some thought to. ■

Abilities Influence Behavior

Individual differences in abilities also influence how we behave and perform.[7] Even the most highly motivated person will not perform well—as a golfer, a company president, or a programmer—unless he or she also has the ability to do the job. Conversely, the most able employee will not perform satisfactorily if not motivated. Some experts summarize this interaction this way: Performance = Ability × Motivation.

There are many types of abilities. Mental abilities include intelligence and its building blocks, such as memory, inductive reasoning, and verbal comprehension. Mechanical ability would be important for mechanical engineers or machinists, who have to visualize how a particular piece of machinery works. Psychomotor abilities include dexterity, manipulative ability, eye-hand coordination, and motor ability: Such abilities might be important for employees who have to put together delicate computer components or who work as croupiers in Las Vegas. People also differ in their visual skills, for example, in their ability to discriminate between colors and between black and white detail (called visual acuity).

In addition to these general abilities that we all have, people also have specific abilities learned through training, experience, or education. We test for these abilities when we are interested in determining the candidate's proficiency on a job such as computer programmer, typist, or chemical engineer.

Self-Concept Influences Behavior

Although it's true that everyone is different, there is one way in which we are all the same: We all have our own self-concepts. As mentioned above, humanist psychologists like Carl Rogers emphasize the role of self-concept in personality. Specifically, who we are and how we behave is largely driven, say humanist psychologists, by the perceptions we have of who we are and how we relate to other people and other things. The very core of personality, say humanists, is to enhance the experiences of life through self-actualization, in other words, to strive to achieve our inborn potential and to become the people we believe we can become. Self-concept, in other words, is how we see ourselves, and how we see ourselves has a big influence on how we act and on how we react to the things that happen to us.

It's hard to underestimate the importance of self-concept in shaping the way we behave. Psychologist Saul Gellerman says that we all are driven in a constant quest to be ourselves or the kinds of individuals we think we should be. In other words,

> the ultimate motivation is to make the self-concept real: to live in a manner that is appropriate to one's preferred role, to be treated in a manner that corresponds to one's preferred rank, and to be rewarded in a manner that reflects one's estimate of [his or her] own abilities. Thus we are all in perpetual pursuit of whatever we regard as our deserved role, trying to make our subjective ideas about ourselves into objective truths.[8]

The next time you're in class or at work, stop and think about how you feel. Of all those people in the class, or in the company cafeteria, or in the office, around whom, more than anyone, does your world revolve, and who most occupies your thoughts? Would it bother you if your classmates or colleagues ignored you? How would you feel if you came to work every day and your boss or your boss's boss seemed to act as if you didn't exist, although you were knocking yourself out 10 hours a day for the company? As a manager or future manager, you should keep in mind that every person you meet views himself or herself as being as special as you view yourself to be; the leader who doesn't recognize and act on that fact will be hampered in dealing effectively with people.

Some people have rigid self-concepts and in response to new experiences are relatively unable to modify the way they view themselves.[9] Experiences that threaten such a person's self-concept will likely be screened out or distorted. Being turned down for promotion might be explained away in terms of politics or the supervisor's incompetence.

To some degree, everyone tries to protect his or her self-concept, and doing so is neither unnatural nor unhealthy, at least up to a point. However, most psychologists would probably agree that "people with healthy self-concepts can allow new experiences into their lives and can accept or reject them."[10] As these experts put it,

> Such people move in a positive direction. With each new experience, their self-concepts become stronger and more defined, and the goal of self-actualization is brought closer.[11]

In this view, *individual development* plays a major role in helping people fulfill their self-concepts. The person with a healthy (and, therefore, somewhat flexible) self-concept is on a voyage of discovery, as the fabric of his or her personality slowly evolves.

Self-Efficacy Influences Behavior

Closely related to self-concept is the idea that people differ in their **self-efficacy,** or their belief about their own capacity to perform a task.[12] For a leader, this individual difference is important because self-efficacy has a big effect on how people perform and even on whether they'll try to accomplish the task.

As a familiar example of self-efficacy, in *My Fair Lady* Professor Higgins convinces a ragged Eliza Doolittle that "she can do it"—and in short order she's speaking and acting like a proper upper-crust English person. However, you don't have to rely on movies for proof that self-efficacy works. Research shows that self-efficacy is associated with high work performance in a wide range of settings: life insurance sales, faculty research productivity, career choice, learning and achievement, and adaptability to new technology, to name a few.[13]

Perception Influences Behavior

The fact that we all differ in terms of things like personality and self-concept helps to explain why we perceive things differently. We all react to stimuli that reach us via our sense organs, but the way we define or perceive these stimuli depends on what we bring with us from past experiences and what our present needs and personalities are.[14] In other words, our behavior is motivated not just by stimuli; it is motivated by our *perceptions* of those stimuli, by the way our personalities and experiences cause us to interpret them. **Perception** is the unique way each person sees and interprets things.

You are probably familiar with the way perceptual distortion clouds our view of inanimate objects. Consider what happens when we try to match the sizes of near objects with those of far ones. When we look down a row of arches, as in the photo below, the farthest one usually looks smaller than the closest one, and its perspec-

Effect of Size Constancy on Perception

tive size is in fact smaller (because it is farthest away). Based on our experience, however, we know that the arches are actually equal in size, so what we *perceive* is a compromise between the perspective size of the arch and its actual size. In the photo, the nearest arch seems about twice the size of the farthest arch. But if you measure the arches you will see that it is actually more than four times the size of the farthest arch. Our desire to see objects as we expect them to be causes us to perceive less difference in height than there really is.

PERCEPTION AND PEOPLE.   Just as we read stable, specific characteristics into objects, we also read them into people. This process is called **stereotyping.** For example, some people tend to associate characteristics like industriousness and honesty with certain socioeconomic classes but not with others. Some managers erroneously assume that women are fit for certain jobs but not for others. Similarly, we tend to stereotype people according to age, sex, race, or national origin and to attribute the characteristics of this stereotype to everyone we meet who is of that age, sex, race, or national origin. In other words, we all learn to associate certain meanings with certain groups of people. This process helps us deduce more quickly (but not always accurately) the important characteristics of the people we meet and to avoid having to make fresh guesses every time.[15] Thus, a manager might jump to the conclusion that an older job candidate would not be as flexible as a younger worker.[16]

FACTORS THAT AFFECT PERCEPTION.   The way we see or perceive the world is influenced by many things. Some important influences are:

- *Personality and needs.* Our needs affect our perceptions. For example, when shown fuzzy and ambiguous pictures of objects, hungry people tend to see them as food whereas others do not. Tell an insecure employee that you want to see him in your office later in the day and he might spend the hours worrying about being fired, although you only wanted to discuss vacation schedules.
- *Self-efficacy and abilities.* Someone confident about doing a job might welcome an assignment, while someone who believes he or she will fail might be devastated by the same assignment. Our abilities influence our perceptions of our own success.
- *Values.* Perceptions are also influenced by values, the basic beliefs a person has about what he or she should or shouldn't do. For example, someone with a strong ethics code might be horrified at the suggestion of taking a bribe, whereas someone of lesser character might think, "That's not a bad idea."
- *Stress.* People who are under stress tend to perceive things less objectively than those who are not. In one experiment, a group of employment interviewers were put under pressure to hire more employees. They subsequently perceived candidates' qualifications as being much higher than did a group of interviewers who were not under pressure.
- *Experience.* Our perceptions are also influenced by our experiences. Based on our experiences, for example, we learn to associate certain groups with certain behaviors (in other words, we stereotype them). We then tend to expect everyone from that group to behave in the same fashion.
- *Position.* A person's position in the organization is another important factor. Production managers tend to see problems as production problems, while sales managers see them as sales problems, for instance.

■ *Attribution*. What people perceive is also strongly influenced by their **attributions,** or the meanings they give to actions. For example, suppose another car cuts you off as you drive to work. If you attribute the driver's actions to his temporarily losing control of his car, you may drive on without giving it further thought. If you attribute his actions to his intentionally cutting you off in anger, you may take evasive action to avoid further encounters with someone you now perceive as a hothead.

In summary, our behavior is prompted by our perceptions, not by "reality," and our perceptions, even of the same event, can be different, since our personalities, values, experiences, and needs will differ as well.[17]

Attitudes Influence Behavior

A person's attitudes can and often will influence his or her performance and behavior at work. An **attitude** is a predisposition to respond to objects, people, or events in either a positive or negative way.[18] When people say things like "I like my job" or "I don't care about my job," they are expressing attitudes, which are important because they can influence the way we behave on the job.

ATTITUDE SURVEYS. Because attitudes are important, many companies conduct periodic (and usually anonymous) attitude or opinion surveys of their workforces. IBM, for example, regularly asks employees their opinions about the company, its management, and their work life. The survey's stated purpose is "to aid management at all levels in identifying and solving problems."[19] An example of a typical attitude survey (not from IBM) is presented in Figure 12.4.

JOB SATISFACTION. **Job satisfaction** is probably the most familiar example of attitudes at work. Job satisfaction reflects an employee's attitude about his or her job; in practice, measuring it usually means measuring several specific aspects of the job. For example, one popular job satisfaction survey, the Job Descriptive Index, measures the following five aspects of job satisfaction:

1. *Pay*. How much pay is received and is it perceived as equitable?
2. *Job*. Are tasks interesting? Are opportunities provided for learning and for accepting responsibility?
3. *Promotional opportunities*. Are promotions and opportunities to advance available and fair?
4. *Supervisor*. Does the supervisor demonstrate interest in and concern about employees?
5. *Co-workers*. Are co-workers friendly, competent, and supportive?[20]

ATTITUDES AND PERFORMANCE. Good (or bad) attitudes do not necessarily translate into good (or bad) performance.[21] Performance can be constrained by many other factors, in which case attitudes might not matter at all. Engineers, for instance, may continue to do their best regardless of how they feel about their employer, because their performance is governed mostly by professional standards of conduct. Similarly, workers on a machine-paced assembly line may have so little discretion over the quantity or quality of what they do that their attitudes might not influence their performance.

This questionnaire is designed to help you give us your opinions quickly and easily. There are no "right" or "wrong" answers—it is your own, honest opinion that we want. Please do not sign your name.

DIRECTIONS:
Check ( ) one box for each statement to indicate whether you agree or disagree with it. If you cannot decide, mark the middle box.

EXAMPLE:

I would rather work in a large city than in a small town .... 2 ☐ 1 ☐ 0 ☐ (Agree ? Disagree)

1. The hours of work here are O.K. .... 2 ☐ 1 ☐ 0 ☐ (Agree ? Disagree)

2. I understand how my job relates to other jobs in my group .... 2 ☐ 1 ☐ 0 ☐ (Agree ? Disagree)

3. Working conditions in GI are better than in other companies .... 2 ☐ 1 ☐ 0 ☐ (Agree ? Disagree)

4. In my opinion, the pay here is lower than in other companies .... 2 ☐ 1 ☐ 0 ☐ (Agree ? Disagree)

5. I think GI is spending too much money in providing recreational programs............. 2 ☐ 1 ☐ 0 ☐ (Agree ? Disagree)

6. I understand what benefits are provided for Glers............. 2 ☐ 1 ☐ 0 ☐ (Agree ? Disagree)

7. The people I work with help each other when someone falls behind, or gets in a tight spot .... 2 ☐ 1 ☐ 0 ☐ (Agree ? Disagree)

8. My supervisor is too interested in her/his own success to care about the needs of other Glers.......................... 2 ☐ 1 ☐ 0 ☐ (Agree ? Disagree)

9. My supervisor is always breathing down our necks; he watches us too closely .... 2 ☐ 1 ☐ 0 ☐ (Agree ? Disagree)

10. My supervisor gives us credit and praise for work well done .... 2 ☐ 1 ☐ 0 ☐ (Agree ? Disagree)

11. I think badges should reflect rank as well as length of service .... 2 ☐ 1 ☐ 0 ☐ (Agree ? Disagree)

12. If I have a complaint to make, I feel free to talk to someone up-the-line .... 2 ☐ 1 ☐ 0 ☐ (Agree ? Disagree)

13. My supervisor sees that we are properly trained for our jobs .... 2 ☐ 1 ☐ 0 ☐ (Agree ? Disagree)

14. My supervisor sees that we have the things we need to do our jobs .... 2 ☐ 1 ☐ 0 ☐ (Agree ? Disagree)

15. Management is really trying to build the organization and make it successful........... 2 ☐ 1 ☐ 0 ☐ (Agree ? Disagree)

16. There is cooperation between my department and other departments we work with..... 2 ☐ 1 ☐ 0 ☐ (Agree ? Disagree)

17. I usually read most of Germox News .... 2 ☐ 1 ☐ 0 ☐ (Agree ? Disagree)

18. They encourage us to make suggestions for improvements here .... 2 ☐ 1 ☐ 0 ☐ (Agree ? Disagree)

19. I am often bothered by sudden speed-ups or unexpected slack periods in my work .... 2 ☐ 1 ☐ 0 ☐ (Agree ? Disagree)

20. Qualified Glers are usually overlooked when filling job openings .... 2 ☐ 1 ☐ 0 ☐ (Agree ? Disagree)

21. Compared with other Glers, we get very little attention from management .... 2 ☐ 1 ☐ 0 ☐ (Agree ? Disagree)

22. Sometimes I feel that my job counts for very little in GI................................. 2 ☐ 1 ☐ 0 ☐ (Agree ? Disagree)

23. The longer you work for GI the more you feel you belong................................. 2 ☐ 1 ☐ 0 ☐ (Agree ? Disagree)

24. I have a great deal of interest in GI and its future .... 2 ☐ 1 ☐ 0 ☐ (Agree ? Disagree)

25. I have little opportunity to use my abilities in GI............... 2 ☐ 1 ☐ 0 ☐ (Agree ? Disagree)

26. There are plenty of good jobs in GI for those who want to get ahead............... 2 ☐ 1 ☐ 0 ☐ (Agree ? Disagree)

27. I often feel worn out and tired on my job................... 2 ☐ 1 ☐ 0 ☐ (Agree ? Disagree)

(PLEASE CONTINUE ON REVERSE SIDE)

(continued)

■ FIGURE 12.4
Attitude Questionnaire of Germox Industries, Inc.

28. They expect too much work from us around here .... Agree 2 □ ? 1 □ Disagree 0 □

29. The company should provide more opportunities for employees to know each other ..... Agree 2 □ ? 1 □ Disagree 0 □

30. For my kind of job, working conditions are O.K. ..... Agree 2 □ ? 1 □ Disagree 0 □

31. I'm paid fairly compared with other Glers ..... Agree 2 □ ? 1 □ Disagree 0 □

32. Compared with other companies, GI benefits are good ..... Agree 2 □ ? 1 □ Disagree 0 □

33. A few people I work with think they run the place ..... Agree 2 □ ? 1 □ Disagree 0 □

34. The people I work with get along well together ..... Agree 2 □ ? 1 □ Disagree 0 □

35. My supervisor has always been fair in his/her dealings with me ..... Agree 2 □ ? 1 □ Disagree 0 □

36. My supervisor gets employees to work together as a team ..... Agree 2 □ ? 1 □ Disagree 0 □

37. I have confidence in the fairness and honesty of management ..... Agree 2 □ ? 1 □ Disagree 0 □

38. Management here is really interested in the welfare of Glers ..... Agree 2 □ ? 1 □ Disagree 0 □

39. Most of the higher-ups are friendly toward us ..... Agree 2 □ ? 1 □ Disagree 0 □

40. I work in a friendly environment ..... Agree 2 □ ? 1 □ Disagree 0 □

41. My supervisor lets us know what is expected of us ..... Agree 2 □ ? 1 □ Disagree 0 □

42. We don't receive enough information from top management ..... Agree 2 □ ? 1 □ Disagree 0 □

43. I know how my job fits in with other work in this organization ..... Agree 2 □ ? 1 □ Disagree 0 □

44. GI does a poor job of keeping us posted on the things we want to know about GI ..... Agree 2 □ ? 1 □ Disagree 0 □

45. I think GI informality is carried too far ..... Agree 2 □ ? 1 □ Disagree 0 □

46. You can get fired around here without much cause ..... Agree 2 □ ? 1 □ Disagree 0 □

47. I can be sure of my job as long as I do good work ..... Agree 2 □ ? 1 □ Disagree 0 □

48. I have plenty of freedom on the job to use my own judgment ..... Agree 2 □ ? 1 □ Disagree 0 □

49. My supervisor allows me reasonable leeway in making mistakes ..... Agree 2 □ ? 1 □ Disagree 0 □

50. I really feel part of this organization ..... Agree 2 □ ? 1 □ Disagree 0 □

51. The people who get promotions in GI usually deserve them ..... Agree 2 □ ? 1 □ Disagree 0 □

52. I can learn a great deal on my present job ..... Agree 2 □ ? 1 □ Disagree 0 □

53. My job is often dull and monotonous ..... Agree 2 □ ? 1 □ Disagree 0 □

54. There is too much pressure on my job ..... Agree 2 □ ? 1 □ Disagree 0 □

55. I am required to spend too much time on the job ..... Agree 2 □ ? 1 □ Disagree 0 □

56. I have the right equipment to do my work ..... Agree 2 □ ? 1 □ Disagree 0 □

57. My pay is enough to live on comfortably ..... Agree 2 □ ? 1 □ Disagree 0 □

58. I'm satisfied with the way employee benefits are handled here ..... Agree 2 □ ? 1 □ Disagree 0 □

59. I wish I had more opportunity to socialize with my associates ..... Agree 2 □ ? 1 □ Disagree 0 □

60. The people I work with are very friendly ..... Agree 2 □ ? 1 □ Disagree 0 □

61. My supervisor welcomes our ideas even when they differ from her/his own ..... Agree 2 □ ? 1 □ Disagree 0 □

62. My supervisor ought to be friendlier toward us ..... Agree 2 □ ? 1 □ Disagree 0 □

63. My supervisor lives up to his promises ..... Agree 2 □ ? 1 □ Disagree 0 □

64. We are kept well informed about GI's business prospects and standing with competitors ..... Agree 2 □ ? 1 □ Disagree 0 □

(PLEASE CONTINUE ON REVERSE SIDE)

(continued)

■ **FIGURE 12.4**
continued

65. Management ignores our suggestions and complaints........ Agree 2 □ ? 1 □ Disagree 0 □

66. My supervisor is not qualified for his/her job well........ Agree 2 □ ? 1 □ Disagree 0 □

67. My supervisor has the work well organized........ Agree 2 □ ? 1 □ Disagree 0 □

68. I have ample opportunity to see the end results of my work........ Agree 2 □ ? 1 □ Disagree 0 □

69. My supervisor has enough authority and backing to perform his job well........ Agree 2 □ ? 1 □ Disagree 0 □

70. I do not get enough instruction about how to do a job........ Agree 2 □ ? 1 □ Disagree 0 □

71. You can say what you think around here........ Agree 2 □ ? 1 □ Disagree 0 □

72. I know where I stand with my supervisor........ Agree 2 □ ? 1 □ Disagree 0 □

73. When terminations are necessary, they are handled fairly........ Agree 2 □ ? 1 □ Disagree 0 □

74. I am very much underpaid for the work I do........ Agree 2 □ ? 1 □ Disagree 0 □

75. I'm really doing something worthwhile in my job........ Agree 2 □ ? 1 □ Disagree 0 □

76. I'm proud to work for GI........ Agree 2 □ ? 1 □ Disagree 0 □

77. Many Glers I know would like to see the union get in........ Agree 2 □ ? 1 □ Disagree 0 □

78. I received fair treatment in my last performance review........ Agree 2 □ ? 1 □ Disagree 0 □

79. During the past six months I have seriously considered getting a job elsewhere........ Agree 2 □ ? 1 □ Disagree 0 □

80. GI's problem-solving procedure is adequate for handling our problems and complaints........ Agree 2 □ ? 1 □ Disagree 0 □

81. I would recommend employment at GI to my friends........ Agree 2 □ ? 1 □ Disagree 0 □

82. My supervisor did a good job in discussing my last performance review with me........ Agree 2 □ ? 1 □ Disagree 0 □

83. My pay is the most important source of satisfaction from my job........ Agree 2 □ ? 1 □ Disagree 0 □

84. Favoritism is a problem in my area........ Agree 2 □ ? 1 □ Disagree 0 □

85. I have very few complaints about our lunch facilities........ Agree 2 □ ? 1 □ Disagree 0 □

86. Most people I know in this community have a good opinion of GI........ Agree 2 □ ? 1 □ Disagree 0 □

87. I usually read most of my division newspaper........ Agree 2 □ ? 1 □ Disagree 0 □

88. I can usually get hold of my supervisor when I need her/him........ Agree 2 □ ? 1 □ Disagree 0 □

89. Most Glers are placed in jobs that make good use of their abilities........ Agree 2 □ ? 1 □ Disagree 0 □

90. I receive adequate training for my needs........ Agree 2 □ ? 1 □ Disagree 0 □

91. I've gone as far as I can in GI........ Agree 2 □ ? 1 □ Disagree 0 □

92. My job seems to be leading to the kind of future I want........ Agree 2 □ ? 1 □ Disagree 0 □

93. There is too much personal friction among people at my level in the company........ Agree 2 □ ? 1 □ Disagree 0 □

94. The amount of effort a person puts into his/her job is appreciated at GI........ Agree 2 □ ? 1 □ Disagree 0 □

95. Filling in this questionnaire is a good way to let management know what employees think........ Agree 2 □ ? 1 □ Disagree 0 □

96. I think some good will come out of filling in a questionnaire like this one........ Agree 2 □ ? 1 □ Disagree 0 □

97 | Please check one term which most nearly describes the kind of work you do: 1 □ Clerical or office   2 □ Production
3 □ Technical   4 □ Maintenance   5 □ Manufacturing   6 □ R & D   7 □ Engineering   8 □ Other

98 | 1 □ Hourly 2 □ Salaried | 99 | 1 □ Male 2 □ Female | 100 | Do you supervise 3 or more Glers? 1 □ Yes 2 □ No

Name of your department:

Please write any comments or suggestions you care to make in the space below.

■ **FIGURE 12.4**
continued

Organizational Behavior in Action

ATTITUDES AND PERFORMANCE

Although the relationship between someone's satisfaction and performance may not always be clear-cut, that doesn't mean job satisfaction isn't important. For example, dissatisfied employees tend to have worse attendance records.[22] Satisfaction may therefore have a cumulative influence on the organization's overall performance.

In one study a researcher from the University of Minnesota studied the relationship between (1) satisfaction and attitudes, and (2) overall organizational performance. The researcher collected performance data for 298 schools and employee satisfaction and attitude data from 13,808 teachers within these schools.[23] Organizational performance was measured in terms of student test scores in reading, mathematics, and social science, and in terms of student behavior such as dropout and attendance rates and percentage of discipline problems.

The researcher concluded that there were strong correlations between employee satisfaction and overall organizational effectiveness. Specifically, ". . . organizations with more satisfied employees tended to be more effective than organizations with less satisfied employees."[24] Therefore, concludes this researcher, even if the relationship between satisfaction and performance *on individual jobs* may tend to be weak, it appears that job satisfaction can have a marked effect on the organization's overall performance, for instance, by boosting overall attendance.[25] ■

Need-Based Approaches to Motivating Employees

We see examples of it all the time: Rocky, the prize fighter down for the count, sees his wife through bleary eyes and rises slowly from the mat, summoning energy from within himself that allows him to attack the challenger and win. During halftime, the lackluster football team is transformed by the coach into screaming, aggressive, and highly motivated players who go on to win the game.

Motivation can be defined as the intensity of a person's desire to engage in some activity. We know that employees can be motivated and that there are few more important leadership tasks than motivating subordinates. In the remainder of this chapter, we'll turn to the organizational behavior studies that help explain what motivates people, and to several specific methods you as a leader can use to motivate subordinates. Let us first, on the next few pages, look at three approaches that help explain what motivates people: need based, process based, and learning/reinforcement based. Each takes a different perspective in explaining how motivation occurs and how to motivate a person, and all are used by managers.

What Are Needs?

The defense attorney paced back and forth in front of the jury and asked, "Ladies and gentlemen, what possible motive would my client have for committing this crime?" That question is crucial: After all, if there is no motive, then why would he do it?

Motives and needs play a central role at work. A **motive** is something that incites the person to action or that sustains and gives direction to action.[26] When we ask why a defendant might have done what he did, or why a football player works to stay in shape all year, or why a sales manager flies all night to meet with a client, we are inquiring about motives.

A motive can be either aroused or unaroused. Everyone carries with him or her **motivational dispositions,** or needs, namely, motives that, like seeds in winter, go unaroused until the proper conditions bring them forth. You may have a motivational disposition to enjoy yourself at the movies, but that motive is dormant until Saturday night when you can put your studies aside. **Aroused motives** are motives that express themselves in behavior.[27] Thus when the conditions are right—when the studies are over and the quiz is done and the weekend has arrived—the movie-attendance motive is aroused and you may be off to your favorite flick.

Need-based approaches to motivating employees focus on the role of needs or motivational dispositions in driving people to do what they do. Which needs or motivational dispositions are most important? How and under what conditions do they become aroused and therefore translated into behavior? These are the sorts of questions studied by psychologists like Abraham Maslow, David McClelland, and Frederick Herzberg.

Maslow's Needs-Hierarchy Theory

Maslow's needs-hierarchy approach to motivation is typical of need-based approaches and is the basis for the others discussed in this section. Maslow proposed that people have five increasingly higher-level needs: physiological, safety, social, self-esteem, and self-actualization. According to Maslow's *prepotency process principle,* people become motivated to satisfy the lower-order needs and then, in sequence, each of the higher-order needs.[28] (Psychologist Clay Alderfer, in a variant of this theory, emphasizes that all the needs may be active to some degree at the same time.)

Maslow's hierarchy can be envisioned as a stepladder, as in Figure 12.5. The lower-level needs (once satisfied) become the foundations that trigger the potency of higher-order needs.[29]

PHYSIOLOGICAL NEEDS. People are born with certain physiological needs. These are the most basic needs, including the needs for food, drink, and shelter.

SAFETY NEEDS. Maslow says that when these physiological needs are reasonably satisfied—when a person is no longer thirsty and has enough to eat, for instance—then the safety needs become potent or aroused. In other words, if you are starving or in the middle of a desert with nothing to drink, the lower-level need for food or water will drive your behavior, and you might even risk your life and safety by pursuing that need. But once you have enough to eat or to drink, your personal safety, security, and protection motivate your behavior.

SOCIAL NEEDS. Once you feel reasonably secure and have had enough to eat and drink, social needs begin to drive your behavior, says Maslow. These are the needs people have for affiliation, for giving and receiving affection, and for friendship.

SELF-ESTEEM. At level four are the self-esteem needs. Psychologist Douglas McGregor says these include the following:

1. those needs that relate to one's self-esteem—needs for self-confidence, independence, achievement, competence, and knowledge

■ FIGURE 12.5
Maslow's Hierarchy
of Needs

SOURCE: *Fundamentals of Organizational Behavior* by Carrell/Jennings/Heavrin, © 1997. Reprinted by permission of Prentice-Hall, Inc., Upper Saddle River, NJ.

2. those needs that relate to one's reputation—needs for status, recognition, appreciation, and the deserved respect of others[30]

Like the social and safety needs, self-esteem needs only begin to motivate behavior when the lower-level needs have been fairly well satisfied, according to Maslow. But McGregor and other psychologists argue there is a big difference between self-esteem needs and lower-level physiological, safety, and social needs: Higher-level needs for things like self-respect and recognition are insatiable—we never get enough of such things. Lower-level needs are relatively easily satisfied.

SELF-ACTUALIZATION NEEDS. Finally, there is an ultimate need that only begins to dominate someone's behavior once all lower-level needs have been reasonably satisfied. This is the need for self-actualization or fulfillment, the need we all have to become the person we feel we have the potential for becoming. Self-actualization needs, as McGregor says, motivate us to realize our own potential, continue self-development, and be creative in the broadest sense of the word.

Herzberg's Two-Factor Approach to Motivation

Frederick Herzberg divides Maslow's hierarchy into a lower-level (physiological, safety, social) and a higher-level (ego, self-actualization) set of needs, and says the best way to motivate someone is to offer to satisfy the person's higher-level needs.

HYGIENES AND MOTIVATORS. Herzberg believes the factors (which he calls *hygienes*) that can satisfy lower-level needs are different from those (which he calls *motivators*) that can satisfy (or partially satisfy) a person's higher-level needs. He says that if hygiene factors (factors outside the job itself, such as working conditions, salary, and supervision) are inadequate, employees will become dissatisfied.

But—and this is extremely important—adding more of these hygiene factors (like salary) to the job is a very bad way to try to motivate someone, because lower level needs (such as physiological and security needs) are quickly satisfied. Next week or next month the employee is again dissatisfied, saying, in effect, "What have you done for me lately? I want another raise." Offering more hygienes is therefore an inefficient way to motivate employees.

On the other hand, says Herzberg, "job content" or "motivator" factors that are intrinsic to the work itself (like opportunities for achievement, recognition, responsibility, and more challenge) can motivate employees. They appeal to employees' higher-level needs for achievement and self-actualization. These are needs that are never completely satisfied and for which most people have an infinite craving. Thus, according to Herzberg, the best way to motivate employees is to build challenge and opportunities for achievement into their jobs. That way even the prospect of doing the job may motivate the employee, much as the thought of doing a favorite hobby may motivate you.

Needs for Affiliation, Power, and Achievement

David McClelland and John Atkinson agree with Herzberg that higher-level needs are most important at work. They have studied three needs they believe are especially important—the needs for affiliation, power, and achievement. To understand the nature of these needs, try the following exercise.

Take a quick look (just 10 to 15 seconds) at Figure 12.6. Now allow yourself up to five minutes to write a short essay about the picture, touching on the following questions:

1. What is happening? Who are the people?
2. What has led up to this situation? That is, what happened in the past?
3. What is being thought? What is wanted? By whom?
4. What will happen? What will be done?

■ **FIGURE 12.6**
What's Happening Here?

Source: David A. Kolb, Irwin M. Rubin, and James M. McIntyre, *Organizational Psychology: An Experiential Approach* (Englewood Cliffs, NJ: Prentice-Hall, 1971), p. 55.

Remember that the questions are only guides for your thinking, so don't just answer each one. Instead, make your story continuous and let your imagination roam, since no one is going to see your essay except you. Once you have finished writing, resume reading with the next paragraph.

The picture is one of a group of pictures making up a test called the Thematic Apperception Test that McClelland and his associates use to identify a person's needs. You will notice that the picture is intentionally ambiguous, so when you wrote your essay you were supposedly reading into the picture ideas that reflected your own needs and drives. McClelland has found that this test can be useful for identifying the level of a person's achievement, power, and affiliation needs.[31]

THE NEED FOR ACHIEVEMENT. People who are high in the need to achieve have a predisposition to strive for success. They are highly motivated to obtain the satisfaction that comes from accomplishing a challenging task or goal. They prefer tasks for which there is a reasonable chance for success and avoid those that are either too easy or too difficult. Such people prefer getting specific, timely criticism and feedback about their performance. People with a high need for achievement like situations in which they can take personal responsibility for finding solutions to problems, prefer to set moderate achievement goals and take calculated risks, and want concrete feedback on how well they are doing.

Achievement motivation is present in your essay when any one of the following three things occurs:

1. Someone in the story is concerned about a standard of excellence: for example, he wants to win or do well in a competition, or has self-imposed standards for a good performance. Standards of excellence can be inferred by the use of words such as *good* or *better* to evaluate performance.
2. Someone in the story is involved in a unique accomplishment, such as an invention or an artistic creation.
3. Someone in the story is involved in a long-term goal, such as having a specific career or being a success in life.

THE NEED FOR POWER. People with a strong need for power desire to influence others directly by making suggestions, giving their opinions and evaluations, and trying to talk others into things. They enjoy roles requiring persuasion, such as teaching and public speaking, as well as positions as leaders and clergymen. How exactly the need for power manifests itself depends on the person's other needs. Thus, a person with a high need for power but a low need for warm, supportive relationships might become dictatorial, while one with high needs for comradeship might become a clergyman or social worker.

Power motivation is present in your essay when any of the following three things occurs:

1. Someone in the story shows affection or is emotionally concerned about getting or maintaining control of the means of influencing a person. Wanting to win a point, to show dominance, to convince someone, or to gain a position of control—as well as wanting to avoid weakness or humiliation—are obvious examples.[32]
2. Someone is actually doing something to get or keep control of the means of influence, such as arguing, demanding or forcing, giving a command, trying to convince, or punishing.
3. Your story involves an interpersonal relationship that is culturally defined as one in which a superior has control of the means of influencing a subor-

dinate. For example, a boss is giving orders to a subordinate, or a parent is ordering a child to shape up.

NEED FOR AFFILIATION.   People with a strong need for affiliation are highly motivated to maintain strong, warm relationships with friends and relations. In group meetings they try to establish friendly relationships, often by being agreeable or giving emotional support.[33] Affiliation motivation is present in your essay when one of the following three things occurs:

1. Someone in the story is concerned about establishing, maintaining, or restoring a positive emotional relationship with another person. Friendship is the most basic example, such as when your story emphasizes that the individuals are friends. Other relationships, such as father-son, reflect affiliation motivation only if they have the warm, compassionate quality implied by the need for affiliation.
2. One person likes or wants to be liked by someone else, or someone has some similar feeling about another. Similarly, affiliation motivation is present if someone is expressing sorrow or grief about a broken relationship.
3. Affiliation motivation is also present if your essay mentions such affiliative activities as parties, reunions, visits, or relaxed small talk, as in a bull session. Friendly actions such as consoling or being concerned about the well-being or happiness of another person usually reflect a need for affiliation.

Remember that this exercise represents only one of several that constitute the Thematic Apperception Test, and it can therefore give you only the most tentative impressions about what your needs are. It should, however, give you a better understanding of what the needs for achievement, power, and affiliation are and how they manifest themselves.

Process Approaches to Motivating Employees

Process approaches to motivating employees explain motivation in terms of the decision-making process through which motivation takes place. Here we'll focus on the work of psychologists J. S. Adams, Edwin Locke, and Victor Vroom.

Adams's Equity Theory

Adams's **equity theory** assumes that people have a need for, and therefore value and seek, fairness at work.[34] People are strongly motivated to maintain a balance between what they perceive as their inputs or contributions, and their rewards. Equity theory states that if a person perceives an inequity, a tension or drive will develop in the person's mind, and the person will be motivated to reduce or eliminate the tension and perceived inequity.

On the whole, empirical findings regarding underpayment, at least, are consistent with Adams's theory. For example, people paid on a piece-rate basis, per item produced, typically boost quantity and reduce quality when they believe they are underpaid. Those paid a straight hourly rate tend to reduce both quantity and quality when they think they're underpaid. Unfortunately, overpayment inequity does not seem to have the positive effects on either quantity or quality that Adams's theory would predict for it.[35] (See Figure 12.7.)

According to equity the-
ory, how a person reacts
to under- or over-pay-
ment depends on whether
he or she is paid on a
piece-rate or salary basis.

	Employee thinks he or she is underpaid	Employee thinks he or she is overpaid
Piece-rate Basis	Quality down Quantity the same or up	Quantity the same or down Quality up
Salary Basis	Quantity or quality should go down	Quantity or quality should go up

Locke's Goal Theory of Motivation

The goal theory of motivation assumes that once someone decides to pursue a goal, the person regulates his or her behavior to try to ensure the goal is reached.[36] Locke and his colleagues contend that a person's goals provide the mechanism through which unsatisfied needs are translated into action.[37] In other words, unsatisfied needs prompt the person to seek ways to satisfy those needs; the person then formulates goals that prompt action.[38] For example: A person needs to self-actualize and wants to be an artist; to do so, she must go to college for a fine arts degree; she sets the goal of graduating from Columbia University's fine arts program; that goal (which is prompted by her need) then motivates her behavior.

Most of the research in this area has been conducted in laboratory settings, with undergraduates as subjects. Although such findings may not necessarily apply to industrial settings, they do tend to support Locke's basic theory. The most consistent finding here is that people who are assigned or who adopt difficult and specific goals outperform people who are simply told to "do their best."[39]

Such findings have recently been extended to field settings. Here the evidence suggests rather strongly that people who are given or who adopt specific and difficult goals tend to outperform people without such performance goals.[40]

Vroom's Expectancy Theory of Motivation

According to Victor Vroom, a person's motivation to exert a certain level of effort is a function of three things, expressed as follows: Motivation = E × I × V,[41] where

E represents the person's **expectancy** (in terms of probability) that his or her effort will lead to performance

I represents **instrumentality,** or the perceived relationship between successful performance and obtaining the reward

V represents **valence,** which represents the perceived value the person attaches to the reward.[42]

Research generally supports Vroom's theory, particularly in studies focusing on job choice. The results suggest that expectations, instrumentalities, and valence combine to influence a person's motivation to choose specific jobs.[43] Recent studies of the expectancy approach also provide moderate to strong support for its usefulness in explaining and predicting work motivation.[44] Note that Vroom makes no mention of needs or motives.

Learning/Reinforcement Approaches to Motivating Employees

Learning can be defined as a relatively permanent change in a person that occurs as a result of experience.[45] For example, we learn as children that being courteous is rewarded by our parents, and so we may be motivated to be courteous throughout our lives. There are several theories about how people learn. In this section we'll focus on what may be called learning/reinforcement approaches to motivating employees, namely, on how people's behavior is molded by the consequences or results of their actions.

Psychologist B. F. Skinner conducted many of the early studies in this area. Let's apply his theory to a simple example. Suppose you wanted to train your dog to roll over. How would you do it? In all likelihood, you would encourage the dog to roll over (perhaps by gently nudging it down and around) and then would reward it with some treat. Fairly quickly, no doubt, your dog would learn that if it wanted a treat it would have to roll over. Before you knew it, Fido would be rolling through your house.

In Skinner's theory, the dog's rolling over would be called **operant behavior,** because it *operates* on its environment, specifically by causing its owner to give it a treat. (So, who's training whom, you might ask!) In operant conditioning the main question is how to strengthen the association between the **contingent reward** (here the treat) and the operant behavior.[46]

Behavior Modification

The principles of operant conditioning are applied at work through behavior modification. **Behavior modification** means changing or modifying behavior through the use of contingent rewards or punishment. It is built on two principles: (1) behavior that appears to lead to a positive consequence (reward) tends to be repeated, whereas behavior that appears to lead to a negative consequence (punishment) tends not to be repeated; and (2) therefore, by providing the properly scheduled rewards, it is possible to get a person to learn to change his or her behavior.[47] There are two elements in behavior modification: the types of reinforcement (reward or punishment) and the schedules of reinforcement.

There are several types of reinforcement. **Positive reinforcement** is a reward, such as praise or a bonus, that is given when the desired behavior occurs. In **extinction,** reinforcement is withheld so that over time the undesired behavior disappears. Extinction is used when someone is inadvertently being rewarded for doing the wrong thing. For example, suppose your subordinate learns that arriving late invariably leads to a scolding by you, which in turn leads to laughter and congratulations from the worker's peers, who think your obvious annoyance is really quite funny. That laughter represents an inadvertent reward to the worker for arriving late. In extinction you would discipline that person in the privacy of your office, thereby removing the attention and the laughter—the reward—the worker gets from his or her friends.

Punishment is another type of reinforcement. For instance, you might reprimand or harass late employees. Punishment is the most controversial method of modifying behavior. Skinner recommends extinction rather than punishment for decreasing the frequency of the undesired behavior. Positive reinforcement is preferred.

The schedule you use to apply the positive reinforcement is important as well. For example, do you reward someone every time he or she does well, or only periodically? Here behavioral science findings suggest the following:

1. In general, the *fastest* way to get someone to learn is not to put him or her on a schedule at all. Instead, reinforce the desired behavior continuously, each and every time it occurs. The person learns quickly that doing the job is rewarded. The drawback is that the desired behavior also diminishes very quickly once you stop reinforcing it.
2. *Variable ratio* reinforcement is the most powerful at sustaining behavior. Here you reinforce the correct behavior not every time the person does the right thing, but every few times he or she does so, around some average number of times. With this schedule people will continue producing the desired behavior for a long time even without reinforcement, because they are always expecting to "hit the jackpot" on the next try.

Motivation in Action: 10 Methods for Influencing Behavior and Motivating Employees

Translating Theory into Practice

As a leader, you'll want to size up the leadership situation and (1) identify what is happening, (2) account for what is happening, and (3) formulate an action or response. Knowledge about things like perception, self-efficacy, self-concept, and the three approaches to motivating employees (need based, process based, and learnng/reinforcement) gives you tools for identifying what is happening and accounting for it. These behavioral tools can then also help you formulate an action or response, using one (or more) of the 10 motivation methods discussed in the next few pages.

One reason these motivation methods are widely used is the fact that they have strong foundations in OB and motivation theory and research. Table 12.1 presents these foundations. For example, *empowering employees* (column 7) is based in part on self-efficacy—namely, on the idea that people differ in their estimates of how they'll perform on a task. Therefore, building their skills and self-confidence by empowering them should bolster their self-efficacy and thus their motivation.

Using Pay for Performance to Motivate Employees

Pay for performance is probably the first thing that comes to mind when most people think about motivating employees. Pay for performance refers to any compensation method that ties pay to the quantity or quality of work the person produces. Piecework pay plans are probably the most familiar: Here earnings are tied directly to what the worker produces in the form of a "piece rate" for each unit he or she turns out. Thus, if Tom Smith gets 40 cents apiece for stamping out circuit boards, he would make $40.00 for stamping out 100 a day and $80.00 for stamping out 200. Sales commissions are another familiar example.

Piecework plans have a firm foundation in motivation theory. Vroom's expectancy approach describes motivation as depending on employees' seeing the link between performance and rewards, and pay for performance plans should emphasize precisely that. Similarly, behavior modification emphasizes that people will

■ TABLE 12.1 *The Motivational Underpinnings of 10 Motivation Methods*

FOUNDATIONS OF BEHAVIOR AND MOTIVATION	Pay for Performance	Merit Raises	
Self-Concept: People seek to fulfill their potential.			
Self-Efficacy: People differ in their estimates of how they'll perform on a task; self-efficacy influences effort.			
Maslow Needs Hierarchy: High level needs are never totally satisfied and aren't aroused until lower level needs are satisfied.		X	
Alderfer: All needs may be active, to some degree, at same time.		X	
McClelland Ach, Pow, Aff: Needs for achievement, power, affiliation are especially important in work setting.			
Herzberg Dual Factor: Extrinsic factors just prevent dissatisfaction; intrinsic factors motivate workers.			
Vroom Expectancy Approach: Motivation is a function of expectancy that effort leads to performance, performance leads to reward, and reward is valued.	X	X	
Locke Goal Setting: People are motivated to achieve goals they consciously set.			
Adams's Equity Theory: People are motivated to maintain balance between their perceived inputs and outputs.		X	
Reinforcement: People will continue behavior that is rewarded and cease behavior that is punished.	X	X	

SOURCE: Copyright © 1997 by Gary Dessler, Ph.D.

continue behavior that is rewarded, and pay for performance plans, of course, tie rewards directly to behavior.

New pay for performance plans are becoming popular. **Variable pay plans,** for example, are essentially plans that put some portion of the employee's pay at risk, subject to the firm's meeting its financial goals. In one such plan at the DuPont Company, employees could voluntarily place up to 6 percent of their base pay at risk.[48] If they then met the department's earnings projections, they would get that 6 percent back plus additional percentages, depending on how much the department exceeded its earnings projections.

Other companies have gainsharing plans, incentive plans that engage many or all employees in a common effort to achieve a company's productivity goals.[49] Implementing a gainsharing plan requires several steps. Specific performance measures, such as cost per unit produced, are chosen, as is a funding formula, such as "47 percent of savings go to employees." Management thus decides how to divide and distribute cost savings between the employees and the company, and among employees themselves. If employees are then able to achieve cost savings in line with their performance goals, they share in the resulting gains.

Pay for performance plans of all types—including those that let employees share in profits by paying them with shares of company stock—are becoming more

MOTIVATION METHODS

Spot Rewards	Skill-Based Pay	Recognition Awards	Job Redesign	Empower Employees	Goal Setting	Positive Reinforcement	Lifelong Learning
	X	X	X	X			X
	X			X			X
X		X	X	X			X
X		X	X	X			X
	X	X	X	X			X
			X	X			X
X		X			X		
				X	X		
X		X					
X		X				X	

popular because they make sense. As Maggie Hughes, President of LifeUSA Holding Inc. of Minneapolis, puts it:

> I find it amusing, frustrating, and, often quite appalling, how few business leaders recognize that people should share in the economic value they create. At LifeUSA, our employees have options on 2 million shares of company stock. It seems like common sense to us. So why is it still so uncommon in most companies?[50]

IMPLEMENTING SUCCESSFUL PAY FOR PERFORMANCE PLANS. Not all pay for performance plans succeed. However, the following five suggestions make success more likely, given what we've discussed about motivation.

1. *Ensure that effort and rewards are directly related.* Your incentive plan should reward employees in direct proportion to their increased productivity. Employees must also perceive that they can actually do the tasks required. Thus the standard has to be attainable and you have to provide the necessary tools, equipment, and training.[51]
2. *Make the plan understandable and easily calculable by the employees.* Employees should be able to calculate easily the rewards they will receive for various levels of effort.

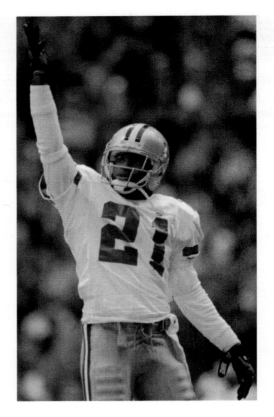

In a well-publicized case of perceived pay inequity, star defensive back Deion Sanders left the San Francisco 49ers, who paid him $1 million a year, for the Dallas Cowboys and their offer of $5 million.

3. *Set effective standards.* The standards should be viewed as fair by your subordinates. They should be high but reasonable; there should be about a fifty-fifty chance of success. The goal should also be specific; this is much more effective than telling someone to "do your best."

4. *Guarantee your standards.* View the standard as a contract with your employees. Once the plan is operational use great caution before decreasing the size of the incentive in any way.[52]

5. *Guarantee a base rate.* It's often advisable to give employees a safety net by providing them with a base rate pay. They'll know that no matter what happens, they can at least earn a minimum guaranteed base rate.[53]

Organizational Behavior in Action

THE MOTHER OF ALL BONUSES

When it comes to pay for performance plans, the recent bonuses at Kingston Technology must qualify for some sort of record. Kingston is the world's largest supplier of add-on memory boards for personal computers and is run by founders John Tu and David Sun.

Their bonus plan is fairly simple: Employees receive, overall, 10 percent of the company's profits. What was a little unusual in 1996, though, is that Japanese conglomerate Softbank Corporation bought Kingston for about $1 billion. And, true to their words, Tu and Sun (who will continue managing Kingston) decided to bestow 10 percent of that—about $100 million—as bonuses to their 523 employees. Some employees got bonuses of up to $300,000, depending on their seniority and individual performance.

It's interesting to note that at Kingston, the bonus plan is just one part of a broader effort to make the company feel more like a family. Blurred lines between jobs give employees freedom to do what they think needs doing, all employees share in free lunches on Friday, and financial seminars were organized to help show employees how to invest their windfalls, for example.[54]   ■

Using Merit Pay to Motivate Employees

Most employees, when they do a good job, expect to be rewarded with at least a merit raise at the end of the year. A merit raise is a salary increase—usually permanent—that is based on the employee's individual performance. It is different from a bonus in that it represents a continuing increment, whereas the bonus represents a one-time payment. Gradually, however, traditional merit raises are being replaced by lump-sum merit raises, which are merit raises awarded in one lump sum that do not become part of the employee's continuing pay.[55]

To the extent that it is actually tied to performance, the prospect of the merit raise may focus the employee's attention on the link between performance and rewards, in line with the expectancy approach to motivation. If it is equitably distributed (which means, among other things, that performance must be evaluated fairly and accurately), a merit raise can enable employees to see the link between their perceived inputs and outputs, in line with Adams's equity approach to motivation.

However, relying too heavily on merit raises for rewards is a bit dangerous. A year is a long time to wait for a reward, so the reinforcement benefits of merit pay are somewhat suspect. You may also have personally experienced the questionable nature of some performance appraisal systems, including the fact that some supervisors take the easy way out and rate everyone's performance about the same, regardless of actual effort. Such problems can undermine the motivational basis for the merit plan and render it useless.[56]

Using Spot Awards to Motivate Employees

As its name implies, a spot award is a financial award given to an employee literally "on the spot" as soon as the laudable performance is observed. Programs like this have actually been around for some time. For example, Thomas J. Watson, Sr., founder of IBM, reportedly wrote checks on the spot to employees doing an outstanding job.[57]

Such cash awards are used increasingly today. Federal Express's Bravo-Zulu voucher program is an example. This program was established to give managers the ability to provide immediate rewards to employees for outstanding performance above and beyond the normal requirements of the job. (Bravo-Zulu is a title borrowed from the U.S. Navy's semaphore signal for "well done.") Bravo-Zulu vouchers average about $50 and may be in the form of a check or some other form of reward, such as dinner vouchers or theater tickets. It's estimated that more than 150,000 times a year a Federal Express manager presents an employee with one of these awards.[58]

Other companies use spot cash incentive awards as well. For example, Victor Kiam, president of Remington Products (who liked Remington shavers so much that "I bought the company"), maintains a $25,000 discretionary fund to give instant cash awards to workers spotted by their supervisors doing an exceptional job. Kiam invites these people to his office and awards them checks ranging from $200 to $500.[59] The Veterans Administration regional office in Philadelphia has managers give $25 on the spot to workers they believe go beyond the call of duty.[60]

Spot rewards like these have a sound basis in what we know about motivation. For example, to the extent that the rewards are both contingent on good performance and awarded immediately, they are certainly consistent with equity theory, the expectancy approach, reinforcing desired behavior, and providing the recognition most people desire.

Using Skill-Based Pay to Motivate Employees

You are probably aware of the fact that in most companies pay is determined by the level of the job's responsibilities. Thus, presidents generally make more than vice presidents, sales managers make more than assistant sales managers, and secretary IVs make more than secretary IIIs, because higher-level jobs are meant to have more responsibility.

Skill-based pay is different in that you are paid for the range, depth, and types of skills and knowledge you are capable of using, rather than for the job you currently hold.[61] The difference is important: It is conceivable that in a company with a skill-based pay plan the secretary III could be paid more per hour than the secretary IV, for instance, if it turns out that the person who happened to be the secretary III had more skills than did the person in the secretary IV job.

A skill-based pay plan was implemented at a General Mills manufacturing facility.[62] In this case, General Mills was trying to boost the flexibility of its factory workforce by implementing a pay plan that would encourage all employees to develop a wider range of skills; in turn, that wider range of skills would make it easier for employees to take over whatever job needed to be done in the plant as the plant's needs changed.

In this plant, therefore, the workers were paid based on their attained skill levels. For each of the several types of jobs in the plant, workers could attain three levels of skill: limited ability (ability to perform simple tasks without direction); partial proficiency (ability to apply more advanced principles on the job); and full competence (ability to analyze and solve problems associated with that job). After starting a job, workers were tested periodically to see whether they had earned certification at the next higher skill level. If so, they received higher pay even though they had the same job: In other words, higher-skilled workers on the same job received higher pay. Workers could then switch to other jobs in the plant, again starting at skill level one and working their way up if they so desired. In this way the workers could earn more pay for more skills (particularly as they became skilled at a variety of jobs), and the company ended up with a more highly skilled and therefore more flexible workforce.

Skill-based pay makes sense in terms of what we know about motivation. People have a vision—a self-concept—of who they can be, and they seek to fulfill their potential. The individual development that is part and parcel of skill-based pay helps employees do exactly that. Skill-based pay also appeals to an employee's sense of self-efficacy in that the reward is a formal and concrete recognition that the person can do the more challenging job and do it well.

FROM HIGH SCHOOL TO $40,000 STARTING SALARY

Our knowledge-based society rewards education. What if you're not motivated to go on to college or can't afford to go? Do you work at McDonald's, deliver pizzas, or clerk at a retail outlet? Many graduates of Rowand High School in Southern California, about 25 miles south of Hollywood's animation epicenter, have another choice. This high school, conventional in all other respects, is home to an innovative training program that has become the fourth-largest supplier of talent to the thriving animation industry. Approximately 50 recent graduates now work for Disney studios, 30 work at Warner Bros., and many others are working at smaller animation studios. It is skill-based development at work.

The entry-level salaries for animator trainees are around $40,000, with scheduled skill-based increases quickly bringing annual pay to upward of $80,000. In the first year of the program, students begin with simple exercises. By their senior year they have their own portfolio, required for job hunting. But students' reputations are so good that the studios come looking for them.

There are also personal links to the studios. Instructor Dave Masters recently left the high school to take over as head animation trainer for Warner Bros. The move led to a teleconferencing link between the high school and Warner's internal training department. While there is some technological support like 3-D systems, the school's key is creativity. As the program's director, Larry Kurnarsky, says: "We've created a place where creativity is nurtured and rewarded. This is not about technology . . . it's about giving the kids the freedom to create and to grow. So much of education just pushes kids down, shuts them off, and closes them out."[63] ∎

Using Recognition to Motivate Employees

Most people like to feel appreciated. In one study, conducted by the Minnesota Department of Natural Resources, respondents said they highly valued day-to-day recognition from their supervisors, peers, and team members; over two thirds said it was important to believe their work was appreciated by others.[64] If you've ever spent half a day cooking a meal for someone who gobbled it up without saying a word about how it tasted, or two weeks doing a report for a boss who didn't even say "Thanks," let alone "Good job," you know how important having your work recognized and appreciated can be.

Being recognized for a job well done—and not necessarily just financially—makes a lot of sense in terms of motivation theory. Immediate recognition can be a powerful reinforcer, for instance, and can provide some immediate outcomes to counterbalance the employees' inputs or efforts. Recognition also underscores the performance-reward-expectancy link, and it helps appeal to and satisfy the need people have to achieve and be recognized for their achievement.

Many companies therefore formalize the commonsense process of saying "Thank you for a job well done." For example, Xerox Corporation gives what it calls bell ringer awards: When an employee is recognized, a bell is rung in the corridor while the person is formally recognized by his or her boss.[65] At Busch Gardens in

Tampa, Florida, the company reportedly gives a "pat on the back"[66] award to employees who do an outstanding job, embodied by a notice of the award in the employee's file. At Metro Motors in Montclair, California, the name of the employee of the month goes up on the electronic billboard over the dealership.[67] Bell Atlantic names cellular telephone sites after top employees.[68]

Using Job Redesign to Motivate Employees

Highly specialized, short-cycle, assembly-line jobs have long had a bad reputation among psychologists. Professor Chris Argyris, for instance, wrote that as people mature into adults they normally move from a position of dependence and narrow interests to one of independence and broad interests and that specialized jobs fly in the face of individual development.[69] In fact, the negative impact of monotonous work has been substantiated. Participants in one recent study were 1,278 blue-collar workers in Israel.[70] The researchers concluded from their study that (1) perceived monotony was moderately related to the objective work conditions, (2) some employees perceived even the same job as more monotonous than did other employees, (3) job satisfaction and psychological distress were related to perceived monotony, and (4) sickness absence was equally related to work conditions and to perceived monotony.

In the face of problems like these, many employers set up programs aimed at redesigning their workers' jobs. **Job design** refers to the number and nature of activities in a job; the basic issue in job design is whether jobs should be more specialized or, at the other extreme, more "enriched" and nonroutine.

JOB ENLARGEMENT AND JOB ROTATION. Initial attempts at job redesign centered on job enlargement and job rotation. **Job enlargement** assigns workers additional same-level tasks to increase the number of tasks they have to perform. For example, if the work is assembling chairs, the worker who previously only bolted the seat to the legs might take on the additional tasks of assembling the legs and attaching the back. **Job rotation** systematically moves workers from job to job. Thus, on an auto assembly line, a worker might spend an hour fitting doors, the next hour installing head lamps, the next hour fitting bumpers, and so on.

Evidence regarding the effects of programs like these is somewhat contradictory. In one study the newly enlarged jobs initially led to improved job satisfaction, reduced boredom, and improved customer satisfaction (because one employee followed the customer's paperwork more or less from beginning to end).[71] However, in a follow-up study two years later, employee satisfaction had leveled off and boredom was on the rise again, suggesting that the motivational value of this technique may be short lived.[72]

JOB ENRICHMENT. Other psychologists, including Frederick Herzberg (recall his two-factor approach to motivating employees), contend that having several boring jobs to do instead of one is not what employees want. Psychologists like Herzberg, Maslow, and Alderfer believe that what employees want from their jobs is a sense of achievement from completing a challenging task successfully and the recognition that comes from using their skills and potential.

Job enrichment is the method Herzberg recommends for applying his two-factor approach to motivation. **Job enrichment** means building motivators like opportunities for achievement into the job by making it more interesting and challenging. This is often accomplished by vertically loading the job, which means giving the worker more autonomy and allowing the person to do much of the planning and inspection normally done by the person's supervisor.

Job enrichment can be accomplished in several ways:[73]

1. *Form natural work groups.* Change the job in such a way that each person is responsible for or "owns" an identifiable body of work. For example, instead of having the typist in a typing pool do work for all departments, make the work of one or two departments the continuing responsibility of each typist.

2. *Combine tasks.* Let one person assemble a product from start to finish, instead of having it go through several separate operations that are performed by different people. Combining tasks in this way is also often called job enlargement.

3. *Establish client relationships.* Let the worker have contact as often as possible with the client of that person's work. For example, let an assistant research and respond to customers' requests, instead of automatically referring all problems to his or her boss.

4. *Vertically load the job.* Have the worker plan and control his or her job, rather than letting it be controlled by others. For example, let the worker set a schedule, do his or her own troubleshooting, and decide when to start and stop working.

5. *Open feedback channels.* Finally, find more and better ways for the worker to get quick feedback on his or her performance.

Under what conditions would a leader want to consider implementing a job enrichment program? To find the answer, says one group of researchers, carefully diagnose the leadership situation, specifically addressing the following questions:[74]

1. Is motivation central to the problem? Or is there some other problem (a poorly designed flow of work in the office, for instance)?

2. Is *the job* low in motivating potential? Is the job the source of the motivation problem identified in step 1? Or, for instance, is it the fact that pay is unusually low, or that several members of the work group continually argue against working harder?

3. What specific aspects of the job are causing the difficulty, if it is the job? Here, consider inadequacies in the following core job dimensions:
   —skill variety: to what degree does the job require the worker to perform activities that challenge his or her skills and abilities?
   —task identity: to what degree does the job require completion of a whole, an identifiable piece of work?
   —task significance: to what degree does the job have a substantial and perceptible effect on the lives of other people in the organization or the world at large?
   —autonomy: to what degree does the job give the worker freedom and independence?
   —knowledge of results: to what degree does the worker get information about the effectiveness of his or her job efforts?

4. How ready are the employees for change? Not all workers will prefer enriched jobs, and in any case some may not be ready to assume more responsibility. It may be futile to proceed with the change if the employees themselves will vigorously resist it.

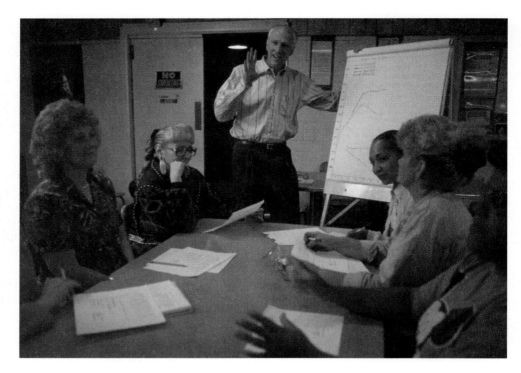

All jobs at Cin-Made are enriched when boss Bob Frey (standing) discusses the company's profit projections with employees. Frey operates under a philosophy of "open-book management," which assumes that if all employees act and think like business people, the company will benefit. In order to do that, employees need the actual financial data Frey provides.

Research results suggest that under the right conditions enrichment programs can be effective, particularly if implemented in association with other changes such as increasing pay in line with the increased levels of responsibilities.[75]

Using Empowerment to Motivate Employees

Empowering employees is a popular phrase today and means giving employees the authority, tools, and information they need to do their jobs with greater autonomy, as well as the self-confidence required to perform the new jobs effectively. Empowering is inherently a motivational approach: It boosts employees' feelings of self-efficacy and enables them to more fully use their potential, satisfying higher-level needs for achievement, recognition, and self-actualization. Figure 12.8 below lists 10 principles for empowering people, including "Tell people what their responsibilities are," and "Give them authority equal to the responsibilities assigned to them." Today, it's often work teams that are empowered.

■ **FIGURE 12.8**
Ten Principles for Empowering People

SOURCE: Diane Tracey, *10 Steps to Empowerment* (New York, William Morrow, 1990), 163. Copyright © 1990 by Diane Tracey. By permission of William Morrow & Co., Inc.

1. Tell people what their responsibilities are.
2. Give them authority equal to the responsibilities assigned to them.
3. Set standards of excellence.
4. Provide them with training that will enable them to meet the standards.
5. Give them knowledge and information.
6. Provide them with feedback on their performance.
7. Recognize them for their achievements.
8. Trust them.
9. Give them permission to fail.
10. Treat them with dignity and respect.

Organizational Behavior in Action

EMPOWERMENT IN PRACTICE

■ **FIGURE 12.9**
Sampling of Saturn Work Team Functions
As you can see from this sampling of the duties, Saturn work teams are empowered. Each unit is responsible for and trained to make many of the decisions formerly made by managers.

SOURCE: Reprinted with permission from *Saturn Work Team Functions,* a company training document.

At Saturn Corporation, for instance, empowered, self-managing work teams are responsible for a variety of duties, as you can see in Figure 12.9. For each team, these duties include resolving its own conflicts, planning its own work schedule, determining its own job assignments, making selection decisions about new members, performing within its own budget, and obtaining its own supplies.

But empowering doesn't just mean assigning broad responsibilities. The teams also get the training, skills, and tools to empower them to do their jobs, such as in consensus decision making. Firms like Saturn also make sure their managers actually let their people do their jobs as assigned.

Not all empowerment programs are so comprehensive. At Scandinavian Air Systems (SAS), for instance, empowering the workforce meant letting employees make more decisions themselves. Thus, ticket agents now have the authority to reticket a

---

Each Saturn team will:

1. Use consensus decision-making: No formal leader [will be] apparent in the process. . . . All members of the work unit who reach consensus must be at least 70% comfortable with the decision, and 100% committed to its implementation.

3. Make their own job assignments: A work unit . . . ensures safe, effective, efficient, and equal distribution of the work unit tasks to all its members.

5. Plan their own work: The work unit assigns timely resources for the accomplishment of its purpose to its customers while meeting the needs of the people within the work unit.

6. Design their own jobs: This should provide the optimum balance between people and technology and include the effective use of manpower, ergonomics, machine utilization, quality, cost, job task analysis, and continuous improvement.

8. Control their own material and inventory: Work directly in a coordinated manner with suppliers, partners, customers, and indirect/product material resource team members to develop and maintain necessary work unit inventory.

9. Perform their own equipment maintenance: Perform those tasks that can be defined as safe, and those they have the expertise, ability, and knowledge to perform effectively.

13. Make selection decisions of new members into the work unit: A work unit operating in a steady state has responsibility for determining total manpower requirements, and selection and movement of qualified new members from a candidate pool will be in accordance with the established Saturn selection process.

14. Constantly seek improvement in quality, cost, and the work environment: The work unit is responsible for involving all work unit members in improving quality, cost, and the work environment in concert with Saturn's quality system.

18. Determine their own methods: The work unit is responsible for designing the jobs of its team members consistent with the requirements of the Saturn production system and comprehending the necessary resources and work breakdown required.

21. Provide their own absentee replacements: The work unit is responsible for the attendance of its members. . . . The work unit will be required to plan for and provide its own absentee coverage.

22. Perform their own repairs: The work unit will have the ultimate responsibility for producing a world-class product that meets the needs and requirements of the customer. In the event a job leaves the work unit with a known or unknown non-conformance to specification, the originating work unit will be accountable for corrective action and repair.

---

passenger or even move the passenger up a class, if they feel the situation warrants it. At one Marriott chain subsidiary, each and every hotel employee, from management to maintenance, is empowered to offer guests a free night's stay if, in the employee's opinion, the hotel has been lax in serving the guest. And at engine maker Pratt & Whitney, salespeople can now authorize multimillion dollar repairs on the spot, instead of having to wait for approvals from up the line. In virtually all such cases, employees find empowerment exciting, while employers find it helps workers to self-actualize and exhibit self-efficacy, and thereby boost motivation and employee commitment.[76]

Using Goal-Setting Methods to Motivate Employees

Have you ever set your sights on some goal—acing a course, graduating from college, or earning enough money for a trip abroad, for instance? What effect did setting the goal have on you? If you're like most people, it proved highly motivating: As Edwin Locke and his associates (discussed earlier) have shown time and again, people are strongly motivated to achieve goals they consciously set. Setting specific goals with employees can be one of the simplest yet most powerful ways of motivating them.

The research on how to set goals that motivate employees is voluminous. Indeed, we discussed much of it in chapter 5 in the context of goal setting for the purpose of planning. Here's a summary.

- *Be clear and specific.* Employees who are given specific goals usually perform better than those who are not.
- *Make goals measurable and verifiable.* Whenever possible, goals should be stated in quantitative terms and should include target dates or deadlines for accomplishment.
- *Make goals challenging but realistic.* According to researcher Gary Yukl, goals should be challenging but not so difficult that they appear impossible or unrealistic.
- *Set goals participatively.* Recall that participatively set goals usually lead to higher performance. The fact that such goals tend to be more difficult seems to account for the higher performance, not that they were participatively set.[77]

Using Positive Reinforcement to Motivate Employees

Positive reinforcement programs (sometimes called behavior management or performance management programs) are widely used. They rely on operant conditioning principles (discussed earlier) to use positive reinforcement to change behavior.

As summarized in Figure 12.10, modifying behavior with reinforcement is much like balancing a scale. Let's say that wearing a safety helmet is the desired behavior and not wearing it is the undesired behavior. One way to increase the desired behavior (wearing the hat) is to add a positive consequence, for instance, by praising the worker each time he or she wears the hat. Another way to do so is to remove the negative consequences of wearing the hat, for instance, by lowering the temperature to cool the plant or by making the hat less cumbersome.

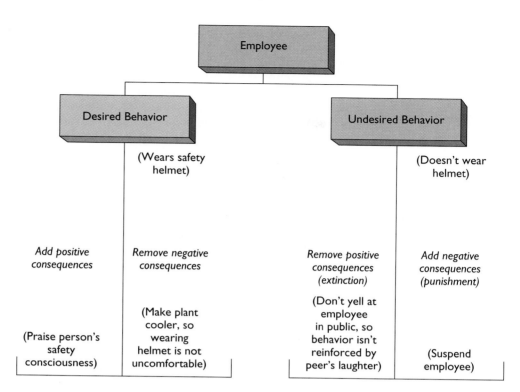

FIGURE 12.10
Options for Modifying Behavior with Reinforcement

Most positive reinforcement/behavior management experts say it's best to focus on improving desirable behaviors rather than on decreasing undesirable ones. If the employee regularly comes in late for work, stress improving the desired behavior (coming to work punctually) rather than reducing the undesirable behavior (coming to work late).

TYPES OF CONSEQUENCES. Obviously you needn't use just tangible rewards in these types of programs. *Social consequences* include peer approval, praise from the boss, letters of thanks from the company president, and a celebratory lunch. *Intrinsic consequences* include such intangibles as the enjoyment the person gets from engaging in a hobby and the sense of achievement from accomplishing a challenging task. *Tangible consequences* include outcomes like bonuses, incentive pay, and merit raises.

Organizational Behavior in Action

BEHAVIOR MODIFICATION PROGRAMS AT WORK

Many employers have implemented positive reinforcement programs, and they have been used successfully in a multitude of applications. Probably the best known application in industry was implemented a number of years ago at Emery Air Freight Company.[78] The program grew out of management's discovery that the containers used to consolidate air freight shipments were not being fully utilized. In the air freight business, small shipments intended for the same destination fly at lower rates when shipped together in containers rather than separately. In this case, the workers used containers only about 45 percent of the time, while they reportedly *thought* they were using them about 90 percent of the time. Management wanted them to boost the actual usage rate to 90 to 95 percent.

A behavior management program was implemented. Included was an elaborate instruction workbook for managers that detailed how to use recognition, rewards, feedback, and various other types of social, intrinsic, and tangible consequences. It enumerated no less than 150 kinds of reinforcement, ranging from a smile to detailed praise like "You're running consistently at 98 percent of standard, and after watching you I can understand why." Intrinsic feedback was used too; for example, the consultants set up a checklist for a dock worker to mark each time he or she used a container. The results of this container usage program were impressive. In 80 percent of the offices in which it was implemented, container usage rose from 45 percent to 95 percent in a single day.

As another example, a positive reinforcement/behavior management program was used to improve worker safety in two departments in a food manufacturing plant.[79] The plant was considered a prime candidate for a safety improvement program: there had been a dramatic increase in the injury rate and a corresponding rise in workers' compensation premiums during the year preceding the study.

After analyzing the safety situation, the consultants recommended several steps, including a formal training program, the use of safety posters, and a behavior management program. For each department, the researchers compiled a list of specific safe practices they could look for when they periodically observed the employees, and discussed these with the employees. Some of these included "When picking up pans from the conveyor belt, no more than two pans are picked up prior to placing the pans on the pan rack" and "When moving conveyor, at least one person is on each end." The researchers then spent several weeks walking through the plant, carefully noting the percentage of safely performed incidents they observed on a graph that all employees could see. Workers could then compare their current safety performance with their previous performance and with a goal the researchers assigned to them. Supervisors recognized workers when they performed the incidents safely; for example, each supervisor was told to comment specifically when he or she saw an employee performing safely.

Safety in the plant subsequently increased markedly. Employees in the two departments improved their safety performance (in terms of percentage of incidents performed safely) from 70 percent to 96 percent in one department and from 78 percent to 99 percent in the other. ∎

Using Lifelong Learning to Motivate Employees

Many employers today face a tremendous dilemma. On the one hand, remaining competitive requires highly committed employees who exercise self-discipline and basically do their jobs as if they owned the company. On the other hand, competitive pressures have forced many companies to continually downsize; this in turn causes employees to question whether it pays for them to work their hearts out for the company.

Lifelong learning is one method increasingly used to address both these issues simultaneously. **Lifelong learning** provides extensive continuing training, from basic remedial skills to advanced decision-making techniques, throughout the employees' careers.

Strategy in Action

LIFELONG LEARNING SUPPORTS A STRATEGY

For example, although the oil industry is constantly changing, Chevron USA has survived by dramatically downsizing. But rather than let trained and talented people go, top management thought of another approach: reeducate and redeploy Chevron's human resources where the jobs were. At Chevron, lifelong learning was thus used to support the firm's strategy of boosting productivity.

Many of the company's bright, qualified employees were in the wrong departments: Some units had too many people, others had too few. The solution was to give employees the opportunity to be trained to take jobs outside their own specialties or in other Chevron companies. Houston-based Chevron Production Co. came up with the idea to mix and match employees from one unit to another. In production operations, many employees are petroleum engineers with college degrees. Chevron's refineries traditionally recruit chemical engineers. So with some training and assistance, the petroleum engineers could fill in.

To implement this plan for the total firm, all companies within Chevron were designated either supply (needed to cut employees) or demand (needed staff). Within every operating company, there were redeployment coordinators identified to help those who wanted to make the change. There were initial concerns: How far would employees try to stretch in order to jump into an entirely new job? Would surplus employees be low performers who supply companies just wanted to get rid of?

Overall the plan has worked very well. Of those who entered the redeployment and relearning program, about 80 percent found work within the companies. The program has saved the company approximately $25 million in severance costs alone and has earned praise from the Department of Labor. Chevron has remotivated an already skilled workforce and changed it into a reskilled, revitalized one, highly motivated by the recognition that they are valued by the firm.[80]

THE BENEFITS OF LIFELONG LEARNING. Implemented properly, lifelong learning programs can achieve three things. *First,* the training and education provide employees with the decision-making and other skills they need to competently carry out the demanding, team-based jobs that increasingly predominate, even on the factory floor. *Second,* the opportunity for lifelong learning is inherently motivational: It enables employees to develop and to see an enhanced possibility of fulfilling their potential; it boosts employees' sense of self-efficacy; and it provides an enhanced opportunity for the employee to self-actualize and gain the sense of achievement that psychologists like Maslow, Alderfer, McClelland, and Herzberg correctly argue is so important. *Third,* although lifelong learning may not cancel out the potential negative effects of downsizing, it might at least counterbalance them to some degree by giving the employee useful and marketable new skills.

AN EXAMPLE. For example, one Canadian Honeywell manufacturing plant in Canada called its lifelong learning program the Honeywell-Scarborough Learning for Life Initiative.[81] It was "a concerted effort to upgrade skill and education levels so that employees can meet workplace challenges with confidence." This lifelong learning program had several components. It began with adult basic education. Here the company, in partnership with the employees' union, offered courses in English as a Second Language, basic literacy, numeracy, and computer literacy.

Next the factory formed a partnership with a local community college. Through that partnership all factory employees—hourly, professional, and managerial—have the opportunity to earn college diplomas and certificates. Included is a 15-hour "skills for success" program designed to refresh adults in the study habits required to succeed academically. All courses take place at the factory after work.

Finally, job training is provided for two hours every other week. These sessions focus on developing skills specifically important to the job, "such as the principles of just-in-time inventory systems, team effectiveness, interpersonal communication skills, conflict resolution, problem solving and dealing with a diverse work force."[82]

It's never easy to evaluate the success of a program like this because not all employees choose to participate, and many other factors will affect factory productivity and employee motivation. However, the evidence suggests that programs like these improve commitment, skills, and motivation, and possibly productivity too.[83]

SUMMARY

1. In sizing up any leadership situation, it's crucial that the leader keep individual differences in mind, since people differ in their personalities, abilities, self-efficacy, values, and needs.

2. Personality may be defined as the characteristic and distinctive traits of an individual and the way the traits interact to help or hinder the adjustment of the person to other people and situations. Psychoanalytic theory, trait theory, and humanistic theory are three theories of how personalities develop.

3. Individual differences in abilities also influence the way we behave and perform. Abilities in which people differ include mental, mechanical, psychomotor, and job-specific abilities.

4. Who we are and how we behave are largely driven by the perceptions we have of who we are and how we relate to other people and other things—in other words, by our self-concepts. Individual development plays a major role in helping people to self-actualize, that is, to fulfill their self-concepts.

5. People also differ in their self-efficacy, namely, in their estimates of their capacity to orchestrate performance on a specific task. Boosting a person's self-efficacy can improve motivation.

6. People's behavior is prompted by their perceptions, not by "reality." Perceptions, even of the same event, may be different among different people because their personalities, values, experiences, and needs differ as well.

7. An attitude is a predisposition to respond to objects, people, or events in either a positive or a negative way. Job satisfaction is probably the most familiar example of attitudes at work; it describes attitudes about five aspects of the job, including pay, the job itself, promotional opportunities, the supervisor, and co-workers.

8. Motivation can be defined as the intensity of the person's desire to engage in some activity. Need-based approaches to motivating employees—such as those of Maslow, Herzberg, and McClelland—emphasize the role played by motivational dispositions or needs such as the need for achievement and for self-actualization.

9. An employee's thought process will also influence his or her motivation, and we discussed three theories here. People want to be treated equitably. Having decided to pursue a goal, they will regulate their behavior to try to ensure the goal is reached. Their expectations—that effort will lead to performance, that performance will lead to the reward, and that the reward is valuable enough to pursue in the first place—also influence motivation.

10. Behavior modification means changing or modifying behavior through the use of contingent rewards or punishment. It assumes, for instance, that behavior that appears to lead to a positive consequence or reward tends to be repeated, whereas behavior that leads to a negative consequence or punishment tends not to be repeated.

11. Methods based on motivational approaches like Maslow's theory and behavior modification include pay for performance, spot awards, merit pay, recognition awards, job redesign, empowerment, goal setting, positive reinforcement, and lifelong learning.

KEY TERMS

law of individual
   differences
personality
psychoanalytic theory
trait theories
humanistic theories
self-concept
authoritarian personality
Machiavellian personality
self-efficacy
perception
stereotyping
attributions

attitude
job satisfaction
motivation
motive
motivational dispositions
aroused motives
equity theory
expectancy
instrumentality
valence
learning
operant behavior
contingent reward

behavior modification
positive reinforcement
extinction
punishment
pay for performance
variable pay plans
job design
job enlargement
job rotation
job enrichment
empowering
lifelong learning

SELF-TEST

TRUE / FALSE QUESTIONS

1 **T** **F** Everyone is motivated by one thing—money.

2 **T** **F** The characteristic and distinctive traits of an individual are called personality.

3 **T** **F** Trait theories assume that all people are motivated by a desire to fulfill their potential.

4 **T** **F** The Murdo-Barnes Test Inventory is one of the most popular tools for measuring personality, especially in a work setting.

5 **T** **F** Motivation equals ability × performance.

6 **T** **F** Our behavior is motivated by our perception of stimuli.

7 **T** **F** Stress is an influence on how we see the world.

8 **T** **F** Motivation is defined as the intensity of the person's desire to engage in some activity.

9 **T** **F** Herzberg's two-factor approach claims that working conditions can be a major motivator.

10 **T** **F** The principles of behavior modification are built on the assumption that the use of positive or negative contingent rewards can cause a person to change behavior.

MULTIPLE-CHOICE QUESTIONS

1 There are three personality theories. Which of these is *not* one of them?
- **a.** psychoanalytic
- **b.** behavioral
- **c.** trait
- **d.** humanistic

2 In Freud's theory there are three basic building blocks of personality. Identify the term *not* included.
- **a.** id
- **b.** ego
- **c.** od
- **d.** superego

3 The _____ personality tends to be oriented toward manipulation and control.
- **a.** McClelland
- **b.** Burkian
- **c.** Allportian
- **d.** Machiavellian

4 To fulfill one's self-concept is to _____.
- **a.** self-actualize
- **b.** materialize
- **c.** conceptualize
- **d.** re-actualize

5 Reading specific, stable characteristics into people is called _____.
- **a.** intuition
- **b.** mind reading
- **c.** perception
- **d.** stereotyping

6 Our behavior is prompted by our _____, not by reality.
- **a.** perceptions
- **b.** ideas
- **c.** sight
- **d.** ego

7 Under Herzberg's two-factor approach, motivation comes from factors _____ to the work itself, such as recognition.
- **a.** external
- **b.** intrinsic
- **c.** beyond
- **d.** none of the above

8 Victor Vroom's expectancy theory of motivation is based on the formula: Motivation = E × I × V. The I stands for _____ and the V stands for _____.
- **a.** innovation; victory
- **b.** inventory; valence
- **c.** instrumentality; valence
- **d.** instrumentality; value

9 A successful pay plan includes which of these directives?
- **a.** Ensure that efforts and rewards are directly related.
- **b.** Pay everyone the same.
- **c.** Use only 360 degree performance appraisals.
- **d.** Guarantee annual pay raises connected to the CPI.

10 If you believe that workers will be motivated by challenging tasks and the recognition that comes from using their skills and potentialities, you will use job _____.
- **a.** enlargement
- **b.** rotation
- **c.** enrichment
- **d.** magnifying

CRITICAL THINKING EXERCISES

1 Are men and women motivated by the same things in the workplace? Are African-American women motivated by the same things that Korean-American men are? Are those who embrace the Muslim religion motivated in the same way that Protestants are? Do CEOs of large corporations want the same rewards as Michael Jordan and Jackie Joyner-Kersey? What do you think and why? How do the theories presented in this chapter influence your answer?

2 It is said the baby boomers (born 1946–1964) "live to work" and that Generation Xers (1965–1981) "work to live." What are the challenges in motivating the two groups? What if they are working on teams together? What job design challenges might you encounter as the team manager?

EXPERIENTIAL EXERCISES

1 Interview four or five friends, workmates, or fellow students about what motivates them. Record their responses. Then match the responses with the theories in the chapter and be prepared to discuss in class what you find.

2 Read the business pages of your local newspaper for a week. Also read the sports pages for the same period. Then compare and contrast examples of motivation. Do you find a difference? How would you describe the differences? Construct a one-page explanation of your findings to share in class.

DIVERSITY CASE

THE HOPPERS AND THEIR INSPIRATIONAL MATRON SAINT

The late Rear Admiral Grace Murray Hopper spent her 43-year career in the Navy, earning recognition as a computer pioneer who contributed to the creation and acceptance of high-level computer languages and assisting in developing the Mark I, the first large-scale digital computer. Hopper coined the term "bug" to describe mysterious program malfunctions after a two-inch moth fouled up one of the Mark I's circuits.

In 1990, the women engineers at Microsoft adopted Hopper as their icon and formed a group in her name. The "Hoppers" help their members advance in a number of ways.

They hold discussions and study groups on a variety of technical subjects, identify emerging Microsoft technologies, school Microsoft women on the realities of performance appraisal, and counsel them on sexual harassment. Some meetings are face to face, but much of the group's business is conducted on-line.

Although the group started out as a gathering of disaffected women, in six years it has evolved to become a virtual partner with management.

Questions

1 How would you characterize the source of Hopper's motivation?
2 How can an icon motivate others?
3 Do you think motivation has been different for the women of Microsoft since they organized?
4 Do you think most companies would encourage groups like the Hoppers to form?

SOURCE: "The Matron Saint," *Fast Company,* June/July 1996, 91.

STRATEGY CASE

"BE KIND, BE HONEST, HAVE FUN"

Doug Greene is founder and CEO of New Hope Communications. Greene believes that there are three principles for relating to people: "Be kind, be kind, be kind." However, the employees found that they were not being authentic when they were being kind, so they changed it to "Be kind, be honest, be kind." Because Greene wanted them to emphasize the joy of business, they changed it to "Be kind, be honest, have fun."

If his employees are not being effective or having fun, Greene encourages them to be aware of this so that he and other managers don't have to find this out too late. At the beginning of employment, each recruit at New Hope is therefore encouraged to consider quitting. Greene says, "We tell people, 'We want you to quit. We want you to leave this company. We are hiring you, but we don't want you to stay forever. If someone wants you to stay forever, run as fast as you can in the other direction. You may stay for forty years or for four hours. We don't know how long you are going to stay. If our needs meet and it fits right, fine. If you quit, I want you to

be as happy the day you quit as the day you joined the company.'"

Questions

1 How do motivational approaches at New Hope Communications differ from those at other companies you have read about?
2 How is fun related to motivation?
3 Do you think there might be some generation conflict over this type of approach to motivation?
4 Would New Hope's motivational approach work on the GM assembly line? In a brokerage house on Wall Street? In the surgery rooms of a large metropolitan hospital?
5 Present concrete examples of how Greene's approach to motivation might help a firm like his implement its strategy. What type of strategy would be especially appropriate for this motivational approach?

SOURCE: Michael Ray and Alan Rinzler, *The New Paradigms of Business* (New York: John Puttnam's Sons, 1993), 100.

ENTREPRENEURIAL CASE

EVERY FOURTH SUNDAY THE EMPLOYEES ARE IN CHARGE

A chronic problem facing small business owners is the high cost of health insurance for the employees. Many just cannot afford it. At his Bucksport, Maine, restaurant, George McLeod found a way. Once a month on a Sunday, a day the restaurant is normally closed, he turns the business over to his employees to run. All the proceeds go toward the employee health plan except for taxes and related expenses.

Since they began a year and a half ago, his 16 employees have made enough every month to cover the cost of the insurance. Another outcome is that McLeod can now attract and retain good employees in a labor market plagued by high turnover. In addition, because employees rotate the job

of manager on each working Sunday, McLeod thinks the program helps to break unproductive work habits and encourage people to think creatively. It has also brought management and workers closer together.

Questions

1 How would you describe the motivational approach McLeod is using?
2 Do you think many companies would use McLeod's approach as a motivational tool? Why or why not?
3 What motivational theories is McLeod actually making use of?

SOURCE: Hands On, "Helping Employees Foot the Bill," *Inc.,* January 1996, 85.

THE BUSINESS TEAM, INC.

LIVE TO WORK OR WORK TO LIVE?

Ruth's parents, Aaron and Betty, have owned and managed a generations-old, hierarchically structured family furniture store that prides itself on well-designed and well-crafted products. The company generally employs about 165 people, from skilled craftspeople to salespeople. Recently, many of the long-standing employees retired, taking years of experience with them. The company will now need to replace about 40 people, and Ruth's parents are asking for help from The Business Team.

Aaron and Betty are concerned that the new workers they recruit may be less committed and less motivated by work, less loyal, and less willing to work under the rules and regulations that have guided the company and set its management style for years. They believe you live to work, while the newer employees work to live. Aaron and Betty are accustomed to working until the job is done, whether that takes 50 hours a week or 90. Aaron just read a Gallup Poll survey that identified some of the most critical factors employees said influenced their job satisfaction and performance:

> employees have the opportunity every day to do the work they do best

employees' opinions are counted

employees have opportunities to learn and grow on the job

companies are "family friendly."

Questions

1 What advice do you think the Business Team should give Ruth's parents?

2 Which motivational theories do you think would be most helpful here? Why?

3 What problems might the management confront as the older generation starts to work with the younger generation?

4 Employees will have to be replaced in all functional areas. What do you think The Business Team should expect to find are the differences in how the furniture business will have to motivate employees in accounting? operations? sales? HR?

SOURCE: Jeffrey L. Seglin, "The Happiest Workers in the World." *Inc.,* 21 May 1996. Special issue: The State of Small Business, 62–74.

YOU BE THE CONSULTANT

MOTIVATING CREATIVE PEOPLE

With increased consolidation in the music industry, getting—and, more importantly, keeping—top-notch artists is becoming more difficult for smaller recording companies like KnitMedia. As the company says, capital restraints have greatly inhibited the company's ability to compete with major record labels in signing artists with large cash advances. As a result, in 1995 the company lost four of its rock artists and one jazz band to major labels. These artists had achieved significant success with the company, and each had contracts expiring in 1995. The artists included Eric Sanko, who signed with Capitol Records for $1 million; Bill Ware and the Groove Collective, who moved to Warner Music, as did Soul Coughing; and The Jazz Passengers, who went to BMG. Similarly, many artists who have performed at the Knitting Factory in the past have gone on to find tremendous success with major record labels, artists including John Zorn, Bill Frisell, Indigo Girls, Vernon Reid, and Sonic Youth.

The idea of KnitMedia is to attract and showcase new

artists at the Knitting Factory Clubs and then to develop these new artists into successful recording artists. However, that plan will obviously fail if KnitMedia can't successfully retain the artists that it identifies as hot prospects.

Team Exercises and Questions

Use what you learned in this chapter to answer the following questions:

1 Based on the concepts discussed in this chapter, how would you describe the motivational needs of recording artists and the other highly creative people that are associated with KnitMedia?

2 Based on this and whatever else you know about the music industry and KnitMedia, develop a statement describing what you think Michael Dorf should do to ensure that he and his colleagues can continue to attract and keep high-potential recording artists.

For the online version of this case, visit our Web site at: <www.prenhall.com/desslermgmt>.

For Internet exercises, interactive study questions, news updates and more, visit the Dessler Web site at

www.prenhall.com/desslermgmt

If you're using the **CD-ROM** that accompanies this text, simply click on the "Web Site" button to access the site.

CHAPTER 13

INFLUENCING INTERPERSONAL AND ORGANIZATIONAL COMMUNICATION

What's Ahead?

Ever since Nathaniel Weiss developed the G-VOX system, his company, Lyrrus, Inc., has been bursting with sales. The G-VOX pickup fits under guitar strings and sends their sound to a belt pack, which transmits them directly to a computer. In building Lyrrus, Weiss says he's learned that listening to employees is crucial. "You want to feel that you're contributing something," he says. "It's very powerful that what you're doing you feel is being taken seriously and is making something happen."[1] What Weiss needs now, as his company grows, are ways to ensure that communications stay as open as they've been from the very beginning. As one employee in Lyrrus's West Coast office says, "We have one big office with a roof 3000 miles long."[2]

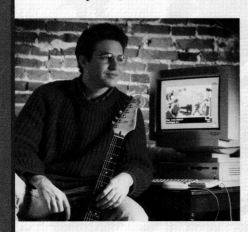

Nathaniel Weiss

Objectives

After studying this chapter, you should be able to

- define communication
- explain how to improve interpersonal communication
- describe special barriers that may undermine organizational communications and ways to avoid them
- discuss how improving communications helps companies manage change.

MANAGEMENT ON THE WEB

COOL COMPANIES

Why do some companies on the cutting edge become winners and others meet a drastically different fate? Find out answers to these questions and more by visiting sites that evaluate and rank company performance, such as *Cool Companies,* which examines 25 technology companies on the cutting edge. What use could Nathaniel Weiss make of this site? ■

http://www.pathfinder.com/@@wltnvAYAXDR2Jo6E/fortune/1997/970707/coo.html

Communication Carries Meaning

Communication Defined

As the exchange of information and the transmission of meaning, **communication** is the very essence of managing.[3] Managers like Nathaniel Weiss operate on the basis of information—about competitors' tactics, supplies of labor and materials, or assembly line delays, for instance. And it's not the events themselves that trigger management action, but the *information* managers receive about them. If that information arrives too late or is erroneous or distorted, then the organization—and its managers—will suffer.

The Manager as Communicator

Much of what managers do is communicate—get information quickly and accurately from one person to another.[4] In fact, most studies of what managers do conclude that they spend most of their time communicating. One study of supervisors in a DuPont lab found that they spent 53 percent of their time in meetings, 15 percent writing and reading, and 9 percent on the phone. If we include meetings, interacting with customers and colleagues, and other ways in which managerial communication takes place, we find that managers spend 60 to 80 percent of their time communicating, mostly face to face.[5] Influencing people through communicating and managing communications is thus an irreplaceable part of what managers do.

A Communication Model

Managing communications is important because without doing so, information will go astray. Problems can arise in any stage of the communication process, which is illustrated in Figure 13.1.[6]

As you can see, there are five basic elements in the communication process. The **encoder/sender** puts a message in understandable terms and then transmits it via a **communication channel,** a vehicle that carries the message. Face-to-face communication is the most familiar and widely used communication channel. However, there are many others. Memos, reports, policies and procedures manuals, videotape reports, and e-mail are also channels.

The information sent is not necessarily the information received. This is so because *all* information channels are subject to "noise," specifically, distortions. A

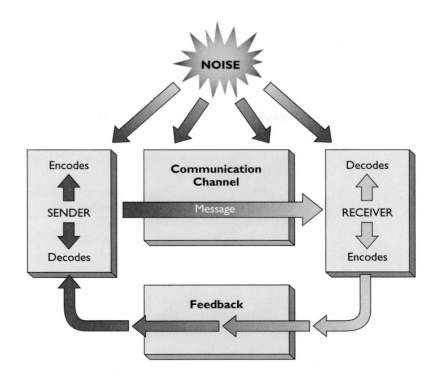

FIGURE 13.1
The Communication Process

SOURCE: *Fundamentals of Organizational Behavior* by Carrell/Jennings/Heavrin, © 1997. Reprinted by permission of Prentice-Hall, Inc., Upper Saddle River, NJ.

face-to-face conversation in a restaurant can lead to misunderstandings when the message is overwhelmed by conversations from surrounding tables. Other kinds of "noise" include ambiguities in the message and preconceptions on the part of the receiver.

The **decoder/receiver** is the person or persons to whom the information is sent. Of course, noise or other barriers like stress or perceptual differences can cause the person to decode the message erroneously.

If that should occur, feedback can save the situation. **Feedback** is the receiver's response to the message that was actually received. Air traffic controllers use feedback when they confirm and get reconfirmation of the messages they send.

Interpersonal and organizational communication barriers, discussed below, can lead to communications problems in any of these five elements. An event (like a big client lunching with one of your competitors) might be misperceived by you, the sender, as a cause for alarm. A restrictive communication channel (like the chain of command) could cause the message you sent about the event to be delayed for several weeks. Noise (perhaps in the form of distractions) may further delay the message. And then the president, shocked at the long delay in receiving the message, might decode it erroneously and act as if it were accurate, although the lunch was innocent and the client was not thinking of switching accounts.

The communication model in Figure 13.1 graphically represents both interpersonal and organizational communications. **Interpersonal communication** occurs between two individuals. **Organizational communication** occurs among several individuals or groups. In this chapter, we'll discuss how managers in their leadership roles can better influence other people through both interpersonal and organizational communication techniques.

Improving Interpersonal Communication

Because managers spend so much time communicating face to face, knowing how to improve interpersonal communication is an important management skill. However, let's look first at interpersonal communication barriers.

Interpersonal Communication Barriers

Several interpersonal communication barriers can distort messages and inhibit communication.[7]

PERCEPTION.   As we saw in chapter 12, our perceptions are influenced by many factors, and it is probably safe to say that no two people will perceive the same stimulus or message in exactly the same way.

For one thing, people tend to perceive things in a manner consistent with what they *believe*. If you believe that people are good, trustworthy, and honest, then you may tend to perceive people's actions and their comments in a supportive way. People also perceive *selectively*. At the moment, for instance, you are probably concentrating on this book (we hope!) and may, therefore, be unaware of the radio blaring in the background. Similarly, people tend to select out messages they don't want to hear or simply tune out low-priority or unwelcome information.

SEMANTICS.   **Semantics,** the meaning of words, is another barrier, because words mean different things to different people. For example, you might tell an employee to "clean up that oil spill as soon as you can," only to find 10 minutes later that it has not been cleaned up and someone has slipped on it. The employee may say, "But you told me to do it as soon as I can, and I was busy." What you meant by "as soon as you can" was not the same thing as what the employee thought you meant.

NONVERBAL COMMUNICATION.   People pick up cues to what you mean not just from your words but from your **nonverbal communication**—your manner of speaking, facial expressions, bodily posture, and so on. Thus, coming to work looking perturbed because you were caught in a traffic jam may communicate to employees that you are dissatisfied with their work, although you don't intend that message to be sent. According to one expert, "It has been estimated that in a conversation involving two people, verbal aspects of a message account for less than 35 percent of the social meaning, whereas nonverbal aspects of a message account for 65 percent of the social meaning."[8]

AMBIGUITY.   Three types of ambiguity can distort messages. Ambiguity of *meaning* occurs when the person receiving the message isn't sure what was meant by the person who said or wrote the message. (For example, you might wonder whether "see me in my office as soon as you can" means immediately or next week, after you've finished your project.) Ambiguity of *intent* means that the words may be clear, but the sender's intentions aren't. (For example, you may ask, "Why does she want to see me in her office *now?*") Finally, ambiguity of *effect* represents the receiver's uncertainty about predicting what the consequences of responding to the message might be. (Thus, you might understand both your boss's note and her intentions but still not be able to gauge how noncompliance will affect you.)

DEFENSIVENESS.   When confronted with information that may clash with their self-concept, many employees react defensively. Defenses, or defense mechanisms, are adjustments people make, often unconsciously, to avoid having to recognize per-

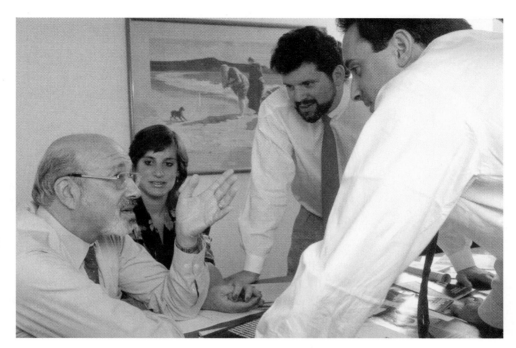

Not all communication is verbal. Gestures, posture, facial expression, and even the distances between people all tell a part of the story.

sonal qualities that might lower their self-esteem. Defense mechanisms are very important. Everyone has a picture, real or not, of who they are and what they deserve, and most people try hard to screen out experiences that don't fit this ideal self-image: Defense mechanisms are one way to do so.

Up to a point, screening can be useful: If people had to absorb the full impact of the problems and tensions of daily living, some might crack under the pressure. Defense mechanisms help people deflect a lot of the things that might otherwise diminish their self-esteem and raise their anxiety.

As a leader you will therefore find defenses to be an important and familiar aspect of interpersonal relations. When someone is accused of poor performance, for instance, his or her first reaction will often be denial. By denying fault, the person avoids having to question or analyze his or her own competence. Still others react to criticism with anger and aggression. This helps them let off steam and postpone confronting the problem until they are better able to cope with it. Still others will react to criticism by retreating into a shell.

Ways to Improve Interpersonal Communications

Leaders depend on interpersonal communication skills to influence others in a variety of situations. The employee who breaks a rule may have to be disciplined; a new employee has to be shown how to improve her performance; a worker has to be persuaded to adopt a remedial plan of action; the sales manager wants to convince the production manager to get the order out a few days sooner—all are situations in which interpersonal communications are the key. The following guidelines should therefore be useful in improving your interpersonal communication skills.

BE AN ACTIVE LISTENER. Communications pioneer Carl Rogers says active listeners try to understand both the facts and the feelings in what they hear. The active listener doesn't just passively hear what the speaker is saying but also tries to understand and respond to the feelings behind the words—fear, anger, confusion, or tension, for instance.[9] The goal is to grasp what the person is saying from his or her point of view, and then convey that you understand. To do this,

- *Listen for total meaning.* For example, if the sales manager says "We can't sell that much this year," the active listener's response wouldn't be "Sure you can." Instead, understand the underlying feelings, such as the pressure the sales manager might be under, and let the person know that his or her problem is understood.
- *Reflect feelings.* Reflecting the speaker's feelings is important because it helps the speaker confront them. Reflecting feelings here might mean something like, "They're pushing you pretty hard, aren't they?"
- *Note all cues.* Remember that not all communication is verbal. Other cues such as facial expression and hand gestures portray the person's feeling, too.
- *Avoid passing judgment.* Being judged is almost invariably threatening to the other person's self-image.

AVOID TRIGGERING DEFENSIVENESS. Criticizing, arguing, even giving advice can trigger defensiveness as the person you're speaking with tries to protect his or her self-image. Attempting to influence someone in this way may, therefore, actually backfire. For the same reason, attacking a person's defenses is unwise. For example, don't try to "explain a person to himself or herself" by saying things like "You know the reason you're using that excuse is that you can't bear to be blamed for anything." Instead, concentrate on the act itself (low sales or poor attendance, for instance). Sometimes the best thing to do is nothing at all—postpone action. A cool-down period could give you a different perspective on the matter.

CLARIFY YOUR IDEAS BEFORE COMMUNICATING. If you mean "immediately," *say* "immediately," rather than "as soon as you can." Keep in mind the underlying meaning of your message, and make sure your tone, expression, and words consistently convey that meaning.

Organizational Communication

While interpersonal communication occurs between two people, organizational communication is the exchange of information and transmission of meaning among several individuals or groups throughout the organization.

Organizational communication can flow downward, laterally, and upward. Downward communications are transmitted from superior to subordinate and consist of messages regarding things like corporate vision, what the job entails, procedures and practices to be followed, and performance evaluations. Lateral or horizontal communications are messages between departments or between people in the same department. Organizational communication can also flow upward. Upward communication (from subordinates to superiors) provides management with valuable insight into how the organization and its employees and competitors are functioning.

We can also distinguish between formal and informal organizational communication. **Formal communications** are messages recognized as official by the organization; they include orders (from superiors to subordinates) and various written and unwritten reports on sales levels, status of projects in progress, and so on. **Informal communication** is not officially sanctioned by the organization; the grapevine (or rumors) is the most familiar example.

Special Barriers to Organizational Communication

Because organizational communication happens between people, it is susceptible to all the interpersonal communication problems discussed earlier. Noise, defensiveness, criticism, semantics, perception, and filtering also undermine organizational communication.

However, organizational communication is also plagued by some special problems because of the number of people involved and because they often work in different departments and at different organizational levels. Barriers that undermine organizational communication are as follows.

DISTORTION. The fact that a message has to be relayed from person to person creates many opportunities for the message to be filtered, embellished, or otherwise distorted. Most people are familiar with the party game in which seven or eight people line up and the first person is given a simple message to relay. Each person whispers the message to the next one in line and the final message usually bears little resemblance to the original one. Much the same phenomenon occurs in organizations. Messages that have to be transferred from person to person tend to be distorted, and the more people involved, the more distortion occurs.

RUMORS AND THE GRAPEVINE. Rumors are a good example of how messages get distorted in organizations. Rumors are spread by the organizational grapevine, often with alarming speed.[10] In one study of 100 employees, the researcher found that when management made an important change in the organization, most employees would hear the news first by grapevine. Hearing news from a supervisor and official memorandums ran a poor second and third respectively.[11]

Researcher Keith Davis says there are at least three reasons why rumors get started: lack of information, insecurity, and conflicts.[12] Lack of information contributes because when employees do not know what is happening in their world they are likely to speculate about a situation, and thus a rumor is born. For example, employees who observe an unscheduled disassembly of a machine may speculate that machines are being transferred to another plant and that workers will be laid off. Insecure, anxious employees are more likely to perceive events negatively and tell others of their worries. Conflicts also foster rumors. For example, conflicts between union and management, or between two strong-willed executives, may trigger rumors as each side tries to interpret or distort the situation in a way most favorable to itself. Davis says the best way to refute a rumor is to release the truth as quickly as possible, because the more the rumor is repeated the more it will be believed and distorted.

INFORMATION OVERLOAD. Sometimes, usually around holidays, you may find that if you try to make a long distance call you only get a rapid busy signal, because all the circuits are busy. In this case, the phone lines leading across the country are overloaded and can handle no more messages. Similar problems occur in organizations. Supervisors can juggle only so many problems and make so many decisions before they become overloaded and incapable of handling any more messages.

NARROW VIEWPOINTS. Organizational communication often connects people from different departments, each of whom has his or her own narrow viewpoint and specialty. Sales managers tend to see problems as sales problems, and production managers see them as production problems, for instance. These narrow viewpoints in turn can undermine organizational communication because they make it more difficult for each person to see or understand the other's point of view.

STATUS. The fact that each person in an organization holds a different status can also undermine organizational communication. On the organization chart, it is apparent that the president has more status than the vice president, who in turn has more status than a sales manager, who in turn has more status than a salesperson.

Status differences can translate into communication breakdowns. Subordinates may prefer not to relate bad news to a boss, and thus hesitate to be candid about problems. The boss in his or her ivory tower may forget that subordinates down the line have a need to know what is happening in their world.

ORGANIZATIONAL CULTURE. The organization's culture—its shared values and traditional ways of doing things—can influence the way messages flow throughout the organization. When Jack Welch took over as GE's CEO, he inherited an organization that he felt did not adequately encourage lower-level employees to speak their minds. One of Welch's first tasks, therefore, was to re-create GE's culture to encourage all employees to communicate quickly, openly, and with candor.[13] He did this by emphasizing the value of open communication and by instituting organizational changes to encourage employees to speak their minds.

STRUCTURAL RESTRICTIONS. The organization chart itself can (and is often meant to) restrict communication to formally sanctioned routes. For example, when Mike Walsh took over as CEO of Union Pacific Railway, he found it sometimes took months for a message about a problem to make its way from one of the railroad yards to top management. Although this example may seem extreme, there's no doubt that the nature of formal organizations—sticking to the chain of command, following procedures, filling out the necessary paperwork in order to pass the request up the chain of command, and so on—can slow the flow of communications, as it did at Union Pacific.

DIVERSITY ISSUES. When many people and groups work together, there's a greater chance that diversity-driven differences in the way messages are interpreted will undermine effective communications. What something means—whether it's a word, tone, hand gesture, or nonverbal behavior—can be dramatically different among different ethnic and cultural groups.

Table 13.1 presents an example, one that underscores the difficulties U.S. and Japanese managers might encounter in discussing some issue. The Japanese, for instance, tend to be indirect and relationship oriented, while the U.S. manager (with his or her more adversarial style) tends to be more direct and task oriented. Another example of miscommunication appears in the following Managing Change feature.

➡️ ➡️ Managing Change ➡️ ➡️

FIT HOW YOU COMMUNICATE TO WHERE YOU ARE

In today's fast-changing world, cross-cultural communication is a fact of business life. So how do you learn how to communicate in a culture not your own? One way is to learn from others' mistakes. Here is a scenario about a U.S.-German partnership that started off on the wrong foot.

JAPANESE *NINGENSEI* STYLE OF COMMUNICATION	U.S. ADVERSARIAL STYLE OF COMMUNICATION
1. Indirect verbal and nonverbal communication	1. More direct verbal and nonverbal communication
2. Relationship communication	2. More task communication
3. Discourages confrontational strategies	3. Confrontational strategies more acceptable
4. Strategically ambiguous communication	4. Prefers more to-the-point communication
5. Delayed feedback	5. More immediate feedback
6. Patient, longer-term negotiators	6. Shorter-term negotiators
7. Uses fewer words	7. Favors verbosity
8. Distrustful of skillful verbal communicators	8. Exalts verbal eloquence
9. Group orientation	9. More individualistic orientation
10. Cautious, tentative	10. More assertive, self-assured
11. Complementary communicators	11. More publicly critical communicators
12. Softer, heartlike logic	12. Harder, analytic logic preferred
13. Sympathetic, empathetic, complex use of pathos	13. Favors logos, reason
14. Expresses and decodes complex relational strategies and nuances	14. Expresses and decodes complex logos, cognitive nuances
15. Avoids decision making in public	15. Frequent decision making in public
16. Makes decisions in private venues, away from public eye	16. Frequent decisions in public at negotiating tables
17. Decisions via *ringi* and *nemawashi* (complete consensus process)	17. Decisions by majority rule and public compromise are more commonplace
18. Uses go-betweens for decision making	18. More extensive use of direct person-to-person, player-to-player interaction for decisions
19. Understatement and hesitation in verbal and nonverbal communication	19. May publicly speak in superlatives, exaggerations, nonverbal projection
20. Uses qualifiers, tentative, humility as communicator	20. Favors fewer qualifiers, more ego-centered
21. Receiver/listening-centered	21. More speaker- and message-centered
22. Inferred meanings, looks beyond words to nuances, nonverbal communication	22. More face-value meaning, more denotative
23. Shy, reserved communicators	23. More publicly self-assertive
24. Distaste for purely business transactions	24. Prefers to "get down to business" or the "nitty gritty"
25. Mixes business and social communication	25. Tends to keep business negotiating more separated from social communication
26. Utilizes *matomari*, or "hints," for achieving group adjustment and saving face in negotiating	26. More directly verbalizes management's preference at negotiating tables
27. Practices *haragei*, that is, belly logic and communication	27. Practices more linear, discursive, analytical logic; greater reverence for cognitive than for affective

SOURCE: Reprinted from *International Journal of Intercultural Relations*, vol. 18, no. 1, A. Goldman, "The Centrality of 'Ningensei' to Japanese Negotiating and Interpersonal Relationships: Implications for U.S.-Japanese Communications," copyright 1994, with permission from Elsevier Science.

The U.S. manager for a company just purchased by a German firm made a trip overseas to meet his new boss. He got to the office four minutes late. Finding the door closed, he knocked on the door and walked in. From his perspective the furniture was too far away from the boss's desk, so he moved the chair closer. Then he leaned over the desk, offered his hand, and said, "Good morning, Hans, it's nice to meet you!"

The U.S. manager was surprised by the German's frosty reaction. But as he was to find out later, he had broken four rules of polite behavior in Germany: punctuality, privacy, personal space, and proper greetings. Both men left the meeting considering the other rude, a common result of cross-cultural miscommunications.[14] ■

BOUNDARY DIFFERENCES. The organizational positions of the sender and receiver can influence the accuracy with which the message is received. Subordinates tend to be somewhat deferential toward their bosses, and may tell them what they want to hear or withhold unwelcome information. Employees also tend to be short-sighted when it comes to interpreting information and understanding organizational problems. Thus, the president's message that "costs are too high" might prompt the sales manager to claim that "production should get their costs under control," while the production manager argues that "we are selling too many products."[15]

In other words, remember (from chapter 8, "Designing Organizations to Manage Change") that boundary differences can inhibit communications. The authority, task, political, and identity boundaries must be pierced if communications are to flow freely.

Improving Organizational Communication

Different techniques exist for improving organizational communications in each direction in which they flow. For example, suggestion systems are useful for encouraging upward communication. And, some firms like Toyota install closed-circuit informational TV systems for enhancing the information that top management can broadcast downward to the company's troops.

Influencing Upward Communication

Many organizations establish special methods through which employees can communicate their feelings and opinions upward to their superiors. Such methods can be beneficial. For example, they provide superiors with feedback about whether subordinates understand orders and instructions. They contribute to an acceptance of top management's decisions by giving subordinates a chance to "blow off steam." And they encourage subordinates to offer ideas of value to themselves and the organization. Special channels like these also provide supervisors with valuable information on which to base decisions,[16] encourage gripes and grievances to surface,[17] and cultivate commitment by giving employees an opportunity to express their ideas and suggestions.[18] Upward communication can help employees "cope with their work problems and strengthen their involvement in their jobs and with the organization."[19]

Many firms also use upward communication to "take their pulse" by seeing how subordinates feel about their jobs, superiors, subordinates, and organization. For example, we saw that some companies periodically administer attitude surveys. In this way, management gets answers to questions like "Are working hours and shift rotations perceived as reasonable?" "Do employees feel the boss has favorites?" and "Do employees consider cafeteria prices fair and the quality good?" Managers can then assess the need for change and correct any problems that need solving.

METHODS FOR ENCOURAGING UPWARD COMMUNICATION. Many techniques are used to encourage upward communication. One expert says that "by far the most effective way of tapping the ideas of subordinates is sympathetic listening in the many day-to-day, informal contacts within the department and outside the workplace."[20] Here are other popular methods.

1. Social gatherings, including departmental parties, outings, picnics, and recreational events, provide good opportunities for informal, casual communication.
2. Union publications (in unionized organizations) can provide management with useful insights into employee attitudes.
3. Scheduled meetings. Particularly where subordinates are numerous, it can be easy to neglect contacting or communicating with them, especially the more introspective ones. For this reason, some experts suggest that supervisors keep a checklist of those subordinates they have spoken with during the month so that meetings can be scheduled with any who might have been missed. Some supervisors formally schedule a monthly meeting with each of or all of their subordinates, in addition to the informal contacts that take place during the month.
4. Performance appraisal meetings usually provide good opportunities for seeking out an employee's opinions about his or her job and job attitudes.

By communicating with employees in the informal atmosphere of lunch, Horst Stormer, director of physical research at AT&T Bell Labs, is successfully enhancing upward communication in his firm.

5. Grievances should be monitored. Grievances are often symptoms of misunderstandings and provide top management with useful insights into problems at the operational level.
6. Attitude surveys can provide supervisors with useful information about employee morale.
7. A formal suggestion system—even one as simple as a suggestion box into which employees can anonymously drop comments—is another good way to encourage upward communication.
8. An "open door" policy, which allows subordinates to transmit concerns through a channel outside the normal chain of command, can act as a useful safety valve. Related to this is a formal appeals process (where no formal grievance process is in effect) that can show subordinates their requests and complaints will receive fair treatment, even if they are not satisfied with the response of their immediate superior.
9. Finally, indirect measures, including monitoring absences, turnover rates, and safety records, can be valuable indicators of unstated, uncommunicated problems that exist at the operational level.

Whichever of these mechanisms are used, at least three principles can boost their effectiveness. First, the system should be formalized—through scheduled meetings, suggestion plans, yearly surveys, and so on. Second, there has to be a culture of trust in the organization, since subordinates are unlikely to speak freely (even anonymously) if they mistrust management's motives.[21] Finally, management should react to the opinions and problems expressed in upward communications, even if just to acknowledge that they have been received. If the problem cannot be solved, it should be made clear why; if the problem can be eliminated, it should be. Case histories of three effective upward communication programs follow.

Managing Change

GENERAL ELECTRIC'S WORK-OUT

Jack Welch knew that to make General Electric more responsive to change, he had to foster a greater sense of open communications among everyone in the company.[22] He therefore initiated a series of classroom sessions with executives in what became known as the "pit." In these sessions, GE executives were encouraged to put aside decorum and engage Welch in the "rough and tumble debate he relishes."[23] Soon, however, Welch became concerned that the candor he was experiencing with his executives in the pit meetings was not carrying over to lower-level GE employees, and the work-out was born.

Like the pit, "work-out" is basically a place. One observer described it as a forum in which participating employees get a mental work-out while engaging in enthusiastic discussions aimed at taking unnecessary work out of their jobs and working out problems together.[24] Welch himself compares his work-outs to New England town meetings. A group of 40 to 100 employees, "picked by management from all ranks and several functions, goes to a conference center or hotel."[25] The three-day sessions are usually kicked off by a talk by the group's boss, who soon leaves. An outside consultant/facilitator then breaks the group into five or six teams, each of which addresses problems, lists complaints, and debates solutions. Later the boss returns and the team spokesperson makes the team's proposals. Under work-out's rules, the boss can make only three responses: He or she can agree on the spot, say no, or ask for more information, "in which case he must charter a team to get it by an agreed upon date."[26]

The work-out sessions are useful for solving problems and for getting employees to express their ideas upward with openness and candor. As one GE electrician responded when told his comments had made his boss "really sweat," "When you've been told to shut up for 20 years and someone tells you to speak up—you're going to let them have it."[27] ■

FEDERAL EXPRESS'S GUARANTEED FAIR TREATMENT PROCEDURE. In brief, the Federal Express guaranteed fair treatment procedure is an upward communication process that contains three steps. In step 1, *management review,* the complainant submits a written complaint to a member of management. The manager reviews all relevant information, holds a conference with the complainant, and makes a decision either to uphold, modify, or overturn the original supervisor's actions.[28]

In step 2, *officer review,* the complainant can submit a written complaint to a vice president or senior vice president of his or her division. That person reviews all relevant information, conducts an additional investigation, and makes a decision to uphold, overturn, or modify management's action.

Finally, in step 3, *executive appeals review,* the complainant can submit a written complaint that goes to an appeals board consisting of Federal Express's CEO, president, and chief personnel officer as well as two other senior vice presidents. They then review all relevant information and make a decision to uphold, overturn, or initiate an investigative board of review. (The latter is used when there is a question of fact.)

TOYOTA'S HOTLINE. Toyota Motor Manufacturing tells its employees, "Don't spend time worrying about something . . . speak up!" At Toyota, the primary upward communication channel is called "Hotline." Its purpose is to give team members an additional channel for bringing questions or problems to the company's attention.

The hotline is available 24 hours a day. Employees are instructed to pick up any phone, dial the hotline extension (the number is posted on the plant bulletin board), and deliver their messages to the recorder. All inquiries received on the hotline are guaranteed to be reviewed by the human resources manager and to be thoroughly investigated. If it is decided that a particular question would be of interest to other Toyota team members, then the question, along with the firm's response, is posted on plant bulletin boards. If a personal response is desired, employees must leave their names when they call. However, employees know that no other attempt will be made to identify a particular hotline caller.[29]

Organizational Behavior in Action

APPRAISING YOUR BOSS

How would you like to appraise your supervisor, and how (if at all) do you think knowing she will be appraised would influence the way she acted? A recent study sheds some interesting light on this upward communication technique.

Supervisors usually seem to react well to having subordinates appraise them, especially when the appraisals are not anonymous.[30] One study examined the effects of such upward feedback by collecting subordinates' ratings for 238 managers in a large corporation at two points in time, six months apart. Subordinates were asked to rate a variety of supervisory behaviors, such as "Regularly challenged me to continuously improve my effectiveness," "Took steps to resolve conflict and disagreement within the team," and "Treated me fairly and with respect."[31]

The study found that the performance of those managers whose initial level of performance was high did not improve significantly in six months. However, there was a marked improvement in performance among managers whose initial level of performance was moderate or low. The researchers conclude that "this is encouraging because these are the managers that most need to improve from the organization's (as well as the subordinates') perspective."[32]

An interesting aspect of the findings was that the managers' performance improved whether or not they received the feedback. It's possible the knowledge that their subordinates would appraise them was enough to get them to improve their behavior at work.

Influencing Downward Communication

In many firms today, the scope of downward communication has been expanded dramatically. The aim is to provide newly empowered employees with information about their companies and tasks so they can do their jobs better. Downward communication includes a variety of essential types of information regarding, for instance, job instructions, rationales for jobs (including how jobs are related to other jobs and positions in the organization), organizational policies and practices, employee performance, and the organization's mission.[33]

In addition to the usual channels (like face-to-face and written messages), firms today use many means to get data "down to the troops." At Saturn Corporation, assemblers describe communications as excellent and say, "We get information continuously via the internal television network and from financial documents."[34] The firm also has monthly town-hall-like meetings, usually with 500 to 700 people attending. The result is that all employees are familiar with Saturn's activities and performance.

Toyota Motor Manufacturing has five-minute team information meetings at job sites twice a day, where employees get the latest plant news. Toyota also puts a television set in each worksite break area, which runs continuously and presents plantwide information from the in-house Toyota Broadcasting Center. The company sponsors quarterly roundtable discussions between top management and selected nonsupervisory staff, and an in-house newsletter. The hotline described earlier is another channel of top-down information, giving management a chance to answer publicly questions team members might have.

Toyota's managers also practice what's become known as "managing by walking around." The plant's top management is often on the shop floor, fielding questions, providing performance information, and ensuring that all general managers, managers, and team members are "aware of Toyota's goal and where we are heading."[35] The following Strategy feature shows how a small business improved its upward and downward communications.

An innovative form of downward communication, the in-house Toyota Broadcasting Center presents company news and information that employees can watch in their worksite break areas.

◎ ◎ ◎ **Strategy in Action** ◎ ◎ ◎

KROY, INC.

Deducing what was wrong at Kroy, Inc., did not require a high-priced consultant. A buyout in the mid-1980s had loaded the company with debt. Sales headed down, to the point where income at this labeling equipment maker was insufficient to cover interest payments. The cash shortage led to neglect of new-product development, making dealers unhappy. The dearth of capital also led to unannounced, seemingly random layoffs. Morale was lower than profits. Rumors were rampant, largely owing to the lack of any form of communication from top management.

The future, if there was to be one, hinged on reducing debt. The firm filed for Chapter 11 bankruptcy to give it a chance to work out its problems. New CEO Howard Klemmer came on board in late 1990. His assessment of Kroy's most critical shortcoming was symbolized by his first move on the job: Communication, he said, would be central to Kroy's strategy of reducing debt, boosting productivity, and returning to financial health. Managers would never again wall themselves off from the rest of the company, even if they wanted. The day he arrived, Klemmer ordered all doors removed from executive offices.

The ensuing days found Klemmer holding companywide meetings at the Scottsdale, Arizona, headquarters. His message made clear that hard work lay ahead, but he made it equally clear that with commitment from every employee, the company would survive. Workers were invited to ask job-related questions. "No" was the answer to their most pressing concern—no one's job was guaranteed. Many left, but the new candor relieved much of the anxiety that had plagued the company.

To institutionalize the new communication channels, managers met regularly with employees. Klemmer was everywhere, keeping employees abreast of the latest developments and helping quash further rumors. Meetings between the CEO, top brass, and employees became a monthly occurrence. Everything from planned cost-cutting measures to proposed staffing reductions was aired. Honesty was the main theme. Employees also got the most up-to-the-minute status reports of the company's position. Workers too shy to broach topics in the open had the option of dropping their questions anonymously into boxes throughout the offices. A manager would then research the answer for announcement the following month without ever identifying the employee.

Howard Klemmer made upward and downward communication his number one priority and the centerpiece of his management strategy at Kroy. His active and ongoing participation in the process made it clear that his commitment to open, honest exchanges between members of the company was more than rhetoric. By the time Kroy emerged from Chapter 11 bankruptcy, employee morale was up and so were profits.[36]

Influencing Horizontal Organizational Communication

Managers also work hard to boost horizontal communication. Doing so facilitates interdepartmental coordination because coordinating almost always depends on communicating. Horizontal interdepartmental communication also enhances organizational responsiveness by helping employees pierce departmental or geographic barriers and get right to the source when quick decisions must be made.

STRUCTURAL DEVICES. Managers traditionally use individuals or committees to bridge departments and improve the flow of communications between them. These are some of the ways bridging works:

- *Liaison personnel.* A sales liaison person may be employed by the sales department, but be physically located in the factory to advise factory management about the sales department's priorities.
- *Committees and task forces.* Interdepartmental committees, task forces, and teams are usually composed of representatives from several interdependent departments; the committees meet periodically to discuss and solve common problems and to ensure interdepartmental communication and coordination occur.
- *Independent integrators.* Some companies boost interdepartmental communication by creating special independent integrators. A new-product development department is one example. This department's entire role is to facilitate communication and coordination among the activities of several other departments such as research and development, sales, engineering, and manufacturing.

ENCOURAGE SOCIAL ACTIVITIES. Many companies encourage horizontal communication by organizing social activities such as bowling teams. Here, employees from several departments intermingle and much horizontal communication can occur. For example, Toyota Motor Manufacturing has an annual picnic.

Influencing Organization-Wide Communications

There are also several ways to influence and improve the flow of communications throughout the organization. Most of these are essentially structural solutions, which we described at length in chapter 8; we summarize them here.

FOSTER INFORMAL COMMUNICATION. There is always some informal communication in organizations—for example, between the sales and production managers. Such communications seemingly violate the pattern of communication mandated by the organization chart. Yet without some informal communication, things might soon slow to a halt—if, for instance, the sales manager had to wait two months for a question to make its way through the chain of command to the production manager.

Therefore (while it may seem a contradiction in terms), managers sometimes encourage informal communications. For example, the president might authorize the sales manager and production manager to communicate directly and make schedule changes, but with the stipulation that the vice presidents for sales and production be informed of such changes within 24 hours. We'll discuss other ways to foster informal communication below.

USE NETWORKS. Many firms superimpose organizational networks over their existing organizational structures. Recall that a network is a system of interconnected or cooperating individuals who can be formally, informally, or electronically linked. Managers from various departments, levels, and geographic areas form a multidisciplinary team whose members communicate across normal organizational boundaries.

ENCOURAGE BOUNDARYLESSNESS. Taken to its logical conclusion, a networked organization results in a boundaryless firm. Boundaryless networked organizations are those in which managers have taken the steps required to pierce the boundaries that often inhibit networked communications and decision making. Boundaries to pierce include the authority, task, identity, and political boundaries.

USE ELECTRONIC NETWORKING. Managers increasingly use various forms of computerized networks to electronically link employees and thereby provide instantaneous communication organization-wide. For example, when Price Waterhouse accounting manager Rick Richardson arrives at his office each morning, he checks his computer to review the average 20 to 25 e-mail messages he gets in a typical day. Price Waterhouse also maintains electronic bulletin boards on more than 1,000 different subjects. About 18,000 Price Waterhouse employees in 22 countries use these electronic bulletin boards to get updates on matters such as how to handle specialized projects on which they are working.[37] Other companies use videoconferencing as a cost-effective way to enable employees in different locations to communicate live and interactively.[38]

How Companies Manage Change by Improving Communication

The methods for improving organizational communications that we've discussed provide a tool box from which managers can choose when they need to influence and improve organizational communications. What follows are some examples of how real companies actually use techniques like these to improve communications and better manage change.

Communicating in the "Intelligent Enterprise"

James Bryan Quinn has studied what he calls "intelligent enterprises." These are companies like those in the rapidly changing computer industry that depend on converting their employees' "intellectual resources" into the services and products demanded by their customers. They are "intelligent" in part because like intelligent people, they can quickly size up situations and arrive at good decisions.

Companies like these, says Quinn, must "leverage"—take maximum advantage of—their intellectual capital by ensuring that ideas and advice can flow quickly and freely among all employees. The electronic bulletin board system used at Price Waterhouse is one way to do this; for example, if a Price Waterhouse Dublin consultant has a question about auditing a cheese plant, he or she can post an inquiry and get an answer from another Price Waterhouse consultant who may be half a world away. In this way Price Waterhouse helps the Dublin consultant take advantage of the other's expertise—to leverage the latter's knowledge, in other words.

Quinn found that many of the intelligent enterprises he studied used systems like these. As the managing director of business systems consulting at Arthur Andersen Consulting said:

> Our group talk system was installed about four years ago and there is no question among our practitioners that it gives us competitive advantage and has made a direct contribution to our sales growth. Our business strategy says that we will leverage the intellectual capital of our people, the intellectual capital of our firm, and the intellectual capital of the business world at large. In order to do that, we made a decision to have a computer in every single professional's hands, and they are obliged to sign on to the bulletin board a minimum of once a week. It allows you to ask questions and get answers to questions from peers all around the world. For each of the 600 people directly on our network, they probably have another ten they relate to closely, so we can essentially network to 6,000 minds.[39]

How Companies Encourage Informal Communications

In their study of "excellent" innovative companies, Tom Peters and Robert Waterman found that these companies used very informal, almost unorthodox, means of communicating to help them remain responsive and manage change.[40] Although some firms subsequently fell off most experts' lists of "excellent" companies, the techniques they used to encourage informal communications provide some useful insights:

> The excellent companies are a vast network of informal, open communications. The patterns and intensity cultivate the right people getting into contact with each other, regularly, and the chaotic/anarchic properties of a system are kept well under control simply because of the regularity of contact and its nature.[41]

In these outstanding and innovative companies, "the name of the success game" is rich, informal communication:

> The astonishing byproduct is the ability to have your cake and eat it, too; that is, rich informal communication leads to more action, more experiments, more

learning, and simultaneously to the ability to stay better in touch and on top of things.[42]

In excellent companies, say Peters and Waterman, the intensity and sheer volume of communications are unmistakable and usually start with a stress on informality.[43] Specifically, they found that several techniques are used to encourage informal communication:

1. *Informality is emphasized.* At the Walt Disney Company, for instance, everyone from the president down wears a name tag with just his or her first name on it. (These are worn in the parks on a regular basis.) At 3M there are endless meetings but few are scheduled; most are characterized by the casual getting together of people from different disciplines who talk about problems in a campuslike, shirt-sleeves atmosphere.

2. *Communication intensity is maintained at an extraordinary level.* At the more successful companies, meetings and presentations are held in which "the questions are unabashed; the flow is free; everyone is involved. Nobody hesitates to cut off the chairman, the president or board members."[44] What is encouraged, in other words, is an open confrontation of ideas in which people are blunt and straightforward in going after the issues. Meetings in these companies are not highly formal and politicized affairs. Instead, they are open, informative discussions in which all points of view can safely be aired.

3. *Communication is given physical support.* Blackboards and open offices facilitate and encourage frequent informal interaction. In one high-tech

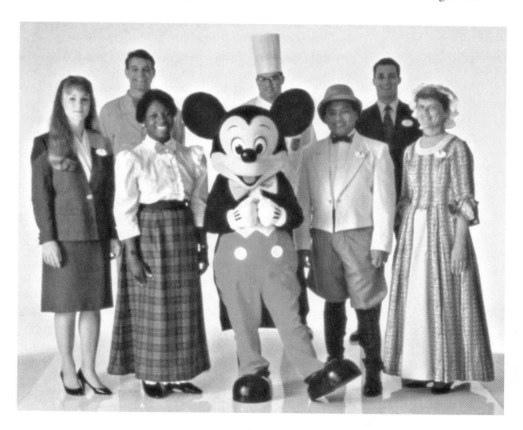

Informal communication at The Walt Disney Co. is exemplified by the employees' first-name-only name tags.

firm, for instance, all employees from the president down work not in offices but in six-foot-high doorless cubicles that encourage openness and interaction among employees. Corning Glass installed escalators rather than elevators in its new engineering building to increase the chance of face-to-face contact.[45] Another company got rid of its four-person dining room tables and substituted long rectangular ones that encourage strangers to come in contact, often across departmental lines. Managers are encouraged to get out of their offices, walk around, and strike up conversations with those both in and outside their own departments.

What all this adds up to, says Peters and Waterman, is "lots of communication." In most of these firms, they say, you cannot wander around for long without "seeing lots of people sitting together in a room with blackboards working casually on problems."[46]

How Other Companies Open Up Communications

UNION PACIFIC RAILWAY, OPENING UP COMMUNICATIONS. When Mike Walsh took over as CEO of Union Pacific Railway, employees routinely addressed each other with the formal "Mr." or "Mrs." and teamwork between departments was almost nonexistent.[47] Walsh viewed the firm as bureaucratic and militaristic.

One of the first things he did to boost communication was to institute so-called town hall meetings throughout the 19-state rail system. In each meeting, Walsh spoke to 300 to 1,000 employees, explaining the firm's new strategy and his vision for it, and how that new vision would affect Union Pacific and its employees. Employees were asked to contribute their ideas.

"FRESH AIR" AT MATTEL TOYS. When John Amerman became CEO of Mattel Toys, he told employees he wanted to let in some "fresh air" and enable employees to have some fun. In a company that was described as "an out-of-control money-loser" that had "spent big to introduce a series of toys that bombed" and whose morale was low, Amerman's ideas triggered a big change in culture.[48]

To put his "fresh air" ideas in place, he began wandering around the firm, eating in the cafeteria, and meeting regularly with employees. Suggestions were soon forthcoming; to his surprise, "many employees recommended that their departments be pruned or totally scrapped."[49]

GETTING PERSONAL AT BROOKS FURNITURE. Bob Crawford, founder and CEO of Brooks Furniture Rental, emphasizes two-way communication. As he says, "People will put every effort into advancing the businesses in which they can communicate their ideas freely."[50] Crawford takes a personal approach to communication. He walks through his company's huge warehouses, greeting every worker by name and chatting about work and personal matters. Crawford emphasizes the importance of listening and says, "The secret of good human dynamics is a balance between talking and listening."[51]

PLANNED NOSINESS AT CHIAT/DAY/MOJO. At advertising agency Chiat/Day/Mojo (CDM), creativity is the hallmark, and "everything and everyone serves that idea."[52] The agency has no organization chart, business cards have no titles, and everyone works out of open, low-partition offices. The whole human resource system from selection through compensation and appraisal is aimed at encouraging a love for work and creativity.

Not surprisingly, employees at CDM emphasize open communication to foster the firm's famous creativity. "Nosiness feeds creative energy," is how one staffer put it. "You can pop in and out of offices and exchange ideas, look at story boards or ads. By being close together, creatives can bounce more ideas off each other. Our physical structure encourages communications. And our philosophy demands not hiding things."[53]

Chiat/Day/Mojo's open-office experience provides some lessons for others contemplating open-office layouts. A big problem turned out to be the openness itself. As one person put it:

> Whenever anybody walked by, they looked at you, you looked at them, and your concentration was gone . . . creative people need quiet places to think, and that was something they never planned for.[54]

The company's space today, therefore, provides for a bit more privacy. A large room full of tables and desktop computers has been added where employees can spread out their materials. Team-sized project rooms were made so account teams could meet and brainstorm. Smaller, more private spaces are available for writers and art directors to concentrate. Balancing open space with some degree of privacy is therefore crucial.

Organizational Behavior in Action

APPLYING COMMUNICATIONS RESEARCH IN PRACTICE

What can research studies by communications experts tell us about staying more responsive by managing communications? Results from two lines of research—on communications networks and on "media richness"—are informative.

COMMUNICATIONS NETWORKS IN ACTION. What happens when organizational communications are restricted to just a few allowable routes, as in more bureaucratic organizations? A classic study by psychologist Harold Leavitt addressed this question.[55]

Groups of five persons were arranged in one of the "communication networks" shown in Figure 13.2. Each person was placed in a compartment at a table in such a way that his or her communication was restricted. Each subject in the all-channel network could communicate with any other subject. Subjects in the wheel network could communicate only with the subject in the central position (hub) of the network, but this central person could communicate with the four remaining subjects in his network. (The lines all show two-way linkages.) All each person knew was to whom messages could be sent and from whom messages could be received.

The researchers found that the best communication network depended on the nature of the problem that had to be solved. Where the problem was simple and amenable to a clear-cut yes or no answer (such as "Is this marble blue?"), the wheel network was best. But for complex, ambiguous problems that required lots of give-and-take among the subjects, the all-channel network was best. Here, for instance, each person was given marbles that were difficult to describe. Two people looking at identical marbles could describe them quite differently; what one might view as "greenish-yellow," another might call "aqua." The person in the center of the wheel network could not him or herself quickly decide what color was common to all the

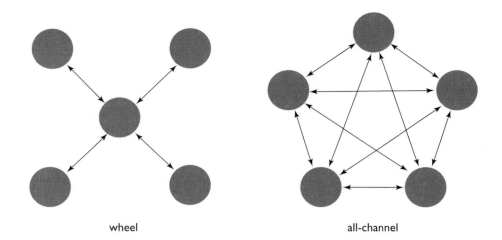

■ FIGURE 13.2
Two Experimental Communications Networks

Note: In the "centralized" wheel networks, each subject could communicate only with the hub subject; in the all-channel "decentralized" network, each subject could communicate with each other subject, so that ambiguous problems could be solved more quickly.

wheel   all-channel

■ FIGURE 13.3
Hierarchy of Media Richness and Application for Managerial Applications

SOURCE: Adapted from Richard L. Daft and Robert H. Lengel, "Information Richness: A New Approach to Managerial Information Processing and Organization Design," in Barry Staw and Larry L. Cummings, eds., *Research in Organizational Behavior*, vol. 6 (Greenwich, CT: JAI Press, 1984), pp. 191–233. Reprinted from R. Daft and R. Steers, *Organizations: A Micro/Macro Approach*, (Glenview, IL: Scott, Foresman, 1986) p. 532.

marbles. Rather, the all-channel network in which communications could flow freely to everyone arrived at the fastest decision for ambiguous problems.

Evidence from studies like Peters and Waterman's (discussed above) support this idea that lots of give and take is best when the company is faced with many ambiguous, unpredictable situations. In their study of fast-changing "organic" companies in the electronics industry, for instance, Burns and Stalker found "a lateral rather than a vertical direction of communication throughout the organization; communication between people of different rank, also resembling consultation rather than command; [and] a content of communication which consists of information and advice rather than instructions."[56]

THE MEDIA RICHNESS MODEL. If you were an emergency room doctor and had to diagnose a patient who was obviously turning green, would you do it face to face or send impersonal notes back and forth?

The question highlights what communications researchers call the media richness model. Richard Daft and Robert Lengel say that the communication media or channels used—which may include face-to-face contact, telephone, personally addressed documents, or unaddressed documents—differ in their "media richness." The idea is summarized in Figure 13.3.[57] Media richness means the capacity of the media to resolve ambiguity. It is determined by four aspects: speed of feedback, number of cues and channels employed, personalness of the source, and richness of the language used.

MEDIA		CHARACTERISTICS		MEDIA RICHNESS	BEST FOR COMMUNICATIONS THAT ARE:
		FEEDBACK	CUES AND CHANNELS		
Face to face	Oral	Immediate	Audio and visual	High	Ambiguous, emotional, divergent in background
Telephone		Rapid	Audio	↕	
Addressed documents	Written	Slow	Limited visual		
Unaddressed documents		Slowest	Limited visual	Low	Clear, rational, official, similar in background

Face-to-face oral communication is the richest medium. As you know from your own experience, it provides instantaneous audio and visual feedback not just through the person's words but through his or her body language and tone as well. At the other extreme, unaddressed documents like companywide memos impersonally distributed to all employees are lowest in media richness.

Do organizations and people rely more on rich media for addressing ambiguous situations? Yes and no. When it comes to traditional forms of communication such as face to face, telephone, and letters and memos, the answer is yes: The more ambiguous the situation to be addressed, the richer the media used in many companies, such as Chiat/Day/Mojo, described earlier. On the other hand, a recent entry in the communication media medley—e-mail—seems frequently to be used for addressing more emotional, ambiguous tasks at firms like Arthur Andersen, although it would seem to be relatively low in media richness.

SUMMARY

1. There are five elements in the communication process, and errors can occur at any one: encoder/sender, communication channel, noise, decoder/receiver, and feedback.

2. Several interpersonal communication barriers can distort messages and inhibit communication. These barriers include ambiguity, defensiveness, errors in perception, semantics, and nonverbal communication.

3. You can improve interpersonal communications by being an active listener, avoiding triggering defensiveness, and clarifying your ideas before communicating.

4. Because organizational communication involves people, it is susceptible to all the problems of interpersonal communication and some special problems, including distortion, rumors and the grapevine, information overload, narrow viewpoints, differences in status, organizational culture, structural restrictions, diversity issues, and boundary differences.

5. Upward communication can be encouraged through techniques like social gatherings, union publications, scheduled meetings, and formal suggestion systems. Federal Express's Guaranteed Fair Treatment Procedure, Toyota's hotline, and General Electric's work-out are other examples. Downward communication is encouraged through usual channels (like face-to-face and written messages), as well as techniques like closed-circuit televisions and top managers "walking around."

6. Lateral organizational communication can often be improved through liaison personnel, committees and task forces, and independent integrators.

7. To influence and improve organization-wide communications, the leader can foster informal communication, use networks, encourage boundarylessness, and use electronic networking.

8. Companies can better manage change by improving communications. For example, Price Waterhouse and Arthur Andersen use electronic networking in their "intelligent enterprises"; other successful companies keep communication systems informal and give communication physical support.

KEY TERMS

communication
encoder/sender
communication channel
decoder/receiver
feedback

interpersonal
  communication
organizational
  communication
semantics

nonverbal communication
formal organizational
  communication
informal organizational
  communication

SELF-TEST

TRUE / FALSE QUESTIONS

1 **T F** The exchange of information and the transmission of meaning is called communication.

2 **T F** In our technology-driven organizations, communication has become less frequent and important.

3 **T F** A communication channel is a vehicle for conveying a message.

4 **T F** Feedback is the receiver's response to the message that the sender actually sent.

5 **T F** People will perceive the same stimulus or message in the same way.

6 **T F** People tend to react defensively when presented with information that conflicts with their self-concept.

7 **T F** One purpose of the organization chart is to restrict communication to formally authorized routes.

8 **T F** Appraising one's boss is an example of horizontal communication.

9 **T F** In an organization, a network is a system of interconnected or cooperating individuals, which may be informal, formal, or electronically based.

10 **T F** Innovative companies tend to rely on formal lines of communication.

MULTIPLE-CHOICE QUESTIONS

1 Which of the following is the most accurate description of the amount of time managers spend communicating?
  a. very little
  b. moderate
  c. half
  d. most

2 Which is not considered one of the five elements in the communication process?
  a. channel
  b. decoder
  c. receiver
  d. player

3 _____ communication describes the manner of speaking, facial expressions, and bodily posture.
  a. Verbal
  b. Linguistic
  c. Nonverbal
  d. Auditory

4 What type of listener is the following: one who tries to understand and respond to the feelings of the speaker, not just the words?
  a. passive
  b. active

  c. neutral
  d. overemotional

5 Organizational communication can flow in which directions?
  a. upward
  b. downward
  c. laterally
  d. all of the above

6 Which of these issues can undermine communication?
  a. diversity
  b. boundary differences
  c. organizational status
  d. all of the above

7 Three principles enhance encouraging upward communication. Which of these is *not* one of them?
  a. scheduled meetings
  b. union publications
  c. attitude surveys
  d. nonformalized channels

8 Apparently, supervisors seem to react _____ to having subordinates appraise or evaluate them.
  a. well
  b. badly
  c. neutrally
  d. none of the above

9 Most rumors spread by _____.
  a. the grapevine
  b. newsletter
  c. monthly reports
  d. none of the above

10 By far the most effective way of encouraging upward communication is _____.
  a. daily listening
  b. formal meetings
  c. the suggestion box
  d. the grapevine

CRITICAL THINKING EXERCISES

1 For many of us, communication brings to mind technology. The uses of the computer, from e-mail to the Internet, shape our thinking patterns and, consequently, our communication. Everything is speeded up with electronic communication. Where will this electronic revolution take communication in the next 10 years? Will we all be e-mailing instead of writing letters, banking and shopping from home computers, doing business through our home pages on the Net and teleconferencing via video computer links? What do you think will be our patterns of communication as technology evolves?

2 Television is a powerful medium of communication, but in general, it is a monologue, not a dialogue. Your challenge as a class is to break up into teams of four to five people. Each team member is then to be assigned one news station to watch all week. For example, you might choose ABC, and another student PBS. At the end of the week, your team is to compare notes as to what news was communicated, how it was presented, who presented the stories, and how balanced they seemed to be. Then be prepared to make a team presentation to the class about your findings and how you see the news shaping our society through the way it is communicated.

EXPERIENTIAL EXERCISES

1 Describe what happened in this conversation by using the concepts presented in this chapter:

A man drove up to a gasoline pump to fill his gas tank. The gas station attendant noticed three penguins in the back seat of the car and, curious, asked about them.

"I don't know how they got there," the driver said. "The penguins were there when I took the car out of the garage this morning."

The attendant thought for a moment. "Why don't you take them to the zoo?"

"Good idea," the driver said and drove away.

The next day, the same man returned to the gas station. In the back seat were the same three penguins, but now they wore sunglasses.

The attendant looked at the car in surprise. "I thought you took them to the zoo!" she exclaimed.

"I did," the driver said. "And they had such a good time that today I decided to take them to the beach."

Review this exercise to clarify the communication problems between the driver and the gas station attendant. Then compose your own version of the story from one of your own experiences with miscommunication.

2 Because actions speak louder than words, nonverbal communication can be confounding. Take international gestures. In Britain, secrecy or confidentiality is conveyed by a tap on one's nose, while in Italy it means a friendly warning. A nod in Bulgaria and Greece signifies "no." In most other countries, it means "yes." Placing your fingers in a circle is widely accepted as the U.S. "okay" sign, except in Brazil, where it's considered vulgar or obscene.[58]

Gather 8 to 10 different gestures that mean different things in different nations. Interview classmates, friends, relatives, and co-workers and then come to class ready to discuss what you discovered. Or brainstorm with a group of four to six classmates, generating a list of 8 to 10 U.S. gestures. Then divide the list and seek out what these gestures communicate in other cultures. Report to the class on your findings.

DIVERSITY CASE

APPROACHING DIVERSITY: BARRIERS OR BREAKTHROUGHS?

You have just been hired by a traditional, paternalistic restaurant chain that has been successfully sued by former employees five times in the last five years for racial and gender discrimination. The company is starting to lose business because of its poor image in the community it serves. Employees are also leaving and others are threatening to sue if conditions do not improve. The workforce is 65 percent women, of which 55 percent are women of color. Twenty-one percent of the male workforce are men of color. Middle management and above are all white males.

The Board of Directors has fired the CEO and replaced her with a young Latina to try to change the company. You are the new Chief Operations Officer. The new CEO has asked you to help her implement a diversity program to reach all aspects of operations. She needs your report by the end of the week.

Questions
1 What communications problems might you expect to unearth in this situation?
2 What means of communication might you use to help the new CEO reach the employees?

3 Given that you are new on the job, how would you collect information to do your analysis in less than a week?

SOURCE: Gillian Flynn, "Do You Have the Right Approach to Diversity?" *Personnel Journal* (October 1995):68–76.

STRATEGY CASE

IF KNOWLEDGE IS POWER, YOU BETTER LEARN HOW TO LOG, SURF, AND DOWNLOAD

The Internet is one of the most powerful forms of communication now at our fingertips and an incredible strategic tool for business. Although the Web is not without problems, it is clearly here to stay and change the way we talk, think, and work.

You are the new kid on the block in a management consulting company that is basically computer illiterate. You love all forms of technology. Your job is to communicate to the rest of the staff the strategic value to the firm of the Internet and the other technological tools available. Because the company is located all over the world, you think a good intranet is needed and believe everyone should have his or her own computer and receive training on a regular basis.

Questions
1 How can a company like this use communications as a strategic tool? List some examples.
2 How would you communicate your ideas to management?
3 What communication barriers might you encounter with other employees if management buys into your ideas?

SOURCE: Samuel Greengard, "Leverage the Power of the Internet," *Workforce*, March 1997, 76–85.

ENTREPRENEURIAL CASE

ROTTEN TO THE CORE, OR, CAN JOBS BRING APPLE BACK TO ITS GLORY DAYS?

Most lists of famous entrepreneurs these days would include the name of Steven Jobs, founder of Apple Computers. Apple's many growth stages have been marked by inventive communication. In the beginning, Apple communicated its entrepreneurial culture by flying a pirate flag atop its Cupertino, California, headquarters. To communicate how this David of the computer world would go up against the Giant, IBM, in the 1980s, Apple portrayed itself in ads as the only athlete able to go up against a formidable opponent and win with guts and determination because it was right. Then Jobs was forced out of the firm.

In the 1990s, with increased competition, defection of talent, and product defects, the company has lost market share, and market analysts are questioning whether this once-vital company is now at death's door.

Reenter Steve Jobs, invited back in 1996 to help revive Apple. What Jobs has brought back is the intangible feeling that Apple is on track and going where it always should have gone.

Questions
1 What is Apple communicating by bringing Steve Jobs back to "save" the firm?
2 What do you think the grapevine is saying about Jobs' return and the company's problems?
3 What communication obstacles might Jobs come up against?
4 What communication changes would you recommend Jobs recommend in this situation?

SOURCE: Peter Burrows, "Apple: What Is Steve Jobs Up To?" *Business Week*, 17 March 1997, 116–7.

THE BUSINESS TEAM, INC.

TO LOG ON OR NOT TO LOG ON: THAT *IS* THE COMMUNICATION QUESTION

The Business Team has decided that one way to grow their business is to create a home page on the Internet. They are excited by the prospect of getting new business, but also a bit concerned. They have prided themselves on their interpersonal skills in face-to-face conversations and over the phone. Logging on and using e-mail draws on a different set of communication skills and abilities. All the team members are computer literate and quite comfortable with technology, but selling their unique multifunction approach over the Internet is new. Also, Maria and Len are both subscribers to America Online (AOL) and have experienced the same frustrations as many other users when demand outstripped the capacity of the system.

Although they want to enter the electronic communications age, they all have some concerns about how it might change their business and their own personal interactions.

Questions

1 What do you think are the advantages and disadvantages of using the Internet for business communications?
2 How might the partners use the Internet to highlight their multifunction approach to solving business problems?
3 What general lessons about communications without the use of technology can you apply to Internet-based communications?

YOU BE THE CONSULTANT

KEEPING THE LINES OF COMMUNICATION OPEN AT KNITMEDIA

As their company grows, Michael Dorf and his colleagues have to make sure they take steps to keep the lines of communication open. One of the primary strengths of Knit-Media's large competitors is also their greatest weakness: size. Due to the enormousness of the multinationals' internal structures, they are restricted in their ability to react quickly to market demands. As we've seen, this can lead to late entry of major record labels into new markets and can also isolate the more ponderous competitors from the consumer and thus undercut their ability to see shifts in the marketplace.

Identifying new trends and supplying products at the early growth stages of these developments are at the heart of what music companies like KnitMedia must do. To do this, they must be sure to institute methods that enhance not only organizational communication, but communication between KnitMedia and both the consumers and the artists. The question is, how should they do this?

Team Exercises and Questions

Use what you learned in this chapter to answer the following questions:

1 Do you think interpersonal and organizational communications at KnitMedia are currently adequate? Please explain your answer.
2 Based on a review of Internet- and non-Internet–based information, compile a list of methods KnitMedia and other music companies use to improve organizational and interpersonal communications, both within their companies and between the companies and their artists and consumers. Which of these techniques do you think KnitMedia should implement, and how would you suggest they do so?

For the online version of this case, visit our Web site at: <www.prenhall.com/desslermgmt>.

For Internet exercises, interactive study questions, news updates and more, visit the Dessler Web site at

www.prenhall.com/desslermgmt

If you're using the CD-ROM that accompanies this text, simply click on the "Web Site" button to access the site.

LEADING GROUPS AND TEAMS

What's Ahead?

In March 1997 the Oxford Health Plans health maintenance organization announced it was creating teams of specialists to treat serious health conditions. Oxford, which instituted the changes after polling its 1.7 million patient-members, said that for certain categories

"ranging from obstetrics to oncology" it would start offering care by teams of physicians, therapists, and other professionals who would be responsible for a patient's treatment from diagnosis through conclusion of care. Over 200 of the teams have already been formed.[1]

Steve Wiggins

Objectives

After studying this chapter, you should be able to

- list and briefly describe the types of teams used at work
- explain the causes and symptoms of unproductive teams
- discuss how to build team performance
- describe the problems of making the transition from supervisor to team leader
- list the values team leaders should have
- use important team-leader coaching skills.

MANAGEMENT ON THE WEB

CENTER FOR THE STUDY OF WORK TEAMS

The Center for the Study of Work Teams is dedicated to the design, implementation, and development of collaborative work systems. Team-related links to organizations, information resources, and practitioners are maintained. You will also find a collection of papers, award-winning conference proceedings, and recommended readings on self-managed teams. How could Oxford make use of this site? ■

http://www.workteams.unt.edu/

Teams: Employee Involvement in Action

Teams like those at Oxford are becoming much more common. For example, at the General Mills cereal plant at Lodi, California, work teams run the plant and productivity has never been higher.[2] In one team, Carmen Gomez, Ruby Liptack, and Bill Gerstner operate the cereal-manufacturing machinery, while Donald Owen, William Walker, and Irma Hills help maintain it. The manager, Denny Perak, is not a manager in the traditional sense at all: instead, he "coaches the team on management techniques and serves as the team's link with headquarters."[3]

At Johnsonville Foods, similar self-managing teams now recruit, hire, evaluate, and fire (if necessary) on their own. Although many of the workers have little or no college background, they also "train one another, formulate and track their own budgets, make capital investment proposals as needed, handle quality control and inspection, develop their own quantitative standards, improve every process and product, and create prototypes of possible new products."[4] Work teams like these can be defined as "a small number of people with complementary skills who are committed to a common purpose, set of performance goals, and approach, for which they hold themselves mutually accountable."[5]

The use of work teams is now widespread throughout the United States. For example, one study concluded that 82 percent of all U.S. firms have organized at least some of their employees into work groups identified as teams. Thirty-five percent of all U.S. organizations also have at least one team classified as self-directed or semi-autonomous (which generally means that the team supervises itself).[6]

Work teams like these are examples of employee involvement programs. An **employee involvement program** is any formal program that lets employees participate in formulating important work decisions or in supervising all or part of their own work activities.[7]

Managers rank such programs as their biggest productivity boosters. For example, the editors of *National Productivity Review* mailed a survey several years ago to subscribers. They found that "increased employee involvement in the generation and implementation of ideas was ranked the highest priority productivity improvement action by the respondents." Employee involvement "was similarly ranked number one as the top cause of improvement over the past two years at these firms." (The other eight causes of improvement, in descending order, were quality programs, improved process methods, top management, equipment, technology, training, computers, and automation.)

■ **FIGURE 14.1**
Eight Levels of Employee Involvement

SOURCE: Jack Osborn et al., *Self-Directed Work Teams* (Homewood, IL: Business One Irwin, 1990), 30.

> **Employee Involvement in Your Company:**
> **An Informal Checklist**
>
> 1. Information sharing: Managers make decisions on their own, announce them, then respond to any questions employees may have.
> 2. Managers usually make the decisions, but only after seeking the views of employees.
> 3. Managers often form temporary employee groups to recommend solutions for specified problems.
> 4. Managers meet with employee groups regularly—once a week or so—to help them identify problems and recommend solutions.
> 5. Intergroup problem solving: Managers establish and participate in cross-functional employee problem-solving teams.
> 6. Ongoing work groups assume expanded responsibility for a particular issue, like cost reduction.
> 7. Employees within an area function full-time with minimal direct supervision.
> 8. Total self-direction: Traditional supervisory roles do not exist; almost all employees participate in self-managing teams.

Levels of Employee Involvement

Several levels or degrees of employee involvement are possible. Based on one study of work team employee involvement programs in the United States, researchers presented the "informal, non-scientific" sample of employee involvement levels summarized in Figure 14.1.[8] As you can see, the levels of employee involvement range from Level 1, information sharing (managers make all important operational decisions, inform employees, and then respond to employee questions) to Level 5, intergroup problem solving (experienced, trained, cross-functional teams meet regularly with a manager to work on problems across several organizational units);[9] up to Level 8, total self-direction ("every employee belongs to a self-directed team, starting with a highly interactive executive group").[10] Level 8 often means establishing a team-based organization. Here the company rearranges its organizational structure and systems around team-based work assignments. The managers then devote their major efforts toward coaching their subordinates to manage themselves.[11]

Group Dynamics: The Building Blocks of Groups

How do groups and teams differ, and how—if at all—are they alike?

Groups and Teams

All teams are groups, but a group is not always a team. Whether we are referring to a football team, a commando team, or a self-managing work team, a **team** is always distinguished by the fact that its members are "committed to a common purpose, set of performance goals, and approach for which they hold themselves mutually accountable."[12] A **group** is defined as two or more persons who are interacting with one another in such a manner that each person influences and is influenced by each other person.[13] Groups in general need not have such unanimity of purpose, but since all teams are groups, we should briefly review some group concepts before moving on. Two aspects of groups are especially important: norms and cohesiveness.

Development and Enforcement of Group Norms

Group norms are "the informal rules that groups adopt to regulate and regularize group members' behavior."[14] They are "rules of behavior, proper ways of acting, which have been accepted as legitimate by members of a group [and that] specify the kind of behaviors that are expected of group members."[15]

Work groups, by enforcing their norms, can have an enormous impact on their members' behavior.[16] In fact, studies show that "group norms may have a greater influence on the individual's performance than the knowledge, skills and abilities the individual brings to the work setting."[17] This fact was first revealed by a research project known as the Hawthorne studies. Here researchers described, for instance, how production that exceeded the group's norms triggered what the workers called binging, in which the producer's hand was slapped by other workers.

Determinants of Group Cohesiveness

In turn, the extent to which a group can influence its members' behavior depends largely on the attraction of the group for its members, or its **group cohesiveness.**[18]

Group cohesiveness depends on several factors. Proximity and contact are prerequisites for group cohesiveness; without them, individuals would have no opportunity to become attracted to one another. On the other hand, proximity is no guarantee that people will discover they have something in common; if the individuals should find they have little in common, the effect could be just the opposite.[19]

Cohesiveness also depends on the interpersonal attraction between the people involved. Similarly, individuals are usually attracted to the group itself because they find its activities or goals attractive, rewarding, or valuable, or because they believe that through the group they can accomplish something they could not accomplish on their own.

Several other things influence group cohesiveness. Intergroup competition can foster cohesiveness (particularly for the winning group), whereas intragroup com-

Cohesiveness is essential to the success of many work teams, as much in traditional business settings as in such high-risk work as capping gushing oil wells.

petition (competition between the group's members) tends to undermine cohesiveness.[20] People join groups in part because they believe the group can help them accomplish their goals; agreement over goals therefore boosts cohesiveness, whereas differences reduce it.[21] Group cohesiveness also tends to decline as group size increases beyond about 20 members.[22] In summary, proximity, interpersonal attractiveness, homogeneity of interests or goals, intergroup competition, and a manageable size tend to foster group cohesiveness and may therefore influence team performance as well.

How to Use Teams at Work

In considering whether and how to rely more heavily on teams in the organization, the head of a company naturally must decide what sorts of teams to use. Here there are many choices, because teams can be used in various ways.

For example, team-expert James Shonk says companies can use four basic types of teams: suggestion teams, problem-solving teams, semi-autonomous teams, and self-managing teams.[23]

Suggestion teams are usually short-term teams that exist to work on given issues such as how to cut costs or increase productivity.

Problem-solving teams "are involved in identifying and researching activities and in developing effective solutions to work-related problems."[24] Most such teams consist of the supervisor and five to eight employees from a common work area; the quality circles described later are an example.

Semi-autonomous teams have a lot of input into managing the activities in their own work area but are still managed by a supervisor. Teams like this might establish their own goals, provide input into solving problems in their work area, and have a lot of input into daily operating decisions such as when to take breaks and which tasks to do first. However, they are still managed by a formal supervisor.

Self-managing teams are also called self-directed work teams. These are like the teams at the Lodi plant of General Mills and are responsible for managing their work on a daily basis. For example, they do their own work scheduling, set their own goals, hire team members, and make operating decisions such as dealing with vendors if some parts are defective. These teams are a major element in helping companies manage change. As Shonk puts it, "self-managing teams are also used where employees need freedom to act."[25] We'll look more closely at several specific types of work teams next.

Quality Circles

Companies have long used decision-making committees at the management level for analysis, advice, and recommendations. Often called task forces, project groups, or audit or safety groups, these committees identify problems or opportunities and recommend courses of action.[26]

Such analysis and recommendation teams have now become common in nonmanagerial ranks as well. The quality circle is the most familiar example. A **quality circle (QC)** is a team of 6 to 12 employees that meets once a week at work to solve problems affecting its work area.[27] Such teams are first trained in problem analysis techniques (including basic statistics). Then the quality circle is set to apply the problem analysis process.[28] In practice, this process has five steps: problem identification, problem selection, problem analysis, solution recommendations, and solution review by top management. One study estimates that "perhaps several hundred thousand U.S. employees belong to QC circles," and that most of these are frontline manufacturing employees.[29]

The original wave of employer enthusiasm and support for quality circle programs began to fade several years ago. Perhaps the biggest reason is that many circles failed to produce measurable cost savings. Some circles' bottom line aims were too vague. In other firms, having the employees choose and analyze their own problems proved incompatible with the autocratic management styles and cultures in existence.[30]

Many firms today are taking steps to make their quality circles more effective. At Honeywell Corporation the firm has replaced about 700 of its original quality circles with about 1,000 new work teams. These new teams are generally not voluntary; instead they include most shop floor employees and, in contrast to the bottom-up approach of quality circles, they work on problems assigned by management.[31]

Project, Development, or Venture Teams

Teamwork is especially important for special projects like developing a new product. The tight coordination and open communications needed here make close-knit teams especially useful. Project and development teams are often composed of professionals (marketing experts or engineers, for example). They team up on specific projects such as designing new processes (process design teams) or products (new-product development teams).

A **venture team** "is a small group of people who operate as a semi-autonomous unit to create and develop a new idea."[32] The classic example was the IBM team organized in Boca Raton, Florida, to develop and introduce IBM's first personal computer. As is usually the case with venture teams, the unit was semi-autonomous in that it had its own budget and leader and the freedom to make decisions within broad guidelines.

As it turns out, IBM's PC venture team illustrates both the pros and cons of the venture team approach. Working semi-autonomously, the team was able to create a new computer system and bring it to market in less than two years. This might have taken IBM many years to accomplish under its usual hierarchical approach to product development.

However, many believe the venture team's autonomy eventually backfired. Not bound by IBM's traditional policy of using only IBM parts, the team went outside IBM, both to Microsoft (for its DOS or disk operating system) and to Intel (for the computer processor). This facilitated the early introduction of the IBM PC. Unfortunately for IBM, it also allowed Intel and Microsoft to sell the same PC parts to any manufacturer and led to the proliferation of IBM clones.[33]

Managing Change

"HOT" GROUPS

If teams in general can be useful for getting things done, imagine how useful a "hot" group can be. A **hot group,** according to two experts, is just what the name implies: "a lively, high-achieving, dedicated group, usually small, whose members are turned on to an exciting and challenging task. Hot groups, while they last, completely captivate their members, occupying their hearts and minds to the exclusion of almost everything else."[34]

A hot group isn't so much a special use for a team as it is an especially vibrant and high-energy team. Thus, quality circles, new-product development, and self-directed work teams may also be hot teams (although hot teams do tend to focus on short-term projects or tasks). The thing that makes a team "hot," to repeat, is the fact that it is high achieving, dedicated, and turned on to an exciting and challenging task.

Hot teams are especially important for 21st-century organizations, these experts say.[35] Tomorrow's organizations will require "both the capacity to keep up with an intense pace of change and the capacity to reshape themselves continually."[36] High-energy dedication helps hot team members challenge and pierce the "accepted organizational propriety" that might otherwise inhibit creative solutions. The hot group that developed Apple's flagship product, the Macintosh, a number of years ago is a classic example. As these experts describe it,

> Apple's early culture was exciting, urgent, flamboyant, defiant, ready to take on Big Blue (IBM) and anyone else in its path. . . . It is not surprising, therefore, that Apple's flagship product, the Macintosh, was developed by a small group consisting of people from all over the company. Led primarily by the aggressive and charismatic Steve Jobs, the group was spurred on by the ennobling challenge of building small computers for the masses.[37]

Hot groups have a number of distinguishing characteristics that leaders should keep in mind:[38]

> *A total preoccupation with an important mission.* The most distinguishing characteristic of a hot group is its total preoccupation with a task that for members has a higher meaning. The mission may be developing a vaccine for AIDS, or something less magnificent like instituting a 24-hour customer service system for a department store. Outsiders may not see the mission the same way, but hot groups always feel that what they are doing is extremely relevant and important, and they think about their task constantly.

> *Intellectual intensity, integrity, and exchange of ideas.* Hot groups work on problems in which all members have to use their heads, intensely and continuously. Debate among members is often loud and passionate.

> *Emotional intensity.* Perhaps the best way to put this is that "hot group members behave like people in love. They are infatuated with the challenge of their task and often with the talent around them."[39] Even once they go home at night they may sacrifice their own personal preferences—say to attend a movie or a play—to continue trying to solve the problem at hand. Hot group members may then come in the next morning with a comment like "I was thinking about that problem in bed last night, and I had an idea. So I got up and tried a few things on my PC, and here's what I got. What do you all think?"[40]

> *Temporary structure/small size.* Hot groups are usually small enough to permit close interpersonal relationships among their members (fewer than 30) and are also temporary and relatively short lived: "They share the happy attribute of dissolving when they finish their work."[41]

Managers can provide several things to encourage the growth of hot groups:

> *Openness and flexibility.* Companies in which hot groups thrive disdain bureaucracy and don't inhibit hot group members from seeking out information and

advice anywhere in the company. Quite the opposite: Hot groups require "easy, informal access across hierarchical levels and across departmental, divisional, and organizational boundaries."[42]

Independence and autonomy. To help keep hot groups hot while they make their contributions, "it is wise to leave them alone for reasonable periods of time."[43] They need the independence and autonomy that IBM's Boca Raton PC development team received, for instance. And, they must not be unduly bound by restrictive company policies and procedures—like requiring hot team members to get approval ahead of time for just about every penny they spend, for instance.

People first. Hot groups tend to thrive in companies that put a premium on putting their people first—on emphasizing respect for the individual and the importance of hiring high-potential people. Management then gives them the elbow room, opportunities, and training they need to become all that they can be.

The search for truth. Hot groups traditionally thrive in research-oriented companies like Bell Labs where the culture values the scientific method and the search for truth. What does this mean? It means valuing open debate of the issues, publicizing results, conducting objective, preferably measurable, studies to support one's conclusions, and accepting the fact that failures are an inescapable feature of the research process.

Transnational Teams

What do you do, as the head of a multinational company, if you have a special project that involves activities in several countries at once? Increasingly, top executives are answering that question by creating **transnational teams,** work groups composed of multinational members whose activities span many countries.[44]

Transnational teams are being used in a variety of ways. For example, Fuji-Xerox sent 15 of its most experienced Tokyo engineers to a Xerox Corporation facility in Webster, New York. There they worked for five years with a group of U.S. engineers to develop a "world copier," a product that proved to be a huge success in the global marketplace.[45] A group of managers and technical specialists from IBM-Latin America formed their own multicountry team to market, sell, and distribute personal computers in 11 Latin American countries. A European beverage manufacturer formed a 13-member transnational team called the European Production Task Force with members from five countries. Its job was to analyze how many factories they should operate in Europe, what size and type they should be, and where they should be located. The common denominator in each case is that a multicountry team contributed to its company's efforts to globalize, that is, to extend the firm's products and operations into international markets.[46]

Transnational teams face some special challenges.[47] They typically work on projects that are highly complex and important compared to most other teams (projects like the world copier or multinational factory placement projects, for example). They are also obviously subject to what several experts have called the special demands of "multicultural dynamics"—in other words, the fact that they are made up of people with different languages, different interpersonal styles, different cultures, and a host of other differences and are dealing with activities in multiple cultures as well.

Characteristics like these make it especially important to design and lead transnational teams carefully. Recommendations here include:

Focus on business strategy. Ensure that the team members understand and buy into the company's strategy and make sure the team understands how the team's mission fits with that overall strategy.

Provide for communications and decision making. Since many transnational teams must communicate and make decisions across vast geographic distances, considerable thought must be given to the technology that will be used to enhance communications and decision making. For example, the communications system must enable geographically dispersed team members to communicate with each other, with others in the company, and with outsiders quickly and in a manner that provides for a full and rich understanding of the issues. Information technology therefore typically includes videoconferencing as well as the more usual telephone, voice mail, e-mail, and fax. Decision support systems—PC-based "groupware" that permits, for instance, simultaneous computerized discussions of issues—are used as well.

Build teamwork. Given the multicultural nature of these groups, facilitating group cohesiveness is particularly important. "Successful teams are characterized by leaders and members who trust each other, are committed to the team's mission, can be counted on to perform their respective tasks, and enjoy working with each other."[48] Team leaders and the company itself therefore have to work hard to provide the training and leadership that foster such group characteristics.

Self-Directed Work Teams

In many firms today, self-directed (also called self-managing) work teams are the ultimate manifestation of employee involvement programs. A **self-directed work team** is a highly trained group of from six to eight employees, on average, fully responsible for turning out a well-defined segment of finished work."[49] The "well-defined segment" might be an entire refrigerator, or an engine, or a fully processed insurance claim. In any case, the distinguishing features of self-directed work teams are that they are empowered to direct their own work and that the work itself is a well-defined item.

These teams usually consist of frontline employees who work together making or doing things full-time. Increasingly, such teams include employees who are responsible for the most basic activities of the business—product assembly, customer sales, and product service.[50] In many cases the work of the whole company is divided up and organized around such teams.

STEPS TO EXPECT IN MOVING TO SELF-DIRECTED TEAMS. Firms typically go through six phases in organizing the company's work around self-directed teams:

1. *Start-up.* First, an executive steering committee should establish the feasibility of a team-based organizational structure: develop a mission statement for the program, select the initial team sites, design a multilevel network of teams (to establish what tasks each of them will do and how the teams will overlap), and assign employees to the teams. Then, at start-up, the teams and supervisors begin working out their specific roles in the new teams. In summary, look at all the work that must be done by the company (or the location that will be "teamed") and decide what kinds of teams will be assigned what tasks.

2. *Training.* Experts contend that "the dominant feature of start-up is intensive training for all involved." Team members must learn how to communicate and how to listen, how to use administrative procedures and budgets, and how to develop other similar skills. Supervisors must learn how to become facilitators and coaches rather than top-down supervisors.[51]

3. *Confusion.* Once the initial enthusiasm wears off, the organization and its teams may enter a period of some confusion. Team members may become concerned about whether their new (probably self-imposed) higher work standards are liable to backfire on them at compensation time; supervisors may become increasingly concerned about their apparently shrinking role in day-to-day operations.

4. *The move to leader-centered teams.* Ideally, the team's confidence should grow as members master their new skills and find better ways to apply their new authority and accomplish their work. The chief danger in this stage, according to experts, is that the teams become too reliant "on their internal leaders." Rather than remaining self-directed, some teams may slip into the habit of letting an elected team member carry out the former supervisor's supervisory role. A way to avoid this is "to make sure everyone continues to learn and eventually exercise leadership skills, . . . [and] allow anyone to exercise leadership functions as needed."[52]

5. *Misplaced loyalty.* The teams, sometimes blinded by their newfound authority and ability to supervise themselves, may allow loyalty to their co-workers to hide problems in the team. For example, team members might hide a poorly performing member to protect the person from outside discipline in a misguided fit of loyalty. Management's job here is to reemphasize both the need for intrateam cooperation and the team's responsibility to adequately supervise its own members.

6. *The move to self-directed teams.* Once the new teams rid themselves of the intense team-oriented loyalties that often accompany building self-directed teams, the organization can move to what researcher Jack Orsburn calls "the period of true self-direction."[53]

The empowerment of self-directed teams can reportedly be a heady experience for all concerned. Here's what one vice president of a midwestern consumer goods company said about organizing his firm around teams: "People on the floor were talking about world markets, customer needs, competitors' products, making process improvements—all the things managers are supposed to think about."[54]

Strategy in Action

THE IMPORTANCE OF TOP-MANAGEMENT TEAMWORK

Most companies are led by CEOs; however, no single individual can formulate and implement a strategy for a complex organization alone.[55] Therefore, creating a cohesive top-management team including the CEO and his or her subordinate officers is a precondition if a firm is to implement its strategy and structure and achieve its goals. Strategy management experts list several reasons why top-management teamwork is crucial for success:[56]

- The CEO has a complex coordinative task and cannot be effective without working closely with the people who are in charge of the company's major activities (such as functions, products, or regions).
- The CEO's subordinate officers usually possess greater expertise about the operating components of the organization and their own fields of expertise than does the CEO.
- The team members can be more understanding of and supportive of the CEO's strategic decisions if they have a voice in shaping those decisions.
- Teamwork among the members of the top-management team enhances communication and coordination among them.
- Technical and administrative innovations will be more likely when team members have more opportunity for cross-functional communication.

Most CEOs therefore spend considerable time molding their subordinates into a cohesive top-management team. For example, former Chairperson and CEO Stephen Wolf of United Airlines' parent UAL Corporation reportedly worked closely on a daily basis with the executives in charge of areas like finance, marketing, and employee relations. His success in turning that company around is partially attributed to his ability to assemble a talented top management team.

Other companies go even further. For example, Xerox created an executive team of six executives who replace the chief operating officer (who in many firms would hold the title "president") and report to the CEO. Similarly, Microsoft's three-person "Office of the President" reports directly to Chairperson William Gates III, and Seattle-based department store Nordstrom is run by six "co-presidents."[57]

Former United Airlines CEO Stephen Wolf is credited with forging a top management team that has helped revive the airline's fortunes.

Requiring several people to work together doesn't make the group a team, and certainly not a productive one. An underperforming team might simply lack the sort of initiative and sense of urgency that coaches traditionally try to ignite during half-time breaks. But a lack of initiative is often just one of the problems with which teams must cope.

Causes of Unproductive Teams

Obviously, many problems can cause unproductive teams. For example, all the things that contribute to cohesiveness—*proximity, interpersonal attraction,* and *attractive goals*—can undermine a team's productiveness if absent.

Similarly, the purpose of a team is to harness divergent skills and talents for specific objectives; however, the *divergent points of view* may lead instead to tension and conflict.[58] *Power struggles*—some subtle, some not—can also undermine the group's effectiveness; for example, individual members may try to undermine potentially productive ideas with the implicit goal of winning their point rather than doing what's best for the team. In addition, some team members may be ignored, thus eliminating a potentially valuable resource.[59]

Irving Janis describes another team problem, one he calls **groupthink:** "the tendency for a highly cohesive group, especially one working on special projects, to develop a sense of detachment and elitism."[60] This sense of detachment, Janis found, can lead the group to press for conformity and hesitate to examine different points of view. The opinions of individual group members thus tend to be ignored or subordinated to the will of the group as groupthink sets in. The group enforces a strong norm of consensus so that just one powerful point of view prevails, even though cogent arguments against it may exist in the group.

Symptoms of Unproductive Teams

Various symptoms make it easy to recognize unproductive teams:[61]

Cautious or guarded communication. When people fear some form of punishment, ridicule, or negative reaction, they may say nothing or be guarded in what they do say.

Lack of disagreement. Lack of disagreement among team members may reflect an unwillingness to share members' true feelings and ideas.

Use of personal criticism. Personal criticism, such as "If you can't come up with a better idea than that, you better keep quiet," is a sign of unhealthy team member relations.

Malfunctioning meetings. Unproductive teams often have malfunctioning meetings characterized by boredom, lack of enthusiastic participation, failure to reach decisions, and dominance by one or two people.

Unclear goals. Productive teams have a clear sense of mission, whereas members of unproductive teams are often unable to recite their own team's objectives.

Low commitment. Without a clear sense of purpose, unproductive teams tend to have low commitment, because it's not clear what they should be committed to.

Conflict within the team. Unproductive teams are often characterized by a suspicious, combative environment and by conflict among team members.

Characteristics of Productive Teams

Of course, it is not unproductive teams you want but productive ones. A team, remember, is "a small number of people with complementary skills who are committed to a common purpose, set of performance goals, and approach for which they hold themselves mutually accountable."[62] The characteristics of productive teams are implicit in this definition. Specifically, based on an extensive study of teams at work, Katzenbach and Smith found that productive teams have five characteristics.

COMMITMENT TO A MISSION. Katzenbach and Smith found that "the essence of a team is a common commitment. Without it, groups perform as individuals; with it, they become a powerful unit of collective performance."[63] Teams must, therefore, have a clear mission to which to be committed, such as Saturn's "Let's beat the Japanese by producing a world-class quality car."[64] Katzenbach and Smith found that the most productive teams then developed commitment around their own definition of what management wanted their teams to do: "The best teams invest a tremendous amount of time and effort exploring, shaping, and agreeing on a purpose that belongs to them both collectively and individually."[65]

SPECIFIC PERFORMANCE GOALS. Productive teams translate their common purpose (such as "build world-class quality cars") into specific performance goals (such as "reduce new-car defects to no more than four per vehicle"). In fact, "transforming broad directives into specific and measurable performance goals is the surest first step for a team trying to shape a purpose meaningful to its members."[66]

RIGHT SIZE, RIGHT MIX. Best-performing teams generally have fewer than 25 people, and usually between 7 and 14 people. Team members also complement each other in terms of their skills. For example, accomplishing the team's mission usually calls for people strong in technical expertise as well as those skilled in problem solving, decision making, and interpersonal relationships.

Organizational Behavior in Action

GROUP COMPOSITION DETERMINES GROUP INNOVATION

A recent study illustrates the importance of the right mix of group members. The researchers studied the innovativeness of proposals made by top-management teams in 27 hospitals. The question was whether the teams' innovativeness reflected the individual innovativeness of their team members. Individual innovativeness was measured with a scale that asked such questions as "I suggest new working methods to the people I work with" and "I try to introduce improved methods of doing things at work."[67]

In this study the level of team innovation, and specifically the radicalness of the innovations introduced by the teams, apparently depended to a large extent on how individually innovative the teams' members were. The implication is that—at least when it comes to innovation—the team you put together had better have a mix that includes at least a few highly innovative people.

A COMMON APPROACH.   Productive teams also agree on a common approach with respect to the way they will work together to accomplish their mission. For example, team members agree about: who will do particular jobs; how schedules will be set and followed; what skills need to be developed; what members will have to do to earn continuing membership in the team; and how decisions will be made and modified.

MUTUAL ACCOUNTABILITY.   The most productive teams also develop a sense of mutual accountability. They believe "we are all in this together" and that "we all have to hold ourselves accountable for doing whatever is needed to help the team achieve its mission." Katzenbach and Smith found that such mutual accountability cannot be coerced. Instead, it emerges from the commitment and trust that come from working together toward a common purpose. The Entrepreneurs in Action box illustrates how one entrepreneur built productive, self-managing teams to help run his newsletter business.

How to Build Team Performance

Good coaches know that productive teams don't emerge spontaneously; they require careful selection, training, and management. Experts have identified the following guidelines companies can use to build effective teams:

Establish urgent, demanding performance standards. All team members need to believe the team has urgent and worthwhile purposes, and they need to know what their performance standards are.

Select members for skill and skill potential. Choose people both for their existing skills and for their potential to improve existing skills and learn new ones.

Pay particular attention to first meetings and actions. Initial impressions always mean a lot. When potential teams first gather, everyone monitors the signals given by others to confirm, suspend, or dispel their assumptions and concerns. If a senior executive leaves the team kickoff to take a phone call 10 minutes after the session begins and never returns, people get the message.

Set some clear rules of behavior. All effective teams develop rules of conduct at the outset to help them achieve their purpose and performance goals. The most critical initial rules pertain to attendance (for example, "no interruptions to take phone calls"), discussion ("no sacred cows"), confidentiality ("the only things to leave this room are what we agree on"), analytic approach ("facts are friendly"), end-product orientation ("everyone gets assignments and does them"), constructive confrontation ("no finger pointing"), and, often the most important, contributions ("everyone does real work").

Move from "boss" to "coach." Self-directed work teams are by definition empowered: They have the confidence, authority, tools, and information to manage themselves. That means the leader's job is not to boss but to support and to coach—to see that team members have the support they need to do their jobs.

Set a few immediate performance-oriented tasks and goals. Most effective teams trace their advancement to key accomplishments. Such accomplishments can be facilitated by immediately establishing a few challenging goals that can be reached early on.

Challenge the group regularly with fresh facts and information. New information (such as on how the company is doing) causes a team to redefine and

Entrepreneurs in Action

PUBLISHED IMAGE, INC.

Almost from the day he founded Published Image, Inc., and organized the newsletter into self-managed teams, Eric Gershman had in mind the day his own position would become superfluous. His viewpoint was that employees capable of preparing their own work schedules, budgets, and bonuses certainly shouldn't have much use for a boss.

Gershman's team approach is nothing new in larger corporations, but it is rare for operations like Published Image, which has a total workforce of only 26. For one thing, it's costly, in both time and tangible resources, to implement successful self-managed work teams. "You have to seriously redesign the organization to make them most effective," says Edward Lawler III, director of the University of Southern California's Center for Effective Organizations.

Gershman has always been something of a contrarian, dating back to his first job at a Boston ad agency. Luckily, he's also resilient. Getting sacked didn't change his viewpoint in the least. "I always felt I had better ways of doing things than my boss," he says.

With the growth of mutual funds, Gershman correctly predicted the need for shareholder newsletters, and he spent his entire savings getting Published Image off the ground. Eleven clients and $600,000 in revenue later, things almost looked rosy, except for a few problems. Turnover was high, morale low, factual errors commonplace, and a third of the clients were opting out annually. In fact the company was about to go bust. Gershman's characteristic certitude led him to the inescapable conclusion that changes had to be made. He came up with a 250-page plan of action.

"We blew up the whole company and totally changed people's thinking about what their job is," Gershman says. Published Image was divided into four virtually independent teams responsible for client relations, sales, editorial content, and production. Everyone performed a speciality, but everyone shared responsibility for daily deadlines as well. "We work like a unit and pitch in to get out on time whatever has to get done," says Shelley Danse. Her day as an account executive can stretch to cover tasks from research to proofreading to laying out artwork.

Not surprisingly, the team approach at Published Image fosters a sense of ownership of the collective output, as well as enhanced appreciation of the work of fellow members. Planning is easier and efficiency has improved. Turnover is down to zero. Clients are also impressed. "We have one group of people who know all facets of our job, and we can contact any of them during the process," says Peter Herlihy, vice president of mutual funds marketing at Fleet Financial Group.

Gershman may soon get his wish of working himself out of a job. Revenue doubled in 1993 to $4 million, and more than a third of the 20 percent rise in profit margin occurred in the fourth quarter. ■

SOURCE: Michael Selz, "Testing Self-Managing Teams, Entrepreneur Hopes to Lose Job," *Wall Street Journal,* 11 January 1994, B-1.

enrich its understanding of the challenges it faces. It thereby helps the team shape its common purpose, set clearer goals, and improve its approach.

Spend lots of time together. Remember that proximity and interaction usually builds cohesiveness. Team members should spend a lot of time together, scheduled and unscheduled, especially in the beginning. This time need not always be spent together physically; electronic, fax, and phone time can also count as time spent together.

Exploit the power of positive feedback, recognition, and reward. Positive reinforcement works as well for teams as elsewhere. There are many ways to recognize and reward team performance beyond money. They include having a senior executive speak directly to the team about the urgency of its mission, and using awards to recognize contributions.

Shoot for the right team size.[68] Create teams with the smallest number of employees required to do the work. Large size can reduce interaction and involvement and boost the need for excessive coordination.

Choose people who like teamwork. Do what companies like Toyota do: recruit and select employees who have a history of preferring to work in teams and of being good team members. Loners and antisocial types don't usually make good team members.

Train, train, train. Make sure team members have the training they need to do their jobs. Training should cover topics such as the philosophy of doing work through teams, how teams make decisions, interpersonal and communications skills for team members, and the technical skills that team members will need to perform their jobs.

Cross-train for flexibility. Ideally, members of most teams should receive cross-training to learn the jobs of fellow team members, either informally or through scheduled rotating assignments. This can help reduce disruptions due to absenteeism and can boost flexibility, since all team members are always ready to fill in when needed.

Emphasize the task's importance. Team members need to know that what they're doing is important for the organization, so communicate that message whenever you can. For example, emphasize the task's importance in terms of its consequences for customers, other employees, the organization's mission, and the business's overall results.

Assign whole tasks. Try to make the team responsible for a distinct piece of work, such as an entire product or project or segment of the business. This can boost team members' sense of responsibility and ownership, in line with Herzberg's theory of job enrichment.

Build team spirit. Teams obviously should have a "can do" attitude and the confidence and sense of self-efficacy that they can and will be effective. Those managing and leading groups therefore have to focus on fostering a positive attitude. And, as we'll see below, they must provide the coaching and support needed to foster the self-confidence that's a big part of empowered work groups.

Encourage social support. Work teams, like any group, are more effective when members support and help each other. Therefore, set a good example by being supportive yourself, and take concrete steps to encourage and reinforce positive interactions and cohesiveness within the team.

Organizational Behavior in Action

CO-WORKER SIMILARITY AND THE PERFORMANCE OF THE TEAM

How diverse should the team be that you put together? Co-worker diversity can be a tricky issue when it comes to team performance.[69] On the one hand, "a team with a variety of members whose skills and experiences differ and complement each other can take on a wide range of tasks."[70] On the other hand, "be on the alert . . . for teams whose membership is excessively varied, because conflict and communications breakdown can result."[71] What is a manager to do?

Part of the answer lies in a recent study conducted by three behavioral scientists at the University of Houston.[72] The study examined the impact of various types of similarities (demographic, value, and behavioral style preference) on co-workers' attitudes and behaviors. The study was conducted in conjunction with a four-week training program for executives and surveyed 43 senior-level managers who were enrolled in the program and assigned to five- or six-person case study teams as part of their training.

Information about various dimensions of co-worker similarity was measured. Demographic characteristics included age, level of education, country of citizenship, and gender. Information about values included the relative importance that individuals placed on, for example, "a world at peace," "happiness," "freedom," and "self-determination." A psychological inventory known as the Myers-Briggs Type Indicator (discussed earlier in this book) was used to measure individuals' behavioral style preferences—for instance, in terms of sensing/intuition and thinking/feeling. Team members also rated such things as how much they liked each team member and their willingness to work with each of them in the future.

The basic research question was, how did co-workers' similarities influence how well they liked each other and how they felt about working with the other team members in the future? Co-worker similarities were important. For example, demographic similarity was the strongest predictor of social liking and co-worker preference, but only at the start of the training: Three weeks after the teams had begun their work, demographic similarity ceased to contribute significantly to social liking and co-worker preference. Apparently, such differences among team members were overcome by the positive effects that came from the team members' working together successfully to analyze their assigned case studies.

After three weeks of working together, however, similarity in personal values still predicted both liking and preference. Therefore, creating teams whose members share personal values—beliefs about what is good or bad and what one should or should not do—seems to be important for building long-term team cohesiveness. Differences in things like age, education, country of citizenship, and gender seem to fade in significance as the team works together successfully. ■

In Summary—Team Traps: What They Are, How to Avoid Them

Obviously, some teams do not succeed, because there's a negative side to each of the team performance-building guidelines above. For example, if the team is too large, if it's staffed with chronic loners, if members haven't the skills or skill potential, or if the required team spirit is lacking, the team might well fail.

One expert says the causes of a decline in team effectiveness can be summed up by three factors: leadership, focus, and capability, a point summarized in Figure 14.2 and to which we now briefly turn.[73]

Leadership. Some problems have their genesis in a lack of leadership—lack of support, of consistency of direction, of vision, budget, or resources. As summarized in Figure 14.2, the way to improve this situation is to ensure demonstrated leadership support, make the budget and resources available, boost communications and contact with the leader, or (if required) change leadership.

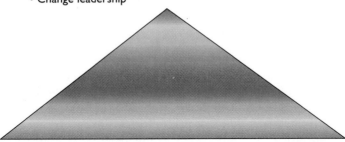

Leadership

Lack of support, consistency of direction, vision, budget, and resources.

Improvement strategy:
- Plan events to ensure demonstrated leadership support
- Increase availability of budget and resources
- Increase communication and contact with leader
- Change leadership

Focus

Lack of clarity about team purpose, roles, strategy, and goals.

Improvement strategy:
- Establish and clarify team charter
- Clarify boundary conditions
- Ensure open channels for communications and information transfer
- Clarify team member roles
- Establish regular team meetings

Capability

Lack of critical skill sets, knowledge, ongoing learning, and development.

Improvement strategy:
- Provide appropriate education and training
- Establish a team development plan
- Establish individual development plans
- Reflect on how group process can be improved
- Regularly assess team effectiveness

▦ **FIGURE 14.2**
Leadership, Focus, and Capability Pyramid
Note: Traps that lead to a decline in team effectiveness typically are related to one of three factors: leadership, focus, or capability. Each of these three factors requires a different improvement strategy to overcome the trap.

SOURCE: Steven Rayner, "Team Traps: What They Are, How to Avoid Them," *National Productivity Review* (Summer 1996), 107. Reprinted by permission of John Wiley & Sons, Inc.

Focus. A lack of clarity or focus about team purpose, roles, strategy, and goals is the basis for several of the other problems that may undermine the team's performance. Improving the situation requires steps like clarifying the team's mission and charter, ensuring open channels of communication, clarifying team members' roles, and establishing regular team meetings.

Capability. Other problems (lack of training or of team member flexibility, for instance) stem from an overall "capability" problem—namely, a lack of critical skills, knowledge, learning, and development. Improvement calls for such things as providing appropriate education and training, establishing a team development plan, establishing individual team member development plans, and regularly assessing team effectiveness.

Managers in their leadership roles can obviously influence their teams' effectiveness. Doing so requires applying team performance-building guidelines like those listed above, and thereby avoiding the three big failings—inadequate leadership, inadequate focus, and inadequate team member capabilities.

Leading Productive Teams

You might say that leading productive teams is like leading anything—only more so. In other words, as we've just seen, leading a team also requires special team-building skills, skills like building mutually supportive team–member relationships,

Rodel, Inc., a manufacturing firm in Delaware, ensures that its people are effective with a rigorous leadership training program aimed at building trust, teamwork, and leadership. The team members pictured here went through the program together.

building team members' self-confidence, and learning how to move from "boss" to "coach." In the remainder of this chapter we will turn briefly to a few of the uniquely team-related aspects of being a leader.

How Do Team Leaders Behave?

We've touched on this elsewhere, but a short review and elaboration is now in order. Team leaders

- coach, they don't boss. They assess their team members' skills and help members use them to the fullest,
- encourage participation. They solicit input into decisions, share decision-making responsibility, and delegate specifically identified decisions to the team—often a great many decisions, as in the case of self-directed, self-managing work teams.
- are boundary managers. The team leader has to manage the interaction of the team with its environment, which means with other teams and with management and those outside the company. As a boundary manager, the team leader must also provide his or her team with high-quality information so the team can make informed choices.[74]
- are facilitators.[75] The best team leaders see themselves as facilitators. They give the other team members the self-confidence, authority, information, and tools they need to get their jobs done. Team leaders don't view themselves as sitting atop an organizational pyramid with team members reporting to them. Instead, they view the pyramid as upside down, with their job being to support and facilitate so their team can get the job done.

From Supervisor to Team Leader: Typical Transition Problems

Moving from being a traditional in-charge supervisor to being a facilitator/coach team leader isn't easy. As one former executive put it:

> Working . . . under the autocratic system was a lot easier, particularly when you want something done quickly and you are convinced you know the right way to do it. It is a lot easier to say, "OK, . . . we're going to Chicago tomorrow,"

rather than sit down and say, "All right, first of all, do we want to go out of town? And where do we want to go—east or west?"[76]

Why is it so difficult to make the transition from supervisor to team leader? For at least four reasons, as follows:

THE PERCEIVED LOSS OF POWER OR STATUS. Making the transition from supervisor to team leader often involves a perceived loss of power or status.[77] One day you are the boss, with the authority to give orders and have others obey; next day the pyramid is upside down and suddenly you're a facilitator/coach, trying to make sure your team members have what they need to do their jobs—to a large extent, without you. We've seen, for instance, that self-managing teams often schedule their own work priorities, hire their own co-workers, and decide themselves when to take their breaks.

What's worse, the perceived loss of power or status sometimes comes along with a real loss of supervisory perks. For example, the former boss (but now team leader) may find that he or she has had to relinquish that special parking spot or office that went along with being boss. This is because the company is now operating in the new egalitarian climate most conducive to self-managing, empowered work teams.

UNCLEAR TEAM LEADER ROLES. Some companies make the mistake of overemphasizing what the former supervisor (now team leader) is *not:* you're not the boss anymore; you are not to control or direct anymore; you are not to make all the hiring decisions anymore. Just telling the new team leaders what they're not, without clarifying what they are, can cause unnecessary transition difficulties. It can exacerbate the new team leader's perceived loss of power or status. And of course it can leave the person with the very real and unnerving question, "What exactly am I supposed to be doing, anyway?"

This problem is easily avoided. We've seen that team leaders do have important duties to perform—for instance, as coaches, facilitators, and boundary managers. The company's job is to ensure that the new team leaders understand what their new duties are, and that they have the training they need to do their new jobs effectively.

JOB SECURITY CONCERNS. Telling some new team leaders they're not in charge anymore understandably undermines their sense of security. After all, it's not unreasonable for someone to ask, "Just how secure is the job of managing a self-managing team?" Some new team leaders will say, "Sure, I know my new duties are to facilitate and coach, but that just doesn't make me feel as irreplaceable as I was when I was in charge."

There is a lot of truth in that. For example, Dana Corporation announced that it had reduced the number of management levels from 14 to 6 by moving responsibilities down in the organization. General Mills claims much of its productivity improvement from self-directed work teams (like those at Lodi) came from eliminating middle managers. Insecurity is therefore not just a figment of supervisors' imaginations as companies move to self-managing teams.

Companies handle this problem in several ways. Many—perhaps most—of the resulting teams will still need someone as facilitator/coach, so many of the supervisors will in fact find new homes as effective team leaders. What happens when there are too many supervisors? As you know, many companies have been downsized, and many former supervisors or managers have unfortunately lost their jobs.

Other companies, reluctant to lose the enormous expertise their supervisors have, take steps to retain these valuable human assets. For example, when Rohm and

Haas's Lousiville, Kentucky, plant changed over to self-directing work teams, the redundant supervisors were turned into training coordinators and made responsible for managing the continuing educational requirements of the plant's new teams.[78] In another company, 15 of the 25 supervisors who were displaced by the move to self-directed work teams were guaranteed their existing salary packages if they became team members; if not, they had the option to transfer elsewhere in the company.

Companies don't take steps to absorb displaced supervisors out of the kindness of their hearts. They want to retain the supervisors' expertise. Many employers know that, realistically, the only way they can get the supervisors to work with the company during the transition to self-managing teams is to let them know they will have employment options with the firm.

THE DOUBLE STANDARD PROBLEM. Many existing supervisors will feel the company is treating them as second-class citizens compared with the employees who are being trained to be team members. In other words, the supervisors see the company as having a double standard. Some companies do make the mistake of treating the supervisory staff as the forgotten people of the company, providing them with little or no attention, training, or clarification of what their new roles will be.

Treating anyone—let alone the company's supervisors—so cavalierly can obviously make them annoyed and resistant. The smarter way to proceed is to create and implement a development and transition plan for the supervisors too, one that clarifies their new team leadership duties, outlines how their security will be ensured, and identifies training they can expect to receive as they make the transition from supervisor to team leader.

What Are Team-Leader Values?

Not everyone is cut out to be an effective leader of self-managing teams. Self-managing teams are empowered to work with a minimum of supervision. Not every leader is philosophically prepared to surrender the trappings of "being a boss" that leading in such a situation requires.

In particular, being a leader of a self-managing team requires a special set of personal values, values that derive from the empowered nature of these teams. What personal values are consistent with building self-confidence, sharing authority, and ensuring the team has the tools and information it requires? Important team-leader values include the following.

PUT YOUR TEAM MEMBERS FIRST. Effective team leaders have an abiding respect for the individual. At Saturn, for instance, team members carry a card that lists the firm's values, one of which is set forth in these words:

> We have nothing of greater value than our people. We believe that demonstrating respect for the uniqueness of every individual builds a team of confident, creative members possessing a high degree of initiative, self-respect, and self-discipline.[79]

You'll find a similar stress on putting people first at companies like Toyota. Here's how one manager puts it:

> In all our meetings and in every way, all Toyota top managers continually express their trust in human nature. Mr. Cho [the chief executive of the company] continually reminds us that the team members must come first and that every other action we take and decision we make must be adapted to that basic idea; I must manage around that core idea.[80]

TEAM MEMBERS CAN BE TRUSTED TO DO THEIR BEST. Some leaders have what Douglas McGregor called "Theory X" assumptions: They believe that people are lazy, need to be controlled, need to be motivated, and are not very smart.

Assumptions like those obviously won't work for leaders of self-managing teams. These leaders need what McGregor called "Theory Y" assumptions about human nature: that people like to work, have self-control, can motivate themselves, and are smart.

What this comes down to is that effective team leaders trust that their team members will do their best. They believe that team members can and want to do a good job, they trust them to do their best, and they focus much of their attention on ensuring that their team members have what they need to do their jobs.

HELP TEAM MEMBERS TO SELF-ACTUALIZE. Effective team leaders understand that team members are driven by the need to fulfill their potential and to have fulfilling lives. They therefore value giving their team members the opportunity and ability to self-actualize.

DEVELOP YOUR TEAM MEMBERS' CAPABILITIES. Effective team leaders understand that team members can't develop the self-confidence and self-efficacy to do their jobs unless they receive the training and development to manage the work of the team. These leaders believe in the wisdom, value, and advisability of providing such training and development.

BELIEVE THAT TEAMWORK IS IMPORTANT. Although it may seem obvious, effective team leaders should believe that teamwork is important. They can't just pay lip service to the value of teamwork, since they really have to "walk the talk." Remember that much of the status and prestige of being a boss is stripped away in the transition from supervisor to team leader. Team leaders have to minimize status differences (like special parking spots and separate lunch rooms) when creating teams, and may even have to forego mammoth salary differentials.[81] At Toyota Manufacturing in Lexington, Kentucky, for instance, none of the managers—not even the president—has a private office; all work in the same large open space. At Ben & Jerry's Ice Cream, the owners believed that the top manager should earn no more than 7 to 10 times what the lowest paid employee earned—a far cry from the 100 to 200 times that's found in many other companies. But to take steps like these, one must believe that teamwork is important.

DELEGATE, DELEGATE, DELEGATE. Self-managing teams can't be led by someone who makes all or most of the decisions himself or herself. Team leaders have to value delegating. They must truly believe that an empowered team can do things—come up with better solutions or build-in better quality, for instance—that those who simply follow orders could not.

BARRIERS TO SUCCESS SHOULD BE ELIMINATED. Team leaders value eliminating barriers to success and are often driven by the desire to do so.[82] At Procter & Gamble, for instance, some team leaders refer to themselves as "barrier busters" because "they recognize the primary importance of removing the things that get in the way of the success of their teams."[83] Probably the single biggest difference between team leaders and supervisors is that team leaders view themselves as there to support their teams and therefore to eliminate barriers to their team's success. They believe that perhaps their primary responsibility is to make sure their teams have the means to get their jobs done. And if any factor is lacking—tools, or

too much red tape involved in getting a purchase approved, for instance—
team leader's responsibility to "bust through the barriers" and get the team t.
port it needs.

How Can Leaders Develop Effective Coaching Skills?

We've seen in this chapter that coaching is a big part of what team leaders do. That's why in his book *Team-Based Organizations*, James Shonk says that leading self-managing teams is a lot like coaching:

> It involves assessing the team's skills and helping them use them to the fullest. Employees tend to more effectively contribute when they are coached to make optimal use of all their strengths and resources.[84]

What is required to coach subordinates? Experts list the following guidelines:[85]

- Know your people. Assess each employee's skills so you can help team members use them to the fullest. As Shonk put it, employees contribute more effectively when coached to use all of their strengths and resources.
- Coach, don't tell. Remember: Your role as coach is to help your people develop their skills and competencies. In other words, your job is not to tell people what to do or to sell your own ideas, but to help others define, analyze, and solve problems. The best way to influence subordinates in a coaching situation is *not* to tell them what to do. Instead, stimulate increased employee initiative and autonomy by raising questions, helping your people identify alternatives, providing general direction, encouraging employees to contribute their own ideas, and supplying feedback.[86]
- Give emotional support. Even top-ranked National Football League coaches know when to back off and be more supportive. Particularly when an employee is new to the task and just developing his or her skills (like how to analyze problems), it's crucial to create a supportive environment. The way to influence employees is to let them know that you're not there to pass judgment or to place blame. Instead, provide the emotional support they need as they develop their skills and competencies.
- Provide specific feedback. Being supportive doesn't mean you shouldn't explain what improvements are required from your point of view. Letting subordinates flounder around trying to figure out where they fall short is no way to influence them; for example, if the team provides you with a recommendation that is lacking, be specific (but supportive) about why it needs improvement. Let them know you are confident they will get it right the next time.
- Use Socratic coaching. Try to refrain from making judgmental statements like, "That won't work." Instead, be Socratic, which means asking the questions that will lead your subordinates to find the answers for themselves. For instance, "What is the problem you want to solve?" or "How will you know when you have solved it?"[87]
- Show you have high expectations. The best coaches communicate the fact that they have high expectations for the team and its members. The heart of empowering employees is giving them not just the authority and tools but also the self-confidence to get the job done. That's why one expert says, "When I think back on people who have been great coaches in my life, they have always had very high expectations of me."[88]

1. Work teams are examples of employee involvement programs, which let employees participate in formulating important work decisions or in supervising all or most of their work activities. Managers rank such programs as their biggest productivity boosters.

2. Several aspects of group dynamics are especially important for leaders grappling with how to build more effective teams. Group norms are important because they're the rules that groups use to control their members. Group cohesiveness determines the attraction of the group for its members and is influenced by things like proximity, interpersonal attractiveness, homogeneity of interests or goals, and intergroup competition.

3. Leaders can use four general types of teams in organizations: suggestion teams, problem-solving teams, semi-autonomous teams, and self-managing teams. Specific examples of teams include quality circles; project, development, or venture teams; transnational teams; and self-directed work teams. Any of these may also be "hot" groups, which are high-achieving groups dedicated to a specific challenging task.

4. Not all teams function effectively, and leaders will find a number of symptoms of unproductive teams. These include cautious or guarded communication, lack of disagreement, use of personal criticism, malfunctioning meetings, unclear goals, low commitment, and conflict within the team. On the other hand, characteristics of productive teams include commitment to a mission, specific performance goals, the right size and mix, a common approach, and mutual accountability.

5. How can a leader go about building a high-performing team? We listed a number of guidelines, including: establish urgent, demanding performance standards; select members for skill and skill potential; set some clear rules of behavior; move from "boss" to "coach"; choose people who like teamwork; train, train, train; assign whole tasks; and encourage social support. When teams do not succeed, the problem often lies in one of three factors: leadership, focus, or capability.

6. Team leaders have some special duties. They coach, encourage participation, are boundary managers, and are facilitators. Moving to team leader can therefore cause transition problems stemming from: the perceived loss of power or status, unclear team leader roles, job security concerns, and the double standard problem. Any of these can undermine the transition from supervisor to team leader.

7. Not everyone is cut out to be an effective leader of self-managing teams; the successful team leader must adhere to the right values. These include putting your team members first, trusting your team members to do their best, helping team members to self-actualize, developing team members' capabilities, emphasizing teamwork, delegating, and eliminating barriers to success.

8. Leaders need to develop effective coaching skills. These skills include knowing how to assess each employee's skills, emphasize developing those skills, give emotional support, provide specific feedback, use Socratic coaching, and show you have high expectations.

KEY TERMS

employee involvement
  program
team
group
group norms
group cohesiveness

suggestion team
problem-solving team
semi-autonomous team
self-managing team
quality circle (QC)
venture team

hot group
transnational team
self-directed work team
groupthink

SELF-TEST

TRUE / FALSE QUESTIONS

1 **T F** Employee involvement can be achieved through the use of self-managed teams.

2 **T F** A few U.S. firms use work groups recognized as teams.

3 **T F** Managers have found employee involvement programs to be a huge productivity booster.

4 **T F** A familiar example of a nonmanagerial group that performs analysis and generates recommendations for the organization is the quality circle.

5 **T F** A hot group is a lively, high-achieving, dedicated group, usually small, whose members are turned on to an exciting and challenging task.

6 **T F** An attribute of hot groups is that they are a permanent fixture in the organization.

7 **T F** Transnational teams face the challenge of working on projects that are highly complex and important.

8 **T F** A self-directed work team is a trained group of 10 to 18 employees responsible for turning out a well-defined segment of completed work.

9 **T F** Divergent points of view may lead to tension and conflict rather than cohesion in a team.

10 **T F** Best-performing teams generally have fewer than 25 people, and commonly from 7 to 14 people.

MULTIPLE-CHOICE QUESTIONS

1 Work groups, by enforcing their _____, can have a great deal of influence over the behavior of their members.
a. norms
b. will
c. status
d. none of the above

2 Group cohesiveness tends to decline when the size of the group goes beyond about _____ members.
a. 5
b. 10
c. 20
d. 50

3 Which of the following are considered teams?
a. suggestion
b. problem-solving
c. semi-autonomous
d. all of the above

4 A _____ team is a small group of people who operate as a semi-autonomous unit to create and develop a new idea.
a. project

b. development
c. venture
d. quality

5 Which of the following describes the distinguishing characteristics of hot groups?
a. total preoccupation with an important mission
b. emotional intensity is very high
c. intellectual intensity, integrity, and exchange of ideas
d. all of the above

6 What type of team is described by the following: work groups composed of multinational members whose activities span multiple countries?
a. ethnocentric
b. global
c. transnational
d. line employees

7 Self-directed work teams are commonly made up of which stakeholders in the organization?
a. middle management
b. first-line supervisors
c. stockholders
d. line employees

8 What is "the tendency for a highly cohesive group, especially one working on special projects, to develop a sense of detachment and elitism"?
  a. arrogance net
  b. groupthink
  c. conflict trap
  d. reality disconnection

9 To build an effective team, all the following approaches are recommended except
  a. Establish urgent, demanding performance standards.
  b. Set some clear rules of behavior.
  c. Move from "boss" to "coach."
  d. Use only experienced team players.

10 _____ similarity is seen as the strongest predictor of initial social liking and co-worker preference, but only at the start of a training process.
  a. Geographic
  b. Work
  c. Demographic
  d. Professional

CRITICAL THINKING EXERCISES

1 Many girls are now expected to participate in sports to the same extent as boys. What type of impact do you think this will have on teamwork in organizations? What are the cultural and gender issues that arise around this trend and teamwork in general? Are teams the key to our economic present and future or just a passing fad?

2 In many of the exercises throughout this book, you have been working in teams. Compare class and team cohesiveness as the semester or quarter has progressed. What factors have changed and which have remained the same? How do students react to teamwork? Are there demographic or values issues you have noted with the use of teams?

EXPERIENTIAL EXERCISES

1 Your class has just been appointed by the university administration to form teams to help address racial conflict and hate crimes against minorities. Your goal is to create a plan to promote cultural awareness among the student body and to make positive links with the surrounding ethnically diverse community.

The administration prefers each team to consist of students from several constituencies. Assume that those represented are to include the African American Honor Society, the Latino Community Outreach Group, the Disabled Students Coalition, the ROTC, the Gay and Lesbian Alliance, Christian Outreach, the Young Republicans, the Asian-Pacific Compact, and the Older Students Awareness Association.

Break into groups of five and select a team leader for each group. Then try to have each remaining member represent, or role-play that they represent, a group such as those from the list above. Now create the plan requested by the administration.

When your plan is complete, be prepared to present it to the class, staying in your role. After role playing, discuss the impact it had on you, others, and the team.

2 Choose something you are interested in, whether it is an NFL team or a new entrepreneurial venture or a Fortune 500 company such as AT&T, and do some research on it. Then, for that organization, build the best top-management team you can assemble from leaders throughout history. Alexander the Great could be your CEO for a Fortune 500 company, for example, with other historical and present-day figures forming your team. Remember, this is a dream team, not one based in reality, but be prepared to justify *why* you chose the people you did. Discuss your research and your dream team in class.

DIVERSITY CASE

WHAT DOES IT TAKE TO MAKE A TEAM?

Your company is a traditional one with many managers in their 40s and 50s who have been with the firm for years. It has just merged with an entrepreneurial firm which is organized around teamwork, not hierarchy and seniority, and with a young and computer-skilled workforce.

The combined company has now received a huge contract and needs people highly skilled in computer applications to meet the contract specifications. You are the leader of a new team made up of recruits to the firm and veteran employees from both the merged companies. Your task is to forge a team and inspire great teamwork from the assembled personnel.

Questions
1 How would you forge a cross-generational team in this firm?
2 What personal challenges would you face in working with people older or younger than you?
3 What problems might arise for the cross-generational team and how would you manage them?

STRATEGY CASE

WHEN A STRIKE PUT EMPLOYEES UP AT BAT

In 1994 the "boys of summer" packed up their gear and headed home, on strike, without finishing the baseball season or playing a World Series. Fans were disappointed, but businesses whose fortunes were tied to baseball were in trouble.

Pinnacle Brands Inc., a trading-card company, found itself looking at a loss of $40 million in revenue. Its competitors were laying off employees; what could Pinnacle do?

Management issued an intriguing challenge to its workforce: Come up with a strategy to replace the lost revenue, and they could keep their jobs. This was no easy task—baseball cards represented 65 percent of Pinnacle's business. But management viewed its employees as revenue producers, not expense items.

The owners encouraged employees by setting up opportunities for them to gather in informal teams, deliberately cross-functional, and discuss ideas. From this rich mix of perspectives, there began to flow all sorts of ideas. The custodian saw that the company spent about $50,000 a year on refrigerated sodas and bottled water for every conference room and most executive offices, so the firm discontinued the practice. The public relations director observed how well pins sell at the Olympics, so with the 1996 games coming up in Atlanta he contacted a licensed manufacturer to make pins. Pinnacle had the distribution channels the pin maker lacked, so a new collaboration was forged.

Pinnacle's mission statement is "to provide unexpected delight in everything we do." As a result of this philosophy and hard, creative teamwork, Pinnacle emerged from the strike victorious, with a sales jump of 80 percent in two years.

Questions

1. How did Pinnacle's management show its commitment to teams?
2. What type of teams are required to pull off what this company did?
3. "Pinacle's strategy both influenced and was influenced by the use of teams." Indicate whether you agree or disagree, and why.

SOURCE: Gillian Flynn, "A Strike Puts Employees Up to Bat," *Personnel Journal* (June 1996):71–4.

ENTREPRENEURIAL CASE

RED STAR RISING: HOW DO YOU BUILD A TEAM IN A NATION BUILT ON SECRECY?

With the breakup of the Soviet Union, challenges to rebuild the "new" countries into democracies and market economies multiplied. How do you manage in a country such as Russia, where the government has planned everything for years and entrepreneurship was unknown?

The answer for U.S. entrepreneur James Hickman was twofold. To start Rustel, a $40 million telephone company based in Moscow, he needed people who knew how to work the old bureaucratic system. But those he hired had the habit of secrecy. They left no records of their contacts when they left Rustel, and the plans they devised were incomplete.

In its second round of hiring, the company found some of its most important employees among the thousands of gypsy cab drivers who work Moscow's streets. Here were the entrepreneurs with the work ethic Rustel needed. They might have lacked skills and training, but motivation and willingness to learn earned them important positions in the expanding Rustel and the growing market economy in Russia.

Questions

1. What barriers do you think there are to building a team in Russia today?
2. The company still hires experienced bureaucrats and new entrepreneurs. What would you do to forge a team between these two very different styles?
3. What are the differences between the United States and Russia in terms of building a team?

SOURCE: James L. Hickman, "Red Star Rising," *Inc.*, August 1995, 19–20.

THE BUSINESS TEAM, INC.

BUILDING THE TEAM AT STATE U.

When Maria got the phone call from the president of her team members' alma mater, State University, the president sounded stressed. Jan Morris had been president for 15 years now, but in the past year everything seemed to be falling apart in all the university's divisions. Two new buildings that had just been finished were uninhabitable because they were leaking so badly they could not pass inspection.

One department had apparently run up a substantial deficit without the controller noticing it. The faculties of two colleges were in the midst of revolting aginst their deans. To make matters worse, enrollments were dropping as more distance-learning–based competitors entered State's urban market. And as all this was occurring, the president's top officers—the vice presidents for academic, administrative, and student affairs, and the head of fundraising—were falling over themselves to fix the blame for the problems on each other. President Morris wants the team to advise her on how to proceed.

Questions

1 What is the first thing you think the team should do?
2 What are some possible causes for such multifunctional problems?
3 Explain specifically the change program you recommend for State U.

YOU BE THE CONSULTANT

TEAMWORK AT KNITMEDIA

As KnitMedia grows, one challenge (as its management has said) will be to "fully integrate all of its various products and services into one single, multifunctional corporation capable of providing the vertical integration required for the growth of its business and for offering recorded, live, film, and interactive entertainment." In 1997, KnitMedia was in a strong position to execute this strategy because, compared to its competitors, it was already small and integrated and with few of the functional boundaries or "smokestacks" preventing departments from talking with each other. One possibility for obtaining even closer cross-functional integration is to use teams more extensively. The question is, how?

Team Exercises and Questions

Use what you know and what you learned in this chapter to answer the following questions:

1 To what extent and in what manner do KnitMedia and its competitors now use teams in accomplishing their missions?
2 What recommendations would you make to Michael Dorf regarding how KnitMedia could make more extensive use of teams at KnitMedia?

For the online version of this case, visit our Web site at: <www.prenhall.com/desslermgmt>.

For Internet exercises, interactive study questions, news updates and more, visit the Dessler Web site at

www.prenhall.com/desslermgmt

If you're using the CD-ROM that accompanies this text, simply click on the "Web Site" button to access the site.

CHAPTER 15

LEADING ORGANIZATIONAL CHANGE

What's Ahead?

It was a revelation of enormous importance for Bill Gates and Microsoft Corporation. Gates obviously wanted Microsoft to maintain its huge lead as the top provider of operating systems for personal computers. But the realization that the Internet itself could be used as a sort of substitute for Microsoft's operating systems meant that big changes were in order for the firm. Given competitor Netscape's advantage as an Internet access provider, Gates had to lead an organizational change of monumental proportions if Microsoft were to become a provider of truly "Internet-friendly" programs.

Bill Gates

Objectives

After studying this chapter, you should be able to

- ■ list the things managers can change in organizations
- ■ explain the main sources of resistance to change and demonstrate how to overcome them
- ■ discuss the 10 steps for leading organizational change, and describe the manager's leadership role in organizational change
- ■ demonstrate how to use organizational development techniques to change organizations
- ■ identify sources of individual, interpersonal, and organizational conflicts and ways to overcome them.

MANAGEMENT ON THE WEB

CONFLICT MANAGEMENT GROUP

Conflict Management Group is dedicated to improving the methods of negotiation, conflict resolution, and cooperative decision making as applied to issues of public concern. How might Bill Gates have used this site to facilitate his changes at Microsoft? ■

http://www.cmonline.org

The Challenge of Organizational Change

Why should Microsoft change?

Because organizations that don't adapt to their environments do not survive.[1] For years General Motors and IBM were run almost like monolopies, growing fat and bureaucratic in an environment characterized by minimal international competition. Today, as we've seen, intense international competition has companies like these changing fast—downsizing and networking their organizations, creating self-managing teams, and opening up communications with techniques like upward appraisals and "work-out" forums. The bottom line is this: Change and adapt, or die. Many managers have chosen to try to change their organizations; the purpose of this chapter is to explain how to lead such organizational change.

What to Change?

Although some aspects of organizations are immutable, managers *can* focus on changing certain things, specifically, the strategy, culture, structure, tasks, technologies, and the attitudes and skills of the organization's people.

STRATEGIC CHANGE. Organizational change often starts with **strategic change,** a change in the firm's strategy, mission, and vision. Strategic change may then lead to other organizational changes, for instance, in the firm's technology, structure, and culture.

The strategic change initiated at Fuji-Xerox by President Yotaro Kobayashi provides an example.[2] In response to declining market share, a dearth of new products, and increasing customer complaints, Kobayashi and his team formulated a new vision for Fuji-Xerox. They called this the New Xerox Movement; the strategy was based on turning Fuji-Xerox into a total-quality–based company. The core values of quality, problem solving, teamwork, and customer focus symbolized this new strategy.

CULTURAL CHANGE. As at Fuji, implementing a strategic change often requires changing the culture, in other words, the firm's shared values and aims. Fuji-Xerox took several steps to implement its own cultural change: for example, Fuji's executive team instituted what two experts referred to as a "dense infrastructure of objectives, measures, rewards, tools, education and slogans, all in service of total quality control and the 'new Xerox.'"[3] To help support implementing the new strategy, they also created a new set of "heroes," individuals and teams who were publicly congratulated whenever their behavior reflected the best of Fuji's new values.

STRUCTURAL (ORGANIZATIONAL) CHANGE. Reorganizing means redesigning the organization's structure, that is, changing the departmentalization, coordination, span of control, reporting relationships, or centralization of decision making. Reorganization is a relatively direct and quick method for changing an organization, one often used to support a change in strategy.

Reorganizing is widely used and often effective, particularly given recent demands for lean and responsive organizations. Before he began the process of building openness, candor, and communications at GE, for instance, Jack Welch collapsed the firm's management structure from nine layers to as few as four, reduced 29 pay levels to 5 broad bands, and reorganized 350 different product lines and business units into 13 big businesses.[4]

The aim today is often to create organic, more responsive, organizations. Here, as we've seen, committed and empowered cross-functional teams supervise their own efforts within the framework of top management's vision. Employees communicate with colleagues horizontally and vertically throughout the often boundaryless firm in these newly redesigned and more responsive structures.[5]

TASK REDESIGN. The tasks and authority of individuals and teams within the organization are often changed as well. For example, to gain employees' commitment to quality, traditional assembly-line jobs were abolished at Saturn. Instead, work teams supervise their own work.

TECHNOLOGICAL CHANGE. Technological changes are modifications to the work methods the organization uses to accomplish its tasks. Such changes include new production technologies, new selection and screening procedures, and new performance appraisal methods, for instance. The new employee compensation plans and appraisal systems instituted by Yotaro Kobayashi at Fuji-Xerox illustrate technological change implemented to support cultural and strategic changes.

CHANGES IN PEOPLE: ATTITUDES AND SKILLS. Sometimes the employees themselves must change.[6] Techniques such as lectures, conferences, and on-the-job training are often used to provide new or present employees with the skills they need to perform their jobs adequately. **Organizational development interventions** (such as the sensitivity training discussed later in the chapter) are aimed at changing employees' attitudes, values, and behavior.

Types of Change

Organizational changes differ in their breadth and urgency. Some changes are limited and *incremental* in nature: They may require reorganizing just one department or establishing work teams in a single plant, for instance. At the other extreme, *strategic organizational changes* affect the entire organization and usually fundamentally change not only the company's strategy but its structure, culture, people, and processes as well.[7] Some changes are *reactive* and reflect a sense of urgency in response to a crisis or threat; others are *anticipatory* and are initiated to better prepare the company for competing in the future. When CEO Gil Amelio took over Apple Computer in 1996, organizational change was urgent, since Amelio had to react quickly to Apple's deteriorating market position. Amelio apparently failed to move fast enough, and was replaced the next year. On the other hand, when he became CEO, Jack Welch had several years to create and implement his vision of a more agile, open, and adaptive General Electric Corporation.

Strategy in Action

IMPLEMENTING STRATEGIC ORGANIZATIONAL CHANGE

Strategic organizational changes—redefining as they do the organization's basic direction—are among the riskiest but most important changes managers can implement. What triggers such changes? Why are they risky? We can summarize some recent research findings as follows.

1. *Strategic organizational changes are usually triggered by factors outside the organization.* External threats or challenges, such as deregulation, intensified global competition, and dramatic technological innovations (like those in the computer and telecommunications industries), are usually the ones that prompt organizations to embark on company-wide, strategic changes.[8]

2. *Strategic organizational changes are often required for survival.* Researchers Nadler and Tushman found that making a strategic organizational change did not guarantee a firm's success, but that firms that failed to change generally failed to survive. In particular, they found that what they called "discontinuous" environmental change—change of an unexpected nature, such as happened when the Internet made obsolete many firms' internal computer networks—required quick and effective strategic change for the firm to survive.

Gil Amelio tried to bring rapid organizational change to Apple Computer in 1996 when it was urgently needed.

3. *Strategic, systemwide changes implemented under crisis conditions are highly risky.* This study concluded that of all organizational changes, strategic, organization-wide ones initiated under crisis conditions and with short time constraints were by far the riskiest. For one thing, such changes usually require a change in core values.[9] Because core values tend to be resistant to change, changing them tends to trigger the most serious resistance from employees.

Sources of Resistance to Change

The hardest part of leading a change is overcoming resistance to it. Niccoló Machiavelli, a shrewd observer of sixteenth-century Italian politics, said that "there is nothing so difficult to implement as change, since those in favor of the change will often be small in number while those opposing the change will be numerous and enthusiastic in their resistance to change."[10] Indeed, even the most effective leaders would agree that implementing wide-scale change is enormously challenging: GE's Jack Welch has said that even after 10 years of almost continual change, he expected it would take at least another 10 years to completely rejuvenate GE's culture.[11]

Just because a change is advisable or even mandatory doesn't mean employees will accept it. As Machiavelli observed, individuals, groups, even entire organizations may resist a change, and this resistance stems from several sources, as follows.[12]

HABIT. People become accustomed to the usual way of doing things; they may then resist change solely because they assume it is more convenient or less costly to keep doing things "the usual way." For instance, many executives resist switching to computerized systems in part because the present way of doing things is familiar, comfortable, and (from their point of view) workable.

RESOURCE LIMITATIONS. Resource limitations can also stymie change. Executives of Russia's Aeroflot Airlines knew they would not be able to compete effectively with their outdated fleet of planes. However, resource limitations made it impossible to rejuvenate it.

THREATS TO POWER AND INFLUENCE. Years ago, Harvard Professor Paul Lawrence pointed out that it is usually not the technical aspects of a change that employees resist, but rather the social consequences, "the changes in their human relationships that generally accompany the technical change."[13] For example, they may see in the change diminished responsibilities for themselves and therefore lower status in the organization and less job security. Such real or perceived threats to our power and influence often underlie our resistance to change.

FEAR OF THE UNKNOWN. Sometimes it is not fear of the obvious consequence of a change but rather apprehension about its unknown consequences that produces resistance. For example, Blockbuster Video recently decided to move its headquarters from Miami to Dallas. The fact that most employees elected not to relocate reflects, in part, their fears about the move's unknown aspects.

CHANGES IN "PERSONAL COMPACT." Each employee has a "personal compact" with his or her company, in other words, a set of reciprocal obligations and mutual commitments, both stated and implied, that define the employee-employer relationship.[14] Employees will understandably resist any change that seems to alter what they view as their personal compact.

There are three aspects to an employee's personal compact: formal, psychological, and social.[15] The *formal dimension* represents the basic tasks and performance requirements for the job as defined by company documents such as job descriptions and employment contracts. It answers questions like "What am I supposed to do for the company?" and "What will I get to do the job?"

The *psychological dimension*

incorporates the elements of mutual expectation and reciprocal commitment that arise from feelings like trust and dependence between employee and employer.[16]

For example, managers expect employees to be loyal and willing to do whatever it takes to get the job done; for their part, employees want to know, as part of the psychological dimension of their personal compact with the company, "How hard will I really have to work? What recognition or other personal satisfaction will I get for my efforts? Are the rewards worth it?"

There's also what we may call a *social dimension* to personal compacts. This social dimension represents the degree to which employees view the firm's values and expectations as consistent with their own, and the degree to which management carries through on the values it espouses. For example, employees notice what the company says about its values (such as "be trusting") and whether the company's actions (such as time clocks) are then consistent with those stated values. Similarly, employees want to know "Are my values similar to those of others in the organization?" and "What are the real rules that determine who gets what in this company?"

In summary, employees and employers have reciprocal obligations and mutual commitments that from the employee's point of view are embodied in what may be called a "personal compact." These compacts have formal, psychological, and social aspects; if any aspect of the compact is threatened by the organizational change, employees can be expected to resist it.

How to Overcome Resistance to Change

SIX METHODS FOR DEALING WITH RESISTANCE TO CHANGE How should leaders overcome resistance to change? In Table 15.1, John Kotter and Leonard Schlesinger have summarized the pros and cons of some methods leaders can use to deal with resistance to change:

- *Education and communication* are appropriate where inaccurate or missing information is contributing to employee resistance to change.
- *Facilitation and support* (which might include training, giving an employee time off after a demanding period, or simply listening and providing emotional support) can reduce resistance brought on by fear and anxiety.
- *Participation and involvement* includes presenting the problem to a group of employees and letting them collect and analyze data and select the solution. This can be useful where management does not have all the information needed to design the change or believes employee resistance may be an especially serious problem.
- *Negotiation and agreement* may be appropriate where one group will clearly lose by the change and that group has considerable power to resist.
- *Manipulation and co-optation* (for instance, giving a key resister a key role in the change) work well where other tactics will not work or are too expensive.

■ TABLE 15.1 *Six Methods for Dealing with Resistance to Change*

APPROACH METHOD	COMMONLY USED IN SITUATIONS	ADVANTAGES	DRAWBACKS
Education + communication	Where there is a lack of information or inaccurate information and analysis.	Once persuaded, people will often help with the implementation of the change.	Can be very time consuming if lots of people are involved.
Participation + involvement	Where the initiators do not have all the information they need to design the change, and where others have considerable power to resist.	People who participate will be committed to implementing change, and any relevant information they have will be integrated into the change plan.	Can be very time consuming if participators design an inappropriate change.
Facilitation + support	Where people are resisting because of fear and anxiety.	No other approach works as well with employee adjustment problems.	Can be time consuming, expensive, and still fail.
Negotiation + agreement	Where someone or some group will clearly lose out in a change, and where that group has considerable power to resist.	Sometimes it is a relatively easy way to avoid major resistance.	Can be too expensive in many cases if it prompts others to negotiate.
Manipulation + co-optation	Where other tactics will not work, or are too expensive.	It can be a relatively quick and inexpensive solution to resistance problems.	Can lead to future problems if people feel manipulated.
Coercion	Where speed is essential, and the change initiators possess considerable power.	It is speedy, and can overcome any kind of resistance.	Can be risky if it leaves people angry at the initiators.

SOURCE: Adapted and reprinted by permission of *Harvard Business Review.* "Six Methods for Dealing with Change," from "Choosing Strategies for Change," by John P. Kotter and Leonard A. Schlesinger, March–April 1979. Copyright © 1979 by the President and Fellows of Harvard College; all rights reserved.

■ *Coercion*—simply forcing the change—can be a fast way of pushing through a change and is widely used, particularly when speed is essential. But it can be risky if it leaves influential employees with a residue of ill will against the company.

LEWIN'S PROCESS FOR OVERCOMING RESISTANCE. Psychologist Kurt Lewin formulated a model of change to summarize what he believed was the basic process for implementing a change with minimal resistance. To Lewin, all behavior in organizations was a product of two kinds of forces: those striving to maintain the status quo and those pushing for change. Implementing change thus meant either reducing the forces for the status quo or building up the forces for change. Lewin's process consisted of these three steps:

1. *Unfreezing.* **Unfreezing** means reducing the forces that are striving to maintain the status quo, usually by presenting a provocative problem or event to get people to recognize the need for change and to search for new solutions. Without such unfreezing, said Lewin, change will not occur. Attitude surveys, interview results, or participatory informational meetings are often used to provide such provocative events. When he took over as CEO of Dutch electronics firm Philips, Jan Timmer invited the company's

top 100 managers to an off-site retreat. Here he gave them a shock: a hypothetical press release that said Philips was bankrupt and that it was up to the 100 managers to bring the company back from the brink.[17] In the fast-changing electronics industry, Timmer then got a shock of his own: Within three years he was replaced by Cor Boostra, who pledged to make the ruthless cost-cutting changes that Timmer—despite his shocking start—was unable to implement.[18]

2. *Moving.* Lewin's second step aims to shift or alter the behavior of the individuals in the department or organization in which the changes are to take place. **Moving** means developing new behaviors, values, and attitudes, sometimes through organizational structure changes and sometimes through the sorts of organizational change and development techniques explained later in this chapter.

3. *Refreezing.* Lewin assumed that organizations tended to revert to their former ways of doing things unless the changes were reinforced. This reinforcement is accomplished by **refreezing** the organization into its new state of equilibrium. Lewin advocated instituting new systems and procedures that would support and maintain the changes that were made. For example, after John Walter took over as president of AT&T, he instituted a new program in which he tried to meet with employees and customers each day to emphasize the culture of trust and customer orientation he was trying to cultivate. (AT&T's directors soon became impatient, and they replaced him within the year.)

The Basic Organizational Change Process: An Overview

Implementing a change is like solving any problem: You have to recognize there's a problem, diagnose the problem, and then formulate a solution and implement it. In the case of organizational change, an overview of that basic process looks like this:

BECOME AWARE OF THE NEED FOR CHANGE.   Most organizational changes are carried out in reaction to or in anticipation of pressures from inside or outside the organization. Outside the organization, technological innovations like "cableless" cable television, microprocessors, and automated factories force managers to confront a constantly changing competitive terrain. Within the firm, conflicts arise, employees retire or resign, and the organization outgrows its old ways of doing things. Pressures like these (or the anticipation of such pressures) demand changes in the strategy, culture, structure, technology, tasks, and people in the organization.

RECOGNIZE AND ACCEPT THE NEED FOR CHANGE.   Even within the same industry, some leaders have been more adept at recognizing and accepting the need for change than others. For example, Bill Gates at Microsoft successfully recognized and accepted the pressures driving the computer industry toward greater reliance on the Internet, and in 1996 revamped all his firms' offerings to make them more "Internet friendly." Ten years earlier, top executives at IBM seemed to let their firm drift, dramatically underestimating the effects the personal computer would have on their industry.

DIAGNOSE THE PROBLEM.   Recognizing that change is required isn't enough: The manager then must diagnose the problem to determine how change may affect the firm and what its consequences will be. After all, you don't want to implement a change that's aimed at solving the wrong problem. (We discussed problem solving in chapter 4, "Decision Making.")

The breadth of the diagnosis will depend on how widespread the problem itself seems to be. In some cases, organizational analysis—in which the organization's goals, plans, environment, practices, and performance are studied—is appropriate. At other times, the problem may occur in just one department, group, or individual, and the diagnosis can appropriately focus there.

FORMULATE THE CHANGE. The next step is to decide what to change and how to change it. We've seen there are several things leaders can change: the company's strategy, culture, structure, technology, and people. The change itself can therefore involve almost anything, such as reorganization, training programs, or new computer systems, for instance.

IMPLEMENT AND LEAD THE CHANGE. Overcoming resistance is a big part of this step, as we've seen. We'll look more closely at how to implement and lead a change in the following section, "a 10-step process for leading organizational change."

FOLLOW UP ON THE CHANGE. Finally, evaluate the effects of the change and institute the procedural modifications that will ensure the change becomes institutionalized. For example, to institutionalize GE's new set of values, Welch made these values a key part of the firm's performance and reward processes:

> We've told the business leaders that they must rank each of their officers on a scale of 1–5 against the . . . characteristics in that [value] statement. . . . We have to know if our people are open and self-confident, if they believe in honest communication and quick action, if the people we hired years ago have changed.[19]

A 10-Step Process for Leading Organizational Change

Implementing and leading an organizational change can be tricky even for a CEO with lots of clout. The change may be complex and require dozens or hundreds of managers to do their parts; resistance may be almost insurmountable; and the change may need to be carried out while the company continues to serve its customers. Here is a 10-step process for actually leading such an organizational change.[20]

Establish a Sense of Urgency

Having become aware of the need to change, most leaders start by creating a sense of urgency. Philips' CEO Jan Timmer knew that to rouse his top managers out of their status-quo thinking, he had to create a sense of urgency; he did this with his hypothetical bankruptcy press release. Psychologists like Kurt Lewin contend that reducing status-quo thinking requires "unfreezing" the old ways of looking at things, and one way to do this is to establish a sense of urgency.

Urgency does more than overcome employees' traditional reasons for resisting change: It can also jar them out of their complacency. In organizations, several things can leave employees feeling "fat and happy."[21] These include the absence of a major and visible crisis, too many visible resources, low overall performance standards, and a lack of sufficient performance feedback from external sources. When complacency sets in (as it did in many companies, including IBM and General Motors, in the 1980s), something must be done to establish a sense of urgency so that employees are open to change.

There are many ways to raise the urgency level.[22] A partial list includes

- creating a crisis by allowing a financial loss or by exposing managers to major weaknesses relative to competitors
- eliminating obvious examples of excess such as company-owned country club facilities, numerous aircraft, or gourmet executive dining rooms
- setting targets for revenue, income, productivity, customer satisfaction, and product development cycle time so high they can't be reached by conducting business as usual
- sending more data about customer satisfaction and financial performance to more employees, especially information that demonstrates weaknesses relative to competition

Mobilize Commitment to Change through Joint Diagnosis of Business Problems

Having established a sense of urgency, many leaders then create one or more task forces to diagnose the business problems. Such teams can produce a shared understanding of what can and must be improved and thereby mobilize the commitment of those who must actually implement the change.

Create a Guiding Coalition

Major transformations—such as Bill Gates accomplished in 1996 to transform Microsoft into an Internet-oriented company—are often associated with one highly visible leader, but no leader can accomplish any significant change alone. That's why most leaders create a guiding coalition of influential people who can be missionaries and implementers of change. The coalition should include people with enough power to lead the change effort, and it's essential to encourage the group to work together as a team.

Choosing the right coalition members is crucial. One reason to create the coalition is to gather political support; the leader will, therefore, want to ensure that there are enough key players on board so that those left out can't easily block progress.[23] In addition, the coalition's members should have the expertise, credibility, and leadership skills to explain and implement the change.

Develop a Shared Vision

In chapter 10 ("Being a Leader") we saw that the leader must provide a direction toward which his or her followers can work. Whether that "direction" is a statement of vision, mission, or objectives depends largely on what the leader wants to achieve and the level at which he or she is acting.

To transform an organization, it's usually a new vision that is required, "a general statement of the organization's intended direction that evokes emotional feelings in organization members." For example, recall from chapter 10 that when Barry Gibbons became CEO of a drifting Spec's Music, its employees, owners, and bankers—all its stakeholders—required a vision of a renewed Spec's around which they could rally. Gibbons's vision of a leaner Spec's offering a diversified blend of concerts and retail music helped to provide the sense of direction they all required.

Communicate the Vision

Change expert John Kotter points out that "the real power of a vision is unleashed only when most of those involved in an enterprise or activity have a common understanding of its goals and direction."[24] In fact, fostering support for the new vision is virtually impossible unless the vision has been effectively communicated.

What are the key elements in effectively communicating a vision?[25] They include

- *Keep it simple.* Eliminate all jargon and wasted words. Here is an example of a good statement of vision: "We are going to become faster than anyone else in our industry at satisfying customer needs."
- *Use multiple forums.* Try to use every channel possible—big meetings and small, memos and newspapers, formal and informal interaction—to spread the word.
- *Use repetition.* Ideas sink in deeply only after they have been heard many times.
- *Lead by example.* "Walk your talk" so that your behaviors and decisions are consistent with the vision you espouse.

Remove Barriers to the Change: Empower Employees

Accomplishing a change that transforms an organization usually requires the assistance of the employees themselves: but to get that assistance, change experts advise empowering the employees. Here's how one expert explains this:

> Environmental change demands organizational change. Major internal transformation rarely happens unless many people assist. Yet employees generally won't help, or can't help, if they feel relatively powerless. Hence the relevance of empowerment.[26]

The next step, therefore, is to empower employees to help make the change and this starts with removing the barriers to empowerment. This idea is summarized in Figure 15.1. By now employees understand the vision and want to make it a reality, but are boxed in: A lack of skills undermines action; formal structures, personnel, and systems make it difficult to act; or bosses may discourage implementing the new vision. It's the leader's job to see to it that such barriers are removed. The employees will then be able to do their parts in implementing the change.

Examples of removing barriers abound. When he took over as CEO of Sony and its loss-making movie studios, Nobuyuki Idei proceeded, "in a most un-Japan-

■ FIGURE 15.1 Barriers to Empowerment

SOURCE: Reprinted by permission of Harvard Business School Press. From *Leading Change* by John P. Kotter. Boston, MA, 1996, p. 102. Copyright © 1996 by the President and Fellows of Harvard College; all rights reserved.

Formal structures make it difficult to act.

Bosses discourage actions aimed at implementing the new vision.

Employees understand the vision and want to make it a reality, but are boxed in.

A lack of needed skills undermines action.

Personnel and information systems make it difficult to act.

ese way," to sweep the old studio executives out of office and to install a team led by a new staff of industry veterans, with a mandate to fix Sony's movie business.[27] At Allied Signal, CEO Lawrence Bossidy put all of his 80,000 people through quality training within two years. He also created area "councils" (for instance, for Asia) so that employees from Allied divisions who were undertaking initiatives in those areas could get together, share market intelligence, and compare notes.[28]

After empowering the employees, it's often advisable to let them then find their own way, rather than forcing the changes down on them. In one successful change, for instance, an engineering department spent nearly a year analyzing how to implement the team concept: The engineers conducted surveys, held off-site meetings, and analyzed various alternatives before deciding on a matrix management approach that the department members felt would work for them.[29]

Generate Short-Term Wins

Transforming a company can take time, but employees need reinforcement periodically to see that their efforts are bearing fruit. This is why maintaining employees' motivation to stay involved in the change requires planning for and creating short-term wins.

The leader can't just hope that short-term wins will materialize: He or she must plan for visible performance improvements.[30] For example, the guiding coalition in one manufacturing company intentionally set its sights on producing one highly visible and successful new product about 20 months after the start of an organizational renewal effort.[31] The new product was selected in part because the coalition knew that its introduction was doable. And, they knew that the introduction would provide the positive feedback required to renew their sense of urgency and motivation.

Consolidate Gains and Produce More Change

As momentum builds and changes are made, the leader has to guard against renewed complacency. That's why it's crucial, while employees are generating short-term wins, to consolidate the gains that have been made and produce even more change. How?

The leader and his or her guiding coalition should use the increased credibility that comes from short-term wins to change all the systems, structures, and policies that don't fit well with the company's new vision. In one company, for example, when a vice president for operations saw the handwriting on the wall and left the firm, the position was left vacant; the two departments that had reported to him—engineering and manufacturing—now reported to the general manager. This helped to formalize the cross-functional nature of the new team approach at this firm.[32]

Other actions can be taken. For example, firms can continue to consolidate gains and produce more change by hiring, promoting, and developing new people who can implement the company's new vision, identifying some employees to champion the continuing changes, and providing additional opportunities for short-term wins by employees.

Anchor the New Ways of Doing Things in the Company's Culture

Few organizational changes will survive without a corresponding change in employees' shared values. For example, a "team-based, quality-oriented, adaptable organization" is not going to happen if the company's shared values still emphasize selfishness, mediocrity, and bureaucratic behavior. The Entrepreneurs in Action box shows how one manager changed his firm's values.

Entrepreneurs in Action

LEEGIN CREATIVE LEATHER PRODUCTS, INC.

His expert management of change brought a surge of new business to Jerry Kohl's Leegin Creative Leather.

Leegin Creative Leather Products, Inc., isn't what it used to be. A decade ago the belt manufacturer's sales stalled around $10 million. Salespeople had to make big trips to write small orders. Staying abreast of the latest designs kept the factory in perpetual disarray. Interdepartmental conflict was the norm. Passing the buck and watching one's back was everyone's priority. Perhaps only to get out of town for a few weeks, company founder Jerry Kohl headed to the Harvard Business School. He returned with a vision for a revitalized firm.

One change was computerization. Kohl's salespeople started carrying computers. On calls, they first inventoried the store's belts and input the data by color and size. Then they did something unusual. They showed the store owner what products were hot and where he or she might increase sales with the next order. The numbers didn't lie. Store owners now knew exactly what to restock, and salespeople didn't waste time pushing belts that didn't move. The result was trust, cooperation, and orders. "Thanks to them," says store owner Don Zuiderma, "we make a lot of money in the small space we use for belts."

The transition was not without problems, and some salespeople quit. But Kohl eased the process with training-and-discussion seminars held several times annually. As he refined his sales approach, Kohl dissolved his small firm's structure. The order-processing, customer-service, and credit-and-collection departments were dissolved. Two account specialists per territory were assigned to perform these functions. More employees left, and Kohl sent the rest to training classes. "You lose some people as they get frustrated," he says, "but we were getting people to feel more a part of the company." The classes and the refinements to computer software never stopped. No expenses were spared in making the job easier. Customers noted both the new expeditiousness and the accuracy. "I can call and place an order, and they ship it right out," says store manager Lottie Shamie. "Another company we deal with, their orders get messed up all the time."

Kohl shook up his factory floor next. In an effort to consolidate the assembly-line-type belt-making process, he selected 20 workers and assigned them the entire manufacturing process on specific belt designs. The piece-rate pay plan was changed to an equivalent hourly wage. Quality increased, but productivity sank and deliveries fell behind. The assembly group was then further divided into four or five smaller teams under an incentive pay scheme. Output climbed back to the former levels and gradually surpassed it. Eventually, 10- to 12-person teams were found to work best. Soon every production line had been replaced by cross-trained workers together creating different types of belts.

Leegin now makes more than a thousand different belts in addition to wallets, handbags, and other small leather goods. The number of accounts the company services has more than tripled to 7,000. Every other aspect of production, quality, delivery time, and pricing has improved. As for those sales that seemed stuck around $10 million—they were soon projected to be $110 million.

SOURCE: John Case, "A Business Transformed," *Inc.,* June 1993, 84–91, and *Personal Communication*, 1997.

We've already discussed at length how to lead a change in organizational culture (see chapter 11). In brief, it means crystallizing those values that are consistent with your vision for the company, usually by issuing a core values statement. The manager then has to "walk the talk" by using signs, symbols, and ceremonies to reinforce the values you want your employees to share.

Monitor Progress and Adjust the Vision as Required

Why spend time creating a more responsive organization if the firm doesn't respond to possible inadequacies in the change plan itself? In other words, it's essential that the company have in place a mechanism for monitoring the effectiveness of the change and for recommending remedial actions as required. One firm appointed an oversight team composed of managers, a union representative, an engineer, and several others to monitor the functioning of its new self-managing teams. In another firm, regular morale surveys were used to monitor employee attitudes.

The Leader's Role in Organizational Change

Organizational changes almost never take place spontaneously; instead, they are driven by leaders. The leader may be the CEO, the factory manager, or just a champion who assumes the role of cajoling, inspiring, and negotiating a new product successfully through the firm until it's produced. Whatever the case, such leaders—called **change advocates**—play a major role in any organizational change.

What Is the Role of Executive Leadership in Strategic Organizational Change?

Nowhere is the role of leadership more obvious or more important than in the sorts of organization-wide strategic changes implemented at firms like Leegin (see the Entrepreneurs box), GE, or Fuji-Xerox. A careful analysis of leaders like theirs suggests three crucial leadership roles for change leaders: charismatic, instrumental, and missionary leadership.[33]

CHARISMATIC LEADERSHIP. Nadler and Tushman say that successful leadership for change requires, first, charismatic leaders, who possess "a special quality that enables the leader to mobilize and sustain activity within an organization."[34]

Charismatic leadership is itself composed of three behaviors: envisioning, energizing, and enabling. As summarized in Figure 15.2, the charismatic leader is an *envisioning* leader who is capable of articulating a compelling vision, setting high expectations, and being a model of behaviors that are consistent with that compelling vision. The charismatic leader is also an *energizing* leader who is able to demonstrate personal excitement, express personal confidence, and seek, find, and use success among his or her colleagues. Finally, the charismatic leader is an *enabling* leader who is able to express personal support, empathy, and confidence in people and thereby inspire them to undertake the required changes.

INSTRUMENTAL LEADERSHIP. Charismatic leadership alone does not explain the sort of success that executives like entrepreneur Jerry Kohl had in transforming Leegin Leather, or that Louis Gerstner has had in turning IBM around. Effec-

■ **FIGURE 15.2**
**What Charismatic
Leadership Is**
Charismatic change lead-
ership plays a major role
in driving through a
change. Its components
are envisioning, energiz-
ing, and enabling leader-
ship.

SOURCE: Copyright © 1990, by
The Regents of the University
of California. Reprinted from
the *California Management Review*, Vol. 32, No. 2. By permission of The Regents.

tive leaders of change must also "build competent teams, clarify required behavior, build in measurements, and administer rewards and punishments so that individuals perceive that behavior consistent with the change is essential for them in achieving their own goals." Nadler and Tushman call this second change-leadership role **instrumental leadership:** the managerial aspect of change leadership that puts the instruments in place through which the employees can accomplish their new tasks.

There are three components of instrumental leader behavior. The first is *structuring.* Leaders must ensure that the necessary structure is in place to carry out the change and so must invest time in building teams, creating new organizational structures, setting goals, establishing standards, and defining roles and responsibilities.[35] Instrumental change leadership also means establishing successful *controlling* mechanisms, "the creation of systems and processes to measure, monitor and assess both behavior and results and to administer corrective action."[36] Finally, instrumental change leadership means *rewarding,* instituting the material (and nonmaterial) rewards and punishments needed to reinforce behaviors consistent with (or discourage behaviors that are inconsistent with) the desired organizational change.[37]

MISSIONARY LEADERSHIP. Few leaders are capable of turning organizations around by themselves; instead, as we've seen, they must enlist the aid of others. They must then depend on this new coalition to be the missionaries who spread the top manager's vision.

In practice, successful executive leaders seek to extend their new visions to three other groups: their own senior team, senior management, and leadership throughout the organization. They generally look first for opportunities to extend and institutionalize their vision for the firm to the group of individuals who comprise their own senior team. (This, in part, is why CEOs seeking to implement major changes often seek out and hire new subordinates whose values and visions are consistent with theirs. For example, Louis Gerstner quickly hired several new senior vice presidents for finance, human resource management, and several other functions within months of assuming the reins at IBM.)

The CEO must then encourage senior managers just below the top executive team to buy into his or her vision and plans and become missionaries for change. Unfortunately, those below the top management level often feel they are not in positions to lead such change. They may even feel more like unwitting participants or observers in the changes occurring around them. As a result, "the [leader's] task is to make this group feel like [top] management, to get them signed up for the change, and to motivate and enable them to work as an extension of the senior team."[38]

Finally, the vision and details of the change need to be spread throughout the organization; this means creating cadres of employees who are capable of helping to lead the changes and eager to do so. GE does this, in part, by annually training hundreds of employees, not just managers but engineers, chemists, and others throughout the firm. In this way, GE provides employees with the values and skills they will need to make their units consistent with Welch's vision of a lean, competitive, agile organization.[39]

Organizational Behavior in Action

TRAINING LEADERS TO LEAD CHANGE

Can leaders be trained to be better leaders of change? The answer, based on one recent study, is yes.

Much of what change leaders do—being charismatic, exercising instrumental leadership, and missionary leadership, for instance—is part of what being a transformational leader is all about. We've seen (in Chapter 10) that transformational leaders can be influential in shaping organizational change. Transformational leadership tends to be positively correlated with subordinates' satisfaction, organizational commitment, and performance, for instance.[40]

But can a person be trained to be more transformational? The results of one study suggest that the answer is a definite yes.[41]

The study took place in one of the five largest banks in Canada. The managers of the 20 branches in one region were randomly assigned either to receive transformational leadership training or not to receive it. The "training" group ended up with five male and four female managers; the "no training" group had six male and five female managers.

There was a two-part training program. The first part consisted of a one-day training session that familiarized participants with the meaning of transformational leadership and explained and illustrated how it might be implemented in the managers' branches. The second part consisted of several one-on-one "booster" sessions; here a trainer met individually with each of the managers to go over the latter's leadership style and to develop personal action plans for the manager to become more of a goal-oriented, transformational leader.

The results of this study clearly indicate that managers can be trained to be transformational leaders. For example, the subordinates of the managers who received the training subsequently perceived their managers as higher on intellectual stimulation, charisma, and individual consideration than did subordinates of managers in the no-training group. (The training program also apparently had positive effects on subordinates' organizational commitment as well as on branch-level financial indicators.) Concepts like charismatic or transformational or instrumental leadership, therefore, aren't just theoretical; behaviors like these can be developed, and developing them begins with an understanding—which you now should have—of what these concepts are and how they can be used. ■

Using Organizational Development to Change Organizations

What Is Organizational Development?

Organizational development (OD) is a special approach to organizational change in which the employees themselves formulate the change that's required and implement it, often with the assistance of a trained consultant. As an approach to changing organizations, OD has several distinguishing characteristics:

1. It is usually based on **action research,** which means collecting data about a group, department, or organization, and then feeding that data back to the employees so they can analyze it and develop hypotheses about what the problems in the unit might be.
2. It applies behavioral science knowledge for the purpose of improving the organization's effectiveness.
3. It changes the attitudes, values, and beliefs of employees so that the employees themselves can identify and implement the technical, procedural, structural, or other changes needed to improve the company's functioning.
4. It changes the organization in a particular direction—toward improved problem solving, responsiveness, quality of work, and effectiveness.[42]

Types of OD Applications

The number and variety of OD applications (also called OD *interventions* or *techniques*) have increased substantially over the past few years. OD got its start with what were called **human process interventions.** These interventions were aimed at helping employees better understand and modify their own and others' attitudes, values, and beliefs, and thereby improve the company.

Today, as illustrated in Table 15.2, a much wider range of applications is available. Indeed, the once-clear lines between OD and other types of organizational change efforts (such as reorganizing) are starting to blur. This is happening because OD practitioners have become increasingly involved not just in changing participants' attitudes, values, and beliefs but also in directly altering the firm's structure, practices, strategy, and culture.

There are four types of OD applications: human process, technostructural, human resource management, and strategic applications. All are based on getting

Interventions	PRIMARY ORGANIZATIONAL LEVEL AFFECTED		
	Individual	Group	Organization
Human Process			
T-Groups	X	X	
Process consultation		X	
Third-party intervention	X	X	
Team building		X	
Organizational confrontation meeting		X	X
Intergroup relations		X	X
Technostructural			
Formal structural change			X
Differentiation and integration			X
Cooperative union-management projects	X	X	X
Quality circles	X	X	
Total quality management		X	X
Work design	X	X	
Human Resource Management			
Goal setting	X	X	
Performance appraisal	X	X	
Reward systems	X	X	X
Career planning and development	X		
Managing workforce diversity	X		
Employee wellness	X		
Strategic			
Integrated strategic management			X
Culture change			X
Strategic change			X
Self-designing organizations		X	X

the employees themselves to collect the required data and to create and implement the solutions.

HUMAN PROCESS APPLICATIONS. The human process OD techniques generally aim first at improving employees' human relations skills. The goal is to provide employees with the insight and skills required to analyze their own and others' behavior more effectively so they can solve interpersonal and intergroup problems more intelligently. **Sensitivity training**, team building, confrontation meetings, and survey research are in this category.

Sensitivity Training. Sensitivity, laboratory, or t-group training (the *t* is for training) was one of the earliest OD techniques; although its use has diminished, it is still found today. Sensitivity training's basic aim is to increase the participant's insight into his or her own behavior and the behavior of others by encouraging an open expression of feelings in the trainer-guided t-group. Typically, 10 to 15 people meet, usually away from the job, and no activities or discussion topics are planned. The focus is on the here and now (specifically, the feelings and emotions of the members in the group). Participants are encouraged to portray themselves as they are in the group rather than in terms of past experiences or future problems. The t-group's success depends largely on the feedback process and in particular on participants' willingness to tell one another how their behavior is being perceived. A climate of "psychological safety" is therefore necessary if participants are to feel safe enough to reveal themselves, to expose their feelings, to drop their defenses, and to try out new ways of interacting.[43]

T-group training is obviously very personal in nature, so it is not surprising that it is a controversial technique and that its use has diminished markedly since its heyday in the 1970s. The personal nature of such training suggests that participation should be voluntary: Some therefore view t-group training as unethical because participation "suggested" by one's superior cannot be considered strictly voluntary.[44] Others argue that it can actually be a dangerous exercise if led by an inadequately prepared trainer.

Team Building. The characteristic OD stress on action research is perhaps most evident in **team building,** which refers to the process of improving the effectiveness of a team. Data concerning the team's performance are collected and then fed back to the members of the group. The participants then examine, explain, and analyze the data and develop specific action plans or solutions for solving the team's problems.

According to experts French and Bell, the typical team-building meeting begins with the consultant interviewing each of the group members and the leader prior to the meeting.[45] They all are asked what their problems are, how they think the group functions, and what obstacles are keeping the group from performing better. The consultant might then categorize the interview data into themes and present the themes to the group at the beginning of the meeting. (Themes like lack of time or lack of cohesion might be culled from such statements as "I don't have enough time to get my job done" or "I can't get any cooperation around here.") The themes are ranked by the group in terms of their importance, and the most important ones become the agenda for the meeting. The group then explores and discusses the issues, examines the underlying causes of the problems, and begins working on some solutions.

Confrontation Meetings. Other human process interventions aim to bring about intergroup or organization-wide change. Organizational **confrontation meetings** can help clarify and bring into the open intergroup misperceptions and problems so that they can be resolved. The basic approach here, as we will see later, is that the participants themselves provide the data for the meeting and then (with the help of a facilitator/moderator) confront and thrash out any misperceptions in an effort to reduce tensions.

Survey research requires that employees throughout the organization fill out attitude surveys. The data are then used as feedback to the work groups who use it as a basis for problem analysis and action planning. In general, such surveys are a convenient and widely used method for unfreezing an organization's management and employees by providing a lucid, comparative, graphic illustration of the fact that the organization does have problems that should be solved.

TECHNOSTRUCTURAL APPLICATIONS. OD practitioners are increasingly involved in efforts to change the structures, methods, and job designs of firms. Compared with human process interventions, these technostructural interventions (as well as the human resource management interventions and strategic interventions described in the following sections) generally focus more directly on productivity improvement and efficiency.

OD practitioners use a variety of technostructural interventions. For example, in a **formal structure** change program the employees collect data on existing formal organizational structures and analyze them. The purpose is to jointly redesign and implement new organizational structures. OD practitioners also assist in implementing employee-involvement programs, including quality circles and job redesign.

HUMAN RESOURCE MANAGEMENT APPLICATIONS. OD practitioners increasingly use action research to enable employees to analyze and change their firm's personnel practices. Targets of change include the firm's performance appraisal system and reward system, and changes might include instituting, for instance, workforce diversity programs aimed at boosting cooperation among a firm's diverse employees.

Strategic Applications. Among the newest OD applications are **strategic interventions,** organization-wide interventions aimed at bringing about a better fit between a firm's strategy, structure, culture, and external environment.

Strategy in Action

USING OD TO CREATE A NEW STRATEGY

Integrated strategic management is one example of using OD to create or change a strategy. This intervention consists of four steps:

1. *Analyze current strategy and organizational design.* Senior managers and other employees utilize models such as the SWOT matrix (explained in chapter 5) to together analyze the firm's current strategy, as well as its organizational design.
2. *Choose a desired strategy and organizational design.* Based on the OD consultant-assisted analysis, senior management formulates a strategic vision, objectives, and plan and an organizational structure for implementing them.
3. *Design a strategic change plan.* The group designs a strategic change plan, which "is an action plan for moving the organization from its current strategy and organizational design to the desired future strategy and design."[46] The plan explains how the strategic change will be implemented, including specific activities as well as the costs and budgets associated with them.
4. *Implement a strategic change plan.* The final step is actually implementing a strategic change plan and measuring and reviewing the results of the change activities to ensure that they are proceeding as planned.[47]

Conflict-Management Techniques

Conflict can be a cause or a result of organizational change. Sometimes, for instance, a conflict makes the need for a change apparent, as when two departments resist working cooperatively to achieve some goal. Sometimes, on the other hand, an organizational change (such as a new strategy) may trigger a conflict, as two or more managers or units see in the change an opportunity or need to get more power or resources for themselves. In any case, conflict management is an important aspect of leading organizational change.

Conflict: Pros and Cons

Conflict, as you probably know, can have dysfunctional effects on the organization and its employees. Opposing parties in conflicts tend to put their own aims above those of the organization, and the organization's effectiveness suffers. Time that could have been used productively is wasted as people hide valuable information from each other and jockey for position, preventing one another from carrying out their assigned tasks. Opponents can become so personally involved in the tensions produced by conflict that they undermine their emotional and physical well-being. Perhaps the most insidious effect of conflict is that it doesn't remain organization-bound for long. Its effects are observed by customers and stockholders and are taken home by the opponents, whose families are caught in the fallout.

Despite its adverse effects, conflict is viewed by most experts today as a potentially useful aspect of organization because it can, if properly channeled, be an engine of innovation and change. This view recognizes the necessity of conflict and explicitly encourages a certain amount of controlled conflict in organizations. The basic case for it is that a lack of active debate can permit the status quo or mediocre ideas to prevail.

This more positive view of conflict is supported by surveys of management practice. In one survey of top and middle managers, for example, managers rated "conflict management" as of equal or slightly higher importance than topics like planning, communication, motivation, and decision making. The managers spent about 20 percent of their time on conflicts, yet they did not consider the conflict level in their organization to be excessive. Instead, they rated it as about right—that is, at the midpoint of a scale running from "too low" to "too high."

Individual, Interpersonal, and Intergroup Organizational Conflict

Three types of conflict—individual, interpersonal, and intergroup organizational conflict—exist in organizations. **Role conflict** is a familiar example of conflict within the individual. Role conflict occurs when a person is faced with conflicting orders, such that compliance with one would make it difficult or impossible to comply with the other. Sometimes role conflict arises out of obviously conflicting orders, as when a corporal receives orders from a captain that would force her to disobey an order from her sergeant. Sometimes, however, the role conflict's source is not so obvious: This obeying an order might force a person to violate his or her own cherished values and sense of right and wrong. In any case, role conflict is a serious problem in organizations, one that can be stressful to the people involved and adversely affect their morale and performance.[48]

Organizational Behavior in Action

HOW ROLE CONFLICT CAN AFFECT A SUPERVISOR'S BEHAVIOR

Although the term "role conflict" can sound theoretical, its effects in practice can be very real. This fact is illustrated by a study that included, among others, 68 supervisors employed by a large midwestern university.[49] Role conflict (like any conflict) understandably puts someone under stress. The basic question in this study was whether the stress resulting from supervisors experiencing role conflict would result in a deliberate inflation of performance ratings for the subordinates they were rating.

To study this, surveys were used to measure two things: the extent to which the supervisors experienced role conflict, and the degree to which their subordinates' performance ratings were inflated. An example of a survey item used to measure the self-reported tendency to deliberately inflate performance ratings included "At times I find it necessary to deliberately inflate performance evaluation ratings of my subordinates." An example of an item used to measure the supervisor's role conflict is, "I receive incompatible requests from two or more people."[50]

The degree to which supervisors experienced role conflict correlated positively with their reported tendency to deliberately inflate subordinates' performance ratings. Taken as a whole, say the researchers, the results

> indicate that role conflict is positively associated with self-reported tendencies to deliberately inflate performance scores in both the sample of university supervisors and the sample of MBA student supervisors.[51]

These findings show the sorts of subtle but serious consequences role conflict can have. In this case role conflict and inflated appraisals went hand in hand. The more supervisors saw themselves as receiving conflicting orders and instructions, the more leniently they tended to appraise their own subordinates. Why might that be the case? It's not clear, but perhaps the supervisors with more role conflict felt their own authority was less clear and secure and so were less apt to take a chance on being strict with their subordinates. ■

Conflicts in organizations can also be **interpersonal** and occur between individuals or between individuals and groups. Sometimes, of course, such conflicts arise from legitimate sources, as when real differences in goals or objectives exist between the parties involved. Often, however, interpersonal conflicts arise not from legitimate differences but from personalities. Some people are more aggressive and conflict prone than others, and some are so hypersensitive that every comment is viewed as an insult that provokes a response.

Finally, there are **intergroup organizational conflicts,** such as between line and staff units or between production and sales departments. Effectively managing intergroup conflict is especially crucial today as firms increasingly try to manage change by moving toward the kinds of boundaryless organizations discussed in chapter 8. We will focus on the causes and management of intergroup conflicts in the remainder of this section.

Causes of Intergroup Conflict

There are many causes of intergroup conflict, but research findings suggest that four factors create most of the problems: interdependencies and shared resources; intergroup differences in goals, values, or perceptions; authority imbalances; and ambiguities.

INTERDEPENDENCIES AND SHARED RESOURCES. Groups that do not have to depend on each other or compete for scarce resources will generally not get involved in intergroup conflict. Conversely, groups who work interdependently or who must compete for scarce resources may eventually come into conflict.[51]

Examples of how interdependency or competition for scarce resources leads to conflict are common. Conflicts are often a way of life for members of quality control and production departments, sales and production departments, and other departments that depend on each other. On the other hand, intergroup conflict is less likely to occur between the finance and quality control departments, since the people in these departments are not so interdependent. Competition for scarce resources, such as when two or more departments must compete for limited funds or for the services of a typing pool, often leads to "office politics," hiding of information, and conflict.

Of course, interdependence doesn't have to lead to conflict; just the opposite can be true. If the situation is managed correctly, or if the groups' overall aims are similar, interdependence can provide an incentive for collaboration rather than conflict. This is one reason why the conflict management techniques we discuss later in this chapter are so important.[52]

INTERGROUP DIFFERENCES IN GOALS, VALUES, OR PERCEPTIONS. Persons who agree in terms of their goals, values, or perceptions are less likely to find themselves arguing than are those with fundamental differences.

Differing goals are one familiar source of intergroup conflict. Researchers Richard Walton and John Dutton, for example, found that the preference of production departments for long, economical runs conflicted with the preference of sales units for quick delivery to good customers and that these differing goals often led to intergroup conflict.[53] Other fundamental differences in goals that have been found to lead to intergroup conflicts include those between flexibility and stability, between short-run and long-run performance, between measurable and intangible results, and between organizational goals and societal needs.[54] In summary, when the goals of two groups are similar or identical, there is little chance of serious conflict arising, but when there is a fundamental difference in goals, conflicts will likely arise.

Researchers Paul Lawrence and Jay Lorsch found that what they call "organizational differentiation" is another source of intergroup conflict.[55] As each department in an organization tries to cope with the unique demands of its own environment, it necessarily develops its own types of procedures, cherished values, and point of view. For example, a research department in a chemical firm might be run very democratically, and its employees might develop a rather long-term time perspective, because most of the things they are working on will not reach fruition for years. On the other hand, the production department might be run more autocratically, and its managers might be expected to put more emphasis on immediate results. Lawrence and Lorsch believe that the greater the differentiation between co-workers' departments, the more potential for conflict there is.

AUTHORITY IMBALANCES. We also know that when a group's actual authority is inconsistent with its prestige, intergroup conflicts are more likely to arise. For example, a researcher found that in one company, the production department had to accept instructions from a production engineering department composed of employees with skills no greater than (and in fact quite similar to) those possessed by production employees. As a result, "production managers spent an inordinate amount of time checking for consistency among the various items produced by production engineering,"[56] in order to catch the engineers in a mistake.

AMBIGUITY. Finally, difficulty in assigning credit or blame between two departments increases the likelihood of conflict between units. For example, if both the quality control and production departments can claim credit for the cost savings resulting from a change in production procedures, a conflict may well result. Similarly, if it is difficult to place the blame for a problem, conflicts may emerge as departments attempt to shed themselves of the blame, say, for a cost overrun or machine breakdown. Conflict can also occur where departmental responsibilities are not clearly delineated. Here power vacuums arise and intergroup conflicts ensue as each department fights to fill those power vacuums by assuming increased responsibilities.

Techniques for Managing Intergroup Conflict

The many techniques for managing or resolving conflicts generally fall into four categories: superordinate goals, structural approaches, conflict-resolution modes or ways of solving problems, and organizational development conflict-resolution techniques.

INSTITUTE COMMON OR SUPERORDINATE GOALS TO MANAGE CONFLICT. One of the most familiar and sensible ways of short-circuiting conflicts is to find some common ground on which the parties can agree. In labor-management negotiations, for example, arbitrators generally begin their work by finding some point on which both sides can agree and then build a solution from that one point of agreement. As another example, national leaders such as Cuba's Fidel Castro often use the ploy of claiming their countries are about to be attacked in order to bring about unification of the opposing factions in their own countries. Invoking such a superordinate ("it's bigger than both of us") goal can be an effective conflict-management tactic.

USE STRUCTURAL APPROACHES TO MANAGE CONFLICT. There are also various conflict-managing methods that are based on using the organization's structure. For example, the most frequent way of resolving disagreements between departments is still to refer them to a common superior. Thus, if the vice presidents for sales and finance cannot reach agreement on some point, they would typically refer their disagreement to the president for a binding decision.

Another structural way to reduce the potential for conflict is to reduce the interdependencies or the need to compete for scarce resources. Sometimes the changes are as simple as separating the units physically, so that the members of one group no longer have to confront members of the other each day.[57] Another change is to increase the available resources so that both groups can get basically what they want.

Lawrence and Lorsch, in the study mentioned earlier, found that many companies have reduced interdepartmental conflict by setting up special liaisons between the warring departments. In the high-technology plastics industry, for example, successful companies set up special "integrator" new-product development departments; their job was to coordinate the work of the research, sales, and manufacturing departments.

USE THE RIGHT CONFLICT-RESOLUTION STYLES. There are different ways to settle an argument. For example, having both parties meet to confront the facts and hammer out a solution is usually more effective than simply smoothing over the conflict by pushing the problems under a rug. Popular conflict-management styles and illustrations are listed below.

- *Confrontation.* "In recent meetings we have had a thrashing around about our needs. At first we did not have much agreement but we kept thrashing around and finally agreed on what was the best we could do."
- *Smoothing.* "I thought I went to real lengths in our group to confront conflict. I said what I thought in the meeting, but it did not bother anybody. I guess I should have been harsher. I could have said I won't do it unless you do it my way. If I had done this, they couldn't have backed away, but I guess I didn't have the guts to do it. I guess I didn't pound the bushes hard enough."
- *Forcing.* "If I want something very badly and I am confronted by a roadblock, I go to top management to get the decision made. If the research managers are willing to go ahead [my way], there is no problem. If there is a conflict, then I take the decision to somebody higher up."[58]
- *Avoidance.* "I'm not going to discuss that with you."
- *Competitive.* "You don't know what you're doing." "You need to get to work; if you can't get your job done, get out." "This is your doing, not mine."
- *Compromise and collaboration.* "I'm sure we can figure out a way to solve this together." "We're all in the same boat in this matter." "Let's see how we can work this out."
- *Accommodating.* "Calm down so we can work this out." "Please tell me what is wrong."[59]

There are several general rules for which style to use, and when. **Avoidance** or **smoothing over** usually won't resolve a conflict and may actually make it worse if bad feelings fester; however, some problems—especially small ones—sometimes do go away by themselves, and avoidance or smoothing over may be your only choices if the other party is highly emotional. **Accommodation** can help calm an opponent who is not uncontrollably irate, but again this is only a stop-gap measure since the disagreement itself remains unresolved.

Other approaches are more direct. **Competition** presumes a win-lose situation and sometimes works best when it's all right to resolve the conflict with a clear winner or loser, such as in sports. However, if you need to continue to work with someone, this approach may leave a residue of ill will. **Compromise** means each person gives up something in return for reaching agreement. This approach can work well but may leave one or both parties feeling they could have done better if they'd bargained harder. **Collaborating**—with both sides "on the same side of the table" to work out the agreement—is often the best approach, especially when differences are confronted and aired in a civil, problem-solving manner. **Forcing** can be effective as a brute show of power, but it can backfire if the person "forced" has the option of wiggling out of the deal.

Realistically, the style you use will depend on several things, including your personality, your success or failure with particular styles, and the response you get (or expect to get) from the other party. The latter is illustrated in Figure 15.3. Note how the effect of the wife using "avoidance" depends on which of three different styles her husband responds with, for example.

Husband confronts wife about her parents giving their children expensive gifts.

Avoidance—Accommodation

W: "I don't want to talk about this."
H: "Alright, maybe we'll talk about it later."

Avoidance—Competitive

W: "I don't want to talk about this."
H: "You never want to talk about anything."
W: "That's not true. You're the one avoiding problems."
H: "Look, if you're not going to discuss this rationally, I don't want to hear from you about it later."
W: "Don't blame me for this."

Avoidance—Collaborative

W: "I don't want to talk about this."
H: "I know you're upset with me, and I can understand why."
W: "There's no problem here. Just drop it."
H: "Does it bother you when I criticize your parents' attitude toward the kids?"
W: "Yes, of course it does."
H: "Why do you think they bring them so much?"
W: "It makes them happy to give the things. After all they don't get to see them very often."
H: "Well, that's true. And certainly they're not to blame for that. Our career choices have caused us to move so far away. I just don't want the kids to misunderstand their love of their grandparents isn't dependent upon gifts."
W: "I think we could find a way to let the children know, without changing my parents, don't you?"

■ **FIGURE 15.3**
Sample Conflict-Resolution Styles

Fundamentals of Organizational Behavior by Carrell/Jennings/Heavrin, © 1997. Reprinted by permission of Prentice-Hall, Inc., Upper Saddle River, NJ.

Organizational Behavior in Action

MANAGING CONFLICT: WHICH CONFLICT-RESOLUTION STYLE IS BEST?

A recent study of how supervisors and subordinates actually handled their conflicts provides an interesting perspective on which conflict-resolution styles are best. The fact is, people usually don't rely on a single conflict-resolution mode. In other words, they don't just confront or smooth over a situation, but rather use these and other approaches together to some degree. When applied to managing conflict, the idea of using several approaches at once is called *conglomerated behavior,* which means using several behaviors together simultaneously.[60]

In this study, the researchers focused on seven possible conflict resolution styles. These and the researchers' definitions are presented in Table 15.3: forcing, confronting, process controlling, problem solving, compromising, accommodating, and avoiding. The basic question the researchers wanted to study was whether some

■ TABLE 15.3 *Conflict-Resolution Modes*

COMPONENT	DEFINITION
Forcing	Contending the adversary do what you say in a direct way
Confronting	Demanding attention to the conflict issue
Process controlling	Dominating the conflict-resolution process to one's own advantage
Problem solving	Reconciling the parties' basic interests
Compromising	Settling through mutual concessions
Accommodating	Giving in to the opponent
Avoiding	Moving away from the conflict issue

Source: Evert Van De Vliert, Martin C. Euwema, and Sipke E. Huismans, "Managing Conflict with a Subordinate or a Superior: Effectiveness of Conglomerated Behavior," *Journal of Applied Psychology 80*, no. 2 (April 1995):271–81. Copyright © 1995 by the American Psychological Association. Reprinted by permission.

combination of these conflict-resolution styles was more effective than others. To answer this question they analyzed videotapes of 116 male police sergeants handling a standardized, scripted conflict with either a subordinate or a superior.

It was clear that to resolve the conflict most effectively the sergeant had to use several conflict-resolution styles at once. For example, problem solving tended to enhance the sergeant's effectiveness, especially if he combined it with much forcing. However, process controlling—dominating the conflict-resolution process to one's own advantage—was even more effective than trying to force the issue by insisting that the adversary do what he or she was told. In this study the sergeants also enhanced their conflict-management effectiveness by being somewhat accommodating.

The bottom line seems to be that for these police sergeants, the use of three conflict-resolution styles together—namely problem solving while being moderately accommodating and still maintaining a strong hand in controlling the conflict-resolution process—was an especially effective combination. Whether this combination would prove equally effective for other types of supervisors would have to be addressed by other studies. ■

USING OD: THE CONFRONTATION MEETING. OD techniques, including team building and the confrontation meeting, are sometimes used to manage conflict. For example, firms use the confrontation meeting to clear the air and resolve intergroup conflicts.[61] Confrontation meetings seem to be especially useful when misperceptions are at the root of the intergroup conflict, such as when each group misperceives or misunderstands the opposing group's true position.

A confrontation meeting is an OD technique in which opposing parties meet and discuss their perceptions of their own and the other group's positions under the guidance of an outside consultant who is skilled in its use. The typical confrontation meeting lasts from four to eight hours and usually begins with the consultant discussing in general terms topics such as organizational communication, the need for mutual understanding, and the need for members of the management team to share responsibility for accomplishing the organization's goals. The discussion might then turn to the causes of the conflict. Thus, in one case, two groups of employees were assigned to separate rooms and asked to discuss three questions: What qualities best describe our group? What qualities best describe the other group? What qualities do we predict the other group would assign to us?[62]

Each group was asked to develop a list of words or phrases that it felt best described its answers to each question. The two groups of employees then met and discussed their own lists as well as those developed by the other group. They questioned each other about the lists, and after several hours "it appeared as if each side moved to a position where they at least understood the other side's point of view."[63]

SUMMARY

1. Thinking like a leader involves reviewing a leadership situation and identifying what is happening, accounting for what is happening (in terms of leadership and other behavioral science theories and concepts), and formulating leader actions. Your knowledge of organizational change and development can be useful tools in that regard.

2. Managers in their leadership roles can focus on various change targets. They can change the strategy, culture, structure, tasks, technologies, or attitudes and skills of the people in the organization.

3. The hardest part of leading a change is overcoming resistance to change. This resistance stems from several sources: habit, resource limitations, threats to power and influence, fear of the unknown, and altering employees' "personal compacts." Methods for dealing with resistance include education and communication, facilitation and support, participation and involvement, negotiation and agreement, manipulation and co-optation, and coercion. Psychologist Kurt Lewin suggests unfreezing the situation, perhaps by using a dramatic event to get people to recognize the need for change.

4. Implementing a change is basically like solving any problem: The manager must recognize that there's a problem, diagnose the problem, and then formulate and implement a solution.

5. A 10-step process for actually leading organizational change would include establishing a sense of urgency; mobilizing commitment to change through joint diagnosis of business problems; creating a guiding coalition; developing a shared vision; communicating the vision; removing barriers to the change and empowering employees; generating short-term wins; consolidating gains and producing more change; anchoring the new ways of doing things in the company's culture; and monitoring progress and adjusting the vision as required.

6. Organizational changes almost never take place spontaneously; instead, they are pushed or driven by leaders. In terms of being the change leader, important roles to keep in mind include the need for charismatic leadership, instrumental leadership, missionary leadership, and being a transformational leader.

7. Organizational development is a special approach to organizational change that basically involves letting the employees themselves formulate and implement the change that's required, often with the assistance of a trained consultant. The once-clear lines between OD and other types of organiza-

tional change efforts (such as reorganizing) are beginning to blur, so that our discussion of OD applications provides a useful overview of the sorts of organizational changes that are possible. Types of OD applications include human process applications, technostructural interventions, human resource management applications, and strategic applications.

8. Conflict exists and can have dysfunctional effects on the organization and the people that it comprises, although conflict can be a positive force as well. At least three types of conflict can be identified in organizations: individual, interpersonal, and intergroup organizational conflict. Intergroup conflicts often stem from interdependencies and shared resources; intergroup differences in goals, values, or perceptions; authority imbalances; or ambiguity. Problems like these can be solved by establishing superordinate goals, eliminating interdependencies, using one or more conflict-resolution modes, or through OD conflict-resolution techniques like confrontation meetings.

KEY TERMS

strategic change
organizational
   development
   interventions
unfreezing
moving
refreezing
change advocates
charismatic leadership
instrumental leadership
organizational
   development (OD)

action research
human process
   interventions
sensitivity training
team building
confrontation meetings
survey research
formal structure change
   program
strategic interventions
integrated strategic
   management

role conflict
interpersonal conflict
intergroup organizational
   conflict
avoidance
smoothing over
accommodation
competition
collaboration
compromise
forcing

SELF-TEST

TRUE / FALSE QUESTIONS

1 **T** **F** The environment must adapt to the organization.

2 **T** **F** A strategic change alters the company's strategy, mission, and vision.

3 **T** **F** Technological changes are typically radical alterations to the work methods used by the organization to complete its tasks.

4 **T** **F** Most strategic organizational changes come from factors internal to the organization.

5 **T** **F** Leading change means overcoming resistance to change.

6 **T** **F** Coercion is never recommended as a way of creating change.

7 **T** **F** One way to create change is to establish a sense of urgency.

8 **T** **F** A key element in the effective communication of a vision is to keep it simple.

9 **T** **F** Some argue that for successful leadership during change, the leader must be charismatic.

10 **T** **F** OD (organizational development) is employee centered.

MULTIPLE-CHOICE QUESTIONS

1 There are different types of change. Which of the following is not one?
- **a.** incremental
- **b.** reactive
- **c.** anticipatory
- **d.** participatory

2 Which is not a source of resistance to change?
- **a.** threats to power and influence
- **b.** fear of the known
- **c.** altering employees' personal compacts
- **d.** habit

3 The first step in Kurt Lewin's approach to overcoming resistance is _____ the forces that are trying to maintain the status quo.
- **a.** unfreezing
- **b.** moving
- **c.** refreezing
- **d.** deep-freezing

4 The real power behind a vision for change is created when the majority have a _____ of its goals and direction.
- **a.** differing perspective
- **b.** powerful idea
- **c.** common understanding
- **d.** strategic grasp

5 Which is not an aspect of instrumental leadership?
- **a.** structuring
- **b.** controlling
- **c.** rewarding
- **d.** organizing

6 Innovations require _____.
- **a.** icons
- **b.** champions
- **c.** philosophers
- **d.** genius

7 Which is not a type of OD application?
- **a.** human process applications
- **b.** technostructural applications
- **c.** human resource management applications
- **d.** quality control techniques

8 When OD practitioners strive to change the structures, methods, and job designs of firms, they are practicing _____.
- **a.** technological interventions
- **b.** human resources planning
- **c.** reengineering
- **d.** virtual management

9 Which is not a type of organizational conflict?
- **a.** individual
- **b.** interpersonal
- **c.** organizational
- **d.** environmental

10 Which of the following is not a conflict-resolution mode?
- **a.** abdication
- **b.** confrontation
- **c.** smoothing
- **d.** forcing

CRITICAL THINKING EXERCISES

1 Edwin Land, founder of Polaroid, had some simple advice on change: You, rather than your competitor, should be the one to make your product obsolete. Do you think most organizations are capable of changing as Land advised? If change equals constant reinvention of your company, how will this affect the firm's human resources?

2 The scene was the General Synod of the Church of England in the 1980s. The topic being debated was the controversial proposition that women be admitted to the priesthood. A speaker from the floor of the Chamber spoke with compassion: "In this matter," he cried, "as in so much else in our great country, why cannot the status quo be the way forward?"[64]

What are the sources of resistance here? Why is change so difficult for many people? Is change inevitable?

EXPERIENTIAL EXERCISES

1 Management guru Peter F. Drucker, who is in his mid-80s, has witnessed, experienced, and analyzed a great deal of organizational change in this century. In a recent interview he was asked a series of questions about the changes he sees in our post-capitalist world, that is, a world based on knowledge as the economic driving force, rather than on assets or brawn.[65] Read the following questions and then interview five people you know between 35 and 60 years old and ask them to respond to the questions. Compare their answers. Be prepared to discuss your findings in class.

▪ If a "man in a gray flannel suit" represents yesterday's typical corporate type, what is today's?

- How does one prepare for this new kind of managerial career?
- What do you think is the biggest challenge in leading organizational change in Drucker's post-capitalist companies?

2   At Shell International, the giant oil and petroleum multinational with headquarters in both The Hague and London, the global scale of operations is evident. In fact, with operations in more than 120 countries, Shell may have more expatriates, or employees stationed outside their native countries, than any other company in the world.

Shell conducted a survey to chart demographic and social trends among expatriates. They noted increasing numbers of women in the workforce, more aged dependents, greater travel opportunities and chances to experience other cultures, and concern about the unknown effects of expatriation on children separated from their parents.[66]

Your team has been asked to advise Shell. Write a two- to three-page report about how the firm might integrate these external trends into its internal management policies and strategies. What is the leadership challenge here? What concepts from this chapter can help Shell management develop an effective way to manage changes?

DIVERSITY CASE

NEW SOCIAL CONTRACT OR GOOD OLD PATERNALISM?

The hotel industry faces the problem of attracting and keeping a trained and disciplined workforce. The Marriott Corporation has decided to meet the challenge head on by evaluating potential employees and filling in the gaps in their background with education and training, from basic literacy to home management skills, citizenship training, English, and instruction in family and childcare issues. Marriott pays $7.40 an hour, which is above the current minimum wage.

Questions

1   What lessons about leading organizational change might others learn from Marriott?

2   Has Marriott taken a stand on a social issue or is this just a case of paternalism where the traditional management people are totally in charge and the workers are only there to follow orders?

3   What change-management problems might you face under Marriott's plan?

Sources: John Case, "The Open Book Revolution," *Inc.,* June 1995, 26–43; and Catherine Yang, Ann Therese Palmer, Seanna Browder, and Alice Cuneo, "Low Wage Lessons," *Business Week,* 11 November 1996, 108–16.

STRATEGY CASE

THE OUTSOURCING OF HUMAN RESOURCES

At the Oakland, California, airport the people behind the American Airlines counter are wearing American's uniform, but they are not airline employees making up to $19 an hour plus benefits. They are from Johnson Control Inc., which has contracted with American for the ticketing jobs.

At 28 second-tier airports, American outsourced these jobs at $7 to $9 an hour plus inferior benefits such as less expensive health insurance. The move was part of a cost-cutting strategy. Other companies are also using outsourcing as a cost-saving strategy. UPS, for example, recently outsourced 5,000 jobs at its 65 customer service centers. The UPS decision was in part driven by computer technology and by a management decision to centralize various functions.

Questions

1   What resistance to change might this outsourcing strategy create?

2   How would you manage the situation if conflict arose between the full-time employees and the outsourced employees?

3   Do you think outsourcing represents a permanent change in the way companies handle human resources? What are the implications for leadership under these conditions?

4   Outline a ten-step change program for achieving the changes required to implement a cost-cutting strategy.

ENTREPRENEURIAL CASE

JOB SURFING: CATCHING THE NEW WAVE

Switching jobs is no longer viewed as irresponsible behavior. In fact, it makes sense to stay mobile and increase your skills whenever you can.

David Friedensohn is a case in point. Over the last decade he has worked for four different employers, including Citicorp and Viacom. In addition, he has been a self-employed consultant. David has continually learned new skills, increased his responsibilities, and bumped up his income. Currently, he is vice president for new business at Prodigy, running a couple of the online service's startup ventures in New York City and earning a steady six-figure income. His advice: "You have to be disciplined to get the skills to stay in the race. You can't force the ocean to throw a good wave at you either. You have to seize opportunities when they come."

Questions

1. What are the implications of David's philosophy for leading organizational change today?
2. Why, do you think, that David does not resist change but rather embraces it?
3. Could you manage your career as does David?
4. Do you think constant change is the wave of the future for most job seekers? Why or why not?

SOURCE: Justin Martin, "Job Surfing: Move On to Move Up." *Fortune*, 13 January 1997, 50–4.

THE BUSINESS TEAM, INC.

WHEN LEADERSHIP STYLES COLLIDE, CONFLICT CAN OCCUR

The Team had read in the business section of the local paper that there was to be a new joint venture between a Japanese firm and a local one. Each firm brought its own expertise to the table. The Japanese firm had extensive worldwide contacts and excellent production facilities in the United Sates and throughout Asia, while the local firm was noted for its creative design and sales teams. Both companies were betting that a merger of their respective strengths would be a winner. Their product was to be new electronic equipment for a wide variety of entertainment purposes.

All seemed to go well initially from top management's perspective, but as middle management and line workers began to work together there were problems concerning who was in charge and how they should do things. The Japanese wanted to work in teams on a consensus basis, gathering input from everyone prior to a decision. The U.S. workers wanted to appoint one leader who would make the final decision, and to work mainly as individual representatives of their departments, coming together as a team only in the final stages of a project. Already both parties were highly frustrated, and they were showing it in their own ways. The Japanese wanted to check in with headquarters in Tokyo for advice, while the U.S. executives wanted to just make the decision and get on with business.

Finally, they agreed to consult with the Business Team as to what to do.

Questions

1. What advice do you think the Business Team should give the two firms?
2. What techniques of change leadership and conflict resolution presented in the chapter might the Team suggest?
3. What special change issues arise when two different cultures clash like this?
4. Could the clash be due to the functional specialties of the Japanese and American managers, rather than just cultural differences?

KNITMEDIA PREPARES FOR CONTINUAL CHANGE

Staying on the leading edge of musical trends is a crucial task for KnitMedia. As their management has said, the company's future success depends in part on its ability to respond and adapt to changes in the marketplace, to technological change, and to changes in consumption and distribution. To do this, KnitMedia will have to develop strong artistic and consumer relations as well as technological innovations and to incorporate such relationships and innovations into its products and services in a cost-effective manner. To accomplish this, companies like KnitMedia must continually guard against becoming lethargic and bureaucratic; the company would therefore like to know if there are any techniques for managing organizational change that it can use to ensure, in a sense, that it keeps its fighting edge.

Team Exercises and Questions

Use what you learned in this chapter to answer the following questions:

1 What evidence is there that any of KnitMedia's larger competitors, such as Warner, are using organizational change techniques like those described in this chapter to increase their responsiveness?
2 Do you think KnitMedia could benefit from a formal organizational change program like one of those described in this chapter, and if so, how would you suggest they proceed?

For the online version of this case, visit our Web site at: <www.prenhall.com/desslermgmt>.

For Internet exercises, interactive study questions, news updates and more, visit the Dessler Web site at

www.prenhall.com/desslermgmt

If you're using the CD-ROM that accompanies this text, simply click on the "Web Site" button to access the site.

LEADING WITH VISION

Michael Dorf is a charismatic leader who inspires his employees to implement the ideas he generates. He has created an organizational culture in which they can be independent, creative, and innovative in making both his ideas and theirs work. He motivates them with his vision of what KnitMedia is and what it will be in the future. His vision of KnitMedia's potential has drawn his employees, as well as investors, to that vision. It is a powerful vision: being a major force in the music business; having Knitting Factory clubs all over the world; producing cyber-concerts; building a global record label; creating a digital KnitMedia community; and being in television, film, and new media.

Michael spends much of his time thinking about how to manage and motivate his staff. "The textbook doesn't teach you how to deal with other human beings and motivate them," says Michael. "I spend hours thinking about that. Managing people is difficult. I've developed a lot of patience." By empowering and inspiring his staff, Michael has motivated them to work for less money than they could earn elsewhere, and for long hours, to make that vision a reality. He has created an environment in which working with him and the music is play, not work. His passion for excellence motivates the staff to excel in their work. Many people are highly motivated by the opportunity to be the best they can be, to excel in their work. Those who join the Knit-Media staff have this opportunity.

Producing excellent work and maintaining a core of artistic integrity are important shared values at KnitMedia. The Knit demonstrates its integrity with the music it promotes and in how it runs the business. Michael is noted in the music business for his integrity.

The staff of KnitMedia also share a love of the music and the chance to hear and meet great musicians; they value being able to share that music with others. The opportunity to work with people who share the same values and goals contributes to the motivation of the people who work at KnitMedia. This is especially important since Knit-Media is not able to motivate its people with financial incentives due to its cash flow problems. Despite these problems, though, Michael is generous with Christmas bonuses, which also serves as a motivating factor.

Communications is an important part of leadership. Michael Dorf has regular Wednesday afternoon meetings with the staff to keep everyone apprised of what each one is doing. He started holding these meetings as a result of an off-site company seminar he held for his managers. As Michael recalls, "one of the elements that came out of a management seminar we did up at my house upstate, which was pretty productive, I think, was people really wanted to hear—and that's why we went into those weekly meetings—they really wanted to hear what I am doing that I'm not telling everybody about. You know, while I'm delegating as much as I can and trying to inspire certain areas: what are the projects that I'm doing when I have a meeting with MTV or a meeting with the investors or thinking of some different festivals, what else are we thinking about doing? And communicating those things so that everyone understands the bigger picture and shares and gets involved with the whole vision of KnitMedia, in a sense. And I think that has helped, in a real positive way." It is sharing the vision.

As CEO of this rapidly growing company, Michael knows that changes in the organization will have important implications for KnitMedia's operations, organizational structure, and culture. These changes will affect his employees. He thinks about how he can keep everyone motivated and retain the unique KnitMedia culture that he built. He wonders "how all of these people can continue to feel the same sort of shared vision and then make sure that they're inspiring everyone underneath" as they take on new areas of responsibility and new people take on their former jobs.

Michael doesn't want the company to be like a large corporation. He says he wants "a big company with a small company feeling, and this balance is always on my mind." By thinking about it now, he feels he can manage the process better than if he just lets it happen. He thinks about what the company should look and feel like and how to retain the KnitMedia culture. Currently Michael shares his office and conference room because they've outgrown their office space. As they expand as a result of their new financing, they will need more space. Michael knows that a company's physical layout can affect the company's culture. Reflecting on the impact of this growth, Steve Smith, Publicity Director, is "curious as to how it will affect us and I think obviously that's going to be some reflection of the physical space itself. I mean, are we going to have offices? Are we going to have doors? Is it going to become more of a professional working environment?"

Michael will need to manage the changes wrought by growth to minimize employee resistance and maintain employee motivation and productivity.

Questions

Based on the cases, the videos, the textbook you've looked at thus far, and your knowledge from other sources, answer the following questions:

1 Assuming you are acting as a consultant to Michael Dorf, what would you advise him to do to manage the changes KnitMedia faces in order to minimize employee resistance and maintain employee motivation and productivity?

2 What techniques would you recommend to Michael Dorf to improve his effectiveness as a leader?

3 Analyze Dorf's ability to motivate his employees. What lessons can we learn from his motivational techniques? What should he do to be even more effective?

SOURCE: End-of-part video cases prepared by d.t. ogilvie, Rutgers University.

CHAPTER 16

CONTROLLING AND BUILDING COMMITMENT

What's Ahead?

Margot Rambert, owner and CEO of Rambert Electronics, Inc., had a serious problem. Her small company's survival was based on protecting its intellectual property—its patents and its trademarks. Every shipment of calculators that left the plant had to include a permanently attached label indicating that the Rambert Electronics material was patent protected. Yet while Margot coaxed, cajoled, and disciplined her employees, order after order left the plant without the required labels.

Objectives

After studying this chapter, you should be able to

- **define** control and explain each of the main steps in the traditional control process

- **distinguish** between traditional control methods and commitment-based control methods

- **explain** how managers use traditional diagnostic, boundary, and interactive control methods

- **identify** unintended human behavioral consequences of controls

- **show** how managers like Margot can use belief systems and employee commitment to maintain better control.

MANAGEMENT ON THE WEB

PERFORMANCE MANAGEMENT NETWORK

Performance Management Network's mission is to add value to public and private sector enterprises through the exchange of ideas on performance management, measurement, and improvement. How could Margot Rambert use this site? ∎

http://www.globalx.net/pmn/index.html

What Is Control?

After plans have been made and the organization has been designed and staffed with motivated employees, it's time to ensure that the plans are being implemented, or, if necessary, revised. **Control,** what Margot is struggling with, is the task of ensuring that activities are providing the desired results. In its most general sense, controlling means setting a target, measuring performance, and taking corrective action as required.

Managers need controls for two reasons. One explanation is that employees must be influenced to do what they are supposed to do:

> If all personnel always did what was best for the organization, control—and even management—would not be needed. But, obviously, individuals are some-times unable or unwilling to act in the organization's best interest, and a set of controls must be implemented to guard against undesirable behavior and to encourage desirable actions.[1]

In today's fast-changing world, however, there's a second need for control. Plans can quickly become outdated as unanticipated events occur; when that happens, con-trol is required to inform management that the plan needs changing. As control expert Kenneth Merchant says, "The goal [of the control system] is to have no unpleasant surprises in the future."[2]

What is the best way to "stay in control"? As we'll see in this chapter, the two basic options are traditional, and commitment-based control methods.

The Traditional Control Process

Whether controlling an assembly line or the New York City budget, control tradi-tionally includes three steps:

1. Establish a standard, goal, or target.
2. Compare actual performance to the standard.
3. Take corrective action.

In practice, of course, control is more complicated. It also requires analyzing the reasons for the deviations, reviewing alternative courses of action, and finally choos-ing and implementing the most promising solutions.[3]

STEP 1: ESTABLISH A STANDARD.   You can express standards in terms of money, time, quantity, or quality (or a combination of these). Thus a salesperson might get a dollar-based quota of $8,000 worth of products per month, or a pro-duction supervisor be told to cut costs by $2,000 per week. Performance standards are also expressed in terms of time—a person might have to meet a certain sales quota in a week or complete a report by May 1.

Some standards are quantity based. For instance production supervisors are usually responsible for producing a specified number of units of product per week. Sometimes standards are qualitative, such as the reject rates in quality control, the grades of products sold (such as "grade A"), or the quality of a student's report.

Whatever the category—quantity, quality, timeliness, dollars—the usual procedure is to choose a specific yardstick and then set a standard, as shown in Figure 16.1. Thus, for quantity, yardsticks include units produced per shift and grievances filed per month.[4] Specific quantitative goals then might be set for each.

STEP 2: MEASURE ACTUAL PERFORMANCE AND COMPARE TO STANDARD. The next step is to measure the actual performance or results. This can be accomplished using both personal and impersonal means.[5] Personal observation is the simplest and most common way of comparing actual performance to standards. For example, while a new employee is getting on-the-job training, her performance is personally observed by a supervisor.

Nothing substitutes for the interactive give-and-take feedback of this kind of personal supervision. However, as the manager assumes more responsibilities, it becomes increasingly difficult to personally monitor everyone. One way to handle this problem is to add supervisors; for example, a hospital director might hire two assistant directors to observe employees on different floors. But from a practical point of view, personal control must at some point be supplemented by formal, more impersonal control reports. Budgetary control reports, quality control reports, and inventory control reports are three examples of tools used to measure and compare actual performance to standards.

STEP 3: TAKE CORRECTIVE ACTION. If there's a discrepancy, then corrective action may be required. Taking corrective action is essentially a problem-solving activity. In some instances the deviation—such as sales that are too low—can be easily explained. However, as we saw in chapter 4 ("Making Decisions"), things are often not what they seem. Perhaps the sales target was too high, or your firm could not supply the products or couldn't supply them on time. The point is that a deviation from the standard merely flags a problem that may (or may not) then require further analysis.

The Timeliness of the Control System

Some control systems provide more timely notice of problems than do others. For example, experts distinguish between steering controls, yes-no controls, and post-action controls.

FIGURE 16.1
Examples of Control Standards

STEERING CONTROLS. With **steering controls,** corrective action is taken before the operation or project has been completed.[6] For example, the flight of a

AREA TO CONTROL	POSSIBLE YARDSTICK	STANDARD/GOAL TO ACHIEVE
Quantity	Number of products produced	Produce 14 units per month
Quality	Number of rejects	No more than 10 rejects per day
Timeliness	Percent sales reports in on time	Return 90% of sales reports on time
Dollars	Percent deviation from budget	Do not exceed budgeted expenses by more than 5% during year

spacecraft aimed for the moon is tracked continuously, since you would not want to find out after the fact that you had missed your mark! Its trajectory is modified so that flight-path corrections can be made days before the spacecraft is due to reach the moon.

Steering controls play a big role in today's organizations. For example, most managers set intermediate milestones so they can check a project's progress long before it is to be completed. Then, if a problem is found, it can be rectified in time to save the project.

YES-NO CONTROLS. A **yes-no control** is one in which work may not proceed until it passes an intermediate control step. For example, most large companies have a rule forbidding employees from entering into contracts with suppliers or customers unless the agreements have been approved ahead of time by the firm's legal staff.

POST-ACTION CONTROLS. A **post-action control** is one in which results are compared to the standard after the project has been finished. Budgets are examples of post-action controls, as are the end-of-term grades you receive. The problem with post-action controls, as with grades, is that you usually can't do much to remedy the situation once the time period is over and the results are in. Most students therefore prefer to find out how they're doing during the semester.

The same is true in organizations. Particularly when things are changing fast, you don't want to find out after the fact—say, at the end of the year—that your plans were ill conceived or your employees incompetent. Companies therefore try to build in the timeliness provided by steering controls. This can help identify problems—such as with the assumptions underlying a plan—before they get out of hand.

Control in an Age of Empowerment

As companies expand worldwide and compete in fast-changing markets, the problems of relying on traditional—set standards/compare actual to standards/take corrective action—controls have become increasingly apparent. In England the great banking firm Barings—almost 400 years old—was virtually destroyed by the trading practices of a lone rogue trader in Singapore named Nicholas Leeson. Sears, Roebuck and Company (as we saw in chapter 3, "Ethics, Diversity, and Social Responsibility") took a $60 million charge against earnings after it admitted that some of its service writers and mechanics recommended unnecessary automobile repairs to customers. Kidder, Peabody & Company lost $350 million recently when a trader allegedly reported fictitious profits.

Problems like these were not—and probably could not have been—anticipated by traditional controls like budgets and accounting reports. Particularly today, when markets change quickly and more employees are empowered, managers need a way to ensure that the employees won't want to let activities slip out of control, or that, if they do, the managers will discover it before catastrophe strikes. Harvard professor and control expert Robert Simons puts it this way:

> A fundamental problem facing managers in the 1990s is how to exercise adequate control in organizations that demand flexibility, innovation, and creativity. . . . In most organizations operating in dynamic and highly competitive markets, managers cannot spend all their time and effort making sure that everyone is doing what is expected. Nor is it realistic to think that managers can achieve control by simply hiring good people, aligning incentives, and hoping for the best. Instead, today's managers must encourage employees to initiate process improvements and new ways of responding to customers' needs—but in a controlled way.[7]

WHY IT'S DANGEROUS TO RELY ON TRADITIONAL CONTROLS TODAY.

At least four specific characteristics of doing business in the "age of empowerment" make it dangerous to try to control activities solely (or even primarily) with traditional controls like budgets:

- *All details cannot be specified in advance.* There was a time when the remarkable quality of Mercedes Benz automobiles was achieved primarily by groups of lab-coated final inspectors at the ends of the car lines carefully inspecting all cars and (if necessary) returning them for repairs. In today's highly competitive and quality-conscious environment, car makers know that they can no longer rely on such a relatively inefficient way of finding quality problems. The better approach is to get the employees themselves to build-in quality with every bolt they turn and every window they install. However, as we've seen in the leadership chapters, doing so requires motivating employees to want to do their jobs as if they owned the company, and that usually means empowering them. The most complete and detailed control handbook could not possibly anticipate every single detail that could go wrong to undermine the quality of a Mercedes Benz, nor could it anticipate something like the aggressive misbehavior of a rogue trader in Singapore. The faster things change, the more difficult it is to anticipate every possible problem. And, the more important it becomes to be able to rely on your employees' self-control.
- *You can't watch everything everyone does.* Whether it's your trader in Singapore or an assembly-line worker turning a bolt, you can't watch everything everyone does, and the faster things change and the more geographically dispersed your employees are, the more that is true. Again, under conditions like these, relying on your employees' self-control becomes more important.
- *Assumptions change.* Particularly when technologies and markets are changing fast, the assumptions on which your plan was built yesterday may no longer apply tomorrow. Until 1996, Bill Gates and Microsoft virtually ignored the Internet and based their plans on supplying operating systems to conventional PCs. In 1996 it dawned on Microsoft's managers that their assumption about the Internet was erroneous. Luckily, they had in place the kind of early warning systems that could show them they had to revise their assumptions and their plans.
- *You cannot legislate creativity.* You can closely watch people on assembly-line type jobs and perhaps control the quantity and even quality of their work. However it's more difficult and at times impossible to dictate that employees be creative and use initiative, and to control their creativity with traditional supervisory methods. Creativity and initiative—two characteristics of empowered jobs in these fast-changing times—require relying more on employees' self-control.

For reasons like these, companies are increasingly relying on their employees' self-control to keep things operating in control, rather than just on traditional controls like budgets. One sign of this is the widespread use of empowerment, wherein self-managing teams get the self-confidence, tools, training, and information they need to do their jobs as if they owned the company. However, being creative and managing yourself is inconsistent with being controlled and monitored: you cannot require or force people to be creative, in other words. Control in an age of empowerment, as Robert Simons puts it, therefore requires new types of commitment-based control tools, to "reconcile the conflict between creativity and control."[8]

While any classification scheme is bound to be somewhat arbitrary, we can conveniently distinguish between traditional control methods and commitment-based control methods:

- **Traditional control methods,** as we've seen, are based on setting standards and then monitoring performance. These control methods include three categories of controls, which have been called diagnostic controls, boundary systems, and interactive controls.[9] **Diagnostic control systems** (such as budgets) allow managers to determine whether important targets were met. **Boundary systems** are the policies that identify the actions and pitfalls that employees must avoid. Ethical rules against accepting gifts from suppliers are an example. **Interactive control systems** basically involve controlling by questioning subordinates face to face, perhaps to learn about competitive threats as conditions change.
- **Commitment-based control methods** rely on getting the employees themselves to want to do things right—they emphasize self-control, in other words. For example, companies like Toyota and Saturn work hard to socialize all employees in the companies' *belief systems* and values, such as the importance of teamwork, quality, and respect for people, to foster self-control. Other companies emphasize building employees' *commitment* to doing what is best for the company, and doing it right.

We'll devote the rest of this chapter to discussing how to use these control methods.

Traditional Control Methods

There are three categories of traditional control methods: diagnostic control systems, boundary control systems, and interactive control systems.

Diagnostic Control Systems

When most people think of controls, they're thinking of *diagnostic control systems*. Such control systems aim to ensure that important goals are being achieved and that variances, if any, are explained. Budgets and performance reports are examples.

One of the main purposes of diagnostic controls is to reduce the need for managers to constantly monitor everything.[10] Once targets have been set managers can (at least in theory) leave the employees to pursue those goals, supposedly secure in the knowledge that if the goals are not being met, the deviations will show up as variances that have to be explained. This idea is at the heart of what management experts call the principle of exception. The **principle of exception** (or "management by exception") holds that to conserve managers' time, only significant deviations or exceptions from the standard, "both the especially good and bad exceptions," should be brought to the manager's attention.[11]

For diagnostic control systems to work effectively, several things must be assumed. One is that the results produced by the employees (like reported sales) are accurate and, in particular, that employees don't work aggressively to get around or fudge the control system. It's also assumed that the goals or targets themselves remain acceptable and valid. If they didn't, what would be the use of comparing the company's actual results to an outdated goal?

Unfortunately (as firms like Barings have learned to their sorrow), assumptions like these are often not valid in today's fast-changing world. Nevertheless, diagnostic control systems remain important and widely used: Budgets and performance reports are among the most familiar examples and are discussed in a later section.

Boundary Control Systems

As their name implies, boundary control systems "establish the rules of the game and identify actions and pitfalls that employees must avoid."[12] They are widely used and are illustrated by things like the standards of ethical behavior and codes of conduct to which employees are encouraged to adhere.

As explained in chapter 3, Johnson & Johnson's ethical credo illustrates the foundation of such a boundary control system. It contains the fundamental ethical guidelines (such as, "We believe our first responsibility is to the doctors, nurses, and patients ... who use our products" and "our suppliers and distributors must have an opportunity to make a fair profit") that are supposed to provide the boundaries over which Johnson & Johnson employees are not to step. For example, selling a product that might be harmful would obviously be out of bounds. This helps account for the fact that when confronted by several bottles of poisoned Tylenol some years back, Johnson & Johnson's managers elected to recall their entire stock of the product.

Ethical or boundary control systems require more than just drawing up a list of ethical guidelines. In chapter 3, for instance, we emphasized that fostering ethics at work has at least these five steps:

1. Emphasize top management's commitment.
2. Publish a "code."
3. Establish compliance mechanisms.
4. Involve personnel at all levels.
5. Measure results.

Boundary control systems are important for any company, but they are especially important for firms that are very dependent on a reputation built on trust.[13] For example, large consulting firms like McKinsey & Company and the Boston Consulting Group must be able to assure clients that the highly proprietary strategic data they will review will never be compromised. They must therefore enforce strict boundaries "that forbid consultants to reveal information—even the names of clients—to anyone not employed by the firm, including spouses."[14]

The "boundaries" a firm lays down don't have to be limited to ethical guidelines. For example, "strategic boundaries focus on ensuring that people steer clear of opportunities that could diminish the business's competitive position."[15] Thus managers at Automatic Data Processing (ADP) use a strategic boundary list that lays out the types of business opportunities ADP managers should avoid. Another company, a large Netherlands-based multinational, has a strategic policy of discouraging its executives from forming joint ventures with firms in the United States because of the heightened possibility of litigation in U.S. courts.

Interactive Control Systems

The typical small, entrepreneurial mom-and-pop company has at least one big control advantage over its huge multinational competitors: Mom and Pop can talk face to face with almost everyone in their firm to find out immediately how everything is going. Of course as companies grow and expand, this kind of direct interaction becomes more difficult because there are so many people, often far away, to keep track of. However, just because it's difficult doesn't mean that interactive, primarily face-to-face controls cannot and should not be implemented, and many firms have implemented them. For example, *interactive strategic control* is a real-time, usually face-to-face method of monitoring both a strategy's effectiveness and the underlying assumptions on which the strategy was built.[16]

Senior managers at *USA Today* use interactive control.[17] Three weekly reports delivered each Friday give senior managers an overview of how they have done in the previous week and what they may expect in the next few weeks. This "Friday packet" information ranges from year-to-date advertising and sales figures to account-specific information regarding particular advertisers.

Weekly face-to-face meetings among senior managers and key subordinates are then an important part of interactive control at *USA Today*. Each week the regular topics of discussion and debate include advertising volume compared to plan and new business by type of client. The senior managers don't just look for unexpected shortfalls; they also look for unexpected successes that may suggest the advisability of putting more emphasis on a particular area, such as appealing to more software suppliers to become advertisers. Several strategic innovations have emerged from these meetings; these include exclusive advertising inserts dedicated to specific customers and products, and a new market-survey service for automotive clients.

How does information like this help *USA Today*'s senior managers? For one thing, it helps them to look at the big picture regarding how the paper is doing versus its competitors. And it helps them to identify trends, such as decreasing or increasing advertising expenditures by specific advertisers, or changing sales patterns in various states.

As at any company using interactive controls for strategic purposes, the basic intention of their use at *USA Today* is twofold: (1) to give senior managers a formal procedure through which they can monitor information of strategic importance to the firm; and (2) to get a feel for the importance of that information by interacting, primarily face to face, with key subordinates. Such controls can thus be very useful for managing change.

Managing Change

TWO INTERACTIVE STRATEGIC CONTROL TOOLS

In some companies, the interactive control system is informal, at least for a while. For example, consider Bill Gates and Microsoft. According to one version of the events, two Microsoft programmers who'd previously worked for Internet providers convinced Gates during face-to-face meetings that Microsoft had to focus its resources more aggressively on giving Microsoft programs Internet capabilities. It was out of these informal, strategy-oriented interactive meetings that Microsoft's new Internet strategy was reportedly born.

Many companies don't leave their interactive controls to chance but instead formalize them using specific tools and procedures like *USA Today*'s weekly meetings. Like these meetings, the aim of an interactive control system is usually to interactively evaluate not just how well the firm is implementing its plan but also the underlying assumptions on which that plan was built. Environmental monitoring and environmental scanning are two other tools used to facilitate interactive control.

ENVIRONMENTAL MONITORING. Strategic plans are formulated based on assumptions regarding what the future holds. **Environmental monitoring** means systematically and continuously checking those assumptions to see whether any of the strategic plan's basic assumptions have changed, which in turn might require modifying the strategy.[18]

Specially qualified individuals and departments are often assigned to monitor environmental information related to matters such as competitors' actions, inflation, and new-product developments. When the environment is not carefully monitored, mistakes can be made. A number of years ago Polaroid Corporation decided to base much of its strategy on creating an "instant" movie film that, like its instant cameras, would produce a viewable moving picture within a minute or so. Unfortunately, the assumptions on which this plan was built did not include the advent of the video-tape machine; if Polaroid had foreseen the videotape, the firm might have cut its losses earlier. FedEx made a similar mistake some time ago, investing hundreds of millions of dollars in "Zapmail," a proprietary satellite network to fax letters for clients from one FedEx office to another. The assumption was that most people couldn't afford fax machines and, of course, FedEx was soon proved wrong.

ENVIRONMENTAL SCANNING. Environmental monitoring focuses your experts' attention on the previously identified assumptions on which the strategic plan was built. **Environmental scanning,** on the other hand, finds previously *un*identified or *un*detected critical events that could influence the company's strategy. Environmental scanning is a more open, less focused activity than monitoring, since the firm is scanning its whole environment to detect unexpected events, ones for which it is not specifically looking.

Environmental scanning starts by dividing the firm's environment into sectors (economic, political, social, and so on), perhaps using a worksheet like that in Figure 16.2. These sectors (such as the economic sector) are then further subdivided into subsectors that may have particular relevance for the company (such as interest rates and employment trends within the economic sector). The sectors and subsectors are then continuously scanned by the company's experts to detect previously unidentified events or trends that could be significant for the company and its strategy.

Such scanning can be accomplished in several ways. Employees can be assigned the responsibility of tracking particular subsectors, perhaps by monitoring publications like the *New York Times, Business Week,* and the *Wall Street Journal,* as well as the Internet, consultants' reports, information services, and industry newsletters. Increasingly, outside experts called environmental scanners (individuals who read and abstract a wide variety of publications) are retained to search for environmental changes that could affect the firm. Internet news services can be used to continuously and automatically screen thousands of news stories and provide precisely the types of stories in which scanners are interested. ∎

Traditional Control Tools

Managers use a variety of specific tools to create traditional control systems. For example, as we've seen, ethical codes of conduct form the heart of many boundary control systems. Environmental monitoring and environmental scanning are popular interactive control tools; the strategy-evaluation assessment matrix, discussed later in this section, is a third interactive control tool. Budgets, zero-based budgeting, and ratio

Economic Trends
(such as: recession; inflation; employment; monetary policies)

_____
_____
_____
_____

Competitive Trends
(such as: competitors' strategic changes; market/customer trends; entry/exit of competitors; new products from competitors)

_____
_____
_____
_____

Political Trends
(such as: national/local election results; special interest groups; legislation; and regulation/deregulation)

_____
_____
_____
_____

Technological Trends
(such as: introduction of new production/distribution technologies; rate of product obsolescence; trends in availability of supplies and raw materials)

_____
_____
_____
_____

Social Trends
(such as: demographic trends; mobility; education; evolving values)

_____
_____
_____
_____

Geographic Trends
(such as: opening/closing of new markets; factors effecting current plant/office facilities location decisions)

_____
_____
_____
_____

■ **FIGURE 16.2**
Worksheet for Environmental Scanning

analysis (discussed next) are among the most widely used diagnostic control tools, and here managers also increasingly use a tool called the corporate scorecard.

Budgets and Performance Reports

Budgets are formal financial expressions of a manager's plans. They show target numbers for such yardsticks as revenues, cost of materials, expenditures, and profits, usually expressed in dollars.

BUDGET FOR MACHINERY DEPARTMENT, JUNE 1997

Budgeted Expenses	Budget
Direct Labor	$2,107
Supplies	$3,826
Repairs	$ 402
Overhead (electricity, etc.)	$ 500
TOTAL EXPENSES	$6,835

■ **FIGURE 16.3**
Example of a Budget

PERFORMANCE REPORT FOR MACHINERY DEPARTMENT, JUNE 1997

	Budget	Actual	Variance	Explanation
Direct Labor	$2,107	$2,480	$373 over	Had to put workers on overtime.
Supplies	$3,826	$4,200	$374 over	Wasted two crates of material.
Repairs	$ 402	$ 150	$252 under	
Overhead (electricity, etc.)	$ 500	$ 500	0	
TOTAL	$6,835	$7,330	$495 over	

■ **FIGURE 16.4**
Example of a Performance Report

Budgets are widely used. Each manager, from first-line supervisor to top manager, usually has his or her own budget.[19] However, creating the budget (as shown in Figure 16.3) is just the standard-setting step in the control process. Actual performance still must be measured and compared to the budgeted standards. Then corrective action can be taken.

The organization's accountants are responsible for collecting data on actual performance. They then compile the financial data and feed them back to the appropriate managers. The most common form of feedback is a performance report, such as the one shown in Figure 16.4. The manager typically receives a report like this for his or her unit at the end of some time period (say, each month). As in Figure 16.4, the performance report shows budgeted or planned targets. Next to these figures, it shows the department's actual performance. The report also lists the differences between budgeted and actual amounts; these are usually called **variances.** A space on the report is sometimes provided for the manager to explain any variances. After reviewing the performance report, the manager can then take any required corrective action.

Zero-Based Budgeting

In traditional budgeting, funding requests are often based on ongoing projects, although sometimes these projects may no longer be needed. For example, many federal government programs are routinely continued from year to year simply because "they've always been in the budget."

Zero-based budgeting is a technique that forces managers to defend all their budgeted programs every year and to rank them in order of priority based on the ratio of their benefits and costs. This exercise gives top management an opportunity to reevaluate ongoing programs, compare ongoing to proposed programs, and consider reducing or eliminating the funding for ongoing programs so that new programs with higher priorities can be implemented.[20]

Ratio Analysis and Return on Investment

Most managers achieve control in part by monitoring various **financial ratios,** which compare one financial indicator to another. The rate of return on investment (ROI) is one such ratio: it is a measure of overall company performance and equals net

NAME OF RATIO	FORMULA	INDUSTRY NORM (ASSUMED MERELY AS ILLUSTRATION)
1. Liquidity Ratios (measuring the ability of the firm to meet its short-term obligations)		
Current ratio	$\dfrac{\text{Current assets}}{\text{Current liabilities}}$	2.6
Acid-test ratio	$\dfrac{\text{Cash and equivalent}}{\text{Current liability}}$	1.0
Cash velocity	$\dfrac{\text{Sales}}{\text{Cash and equivalent}}$	12 times
Inventory to net working capital	$\dfrac{\text{Inventory}}{\text{Current assets} - \text{Current liabilities}}$	85%
2. Leverage Ratios (measure the contributions of financing by owners compared with financing provided by creditors)		
Debt to equity	$\dfrac{\text{Total debt}}{\text{Net worth}}$	56%
Coverage of fixed charges	$\dfrac{\text{Net profit before fixed charges}}{\text{Fixed charges}}$	6 times
Current liability to net worth	$\dfrac{\text{Current liability}}{\text{Net worth}}$	32%
Fixed assets to net worth	$\dfrac{\text{Fixed assets}}{\text{Net worth}}$	60%
3. Activities Ratios (measuring the effectiveness of the employment of resources)		
Inventory turnover	$\dfrac{\text{Sales}}{\text{Inventory}}$	7 times
Net working capital turnover	$\dfrac{\text{Sales}}{\text{Net working capital}}$	5 times
Fixed-assets turnover	$\dfrac{\text{Sales}}{\text{Fixed assets}}$	6 times
Average collection period	$\dfrac{\text{Receivables}}{\text{Average sales per day}}$	20 days
Equity capital turnover	$\dfrac{\text{Sales}}{\text{Net worth}}$	3 times
Total capital turnover	$\dfrac{\text{Sales}}{\text{Total assets}}$	2 times

■ **FIGURE 16.5**
Widely Used Financial Ratios

(continued)

NAME OF RATIO	FORMULA	INDUSTRY NORM
4. Profitability Ratios (indicating degree of success of achieving desired profit levels)		
Gross operating margin	$\dfrac{\text{Gross operating profit}}{\text{Sales}}$	30%
Net operating margin	$\dfrac{\text{Net operating profit}}{\text{Sales}}$	6.5%
Sales margin	$\dfrac{\text{Net profit after taxes}}{\text{Sales}}$	3.2%
Productivity of assets	$\dfrac{\text{Gross income less taxes}}{\text{Total assets}}$	10%
Return on investment	$\dfrac{\text{Net profit after taxes}}{\text{Total investment}}$	7.5%
Net profit on working capital	$\dfrac{\text{Net operating profit}}{\text{Net working capital}}$	14.5%

■ **FIGURE 16.5**
continued

income divided by total investment. Return on investment views profit (net income) not as an absolute figure, but rather in relation to the total investment in the business; thus, a $1 million profit would be more impressive in a business with a $10 million investment than in one with a $100 million investment. Figure 16.5 presents some commonly used financial ratios.

Figure 16.6 shows how some companies combine these ratios for control. For example, sales by itself is less informative than the ratio of sales to total investment (or capital turnover). Similarly, sales divided by earnings (the profit margin) reflects management's success or failure in maintaining satisfactory cost controls. As another example, note how ROI can be influenced by factors like excessive investment. In turn, excessive investment might reflect inadequate inventory control, accounts receivable, or cash.

Strategy in Action

THE STRATEGY-EVALUATION MATRIX

When it comes to using traditional diagnostic control techniques, few things are more important than controlling the results and direction of the company's strategy. Budgets, financial plans, and financial ratios are extremely important, of course, and are therefore among the most important tools that managers use. However, if the company's basic direction is wrong—if, for instance, Microsoft had continued to ignore the Internet—then it would do its managers little good to have the right short-term budget results while companies like Netscape were eating up their market over the long run.

As a result, managers also need strategy-control tools, and the strategy-evaluation matrix is a popular one.[21] The framework is illustrated in Table 16.1 and is often used in conjunction with environmental monitoring and environmental scanning.

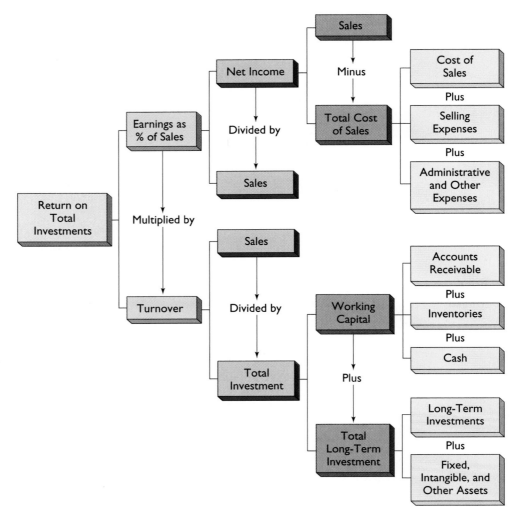

■ **FIGURE 16.6**
Relationship of Factors Affecting Return on Investment
The firm's overall profitability—its return on total investments—can be better understood by analyzing its components, including earnings as a percentage of sales and turnover.

As you may recall from chapter 6 ("Strategic Management"), many internal and external factors are considered in creating a company's strategy. Internal strengths include, for instance, patented products, proprietary production facilities, economies of scale, and world-class managers. Weaknesses might include inadequate funding, inexperienced management, and aging technology. External threats and opportunities might include new competitors and the opportunity to expand abroad.

Controlling the direction and effectiveness of a company's strategy using this tool, therefore, starts with asking questions such as the following:

1. Are our internal strengths still strengths?
2. Have we added internal strengths? If so, what are they?
3. Are our internal weaknesses still weaknesses?
4. Do we now have other internal weaknesses? If so, what are they?
5. Are our external opportunities still opportunities?
6. Are there other external opportunities? If so, what are they?
7. Are our external threats still threats?
8. Are there other external threats? If so, what are they?
9. Are we vulnerable to a hostile takeover?[22]

■ **TABLE 16.1** *A Strategy-evaluation Assessment Matrix*

HAVE MAJOR CHANGES OCCURRED IN THE FIRM'S INTERNAL STRATEGIC POSITION?	HAVE MAJOR CHANGES OCCURRED IN THE FIRM'S EXTERNAL STRATEGIC POSITION?	HAS THE FIRM PROGRESSED SATISFACTORILY TOWARD ACHIEVING ITS STATED OBJECTIVES?	RESULT
No	No	No	Take corrective actions
Yes	Yes	Yes	Take corrective actions
Yes	Yes	No	Take corrective actions
Yes	No	Yes	Take corrective actions
Yes	No	No	Take corrective actions
No	Yes	Yes	Take corrective actions
No	Yes	No	Take corrective actions
No	No	Yes	Continue present strategic course

Source: *Strategic Management* 6/E by Fred R. Davis. Copyright © 1994. Adapted by permission of Prentice-Hall, Inc., Upper Saddle River, NJ.

The strategy-evaluation assessment matrix is used to consolidate answers to the questions. In the matrix presented in Table 16.1, for instance, corrective actions are not required if (1) there have been no major changes in the firm's internal strategic position, (2) there have been no major changes in the firm's external strategic position, and (3) the firm has progressed satisfactorily toward achieving its stated objectives. In other words, the matrix presents all possible combinations of internal changes, external changes, and satisfactory progress and indicates whether or not corrective action is required for that particular combination of events.

The Corporate Scorecard

As the head of a company, how would you like to have the equivalent of a set of cockpit displays that you could use to help you pilot your company? Today, more and more companies are experimenting with a control tool called a corporate scorecard. Its basic purpose is to provide managers with an overall impression of how their companies are doing.[23]

Corporate scorecards (which are usually computerized models) put a new twist on traditional control tools. Like other traditional diagnostic control tools, they measure how the company has been doing and help managers diagnose exactly what (if anything) has gone wrong. However, they differ from their simpler control cousins, such as budgets, in several ways. First, they mathematically trace a multitude of performance measures simultaneously, and show the interactions between these various measures. Second, the manager generally gets several measures of overall performance, rather than just one or two. At Shell Oil, for instance, the Shell Business Model (as their scorecard is called) shows revenue growth, overall company market value, rate of return compared to the cost of borrowing money, and rate of return of the firm as a whole.

Like your car's dashboard, the corporate scorecard can help a manager better analyze and control what's happening in his or her company. For example, before using their model, Shell's managers did not understand the mathematical link between revenue growth and shareholder value. As a result, they often did not try to rush a new oil rig—say, in the Gulf of Mexico—into operation, because fast growth was not so important to them. With their new scorecard model, they can see that faster growth translates into higher shareholder value, so they're more anxious to get those oil rigs on-line fast.

Human Responses to Control

Control: A Central Issue in Managing

Every organization has to ensure that its employees are performing as expected. For this reason, maintaining control lies at the core of a manager's job. Every day managers are faced with questions like "How can I make sure that Marie files her sales reports on time?" and "How can I make sure John doesn't close the store before 10:00 P.M.?" To a large extent, the answer to both questions is "By imposing controls."

But if tightly controlling employees were the only (or the best) way to ensure effective performance, we could disregard more than half this book. For example, we would not need to know very much about what motivates people, what leadership style is best, or how to win employees' commitment.

But the fact is that managers can't rely just on controls for keeping employees' performance in line, as we said earlier in this chapter. For one thing, it is virtually impossible to have a system of rules and controls so complete that you can keep track of everything your employees say or do. This is one reason why as a manager you will have to rely more on self-control, such as can be fostered with motivational practices like those in chapter 12.

Furthermore, a manager cannot rely just on controls because employees can and will retaliate against controls, using what will often seem to be extraordinarily ingenious techniques. Consider this true story. The owner of a chain of dry cleaning stores tried to control stealing by requiring store managers to give a cash register receipt to each and every customer. To reinforce this policy, the owner placed a large sign by the register that said, "If you don't get a cash receipt, your order is free. Please call us at 555-6283." Sure that he could now account for all the cash coming into the store, the owner happily went home every night, handing over the store to his store manager at 5:00 P.M. But every evening at 5:15 sharp, the store manager pulled out his own cash register, which he had secreted away during the day, and spent about an hour happily taking in cash and giving each satisfied customer a cash register receipt. Then he replaced the owner's cash register and pocketed his loot.[24]

Some Unintended Behavioral Consequences of Controls

As you can see, a big problem with overrelying on traditional controls is that they can lead to unintended, undesirable, and often harmful employee reactions. Professor Kenneth Merchant classifies these reactions as behavioral displacement, gamesmanship, operating delays, and negative attitudes.[25] Reduced empowerment is a fifth unwanted reaction. Before discussing these, let's consider how personality may affect how people react to being controlled.

Organizational Behavior in Action

PERSONALITY AND HOW PEOPLE REACT TO CONTROL

While it is reasonable to expect that almost everyone at some point will react negatively to being "controlled," there's also little doubt that some will react more negatively than others. You have probably noticed, for instance, that some people are just more laid back and less likely to take offense than are others, and so might be willing to put up with controls that others might view as total nonsense.

Many psychologists also believe that a person's locus of control helps determine the degree to which the person will put up with having someone else control his or her behavior. To psychologists like Julian Rotter, who first studied this phenomenon, **locus of control** refers to the extent to which individuals believe that they control their lives.[26] Some people, called internals, "have an internal locus of control and believe that they can control what happens to them. Others, called externals, have an external locus of control and tend to think that what happens to them is determined by fate or luck."[27] To psychologists, locus of control is basically a personality trait—people are either "internals" or "externals," for instance. To examine locus of control, Rotter developed a test consisting of a series of statements about oneself and other people. Here is a sampling. With which statement in each pair do you agree?

With enough effort, we can wipe out political corruption.	vs.	It is difficult to have much control over the things politicians do in the office.
There is a direct connection between how hard I study and the grade I get.	vs.	Sometimes I can't understand how teachers arrive at the grades they give.
What happens to me is my doing.	vs.	Sometimes I feel that I don't have enough control over the direction my life is taking.
People's misfortunes result from the mistakes they make.	vs.	Many of the unhappy things in people's lives are partly due to bad luck.[28]

Statements like these, according to Rotter, help distinguish between internals and externals. Internals tend to agree with the statements on the left, whereas externals agree with those on the right. Internals generally feel they need to control their environments; externals believe they have little control over their lives.

You are probably thinking that a clever manager can influence the degree to which his or her employees react badly to being controlled by choosing his or her employees more carefully; if so, you are right. For example, internals tend to be more independent and more reliant on their own judgment. They may be more prone to resist a manager's attempts to closely supervise their work.[29] On the other hand, internals also tend to exercise more self-control and to display greater work motivation. Therefore, as several experts have said,

To reduce any tensions, management may assign internals to a job requiring high initiative and low compliance. Externals may be assigned to highly structured jobs requiring greater compliance. Becoming directly involved in workplace decisions can also bolster the attitudes and performance of internals.[30]

BEHAVIORAL DISPLACEMENT. Behavioral displacement is one of the unintended ways in which employees react to being controlled. Employees who feel pressured to look good in terms of the control standards may concentrate their efforts where results are measured, disregarding the company's more important goals. **Behavioral displacement** occurs when the behaviors encouraged by the controls are inconsistent with what the company actually wants to accomplish.

This problem stems mostly from focusing too narrowly on one or two control standards. For example, Nordstrom, a retailer famed for its extraordinary customer service, recently found itself involved in a series of lawsuits related to its policy of controlling sales per hour of performance.[31] Nordstrom is known for empowering its employees. For example, its employee handbook reportedly includes only one policy, "Use your best judgment." Unfortunately, tracking the performance of its empowered salespeople by simply monitoring sales per hour backfired on Nordstrom. Without other, counterbalancing measures the sales per hour system blew up: Some employees claimed that first-line supervisors were pressuring them to underreport their hours on the job to boost reported sales per hour. Nordstrom ended up settling those claims for over $15 million.

GAMESMANSHIP. **Gamesmanship** refers to management actions aimed at improving the manager's performance in terms of the control system without producing any economic benefits for the firm. For example, there was the manager who depleted his stocks of spare parts and heating oil at year's end although he knew these stocks would have to be replenished shortly thereafter at higher prices. By reducing his stocks the manager reduced his expenses for the year and made his end-of-year results look better, although in the long run the company lost out.[32] In another example, a division overshipped products to its distributors at year-end. The aim was to ensure that management could meet its budgeted sales targets, even though the managers knew the products would be returned.[33]

OPERATING DELAYS. Operating delays can be another unfortunate and unintended consequence of many control systems, and are especially dangerous when quick, responsive decisions are required. When he became CEO of General Electric, for instance, Jack Welch knew that it sometimes took a year or more for division managers to get approval to introduce new products because a long list of approvals was required by GE's planning and control approval system. Similarly, when he took over as CEO of Union Pacific Railway, Mike Walsh discovered that even the simplest requests from railway yard supervisors often waited a year for a response because they required approval at a dozen or more steps up and then down the chain of command. Flattening the organization and streamlining the approval process are two ways to ameliorate this problem.

NEGATIVE ATTITUDES. In addition to displacement, gamesmanship, and operating delays, controls can have a more insidious effect by undermining employees' attitudes. In one study that focused on first-line supervisors' reactions to budgets, Professor Chris Argyris found the budgets were viewed as pressure devices. The supervisors came to see budgets as prods by top management and in turn used them to prod their own subordinates. As a result of this pressure, employees formed anti-management work groups and the supervisors reacted by increasing their compliance efforts.[34]

"Intelligent" employee ID badges may provide one contemporary example of a control tool that may elicit negative attitudes. Italy's Olivetti holds the basic patent on the Active-Badge System and began marketing it commercially around the beginning of 1993. When asked how many people will be wearing Active Badges in 5 to 10 years, one Olivetti lab director responded, "Everybody." The Active Badge looks like a clip-on ID card. But it's actually a small computer that emits infrared signals to strategically located sensors, which can then effectively track the wearer anywhere within an equipped facility. The system can also keep tabs on most visitors, revealing who they are and when they stopped by.

This may sound like a dream come true for companies trying to safeguard technological secrets, but could become an Orwellian nightmare for employees. The inventor, Roy Want, agrees. "It's great technology in the right hands. But if you've got a bad manager he's going to make your life hell." Besides Olivetti, Digital Equipment Corp., Xerox, and the Media Laboratory of MIT also currently use some variation of the system, and they find there are advantages. Knowing where people are avoids interruptions, wasted phone calls, and useless trips to empty offices.

But questions remain: How much privacy can managers expect employees to surrender in the name of control? How much control is too much? And what effect will these badges have on employee morale and performance? Proponents say effective safeguards can be implemented. Critics fear that once such a system is in place, there will be no defense against capricious abuse, and no turning back.[35]

Xerox uses a form of the Active Badge as a management control device. The badges allow managers to find employees quickly for meetings and phone calls, but they can be viewed as an invasion of privacy.

Organizational Behavior in Action

ELECTRONIC PERFORMANCE MONITORING AND CONTROL

When it comes to monitoring employees electronically, computerized ID badges are just the tip of the iceberg. As two researchers recently put it:

> Organizations now use computer networks, sophisticated telephone systems, and both wireless audio and video links to monitor and record the work activities of employees. Recent estimates indicate that as many as 26 million workers in the United States are subject to electronic performance monitoring (EPM) on the job.[36]

Studying the effects of electronic performance monitoring is important because it gets to the heart of how controls can backfire. Most people like to feel that they have some personal control over their job and environment; the research evidence suggests that when people believe they don't—as is often the case when their performance is electronically monitored—it lowers their morale and their performance.[37] On the other hand, making people believe that they do have personal control leads to faster learning, better task performance, and higher job satisfaction. Researchers found that "job satisfaction and performance improved when employees had more perceived control over their work environments."[38]

There's considerable research evidence that electronic performance monitoring is associated with lower feelings of personal control.[39] Using EPM—such as having supervisors monitor through electronic means the amount of computerized data an employee is processing per day—can make workers feel they can't control their own performance or work conditions, such as the pace at which they work or their ability to correct errors.

Does EPM adversely affect employee performance? Jeffrey Stanton and Janet Barnes-Farrell recently studied the effects of electronic performance monitoring on individuals working on computers in an officelike environment.[40] The 108 participants in this study were recruited from introductory psychology classes. All had prior computer experience, and all performed the experiment with the same equipment in the same room. The workers were paired off, with one as supervisor and one as worker. The worker used a computer that was connected to the supervisor's computer. Basically, the worker had to cross-check database records against corresponding records from a stack of paper forms and correct discrepancies in the computerized version.

The researchers wanted to study several things: one was whether a worker's feelings of personal control were affected by having the ability to lock out the performance monitoring; another was whether informing the person he or she was being monitored affected the person's performance.

In this study, personal control was measured by responses, on a five-point scale ranging from strongly disagree to strongly agree, to the following questions:[41]

1. I really had control over my work situation during that task.
2. There was too much pressure on me while I did that task.
3. While I was correcting those orders I felt pressures to work harder.
4. I felt that I was able to control my work rate.
5. The pace of this work was too fast.

6. I had to sacrifice quality in favor of quantity on the task I just did.
7. I felt that I couldn't slow down when I needed to.

The results show why it's important for employees to believe they have some personal control over their environments. "Participants with the ability to delay or prevent electronic performance monitoring indicated higher feelings of personal control and demonstrated superior task performance."[42] The findings also suggest that if you are going to monitor employees' performances electronically, it's probably best not to let them know when they're actually being monitored: The participants who knew exactly when they were being monitored actually expressed lower feelings of personal control than did those who were not told when they were being monitored. ■

REDUCED EMPOWERMENT.   If controls can reduce employees' feelings of personal control, they can obviously also undermine a company's empowerment efforts. As a result, to paraphrase Professor Robert Simons, maintaining control in an age of empowerment can be a very tricky matter. On the one hand, too much control or the wrong controls can actually undermine your empowerment efforts: After all, empowerment basically means the employees self-manage their jobs, and they can hardly do this (or be motivated to do so) if someone is closely monitoring every decision that they make. But empowerment without control can be equally deadly: Recall the overenthusiastic Nordstrom supervisors, for instance, whose empowerment and lack of oversight may have allowed them to pressure subordinates to underreport actual hours worked.

What is a manager to do? The answer is that in an age of empowerment, managers can no longer rely just on traditional diagnostic, boundary, or even interactive control techniques, because doing so might actually be counterproductive. In an age of empowered employees, managers have to emphasize employees' self-control and their commitment to do their best for the company, even if they're half a world away and out of sight of the headquarters staff.

Management writer Tom Peters put it this way:

> You are out of control when you are "in control." You are in control when you are "out of control." [The executive] who knows everything and who is surrounded by layers of staffers and inundated with thousands of pages of analyses from below may be "in control" in the classical sense but in fact really only has the illusion of control. The manager has tons of after-the-fact reports on everything, but (almost) invariably a control system and organization that's so ponderous that it's virtually impossible to respond fast enough even if a deviation is finally detected. . . . In fact, you really are in control when thousands upon thousands of people, unbeknownst to you, are taking initiatives, going beyond job descriptions and the constraints of their box on the organization chart, to serve the customer better, improve the process, [or] work quickly with a supplier to nullify a defect.[43]

Commitment-Based Control Methods

Managers use at least three methods for encouraging such self-control and employee commitment: motivation techniques, belief systems, and building employee commitment. Obviously, highly motivated employees are more likely to do their jobs right than are unmotivated ones; we discussed motivation techniques at length in chapter 12. In the remainder of this chapter we'll focus on using *belief systems* and on *building employee commitment* for encouraging self-control.

Using Belief Systems and Organizational Culture to Maintain Control

As we saw in chapter 11 ("Influencing Organizational Culture and Shared Values"), shared values can make it easier for responsive companies to maintain control. Shared values like Wal-Mart's "hard work, honesty, neighborliness, and thrift" provide a common ideology, one that gives all employees the direction and sense of purpose that's required to do the job right, no matter how far away from headquarters they are, and without a rule book or a supervisor to watch their every move.

BELIEF SYSTEMS IN ACTION. The idea that shared values facilitate self-control and thus enable firms to be more responsive has been confirmed in practice. For example, Burns and Stalker, in their study of British industry, found that organic (highly innovative) organizations achieved coordinated action in the absence of formal rules and a chain of command by relying

> on the development of a common culture, of a dependable constant system of shared values about the common interests of the working community and about the standards and criteria used in it to judge achievement, individual contributions, expertise, and other matters by which a person or a combination of people are evaluated. A system of shared values of this kind is expressed and visible in a code of conduct, a way of dealing with other people.[44]

In a recent study of successful and long-lived companies, James Collins and Jerry Porras made precisely the same observations. In their book *Built to Last* they describe how firms like Boeing, Disney, General Electric, Merck, and Motorola put enormous effort into creating shared values among employees, values that answer questions such as What are we trying to achieve together? and What does this organization stand for?[45] As they say,

> More than at any time in the past companies will not be able to hold themselves together with the traditional methods of control: hierarchy, systems, bud-

Shared values are a highly effective means of control. Employees at Smith & Hawken use the firm's gardening products to work together in the official company garden, producing flowers and vegetables they donate to charity.

gets, and the like. Even "going into the office" will become less relevant as technology enables people to work from remote sites. The bonding glue will increasingly become *ideological.*[46]

In explaining why shared values are so important for managing change, these writers (like Burns and Stalker before them) emphasize that a strong set of shared values "allows for coordination without control, adaptation without chaos."[47] In other words, employees who share and "buy into" your company's values don't need to be coaxed, prodded or controlled into doing the right thing: they'll do the right thing because they believe it's the right thing to do.

What sorts of shared values and beliefs do change-oriented, responsive companies encourage? Core values in firms like these emphasize caring deeply about not just customers, but stockholders and employees too, and valuing the processes—such as empowerment—that can create useful change. They also value willingly initiating change when needed, even if this might entail some risks. Teamwork, openness, candor, trust, and being number one are other values that are stressed.

Organizational Behavior in Action

HOW TO CHANGE A COMPANY'S CULTURE

Imagine you are swept into the CEO's position in a company long known for its culture of backbiting, bureaucratic behavior and disdain for the clients: What steps would you take to change your company's culture?

We discussed that question at length in chapter 11, but management expert Edgar Schein has proposed a sort of shorthand list of mechanisms leaders can use to establish, embed, and reinforce organizational culture.[48]

Schein advocates five "primary embedding mechanisms" to change a company's culture. To change culture, says Schein, you should

1. *Make it clear to your employees what you pay attention to, measure, and control.* For example, you can direct the attention of your employees toward controlling costs or serving customers if those are the values you want to emphasize.
2. *React appropriately to critical incidents and organizational crises.* For example, if you want to emphasize the value that "we're all in this together," don't react to declining profits by laying off operating employees and middle managers while leaving your top managers intact.
3. *Deliberately role model, teach, and coach the values you want to emphasize.* For example, Wal-Mart founder Sam Walton truly embodied the values "hard work, honesty, neighborliness, and thrift" that he wanted all Wal-Mart employees to follow. Although he was one of the richest men in the world, he drove a pickup truck, a preference he explained by saying "If I drove a Rolls Royce, what would I do with my dog?"
4. *Communicate your priorities by the way you allocate rewards and status.* Leaders communicate their priorities by the way they link pay raises and promotions (or the lack thereof) to particular behaviors. For example, when the top management at General Foods decided several years ago to reorient its strategy from cost control to diversification and sales growth, it

■ **TABLE 16.2** *Mechanisms for Embedding and Reinforcing Organizational Culture*

PRIMARY EMBEDDING MECHANISMS

1.	What leaders pay attention to, measure, and control
2.	Leader reactions to critical incidents and organizational crises
3.	Deliberate role modeling, teaching, and coaching
4.	Criteria for allocation of rewards and status
5.	Criteria for recruitment, selection, promotion, retirement, and excommunication

SECONDARY ARTICULATION AND REINFORCEMENT MECHANISMS

1.	Organization design and structure
2.	Organizational systems and procedures
3.	Design of physical space, facades, buildings
4.	Stories about important events and people
5.	Formal statements of organizational philosophy, creeds, charters

SOURCE: Reprinted with permission from E. H. Schein, *Organizational Culture and Leadership.* Copyright © 1985 Jossey-Bass Inc., Publishers. All rights reserved.

revised the compensation system to link bonuses to sales volume (rather than just to increased earnings) and to new-product development.

5. *Make your HR procedures and criteria consistent with the values you espouse.* When he became Chairperson and CEO of IBM, Louis Gerstner brought in a new top management team whose values were consistent with shaking up IBM's traditionally bureaucratic and politicized culture.

Schein suggests not stopping there. As you can see in Table 16.2, he also recommends using secondary mechanisms—such as a redesign of the organizational structure, new organizational systems, and a redesign of physical space—to further reinforce the desired cultural changes. However, Schein believes that these secondary mechanisms are just that—secondary, because they work only if consistent with the five primary mechanisms listed above. ■

How to Use Employee Commitment to Maintain Control

Most experts would probably agree that the most powerful way for a firm to get things done is to synchronize its goals with those of its employees until the two sets of goals are essentially the same. Creating such a synthesis is essentially what building commitment is all about.[49] Researcher Richard Steers defines commitment as the relative strength of an individual's identification with and involvement in an organization. He says commitment is characterized by a strong belief in and acceptance of the organization's goals and values, a willingness to exert considerable effort on behalf of the organization, and a strong desire to maintain membership in the organization.[50] Employee commitment therefore exists when an employee comes to think of the organization's goals in personal terms and to incorporate them into his or her own goals.

Creating commitment means taking those steps needed to synthesize employee and company goals and create self-motivated employees. It requires a multifaceted approach, one that depends on using virtually all the management skills you've learned in this book. Steps for building employee commitment are discussed in the following sections.

Foster People-First Values

Building employee commitment usually starts by establishing a strong foundation of "people-first values." Firms that hold to these values literally put their people first: They trust them, assume that their employees are their most important assets, believe strongly in respecting their employees as individuals and treating them fairly, and maintain a relentless commitment to each employee's welfare. Research indicates that firms do at least four things to institutionalize such values: "they clarify what they want, they codify it, they hire and indoctrinate, and they walk the talk."

CLARIFY WHAT YOU WANT. Clarifying that you want people-first values is first. Here is how one United Auto Workers (UAW) officer at Saturn Corporation's Spring Hill, Tennessee, plant put it:

> Our philosophy is, we care about people—and it shows. We involve people in decisions that affect them. I came from the Mesina, New York GM foundry and managers there, like a lot of the other managers you'll come across, take the position that "I'll tell you what to do, and that's what you'll do." In fact, some of those managers from the foundry are here now. But on the whole those who are here now are different, and the basic difference is wrapped up in the question, "Do you really believe in people?" Saturn's commitment really comes

People-first values lie behind many employers' efforts to provide on-site day care for employees' children, like this free center for kids at Apple's Cupertino offices.

down to how you feel about people—your attitudes—more than anything, because all the other Saturn programs—the work teams, the extensive training, the way people are paid—all stem from these people attitudes.[51]

CODIFY. Second, these firms codify their people-first values by frequently mentioning them in company brochures, handbooks, and handouts. For example, Saturn employees carry a card that lists the firm's values, one of which is expressed in these words:

> Trust and respect for the individual: We have nothing of greater value than our people. We believe that demonstrating respect for the uniqueness of every individual builds a team of confident, creative members possessing a high degree of initiative, self-respect, and self-discipline.[52]

HIRE AND INDOCTRINATE. The UAW officer's comment that "commitment really comes down to what you feel about people" underscores a third way in which people-first values are institutionalized throughout these kinds of firms: The firms hire managers who have people-first values from the start, and then promote them in part based on their people skills. In fact, it is almost impossible for antisocial "Theory X" people to move into management at such firms—or to stay.

WALK THE TALK. Managers in these firms walk the talk, in that people-first values permeate everything they say and do. The idea that the firm's people-first values should be applied to every one of its decisions was summed up by one officer at retailer JCPenney this way:

> Our people's high commitment stems from our commitment to them, and that commitment boils down to the fundamental "respect for the individual" that we all share. That respect goes back to the Penney idea—"To test every act in this wise: Does it square with what is right and just?" As a result, the value of respect for the individual is brought into our management process on a regular basis and is a standard against which we measure each and every decision that we make.[53]

Encourage Extensive Two-Way Communications

Commitment is built on trust, and trust requires two-way communication. Managers in firms like Saturn, Federal Express, and GE thus do more than express a willingness to hear and be heard. They also establish programs that guarantee two-way communications. As explained in chapter 13 (Communications), at least four types of communications programs are typically employed here: guaranteed fair treatment programs for filing grievances and complaints, "speak up" programs for voicing concerns and making inquiries, periodic survey programs for expressing opinions, and various top-down programs for keeping employees informed.

Build a Sense of Shared Fate and Community

Firms that score high on commitment also work hard to encourage a sense of community and shared fate. They do so by pursuing what Rosabeth Moss Kanter calls commonality, communal work, and regular work contact and ritual, which combine to create a sense of shared fate and community.

EMPHASIZE COMMONALITY. First, they emphasize a sense of commonality, in other words, a sense that "we're all in this together, and no one is better than anyone else." For example, for many years Ben & Jerry's had a policy of paying executives no more than seven times the firm's lowest entry-level wage. This helped ensure that employees and managers didn't develop an "us versus them" mentality. Another way to avoid the status differences that often set top management apart from employees can be found at Toyota Motor Manufacturing in Tennessee. Here the whole office staff works in one huge open room, without offices, walls, or partitions. President Fujio Cho is there, along with secretaries, public relations people, vice presidents, and data entry clerks. Executives at Ben & Jerry's have private offices, but they are spartan compared with those you will find in most firms, and until a few years ago the company's founders worked in a trailer at the foot of the hill on which the plant is situated. Similarly, few firms that take commitment seriously have executive parking spots.

ENCOURAGE COMMUNAL WORK. The sense of community can be further emphasized by encouraging joint effort and communal work. In early communes (and in some communities today), all the citizens would gather for a "house raising," in which everyone in the community worked together to build a new community member's house. In companies, this sense of joint effort and communal work can be accomplished in several ways. At Toyota, new employees are quickly steeped in the terminology and techniques of teamwork: There are no employees in the plant, only team members, working together on their "communal tasks" (like installing all dashboard components). Team training begins during the employee's initial orientation, as new members meet their teams and are trained in the interpersonal techniques that make for good teamwork. The resulting closeness is then enhanced by empowering work teams to recruit and select their own new members. Periodic job rotation reinforces the sense that everyone is sharing all the work.

ENSURE REGULAR CONTACT. Rosabeth Moss Kanter found that the feeling of "we're all in this together" is further enhanced by activities that bring individual employees into regular contact with the group as a whole.[54] Ben & Jerry's hosts monthly staff meetings in the receiving bay of its Waterbury, Vermont, plant. Ben & Jerry's also has a "joy gang," whose function is to organize regular "joy events," including Cajun parties, ping-pong contests, and "manufacturing appreciation day." All are aimed at getting everyone together and fostering a sense of sharing and communion.

Provide a Vision

Committed employees need missions and visions to which to be committed, missions and visions that they can say "are bigger than we are, that are greater than ourselves." Having such missions, workers at firms like Saturn and Ben & Jerry's become not just workers but almost soldiers in a crusade that allows them to redefine themselves in terms of an ideology and a mission. In that way, says Kanter, the employee can "find himself anew in something larger and greater."[55] The commitment in high-commitment firms thus derives in part from the power of the firm's mission and from the willingness of the employees to acquiesce, if need be, to the needs of the firm for the good of achieving its mission.

Many firms therefore create a sense of "institutional charisma": they link their firm's missions and values to a higher calling. Ben & Jerry's is a good example. The company's mission symbolizes its founders' idea of what a business should be and provides the firm and its employees with an ideology that represents a higher calling to which employees can commit themselves. Ben & Jerry's mission (including its unique social mission to recognize "the central role that business plays in the structure of a society") is presented in Figure 16.7. Ben & Jerry's employees don't just make ice cream, in other words: They are, in a real sense, out to change the world.

■ **FIGURE 16.7**
Some Elements of Ben & Jerry's Mission
Ben & Jerry's mission is "charismatic" in that it links employees' actions with the transcendent goal of helping humankind.

SOURCE: Adapted from Ben & Jerry's Homemade, Inc., *Employee Handbook*

Ben & Jerry's mission consists of three interrelated parts:
Product Mission: Making, selling, and distributing the best all natural ice cream and related products in a wide variety of innovative flavors made from Vermont dairy products.
Social Mission: Operating the company in a way that actively recognizes the central role that business plays in the structure of a society by initiating new ways to improve the quality of life of the broad community, including local, national, and international.
Economic Mission: Operating the company on a sound financial basis of profitable growth, increasing value for our shareholders and creating career opportunities and financial rewards for our employees.

Use Value-Based Hiring

In *Thriving on Chaos,* Tom Peters makes this observation:

> The task of transforming raw recruits into committed stars, able to cope with the pace of change that is becoming normal, begins with the recruiting process per se. The best three tenets, unfortunately ignored by most: (1) spend time, and lots of it; (2) insist that line people dominate the process; and (3) don't waffle about the qualities you are looking for in candidates.[56]

Indeed, as we saw in chapter 9 (Staffing), many firms today practice **value-based hiring.** Instead of looking just at an applicant's job-related skills, they try to: get a sense of the individual and his or her personal qualities and values; identify common experiences and values that may signal the applicant's fit with the firm; give their applicants realistic previews of what to expect; and usually end up rejecting large numbers of applicants. In short, they foster commitment in part by putting enormous effort into interviewing and screening to find people whose values are consistent with the firm's. As one Toyota USA vice president put it:

> You might be surprised, but our selection or hiring process is an exhaustive, painstaking system designed not to fill positions quickly, but to find the right people for these positions. What are we looking for? First, these people must be able to think for themselves . . . be problem solvers . . . and, second, work in a team atmosphere. Simply put, we need strong minds, not strong backs. . . . We consider the selection of a team member as a long-term investment decision. Why go to the trouble of hiring a questionable employee only to have to fire him later?[57]

Stress Job Security without Guarantees

Job security and employee commitment go hand in hand. For one thing, with the costs involved in value-based hiring and in extensively training, empowering, and building employees' capabilities, it just makes sense to keep employees around. That is why Toyota's president has been quoted as saying, "At Toyota we hire people who will stick around for 30 to 40 years or the remainder of their working years. So we always try to remember that hiring a 30-year employee who will earn $30,000 or $40,000 a year is really a million dollar plus decision for us."[58] Commitment is also a two-way street: Employees become committed to companies that are committed to them, and few things express an employer's commitment like job security.

A high-commitment firm like Federal Express is thus dedicated to "providing the maximum job security for all of our employees."[59] However, at Federal Express (as at other firms that try to hire for the long term), job security is a commitment, not an ironclad policy. Although it offers no guarantees, the firm is on record as having a strong commitment not to lay off personnel except in the most extreme economic circumstances as determined by the chief executive officer.[60] In fact, Federal Express has avoided layoffs since its incorporation on June 24, 1971. The most notable example occurred when the firm discontinued its facsimile products (Zapmail) business in the early 1980s. More than 1,000 employees assigned to that area were retained and reassigned without a loss in pay.

Use Financial Rewards and Profit Sharing

Although you may not be able to buy commitment, most firms don't try to build it without good financial rewards. Intrinsic motivators like work involvement, a sense of achievement, and the feeling of oneness that communion brings are not enough. To paraphrase psychologist Abraham Maslow, you can't appeal to someone's need to achieve until you've filled his or her belly and made the person secure. That is why Rosabeth Moss Kanter says that "entrepreneurial incentives that give teams a piece of the action are highly appropriate in collaborative companies."[61]

When it comes to pay, for instance, the JCPenney Company may have one of the best kept secrets in retailing, a tradition that goes back to 1902. On April 14 of that year, James Cash Penney, age 26, opened The Golden Rule, a dry goods and clothing store in Kemmerer, Wyoming, in partnership with his former employers, merchants Thomas Callahan and William Johnson. In 1903, Penney's partners offered him a one-third partnership in their new Rock Springs, Wyoming, Golden Rule store and asked him to supervise it. At the same time, Penney recommended they open a new Golden Rule store in nearby Cumberland, Wyoming, and also became its one-third partner.

By 1907 Johnson and Callahan had sold Penney their interests in the Kemmerer, Cumberland, and Rock Springs stores, and Penney and his new partners (all former sales clerks) began building their own chain of Golden Rule stores. As the chain spread across the country, Penney followed the same practice of giving hard-working clerks the opportunity to manage the stores, also with a one-third partnership—the same opportunity Johnson and Callahan had given him back in 1902. When the JCPenney Company was incorporated in 1913, the partnership incentive was retained by offering one-third stock interests in new stores to managers. If the purpose of commitment is to synchronize the employees' goals with those of the firm, the Penney's one-third partnership concept helped fill that bill.

Although the structure of the plan has changed, the heavy incentive value of the partnership concept remains intact today at JCPenney. Entry-level merchandise manager trainees straight out of college start off at perhaps $20,000 to $25,000 per year. But after three years or so they usually find themselves making more than other middle managers in the industry and the gap continues to widen as they move up the chain of command.[62] For store managers in the largest JCPenney's stores, for instance, 90 percent of annual pay typically comes from bonus and only 10 percent from salary, with a total annual pay of well over $150,000 per year.

Encourage Self-Actualizing

Most people come to a point at which they ask themselves whether they've achieved all they could have achieved, given their skills, gifts, and dreams, and woe to the firm that prevented them from doing so. Few needs are as strong as the need to fulfill our dreams, to become all we are capable of being. In chapter 12 (Individual Behavior and Motivation) we saw that Abraham Maslow said the ultimate need is "the desire to become more and more what one is, to become everything that one is capable of becoming." Self-actualization, to Maslow, meant that "what man *can* be, he *must* be . . . it refers to the desire for self-fulfillment, namely, to this tendency for him to become actualized in what he is potentially."[63]

Firms do at least three things to "actualize employees": They commit to the goal of actualizing all employees and carry through on doing so; they aggressively promote employees from within; and they empower employees at work. Obviously, actualizing does not just mean promotions. Certainly, promotions are important. But the real question is whether employees get the opportunity to develop and use all their skills and become, as Maslow would say, all they can be. Training employees to expand their skills and to solve problems at work, enriching their jobs, empowering employees to plan and inspect their own work, and helping them to continue their education and to grow are some other ways to accomplish employee self-actualization, as we've seen in earlier chapters.

Explicitly committing to the goal of helping workers to self-actualize is an especially important part of the process. Here's how one Saturn assembler put it:

> I'm committed to Saturn in part for what they did for me; for the 300 hours of training in problem solving and leadership that help me expand my personal horizons; for the firm's Excel program that helps me push myself to the limit; and because I know that at Saturn I can go as far as I can go—this company wants its people to be all that they can be. But I'm also committed to Saturn for what I saw where I came from: the burned out workers, the people who were so pressed down by the system that even if they saw their machines were about to break from poor maintenance, they'd say, "Leave it alone. Let management handle it." This is like a different world.[64]

Similarly, one Federal Express manager described his firm's commitment to actualizing employees as follows:

> At Federal Express, the best I can be is what I can be here. I have been allowed to grow with Federal Express. For the people at Federal Express, it's not the money that draws us to the firm. The biggest benefit is that Federal Express made me a man. It gave me the confidence and self-esteem to become the person I had the potential to become.[65]

In summary, "achieving control in an age of empowerment" depends on fostering employees' self-control. Motivation techniques (like those in chapter 12) and building belief systems are two important ways to tap such self-control. Another powerful way to do so is to get the employees to actually think of the company's goals as their own—to get their commitment to the company and its mission, in other words. Doing so isn't easy; it will require most of your management skills, since you must

> foster people-first values
> encourage extensive two-way communications
> build a sense of shared fate and community
> provide a vision
> use value-based hiring
> stress job security without guarantees
> use financial rewards and profit sharing
> encourage self-actualizing

Doing so is obviously not as easy as just monitoring everything employees do, or raking them over the coals when they don't reach their budgets or when some other problem—like too many defects—means that "things are out of control." But in an age of self-managing teams fostering self-control is an increasingly important technique for ensuring that activities produce the desired results. The Entrepreneurs in Action box shows how one small organization obtains commitment.

Entrepreneurs in Action

CHILDREN'S MEDICAL CENTER OF DALLAS

Joan McGuigan's job usually isn't pleasant. As a registered nurse at the Small Children's Medical Center of Dallas, she spends her days caring for children who are in some of the worst conditions imaginable. Sometimes their parents are in even worse shape. It's a high-stress, often sad job, yet she says she loves it.

McGuigan could easily work someplace else. But she's been at Children's Medical Center for more than eight years, working 24-hour shifts, because she likes being on the cutting edge of children's health care. She might be an anachronism, but McGuigan says she's committed to her employer because the hospital enables her to be the best at what she does.

An employee like McGuigan sounds like a dream come true, but unfortunately, such people don't come around that often. In a business environment where most companies are reducing human resources budgets, prospective employees are increasingly looking out for themselves. Factors contributing to this attitude include company downsizings, low compensation, and even policies relating to child care and family leave issues. "It's earned loyalty—in both directions," says Suzanne Kenney, manager of the Employee Listening Practice for the Hewitt Associates consulting firm. "Employees are now asking, Is my company loyal to me?"

Children's Medical Center seems to have overcome the sorts of loyalty-based problems that plague most hospitals. For example, the rate of turnover for registered nurses in general is notoriously high, for reasons ranging from stress and burnout to the need to be home with a family. But the Dallas hospital took steps to encourage nurses to stay on board. They were given the opportunity to participate and grow—in a sense, to become partners in the hospital's achievements.

The hospital established a "clinical ladder," which offers the potential for career enhancement for nurses. Research, in-service work, and other projects all can result in increased salary levels. If a nurse spots a case where a new diagnosis is possible, he or she can put together the data and present it.

Offering employees greater involvement in decision making also helps engender loyalty to the medical center. Teams formed by the nursing department coordinate care methods at the patient level. Under a program called "independent practice," standout nurses are urged to exercise their own judgment regarding the most appropriate types of treatment. The result is better care, better nurses, and a feeling on the part of the staff that their abilities are being utilized for maximum benefit. They also have an enhanced sense of recognition and purpose.

The medical center, in conjunction with a consulting firm, also spelled out the organization's mission and communicated it to the nurses. Letting employees know where the hospital was headed and what their individual roles were in that mission provided an inspirational bond for employees. Shirley Lopez, a vice president of human resources, summed it up: "If I work for a company that knows where it's going and can share that with me, then I'm going to be more committed to that as a direction." ■

SOURCE: "The Loyalty Factor," *Personnel Journal* (September 1992): 52.

1. Control is the task of ensuring that activities are providing the desired results. In its most general sense, controlling therefore means setting a target, measuring performance, and taking corrective action as required. Experts distinguish between steering controls, yes-no controls, and post-action controls.

2. As companies expand worldwide and compete in fast-changing markets, the problems of relying on the traditional (set standards/compare actual to standard/take corrective action) controls have become increasingly apparent. Companies have had to become more empowered in order to be more responsive. As a result, a fundamental problem facing managers in the 1990s is how to exercise adequate control in empowered organizations that demand flexibility, responsiveness, and creativity.

3. While the classification is somewhat arbitrary, this chapter explained three types of traditional control methods. Diagnostic control systems like budgets and performance reports are intended to ensure that goals are being achieved and that variances, if any, are explained: they follow the traditional process of setting standards, comparing actual results to standards, and taking corrective action. Boundary control systems establish the rules of the game and identify actions and pitfalls that employees must avoid. Interactive control systems are real-time, usually face-to-face methods of monitoring both the plan's effectiveness and the underlying assumptions on which the plan was built.

4. Budgets, zero-based budgeting, and ratio analysis are among the diagnostic control tools that are most widely used. Budgets are formal financial expressions of a manager's plans and show targets for yardsticks such as revenues, cost of materials, and profits, usually expressed in dollars. Zero-based budgeting is a technique that forces managers to defend all their programs every year and to rank them in order of priority. Most managers also achieve control by monitoring various financial ratios, such as the trend of sales divided by earnings (the profit margin).

5. A big problem with overrelying on traditional controls is that they can lead to unintended, undesirable, and often harmful employee reactions, such as behavioral displacement, gamesmanship, operating delays, negative attitudes, and reduced empowerment.

6. "Achieving control in an age of empowerment" relies on employees' self-control. Motivation techniques (like those in chapter 12) and building belief systems are two important ways to tap such self-control. Another powerful way is to get the employees to actually think of the company's goals as their own—to get their commitment.

KEY TERMS

control
steering control
yes-no control
post-action control
traditional control
    methods
diagnostic control systems
boundary systems

interactive control
    systems
commitment-based
    control methods
principle of exception
environmental
    monitoring
environmental scanning

budgets
variances
zero-based budgeting
financial ratios
locus of control
behavioral displacement
gamesmanship
value-based hiring

SELF-TEST

TRUE / FALSE QUESTIONS

1 **T F** Control is the task of monitoring activities to make sure the company is getting the desired results.

2 **T F** The goal of a control system is to have no undesirable surprises in the future.

3 **T F** Steering controls are used to take corrective action after the operation or project has been completed.

4 **T F** A fundamental problem facing managers in this decade is how to exercise control while still demanding flexibility, innovation, and creativity.

5 **T F** Commitment-based control methods rely on the supervisor's control of the employee.

6 **T F** Under the principle of exception, minor and major deviations are brought to the manager's attention.

7 **T F** Environmental monitoring means regularly checking on the assumptions on which your strategic plan is constructed.

8 **T F** Zero-based budgeting is a technique used to force managers into justifying and prioritizing all programs on the basis of costs and benefits.

9 **T F** Locus of control is important for determining how much a person will allow her or his behavior to be controlled.

10 **T F** If employees share the company's values, they will tend to do the right thing automatically.

MULTIPLE-CHOICE QUESTIONS

1 The three basic aspects of control include all but which of these?
  a. setting a goal or standard
  b. measuring performance
  c. relying on feedback
  d. taking corrective action

2 Post-action control is based on _____ .
  a. feedback
  b. preemption
  c. empowerment
  d. reengineering

3 Which is not a factor in the control function?
  a. All details are specified in advance.
  b. You can't watch everything everyone does.
  c. Assumptions change.
  d. You cannot legislate creativity.

4 _____ control systems are based on policies that identify the actions and traps employees must avoid.
  a. Interactive
  b. Boundary
  c. Diagnostic
  d. Behavioral

5 Environmental _____ identifies critical events that might influence the company's strategy.
  a. monitoring
  b. measuring
  c. norming
  d. scanning

6 Which is not a traditional control method?
  a. budgets
  b. performance reports
  c. rate of return on investment
  d. virtual measurements

7 Unintended consequences of imposing controls include
  a. gamesmanship
  b. operating delays
  c. negative attitudes
  d. all of the above

8 Behavioral _____ takes place when the behaviors encouraged by the controls are inconsistent.
  a. gamesmanship
  b. displacement
  c. delays
  d. sabotage

9 In an age of technologically based work, how much _____ can managers expect employees to give up?
  a. privacy
  b. creativity
  c. compensation
  d. ambition

10 Commitment is built on _____, which requires two-way communication.
  a. money
  b. drive
  c. trust
  d. fate

CRITICAL THINKING EXERCISES

1 The budget is a traditional means of control, usually established by the top management. Now think about establishing a budget for a company by using committed and empowered employees to develop it. Who would be involved and why? How would your approach differ from traditional budgeting?

2 We are increasingly dependent on technology and the flow of information provided by means such as the Internet. Yet there is ongoing debate about the control and privacy aspects of both the Internet and intranets. What do you think about using electronic monitoring technology as a control device? What about the privacy issues? Should anyone be able to monitor us and our use of computers?

EXPERIENTIAL EXERCISES

1 You are one of the founding engineers in your 6-month-old firm, and you brought to the firm values of environmental awareness, quality, and excellence. These values have united the original members, but you are concerned that they might change with the addition of 50 new people needed by your fast-growing company to meet demand. What type of control system would you develop to ensure your values are adhered to, based on the concepts in this chapter?

2 When you next eat at a fast food restaurant, or go to the gas station to fill up your tank or get service, or go shopping at the grocery store, note the control systems in place. Then be prepared to discuss them in class in terms of what you have read in this chapter.

DIVERSITY CASE

WHEN LEADERS DON'T CONTROL THEMSELVES

In 1994 a group of senior Texaco executives gathered to discuss a class-action discrimination suit brought by almost 1,400 black professionals and middle managers. The claimants charged that they were denied promotions because of their race. The meeting was secretly recorded by one participant, who handed over the tape to the suing employees' attorneys when he was laid off a year later. After reading transcripts of the tape, the *New York Times* reported that Texaco's executives had used racial insults and belittled the African-American holiday Kwanzaa. These affronts were in addition to an alleged conspiracy, apparent on the tape, to destroy documents required by the discrimination suit.

The employees won their suit, costing the company $175 million as well as a great deal of bad publicity, internal turmoil, and demands for changes in values and attitudes.

Questions

1 What control issues are presented by this case, and how would you design a new control so this problem didn't occur again?

2 According to a 1995 survey by the American Management Association, small firms provide better job opportunities for minorities than big firms. Why do you think this is the case?

3 What boundary system issues are present here?

4 How would you feel as a minority at Texaco prior to the suit and afterward?

SOURCE: Shari Caudron, "Don't Make Texaco's $175 Million Mistake," *Workforce,* March 1997, 58–66.

STRATEGY CASE

FINDING GOLD IN A GUTTER

In Nairobi, Kenya, 25 years ago, travel-weary Ken Thuerbach was looking for something to read. Discarded on the street was a magazine, which he picked up. When he read that by 1990 the art of building authentic log homes would disappear, a business was born and a strategy was created.

When he returned to the States, Thuerbach scoured the American West to find the few remaining log craftsmen. The journey took him to Alpine Log Homes, which was doing poorly and had not paid its employees for six months. For $3,000 Thuerbach purchased the company and then spent the next few years learning all he could about the business. His real strategic breakthrough came when he recognized he could save on inventory and labor costs by having Alpine construct all lodgings in one location, dismantle them, and send them to their destination like a Tinkertoy set.

Among the proud owners of Thuerbach's log homes, which can cost up to $9 million, are 200 top officers of Fortune 500 companies. The company brought in sales of $15 million in 1996 and had no debt.

Questions

1. What control problems does Ken Thuerbach face in keeping his company on track?
2. Are control problems different in a small business like Ken's than in a large company? Why or why not?
3. What lessons about strategic control can you learn from this case?

SOURCE: Linda Grant, "The Man Who Found Gold in the Gutter," *Fortune,* 3 February 1997, 126.

ENTREPRENEURIAL CASE

BUILDING ORGANIZATIONAL STRENGTH

One of the most difficult aspects to control in any company's budget is the cost of health care insurance. Alamco, a $12 million Clarksburg, West Virginia, oil and gas company, has found some effective answers to addressing health care costs: incentive rewards for maintaining a healthy lifestyle.

The company recently won a Wellness Council of America award for encouraging healthful lifestyles among its 96 employees. Employees are offered cash incentives for six healthful behaviors or conditions (which they report on their honor): not smoking or chewing tobacco ($100), wearing a seat belt ($25), having a cholesterol level below 150 ($100), having blood pressure below 135/85 ($50), having a waist-to-hip ratio of .8 or less for women and .95 for men ($50), and getting 30 minutes of exercise three times a week ($25).

Spouses are able to earn half the incentive amounts. Alamco arranges for guest speakers on health-related issues and sponsors two health fairs annually.

In 1996 the company handed out $19,000 in incentives, and its insurance premiums have stayed steady for five years. Other positive consequences are improved morale, lower absenteeism, and a greater feeling of teamwork and camaraderie.

Questions

1. What types of controls are being used here?
2. What unintended consequences could have occurred in this case that might lead to the need to boost control?
3. Could this approach be used to control other behaviors, and, if so, which ones?

SOURCE: Donna Fenn, "Healthful Habits Pay Off." *Inc.,* April 1996, 111

THE BUSINESS TEAM, INC.

STAYING IN CONTROL

The Business Team has been up and running for some time now. At first, its members did not pay much attention to control issues. They were just excited to be out of school and on their own and, in any case, while they were small, they could stay in control by just interacting with each other. The work, though cyclical, continued to pour in. Their reputation in their own community as well as nationally and globally was growing.

At the first annual meeting of the team, the strategic issues of where they had been and where they wanted to go were at the top of the agenda. To address these issues, each partner had assessed her or his own area as well as the area of

one other partner. Each was to present a report with an analysis showing where they were achieving their targets and recommending any corrective action that might be warranted.

Each partner came to the table with the same conclusions: They were unsure of their targets; they had not really developed performance measures except cashflow.

Questions

1. What control processes should the team use?
2. How do you think each of the partners will differ in their ideas? Why?
3. What mistakes do you think the team has made so far, and how would you remedy them?

KEEPING THINGS UNDER CONTROL AT KNITMEDIA

KnitMedia's plans to establish a global club network (called the "Knitwork") modeled on the operation of the New York Knitting Factory Club will mean that it will need sophisticated new methods for maintaining control. The company planned to open its first wholly-owned Knitting Factory in Los Angeles in 1997 and then to open additional clubs through 1997 and 1998 through joint ventures and limited partnerships in the United States, Europe, and Asia. The company's management has said that "to effectively monitor the finances of each club, the company will employ a sophisticated asset management system, using software for inventory monitoring and control." In particular, each individual club will report to the company headquarters in New York the exact ticket, merchandise, and bar sales on a nightly basis. These totals will be monitored daily to keep a firm control on revenues generated through each club. The company may use a sophisticated global network to help accomplish this. Michael Dorf has asked you for recommendations about how he can maintain better control over his soon-to-be global network of Knitting Factory Clubs, when he is based in New York. He needs your recommendations as soon as possible.

Team Exercises and Questions

Use what you learned in this chapter to answer the following questions:

1 How do other companies (including, for instance, restaurant chains) maintain control over their networks of globalized locations?

2 What control techniques described in this chapter do you think would be most appropriate for maintaining control of the new Knitting Factory network, and why? How would you suggest Michael Dorf go about instituting those types of controls?

3 KnitMedia is considering the possibility of franchising Knitting Factory Clubs. At least from the point of view of control, what are the pros and cons of franchising clubs like these?

For the online version of this case, visit our Web site at <www.prenhall.com/desslermgmt>.

For Internet exercises, interactive study questions, news updates and more, visit the Dessler Web site at

www.prenhall.com/desslermgmt

If you're using the CD-ROM that accompanies this text, simply click on the "Web Site" button to access the site.

MANAGING OPERATIONS AND SERVICES: COMBINING TECHNOLOGY AND PEOPLE

CHAPTER 17

What's Ahead?

With more of its customers buying competitors' jeans at stores like the Gap, Levi Strauss knew it needed a new competitive advantage. It therefore hit on the idea of custom-made jeans: Cus-

tomers could visit a Levi's store and have several special measurements taken. The information would be zapped electronically to Levi's, where computerized machines would design the jeans, plan their production, and control their progress from machine to machine. The new project was called the "Personal Pairs" program. However, implementing Personal Pairs would require changing many of the company's personnel, production, and operations management systems.[1]

Objectives

After studying this chapter, you should be able to

- **define operations management and explain what is meant by a production system**

- **identify the four production design decisions that operations managers must make**

- **describe several important production scheduling, planning, and control methods**

- **demonstrate how to use two basic inventory management systems**

- **compare and contrast five tools that are used to improve quality**

- **explain how to use world-class manufacturing to help manage change.**

MANAGEMENT ON THE WEB

JOURNAL OF MANAGEMENT INFORMATION SYSTEMS

This journal presents research that advances the practice and understanding of organizational information systems. It serves those investigating new modes of information delivery and the changing landscape of information policy making, as well as practitioners and executives managing the information resource. A vital aim of this quarterly journal is to bridge the gap between theory and practice of management information systems. How could Levi's use this site to help perfect its Personal Pairs program? ■

http://rmm-java.stern.nyu.edu/jmis

Basics of Operations Management

Operations Management Defined

Levi's marketers had an appealing new idea. Now what management needed to make Personal Pairs a success was good operations management. **Operations management** is the process of managing the resources required to produce the organization's goods and services.[2] Like any managers, operations managers plan, organize, lead, and control. However, unlike other managers, operations managers focus on the direct production resources of a firm, often called the five P's of operations and production management: people, plants, parts, processes, and planning and control systems. The people include the direct and indirect workforce, such as assembly workers, inventory clerks, and clerical staff. Plants are the factories or service branches where the product or service is produced. Parts include the raw materials and other inputs that will be transformed into finished products or services. Processes represent the technology, the equipment, and the steps required to accomplish production. The planning and control systems are the procedures that management uses to operate the system (such as the methods used to schedule the work) and to control quality.[3]

We'll see in this chapter that the "people" component is more than just one of the five P's—it's more like a first among equals. In a recent study of computerized factories, for instance, a researcher found that many firms had wasted their money on technology because the employees themselves were unable or unwilling to make the systems work as they should.[4] That's why smart managers today make sure they focus on combining technological improvements like computerization with behavioral efforts such as team building, worker empowerment, and employee commitment.

Strategy in Action

PRODUCTION AND OPERATIONS STRATEGY SHOULD BE CONSISTENT WITH COMPETITIVE STRATEGY

Managers designing a production system must take their company's strategy into account. In chapter 6, for instance, we saw that most businesses try to achieve competitive advantage by pursuing either a low-cost, differentiator, or focus ("niche") competitive strategy.

Table 17.1 illustrates the need for consistency between competitive strategy and production and operations strategies. For example, a differentiator such as Rolex watches would emphasize quality in operations, even at high cost; a low-cost leader like Casio would emphasize operations efficiencies, economies of scale, and substituting automated machines for labor. Similarly, the design of the production system itself, the location of the facility, the type of production process (for instance, custom-made versus mass production), and the company's inventory policy are some of the other production decisions that should be guided by the firm's overall and operations management functional strategy.

The Production System

At the heart of operations management is a production system, which always has three main components: inputs, a "conversion system," and outputs. These are summarized in Figure 17.1. **Inputs** are all the resources required to manufacture the product or service. These include primary inputs like materials and supplies, personnel, and capital. Market inputs include data on the competition, the product, and the customer. Environmental inputs include data on the legal aspects of doing business, social and economic trends, and technological innovations.

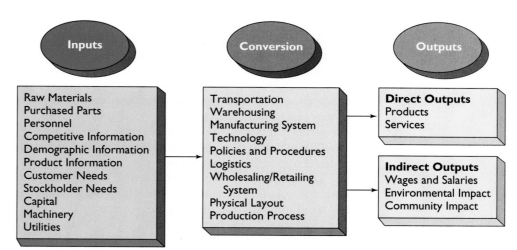

■ **FIGURE 17.1**
The Basic Production System
Every production system is built around a conversion that takes various inputs and converts these into outputs such as products or services

■ TABLE 17.1 Fitting Production/Operations Management to the Firm's Strategy

STRATEGY	PURCHASING & MATERIALS MANAGEMENT	PRODUCTION/OPERATIONS MANAGEMENT
Niche—low-cost	Purchase at low costs through networks and contacts with domestic and foreign suppliers. Operate storage and warehouse facilities and control inventory efficiently.	Emphasize low initial investments in plants, equipment, and outlets. Emphasize low operation costs.
Niche—differentiation	Purchase high-quality inputs, even if they cost more. Conduct storage, warehouse, and inventory activities with utmost care, even if at higher costs (e.g., fine wine must be kept in high-cost storage with correct lighting and air-conditioned space).	Emphasize specialized quality in operations even at high cost, such as the hand crafting of products.
Niche—low-cost/ differentiation	Purchase high-quality inputs, if possible, at low costs. This may be done through the development of organizational expertise, as Porsche has done. Conduct storage, warehouse, and inventory activities with utmost care, if possible, at low costs.	Emphasize specialized quality of operations, if possible, at low costs.
Low-cost	Purchase at low costs through quantity discounts. Operate storage and warehouse facilities and control inventory efficiently.	Emphasize operation efficiencies through learning, economies of scale, and capital-labor substitution possibilities.
Differentiation	Purchase high-quality inputs, even if they cost more. Conduct storage, warehouse, and inventory activities with extensive care, even if at higher costs.	Emphasize quality in operations, even if at high cost.
Low-cost— differentiation	Purchase high-quality inputs, if possible, at low costs. Conduct storage, warehouse, and inventory activities with care, if possible, at low costs.	Emphasize quality in operations, if possible, at low costs.
Multiple	Mixed	Mixed

SOURCE: Adapted from Peter Wright, Mark Kroll, and John Parnell, *Strategic Management Concepts* (Englewood Cliffs, NJ: Prentice-Hall, 1996), 174–175.

Any production system takes inputs and converts these into products or services called outputs. The **conversion system** (also called the production process or technology) has several components. These include the production machinery and its physical layout, the transport services that bring in the inputs and deliver the final products to customers, and storage services for goods awaiting shipment. The production system's **outputs** may be divided into direct outputs (the firm's actual products or services) and indirect outputs (such as taxes, wages, and salaries).

Production system design can be especially important for a small, fledgling firm, as the Entrepreneurs box shows.

The input-conversion-outputs sequence remains basically the same whether the output is tangible (such as a car) or intangible (such as a service). The primary inputs for an automobile factory include purchased parts, raw materials, supplies, paints, and personnel.[5] This factory's conversion system would include the assembly lines of machines that transform steel and other raw materials into finished cars. The output, of course, would be cars.

Entrepreneurs in Action

ALADAN CORPORATION INSTALLS NEW MACHINES

Julian H. Danielly might agree with the saying that timing is everything. The widespread AIDS awareness that arose in the late 1980s brought with it a shortage of protective gloves. With little in the way of other job options, Danielly combined this growing health concern with his own background as an executive at a latex-glove manufacturing company to find financing for his own start-up firm, Aladan. An old friend and colleague, Larry Povlacs, worked up plans for a $3 million glove-manufacturing machine that would outperform competitors in both quantity and quality. Danielly began looking for ways to obtain the money to build a factory where his partner could install the innovative machine.

Danielly sold investors $2 million in stock. He was also convincing enough to obtain $3 million in tax-free, industrial-development bond financing, a rare feat for a fledgling company. But he first had to get a bank to back the bond issue. Before South Trust Bank would agree to underwrite it, it insisted that Danielly sign customers to long-term contracts. He shortly returned with one $25 million order and several others that extended as long as five years. July 1987 marked the ground breaking for Aladan's first plant in Dothan, Alabama. That particular site was selected because of tax incentives and a nearby airport. It was also Povlacs's home.

Latex gloves are essential for people in the medical field, but profit margins are slim and manufacturing and selling the gloves is therefore risky. Since 1986 the price for 100 gloves has ranged from $2 to $12. In that same period, the market tripled in size to around $300 million. Danielly had performed miracles getting his factory built. He knew keeping it running would require staying on top of the latest manufacturing technology, developing good marketing strategy, and reducing risks through product diversification. Foreign competition posed the great-est immediate threat. Povlacs would have to design factory equipment efficient enough to outproduce the Pacific Rim companies, where labor was cheaper.

"A lot of what we've done here is incorporate improvements we had thought of over the years, but never had the opportunity to build," says Povlacs. "Starting from scratch was a real advantage for us from a manufacturing standpoint." The yearly output for each of Povlacs's machines totaled 200 million gloves. Aladan pioneered triple-dipping, a process that vastly increased the impenetrability of the gloves, exceeding the Food and Drug Administration standard. Competitors had no choice but to match the product quality level or be left behind. Povlacs even designed and built Aladan's drying equipment in-house. His machines were twice as expensive as others available, but they also were six times as efficient.

Aladan has spearheaded other improvements. After an investment of $1 million, it reduced the labor requirements of the most expensive powder-free gloves, making the product feasible for a vastly expanded market.

Aladan has funneled $30 million into company plant and equipment. Danielly used ingenuity in raising funds for the construction of the first factory. Povlacs applied innovation in the design of equipment, and the quality of the product is the standard the rest of the industry strives to attain. Sales per employee were $126,000 in 1993, and profit margins range between 10 and 20 percent. Aladan took advantage of rising demand for its principal product, but it was obviously more than good timing that turned the company into an industry leader. The partners' knowledge of operations management also helped turn Aladan into a winner. ∎

SOURCE: Teri Lammers, "What's Luck Got to Do With It?" *Inc.*, December 1993, 90–8.

PRODUCTION SYSTEM	PRIMARY INPUTS	PURPOSE OF CONVERSION SUBSYSTEM	OUTPUTS
1. Pet food factory	Grain, water, fish meal, personnel, tools, machines, paper bags, cans, buildings, utilities	Converts raw materials into finished goods	Pet food products
2. Hamburger stand	Meat, bread, vegetables, spices, supplies, personnel, utilities, machines, cartons, napkins, buildings, hungry customers	Transforms raw materials into fast-food products and packages	Satisfied customers and fast-food products
3. Automobile factory	Purchased parts, raw materials, supplies, paints, tools, equipment, personnel, buildings, utilities	Transforms raw materials into finished automobiles through fabrication and assembly operations	Automobiles
4. Public accounting firm	Supplies, personnel, information, computers, buildings, office furniture, machines, utilities	Attracts customers, compiles data, supplies management information, computes taxes	Management information, tax services, and audited financial statements
5. College or university	Students, books, supplies, personnel, buildings, utilities	Transmits information and develops skills and knowledge	Educated persons

SOURCE: Adapted from Norman Gaither, *Production and Operations Management*, 5th ed. (Fort Worth, TX: The Dryden Press, 1992), 22–3.

The same sequence applies to a service business like a university. Here inputs would include students, books, supplies, professors, and buildings. The conversion system consists of the technology used to transmit information to the students (lectures, exams, computerized instruction, and so forth). The output would be educated persons. Examples of inputs, conversion subsystems, and outputs for several other products and services are shown in Table 17.2.

Designing Production Systems

Designing any production system means making four basic decisions: Where will the facility be located? What type of production process will be used? What will be the layout of the plant or facility? And what will be the layout of the production system itself? We'll look at each in turn.

The Facility Location Decision

Deciding where to locate the facility is always a crucial step. For a service firm like a retail store or fast-food restaurant, even placing the facility on the wrong side of the road can spell disaster if the location is inaccessible. For a manufacturer, plant location will influence factors like transportation costs and labor availability.

Locating a factory requires managers to apply both subjective and objective criteria. On the subjective side are things like the owner's personal preference. If Mr. Suarez loves to sail and his whole family lives in Miami, then the plant may be located in nearby Hialeah, even if transportation costs there are somewhat higher.

■ **TABLE 17.3** *Some Considerations and Factors That Affect Location Decisions*

COUNTRY DECISION

1. Government rules, attitudes, stability, incentives
2. Cultural and economic issues
3. Location of markets
4. Labor availability, attitudes, productivity, costs
5. Availability of supplies, communications, energy
6. Exchange rate

REGION/COMMUNITY DECISION

1. Corporate desires
2. Attractiveness of region (culture, taxes, climate, etc.)
3. Labor availability, costs, attitudes toward unions
4. Cost and availability of utilities
5. Environmental regulations of state and town
6. Government incentives
7. Proximity to raw materials and customers
8. Land/construction costs

SITE DECISION

1. Site size and cost
2. Air, rail, highway, waterway systems
3. Zoning restrictions
4. Nearness of services/supplies needed
5. Environmental impact issues

SOURCE: Jay Heizer and Barry Render, *Production & Operations Management* (Upper Saddle River, NJ: Prentice-Hall, 1996), 347.

As production becomes more globalized, selecting a site tends to rest on a variety of country-, region-, and site-specific objective criteria like labor costs, exchange rates, and outbound and inbound transportation costs.[6] Some facility location factors are summarized in Table 17.3. They include labor availability, government rules, land and construction costs, zoning restrictions, communications, the tax structure, and property costs.

Basic Types of Production Processes

We can distinguish between two broad types of production systems: intermittent production systems and continuous production systems.

INTERMITTENT PRODUCTION. In **intermittent production** systems, production is performed on the product on a start-and-stop basis.[7] Manufacturing operations like automobile repair shops, custom cabinet shops, and construction contractors are examples. They are generally characterized by made-to-order products and relatively low product volumes, as well as frequent schedule changes and the use of general-purpose equipment that can make a variety of models or products.

Mass production is a special type of intermittent production process in which standardized methods and single-use machines produce long runs of standardized items. Most mass production processes use assembly lines. An assembly line is a fixed sequence of specialized (single-use) machines. In a typical assembly line, the product moves from station to station where one or more employees and/or specialized machines perform tasks such as inserting bumpers or screwing on doors. While mass production systems are intermittent production processes, they may in fact run more or less continuously and may stop and start very few times over the course of a year.

CONTINUOUS PRODUCTION. **Continuous production** processes run for very long periods without the start-and-stop behavior associated with intermittent production. Chemical plants, paper plants, and petroleum refineries are examples of continuous production process plants. Enormous capital investments are involved in building highly automated continuous process facilities such as these. They are therefore usually designed for high product volume and use special-purpose equipment.

As we will see later in this chapter, the traditional dividing line between intermittent and continuous processes is beginning to blur. For example, computer-assisted manufacturing processes at Mead Corporation, which produces and sells paper, merge the flexibility of intermittent production with the efficiency of continuous production.

Facility Layout

Facility layout refers to the configuration of the total facility—not just the machines, but also the employee work stations, storage areas, internal walls, and so forth that constitute the production facility. Important objectives here usually include reducing materials-handling costs, providing sufficient capacity, and allowing for safe equipment operation and ease of maintenance.

Facility layout is also important for service firms. Retailers lay out their stores to improve sales, raise customer satisfaction, and increase convenience, for instance. Similarly, office managers seek to promote communication between departments and to provide adequate privacy.

Production System Layout

There are basically four ways to lay out the production (conversion) system itself. In a **product layout,** every item to be produced follows the same sequence of operations from beginning to end, moving from one specialized tool and operation to another. An assembly, or production, line is one example. However, product layouts are not restricted to manufacturing. For example, automatic car washes use product layouts, as Figure 17.2 illustrates.[8]

In a **process layout,** similar machines or functions are grouped together; for example, all drill presses may be positioned in one area and all lathes in another. As Figure 17.3 illustrates,[9] universities and hospitals are usually organized around process layouts; separate locations exist for classrooms, libraries, offices, and computer centers, for instance. In a **fixed-position layout,** the product stays at one loca-

Product Layout of Car Wash

Exit

FIGURE 17.2
Product Layout

A car wash is an example of an assembly-line-type product layout, where each special-purpose machine performs its function as the product moves from station to station.

SOURCE: Everett Adam, Jr. and Ronald Ebert, *Production and Operations Management* (Englewood Cliffs, NJ: Prentice-Hall, 1992), 254.

tion and the manufacturing machines and tools required to build the product are brought to that location as needed. Bulky or heavy products such as ships are built in this way.

In **cellular manufacturing,** machines are grouped into cells, each of which contains all the tools and operations required to produce a particular product or family of products. This is shown in Figure 17.4.[10] Cellular manufacturing layouts may combine aspects of both process and product layouts. As in product layouts, each cell is usually dedicated to producing particular parts or products. But, as in process layouts, each cell is also sometimes designed to perform a specific set of manufacturing operations (such as all the grinding and buffing needed to produce one of the valves that goes into the company's car engines).

FIGURE 17.3
Process Layout

In a process layout like this, each process has its own area, and the "product" (in this case the patient) is directed to the processes (such as X-ray and pediatrics) that are appropriate.

SOURCE: Everett Adam, Jr. and Ronald Ebert, *Production and Operations Management* (Englewood Cliffs, NJ: Prentice-Hall, 1992), 254.

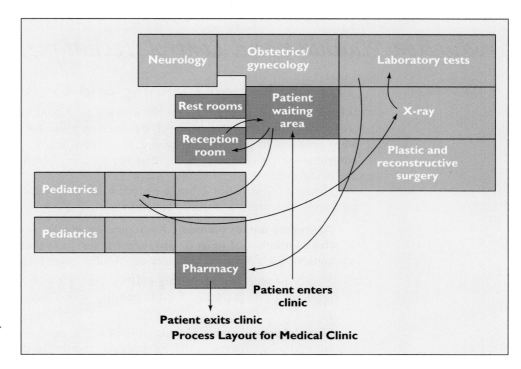

Process Layout for Medical Clinic

FIGURE 17.4
Improving Layouts by Moving to the Work Cell Concept

SOURCE: *Principles of Operations Management*: 2/E by Render/Heizer, © 1997. Reprinted by permission of Prentice-Hall, Inc., Upper Saddle River, NJ.

Note in both **(a)** and **(b)** that U-shaped work cells can reduce material and employee movement. The U shape may also reduce space requirements.

(a) Current layout—workers in small closed areas. Cannot increase ouput without a third worker.

(b) Current layout—straight lines are hard to balance.

Improved layout—workers can assist each other. May be able to add a third worker.

Improved layout—in U shape, workers have better access. Four workers were reduced to three.

Production Planning and Control Techniques

The Production Planning and Control Process

Whether you are producing cars or a Broadway show, a system for planning and controlling production is required. **Production planning** is the process of deciding what products to produce and where, when, and how to produce them. **Production control** is the process of ensuring that the specified production plans and schedules are being met.

Figure 17.5 provides a bird's-eye view of the production planning and control process.[11] The process includes several steps:

Aggregate output planning. Aggregate output planning shows the aggregate (total) number of units or products (or services) that must be produced to achieve each product's (or service's) dollar sales forecast.

Master production scheduling (MPS). The MPS shows the numbers of all products to be produced for the coming period, and the dates they are to be produced.

Material requirements planning (MRP). The materials requirements plan is a computer-based system that reviews the master production schedule and specifies the required raw materials, parts, subassemblies, and assemblies needed

■ FIGURE 17.5
The Operations Planning and Control System

SOURCE: Adapted from Everett Adam, Jr. and Ronald Ebert, *Production and Operations Management* (Englewood Cliffs, NJ: Prentice-Hall, 1992), 374.

each week to meet the master production schedule. The system contains computerized records or **bills of materials** listing the required parts and materials for each product and where they can be purchased or produced.

Shop floor control. Overseeing the weekly and daily production schedules to most effectively implement the master production schedule on a week-by-week basis is called shop floor control. It consists of several elements. **Loading and sequencing** means assigning individual jobs to machines and work centers. This is based on a **load schedule,** which compares the labor and machine hours needed to carry out the master production schedule with the labor and machine hours actually available each week.[12] Detailed scheduling means specifying the actual start times and finishing times for all jobs at each machine or work center, as well as each job's labor assignments. Finally, the movement of products and materials from operation to operation must be monitored and adjusted, a process known as **expediting.** We'll turn to some important production planning and control tools used to schedule and control production (such as scheduling charts in later sections of this chapter).

Organizational Behavior in Action

THE FACTORY THAT MANAGES ITSELF

In most factories it's the managers who control the production schedule, but things are different in the plant that Lynn Mercer runs for Lucent Technologies.[13] Ms. Mercer runs the plant, which produces cellular phone equipment, on the assumption that the workers themselves are in the best position to know how to do their jobs. She, therefore, sets only broad performance goals for the plant and leaves it to her workers to decide how to reach them. Her management principles are as follows:

1. Hire attitude over aptitude. The work is technical but teachable. What's not teachable are attitudes and values like initiative, curiosity, and teamwork. Ms. Mercer, therefore, tests applicants to weed out loners and malcontents.
2. Create mission from above, methods from below. Ms. Mercer distributes a one-page list of "working principles" that all employees must sign. These include speed, candor, and deep respect for colleagues. She sets the overall direction and goals; the employees then work together (with engineers when necessary) to continually improve how things are done.
3. Foster feedback. Operating statistics are displayed everywhere. Where performance is lagging behind goal, the chart hangs behind a sheet of red see-through plastic.
4. Unite the inside and outside. In other words, Ms. Mercer gets workers in contact with customers. Assemblers know the destination of every product they touch and sign off on it when it's finished. Many assemblers attend trade shows where they meet and talk with customers.
5. Reward teamwork. The yearly bonus is equal to 15 percent of regular pay and is based on individual achievement and team performance.

In most plants it's the managers who still control the production process and schedule. However, in Lynn Mercer's plant, the factory to a large extent manages itself, thanks to the motivated workers. ■

Scheduling and Gantt Charts

Production schedules like the master production schedule can be presented on charts that show specifically what operations are to be carried out and when. The **Gantt chart** shown in Figure 17.6 is one example.

Henry Gantt, a management pioneer, actually devised several versions of his chart. In the example shown in Figure 17.6, time is presented on the horizontal scale, and for each order, the start and stop times for each operation are shown sequentially. In another type of Gantt chart, each operation is listed separately in the left column one under the other, while time is again shown horizontally. That way, the start and stop times for all operations in a complex project can be scheduled and visually tracked.

In practice, schedulers work from the required delivery date backward. They determine how long each assembly will take, how long it will take to obtain raw materials, and so forth. Based on the results, schedulers can determine whether the required delivery date can be met and what bottlenecks they must prepare to unclog.

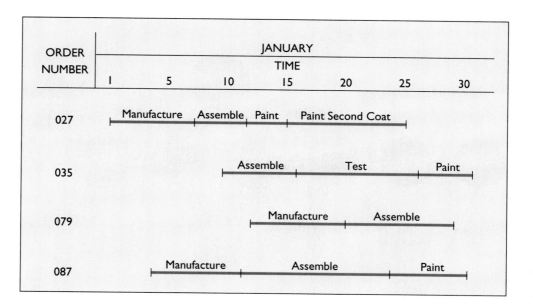

■ FIGURE 17.6
A Gantt Chart
This particular Gantt Chart shows the step and timing of each step for each order.

Network Planning and Control Methods

Versions of the Gantt chart are adequate for managing a relatively simple project (with not too many subassemblies or activities). However, more complex projects usually require computerized network charting methods to show how one activity affects the others.

Network planning and control methods are methods for planning and controlling projects by graphically representing the project's steps and the timing and linkages amongst those steps. A project is a series of interrelated activities aimed at producing a major, coordinated product or service. Examples of a project include introducing a new Taurus automobile or planning a wedding reception.

PERT and CPM are the two most popular network planning and control methods. PERT (program evaluation review technique) and CPM (critical path method) were invented at about the same time and are similar, although several details (including the cost of each step) set PERT apart from CPM.

Events and activities are the two major components of PERT networks. As Figure 17.7 shows, **events,** depicted by circles, represent specific accomplishments such as "foundation laid." **Activities** are the time-consuming aspect of the project (like laying the foundation) and are represented by arrows. (Actually, a Gantt chart would usually suffice for something as "simple" as building a house: PERT charts are reserved for products with thousands of events and activities.) By studying the PERT chart, the scheduler can determine the **critical path,** the sequence of critical events that in total requires the most time to complete.

Developing a PERT chart involves four steps.

1. Identify all the individual activities required to complete the project and the order in which they must be completed.
2. Place each event in its proper sequence relative to all other events. (You must be able to visualize these tasks in a network, as shown in Figure 17.7.)
3. Estimate how long it will take to complete each activity. (Some estimators make three estimates: optimistic, pessimistic, and expected.) In our example in Figure 17.7, the scheduler estimates it will take nine days from

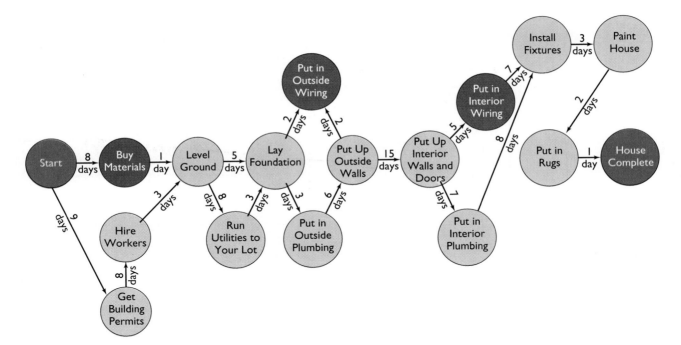

■ **FIGURE 17.7**
PERT Chart for
Building a House
In a PERT Chart like this
one, each event is shown
in its proper relationship
to the other events. The
darkened circles show the
critical—or most time-
consuming—path.

the time the foundation is laid to put up the walls. (Notice that the plumbing must go in before completing the walls, so the wall job will actually take at least nine days altogether to complete.) Before an event like laying the foundation can be completed, *all* prior activities (running utilities, leveling ground, and so forth) must be completed.

4. Compute the critical path by adding up the times for all possible sequences of events. This will show where to direct resources (like adding more personnel) to speed the project's completion. Computerized programs (as in the accompanying picture on page 577) are used to create PERT networks for very complex projects.[14]

Purchasing

Purchasing departments buy all the materials and parts the firm needs to conduct its business. These materials and parts include the raw materials that go into the firm's products, as well as machinery, tools, purchased components, and even paper clips and computer paper.

Purchasing is a more important function than many managers realize. Some experts estimate that 60 percent of a manufacturer's sales dollars are paid to suppliers for purchased materials.[15] Furthermore, manufacturers striving to maintain world-class quality levels know that the quality of their finished products can't be any better than the quality of their components. This point was illustrated several years ago when Saturn had to recall tens of thousands of cars due to faulty alternators. Purchasing departments can therefore affect a firm's cost-effectiveness as well as its quality reputation. Today, in fact, many firms work closely with their suppliers to create better-quality parts. Many firms, such as Ford, send out engineers to help their suppliers boost their quality-management systems.

Purchasing managers engage in several activities.[16] They maintain a database of available suppliers to facilitate supplies and materials purchases. They also are responsible for selecting suppliers and negotiating supply contracts with them.

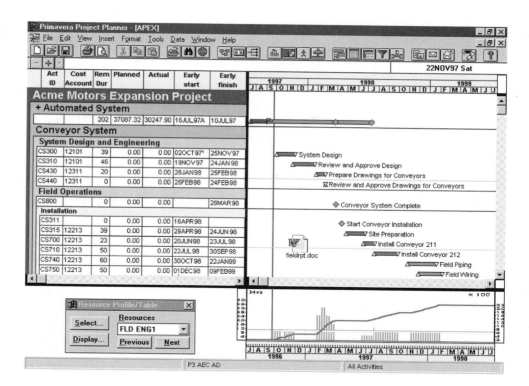

Example of a network
planning report

Purchasing managers try to minimize the costs of materials and supplies, but it would be an oversimplification to say that this is their only (or even their main) concern. For many firms high-quality, reliable, on-time deliveries outweigh costs. The purchasing manager working in these firms might well choose a somewhat more expensive (but much more reliable) supplier.

Inventory Management Techniques

The Role of Inventory Management

Firms keep inventories of five types of items.[17] *Raw materials* and purchased parts are obtained from outside suppliers and used in the production of the firm's finished products. *Components* are subassemblies that are awaiting final assembly. *Work in process* refers to all materials or components on the production floor in various stages of production. *Finished goods* are final products waiting to be purchased or about to be sent to customers. Finally, *supplies* are all items the firm needs that are not part of the finished product, such as paper clips, duplicating machine toner, and tools.

Inventory management is the process of ensuring that the firm has adequate inventories of all parts and supplies needed, within the constraint of minimizing total inventory costs.

In practice, inventory managers must address four specific costs. **Ordering or setup costs** are the costs of placing the order or setting up machines for the production run. For purchased items, ordering costs might include clerical order-processing costs and the cost of inspecting goods when they arrive. For items made in-house, setup costs are usually incurred when manufacturing a product and include the labor involved with setting up the machine and the cost of preparing the paperwork for scheduling the production run.

Ordering or setup costs are usually fixed, meaning that they are independent of the size of the order. On the other hand, **acquisition costs,** the total costs of all units bought to fill an order, vary with the size of the order. For example, ordering required parts in larger quantities may reduce each unit's cost thanks to quantity discounts. This in turn will lower the total acquisition costs of the order, whereas ordering smaller quantities may raise the unit cost.

Inventory managers focus on two other inventory costs. **Inventory-holding** (or carrying) **costs** are all the costs associated with carrying parts or materials in inventory. The biggest specific cost here is usually the firm's cost of capital, which in this case is the value of a unit of the inventory times the length of time it is held times the interest rate at which the firm borrows money.[18] **Stockout costs** are the costs associated with running out of raw materials or finished-goods inventory. For example, if a company cannot fill a customer's order, it might lose both the current order and any profits or future sales the customer may have delivered.

Inventory managers want to avoid three basic problems. The first is overinvestment in inventories, which ties up money, crowds available space, and hikes losses when stored products deteriorate or become obsolete. At the other extreme, inventory managers want to avoid underinvestment, which leaves the firm unable to fill production orders and discourages customers. The third problem is unbalanced inventory, which means some items are understocked while others are overstocked.

Basic Inventory Management Systems

Many quantitative and nonquantitative systems are available for managing inventory. The ABC and EOQ systems are two of the most popular.

ABC INVENTORY MANAGEMENT. Most firms find that a small proportion (25 to 30 percent) of the parts in their inventory accounts for a large proportion (70 or 80 percent) of their annual dollar volume of inventory usage. (A part's annual dollar volume is computed by multiplying its cost per part by the number of parts used in a year.) When using the ABC system, the manager divides the inventory into three dollar-volume categories—A, B, and C—with the A parts being the most active. The inventory manager then concentrates most of his or her checking and surveillance on the A parts. For example, the A parts are ordered most often so that their total in inventory is minimized and so that they are not in the inventory bins too long.

At the other extreme, the inventory manager might find that perhaps 50 percent of the parts in inventory account for, say, 15 percent of annual dollar volume. Why spend as much time closely monitoring all those parts when in total they account for only 15 percent of the firm's annual dollar volume of inventory usage? The idea, instead, is to focus on the high-annual-dollar-volume A inventory items, and to a lesser extent on the B items and even less on the C items.

THE ECONOMIC ORDER QUANTITY INVENTORY MANAGEMENT SYSTEM. The idea behind the **economic order quantity (EOQ)** system or model is to determine the most economic quantity to order, in other words the quantity that will minimize total inventory costs. EOQ is the best-known and probably the oldest inventory system.

Figure 17.8 illustrates the relationships involved. As shown, the two major costs, inventory carrying costs and ordering costs, vary inversely with each other. For

■ FIGURE 17.8
The Economic Order Quantity Model

As in this example, when order size goes up, ordering costs per order go down, but carrying costs go up because more items are left longer in inventory. The Economic Order Quantity (EOQ) is that order size at which total costs are minimized. NOTE: As the order size goes up, costs per order go down—due to reduced ordering costs and other factors. But as order size goes up, the inventory manager will order less often and carry more inventory, which means that carrying costs will go up.

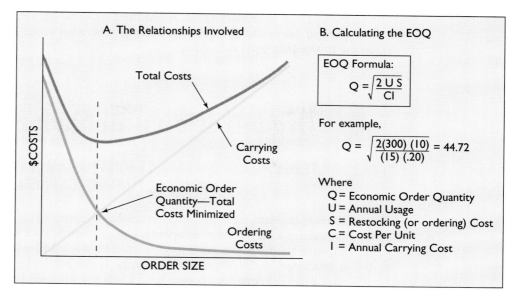

example, ordering in large quantities usually allows the firm to order more economically, but it means higher storage costs (because the firm would have, on average, more inventory in stock).

In its simplest form the economic order quantity is

$$Q = \sqrt{2US/CI}$$

where Q is the economic order quantity (the most economical quantity to order), U is the annual usage of the item, S is the restocking or ordering costs, C is the cost per unit, and I is the annual carrying costs.

This EOQ equation is widely used, but it is based on some simplifications. For example, it assumes that the same number of units are taken from inventory periodically, such as ten units per day. It also assumes that the supplier does not offer quantity discounts for ordering in large batches. More sophisticated EOQ versions are available for handling these and other complications.[19]

Controlling for Quality and Productivity

Quality Defined

Quality can be defined as the totality of features and characteristics of a product or service that bears on its ability to satisfy given needs. To put this another way, "quality measures how well a product or service meets customer needs."[20]

This definition highlights several important characteristics of quality. First, the customer's needs are the basic standard for measuring something's quality: thus an airplane seat in coach can be as high quality as one in first class, in terms of the coach passenger's expectations and the competitor's services. Second, high quality does not have to mean high price. Again, the basic consideration should be the extent to which the product or service meets the customer's expectations.

Quality standards today are international. Doing business in Europe often means the firm must show it complies with **ISO 9000,** the quality standards of the

European Community (EC). If required to do so by a customer, the vendor would have to prove that its quality manuals, procedures, and job instructions all comply with the ISO 9000 standards.

Organizational Behavior in Action

TEAMWORK ENHANCES CUSTOMER SATISFACTION AND MANUFACTURING CAPABILITY

Teamwork plays an increasingly crucial role in achieving quality standards at many companies today. To stay competitive, most companies know they must continuously improve their operations, banish wasted efforts, and build-in quality as the product is produced, not try to catch the errors as the product goes out the door. To paraphrase two experts, the people who are best equipped to recognize and make such improvements are the work teams who actually accomplish the tasks, for they are the ones closest to the process, be it design, manufacturing, service, or support. "If they are motivated, trained, and sensitized to recognize opportunities for improvements, and then trained how and empowered to make the required changes, the company or organization will realize an organizational effectiveness that it never imagined."[21]

The experience of the Kent-Moore Company of Warren, Michigan, shows how companies use teams in manufacturing.[22] The company makes specialty service tools and diagnostic equipment for vehicle manufacturers and dealers in the transportation industry. It established what it called a team-based total quality improvement (TQI) program to boost customer satisfaction and manufacturing capability. Implementing TQI included taking the following steps.

A TQI steering committee was organized to begin organizing TQI teams, among other things. Like all subsequent teams, the TQI steering committee members (primarily senior managers) were given extensive training in team building, and learned decision-making techniques and the importance of group dynamics and personality in teams. They also got instruction in problem-solving processes, communication principles, and ways to facilitate effective meetings. The importance of consensus decision making was stressed.

The TQI steering committee then identified two processes that needed improvement. The first was the process for identifying and coding the origin of products scheduled for export; the second concerned the manufacture of stainless steel bushings (tubular separators) used in the equipment.

A 10-member team was organized to address the export documentation problem. (Kent-Moore export shipments were occasionally held by customs officials because of oversights regarding country-of-origin documentation. The problem meant delays for the customer and needless expense for the company.)

The team consisted of 10 Kent-Moore employees, including the automotive sales and marketing manager, product development supervisor, automotive sales engineer, export clerk, and export services manager. Their goal was to develop a consistent and efficient process to properly identify a product's country of origin and its "harmonized system commodity code," a universally used coding system for describing a product for export. Meeting at weekly two-hour sessions over a period of 16 months, the team members drafted a mission statement for their team, developed an action plan, and flowcharted the existing process. They also gathered information from sources like the U.S. Department of Commerce, the United Nations, and a Canadian customs broker.

Out of this process emerged several recommendations. These included having Kent-Moore suppliers identify the origin of all products shipped to Kent-Moore, daily coding all products scheduled for shipment, and electronically transmitting export documentation to customs.[23]

The results of this team effort were impressive. Kent-Moore has been 100 percent successful in meeting customer requests for completed export documentation, and the amount of time needed to respond to those requests has been cut by 50 percent. In addition, the risk of having shipments held by customs officials has been reduced, customers now save an estimated $250,000 annually in lowered duty rates, and it's become easier to ship products into specific countries.

Kent-Moore organized a second team to analyze and solve its problems with the stainless steel bushings. These bushings are used in rebuilding diesel engines and are basically spacers used to set the height of one component relative to another. At the time, the bushing manufacturing process suffered significant variances, in part because so many different suppliers were being used that the component parts could not be sufficiently standardized.

A seven-member team was organized and included an accounting manager, operations manager, stainless steel bushing unit employee, and project engineer. They met for an average of twice a month for two to six hours at a time, researching and flowcharting the existing process. They made several recommendations, including changing the physical layout of the work center where stainless steel bushings were produced, rerouting materials through the work center, and changing the sequence in which the materials were routed.

These recommendations also led to impressive savings. Daily production increased by 25 percent, which translated into a cost saving of over $50,000 a year. The unit price of the bushings dropped by 11 percent.

Actually, financial benefits like these are only part of what companies gain when they involve work teams in improving the company's processes. As two managers involved in the Kent-Moore teamwork effort put it:

> Kent-Moore's decision to implement a total quality improvement initiative continues to provide significant benefits for the company. By reducing costs and improving quality and delivery performance, the firm is not only able to retain existing customers but also to attract new ones. The company's experiences with team problem solving point up the fact that in striving to attain its goal of offering top-notch service to its customers, Kent-Moore has succeeded not only in delighting them, but also in strengthening the company's overall performance and securing its future.[24]

Total Quality Management Programs and the Malcolm Baldrige Award

Total quality management (TQM) programs are organization-wide programs that aim to integrate all functions of the business such that all aspects of the business including design, planning, production, distribution, and field service are aimed at maximizing customer satisfaction through continuous improvements.[25] In the

United States, this approach is also often called *continuous improvement, zero defects,* or *six sigma;* in Japan it is known as *Kaizen.*[26]

W. Edwards Deming, who is credited with bringing quality control to Japan in the 1950s, is generally regarded as the intellectual father of total quality management. His concept of total quality is based on the following 14-point system, which he says must be implemented at all organizational levels.

1. Create consistency of purpose toward improvement of product and service and translate that into a plan.
2. Adopt the new philosophy of quality.
3. Cease dependence on inspection to achieve quality. In particular, eliminate the need for inspection on a mass basis by building quality into the product from the beginning.
4. End the practice of choosing suppliers based solely on price. Move toward a single supplier for any one item and toward a long-term relationship of loyalty and trust.
5. Improve constantly and forever the production and service system in order to improve quality and productivity and thus constantly decrease cost. In other words, aim for continuous improvement.
6. Institute extensive training on the job.
7. Shift your focus from production numbers to quality.
8. Drive out fear, so that everyone may work effectively for the company.
9. Break down barriers between departments. People in research, design, sales, and production must work as a team to foresee problems of production as well as problems that may occur after sale when the product or service is actually used.
10. Eliminate slogans and targets for the workforce for zero defects and new levels of productivity, particularly where new methods for achieving these targets are not put in place.
11. Eliminate work standards (quotas) on the factory floor.
12. Remove barriers that rob employees of their right to pride of workmanship. Among other things, this means abolishing the annual merit rating and all forms of management by objectives or management by numbers.
13. Institute a vigorous program of education and self-improvement.
14. Create a structure within top management that will push every day for each of the preceding 13 points. Make sure to put everybody in the company to work to accomplish the transformation.[27]

In 1987, the U.S. Department of Commerce created the **Malcolm Baldrige Award,** in part to recognize organizations that adhere to Deming-type quality principles. The award is named after former President Reagan's Secretary of Commerce, who died while in office. Most U.S. manufacturing firms, service firms, and small business are eligible to apply for the Baldrige. Winners include Motorola, Inc., Federal Express, Cadillac Motor Car Company, and Xerox Business Products and Systems.

In choosing the Baldrige Award winners, several agencies (including the National Institute of Standards and Technology of the U.S. Department of Commerce and a Board of Examiners consisting of quality experts) evaluate and visit the applicants' sites. Overall, applicants are judged on the extent to which they are continually improving value to customers while maximizing their overall productivity and effectiveness.[28] The judges focus on a number of core issues, which are grouped into seven categories. These seven categories represent the core of the

Baldrige application and are also illustrative of the elements in any total quality management program.[29] The seven Baldrige categories are summarized in Figure 17.9. Implementing a Baldrige-type program thus involves these seven steps:

EXHIBIT SENIOR EXECUTIVE LEADERSHIP. Show top management's symbolic commitment to quality and the day-to-day quality leadership of senior staff. Symbolic gestures might include taking the same courses lower-level employees take in preparation for the TQM programs, talking to customers about quality, and meeting with employees regarding quality.

OBTAIN QUALITY INFORMATION AND ANALYSIS. Show that you have gathered and used data that demonstrate both quality performance and continuous improvement. Applicants are expected to have a very adequate system for collecting statistical data on matters such as product or service quality and customer satisfaction.

Benchmarking refers to the process of comparing one's own firm's statistical results in key areas with those of other firms. The firm is expected to report which companies it benchmarked, what has been learned, and how the information was used.[30]

ENGAGE IN STRATEGIC QUALITY PLANNING. Strategic quality planning refers to the adequacy of the firm's planning process and how well key quality goals are integrated into the firm's overall planning process. In practice, examiners typically review two or three goals the firm has set to determine how well it has met them. For example, goals might include answering all customer telephone calls by the second ring or increasing on-time customer deliveries by 80 percent.

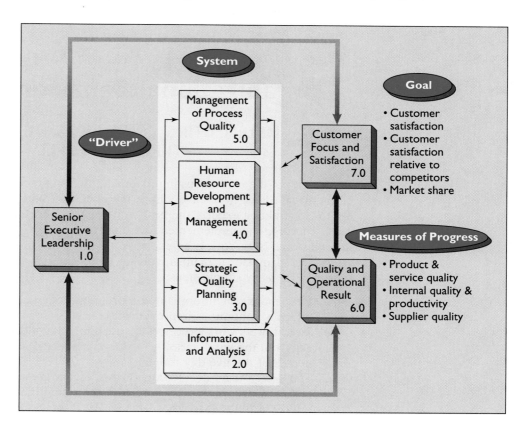

■ **FIGURE 17.9 Baldrige Award Criteria Framework**
Senior executive leadership is the "driver" of total quality management, with each of the other six elements, or Baldrige categories, playing a crucial role.

Source: U.S. Department of Commerce, 1992.

DEVELOP HUMAN RESOURCES. In practical terms, in this category examiners tend to focus on the extent to which human resource management and organizational behavior techniques (such as enrichment, empowerment, training, and career development) are used to fully tap each employee's potential. For example, employees should be trained to use problem-solving tools and group decision-making skills. The teams and employees should also have enriched and empowered jobs.[31]

MANAGE THE ENTIRE QUALITY PROCESS. Rather than viewing design, production, and sales as separate entities, top firms usually recognize the integrated nature of the departments' work. Representatives from design, production, and sales might work together on the initial design to facilitate production and maximize customer satisfaction. Many Baldrige winners develop process-flow diagrams, identify bottleneck areas, and use statistical and other approaches to develop solutions.[32]

MEASURE OPERATIONAL RESULTS. Firms should provide statistical data on quality levels, quality improvement trends, operational performance, and supplier quality. One aim here is to show that the firm is achieving *continuous improvement* in critical operational areas, such as in service quality. This means that all employees are continually reviewing quality levels and customer feedback to continually improve how things are done.

EXHIBIT A CUSTOMER FOCUS. This criterion measures whether firms provide objective, validated data regarding their "focus on the customer" and "customer satisfaction." The firm will be expected to have used sources such as sales calls, customer surveys, and telephone hotlines to generate the data. The overall emphasis is on how the company assesses customer satisfaction and on current trends and levels of satisfaction.

Organizational Behavior in Action

IMPLEMENTING CONTINUOUS IMPROVEMENT THROUGH PEOPLE

Implementing the continuous improvement philosophy required by a Baldrige-type effort doesn't have to involve a huge investment of time or money. In fact, according to two training experts, the best improvement efforts are low-cost and immediate.[33] The program implemented at Cummins Engine Company's Jamestown plant in Lakewood, New York is an example.

At the Jamestown plant, involving employees in "continuous improvement" took several fairly simple steps:

1. First, management appointed a program design group. Its goal was to start to apply continuous improvement concepts (see pages 581–584) to Jamestown's work processes by implementing a training program; employees from the work areas were directly involved in creating the actual details of the five-day training.
2. The design team decided that cross-functional teams of technical and nontechnical people should coordinate the actual (continuous improvement effort) in their work areas. This meant gaining a commitment from the

plant's top management to eliminate barriers and provide resources to the teams, and also empowering teams to make immediate improvements when they identified better ways of doing things.

3. The design group laid out the actual content of a five-day continuous improvement training program. Among the continuous improvement rules to be emphasized were these:

   ■ Discard convention and fixed ideas about doing work.
   ■ Think of how to do it rather than why it cannot be done.
   ■ Start by questioning current practices.
   ■ Begin to make improvements immediately, even if only 50 percent of them can be completed.
   ■ Correct mistakes immediately.
   ■ Gain wisdom from facing hardships.
   ■ Ask "why" five times and seek root causes.
   ■ Seek the wisdom of ten, not the wisdom of one.

4. A recognition and reward program was set up to reinforce participants' active involvement.

The program seems to be a success. Two hundred twenty-three plant employees have completed the training program. Sixty-one process improvements have been documented, with tangible results such as higher quality, lower cost, reduced cycle times, improved safety, less inventory, and more efficient use of personnel. Therefore, the program apparently has had the desired effect of boosting Cummins's product quality and processes, primarily (as expected) by reducing the sort of wastes that would otherwise reduce the plant's performance. ■

Quality Control Methods

In addition to building a plantwide commitment to quality, companies use various tools and techniques to monitor product quality. First, most firms have a formal inspection procedure, in which inspectors test and measure the product against quality standards. Sometimes (such as when producing heart pacemakers), a 100 percent inspection is typical, and every unit is inspected. More common is **acceptance sampling,** in which only a portion of the items are inspected, perhaps 2 or 5 percent.

Firms also use quality control charts like the one in Figure 17.10. There are many types, but the basic idea is always the same. First, upper and lower control limits are drawn to show the range within which some measurable characteristic of the product are to fall. Then the chosen characteristic, such as its length or weight, is inspected and measured. (Thus, Kellogg's might want to make sure each box of corn flakes contains no more than 20 ounces and no fewer than 19.5 ounces.) If the measures begin to move toward the upper or lower control limits, then quality may be going out of control, and the reason for the trend must be ascertained.

To help teams of employees monitor quality problems, they typically use several tools. Some of these are summarized in Figure 17.11 (on page 587).[34] For example, a scatter diagram is a graph that shows the magnitude of one trait (such as the number of defects) versus a second trait (such as time). A cause and effect (or fishbone) diagram outlines the four main categories of problems—machine, human (personnel), method, and material—and helps to analyze the problem and devise solutions.

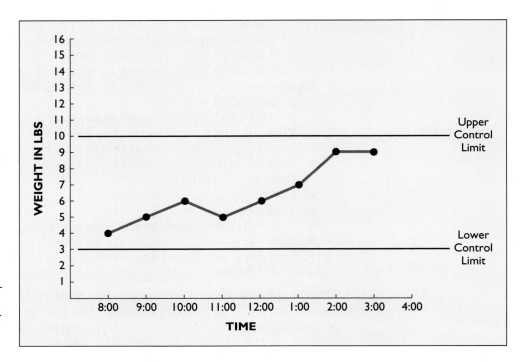

■ **FIGURE 17.10**
Example of Quality Control Chart
The idea behind any quality control chart is to track quality trends to ensure they don't go out of control.

Design for Manufacturability

Designing for manufacturability means designing products with ease of manufacturing in mind. Its aims are to develop a product that can

- exhibit the desired level of quality and reliability
- be designed in the least time with the least development cost
- make the quickest and smoothest transition into production
- be produced and tested with the minimum cost in the minimum amount of time
- satisfy customer's needs and compete in the marketplace[35]

Designing for manufacturability is increasingly important. As one expert points out, "by the time a product has been designed, only about 8 percent of the total product budget has been spent. But by that point, the design has determined 80 percent of the cost of the product!"[36] For example, Hewlett-Packard's Laser Jet III printer has dozens of parts more than does the IBM laser printer. Because IBM's printers have fewer points where assembly errors can occur, they can be manufactured more quickly, less expensively, and with fewer initial defects. As one expert said,

> The design determines the manufacturability. It is not determined by the factory, no matter how sophisticated it may be. In fact, the more advanced the factory is, the more it depends on good designs. Automation places many constraints on the design, which design for manufacturing accounts for.[37]

Designing for manufacturability often means designing products in multidisciplinary teams with representatives from sales, product design, and manufacturing, for instance. This team approach is also called simultaneous design or **concurrent engineering.** It ensures that all departments involved in the product's success contribute to its design.[38]

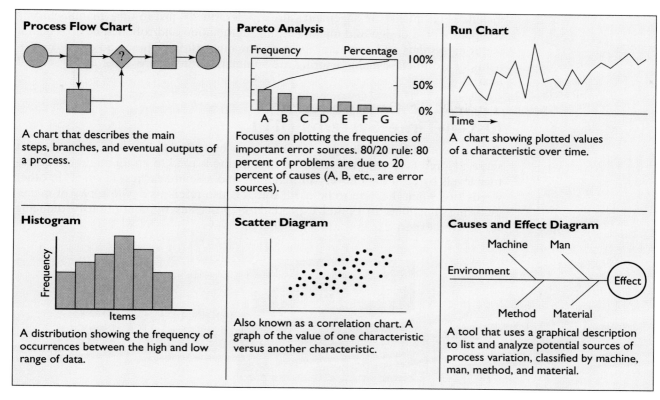

■ **FIGURE 17.11** **Tools Commonly Used for Problem Solving and Continuous Improvement**
A selection of tools employee teams can use to monitor and analyze quality.

SOURCE: Adapted from Richard Chase and Nicholas Aquilero, *Production and Operations Management*, 6th ed. (Homewood, IL: Irwin, 1992), 197.

World-Class Manufacturing and Managing Change

The World-Class Manufacturer

Today, no firm—not even one in the heartland of the United States—can assume it will be immune from global competitors.[39] Virtually every firm today finds its industry globalized, which means it faces not only local competitors but foreign ones as well. This globalization means intensified competition as firms around the world strive to improve quality, lead time, customer service, and costs in the hope of gaining a stronger competitive advantage.

World-class companies are those that can compete based on quality and productivity in an intensely competitive global environment. Firms such as UPS, Sony, and Motorola, to name a few, set the performance standards for their industries and are able to respond swiftly and effectively to changing conditions. As two experts put it, "being world-class in manufacturing means that the company can compete successfully and make a profit in an environment of international competition, not only now, but also in the future."[40]

World-class manufacturers are world class in part because they use modern production techniques and management systems to boost manufacturing productivity, quality, and flexibility. These production techniques and management systems include total quality management (already described), just-in-time manufacturing, computer-aided design and manufacturing, automation and robotics, flexible manufacturing systems, and computer-integrated manufacturing. These and other components of world-class manufacturing are summarized in Figure 17.12 and discussed next.

The Basic Components of Just-in-Time Systems (JIT)

The concept called **just-in-time (JIT)** has two related definitions. In the narrowest sense, JIT refers to the production control methods used to attain minimum inventory levels by ensuring delivery of materials and assemblies "just in time," in other words, just when they are to be used. But JIT also refers to a *philosophy* of manufacturing that aims to optimize production processes by continuously reducing waste. One expert explains JIT's benefits this way:

■ **FIGURE 17.12   Components of World-Class Manufacturing**
Shown here are components of world-class manufacturing and how they interact. A basic aim is to reduce the lot sizes needed for economic production, while reducing setup time, so that the firm gains the advantages of mass production costs, but small-lot-size flexibility.

SOURCE: Adapted from Harold Steudel and Paul Desruelle, *Manufacturing in the 90s* (New York: Van Nostrand Reinhold, 1992), 11.

JIT streamlines production, based on demand-driven, just-in-time arrival of components at each assembly's stage. JIT strives to simplify manufacturing and reduce material burden by operating with minimum lot sizes, no queues (products waiting in line to be used), and minimum inventory levels. . . . JIT means producing each day only that day's demand so material "flows" through production. [But] JIT also can serve as a focal point for other approaches to world-class manufacturing. . . . JIT demands zero defects and other total quality management efforts to eliminate waste. It calls for individual responsibility and empowerment. The ideal of continuous improvements—making products ever better, cheaper and faster—is likewise the mission of JIT.[41]

Reducing seven main wastes lies at the heart of the JIT philosophy. As summarized in Figure 17.13,[42] these are the wastes of overproduction, waiting, transportation, processing, stock, motion, and making defective products. As you can see from this comprehensive list, JIT is a thorough management approach. It is also sometimes called **lean manufacturing** or **value-added manufacturing** (meaning that any manufacturing process that does not add value to the product for the customer is wasteful).[43]

As a management philosophy, JIT has eight basic components, starting with focused factories.

FOCUSED FACTORIES. The Japanese business community (where JIT was invented) tends to build small, specialized plants rather than large ones. This is so because it is easier to manage small plants, and it is easier to organize the work flow and to staff highly specialized plants. Few Japanese plants have as many as 1,000 employees; most have fewer than 30.[44]

GROUP TECHNOLOGY. Inside their plants, the Japanese tend to lay out the facilities around the cell or group technology discussed earlier. The process-oriented departments that form the core of many U.S. firms—such as those specialized in

■ FIGURE 17.13
The Seven Wastes JIT Aims to Eliminate

Just-in-time is aimed at eliminating the seven wastes: over-production, waiting, transportation, processing, stocks, motion, and defective products.

SOURCE: R. Hall, *Attaining Manufacturing Excellence* (Homewood, IL: Dow Jones-Irwin, 1987), 26.

1. *Waste of overproduction.* Eliminate by reducing setup times, synchronizing quantities and timing between processes, compacting layout, visibility, and so forth. Make only what is needed now.

2. *Waste of waiting.* Eliminate through synchronizing work flow as much as possible, and balance uneven loads by flexible workers and equipment.

3. *Waste of transportation.* Establish layouts and locations to make transport and handling unnecessary if possible. Then rationalize transport and material handling that cannot be eliminated.

4. *Waste of processing itself.* First question why this part or product should be made at all, then why each process is necessary. Extend thinking beyond economy of scale or speed.

5. *Waste of stocks.* Reduce by shortening setup times and reducing lead times, by synchronizing work flows and improving work skills, and even by smoothing fluctuations in demand for the product. Reducing all the other wastes reduces the waste of stocks.

6. *Waste of motion.* Study motion for economy and consistency. Economy improves productivity, and consistency improves quality. First improve the motions, then mechanize or automate. Otherwise there is danger of automating waste.

7. *Waste of making defective products.* Develop the production process to prevent defects from being made so as to eliminate inspection. At each process, accept no defects and make no defects. Make processes failsafe to do this. From a quality process comes a quality product—automatically.

grinding, drilling, pressing, and so forth—are not used in JIT firms. Instead, cells are formed in which *all the processes required to complete a major part of the product are grouped together.* One employee can then perform all the processes needed. The worker will have to be more highly trained and flexible, but the moving and waiting time between processes is reduced or eliminated.

JIDOKA: QUALITY AT THE SOURCE. JIT-based firms function on the idea that every worker is personally responsible for the quality of the item he or she produces. Thus, quality goes in "at the source," when the product is actually made. These firms do not rely on end-of-the-line quality inspectors to catch defects. **Jidoka** means "stop everything when something goes wrong." Defects don't just continue down the line. If a defect is found, the entire line is stopped (usually by the employees, who have pushbuttons or cords to signal the need for a stop).

JUST-IN-TIME PLANNING AND CONTROL. The aim of just-in-time planning and control methods is to reduce the waiting time for parts and materials to zero. In this way the firm hopes to minimize inventory investment and to shorten production lead times.

KANBAN PRODUCTION CONTROL SYSTEM. Just-in-time production is a pull system. This means that whenever an item, such as a car, is sold, it pulls the need for another item, such as an engine, which in turn pulls the need for engine components, and so forth. At Toyota, the control system is called **Kanban,** from the Japanese word "card." When a part is used, a Kanban card goes back to the parts depot requesting a new part. Containers for the parts travel with the Kanbans requisitioning the parts and are returned with them.

UNIFORM PLANT LOADING. Just-in-time systems depend on minimizing wide swings in production levels. Many Japanese plants therefore use **uniform plant loading.** This usually means that monthly production plans are established for the plant and then are strictly adhered to. For example, the monthly production quantities of each model of the items to be produced are set and then daily production quantities are computed. From these data the plant manager determines the cycle time, or the amount of time that elapses between identical units coming off the production line. The plant management uses this information to compute the amounts and types of parts and materials and labor required each hour.

MINIMIZE SETUP TIMES. Uniform plant loading allows plant managers to focus on small daily production lots. However, it can also mean that in one day a plant must produce several models—say sedans, coupes, and convertibles—requiring several machinery setups and changes. Many JIT-based Japanese firms therefore use industrial engineering and behavioral science methods to reduce machinery changeover times. For example, a well-trained team might be able to change the tooling on an 800-ton press in 10 minutes in Japan, a job that might take six hours in the United States and four hours in Germany.[45] Superior training, commitment, and the use of self-management are some of the factors accounting for the JIT firm's looser setup times.

BUILD EMPLOYEE COMMITMENT AND TEAMWORK. The productivity and quality improvements obtained by JIT firms require committed employees and teamwork. This commitment depends in part on a strong value of "respect for people" instilled in these firms, as well as on such things as creating a sense of community, as we've seen.

Organizational Behavior in Action

IMPLEMENTING JIT IN AMERICA

When Dana Corporation managers traveled to Japan to see just-in-time (JIT) manufacturing processes in action, some of the Japanese businesspeople told them they didn't think most U.S. workers would ever excel at it. Americans, they were told, were terrific innovators but made poor team members. JIT methods ran contrary to the typical individualistic company culture in the United States, and changing culture is difficult, Dana's managers were told.

Upon their return, the managers did discover that implementing the components of JIT was easier said than done. Management leadership, employee education, eliminating waste, cellular manufacturing, Kanban pull systems, quick changeover and computer-aided design (discussed in the next section) were all sound principles. But, as Dana managers discovered, to make them work together, they first had to win the hearts and minds of both supervisors and employees by getting them as committed to JIT as the managers were themselves.

Dana began at its Minneapolis valve plant. A vision of what the JIT manufacturing system could be was explained to every employee. The reasons behind the changes—intense competition and the need for improved quality, productivity, and responsiveness—were spelled out. Plant leaders made clear their own commitment to carrying through on the required changes in the plants' systems and procedures. Everyone was to participate in continuing education and be expected to actively support his or her respective team.

Contrary to (and perhaps because of) their Japanese hosts' warnings, Dana managers made work teams the driving force of the entire JIT implementation, and built their teams on a sense of commitment to what the firm was doing. The transformation was neither painless nor easy. But despite those dire predictions, Dana's Minneapolis valve plant was awarded the Shingo Prize for excellence in manufacturing, thanks in large part to its successful implementation of JIT.[46] ■

Computer-Aided Design and Computer-Aided Manufacturing

Computer-aided design (CAD) is a computerized process for designing new products or modifying existing ones. Designers actually sketch and modify their designs on a computer screen, usually with an electronic pencil. CAD is very beneficial: It facilitates the actual design of the item, makes it easier to modify existing products, and lets designers expose their designs to simulated stresses such as wind resistance.

Computer-aided manufacturing (CAM) uses computers to plan and program the production equipment. For example, CAM allows for computerized control of tool movement and cutting speed so that a machine can carry out several sequential operations on a part, all under the guidance of the computer-assisted system.

CAD and CAM are often used together. For example, with the design already in place within the CAD system, the computer "knows" a component's specifications and can thereby "tell" the production equipment how to cut and machine it.

Automated quality control testing at Hewlett-Packard

Automation and Robotics

Automation can be defined as the automatic operation of a system, process, or machine. A robot is a programmable machine capable of manipulating items and designed to move materials, parts, or specialized devices through programmed motions.

The accompanying photos suggest the range of applications for automation today. The first shows automated quality-control testing at Hewlett-Packard in Grenoble, France. The next shows automated process control at Warren Papers in Michigan; here a worker monitors an automated process-control system, which controls a system that produces paper from wet pulp to the finished product.

Managing Change

FLEXIBLE MANUFACTURING SYSTEMS

In many firms today flexible manufacturing systems are at the heart of managing change. A **flexible manufacturing system (FMS)** is "a system in which groups of production machines are connected by automated materials-handling and transfer

Automated production
process control at Warren
Papers

machines, and integrated into a computer system."[47] Computers route parts and
components to the appropriate machines, select and load the proper machine tools,
and then direct the machines to perform the required operations. The items are then
moved from machine to machine by computerized automated guided vehicles
(AGV). These form a computer-guided cart system that picks up and delivers tools
and parts from multiple workstations.

Several things combine to provide a flexible manufacturing system with its flexibility: Machine setup times are reduced by computerized instructions; each machine
can be quickly retooled to produce a variety of parts; reduced setup times cut
required manufacturing lead times; automated guided vehicles move parts with relative speed and efficiency; and the firm can respond more quickly to new competing products or changing consumer tastes by using CAD to redesign products and
CAM to reprogram its machines. In fact, says Toshiba President Funio Sato, the aim
of flexible manufacturing at his firm "is to push Toshiba's two dozen factories to
adapt faster to markets ... customers wanted choices. They wanted a washing
machine or TV set that was precisely right for their needs. We needed variety, not
mass production."[48]

SOME EXAMPLES. Flexible manufacturing lets Toshiba and other firms combine
the advantages of customized, one-at-a-time production with mass production's
efficiency. At the Toshiba plant in Ome, Japan, for instance, workers efficiently

assemble nine word processor models on one line and 20 laptop computer models on another.[49] Such flexibility lets Toshiba be very responsive to customer requirements.

The National Bicycle Industrial Company, a subsidiary of electronics giant Matsushita, is another example.[50] With only 20 employees, National Bicycle's factory can produce more than a million variations of 18 bicycle models, each custom-made to a customer's unique requirements. At the retail store, the customer sits on a special frame, and the shopkeeper measures him or her and faxes the person's measurements to the factory. There the information goes into a computer-assisted design system, which creates a computerized blueprint for the custom-made bike. A bar code is printed for the bike and each of its parts, and from there on every part that goes into the bicycle moves from workstation to workstation on computerized automated guided vehicles.

Firms like General Motors are taking further advantage of their increasingly flexible facilities by running them on round-the-clock schedules. For example, instead of closing GM's unprofitable Lordstown, Ohio, assembly plant, managers there boosted output from 260,000 to 400,000 cars a year by running the plant all night; the goal was recently raised to 450,000 cars a year.[51]

As these examples show, flexible manufacturing's goal is not just developing adaptable production processes, but maximizing the responsiveness of the whole company—including its sales effort—to customer demand. ■

Computer-Integrated Manufacturing (CIM)

Many firms aim to integrate automation, JIT, flexible manufacturing, and CAD/CAM into one self-regulating production system. **Computer-integrated manufacturing (CIM)**, defined as the total integration of all production-related business activities through the use of computer systems,[52] gives the firm a manufacturing competitive advantage based on speed, flexibility, quality, and low cost. This process is summarized in Figure 17.14.

CIM's advantages usually exceed that of the sum of its component parts. In other words, CIM can yield synergistic results. For example, computer-aided design facilitates computer-aided manufacturing by feeding design changes directly to the machinery tools. Automated guided vehicles can facilitate just-in-time systems by eliminating human variabilities from the system.[53]

Eventually, some firms link CIM with their other systems. Caterpillar, Inc., is working on a computer system that will link its plants, suppliers, and dealers into a worldwide electronic information network that will help make the firm one of the most efficient producers of earth-moving equipment. As part of its plan, the firm is junking its existing production methods in favor of a flexible manufacturing system aimed at cutting Caterpillar's manufacturing costs by 20 percent, which amounts to about $1.5 billion a year.[54]

Why is an integrated approach important? As one Japanese executive put it, "In the past, manufacturing was characterized by large (production run) quantities, with few varieties. Today's customers are asking for small quantities in very many varieties. CIM adds flexibility to help make those very short production runs economical."[55] CIM can thus be an essential part of managing change.

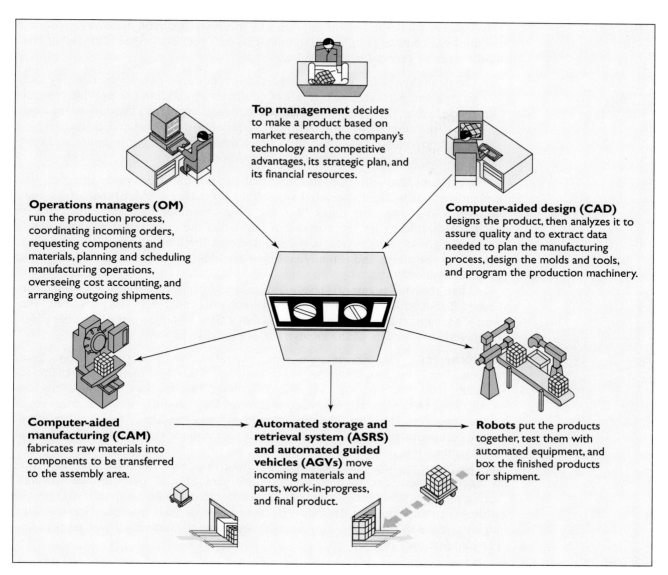

FIGURE 17.14   The Elements of Computer-Integrated Manufacturing (CIM)

SOURCE: *Principles of Operations Management*: 2/E by Render/Heizer, © 1997. Reprinted by permission of Prentice-Hall, Inc., Upper Saddle River, NJ.

Organizational Behavior in Action

COMBINING COMPUTERS AND PEOPLE TO BUILD FLEXIBILITY

Unfortunately, many CIM installations fail. Some companies spend millions of dollars installing computer-integrated manufacturing systems, only to discover that their plants are no more productive or flexible than they were before CIM.

A recent study sheds some light on why this is so. The main discovery concerned the important role of people—both managers and operators. Specifically, what Harvard Professor David Upton found was that

> The flexibility of the plants depended much more on people than on any technical factor. Although high levels of computer integration can provide critically needed advantages in quality and cost competitiveness, all the data in my study point to one conclusion: operational flexibility is determined primarily by a plant's operators and the extent to which managers cultivate, measure, and communicate with them. Equipment and computer integration are secondary.[56]

Specifically, Professor Upton found that the degree of computer integration in a plant was not in itself associated with either producing a wider range of products or improved changeover times. "Indeed, even computer hardware and software designed specifically for the purpose of improving the changeover process, such as automatic grade-change systems, did not decrease the time required to make grade changes in the plants and actually inhibited the ability of plants to produce a broad range of grades."[57]

After studying many of these manufacturing facilities, Professor Upton's conclusion is that building flexibility requires combining computers and people. In other words, trying to computerize a plant or install a CIM system is probably futile unless the behavioral aspects of the change are attended to as well.

AN EXAMPLE. The experience of paper manufacturer Mead Corporation's Escanaba mill, in Escanaba, Michigan, is an example.[58] Like most managers in the paper industry, Escanaba's managers had long assumed that the key to competitiveness was to achieve the lowest possible costs through long production runs and few product changeovers. However, like managers in industries suddenly faced with international competition, they had to rethink their assumptions and find new ways to beat their competitors.

The answer, they decided, was to be more responsive to customers than their competitors were, and their successful implementation of computerized manufacturing provides some insights into the right way to combine computers and people with the goal of building flexibility. Because some of their machines were already highly computer-integrated, they knew that computerization itself was no panacea. Here's what they did:

- They replaced their existing computer systems with a new system called Quality and Information for Decisions. "The system was designed from the outset to help workers make better decisions rather than to cut them out of the decision making process."[59] The system (nicknamed QUPID) was custom designed to support the machine operators who actually ran the manufacturing process. They would be free to make production changes depending on what they saw happening on the production line.
- From the outset, the plant's managers insisted that operators be very much involved in the system's design and development.
- The plant managers saw to it that the computer system was designed mostly in-house. In particular, the people at each work function in the plant designed their own computer interface to ensure that operators got the information they felt they needed to do their jobs, and in the format that was easiest for them to understand.
- Management spent a great deal of time designing and redesigning its training programs. For example, they created one training program to help

workers understand what they had to do to satisfy customers. "The program explained why quick changeovers were critical to the mill's long-term success. And it emphasized that the systems were only a tool to help them perform their jobs better. Operators who had long assumed that keeping the machines running was all that mattered began to look at their work differently."[60]

■ Managers set up a new measurement and incentive system. For example, current measures and incentives aimed at maximizing capacity utilization and output and at minimizing costs were deemphasized. Measures and incentives aimed at maximizing responsiveness and customer satisfaction were emphasized.

■ Each year the plant surveys customers to identify what it is doing well and how it needs to improve. A team drawn from managers and employees throughout the plant then uses this survey to generate specific operating goals: "For example, the team might challenge Escanaba to reduce changeover losses by 25 percent within six months."[61]

The program has apparently been highly successful. The plant's responsiveness and customer satisfaction have increased dramatically, and the plant recently sold the most paper in its history. Escanaba is now the most productive mill in Mead's fine-paper group and has dramatically increased its market share. This plant's experience and results underscore the necessity of combining computers and people when a plant sets out to computerize in order to build flexibility. ■

Mass Customization

A customer can now walk into a Levi's Jeans store, have computer and optical equipment take his or her measurements, and get a new custom-made set of Levi's "mass produced-priced" Personal Pairs jeans within a few days. The philosophy behind the Levi's program is called **mass customization:** it means designing, producing and delivering products in such a way that customers get customized products for at or near the cost and convenience of mass produced items.[62]

Companies like Hewlett-Packard make good use of mass customizing for products such as computers, printers, and medical equipment.[63] At Hewlett-Packard, for instance, mass customization is built on three building blocks, as follows:

1. *Modular product design.* Products consist of independent modules, so they can be assembled into different forms of the product easily. For example, instead of designing its printers with standard power supplies, they're designed to have a separate power supply inserted later, so customers around the globe can get the power they need.

2. *Modular process design.* Similarly, production is designed to be performed in modules or parts. That's the heart of the Levi's Personal Pairs program: They're designed at the store, sewn at the factory, and picked up back at the store.

3. *Agile supply networks.* The whole chain from production to distribution is designed to be flexible. For example, some companies now let their warehouses do some light, last-minute product assembly. That way a customer can really be sure of getting quick service on just the product he or she needs. The right product modules (like the printer's power supply) is simply added at the last minute before the product is shipped.

SUMMARY

1. Operations management is the process of managing the resources required to produce an organization's goods and services. The direct production resources of a firm are often called the five P's of operations and production management: people, plants, parts, processes, and planning and control systems.

2. Any production system consists of inputs, a conversion system, and outputs. Inputs are the primary resources used in the direct manufacture of the product or service. The conversion system converts those inputs into useful products or services called outputs.

3. The production system is the heart of the operation. Four production design system decisions include the facility or plant location, the type of production processes that will be used, the layout of the plant or facility, and the layout of the production system itself.

4. Production planning is the process of deciding what products to produce, and where, when, and how to produce them. Production control is the process of ensuring that the specified production plans or schedules are being met. Several elements make up the production planning and control process: aggregate output planning, master production scheduling, material requirements planning, and shop floor control.

5. The production schedule is often presented on a chart that shows specifically what operations are to be carried out and when. Network planning and control methods are used to plan and control projects, usually by graphically representing the project steps and the timing and interrelationships between these steps. Purchasing departments buy the materials and parts the firm needs to conduct its business.

6. Inventory management ensures that the firm has adequate inventories of all parts and supplies needed, within the constraint of minimizing total inventory costs. Many quantitative and nonquantitative systems are available for managing inventory; ABC and EOQ systems are two of the most popular.

7. Quality reflects how well a product or service meets customer needs. Many firms use a process called designing for manufacturability to improve quality. Quality control in many firms today involves a total, companywide effort. A number of quality-control techniques are used to monitor and control product quality, including inspection procedures and acceptance sampling.

8. World-class companies can compete based on quality, productivity, and responsiveness in an intensely competitive global environment. World-class manufacturers use modern production techniques and progressive management systems to boost manufacturing productivity, quality, and flexibility. These production techniques and management systems include total quality management, just-in-time manufacturing, computer-aided design and manufacturing, automation and robotics, flexible manufacturing systems, computer-integrated manufacturing, and mass customization.

KEY TERMS

operations management
inputs
conversion system
outputs
intermittent production
mass production
continuous production
facility layout
product layout
process layout
fixed-position layout
cellular manufacturing
production planning
production control
aggregate output planning
master production
    scheduling (MPS)
material requirements
    planning (MRP)
bills of material
shop floor control
loading and sequencing
load schedule

expediting
Gantt chart
network planning and
    control methods
events
activities
critical path
inventory management
ordering or setup costs
acquisition costs
inventory-holding costs
stockout costs
economic order quantity
    (EOQ)
quality
ISO 9000
total quality management
    (TQM) program
Malcolm Baldrige Award
benchmarking
acceptance sampling
designing for
    manufacturability

concurrent engineering
world-class companies
world-class manufacturers
just-in-time (JIT)
lean manufacturing
value-added
    manufacturing
jidoka
Kanban
uniform plant loading
computer-aided design
    (CAD)
computer-aided
    manufacturing (CAM)
automation
flexible manufacturing
    system (FMS)
computer-integrated
    manufacturing (CIM)
mass customization

SELF-TEST

TRUE / FALSE QUESTIONS

1 T F Operations management is the process of managing organizational resources for goal attainment.

2 T F Production is the most important P in the five P's of operations management.

3 T F There needs to be a harmony between the competitive and production strategies.

4 T F There are two broad types of production processes: intermittent and final.

5 T F The letters PERT stand for a popular network planning and control method: Personal Evaluation Report Technique.

6 T F ABC is a type of incentive management.

7 T F The quality standards of the European Community (EC) are the ISO 9000.

8 T F The Japanese are credited with inventing TQM.

9 T F We call companies world-class manufacturers when they use modern production techniques and management systems to promote productivity, quality, and flexibility

10 T F Jidoka means quality at the source, that is, "stop everything when something goes wrong."

MULTIPLE-CHOICE QUESTIONS

1 Which of the following is *not* one of the five P's of operations management?
   a. people
   b. plants
   c. planning
   d. plotting

2 A good example of mass production is _____.
   a. batch production
   b. assembly-line production
   c. team production
   d. cluster production

3 Material requirements planning, or MRP, is a type of plan that is _____.
   a. hand calculated
   b. computer based
   c. slide-rule bound
   d. none of the above

4 One of the best-known production scheduling devices presented on a chart that specifically shows what operations are to be done and when is the _____ chart.
   a. Taylor
   b. Weber
   c. Deming
   d. Gantt

5 CPM, or _____, is a popular network planning and control method.
   a. critical path method
   b. critical planning method
   c. complete planning method
   d. comprehensive plants model

6 Purchasing departments can affect both the firm's cost-effectiveness and its ___ reputation.
   a. quantity
   b. just-in-time
   c. quality
   d. personnel

7 _____ measures how well a product or service meets customer needs.
   a. Quality
   b. Culture
   c. Inventory
   d. Materials

8 Deming recommends as one of his 14 points that in a long-term relationship with a supplier firms move beyond _____ to _____.
   a. trust; money
   b. loyalty; price
   c. price; trust
   d. price; buy-in partnership

9 What traditional numerical measure would Deming remove on the factory floor?
   a. quality measures
   b. quotas
   c. total quantity measures
   d. cost

10 Among the tools used by teams of employees who monitor quality problems is a _____.
   a. fishbone diagram
   b. shotgun chart
   c. military maneuver
   d. design diagram

CRITICAL THINKING EXERCISES

1 When W. Edwards Deming and John Juran advised U.S. companies soon after World War II, their ideas about TQM and JIT inventory were largely ignored. Unable to make managers here listen to their message, they and other quality experts went to Japan, which was rebuilding after losing the war. There the managers, from CEOs on down, listened. Not until the 1980s did Deming's or Juran's ideas break through in the United States. Why do you think it took so long? What have been some of the consequences of ignoring Deming's 14 points?

2 Quality has become the watchword of the 1990s. Why is it such an important issue now, when it was not thought so important 20 years ago?

EXPERIENTIAL EXERCISES

1 Design a PERT chart for building a quality program for the School of Business at your university, working in a team of five.

2 Go to the library on campus, or a food service, or the career planning center. Observe how they operate, then write up a description of actual operations, making recommendations based on this chapter to improve their quality.

DIVERSITY CASE

BYPASSING THE PHONE RIGHT TO A VOICE PAGER IN CHINA

In a China market of 1.2 billion people, fewer than one in 20 people have a phone, while an astonishing one in 71 have a pager. Sinoamerican Telecom, with revenues of $12 million and 130 employees, has done well in China. The pager it sells allows you to receive a short voice message in Chinese without the aid of a telephone.

Allen Yuen, who invented the new pager, worked for ITT as an electrical engineer and then started his own factory in one of China's Shenzen economic zones just across from Hong Kong. The People's Liberation Army, which operates what is probably the largest collection of businesses in China, turned out to be his biggest customer. Yuen needs $30 million worth of equipment to build his Chinese network, so while the prospects are great, so are the challenges.

Questions
1 What issues of control would Yuen need to be careful about in terms of production and operations because of the fact that he is manufacturing in China?
2 Would Deming's 14 points translate well in China?
3 What potential quality problems might Yuen face?

SOURCES: Louis Kraar, "A World of Cool Companies," *Fortune*, 28 October 1996, 162–8; Irene Yeung and Rosalie Tung, "The Importance of Guanxi (Connections)," *Organizational Dynamics* (Autumn 1996): 54–65.

STRATEGY CASE

CAN UNIONS AND MANAGEMENT COOPERATE?

As unions have started to lose membership in the traditional production trades, they have pursued a strategy of embracing partnerships with management to boost productivity. At Aluminum Co. of America, which makes products for the packaging industry, there has been a big change in the traditional way of managing production since 1994. That year the International Association of Machinists union (IAM), representing 170 of the workers at the Denver plant, asked to help create a high-performance work system. Union leaders and management attended union-sponsored training in Maryland to help build partnerships, spur productivity, and in the process protect jobs.

To meet their goal of protecting workers' jobs and pay by making employees more productive, unions want more say in how work is accomplished and how companies are run. In line with that, the steelworkers persuaded major steel makers to appoint a union-designated board of directors member and to train union leaders in business skills so they can sit on union/management councils.

Questions
1 What tools discussed in the chapter would help the union better implement its new union-management strategy?
2 Do you think unions and management can work together in industries where there has been a history of acrimony, such as the auto and airline industries?
3 Should unions have decision-making power over the quality and production issues of a business? Why?

SOURCE: Aaron Berstein, "Look Who's Pushing Productivity," *Business Week*, 7 April 1997, 72–5.

ENTREPRENEURIAL CASE

A DO-IT-YOURSELF FACTORY WITH START-UP CAPITAL OF $500

Tom Buschman seized an opportunity and capitalized on it with old-fashioned hard work. In 1978 his employer, paper manufacturer Avery International, was experiencing a 50 percent failure rate for metering rods, critical components of the paper-coating system. So Buschman said he could produce a better rod and Avery said it would buy it.

With very little money, but a knack for machinery, Buschman scoured junkyards in his off hours to find the material to construct a little factory. Within a few months he was selling Avery rods with just a 2 percent failure rate. Then he quit his job and started to advertise. It wasn't easy at first. Buschman labored in the basement and his wife did the books. Then he expanded to a rundown house that he fixed almost single-handedly.

Today he employs 20 people. His 1994 revenues were $2.7 million, and he still builds his machinery in-house.

Questions

1 What could large firms having quality problems learn from Tom Buschman?
2 What techniques in this chapter can Buschman consider using to expand his company?
3 What kind of dialogue might W. Edwards Deming and Tom Buschman have on work and quality?

_____

SOURCE: "Started with $1,000 or Less," *Inc.,* August 1995, 32–3.

THE BUSINESS TEAM, INC.

AFTERMATH OF THE 1996 OLYMPICS FOR VENDORS

Before the Olympics arrived in Atlanta in the summer of 1996, many vendors had dollar signs in their eyes. In addition to their high hopes for revenue from the Games, they also banked on the redevelopment of Atlanta to continue once the Olympic torch had been extinguished. But small business can be a hard business. Take Bill, an old friend of Len's from high school days. Bill was not interested in college. Instead, he decided to make his fortune in the bagel business. His grandfather and his father had both been bakers in the East, and Bill decided to move their traditions to the South in the form of Bill's Bagel Works.

During the Olympics, business boomed. Before that, business had been expanding so rapidly that Bill called the Business Team for some quick advice. Production and operations were the areas where he needed the most help, so Hal gave him some advice over the phone (Bill's budget could not stretch to the full Team's consulting fees).

Bill took Hal's advice and streamlined production by diverting some of his profits back into the business in new state-of-the-art equipment. Technology was now his friend. He used it where he thought it could improve production and service. While the Olympics were in Atlanta, Bill and his quickly expanding crew had no time to think about the human impact of the new technology. They were just grateful for the tremendous business they were handling.

Now the Olympics are over and the immense crowds are gone. Business is down and Bill has had to lay off half the crew. The remaining workers fear for their jobs if things get any slower, and Bill has decided he can purchase more technology to rid himself of overhead, that is, the workers. He's not sure the market warrants the investment, however.

Bill has called his old friend Len again and asked that the Team come in at a reduced fee and give him some advice.

Questions

1 What advice do you think the multi-function Business Team should give Bill?
2 How would you recommend that Bill handle his employees' concerns about technology displacement?
3 What people strategies might you suggest to Bill before technological changes are put in place?

KNITMEDIA GETS THE PRODUCTS OUT FASTER

By its nature, leading edge, avant-garde music has a fickle audience, so that what is popular today may not be popular next week. The company, therefore, shares a challenge with many manufacturing companies who have to ensure that they can design, develop, and introduce a new product fast, since (as in industries such as computer chips and personal computers) the whole life cycle of a new product may be less than one year.

KnitMedia's management, therefore, intends to employ a very short new-product development cycle in an attempt to offer consumers the products they desire when they are desired. KnitMedia's people really have to "keep their ears to the ground" to identify new trends: As new trends arise, their product development (identifying and signing a band, recording their records, promoting them, and so on) then has to be super-swift. It's apparent to Michael Dorf and his colleagues that they share many of the challenges facing managers in manufacturing companies, who have instituted state-of-the-art operations manage-

ment techniques to ensure fast development and introduction of products. KnitMedia's managers are relying on you to make recommendations to them regarding what state-of-the-art operations management techniques KnitMedia should use.

Team Exercises and Questions:
Use what you learned in this chapter to answer the following question:

l In this chapter, we discussed a number of world-class manufacturing methods including just-in-time systems and computer-aided design and computer-aided manufacturing. Based on your knowledge of the techniques in this chapter and on a review of what KnitMedia's larger competitors are doing, develop a report for Michael Dorf explaining how KnitMedia can use world-class operations management techniques to shorten product development cycle times and get their products out faster.

For the online version of this case, visit our Web site at: <www.prenhall.com>.

For Internet exercises, interactive study questions, news updates and more, visit the Dessler Web site at

www.prenhall.com/desslermgmt

If you're using the CD-ROM that accompanies this text, simply click on the "Web Site" button to access the site.

APPENDIX

Managing Services

THE CHALLENGE OF SERVICE MANAGEMENT

It's likely that after college you will go to work for a service firm. The number of people employed in goods-producing industries (including manufacturing, construction, mining, and agriculture) will stay about the same—at about 27.6 million people—through the year 2000. But the number of people employed in service-producing industries is exploding, from about 51.5 million in 1972 to about 75 million in 1990. By 2000 almost 96 million people will work in service-producing industries like transportation, communications, wholesale and retail trade, finance and insurance, government, and in the legal, educational, and health sectors. In fact, just about every new job added in the U.S. economy over the next few years will be in service-producing industries. Currently, about 75 percent of the people working are employed in the service-producing sector. Managing services is therefore going to be quite a "growth industry" itself.

Organizational Behavior in Action

EMPOWERMENT HELPS SAS TAKE OFF

When it comes to managing services, few people equal the exploits of Jan Carlson, president of Sweden's Scandinavian Airlines System (SAS). Taking over the airline in 1980 (at the relatively young age of 39), Carlson spent the next decade building it into a world-class competitor using top-notch service as the airline's competitive edge.[1]

Carlson had inherited an undistinguished, unprofitable airline during a period in which the world economy was being pummeled by the second oil shock. His airline had already lost money two years running and was pointing nose down toward an imminent crash landing. Due to relatively high wage rates, Carlson knew he had no chance to compete with other airlines based on low prices.

Carlson's greatest insight was recognizing that his country's reputation for high-quality products meant he could make high-quality service the centerpiece of his airline's turnaround strategy. He decided to reposition SAS as the airline of choice for business travelers and to focus all his people's efforts on boosting the quality of service travelers would get.

Carlson's service management effort at SAS was a companywide approach to maximizing the quality of service for service-conscious business travelers. Carlson and his staff had first-class cabins removed on most flights; they replaced them with enlarged business-class service so that more businesspeople could afford to travel in plush, leather-lined style. To make sure these business travelers kept coming back, Carlson and his people had meeting after meeting with employees emphasizing the importance of treating the customers right. Carlson even coined the term "the moments of truth," by which he meant all the key points at which a traveling customer interacts with an SAS employee or activity. Carlson emphasized to employees that the traveler's overall perception of the quality of service he or she was getting would be molded by all these moments of truth (such as when a hassled passenger got some extra friendly help during check-in).

THE ROLE OF EMPOWERMENT. Carlson knew, though, that to get his employees to provide such top-notch service, he had to give them the power to carry out their jobs. For example, what good would it do to encourage an SAS ticket agent to smile and try to be friendly to a traveler who was going to miss her plane anyway because the agent hadn't the power to reroute her or to write a new ticket? Carlson therefore empowered his employees, granting them much broader authority to do things like write new tickets than other airline employees ever had.

To do this he had to make many of the SAS systems more customer oriented. For example, the procedures had to be changed to allow clerks to give vouchers to disgruntled passengers, or to let flight attendants distribute free drinks if their planes were delayed. On the ground, new systems had to be instituted to speed up check-ins at the airport and to make business facilities (like fax machines) more widely available for traveling customers. Boosting customer service required, in other words, a multifaceted approach. ▪

SERVICE MANAGEMENT DEFINED. This example illustrates why Karl Albrecht, a famous service management expert, defines service management as "a total organizational approach that makes quality of service, as perceived by the customer, the number one driving force for the operation of the business."[2]

Service management thus means more than just managing a service firm. Certainly, Jan Carlson was a service manager insofar as he was the president of SAS, which is a service firm. But "service management" also means managing an enterprise (whether it is a service firm like SAS or a manufacturing firm like Honda) in such a way that *quality of service* becomes the basic standard for evaluating everything the company does or should do.

WHY SERVICE MANAGEMENT IS IMPORTANT

Service management is important because of the intense global competition all enterprises face today. As we've explained throughout this book, deregulation and the growth of global competitors have increased the level of competition for virtually all companies and organizations. That means everyone has to fight harder for customers than ever before. Therefore, service management is important today for at least three specific reasons:

SERVICE IS A COMPETITIVE ADVANTAGE. Back in chapter 6 ("Strategic Management"), we explained that one way for a company to compete is to differentiate its product or service by creating something that is perceived as unique.[3] Many firms today differentiate themselves, at least in part, on customer service. For example, Mercedes-Benz North America offers its customers an 800 number they can call 24 hours a day, seven days a week if they need road assistance. Crown Cork and Seal custom-builds a can manufacturing plant near each of its major customers, thereby providing customized services for each one of them. Microsoft provides a 24-hour telephone help line.

BAD SERVICE LEADS TO LOST CUSTOMERS. Good service is also important because companies never hear from most of their dissatisfied customers; they just lose them.

This point is illustrated by a series of studies undertaken by the Technical Assistance Research Program, Inc. (TARP), in Washington, D.C.[4] TARP found that the average business never even hears from 96 percent of its unhappy customers. In other words, if four people complain to a company, there are probably another 96 or so unhappy customers who don't. However, TARP also found that while the company may not hear from these unhappy customers directly, they are out there spreading the word nevertheless. Each of them will tell an average of nine or ten people about the problems that they had with the firm. So in addition to reducing its competitive edge, bad service will siphon off many of the firm's current and potential customers.

CUSTOMER DEFECTIONS DRAIN PROFITS. Effective service management is also crucial because in most industries the longer a firm keeps a customer, the more profit it stands to make from that customer.[5]

There are three reasons for this. First, long-term customers tend to spend more than new customers. Second, they tend to generate profits in other ways, such as referrals. Third, customers generally become more profitable over time. For example, it usually costs a credit card company about $51 to recruit a new customer. If that customer then stays only about a year and uses the card once or twice before leaving in disgust over an error on her bill, the credit card company might not even earn back the $51 acquisition cost. On the other hand, if the company can keep that customer for several years, her value to the company rises because the customer generates a profit in each of those years through credit card fees.

Why Managing Services Is a Special Challenge

Managing services is especially challenging because it's different from managing the creation of tangible products.[6] First, a service is generally created the instant it is used; it cannot be produced and held in stock awaiting demand. Second, most services are provided with little or no supervision. Usually no production supervisor or quality-control clerk is hovering around the arrogant waiter who ruins a customer's meal, for example.

KARL ALBRECHT'S SERVICE TRIANGLE

The actual techniques of service management focus on three core concepts: the moment of truth, service cycles, and the service triangle.[7]

The Moment of Truth

The core concept in service management is the **moment of truth,** which service management expert Karl Albrecht defines as "that precise instant when the customer comes into contact with any aspect of your business and, on the basis of that contact, forms an opinion about the quality of your service and, potentially, the quality of your product."[8]

The moment of truth plays a central role in service management because it is, as Albrecht says, "the basic atom of service, the smallest indivisible unit of value delivered to the customer."[9] When you as a customer call Federal Express or go to a movie or theater or supermarket, you experience moments of truth—precise instants when you come into contact with any aspect of the business. On the basis of those accumulated moments of truth you then form an opinion about the quality of the service you have received and, potentially, about the quality of the product as well.

For example, here are some typical moments of truth in a supermarket shopping experience:

1. You look for a place to park in the supermarket's lot.
2. You walk to the supermarket from your car.
3. You look for a shopping cart.
4. You get your check approved.
5. You ask a clerk how to find a product.
6. You pick up your item.
7. You wait in the checkout line.
8. Your order is added up.
9. Your items are placed in the bag.
10. You take your purchases back to your car.

This is a simplified example, of course, but consider how many opportunities the supermarket's management has to create a good (or bad) service quality impression with you. In fact, if your supermarket were really interested in improving quality, it would have to manage the service experience in such a way that each of those moments of truth proved to be as positive an experience as possible. How might management do this? By taking actions like reducing waiting time at the checkout lines, expediting the check approval process, and ensuring that stock clerks are ready and eager to answer your questions.

One of the main points service management experts like Albrecht make is that when the moments of truth go unmanaged, the quality of service quickly declines. In other words, if the supermarket manager does not actually sit down and consider what his or her customer's typical moments of truth are and then see to it that they are positive, they will likely be unhappy experiences. And for the supermarket (or almost any other business, for that matter), the accumulation of negative experiences embodied by the bad moments of truth will undermine the customer's perceptions of the quality of the service of the firm.

In today's highly competitive world, that could be deadly. To take our supermarket example, management may stock the shelves with the finest products and perhaps even offer competitive prices. But if the moments of truth go unmanaged and the customer's experience is sufficiently bad, the market will lose out to its competitors down the road.

The Cycle of Service

Albrecht therefore suggests thinking of the organization's moments of truth in terms of a **cycle of service.** Start with the first instance in which a customer comes into contact with any aspect of the organization, and then proceed through every other contact.

The manager and his or her team will want to map out a cycle of service for three reasons. First, by carefully thinking through each contact from beginning to end, they can identify a complete list of all the moments of truth. Second, once identified, the most critical moments of truth can be focused on. Finally, with a list of moments of truth (and particularly the critical ones), management can turn to actually managing the service experience. But such service management also means creating a service strategy and attending to the service people and the service system. We discuss these elements next.

The Service Triangle

Albrecht says it's useful to think of a successful service management effort in terms of a triangle, as presented in Figure 17A.1. As you can see, three key factors form the corners of the service triangle:

1. a vision, or strategy, for the service effort
2. customer-oriented front-line people
3. customer-friendly systems[10]

Service management experts know these three factors must work together to achieve service quality. Here's how Albrecht describes each of them:

A well-conceived strategy for service. The outstanding organizations have discovered, invented, or evolved a unifying idea about what they do. This service concept, or service strategy ... directs the attention of the people in the organization toward the real priorities of the customer. This guiding concept finds its way into all that people do. It becomes a rallying cry, ... and the nucleus of the message to be transmitted to the customer. For example, McDonald's focuses on "quality, service, cleanliness, and price."

Customer-oriented front-line people. By some means the managers of such organizations have [also] encouraged and helped the people who deliver the service to keep their attention fastened on the needs of the customer. ... This leads to a level of responsiveness, attentiveness, and willingness to help that marks the service as superior in the customer's mind and makes him or her want to tell others about it and then come back for more.

Customer-friendly systems. The delivery system that backs up the service people is truly designed for the convenience of the customer rather than the convenience of the organization. The physical facilities, policies, procedures, methods, and communication processes all say to the customer, "This apparatus is here to meet your needs."[11]

■ **FIGURE 17A.1**
Three Service Management Components
Successful service management means formulating an effective service strategy, creating customer-oriented front-line people, and then building customer-friendly systems.

SOURCE: Karl Albrecht and Ron Zemke, *Service America: Doing Business in the New Economy* (Homewood, IL: Dow Jones-Irwin, 1985), 41. © 1984 Karl Albrecht.

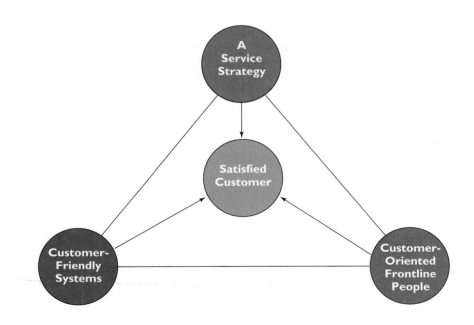

Jan Carlson and his efforts at SAS provide an example. Recall that on becoming CEO, Carlson decided to build SAS's competitive advantage around customer service. He therefore formulated a service strategy that aimed at giving business travelers the top-notch service for which they were willing to pay top-notch prices—the special business-class seats and service, for instance. But he knew that to implement his strategy, he had to modify both the people and the systems at SAS. For example, the SAS *people* had to be trained and retrained and empowered to cut through red tape to help the customers. In terms of the *systems,* Carlson had to eliminate first-class service, expand business-class service, institute new check-in systems for business customers, and install business equipment like fax machines that his customers could use.

FIVE STEPS IN IMPLEMENTING A SERVICE MANAGEMENT PROGRAM

What is the overall process involved in creating a service-oriented, customer-driven organization? Service management experts Karl Albrecht and Ron Zemke say it has five steps.[12]

Step 1: The Service Audit

The first step in making a company service oriented is to conduct a service audit, often using a **customer report card.** The customer report card lists the service attributes for which your customers are looking, as well as the relative weights or priorities of each attribute and how the customers score your company on each of them. If the information can be obtained, it's also useful to add your competitors' scores on each attribute for comparison purposes. One way to obtain the information required to compile the report card is to conduct in-depth interviews with a sample of the company's customers.[13]

An example of a report card for the Downtown Ten-Plex Movie Theater is presented in Table 17A.1. As you can see, the movie theater's customer research found eight service attributes that typical theatergoers look for in the Ten-Plex Theater. These service attributes include convenient parking, first-run movies, and a clean

■ TABLE 17A.1 Report Card for Downtown Ten-Plex Movie Theater

DESIRABLE SERVICE ATTRIBUTES	CUSTOMER PRIORITY	OUR SCORE (BASED ON AUDIT)
Convenient parking	High	Medium
Safe parking	High	Low
First-run movies	High	High
Clean theater	High	Medium
Unobstructed view	High	High
Comfortable seats	Medium	Medium
Courteous clerks	Low	Low
Short waits for tickets	Medium	Low

theater. In the next column, each of these attributes is given a priority ranking, to reflect the fact that some attributes are more important than others. For example, convenient parking, safe parking, and first-run movies are all high-priority services, while courteous clerks (although a significant service attribute) is rated lower. Finally, the customer report card includes a space called "Our Score" toward the right. Management can use this space to record how customers rated the Downtown Ten-Plex Movie Theater on each of these service attributes. While the report card for Ten-Plex does not include one, a column can be added on the right to list the competitors' scores. This can provide important information when formulating a service strategy for the Ten-Plex Theater.

Step 2: Strategy Development

The second step is to formulate a service strategy, which has been defined as "a distinctive formula for delivering service; such a strategy is keyed to a well-chosen benefit premise that's valuable to the customer and that establishes an effective competitive position."[14] In the simplest terms, the service strategy should answer the question "Why should the customer choose us?" It should be clear and brief enough to be easily communicated to and grasped by all the company's employees. McDonald's Corporation's strategic emphasis on "quality, service, cleanliness, and price" and Carlson's SAS strategy emphasizing "high-quality service for business travelers" are examples.

Step 3: Education

The next step in implementing a service program is to spread the gospel of service throughout the organization. As at companies like SAS, "wall-to-wall training" is often the method of choice here. This means doing short bursts of 100 percent participation training: A service management program is kicked off by bringing together every employee in the organization (perhaps in large groups). Everyone is trained at about the same time during a one- or two-day period.

Step 4: Implementation

The next phase is the "implementation of grass-roots improvements in the way the organization produces and delivers its service products."[15]

Several activities take place here. Service quality teams are often created, each of which serves as a source of specific recommendations on how to improve service and also functions as a conduit of information back to the departments. The application lab is another implementation technique. Here, a trainer (often a member of the firm's human resources department) is invited to meet with a department to discuss the group's service mission and to identify operational aspects that the department would like to improve. Other companies use service quality circles, small groups of employees who meet on a regular basis to identify and solve service problems. Useful tools include the service report card and an analysis of the moments of truth and the cycle of service.

The most important implementation activity is redesigning service systems using what you know about the moments of truth. For example, in one bank the system required that you stand in one line to get the check approved and then stand in a second, longer line to pick up your money. A system like this would undermine the customers' service experience even with the most service-oriented employees.

Redesigning service systems can involve many changes. Grass-roots improvements might include modifying: organizational structures, data systems (to avoid having to respond to customer concerns with "Sorry, the computer can't do that"), customer rules, and serial procedures (the actual sequence of steps the company uses to handle the customer's problem).

Step 5: Maintenance—Making the Change Permanent

Making the change permanent requires all your planning, organizing, leading, and controlling skills. For example, making high-quality service the norm means the firm must continually poll customers to ensure that the service attributes (such as speed of delivery) do not have to be revised, and to continually assess each attribute's relative importance. Employees need to be empowered and reminded that the customer comes first. Employee selection and training must be effective so that the emotionally laden customer-contact jobs are properly staffed. Top managers have to walk their talk and show by word and deed that they do take service seriously. Service standards must be set, performance measured, and rewards distributed to ensure that customer service remains top-notch. It requires, in other words, effective management.

KEY TERMS

moment of truth   service triangle
cycle of service   customer report card

CHAPTER 18

MANAGING CHANGE WITH INFORMATION TECHNOLOGY

What's Ahead?

When Jim McCann bought 1-800-FLOWERS, it was $7 million in debt and its expenses were much too high. Today the company is profitable, thanks in part to a new information system Jim had installed. Among other things, the computerized system cut order-processing time in half, let telephone sales reps see various floral arrangements, and linked the company's 2,500 participating florists. Now Jim has to decide how else the computer can help him stay competitive.

Jim McCann

Objectives

After studying this chapter, you should be able to

- **define** information technology and list the characteristics of good-quality information
- **explain** why managers at different organizational levels require different types of information
- **discuss** and give examples of information systems used by managers
- **define** telecommunication and illustrate its role in managing organizations
- **explain** how computerization and information technology can help managers manage change and compete more effectively.

MANAGEMENT ON THE WEB

INFORMATION TECHNOLOGY & PEOPLE

Information Technology & People is an online interdisciplinary, international journal covering social and organizational issues in the design and use of information technology. How could Jim McCann use this site? ■

http://www.mcb.co.uk/itp.htm

Management in the Information Age

As with 1-800-FLOWERS, companies needn't be high-tech businesses to profit from information technology. **Information technology** refers to any processes, practices, or systems that facilitate processing and transporting information. You are no doubt already very familiar with information technology's modern components. For example, you may use a personal computer and be familiar with management information systems from the work you do. You probably use cellular phones, facsimile machines, and the increasingly ubiquitous e-mail and voice-mail answering systems. Information technologies like these have dramatically altered the way people do their jobs and the way organizations are managed. How information technology affects managing is the subject of this chapter.

The Nature of Information

Information is data presented in a form that is meaningful to the recipient.[1] "Information," as Peter Drucker has said, "is data endowed with relevance and purpose."[2] Knowledge, on the other hand, has been defined as "information . . . distilled via study or research and augmented by judgment and experience."[3]

To put these definitions into managerial terms, consider this example. PepsiCo, Inc., wants to determine why consumers are not buying its new Pepsi Light clear drink. To search for an answer, the company's market researchers conduct a survey containing 25 multiple-choice questions. The answers to the questions are put on computer disks, where by themselves they would appear to the untrained eye as nothing but long streams of unrelated numbers.

When market researchers summarize this *data* for presentation to management, though, the result is *information,* such as graphs showing average responses by age level and other demographic traits for each question. The marketing department can then apply its *knowledge* to draw meaningful conclusions, such as, in PepsiCo's case, a hypothesis about why older consumers seem less inclined to purchase Pepsi Light than are younger ones.

What Is "Information Quality"

High-quality information has several characteristics.[4] As in the PepsiCo example, good information must be *pertinent* and related to the problem at hand. It must also be *timely.* For example, the Pepsi Light survey information would be useless if it came rolling in two years after the product was pulled off the shelf. Good information must also be *accurate,* and finally, good information reduces *uncertainty,* which we can define as the absence of information about a particular area of concern.[5] In the PepsiCo example, to meet these last criteria, the survey information should help the marketing manager answer the question "Why aren't people buying Pepsi Light the way we thought they would?"

Yet, even good information is relatively useless without the knowledge that comes from analysis, interpretation, and explanation.[6] Managers today are, if anything, deluged by information—on competitors' practices, consumers' buying habits, machinery breakdowns, and many other relevant issues. The role of organizational information technology is thus not just to generate and transfer more (or even better-quality) information. It is to contribute to the manager's knowledge of what is happening, through analysis, interpretation, and explanation.

DATA MINING. "Data mining" is one example.[7] This means using special computer software to analyze vast amounts of customer data stored in a company's data banks to obtain information the firm can use to be more competitive. When it comes to making decisions, managers usually don't want to be deluged by truckloads of numbers; they want to receive reports that let them see meaningful patterns and relationships. New data-mining software products like Intelligent Miner from IBM let them do just that. For example, like most phone companies, MCI Communications Corp. wants to keep its best customers. To do this, it's helpful to identify early those MCI customers who might be thinking of jumping to another long-distance carrier. But how do you screen telephone data on over 100 million households to try to find patterns in characteristics like lifestyle and past calling habits that may suggest the customer is a likely candidate for switching phone companies? In this case, MCI uses its IBM supercomputer and special data-mining software to analyze a set of 22 detailed and highly secret statistical profiles of customers to monitor the patterns that MCI believes can help identify customers' intentions.

Strategy in Action

USING INFORMATION TECHNOLOGY FOR STRATEGIC ADVANTAGE

Data mining is just one example of how companies today are using information technology to gain a strategic advantage against their competitors. Other examples are discussed below.[8]

HELPING UPS COMPETE GLOBALLY. UPS is the world's largest air and ground package distribution company, delivering close to three billion parcels and documents each year in the United States and over 185 countries abroad. Critical to its success has been the $1.8 billion UPS invested between 1992 and 1996 in information technology. UPS drivers use a hand-held computer called a Delivery Information Acquisition Device to capture customers' signatures along with pick-up, delivery, and time card information and automatically transmit this information back to headquarters via a cellular telephone network. Through TotalTrack, its automated

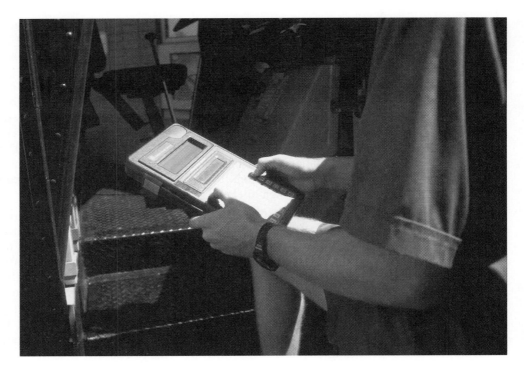

UPS's portable scanners relay information about each delivery back to headquarters via cellular phone linkups and allow the firm to monitor the whereabouts of every package it ships.

package-tracking system, UPS can monitor packages throughout the delivery process. And with its own global communication network called UPSnet, UPS not only tracks its packages but electronically transmits documentation on each shipment directly to customs officials prior to arrival. The shipments are, therefore, either cleared for shipment or flagged for inspection when they arrive. Soon, UPS expects to be able to intercept packages prior to delivery and have them returned or rerouted if necessary, and the company may even use its information technology systems to transmit electronic messages directly between customers.

NEW PRODUCTS FOR NEW STRATEGIES.   Other companies use information and information technology to create new products or services around which the firms create new strategies. In the late 1970s, for instance, Merrill Lynch, then the nation's largest retail brokerage firm, developed a new financial product called a Cash Management Account, based on a sophisticated proprietary software program. The Cash Management Account made it easy for customers to transfer money freely from stocks to bonds and to money market funds and to write checks against these funds cost-free. The flexibility provided by the Cash Management Account proved attractive to customers and helped Merrill Lynch change from the stock brokerage business to the financial services business.

Levi Strauss's new Personal Pairs program uses information technology to let customers design jeans to their own specifications, and could prove a key advantage for Levi-owned stores in the next few years.

In Arizona, entrepreneur Steve Wunsch has used a proprietary system to create a new computerized stock exchange. The exchange is an electronic, online stock auction where buyers and sellers can "meet" to buy and sell stocks at prices preset by Wunsch's computers. If it succeeds, Wunsch's system will be the first true online stock auction, where computers actually set a price that traders then bid for. (Existing electronic trading systems don't set specific target prices; they just let buyers and sellers list the prices for which they're willing to buy and sell.)[9] Look for it on the Arizona Stock Exchange (AZS) Web site, which went online in 1997.

And, of course, tens of thousands of companies are using the Internet to sell their products—a strategic change of major proportions for many companies. Wal-Mart and its competitors have begun to build massive online bazaars intended to lower operating costs and produce savings for the consumer, for instance.[10]

LOCK IN CUSTOMERS. Other companies are using information technology to lock in customers so they won't want to switch to competitors. For example, Baxter Health Care International, Inc. (which supplies almost two thirds of all products used by U.S. hospitals) uses a "stockless inventory" and ordering system to lock in its hospital customers. Terminals tied to Baxter's own computers are installed in hospitals, which can then easily place an order via direct telecommunications links. The system generates shipping, billing, and inventory information and informs customers via their hospital terminals what their estimated delivery dates will be.[11]

LOWERING COSTS. Other firms use information technology to help them compete as low-cost leaders. Wal-Mart, for instance, has grown in part because its "continuous replenishment system" uses point-of-sale cash registers to read bar codes and continuously update inventory information, and to notify suppliers when particular styles of specific products are going to be needed. Partly because of systems like these, Wal-Mart pays only 15% of sales revenue for overhead, compared with 30% for Sears and 21% for Kmart.[12]

Management's Requirement for Information

Managers at different levels in the organization require different types of information.[13] First-line managers (like Ford production supervisors or the front-desk manager at a Hilton Hotel) tend to focus on short-term, operational decisions. At this level, information should emphasize operational activities such as accounts receivables information, order entry information, inventory control information, and cash management information.

Middle managers tend to focus more on intermediate-range decisions, like those events that might affect the company in the coming year or so. They therefore require information for use in budget analysis, short-term forecasting, and variance analysis.

Top managers (including the CEO and the firm's top vice presidents) focus more on long-range, strategic decisions. They therefore need information that will enable them to make, for example, factory location decisions, merger and acquisition decisions, and new-product planning decisions. We will see in the next section that these different information requirements translate into requirements for different types of information systems at each level of the organization.

Information Systems for Managing Organizations

What Is an Information System?

An **information system** can be defined as a set of people, data, technology, and organizational procedures that work together to retrieve, process, store, and disseminate information to support decision making and control.[14] Specifically, we'll focus on *managerial* information systems, which are systems that support managerial decision making and control.

Information systems are more than computers. The information system also usually includes the organization or major parts of it, such as the employees who input data into the system and retrieve its output. Managers are (or should be) part of the information system, since it's their specific needs for information (like the MCI managers' need for information about customers' calling patterns) that the information system is designed to serve.

Organizational Behavior in Action

INFORMATION SYSTEMS = TECHNOLOGY + PEOPLE + ORGANIZATIONS

Recent changes at Schneider National, North America's biggest carrier of full truckload cargoes, help show why information systems include technology, people, and organizations.

After deregulation revolutionized the trucking industry, Schneider National knew it had to do something quickly to get itself into more competitive shape.[15] The regulations that had made it difficult for customers to change carriers were gone, so the firm suddenly faced more competition than ever before.

Schneider National managers decided on a two-pronged strategy. First, to prepare the organization for other changes to come, management focused on making sweeping changes in its corporate culture. The main aim was to replace its "regulated-utility" mentality with a sense of urgency to get things done fast. The company's CEO took several steps to change the culture and values of the company: He encouraged everyone from drivers on up to suggest ways to improve operations, eliminated status symbols like reserved parking spaces, began calling all employees "associates," and drew attention to the new emphasis on performance by awarding bonus paychecks based solely on performance.

Information technology changes were then built on this new cultural foundation. All trucks were equipped with computers and rotating antennas, so that a satellite could track every rig, making sure it stuck to its schedule. When a customer called to request a pick-up, dispatchers knew exactly which truck to assign to the job, and the order was sent directly to that driver's on-board terminal, complete with directions to the destination and instructions about what gate to use.

The new information system has been very successful. However, it's doubtful that it would have been so successful if management hadn't had the wisdom to design the system around the people—by changing the culture, by making sure the drivers who had to use the system were made to feel like involved participants in the process, and by designing a system the drivers wanted to use. ■

LEVELS OF INFORMATION SYSTEMS. There is a hierarchy of information systems because information requirements at each organizational level tend to be unique to that level.[16] As in Figure 18.1, **executive support systems** provide infor-

	SALES	MANUFACTURING	ACCOUNTING	FINANCE	PERSONNEL
EXECUTIVE SUPPORT SYSTEMS (ESS)	**STRATEGIC-LEVEL SYSTEMS**				
	5-year sales trend forecasting	5-year operating plan	5-year budget forecasting	Profit planning	Personnel planning

	SALES	MANUFACTURING	ACCOUNTING	FINANCE	PERSONNEL
MANAGEMENT INFORMATION SYSTEMS (MIS)	**MANAGEMENT CONTROL-LEVEL SYSTEMS**				
	Sales management	Inventory control	Annual budgeting	Capital investment analysis	Relocation analysis
DECISION SUPPORT SYSTEMS (DSS)	Sales region analysis	Production scheduling	Cost analysis	Pricing/ profitability analysis	Contract cost analysis

	SALES	MANUFACTURING	ACCOUNTING	FINANCE	PERSONNEL
TRANSACTION PROCESSING SYSTEMS (TPS)	**OPERATIONAL-LEVEL SYSTEMS**				
		Machine control	Payroll	Auditing	Compensation
	Order tracking	Plant scheduling	Accounts payable	Tax reporting	Training & development
	Order processing	Material movement control	Accounts receivable	Cash management	Employee recordkeeping

■ **FIGURE 18.1**
Objectives of Information Systems of Each Organizational Level

Managers at each level of the organization have unique information requirements. Various types of information systems have thus been developed to serve the needs at each management level.

SOURCE: Adapted from *Management Information Systems* 4/E by Laudon/Laudon, (Upper Saddle River, NJ; Prentice-Hall, 1996).

mation for strategic-level decisions on matters such as five-year operating plans. **Management information systems** and **decision support systems** provide middle managers with reports regarding matters such as current versus historical sales levels. **Transaction processing systems** provide detailed information about the most short-term, daily activities, such as accounts payables and order status. The Entrepreneurs in Action feature shows how one small business designed an information system to boost its business. We'll look more closely at each type of system.

Transaction Processing Systems

A *transaction* is an event that affects the business. Hiring an employee, selling merchandise, paying an employee, and ordering supplies are transactions. In essence, transaction processing systems collect and maintain detailed records regarding the organization's transactions. For example, a university must know which students have registered, which have paid fees, which members of the faculty are teaching, and what secretaries are employed in order to conduct its business.

The collection and maintenance of such day-to-day transactions were two of the first procedures to be computerized in organizations. As is still the case today, early transaction processing systems automated the collection, maintenance, and processing of mostly repetitive transactions. Examples include computing withholding taxes and net pay, and processing accounts payable checks.

Transaction processing systems (TPS) can be put to five uses.[17] It may have to classify data based on common characteristics of a group (such as finding all sales employees with five years' service, for instance). Such systems are used to do routine calculations (such as computing net pay after taxes and deductions for each employee) and can be used for sorting (for instance, grouping invoices by zip code to more efficiently distribute them). The TPS can also be used for summarization (such as summarizing for each department's manager what his or her average payroll is compared to the other departments). Finally, the TPS can be used for storage (for example, storing payroll information for, say, the past five years).

Management Information Systems

A management information system (MIS) provides decision support for managers by producing standardized, summarized reports on a regular basis.[18] It generally produces reports for longer-term purposes than typical transaction processing systems.

Entrepreneurs in Action

COMPUTERS ADD VALUE AT BISSETT NURSERY

Back in the early 1980s, Long Island, New York, was in the midst of a building boom, and Bissett Nursery couldn't have handled any more business. Bissett's son Jimmy spent his days sprinting around the shop trying to serve customers, many of whom had to wait up to 25 minutes for a handwritten invoice. Bookkeeping was a month behind, receivables sometimes took 90 days to meander back, and inventory control didn't exist.

Both Bissetts knew booms invariably turned to busts and the company, a wholesaler of nursery materials, hard goods, and lumber, would have to change to make it through tougher times. The younger Bissett had ideas about expanding through vertical integration without taking on big labor costs. He thought the best way to do so would be with the help of brother-in-law Bob Pospischil, an ex-fighter pilot who knew both sophisticated computer hardware and the financial data it could produce. "My goal was not to change the business," says Pospischil, "but to use technology to meet the business needs." The elder Bissett was skeptical. He'd seen competitors go the same route only to find it an expensive mistake, but he finally relented.

Pospischil signed on as the company's chief financial officer. He spent 60 days getting a handle on buying, sales, shipping, and accounting and then spent $135,000 on the company's first big computer. Order-entry employees took turns visiting the software vendor to learn the new system. After the first

30 minutes of operations, the network crashed. Convinced the curse of computers had finally descended on his house, a frantic Jim Bissett insisted everyone return to the old manual system. The trouble was ironed out in 15 minutes and the elder Bissett gradually became accustomed to the new technology.

What Jim Bissett senior soon gained from the information system was a new perspective on practically every phase of his business operation. Instead of doing haphazard strategic planning, he could order with precision based on his customers' historical needs. He was also able to make Bissett Nursery indispensable to them while at the same time providing better service. He could easily show small contractors their annual needs for nonperishable goods, enabling them to purchase in bulk and save money. When water conservation became an issue in the region, Bisset was out in front steering clients to heartier plants that thrived in drier conditions. Bissett Nursery's customer base shot from 600 to 7,500, and Pospischil was only beginning to hit his stride.

Marketing was costing Bissett $130,000 annually, and better than 60 percent of that budget went to producing ads and catalogs. Pospischil had an easier time selling the elder Bissett on the idea he could do more timely promotions with an in-house desktop publishing system. The price tag was $40,000, but the company never felt a ripple. "With the first catalog we saved enough to pay for the system," says Pospischil.

The next technological innovation was the greatest challenge. It also provided the nursery's customers their biggest competitive advantage. Landscapers face big barriers with homeowners because they have to sell the aesthetics of their products either by driving potential clients by past jobs or through the use of pictures. It's not always easy to get a customer to visualize how a tree or row of shrubbery six blocks away would look in their own front yard. That changed when a software company sold Bissett on an imaging system that could produce a rendering of how the planned trees and plants would look in front of the customer's house.

The new technology gave Bissett Nursery a huge edge when the building boom turned into a recession. More than 95 percent of landscape contractors who used Bissett's computer-generated images sold the job and came back to fill orders at the nursery. "We were a very strong company going into the recession," says the younger Bissett, "and I feel we've stayed fairly strong."

Despite the fact that the nursery and landscape businesses are generally not regarded as being in the vanguard of high technologies, the Bissetts have proved otherwise. Using the latest information systems, they have managed the enviable feat of producing more efficiently, providing better service, and making themselves indispensable to customers.

Although the firm's first computer crashed, technology eventually transformed the operations of Long Island's Bissett Nursery Corp.

SOURCE: Donna Fenn, "Picture the Image," *Inc.,* February 1994, 66–71.

In a university, for instance, a TPS is used to print class rolls and grade rolls. An MIS, in contrast, can measure and report class size and enrollment trends by department and by college. The deans and academic vice presidents can then use the MIS reports to increase or decrease the class sizes or to drop some courses from next semester's schedule while adding others. Management information systems condense, summarize, and manipulate information derived from the organization's transaction processing systems. They then present the results in the form of routine summary reports to management, often with exceptions flagged for control purposes.[19]

Decision Support Systems

Decision support systems (DSS) "assist management decision making by combining data, sophisticated analytical models, and user-friendly software into a single powerful

TABLE 18.1 Examples of DSS Systems Uses

American Airlines	Price and route selection
Champlin Petroleum	Corporate planning and forecasting
Equico Capital Corporation	Investment evaluation
Frito-Lay, Inc.	Price, advertising, and promotion selection
General Dynamics	Price evaluation
Juniper Lumber	Production optimization
Kmart	Price evaluation
National Gypsum	Corporate planning and forecasting
Southern Railway	Train dispatching and routing
Texas Oil and Gas Corporation	Evaluation of potential drilling sites
United Airlines	Flight scheduling
U.S. Department of Defense	Defense contract analysis

system that can support semi-structured or unstructured decision making."[20] In other words, systems like these can help managers make decisions that are relatively unstructured when compared to those addressed by the typical MIS. At the university, for instance, an MIS is used to make course addition and deletion decisions, decisions that are fairly routine. However, suppose the university's faculty threatens to strike. The university could use a decision support system to estimate the impact on university revenues of having to drop various combinations of classes.

An MIS differs from a DSS in several ways.[21] A DSS is more capable of analyzing various alternatives, in part because decision support systems let the user (in this case, the vice president for academic affairs) include different subprograms showing how various components of the university (such as revenues and enrollments in various courses) are related. Furthermore, a DSS does not just rely on internal information from the transaction processing system the way the MIS typically does. Instead, a DSS is built to absorb new external information into the analysis. Thus, our university's academic vice president, faced with a strike, may want to include in her or his analysis an estimate of the likelihood that a number of the university's students will move across town to a competing university, given the competing university's ability (or inability) to expand its class offerings.

Table 18.1 gives some examples of how companies use their DSS systems. For example, American Airlines uses its system for price and route selection, General Dynamics for price evaluation, and Southern Railway for train dispatching and routing.

Executive Support Systems

Executive support systems (ESS) are information systems designed to help top-level executives acquire, manipulate, and use the information they need to maintain the overall effectiveness of the company. Such systems often focus on providing top management with information for making strategic decisions. They help top management match changes in the firm's environment with the firm's existing and potential strengths and weaknesses.[22]

Executive support systems perform several specific tasks. Executives such as Cypress Semiconductor's Tom Rogers use their ESS for keeping informed about and monitoring the pulse of their organizations. Rogers monitors the weekly compliance of all 4,000 Cypress employees (for instance, how each worker stands in terms of project progress or sales productivity). Second, executives use ESS to quickly identify and understand evolving situations. A university president could thus use an ESS to keep tabs on and analyze the following questions:

Is the average student taking fewer courses?

Are costs for maintenance labor substantially higher than they have been in the past?

Is there a significant shift in the zip codes from which most of our students come?

An ESS also makes it easy for executives to browse through the data. One executive describes the capability this way:

I like to take a few minutes to review details about our customers, our manufacturers or our financial activities first hand. Having the details flow across the screen gives me a feel for how things are going. I don't look at each record, but glance at certain elements as they scroll by. If something looks unusual, it will almost jump out at me and I can find out more about it. But if nothing is unusual, I will know that, too.[23]

The top executive can also use an ESS to monitor a situation. Thus, a university president could use an ESS to monitor the new dining facilities management firm running the student cafeteria by reviewing information such as student usage, student complaints, and revenues. Executives also use ESS to facilitate environmental scanning. For example, a wealth of information is available in commercial computerized data banks, including financial information on tens of thousands of U.S. companies. Executives can use an ESS to tap into such data banks in order to glean competitive data regarding other firms in their industry. An ESS can also support analytical needs. For example, it may allow our university president to create "what if" scenarios that show the probable effects on university revenues of increasing faculty salaries or adding new programs. Finally, an ESS may enable the executive to get at data directly. Using their terminals and telephone lines, executives can use an executive support system to tap directly into the company's data files in order to get specific information that may be of interest, without waiting for others to assemble it.[24]

Expert Systems and Artificial Intelligence

An **expert system** is an information system in which computer programs store facts and rules (often called a knowledge base) to replicate the abilities and decisions of true human experts. For example, one early application identified an investment advisor's criteria for recommending investments to clients who were in various demographic and risk-propensity categories. Those observations were then used to develop a computer program that replicated most of the investment decisions the investment officer (the "expert") would have made.

Expert systems are used in all fields of business, from manufacturing to sales to finance. Increasingly, though, some of the most well-publicized uses have been in the area of finance and investments. For example, Countrywide Funding Corp. in Pasadena, California, uses a microcomputer-based expert system to help its loan underwriters in 150 offices around the country analyze loan applications. The system makes preliminary creditworthiness decisions on loan requests using the same criteria and decision-making habits as professional loan underwriters. The system was refined until it agreed with the underwriter in 95 percent of the cases.[25]

Countrywide does not depend solely on the expert system, and underwriters still review or reject loans and make the final decisions. However, the system does speed the process: Underwriters who could previously handle only six or seven applications a day can now evaluate at least 16 per day.

The term "artificial intelligence" is often used in association with expert systems because they both are related to replicating human thought processes. However, expert systems are relatively straightforward information systems made up of programs that contain decision rules. These decision rules (when combined with the facts of the situation) allow the expert system to mimic the expert's decision-making style.

Artificial intelligence leaps beyond this sort of logical problem solving. **Artificial intelligence (AI)** can be defined as a computer's ability "to accomplish tasks in a manner that is considered 'intelligent,' and is characterized by learning and making decisions."[26] Ultimately, says one expert,

> Such systems would be able to learn natural languages; accomplish coordinated physical tasks (robotics); develop and utilize a perceptual apparatus that informs their physical behavior and language; and, finally, exhibit logic, reasoning, intuition, and just plain common sense—qualities that we associate with human beings.[27]

Dramatic as this sounds, many experts today believe that such thinking machines are a long way off. One contends that "artificial intelligence is the snake oil of the information age."[28] Others simply throw up their hands and conclude that "the truth is, nobody knows what AI means."[29] In any case, it would seem that we are some years away from being able to replace either faculty members or students with so-called thinking machines.

Organizational Behavior in Action

THE BEHAVIORAL SIDE OF BUSINESS REENGINEERING

Facing the need to be faster, leaner, and quicker to respond to customers, many companies today are engaging in business reengineering. **Business reengineering** has been defined as "the radical redesign of business processes, combining steps to cut waste and eliminate repetitive, paper-intensive tasks in order to improve cost, quality, and service, and to maximize the benefits of information technology."[30] The approach is to (1) identify a business process to be designed (such as approving a mortgage application), (2) measure the performance of the existing processes, (3) identify opportunities for applying information technology to improve these processes, and (4) then redesign and implement a new way of doing the work.

A new system implemented at Banc One Mortgage provides an example. As illustrated in Figure 18.2, Banc One redesigned its mortgage application process so that it required fewer steps and reduced mortgage processing time from 17 days to two. In the past, a mortgage applicant completed a paper loan application that the

Shifting from a traditional approach helped Banc One Mortgage slash processing time from 17 days to two

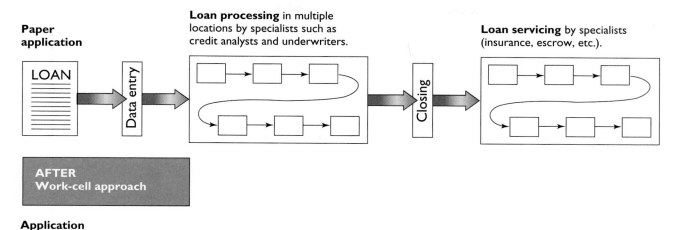

BEFORE
Desk-to-desk approach

Paper application

Loan processing in multiple locations by specialists such as credit analysts and underwriters.

Loan servicing by specialists (insurance, escrow, etc.).

LOAN

Data entry

Closing

AFTER
Work-cell approach

Application on laptop computer

Regional production center: Teams process open applications.

Servicing: Specialists work together as a team.

LOAN

Closing

LOAN

Dial-up network

■ **FIGURE 18.2**

Redesigning Mortgage Processing at Banc One

By redesigning their mortgage processing system and the mortgage application process, Banc One will be able to handle the increased paperwork as they move from processing 33,000 loans per year to processing 300,000 loans per year.

SOURCE: Adapted from Mitch Betts, "Banc One Mortgage Melts Paper Blizzard," *Computerworld,* December 14, 1992. Copyright (December 14, 1992) by Computerworld, Inc., Framingham, MA 01701. Reprinted from *Computerworld.* Reprinted by permission.

bank then entered in its computer system. A series of specialists such as credit analysts and underwriters evaluated the application individually as it moved step-by-step through eight different departments.

Banc One redesigned the process, replacing the sequential operation with a *work cell* or team approach. Loan originators in the field now enter the mortgage application directly into laptop computers, where software checks it for completeness. The information is then transmitted electronically to regional production centers where specialists like credit analysts and loan underwriters convene electronically, working as a team to review the mortgage together—at once. Then, after the loan has been formally closed, another team of specialists sets up the loan for servicing.

While reengineering processes with the aid of information technology has had its share of successes, some estimate reengineering failure rates to be as high as 70 percent.[31] When reengineering efforts do fail, it is often due to behavioral factors. Sometimes (as in other change efforts) employees resist the change, deliberately undermining the revised procedures. And if business processes are reengineered without consideration of the new skill requirements, training, and reporting relationships involved, the usual employee resistance problems can be exacerbated. As John Champy, a long-time reengineering proponent, has said:

In short, reducing hierarchy, bureaucracy, and the rest of it is not just a matter of rearranging the furniture to face our customers and markets. It is a matter of rearranging the quality of people's attachments—to their work and to each other. These are *cultural* matters. . . . If that's true, and it is, then values become the most important structural elements in the enterprise. Why? Values are the links between emotion and behavior, the connection between what we feel and what we do. . . . They are business navigational devices as well. As hierarchies flatten, and power, control, and responsibility get pushed out from HQ to the trenches, from staff to line, we need to know that the people "out there" will do the right thing at the moment of truth.[32]

What kind of values does Champy see as consistent with reengineering a corporation? Here's his list:

1. To perform up to the highest measure of competence, always.
2. To take initiatives and risks.
3. To adapt to change.
4. To make decisions.
5. To work cooperatively as a team.
6. To be open, especially with information, knowledge, and news of forthcoming or actual "problems."
7. To trust, and be trustworthy.
8. To respect others (customers, suppliers, and colleagues) and oneself.
9. To answer for our actions, to accept responsibility.
10. To judge and be judged, reward and be rewarded, on the basis of our performance.[33]

The New Telecommunications and Computerized Networks for Managing Organizations

Telecommunication is the electronic transmission of data, text, graphics, voice (audio), or image (video) over literally any distance. In practice, the transmission may travel from machine to machine within an office, from office to office, between cities, around the globe, or even further, such as between NASA headquarters and the transmitter on the Venus probe.[34]

A **telecommunications system** is a set of compatible communications devices that link geographically separated information processing devices[35] (such as personal computers, telephones, and video displays) for the purpose of exchanging data and information.[36]

As in the simple system in Figure 18.3, several common elements exist in any telecommunications system.[37] The **telecommunications lines** or **links** are the medium through which signals are transmitted. They might be copper wires, coaxial cables, optical fibers, or microwave transmissions, for instance. **Terminals** are input-output devices that send or receive data. **Line adapters** modify the signal from the terminal and computer so that it matches the characteristics of the telecommunications line. (This is important because many popular telecommunications links, such as telephone lines, are not suited for the type of signal produced by computerized input and output devices.) The most familiar line adapter is called a **modem**.[38] Finally, **telecommunications software** is the computer program that controls input and output activities and other communications network functions.

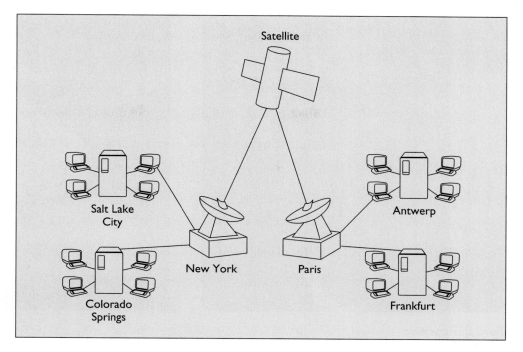

■ **FIGURE 18.3**
A Telecommunications System

A telecommunications system like this one is a set of compatible telecommunications devices like lines, adapters, and computers that link geographically separated devices.

SOURCE: Carroll Frenzel, *Management of Information Technology* (Boston: Boyd & Frazer, 1992), 164.

How Managers Use Telecommunications

Telecommunications plays an important role in managing organizations today. For example, apparel manufacturer Levi Strauss uses a sophisticated telecommunications system to link its own inventory and manufacturing facilities with point-of-sale processing devices at retail stores. Detailed sales information is transmitted directly to headquarters, where it is analyzed for trends and buying patterns. Management can then make decisions regarding inventories and production plans. Similarly, retailers such as JCPenney use telecommunications to manage in-store inventories. Its buyers get instant access to sales information from the stores and can modify their purchasing actions accordingly.

As another example, Ford designers at its Dearborn, Michigan, headquarters use computers to develop designs for new cars such as the Lincoln Continental. As you can see in the photos on page 628, digitized designs are sent via telecommunications and are reproduced at Ford's design facility in Turin, Italy, where styrofoam mockups are made automatically to reproduce Dearborn's design 4,284 miles away.

Telecommunications is also important to managers because more and more managerial computer systems applications rely on it. For example, Levi depends on telecommunications in its computerized inventory control systems; radiologists rely on telecommunications for X-rays taken by their technologists, which can then be read from remote locations; your college or university may use telecommunications to allow you to access library information from your office or home; computer-assisted manufacturing systems rely on telecommunications to transmit information from one location in the plant to another; and banks depend on telecommunications to make their remote automatic teller machines operational. Telecommunications also fosters the use of newer management computer systems applications, such as those we now turn to.

Ford designers in Dearborn, Michigan, send design via telecommunications to Turin, where mockups are produced.

Work Group Support Systems

Work groups and teams play an increasingly important role in managing organizations, as we have seen in previous chapters. The team might be a door-assembly team at Saturn cars, the sales department at a Levi Strauss subsidiary, or a project team set up in a manufacturing plant to solve a quality-control problem. It might be relatively permanent (as it would be if it were a sales department) or temporary (such as a group formed to solve a one-time quality problem). The team's members might all be at a single site, or they might be dispersed around the city or even around the world. (For example, a team might consist of the IBM representatives from various countries devoted to advising Ford on its worldwide computerized systems.) In any event, the aim of all the following work group support systems is to facilitate communication among a team's members.

ELECTRONIC MAIL.   As everyone knows, electronic mail (e-mail) is a computerized information system that lets group members electronically create, edit, and disseminate messages to each other, using electronic "mail boxes." E-mail's aim is to speed and facilitate intragroup communication and thereby bolster intragroup coordination. An **electronic bulletin board** is another example. It lets one or more group members file messages on various topics to be picked up later by other group members.

E-mail systems are not just for messages anymore. For example, e-mail software called Eudora Pro helps Jim Le Goullon manage his sales operation. It lets him set up one computer to check all customer's accounts every 10 minutes so he never misses a rush order. And, it lets him sort messages based on key words like "brochure," (the requests for brochures are automatically routed to the person in charge of mailing them).[39]

VIDEOCONFERENCING.   Videoconferencing is an example of group conferencing, that is, telecommunications-based methods that let group members interact directly with or leave messages for a number of other group members via television links. Firms such as International Open Systems (IOS) of Peabody, Massachusetts, provide videoconferencing via desktop personal computers. It lets users send live video and audio messages (with a few seconds delay).[40]

Videoconferencing can significantly improve communications and coordination among group members and thereby help a work group achieve its aims more quickly than the group could otherwise. For example, the team developing the Boeing 777 made extensive use of videoconferencing for meetings with engine suppliers and key airlines regarding the new aircraft's design.[41]

GROUP DECISION-SUPPORT SYSTEMS. A group decision-support system (GDSS) is an interactive computer-based system to facilitate the solution of unstructured problems by a team of decision makers.[42] The general aim of a GDSS is to allow a team of decision makers to get together (often in the same room) in order to facilitate making a particular decision or completing a particular task. To that end, the GDSS (as pictured in Figure 18.4) allows team members to interact via their microcomputers and to use a number of software tools aimed at assisting them in their decision making or project completion. Typical GDSS software tools include electronic questionnaires, electronic brainstorming tools, idea organizers (to help team members synthesize ideas generated during brainstorming), and tools for voting or setting priorities (so recommended solutions can be weighted and prioritized).

Using GDSS helps a group avoid a lot of the group decision-making barriers that often occur in face-to-face groups. For example, there's less likelihood that one assertive person will hog the whole meeting, since all the brainstorming and listing of ideas—and the voting—is governed by the computerized GDSS programs.

OTHER WORK GROUP SUPPORT SYSTEMS. Other work group support systems are also available. For example, **collaborative writing systems** let a work group's members create long written documents (such as proposals) while working simultaneously at one of a number of interconnected or network computers. As team members work on different sections of the proposal, each member has automatic

■ **FIGURE 18.4**
A Group Decision-Support System
The Ventana Corporation demonstrates the features of its GroupSystems for Windows electronic meeting software, which helps people create, share, record, organize, and evaluate ideas in meetings, between offices, or around the world.

access to the rest of the sections and can modify his or her section to be compatible with the rest. A **group scheduling system** lets each group member put his or her daily schedule into a shared database, which enables group members to identify the most suitable times for meetings to be scheduled or to attend currently scheduled meetings. The **work flow automation system** uses an e-mail-type system to automate paperwork flow.[43] For example, if a proposal requires four signatures, it can be sent electronically from mailbox to mailbox for the required signatures.

TELECOMMUTING. Today, millions of people around the world do most of their work at home and commute to their employers electronically. **Telecommuting** has been defined as the substitution of telecommunications and computers for the commute to a central office.[44]

The typical telecommuter falls into one of three categories. Some are not employees at all but are independent entrepreneurs who work out of their homes— perhaps developing new computer applications for consulting clients, for instance. The second (and largest) group of telecommuters includes professionals and highly skilled people who work at jobs that involve a great deal of independent thought and action. These employees—computer programmers, regional salespersons, textbook editors, or research specialists, for instance—typically work at home most of the time, coming into the office only occasionally, perhaps for monthly meetings.[45] The third telecommuter category includes workers who carry out relatively routine and easily monitored jobs such as data entry or word processing.[46]

Networks

Organizations make extensive use of networks to better manage their operations. A **network** "is a group of interconnected computers, work stations or computer devices (such as printers and data storage systems)."[47] Local area networks (LANs), wide area networks (WANs), and distributed networks are three examples of managerial networks.

LOCAL AREA NETWORKS. A **local area network (LAN)** spans a limited distance, such as a building or several adjacent buildings, using the company's own telecommunications links (rather than common-carrier links such as those provided by AT&T's phone lines). In an office, a LAN may be used to support a work group information system such as e-mail, and a factory may use a LAN to link computers with computer-controlled production equipment.

More generally, LANs are used for one or more of the following reasons: to distribute information and messages (including e-mall); to drive computer-controlled manufacturing equipment; to distribute documents (such as engineering drawings from one department to another); to interconnect the LAN's computers with those of a public network such as Prodigy or the Internet; and, given the high cost of certain equipment such as laser printers, to make equipment sharing possible (including not just printers but disk storage file servers, for instance).

WIDE AREA NETWORKS. **Wide area networks (WANs)** are networks that serve microcomputers over larger geographic areas, spanning distances that can cover a few miles or circle the globe. Early WANs utilized common carrier networks, such as the telephone links provided by AT&T and MCI. However, many firms today own their own wide area networks, which are essentially private, computerized telecommunications systems. For example, the Benetton retail store chain uses its WAN to enable both store managers and headquarters staff to identify local trends and improve inventory and production management. The stores accumulate sales data during the day and keep them on computer disks. At night, another, larger computer at corporate headquarters polls the individual retail stores' computers, accessing data that are then transmitted over telephone lines back to headquarters. Here, the information is processed and a summary of sales trends is forwarded to headquarters and individual store managers.[48]

DISTRIBUTED NETWORKS. As at Benetton, wide area networks are often used to achieve distributed processing. **Distributed processing** generally uses small local computers (such as point-of-sale systems) to collect, store, and process information, with summary reports and information sent to headquarters as needed.[49]

The Internet

While you are reading this page, hundreds of thousands—perhaps millions—of people are "on the Internet" searching through libraries, talking to friends, and buying and selling products and services. For example, small investor Ed Harrison makes several spot trades a week, but instead of using a conventional brokerage firm like Merrill Lynch, he does his trading on the Internet.[50] A company called PointCast sends full articles, Web pages, and animations to subscribers' TVs via the Internet and has more than one million regular viewers—and some 15,000 people joining the service each day.[51]

The Internet is not simply a computer network: It is "an international network of networks connecting more than 20 million people from 100 countries and is currently the largest 'information superhighway' in the world."[52] The value of the Internet lies in its ability to easily and inexpensively connect so many people from so many places; the miracle of the Internet is that no one owns it and it has no formal management organization. Instead, to become part of the Internet, an existing network simply pays a small registration fee and agrees to comply with certain electronic standards, Transmission Control Protocol/Internet Protocol (TCP/IP), that were originally developed by the U.S. Department of Defense and are still used.

The Internet has many communications capabilities, such as e-mail, discussion groups on electronic bulletin boards, interactive conversations, and FTP (transferring files from computer to computer).

However, the World Wide Web is perhaps the biggest Internet capability. The "Web" is essentially a universally accepted set of standards for storing, retrieving, formatting, and displaying information via the Internet. Technically speaking, a **Web site** is an Internet system that holds a Web server; a **Web server** is the software on a site that enables a Web browser to access the documents sitting on the Web site. Web sites like the one shown in the picture on page 632 are perhaps the most familiar feature of the World Wide Web; they can be accessed by means of Web browser software such as Netscape Navigator or Microsoft's Internet Explorer.

HOW MANAGERS USE THE INTERNET. The Internet can provide enormous benefits to organizations. Because companies can, in a sense, get a "free ride" on the Internet, they can substantially reduce their communications' costs. For instance, FedEx's clients can track their own packages using FedEx's Web site instead of inquiring by telephone, thus saving the company millions of dollars per year.[53] Similarly, the Internet makes it easier and less expensive for companies to coordinate the work of small teams that may, for instance, be opening new markets in isolated places. And, of course, the World Wide Web is already facilitating electronic commerce. For example, listing your home for sale on the Web could let you include pictures and floor plans and save the lion's share of the six percent commission that

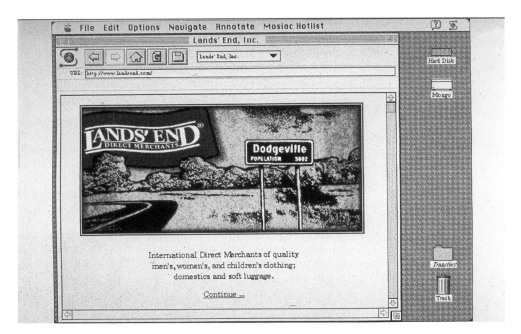

Information technology provides many new opportunities for savvy firms. Lands' End customers can browse the company's catalog and place orders on the World Wide Web, for example.

real estate agents often charge.[54] And Prodigy, an Internet service, offers online catalogs from Sears and other merchants through which Internet "surfers" can purchase items directly.[55]

The Information Superhighway

The **information superhighway** is a high-speed digital communications network that may combine telephone lines, cable lines, microwave transmissions, and fiber optics to let anyone anywhere use interactive television, telephones, PCs, or other devices to interact with databases around the world.

In some respects, the information superhighway is still a sort of "masterpiece in progress." Some big elements—such as the Internet—already exist. And most cable television systems already offer video-on-demand services, as do satellite-based television service firms.

Other components of the superhighway are falling into place. For example, the U.S. government has provided $3 billion for the development of supercomputer centers in the United States and a very high-capacity network called the National Research Education Network, capable of delivering data, voice, and video images to households much more rapidly than is now possible by just the Internet. Full-text retrieval would be possible from libraries, patient medical records could be transferred anywhere they were needed, and students could more easily learn at home, for example.[56] The information superhighway may, in essence, merge the telephone's convenience, the computer's Internet power, and the television's clarity to make "being there" and "doing that" as easy as picking up your phone. One company, Web TV, already sells a $350 device that basically lets you make the Internet just another channel on your TV.[57]

Computer Security

Security-conscious organizations like banks and the armed forces have long understood the need to protect their computer systems from outside intrusion. However, more and more firms are finding that, with the increased use of interactive networks, additional computer security steps are not just wise, but mandatory. Part of the reason is today's widespread ownership of PCs with modems, which make it relatively easy for outsiders to sign on to company networks. Another is the change in the nature of most firms' computer centers. The old computer center was often a large and highly secure complex of rooms. Today, the "computer centers" are more likely to be vast networks of desktop computers, each connected to the Internet and each thus providing a potential doorway into the firm's computer databases.

A firm's computer system (and its computer networks in particular) are subject to two types of security threats.[58] **Passive threats** come from unauthorized individuals or organizations who monitor the firm's data transmission in order to obtain unauthorized information. **Active threats** consist of attempts to alter, destroy, or divert data or to act as an authorized network terminal point, thus illegally exchanging information with legitimate sites and obtaining free network services.[59] Firms are taking a number of steps to boost computer security and protect themselves against either threat. These steps fall into one of four categories:[60]

physical security and isolation of certain computer equipment and data media

authentication of authorized users

careful definition of what users are and are not authorized to do

audit trails, coupled with meaningful accountability

Organizational Behavior in Action

DOWNSIZING: DO COMPUTERS REPLACE PEOPLE?

Information systems applications such as reengineering, decision support systems, and telecommuting lead many people to wonder whether technology caused the massive workforce reductions occurring in the mid-1990s.[61] Two MIS experts conclude, after reviewing much of the evidence, that "technology does not appear to be key to the large corporate workforce reductions occurring in the mid-1990s."[62] Perhaps not directly. Yet during the 1980s, U.S. companies spent over $1 trillion investing in information systems technology. In the past few years these technological investments seemed to be paying off in higher productivity, and therefore in the ability of companies to downsize their workforces.

There are many examples. Companies like Banc One and GTE Corporation have used reengineering to merge operations, redesign processes, and eliminate many employees. For instance, GTE was able to eliminate 17,000 jobs by 1996, in part by merging 12 operations' centers into a single center to monitor the company's entire nationwide telephone network. Apple Computer Company eliminated most of its receptionist jobs by replacing them with voice mail and pagers. Aetna Insurance is eliminating 4,000 jobs (about 10 percent of its workforce) by automating the policy issuing function. AT&T is using computer-based automation to reduce the number of its long-distance operators from 44,000 to 15,000 in just one year.

Perhaps information technology is not the only reason for these dramatic workforce reductions. However, the apparent link between technology and workforce reduction still raises several issues. For one thing, what, if any, responsibility does management bear for the effects of the permanent elimination of jobs when it reengineers or replaces people power with information technology? And how will the company handle the impact on remaining employees when technology replaces their former colleagues?

As we've seen in this chapter, information technology can be enormously beneficial to companies; however, managers need to remember that information systems include the managers, organizations, and people, too. Trying to implement a technological change without anticipating how the managers and other employees will be affected by any subsequent downsizing can be a recipe for disaster. ■

How Information Technology Can Help Manage Change

Information technology opens up a whole new world of options for managers seeking to manage change: using group decision support systems to facilitate teamwork (even for teams that are globally dispersed); letting customers track the progress of their shipments via the company's Web site; helping companies reengineer processes and thereby squeeze out wasted activities; and using expert systems to speed review of mortgage applications. These are just a few of the examples we've discussed so far. Some other examples of how information technology helps manage change follow.

Flatter Structures with Centralized Control Monitoring

Early predictions suggested that computerized organizations "would become more centralized, and that middle management would tend to disappear over time because computers would give central, high-level managers all of the information they require to operate the organization without middle-management intervention."[63] In practice, computerization and information technology has not had quite this effect: In many ways its effect has been just the opposite. On the one hand, the flattening of the hierarchy has occurred: Computerization does seem to have reduced the need for so many layers of middle management. As Peter Drucker has said, "It turns out that whole layers of management neither make decisions nor lead. Instead, their main, if not their only function, is to serve as 'relays,' human boosters for the faint unfocused signals that pass for communications in the traditional pre-information organization."[64] These management layers have been eliminated in many firms.

Yet it does not appear that computerization has led to the sort of centralized decision making that early writers predicted. On the contrary, information technology has actually led to an increase in the depth and range of decisions that lower-level operational employees can make—and thus made it easier to empower them— in part because it gives top managers the security of monitoring subordinates' progress as it occurs. As information technology expert Carroll Frenzel puts it:

> Information technology, especially telecommunications systems, offers executives the potential to have the best of both worlds. Decision-making and operational control can be delegated to organizational units; control information can be available to headquarters on a real-time basis.[65]

Information Technology's Role in Strategic Alliances

Firms wishing to capitalize on today's business opportunities often don't have the time or in-house capabilities to design and launch the required products quickly enough to satisfy fast-changing needs. Therefore, virtual corporations are, as we've seen, increasingly important. A virtual corporation, you may recall, is "a temporary network of independent companies—suppliers, customers, even erstwhile rivals— linked by information technology to share skills, costs, and access to one another's market."[66]

Such business alliances would be impossible without information technology. For example, consider an actual alliance organized to build a new generation of jet engine. It consists of five companies, one each in the United States, Japan, Italy, Great Britain, and Germany. The alliance was organized to build engines for 2,000 new aircraft over the next 20 years. According to one expert, a highly complex and geographically dispersed effort like this relies for its very existence on information technology. Specifically, "it is possible only because a 24-hour communications network transfers data on design control, bills of material, parts catalogues, tool design, and many other items among the firms."[67]

Custom Manufacturing

Manufacturers for many years had to make a choice: either use mass production to make vast numbers of the same product relatively cheaply, or produce small numbers of special orders at much higher costs. Today, that convenient distinction doesn't work so well anymore. Today's consumers are very choosy and want the quality, value, and (especially) individuality of custom-tailored products—which is just what firms are aiming to provide, like Levi Strauss with its Personal Pairs program.

Custom manufacturing lets manufacturers get the best of both worlds: They use advanced information technology such as CAD/CAM and automation to gain the cost advantages of mass production, with the customizing advantages of made-to-order production. As we saw in chapter 17, custom manufacturing uses special software and computer networks to link not only the manufacturing machines but the design and transportation functions, too. The result, say two MIS experts, is:

> A dynamically responsive environment in which products can be turned out in greater variety and easily customized with no added cost for small production runs. Huge manufacturers can be as agile as small firms.[68]

Many firms already have custom manufacturing systems. The John Deere Harvester Works manufacturing plant in Moline, Illinois, for instance, now produces a wide variety of crop planters with less than 7 percent of the plant inventory it previously required; production lines at IBM's Charlotte, North Carolina, plant can produce as many as 27 different products at once; and Caterpillar Inc.'s, Aurora, Illinois, plant spent $250 million on new information systems and equipment to enable it to "customize" its production with the aid of automatically guided cranes and a monorail system to deliver parts as needed all over the plant.[69]

Managerial Applications of Information Technology

The following examples outline some more managerial applications of information technology.

Dell: Getting Closer to Its Customers

Dell Computer, the direct-sales computer firm, relies heavily on information technology to stay close to its customers and their changing needs.[70] Dell gets about 35,000 calls or e-mail messages every day. Employees who take these calls work on PCs linked by a network to a large central computer that contains the company's customer database. As the calls come in, the telephone representatives input the information to the database and follow up inquiries by triggering the mailing of customized sales letters to inquiring customers.

Dell uses its information systems in other ways, too. For example, it fine-tunes its mailing lists to target specific customer needs. (Why send information on office networking to a customer who is obviously an at-home user?) The database also helps Dell boost add-on sales, for instance, by alerting telephone reps to sell extended warranties to all those ordering computers above a particular dollar amount.

American Express: Telecommuting

When you call American Express for travel advice, chances are your travel counselor will not be at Amex headquarters, but back home keeping one eye on the kids.[71] For a company that spends over $1 billion annually on information technology, it is probably not surprising that many of Amex's travel counselors in 15 locations have shifted to "homework."

American Express connects its homeworkers to its phone lines and data lines for a small one-time expense of about $1,300 each, including hardware. After that, the travel counselors easily bounce information from their homes to the nearest reservation center and check fares and book reservations on their home PCs. Supervisors continue to monitor agents' calls, thus ensuring good control.

This has been good for both American Express and its counselors. The homeworker counselors handle 26 percent more calls at home than in the office, resulting in about $30,000 more in annual bookings each. For the counselors, working at home means saving three hours a day on commuting and less wear and tear on both the travel counselor and her or his family.[72]

Winning the Job with Groupware

Figure 18.5 summarizes how a Price Waterhouse team won a consulting job by using groupware.[73] The four Price Waterhouse executives who needed to write the proposal (which was due in three days) were in three different states. But they were able to use their Lotus Notes Groupware to conduct a four-way dialogue on their screens and extract key proposal components from various Price Waterhouse databases. For example, they could pull up résumés of the key Price Waterhouse experts from around the world to include in the proposal, and borrow passages from similar proposals. Then they could use Notes to fine-tune the proposal and put it into final form. The team met the deadline and won the contract.

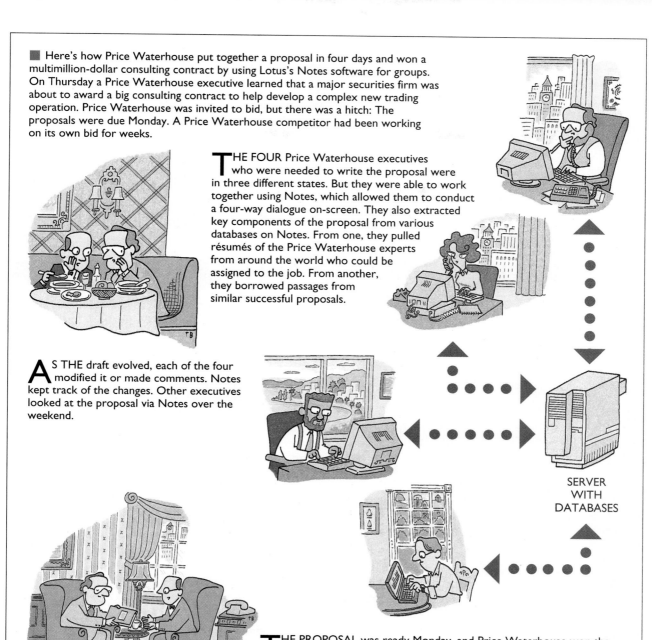

Here's how Price Waterhouse put together a proposal in four days and won a multimillion-dollar consulting contract by using Lotus's Notes software for groups. On Thursday a Price Waterhouse executive learned that a major securities firm was about to award a big consulting contract to help develop a complex new trading operation. Price Waterhouse was invited to bid, but there was a hitch: The proposals were due Monday. A Price Waterhouse competitor had been working on its own bid for weeks.

THE FOUR Price Waterhouse executives who were needed to write the proposal were in three different states. But they were able to work together using Notes, which allowed them to conduct a four-way dialogue on-screen. They also extracted key components of the proposal from various databases on Notes. From one, they pulled résumés of the Price Waterhouse experts from around the world who could be assigned to the job. From another, they borrowed passages from similar successful proposals.

AS THE draft evolved, each of the four modified it or made comments. Notes kept track of the changes. Other executives looked at the proposal via Notes over the weekend.

SERVER WITH DATABASES

THE PROPOSAL was ready Monday, and Price Waterhouse won the deal. Its competitor didn't even meet the deadline. A year later, the client hired Price Waterhouse to audit the new operation. That contract will probably last for years.

■ **FIGURE 18.5**
Winning the Job with Groupware

Source: David Kirkpatrick, "Groupware Goes Boom" *Fortune,* December 27, 1993, 100–101.

Networking the Organization with Groupware

Groupware also helps "network" the organization structure at many firms. As one New York insurance manager put it, groupware networks the corporate hierarchy "because even non-supervisory office workers plugged into groupware networks have information and intelligence previously available only to their bosses." Similarly, "networks . . . can give the rank and file new access: the ability to join in online discussions with senior executives. In these interactions, people are judged more by what they say than by their rank on the corporate ladder."[74]

For example, when Mary Joe Dirkes, a young insurance firm employee, posted a well-done memo on the network about the firm's workers compensation efforts, her good work was immediately noticed by top management in New York and her responsibilities were soon broadened. Her message and the network also altered the chain of command helping make the whole company more responsive:

> She now gets requests for help from around the firm via the network. When a client in Ohio needed someone with experience in cutting workplace injuries in plastics factories, Ms. Dirkes clicked into a groupware database to find an expert that could help. "Before, people would have called or sent a memo to my boss, then he'd assign it to me. . . . Now I do it on my own."[75]

SUMMARY

1. Information technology refers to any processes, practices, or systems that facilitate the processing and transportation of data and information. The increasingly rapid deployment of information technology in organizations has sped the transformation of many businesses today into information-based organizations.

2. Information is data presented in a form that is meaningful to the recipient. Knowledge, on the other hand, has been defined as information distilled via study or research and augmented by judgment and experience. Good-quality information must be pertinent, timely, and accurate and reduce uncertainty. But even good information is relatively useless without knowledge. The role of information technology at work is to contribute to the manager's knowledge of what is happening through analysis, interpretation, and explanation.

3. Managers at different levels in the organization require different types of information. First-line managers tend to focus on short-term, operational decisions and therefore need information that focuses on operational activities. Middle managers tend to concentrate on the intermediate range and so require information for use in such tasks as budget analysis, short-term forecasting, and variance analysis. Top managers make long-range plans and, therefore, require information that will enable them to make better strategic decisions.

4. Information systems are people, data, hardware, and procedures that work together to retrieve, process, store, and disseminate information to support decision making and control. The hierarchy of information systems used in management includes executive support systems, management information and decision support systems, and transaction processing systems. An expert system uses computer programs to store facts and rules and replicate the abilities and decisions of human experts. Artificial intelligence may allow computers to accomplish tasks in a manner that is considered intelligent and is characterized by learning and making decisions.

5. Telecommunication is the electronic transmission of data, text, graphics, voice, or image over any distance. Telecommunications systems connect geographically separated devices through the use of lines or links, terminals,

computers, line adapters, and software. They have fostered the development of numerous new computer systems applications, such as work group support systems, networks, and the information superhighway. The increasing use by businesses of interactive networks underscores the importance of computer security.

6. Computerization and information technology have reduced the need for management layers. They have also boosted the depth and range of decisions that lower-level operational employees can make, thereby giving top-level managers the security of decentralizing decision making while still monitoring the progress of subordinates. Certain types of strategic alliances, such as the virtual corporation, would be impossible without information technology.

KEY TERMS

information technology
information
information system
executive support systems
management information systems
decision support systems
transaction processing systems
expert system
artificial intelligence (AI)
telecommunication
business reengineering

telecommunications system
telecommunications lines (links)
terminals
line adapters
modem
telecommunications software
electronic bulletin board
collaborative writing systems
group scheduling system

work flow automation system
telecommuting
network
local area network (LAN)
wide area network (WAN)
distributed processing
Web site
Web server
information superhighway
passive threats
active threats

SELF-TEST

TRUE / FALSE QUESTIONS

1 T F Information technology refers only to systems that facilitate the processing of information.

2 T F Information is defined as that which has been derived by study or research and amplified by judgment.

3 T F Information and information systems are used as strategic tools to help companies be competitive.

4 T F Management at all levels of the organization requires the same information.

5 T F Information systems are basically computers.

6 T F Transaction processing systems (TPS) and management information systems (MIS) are fundamentally identical processes.

7 T F Artificial intelligence (AI) systems attempt to replicate human thought processes.

8 T F Business reengineering is an incremental process to help redesign an organization.

9 T F Telecommunications is the electronic transmission of data, text, graphics, audio, or video over any distance.

10 T F An electronic bulletin board is an example of videoconferencing.

MULTIPLE-CHOICE QUESTIONS

1 Which is not a characteristic of good-quality information?
- **a.** pertinence
- **b.** accuracy
- **c.** uncertainty
- **d.** timely

2 Data mining is used for many things, among them:
- **a.** helping firms compete globally
- **b.** locking in customers
- **c.** lowering costs
- **d.** all of the above

3 Transaction processing systems (TPS) are put to all of the following uses except _____.
- **a.** classifying data
- **b.** doing routine calculations
- **c.** storing data
- **d.** training employees

4 One major advantage of a DSS over an MIS is its _____.
- **a.** complexity
- **b.** cost
- **c.** flexibility
- **d.** none of the above

5 Business reengineering's basic approach includes identifying a business process, measuring performance, identifying opportunities for applying technology to work, and _____.
- **a.** recycling older patterns of work
- **b.** redesigning new ways of working
- **c.** enriching and enlarging current work
- **d.** flattening the organization to only three levels

6 What does GDSS, an interactive computer-based system to facilitate the solution of unstructured problems by a team of decision makers, stand for?
- **a.** group decision standards systems
- **b.** group decision systematic standards
- **c.** group decisions-support systems
- **d.** generated decisions-supplemental systems

7 The N in LAN stands for _____.
- **a.** new
- **b.** network
- **c.** novice
- **d.** new age

8 The number of people connected by the Internet is about _____.
- **a.** 500,000
- **b.** 3 million
- **c.** 20 million
- **d.** 2 billion

9 The _____ is a universally accepted set of standards for storing, retrieving, formatting, and displaying information via the Internet.
- **a.** Web
- **b.** Bug
- **c.** Surf
- **d.** Downloader

10 The Internet is the largest "information super _____ " in the world.
- **a.** road
- **b.** highway
- **c.** tunnel
- **d.** bridge

CRITICAL THINKING EXERCISES

1 Technology is obviously a great boon to production and productivity. But what about those replaced by computers and other sophisticated machinery? What do you think is the organization's responsibility, if any, to these displaced workers and managers? Does society have any responsibility, and if so, what? If you think there is some responsibility, what recommendations would you make to companies based on what you have learned in this text?

2 How have the tools and techniques presented in this chapter changed the way you do things? Are you currently using many of the processes presented here, or are you at least familiar with their applications to work? If not, start thinking about how you might want to acquire these and other evolving techniques in order to be competitive. Explain two new ways you could use information technology where you work or study.

DIVERSITY CASE

KNOWLEDGE ENGINEERING

Meet Lim Kwee Enn, CEO of Knowledge Engineering, Singapore, who uses artificial intelligence for such assignments as helping clients manage factory production and transportation fleets. Her software programs have outgunned Sun, EDS, and IBM for contracts. Lim contends that since Knowledge Engineering is a new company it uses the latest technology, while its competitors are sometimes at least five years behind. Her company is also small and very flexible.

As an example, Lim has developed an intelligent gate-management system for airports. Now her software helps keep Singapore's Changi airport's 400 daily flights running smoothly. Having kept the intellectual property rights to her software, she is now offering it to international airports in Sydney, Paris, and Kuala Lumpur (Malaysia).

Questions

1 How exactly do you think airlines and shipping companies might use Lim's artificial intelligence programs?
2 Based on this case, what do you think are some possible future applications of AI?
3 Do you see any cultural differences influencing the use of AI in Asia and America? Why?

SOURCE: Louis Kraar, "Knowledge Engineering," *Fortune,* 28 October 1996, 163–4.

STRATEGY CASE

HOW FEDEX RUNS ON TIME

Every morning at 8:30 there is a 60-minute daily operations review at FedEx. Fifteen to 30 representatives of key departments like Air Operations, Computer Systems, and Meteorology attend in person or participate via conference call. The purpose of the meeting is to see what happened last night and figure out what needs to be done today to make sure that things run as smoothly as possible. The reason this is so important? Customer service is all FedEx offers and the heart of their strategy, and the meeting is designed to ensure that it's reliable.

Every weekday at 5 A.M. a taped recap of the night's performance is made available by voice mail so that participants can check in before meeting and review any problems they will need to discuss and solve.

Questions

1 What concepts discussed in this chapter is FedEx using, and how do these affect the management of its operations?
2 How would you describe the way technology has shaped this company's strategy and its thinking?
3 How do you think FedEx will need to use technology in the future in order to maintain its competitive edge?

SOURCE: Matt Goldberg, "How FedEx Runs on Time," *Fast Company,* p. 38.

ENTREPRENEURIAL CASE

WANTED: CHIEF IMAGINATION OFFICERS

At Gateway 2000, a $5 billion South Dakota computer supplier, Tom Grueskin, former senior marketing manager, is the industry's first Chief Imagination Officer. Among the concepts created through imagination are the cow-patterned boxes Gateway ships around the globe. The idea was suggested by a combination of the cattleman's rugged independence and high-tech engineering.

Tom's job is to try to stop the intellectual atrophy that often occurs as organizations grow and people's roles get more specialized. His charge is to supply the building blocks of creativity. Tom says he does his best imagining on his skis or his bike.

Questions

1 What tools presented in this chapter might Tom use as creativity enhancers?
2 How compatible are technology and creativity?
3 How do you think Tom and his work can help Gateway remain entrepreneurial even though it is huge?
4 Where do you do your best creative imagining? Why?

SOURCE: "Job Titles of the Future," *Fast Company,* April–May 1997, 8.

THE BUSINESS TEAM, INC.

TELECOMMUTING AND THE BUSINESS TEAM

Ruth has just had her first child and is adjusting and recovering slowly. To make matters more complex, her husband, John, has just received a huge promotion that requires him to be 60 miles away at headquarters three times a week. Ruth would like to try telecommuting for the next six months to see whether it is better for her family.

Hal's first son was born six months ago and appears to need more care than most kids. He is chronically ill and in need of many doctors' visits each week. Hal and his wife, Jane, have worked out a plan. Each will telecommute, Hal three days a week and Jane two. Jane is an attorney and has to appear in court on a regular basis. Hal wants to telecommute when Jane cannot stay at home with their son.

The Business Team must decide how to handle Ruth and Hal's requests. The partners know that telecommuting is becoming very popular and has many advantages as well as some disadvantages. The physical absence of both Ruth and Hal part of the time will be a change and require adjustments from everyone. So will electronic communication.

Questions

1 What do you think the Team should do about the two requests?
2 What effect do you think telecommuting will have on the Team's viability as a business? Why?
3 How do you feel about being a telecommuter yourself in the future? Or, if you already have experience as a telecommuter, how might you help the Business Team members come to a decision?
4 How could the Business Team use information technology to emphasize its competitive advantage of providing a multifunctional approach to solving business problems?

YOU BE THE CONSULTANT

INFORMATION TECHNOLOGY WINS THE DAY FOR KNITMEDIA

KnitMedia had already gone interactive in 1995. Sponsored by MCI and Apple, the Knitting Factory presented what was billed as "the biggest live event the Internet has ever experienced." This festival, called GIG (for Global Internet Gathering), presented interactive virtual live music from London, Tokyo, Cologne, Paris, Toronto, San Francisco, Amsterdam, and Hong Kong. The company used a central Web site linking multiple live musical venues so that, for instance, Steve Lacy in Paris played and interacted visually with a rhythm section in New York. All the Knitting Factory Clubs, as they go online, will become part of this Internet network. Outlets for these Internet broadcasts already include the Electronic Cafe in Tokyo, the Cafe @ Boat Quay in Singapore, and Amsterdam's Paradiso. Michael Dorf knows this is only the start: What he needs are more suggestions about how he and KnitMedia can use information technology to bring consumers the music they want to hear.

Team Exercises and Questions

Use what you learned in this chapter to answer the following questions:

1 Answer the question "How are music-related companies using information technology today?" by compiling a list of information technology applications used by KnitMedia's competitors.
2 If you were advising Michael Dorf, how would you suggest he use information technology for improving the performance of KnitMedia and its various businesses?

For the online version of this case, visit our Web site at: <www.prenhall.com/desslermgmt>.

For Internet exercises, interactive study questions, news updates and more, visit the Dessler Web site at

www.prenhall.com/desslermgmt

If you're using the CD-ROM that accompanies this text, simply click on the "Web Site" button to access the site.

CONTROLLING FOR QUALITY AND PROFITABILITY

Control systems are an important part of the KnitMedia management system. Requiring that all policy changes and new ideas be put in writing acts as a control system to prevent miscommunication problems. Meetings are a control system. Wednesday management meetings are held so each area can tell the others what's going on. Club operations staff meetings ensure better control over the shows, staffing, operational issues, and so on. Michael Dorf, founder of KnitMedia and the Knitting Factory, meets daily with his Business Manager, Rachel McBeth, to monitor and control the company's financial operations. These meetings enable staff to prevent problems from becoming insurmountable.

Providing a quality music experience to the consumer is a shared value at KnitMedia. According to Dorf, "the Knitting Factory is a conduit . . . between an artist and the consumer. And if we look at the whole business and everything that we do, from everybody who's working here, it's ultimately about that. We need to make sure that the connection between the artist and the consumer is as good as possible . . . , we need to make that experience that the consumer has with the artist, and the artist with the consumer as good at possible. . . . That medium needs to be the ideal. For the consumer it should be nice air conditioning and . . . clean bathrooms and a nice beer selection. . . . These are the things that make the experience for the consumer as good as possible. For the artist we want to have a great sound system. We want to have a great backstage. We also want to have a good tap-beer selection. You know, we want to have things that make their experience better, and thus, when the two meet, it's the ideal opportunity . . . for both of them to interface and to ultimately make better art."

The quest for quality doesn't stop there. Michael continues, "Then you have the medium of the label, where what we're trying to do is get to the consumer, obviously, with the best product we can, . . . as full of art as we can from the label. And the festivals are the same and the radio work is the same and the Internet. . . . We just want it to be as good as possible because what we're about is—and this is from the technology world—we're the content side, where we're just making sure that that conduit is as clean as possible. And as efficient as possible."

Ed Greer, Club Operations Manager, plays a critical role in making sure the club customer has a great experience. He explains, "My job starts before I come through the door because I'm responsible for . . . shows and show production . . . the proper functioning of the bars, and . . . for the physical building itself—for the plant. So I always like to think of my job as starting before I come through the doors. I want to see how the club looks. I want to see, is the sidewalk swept? I want to see how many bottles or candy wrappers there are in our planters outside. And, just . . . thinking of it as how a stranger would approach it. What's the first thing we see as we come through the door? Is it just an ugly pile of stuff, or is there some semblance of order, and is it conducive to people wanting to buy a ticket, . . . coming to see a show and feeling that they'd like to come back. . . . I walk through the entire club just to see what shape we're in that day and also because I don't want to be hit by a surprise when it's show time. I want everything to be cool by that time. So, for my own peace of mind, I do it. I do it to make sure that I'm not gonna be faced with an ugly situation later on that nobody has spotted."

Technology will enable the new clubs to have a dual management system. They will, says Executive Vice President and Chief Operating Officer, Ken Ashworth, "be managed locally . . . but they'll [also] be managed entirely by us here [in New York]. We will hire all the local managements within each city, and we will oversee all that management on a financial basis. We'll have financial controls in place that we'll monitor . . . inflow and outflow on a weekly, monthly basis. We will have a Director of Clubs, who will go and build each one of these and then will be involved . . . in hiring all the people; watching the systems; . . . setting up the systems; and monitoring them on a regular basis. And . . . we will have to start having . . . more regional managers who oversee a number of different clubs."

Michael acknowledges that there have to be control systems in place to manage KnitMedia's growth. "There has to be some sort of rigidity to the communication process and the reporting process that's going to allow us to grow and have controls. We're really going to invest in a real accounting software program that is custom for our business, and scalable for the growth that we plan. So we can plug a club into LA and we get a download every hour of their ticket sales, and of our bar sales; we are thinking about it in these ways. And if we do it right I think it's very, very manageable. But we have to make sure that we're completely on top of the controls."

According to Ken, "We have a global banking account so we can . . . see what our bank accounts are in Amsterdam, London, . . . Los Angeles, New York—on any given day, on any basis, so our Financial Controller has complete control over the amount of . . . money that's coming in and going out. We can . . . make all our check payments through the bank, and we don't have to rely as much on . . . local bookkeepers and controllers to know what's going on. We're able to get greater efficiency out of our long-term . . . cash assets that way as well." That means, says Ed, that "we want to be able to have some sense of central management control here, which is where the headquarters will always be."

Questions

Based on the cases, the videos, the textbook you've looked at thus far, and your knowledge from other sources, answer the following questions:

1 Using the categorizations in the textbook, name the types of control systems used by KnitMedia. Why are or why aren't these control systems appropriate to the type of organization KnitMedia is? What

other control systems would you suggest be used? Why?

2 Perform a service audit on KnitMedia, and indicate how it is meeting the service challenge and how it fares on Albrecht's service triangle. What recommendations would you make to Michael Dorf as a result of your analysis?

3 Discuss KnitMedia's use of technology to manage KnitMedia more effectively. What techniques do you think are working well, and why? Discuss any holes you see and what should be done about them.

SOURCE: End-of-part video cases prepared by d.t. ogilvie, Rutgers University.

Answers to Chapter Tests

CHAPTER 1
True/False 1. F 2. T 3. T 4. F 5. F 6. T 7. T 8. T 9. T 10. T
Multiple Choice 1. C 2. D 3. C 4. B 5. D 6. D 7. A 8. C 9. C 10. A

CHAPTER 2
True/False 1. F 2. F 3. F 4. T 5. F 6. F 7. F 8. T 9. F 10. F
Multiple Choice 1. B 2. D 3. D 4. C 5. A 6. A 7. A 8. D 9. B 10. A

CHAPTER 3
True/False 1. T 2. F 3. F 4. F 5. T 6. F 7. T 8. T 9. T 10. F
Multiple Choice 1. B 2. D 3. B 4. A 5. C 6. D 7. D 8. C 9. A 10. D

CHAPTER 4
True/False 1. T 2. F 3. F 4. F 5. T 6. T 7. F 8. T 9. T 10. T
Multiple Choice 1. B 2. D 3. D 4. D 5. B 6. C 7. C 8. A 9. C 10. B

CHAPTER 5
True/False 1. T 2. F 3. F 4. T 5. T 6. T 7. T 8. F 9. T 10. T
Multiple Choice 1. D 2. D 3. B 4. A 5. B 6. C 7. D 8. A 9. A 10. D

CHAPTER 6
True/False 1. T 2. F 3. F 4. F 5. T 6. T 7. T 8. T 9. F 10. T
Multiple Choice 1. A 2. C 3. B 4. D 5. D 6. A 7. C 8. B 9. C 10. B

CHAPTER 7
True/False 1. F 2. T 3. F 4. T 5. T 6. T 7. T 8. T 9. F 10. F
Multiple Choice 1. C 2. A 3. D 4. C 5. D 6. C 7. B 8. D 9. B 10. C

CHAPTER 8
True/False 1. T 2. T 3. F 4. F 5. T 6. T 7. F 8. T 9. F 10. F
Multiple Choice 1. D 2. C 3. B 4. C 5. C 6. D 7. D 8. A 9. D 10. D

CHAPTER 9
True/False 1. T 2. F 3. T 4. F 5. T 6. F 7. F 8. F 9. T 10. F
Multiple Choice 1. D 2. B 3. D 4. D 5. B 6. C 7. C 8. D 9. D 10. D

CHAPTER 10
True/False 1. T 2. T 3. F 4. F 5. T 6. T 7. T 8. F 9. T 10. F
Multiple Choice 1. D 2. A 3. B 4. D 5. A 6. D 7. D 8. A 9. B 10. A

CHAPTER 11
True/False   1. T 2. F 3. F 4. T 5. T 6. T 7. T 8. T 9. T 10. F
Multiple Choice   1. A 2. C 3. B 4. A 5. D 6. C 7. C 8. D 9. D 10. A

CHAPTER 12
True/False   1. F 2. T 3. F 4. F 5. F 6. T 7. T 8. T 9. F 10. T
Multiple Choice   1. B 2. C 3. D 4. A 5. D 6. A 7. B 8. C 9. A 10. C

CHAPTER 13
True/False   1. T 2. F 3. T 4. F 5. F 6. T 7. T 8. F 9. T 10. F
Multiple Choice   1. D 2. D 3. C 4. B 5. D 6. D 7. D 8. A 9. A 10. A

CHAPTER 14
True/False   1. T 2. F 3. T 4. T 5. T 6. F 7. T 8. F 9. T 10. T
Multiple Choice   1. A 2. C 3. D 4. C 5. D 6. C 7. D 8. B 9. D 10. C

CHAPTER 15
True/False   1. F 2. T 3. F 4. F 5. T 6. F 7. T 8. T 9. T 10. T
Multiple Choice   1. D 2. B 3. A 4. C 5. D 6. B 7. D 8. A 9. D 10. A

CHAPTER 16
True/False   1. T 2. T 3. F 4. T 5. F 6. F 7. T 8. T 9. T 10. T
Multiple Choice   1. C 2. A 3. A 4. B 5. D 6. D 7. D 8. B 9. A 10. C

CHAPTER 17
True/False   1. T 2. F 3. T 4. F 5. F 6. T 7. T 8. F 9. T 10. T
Multiple Choice   1. D 2. B 3. B 4. D 5. A 6. C 7. A 8. C 9. B 10. A

CHAPTER 18
True/False   1. F 2. F 3. T 4. F 5. F 6. F 7. T 8. F 9. T 10. T
Multiple Choice   1. C 2. D 3. D 4. C 5. B 6. C 7. B 8. C 9. A 10. B

Endnotes

Chapter 1

1 Michael H. Martin, "Kinko's: Business Technology Services," *Fortune*, 8 July 1996, 102.

2 Katherine Arnst, "This is Not a Fun Business to Be In Now," *Business Week*, 6 July 1992, 68.

3 Wendy Zellner, Andrea Rothman, and Erik Shine, "The Airline Mess," *Business Week*, 6 July 1992, 51.

4 Thomas Stewart, "Welcome to the Revolution," *Fortune*, 13 December 1993, 68.

5 Rick Tetzeli, "What It's Really Like to Be Mark Andreesen," *Fortune*, 9 December 1996, 137–54.

6 Michael Martin, "The Next Big Thing: A Bookstore," *Fortune*, 9 December 1996, 169–70.

7 Henry Goldblatt, "Industry.Net: Online Shopping for Manufacturers," *Fortune*, 8 July 1996, 90.

8 Stewart, "Welcome to the Revolution," 66.

9 Ibid., 67.

10 "A Portrait of America: How the Country is Changing," *Business Week*, 1992, 51.

11 "Grabbing New World Orders," *Business Week*, Reinventing America, 1992, 110–11.

12 Charles W. Hill, *International Business* (Burr Ridge, IL: Irwin, 1994), 6.

13 Ibid., 9.

14 Amy Barrett, Peter Elstrom, and Catherine Arnst, "Vaulting the Walls with Wireless," *Business Week*, 20 January 1997, 85, 88.

15 Francis Fukuyama, "Are We at the End of History?" *Fortune*, 15 January 1990, 75–78.

16 Ibid., 78.

17 Philip Zweig, "Goldman's Spectacular Roadtrip," *Business Week*, 1 November 1993, 110.

18 Thomas Stewart, "How to Manage in the New Era," *Fortune*, 15 January 1990, 68.

19 Ronald Kucher, "Overview and Implications of the Projections to 2000," *Monthly Labor Review*, September 1987, 3–9.

20 Bryan O'Reilly, "Your New Global Workforce," *Fortune*, 14 December 1992, 52–66.

21 Richard Crawford, *In the Era of Human Capital* (New York: Harper, 1991), 10.

22 Ibid.

23 Ibid., 31.

24 James Brian Quinn, *Intelligent Enterprise* (New York: The Free Press, 1992), 3.

25 Ibid., 26.

26 Fukuyama, "Are We at the End of History?"

27 Thomas Stewart, "Brain Power," *Fortune*, 3 June 1991, 44. See also Thomas Stewart, "Brain Power," *Fortune*, 17 March 1997, 105–10.

28 Peter Drucker, "The Coming of the New Organization," *Harvard Business Review*, January–February 1988, 45.

29 Henry Mintzberg, "The Manager's Job: Folklore and Fact," *Harvard Business Review*, July–August 1975, 489–561.

30 See, for example, ibid.; and George Copeman, *The Chief Executive* (London: Leviathan House, 1971), 271.

31 Drucker, "The Coming of the New Organization," 44.

32 These are based on Henry Mintzberg, "The Manager's Job: Folklore and Fact," 54–59.

33 Noel Tichy and Ram Charan, "The CEO as Coach: An Interview with Allied-Signal's Lawrence A. Bossidy," *Harvard Business Review*, March–April 1995, 69–78.

34 Ibid., 70.

35 Ibid., 73.

36 Ibid., 70.

37 Ibid.

38 Ibid., 76.

39 Sumantra Ghoshal and Christopher Bartlett, "Changing the Role of Top Management: Beyond Structure to Processes," *Harvard Business Review*, January–February 1995, 86–96.

40 Ibid., 89.

41 Ibid., 91.

42 Ibid., 96.

43 Ibid., 94.

44 Renato Tagiuri, "Managing People: Ten Essential Behaviors," *Harvard Business Review*, January–February 1995, 10–11.

45 John Newstrom and Keith Davis, *Organizational Behavior: Human Behavior at Work* (New York: McGraw-Hill, 1997), 5.

46 John Holland, *Making Vocational Choices: A Theory of Careers* (Englewood Cliffs, NJ: Prentice-Hall, 1973); see also John Holland, *Assessment Booklet: A Guide to Educational and Career Planning* (Odessa, FL: Psychological Assessment Resources, Inc., 1990).

47 Edgar Schein, *Career Dynamics: Matching Individual and Organizational Needs* (Reading, MA: Addison-Wesley, 1978), 128–29.

48 A. Howard and D. W. Bray, *Managerial Lives in Transition: Advancing Age and Changing Times* (New York: Guilford, 1988); discussed in Dwayne Schultz and Sydney Ellen Schultz, *Psychology and Work Today* (New York: Macmillan Publishing Co., 1994), 103–4.

49 Ibid., Schultz and Schultz, 104.

50 Ibid.

51 Rosabeth Moss Kanter, *When Giants Learn to Dance* (New York: Touchstone, 1989).

52 Drucker, "The Coming of the New Organization," 45–54.

53 John Byrne, "Paradigms for Post Modern Managers," *Business Week*, Reinventing America, 1992, 62–63.

54 Tom Peters, *Liberation Management* (New York: Alfred Knopf, 1992), 9.

55 Ibid.

56 David Kirkpatrick, "Could AT&T Rule the World?" *Fortune*, 17 May 1993, 55–66.

57 Ibid., 62.

58 Ibid., 55.

59 Ibid., 64.

60 John Keller, "AT&T's New President is Wasting No Time in Shaking Things Up," *Wall Street Journal*, 24 December 1996.

61 Bryan Dumaine, "What the Leaders of Tomorrow See," *Fortune*, 3 July 1989, 58.

62 These are based on Walter Kiechel III, "How We Will Work in the Year 2000," *Fortune,* 17 May 1993, 79.

63 Dumaine, "What the Leaders of Tomorrow See," 51.

64 Rosabeth Moss Kanter, "The New Managerial Work," *Harvard Business Review,* November–December 1989, 88.

65 Ibid.

66 Drucker, "The Coming of the New Organization," 45.

67 Peters, *Liberation Management.*

68 Bryan Dumaine, "The New Non-Managers," *Fortune,* 22 February 1993, 81.

69 Thomas Stewart, "How GE Keeps Those Ideas Coming," *Fortune,* 12 August 1991, 42.

70 Drucker, "The Coming of the New Organization," 43.

71 Stratford Sherman, "A Master Class in Radical Change," *Fortune,* 13 December 1993, 82.

Chapter 1 APPENDIX

1   Alvin Toffler, *Future Shock* (New York: Bantam Books, 1971), 43.

2   Adam Smith, *An Inquiry Into the Nature and Causes of Wealth of Nations,* ed., Edward Cannan, 4th ed. (London: Methuen, 1925). Published originally in 1776.

3   Alfred Chandler, *Strategy and Structure* (Cambridge, MA: MIT Press); see also Daniel Wren, *The Evolution of Management Thought* (New York: John Wiley, 1979).

4   D. S. Pugh, *Organization Theory* (Baltimore: Penguin, 1971), 126–27.

5   Claude George, Jr., *The History of Management Thought* (Englewood Cliffs, NJ: Prentice-Hall, 1972), 99–101.

6   Richard Hopeman, *Production* (Columbus, OH: Charles Merrill, 1965), 478–85.

7   Henri Fayol, *General and Industrial Management,* translated by Constance Storrs (London: Sir Isaac Pitman, 1949), 42–43.

8   Based on Richard Hall, "Intra-Organizational Structural Variation: Application of the Bureaucratic Model," *Administrative Science Quarterly, 7,* no. 3 (December 1962): 295–308.

9   William Scott, *Organization Theory* (Homewood, IL: Richard D. Irwin, 1967).

10 F. L. Roethlisberger and William Dickson, *Management and Worker* (Boston: Graduate School of Business, Harvard University, 1947), 21.

11 Chandler, *Strategy and Structure,* 19–51.

12 Warren G. Bennis, "Organizational Development and the Fate of Bureaucracy." Address at the Division of Industrial and Business Psychology, American Psychological Association, September 5, 1964. Reprinted in L. L. Cummings and W. E. Scott, Jr., *Organizational Behavior and Human Performance* (Homewood, IL: Richard D. Irwin and Dorsey, 1969), 436.

13 Douglas McGregor, "The Human Side of Enterprise," Edward Deci, B. Von haller Gilmer, and Harry Kairn, *Readings in Industrial and Organizational Psychology* (New York: McGraw-Hill, 1972), 123.

14 R. Likert, *New Patterns of Management* (New York: McGraw-Hill, 1961), 6.

15 Ibid., 103.

16 Chris Argyris, *Integrating the Individual and the Organization* (New York: John Wiley, 1964).

17 Likert, *New Patterns of Management,* 91.

18 Ibid., 100.

19 Ibid.

20 Ibid.

21 Chester Barnard, *The Functions of the Executive* (Cambridge: Harvard University Press, 1968), 84.

22 Ibid., 167.

23 Ibid., 143.

24 Herbert A. Simon, *Administrative Behavior* (New York: Free Press, 1976), 11.

25 C. West Churchman, Russell Ackoff, and E. Linard Arnoff, *Introduction to Operations Research* (New York: John Wiley, 1957), 18.

26 Daniel Wren, *The Evolution of Management Thought* (New York: John Wiley, 1979), 512.

27 C. West Churchman, *The Systems Approach* (New York: Delta, 1968).

28 Joan Woodward, *Industrial Organizations: Theory and Practice* (London: Oxford University Press, 1965), 64–65.

Chapter 2

1   Kambiz Foroohar, "Rich Man, Poor Man," *Forbes,* 24 March 1997, 120–24.

2   Charles Hill, *International Business* (Burr Ridge, IL: Irwin, 1994), 4; Dawn Anfuso, "Colgate's Global HR United under One Strategy," *Personnel Journal 74,* no. 10 (October 1995):44ff.

3   For a discussion see, for example, Arvind Phatak, *International Dimensions of Management* (Boston: PWS-Kent, 1989), 2.

4   John Daniels and Lee Radebaugh, *International Business* (Reading, MA: Addison-Wesley, 1994), 8; Richard Robinson, *Internationalization of Business: An Introduction* (Hinsdale, IL: Dryden Press, 1984), 271–72.

5   Theodore Levitt, "The Globalization of Markets," *Harvard Business Review,* May–June 1983, 92–102.

6   For a discussion see, for example, Michael Czinkota, Pietra Rivoli, and Ilka Ronkinen, *International Business* (Fort Worth: The Dryden Press, 1992), Chapter 2.

7   Ibid., 116.

8   Daniels and Radebaugh, *International Business,* 409.

9   Paul Dickens, *Global Shift* (New York: Guilford Press, 1992), 45; reprinted in Hill, *International Business,* 14.

10 *The Economist Book of Vital World Statistics* (New York: Random House, 1990); and Hill, *International Business,* 13.

11 See, for example, Susan Lee, "Are We Building New Berlin Walls?" *Forbes,* 7 January 1991, 86–89; Tom Reilly, "The Harmonization of Standards in the European Union and the Impact on U.S. Business," *Business Horizons,* March/April 1995.

12 Daniels and Radebaugh, *International Business,* 9–10.

13 Ted Rakstis, "Going Global," *Kiwanis Magazine,* October 1981, 39–43.

14 Thomas Clasen, "An Exporter's Guide to Selecting Foreign Sales Agents and Distributors," *The Journal of European Business 3,* no. 2 (November–December 1991):28–32.

15 Albert G. Holzinger, "Paving the Way for Small Exporters," *Nation's Business,* June 1992, 42–43.

16 Hill, *International Business,* 402.

17 Art Garcia, "It's in the Mail," *World Trade,* April 1992, 56–62.

18 See, for example, Daniels and Radebaugh, *International Business,* 544.

19 Czinkota et al., *International Business,* 278.

20 Hill, *International Business,* 411.

21 Daniels and Radebaugh, *International Business,* G-19.

22 Kenichi Ohmae, "The Global Logic of Strategic Alliances," *Harvard Business Review,* March–April 1989, 143–54.

23 Katherine Rudie Harrigan, "Joint Ventures and Global Strategies," *Columbia Journal of World Business 19* (Summer 1984):7–16; Czinkota et al., *International Business,* 320.
24 Ohmae, "The Global Logic," 143.
25 A. DePalma, "Still Under Construction," *Wichita Eagle Beacon,* 10 July 1994, 1E–2E; Kamel Fatehi, *International Management* (Upper Saddle River, NJ: Prentice Hall, 1996), 172.
26 Robert Neff, "Guess Who's Selling Barbies in Japan Now?" *Business Week,* 9 December 1991, 72, 74, 76.
27 Jeremy Main, "How to Go Global—and Why," *Fortune,* 28 August 1989, 70.
28 Hill, *International Business,* 5–6.
29 "Grabbing New World Orders," *Business Week/Reinventing America,* 1992, 110–11.
30 David Francis, "Global Frontiers of Business," *The Christian Science Monitor,* 11 April 1991, 9.
31 Based on Rick Yan, "To Reach China's Consumers, Adapt to Quo Qing," *Harvard Business Review,* September–October 1994, 66–74.
32 Hill, *International Business,* 6; and Michael McGrath and Richard Hoole, "Manufacturing's New Economies of Scale," *Harvard Business Review,* May–June 1992, 94.
33 Based on ibid., 94–102.
34 Regina Fazio Maruca, "The Right Way to Go Global: An Interview with Whirlpool CEO David Whitman," *Harvard Business Review,* March–April 1994, 136.
35 Based on Brian O'Reilly, "Your New Global Workforce," *Fortune,* 14 December 1992, 52–66.
36 Ibid., 64. See also Shirley R. Fishman, "Developing a Global Workforce," *Canadian Business Review 23,* no. 1 (Spring 1996):18–21.
37 See Mariah E. DeForest, "Thinking of a Plant in Mexico?" *Academy of Management Executive 8,* no. 1 (February 1994):33–40.
38 Ibid., 34.
39 Ibid., 37.
40 Ibid., 38. See also Randall S. Schuler, Susan E. Jackson, Ellen Jackofsky, and John W. Slocum, "Managing Human Resources in Mexico: A Cultural Understanding," *Business Horizons 39,* no. 3 (May 1996):55–61.
41 Robert Reich, "Who Is Them?" *Harvard Business Review,* March–April 1991, 77–88.
42 Philip Harris and Robert Moran, *Managing Cultural Differences* (Houston: Gulf Publishing Company, 1979), 1.
43 Marlene Piturro, "Super Manager!" *World Trade, International Business,* Annual Editions, 1982, 80–82. See also Leigh Ann Colli Allard, "Managing Globe-trotting Expats," *Management Review 85,* no. 5 (May 1996):39–43.
44 See "Doing Business in Japan," in Michael Carrell, Daniel Jennings, and Christina Heavrin, *Fundamentals of Organizational Behavior* (Upper Saddle River, NJ: Prentice Hall, 1997). For a recent discussion of this phenomenon see, for example, Richard Lewis, *When Cultures Collide* (London: Nicholas Brealey, 1967).
45 Gretchen Spreitzer, Morgan McCall, Jr., and Joan Mahoney, "Early Identification of International Executive Potential," *Journal of Applied Psychology 82,* no. 1 (February 1997) 6–29.
46 Note that there are few, if any, "pure" market economies or command economies anymore. For example, much of the French banking system is still under government control. And it was only several years ago that the government of England privatized (sold to private investors) British Airways.
47 "GDP Growth," *Fortune,* Special Issue, Autumn–Winter 1993, 77.
48 Ibid., 65.
49 Bryan Moskal, "The World Trade Topography: How Level Is It?" *Industry Week,* 18 May 1992, 24–36.
50 Daniels and Radebaugh, *International Business,* 138.
51 Czinkota et al., *International Business,* 640.
52 Benjamin Weiner, "What Executives Should Know About Political Risk," *Management Review,* January 1992, 19–22.
53 Laura Pincus and James Belohlav, "Legal Issues in Multinational Business Strategy: To Play the Game, You Have to Know the Rules," *Academy of Management Executive 10,* no. 3 (November 1996):52–61.
54 Ibid., 53–54.
55 Ibid., 53.
56 Harris and Moran, *Managing Cultural Differences,* 227–28. See also Jack N. Behrman, "Cross-cultural Impacts on International Competitiveness," *Business and the Contemporary World 7,* no. 4 (1995):93–113 and Lorna Wrighte, "Building Cultural Competence," *Canadian Business Review 23,* no. 1 (Spring 1996):29ff.
57 Geert Hofstede, "Cultural Dimensions in People Management," in *Globalizing Management,* eds. Vladimir Pucik, Noel Tichy, and Carole Barnett (New York: John Wiley & Sons, Inc., 1992), 139–58.
58 Ibid., 143.
59 Ibid.
60 Ibid., 147.
61 Ibid.
62 Czinkota et al., *International Business,* 205.
63 United Nations, *Draft International Code of Conduct on the Transfer of Technology* (New York: United Nations, 1981), 3; quoted in Czinkota et al., *International Business,* 313.
64 Czinkota et al., *International Business,* 314.
65 Phatak, *International Dimensions of Management,* 46–49.
66 John Rossant, "After the Scandals," *Business Week,* 22 November 1993, 56–57.
67 Anant Negandhi, *International Management* (Newton, MA: Allyn & Bacon, Inc., 1987), 61. See also Keith W. Glaister and Peter J. Buckley, "Strategic Motives for International Alliance Formation," *Journal of Management Studies 33,* no. 3 (May 1996):301–22.
68 Richard D. Robinson, *Internationalization of Business: An Introduction* (Hillsdale, IL: The Dryden Press, 1984), 227–28.
69 *PR Newswire,* 27 March 1997, "Reynolds Metal Announces Organizational and Management Changes."
70 See also S. M. Davis, "Managing and Organizing Multinational Corporations," in *Transnational Management,* eds. C. A. Bartlett and S. Ghoshal (Homewood, IL: Richard D. Irwin, 1992); and Phatak, *International Dimensions of Management,* 78–104.
71 Paul Blocklyn, "Developing the International Executive," *Personnel* (March 1989):44. Overseas assignments can also be risky for the manager who's sent abroad, with one recent study concluding that their employers don't reward their international experience. See Linda Grant, "That Overseas Job Could Derail Your Career," *Fortune,* 14 April 1997, 167. See also Martha I. Finney, "Global Success Rides on Keeping Top Talent," *HRMagazine 41,* no. 4 (April 1996):69–72 and Reyer A. Swaak, "Expatriate Failures: Too Many, Too Much Cost, Too Little Planning," *Compensation and Benefits Review 27,* no. 6 (November 1995):47–55.
72 Jackqueline Heidelberg, "When Sexual Harassment Is a Foreign Affair," *Personnel Journal* (April 1996).
73 Madelyn Callahan, "Preparing the New Global Manager," *Training and Development Journal* (March 1989): 30. See also Charlene Marmer Solomon, "Big Mac's McGlobal HR Secrets," *Personnel Journal 75,* no. 4 (April 1996):46ff and Lorna Wrighte, "Building Cultural Competence," *Canadian Business Review 23,* no. 1 (Spring 1996):29ff.

74 Joseph Fucini and Suzy Fucini, *Working for the Japanese* (New York: The Free Press, 1990), 122–23. See also Richard Kustin and Robert Jones, "The Influence of Corporate Headquarters on Leadership Styles in Japanese and US Subsidiary Companies," *Leadership Organizational Development Journal 16,* no. 5 (1995): 11–15.

Chapter 3

1 Robyn Meredith, "VW agrees to pay GM $100 million in Espionage Suit," *New York Times,* 10 January 1997, A1, D3; Peter Elkind, "Blood Feud," *Fortune,* 14 April 1997, 90–102.

2 Roger Bennett, "Profile of Harry Crown, Founder of General Dynamics, Inc.," *New York Times,* 16 June 1985, 26F; as presented in Laroue Tone Hosmer, *The Ethics of Management* (Homewood, IL: Irwin, 1987), 16; Ken Western, "Ethical Spying," *Business Ethics 9,* no. 5 (September 1995): 22–23.

3 Manuel Velasquez, *Business Ethics: Concepts and Cases* (Englewood Cliffs, NJ: Prentice-Hall, 1992), 9; Kate Walter, "Ethics Hot Lines Tap into More Than Wrongdoing," *HRMagazine 40,* no. 9 (September 1995): 79–85.

4 The following, except as noted, is based on Velasquez, *Business Ethics,* 9–12.

5 Ibid., 9.

6 This is based on ibid., 12–14.

7 Ibid., 12. For further discussion see Kurt Baier, *Moral Points of View,* abbr. ed. (New York: Random House, 1965), 88.

8 For further discussion of ethics and morality see Tom Beauchamp and Norman Bowe, *Ethical Theory and Business* (Englewood Cliffs, NJ: Prentice-Hall, 1993), 1–19.

9 See Michael McCarthy, "James Bond Hits the Supermarket: Stores Snoop on Shoppers' Habits to Boost Sales," *The Wall Street Journal,* 25 August 1993, B12.

10 Sar Morris et al., "A Test of Environmental, Situational, and Personal Influences on the Ethical Intentions of CEOs," *Business and Society 34,* no. 2 (August 1995):119–47.

11 Justin Longnecker, Joseph McKinney, and Carlos Moore, "The Generation Gap in Business Ethics," *Business Horizons,* September–October 1989, 9–14.

12 Ibid., 10. For a discussion of the development of a scale for measuring individual beliefs about organizational ethics, see Kristina Froelich and Janet Kottke, "Measuring Individual Beliefs About Organizational Ethics," *Educational and Psychological Measurement 51* (1991), 377–83.

13 Thomas Tyson, "Does Believing that Everyone Else Is Less Ethical Have an Impact on Work Behavior?" *Journal of Business Ethics 11* (1992), 707–17.

14 Lynn Sharp Paine, "Managing for Organizational Integrity," *Harvard Business Review,* March–April 1994, 106.

15 Ibid., 107–17.

16 Ibid., 108.

17 Ibid., 107–8.

18 Ibid., 108. For a recent analysis of the financial consequences of illegal corporate activities, see Melissa Baucus and David Baucus, "Paying the Piper: An Empirical Examination of Longer-term Financial Consequences of Illegal Corporate Behavior," *Academy of Management Journal 40,* no. 1 (February 1997):129–51; Dale Kurschner, "Five Ways Ethical Business Creates Fatter Profits," *Business Ethics 10,* no. 2 (March 1996):20ff. James Hunter, "Good Ethics Means Good Business," *Canadian Business Review 23,* no. 1 (Spring 1996):14–17.

19 This is from Saul Gellerman, "Why Good Managers Make Bad Ethical Choices," *Harvard Business Review,* July–August 1986, 86. Some experts argue that a mature organization sometimes needs a crisis to shake itself out of its ethical lethargy. See, for example, Christopher Boult, Stephen Drew, Alan Pearson, Guy Saint-Pierre, James C. Rush, and Brenda Zimmerman, "Crisis and Renewal: Ethics Anarchy in Mature Organizations," *Business Quarterly 60,* no. 3 (Spring 1996):24–32.

20 Gellerman, ibid.

21 Ibid.

22 For a discussion, see Steen Brenner and Earl Molander, "Is the Ethics of Business Changing?" *Harvard Business Review,* January–February 1977, 57–71; Robert Jackyll, "Moral Mazes: Bureaucracy and Managerial Work," *Harvard Business Review,* September–October 1983, 118–30; see also Ishmael P. Akaah, "The Influence of Organizational Rank and Role of Marketing Professionals' Ethical Judgments," *Journal of Business Ethics 15,* no. 6, (June 1996):605–14.

23 From Guy Brumback, "Managing Above the Bottom Line of Ethics," *Supervisory Management,* December 1993, 12.

24 John Kotter and James Heskett, *Corporate Culture and Performance* (New York: The Free Press, 1992), 141.

25 Deon Nel, Leyland Pitt, and Richard Watson, "Business Ethics: Defining the Twilight Zone," *Journal of Business Ethics 8* (1989):781; Brenner and Molander, "Is the Ethics of Business Changing?"

26 Robert Sweeney and Howard Siers, "Survey: Ethics in Corporate America," *Management Accounting,* June 1990, 34–40.

27 Ibid., 34.

28 Ibid., 35.

29 Rochelle Kelin, "Ethnic versus Organizational Cultures: The Bureaucratic Alternatives," *International Journal of Public Administration 19,* no. 3 (March 1996):323–44.

30 Paine, "Managing for Organizational Integrity," 110.

31 This is based on James Weber, "Influences upon Managerial Moral Decision Making: Nature of the Harm and Magnitude of Consequences," *Human Relations 49,* no. 1 (1996):1–21.

32 *Corporate Ethics: A Prime Business Asset* (New York: The Business Round Table, February 1988), 81.

33 Ibid., 78.

34 Ibid., 79.

35 Ibid.

36 For a discussion see, for example, Alan Rowe et al., *Strategic Management: A Methodological Approach* (Reading, MA: Addison-Wesley Publishing Co., 1994), 101.

37 Ibid., 118.

38 Ibid., 122.

39 Kenneth Andrew, "Ethics in Practice," *Harvard Business Review,* September–October 1989, 99–104; Rowe et al., 101.

40 Rowe et al., 101.

41 Ibid., 4.

42 Ibid., 6.

43 Kate Walters, "Ethics Hot Lines tap into more than wrongdoing," *HRMagazine 40,* no. 9 (September 1995): 79–85.

44 Rowe et al., 7; see also John J. Quinn, "The Role of 'Good Conversation' in Strategic Control," *Journal of Management Studies 33,* no. 3 (May 1996):381–95.

45 Ibid., 9.

46 Sandra Gray, "Audit Your Ethics," *Association Management 48,* no. 9 (September 1996):188.

47 Robert Hartley, *Business Ethics* (New York: Wiley, 1993), p. 147–45. For a discussion of ethics as it relates to various facets of social responsibility, see Velasquez, *Business Ethics,* 211–371. See also "Civics 101," *The Economist,* 11 May 1996, 61, and

Dale Kurschner, "The 100 Best Corporate Citizens," *Business Ethics 10*, no. 3 (May 1996):24–35.

48 Milton Friedman, *Capitalism and Freedom* (Chicago: University of Chicago Press, 1962), 133.

49 Beauchamp and Bowie, *Ethical Theory and Business*, 49–52.

50 Ibid., 79.

51 Ibid., 60.

52 Ibid., 54.

53 William Evan and R. Edward Freeman, "A Stakeholder Theory of the Modern Corporation: Kantian Capitalism," *Ethical Theory of Business*, 82. See also Kenneth Goodpaster, "Business Ethics and Stakeholder Analysis," *Business Ethics Quarterly 1* (January 1991):53–73.

54 John Simon, Charles Powers, and John Gunnermann, "The Responsibilities of Corporations and Their Owners," in *The Ethical Investor: Universities and Corporate Responsibility* (New Haven, CT: Yale University Press, 1972); reprinted in Beauchamp and Bowie, *Ethical Theory of Business*, 60–65.

55 Ben & Jerry's Homemade, Inc., Employee Handbook.

56 Ben & Jerry's Public Relations Release, 5 October 1990.

57 Jo-Ann Johnston, "Social Auditors: The New Breed of Expert," *Business Ethics 10*, no. 2 (March 1996):27.

58 Karen Paul and Steven Ludenberg, "Applications of Corporate Social Monitoring Systems: Types, Dimensions and Goals," *Journal of Business Ethics 11* (1992):1–10.

59 Karen Paul, "Corporate Social Monitoring in South Africa: A Decade of Achievement, An Uncertain Future," *Journal of Business Ethics 8* (1989):464.

60 Ibid. See also John S. North, "Living Under a Social Code of Ethics: Eli Lilly in South Africa Operating Under the Sullivan Principles," *Business and the Contemporary World 8*, no. 1 (1996):168–80; and S. Prakash Sethi, "Working With International Codes of Conduct: Experience of U.S. Companies Operating in South Africa Under the Sullivan Principles," *Business and the Contemporary World 8*, no. 1 (1996):129–50.

61 Janet Near, "Whistle-blowing: Encourage It!" *Business Horizons*, January–February, 1989, 5. See also Robert J. Paul and James B. Townsend, "Don't Kill the Messenger! Whistle-blowing in America: A Review with Recommendations," *Employee Responsibilities and Rights 9*, no. 2 (June 1996):149–61.

62 Near, op. cit.

63 Ibid., 6.

64 See also S. Gellerman, "Why Good Managers Make Ethical Choices," *Harvard Business Review*, July–August 1986, 85–90.

65 See, for example, Taylor Cox, Jr., *Cultural Diversity in Organizations* (San Francisco: Berrett-Koehler Publishers, Inc., 1993), 3.

66 Ibid. See also T. Horowitz and C. Forman, "Clashing Cultures," *The Wall Street Journal*, 14 August 1990, A1.

67 Cox, 3–4.

68 Cox, 11.

69 Michael Carrell, Daniel Jennings, and Christina Heavrin, *Fundamentals of Organizational Behavior* (Upper Saddle River, NJ: Prentice-Hall, 1997), 282–83.

70 George Kronenberger, "Out of the Closet," *Personnel Journal* (June 1991):40–44.

71 Cox, 88.

72 Cox, 89.

73 J. H. Greenhaus and S. Parasuraman, "Job Performance Attributions and Career Advancement Prospects: An Examination of Gender and Race Affects," *Organizational Behavior and Human Decision Processes 55*, no. 2 (July 1993):273–98.

74 Adapted from Cox, 64.

75 Cox, 179–80.

76 Madeleine Heilmann and Lewis Saruwatari, "When Beauty Is Beastly: The Effects of Appearance and Sex on Evaluation of Job Applicants for Managerial and Nonmanagerial Jobs," *Organizational Behavior and Human Performance 23* (June 1979):360–72; see also Tracy McDonald and Milton Hakel, "Effects of Applicant Race, Sex, Suitability, and Answers on Interviewer's Questioning Strategy and Ratings," *Personnel Psychology 38*, no. 2 (Summer 1985):321–34.

77 Cox, 236.

78 K. Kram, *Mentoring at Work* (Glenview, IL: Scott Foresman, 1985); Cox, 198.

79 See, for example, G. F. Dreher and R. A. Ash, "A Comparative Study of Mentoring among Men and Women in Managerial, Professional, and Technical Positions," *Journal of Applied Psychology 75*, no. 5 (1990):1–8.

80 Charles Van Doren, *A History of Knowledge* (New York: Ballantine, 1991), 75.

81 Benjamin Hoff, *The Te of Piglet* (New York: Dutton, 1992), 109–10.

82 Ibid.

Chapter 4

1 Mark Fefer, "Micro Vision," *Fortune*, 8 July 1996, 9.

2 Max Bazerman, *Judgment in Managerial Decision Making* (New York: John Wiley & Sons, Inc., 1994), 3.

3 See, for example, Herbert Simon, *The New Science of Management Decision* (Englewood Cliffs, NJ: Prentice Hall, 1971), 45–47.

4 Larry Long and Nancy Long, *Computers*, (Upper Saddle River, NJ: Prentice-Hall, 1996), M-7.

5 Mairead Browne, *Organizational Decision Making and Information* (Norwood, NJ: Ablex Publishing Corporation, 1993), 6.

6 Richard Evans, "Advanced RISC Machines," *Fortune*, 28 October 1996, 162–68.

7 Bazerman, 5.

8 For a discussion see, for example, Bazerman, 4–5.

9 Ibid., 4.

10 Ibid.

11 James G. Miller, "Adjusting to Overloads of Information," in Joseph A. Litterer, *Organizations: Structure and Behavior* (New York: John Wiley, 1969), 313–22.

12 See Jerald Greenberg and Robert Baron, *Behavior in Organizations* (Englewood Cliffs, NJ: Prentice-Hall, 1995), 357–80.

13 Dewitt Dearborn and Herbert A. Simon, "Selective Perception: A Note on the Departmental Identification of Executives," *Sociometry 21*, (1958):140–44. For a recent study of this phenomenon, see Mary Waller, George Huber, and William Glick, "Functional Background as a Determinant of Executives' Selective Perception," *Academy of Management Journal 38*, no. 4 (August 1995):943–94. While not completely supporting the Dearborn findings, these researchers did also conclude that managers' functional backgrounds affected how they perceived organizational changes.

14 Kenneth Laudon and Jane Price Laudon, *Management Information Systems* (Upper Saddle River, NJ: Prentice Hall, 1996), 125. See also Bob F. Holder, "Intuitive Decision Making," *CMA 69*, no. 8 (October 1995):6.

15 Bazerman, 6–8.

16 Ibid., 38.

17 Lester Lefton and Laura Valvatne, *Mastering Psychology* (Boston: Allyn and Bacon, 1992), 248–49.

18 Ibid.
19 For a recent discussion, see Chris Argyris, "Good Communication That Blocks Learning," *Harvard Business Review,* July–August 1994, 77–86.
20 See, for example, Bazerman, 5.
21 James March and Herbert Simon, *Organizations* (New York: John Wiley, 1958), 140–41.
22 For a discussion of the importance of feedback and experience in decision making see, for example, J. H. Kagel and D. Levin, "The Winner's Curse and Public Information in Common Value Auctions," *American Economic Review 76,* (1986):917, and S. B. Ball, M. H. Bazerman, and J. S. Carroll, "An Evaluation of Learning in the Bilateral Winners' Curse," *Organizational Behavior and Human Decision Processes 48,* (1991):1–22. See also Gwen Ortmeyer, "Making Better Decisions Faster," *Management Review 85,* no. 6 (June 1996):53–56.
23 B. Fischhoff, "Cognitive Liabilities and Product Liability," *Journal of Products' Liability 1,* (1978):207–20; S. Lichtenstein and B. Fischhoff, "Training for Calibration," *Organizational Behavior and Human Performance 26,* (1980):149–71; Bazerman, 196–97. See also Greg Oldham and Anne Cummings, "Employee Creativity: Personal and Contextual Factors at Work," *Academy of Management Journal 39,* no. 3 (June 1996):607–34.
24 Bazerman, 93.
25 Quoted from ibid., 105–6.
26 Ibid., 108.
27 Quoted in Robert L. Heilbroner, "How to Make an Intelligent Decision," *Think,* December 1990, 2–4.
28 Ibid. See also, Theodore Rubin, *Overcoming Indecisiveness: The Eight Stages of Effective Decision Making* (New York: Avon Books, 1985).
29 See, for example, William Taggart and Enzo Valenzi, "Assessing Rational and Intuitive Styles: A Human Information Processing Metaphor," *Journal of Management Studies 27,* no. 2, (March 1990):150–71; Christopher W. Allinson and John Hayes, "The Cognitive Style Index: A Measure of Intuition—Anaylsis for Organizational Research," *Journal of Management Studies 33,* no. 1 (January 1996):119–35.
30 Henry Mintzberg, "Planning on the Left Side and Managing on the Right Side," *Harvard Business Review* (July–August 1976):49–58; for a recent discussion of the use of intuition in management, see Jagdish Parikh, *Intuition: The New Frontier of Management* (Cambridge, MA: Blackwell, 1994).
31 Peter Wright, Mark Kroll, and John Parnell, *Strategic Management Concepts* (Englewood Cliffs, NJ: Prentice Hall, 1996), 10.
32 This and the following guideline are from Heilbroner.
33 James Bowditsch and Anthony Buono, *A Primer on Organizational Behavior* (New York: John Wiley & Sons Inc., 1994) 171–72.
34 Michael Carrell, Daniel Jennings, and Christine Heavrin, *Fundamentals of Organizational Behavior* (Upper Saddle River, NJ: Prentice Hall, 1997) 346.
35 For a discussion of these and the following points see, for example, ibid.
36 Irving Janis, *Groupthink: Psychological Studies of Policy Decisions and Fiascos,* 2d edition (Boston: Houghton Mifflin, 1982).
37 See C. Manz and H. P. Sims, Jr., *Business Without Bosses* (New York: John Wiley & Sons, 1993); discussed in Jerald Greenberg and Robert Baron, *Behavior in Organizations,* (Englewood Cliffs, NJ: Prentice Hall, 1995), 312–13.
38 For an additional perspective on many of these see Randy Hirokawa and Marshall Scott Poole, *Communication and Group Decision Making* (Thousand Oaks, CA: Sage Publications, Inc., 1996), 354–64. See also John O. Whitney and E. Kirby Warren, "Action Forums: How General Electric and Other Firms Have Learned to Make Better Decisions," *Columbia Journal of World Business 30,* no. 4, (Winter 1995): 18–27; Steven G. Rogelberg and Steven M. Rumery, "Gender Diversity, Team Decision Quality, Time on Task, and Interpersonal Cohesion," *Small Group Research 27,* 27, no. 1 (February 1996):79–90; Beatrice Shultz, Sandra M. Ketrow, and Daphne M. Urban, "Improving Decision Quality in the Small Group: The Role of the Reminder," *Small Group Research 26,* no. 4 (November 1995):521–41.
39 See, for example, Lefton and Valvatne, 249.
40 Greenberg and Baron, 393.
41 See Ron Zemke, "In Search of Good Ideas," *Training,* January 1993, 46–52; R. Brent Gallupe, Lana Bastianutti, and William Cooper, "Unblocking Brainstorms," *Journal of Applied Psychology* (January 1991):137–42.
42 R. B. Gallupe, A. R. Dennis, W. H. Cooper, J. S. Valacich, J. S. Bastianutti, and J. F. Nunamaker, "Electronic Brainstorming and Group Size," *Academy of Management Journal 35,* (1992):350–69.
43 The following example is based on Joseph Fucini and Suzy Fucini, *Working for the Japanese* (New York: The Free Press, 1990), 72–74.
44 Ibid., 73.
45 Ibid.
46 See, for example, Greenberg and Baron, 399–400.
47 See S. G. Rogelberg, J. L. Barnes-Farrell, and C. A. Lowe, "The Stepladder Technique: An Alternative Group Structure Facilitating Effective Group Decision Making," *Journal of Applied Psychology 57* (1992):730–37.
48 Norman R. F. Maier and E. P. McRay, "Increasing Innovation in Change Situations Through Leadership Skills," *Psychological Reports 31,* (1972):30–43.
49 Quoted in John Aram, *Presumed Superior: Individualism and American Business* (Englewood Cliffs, New Jersey: Prentice Hall, 1993), 2.
50 Nancy J. Adler, *International Dimensions of Organizational Behavior* (Boston: PWS- Kent, 1991), 77, 79.
51 This example is based loosely on an example presented in Bazerman, 78.

Chapter 4   APPENDIX

1 The breakeven point is also sometimes defined more technically as the quantity of output or sales that will result in a zero level of earnings before interest or taxes. See for example J. William Petty et al., *Basic Financial Management* (Englewood Cliffs, NJ: Prentice Hall 1993), 932.
2 Jay Heizer and Barry Render, *Production and Operations Management* (Upper Saddle River, NJ: Prentice Hall, 1996), 240–50.

Chapter 5

1 Michael Martin, "The Next Big Thing: A Bookstore," *Fortune,* 9 December 1996, 169–74.
2 George L. Morrisey, *A Guide to Tactical Planning* (San Francisco: Jossey-Bass, 1996), 61.
3 Leonard Goodstein, Timothy Nolan, and Jay William Pfeiffer, *Applied Strategic Planning* (New York: McGraw-Hill, Inc., 1993), 3.

4   Harold Koontz, Cyril O'Donnell, and Heinze Weihrich, *Management* (New York: McGraw-Hill, Inc., 1993), 3.

5   Harvey Kahalas, "A Look at Planning and Its Components," *Managerial Planning,* January–February 1982, 13–16; reprinted in Phillip DuBose, *Readings in Management* (Englewood Cliffs, NJ: Prentice Hall, Inc., 1988), 49–50. See also Mary M. Crossan, Henry W. Lane, Roderick E. White, and Leo Klus, "The Improvising Organization: Where Planning Meets Opportunity," *Organization Dynamics 24,* no. 4 (Spring 1996):20–35.

6   Ronald Henkoff, "How to Plan for 1995," *Fortune,* 31 December 1990, 74.

7   Kahalas, 49.

8   Peter Drucker, "Long Range Planning," *Management Science 5,* (1959), 238–49.

9   Harold Koontz and Cyril O'Donnell, *Principles of Management* (New York: McGraw-Hill, 1964), 85.

10   See, for example, Bill Vlasic, "Can Chrysler Keep It Up?" *Business Week,* 25 November 1996, 108–20.

11   This is from George Morrisey, *A Guide to Long-Range Planning* (San Francisco: Jossey-Bass, 1996), 72–73.

12   Goodstein, Nolan, and Pfeiffer, 170.

13   Peter F. Drucker, *The Effective Executive* (New York: Harper & Row, 1966); quoted in Keith Curtis, *From Management Goal Setting to Organizational Results* (Westport, CT: Quorum Books, 1994), 101.

14   Peter F. Drucker, *The Practice of Management* (New York: Harper & Row, 1954), 65–83, 100.

15   Morrisey, 25.

16   Gary Latham and J. James Baldes, "The Practical Significance of Locke's Theory of Goal Setting," *Journal of Applied Psychology 60,* no. 1 (February 1975).

17   See, for example, Gary Latham and Gary Yukl, "A Review of Research on the Application of Goal Setting in Organizations," *Academy of Management Journal 18,* no. 4 (1964):824; Gary Latham and Terrance A. Mitchell, "Importance of Participative Goal Setting and Anticipated Rewards on Goal Difficulty and Job Performance," *Journal of Applied Psychology 63,* (1978):163–71; and Sondra Hart, William Moncrief, and A. Parasuraman, "An Empirical Investigation of Sales People's Performance, Effort, and Selling Method During a Sales Contest," *Journal of the Academy of Marketing Science 17,* no. 1, (Winter 1989): 29–39.

18   The rest of this section, except as noted, is based on Gary Yukl, *Skills for Managers and Leaders* (Englewood Cliffs, NJ: Prentice Hall, 1991), 132–33.

19   Ibid., 133; and Miriam Erez, Daniel Gopher, and Nira Arzi, "Effects of Goal Difficulty, Self-Set Goals, and Monetary Rewards on Dual Task Performance," *Organizational Behavior & Human Decision Processes 47,* no. 2 (December 1990):247–69.

20   See, for example, Stephan Schiffman and Michele Reisner, "New Sales Resolutions," *Sales & Marketing 33,* no. 1 (January 1992):15–16; and Steve Rosenstock, "Your Agent's Success," *Manager's Magazine 66,* no. 9 (September 1991):21–23.

21   Yukl, 133.

22   Gary Latham and Lise Saari, "The Effects of Holding Goal Difficulty Constant on Assigned and Participatively Set Goals," *Academy of Management Journal 22,* (1979):163–68; and Mark Tubbs and Steven Ekeberg, "The Role of Intentions in Work Motivation: Implications for Goal Setting Theory and Research," *Academy of Management Review 16,* no. 1 (January 1991):180–99.

23   See Latham and Saari, 163–68.

24   Gary Latham, Terence Mitchell, and Denise Dorsett, "Importance of Participative Goal Setting and Anticipated Rewards on Goal Difficulty and Job Performance," *Journal of Applied Psychology 63* (1978):170.

25   See, for example, Anthony Mento, Norman Cartledge, and Edwin Locke, "Maryland Versus Michigan Versus Minnesota: Another Look at the Relationship of Expectancy and Goal Difficulty to Task Performance," *Organizational Behavior and Human Performance 25,* no. 3 (June 1980):419–40.

26   William Werther, "Workshops Aid in Goal Setting," *Personnel Journal 68* (November 1989), 32–38.

27   Keith Hammonds, Nicole Harris, and Bill Koenig, "Medical Lessons from the Big Mac," *Business Week,* 10 February 1997, 94, 98.

28   Steven Carroll and Henry Tosi, *Management by Objectives* (New York: Macmillan, 1973).

29   Mark McConkie, "A Clarification of the Goal Setting and Appraisal Processes in MBO," *Academy of Management Review 4* (December 1991):29–40.

30   Peter Drucker, *People and Performance: The Best of Peter Drucker* (New York: Harper, 1977), 65.

31   Duane Schultz and Sydney Ellen Schultz, *Psychology and Work Today* (New York: Macmillan, 1994), 268.

32   Ibid., 268.

33   Ibid., 268.

34   L. A. Hill and J. Elias, "Retraining Mid-career Managers: Career History and Self-Efficacy Beliefs," *Human Resources Management 29* (1991):197–217. For a discussion of goal-setting studies and how to set objectives, see Keith Curtis, *From Management Goal Setting to Organizational Results* (Westport, CT: Quorum Books, 1994).

35   *Webster's Collegiate Dictionary of American English* (New York: Simon & Schuster, Inc., 1988).

36   Thomas E. Milne, *Business Forecasting: A Managerial Approach* (London: Longman, 1975), 2. See also Jae Shim, Joel Siegal, and C. J. Liew, *Strategic Business Forecasting* (Chicago: Probus Publishing Co., 1995).

37   Thomas W. Moore, *Handbook of Business Forecasting* (New York: Harper & Row, 1989), 5.

38   Murray R. Spiegel, *Statistics* (New York: Schaum Publishing, 1961), 283.

39   See, for example, Moore, 5.

40   George Kress, *Practical Techniques of Business Forecasting* (Westport, CT: Quorum Books, 1985), 13.

41   A. Chairncross, quoted in Thomas Milne, *Business Forecasting,* 42.

42   John Chambers, Santinder Mullick, and Donald Smith, "How to Choose the Right Forecasting Technique," *Harvard Business Review,* (July–August 1971):45–74; and Moore, *Handbook of Business Forecasting,* 265–90.

43   Moore, *Handbook of Business Forecasting,* 271.

44   Herman Kahn and Anthony Weiner, *The Year 2000: A Framework for Speculation on the Next Thirty-Three Years* (New York: Macmillan, 1967), 6; quoted in George A. Steiner, *Strategic Planning: What Every Manager Must Know* (New York: The Free Press, 1979), 237; and Nikcholas Georgantzas and William Acar, *Scenario-Driven Planning* (Westport, CT: Quorum Books, 1995).

45   Adam Kahane, "Scenarios for Energy: Sustainable World vs. Global Mercantilism," *Long-Range Planning 25,* no. 4 (1992):38–46.

46   Philip Kotler, *Marketing Management* (Upper Saddle River, NJ: Prentice Hall, 1997), 113.

47   E. Jerome McCarthy and William Perreault, Jr., *Basic Marketing* (Homewood, IL: Irwin, 1990), 131–32.

48   Stan Crock et al., "They Snoop to Conquer," *Business Week,* 28 October 1996, 172.

49 Edmund Andrews, "VW President Resigns Under G.M. Pressure," *New York Times,* 30 November, 1996, 21.

50 Ronald Henkoff, "How to Plan for 1995," *Fortune,* 31 December 1990, 72.

51 Arthur Little, *Global Strategic Planning* (New York: Business International Corporation, 1991), 3.

52 Ibid.

53 See, for example, Craig Galbraith and Gregory Merrill, "The Politics of Forecasting: Managing the Truth," *California Management Review 38,* no. 2 (Winter 1996):29–43.

54 For a good discussion and definition of group cohesiveness, see, for example, James Bowditch and Anthony Buono, *A Primer on Organizational Behavior* (New York: John Wiley & Sons, Inc., 1994), 173–74.

55 These are based on Marvin E. Shaw, *Group Dynamics* (New York: McGraw-Hill, 1976), 84–95; Bowditch and Buono, 173–75; Greenberg and Baron, 295–97; and Schultz and Schultz, 322–23.

56 For a good discussion of how to facilitate effective planning in groups, see Terrence B. Goodwin, *Write on the Wall: A How-to Guide for Effective Planning in Groups* (Alexandria, VA: American Society for Training and Development [ASTD], 1994).

57 This is based on Little, 60–63.

58 Ibid., 62.

59 Ibid., 63.

60 Teri Lammers, "The One-Page Strategy Guide," *Inc.,* September 1992, 135–138.

61 Eric Matson, "Now That We Have Your Complete Attention," *Fast Company,* February/March 1997.

Chapter 6

1 "Sun Microsystems. . . ," PR Newswire, 28 March 1997.

2 Peter Drucker, *Management: Tasks, Responsibilities, Practices* (New York: Harper & Row, 1974), 611. For an interesting point of view on strategic management, see Daniel W. Greening and Richard A. Johnson, "Do Managers and Strategies Matter? A Study in Crisis," *Journal of Management Studies 33,* no. 1 (January 1996):25–52.

3 See, for example, Allan J. Rowe, et al., *Strategic Management* (Reading, MA: Addison-Wesley Publishing Co., 1989), 2; James Higgins and Julian Vincze, *Strategic Management* (Fort Worth: The Dryden Press, 1993), 5; Peter Wright, Mark Kroll, and John Parnell, *Strategic Management Concepts* (Englewood Cliffs, NJ: Prentice Hall, 1996), 1–15.

4 Arthur Thompson and A. J. Strickland, *Strategic Management* (Homewood, IL: Irwin, 1992), 4; Fred R. David, *Concepts of Strategic Management* (Upper Saddle River, NJ: Prentice Hall, 1997) 1–27. See also Bob Dust, "Making Mission Statements Meaningful," *Training & Development Journal 50,* no. 6 (June 1996):53.

5 Higgins and Vincze, *Strategic Management,* 5.

6 Warren Bennis and Bert Manus, *Leaders: The Strategies for Taking Charge* (New York: Harper & Row, 1985); quoted in Andrew Campbell and Sally Yeung, "Mission, Vision and Strategic Intent," *Long-Range Planning 24,* no. 4, 145.

7 Thompson and Strickland, 4. See also George Morrisey, *A Guide to Strategic Planning* (San Francisco: Jossey-Bass, 1996), 7.

8 Ibid., 8.

9 "Silicon Valley Survey," *The Economist,* 29 March 1997, 110.

10 Ibid.

11 "Novell: Triple Whammy?" *The Economist,* 29 March 1997, 71.

12 Thompson and Strickland, 67.

13 This is quoted from, and this section is based on, Allan J. Rowe, Richard O. Mason, Carl E. Dickel, Richard B. Mann, and Robert J. Mockler, *Strategic Management: A Methodological Approach* (Reading, MA: Addison-Wesley Publishing Co., 1994), 114–16.

14 Ibid., 114.

15 This is based on Ibid., 116; and Stephen George and Arnold Weimerskirch, *Total Quality Management* (New York: John Wiley & Sons, 1994), 207–21.

16 Ibid., 38.

17 This is based on Higgins and Vincze, 200–04.

18 Rowe, et al., 246–47.

19 Thompson and Strickland, 169. See also Michael Lubatkin and Sayan Chatterjee, "Extending Portfolio Theory into the Domain of Corporate Diversification: Does It Apply?" *Academy of Management Journal 37,* no. 1, (February 1994):109–36.

20 Steven Tarr and William Juliano, "Leading a Team Through Downsizing," *HR Magazine,* October 1992, 91; and "U.S. West to Slash 9,000 Jobs," *Reuters,* 18 September 1993.

21 Higgins and Vincze, 304.

22 John Byrne, Richard Brandt, and Otis Port, "The Virtual Corporation," *Business Week,* 8 February 1993, 99.

23 See also J. Carlos Jarillo, "On Strategic Networks," *Strategic Management Journal 9* (1988), 31–41; and William Davidow and Michael Malone, "The Virtual Corporation," *California Business Review,* 12 November 1992, 34–42.

24 Bryne et al., 99.

25 Ibid., 100.

26 Ibid.

27 Virtual corporations should not be confused with the Japanese Keiretsus strategy. Keiretsus are tightly knit groups of firms governed by a supra-board of directors concerned with establishing the long-term survivability of the Keiretsus organization. Interlocking boards of directors and shared ownership help distinguish Keiretsus from other forms of strategic alliances, including virtual corporations. See, for example, Byrne et al., 101; Thompson and Strickland, 216; and Kenichi Ohmae, "The Global Logic of Strategic Alliances," *Harvard Business Review,* March–April 1989, 143–54.

28 Unless otherwise noted, the following is based on Michael E. Porter, *Competitive Strategy* (New York: The Free Press, 1980); and Michael E. Porter, *Competitive Advantage* (New York: The Free Press, 1985).

29 Porter, *Competitive Advantage,* 14.

30 Michael Porter, *Competitive Strategy: Techniques for Analyzing Industries and Competitions* (New York: The Free Press, 1980).

31 Porter, *Competitive Strategy,* 17.

32 Based on Tomima Edmark, "Power Play," *Entrepreneur,* March 1977, 104–07.

33 See, for example, Adam Bryant, "Delta Air and Continental are Reported in Merger Talks," *New York Times,* 4 December 1996, C1, C2.

34 R. E. Miles and C. C. Snow, *Organizational Strategy, Structure and Process* (New York: McGraw-Hill, 1978); see also Donald Hambrick, "Some Tests of the Effectiveness and Functional Attributes of Miles and Snow's Strategic Types," *Academy of Management Journal 26,* no. 1 (March 1983):5–26.

35 Michael E. Porter, "What is Strategy?" *Harvard Business Review,* November–December 1996, 61–80.

36 This example is based on ibid., 70–75.

37 Ibid., 64.

38 For a discussion of core competencies see, for example, C. K. Prahalad and Gary Hamell, "The Core Competence of a Corporation," *Harvard Business Review,* May–June 1990, 80–82.

39 Gary Hamel and C. K. Prahalad, "Strategy as Stretch and Leverage," *Harvard Business Review,* March–April 1993, 75–84.

40 Ibid., 77.

41 Ibid., 78.

42 C. K. Prahalad and Gary Hamel, "The Core Competence of a Corporation," 82.

43 Ibid., 82.

44 Ibid., 81.

45 Brian Dumaine, "The Bureaucracy Busters," *Fortune,* 17 June 1991, 42.

46 Gary Yukl, *Managerial Leadership,* 269: "A Review and Theory of Research," *Journal of Management 15,* no. 2 (1989).

47 Except as noted, the next several leader characteristics are based on Michael E. Porter, "What is Strategy?" 77.

48 Ibid., 77.

49 See, for example, Clay Carr, "Seven Keys to Successful Change," *Training,* February 1994, 55–60; Guvenc G. Alpander and Carroll R. Lee, "Culture, Strategy and Teamwork: The Keys to Organizational Change," *Journal of Management Development 14,* no. 8 (1995):418.

50 Thomas Cummings and Christopher Worley, *Organization Development and Change* (Minneapolis: West Publishing Company, 1993).

Chapter 7

1 Jennifer Reese, "Starbucks," *Fortune,* 9 December 1996, 190–200.

2 *Organizing for International Competitiveness: How Successful Corporations Structure Their Worldwide Operations* (New York: Business International Corp., 1988), 52–7.

3 Thomas Steward, "Brain Power," *Fortune,* 17 March 1997, 106–7.

4 "How Can Big Companies Keep the Entrepreneurial Spirit Alive?" *Harvard Business Review,* November–December 1995, 188–9.

5 Ernest Dale, *Organization* (New York: AMA, 1967), 109.

6 See, for example, Lawton Burns and Douglas Wholey, "Adoption and Abandonment of Matrix Management Programs: Effects of Organizational Characteristics and Interorganizational Networks," *Academy of Management Journal 36,* no. 1 (February 1993):106–34.

7 *Organizing for International Competitiveness,* 117.

8 Burns and Wholey, 106.

9 For a discussion of this type of organization and its problems, see Stanley Davis and Paul Lawrence, *Matrix* (Reading, MA: Addison-Wesley, 1967); and Davis and Lawrence, "Problems of Matrix Organizations," *Harvard Business Review* (May–June 1978):131–42.

10 Rob Walker, "Down on the Farm," *Fast Company,* February–March 1997, 112–22.

11 For a discussion, see James Thompson, *Organizations in Action* (New York: McGraw-Hill, 1967).

12 Jay Galbraith, "Organizational Design: An Information Processing View," *Interfaces 4,* no. 3 (1974):28–36; and *Organizational Design* (Reading, MA: Addison-Wesley, 1977).

13 Henry Mintzberg, *Structure in Fives: Designing Effective Organizations* (Englewood Cliffs, NJ: Prentice-Hall, 1983), 4–9.

14 Mintzberg, 4.

15 Paul Lawrence and Jay Lorsch, *Organization and Environment* (Cambridge, MA: Harvard University Press, 1967).

16 Ibid., 6.

17 Christopher A. Bartlett and Sumantra Ghoshal, "Matrix Management: Not a Structure, a Frame of Mind," *Harvard Business Review* (July–August 1990):138–45.

18 Ibid., 143–44.

19 John Katzenbach and Douglas Smith, "The Discipline of Teams," *Harvard Business Review* (March–April 1993):118.

20 Jennifer Laabs, "Team Training Goes Outdoors," *Personnel Journal* (June 1991):56–63.

21 Quoted in Sanford Dornbusch and W. Richard Scott, *Evaluation and the Exercise of Authority* (San Francisco: Jossey Bass, 1975), 31.

22 Robert Peabody, "Perceptions of Organizational Authority: A Comparative Analysis," *Administrative Science Quarterly 6,* no. 4 (1962):514.

23 John R. P. French, Jr., and Bertram Raven, *Studies in Social Power* (Ann Arbor, MI: Institute for Social Research, 1959); reprinted in Henry Tosi and W. Clay Hamner, *Organizational Behavior and Management* (Chicago: St. Clair Press, 1977), 442–56.

24 Michael Carrell, Daniel Jennings, and Christina Heavrin, *Fundamentals of Organizational Behavior* (Upper Saddle River, NJ: Prentice-Hall, 1997), 329.

25 These are based on Jerald Greenberg and Robert Baron, *Behavior in Organizations* (Englewood Cliffs, NJ: Prentice-Hall, 1995), 473–74; Andrew J. DuBrin, *Winning at Office Politics* (New York: Ballantine Books, 1978); and Patricia Sellers, "Women, Sex & Power," *Fortune,* 5 August 1996, 42–57.

26 Kenneth MacKenzie, *Organizational Structure* (Arlington Heights, OH: AHM 1978), 198–230.

27 Ibid.

28 "A Circus Juggles HR Worldwide," *Workforce,* February 1997, 50.

29 The foundation study for this conclusion is Alfred Chandler, *Strategy and Structure* (Cambridge: MIT Press, 1962); for a recent literature review and test of the strategy-structure link see Terry Amburgey and Tina Dacin, "As the Left Foot Follows the Right? The Dynamics of Strategic and Structural Change," *Academy of Management Journal 37,* no. 6 (1994):1427–52.

30 Amburgey and Dacin, "Left Foot."

31 Chandler, 14.

32 Ibid., 366.

33 Judith H. Dobrzynski, "Jack Welch: How Good a Manager?" *Business Week,* 14 December 1987, 94. See also Thomas Stewart, "Brain Power," *Fortune,* 17 March 1997, 105–10.

34 See, for example, Brian Dumaine, "The Bureaucracy Busters," *Fortune,* 17 June 1991, 36–40; and Todd Vogel, "Where 1990s Style Management Is Already Hard at Work," *Business Week,* 23, October 1989, 92–7.

35 James Worthy, "Organization Structure and Employee Morale," *American Sociological Review 15* (1950):169–79.

36 For findings that cast some doubt on the generalizability of this conclusion, see Lyman Porter and Edward Lawler III, "The Effects of Tall versus Flat Organization Structures on Managerial Job Satisfaction," *Personnel Psychology 17* (1964):135–48.

37 See, for example, Henri Fayol, *General and Industrial Management,* trans. Constance Storrs (London: Sir Isaac Putnam, 1949).

38 For a discussion of the contingencies affecting span of control (task uncertainty, professionalism, and interdependence), see, for example, Daniel Robey, *Designing Organizations,* 3rd ed. (Homewood, IL: Irwin, 1991), 258–9.

39 For the definition of stress see, for example, James Bowditch and Anthony Buono, *A Primer on Organization Behavior* (New York: John Wiley, 1994), 439.

40 Greenberg and Baron, 244.

41 J. D. Quick, R. S. Horn, and J. C. Quick, "Health Consequences of Stress," *Journal of Organizational Behavior Management 8* (1986):19–36.

42 Robert Vecchio, *Organizational Behavior* (Chicago: Dryden Press, 1991), quoted in Carrell, Jennings, and Heavrin, *Fundamentals of Organizational Behavior,* 144.

43 David Myers, *Social Psychology,* 3rd ed. (New York: McGraw-Hill, 1990), 178–9.

Chapter 8

1 George Stalk, Phillip Evans, and Lawrence E. Shulman, "Competing on Capabilities: The New Rules of Corporate Strategy," *Harvard Business Review* (March–April 1992):87–94.

2 Tom Peters, *Liberation Management* (New York: Alfred Knopf, 1992), 9. See also Bart Ziegler, "Gerstner's IBM Revival: Impressive Incomplete," *Wall Street Journal,* 27 March 1997, 81, 84.

3 Rob Walker, "Down on the Farm," *Fast Company,* February–March 1997, 112–22.

4 Tom Burns and G. M. Stalker, *The Management of Innovation* (London: Tavistock, 1961), 1.

5 Ibid., 80.

6 Emery and Trist, two other British researchers, referred to this innovative environment as a "turbulent field" environment because changes often come not from a firm's traditional competitors, but from out of the blue: Often, in fact, the changes seem to "arise from the field itself," in that they result from interaction between parts of the environment. The very "texture" of a firm's environment changes because previously unrelated or (from the point of view of the firm) irrelevant elements in its environment become interconnected. F. E. Emery and E. C. Trist, "The Causal Texture of Organizational Environments," *Human Relations 18* (August 1965):20–6. As another example, after 1970 (when digital watches were introduced), calculator firms like Texas Instruments suddenly and unexpectedly became competitors in the watch industry.

7 Burns and Stalker, 92.

8 Ibid.

9 Adapted from ibid., 119–22.

10 Peter Blau, Cecilia Falbe, William McKinley, and Phelps Tracy, "Technology and Organization in Manufacturing," *Administrative Science Quarterly* (March 1976).

11 However, Allen found that "characteristics, beliefs, and strategies of top management groups were found to be fully as important as contextual factors in predicting organizational choices." Stephen A. Allen, "Understanding Reorganizations and Divisionalized Companies," *Academy of Management Journal, 22,* no. 4 (December 1979):641–71.

12 How can we explain the fact that an organization's environment and technology influence its structure? One plausible explanation is that some environments and technologies require managers to handle more unforeseen problems and decisions than do others. And, since each person's capacity for juggling problems and making decisions is limited, an overabundance of problems forces managers to respond—often by reorganizing. Thus, when a manager finds himself or herself becoming overloaded with problems, one reasonable response is to give subordinates more autonomy, to decentralize (thus letting employees handle more problems among themselves), and to reorganize around self-contained divisions. By reorganizing in these ways, the manager may surrender some direct control, but at least the organization avoids becoming unresponsive, as might otherwise have been the case.

13 Peters, *Liberation Management,* 310.

14 Except as noted, this section is based on Tom Peters, *Thriving on Chaos* (New York: Harper & Row, 1987), 425–38; and Peters, *Liberation Management,* 90–5.

15 Peters, *Liberation Management,* 88.

16 Ibid., 90.

17 "How Can Big Companies Keep the Entrepreneurial Spirit Alive?" *Harvard Business Review,* (November–December 1996):188–9.

18 Walker, 112–22.

19 Peters, *Liberation Management,* 49–50.

20 James O'Toole, *Work and the Quality of Life: Resource Papers for Work in America* (Boston: MIT Press, 1974), 18–29.

21 Todd Vogel, "Where 1990s-Style Management Is Already Hard at Work," *Business Week,* 23 October 1989, 92–100.

22 Peters, *Thriving on Chaos,* 256.

23 Peters, *Liberation Management,* 238.

24 William H. Miller, "Chesebrough-Pond's at a Glance," *Industry Week,* 19 October 1992, 14–5.

25 Except as noted, the remainder of this section is based on James Shonk, *Team-Based Organizations* (Chicago: Irwin, 1997).

26 Ibid., 35–8.

27 Ibid., 133–40.

28 Ibid., 133.

29 *Webster's New World Dictionary,* 3rd College ed. (New York: Simon and Schuster, Inc., 1988), 911. For a discussion of networked organizations, see James Brian Quinn, *Intelligent Enterprise* (New York: Free Press, 1992), 213–40.

30 Ram Charan, "How Networks Reshape Organizations—For Results," *Harvard Business Review* (September–October 1991):104–15.

31 Ibid., 106–07.

32 Ibid., 106.

33 Ibid., 108.

34 Christopher Bartlett and Sumantra Ghoshal, "What Is a Global Manager?" *Harvard Business Review* (September–October 1992):62–74.

35 Tom Lester, "The Rise of the Network," *International Management,* June 1992, 72.

36 Paul Evans, Yves Doz, and Andre Laurent, *Human Resource Management in International Firms* (London: Macmillan, 1989), 123.

37 Chandler Harrison Stevens, "Electronic Organization and Expert Networks: Beyond Electronic Mail and Computer Conferencing," Sloan School of Management Working Paper No. 1794-86, Massachusetts Institute of Technology, Management in the 1990s Research Program, May 1986. Reprinted in Peters, *Liberation Management,* 123–4.

38 David Kilpatrick, "Groupware Goes Boom," *Fortune,* 27 December 1993, 99–101.

39 Kenneth Laudon and Jane Laudon, *Essentials of Management Information Systems* (Upper Saddle River, NJ: Prentice-Hall, 1997), 413–6.

40 Mary Anne Devanna and Noel Tichy, "Creating the Competitive Organization of the 21st Century: The Boundaryless Corporation," *Human Resource Management, 29,* no. 4 (Winter 1990):455–71.

41 Larry Hirschhorn and Thomas Gilmore, "The New Boundaries of the 'Boundaryless' Company," *Harvard Business Review,* May–June 1992, 104. See also Daniel Denison, Stuart Hart, and Joel Kahn, "From Chimneys to Cross-Functional Teams: Developing and Validating a Diagnostic Model," *Academy of Management Journal, 39,* no. 4 (August 1996):1005–23.

42 This is based on Hirschhorn and Gilmore, 104–8.

43 Except as noted, the remainder of this section is based on Hirschhorn and Gilmore, "The New Boundaries," 107–8.

44 Hirschhorn and Gilmore, 107.
45 Ibid., 108.
46 Ibid., 109.
47 Gary Dessler, *Winning Employee Commitment: How to Build and Keep a Competitive Workforce* (New York: McGraw Hill, 1992).
48 Except as noted, this section is based on John A. Byrne, "The Horizontal Corporation," *Business Week*, 20 December 1993, 76–81.
49 Michael Hammer and James Champy, *Reengineering the Corporation* (New York: Harper Business, 1994), 35.
50 Ann Majchrzak and Quinwei Wang, "Breaking the Functional Mind-Set of Process Organizations," *Harvard Business Review* (September–October 1996):93–9.
51 Ibid., 96–9.
52 Frederick Herzberg, *One More Time, How Do You Motivate Workers?* See also Judith A. Kolb, "Let's Bring Structure Back: A Commentary," *Management Communications Quarterly, 9*, no. 4, (May 1996):452–65.
53 *Changing Nature of Work*, 1993. American Psychological Society Observer Special Issue: HCI Report I. See also Jeffrey Edwards, "An Examination of Competing Versions of the Person–Environment Fit Approach to Stress," *Academy of Management Journal, 39*, no. 2, (April 1996):292–339.
54 Except as noted, this section is based on Jia Lin Xie and Gary Johns, "Job Scope and Stress: Can Job Scope Be Too High?" *Academy of Management Journal 38*, no. 5 (1995):1288–1309.
55 Rosabeth Moss Kanter, Barry Stein, and Todd Jick, *The Challenge of Organizational Change* (New York: The Free Press, 1992), 225.
56 William R. Pape, "Virtual Manager: Guide to Hiring the Best Virtual Workers," *Inc. Technology*, November 1996, 23–4.
57 John Case, "The Open-book Management Revolution," *Inc.*, June 1995, 26–43.

Chapter 9

1 Catherine Truss and Lynda Gratton, "Strategic Human Resource Management: A Conceptual Approach," *International Journal of Human Resource Management, 5* no. 3 (September 1994):663.
2 Based on Gary Dessler, *Human Resource Management*, 7th ed. (Upper Saddle River, NJ: Prentice-Hall, 1997), 20–2.
3 See Wade Lambert and Arthur Hayes, "Overqualified Ruling May Presage Suits," *Wall Street Journal*, January 29, 1991, B6.
4 David Terpstra and Susan Cook, "Complainant Characteristics and Reported Behaviors as Consequences Associated with Formal Sexual Harassment Charges," *Personnel Psychology, 38*, no. 2 (Autumn 1985):559–74.
5 "Stanford Doctor to Face Charges," *New York Times*, June 28, 1991, A9.
6 This section is based on Gary Dessler, *Human Resource Management*, 7th ed. (Upper Saddle River, NJ, Prentice-Hall, 1997) 40–2; see also Commerce Clearing House, *Sexual Harassment Manual*, p. 8.
7 Rebecca Thacker and Stephen Gohmann, "Male/Female Differences in Perceptions and Effects of Hostile Environment Sexual Harassment: 'Reasonable' Assumptions?" *Public Personnel Management, 22*, no. 3 (Fall 1993):461–72.
8 Ibid., 464–5.
9 Ibid., 467–8.
10 Ibid., 467.
11 For a discussion see Dessler, *Human Resource Management*, 7th ed., 632–3.
12 Wayne Cascio, *Applied Psychology in Personnel Management* (Reston, VA: Reston, 1978), 132.
13 See, for example, William Bridges, "The End of the Job," *Fortune*, September 19, 1994, 64.
14 See Dessler, *Human Resource Management*, 108–10.
15 Donald Harris, "A Matter of Privacy: Managing Personnel Data in Company Computers," *Personnel*, February 1987, 37.
16 Harold E. Johnson, "Older Workers Help Meet Employment Needs," *Personnel Journal* (May 1988):100–5.
17 Based on Robert W. Goddard, "How to Harness America's Gray Power," *Personnel Journal* (May 1987):33–40.
18 See, for example, Elaine Appleton, "Recruiting on the Internet," *Datamation*, August 1995, 39–41.
19 This section is based on Jerald Greenberg and Robert Baron, *Behavior in Organizations* (Englewood Cliffs, NJ: Prentice-Hall, 1995), 423–4; and Laurie Weingart, Rebecca Bennett, and Jeanne Brett, "The Impact of Consideration of Issues and Motivational Orientation on Group Negotiation Process and Outcome," *Journal of Applied Psychology, 78*, no. 3 (June 1993):504–17.
20 Stephen J. Vodanovich and Rosemary H. Lowe, "They Ought to Know Better: The Incidence and Correlates of Inappropriate Application Blank Inquiries," *Public Personnel Management, 21*, no. 3 (Fall 1992):363.
21 See Paul Blocklyn, "Pre-Employment Testing," *Personnel* (February 1988):66–8.
22 Mel Kleiman, "Employee Testing Essential to Hiring Effectively in the '90s," *Houston Business Journal, 22*, no. 38 (February 8, 1993):31; and Gerald L. Borofsky, "Pre-Employment Psychological Screening," *Risk Management, 40*, no. 1 (January 1993):47.
23 Louis Olivas, "Using Assessment Centers for Individual and Organizational Development," *Personnel, 57*, (May–June 1980):63–7; Tim Payne, Neil Anderson, and Tom Smith, "Assessment Centres, Selection Systems and Cost-Effectiveness: An Evaluative Case Study," *Personnel Review, 21*, no. 4 (Fall 1992):48; and Roger Mottram, "Assessment Centres Are Not Only for Selection: The Assessment Centre as a Development Workshop," *Journal of Managerial Psychology, 7*, no. 1 (January 1992):A1.
24 This is based on Daniel Goleman, "Forget Money; Nothing Can Buy Happiness, Some Researchers Say," *Wall Street Journal*, August 16, 1996, B5, B9. See also Shari Caudron, "Hire for Attitude," *Staffing: A Workforce Supplement*, August 1997, pp. 20–26.
25 Golemon, B9.
26 Source for questions: Goleman, "Forget Money"; and Dr. Richard Davidson, University of Wisconsin.
27 For a full discussion of this, see Gary Dessler, *Human Resource Management*, 6th ed. (Englewood Cliffs, NJ: Prentice-Hall, 1994), chapter 6.
28 R. E. Carlson, "Selection Interview Decisions: The Effects of Interviewer Experience, Relative Quota Situation, and Applicant Sample on Interview Decisions," *Personnel Psychology, 20* (1967):259–80.
29 William Tullar, Terry Mullins, and Sharon Caldwell, "Effects of Interview Length and Applicant Quality on Interview Decision Time," *Journal of Applied Psychology, 64* (December 1979):669–74.
30 Edwin Walley, "Successful Interviewing Techniques," *The CPA Journal* (September 1992):29.
31 Pamela Paul, "Interviewing Is Your Business," *Association Management* (November 1992):29.
32 Gary Dessler, *Human Resource Management*, 7th ed. (Upper Saddle River, NJ: Prentice-Hall, 1997), 242–43.

33 John Jones and William Terris, "Post-Polygraph Selection Techniques," *Recruitment Today,* (May–June 1989):25–31.

34 Gilbert Fuchsberg, "Prominent Psychologists Group Gives Qualified Support to Integrity Tests," *Wall Street Journal,* March 7, 1991, B2, B7.

35 Ian Miners, Nick Nykodym, and Diane Samerdyke-Traband, "Put Drug Detection to the Test," *Personnel Journal, 66,* no. 8 (August 1987):191–97.

36 Eric Rolf Greenberg, "Workplace Testing: Who's Testing Whom," *Personnel* (May 1989):39–45.

37 This is based on Joseph J. Fucini and Suzy Fucini, *Working for the Japanese* (New York: The Free Press, 1990), 1–2; 49–52.

38 *Ibid.*

39 For a complete discussion on these matters, see Fucini and Fucini, 58–9.

40 Jennifer Reese, "Starbuck," *Fortune,* 9 December 1996, 190–200.

41 See, for example, Anne Fields, "Class Act," *Inc. Technology, 1* (1977): 55–7.

42 Based on Fucini and Fucini, *Working for the Japanese,* 67–87.

43 Ibid., 67.

44 Ibid.

45 Ibid., 68–9.

46 See Gary Dessler, *Winning Commitment* (New York: McGraw-Hill, 1993), 84–5.

47 Joseph Boyett and Henry Conn, *Workplace 2000* (New York: Dutton, 1991), 56–7.

48 This is based on Dessler, *Human Resource Management,* 7th ed. 341–415.

49 Barry W. Thomas and Madelyn Hess Olson, "Gainsharing: The Design Guarantees Success," *Personnel Journal* (May 1988):73–9.

50 Matt Rothman, "Into the Black," *Inc.,* January 1993, 59–65. For a good discussion of what other employers are doing to improve benefits, see, for example, Kimberly Seals McDonald, "Your Benefits," *Fortune,* 3 March 1997, 199–201.

51 "AT&T's Intriguing Executive Shuffle," *Fortune,* 3 March 1997, 142.

52 John Aram, *Presumed Superior.* (Englewood Cliffs, NJ: Prentice Hall, 1993)

53 "Transplanting Corporate Cultures Globally," *Personnel Journal,* (October 1993).

54 Gillian Flynn, "It Takes Values to Capitalize on Change," *Workforce,* April 1997, 27–34.

Chapter 10

1 Jeffrey McNally, Stephen Gerras, and R. Craig Bullis, "Teaching Leadership at the U.S. Military Academy at West Point," *Journal of Applied Behavioral Science, 32,* no. 2 (June 1996):181.

2 For example, see Renato Tagiuri, "Managing People: Ten Essential Behaviors," *Harvard Business Review* (January–February 1995):10–1.

3 McNally et al., 178.

4 Shelley Kirkpatrick and Edwin A. Locke, "Leadership: Do Traits Matter?" *Academy of Management Executive 5,* no. 2 (May 1991):49. See also Edwin A. Locke and Associates, *The Essence of Leadership: The Four Keys to Leading Successfully* (New York: Lexington/Macmillan, 1991). See also Ruth Tait, "The Attributes of Leadership," *Leadership and Organization Development Journal 17,* no. 1 (1996):27–31; and David L. Cawthon, "Leadership: The Great Man Theory Revisited," *Business Horizons, 39,* no. 3 (May 1996):1–4.

5 Chester Barnard, *The Functions of the Executive* (Cambridge, MA: Harvard University Press, 1938). See also Roger Dawson, *Secrets of Power Persuasion* (Englewood Cliffs, NJ: Prentice-Hall, 1992); Sydney Finkelstein, "Power in Top Management Teams: Dimensions, Measurement, and Validation," *Academy of Management Journal* (August 1992); and Jeffrey Pfeffer, *Managing with Power: Politics and Influence in Organizations* (Boston: Harvard Business School Press, 1992).

6 Kirkpatrick and Locke, 49.

7 Ibid., 50.

8 Except as noted, this section is based on ibid., 48–60.

9 Ibid., 53.

10 Ibid., 54.

11 Ibid., 55.

12 Ibid.

13 Ibid., 55–6.

14 Ernest Hilgard, *Introduction to Psychology* (New York: Harcourt, Brace and World, 1962) 635; see also Lester Lefton and Laura Valvatne, *Mastering Psychology* (Boston: Allyn and Bacon, 1992), 419.

15 R. B. Cattell, *Personality* (New York: McGraw-Hill, 1950), 37–41.

16 Grant Marshall et al., "The Five-Factor Model of Personality as a Framework for Personality-Health Research," *Journal of Personality and Social Psychology 67,* no. 2 (1994):278–86.

17 See, for example, Kirkpatrick and Locke, 49.

18 Ibid., 56.

19 Tagiuri, 10–1.

20 M. S. Lel-Namaki, "Creating a Corporate Vision," *Long-Range Planning 25,* no. 6 (1979):25.

21 Ibid.

22 Arthur Thompson and A. J. Strickland, *Strategic Management* (Homewood, IL: Irwin, 1992), 7.

23 For a discussion of this issue, see Peter Wissenberg and Michael Kavanagh, "The Independence of Initiating Structure and Consideration: A Review of Evidence," *Personnel Psychology 25* (1972):119–30. See also Gary A. Yukl, *Leadership in Organizations,* 3rd ed. (Englewood Cliffs, NJ: Prentice-Hall, 1994). For an interesting example of what can go wrong when the leader uses the wrong leadership style, see Thomas Ricks, "Army at Odds: West Point Posting Becomes a Minefield for 'Warrior' Officer," *Wall Street Journal,* March 13, 1997, A1, A9.

24 Ralph Stogdill and A. E. Koonz, "Leader Behavior: Its Description and Measurement" (Columbus: Bureau of Business Research, Ohio State University, 1957). See also Bernard M. Bass, *Bass & Stogdill's Handbook of Leadership: Theory, Research, & Managerial Applications,* 3rd ed. (New York: The Free Press, 1990).

25 Ralph Stogdill, *Managers, Employees, Organizations* (Columbus: Bureau of Business Research, Ohio State University, 1965).

26 Gary Yukl, "Towards a Behavioral Theory of Leadership," *Organizational Behavior and Human Performance 6,* no. 4 (July 1971):414–40. See also Gary A. Yukl, *Leadership in Organizations,* 3rd ed. (Englewood Cliffs, NJ: Prentice-Hall, 1994).

27 Chester Schriesheim, Robert J. House, and Steven Kerr, "Leader Initiating Structure: A Reconciliation of Discrepant Research Results and Some Empirical Tests," *Organizational Behavior and Human Performance 15,* no. 2 (April 1976). See also Bernard M. Bass, *Bass & Stogdill's Handbook of Leadership: Theory, Research, & Managerial Applications,* 3rd ed. (New York: The Free Press, 1990).

28 Victor Vroom and Arthur Jago, "On the Validity of the Vroom-Yetton Model," *Journal of Applied Psychology 63,* no. 2

(1978):151–62; Madeleine Heilman et al., "Reactions to Pre-scribed Leader Behavior as a Function of Role Perspective: The Case of Vroom-Yetton Model," *Journal of Applied Psychology 69,* no. 1 (February 1984):50–60. See also Donna Brown, "Why Participative Management Won't Work Here" *Management Review* (June 1992).

29 Vroom and Jago, 151–62.

30 See, for example, Mark Tubbs and Steven Akeberg, "The Role of Intentions in Work Motivation: Implications for Goal Setting Theory and Research," *Academy of Management Review 16,* no. 1 (January 1991):180–99.

31 Geoffrey Smith, "Democratic? No. Effective? Yes," *Business Week,* 7 April 1997, 94.

32 Rensis Likert, *New Patterns of Management* (New York: McGraw-Hill, 1961).

33 Robert Day and Robert Hamblin, "Some Effects of Close and Punitive Styles of Leadership," *American Journal of Psychology 69,* (1964):499–510.

34 See, for example, Nancy Morse, *Satisfactions in the White Collar Job* (Ann Arbor, MI: Survey Research Center, University of Michigan, 1953).

35 Frederick E. Fiedler, *A Theory of Leadership Effectiveness* (New York: McGraw-Hill, 1967), 147.

36 Ibid.

37 See, for example, Robert J. House and J. V. Singh, "Organizational Behavior: Some New Directions for I/O Psychology," *Annual Review of Psychology 38,* (1987):669–718; L. H. Peters, D. D. Hartke, and J. T. Pohlmann, "Fiedler's Contingency Theory of Leadership: An Application of the Meta-Analytic Procedures of Schmidt and Hunter," *Psychological Bulletin 97,* (1985): 274–85.

38 Fred Fiedler and J. E. Garcia, *New Approaches to Effective Leadership: Cognitive Resources and Organizational Performance* (New York: John Wiley and Sons, 1987); and Robert T. Vecchio, "Theoretical and Empirical Examination of Cognitive Resource Theory," *Journal of Applied Psychology* (April 1990):141–7. See also Robert Vecchio, "Cognitive Resource Theory: Issues for Specifying a Test of the Theory" *Journal of Applied Psychology* (June 1992).

39 Robert J. House and Terrence Mitchell, "Path-Goal Theory of Leadership," *Contemporary Business 3* (1974):81–98; and Abraham Sagie and Meni Koslowsky, "Organizational Attitudes and Behaviors as a Function of Participation in Strategic and Tactical Change Decisions: An Application of Path-Goal Theory," *Journal of Organizational Behavior* (January 1994):37–48.

40 Gary Yukl, "Managerial Leadership: A Review of Theory and Research," *Journal of Management 15,* no. 2 (1989):263–5.

41 J. Fulk and E. R. Wendler, "Dimensionality of Leader-Subordinate Interactions: A Path-Goal Investigation," *Organizational Behavior and Human Performance 30,* (1982):241–64.

42 G. B. Graen and T. A. Scandura, "Toward a Psychology of Daidic Organizing." In *Research in Organizational Behavior,* vol. 9, edited by L. L. Cummings and B. M. Staw. Greenwich, CT: J.A.I. Press, 1987, 208.

43 Antoinette Phillips and Arthur Bedeian, "Leader-Follower Exchange Quality: The Role of Personal and Interpersonal Attributes," *Academy of Management Journal, 37,* no. 4 (1994):990–1001.

44 Jerald Greenberg, *Managing Behavior in Organizations,* (Upper Saddle River, NJ: Prentice-Hall, 1996), 215.

45 Phillips and Bedeian, "Leader-Follower Exchange Quality."

46 See Robert P. Vecchio, "Situational Leadership Theory: An Examination of a Prescriptive Theory," *Journal of Applied Psychology* (August 1987):444–51; and Jerald Greenberg, *Managing Behavior in Organizations* (Upper Saddle River, NJ: Prentice-Hall, 1996), 226.

47 J. M. Burns, *Leadership* (New York: Harper, 1978).

48 For a discussion, see Ronald Deluga, "Relationship of Transformational and Transactional Leadership with Employee Influencing Strategies," *Group and Organizational Studies 1,* no. 4 (December 1988):457–8. See also Philip M. Podsakoff, Scott B. MacKenzie, and William H. Bommer, "Transformational Leader Behaviors as Determinants of Employee Satisfaction, Commitment, Trust, and Organizational Citizenship Behaviors," *Journal of Management 22,* no. 2 (1996):259–98.

49 Joseph Seltzer and Bernard Bass, "Transformational Leadership: Beyond Initiation and Consideration," *Journal of Management 4,* (1990):694. See also Bernard M. Bass, "Theory of Transformational Leadership Redux," *Leadership Quarterly 6,* no. 4 (Winter 1995):463–78.

50 Gary Yukl, "Managerial Leadership," 269.

51 N. M. Tichy and M. A. Devanna, *The Transformational Leader* (New York: John Wiley & Sons, 1986).

52 Seltzer and Bass, 694.

53 Deluga, 457.

54 Frances Yamarino and Bernard Bass, "Transformational Leadership and Multiple Levels of Analysis," *Human Relations, 43,* no. 10 (1990):976.

55 J. A. Conger, "Inspiring Others: The Language of Leadership," *Academy of Management Executive 5,* (1991):31–45.

56 Bernard Bass, *Leadership and Performance Beyond Expectations* (New York: The Free Press, 1985); and Deluga, 457–8.

57 Deluga, 457.

58 Ibid.

59 Yamarino and Bass, 981.

60 Tim Smart, "Jack Welch's Encore," *Business Week,* 28 October 1996, 154–60.

61 Thomas Stewart, "How to Lead a Revolution," *Fortune,* 28 November 1994, 61.

62 For a review, see Robert Keller, "Transformational Leadership and the Performance of Research and Development Project Groups," *Journal of Management 18,* no. 3 (1992):489–501.

63 J. J. Hater and Bernard Bass, "Superiors' Evaluations and Subordinates' Perceptions of Transformational and Transactional Leadership," *Journal of Applied Psychology 73* (1988):695–702.

64 J. M. Howell and C. A. Higgins, "Champions of Technological Innovation," *Administrative Science Quarterly 35* (1990):317–41.

65 Yamarino and Bass, 981.

66 C. M. Solomon, "Careers Under Glass," *Personnel Journal, 69,* no. 4 (1990):96–105.

67 See, for example, James Bowditch and Anthony Buono, *A Primer on Organizational Behavior* (New York: John Wiley, 1994), 238.

68 Russell Kent and Sherry Moss, "Effects of Sex and Gender Role on Leader Emergence," *Academy of Management Journal, 37,* no. 5 (1994):1335–46; Jane Baack, Norma Carr-Ruffino, and Monica Pelletier, "Making It to the Top: Specific Leadership Skills," *Women in Management Review, 8,* no. 2 (1993):17–23.

69 S. M. Donnel and J. Hall, "Men and Women as Managers: A Significant Case of No Significant Difference," *Organizational Dynamics, 8,* (1980):60–77. See also Jennifer L. Berdahl, "Gender and Leadership in Work Groups: Six Alternative Models," *Leadership Quarterly, 7,* no. 1 (Spring 1996):21–40.

70 M. A. Hatcher, "The Corporate Woman of the 1990s: Maverick or Innovator?" *Psychology of Women Quarterly, 15,* (1991):251–9.

71 D. G. Winter, *The Power Motive* (New York: The Free Press, 1975).

72 L. McFarland Shore and G. C. Thornton, "Effects of Gender on Self and Supervisory Ratings," *Academy of Management Journal, 29,* no. 1 (1986):115–29; quoted in Bowditch and Buono, 238.

73 G. H. Dobbins and S. J. Paltz, "Sex Differences in Leadership: How Real Are They?" *Academy of Management Review, 11* (1986):118–27; R. Drazin and E. R. Auster, "Wage Differences Between Men and Women: Performance Appraisal Ratings versus Salary Allocation as the Locus of Bias," *Human Resource Management, 26* (1987):157–68. See also Nancy DiTomaso and Robert Hooijberg, "Diversity and the Demands of Leadership," *Leadership Quarterly, 7,* no. 2 (Summer 1996):163–87 and Chao C. Chen and Ellen Van Velsor, "New Directions for Research and Practice in Diversity Leadership," *Leadership Quarterly, 7,* no. 2 (Summer 1996):285–302.

74 M. Jelinek and N. J. Alder, "Woman: World-Class Managers for Global Competition," *Academy of Management Executive 2,* no. 1 (1988):11–9; J. Grant, "Women as Managers: What Can They Offer to Organizations?" *Organizational Dynamics 16,* no. 3 (1988):56–63. On the other hand, one author suggests that women should be more Machiavellian: "War favors the dangerous woman. Women may love peace and seek stability, but these conditions seldom serve them." Harriet Rubin, *The Princessa: Machiavelli for Women* (New York: Doubleday/Currenly, 1997), quoted in Anne Fisher, "What Women Can Learn from Machiavelli," *Fortune,* 14 April 1997, 162.

75 Andrew Dubrin, *Leadership: Research Findings, Practice, and Skills* (Boston: Houghton-Mifflin, 1995), 10–1.

76 Adapted from "Development and Application of New Scales to Measure the French and Raven (1959) Bases of Social Power," by Thomas R. Hinkin and Chester A. Schriesheim, *Journal of Applied Psychology* (August 1989):567. Copyright 1989 by the American Psychological Association. Adapted by permission. Found in Andrew DuBrin, *Leadership: Research in Findings, Practice, and Skills* (Boston: Houghton-Mifflin, 1995), 146–7. (The actual scale presents the items in random order. They are classified here according to the power source for your convenience.)

77 Steve Kerr and J. M. Jermier, "Substitutes for Leadership: Their Meaning and Measurement," *Organizational Behavior and Human Performance 22* (1978):375–403. See also Philip M. Podsakoff and Scott B. MacKenzie, "An Examination of Substitutes for Leadership Within a Levels-of-Analysis Framework," *Leadership Quarterly 6,* no. 3 (Fall 1995):289–328.

78 David Alcorn, "Dynamic Followership: Empowerment at Work," *Management Quarterly 33,* no. 1 (Spring 1992):11–3.

79 Jon Howell, David Bowen, Peter Dorfman, Steven Kerr, and Philip Podsakoff, "Substitutes for Leadership: Effective Alternatives to Ineffective Leadership," *Organizational Dynamics,* (Summer 1990):23.

80 Ibid.

81 See, for example, P. M. Podsakoff, P. B. Niehoff, S. B. MacKenzie, and M. L. Williams, "Do Substitutes for Leadership Really Substitute for Leadership? An Empirical Examination of Kerr and Jermier Situational Leadership Model," *Organizational Behavior and Human Decision Processes 54* (1993):1–44.

82 "What It Means to Lead," *Fast Company,* February–March 1997.

Chapter 11

1 David Stamps, "Culture Change at the Post Office Fizzles," *Training 33,* no. 7 (July 1996):26–34.

2 James G. Hunt, *Leadership* (Newbury Park, CA: Sage Publications, 1991), 220–4. One somewhat tongue-in-cheek writer describes culture as a sort of "organizational DNA," since "it's the stuff, mostly intangible, that determines the basic character of a business." See James Moore, "How Companies Have Sex," *Fast Company,* October–November 1997, 66–8.

3 Hunt, 221. For a recent discussion of types of cultures see, for example, "A Quadrant of Corporate Cultures," *Management Decision 34,* no. 5 (September 1996):37–40.

4 *Blueprints for Service Quality: The Federal Express Approach* (New York: AMA Membership Publications, 1991), 13.

5 Example is based on Daniel Denison, *Corporate Culture and Organizational Effectiveness* (New York: John Wiley and Sons, 1990), 147–74.

6 Ibid., 148.

7 Ibid.

8 Ibid., 151.

9 Ibid.

10 Ibid.

11 Ibid.

12 Ibid., 152.

13 Ibid., 153.

14 Ibid., 154.

15 Ibid., 155.

16 John Dessauer, *My Years with Xerox* (Garden City, NJ: Doubleday, 1971), quoted in John Kotter and James Heskett, *Corporate Culture and Performance* (New York: The Free Press, 1992), 76. For a recent discussion of culture see, for example, Mary Jo Hatch, "The Dynamics of Organizational Culture," *Academy of Management Review 18,* no. 4 (October 1993):657–93.

17 Kotter and Heskett, 76.

18 Ibid., 76–7. For a discussion of how culture also affects employee retention rates, see John Sheridan, "Organizational Culture and Employee Retention," *Academy of Management Journal 35* (December 1992):1036–57.

19 Dave Francis and Mike Woodcock, *Unblocking Organizational Values* (Glenview, IL: Scott, Foresman and Co., 1990).

20 The following is quoted from Francis and Woodcock, 27–30.

21 Richard Osbome, "Core Value Statements: The Corporate Compass," *Business Horizons,* September–October 1991, 29.

22 Ibid., 29.

23 Kotter and Heskett, 54.

24 Edgar Schein, *Organizational Culture and Leadership,* 2nd ed. (San Francisco: Jossey-Bass Publications, 1992), 211–2. See also Edgar Schein, "Culture: The Missing Concept in Organization Studies," *Administrative Science Quarterly 41,* no. 2 (June 1996):229–40.

25 Sam Walton and John Huey, *Sam Walton: Made in America, My Story* (New York: Doubleday, 1992), 14.

26 Ibid., 14. For a discussion of culture's role in ethics, see, for example, Ishmael Akaah, "Organizational Culture and Ethical Research Behavior," *Journal of the Academy of Marketing Science* (Winter 1993):59–64.

27 Walton and Huey, 171.

28 Ibid., 161.

29 Thomas J. Peters and Robert Waterman, *In Search of Excellence* (New York: Harper & Row, 1982), 81.

30 Gary Dessler, *Winning Commitment: How to Build and Keep a Competitive Work Force* (New York: McGraw-Hill, 1993), 85.

31 Ibid., 85.

32 Denison, *Corporate Culture,* 12. For a recent discussion see also Daniel Denison, "What Is the Difference between Organizational Culture and Organizational Climate? A Native's Point of View on a Decade of Paradigm Wars," *Academy of Management Review 21,* no. 3 (July 1996):619–54.

33 J. Lorsch, "Managing Culture: The Invisible Barrier to Strategic Change," *California Management Review 28,* no. 2

(1986):95–109, quoted in Fred R. David, *Strategic Management* (Upper Saddle River, NJ: Prentice-Hall, 1997), 144.

34 Thomas Wheelen and J. David Hunger, *Management* (Reading, MA: Addison-Wesley Publishing Co., 1995), 124.

35 Fred R. David, *Strategic Management* (Englewood Cliffs, NJ: Prentice-Hall, 1995), 161.

36 "Why Too Many Mergers Miss the Mark," *The Economist,* 4 January 1997, 58.

37 Ibid., 58.

38 Peter Truell, "A Cross Cultural Match in the Financial World," *New York Times,* 8 February 1997, 35, 36.

39 Ibid., 36.

40 Denison, *Corporate Culture,* 12.

41 Quoted in Gideon Kunda, *Engineering Culture: Control and Commitment in a High-Tech Corporation* (Philadelphia: Temple University Press, 1992), 10.

42 Ibid., 11.

43 Kotter and Heskett, 44.

44 Ibid., 50.

45 Ibid.

46 Ibid., 53–4.

47 Ibid., 53. For another view of culture's impact, see Raymond Zammuto and Edward O'Connor, "Gaining Advanced Manufacturing Technologies, Benefits: The Roles of Organization Design and Culture," *Academy of Management Review* (October 1992):701–29.

48 J. Rampey and H. Roberts, "Perspectives on Total Quality," *Proceedings of Total Quality Forum IV,* Cincinnati, Ohio, November 1992.

49 Greg Bounds, Lyle Yorks, Mel Adams, and Gipsie Ranney, *Beyond Total Quality Management* (New York: McGraw-Hill, 1994), 90–3.

50 Ibid., 90.

51 Ibid., 91.

52 Andrew DuBrin, *Leadership: Research Findings, Practice, and Skills* (Boston: Houghton Mifflin Co., 1995), 312.

53 Wilham Echikson, "Phillips Electronics: How Hard It Is to Change Culture," *Fortune 130* (November 14, 1994):52–68. See also Lewis Young, "European-Style Restructuring," *Electronic Business Today 23* (February 1997):36(5).

54 Hunt, 234–6.

55 Kotter and Heskett, 85.

56 Ibid., 84.

57 Ibid.

58 Ibid.

59 Richard Osborne, "Core Value Statements: The Corporate Compass," *Business Horizons,* September–October 1991, 29.

60 Judith Dobrzynski, "Jack Welch: How Good a Manager?" *Business Week,* 14 December 1987, 92–98.

61 General Electric Company 1996 Annual Report, 1.

62 Stephanie L. Gruner, "Why Open the Books?," *Inc.,* November 1996, 95.

63 Matthew J. Kiernan, "Get Innovated or Get Dead," *Business Quarterly* (Autumn 1996).

Chapter 12

1 R. Cattel, *The Scientific Analysis of Personality* (Baltimore, Penguin Books, 1965). See also G. Northcraft and M. Neale, *Organizational Behavior* (Hinsdale, IL: Dryden Press, 1994), 64–240.

2 J. M. Digman, "Personality Structure: Emergence of the Five Factor Model," *Annual Review of Psychology 41* (1990):417–40.

3 Ibid.

4 The discussion of personality theories, except as noted, is based on Lester Lefton and Laura Valvatne, *Mastering Psychology* (Boston: Allyn and Bacon, 1992), 398–420; and Michael Carrell, Daniel Jennings, and Christina Heavrin, *Fundamentals of Organizational Behavior* (Upper Saddle River, NJ: Prentice-Hall, 1997), 106–10.

5 James Bowditch and Anthony Buono, *A Primer on Organizational Behavior* (New York: John Wiley, 1994), 115.

6 Discussed in Anne Fisher, "Are You Afraid of Success?" *Fortune,* 8 July 1996, 105–10.

7 Based on Ernest J. McCormick and Joseph Tiffin, *Industrial Psychology* (Englewood Cliffs, NJ: Prentice-Hall, 1974), 136–74. See also Marilyn Gist and Terence Mitchell, "Self-Efficacy: A Theoretical Analysis of its Determinants and Malleability," *Academy of Management Review 17,* no. 2 (April 1992):183–202.

8 Saul Gellerman, *Motivation and Productivity* (New York: AMACOM).

9 Lefton and Valvatne, 412.

10 Ibid.

11 Ibid.

12 Gist and Mitchell, 183.

13 For a review and listing of these studies, see Gist and Mitchell, 183–211.

14 Ernest R. Hilgard, *Introduction to Psychology* (New York: Harcourt Brace and World, 1962), 186.

15 Timothy Costello and Sheldon Zalkind, *Psychology in Administration* (Englewood Cliffs, NJ: Prentice-Hall, 1963), 315–6.

16 Benson Rosen and Thomas Jerdee, "The Influence of Age Stereotypes on Managerial Decisions," *Journal of Applied Psychology 61,* no. 4 (August 1976):428–32.

17 Hilgard, 476. See also R. Heneman et al., "Attributions and Exchanges: The Effects of Interpersonal Factors on the Diagnosis of Employee Performance," *Academy of Management Journal 32* (June 1989):466–78; and Mary Ann Glynn, "Effects of Work Task Cues and Play Task Cues on Information Processing, Judgment and Motivation," *Journal of Applied Psychology 79* (February 1994):34–46.

18 Martin Fishbein and Icek Ajzen, *Attitude, Intention and Behavior: An Introduction to Theory and Research* (Reading, MA: Addison-Wesley, 1975).

19 All About Your Company, IBM Employee Handbook, 184.

20 The Job Descriptive Index is copyrighted by Bowling Green State University, and can be obtained from Dr. Patricia C. Smith, Department of Psychology, Bowling Green State University, Bowling Green, Ohio, 43403.

21 See, for example, M. T. Iaffaldano and M. P. Muchinsky, "Job Satisfaction and Job Performance: A Meta-Analysis," *Psychological Bulletin,* March 1985, 251–73.

22 For a discussion, see Cheri Ostroff, "The Relationship Between Satisfaction, Attitudes, and Performance: An Organizational-Level Analysis," *Journal of Applied Psychology 77,* no. 6 (December 1992):963–74.

23 Ibid.

24 Ibid., 968–9.

25 Ibid. See also Adrian Furnham, "Attitudinal Correlates and Demographic Predictions of Monetary Beliefs and Behaviors," *Journal of Organizational Behavior* 17 no. 4, July 1996, 375–388. See also "The Congruence between the Importance of Job Satisfaction and the Perceived Level of Achievement," *Journal of Management Development* 15, no. 6, 1996, 18–27.

26 Hilgard, 124–5.

27 Ibid., 124.

28 See, for instance, Kanfer, "Motivation Theory," in *Handbook of Industrial and Organizational Psychology,* 1990. See also Robert Hersey, "A Practitioner's View of Motivation," *Journal of Managerial Psychology* (May 1993):110–5, and Kenneth Kovatch, "Employee Motivation: Addressing a Crucial Factor in Your Organization's Performance," *Employment Relations Today 22* (Summer 1995):93–107.

29 See Douglas M. McGregor, "The Human Side of Enterprise," in *Management Classics* ed. Michael Matteson and John M. Ivancevich (Santa Monica, CA: Goodyear, 1977), 43–9.

30 McGregor, 45.

31 This is based on David Kolb, Irwin Rubin, and James McIntyre, *Organizational Psychology: An Experiential Approach* (Englewood Cliffs, NJ: Prentice-Hall, 1971), 65–9.

32 These are all from Kolb et al.

33 George Litwin and Robert Stringer, Jr., *Motivation and Organizational Climate* (Boston: Harvard University, 1968), 20–4.

34 Kanfer, 102. See also Robert Bretz and Steven Thomas, "Perceived Equity, Motivation, and Final-Offer Arbitration in Major League Baseball," *Journal of Applied Psychology* (June 1992):280–9.

35 See, for example, J. Greenberg, "A Taxonomy of Organizational Justice Theories," *Academy of Management Review 12* (1987):9–22.

36 For a discussion, see Kanfer, 124.

37 Edwin A. Locke and D. Henne, "Work Motivation Theories," in *International Review of Industrial and Organizational Psychology* eds. C. L. Cooper and I. Robertson (Chichester, England: Wiley, 1986), 1–35.

38 Kanfer, 125.

39 A. J. Mento, R. P. Steel, and R. J. Karren, "A Meta-analytic Study of the Effects of Goal Setting on Task Performance: 1966–1984," *Organizational Behavior and Human Decision Processes 39* (1987):52–83.

40 Gary Latham and T. W. Lee, "Goal Setting," in *Generalizing from Laboratory to Field Settings,* ed. Edwin A. Locke (Lexington, MA: Lexington Books, 1986), 101–19.

41 Kanfer, 113.

42 For a discussion, see John P. Campbell and Robert Pritchard, "Motivation Theory in Industrial and Organizational Psychology," in *Industrial and Organizational Psychology,* ed. Marvin Dunnette, 74–5; and Kanfer, 115–6.

43 See, for example, Terrence Mitchell, "Expectancy-Value Models in Organizational Psychology," in *Expectations and Actions: Expectancy-Value Models in Psychology,* ed. N. P. Feather (Hillsdale, NJ: Erlbaum, 1982), 293–312. See also Mark Tubbs et al., "Expectancy, Valence, and Motivational Force Functions in Goal Setting Research: An Empirical Test," *Journal of Applied Psychology* (June 1993):36–49.

44 Mark Tubbs, Donna Boehne, and James Dahl, "Expectancy, Valence, and Motivational Force Functions in Goal Setting Research: An Empirical Test," *Journal of Applied Psychology 78,* no. 3 (June 1993):361–73; Wendelien Van Eerde and Hank Thierry, "Vroom's Expectancy Models and Work-Related Criteria: A Meta-Analysis," *Journal of Applied Psychology 81,* no. 5 (October 1996):575–86.

45 For a definition of learning, see Lefton and Valvatne, 161.

46 For a recent review of operant conditioning, see Fred Luthans and R. Kreitner, *Organizational Behavior Modification and Beyond: An Operant and Social Learning Approach* (Glenview, IL: Scott, Foresman, 1985).

47 W. Clay Hamner, "Reinforcement Theory in Management and Organizational Settings," in *Organizational Behavior and Management: A Contingency Approach,* Henry Tosi and W. Clay

Hamner (Chicago: Saint Claire, 1974), 86–112. See also Donald J. Campbell, "The Effects of Goal-Contingent Payment on the Performance of a Complex Task," *Personnel Psychology 37,* no. 1 (Spring 1984):23–40.

48 Robert McNutt "Sharing Across the Board: DuPont's Achievement Sharing Program," *Compensation & Benefits Review 22* (July–August 1990):17–24.

49 Barry Thomas and Madeline Hess Olson, "Gainsharing: The Design Guarantees Success," *Personnel Journal 67* (May 1988):73–9. One of the most well-known and well-established plans of this type is in place at the Lincoln Electric Company. See, for example, Kenneth Chilton, "Lincoln Electric's Incentive System: A Reservoir of Trust," *Compensation and Benefits Review 26,* no. 6 (November 1994):29–34.

50 "The Fast Company Unit of One Anniversary Handbook," *Fast Company,* February–March 1997, 99.

51 See, for example, James Gutherie and Edward Cunningham, "Pay for Performance: The Quaker Oats Alternative," *Compensation & Benefits Review 24,* no. 2 (March–April 1992):18–23.

52 See, for example, Graham O'Neill, "Linking Pay to Performance: Conflicting Views and Conflicting Evidence," *Asia Pacific Journal of HRM 33,* no. 2 (Winter 1995):20–35.

53 See, for example, Kent Romanoff, "The Ten Commandments of Performance Management," *Personnel 66,* no. 1 (January 1989):24–8.

54 Carey Goldberg, "Windfall Sets Off a Blizzard of Bonuses for a Company," *New York Times,* 25 December 1996, A16.

55 For a discussion see, for example, Gary Dessler, *Human Resource Management* (Upper Saddle River, NJ: Prentice-Hall, 1997), 466–7.

56 James Brinks, "Is There Merit in Merit Increases?" *Personnel Administrator 25* (May 1980):60. See also Atul Migra et al., "The Case of the Invisible Merit Raise: How People See Their Pay Raises," *Compensation and Benefits Review 27,* no. 3 (May 1995):71–6.

57 Bob Nelson, *1001 Ways to Reward Employees* (New York: Workmen Publishing, 1994), 47.

58 *Blueprints for Service Quality,* Federal Express Corporation, 34–5.

59 Nelson, 52.

60 Ibid., 48.

61 Gerald Ledford, Jr., "Three Case Studies on Skill-Based Pay: An Overview," *Compensation & Benefits Review 23* (March–April 1991):11–23.

62 Gerald Ledford, Jr., and Gary Bergel, "Skill-Based Pay Case No. 1: General Mills," *Compensation & Benefits Review 23* (March–April 1991):24–38.

63 Hal Plotkin, "Hollywood Lures High School Animators with Sweet Deals," *Inc.,* January 1997, 20.

64 Nelson, 19.

65 Nelson, 6. See also Bob Nelson, "Dump the Cash, Load on the Praise," *Personnel Journal 75,* no.7, July 1996, 65ff.

66 Ibid., 5.

67 Ibid., 5.

68 Ibid., 6.

69 Chris Argyris, *Integrating the Individual and the Organization* (New York: John Wiley, 1964).

70 Samuel Melamed, Irit Ben-Avi, Jair Luz, and Manfred Green, "Objective and Subjective Work Monotony: Effects on Job Satisfaction, Psychological Distress, and Absenteeism in Blue Collar Workers," *Journal of Applied Psychology 80,* no. 1 (February 1995):29–42.

71 M. A. Campion and C. L. McClelland, "Interdisciplinary Examination of the Costs and Benefits of Enlarged Jobs: A Job Design Quasi-experiment," *Journal of Applied Psychology 76* (1991):186–98.

72 M. A. Campion and C. L. McClelland, "Follow-up and Extension of the Interdisciplinary Costs and Benefits of Enlarged Jobs," *Journal of Applied Psychology 78* (1993):339–51.

73 See, for example, J. Richard Hackman et al., "A New Strategy for Job Enrichment," *California Management Review 17,* no. 4 (1973):57–71.

74 Ibid.

75 See, for example, J. Richard Hackman and Greg Oldham, "Motivation Through the Design of Work: Test of a Theory," *Organizational Behavior and Human Performance 16,* no. 2 (August 1976):250–79; and J. R. Hackman and G. Oldham, *Work Redesign* (Reading, MA: Addison-Wesley, 1980).

76 See, for example, Kenneth Thomas and Betty Velthouse, "Cognitive Elements of Empowerment: An Interpretive Model of Intrinsic Task Motivation," *Academy of Management Review 15,* no. 4 (1990):666–81. See also Allan J. H. Thorlackson and Robert P. Murray, "An Empirical Study of Empowerment in the Workplace," *Group and Organization Management 21,* no. 1 (March 1996):670–83.

77 See, for example, Anthony Mento et al., "Maryland vs. Michigan vs. Minnesota: Another Look at the Relationship of Expectancy and Goal Difficulty to Task Performance," *Organizational Behavior and Human Performance 25,* no. 3 (June 1980):419–40.

78 This is based on W. Clay Hamner and Ellen Hamner, "Behavior Modification on the Bottom Line," *Organizational Dynamics* (Spring 1976). For recent applications, see Greg LaBar, "Safety Incentives: Q & A Reveals Best Practices," *Occupational Hazards 58,* no. 11, November 1996, 51–56.

79 Judi Komaki, Kenneth Barwick, and Lawrence Scott, "A Behavioral Approach to Occupational Safety: Pinpointing and Reinforcing Safe Performance in a Food Manufacturing Plant," *Journal of Applied Psychology 63,* no. 4 (1978):434–45.

80 Gillian Flynn, "New Skills Equals New Opportunities," *Personnel Journal* (June 1996):77–9.

81 This is based on Norman Nopper, "Reinventing the Factory with Lifelong Learning," *Training,* May 1993, 55–7.

82 Ibid., 57. For other examples see Kevin Kelly and Peter Burrows, "Motorola: Training for the Millennium," *Business Week,* 28 March 1994, 158–60; and "Some Nuts and Bolts of Lifelong Learning," *Training,* March 1994, 30.

83 Nopper, "Reinventing the Factory"; and Dessler, *Winning Commitment: How to Build and Keep a Competitive Workforce* (New York: McGraw-Hill, 1993), 133–50.

Chapter 13

1 Marianne Detwiler, "Interview with: Nathaniel Weiss—Lyrrus, Inc.," *Entrepreneurial Edge on Line* (1997): Internet (www.edgeonline.com).

2 Personal communication.

3 Daniel Katz and Robert Kahn, *The Social Psychology of Organizations* (New York: John Wiley & Sons, 1966).

4 George Miller, *Language and Communication* (New York: McGraw-Hill, 1951), 10, discussed in Gary Hunt, *Communication Skills in the Organization,* 2nd ed. (Englewood Cliffs, NJ: Prentice-Hall, 1989), 29.

5 This is discussed in and based on Fred Luthans and Janet Larsen, "How Managers Really Communicate," *Human Relations 39,* no. 2 (1986):162.

6 This model is based on the classic and best-known communication model by Claude E. Shannon and Warren Weaver and is adapted by using several improvements suggested by Sanford,

Hunt, and Bracey. Both models are presented in Hunt, *Communication Skills,* 34–6.

7 This section on dealing with communication barriers is based on R. Wayne Pace and Don Faules, *Organizational Communication,* (Englewood Cliffs, NJ: Prentice Hall, 1989), 150–62, unless otherwise noted. See also Tom Geddie, "Leap Over Communications Barriers," *Communication World,* April 1994, 12–7.

8 Pace and Faules, 153.

9 For instance, see Jay Knippn and Thad Green, "How the Manager Can Use Active Listening," *Public Personnel Management 23,* no. 2 (Summer 1994):357–9.

10 Bob Smith, "Care and Feeding of the Office Grapevine," *American Management Association,* February 1996, 6.

11 Eugene Walton, "How Efficient Is the Grapevine?" *Personnel,* March/April 1961, 45–9, reprinted in Davis, *Organizational Behavior, a Book of Readings.*

12 Keith Davis, "Cut Those Rumors Down to Size," *Supervisory Management,* June 1975, 206.

13 Thomas Stewart, "How G.E. Keeps Those Ideas Coming," *Fortune,* 12 August 1991, 41–9.

14 Valerie Frazee, "Establishing Relations in Germany," *Global Workforce,* April 1997, 16–7.

15 For further discussion, see Pace and Faules, 157–60.

16 Jitendra Sharma, "Organizational Communications: A Linking Process," *The Personnel Administrator 24,* (July 1979):35–43. See also Victor Callan, "Subordinate-Manager Communication in Different Sex Dyads: Consequences for Job Satisfaction," *Journal of Occupational and Organizational Psychology* (March 1993):13–28.

17 William Convoy, *Working Together . . . Communication in a Healthy Organization,* (Columbus, OH: Charles Merrill, 1976). See also David Johnson et al. "Differences Between Formal and Informal Communication Channels," *Journal of Business Communication* (April 1994):111–24.

18 Dessler, *Winning Commitment: How to Build and Keep a Competitive Workforce* (New York: McGraw-Hill, 1993).

19 Pace and Faules, 105–6. See also Joanne Yates and Wanda Orlinkowski, "Genres of Organizational Communication: A Structurational Approach to Studying Communication and Media," *Academy of Management Review 17* (April 1992):299–327.

20 Earl Plenty and William Machaner, "Stimulating Upward Communication," in *Readings in Organizational Behavior,* eds. Jerry Gray and Frederick Starke (Columbus: Merrill, 1977), 229–40. See also Pace and Faules, 153–60.

21 For a discussion of this see Karlene Roberts and Charles O'Reilly III. "Failures in Upward Communication in Organizations: Three Possible Culprits," *Academy of Management Journal 17,* no. 2 (June 1974):205–15.

22 Based on Stewart, "How G.E. Keeps Those Ideas Coming."

23 Ibid., 42.

24 Ibid.

25 Ibid.

26 Ibid., 43.

27 Ibid.

28 *Federal Express Employee Handbook,* 89.

29 *Team-Member Handbook,* Toyota Motor Manufacturing, USA, February 1988, 52–3.

30 For a recent review and a discussion of the current study see James SmithER et al., "An Examination of the Effects of an Upward Feedback Program Over Time," *Personnel Psychology 48* (1995):1–34.

31 Ibid., 10–1.

32 Ibid., 27.

33 Pace and Faules, 99–100.

34 Personal interview, March 1992.

35 Personal interview, March 1992.

36 Suellyn McMillan, "Squelching the Rumor Mill," *Personnel Journal,* October 1991, 95–101.

37 David Kirkpatrick, "Groupware Goes Boom," *Fortune,* 27 December 1993, 99–101; see also Samuel Greengard, "E-mail: Using Your Connections," *Personnel Journal 74,* no. 9 (September 1995):161–5.

38 Lorraine Parker, "Make the Most of Teleconferencing," *Training and Development Journal 50,* no. 2 (February 1996):28–9.

39 James Bryan Quinn, *Intelligent Enterprise* (New York: The Free Press, 1992), 266. See also James Bryan Quinn, Phillip Anderson, and Sydney Finkelstein, "Leveraging Intellect." *Academy of Management Executive 10,* no. 3 (November 1996):7–27.

40 This is based on Tom Peters and Robert Waterman, *In Search of Excellence* (New York: Harper and Row), 119–218.

41 Ibid., 122.

42 Ibid., 124.

43 Ibid., 218–20, 122–3.

44 Ibid., 219.

45 Ibid., 22.

46 Ibid., 122–3.

47 Faye Rice, "Champions of Communication," *Fortune,* 3 June 1991, 111–20.

48 Ibid., 43.

49 Ibid.

50 Ibid., 112.

51 Ibid., 116.

52 Tom Peters, *Liberation Management* (New York: Alfred A. Knopf, 1992), 172–5.

53 Ibid., 174.

54 Ronald Lieber, "Cool Offices," *Fortune,* 9 December 1996, 208.

55 Harold Leavitt, "Some Effects of Certain Communication Patterns on a Group Performance," *Journal of Abnormal and Social Psychology 46* (1972):38–50.

56 Tom Burns and G. M. Stalker, *The Management of Innovation* (London: Tavistock Publications, 1961), 120–5.

57 R. L. Daft and R. H. Lengel, "Information Richness: A New Approach in Managerial Behavior and Organization Design," in *Research in Organizational Behavior,* eds. Larry Cummings and Barry Staw (Greenwich, CT: JAI Press, 1984), 190–233, discussed in Janet Fulk and Bryan Boyd, "Emerging Theories of Communication in Organizations," *Journal of Management 17,* no. 2 (1991):409–11. See also Susan Strauss and Joseph McGrath, "Does the Medium Matter? The Intersection of Task Type and Technology on Group Performance and Member Reactions," *Journal of Applied Psychology* (February 1994):87–99.

58 Roger E. Axtell, ed., *Do's and Taboos Around the World* (New York: John Wiley & Sons, Inc., 1985), 37–48.

Chapter 14

· ·

1 "Oxford, Responding to Consumers, Reorganizes Services," Infoseek/Reuters (March 25, 1997): Internet (http://www.infoseek.com).

2 Brian Dumaine, "Who Needs a Boss?" *Fortune,* 7 May 1990, 52–60.

3 Ibid., 52. For further discussion of employee involvement, see Fritz Pil and John MacDuffie, "The Adoption of High-Involvement Work Practices," *Industrial Relations 35,* no. 3 (July 1996):423–55.

4 Tom Peters, *Liberation Management* (New York: Alfred Knopf, 1992), 238–9.

5 John Katzenbach and Douglas Smith, "The Discipline of Teams," *Harvard Business Review* (March–April 1993):112.

6 Jack Gordon, "Work Teams: How Far Have They Come?" *Training,* October 1992, 60–5.

7 For employee involvement survey data, see Lee Towe, "Survey Finds Employee Involvement a Priority for Necessary Innovation, " *National Productivity Review 9,* no. 1 (Winter 1989–90):3–15.

8 Jack Orsburn, Linda Moran, Ed Musselwhite, John Zenger, and Craig Perrin, *Self-Directed Work Teams: The New American Challenge* (Homewood, IL: Business One Irwin, 1990), 30–4.

9 Ibid., 33.

10 Ibid.

11 Ibid., 34. See also Charles Manz, "Self-Leading Work Teams: Moving Beyond Self-Management Myths," *Human Relations 45,* no. 11 (1992):1119–41.

12 See, for example, Katzenbach and Smith, 112–3. Note that many researchers do not, however, distinguish between groups and teams. See, for example, Gary Coleman and Eileen M. VanAken, "Applying Small-Group Behavior Dynamics to Improve Action-Team Performance," *Employment Relations Today* (Autumn 1991):343–53.

13 These definitions are from Marvin E. Shaw, *Group Dynamics: The Psychology of Small Group Behavior* (New York: McGraw-Hill, 1976), 11.

14 Daniel Feldman, "The Development and Enforcement of Group Norms," *Academy of Management Review 9,* no. 1 (1984):47–53.

15 A. P. Hare, *Handbook of Small Group Research* (New York: The Free Press, 1962), 24. See also S. Barr and E. Conlon, "Effects of Distribution of Feedback in Work Groups," *Academy of Management Journal* (June 1994):641–56.

16 See Stephen Worchel, Wendy Wood, and Jeffrey Simpson, *Group Process and Productivity* (Newbury Park, CA: Sage Publications, 1992), 245–50.

17 Ibid., 245.

18 For a discussion of the difficulty of measuring and defining cohesiveness, see Peter Mudrack, "Group Cohesiveness and Productivity: A Closer Look," *Human Relations 42,* no. 9 (1989):771–85. See also R. Saavedra et al., "Complex Interdependence in Task-Performing Groups," *Journal of Applied Psychology* (February 1993):61–73.

19 See Marvin Shaw, *Group Dynamics* (New York: McGraw-Hill, 1976), Chapter 4.

20 Robert Blake and Jane Mouton, "Reactions to Inter-Group Competition under Win-Lose Conditions," *Management Science 7* (1961):432.

21 John R. P. French, Jr., "The Disruption and Cohesion of Groups," *Journal of Abnormal and Social Psychology 36* (1941):361–77.

22 Stanley C. Seashore, *Group Cohesiveness in the Industry Work Group* (Ann Arbor, MI: Survey Research Center, University of Michigan, 1954), 90–5, and Joseph Litterer, *The Analysis of Organizations* (New York: Wiley, 1965), 91–101; and J. Haleblian and S. Finkelstein, "Top Management Team Size, CEO Dominance, and Firm Performance: The Moderating Roles of Environmental Turbulence and Discretion," *Academy of Management Journal* (August 1993):844–64.

23 This material is based on James H. Shonk, *Team-Based Organizations* (Chicago: Irwin, 1997), 27–33.

24 Ibid., 28.

25 Ibid., 29.

26 Katzenbach and Smith, 116–8.

27 Everett Adams, Jr., "Quality Circle Performance," *Journal of Management 17,* no. 1 (1991):25–39.

28 Ibid.

29 Eric Sundstrom, Kenneth DeMeuse, and David Futrell, "Work-teams: Applications and Effectiveness," *American Psychologist,* February 1990, 120.

30 See, for example, Adams, "Quality Circle Performance"; and Gilbert Fuchsberg, "Quality Programs Show Shoddy Results," *Wall Street Journal,* 14 May 1992, B-1, B-4.

31 Gopal Pati, Robert Salitore, and Saundra Brady, "What Went Wrong with Quality Circles?" *Personnel Journal* (December 1987):83–9.

32 Philip Olson, "Choices for Innovation Minded Corporations," *Journal of Business Strategy* (January–February 1990):86–90.

33 In many firms, the concept of a venture team is taken to what may be its natural conclusion in that new-venture units and new-venture divisions are established. These are separate divisions devoted to new-product development. See, for example, Christopher Bart, "New Venture Units: Use Them Wisely to Manage Innovation," *Sloan Management Review 35* (Summer 1988):35–43; and Robert Burgelman, "Managing the New Venture Division: Research Findings and Implications for Strategic Management," *Strategic Management Journal 6* (1985):39–54.

34 Harold J. Leavitt and Jean Lipman-Blumen, "Hot Groups," *Harvard Business Review* (July–August 1995):109.

35 Ibid., 165.

36 Ibid.

37 Ibid., 113.

38 The remainder of this section is based on Leavitt and Lipman-Blumen, 110–6.

39 Ibid., 111.

40 Ibid.

41 Ibid., 112.

42 Ibid.

43 Ibid., 113.

44 Charles Snow, Scott Snell, Sue Canney Davison, and Donald Hambrick, "Use Transnational Teams to Globalize Your Company," *Organizational Dynamics* (Spring 1996):50–67.

45 Ibid., 50.

46 Ibid.

47 Ibid., 53–57.

48 Ibid., 61.

49 Jack Orsburn et al., 8.

50 Katzenbach and Smith, 116; and Sundstrom, DeMeuse, and Futrell, 121.

51 Orsburn et al., 20–7.

52 Ibid., 21.

53 Ibid., 22.

54 Ibid., 22–23.

55 For a discussion, see Peter Wright, Mark Kroll, and John Parnell, *Strategic Management Concepts* (Englewood Cliffs, NJ: Prentice-Hall, 1996), 224–5.

56 Ibid.

57 Ibid., 225.

58 Based on Erin Neurick, "Facilitating Effective Work Teams," *SAM Advanced Management Journal* (Winter 1993):22–6.

59 Ibid., 23.

60 Ibid.

61 The following, except as noted, is based on Glenn H. Varney, *Building Productive Teams: An Action Guide and Resource Book* (San Francisco: Jossey-Bass Publishers, 1989), 11–8. See also P. Bernthal and C. Insko, "Cohesiveness without Group Think: The Interactive Effects of Social and Task Cohesion," *Group and Organization Management* (March 1993):66–88.

62 Katzenbach and Smith, 112. See also C. Meyer, "How the Right Measures Help Teams Excel," *Harvard Business Review* (May–June 1994):95–106.

63 Katzenbach and Smith, 112.

64 See G. T. Shea and R. A. Guzzo, "Groups as Human Resources," in *Research in Personnel and Human Resources Management,* Vol. 5, eds. K. M. Roland and G. R. Ferris. (Greenwich, CT: JAI Press, 1987), 323–56. See also Sundstrom, DeMeuse, and Futrell, 123.

65 Katzenbach and Smith, 113.

66 Ibid. The evaluation process is important as well. See R. Saavedra and S. Kwun, "Peer Evaluation in Self-Managing Work Groups," *Journal of Applied Psychology* (June 1993):450–63.

67 Michael West and Neil Anderson, "Innovation in Top Management Teams," *Journal of Applied Psychology 81,* no. 6 (December 1996):680–93.

68 The remaining items in this section, except as noted, are quoted from or based on Michael A. Campion and A. Catherine Higgs, "Design Work Teams to Increase Productivity and Satisfaction," *HR Magazine,* October 1995, 101–7. See also Steven G. Rogelberg and Steven M. Rumery, "Gender Diversity, Team Decision Quality, Time on Task, and Interpersonal Cohesion," *Small Group Research 27,* no. 1 (February 1996):79–90; Steven E. Gross and Jeffrey Blair, "Reinforcing Team Effectiveness Through Pay," *Compensation and Benefits Review 27,* no. 5 (September 1995):34–8; and Joan M. Glaman, Allan P. Jones, and Richard M. Rozelle, "The Effects of Co-Worker Similarity on the Emergence of Affect in Work Teams," *Group and Organization Management 21,* no. 2 (June 1996):192–215.

69 See Campion and Higgs, 102–3. See also Michael Campion, Ellen Papper, and Gina Medsker, "Relations Between Work Team Characteristics and Effectiveness: A Replication and Extension," *Personnel Psychology 49,* no. 2 (Summer 1996):429–52.

70 Ibid., 102.

71 Ibid., 103–4.

72 Joan Glaman, Allan Jones, and Richard Rozelle, "The Effects of Co-Worker Similarity on the Emergence of Affect in Work Teams," *Group & Organization Management 21,* no. 2 (June 1996):192–215.

73 This is based on Steven Rayner, "Team Traps: What They Are, How to Avoid Them," *National Productivity Review* (Summer 1996):101–15.

74 These are based on Shonk, 133–8.

75 Kimball Fisher, *Leading Self-Directed Work Teams* (New York: McGraw-Hill, 1993), 151–3.

76 Ibid., 44.

77 These are based on Fisher, 48–56.

78 Ibid., 53.

79 Gary Dessler, *Winning Commitment* (New York: McGraw-Hill, 1992), 28.

80 Ibid., 30.

81 For a discussion see Fisher, 106.

82 Ibid., 110–1.

83 Ibid., 110.

84 Shonk, 133.

85 See Shonk, 133–8; Andrew DuBrin, *Leadership: Research Findings, Practice and Skills* (Boston: Houghton-Mifflin, 1995), 224–7.

86 Shonk, 133.

87 Fisher, 143–4.

88 Ibid., 143.

Chapter 15

1 See for example, Martha Peak, "An Era of Wrenching Corporate Change," *Management Review 85,* no. 7 (July 1996):45–9.

2 Based on David Nadler and Michael Tushman, "Beyond the Charismatic Leader: Leadership and Organizational Change," *California Management Review* (Winter 1990):77–97.

3 Ibid., 78. See also Guvenc G. Alpander and Carroll R. Lee, "Culture, Strategy and Teamwork: The Keys to Organizational Change," *Journal of Management Development 14,* no. 8 (1995):4–18; and Benjamin Schneider, Arthur P. Brief, and Richard A. Guzzo, "Creating a Climate and Culture for Sustainable Organizational Change," *Organizational Dynamics 24,* no. 4 (Spring 1996):7–19.

4 Stewart Thomas, "G.E. Keeps Those Ideas Coming," *Fortune,* 12 August 1991, 42.

5 See, for example, Brian Dumaine, "The Bureaucracy Busters," *Fortune,* 17 June 1991, 36–50.

6 Roger Harrison, "Choosing the Depth of Organization Intervention," *Journal of Applied Behavioral Science 2,* (April-May-June 1970):181–202.

7 Nadler and Tushman, 79.

8 Ibid., 80; and Alfred Marcus, "Responses to Externally Induced Innovation: To their Effects on Organizational Performance," *Strategic Management Journal 9,* (1988):194–202.

9 Nadler and Tushman, "Beyond the Charismatic Leader."

10 Niccolo Machiavelli, *The Prince,* trans. W. K. Marriott (London: J. M. Dent & Sons, Ltd., 1958).

11 Richard Osborne, "Core Values Statements: The Corporate Compass," *Business Horizons* (September–October 1991):28–34.

12 Based on Gregory Northcraft and Margaret Neale, *Organizational Behavior* (Fort Worth: The Dryden Press, 1990), 716–20.

13 Paul Lawrence, "How to Deal with Resistance to Change," *Harvard Business Review* (May–June, 1954). See also Andrew W. Schwartz, "Eight Guidelines for Managing Change," *Supervisory Management* (July 1994): 3–5; Thomas J. Werner and Robert F. Lynch, "Challenges of a Change Agent" *Journal for Quality and Participation* (June 1994): 50–4; Larry Reynolds, "Understand Employees' Resistance to Change," *HR Focus* (June 1994): 17–8; and Kenneth E. Hultman, "Scaling the Wall of Resistance," *Training & Development Journal 49,* no. 10 (October 1995):15–8.

14 Paul Strebel, "Why Do Employees Resist Change?" *Harvard Business Review* (May–June 1996):86–92.

15 Ibid., 87.

16 Ibid.

17 Kurt Lewin, "Group Decision and Social Change," in *Readings in Social Psychology* eds. T. Newcomb and E. Hartley (New York: Holt Rinehart & Winston, 1947). See also Thomas Cummings and Christopher Worley, *Organization Development and Change* (Minneapolis: West Publishing Company, 1993), 53.

18 Charles Philips, "Can He Fix Philips?" *Fortune,* 31 May 1997, 98–100.

19 Noel Tichy and Rarn Charan, "Speed, Simplicity, Self-Confidence: An Interview with Jack Welch," *Harvard Business Review* (September–October 1989):112–20, reprinted in Richard Osborne, "Core Values Statements: The Corporate Compass," *Business Horizons* (September–October 1991):32.

20 The ten steps are based on Michael Beer, Russell Eisenstat, and Burt Spector, "Why Change Programs Don't Produce Change," *Harvard Business Review* (November–December 1990):158–66; Thomas Cummings and Christopher Worley, *Organization Development and Change* (Minneapolis: West Publishing Company, 1993); John P. Kotter, "Leading Change: Why Transformation Efforts Fail," *Harvard Business Review* (March–April 1995):59–66; and John P. Kotter, *Leading Change* (Boston: Harvard Business School Press, 1996).

21 Kotter, *Leading Change,* 40–1.

22 Ibid., 44.

23 Ibid., 57.

24 Ibid., 85.

25 Ibid., 90–1.

26 Ibid., 101–2.

27 Kathryn Harris, "Mr. Sony Confronts Hollywood," *Fortune,* 23 December 1996, 36.

28 Noel Tichy and Ram Charan, "The CEO as Coach: An Interview with Allied Signal's Lawrence A. Bossidy," *Harvard Business Review* (March–April 1995): 77.

29 Beer, Eisenstat, and Spector, 163.

30 This is based on Kotter, "Leading Change: Why Transformation Efforts Fail," 61–6.

31 Ibid., 65.

32 Beer, Eisenstat, and Spector, 164.

33 The following is based on Nadler and Tushman, 77–97.

34 Ibid., 82.

35 Ibid., 85.

36 Ibid.

37 The perceptive reader will note that Nadler and Tushman's concept of instrumental leadership is in some respects the same as saying that the successful executive leader of change is really a successful manager in that he or she is able to successfully plan, organize, staff, lead, and control the various elements of the change.

38 Ibid., 92.

39 Ibid., 93–4. See also Thomas Stewart, "Brain Power," *Fortune,* 17 March 1997, 105–10.

40 For a discussion see Julian Barling, Tom Weber, and E. Kevin Kelloway, "Effects of Transformational Leadership Training on Attitudinal and Financial Outcomes: A Field Experiment," *Journal of Applied Psychology 81,* no. 6 (December 1996):827–32.

41 Ibid.

42 Cummings and Worley, 3.

43 Based on J. T. Campbell and M. D. Dunnette, "Effectiveness of T-Group Experiences in Managerial Training and Development" *Psychological Bulletin 7,* (1968): 73–104, reprinted in W. E. Scott and L. L. Cummings, *Readings in Organizational Behavior and Human Performance* (Homewood, IL: Irwin, 1973), 571.

44 Robert J. House, *Management Development* (Ann Arbor, MI: Bureau of Industrial Relations, University of Michigan, 1967), 71; Louis White and Kevin Wooten, "Ethical Dilemmas in Various Stages of Organizational Development," *Academy of Management Review 8,* no. 4 (1983): 690–7.

45 Wendell French and Cecil Bell, Jr., *Organization Development* (Englewood Cliffs, NJ: Prentice-Hall, 1995), 171–93.

46 Cummings and Worley, 501.

47 For a description of how to make OD a part of organizational strategy, see Aubrey Mendelow and S. Jay Liebowitz, "Difficulties in Making OD a Part of Organizational Strategy," *Human Resource Planning 12,* no. 4 (1995):317–29.

48 See, for example, John Rizzo, Robert J. House, and Sydney I. Lirtzinan, "Role Conflict and Ambiguity in Complex Organizations," *Administrative Science Quarterly 15,* (June 1970): 150–63. For additional views on sources of conflict, see Patricia A. Gwartney-Gibbs and Denise H. Lach, "Gender Differences in Clerical Workers' Disputes Over Tasks," *Human Relations* (June 1994):611–40; and Kevin J. Williams and George Alliger, "Role Stressors, Mood Spillover, and Perceptions of Work-Family Conflict in Employed Parents," *Academy of Management Journal* (August 1994):837–69.

49 Yitzhak Fried and Robert B. Tiegs, "Supervisors' Role Conflict and Role Ambiguity: Differential Relations with Performance

Ratings of Subordinates and the Moderating Effect of Screening Ability," *Journal of Applied Psychology 80,* no. 21 (April 1995):282–91.

50 Ibid., 291.

51 See, for example, Richard Walton and John Dutton, "The Management of Interdepartment Conflict: A Model and Review," *Administrative Science Quarterly 14,* no. 1, (March 1969):73–84.

52 Ibid.

53 John Dutton and Richard Walton, "Interdepartmental Conflict and Cooperation: Two Contrasting Studies," *Human Organization 25,* (1966):207–20.

54 H. A. Lansberger, "The Horizontal Dimensions in a Bureaucracy," *Administrative Science Quarterly 6* (1961):298–333.

55 Paul Lawrence and Jay Lorsch, *Organization and Environment* (Boston: Harvard University, Graduate School of Business Administration, Division of Research, 1967).

56 John A. Seiler, "Diagnosing Interdepartmental Conflict," *Harvard Business Review,* (September–October 1963):121–32.

57 Eric Neilson, "Understanding and Managing Intergroup Conflict," in Paul Lawrence and Jay Lorsch, *Organizational Behavior and Administration* (Homewood, IL: Irwin, 1976), 294. See also Robin L. Pinkley and Gregory B. Northcraft, "Conflict Frames of Reference: Implications for Dispute Processes and Outcomes," *Academy of Management Journal* (February 1994):193–206.

58 Lawrence and Lorsch, *Organization and Environment,* 74–5.

59 Kenneth Thomas, "Conflict and Conflict Management," in Marvin Dunnette, *Handbook of Industrial and Organizational Psychology* (Chicago: Rand McNally, 1976), 900–2; and Michael Carrell, Daniel Jennings, and Christina Heavrin, *Fundamentals of Organizational Behavior* (Upper Saddle River, NJ: Prentice-Hall, 1997), 505–9.

60 This section is based on Evert Van De Vliert, Martin Euwema, and Sipke Huismans, "Managing Conflict with a Subordinate or a Superior: Effectiveness of Conglomerated Behavior," *Journal of Applied Psychology 80,* no. 2 (April 1995):271–81.

61 Warren Bennis, *Organization Development: Its Nature, Origins and Prospects* (Reading, MA: Addison-Wesley, 1969), 4–6.

62 Ibid.

63 Ibid. For a discussion of additional third-party interventions, see Donald E. Conlon, Peter J. Carnevale, and Keith J. Murnighan, "Intravention: Third-Party Intervention with Clout" *Organizational Behavior & Human Decision Processes* (March, 1994):387–41.

64 Charles Handy, *The Age of Unreason.* (Boston: Harvard Business School Press, 1989), 3.

65 T. George Harris, "The Post-Capitalist Executive: An Interview with Peter F. Drucker," *Harvard Business Review* (May–June 1993):115–22.

66 Charlene Marmer Solomon, "Expats Say: Help Make Us Mobile," *Personnel Journal* (July 1996):47–52.

Chapter 16

1 Kenneth Merchant, "The Control Function of Management," *Sloan Management Review* (Summer 1982): 43.

2 Ibid., 44.

3 Glenn A. Welsch, *Budgeting: Profit Planning and Control* (Englewood Cliffs, NJ: Prentice-Hall, 1988), 16.

4 Thomas Connellan, *How to Improve Human Performance: Behaviorism in Business and Industry* (New York: Harper & Row, 1978), 68–73.

5 For a discussion, see Joan Woodward, *Industrial Organization: Behavior and Control* (London: Oxford, 1970), 37–56.

6 This section is based on William Newman, *Constructive Control* (Englewood Cliffs, NJ: Prentice-Hall, 1975), 6–9.

7 Robert Simons, *Levers of Control: How Managers Use Innovative Control Systems to Drive Strategic Renewal* (Boston: Harvard Business School Press, 1995), 80.

8 Ibid.

9 This classification is based on Simons, 81.

10 For example, see Simons, 82.

11 Daniel Wren, *The Evolution of Management Thought* (John Wiley & Sons, 1994), 115.

12 Simons, 81.

13 Ibid., 84.

14 Ibid., 84–95.

15 Ibid., 86.

16 These characteristics are based on Simons, 87.

17 This discussion is based on Simons, 87–8.

18 John Preble, "Environmental Scanning for Strategic Control," *Journal of Managerial Issues 4,* no. 2 (Summer 1992): 254. For a discussion of the emphasis on self-control in various countries, see Paul Boreham, "The Myth of Post-Fordist Management: Work Organization and Employee Discretion in Seven Countries," *Management Decisions 30,* no. 6 (November 1990): 100–9.

19 Charles Horngren, *Accounting for Management Control* (Englewood Cliffs, NJ: Prentice-Hall, 1975), 188.

20 Mark Dirsmith and Stephen Jablonski, "Zero Based Budgeting as a Management Technique and Political Strategy," *Academy of Management Review 4,* no. 4 (October, 1979): 355–65.

21 Fred R. David, *Strategic Management* (Upper Saddle River, NJ: Prentice-Hall, 1997), 281–3.

22 Ibid., 283.

23 Joel Kurtzman, "Is Your Company Off Course? Now You Can Find Out Why," *Fortune,* 17 February 1997, 128–30.

24 As described by the owner of a chain of dry cleaning stores to the author. For a discussion of how to evaluate standards, see Dennis Arter, "Evaluate Standards and Improve Performance with a Quality Audit," *Quality Progress 22,* no. 9 (September 1989): 41–3.

25 The following, except as noted, is based on Kenneth Merchant, *Control in Business Organizations* (Boston: Pitman, 1985), 71–120. See also Robert Kaplan, "New Systems for Measurement and Control," *The Engineering Economist 36,* no. 3 (Spring 1991): 201–18.

26 Lester Lefton and Laura Valvatne, *Mastering Psychology* (Boston: Allyn and Bacon, 1992), 426–7.

27 Michael Carrell, Daniel Jennings, and Christina Heavrin, *Fundamentals of Organizational Behavior* (Upper Saddle River, NJ: Prentice-Hall, 1997), 107.

28 Quoted from Lefton and Valvatne, 427.

29 Carrell, Jennings, and Heavrin, 107–8.

30 Ibid., 108.

31 This is based on Simons, 81–2.

32 Merchant, 98.

33 "Did Warner-Lambert Make a $468 Million Mistake?" *Business Week,* 21 November 1983, 123; quoted in Merchant, 98–9.

34 Chris Argyris, "Human Problems with Budgets," *Harvard Business Review 31,* no. 1 (January–February 1953): 97–110.

35 Peter Coy, "Big Brother, Pinned to Your Chest," *Business Week,* 17 August 1992, 38.

36 Jeffrey Stanton and Janet Barnes-Farrell, "Effects of Electronic Performance Monitoring on Personal Control, Task Satisfaction, and Task Performance," *Journal of Applied Psychology 81,* no. 6 (December 1996): 738.

37 This review is based on Stanton and Barnes-Farrell, 739.
38 Ibid. See also D. B. Greenberger, S. Strasser, and R. B. Dunham, "The Impact of Personal Control on Performance and Satisfaction," *Organizational Behavior and Human Decision Processes* 43, (1989): 29–51.
39 See, for example, Greenberger, Strasser, and Dunham; and M. J. Smith et al., "Employee Stress and Health Complaints in Jobs with and without Electronic Performance Monitoring," *Applied Ergonomics 23* (1992): 17–27.
40 Stanton and Barnes-Farrell, 738–45.
41 Stanton and Barnes-Farrell, 745. Note that items 2, 3, 5, 6, and 7 were reverse scored.
42 Ibid., 738.
43 Tom Peters, *Liberation Management* (New York: Alfred A. Knopf, 1992), 465–6.
44 Tom Burns and G. M. Stalker, *The Management of Innovation* (London: Tavistock, 1961), 119.
45 This quote is based on William Taylor, "Control in an Age of Chaos," *Harvard Business Review,* (November–December 1994): 70–1. James Collins and Jerry Porras, *Built to Last: Successful Habits of Visionary Companies* (New York: Harper and Row, 1994).
46 Ibid., 71.
47 Ibid., 72.
48 Edgar Schein, *Organizational Culture and Leadership* (San Francisco: Jossey-Bass, 1985), 224–37, and Peter Wright, Mark Kroll, and John Parnell, *Strategic Management Concepts* (Englewood Cliffs, NJ: Prentice-Hall, 1996), 233–6.
49 Except as noted, this section is based on Gary Dessler, *Winning Commitment: How to Build and Keep a Competitive Work Force* (New York: McGraw-Hill, 1993).
50 Richard Steers, "Antecedents and Outcomes of Organizational Commitment," *Administrative Science Quarterly 22* (March 1977). For an additional view, see R. Hackett et al., "Further Assessments of Meyer and Allen's (1991) Three Component Model of Organizational Commitment," *Journal of Applied Psychology 79* (February 1994): 15–24.
51 Personal interview. See Gary Dessler, *Winning Commitment,* 27–8.
52 Ibid., 28.
53 Ibid., 30.
54 See Dessler, 64.
55 Ibid., 69.
56 Peters, 379.
57 Dessler, 89.
58 Fujio Cho speech.
59 *Federal Express Employee Handbook,* 103.
60 Ibid., 21.
61 Kanter, 91.
62 Personal interview with JCPenney's compensation manager, December, 1991.
63 Abraham Maslow, *Motivation and Personality* (New York: Harper & Row, 1954), 336.
64 Interview with assembler Dan Dise, March 1992.
65 Personal interview, March 1992.

Chapter 17
. . . .

1 Jennifer Steinhauer, "Squeezing Into the Jeans Market," *New York Times,* 14 March 1997, C1, C15.
2 Richard Chase and Nicholas Aquilero, *Production & Operations Management* (Homewood, IL: Irwin, 1992), 5.
3 Ibid.
4 David Upton, "What Really Makes Factories Flexible?" *Harvard Business Review* (July–August 1995): 74–86.
5 Norman Gaither, *Production and Operations Management* (Fort Worth, TX: The Dryden Press, 1992), 22.
6 For a discussion of the strategic aspects of foreign factory placement and assignment, see Kasra Ferdows, "Making the Most of Foreign Factories," *Harvard Business Review* (March–April 1997): 73–91.
7 Gaither, 132–3.
8 Everett Adam, Jr., and Ronald Ebert, *Production & Operations Management* (Englewood Cliffs, NJ: Prentice-Hall, 1992), 254.
9 Ibid., 254.
10 Gaither, 135.
11 Adam and Ebert, 374.
12 Gaither, 869.
13 Thomas Petzinger, Jr., "How Lynn Mercer Manages a Factory That Manages Itself," *Wall Street Journal,* 17 March 1997, B1.
14 Barry Render and Jay Heizer, *Principles of Operations Management* (Upper Saddle River, NJ: Prentice-Hall, 1997), 483.
15 Ibid., 551.
16 Ibid., 551–3.
17 James Evans et al. *Applied Production and Operations Management* (St. Paul: West Publishing Co., 1984), 500–501.
18 Ibid., 511.
19 See, for example, Steven Replogle, "The Strategic Use of Smaller Lot Sizes through a New EOQ Model," *Production and Inventory Management Journal* (Third Quarter 1988): 41–4; T. C. E. Cheng, "An EOQ Model with Learning Effect on Set-Ups," *Production and Inventory Management Journal* (First Quarter 1991): 83–91.
20 Evans et al., 39.
21 Bob Carroll and Sam Tomas, "Team Competition Spurs Continuous Improvement at Motorola," *National Productivity Review* (Autumn 1995): 1.
22 Paul Zuech and Nancy Finley, "Teamwork Enhances Customer Satisfaction and Manufacturing Capability at Kent-Moore," *National Productivity Review* (Spring 1996): 101–5.
23 Ibid., 103.
24 Ibid., 105.
25 Based in part on Joel E. Ross, *Total Quality Management: Text, Cases and Readings* (Delray Beach, FL: St. Lucie Press, 1993), 1.
26 Render and Heizer, 96.
27 Ross, 2–3, 35–6.
28 Richard M. Hodgetts, *Blueprints for Continuous Improvement: Lessons from the Baldrige Winners* (New York: American Management Association, 1993), 13.
29 Except as noted, the following is based on Hodgetts, 15–22; and Ross, 4–5.
30 Hodgetts, 19.
31 Ross, 4.
32 Hodgetts, 21.
33 David Taylor and Ruth Karin Ramsey, "Empowering Employees to 'Just Do It,'" *Training & Development,* May 1993, American Society for Training and Development. Based on Michael Carrell, Daniel Jennings, and Christina Heavrin, *Fundamentals of Organizational Behavior* (Upper Saddle River, NJ: Prentice-Hall, 1997), 324–5.
34 Chase and Aquilero, 197.
35 These traits are quoted from David Anderson, *Design for Manufacturability* (Lafayette, CA: CI Press, 1990), 9.

36 Ibid., 16.

37 Anderson, 15. See also F. Robert Jacobs and Vincent Mabert, *Production Planning, Scheduling, and Inventory Control* (Norcross, GA: Industrial Engineering and Management Press, 1986), 96–100; and Otis Port, Zachary Shiller, Gregory Miles, and Amy Schulman, "Smart Factories, America's Turn," *Business Week,* 8 May 1989, 142–8.

38 See, for example, Joseph Martinich, *Production and Operations Management* (New York: Wiley, 1997), 215–6.

39 Valerie Reitman, "Global Money Trends Rattle Shop Windows in Heartland America," *Wall Street Journal,* 26 November 1993, A-1.

40 Harold Stradel and Paul Desruelle, *Manufacturing in the 90s* (New York: Van Nostrand Reinhold, 1992), 2.

41 David Mandel, "JIT: Strategic Weapon for Aerospace and Defense?" *Industrial Engineering* (February 1993): 48. Just-in-time can also be used to improve performance of service organizations. See, for example, W. Calvin Waco, Robert Stonehocker, and Larry Feldman, "Success with JIT and MRP II in a Service Organization," *Production & Inventory Management Journal* (Fourth Quarter) 1991, 15–22.

42 Adam and Ebert, 568.

43 These elements are based on Kenneth Wantuck, *The Japanese Approach to Productivity* (Southfield, MI: Bendix Corporation, 1983); and Chase and Aquilero, 261–72.

44 Chase and Aquilero, 261.

45 Ibid., 270.

46 Hank Rogers, "What Dana Learned from Japan," *Industry Week,* 15 July 1991, 36–40.

47 Adapted from Gaither, 6–8. See also David Woodruff, "A Dozen Motor Factories—Under One Roof," *Business Week,* 20 November 1989, 93–4.

48 Thomas Stewart, "Brace for Japan's Hot New Strategy," *Fortune,* 21 September 1992, 64.

49 Ibid.

50 Susan Moffat, "Japan's New Personalized Production," *Fortune,* 22 October 1990, 132–5.

51 James Treece and Patrick Oster, "General Motors: Open All Night," *Business Week,* 1 June 1992, 82–3.

52 Mark Vonderem and Gregory White, *Operations Management* (St. Paul, MN: West Publishing, 1988), 44–5. For more information on computer-integrated manufacturing, see Michael Baudin, *Manufacturing Systems Analysis* (Englewood Cliffs, NJ: Prentice-Hall, 1990), 2–5.

53 For additional information, see, for example, Alan Luber, "Living in the Real World of Computer Interfaced Manufacturing" *Production & Inventory Management* (September, 1991): 10–1; and Jeremy Main, "Computers of the World, Unite!" *Fortune,* 24 September 1990, 115–22. See also John Teresko, "Japan's New Idea," *Industry Week,* 3 September 1990, 62–6.

54 Bryan Bremner, "Can Caterpillar Inch Its Way Back to Heftier Profits?" *Business Week,* 25 September 1989, 77–8.

55 John Teresko, "Manufacturing in Japan," *Industry Week,* 4 September 1989, 35–79.

56 David Upton, "What Really Makes Factories Flexible?" *Harvard Business Review* (July–August 1995): 75.

57 Ibid., 77.

58 Ibid., 80–1.

59 Ibid., 80.

60 Ibid., 81.

61 Ibid.

62 See, for example, James Gilmore and B. Joseph Pine, II, "The Four Tales of Mass Customization," *Harvard Business Review* 75 (January–February 1997): 91–101.

63 Edward Feitzinger and Jan Lee, "Mass Customization at Hewlett-Packard: The Power of Postponement," *Harvard Business Review* 75 (January–February 1997): 116–21.

Chapter 17 APPENDIX

1 Based on Kenneth Labich, "An Airline That Soars on Service," *Fortune,* 31 December 1990, 94–6.

2 Karl Albrecht, *At America's Service: How Corporations Can Revolutionize the Way They Treat Their Customers* (Homewood, IL: Dow Jones-Irwin, 1988), 20. For an analysis of how to organize and manage service businesses, see also James Brian Quinn, *Intelligent Enterprise* (New York: The Free Press, 1992).

3 Michael E. Porter, *Competitive Strategy: Techniques for Analyzing Industries and Competitors* (New York: The Free Press, 1980), 37.

4 Based on a discussion in Karl Albrecht and Ron Zemke, *Service America!: Doing Business in the New Economy* (Homewood, IL: Dow Jones-Irwin, 1985), 6.

5 Based on Frederick F. Reichheld and W. Earl Sasser, Jr., "Zero Defections: Quality Comes to Service," *Harvard Business Review* (September–October 1990): 105–11.

6 Based on Philip Sadler, *Managerial Leadership in the Post-Industrial Society* (Gower), as summarized in "When the Product Is Service," *The Economist,* 7 January 1989, 60.

7 Based on Albrecht and Zemke, *Service America!,* 31–47. Albrecht, *At America's Service,* 20–42; and Karl Albrecht and Lawrence J. Bradford, *The Service Advantage: How to Identify and Fulfill Customer Needs* (Homewood, IL: Dow Jones-Irwin, 1990), 24–49.

8 Albrecht and Bradford, 30.

9 Albrecht, *At America's Service,* 26.

10 Based on Albrecht, *At America's Service,* 31–2.

11 Ibid., 32.

12 Based on Albrecht and Zemke, *Service America!,* 169–79; and Albrecht, *At America's Service,* 157–223.

13 Albrecht, *At America's Service,* 162–3; Albrecht and Bradford, *The Service Advantage,* 88–91.

14 Albrecht and Zemke, *Service America!,* 174.

15 Albrecht, *At America's Service,* 198.

Chapter 18

1 James Senn, *Information Systems in Management* (Belmont, CA: Wadsworth Publishing Co., 1990), 58.

2 Peter F. Drucker, "The Coming of the New Organization," *Harvard Business Review* (January–February 1988): 45.

3 Carroll Frenzel, *Management of Information Technology* (Boston: Boyd & Fraser, 1992), 10.

4 See, for example, David Kroenke and Richard Hatch, *Management Information Systems* (New York: McGraw-Hill, 1994), 20.

5 Senn, 58.

6 Kenneth Laudon and Jane Price Laudon, *Management Information Systems* (New York: Macmillan Publishing, 1991), 25.

7 The following is based on Kenneth Laudon and Jane Price Laudon, *Management Information Systems* (Upper Saddle River, NJ: Prentice-Hall, 1996), 11, 41–6. See also John Verity, "Coaxing Meaning out of Raw Data," *Business Week,* 3 February 1997, 134, 138.

8   Ibid., 54. For another good example, see Christopher Caggiano, "Thriving on Bureaucracy," *Inc. Technology,* no. 1 (1997): 63–6.

9   John Wyatt, "E*Trade: Is This Investing's Future?" *Fortune,* 3 March 1997, 190–2.

10 Dan Kennedy, "Who's on Line?" *Inc. Technology,* no. 1 (1997): 34–9.

11 Laudon and Laudon, 1996, 54

12 Ibid, 54.

13 Frenzel, 11.

14 Based on Senn, 8; and Laudon and Laudon, *Management Information Systems,* 5.

15 Kenneth Laudon and Jane Laudon, *Essentials of Management Information Systems,* (Upper Saddle River, NJ: Prentice-Hall, 1997), 73.

16 Laudon and Laudon, *Management Information Systems,* 7.

17 Senn, 14–5.

18 See, for example, Kroenke and Hatch, 51.

19 Laudon and Laudon, *Management Information Systems* (Upper Saddle River, NJ: Prentice Hall, 1996), 24.

20 Laudon and Laudon, *Essentials,* 405.

21 See, for example, Laudon and Laudon, *Management Information Systems,* 24.

22 Larry Long and Nancy Long, *Computers* (Upper Saddle River, NJ: Prentice-Hall, 1996), 18.

23 Senn, 576.

24 This discussion is based on Senn, 576–7.

25 Laudon and Laudon, *Essentials,* 385.

26 Senn, A-11.

27 Laudon and Laudon, *Essentials,* 662.

28 Herb Grosch, "The Artificial Intelligence Scam," *Management Technology,* March 1984; reprinted in Laudon and Laudon, *Essentials,* 663.

29 Kroenke and Hatch, 745.

30 Laudon and Laudon, *Essentials,* 526.

31 Michael Hammer and Steven Stanton, *The Reengineering Revolution* (New York: Harper Collins, 1995).

32 John Champy, *Reengineering Management: The Mandate for New Leadership* (New York: Harper Business, 1995), 78–9.

33 Ibid., 79.

34 For the definition of telecommunications, see G. Michael Ashmore, "Telecommunications Opens New Strategic Business," *Journal of Business Strategy* (March–April 1990): 58.

35 Laudon and Laudon, *Management Information Systems,* 321.

36 Frenzel, 159–60.

37 Ibid., 160.

38 The term *modem* is derived from the functions of modulation and demodulation. A modem's function is to modulate or superimpose on the telephone line's analog signal the digital information from the computer input device. See, for example, Frenzel, 161.

39 Sarah Schafer, "E-mail Grows Up," *Inc. Technology,* 1, (1997): 87–8.

40 Stephen Loudermilk, "Desk Top Video Conferencing Getting Prime Time," *PC Week,* 19 October 1992, 81.

41 Paul Saffo, "The Future of Travel," *Fortune,* Autumn 1993, 119.

42 Laudon and Laudon, *Essentials,* 413.

43 Kroenke and Hatch, 359.

44 Robert Ford and Michael Butts, "Is Your Organization Ready for Telecommuting?" *SAM Advanced Management Journal* (Autumn 1991): 19; and Laudon and Laudon, *Essentials,* 413–6.

45 Ibid.

46 See Sandra Atchison, "The Care and Feeding of Loan Eagles," *Business Week,* November 15, 1993, 58.

47 Senn, 415.

48 See, for example, Senn, 418.

49 Ibid., 427.

50 Leah Nathans Spiro and Linda Himelstein, "With the World Wide Web, Who Needs Wall Street?" *Business Week,* 29 April 1996.

51 Amy Cortese, "A Way Out of the Web Maze," *Business Week,* 24 February 1997, 97.

52 Laudon and Laudon, *Essentials,* 531.

53 David Kirkpatrick, "Hot New PC Services," *Fortune,* 2 November 1992, 108. See also Amy Cortese, "Here Comes the Intranet," *Business Week,* 26 February 1996.

54 Mark Lewyn, "The Information Age Isn't Just for the Elite," *Business Week,* 10 January 1994; Computer Systems Policy Project, "Perspectives on the National Information Infrastructure," 12 January 1993, Telecommunications Policy Round Table, 1994; and Laudon and Laudon, *Essentials,* 118.

55 Frenzel, 476–9.

56 Ibid., 476.

57 Frank Rose, "The End of TV as We Know It," *Fortune,* 26 December 1996, 58–68.

58 Kenneth Weiss, "Controlling the Threat to Computer Security," *Management Review,* (June 1990): 55–6; and Frenzel, 476–9.

59 Laudon and Laudon, *Management Information Systems,* 164–5.

60 Ibid.

61 Laudon and Laudon, *Essentials,* 164–5.

62 Ibid., 164.

63 Frenzel, 498.

64 Peter F. Drucker, "The Coming of the New Organization," *Harvard Business Review* (January–February 1988): 46.

65 Frenzel, 498.

66 John A. Byrne, Richard Brandt, and Otis Port, "The Virtual Corporation," *Business Week,* 8 February 1993, 99.

67 Wayne Ryerson and John Pitts, "A Five-Nation Network for Aircraft Manufacturing," *Telecommunications* (October 1989): 45; and Frenzel, 402.

68 Laudon and Laudon, *Management Information Systems,* 95.

69 Ibid., 95; Jeff Moad, "Let Customers Have It Their Way," *Datamation,* 1 April 1995; Jean Bylinsky, "The Digital Factory," *Fortune,* 14 November 1994.

70 Stratford Sherman, "How to Bolster the Bottom Line," *Fortune,* Autumn, 1993, 18.

71 Ibid., 24–5.

72 Ibid., 28.

73 David Kirkpatrick, "Groupware Goes Boom," *Fortune,* December 27, 1993, 100–101.

74 John Wilke, "Computer Links Erode Hierarchical Nature of Workplace Culture," *Wall Street Journal,* 9 December 1993, A-7.

75 Ibid.

Glossary

A

acceptance sampling a method of monitoring product quality that requires the inspection of only a small portion of the produced items.

accommodation giving in to the opponent in an attempt to end a conflict.

acquisition costs the total costs of all units bought to fill an order, usually varying with the size of the order.

action research the process of collecting data from employees about a system in need of change, then feeding that data back to the employees so they can analyze it, identify problems, develop solutions, and take action themselves.

active threats security threats to a company's computer system consisting of attempts to alter, destroy, or divert data or to illegally act as an authorized network terminal point.

activities the time-consuming aspects of a project, represented by arrows in a PERT chart.

affirmative action a legislated requirement that employers make an extra effort to hire and promote those in a protected (women or minority) group.

aggregate output planning a production plan that shows the aggregate (overall) volume of products or services that need to be produced to achieve the sales forecast for each product or service.

application blank a form that requests information such as education, work history, and hobbies from a job candidate as a means of quickly collecting verifiable historical data.

appraisal a manager's evaluation of and feedback on an employee's work performance.

aroused motives motives that express themselves in behavior.

artificial intelligence (AI) a computer's ability to accomplish tasks in a manner that is considered intelligent, and is characterized by learning and making decisions.

attitude a predisposition to respond to objects, people, or events in either a positive or negative way.

attributions the meanings people give to the causes of actions and outcomes.

authoritarian personality a personality type characterized by rigidity, intolerance of ambiguity, the tendency to stereotype others as being good or bad, and conformity to the requirements of authority.

authority the right to take action, to make decisions, and to direct the work of others.

authority boundary the boundary represented by differences in organizational level or status across which communications may be distorted or constrained due to the status difference.

automation the automatic operation of a system, process, or machine.

availability heuristic basing a decision on the aspects of the situation that are most readily available in memory.

avoidance moving away from or refusing to discuss a conflict issue.

B

benchmarking a process through which a company learns how to become the best in one or more areas by analyzing and comparing the practices of other companies that excel in those areas.

behavior modification the technique of changing or modifying behavior through the use of contingent rewards or punishments.

behavioral displacement a reaction to being controlled in which employees concentrate too narrowly on the company's control standards and thereby miss the company's more important objectives.

bills of material computerized records listing the required parts and materials for each manufactured product and where they can be purchased or made.

boundary systems policies, such as codes of conduct, that establish rules and identify the actions and pitfalls that employees must avoid.

boundaryless organization an organization in which the widespread use of teams, networks, and similar structural mechanisms means that the boundaries separating organizational functions and hierarchical levels are reduced and more permeable.

bounded rationality the boundaries on rational decision-making imposed by one's values, abilities, and limited capacity for processing information.

brainstorming a creativity-stimulating technique in which prior judgments and criticisms are specifically forbidden from being expressed and thus inhibiting the free flow of ideas which are encouraged.

breakeven analysis A financial analysis decision-making aid that enables a manager to determine whether a particular volume of sales will result in losses or profits.

business reengineering the radical redesign of business processes to cut waste, to improve cost, quality, and service, and to maximize the benefits of information technology, generally by questioning how and why things are being done as they are.

C

career anchor a dominant concern or value that directs an individual's career choices and which the person will not give up if a choice must be made..

cash cows businesses with high relative market shares in low-growth industries such that minimal investments can and need be made to continue to withdraw relatively high quantities of cash.

causal forecasting estimating a company factor (such as sales) based on other influencing factors (such as advertising expenditures or unemployment levels).

causal methods forecasting techniques that develop projections based on the mathematical relationship between a certain factor and the variables believed to influence or explain that factor.

cellular manufacturing usually a combination of process and product layouts, in which machines and personnel are grouped into cells containing all the tools and operations required to produce a particular product or family of products.

certainty the condition of knowing in advance the outcome of a decision.

chain of command the path a directive and/or answer or request should take through each level of an organization; also, called a scalar chain or the line of authority.

change advocates leaders who champion organizational change, often by cajoling, inspiring, and negotiating it.

charismatic leadership guidance from leaders who possess envisioning, energizing, and enabling qualities that mobilize and sustain activity within an organization.

close supervision a leadership style involving close, hands-on monitoring of subordinates and their work.

coercive power based on the real or imagined expectation that one will be punished for failing to conform to the powerful person's attempts at influence.

cognitive biases standard errors in judgment that influence how people make decisions.

cohesiveness the attraction of the group for its individual members.

collaboration a conflict-management style in which both sides work together to achieve agreement.

collaborative writing systems a computerized support system that lets group members work simultaneously on a single document from a number of interconnected or network computers.

commitment-based control methods a category of control tools that rely on the employees' self-control and commitment to doing things right to make sure things stay in control.

common market when no barriers to trade exist among member countries; a common external trade policy is in force; governing trade with nonmembers, and factors of production, such as labor, capital, and technology, are mobile among members.

communication the exchange of information and the transmission of meaning.

communication channel the vehicle that carries the message in the communication process.

competition an approach to conflict management and negotiating that presumes a win-lose situation.

competitive advantage the basis for superiority over competitors and thus for hoping to claim certain customers.

competitive intelligence systematic techniques used to obtain and analyze public information about competitors.

competitive strategy identifies how to build and strengthen the business's long-term competitive position in the marketplace.

competitors in negotiations or conflict management, people whose primary motive is to win or to outdo others.

compromise settling a conflict through mutual concessions.

computer-aided design (CAD) a computerized process for designing new products, modifying existing ones, or simulating conditions that may affect the designs.

computer-aided manufacturing (CAM) a computerized process for planning and programming actual production processes and equipment.

computer-integrated manufacturing (CIM) the total integration of all production-related business activities through the use of computer systems, usually including automation and automatic guided vehicles.

concurrent engineering designing products in multidisciplinary teams so that all departments involved in the product's success contribute to its design.

confrontation meetings organizational meetings aimed at clarifying and revealing intergroup misperceptions, tensions, and problems so that they can be resolved.

conglomerate diversification diversifying into other products or markets that are not related to a firm's present businesses.

consideration leader behavior indicative of mutual trust, friendship, support, respect, and warmth.

contingent reward a reward that is contingent or dependent on performance of a particular behavior.

continuous production production processes, such as those used by chemical plants or refineries, that run for very long periods without the start-and-stop behavior associated with intermittent production.

control the task of ensuring that activities are getting the desired results.

conversion system any production system that converts inputs (material and human resources) into outputs (products or services); sometimes called the production process or technology.

cooperators people whose primary concern in negotiating or managing conflicts is to maximize outcomes for themselves and others.

coordination the process of achieving unity of action among interdependent activities.

core competencies the collective learning in an organization, especially the knowledge of how to coordinate diverse design and production skills and integrate multiple streams of technologies.

corporate-level strategy a plan that identifies the portfolio of businesses that comprise a corporation and how they will relate to each other.

corporate social audit a rating system used to evaluate a corporation's performance with regard to meeting its social obligations.

corporate stakeholder Any person or group which is important to the survival and success of the corporation.

cost leadership a competitive strategy by which a company aims to be the low-cost leader in its industry.

critical leadership thinking skills the ability to identify what is happening in a leadership situation, account for what is happening, and decide on the actions to be taken.

critical path the sequence of events in a project that in total requires the most time to complete.

cultural artifacts the obvious signs and symbols of corporate culture, such as organizational structure, policies, and dress codes.

customs union trade barriers among members are removed and a common trade policy exists with respect to nonmembers.

customer departmentalization similar to product-divisional organization except that generally self-contained departments are organized to serve the needs of specific groups of customers.

D

decentralized organization an organization in which department heads have authority for most decisions in their divisions, while the company's headquarters office focuses on controlling essential company-wide matters.

decision a choice made between available alternatives.

decision making the process of developing and analyzing alternatives and choosing from among them.

decision support systems information systems that assist management in semi-structured or unstructured decision making by combining data, analytical models, and user-friendly software.

decision tree a technique for facilitating how decisions under conditions of risk are made, whereby an expected value and gain or loss can be applied to each alternative.

decoder/receiver generally, the person or persons to whom the information is sent in the communication process, although this may also refer to any device that converts a message into a usable form.

delegation the act of passing down authority from supervisor to subordinate.

departmentalization the process through which an organization's activities are grouped together and assigned to managers; the organization-wide division of work.

descriptive plans plans that state in words what is to be achieved and how.

designing for manufacturability designing products with ease of manufacturing and quality in mind.

diagnostic control systems control methods, such as budgets, which ensure that standards are being met and that variances are diagnosed and explained.

differentiation strategy a competitive strategy aimed at distinguishing a company from its competitors by focusing on the attributes of its products or services that consumers perceive as important.

discipline without punishment a multistage displinary technique that uses oral reminders of the violated rule; then written reminders; followed by mandatory one-day leaves; and finally, if the behavior is not corrected, dismissal.

discrimination a behavioral bias toward or against a person based on the group to which the person belongs.

dismissal the involuntary termination of an employee's employment with a firm.

distributed processing computerized networks that use small local computers to collect, store, and process information which is sent periodically to headquarters for analysis and review.

diverse describes a workforce comprised of two or more groups, each of which can be identified by demographic or other characteristics.

diversification a corporate strategy whereby managers try to better utilize their organizational resources by developing new products and new markets.

divestment selling or liquidating the individual businesses of a larger company.

divisionalization (product departmentalization) a form of organization in which the firm's major departments are organized so that each can manage all or most of the activities needed to develop, manufacture, and sell a particular product or product line.

dogs businesses in low-growth, unattractive industries that also have low relative market shares. and thus should usually be divested.

downsizing dramatically reducing the size of a company's workforce.

E

economic integration attempts by two or more nations to obtain the advantages of free trade by minimizing trade restrictions.

economic order quantity (EOQ) an inventory management system based on a simple formula which is used to determine the most economic quantity to order so that the total of inventory and set-up costs is minimized.

electronic bulletin board an example of e-mail–based communications that allows one or more group members to file messages on various topics to be picked up by other group members via television links.

employee benefits any supplements to wages or pay that employees get based on their working for the organization.

employee compensation all forms of pay or rewards that go to employees and arise from their employment.

employee involvement program any formal program that lets employees participate in formulating important work decisions or in supervising all or part of their own work activities.

employee oriented a leadership style that focuses on the needs of employees and emphasizes building good interpersonal relationships.

empowering employees authorizing and enabling employees to do their jobs with greater autonomy.

empowerment the act of giving employees the authority, tools, and information they need to do their jobs with greater autonomy and confidence.

encoder/sender the element or person in the communication process that puts a message in a form suitable for transmission.

environmental monitoring a strategic control method of tracking previously identified events, trends, and premises to see if any of the plan's basic assumptions have changed or require modification.

environmental scanning a strategic control method aimed at identifying previously unidentified or undetected critical events that could influence the company's strategy.

equalizers people whose primary concern in negotiating or managing conflicts is to equalize outcomes for everyone involved in a situation.

equity theory J. S. Adams's theory that people have a need for, and therefore value and seek, fairness in employer-employee relationships.

ethics the study of standards of conduct and moral judgment; also, the standards of right conduct.

ethnocentric a management philosophy that leads to the creating of home market–oriented firms.

events the specific accomplishments in a project, represented by circles in a PERT chart.

exchange rate the rate at which one currency can be exchanged for another between two countries.

executives managers at the top management level of an organization.

executive recruiters agencies retained by employers to seek out top management talent.

executive support systems information systems designed to help top level executives acquire, manipulate, and use the information they need to maintain the company's overall effectiveness.

expectancy in motivation, the probability that a person's efforts will lead to performance.

expected value a calculated value that equals (1) the probability of the outcome multiplied by (2) the benefit or cost of that outcome.

expediting the process of monitoring and adjusting the movement of products and materials from operation to operation.

expert power power that is derived from a person's perceived expertise in some area and the dependence of others on the expert's advice and counsel.

expert system an information system in which computer programs store facts and rules (often called a knowledge base) and which can replicate the abilities and decisions of true human experts.

exporting selling abroad, either directly to target customers, or indirectly by retaining foreign sales agents and distributors.

extinction the behavioral modification technique of withholding positive reinforcement so that over time the undesired behavior disappears.

facility layout refers to the configuration of all the machines, employee work stations, storage areas, internal walls, and so forth that constitute the facility used to create a firm's product or service.

feedback the receiver's response to the message that was actually received in the communication process.

financial incentive any financial reward that is contingent on a worker's performance, such as commissions or piecework.

financial ratios an arithmetic comparison of one financial measure to another, generally used to monitor and control financial performance.

first-line managers managers at the bottom management level of an organization, also called supervisors, who have non-supervisors as subordinates.

fixed-position layout a production system arrangement in which the product being built or produced stays at one location and the machines and tools required to build the product are brought to that location as needed, as for the building of ships or other bulky products.

fixed salary compensation based on an agreed rate for a set period of time.

flexible manufacturing system (FMS) the organization of groups of production machines which are connected by automated materials-handling and transfer machines, and integrated into a computer system for the purpose of combining the benefits of made-to-order flexibility and mass-production efficiency.

focus strategy when a business selects a narrow market segment and builds its strategy on serving those in its target market better or more cheaply than its generalist competitors.

forcing a direct, contentious method of resolving conflict that forces the adversary's hand.

forecast to estimate or calculate in advance or to predict.

foreign direct investment operations in one country that are controlled by entities in a foreign country.

formal communication messages that are recognized as official by the organization, i.e., orders from superiors to subordinates, sales reports, and status reports.

formal organizational network a formally assigned, permanent group of managers or other employees drawn from across a company's functions, geographic areas, and hierarchical levels to take the initiative in finding and solving problems.

formal structure change program an intervention technique in which employees collect information on existing formal organizational structures and analyze it for the purpose of redesigning and implementing new organizational structures.

framing in decision making, the idea that the way a problem is presented can influence decisions.

free trade the unrestricted exchange of goods among participating countries.

free trade area a type of economic integration in which all barriers to trade among members are removed.

functional authority narrowly limited power to issue orders down the chain of command in a specific functional area such as personnel testing.

functional departmentalization a form of organization that groups a company's activities around essential functions such as manufacturing, sales, or finance.

functional fixedness in decision making, the inability to see other possibilities for an ob-

ject or idea beyond an object's or idea's stated or usual functions.

functional plan a tactical short-term plan showing how each department of a business will contribute to top management's plans.

functional strategy the overall course or courses of action and basic policies that each department is to follow in helping the business accomplish its strategic goals.

G

gainsharing plan an incentive plan that engages many or all employees in a common effort to achieve a company's productivity objectives and in which they share in the gains.

gamesmanship management actions that try to improve the manager's apparent performance in terms of the control system without producing any economic benefits for the company.

Gantt chart a production scheduling chart (named after management pioneer Henry Gantt) that plots time on a horizontal scale and generally shows, for each order, the start and stop times of each operation.

gender-role stereotypes usually, the association of women with certain behaviors and possibly (often lower-level) jobs.

general leader a leader who takes a middle-ground approach between close supervision and laissez-faire leadership.

geocentric see *regiocentric*

geographic expansion a strategic growth alternative of aggressively expanding into new domestic and/or overseas markets.

global corporation sells essentially a standardized product throughout the world, components of which may be made in or designed in different countries.

globalization the extension of a firm's sales or manufacturing to new markets abroad.

global mercantilism in planning, a scenario in which geopolitical change and international economic tensions lead to more government intervention in managing international trade.

goal commitment the strength of one's determination to reach a goal.

goals specific results to be achieved; the end results of a plan.

goal setting studies organizational behavior research that provides useful insights into how to set effective goals.

graphic plans plans that show graphically or in charts what is to be achieved and how.

grievance a complaint that an employee lodges against an employer, usually one regarding wages, hours, or some condition of employment, such as unfair supervisory behavior.

group two or more persons interacting in such a manner that each person influences and is influenced by the other, and who may or may not have unanimity of purpose.

group cohesiveness the degree of interpersonal attractiveness within a group, dependent on factors like proximity, attraction amongst the individual group members, group size, intergroup competition, and agreement over goals.

group norms the informal rules that groups adopt to regulate and regularize group members' behavior.

group scheduling system a computerized support system that allows each group member to put his or her daily schedule into a shared database so that each can identify the most suitable times to schedule meetings or to attend currently scheduled meetings.

groupthink the mode of thinking in a cohesive group in which the desire to achieve group consensus overrides potentially valuable individual points of view of its members.

H

heuristics rules of thumb and approximations applied as shortcuts to decision making.

hierarchy of plans includes the enterprise-wide plan, and the derivative plans of subsidiary units required to help achieve the enterprise-wide plan.

horizontal corporation a structure that is organized around customer-oriented processes performed by multidisciplinary cross-functional teams rather than formal functional departments.

horizontal integration acquiring ownership or control of competitors who are competing in the same or similar markets with the same or similar products.

hot group an energetic, high-achieving work group, usually small, whose members are excited by or obsessed with completing a challenging task.

hourly wage compensation based on a set hourly pay rate for work performed.

human process interventions organizational change techniques aimed at enabling employees to develop a better understanding of their own and others' behaviors for the purpose of improving that behavior in such a way that the organization benefits.

human resource management the management function devoted to acquiring, training, appraising, and compensating employees.

humanistic theories personality theories that assume people are motivated by the desire to fulfill the potential they see themselves as having.

I

identity boundary the tendency to identify with those groups with which we have shared experiences and with which we believe we share fundamental values.

independent integrator an individual or group that coordinates the activities of several interdependent departments, but is independent of them.

individualists in negotiations or conflict management, people whose primary motive is to gain as much as possible for themselves.

informal communication communication not officially sanctioned by the organization, i.e., rumors heard through "the grapevine."

informal organization informal contacts, communications, and habitual ways of doing things that employees develop.

informal organizational network cooperating individuals who are interconnected only informally to share information and help solve each other's problems.

information data presented in a form that is meaningful to the recipient.

information superhighway a high-speed digital communications network that may combine telephone lines, cable lines, microwave transmissions, and fiber optics to let anyone anywhere use interactive television, telephones, PCs, or other devices to interact with databases around the world.

information system a set of people, data, and procedures that work together to retrieve, process, store, and disseminate information to support decision making and control.

information technology any processes, practices, or systems that facilitate the processing and transportation of data information.

initiating structure the leadership factor of being able to organize the work to be done and to define relationships or roles, the channels of communication, and the ways of getting jobs done.

Input Devices devices that receive instructions and data, convert them into electrical impulses, and then transfer the impulses to the computer's storage unit.

inputs all the resources required for the manufacture of a product or service.

instrumental leadership the managerial role of building and clarifying organizational changes so that employees can accomplish their new tasks.

instrumentality the perceived correlation between successful performance and obtaining the reward.

integrated strategic management an organizational development program to create or change a company's strategy by analyzing the current strategy, choosing a desired strategy, designing a strategic change plan, and implementing the new plan.

interactive control systems control methods that involve direct, face-to-face interaction with employees so as to monitor rapidly changing information and respond proactively to changing conditions.

intergroup behavior the interactive personal dynamics between groups or departments within an organization.

intergroup organizational conflict a disagreement between organizational units such as production and sales departments or between line and staff units.

intermittent production a system in which production is performed on a start-and-stop basis, such as for the manufacture of made-to-order products.

international business any firm that engages in international trade or investment; also refers to those business activities that involve the movement of resources, goods, services, and skills across national boundaries.

international management the performance of the management process across national boundaries.

international trade the export or import of goods or services to consumers in another country.

interpersonal behavior how individuals in an organization relate to each other.

interpersonal communication communication that occurs between two individuals.

interpersonal conflict a conflict occurring between individuals or between individuals and groups.

inventory-holding costs all of the costs associated with carrying parts or materials in inventory.

inventory management the process of ensuring that the firm has adequate inventories of all parts and supplies needed, within the constraint of minimizing total inventory costs.

ISO 9000 the quality standards of the European Community (EC).

J

jidoka a Japanese term that means "stop everything when something goes wrong" so that discovered defects don't continue down the line.

job analysis the procedure used to determine the duties of particular jobs and the kinds of people (in terms of skills and experience) who should be hired for them.

job analysis questionnaire a form used by managers to determine the duties and functions of a job through a series of questions that employees answer.

job centered a leadership style that focuses on production and on a job's technical aspects.

job description identifies a particular job, provides a brief job summary, and then lists specific responsibilities and duties of the job.

job design the number and nature of specific tasks or activities in a job.

job enlargement an increase in the number of similar tasks assigned to a job.

job enrichment the inclusion of opportunities for achievement and other motivators in a job by making the job itself more challenging.

job rotation the systematic movement of a worker from job to job to improve job satisfaction and reduce boredom.

job satisfaction the measure of an employee's attitude about his or her job.

job specification the human qualifications in terms of traits, skills, and experiences required to accomplish the job.

joint venture the participation of two or more companies in an enterprise such that each party contributes assets, owns the entity to some degree, and shares risk.

jury of executive opinion a qualitative forecasting technique in which a panel of executives are given pertinent data and asked to make independent sales forecasts, which are then reconciled in an executive meeting or by the company president.

just-in-time (JIT) the production control methods used to attain minimum inventory levels by ensuring delivery of materials and assemblies just when they are to be used; also refers to a philosophy of manufacturing that aims to optimize production processes by continuously reducing waste.

K

Kanban from the Japanese word for "card," a production control system that operates on the theory that whenever an item is used, it pulls the need for another item (as evidenced by a card containing the part number), which in turn pulls the need for another, and so on.

L

laissez-faire leader a leader who takes a completely hands-off approach toward supervising subordinates.

law of individual differences a psychological term representing the fact that people differ in their personalities, abilities, values, and needs.

leader-member exchange (LMX) theory the theory that leaders may use different leadership styles with different members of the same work group, based in part on perceived similarities and differences with the leader.

leadership one person influencing another to willingly work toward a predetermined objective.

leading getting others to get the job done, maintaining morale, and motivating subordinates.

lean manufacturing a management philosophy that assumes that any manufacturing process that does not add value to the product for the customer is wasteful; also called *value-added manufacturing*.

learning a relatively permanent change in a person that occurs as a result of experience.

legitimate power authority that is based on a general acceptance of someone's right to influence others who in turn feel an

obligation to accept this influence; the actual source of legitimate power might be tradition or the higher position of the one in power.

leverage to gain a competitive edge by concentrating a company's resources on key strategic goals or competencies

lifelong learning the organizational program of providing continuing education and training to employees throughout their careers.

line adapters devices that modify the signal from the terminal and computer to match the characteristics of the telecommunications line; a modem is one example.

linear programming a mathematical method used to solve resource allocation problems.

line manager a manager authorized to issue orders to subordinates down the chain of command.

line-staff conflict disagreements between a line manager and the staff manager who is giving him or her advice.

load schedule a plan that compares (1) the labor and machine hours needed to carry out the master production schedule with (2) the labor and machine hours actually available each week.

loading and sequencing assigning individual jobs to machines and work centers.

local area network (LAN) a communications network that spans a limited distance, such as a building or several adjacent buildings, using the company's own telecommunications links.

locus of control the degree of control that individuals believe they have over their lives.

M

Machiavellian personality a personality type oriented toward manipulation and control, with a low sensitivity to the needs of others, the name of which refers to the 16th-century political advisor Nicolo Machiavelli.

Malcolm Baldrige Award a prize created in 1987 by the U.S. Department of Commerce to recognize outstanding achievement in quality control management.

management the managers of an organization; or, the study of what managers do.

management assessment center a development and/or selection device wherein management candidates spend two or three

days performing realistic management tasks under the observation of appraisers.

management by objectives (MOB) a technique in which supervisor and subordinate jointly set goals for the latter and periodically assess progress toward those goals.

management information systems information systems that provide decision support for managers by producing standardized, summarized reports on a regular basis.

management process refers to the manager's four basic functions of planning, organizing, leading, and controlling.

manager a person who plans, organizes, leads, and controls the work of others so that the organization achieves its goals.

managerial competence the motivation and skills required to gain a management position, including intellectual, emotional, and interpersonal skills.

managing diversity planning and implementing organizational systems and practices to manage people in a way that maximizes the potential advantages of diversity while minimizing its potential disadvantages.

market penetration a growth strategy to boost sales of present products by more aggressively permeating the organization's current markets.

marketing channel the means through which a manufacturer distributes its products to its ultimate customers.

marketing-channel departmentalization arranging departments of an organization to focus on particular marketing channels such as drugstores or grocery stores.

marketing research the procedures used to develop and analyze current customer-related information to help managers make decisions.

mass customization designing, producing, and delivering customized products for or near the cost and convenience of mass-produced items.

mass production a special type of intermittent production process usually involving an assembly line in which standardized methods and specialized machines produce long runs of standardized items.

master production scheduling (MPS) planning the amounts of all products to be produced for the coming period, and the dates for which they are to be produced.

material requirements planning (MRP) a computer-based system that reviews the master production schedule and specifies the required raw materials, parts, subassemblies, and assemblies needed each week to meet the master production schedule.

matrix organization (matric management) the superimposing of one or more forms of departmentalization on top of an existing one.

mechanistic organization an organizational structure characterized by close adherence to the established chain of command, highly specialized jobs, and vertical communications.

mentoring a relationship between two people in which the more experienced mentor provides support, guidance, and counseling to enhance the protege's success at work in other areas of life.

mission statement broadly outlines the enterprise's purpose and serves to communicate "who we are, what we do, and where we're headed."

mixed economy an economy of which some sectors are left to private ownership and free market mechanisms, while others are largely owned and managed by the government.

modem the most familiar means of converting telecommunications signals from one type of signal to a more compatible one for the device.

moral minimum the standard that corporations should be free to strive for profits so long as they commit no harm.

morality a society's accepted norms of behavior.

motivation the intensity of a person's desire to engage in some activity.

motivational dispositions or needs motives that lie dormant until the proper conditions arise to bring them forth or make them active.

motive something that incites a person to action or that sustains and gives direction to action.

moving a step in psychologist Kurt Lewin's model of change aimed at using techniques and actually altering the behaviors, values, and attitudes of the individuals in an organization.

multinational corporation (MNC) an internationally integrated company over which equity-based control is exercised by a parent corporation that is owned and managed essentially by the nationals of the country in which it is domiciled.

mutual adjustment achieving coordination through personal interactions and communicated responses to a situation.

network planning and control methods ways of planning and controlling projects by graphically representing the projects' steps and the timing and links between these steps.

nonprogrammed decision a decision that is unique and novel.

nonverbal communication the nonspoken aspects of communication, such as a person's manner of speaking, facial expressions, or body posture, that express meaning to others.

normative control a characteristic of control processes in more responsive organizations in which members are guided in their behavior by a strong set of shared values, beliefs, and traditions rather than by rules, procedures, and close supervision.

normative judgment a comparative evaluation stating or implying that something is good or bad, right or wrong, better or worse.

norms the informal rules that groups adopt to regulate and regularize the behavior of group members.

objectives specific results toward which effort is directed.

operant behavior behavior that appears to operate on or have an influence on the subject's environment.

operational planning short-term plans that show the detailed daily steps of business operations.

operations management the process of managing the resources that are needed to produce an organization's goods and services.

ordering or setup costs the costs, usually fixed, of placing an order or setting up machines for a production run.

organic organization an organizational structure characterized by flexible lines of authority, less specialized jobs, and decentralized decisions.

organization a group of people with formally assigned roles who work together to achieve the stated goals of the group.

organization chart illustrates the organization-wide division of work by charting who is accountable to whom and who is in charge of what department.

organizational behavior (OB) the study and application of how people behave, individually and as a group, within organizations.

organizational communication communication that occurs among several individuals or groups.

organizational culture the characteristic set of values and ways of behaving that employees in an organization share.

organizational development (OD) an approach to organizational change in which the employees themselves formulate the change that's required and implement it, usually with the aid of a trained consultant.

organizational development interventions in-depth human process interventions such as sensitivity training aimed at changing employees' attitudes, values, and behavior.

organizing to arrange the activities of the enterprise in such a way that they systematically contribute to the enterprise's goals.

orientation the process of providing new employees with basic information about the employer, such as company policies, working hours, or parking arrangements.

outputs all the direct outcomes (actual products and services) or indirect outcomes (taxes, wages, salaries) of a production system.

P

passive threats security threats to a computer system that come from unauthorized individuals or organizations who monitor the firm's data transmissions in order to obtain unauthorized information.

patterns of behavior in organizational behavior, the ceremonial events, written and spoken comments, and actual behaviors of an organization's members which contribute to creating the organizational culture.

pay for performance any compensation method based on merit or performance rather than across-the-board non-output-based pay.

perception the unique way each person defines stimuli, depending on the influence of past experiences and what the person's present needs and personality are.

personality the characteristic and distinctive traits of an individual, and the way these traits interact to help or hinder the adjustment of the person to other people and situations.

personality trait any readily identifiable and measurable characteristic of an individual.

planning the process of setting goals and courses of action, developing rules and procedures, and forecasting future outcomes.

planning premises assumptions about the future on which plans are based.

plans methods formulated beforehand for doing or making something and consisting of a goal and a course of action.

policies standing plans that set broad guidelines for the enterprise.

political boundary the special interests or agendas within an organization that may oppose each other.

politics the acquisition and use of power.

polycentric a management philosophy oriented toward pursuing a limited number of individual foreign markets.

positive reinforcement the act of rewarding desired behavior; or the actual rewards, such as praise or bonuses, given each time the desired behavior occurs.

post-action control any control tool in which the project or operation being controlled is completed first, and then results are measured and compared to the standard.

power the ability of one person to influence another to do something the latter would not otherwise do.

prejudice a bias that results from prejudging someone on the basis of the latter's particular trait or traits.

primary data information specifically collected to address a current problem.

principle of exception sometimes called management by exception, this rule holds that employees should be left to pursue the standards set by management and only significant deviations from the standard should be brought to a manager's attention.

problem-solving teams groups formed to identify and solve work-related problems.

procedures plans that specify how to proceed in specific situations that routinely arise.

process layout a production system design in which similar machines or functions are grouped together.

product development the strategy of improving products for current markets to maintain or boost growth.

product layout a production system design in which every item to be produced follows the same sequence of operations from beginning to end, such as an assembly line.

production control the process of ensuring that the specified production plans and schedules are being adhered to.

production planning the process of deciding what products to produce and where, when, and how to produce them.

programmed decision a decision that is repetitive and routine, and can therefore be made using a definite, systematic procedure.

programs plans that lay out all the steps in proper sequence to a single-use, often one-time business project.

promotion rewarding an employee's efforts by moving that person to a job with increased authority and responsibility.

psychoanalytic theory the personality theory, developed by Sigmund Freud, which emphasizes the role of past experiences, sexual frustrations, and the unconscious in the determination of personality.

psychological set the tendency to rely on a rigid strategy or approach when solving a problem.

punishment a behavioral modification option that applies penalties for the undesired behavior to reduce the possibility that it will recur.

Q

qualitative forecasting predictive techniques that emphasize logical, unbiased human judgment and may include both technological and judgmental methods.

quality the extent to which a product or service is able to meet customer needs and expectations.

quality circle a team of 6 to 12 employees that meets about once a week on company time to solve problems affecting its work area.

quantitative forecasting a type of forecasting in which statistical methods are used to examine data and find underlying patterns and relationships; includes time series methods and causal models.

question marks in strategic planning, businesses in high-growth industries, but with low relative market shares.

R

recruiting attracting a pool of viable job applicants.

referent power power that stems from one person's identification with or attraction toward another.

refreezing a step in psychologist Kurt Lewin's model of change aimed at preventing a return to old ways of doing things by instituting new systems and procedures that reinforce the new organizational changes.

regiocentric a management philosophy oriented toward larger areas, including the global marketplace.

related diversification a strategy of expanding into other industries or markets related to a company's current business lines.

retrenchment the reduction of activities or operations to reduce investment.

reward power power based on the ability to raise positive rewards or reduce negative rewards.

risk the chance that a particular outcome will or will not occur.

rites and ceremonies traditional culture-building events or activities that symbolize the firm's values and help convert employees to these values.

role ambiguity a lack of clarity about what or how a person is to do a job.

role conflict a situation in which an employee has conflicting orders, such that compliance with one would make it difficult or impossible to comply with the other.

rule a highly specific guide to action.

S

sales force estimation a forecasting technique that gathers and combines the opinions of the sales force on what they predict sales will be in the forthcoming period.

satisfice to stop the decision-making process when satisfactory alternatives are found, rather than reviewing solutions until an optimal alternative is discovered.

scenarios hypothetical sequences of events constructed for the purpose of focusing attention on causal processes and decision points.

secondary data information for analyzing a situation that has already been collected or published.

self-concept the perceptions people have of themselves and their relationships to people and other aspects of life.

self-directed work team a highly trained group of employees, from 6 to 18 people on average, who are fully responsible for turning out a well-defined segment of finished work.

self-efficacy being able to influence important aspects of one's world; the belief that one can accomplish what one sets out to do.

self-managing teams see *self-directed work teams.*

semantics the meaning of words.

semi-autonomous teams work groups that have considerable input into managing the activities in their own work area but are still headed by a supervisor.

sensitivity training also called laboratory or t-group training, the basic aim of this organizational development technique is to increase participants' insight into their own behavior and that of others by encouraging an open expression of feelings in a trainer-guided group.

shop floor control (SFC) the process of overseeing the weekly and daily production schedules to most effectively implement the master production schedules on a week-by-week basis.

signs and symbols practices and actions that create and sustain a company's culture.

similarity heuristic the tendency to base a decision on the aspects of a person or situation that are most familiar or similar to one's own past experience.

simple smoothing average forecast for the next period, based on the average sales of the past specified number of periods.

smoothing methods methods used to average the date from a time series so as to remove seasonal and random variations.

smoothing over in conflict management, the act of diminishing or avoiding a conflict issue.

social responsibility the extent to which companies should or do channel resources toward improving the quality of life of one or more segments of society other than the firm's own stockholders.

socializing the process of transforming new employees into committed organizational members by steeping them in the organization's values and traditions.

span of control the number of subordinates reporting directly to a supervisor.

staff manager a manager without the authority to give orders down the chain of command (except in his or her own department); generally can only assist and advise line managers in specialized areas such as human resource management.

staffing refers to actually filling a firm's open positions; also, the HR/personnel process that includes six steps: job analysis, personnel planning; recruiting, interviewing, testing and selection, and training and development.

standing plans plans established to be used repeatedly, as the need arises.

stars in strategic planning, businesses in high-growth industries that also enjoy a high relative market share.

statistical decision theory techniques techniques used to solve problems for which information is incomplete or uncertain.

steering controls a control system that predicts results and takes corrective action before the operation or project is completed.

stereotyping the process of attributing specific behavioral traits to individuals on the basis of their apparent membership in a group.

stockout costs the costs associated with running out of raw materials, parts, or finished-goods inventory.

stories the repeated tales and anecdotes that contribute to a company's culture by illustrating and reinforcing important company values.

strategic alliances any agreements between potential or actual competitors to achieve common objectives.

strategic change a change in a firm's strategy, mission, and/or vision.

strategic control the process of assessing the firm's progress toward its strategic objectives and taking corrective action as needed to ensure optimal implementation.

strategic human resource management the linking of the human resource function with the company's strategies to accomplish that strategy.

strategic interventions organization development applications aimed at effecting a suitable fit among a firm's strategy, structure, culture, and external environment.

strategic management the process of identifying and pursuing the organization's strategic plan by aligning internal capabilities with the external demands of its environment, and then ensuring the plan is being properly executed.

strategic plan outlines the course of action a firm plans to pursue in becoming the sort of enterprise it wants to be, given the firm's external opportunities and threats and its internal strengths and weaknesses.

strategic planning the process of identifying the current business of a firm and the business it wants for the future, and the course of action or strategy it will pursue.

strategy a course of action which explains how an enterprise will move from the business it is in now to the business it wants to be in.

suggestion teams short-term teams formed to work on given issues such as increasing productivity.

survey research the process of collecting data from attitude surveys filled out by employees of an organization, then feeding the data back to work groups to provide a basis for problem analysis and action planning.

sustainable world a scenario in which economic frictions are resolved and economic trade flows freely, but concern about the environment leads to tightened emissions regulation and higher quality standards for energy products.

SWOT a strategic planning tool for analyzing a company's strengths, weaknesses, opportunities, and threats.

T

tactical plans plans that show how top management's plans are to be carried out at the departmental, short-term level.

task boundary the perceived limited actions of a specific organizational position.

team a group of people committed to a common purpose, set of performance goals, and approach for which they hold themselves mutually accountable.

team building the process of improving the effectiveness of a team through action research or other techniques.

technology transfer the transfer, often to another country, of systematic knowledge for the manufacturing of a product, for the application of a process, or for the rendering of a service; does not extend to the mere sales or lease of goods.

telecommunication the electronic transmission of data, text, graphics, voice (audio), or image (video) over literally any distance.

telecommunications lines (links) the medium through which signals are transmitted in a telecommunications system; for example, copper wires, optical fibers, or microwave transmissions.

telecommunications software the computer program that controls input and output activities and other communications network functions.

telecommunications system a set of compatible telecommunications devices that link separate information processing devices for the purpose of exchanging data.

telecommuting the substitution of telecommunications and computers for the commute to a central office.

terminals input-output devices that send or receive data.

time series a set of observations taken at specific times, usually at equal intervals, to identify fundamental patterns.

tokenism symbolically appointing a small number of minority-group members to high-profile positions instead of more aggressively achieving full representation for that group.

total quality management (TQM) an organization-wide management system that focuses all functions of the business on maximizing customer satisfaction at continually lower real costs.

total quality management (TQM) program specific organization-wide programs that integrate all the functions and related processes of a business such that they are all aimed at maximizing customer satisfaction through ongoing improvements.

trade controls governmental influences that are usually aimed at reducing the competitiveness of imported products or services.

traditional control methods control procedures that are based on maintaining control generally through external means, by setting standards, comparing the actual results to the standard, and then taking corrective action, and including diagnostic, boundary, and interactive control systems.

training program the process of providing new employees with information they need to do their jobs satisfactorily.

trait theories theories that an individual's personality reflects or is comprised of relatively enduring traits.

trait theory in leadership, the theory that leaders have basic identifiable traits or characteristics that contribute to their success as leaders.

transaction processing systems information systems that provide detailed information about short-term, daily activities.

transactional behaviors leadership actions that focus on accomplishing the tasks at hand and on maintaining good working relationships by exchanging promises of rewards for performance.

transformational leadership the leadership process that involves influencing major changes in the attitudes and assumptions of organization members and building commitment for the organization's mission, objectives, and strategies.

transnational team work teams composed of multinational members whose activities span many countries.

21st-century managing a management approach to the rapidly changing business world that emphasizes responsiveness and effective leadership.

U

uncertainty the absence of information about a particular area of concern.

unemployment insurance legally mandated insurance that is paid by state agencies to workers who are terminated through no fault of their own (the funds come from a tax on the employer's payroll).

unfreezing a step in psychologist Kurt Lewin's model of change that involves reducing the forces for the status quo, usually by presenting a provocative problem or event to get people to recognize the need for change and to search for new solutions.

uniform plant loading establishing monthly production plans and strictly adhering to them so that wide swings in production levels are minimized.

V

valence in motivation, the perceived value a person ascribes to the reward for certain efforts.

value-added manufacturing a management approach that emphasizes the idea that any manufacturing process that does not add value to the product for the customer is wasteful; also called *lean manufacturing*.

value-based hiring the practice of screening and hiring people whose values are consistent with those of the company, rather than looking just at an applicant's job-related skills.

values basic beliefs about what is important and unimportant, and what one should and should not do.

values and beliefs the guiding standards of an organization such as "the customer is always right" or "don't be bureaucratic" that affirm what should be practiced, as distinct from what is practiced.

variable pay plans compensation plans that may reduce or increase some portion of the individual employee's pay, depending on whether or not the company meets its financial goals.

variances the difference between budgeted and actual amounts.

venture team a small group of people who operate as a semi-autonomous unit to create and develop a new idea.

vertical integration a growth strategy in which a company owns or controls its own suppliers and/or distribution channels.

vision a general statement of an organization's intended direction that evokes emotional feelings in its members.

waiting line/queuing techniques mathematical techniques used to solve waiting line problems such that the optimal balance of employees available to waiting customers is attained.

whistle-blowing the activities of employees who try to report organizational wrongdoing.

wide area networks (WAN) networks that serve microcomputers over large geographic areas, spanning distances from a few miles to around the globe, and which may use common carrier networks or private telecommunications systems.

work flow automation system an e-mail type system that automates the flow of paperwork from person to person.

worker's compensation a legally mandated benefit that pays income and medical benefits to work-related accident victims or their dependents, regardless of fault.

world-class companies organizations that can compete successfully based on quality and productivity in an intensely competitive global environment.

world-class manufacturers organizations that use modern production techniques and management systems to boost manufacturing productivity, quality, and flexibility in an environment of international competition.

yes-no control a control system in which work may not proceed to the next step until it passes an intermediate checkpoint step.

Z

zero-based budgeting a control technique that requires all of a company's budgeted programs to be reviewed every year based on the ratio of their benefits and costs.

Photo Credits

Name Index

Mobil Oil Co., 186
Montgomery Ward, 186
Morgan Stanley, 377
Morris, June, 5
Morris Air, 4, 5, 377
Morrisey, George, 155–56
Motorola, 56, 112, 548, 582, 587
MovieFone, 194–95
Murdock, Rupert, 178

N

Nacchio, Joe, 321
Nadler, 494, 504, 505
National Bicycle Industrial Co., 594
NationsBank, 377
NBC, 193
NCNB, 377
Netscape Communications, 180, 183,
    185, 201, 539
    Netscape Navigator, 3, 631
New Jersey Bell Telephone Co., 39
Newmark, Evan, 6
Newton, 112
New United Motor Manufacturing
    (NUMMI), 52, 53
Nissan, 383
Nordstrom, 473, 544, 547
Norton Co., 86, 88
Notes Groupware, 636
Novell, 180

O

O'Donnell, 148
Ohmae, Kenichi, 52
Olivetti, 266
    Active Badge System, 545
1–800-FLOWERS, 613, 614
Orfalea, Paul, 1, 2
Orsburn, Jack, 472
Otis Elevator, 339
Outward Bound, 230–31
Owen, Donald, 464
Oxford Health Plans, 463, 464

P

Pan Am, 2, 187
Patton, William, 181
Pawley, Dennis (Chrysler), 148–49
Pawley, Denny (Mazda), 68
A Pea in the Pod, 193
Penney, James Cash, 555
JCPenney, 83, 193, 223, 376, 552, 555,
    627
People's Express, 4
Pepperidge Farm Cookies, 186

Pepsi, 185
PepsiCo Corp.
    Frito-Lay, 185
    Pepsi, 185
    Pepsi Light, 614–15
    Pizza Hut, 185
Pepsi Light, 614–15
Perak, Denny, 464
Personal Pairs, 563, 564, 597, 616, 635
Peters, Tom, 20, 23–25, 232, 256, 375,
    378, 452–54, 547, 554
Philips Electronics, 3, 198, 266,
    381–82, 497–99
Piech, Ferdinand, 75, 76
Piedmont, 4
Pizza Hut, 185
PointCast, 631
Polaroid Corp., 178, 535
Pollo Tropical, 43, 44
Pontiac LeMans, 4
Porras, Jerry, 548–49
Porter, Michael, 191, 193–95, 197, 202
Pospischil, Bob, 620
Povlacs, Larry, 567
PowerBook, 188
Prahalad, C. K., 198–200
Pratt & Whitney, 240, 261, 425
Price Club, 377
Price Waterhouse, 265, 451, 452, 636
Procter, William, 369
Procter & Gamble (P&G), 369–70,
    376, 484
    Folger's coffee, 370
Prodigy, 630, 632
Published Image, 477

Q

Quaker Oats, 377
Quicken, 82
Quinn, James Brian, 7, 452

R

Rain Forest Crunch, Ben & Jerry's,
    92
Rambert, Margot, 527, 528
Rambert Electronics, 527
Reagan, Ronald, 582
Relsed Americas Corp., 57
Remington Products, 417
Revlon, 221–22
R. J. Reynolds, 183
Reynolds Metals, 66
Rheem, 159
Richardson, Rick, 451
Ricoh, 55
Roffman, Harvey, 50
Rogers, Carl, 394–96, 398, 439–40

Rogers, Tom, 22, 623
Rohm and Haas, 482–83
Rolex, 565
Rosenbluth, Hal, 225, 250, 258, 375
Rosenbluth International, 375
Rosenbluth Travel, 225, 236, 241, 250,
    258
Rotter, Julian, 543
Royal Dutch Shell
    Shell Oil Co., 160–61, 186, 264–65,
        541–42
    Shell Switzerland, 66
    Shell U.S.A., 66
Runyon, Marvin, 365, 366
Rutkowski, Richard, 107
Ryder Systems, 270

S

SABER, 194
Safari, 188
Samsung, 112
Sato, Funio, 593
Saturn Corp., 20–22, 184, 229–30,
    250, 261, 376, 422–23, 448, 493,
    532, 551–52, 556, 576, 628
Scandinavian Air Systems (SAS),
    258, 425, 604–5, 609, 610
Scanlon, Joseph, 319
Schein, Edgar, 18, 373–74, 549–50
Schlesinger, Leonard, 496–97
Schneider National, 618
Schultz, Howard, 211, 319–20
Schwartzkopf, Norman, 335
Schweser, Fred, 50
Sears, Roebuck and Co., 80–83, 88,
    240, 530, 617, 632
Shamie, Lottie, 503
Sharper Image, 50
Shell Oil Co., 160–61, 186, 264–65,
    541–42
Shell Switzerland, 66
Shell U.S.A., 66
Shonk, James, 467, 485
Simon, Herbert, 39–40, 117, 120–21
Simons, Robert, 530, 531, 547
Skinner, B. F., 412
Smith, Adam, 31–32, 45
Smith, Fred, 370
Snapple Beverages, 377
Snow, C. C., 195–96
Softbank Corp., 416
Sony Corp., 49, 188, 198, 501–2, 587
    Walkman, 45
Southern Railway, 622
South Trust Bank, 567
Southwest Airlines, 5, 192, 197, 202,
    377
Spec's Music Stores, 329, 330, 338,
    339, 500

Subject Index

organizational communication and encouraging boundarylessness, 451

overview of, 265–66

Bounded rationality, decision making and, 120–21

Brainstorming, 129

Breakeven analysis, decision making and, 138–39

Breakeven charts, 138

Breakeven formula, 138–39

Breakeven point, 138

Budgets, 145, 536–37
zero-based budgeting, 537–38

Built to Last (Collins and Porras), 548–49

Bureaucracy, 35

Business reengineering, 624–26

Business Week, 535

C

California Civil Rights Initiative, 7

Career anchor, 18

Carrying (inventory-holding) costs, 578

Cash cows, businesses as, 190

Causal forecasting methods, 159–60

Cellular manufacturing layout, 571

Center for Effective Organizations, University of Southern California, 477

Center for the Study of Work Teams web site, 464

CEO
personality of, strategic management and, 195–96
teamwork, building, 472–73

Ceremonies, organizational culture and, 376

Certainty, decision making and, 140

Chain of command, 212–13

Challenger, space shuttle, 128

Change, designing organizations to manage, 249
boundaryless organizations, 265–74
case example, 267
factors affecting organizational structure, 250–55
job enrichment, 272–74
moving beyond organic organizations, 255–59
network-based organizations, 262–66
overview of, 250
team-based organizations, 259–62

Change, improving communication and managing
how companies succeed in, 452–57

intelligence enterprises, 452
overview of, 451–52

Change, information technology and managing
custom manufacturing, 635
flatter structures with centralized control monitoring, 634
overview of, 634
strategic alliances, 635

Change, organizational (structural), 491
attitudes, changes in, 493
case example, 503
coalition to guide, 500
commitment to, 500
conflict management, 511–18
cultural change, 381–84, 492, 502, 504, 549–50
defined, 493
empowerment and, 501–2
gains, consolidating, 502
leader's role in, 504–7
monitoring, 504
organizational development and, 507–10
overview of, 492, 498–99
process for leading, 499–502, 504
resistance, overcoming, 496–98, 501–2
resistance, sources of, 495–96
short-term wins, generating, 502
skills, changes in, 493
strategic change, 179–80, 201–3, 492–95
task redesign, 493
technological change, 493
types of, 493
urgency and, 499–500
vision and, 500–501, 504
what to change, 492–93

Change, strategic, 179–80
defined, 492
leadership and, 201–3

Charismatic leadership, 504

Chelsea (Mass.) School District, 342

Chemical Engineering, 297

Chicago Bulls, 330

Citadel, the, 6, 288

Civil Rights Act of 1964, Title VII of, 286

Clarification of ideas, 440

Classical school of management, 32–35

Close supervision style of leadership, 345

Coaching skills, developing, 485

Coalition, to guide organizational change, 500

Cocaine National Help Line, 310

Codes of ethics
examples of, 86, 88
role of, 86–87
survey conclusions, 83–84

Coercive (punishment) power, 230, 334

Cognitive biases, 118

Cohesiveness, group, 126, 466–67

Collaborating, conflict managment and, 515

Collaborative writing systems, 629–30

Commercial News USA, 50

Commissions, 319

Committees, coordination through, 229

Common ground, conflict management and, 514

Common market, 47

Communication, 435
cultural differences in, 58, 442, 444
defined, 436
manager as communicator, 436
model for, 436–37

Communication, interpersonal
active listening, 439–40
ambiguity and, 438
barriers to, 438–39
clarification of ideas, 440
defense mechanisms and, 438–40
defined, 437
improving, 439–40
nonverbal, 438
perception and, 438
semantics and, 438

Communication, organizational
appraisals, manager, 447–48
barriers to, 441–442, 444
boundary differences and, 444
boundarylessness, encouraging, 451
case examples, 446–47, 449–50, 454–55
change, improving communication and managing, 451–57
controls and two-way, 552
defined, 437, 440
distortion and, 441
diversity issues and, 442
downward, 448–50
electronic networking, 265, 451
formal, 440
horizontal, 450
improving, 444–57
informal, 441, 451–54
information overload and, 441
intelligence enterprises, 452
media richness model, 456–57
networks, 265, 451, 455–56
organizational culture and, 442
organization-wide, 451
rumors and, 441
status and, 442

Critical path, PERT, 575
Cultural artifacts, 367–68
Cultural differences, 58, 64–65
　communication and, 58, 442, 444
Culture, organizational, 81–83, 365
　belief systems, controls and,
　　548–49
　case examples, 369–70, 383–84
　ceremonies and, 376
　changing, 381–84, 492, 502, 504,
　　549–50
　communication and, 442
　core values statement, 373
　defined, 366
　how to create and sustain,
　　373–77
　leadership and, 373–76
　overview of, 366–68
　responsiveness and, 377–79
　rites and, 376
　signs and, 376
　stories and, 376
　strategy and, 376–77
　symbols and, 376
　total quality management (TQM),
　　building, 379–81
　unhealthy, 370–72
　values and, 81–83, 368–70, 372–73,
　　377–78, 548–49, 551–52
Customer departmentalization
　advantages of, 221
　defined, 220
　disadvantages of, 221
Customer report card, 609–10
Customization, mass, 597
Custom manufacturing, information
　technology and, 635
Customs union, 47
Cycle of service, 607

D

Data mining, 615
DEA (Drug Enforcement Agency),
　163
Debiasing your judgment, 122, 353
Decentralization, 255
　defined, 37, 236
　delegation and, 236, 238
　technology and, 257
Decision making, 107
　biases and, 118, 122
　breakeven analysis and, 138–39
　case examples, 110, 112, 113,
　　128–30
　creativity and, 122–24
　debiasing your judgment, 122, 353
　decision, defined, 108
　decision tree, 141
　defined, 108

escalation of commitment and, 119
　ethics and, 84–86
　finality of, 125
　framing and, 118–19
　functional fixedness and, 119
　group, 126–32
　how to make better decisions,
　　121–25
　intuitive, 117–18, 124
　knowledge and, 122
　leadership actions, deciding on,
　　333–34
　leadership and good, 336
　leadership styles and, 342–44
　linear programming and, 139–40
　nonprogrammed decisions, 108,
　　111–13
　organizational barriers to, 120
　overview of, 108
　programmed decisions, 108–13
　psychological set and, 119–20
　quantitative aids to, 138–41
　rational, 113–14, 116–21
　satisficing, 121
　shortcuts (heuristics), 118
　statistical decision theory
　　techniques, 140–41
　strategic, 125
　systematic, 117
　timing and, 125
　waiting-line/queuing techniques,
　　decision making and, 140
Decision support systems (DSS)
　defined, 619, 621–22
　management information systems
　　compared to, 622
　using, 622
Decision tree, 141, 344
Decoder/receiver, 437
Defense mechanisms
　defined, 438–39
　interpersonal communications and,
　　438–40
Delegation, 255
　case examples, 237, 238
　decentralization and, 236, 238
　defined, 236
　empowerment and, 236
　teams and, 484
Delphi Technique, 130
Deming Award, 380
Demographics and the new global
　workforce, 6–7
Departmentalization, 253
　case examples, 217, 219, 225
　customer, 220–21
　defined, 214
　functional, 214–16
　geographic, 222–23
　hybrid, 224–25
　marketing-channel, 221–22

matrix, 223–24
　product (divisionalization), 216–17,
　　219–20, 228–29
　technology and, 257
DePaul University Institute for
　Business and Professional Ethics
　web site, 76
Deregulation, 4
Descriptive plans, 145
Designing for manufacturability, 586
Development, organizational (OD)
　confrontation meetings, 509,
　　517–18
　defined, 507
　human resource management and,
　　510
　integrated strategic management,
　　510
　types of applications, 507–10
Development teams, 468
Devil's-advocate approach to
　decision making, 130
Diagnostic control systems, 532–33
Differences, individual, 392
Differentiation strategy, 192
Direct supervision, coordination
　through, 228
Disabilities, workforce diversity and,
　94, 286
Discipline, employee, 320–21
Discrimination
　defined, 94
　nondiscrimination in practice,
　　286–87
Dismissal, employee, 321
Distortion, organizational
　communication and, 441
Distributed networks/processing,
　631
Diversification
　conglomerate, 186
　defined, 186
　related, 186
Diversification stage, 37
Diversity, managing
　age, 94, 286, 298
　barriers to, 94–95
　bases for, 93–94
　boosting performance by, 95–97
　defined, 93
　disabilities, 94, 286
　ethnicity, 93, 94, 286
　gender, 93–95, 286–90
　leadership and, 96
　nondiscrimination in practice,
　　286–87
　organizational communication and,
　　442
　overview of, 93
　race, 93, 286
　sexual orientation, 94

Post-action controls, 530
Postentrepreneurial organization, 19
Postmodern organization, 19
Power
  coercive (punishment), 232, 334
  defined, 232
  expert, 233, 334
  leadership and, 334–35, 356–57
  legitimate (position), 233, 334
  need for, 409–10
  Rating a Manager's Power self-assessment exercise, 356–57
  referent, 233, 334
  reward, 232, 334
Pregnancy Discrimination Act of 1978, 286
Prejudice, 94
Prepotency process principle, 406
Primary data, 162
Prince, The (Machiavelli), 335
Privacy Act of 1974, 292
Problem, 108
Problem-solving teams, 467
Procedures
  coordination through rules and, 228
  defined, 145
Process approaches to motivation
  equity, 410
  expectancy, 346, 411
  objectives, 411
Process layout, 570
Product departmentalization (divisionalization)
  advantages of, 219
  case examples, 217, 219
  coordination through, 228–29
  defined, 216–17
  disadvantages of, 220
Product development, 186
Product layout, 570
Production/production system(s)
  case example, 567
  continuous, 570
  designing, 568–71
  intermittent, 569–60
  international, 55–56
  layout, 570–71
  location decision, 568–69
  mass, 570
  overview of, 565–66, 568
  types of processes, 569–70
Production planning and control
  aggregate output planning, 572
  case example, 574
  defined, 572
  Gantt charts, 574
  master production scheduling (MPS), 572
  material requirements planning (MRP), 572–73

network methods of, 575–76
  process of, 572–73
  purchasing, 576–77
  scheduling, 574
  shop floor control, 573
Profit sharing, controls and, 555
Programmed decisions, 108–13
Programs (planning), 145
Project teams, 468
Promotions, 320
Psychoanalytic theory, 393–94
Psychological needs, 406
Psychological set, decision making and, 119–20
Punishment, behavior modification and, 412
Punishment (coercive) power, 232, 334
Purchasing, 576–77

Q

Qualitative forecasting methods, 158, 160
Quality, defined, 579–81
Quality circles (QC)
  defined, 467
  using, 467–68
Quality control
  Malcolm Baldrige Award, 380, 582–84
  benchmarking, 184, 583
  case examples, 580–81, 584–85
  designing for manufacturability, 586
  ISO 9000, 380, 579–80
  methods of, 585
  quality, defined, 579–81
  quality circles (QC), 467–68
  strategic quality planning, 583
  total quality improvement (TQI), 580–81
  total quality management (TQM), 379–81, 581–83
Quantitative aids to decision making, 138–41
Quantitative forecasting methods, 158–60
Quantitative school of management, 40–41
Question marks, businesses as, 189–90

R

Race, workforce diversity and, 93, 286
Rating a Manager's Power self-assessment exercise, 356–57

Rational decision making
  bounded rationality, 120–21
  defined, 113–14
  limits to, 116–20
  steps in, 114, 116
Receiver/decoder, 437
Recognition, motivation and, 419
Recruiting
  advertising and, 297
  age and, 298
  defined, 297
  employment agencies and, 297
  executive recruiters and, 298
  internal sources of candidates, 297
  Internet and, 298
  referrals and, 298
  walk-ins and, 298
Reengineering, business, 624–26
References, checking, 309–10
Referent power, 233, 334
Referrals, recruiting and, 298
Refreezing, 498
Regiocentric philosophy, 59
Reinforcement/learning approaches to motivation. *See* Learning/reinforcement approaches to motivation
Related diversification, 186
Renewal process, 14–15
Responsiveness, organizational culture
  unresponsive versus responsive cultures, 378–79
  values and, 377–78
Retrenchment, 187
Return on investment (ROI), 538–39
Reward, contingent, 412
Reward power, 232, 334
Risk, decision making and, 141
Rites, organizational culture and, 376
Robotics/automation, 592–94
Rockefeller Foundation, 39
Role ambiguity, 242
Role conflict, 242, 511–12
Rowand High School (Southern California), 418–19
Rules
  coordination through procedures and, 228
  defined, 145
Rumors, organizational communication and, 441

S

Sacred Hoops: Spiritual Lessons of a Hardwood Warrior (Jackson), 330
Safety. *See* Occupational safety and health
Safety needs, 406

St. Francis Hospital (Beech Grove, Ind.), 156
Salary/wage, 318
Sales force estimation, 160
Sales forecasting techniques
  causal methods, 159–60
  competitive intelligence (CI), 162–64
  jury of executive opinion technique, 160
  qualitative methods, 158, 160
  quantitative methods, 158–60
  sales force estimation, 160
  time-series analysis, 159
Sales Management, 297
Sampling, acceptance, 585
Satisfactory alternatives, 121
Satisficing, 121
Scenario planning, 160–61
Scenarios, defined, 160–61
Scheduling
  group scheduling systems, 630
  production, 574
Scientific management, 31–35
Secondary data, 162
Security, computer, 632–33
Self-actualization needs, 407
Self-actualizing, controls and, 555–57
Self-assessment exercises
  Are you ready to be a leader? 352–53
  Do you really want to succeed? 394–95
  Rating a manager's power, 354–55
Self-concept
  behavior and, 394–95, 398
  defined, 394
Self-directed teams
  defined, 467, 471
  organizing, 471–72
Self-efficacy
  behavior and, 401
  defined, 158, 401
Self-esteem needs, 408–9
Semantics, 438
Semi-autonomous teams, 467
Sender/encoder, 436
Sensitivity training, 508–9
Service and knowledge work, shift to, 7–8
Service management
  case example, 604–5
  cycle of service, 607
  defined, 605
  empowerment and, 604–5
  moment of truth, 606–7
  overview of, 604
  service triangle, 608–9
  steps in implementing a program, 609–11

why it is challenging, 606
why it is important, 605–6
Service triangle, 608–9
Setup costs, 577–78
Sexual harassment
  avoiding and dealing with, 288–89
  defined, 288
  perceptions of, 289–90
Sexual orientation, workforce diversity and, 94
Shared fate and commonality, controls and, 552–53
Shingo Prize, 591
Shop floor control, 573
Signs, organizational culture and, 376
Similarity heuristic, 118
Simple smoothing average, 159
Single Europe Act, 47
Situational leadership model, 348
Situational theories of leadership
  contingency theory, 345–46
  leader-member exchange (LMX) theory, 347–48
  overview of, 345
  path-goal theory, 346–47
  situational leadership model, 348
  transformational leadership, 350–51
Situational theory of management, 41–42
Situation analysis
  benchmarking, 184
  environmental scanning, 182–84
  overview of, 181–82
  SWOT analysis, 182
Six sigma. *See* Total quality management
Skill-based pay, motivation and, 418–19
Skills
  changes in, 493
  coordination through standardized, 229–30
Small Children's Medical Center (Dallas), 557
Smoothing methods, 159
Smoothing over, conflict management and, 515
Social audit, corporate, 92
Socializing, defined, 313
Social needs, 406
Social responsibility
  defined, 89
  how to improve, 92–93
  theories of corporate, 90–92
Social Security, 319
Society for Human Resource Management web site, 282
Sociocultural environment of international business, 64–65

Span(s) of control, 253
  defined, 239
  technology and, 255
  widening, 258
Specialization of jobs, 253, 255
Spokesperson role, 13
Spot awards, motivation and, 417
Stable environment, 251
Staff assistants, coordination through, 229
Staff authority/managers
  defined, 234
  line conflict with, 234
Staffing, 281
  application blanks, 300
  case examples, 311–13
  defined, 292
  drug abuse and, 310
  health exams, 310
  international, 56–57, 67
  interviews, 302, 305, 307–9
  job analysis, 292–93
  personnel planning, 296–97
  recruiting, 297–98
  references, checking, 309–10
  selection and placement techniques, 298–302, 305, 307–13
  testing for employee selection, 300–2, 310
  value-based, 554
Stakeholder, corporate, 91
Standing plans, 145
Stanford-Binet test, 300
Stanford University School of Medicine, 288
Stars, businesses as, 189
Statistical decision theory techniques, 140–41
Status, organizational communication and, 442
Status quo strategies, 186–87
Steering controls, 529–30
Stepladder technique, 131
Stereotyping
  defined, 94, 400
  gender-role, 95
Stockout costs, 578
Stories, organizational culture and, 376
Strategic alliances, 52, 187–88
  information technology's role in, 635
Strategic business unit (SBU), 196
Strategic change, 179–80, 201–3
  defined, 492, 493
  implementing, 494–95
Strategic control, 179
Strategic decision making, 125
Strategic interventions, 510

GARY DESSLER, MANAGEMENT: Leading People and Organizations in the 21st Century

Prentice-Hall, Inc.

YOU SHOULD CAREFULLY READ THE TERMS AND CONDITIONS BEFORE USING THE DISKETTE PACKAGE. USING THIS DISKETTE PACKAGE INDICATES YOUR ACCEPTANCE OF THESE TERMS AND CONDITIONS.

Prentice-Hall, Inc. provides this program and licenses its use. You assume responsibility for the selection of the program to achieve your intended results, and for the installation, use, and results obtained from the program. This license extends only to use of the program in the United States or countries in which the program is marketed by authorized distributors.

LICENSE GRANT You hereby accept a nonexclusive, nontransferable, permanent license to install and use the program ON A SINGLE COMPUTER at any given time. You may copy the program solely for backup or archival purposes in support of your use of the program on the single computer. You may not modify, translate, disassemble, decompile, or reverse engineer the program, in whole or in part.

TERM The License is effective until terminated. Prentice-Hall, Inc. reserves the right to terminate this License automatically if any provision of the License is violated. You may terminate the License at any time. To terminate this License, you must return the program, including documentation, along with a written warranty stating that all copies in your possession have been returned or destroyed.

LIMITED WARRANTY THE PROGRAM IS PROVIDED "AS IS" WITHOUT WARRANTY OF ANY KIND, EITHER EXPRESSED OR IMPLIED, INCLUDING, BUT NOT LIMITED TO, THE IMPLIED WARRANTIES OR MERCHANTABILITY AND FITNESS FOR A PARTICULAR PURPOSE. THE ENTIRE RISK AS TO THE QUALITY AND PERFORMANCE OF THE PROGRAM IS WITH YOU. SHOULD THE PROGRAM PROVE DEFECTIVE, YOU (AND NOT PRENTICE-HALL, INC. OR ANY AUTHORIZED DEALER) ASSUME THE ENTIRE COST OF ALL NECESSARY SERVICING, REPAIR, OR CORRECTION. NO ORAL OR WRITTEN INFORMATION OR ADVICE GIVEN BY PRENTICE-HALL, INC., ITS DEALERS, DISTRIBUTORS, OR AGENTS SHALL CREATE A WARRANTY OR INCREASE THE SCOPE OF THIS WARRANTY.

SOME STATES DO NOT ALLOW THE EXCLUSION OF IMPLIED WARRANTIES, SO THE ABOVE EXCLUSION MAY NOT APPLY TO YOU. THIS WARRANTY GIVES YOU SPECIFIC LEGAL RIGHTS AND YOU MAY ALSO HAVE OTHER LEGAL RIGHTS THAT VARY FROM STATE TO STATE.

Prentice-Hall, Inc. does not warrant that the functions contained in the program will meet your requirements or that the operation of the program will be uninterrupted or error-free.

However, Prentice-Hall, Inc. warrants the diskette(s) on which the program is furnished to be free from defects in material and workmanship under normal use for a period of ninety (90) days from the date of delivery to you as evidenced by a copy of your receipt.

The program should not be relied on as the sole basis to solve a problem whose incorrect solution could result in injury to person or property. If the program is employed in such a manner, it is at the user's own risk and Prentice-Hall, Inc. explicitly disclaims all liability for such misuse.

LIMITATION OF REMEDIES Prentice-Hall, Inc.'s entire liability and your exclusive remedy shall be:

1. the replacement of any diskette not meeting Prentice-Hall, Inc.'s "LIMITED WARRANTY" and that is returned to Prentice-Hall, or

2. if Prentice-Hall is unable to deliver a replacement diskette that is free of defects in materials or workmanship, you may terminate this agreement by returning the program.

IN NO EVENT WILL PRENTICE-HALL, INC. BE LIABLE TO YOU FOR ANY DAMAGES, INCLUDING ANY LOST PROFITS, LOST SAVINGS, OR OTHER INCIDENTAL OR CONSEQUENTIAL DAMAGES ARISING OUT OF THE USE OR INABILITY TO USE SUCH PROGRAM EVEN IF PRENTICE-HALL, INC. OR AN AUTHORIZED DISTRIBUTOR HAS BEEN ADVISED OF THE POSSIBILITY OF SUCH DAMAGES, OR FOR ANY CLAIM BY ANY OTHER PARTY.

SOME STATES DO NOT ALLOW FOR THE LIMITATION OR EXCLUSION OF LIABILITY FOR INCIDENTAL OR CONSEQUENTIAL DAMAGES, SO THE ABOVE LIMITATION OR EXCLUSION MAY NOT APPLY TO YOU.

GENERAL You may not sublicense, assign, or transfer the license of the program. Any attempt to sublicense, assign or transfer any of the rights, duties, or obligations hereunder is void.

This Agreement will be governed by the laws of the State of New York.

Should you have any questions concerning this Agreement, you may contact Prentice-Hall, Inc. by writing to:

Director of New Media
Higher Education Division
Prentice-Hall, Inc.
1 Lake Street
Upper Saddle River, NJ 07458

Should you have any questions concerning technical support, you may write to:

New Media Production
Higher Education Division
Prentice-Hall, Inc.
1 Lake Street
Upper Saddle River, NJ 07458

YOU ACKNOWLEDGE THAT YOU HAVE READ THIS AGREEMENT, UNDERSTAND IT, AND AGREE TO BE BOUND BY ITS TERMS AND CONDITIONS. YOU FURTHER AGREE THAT IT IS THE COMPLETE AND EXCLUSIVE STATEMENT OF THE AGREEMENT BETWEEN US THAT SUPERSEDES ANY PROPOSAL OR PRIOR AGREEMENT, ORAL OR WRITTEN, AND ANY OTHER COMMUNICATIONS BETWEEN US RELATING TO THE SUBJECT MATTER OF THIS AGREEMENT.